Lecture Notes in Artificial Intelligence 12815

Subseries of Lecture Notes in Computer Science

More information about this subseries at http://www.springer.com/series/1244

Han Qiu · Cheng Zhang ·
Zongming Fei · Meikang Qiu ·
Sun-Yuan Kung (Eds.)

Knowledge Science, Engineering and Management

14th International Conference, KSEM 2021
Tokyo, Japan, August 14–16, 2021
Proceedings, Part I

Springer

Editors
Han Qiu
Tsinghua University
Beijing, China

Zongming Fei
University of Kentucky
Lexington, KY, USA

Sun-Yuan Kung
Princeton University
Princeton, NJ, USA

Cheng Zhang
Ibaraki University
Hitachi, Japan

Meikang Qiu
Texas A&M University – Commerce
Commerce, TX, USA

ISSN 0302-9743 ISSN 1611-3349 (electronic)
Lecture Notes in Artificial Intelligence
ISBN 978-3-030-82135-7 ISBN 978-3-030-82136-4 (eBook)
https://doi.org/10.1007/978-3-030-82136-4

LNCS Sublibrary: SL7 – Artificial Intelligence

This Springer imprint is published by the registered company Springer Nature Switzerland AG
The registered company address is: Gewerbestrasse 11, 6330 Cham, Switzerland

Preface

The three-volume set contains the papers presented at the 14th International Conference on Knowledge Science, Engineering, and Management (KSEM 2021), held during August 14–16, 2021, in Tokyo, Japan.

There were 492 submissions. Each submission was reviewed by at least 3 reviewers, and on average 3.5 Program Committee members. The committee decided to accept 164 full papers, resulting in an acceptance rate of 33%. We have separated the proceedings into three volumes: LNCS 12815, 12816, and 12817.

KSEM 2021 was the 14th edition in this conference series which started in 2006. The aim of this interdisciplinary conference is to provide a forum for researchers in the broad areas of knowledge science, knowledge engineering, and knowledge management to exchange ideas and to report state-of-the-art research results. KSEM is in the list of CCF (China Computer Federation) recommended conferences (C series, Artificial Intelligence).

KSEM 2021 was held in Tokyo, Japan, following the traditions of the 13 previous successful KSEM events in Guilin, China (KSEM 2006); Melbourne, Australia (KSEM 2007); Vienna, Austria (KSEM 2009); Belfast, UK (KSEM 2010); Irvine, USA (KSEM 2011); Dalian, China (KSEM 2013); Sibiu, Romania (KSEM 2014); Chongqing, China (KSEM 2015), Passau, Germany (KSEM 2016), Melbourne, Australia (KSEM 2017), Changchun, China (KSEM 2018); Athens, Greece (KSEM 2019), and Hangzhou, China (KSEM 2020).

We would like to express our gratitude to the honorary general and Steering Committee chairs, Ruqian Lu (Chinese Academy of Sciences, China), and Dimitris Karagiannis (University of Vienna, Austria), and the members of the Steering Committee, who provided insight and guidance at all stages. The KSEM 2021 general co-chairs, Meikang Qiu (Texas A&M University-Commerce, USA), and Sun-Yuan Kung (Princeton University, USA) were extremely supportive in the conference organizing, call for papers, and paper review process, and played an important role in the general success of the conference.

The objective of KSEM 2021 was to bring together researchers and practitioners from academia, industry, and government to advance the theories and technologies in knowledge science, engineering, and management. KSEM 2021 focused on three broad areas: Knowledge Science with Learning and AI (KSLA), Knowledge Engineering Research and Applications (KERA), and Knowledge Management with Optimization and Security (KMOS).

We would like to thank the conference sponsors: Springer LNCS, Waseda University, the North America Chinese Talents Association, and the Longxiang High Tech Group Inc.

August 2021

Han Qiu
Cheng Zhang
Zongming Fei
Meikang Qiu
Sun-Yuan Kung

Organization

Honorary General Chairs

Ruqian Lu	Chinese Academy of Sciences, China
Dimitris Karagiannis (Chair)	University of Vienna, Austria

General Chairs

Meikang Qiu	Texas A&M University-Commerce, USA
Sun-Yuan Kung	Princeton University, USA

Program Chairs

Han Qiu	Tsinghua University, China
Cheng Zhang	Waseda University, Japan
Zongming Fei	University of Kentucky, USA

Steering Committee

Ruqian Lu (Honorary Chair)	Chinese Academy of Sciences, China
Dimitris Karagiannis (Chair)	University of Vienna, Austria
Hui Xiong	The State University of New Jersey, USA
Yaxin Bi	Ulster University, UK
Zhi Jin	Peking University, China
Claudiu Kifor	Sibiu University, Romania
Gang Li	Deakin University, Australia
Yoshiteru Nakamori	Japan Advanced Institute of Science and Technology, Japan
Jorg Siekmann	German Research Centre of Artificial Intelligence, Germany
Martin Wirsing	Ludwig-Maximilians-Universität München, Germany
Bo Yang	Jilin University, China
Chengqi Zhang	University of Technology Sydney, Australia
Zili Zhang	Southwest University, China
Christos Douligeris	University of Piraeus, Greece
Xiaoyang Wang	Zhejiang Gongshang University, China

Publicity Chair

Peng Zhang	Stony Brook University, USA

Finance Chair

Hui Zhao	Henan University, China

Technical Committee

Chao Feng	National University of Defense Technology, China
Zhong Ming	Shenzhen University, China
Hiroyuki Sato	The University of Tokyo, Japan
Shuangyin Ren	Chinese Academy of Military Science, China
Thomas Austin	San Jose State University, USA
Zehua Guo	Beijing Institute of Technology, China
Wei Yu	Towson University, USA
Keke Gai	Beijing Institute of Technology, China
Chunxia Zhang	Beijing Institute of Technology, China
Hansi Jiang	SAS Institute Inc., USA
Weiying Zhao	University College London, UK
Shangwei Guo	Chongqing University, China
Jianlong Tan	Chinese Academy of Sciences, China
Songmao Zhang	Chinese Academy of Sciences, China
Bo Ning	Dalian Maritime University, China
Leilei Sun	Beihang University, China
Tong Xu	University of Science and Technology of China, China
Ye Zhu	Monash University, Australia
Jianye Yang	Hunan University, China
Lifei Chen	Fujian Normal University, China
Fan Zhang	Guangzhou University, China
Xiang Zhao	National University of Defense Technology, China
Massimo Benerecetti	University di Napoli "Federico II", Italy
Knut Hinkelmann	FHNW University of Applied Sciences and Arts Northwestern Switzerland, Switzerland
Shuang Li	Beijing Institute of Technology, China
Yuliang Ma	Northeastern University, China
Xin Bi	Northeastern University, China
Cheng Li	National University of Singapore, Singapore
Hechang Chen	Jilin University, China
Chen Chen	Zhejiang Gongshang University, China
Mouna Kamel	IRIT, Paul Sabatier University, France
Yuan Li	North China University of Technology, China
Shu Li	Chinese Academy of Sciences, China
Serge Autexier	DFKI, Germany
Huawen Liu	Zhejiang Normal University, China

Bo Ma	Chinese Academy of Sciences, China
Zili Zhang	Deakin University, Australia
Long Yuan	Nanjing University of Science and Technology, China
Shuiqiao Yang	UTS, Australia
Robert Andrei Buchmann	Babeş-Bolyai University of Cluj Napoca, Romania
Yong Deng	Southwest University, China
Dawei Cheng	Tongji University, China
Jun-Jie Peng	Shanghai University, China
Oleg Okun	Cognizant Technology Solutions GmbH, USA
Jianxin	Deakin University, Australia
Jiaojiao Jiang	RMIT University, Australia
Guangyan Huang	Deakin University, Australia
Li Li	Southwest University, China
Ge Li	Peking University, China
Ximing Li	Jilin University, China
Daniel Volovici	Lucian Blaga University of Sibiu, Romania
Zhenguang Liu	Zhejiang Gongshang University, China
Yi Zhuang	Zhejiang Gongshang University, China
Bo Yang	Jilin University, China
Maheswari N.	VIT University, India
Min Yu	Chinese Academy of Sciences, China
Krzysztof Kluza	AGH University of Science and Technology, Poland
Jia Xu	Guangxi University, China
Jihe Wang	Northwestern Polytechnical University, China
Shaowu Liu	University of Technology, Sydney, Australia
Wei Luo	Deakin University, Australia
Yong Lai	Jilin University, China
Ulrich Reimer	University of Applied Sciences St. Gallen, Switzerland
Klaus-Dieter Althoff	DFKI/University of Hildesheim, Germany
Jiali Zuo	Jiangxi Normal University, China
Hongtao Wang	North China Electric Power University, China
Salem Benferhat	University d'Artois, France
Xiaofei Zhou	Hangzhou Dianzi University, China
Shiyu Yang	East China Normal University, China
Zhisheng Huang	Vrije Universiteit Amsterdam, the Netherlands
Guilin Qi	Southeast University, China
Qingtian Zeng	Shandong University of Science and Technology, China
Jing Wang	The University of Tokyo, Japan
Jun Zheng	New Mexico Institute of Mining and Technology, USA
Paolo Trunfio	University of Calabria, Italy
Kewei Sha	University of Houston-Clear Lake, USA
David Dampier	University of Texas at San Antonio, USA
Richard Hill	University of Huddersfield, UK
William Glisson	University of South Alabama, USA
Petr Matousek	Brno University of Technology, Czech Republic

Javier Lopez	University of Malaga, Spain
Dong Dai	Texas Tech University, USA
Ben Martini	University of South Australia, Australia
Ding Wang	Peking University, China
Xu Zheng	Shanghai University, China
Nhien An Le Khac	University College Dublin, Ireland
Tan Guo	Chongqing University of Posts and Telecommunications, China
Shadi Ibrahim	Rennes Bretagne Atlantique Research Center, France
Neetesh Saxena	Bournemouth University, UK

Contents – Part I

Contents – Part II

Contents – Part III

Knowledge Science with Learning and AI (KSLA)

Research on Innovation Trends of AI Applied to Medical Instruments Using Informetrics Based on Multi-sourse Information

Xingwang Wang(✉) and Tingting Yu

Shanghai Jiao Tong University, Shanghai 200240, China
wxwks@sjtu.edu.cn

Abstract. COVID-19 accelerates the application of AI in medical field, and the global research and development on AI technology applied to medical instruments also become more important and noticeable. The innovation trends of AI applied to medical instruments is analyzed using informetrics methods based on two sources of information, and revealed from four aspects, innovation focuses of fundamental research and technology R & D, innovation fronts of fundamental research and technology R & D. The research results show that the main innovation trends of AI applied to medical instruments include intelligent expert systems for medical diagnosis and treatment, miniaturized and portable medical diagnosis and treatment equipment, tumor and cancer detection and diagnosis devices and instruments, and so on. The research results provide a reference for further R & D on the AI technology applied to medical instruments, and can guide the further innovation of it.

Keywords: Innovation trends · Artificial intelligence · Medical instruments · Informetrics · Multi-sourse information

1 Introduction

In whole 2020, COVID-19 spread all over the world, and had changed the world deeply. In the process of prevention and control of COVID-19, artificial intelligence (AI) technologies played a huge role, and the application of AI in medical field has received more and more attention.

In fact, the application of artificial intelligence in medical field has a long history. In 1972, AAP Help system was developed by University of Leeds as the first artificial intelligence system in medical field, and it mainly was used for the auxiliary diagnosis of abdominal pain and the related needs of surgery [1]. Subsequently, INTERNISTI was developed by University of Pittsburgh, which is mainly used for the auxiliary diagnosis of complex internal diseases; MYCIN was developed by Stanford University, which can diagnose patients with infectious diseases and prescribe antibiotics [2]. In the 1980s, some commercial application systems appeared, such as QMR (Quick Medical Reference), and DXplain developed by Harvard Medical School [3]. In the past ten years, international business giants enter the AI-Medicine industry one after another, the

H. Qiu et al. (Eds.): KSEM 2021, LNAI 12815, pp. 3–12, 2021.
https://doi.org/10.1007/978-3-030-82136-4_1

well-known IBM Watson quickly became an oncologist in a short time through acquiring mass medical knowledge, and it was able to screen 1.5 million patient records in decades of cancer treatment history in a few seconds, and provide evidence-based treatment options for doctors [4]. In recent years, the application research of AI in medical field has been continuously deepened, some representative works include: smart personal health advisor (SPHA) for comprehensive and intelligent health monitoring and guidance [5], hybrid model based on the random vector functional link (RVFL) network [6], improved fuzziness based random vector functional link (IF-RVFL) algorithm for liver disease detection [7], using multilayer convolutional neural networks to analyze EEG signals to help doctors quickly diagnose Parkinson's disease [8], auxiliary diagnostic system based on the transfer learning and deep learning technology which can achieve higher prediction accuracy than human experts in some ophthalmic diseases [9], using deep convolutional neural networks to do the breast cancer screening exam classification [10], Al system for breast cancer screening [11], and so on.

The application of artificial intelligence in medical field is mainly depends on medical instruments. The advanced level of medical instruments affects the overall level of the medical industry greatly. Therefore, the application of AI technology in medical instruments represents the future development direction.

This article will research the innovation trends of AI technology applied to medical instruments (abbreviated AI-Medical Instruments below) using informetrics method based on multi-sourse information, and introduce them from four aspects: innovation focuses of fundamental research and technology R & D, which represent the current scientific and technological innovation trends respectively; innovation fronts of fundamental research and technology R & D, which represent the future scientific and technological innovation trends respectively.

2 Research Methods and Data Source

The innovation situation of science and technology are mainly recorded in scientific and technological literatures, so innovation trends can be found by analyzing scientific and technological literatures, and the core of innovation trends analysis is to discover the innovation focuses and fronts. The research framework of innovation trends is shown as Fig. 1.

Innovation focuses can be revealed by means of informetrics, that is, reveal the hot directions or focus issues of scientific and technological innovation through quantitative analyzing the research topics of recent scientific and technological literatures. Informetrics methods mainly include co-word analysis, co-citation analysis, and text clustering, etc., which can reveal research focuses from different perspectives. This paper will use co-word analysis and text clustering methods (co-citation analysis has time lag), and take groups of clustered words as the candidates for innovation focus fields, and confirms several innovation focus fields through consulting the experts of relevant scientific and technological field.

Innovation fronts also can be revealed by means of informetrics, that is, reveal the frontier directions of scientific and technological innovation through quantitative analyzing the research topics of recent scientific and technological literatures. This paper

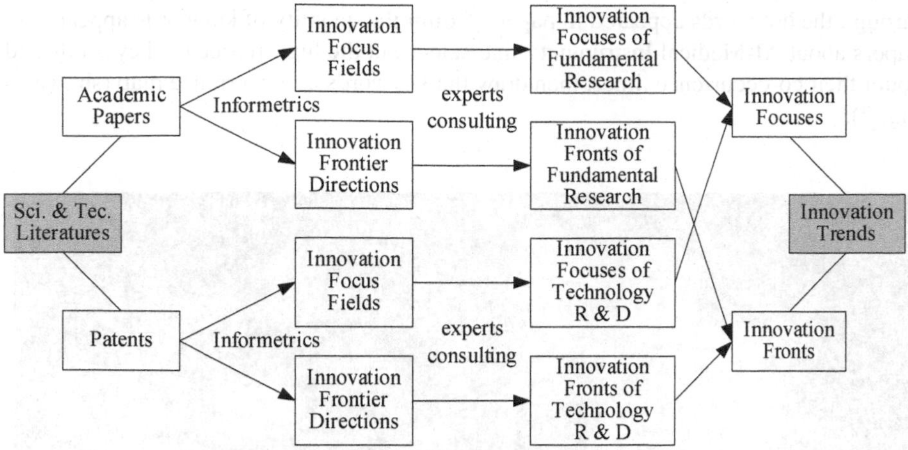

Fig. 1. Research framework of innovation trends.

will use words frequency analysis method and Kleinberg burst detection algorithm [12] to identify the burst words. Burst detection identifies time periods in which a target event is uncharacteristically frequent, or "bursty". Burst detection can be used to detect bursts in a continuous stream of events (such as receiving emails) or in discrete batches of events (such as poster titles submissions to an annual conference). The burst detection algorithm designed by Kleinberg can be used to identify the frontiers of emerging research terminologies.

The identified burst words will be taken as the candidates for innovation frontier directions, and confirms several innovation frontier directions through consulting the experts of relevant scientific and technological field.

At the same time, visualization tools based on informetrics are used to display the analysis results visually, including BibExcel [13], VOSviewer [14] and CiteSpace [15].

The data of scientific and technological literatures about AI-Medical Instruments in this paper come from two kinds of literature databases. Academic papers and patents are retrieved from Scopus of Elsevier and Derwent Innovations Index of Clarivate respectively. The search theme is AI technology applied to medical instruments, and 5,435 papers and 4,536 patents published in 2014–2019 are found and selected as the analysis data.

3 Research Results

Through the analysis on the data what is obtained above, the innovation trends analysis results about AI-Medical Instruments are obtained as follows.

3.1 Innovation Focuses of AI-Medical Instruments

Innovation Focuses of Fundamental Research. Generally, academic papers focus on fundamental research, and the innovation focuses of fundamental research can be found through the hot words appeared in papers. Count the quantity of keywords appeared in papers about AI-Medical Instruments, and select out the high-frequency keywords and count their co-occurrence times, then draw the keywords co-occurrence map (shown as Fig. 2).

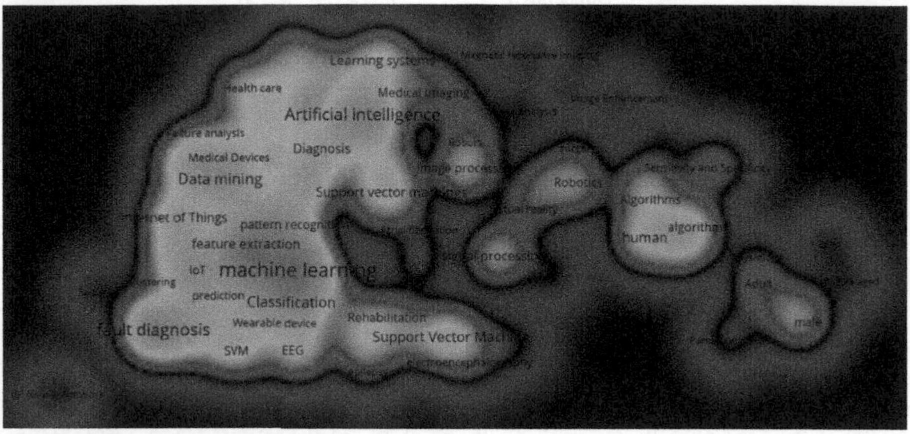

Fig. 2. AI-Medical Instruments papers keywords co-occurrence map.

According to Fig. 2, we can find the innovation focuses of fundamental research of AI-Medical Instruments, and they are three main aspects as follow.

(1) Application of machine learning in medical diagnosis and treatment. The main research is to use AI algorithms and technologies to assist the development of intelligent diagnosis and treatment instruments. The AI algorithms and technologies include learning system, support vector machine, neural network, data mining, deep learning, pattern recognition, etc. The intelligent diagnosis and treatment instruments include wearable device, computer aided diagnosis equipment, computer aided image processing equipment, biomedical equipment, etc.
(2) Application of artificial intelligence in medical diagnosis and treatment. The main application areas include clinical decision support system, computer aided tomography, MRI, wearable technology, computer aided diagnosis, virtual reality, computer vision, mobile device, biomedical equipment, biological model, robotics, medical computing, computer-assisted signal processing, computer-aided image analysis, etc. These applications are used for patient treatment, patient monitoring, telemedicine, patient rehabilitation, medical care, equipment failure analysis, failure detection, etc.
(3) Application of Support Vector Machine in medical diagnosis and treatment. The involved research areas include biomedical signal processing, computer-aided diagnosis, pattern recognition, classifier, wearable sensor, image analysis, etc.

Innovation Focuses of Technology R & D. Generally, patents focus on technology research and development, and the innovation focuses of technology R & D can be found through the hot words appeared in patents or patent classifications, such as Derwent Manual Code (MC), which represent the technology innovation of a patent as the keyword of a paper. Count the quantity of MCs of patents about AI-Medical Instruments, and select out the high-frequency MCs and count their co-occurrence times, then draw the MCs co-occurrence map (shown as Fig. 3).

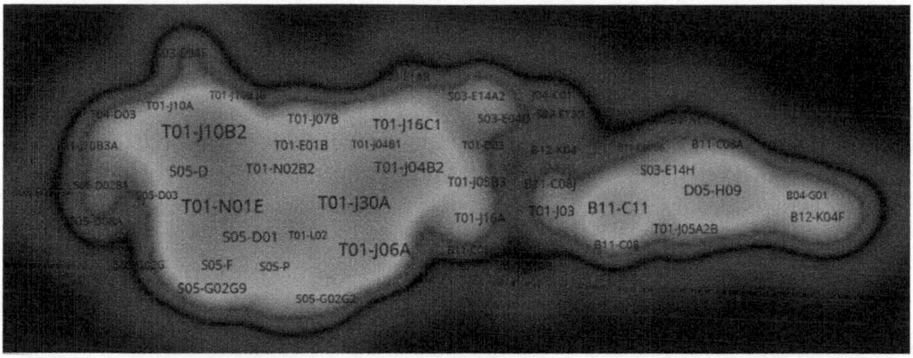

Fig. 3. AI-Medical Instruments patents MCs co-occurrence map.

According to Fig. 3 combined with the meaning of Derwent manual code, we can find the innovation focuses of technology R & D of AI-Medical Instruments, and they are four main aspects as follow.

(1) Application of artificial intelligence in tumors and cancers diagnosis. The involved MCs include D05-H09 (Testing and Detection), T01-J03 (For Evaluating Statistical Data), S03-E09F (Immunoassay Techniques and Biological Indicators), B12-K04G (Diagnosis of Diseases or Conditions in Animals General), B12-K04F (Tests Involving Nucleic Acid, Hybridisation Probes, etc.), B12-K04G2A (Diagnosis of Tumors, Cancer), etc. Through these MCs, we can find the applications mainly involve the tools, devices and optical instruments for the diagnosis, detection and testing of tumor and cancer.
(2) Intelligent medical system. The involved MCs include T01-N01E (On-line Medicine), T01-S03 (Claimed Software Products), T01-J06A1 (Medical Information Systems), T01-N01E1 (On-line Medical Information Systems), S05-D01 (Measuring and Recording Systems), T01-J16A (Expert Systems), etc. Through these MCs, we can find the focuses mainly involve such as medical information systems, electronic medical record, expert system, data modeling, medical simulation, etc.
(3) Telemedicine. The involved MCs include T01-J05B2 (Storage), T01-J16C1 (Neural Networks), T01-N01B3A (Remote Examination/Testing), T01-N01D2 (Document Transfer), T01-N01D (Data Transfer), etc. Through these MCs, we can find the focuses mainly involve the technical means related to telemedicine, such as data transmission, data storage, remote inspection, remote testing, etc.

(4) Application of artificial intelligence in medical imaging assisted diagnosis. The involved MCs include T01-J10B2 (Image Analysis), T01-J30A (Educational Aids), S05-D (Electrical Diagnosis), T01-J10B1 (Image Enhancement), T01-N01D1B (Video Transfer), T01-J05B4F (Image And Video Databases), S05-D08A (General Image Processing), etc. Through these MCs, we can find the applications mainly involve medical image recognition, such as graphic analysis, image processing, image enhancement, electronic diagnosis, etc.

3.2 Innovation Fronts of AI-Medical Instruments

Innovation Fronts of Fundamental Research. In the same way, the innovation fronts of fundamental research can be found through analyzing the words appeared in academic papers. Through detecting the burst terms appeared in the title or abstract or keywords or topic (including title, abstract and keywords) of papers about AI-Medical Instruments, the results are as follows.

(1) No burst term was obtained only by detecting the titles of papers.
(2) 22 valid burst terms were obtained only by detecting the abstracts of papers as follows: classification algorithm, clinical data, control system, data analysis, deep learning, deep neural network, fault diagnosis method, fault feature, heart rate, image processing, intelligent system, learning approach, machine learning algorithm, medical informatics, mobile application, mobile device, photo-optical instrumentation engineers, previous study, second stage, svm classifier, things iot, vital signs.
(3) No burst term was obtained only by detecting the keywords of papers.
(4) 20 valid burst terms were obtained by detecting the topics of papers as follows: activity recognition, breast cancer, classification algorithm, clinical application, computational complexity, daily activity, data mining technique, diagnosis system, elderly people, electrical activity, human body, image processing, mathematical model, medical informatics, mobile application, mobile device, monitoring system, overall accuracy, power system, training data.

Integrating above results, 40 burst terms were obtained as frontier terms candidates, which represent the innovation frontier directions of fundamental research about AI-Medical Instruments.

Innovation Fronts of Technology R & D. In the same way, the innovation fronts of technology research and development can be found through analyzing the words appeared in patents. Through detecting the burst terms appeared in the title or/and abstract of patents about AI-Medical Instruments, the results are as follows.

(1) 12 valid burst terms were obtained only by detecting the titles of patents as follows: biological sample, blood sample, breast cancer, computer-implemented method, decision tree, detection method, electric signal, expert system, genetic algorithm, lung cancer, medical imaging, wearable device.

(2) 16 valid burst terms were obtained only by detecting the abstracts of patents as follows: average value, biological sample, characteristic parameter, computer system, computer-implemented method, c-reactive protein, decision tree, electric signal, extracting process, genetic algorithm, principal component analysis, processing unit, second set, support vector machine, unknown sample, user interface.
(3) 20 valid burst terms were obtained by detecting the titles and abstracts of patents as follows: average value, biological sample, breast cancer, characteristic parameter, computer system, computer-implemented metho, c-reactive protein, decision tree, electric signal, expert system, heart rate, infrared spectrum, lung cancer, main body, pressure sensor, principal component analysis, processing unit, support vector machine, unknown sample, user interface.

Integrating the above results, 28 burst terms were obtained as frontier terms candidates, which represent the innovation frontier directions of technology R & D about AI-Medical Instruments.

3.3 Innovation Trends of AI-Medical Instruments

According to the above analysis results, several innovation focus fields and frontier directions were selected and confirmed after consulting experts in relevant R & D fields from two aspects: fundamental research and technology R & D (shown as Table 1).

Table 1. Innovation Focus Fields and Frontier Directions about AI-Medical Instruments.

Innovation trends	Fundamental research	Technology R & D
Innovation focus fields	(1) Using machine learning algorithms and technologies such as learning systems, neural networks, and deep learning to assist the development of AI-Medical Instruments (2) Application of AI in medical fields such as clinical decision support system, computer aided diagnosis, and biomedical equipment (3) Application of support vector machine in medical fields such as biomedical signal processing, automatic pattern recognition, and wearable sensor	(1) Application of AI in the tools, devices and instruments for the detection and diagnosis of tumor and cancer (2) Intelligent medical system such as medical information systems, electronic medical records, and expert systems (3) Telemedicine technologies such as data transmission, data storage, remote inspection and remote testing (4) Medical image recognition technologies such as graphic analysis, image processing and image enhancement

(*continued*)

Table 1. (*continued*)

Innovation trends	Fundamental research	Technology R & D
Innovation frontier directions	(1) Intelligent system related to medical diagnosis and treatment (2) Application of deep neural network in medical diagnosis and treatment (3) Application of deep learning technology and approach in medical diagnosis and treatment (4) Application of support vector machine classifier technology in medical diagnosis and treatment (5) Application of Internet of Things technology related to big data and 5G in medical diagnosis and treatment (6) Miniaturized and portable mobile medical device (7) Application of AI in breast cancer diagnosis and treatment (8) Application of activity recognition technology (automatic recognition and detection of different postures of the human body) in medical diagnosis and treatment	(1) Expert system for medical diagnosis and treatment (important platform for artificial intelligence and big data analysis) (2) Application of decision tree in medical diagnosis and treatment (3). Application of principal component analysis in medical diagnosis and treatment (4) Application of AI in breast cancer diagnosis and treatment (5) Application of characteristic parameter (for characteristic extraction) in medical diagnosis and treatment (6) Application of AI in lung cancer diagnosis and treatment (7) Smart wearable device for medical diagnosis and treatment

We can see (from Table 1) that there are a lot of similarities between innovation focus fields and frontier directions, between fundamental research and technology R & D about AI-Medical Instruments, although there are certain differences between them each other.

These innovation focus fields and frontier directions can represent the innovation trends of AI-Medical Instruments. The main innovation trends of that include: intelligent expert systems for medical diagnosis and treatment, medical image processing technologies (image analysis, processing, and enhancement, etc.), miniaturized and portable medical diagnosis and treatment equipment (mobile terminals and wearable devices), the application of machine learning algorithms (neural networks, deep learning, decision trees, etc.) in medical diagnosis and treatment, the application of behavior feature recognition and analysis technology in medical diagnosis and treatment, tumor and cancer detection and diagnosis devices and instruments, and so on.

4 Conclusions

According to above research results, the innovation trends of AI technology applied to medical instruments were presented from four aspects. Innovation focuses of fundamental research and technology R & D represent the current scientific and technological innovation trends respectively. Innovation fronts of fundamental research and technology R & D represent the future scientific and technological innovation trends respectively.

In 2021, COVID-19 continues to spread in some parts of the world. The application of AI in medical field has accelerated by COVID-19 in the last year, and it will become more wide and deep in the future. The global research and development on AI applied to medical instruments also will become more and more.

This article analyses the innovation trend of AI technology applied to medical instruments using informetrics method based on two kind of information, and reveals the trends of scientific and technological innovation. The research results in this article provide a reference for further research and development on AI technology applied to medical instruments, and can guide the further innovation of AI technology applied to medical field. At the same time, there are some aspects need to be improved in the next study, such as optimizing the quantitative data analysis algorithm, and considering more expert opinions to improve the analysis effect, and so on.

Acknowledgements. This work was supported by the Key Project of Shanghai Soft Science Research (20692110900), and the Guiding Project of Think Tank Research of Shanghai Jiaotong University (ZKYJ-2020009).

References

1. China Health Industry Innovation Platform WeChat Official Account. https://mp.weixin.qq.com/s?__biz=MzA3OTk0OTQxMg==&mid=2651225761&idx=1&sn=922a4d50927453e01ad0e86be19b478f&chksm=845965aab32eecbcd7f99bc2ec9cd2c832145b181d7f821ef208e8f388224aafaf400862c141&scene=0#rd. Accessed 31 Dec 2020
2. Sotos, J.G.: MYCIN, NEOMYCIN: two approaches to generating explanations in rule-based expert systems. Aviat. Space Environ. Med. **61**(10), 950–954 (1990)
3. Barnett, G.O., Hoffer, E.P., Packer, M.S., et al.: DXplain—Demonstration and discussion of a diagnostic clinical decision support system. In: Proceedings of the Annual Symposium on Computer Application in Medical Care, p. 878 (1991)
4. Miller, A.: The future of health care could be elementary with Watson. CMAJ **185**(9), E367–E368 (2013)
5. Chen, M., Zhang, Y., Qiu, M., et al.: SPHA: smart personal health advisor based on deep analytics. IEEE Commun. Mag. **56**(3), 164–169 (2018)
6. Dai, P., Gwadry-Sridhar, F., Bauer, M., et al.: Healthy cognitive aging: a hybrid random vector functional-link model for the analysis of Alzheimer's disease. In: AAAI Conference on Artificial Intelligence, pp.4567–4573 (2017)

7. Cao, W., Yang, P., Ming, Z., et al.: An improved fuzziness based random vector functional link network for liver disease detection. In: IEEE 6th International Conference on Big Data Security on Cloud (BigDataSecurity), IEEE International Conference on High Performance and Smart Computing, (HPSC) and IEEE International Conference on Intelligent Data and Security (IDS), pp.42–48 (2020)
8. Oh, S.L., Hagiwara, Y., Raghavendra, U., et al.: A deep learning approach for Parkinson's disease diagnosis from EEG signals. Neural Comput. Appl. **32**, 10927–10933 (2020)
9. Kermany, D.S., Goldbaum, M., Cai, W., et al.: Identifying medical diagnoses and treatable diseases by image-based deep learning. Cell **172**(5), 1122–1131 (2018)
10. Wu, N., Phang, J., Park, J., et al.: Deep neural networks improve radiologists' performance in breast cancer screening. IEEE Trans. Med. Imaging **39**(4), 1184–1194 (2020)
11. McKinney, S.M., Sieniek, M., Godbole, V., Godwin, J., Antropova, N., et al.: International evaluation of an Al system for breast cancer screening. Nature **577**, 89–94 (2020)
12. Kleinberg, J.: Bursty and hierarchical structure in streams. In: Eighth ACM SIGKDD International Conference on Knowledge Discovery and Data Mining, pp. 91–101. Association for Computing Machinery, New York (2002)
13. BibExcel Homepage. http://www8.umu.se/inforsk/Bibexcel. Accessed 20 Feb 2016
14. VOSviewer Homepage. http://www.vosviewer.com. Accessed 03 Apr 2019
15. CiteSpace Homepage. http://cluster.ischool.drexel.edu/~cchen/citespace/. Accessed 15 Oct 2019

Extracting Prerequisite Relations Among Wikipedia Concepts Using the Clickstream Data

Cheng Hu[1], Kui Xiao[1(✉)], Zesong Wang[1], Shihui Wang[1], and Qifeng Li[2]

[1] School of Computer Science and Information Engineering, Hubei University, Wuhan, China
xiaokui@hubu.edu.cn

[2] Academic Affairs Office of Hubei University, Wuhan, China

Abstract. A prerequisite relation describes a basic dependency relation between concepts in education, cognition and other fields. Especially, prerequisite relations among concepts play a very important role in various intelligent education applications, such as concept map extraction, learning object sequencing, reading order list generation. In this paper, we investigate the problem of extracting prerequisite relations among Wikipedia concepts. We take advantage of Wikipedia clickstream data and related concept sets to discover prerequisite relations among Wikipedia concepts. Evaluations on two datasets that include nine domains show that the proposed method can cover most of the concept pairs, and achieves significant improvements (+1.7–31.0% by Accuracy) comparing with existing methods.

Keywords: Prerequisite relation · Wikipedia concept · Clickstream data · Set of related concepts · User navigation

1 Introduction

In a textbook, each chapter contains some important knowledge concepts. Similarly, in a MOOC, each video lecture also introduces several main concepts. There are usually some prerequisite relations between the concepts from different chapters or video lectures, which determine the order of the chapters in a textbook or the order of video lectures in a MOOC. Given a pair of concepts (A, B), if a learner has to understand the meaning of concept A before he or she learns concept B, then we say that A is a prerequisite of B. In this paper, we study the problem of prerequisite relation extraction among concepts in Wikipedia.

When users browse the content of a Wikipedia article, they usually cannot understand the content of the article due to lack of background knowledge. But the background knowledge is often contained in other Wikipedia articles. If users know the prerequisite relations between articles, they will be able to quickly find out the articles in which the background knowledge is located. Here a Wikipedia concept refers to the title of a Wikipedia article. If concept A is a prerequisite of

H. Qiu et al. (Eds.): KSEM 2021, LNAI 12815, pp. 13–26, 2021.
https://doi.org/10.1007/978-3-030-82136-4_2

concept B, it means the article of A contains some background knowledge needed to understand the content of the article of B. In addition, some researchers have extracted Wikipedia concepts from learning resources such as textbooks [1–3], MOOCs [4–6], university course introductions [7–9], and scientific reports [10], and inferred precedence relations between learning resources by using concept prerequisite relations.

User navigation data in Wikipedia, i.e. clickstream data, is helpful for discovering concept prerequisite relations. Intuitively, users visit an article they are interested in so that they can understand the corresponding concept. Meanwhile, they will follow links to other articles they believe will support that objective. For example, a user browses the article of concept B, then follows links from the article of B to the article of concept A. This may be because A is a prerequisite of B. Clickstream data refers to the number of times users followed links from one article to the other [14]. Normally, Wikipedia provides clickstream data for the last 30 months for users to download and use.

In this paper, we propose an approach for extracting concept prerequisite relations in Wikipedia based on clickstream data. Clickstream data was used to define different kinds of features for concept pairs, and then we predicted prerequisite relations between concepts with the features. On the other hand, the number of concept pairs covered by clickstream data is always low. To solve this problem, we used the related concept set of every Wikipedia concept, which significantly improved the coverage of concept pairs.

Our main contributions include: (1) A novel metric to extract prerequisite relations among concepts based on clickstream data that outperforms existing baseline methods. (2) A new method to improve the concept pair coverage of clickstream data with the related concept sets of each Wikipedia concept.

The rest of this article is organized as follows. In Sect. 2 we discuss some related work. In Sect. 3, we describe the proposed method for prerequisite relation extraction. Section 4 elaborates our approach for the evaluation. Finally, we conclude our work in Sect. 5.

2 Related Work

Talukdar and Cohen proposed an early attempt to model the prerequisite structure of Wikipedia concepts [11]. For a pair of concepts, the authors used Hyperlinks, Edits and PageContent to define features, and then employed the MaxEnt classifier to infer prerequisite relations between concepts. Liang et al. [12] proposed a hyperlink-based method for inferring prerequisite relations among Wikipedia concepts. They compute prerequisites based on reference distance (RefD), where Wikipedia hyperlinks serve as "reference relations" among concepts. Zhou and Xiao [13] created four groups of features for prerequisite discovering, including link-based features, category-based features, content-based features, and time-based features.

Most of the related methods extracted concept prerequisite relations by using the features based on Wikipedia article content. In contrast, Sayyadiharikandeh et al. [14] proposed a measure for extracting concept prerequisite relations based on the Wikipedia clickstream data. This is the first time that user navigation information is used to predict prerequisite relations. we will use this method as a baseline method.

In addition, there are also some other studies similar to this article. Liang et al. [15,16] used the Active learning technology in prerequisite relations extraction tasks. Chen et al. [17] studied how to incorporate the knowledge structure information, especially the prerequisite relations between pedagogical concepts, into the knowledge tracing model. Qiu et al. [18–20] proposed an algorithm that integrates syntactic and semantic validations in system integration tasks, which was used in smart personal health advisor systems for comprehensive and intelligent health monitoring and guidance.

3 Concept Prerequisite Extraction

For a pair (A, B), there may be several situations in the relationship between them, including 1) B is a prerequisite of A , 2) A is a prerequisite of B , 3)the two concepts are related, but they don't have any prerequisite relation between them, 4)the two concepts are unrelated [11]. In most of the previous studies, extracting concept prerequisite relations is treated as a binary classification task. In other words, the authors only distinguished whether or not B is a prerequisite of A [11–14]. In this paper, we will also treat this task as a binary classification task.

Given a set of concept pairs $(A_1, B_1), (A_2, B_2), \cdots, (A_n, B_n)$, Wikipedia clickstream data usually cannot cover all concept pairs. In other words, there is a low likelihood that we will have clickstream data for all pairs of concepts in the datasets. Because some concept pairs are not so concerned. In this paper, we use the set of related concepts of each concept to improve the concept pair coverage in clickstream data. Before going into details, we define some basic elements used in this section. The details are shown in Table 1.

Table 1. Definition of basic elements

Terms	Explanation
A	A Wikipedia concept, which is the title of a Wikipedia article
RA	A related concept of A, i.e.the article of A contains a link to the article of RA
$f_L^{(A)}$	Set of related concepts of A
TA	A target concept of A, i.e. users followed links from the article of A to the article of TA in the recorded months of clickstream data
$f_C^{(A)}$	Set of target concepts of A

According to [12], a concept could be represented by its related concepts in the concept space. Related concepts are the concepts linked out in Wikipedia by the current concepts, and the related concepts can be obtained via Wikipedia

APIs[1]. Therefore, the prerequisite relation between $f_L^{(A)}$ and $f_L^{(B)}$ also represents the prerequisite relation between A and B. In order to increase the coverage of concept pairs, besides $''A - B''$, we also consider the clicks between the related concepts of A and B, namely $''RA - B''$, and the clicks between A and the related concepts of B, namely $''A - RB''$, as well as the clicks between the related concepts of A and the related concepts of B, namely $''RA - RB''$. In this way, we can significantly increase the coverage of concept pairs.

With the different types of Wikipedia clickstream data, we define four groups of features for concept pairs.

3.1 Features of $''A - B''$

The concept pair features based on the clickstream data of $''A - B''$ indicate the prerequisite relation between concept A and concept B. In this paper, we use 8 features for this group, all of which were proposed by Sayyadiharikandeh et al. [14]. The details of the features are as follows:

- $Weight_1(A, B)$. Total number of clicks from the article of A to the article of B.
- $Weight_1(B, A)$. Total number of clicks from the article of B to the article of A.
- $Sum_1(A, B)$. Sum of $Weight_1(A, B)$ and $Weight_1(B, A)$.
- $Diff_1(A, B)$. Absolute difference between $Weight_1(A, B)$ and $Weight_1$ (B, A).
- $Norm_1(A)$. Normalized value of $Weight_1(A, B)$.

$$Norm_1(A) = \frac{Weight_1(A, B)}{1 + Sat_1(A)} \tag{1}$$

Here, $Sat_1(i)$ is the sum of clicks from i to all its target concepts. A "1" is added to the denominator to prevent the denominator from being zero.

$$Sat_1(i) = \sum_{t \in f_c^{(i)}} Weight_1(i, t) \tag{2}$$

- $Norm_1(B)$. Normalized value of $Weight_1(B, A)$.
- $Gtm_1(A, B)$. A binary feature indicating whether $Weight_1(A, B)$ is greater than $Mean_1(A)$.

$$Gtm_1(A, B) = \begin{cases} 1, \text{ if } Weight_1(A, B) > Mean_1(A) \\ 0, \text{ else} \end{cases} \tag{3}$$

Here, $Mean_1(i)$ is the average number of clicks from i to all its target concepts.

$$Mean_1(i) = \frac{Sat_1(i)}{1 + |f_c^{(i)}|} \tag{4}$$

- $Gtm_1(B, A)$. A binary feature indicating whether $Weight_1(B, A)$ is greater than $Mean_1(B)$.

[1] https://en.wikipedia.org/w/api.php.

3.2 Features of $''RA - B''$

The features based on the clickstream data of $''RA - B''$ reflect the prerequisite relations between the concepts in $f_L^{(A)}$ and concept B. We define 8 features for this group, which are as follows:

- $Weight_2(A, B)$. The average number of clicks from the concepts in $f_L^{(A)}$ to B.

$$\begin{aligned} &Weight_2(A, B) = \overline{Weight_1(r, B)} \\ &\text{where } r \in f_L^{(A)} \text{ and } Weight_1(r, B) > 0 \end{aligned} \tag{5}$$

- $Weight_2(B, A)$. The average number of clicks from concept B to the concepts in $f_L^{(A)}$.

$$\begin{aligned} &Weight_2(B, A) = \overline{Weight_1(B, r)} \\ &\text{where } r \in f_L^{(A)} \text{ and } Weight_1(B, r) > 0 \end{aligned} \tag{6}$$

- $Sum_2(A, B)$. Sum of $Weight_2(A, B)$ and $Weight_2(B, A)$.
- $Diff_2(A, B)$. Absolute difference between $Weight_2(A, B)$ and $Weight_2$ (B, A).
- $Norm_2(A)$. Normalized value of the sum of $Weight_1(r, B)$ of the concepts in $f_L^{(A)}$.

$$Norm_2(A) = \frac{\sum_{r \in f_L^{(A)}} Weight_1(r, B)}{1 + \sum_{r \in f_L^{(A)}} Sat_1(r)} \tag{7}$$

- $Norm_2(B)$. Normalized value of $Weight_2(B, A)$.

$$Norm_2(B) = \frac{Weight_2(B, A)}{1 + Sat_1(B)} \tag{8}$$

- $Gtm_2(A, B)$. A binary feature indicating whether $Weight_2(A, B)$ is greater than $Mean_2(A)$.

$$Gtm_2(A, B) = \begin{cases} 1, \text{ if } Weight_2(A, B) > Mean_2(A) \\ 0, \text{ else} \end{cases} \tag{9}$$

  Where, $Mean_2(A)$ is the average number of clicks from the concepts in $f_L^{(A)}$ to their target concepts.

$$Mean_2(A) = \frac{\sum_{r \in f_L^{(A)}} Sat_1(r)}{1 + \sum_{r \in f_L^{(A)}} |f_C^{(r)}|} \tag{10}$$

- $Gtm_2(B, A)$. A binary feature indicating whether $Weight_2(B, A)$ is greater than $Mean_1(B)$.

$$Gtm_1(B, A) = \begin{cases} 1, \text{ if } Weight_2(B, A) > Mean_1(B) \\ 0, \text{ else} \end{cases} \tag{11}$$

3.3 Features of $''A-RB''$

The features based on the clickstream data of $''A-RB''$ imply the prerequisite relations between A and the concepts in $f_L^{(B)}$. We also define 8 features for this group, which are as follows:

- $Weight_3(A,B)$. The average number of clicks from concept A to the concepts in $f_L^{(B)}$.

$$\begin{aligned} &Weight_3(A,B) = \overline{Weight_1(A,r)} \\ &\text{where } r \in f_L^{(B)} \text{ and } Weight_1(A,r) > 0 \end{aligned} \tag{12}$$

- $Weight_3(B,A)$. The average number of clicks from the concepts in $f_L^{(B)}$ to concept A.

$$\begin{aligned} &Weight_3(B,A) = \overline{Weight_1(r,A)} \\ &\text{where } r \in f_L^{(B)} \text{ and } Weight_1(r,A) > 0 \end{aligned} \tag{13}$$

- $Sum_3(A,B)$. Sum of $Weight_3(A,B)$ and $Weight_3(B,A)$.
- $Diff_3(A,B)$. Absolute difference between $Weight_3(A,B)$ and $Weight_3$ (B,A).
- $Norm_3(A)$. Normalized value of $Weight_3(A,B)$.

$$Norm_3(A) = \frac{Weight_3(A,B)}{1 + Sat_1(A)} \tag{14}$$

- $Norm_3(B)$. Normalized value of the sum of the number of clicks from the concepts in $f_L^{(B)}$ to concept A.

$$Norm_3(B) = \frac{\sum_{r\in f_L^{(B)}} Weight_1(r,A)}{1 + \sum_{r\in f_L^{(B)}} Sat_1(r)} \tag{15}$$

- $Gtm_3(A,B)$. A binary feature indicating whether $Weight_3(A,B)$ is greater than $Mean_1(A)$.

$$Gtm_3(A,B) = \begin{cases} 1, \text{if } Weight_3(A,B) > Mean_1(A) \\ 0, \text{else} \end{cases} \tag{16}$$

- $Gtm_3(B,A)$. A binary feature indicating whether $Weight_3(B,A)$ is greater than $Mean_3(B)$.

$$Gtm_1(B,A) = \begin{cases} 1, \text{if } Weight_3(B,A) > Mean_3(B) \\ 0, \text{else} \end{cases} \tag{17}$$

Here, $Mean_3(B)$ is the average number of clicks from the concepts in $f_L^{(B)}$ to their target concepts.

$$Mean_3(B) = \frac{\sum_{r\in f_L^{(B)}} Sat_1(r)}{1 + \sum_{r\in f_L^{(B)}} |f_C^{(r)}|} \tag{18}$$

3.4 Features of "$RA - RB$"

The features based on the clickstream data of "$RA - RB$" represent the prerequisite relations between the concepts in $f_L^{(A)}$ and the concepts in $f_L^{(B)}$. We define 8 features for this group, too. The features are as follows:

- $Weight_4(A, B)$. The average number of clicks from the concepts in $f_L^{(A)}$ to the concepts in $f_L(B)$.

$$\begin{aligned} &Weight_4(A, B) = \overline{Weight_1(r_1, r_2)} \\ &\text{where} r_1 \in f_L^{(A)} \text{and} r_2 \in f_L^{(B)} \text{and} Weight_1(r_1, r_2) > 0 \end{aligned} \tag{19}$$

- $Weight_4(B, A)$. The average number of clicks from the concepts in $f_L^{(B)}$ to the concepts in $f_L^{(A)}$.

$$\begin{aligned} &Weight_4(B, A) = \overline{Weight_1(r_2, r_1)} \\ &\text{where } r_1 \in f_L^{(A)} \text{ and } r_2 \in f_L^{(B)} \text{ and } Weight_1(r_2, r_1) > 0 \end{aligned} \tag{20}$$

- $Sum_4(A, B)$. Sum of $Weight_4(A, B)$ and $Weight_4(B, A)$.
- $Diff_4(A, B)$. Absolute difference between $Weight_4(A, B)$ and $Weight_4(B, A)$.
- $Norm_4(A)$. Normalized value of the sum of the number of clicks from the concepts in $f_L^{(A)}$ to the concepts in $f_L^{(B)}$.

$$Norm_4(A) = \frac{\sum_{r_1 \in f_L^{(A)}, r_2 \in f_L^{(B)}} Weight_1(r_1, r_2)}{1 + \sum_{r_1 \in f_L^{(A)}} Sat_1(r_1)} \tag{21}$$

- $Norm_4(B)$. Normalized value of the sum of the number of clicks from the concepts in $f_L^{(B)}$ to the concepts in $f_L^{(A)}$.

$$Norm_4(B) = \frac{\sum_{r_1 \in f_L^{(A)}, r_2 \in f_L^{(B)}} Weight_1(r_2, r_1)}{1 + \sum_{r_2 \in f_L^{(B)}} Sat_1(r_2)} \tag{22}$$

- $Gtm_4(A, B)$. A binary feature indicating whether $Weight_4(A, B)$ is greater than $Mean_2(A)$.

$$Gtm_4(A, B) = \begin{cases} 1, \text{ if } Weight_4(A, B) > Mean_2(A) \\ 0, \text{ else} \end{cases} \tag{23}$$

- $Gtm_4(B, A)$. A binary feature indicating whether $Weight_4(B, A)$ is greater than $Mean_3(B)$.

$$Gtm_4(B, A) = \begin{cases} 1, \text{ if } Weight_4(B, A) > Mean_3(B) \\ 0, \text{ else} \end{cases} \tag{24}$$

It is clear that the four group of features have great similarities. The first group of features represent the direct relation between A and B, and the other three groups of features represent the indirect relations between them. On the other hand, features like $f_1(\cdot,\cdot)$ can only cover a few concept pairs. For many concept pairs, the feature $f_1(\cdot,\cdot)$ may not exist, but $f_2(\cdot,\cdot)$, $f_3(\cdot,\cdot)$ and $f_4(\cdot,\cdot)$ may exist. Therefore, we merge these similar features so as to improve the coverage of concept pairs. We define a new type of features as

$$\begin{aligned} f(\cdot,\cdot) = \alpha_1 f_1(\cdot,\cdot) + \alpha_2 f_2(\cdot,\cdot) + \alpha_3 f_3(\cdot,\cdot) + \alpha_4 f_4(\cdot,\cdot) \\ \text{st.}\alpha_1 + \alpha_2 + \alpha_3 + \alpha_4 = 1 \\ 0 \le \alpha_1, \alpha_2, \alpha_3, \alpha_4 \le 1 \end{aligned} \tag{25}$$

Here, α_1, α_2, α_3, α_4 are the weights of the four similar features, and the four weights should subject to two constraints, α_1+α_2+α_3+α_4=1 and $0 \le \alpha_1, \alpha_2, \alpha_3,$ $\alpha_4 \le 1$. At last, six new features are created in this way, including $Weight(A,B)$, $Weight(B,A)$, $Sum(A,B)$, $Diff(A,B)$, $Norm(A)$, $Norm(B)$.

In addition, since the value of the features $Gtm_*(A,B)$ can only be 0 or 1, it may not be able to get an integer result if combined in the previous manner. Therefore, we define the new feature $Gtm(A,B)$ as

$$Gtm(A,B) = \begin{cases} 1, \text{ if } Gtm_1(A,B) + Gtm_2(A,B) + Gtm_3(A,B) + Gtm_4(A,B) > 2 \\ 0, \text{ else} \end{cases} \tag{26}$$

In a similar way, we also define the feature $Gtm(B,A)$.

Thus, we have 8 new features for each concept pair, including $Weight(A,B)$, $Weight(B,A)$, $Sum(A,B)$, $Diff(A,B)$, $Norm(A)$, $Norm(B)$, $Gtm(A,B)$ and $Gtm(B,A)$. After that, we can use these features to predict the prerequisite relations among Wikipedia concepts.

4 Experiment

4.1 Dataset

In this paper, we use two datasets to evaluate the proposed method. The first one is the CMU dataset created by Talukdar and Cohen [11], which contains 1,547 pairs of Wikipedia concepts in five domains: Global warming, Meiosis, Newton's laws of motion, Parallel postulate, and Public-key cryptography. The second one is the AL-CPL dataset created by Liang et al. [15], which contains 6,529 pairs of Wikipedia concepts in four domains: Data mining, Geometry, Physics and Pre-calculus.

We first obtain clickstream data from November 2017 to April 2020 from the Wikipedia website[2], and then calculated the coverage of concept pairs for each domain. The results are shown in Table 2. The third column in the table is the domain name, the fourth column denotes the number of concept pairs in each

[2] https://dumps.wikimedia.org/other/clickstream/.

domain, the fifth column stands for the concept pair coverage of the clickstream data of $''A-B''$, the sixth column and the seventh column are the concept pair coverage based on paths with one and two intermediate nodes respectively, for example, $A-M1-B$ and $A-M1-M2-B$. Here, the $M1$ and $M2$ are the intermediate nodes. It is said that intermediate nodes can also help improve concept pair coverage [14]. And the last column is the concept pair coverage of $''A-B''$, $''RA-B''$, $''A-RB''$ and $''RA-RB''$.

It can be seen from the last column that, after using related concept sets, the clickstream data in seven domains cover more than 90% of the concept pairs. Compared with not using related concepts, i.e. the fifth column, the coverage has been greatly improved. On the AL-CPL dataset, however, the concept pair coverage based on related concept sets is slightly lower than the coverage based on one or two intermediate nodes. We suppose it is because the Wikipedia concepts in the AL-CPL dataset are selected from textbooks. Intermediate nodes strengthen the link between concepts, and increase the coverage of concept pairs.

4.2 Evaluation Results

For each domain, we apply 5-fold cross validation to evaluate the performance of the proposed method. In our experiments, we employ 7 different binary classifiers, including Random Forest (RF), NaïveBayes (NB), C4.5 Decision Tree (C4.5), Multi-Layer Perceptron (MLP), SVM with rbf kernel (SVM), Logistic Regression (LR) and AdaBoost (Ada). We measure performance of classifiers on the CMU and AL-CPL datasets in terms of the precision, recall, and F1 scores. In addition, each of the four weights $\alpha_1, \alpha_2, \alpha_3, \alpha_4$ is set to 0.25.

Table 2. Comparison of different kinds of concept pair coverage

Datasets	ID	Domains	#pairs	A-B(%)	A-M1-B(%)	A-M1-M2-B(%)	A-B/RA-B/A-RB/RA-RB(%)
CMU	D1	Global warming	400	27.25	80.50	82.00	72.25
	D2	Meiosis	347	40.35	90.20	90.78	99.71
	D3	Newton's laws of motion	400	37.75	82.75	84.25	97.00
	D4	Parallel postulate	200	29.00	79.00	79.50	94.50
	D5	Public-key cryptography	200	38.50	84.00	86.50	91.00
	Total		**1547**	**34.58**	**83.52**	**84.81**	**90.11**
AL-CPL	D6	Data mining	826	36.44	91.40	93.70	87.18
	D7	Geometry	1681	25.46	93.46	94.11	93.63
	D8	Physics	1962	29.61	98.01	98.57	95.01
	D9	Pre-calculus	2060	29.17	97.28	97.82	96.02
	Total		**6529**	**29.27**	**95.77**	**96.57**	**93.98**

Table 3 shows the evaluation results on the two datasets. It can be seen that RF outperforms other classifiers on four domains, including Meiosis (CMU), Parallel postulate (CMU), Physics (AL-CPL) and Pre-calculus (AL-CPL). Similarly, Ada performs better than other classifiers on Data mining (AL-CPL) and Geometry (AL-CPL); LR performs better than other classifiers on Newton's laws of motion (CMU). For another two domains, Global warming (CMU) and Public-key cryptography (CMU), different classifiers achieve the best P, R and F1 values. Overall, RF performs best in the concept prerequisite relations prediction tasks. On the CMU dataset, its average F1 outperforms NB, C4.5, MLP, SVM, LR and Ada by 12.7%, 8.3%, 9.5%, 2.1%, 4.9% and 0.3% respectively. On the AL-CPL dataset, its average F1 outperforms NB, C4.5, MLP, SVM, LR and Ada by 9.2%, 8.1%, 14.7%, 8.2%, 6.1% and 2.2% respectively. Consequently, we use RF in the following experiments.

Table 3. Classification results of the proposed method (%)

Classifiers		CMU					AL-CPL			
		D1	D2	D3	D4	D5	D6	D7	D8	D9
RF	P	75.9	**91.2**	77.3	**89.3**	71.8	66.0	72.8	**78.6**	**76.1**
	R	81.9	**92.2**	84.3	**90.6**	82.2	67.2	74.2	**81.6**	**76.8**
	F1	78.5	**91.7**	80.5	**89.8**	76.6	65.4	72.8	**78.8**	**76.4**
NB	P	41.7	74.2	80.2	79.5	77.3	46.8	63.8	70.6	64.6
	R	28.5	81.6	83.3	84.0	82.2	55.6	70.2	76.7	71.2
	F1	20.8	77.0	81.0	80.8	**79.1**	46.2	63.0	72.1	63.5
C4.5	P	77.4	76.8	77.7	73.4	77.1	64.0	70.1	73.4	70.2
	R	74.8	75.3	77.8	71.1	75.1	61.9	70.4	73.4	69.8
	F1	75.6	75.9	77.4	71.1	75.7	62.4	70.2	73.3	69.9
MLP	P	74.6	74.6	79.1	75.5	**78.8**	64.3	62.5	71.1	64.0
	R	84.1	76.6	75.1	82.7	79.6	56.5	63.7	72.6	61.3
	F1	78.9	74.3	76.3	78.6	78.7	57.7	60.2	70.5	60.7
SVM	P	73.9	71.4	76.3	80.5	72.1	48.1	64.1	69.6	67.1
	R	**85.8**	84.5	86.4	87.2	**84.8**	68.9	71.1	79.5	71.8
	F1	79.4	77.4	80.6	82.2	77.9	56.5	60.1	70.7	60.8
LR	P	77.2	71.3	**84.1**	82.5	74.4	58.9	68.7	74.3	67.1
	R	85.5	83.2	**87.0**	87.2	84.2	68.0	71.7	79.1	72.0
	F1	**80.3**	76.7	**82.6**	82.9	78.5	57.6	62.8	70.7	62.3
Ada	P	**78.6**	77.5	76.6	80.0	72.9	**69.0**	**73.4**	76.6	74.1
	R	85.1	82.0	84.3	84.0	80.9	**69.8**	**74.5**	79.9	75.2
	F1	80.1	78.6	79.9	81.5	76.6	**66.2**	**73.5**	75.6	74.2

4.3 Comparison with Baselines

We further compare our approach with two representative methods. The first method is the RefD method proposed by Liang et al. [12]. The authors used two different weights for the related concepts of a Wikipedia concept, namely Equal and Tf-idf. In our experiments, we will compare our approach with both of them, i.e. RefD-Equal and RefD-Tfidf.

Another baseline method is proposed by Sayyadiharikandeh et al. [14]. The authors also identified concept prerequisite relations with Wikipedia clickstream data. They used intermediate nodes to improve concept pair coverage, and there were three strategies in their work: Direct link (no intermediate node), 1 intermediate node, and 2 intermediate nodes. In this paper, we will compare our approach with all of the three strategies.

Table 4 shows the comparison results of the proposed method and the baseline methods in terms of accuracy. We find that our method outperforms all the baseline methods on seven of the nine domains. Furthermore, the average accuracy of our method on CMU outperforms RefD-Equal, RefD-Tfidf, Direct link, 1 intermediate node, and 2 intermediate nodes by 31%, 29.5%, 20%, 13.1% and 12.5%, respectively. On the AL-CPL dataset, our method also beats others with best average accuracy. Its average accuracy outperforms RefD-Equal, RefD-Tfidf, Direct link, 1 intermediate node, and 2 intermediate nodes by 10.3%, 9%, 14.7%, 3.1% and 1.7%, respectively.

Table 4. Comparison with baselines (%)

Methods	CMU					AL-CPL			
	D1	D2	D3	D4	D5	D6	D7	D8	D9
RefD-Equal	57.4	53.0	63.7	70.5	55.2	**70.1**	57.1	68.4	72.7
RefD-Tfidf	60.1	55.7	64.6	67.9	57.7	68.4	57.2	66.4	**78.9**
Direct link	81.3	59.3	72.0	72.7	66.7	58.3	58.8	62.1	67.5
1 Intermediate node	78.0	75.4	84.2	70.0	72.7	68.9	75.8	72.4	76.3
2 Intermediate nodes	76.3	75.4	84.2	83.3	66.7	68.8	75.5	78.3	75.4
Proposed method	**91.8**	**92.2**	**89.7**	**90.6**	**83.3**	69.4	**76.4**	**81.6**	76.8

4.4 Feature Contribution Analysis

In order to investigate the importance of each feature in the proposed method, we perform a contribution analysis with different features. Here, we run our approach 8 times on the Pre-calculus (AL-CPL) dataset. In each time, one feature is removed. We record the decrease of accuracy for each removed feature. Table 5 lists the evaluation results after ignoring different features.

According to the decrement of accuracy, we find that all the proposed features are useful in inferring concept prerequisite relations. Especially, we observe that

$Norm(B)$, decreasing our accuracy by 7.3%, plays the most important role. In fact, $Norm(B)$ represents the proportion of the number of clicks from B (or related concepts of B) to A (or related concepts of A) in the number of clicks from B (or related concepts of B) to all their target concepts. The larger the proportion, the stronger the dependence of concept B on concept A. Therefore, after removing this feature, the overall concept prerequisite relations prediction accuracy drops the most. All the relevant code and data of the experiment have been released on github[3].

Table 5. Contribution analysis of different features (%)

Features	Accuracy
$Weight(A, B)$	74.5%(–2.3%)
$Weight(B, A)$	73.7%(–3.1%)
$Sum(A, B)$	74.5%(–2.3%)
$Diff(A, B)$	73.3%(–3.5%)
$Norm(A)$	73.2%(–3.6%)
$Norm(B)$	**69.5%(–7.3%)**
$Gtm(A, B)$	74.1%(–2.7%)
$Gtm(B, A)$	73.8%(–3.0%)

5 Conclusion

This paper studies the problem of concept prerequisite relation extraction in Wikipedia. We used Wikipedia clickstream data and related concept sets to define concept pair features, and then inferred whether there was a prerequisite relation between two concepts. Experiments show that, the proportion of concept pairs covered by clickstream data has been significantly improved. And at the meanwhile, we can also accurately identify prerequisite relations.

However, our current work is only appropriate for Wikipedia concepts. Some of the main concepts of learning resources may not exist in Wikipedia. In the future, we will study the method of prerequisite relation extraction that can be used for both Wikipedia concepts and non-Wikipedia concepts. And then build concept graphs with concept prerequisite relations. The concept graphs can help us improve various intelligent tutoring systems.

Acknowledgement. This work is supported by the National Natural Science Foundation of China (No. 61977021), the Technology Innovation Special Program of Hubei Province (Nos. 2018ACA133 and 2019ACA144).

[3] https://github.com/Little-spider2001/Data-set-and-code-program-of-KSEM-2021-paper.

References

1. Wang, S., et al.: Using prerequisites to extract concept maps from textbooks. In: Proceedings of the 25th ACM International on Conference on Information and Knowledge Management, pp. 317–226 (2016)
2. Wang, S., Liu, L.: Prerequisite concept maps extraction for automaticassessment. In: Proceedings of the 25th International Conference Companion on World Wide Web, pp. 519–521 (2016)
3. Lu, W., Zhou, Y., Yu, J., Jia, C.: Concept extraction and prerequisite relation learning from educational data. In: Proceedings of the AAAI Conference on Artificial Intelligence, pp. 9678–9685 (2019)
4. Pan, L., Li, C.J., Li, J.Z., Tang, J.: Prerequisite relation learning for concepts in moocs. In: Proceedings of the 55th Annual Meeting of the Association for Computational Linguistics, pp. 1447–1456 (2017)
5. Pan, L., Wang, X., Li, C., Li, J., Tang, J.: Course concept extraction in moocs via embedding-based graph propagation. In: Proceedings of the Eighth International Joint Conference on Natural Language Processing, pp. 875–884 (2017)
6. Roy, S., Madhyastha, M., Lawrence, S., Rajan, V.: Inferring concept prerequisite relations from online educational resources. In: Proceedings of the AAAI Conference on Artificial Intelligence, pp. 9589–9594 (2019)
7. Yang, Y., Liu, H., Carbonell, J., Ma, W.: Concept graph learning from educational data. In: Proceedings of the Eighth ACM International Conference on Web Search and Data Mining, pp. 159–168 (2015)
8. Liu, H., Ma, W., Yang, Y., Carbonell, J.: Learning concept graphs from online educational data. J. Artif. Intell. Res. **55**, 1059–1090 (2016)
9. Liang, C., Ye, J., Wu, Z.H., Pursel, B., Giles, C.L.: Recovering concept prerequisite relations from university course dependencies. In: Thirty-First AAAI Conference on Artificial Intelligence (2017)
10. Gordon, J., Zhu, L.H., Galstyan, A., Natarajan, P., Burns, G.: Modeling concept dependencies in a scientific corpus. In: Proceedings of the 54th Annual Meeting of the Association for Computational Linguistics, pp. 866–875 (2016)
11. Talukdar, P., Cohen, W.: Crowdsourced comprehension: predicting prerequisite structure in Wikipedia. In: Proceedings of the Seventh Workshop on Building Educational Applications Using NLP, pp. 307–315. Association for Computational Linguistics (2012)
12. Liang, C., Wu, Z.H., Huang, W.Y., Giles, C.L.: Measuring prerequisite relations among concepts. In: Proceedings of the 2015 Conference on Empirical Methods in Natural Language Processing, pp. 1668–1674 (2015)
13. Zhou, Y., Xiao, K.: Extracting prerequisite relations among concepts in Wikipedia. In: 2019 International Joint Conference on Neural Networks (IJCNN), pp. 1–8. IEEE (2019)
14. Sayyadiharikandeh, M., Gordon, J., Ambite, J.L., Lerman, K.: Finding prerequisite relations using the Wikipedia clickstream. In: Companion Proceedings of the 2019 World Wide Web Conference, pp. 1240–1247 (2019)
15. Liang, C., Ye, J., Wang, S., Pursel, B., Giles, C.L.: Investigating active learning for concept prerequisite learning. In: Thirty-Second AAAI Conference on Artificial Intelligence (2018)
16. Liang, C., Ye, J., Zhao, H., Pursel, B., Giles, C.L.: Active learning of strict partial orders: a case study on concept prerequisite relations. arXiv preprint arXiv:1801.06481(2018)

17. Chen, P., Lu, Y., Zheng, V.W., Pian, Y.: Prerequisite-driven deep knowledge tracing. In: 2018 IEEE International Conference on Data Mining (ICDM), pp. 39–48. IEEE (2018)
18. Chen, M., Zhang, Y., Qiu, M.K., Guizani, N., Hao, Y.X.: SPHA: smart personal health advisor based on deep analytics. IEEE Commun. Mag. **56**(3), 164–169 (2018)
19. Tao, L.X., Golikov, S., Gai, K.K., Qiu, M.K.: A reusable software component for integrated syntax and semantic validation for services computing. In: IEEE Symposium on Service-Oriented System Engineering, pp. 127–132. IEEE (2015)
20. Gai, K., Qiu, M.: Reinforcement learning-based content-centric services in mobile sensing. IEEE Netw. **32**(4), 34–39 (2018)

Clustering Massive-Categories and Complex Documents via Graph Convolutional Network

Qingchao Zhao[1(✉)], Jing Yang[1(✉)], Zhengkui Wang[2(✉)], Yan Chu[1(✉)], Wen Shan[3(✉)], and Isfaque Al Kaderi Tuhin[2(✉)]

[1] Harbin Engineering University, Harbin, China
{zhaoqc418,yangjing,chuyan}@hrbeu.edu.cn
[2] Singapore Institute of Technology, Singapore, Singapore
{zhengkui.wang,tuhin.kaderi}@singaporetech.edu.sg
[3] Singapore University of Social Sciences, Singapore, Singapore
viviensw@suss.edu.sg

Abstract. In recent years, a significant amount of text data are being generated on the Internet and in digital applications. Clustering the unlabeled documents becomes an essential task in many areas such as automated document management and information retrieval. A typical approach of document clustering consists of two major steps, where step one extracts proper features to model documents for clustering and step two applies the clustering methods to categorize the documents. Recent research document clustering algorithms are mostly focusing on step one to finding high-quality embedding or vector representation, after which adopting traditional clustering methods for the second step. Or infer the document representation based on the predetermined k clusters. However, the traditional clustering methods are designed with simplistic assumption of the data distribution that fails to cope with the documents with complex distribution and a small number of clusters i.e. , less than 50. In addition to this, the previous need a predetermined k. In this paper, we introduce Graph Convolutional Network into the document clustering (instead of using the traditional clustering methods) and propose a supervised GCN-based document clustering algorithm, DC-GCN which is able to handle documents in noisy, huge and complex distribution by a learnable similarity estimator. Our proposed algorithm first adopts a GCN-based confidence estimator to learn the document position in a cluster via the affinity graph, and then adopts a GCN-based similarity estimator to learn the document similarity by constructing the doc-word graphs integrating the local neighbor documents and its keywords. Based on the confidence and similarity, the document clusters are finally formed. Our experimental evaluations show that DC-GCN achieves 21.88%, 17.35% and 15.58% performance improvement on F_p over the best baseline algorithms in three different datasets.

Keywords: Graph Convolutional Network · Document clustering · Supervised clustering · Massive-categories · Supervised learning

H. Qiu et al. (Eds.): KSEM 2021, LNAI 12815, pp. 27–39, 2021.
https://doi.org/10.1007/978-3-030-82136-4_3

1 Introduction

Document clustering or text clustering is an important task in data mining. It aims to partition a pool of text documents into distinctive clusters based on the content similarity such that the documents in a cluster contain similar property in comparison to documents in other clusters. It has been extensively used in many applications such as topic tracking and detection, information retrieval, public opinion analysis and monitoring, and news recommend system, etc. [1].

Traditional document clustering methods are generally conducted in two steps. The first step is the vector representation of document features, which represents the high-dimensional, variable-length documents with low-dimensional fixed-length vectors. Two commonly used feature extraction approaches are proposed either based on topic models e.g. Latent dirichlet allocation (LDA) or the embedding e.g. Doc2vec, FastText [10]. Recently, there are also some clustering methods that extract document features based on the clustering task e.g. , Graph Theory [2], CNN [15], autoencoder [13,19], contractive learning [8,9]. The second step of the document clustering method aims to cluster all the documents based on the extracted features. In this stage, traditional clustering are normally adopted to cluster the documents, such as K-means, DBSCAN, Spectral, Single-Pass, etc.

The existing document clustering approaches focused more on how to get high-quality embedding in the first step. However, in the second step, they adopt the traditional clustering methods that usually result in unsatisfactory performance for the documents with complex distribution and a large number of categories, as they are designed based on simplistic assumption of data distribution with a small number of categories [2,8,9,13,15,19]. For example, K-means-based is only suitable for data distribution around the cluster center. DBSCAN is designed for clusters with uniform density. Spectral is suitable for clusters with similar cluster sizes. The Single-Pass is sensitive to the input order of clustered instances [4,16]. Moreover, most clustering methods require to know the predetermined number of clusters k in order to make accurate clusters [8,15]. Existing approaches work well when the number of clusters is small and provided, and the documents are in a particular distribution. However, there are many application scenarios which contain massive categories of documents with complex data distribution. For example, personalized recommendations for decentralized we-media content need massive categories of text which can not be just a few categories. Meanwhile, the different sizes of clusters and the richness of the contents lead to complex data distributions. The data in these domains have different characteristics compared with the datasets that have been studied before. First, the data is highly noised with a complex distribution such as a lot of non-convex clusters. Second, the number of clusters is large, which is almost impossible to pre-determine. These characteristics have made existing document clustering algorithms ineffective and inefficient unfortunately. This calls for a new approach to tackle the challenges.

To tackle the issues of massive document clustering with complex distribution in the second step of the document clustering, we convert the clustering problem into a structural pattern learning problem using Graph Convolutional Network (GCN). GCN has been proven effective in learning the patterns in the affinity graphs [14,17,18]. In this paper, we model all the documents as an affinity graph. Based on this, we propose a GCN-based clustering algorithm, DC-GCN which enables effective clustering for complex documents with massive categories. We define confidence based on the characteristic of clusters in the affinity graph. The high confidence of a document node defines the distance between the document to the cluster center where more neighbors have the same label. DC-GCN consists of two important steps. In the first step, we learn the confidence of each document node through its context structure using a GCN-based confidence estimator. In the second step, we learn the similarity of two documents via a GCN-based similarity estimator based on doc-word graphs including both documents and keywords relationship information. Based on predicted confidence and similarity, all the documents can be easily grouped into clusters.

Our key contributions of this paper are three-fold. (1) We make the first attempt to introduce Graph Convolutional Network into the document clustering problem. (2) We propose an innovative supervised GCN-based document clustering algorithm, DC-GCN which enables effective and efficient clustering for massive-category documents with complex distribution. DC-GCN does not require the data with a particular distribution and pre-determined cluster number. It is an intelligent learnable model integrating both documents and its keywords information to cluster massive-categories documents. (3) We provide experimental evaluations based on real datasets with various baseline clustering methods. The results confirm the effectiveness of DC-GCN.

The rest of the paper is organized as follows. Section 2 introduces the related works. In Sect. 3, we present our proposed solution. Section 4 and Sect. 5 provide the experimental evaluations and conclusion respectively.

2 Related Works

Document Features Extraction. Much research effort has been devoted to identify the best document feature representations and extractions as the first step of the document clustering algorithm. The simplest method is to use document word frequency to filter out irrelevant features. For example, the main idea of Term Frequency–Inverse Document Frequency (TF-TDF). The purpose of Latent Semantic Analysis (LSA) is to discover hidden semantic dimensions-namely "topic" or "Concept" from the document by singular value decomposition (SVD), then pLSA and Latent Dirichlet Allocation (LDA) were developed Later. There are also neural network-based methods. For example, Doc2vec is an unsupervised learning algorithm based on Word2vec. The algorithm predicts a vector based on the context of each word to represent different documents. The structure of the model potentially overcomes the lack of semantics of the word bag model Shortcomings like LDA. Recently, Xu, Jiaming proposed STC2 which uses CNN to fit the text and use the unsupervised learning method to get the text label. After fitting, K-means is used to cluster the hidden layer variables, and finally the result is obtained [15]. Autoencoder-based methods combine the loss of K-means essentially. Given that there are k clusters, Dejiao Zhang proposed a MIXAE architecture. This model optimizes two parts at the same time: a set of autoencoders where each learns the distribution similar objects; a mixture assignment neural network, which inputs the concatenated latent vectors from the autoencoders set and infers the distribution over clusters [21]. By using the sample augmentations, Bassoma Diallo propose a deep embedding clustering framework based on contractive autoencoder (need a k) with Frobenius norm [8]. These methods still needs a predetermined cluster number k and suit for less-categories data (usually less than 20). Different to these works that aims to tackle the issues in document extraction, our work is orthogonal to them by investigating how to improve the second step of clustering performance without a predetermined k.

Clustering Methods. After the document feature extraction, the document clustering algorithm adopts clustering method to categorize the documents. The first kind is based on agglomerative methods such as Hierarchical Agglomerative Clustering (HAC). HAC has been studied extensively in the clustering literature for document data, and FastHAC is proposed to reduce the calculation [7]. K-medoid and K-means are two classic distance-based partitioning algorithms. There are also some based on the density, such as DBcsan, MeanShift, Density Peak clustering [5,6,11]. Spectral clustering is a Graph-based method. Spectral clustering can also be extended to social networks or Web-based networks [12]. However, all these commonly used clustering algorithms are based on simplistic assumption on the data distribution that fails to cope with the complex distribution or required canedetermine datasets cluster number. Differently, DC-GCN is able to handle any complex distribution with unknown cluster number enabled by its learnable model.

3 Problem Formulation and Our Solution

3.1 Framework Overview

Our proposed GCN-based clustering algorithm, DC-GCN consists of the two similar steps (feature extraction step followed by clustering step) as other document clustering algorithm. In DC-GCN, we first adopt the most popular vector representation, Doc2vec to extract the features for each document. As how to extract features is not our focus, we will omit the detail here. Note that DC-GCN is a general framework which can incorporate any feature representation.

After extracting the document features, in the next step, we construct the affinity graph by calculating the affinity (cosine similarity) between document features. The affinity graph $G(V, E)$ consists of all the documents as the nodes in V and the edges in E that are constructed between any vertex with its k nearest neighbors. Figure 1 provides the whole framework overview. Intuitively, our algorithm tackles the clustering problem by predicting the confidence of the nodes and the similarity of the two nodes. We first adopt GCN to develop a confidence estimator to predict the confidence of each document indicating the position of the document in the cluster. A document with high confidence is close to the cluster center. Otherwise, it is far away from the cluster center. We further propose a similarity estimator to predict the similarity of two documents, where similarity indicates the probability for two documents belonging to the same cluster. Consider that the keywords inside documents provide valuable evidence of the similarity of two documents. We further add the keywords into the learning graph to make an accurate document similarity prediction. After the obtaining the confidence and similarity, we find a path from each node to the cluster center and get final clusters easily.

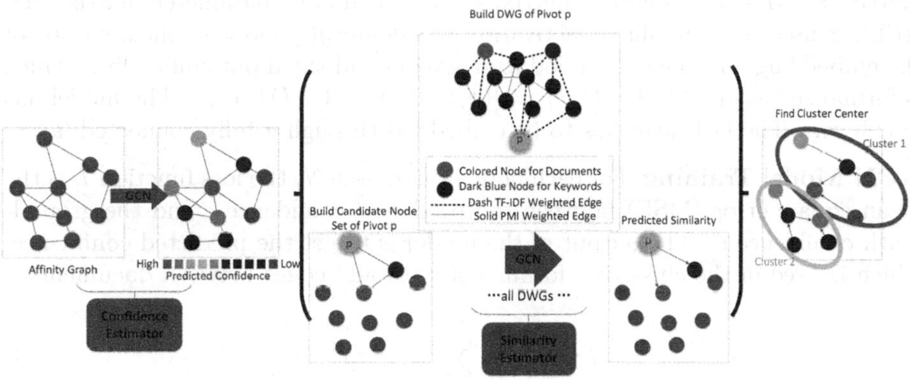

Fig. 1. Overview of DC-GCN framework. (Color figure online)

3.2 Confidence Estimator

According to the observation, when a document is close to the cluster center, its neighbor documents are usually more similar and in the same cluster. For a document at the margin of a cluster, there are usually other labeled documents in its neighbors. We define the confidence of a document as follows.

Definition: Confidence. The confidence C_i of document i is defined as the position of i in its cluster and formally calculated by:

$$c_i = \frac{1}{|N_i|} \sum_{v_j \in N_i} \begin{cases} a_{ij} & l_i = l_j \\ -a_{ij} & l_i \neq l_j \end{cases} \tag{1}$$

where N_i is the neighborhood of document i , a_{ij} is the affinity value (cosine similarity) between two documents i and j. l_i is the ground-truth label of document i. A higher the value of c indicates that the node is close to the cluster center. To calculate the confidence of each document, we first build an affinity graph. For each document, we select its k nearest documents based on their extracted features and build the edge among them. This affinity graph with the original feature is the input of confidence estimator GCN model.

GCN-Based Confidence Learning Model. In order to learn the structural patterns of nodes with similar confidence, the confidence estimator is empowered by a GCN model. The input of the GCN model is the adjacency matrix of the affinity graph and the node feature matrix, while the output is the confidence of each node. The formal representation of each layer of the model is:

$$F_{l+1} = \mathrm{RELU}(g(\tilde{D}^{-1}(A+I), F_l)W_l) \tag{2}$$

where $\tilde{D}_{ii} = \Sigma_j(A+I)_j$ is the diagonal matrix, A is the initial adjacency matrix, and I is the identity matrix. W_l is a trainable parameter matrix, and RELU is used as the nonlinear activation. We define $g(\cdot,\cdot)$ as the concatenation of the embedding after neighborhood aggregation and the input embedding, which is formalized as $g(\tilde{D}^{-1}(A+I), F_l) = [(F_l)^\top, (\tilde{D}^{-1}(A+I)F_l)^\top]^\top$. The model has four layers. The last layer has to be embedded through a fully connected layer.

GCN Model Training. For each node in node-set N, the loss function L is the mean square error (MSE) between the predicted confidence c and the ground-truth confidence c'. The output of the model is to get the predicted confidence, which is used in the clustering forming step to add edges between documents.

$$Loss = \frac{1}{N}\sum_{i=1}^{N}|c_i - c_i'|^2 \tag{3}$$

3.3 Similarity Estimator

The aim of the similarity estimator is to learn the similarity of the documents, which is defined as the probability (a value between 0 and 1) of them with the same label. In ground truth, if two documents are with two different labels/clusters, the similarity is 0. If they are with same labels, it is 1.

To obtain the accurate similarity between documents, both the local context and the keywords information play an important role in determining the similarity. The local context of a document refers to the nearest neighbor documents that are close to each other. The keywords appeared in each document are essential information for us to determine the similarity. Therefore, in our similarity estimator, our GCN-based model is proposed to learn the similarity based on heterogeneous learning graphs, namely doc-word graphs that include both the documents and keywords. Our heterogeneous learning doc-word graphs are constructed via below three steps.

Step 1: Node candidates of doc-word graphs. For a given document p, we form a pivoted learning doc-word graph $DWG_p = G(V_p, E_p)$ of it, which consists of p's n nearest neighbor documents and the keywords of each document in V_p, and the edge set E_p. The nearest neighbor documents are those needed to measure the similarity. And, we unfold the document by capturing its keywords to enrich its semantic meaning of the doc-word graph. These keywords provide detail measures to determine the similarity of the documents instead of using only the Doc2vec information.

Step 2: Build the input adj matrix. Since DWG_p is a heterogeneous graph, we design two types of edges: the edge between the document and the keyword (doc-word edge) and the edge between words (word-word edge). It is worth noting that they are different from the affinity graph in confidence estimator, the doc-word graph does not have the doc-doc edge. For doc-word edge, we assign an edge weight with TF-IDF. For the word-word edge, the point-wise mutual information (PMI) calculates the edge weight between words like TextGCN [20]. Finally, based on the E_p and the edge weight in the sub-graph. The formal description of the element A_{ij} of the adjacency matrix A is as follows:

$$A_{ij} = \begin{cases} PMI(i;j) & i,j \; are \; words, \; PMI(i,j) > 0 \\ TF-IDF_{ij} & i \text{ is document, } j \text{ is word} \\ 1 & i = j \\ 0 & otherwise \end{cases} \tag{4}$$

Step 3: Build the feature matrix. We design a pseudo-one-hot encoding to build the nodes' feature which is more efficient than the one-hot encoding. First, we collect all the keywords, and set the feature of the keywords into one-hot vectors like an identity matrix I whose dimension is equal to the number of keywords. The document node feature is a normalized vocabulary vector. For example, the vectors of the three keywords in corpus w_1, w_2, w_3 are (1,0,0), (0,1,0), (0,0,1). The document d_1 contains the words w_1 and w_3, and the vocabulary vector after the normalization of the document d_1 is (0.5, 0, 0.5).

GCN-Based Similarity Learning Model. Based on the constructed doc-word graphs, we adopt a two-layer GCN model to learn the document classification task. The formal expression is provided as follows.

$$Z = \mathbf{softmax}(\tilde{A}\mathbf{ReLU}(\tilde{A}XW_0)W_1) \tag{5}$$

Where X is pseudo-one-hot encoding of the documents and words, $\tilde{A} = D^{-\frac{1}{2}}AD^{-\frac{1}{2}}$. W_0 and W_1 are the trainable parameter matrix and $\text{softmax}(x_i) = \frac{1}{Z}exp(x_i)$, $Z = \sum_i exp(x_i)$.

Training of Similarity Estimator. For a pivot node i, if a neighbor j shares the same label with i, the label is set to 1, otherwise it is 0.

$$r_{ij} = \begin{cases} 1, \; l_i = l_j \\ 0, \; l_i \neq l_j \end{cases}, v_j \in G_i \tag{6}$$

Where G_i is the sub-graph of pivot i, l_i is the label of the node v_i. The model predicts the similarity that reflects whether two nodes have the same label. The loss function is MSE.

$$L_E(G_i) = \sum_{v_i \in G_i} \left| r_{ij} - r'_{ij} \right|^2 \tag{7}$$

3.4 Form Clusters via Confidence and Similarity

Recall that the document confidence reflects its position in a cluster and the similarity of two documents indicates the probability of them in one cluster. For each node, we locate all its neighbors with higher confidence and add an edge with the most similar neighbor. In this way, each node could locate another similar node which has a higher confidence with the position closer to the cluster center. By so doing, we can find a path from each document to the cluster center and form the clusters easily.

3.5 Complexity Analysis and Discussion

The time complexity of the whole algorithm consists of three parts: confidence estimator, similarity estimator, and clustering. In confidence estimator, building affinity graph costs $O(n\log n)$. The graph convolution can be efficiently implemented as the sparse-dense matrix multiplication, a complexity $O(|\epsilon|)$. In similarity estimator, the cost of the preparation of similarity estimator is $O(n' m \log m)$, where m is the number of the candidate documents and keywords which is far less than the number of keywords in the corpus, and n' is the number of pivots with high confidence we choose. With the affinity graph in confidence estimator, the last step of forming clusters is $O(n \cdot k)$, where k is the number of neighbor documents which is far less than n.

4 Experiments and Performance Analysis

Dataset. Most of the available document datasets are all designed for the classification task with a small number of (i.e., below 20) categories, which can not represent the application with massive categories. To evaluate the capability of DC-GCN handling the massive categories, we use the crawled Wikipedia dataset which includes more than 4000 categories. To verify scalability of method, we use three different scale datasets as shown in Table 1 and there is no overlap between the training and test datasets.

Method Comparison and Metrics. Recall that the most recent document clustering algorithms all aim to improve the quality of the document feature extraction following by using the classic clustering methods [2,8,9,13,15,19]. DC-GCN is orthogonal to recent document clustering algorithm (focus on feature extraction with K) and aims to change the second step on the clustering performance. We compare the proposed method with a series of clustering baselines, which includes the classic clustering methods widely used in recent document clustering algorithms i.e. K-means, mini-batch K-means (MK-means), DBSCAN, HAC, MeanShift, Spectral [5,6,11]) and the streaming document clustering algorithm Single-Pass (S-pass). Additionally, to study the performance improvement of the proposed GCN-based similarity estimator over the existing similarity calculation approach, we develop another method (CE) that only includes the proposed GCN-based confidence estimator and Euclidean distance evaluation to

Table 1. Wikipedia datasets introduction

	#Clusters	#Instances	Domain
Training dataset	1851	10805	Society, Geography, Universe, Politics, Concepts, Events, Government, Economy, Education, Energy, Engineering, Entities, Ethics, Business
Test dataset1	2660	15623	Technology, Health, Culture, Nature, Sports, Science, Entertainment, Religion, Philosophy, Belief, Mathematics, World
Test dataset2	2228	13094	Technology, Health, Culture, Nature, Sports, Science Entertainment
Test dataset3	1688	9921	Technology, Health, Culture, Nature, Sports

form the clusters. For fair comparison, we use unsupervised Doc2vec extracted features that do not require a predetermined K instead of previous document-clustering-based feature extraction.

We adopt three most popular evaluation metrics to evaluate the effect of clustering, namely Normalized Mutual Information (NMI), Pair-wise F-score and BCubed F-score [3]. Meanwhile, we also compare the inferring running time of different methods after the one-off training time.

Clustering Effectiveness and Runtime Analysis. For all baseline methods, we report the best results by tuning the hyper-parameter. Table 2 provides the detail results in three datasets. From the results, we have the following observations: (1) Among all the baseline algorithms, K-means performs nearly the best with the longest inferring time when K is set as the ground-truth number. However, K-means is highly depending on the predefined number of clusters k. The performance will highly decrease if the k is set as the wrong number. We also can infer that all K-means-based methods converge very slowly when the number of categories increases. (2) The sampling method of mini-batch K-means (MK-means) can speed up calculations by losing part of the accuracy. (3) The effect of spectral clustering is second to K-means in all baselines, and the computational efficiency is much higher than K-means. But, solving features Value decomposition leads to a large number of calculations and memory requirements, thereby limiting the application of spectral clustering. (4) DBSCAN is almost the most efficient among all algorithms when given the similarity matrix, but it assumes that the density of each cluster is similar. Therefore, when the cluster distribution is complex, DBSCAN loses efficiency. (5) Although HAC does not require a pre-determined number of clusters, the iterative merging process involves a lot of computational budgets and outliers can have a great impact. (6) The overall result of MeanShift is worse than K-means and spectral clustering, but it has a slow convergence speed and only faster than K-means in all baselines. (7) The effect of single-pass is also good among the baselines, but single-pass is sensitive to the input order of documents. The outliers also have a great influence on the results. (8) Confidence Estimator is better than half of the baseline results. Through more than one thousand classes of training, the results of two thousand clusters can be predicted, which proves its effectiveness and scalable in capturing important structural characteristics of nodes. (9) DC-GCN outperforms other algorithms in all the different datasets and metrics with comparable inferring time. The final column of Table 2 provides the DC-GCN's percentage of performance improvement over the best baseline (underlined) for that metric. This confirms the effectiveness and efficiency of the proposed approach empowered by the learning capability of confidence and similarity estimators.

Table 2. Performance comparison results

	Methods	K-means	MK-means	Spectral	HAC	DBSCAN	MeanShift	S-pass	CE	DC-GCN	Δ(%)
Wiki test set1	F_P	0.2248	0.1359	0.1945	0.0008	0.0009	0.0140	0.0430	0.1496	**0.2740**	21.88
	F_B	0.4172	0.3894	0.3589	0.3619	0.4437	0.3922	0.3766	0.3539	**0.4675**	5.36
	NMI	0.8461	0.8196	0.8325	0.4112	0.5454	0.8056	0.7715	0.8120	**0.8714**	2.99
	Clusters	2661	2633	2658	3250	4639	4533	2935	1881	4677	–
	Time	2041 s	123 s	169 s	25 s	2 s	839 s	93 s	2 s	423 s	–
Wiki test set2	F_P	0.2432	0.1660	0.2024	0.0009	0.0012	0.0188	0.0437	0.1424	**0.2854**	17.35
	F_B	0.4300	0.4061	0.3701	0.3836	0.4600	0.4028	0.3547	0.3533	**0.4792**	4.17
	NMI	0.8481	0.8254	0.8323	0.4430	0.5813	0.8126	0.7616	0.8057	**0.8713**	2.73
	Clusters	2228	2220	2225	2908	4108	3979	2642	1446	3813	–
	Time	991 s	99 s	237 s	29 s	2 s	724 s	81 s	2 s	173 s	–
Wiki test set3	F_P	0.2688	0.1862	0.2231	0.0009	0.0017	0.0274	0.0725	0.2260	**0.3107**	15.58
	F_B	0.4538	0.4310	0.3865	0.3836	0.4736	0.4348	0.4138	0.4209	**0.4941**	4.32
	NMI	0.8504	0.8283	0.8322	0.4430	0.6004	0.8155	0.7894	0.8340	**0.8710**	2.42
	Clusters	1688	1675	1686	2908	3153	3063	2039	1523	2787	–
	Time	812 s	59 s	118 s	13 s	3 s	402 s	44 s	2 s	78 s	–

Candidate Document Selection in Doc-Word Graph. In this experiment, we study the impact of the different candidate documents selection schemes in DC-GCN. We design two different schemes to select the candidate documents adding to the doc-word graph of a given pivot document p. The first scheme (KNN-DWG) adds all the k nearest neighbor documents of the pivot p to its DWG, while the second scheme (FC-DWG) only adds the nearest neighbor documents whose confidence is bigger than p. The second scheme filters out those documents in the nearest neighbor with low confidence value, which results in less nodes in the DWG and improves the calculation efficiency. Table 3 shows the comparison results of these two methods. As expected, FC-DWG is faster than KNN-DWG, as FC-DWG generates smaller size of Doc-word graphs. Interestingly, we also find that FC-DWG is able to generate comparable performance

Table 3. Results of different candidate selection approaches

Methods	Wiki test set1		Wiki test set2		Wiki test set3	
	KNN-DWG	FC-DWG	KNN-DWG	FC-DWG	KNN-DWG	FC-DWG
F_P	0.2615	**0.2740**	0.2746	**0.2854**	0.2974	**0.3107**
F_B	0.4579	**0.4675**	0.4708	**0.4792**	0.4845	**0.4941**
NMI	0.8710	**0.8714**	0.8706	**0.8713**	0.8700	**0.8710**
Clusters	4897	4677	3959	3813	2901	2787
Time	587 s	423 s	190 s	173 s	97 s	78 s

with KNN-DWG, which indicates that remaining those high-confidence documents in the doc-word graphs is sufficient for the learning problem.

Comparison Between Static and Dynamic Affinity Graphs. In DC-GCN, there are two possible approaches based on static affinity graph or dynamic affinity graph in calculating the confidence and similarity. The static affinity graph uses original affinity graph in each layer of the GCN, and finding the k nearest neighbor documents for doc-word graph generation is also based on original affinity graph and Doc2vec features. Differently, the dynamic approach rebuilds the affinity graph after each graph covolutional layer in GCN, and the finding KNN documents is also based on the updated affinity graph and updated features. This experiment aims to study the performance difference between the static approach in calculating the confidence (CE(s)) and similarity (SE(s)), and the dynamic approach (CE(d) and SE(d)). As shown in Table 4, in the confidence estimator, two kinds of methods surpass each other in different testing datasets. In the similarity estimator, using the original feature to locate the candidate documents can get a better result. Moreover, on a large-scale graph with millions of nodes, rebuilding the affinity graph by the hidden feature results in an excessively high computational budget. These observations indicate that the dynamic approach is not superior compared to the static one.

Table 4. Results on static and dynamic affinity graphs

Methods	Wiki test set1				Wiki test set2				Wiki test set3			
	CE(s)	CE(d)	SE(s)	SE(d)	CE(s)	CE(d)	SE(s)	SE(d)	CE(s)	CE(d)	SE(s)	SE(d)
F_P	0.1496	0.1855	0.2740	0.2555	0.1424	0.1907	0.2854	0.2655	0.2260	0.1925	0.3107	0.3055
F_B	0.3539	0.3944	0.4675	0.4544	0.3533	0.3987	0.4792	0.4644	0.4209	0.3872	0.4941	0.4844
NMI	0.8120	0.8308	0.8714	0.8608	0.8057	0.8284	0.8713	0.8608	0.8340	0.8186	0.8710	0.8608
Clusters	1881	2501	4677	4897	1446	1994	3813	3841	1523	1165	2787	2501
Time	2 s	2 s	423 s	514 s	2 s	2 s	173 s	203 s	2 s	2 s	78 s	98 s

5 Conclusion

This paper made the first attempt to introduce Graph Convolutional Network (GCN) into the document clustering task. We proposed a GCN-based document clustering algorithm, DC-GCN that provides effective clustering for massive-category documents with complex distribution. DC-GCN transfers the clustering task into two major learning components (learning the document confidence and similarity) by powerful GCN. It integrates both the document and its keywords into the learning framework. Our experimental results indicated that our proposed method outperforms the existing document clustering algorithms, w.r.t. the accuracy and efficiency. Meanwhile, DC-GCN does not required any predetermined cluster numbers and copes well with the large-scale and high-noise document clustering. We expect DC-GCN can be applied in wider applications with complex data distributions.

Acknowledgement. This research was supported by Singapore MOE TIF grant (MOE2017-TIF-1-G018), the National Natural Science Foundation of China (61672179, 61370083) and China Postdoctoral Science Foundation (2019M651262).

References

1. Aggarwal, C.C., Zhai, C.: A survey of text clustering algorithms. In: Mining Text Data, pp. 77–128. Springer, Boston (2012). https://doi.org/10.1007/978-1-4614-3223-4_4
2. Ali, I., Melton, A.: Semantic-based text document clustering using cognitive semantic learning and graph theory. In: ICSC, pp. 243–247. IEEE (2018)
3. Amigó, E., Gonzalo, J., Artiles, J., Verdejo, F.: A comparison of extrinsic clustering evaluation metrics based on formal constraints. Inf. Retrieval **12**(4), 461–486 (2009)
4. Berkhin, P.: A survey of clustering data mining techniques. In: Grouping Multidimensional Data, pp. 25–71. Springer, Berlin (2006). https://doi.org/10.1007/3-540-28349-8_2
5. Bohm, C., Railing, K., Kriegel, H.P., Kroger, P.: Density connected clustering with local subspace preferences. In: ICDM 2004, pp. 27–34. IEEE (2004)
6. Cheng, Y.: Mean shift, mode seeking, and clustering. IEEE Trans. Pattern Anal. Mach. Intell. **17**(8), 790–799 (1995)
7. Dash, M., Liu, H., Scheuermann, P., Tan, K.L.: Fast hierarchical clustering and its validation. Data Knowl. Eng. **44**(1), 109–138 (2003)
8. Diallo, B., Hu, J., Li, T., et al.: Deep embedding clustering based on contractive autoencoder. Neurocomputing **433**, 96–107 (2021)
9. Hu, W., Miyato, T., Tokui, S., et al.: Learning discrete representations via information maximizing self-augmented training. In: ICML, pp. 1558–1567 (2017)
10. Joulin, A., Grave, E., Bojanowski, P., et al.: Fasttext. zip: compressing text classification models. arXiv:1612.03651 (2016)
11. Rodriguez, A., Laio, A.: Clustering by fast search and find of density peaks. Science **344**(6191), 1492–1496 (2014)
12. Von Luxburg, U.: A tutorial on spectral clustering. Stat. Comput. **17**(4), 395–416 (2007)

13. Wang, X., Peng, D., Hu, P., et al.: Adversarial correlated autoencoder for unsupervised multi-view representation learning. KBS **168**, 109–120 (2019)
14. Wang, Z., Zheng, L., Li, Y., Wang, S.: Linkage based face clustering via graph convolution network. In: CVPR, pp. 1117–1125 (2019)
15. Xu, J., Xu, B., Wang, P., et al.: Self-taught convolutional neural networks for short text clustering. Neural Netw. **88**, 22–31 (2017)
16. Xu, R., Wunsch, D.: Survey of clustering algorithms. IEEE Trans. Neural Netw. **16**(3), 645–678 (2005)
17. Yang, L., Chen, D., Zhan, X., et al.: Learning to cluster faces via confidence and connectivity estimation. In: CVPR, pp. 13369–13378 (2020)
18. Yang, L., Zhan, X., Chen, D., et al.: Learning to cluster faces on an affinity graph. In: CVPR, pp. 2298–2306 (2019)
19. Yang, L., Cheung, N.M., et al.: Deep clustering by gaussian mixture variational autoencoders with graph embedding. In: ICCV, pp. 6440–6449 (2019)
20. Yao, L., Mao, C., Luo, Y.: Graph convolutional networks for text classification. AAAI **33**, 7370–7377 (2019)
21. Zhang, D., Sun, Y., Eriksson, B., Balzano, L.: Deep unsupervised clustering using mixture of autoencoders. arXiv preprint arXiv:1712.07788 (2017)

Structure-Enhanced Graph Representation Learning for Link Prediction in Signed Networks

Yunke Zhang[1], Zhiwei Yang[2], Bo Yu[1], Hechang Chen[1(✉)], Yang Li[3], and Xuehua Zhao[4(✉)]

[1] School of Artificial Intelligence, Jilin University, Changchun, China
chenhc@jlu.edu.cn

[2] College of Computer Science and Technology, Jilin University, Changchun, China

[3] Aviation University of Air Force, Changchun, China

[4] School of Digital Media, Shenzhen Institute of Information Technology, Shenzhen, China
lcrlc@sina.com

Abstract. Link prediction in signed networks has attracted widespread attention from researchers recently. Existing studies usually learn a representation vector for each node, which is used for link prediction tasks, by aggregating the features of neighbour nodes in the network. However, how to incorporate structural features, e.g., community structure and degree distribution, into graph representation learning remains a difficult challenge. To this end, we propose a novel Structure-enhanced Graph Representation Learning method called SGRL for link prediction in signed networks, which enables the incorporation of structural features into a unified representation. Specifically, the feature of community structure is described by introducing two latent variables to submit to Bernoulli distribution and Gaussian distribution. Moreover, the degree distribution of each node is described by a hidden variable that submits to the Dirichlet distribution by using the community feature as the parameter. Finally, the unified representation obtained from the Dirichlet distribution is further employed for the link prediction based on similarity computation. The effectiveness of the SGRL is demonstrated using benchmark datasets against the state-of-the-art methods in terms of signed link prediction, ablation study, and robustness analysis.

Keywords: Representation learning · Structure feature · Signed network · Link prediction

This work is partially supported by the National Natural Science Foundation of China through grants No.61902145 and No. 61902144, the Guangdong Natural Science Foundation (2018A030313339,2021A1515011994), the Scientific Research Team Project of Shenzhen Institute of Information Technology (SZIIT2019KJ022).

H. Qiu et al. (Eds.): KSEM 2021, LNAI 12815, pp. 40–52, 2021.
https://doi.org/10.1007/978-3-030-82136-4_4

1 Introduction

Signed networks can well describe complex relationships using positive and negative links between their entity nodes, e.g., friendly and antagonistic relationships [1]. As a fundamental problem in a signed network, link prediction attempts to predict their signed types between any two nodes, which has been studied for various tasks, including recommendation [2], user characteristic analysis and clustering [3], and research on protein and metabolism Network [4].

Existing studies on link prediction in signed networks are roughly divided into two categories, i.e., supervised learning based methods and unsupervised learning based methods. For supervised learning based methods, Leskovec et al. [5–7] use local features based on balance theory [8], such as in-degrees and tuple relations, and train them through logistic regression. Zolfahar et al. [9,10] employ user interaction behaviour and context information from signed network topology and user behaviour to construct feature sets [11]. For unsupervised learning based methods, link prediction methods often predict potential links by analyzing the topological structure of the network and the interaction between nodes. Guha et al. [12–14] propose to convert a signed network into a matrix first and then complete the matrix through trust propagation, matrix decomposition, or matrix filling methods. Due to the high computational complexity and difficulty of the above method, which limits the application of this type of method in large networks, link prediction methods for signed networks based on node similarity appeared. For example, Tyler et al. [15–20] use node similarity to predict whether there is a potential link between two nodes, which leverage deep neural networks or graph convolutional networks to learn node representation for similarity measuring.

However, these methods usually ignore the structural features of signed networks, e.g., community structure and degree distribution of nodes. Nodes in an identical community tend to have a positive link and a closer distance. On the contrary, nodes in different communities tend to have a negative link and a farther distance. Besides, recent studies have defaulted that the degree distribution of nodes in the signed network is uniformly distributed, but the degree distribution of nodes usually follows power-law distribution in signed networks, i.e., most of the nodes have a small number of links, but a few nodes have a large number of links. Therefore, it will be beneficial to link prediction tasks by incorporating the information of the community structure and degree distribution of nodes.

In view of this, we propose a Structure-enhanced Graph Representation Learning framework, SGRL, for link prediction in signed networks, which enhances the task performance by explicitly incorporating community structure and degree distribution. In our model, first, we use signed graph attention networks (SiGAT) [20] as an encoder to encode Bernoulli and Gaussian distribution parameters. The SiGAT has great effectiveness ability so that we can easily construct the parameter of the distribution. Then, we learn node representation, including community structure and degree distribution, by dividing representation learning into two-stage. In Stage one, we learn the community structure by using two variables submitting Bernoulli distribution and Gaussian distribution, respectively. In Stage two, two variables are merged as a Dirichlet distribution parameter to obtain the representation. In this way, the features of network structure and degree distribution are preserved explicitly. In the experiment, our proposed SGRL outperforms five state-of-the-art methods on four benchmark datasets in terms of link prediction. In summary, the main contributions of this study are as follows:

- A novel link prediction method called SGRL is proposed, which is capable of learning more powerful node representations in signed networks by incorporating community structures and degree distribution features.
- In this method, the Bernoulli and Gaussian distributions are adopted to capture the community structure in the signed network. Moreover, the feature of degree distribution is incorporated by introducing Dirichlet distribution.
- The superiority of the SGRL is demonstrated comparing with the state-of-the-art methods using real-world datasets, and in-depth analysis gives the rationality and robustness of the proposed method.

The following sections are organized as follows: In Sect. 2, the problem formulation for this task is described. Next, in Sect. 3, we introduce the details of the Structure-enhanced Graph Representation Learning method for link prediction in signed networks namely SGRL. After that, in Sect. 4, we show the detailed experimental verifications of the proposed method. Finally, in Sect. 5, we provide the summarization and the future work.

2 Problem Formulation

This section, we introduce the notations in the signed network and the implication of three distributions adopted to describe the structure feature.

We denote a signed network by $\boldsymbol{G} = (V, A)$, where $V = \{1, 2, ..., n\}$ is the node set, and $A = \{-1, 1\}$ is the sign set, where $\mathbf{A}_{ij} = 1$ if there exists a positive link between Node i and Node j, while $\mathbf{A}_{ij} = -1$ if there exists a negative link between Node i and Node j. To describe the structure of the communities in the network satisfying Bernoulli distribution, we denote a binary variable $\mathbf{B} = \{0, 1\}^K$, where K denotes the number of communities, $\mathbf{b}_i \in \mathbf{B}$, and $b_{ik} = 1$ indicates Node i belongs to Community k, while $b_{ik} = 0$ means Node i does not belong to Community k. In addition, a variable $\mathbf{Z}$ satisfying Gaussian distribution is denoted as the strength of node i belongs to Community k, where $z_{ik} \in \mathbb{R}$. And a variable $\mathbf{D}$ satisfying Dirichlet distribution is adopted to capture the degree distribution of the node. $d_i \in \mathbf{D}$ represents the relative degree of Node i, where $d_i \in \mathbb{R}$. Finally, we estimate $p(\tilde{\mathbf{A}}_{ij}|\mathbf{B}, \mathbf{Z}, \mathbf{D}) = f(d_i^T \cdot d_j)$ for link prediction in signed network.

3 Methodology

In this section, we propose a structure-enhanced graph representation learning method for link prediction in signed networks. To intuitively understand the method, we first introduce the overall framework of the algorithm, and then elaborate the encoding methods for latent parameters, the representation learning method based on structure enhancement and the link prediction, respectively.

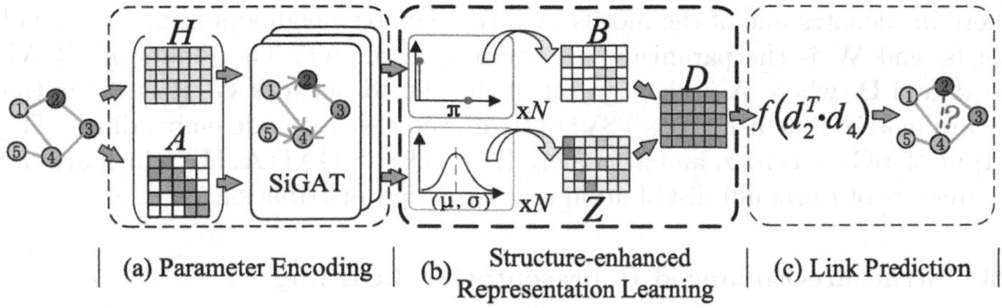

Fig. 1. An architecture of the proposed SGRL model. There are three parts of the model: (a) Parameter encoding. (b) Structure-enhanced representation learning. (c) Link prediction. The green node and yellow node denote the objective nodes, which are predicted signed link. Blue nodes denote neighbours, red edges describe positive links, and grey edges describe negative links. (Color figure online)

3.1 The SGRL Framework

The framework of the SGRL consists of three parts: parameter encoding, structure-enhanced representation learning, and link prediction, as shown in Fig. 1. For part one, a signed graph convolutional neural network is adopted to learn parameter encoding for Bernoulli distribution and Gaussian distribution. For part two, we design a two-stage method to learning the representation incorporating structure features: 1) variables **B** and **Z** that obey the Bernoulli and Gaussian distributions are sampled after parameter encoding; 2) the variables **B** and **Z** are fused as a unified probability parameter of the Dirichlet distribution, from which a variable **D** can be sampled after that. For part three, the inner product for each node pair can be calculated based on the obtained variable representing **D**, which determines the probability of the node on positive and negative edges.

3.2 Latent Parameter Encoding

In the SGRL framework, we use signed graph attention networks (SiGAT) as the encoder to encode parameters for Bernoulli distribution and Gaussian distribution. The SiGAT sets up various motifs to find different kinds of neighbours, using attention mechanism to aggregate information from neighbours. Therefore, the SiGAT has the effectiveness ability to encode the parameters by refining nodes with collecting local neighbours information. This method is formulated as follows:

$$\alpha_{uv}^{m_i} = \frac{\exp(\text{LeakyReLU}(\mathbf{a}_{m_i}^T[\mathbf{W}_{m_i}\mathbf{H}(u)||\mathbf{W}_{m_i}\mathbf{H}(v)]))}{\sum_{k\in\mathcal{N}_{m_i}(u)}\exp(\text{LeakyReLU}(\mathbf{a}_{m_i}^T[\mathbf{W}_{m_i}\mathbf{H}(u)||\mathbf{W}_{m_i}\mathbf{H}(k)]))} \tag{1}$$

$$\mathbf{H}_{m_i}(u) = \sum_{v\in\mathcal{N}_{m_i(u)}} \alpha_{uv}^{m_i}\mathbf{W}_{m_i}\mathbf{H}(v) \tag{2}$$

where m_i denotes one of the motifs, $\mathcal{N}_{m_i}(u)$ denotes neighbors from i^{th} type of motifs, and $\mathbf{W}$ is the parameter for training in SiGAT. The inputs of SiGAT are $\mathbf{A}$ and $\mathbf{H}$, where $\mathbf{A}$ is the sign set of the signed network $\boldsymbol{G}$, $\mathbf{H}$ is the initial feature matrix that using the TSVD [21] method to get node embeddings. The output of SiGAT is μ, σ, and π, namely $\{\mu, \sigma, \pi\} = \text{SiGAT}(\mathbf{A}, \mathbf{H})$, which are the parameters of Bernoulli distribution and Gaussian distribution.

3.3 Structure-Enhanced Representation Learning

In the SGRL framework, we propose to incorporate the features of community structure and degree distribution when learning node representations in a two-stage manner.

Stage I: We use the results from SiGAT as the variational posterior parameters to obtain Bernoulli posterior distribution and Gaussian posterior distribution, respectively:

$$q_\phi(\mathbf{B}|\mathbf{A}, \mathbf{H}) = \text{Bernoulli}(\pi) \tag{3}$$

$$q_\phi(\mathbf{Z}|\mathbf{A}, \mathbf{H}) = \text{Gaussian}(\mu, \sigma) \tag{4}$$

Accordingly, the variables $\mathbf{B}$ and $\mathbf{Z}$ that submit to their distribution respectively are sampled. As it is hard to train the model using the gradient descent method for sampling due to the sampling action is not continuous, we use the reparameterization trick to obtain the variables $\mathbf{B}$ and $\mathbf{Z}$. According to the research of [22,23], we use a parameter π to reparameterize the Bernoulli distribution to obtain $\mathbf{B}$:

$$u \sim \text{Uniform}(0, 1)$$

$$L \overset{d}{=} \log(u) - \log(1 - u)$$

$$\mathbf{B} \overset{d}{=} \begin{cases} 1 & \text{if} \quad L + \log \pi \geq 0 \\ 0 & \text{otherwise} \end{cases} \tag{5}$$

Similarly, according to the research of [24], we use the parameters μ and σ to reparameterize the Gaussian distribution to get $\mathbf{Z}$:

$$\mathbf{Z} = \mu + \sigma \tag{6}$$

Stage II: We naturally choose the dependent variable to be used from stage I since the degree distribution of nodes depends on the community structure. Specifically, we first fuse $\mathbf{B}$ and $\mathbf{Z}$ as a parameter to obtain the Dirichlet posterior distribution, and then sample from it to obtain the embedding $\mathbf{D}$ that obeys the Dirichlet distribution.

$$q_\phi(\mathbf{D}|\mathbf{B}, \mathbf{Z}; \mathbf{A}, \mathbf{H}) = \text{Dirichlet}(\mathbf{B} \circ \mathbf{Z}) \tag{7}$$

According to the research of [25–27], we use $\mathbf{B} \circ \mathbf{Z}$ as a parameter to reparameterize the Dirichlet distribution to obtain $\mathbf{D}$:

$$\tilde{d}_i \sim \text{Beta}(\alpha_i, \sum_{j=i+1}^{n} \alpha_j) \quad \text{for} \quad i = 1, ..., n-1$$

$$d_1 = \tilde{d}_1; \quad d_n = \prod_{j=1}^{n-1}(1 - \tilde{d}_j)$$
$$d_i = \tilde{d}_i \prod_{j=1}^{i-1}(1 - \tilde{d}_j) \quad \text{for} \quad i = 2, ..., n-1 \tag{8}$$

where α denotes the parameter of Dirichlet distribution, namely $\mathbf{B} \circ \mathbf{Z}$.

3.4 Signed Link Prediction

In order to obtain the distribution of the positive and negative links, we use the node representation $\mathbf{D}$ obtained in Sect. 3.3 to perform the inner product operation like VGAE [28]:

$$p(\mathbf{A}_{ij} = 1|\mathbf{B}, \mathbf{Z}, \mathbf{D}) = f(d_i^T \cdot d_j) \tag{9}$$
$$p(\mathbf{A}_{ij} = -1|\mathbf{B}, \mathbf{Z}, \mathbf{D}) = 1 - f(d_i^T \cdot d_j) \tag{10}$$

which $\mathbf{A}_{ij}$ is the element in the adjacency matrix $\mathbf{A}$ and f is the logistic sigmoid function. According to the proportion of positive and negative links, we set 0.3 as the threshold, i.e., if $p(\mathbf{A}_{ij} = 1|\mathbf{B}, \mathbf{Z}, \mathbf{D}) > 0.3$, we get a positive link; otherwise, we get a negative link.

We use the stochastic gradient variational bayes algorithm [24] to infer the parameters of the variational distribution. Formally, we define the loss function as $\mathcal{L}$, which can be solved by maximizing the lower limit of variation:

$$\begin{aligned}
\log p(\tilde{\mathbf{A}}) &\geq \mathcal{L}(\theta, \phi; \mathbf{A}, \mathbf{H}) \\
&= \mathbb{E}_{q(\mathbf{B},\mathbf{Z},\mathbf{D}|\mathbf{A},\mathbf{H})}[\log p(\tilde{\mathbf{A}}|\mathbf{B}, \mathbf{Z}, \mathbf{D})] - D_{KL}(q(\mathbf{B}, \mathbf{Z}, \mathbf{D}|\tilde{\mathbf{A}}, \mathbf{H})||p(\mathbf{Z}, \mathbf{D})) \\
&= \mathbb{E}_{q(\mathbf{B},\mathbf{Z}|\tilde{\mathbf{A}},\mathbf{H})}[E_{q(\mathbf{D}|\mathbf{B},\mathbf{Z};\tilde{\mathbf{A}},\mathbf{H})} \log p(\tilde{\mathbf{A}}|\mathbf{B}, \mathbf{Z}, \mathbf{D})] \\
&- E_{q(\mathbf{B},\mathbf{Z}|\tilde{\mathbf{A}},\mathbf{H})}[D_{KL}(q(\mathbf{D}|\mathbf{B}, \mathbf{Z}; \tilde{\mathbf{A}}, \mathbf{H})||p(\mathbf{D}|\mathbf{B}, \mathbf{Z}))] \\
&- D_{KL}(q(\mathbf{B}, \mathbf{Z}|\tilde{\mathbf{A}}, \mathbf{H})||p(\mathbf{B}, \mathbf{Z}))
\end{aligned} \tag{11}$$

In the loss function $\mathcal{L}$, there are three variables to be optimized simultaneously, i.e., $\mathbf{B}$, $\mathbf{Z}$, and $\mathbf{D}$, indicating Bernoulli variable, Gaussian variable, and Dirichlet variable, respectively. Please refer to Algorithm 1 for more details.

Algorithm 1. Structure-enhanced Graph Representation Learning (SGRL)

Input: signed network initial feature matrix $\mathbf{H}$; sign set $\mathbf{A}$; training epoch N;
Output: link prediction $\tilde{\mathbf{A}}$
for 1 To N: **do**
 π^n, μ^n, $\sigma^n \sim$ SiGAT($\mathbf{A}, \mathbf{H}$); ▷ Latent parameter encoding
 $\mathbf{B}^n \sim$ Bernoulli(π^n); ▷ First stage of representation learning
 $\mathbf{Z}^n \sim$ Gaussian($\mu^n, {\sigma^n}^2$);
 $\mathbf{D}^n \sim$ Dirichlet($\mathbf{B}^n \circ \mathbf{Z}^n$); ▷ Second stage of representation learning
 $p(\tilde{A}_{ij} = 1) = f(d_i^{nT} \cdot d_j^n)$;
 $p(\tilde{A}_{ij} = -1) = 1 - f(d_i^{nT} \cdot d_j^n)$; ▷ Link prediction generating
end for; **return** $\tilde{\mathbf{A}}$

Table 1. The statistics of datasets.

Datasets	Nodes	Positive links	Negative links
Bitcoin-Alpha	3,775	12,721	1,399
Bitcoin-OTC	5,875	18,230	3,259
Slashdot	37,626	313,543	105,529
Epinions	45,003	513,851	102,180

4 Experiment

In this section, we first introduce the experiment settings, including datasets, baselines, evaluation metrics, and experiment settings. Then we evaluate the effectiveness of the SGRL in link prediction. In general, we seek to answer the following questions:

- **Q1:** Is the node representation learned incorporating structural features beneficial to link prediction in signed networks?
- **Q2:** Are these three latent variables, i.e., the Bernoulli distribution, Gauss distribution, and Dirichlet distribution, contributing to the proposed model?
- **Q3:** Is the proposed SGRL model sensitive to the main parameters, e.g., the learning range and split ratio?

4.1 Experiment Setting

Datasets Description: We conduct experiments on four real-world signed social network datasets, i.e., Bitcoin-Alpha, Bitcoin-OTC, Slashdot, and Epinions. **Bitcoin-Alpha** and **Bitcoin-OTC** [29] datasets come from two websites that users trade with others using Bitcoin. Due to the Bitcoin accounts being anonymous, the two websites' users have built online trust networks to protect their security. The members take positive (or negative) scores to whom they trust (or distrust). **Slashdot** [30] is a technology news site where users can tag each other as friends or foes. **Epinions** [31] is a product review site. Members can rate other people's evaluations of goods as correct or incorrect. We summarized the number of nodes, positive and negative links in four datasets. Please refer to Table 1 for more details.

Baselines: Here we present some existing state-of-the-art link prediction methods for signed networks, proving that we learn a powerful representation to predict node pair link.

- `SiNE` [16]:[1] This model uses a deep neural network to make information transfer from neighbours with balance theory [8].

[1] https://github.com/benedekrozemberczki/SINE.

Table 2. Accuracy of link prediction in signed networks (AUC).

Methods	SIDE	SiNE	SGCN	SNEA	SiGAT	SGRL
Bitcoin-Alpha	0.642	0.781	0.801	0.816	0.880	**0.891**
Bitcoin-OTC	0.632	0.782	0.804	0.818	0.895	**0.902**
Slashdot	0.554	0.785	0.786	0.799	**0.884**	0.875
Epinions	0.617	0.831	0.849	0.861	0.923	**0.929**

Table 3. Accuracy of link prediction in signed networks (F1).

Methods	SIDE	SiNE	SGCN	SNEA	SiGAT	SGRL
Bitcoin-Alpha	0.753	0.895	0.915	0.927	0.968	**0.971**
Bitcoin-OTC	0.728	0.876	0.908	0.924	0.935	**0.949**
Slashdot	0.624	0.850	0.859	0.868	0.883	**0.897**
Epinions	0.725	0.902	0.920	0.933	0.945	**0.948**

- `SIDE` [15]:[2] It develops the possibility of direct and indirect signed connection and provides balance theory to search relationship between links and nodes.
- `SGCN` [18]:[3] The first time that the graph convolutional neural network [32] is extended to the signed network using balance theory.
- `SNEA` [19]:[4] It uses the masked self-attention layer to aggregate information from neighbouring nodes to generate node embeddings based on balance theory.
- `SiGAT` [20]: It uses balance theory and status theory to extend graph attention network [33] to signed network.

For seek of fairness, we set the final embedding dimension as 20 for all the methods. We use released code for SiNE, SIDE, SGCN, SNEA, and SiGAT.

Evaluation Metrics and Experiment Settings: We use the Area Under the ROC Curve (AUC) and F1 score [34] to compare our model with the other baselines in terms of link prediction. For the task of signed link prediction, we randomly choose 80% links for training and 20% links for testing. PyTorch and Adam optimizer are used on our model (Learning Rate = 0.00005, Weight Decay = 0.0001, Batch Size = 500). We report the average results of AUC and F1 score by running the model 10 times.

4.2 Results and Analysis (Q1)

To address the first question (**Q1**), we conduct experiments to measure the link prediction quality and compare it with the other baseline methods. As shown in

[2] https://datalab.snu.ac.kr/side/.
[3] https://github.com/benedekrozemberczki/SGCN.
[4] https://github.com/huangjunjie95/SiGAT.

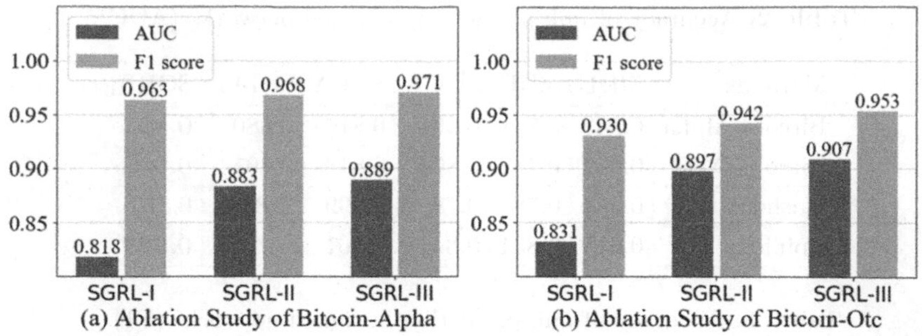

Fig. 2. Ablation study of the SGRL.

Table 2 and Table 3, our proposed SGRL model can successfully predict the link of signed network and almost perform better than all these Baselines. Firstly, SINE and SIDE use deep neural networks to extract the features of nodes, and these two methods do not consider the graph structure. Thus, the ability to extract features is not strong. Secondly, the SGCN, SNEA, and SiGAT all use graph convolutional network to extract node features, considering the hidden relationships between nodes. Moreover, signed graph convolution models have a significant improvement in link prediction. It indicates that the graph convolution neural network has a strong ability of expression on signed networks. Finally, our model uses a graph convolutional network to extract graph structure information of nodes. Besides, three probability distributions are proposed to explore community structure and degree distribution. The proposed algorithm achieves the best results in our experiments. It demonstrates that the latent structure of the signed network can be successfully extracted by using three distributions, i.e., the latent structure plays an important role in improving link prediction ability in signed networks.

4.3 Ablation Study (Q2)

To answer the second question (**Q2**), we will verify whether these three distributions introduced are beneficial to the effectiveness of the model. In the experiment, we design three variants of the proposed model:

- **SGRL(I):** introducing only Bernoulli distribution;
- **SGRL(II):** introducing Bernoulli and Gaussian distributions;
- **SGRL(III):** introducing Bernoulli, Gaussian, and Dirichlet distributions.

We measure the accuracy of these three variants by AUC and F1 in terms of link prediction. As Fig. 2 shows, our model performs the best when all latent variables are introduced. The performance of the SGRL(I) has surpassed SIDE, SiNE, SGCN, and SNEA algorithms after the addition of the Bernoulli distribution. It shows that Bernoulli distribution has a good effect on the link prediction model in this paper. Then, based on the previous step, the SGRL(II)

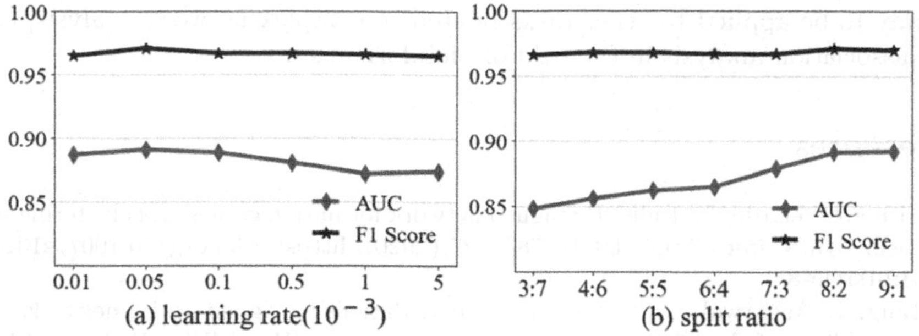

Fig. 3. Parameter sensitivity analysis on Bitcoin-Alpha datasets.

with the Gaussian distribution was further improved. Therefore, the submitting Gaussian variable plays a role in describing the distance between nodes. Finally, after adding the Dirichlet distribution, the results of the SGRL(III) continue to improve. The Dirichlet distribution can also effectively describe the degree distribution of nodes to improve the link prediction ability of the model.

4.4 Sensitivity Analysis (Q3)

In this subsection, we test the robustness of the model and verify whether hyper-parameter settings impact the model. We conduct two groups of experiments, i.e., the learning rates (0.00001, 0.00005, 0.0001, 0.0005, 0.001) and the split ratio of the training set and testing set (2:8, 3:7, 4:6, 5:5, 6:4, 7:3, 8:2). Learning rate controls gradient descent and Batch size controls the size of allocated resources. In order to study the uncertainty of the model output, we adopted a single-parameter sensitivity analysis method, changing one parameter at a time while fixing other parameters at the same time. As shown in Fig. 3, our model still keeps a high accuracy between 0.85 and 0.90 under the change of learning rates and split ratio, and the performance in terms of F1 Score varies in a narrow range. It implies that the proposed SGRL model is not sensitive to these main parameters, and thus has good robustness.

5 Conclusion

In this paper, we proposed a novel framework for link prediction in the signed network, namely SGRL, which encodes the features of community structure and degree distribution to learn a powerful representation for link prediction. Specifically, we introduced a two-stage method to capture these two structural features. First, we encoded the community structural feature by employing Bernoulli distribution and Gaussian distribution. Then, we combined the community structure to obtain Dirichlet distribution, where we can encode the degree distribution of nodes. The experimental results on real-world signed network datasets verified the effectiveness of the proposed framework for link prediction. The SGRL is ready to be applied to other tasks related to complex network analysis, e.g., gene association analysis in the field of bioinformatics.

References

1. Cisneros-Velarde, P., Bullo, F.: Signed network formation games and clustering balance. Dyn. Games Appl. **10**(4), 783–797 (2020). https://doi.org/10.1007/s13235-019-00346-8
2. Tang, J., Aggarwal, C., Liu, H.: Recommendations in signed social networks. In: Proceedings of the 25th International Conference on World Wide Web, pp. 31–40 (2016)
3. Kunegis, J., Schmidt, S., Lommatzsch, A., Lerner, J., De Luca, E.W., Albayrak, S.: Spectral analysis of signed graphs for clustering, prediction and visualization. Genomics Proteomics Bioinformations **14**(1), 62–71 (2016)
4. Ge, M., Li, A., Wang, M.: A bipartite network-based method for prediction of long non-coding RNA-protein interactions. Bioinformatics **33**(4), 608–611 (2017)
5. Yang, S.H., Smola, J.A., Long, B., Zha, H., Chang, Y.: Friend or frenemy? Predicting signed ties in social networks. In: Proceedings of the ACM Special Interest Group on Information Retrieval (SIGIR), pp. 555–564 (2012)
6. Chiang, K.Y., Natarajan, N., Tewari, A., Dhillon, S.I.: Exploiting longer cycles for link prediction in signed networks. In: Proceedings of the ACM International Conference on Information and Knowledge Management (CIKM), pp. 1157–1162 (2011)
7. Patidar, A., Agarwal, V., Bharadwaj, K.K.: Predicting friends and foes in signed networks using inductive inference and social balance theory. In: Proceedings of the IEEE/ACM International Conference on Advances in Social Network Analysis and Mining (ASONAM), pp. 384–388 (2012)
8. Cygan, M., Pilipczuk, M., Pilipczuk, M., Wojtaszczyk, J.O.: Sitting closer to friends than enemies, revisited. In: Rovan, B., Sassone, V., Widmayer, P. (eds.) MFCS 2012. LNCS, vol. 7464, pp. 296–307. Springer, Heidelberg (2012). https://doi.org/10.1007/978-3-642-32589-2_28
9. Zolfaghar, K., Aghaie, A.: Mining trust and distrust relationships in social web applications. In: Proceedings of the International Conference on Intelligent Computer Communication and Processing (ICCP), pp. 73–80E (2010)
10. Borzymek, P., Sydow, M.: Trust and distrust prediction in social network with combined graphical and review-based attributes. In: KES-AMSTA 2010. LNCS (LNAI), vol. 6070, pp. 122–131. Springer, Heidelberg (2010). https://doi.org/10.1007/978-3-642-13480-7_14
11. Yang, Z., Chen, H., Zhang, J., Ma, J., Yi, C.: Attention-based multi-level feature fusion for named entity recognition. In: Proceedings of the 29th International Joint Conference on Artificial Intelligence (IJCAI), pp. 3594–3600 (2020)
12. Guha, V.R., Raghavan, P., Tomkins, A., Kumar, R.: Propagation of trust and distrust. In: Proceedings of the International Conference on World Wide Web (WWW), pp. 403–412 (2004)
13. Kunegis, J., Schmidt, S., Lommatzsch, A., Lerner, J., Luca, W.D.E., Albayrak, S.: Spectral analysis of signed graphs for clustering, prediction and visualization. In: Proceedings of the SIAM International Conference on Data Mining (SDM), pp. 559–570 (2010)

14. Zhang, H., Wu, G., Ling, Q.: Distributed stochastic gradient descent for link prediction in signed social networks. EURASIP J. Adv. Sig. Process. **2019**(1), 1–11 (2019). https://doi.org/10.1186/s13634-019-0601-0
15. Kim, J., Park, H., Lee, J.E., Kang, U.: Side: representation learning in signed directed networks. In: Proceedings of the International Conference on World Wide Web (WWW), pp. 509–518 (2018)
16. Wang, S., Tang, J., Aggarwal, C., Chang, Y., Liu, H.: Signed network embedding in social media. In: Proceedings of the SIAM International Conference on Data Mining (SDM), pp. 327–335 (2017)
17. Islam, M.R., Aditya Prakash, B., Ramakrishnan, N.: SIGNet: scalable embeddings for signed networks. In: Phung, D., Tseng, V.S., Webb, G.I., Ho, B., Ganji, M., Rashidi, L. (eds.) PAKDD 2018. LNCS (LNAI), vol. 10938, pp. 157–169. Springer, Cham (2018). https://doi.org/10.1007/978-3-319-93037-4_13
18. Derr, T., Ma, Y., Tang, J.: Signed graph convolutional networks. In: Proceedings of the IEEE International Conference on Data Mining (ICDM), pp. 929–934 (2018)
19. Li, Y., Tian, Y., Zhang, J., Chang, Y.: Learning signed network embedding via graph attention. In: Proceedings of the AAAI Conference on Artificial Intelligence (AAAI), pp. 4772–4779 (2020)
20. Huang, J., Shen, H., Hou, L., Cheng, X.: Signed graph attention networks. In: Tetko, I.V., Kůrková, V., Karpov, P., Theis, F. (eds.) ICANN 2019. LNCS, vol. 11731, pp. 566–577. Springer, Cham (2019). https://doi.org/10.1007/978-3-030-30493-5_53
21. Eckart, C., Young, G.: The approximation of one matrix by another of lower rank. Psychometrika **1**(3), 211–218 (1936)
22. Maddison, J.C., Mnih, A., Teh, W.Y.: The concrete distribution: a continuous relaxation of discrete random variables. In: Proceedings of the International Conference on Learning Representations (ICLR), pp. 1–20 (2017)
23. Jang, E., Gu, S., Poole, B.: Categorical reparameterization with gumbel-softmax. In: Proceedings of the International Conference on Learning Representations (ICLR), pp. 1–13 (2017)
24. Kingma, D.P., Welling, M.: Auto-encoding variational bayes. In: Proceedings of the International Conference on Learning Representations (ICLR), pp. 1–14 (2014)
25. Ruiz, J.R.F., Titsias, K.M., Blei, M.D.: The generalized reparameterization gradient. In: Proceedings of the International Conference on Neural Information Processing Systems (NIPS), pp. 460–468 (2016)
26. Srivastava, A., Sutton, A.C.: Autoencoding variational inference for topic models. In: Proceedings of the International Conference on Learning Representations (ICLR), pp. 1–12 (2017)
27. Figurnov, M., Mohamed, S., Mnih, A.: Implicit reparameterization gradients. In: Proceedings of the International Conference on Neural Information Processing Systems (NIPS), pp. 439–450 (2018)
28. Kipf, T.N., Welling, M.: Variational graph auto-encoders. In: Proceedings of the International Conference on Neural Information Processing Systems (NIPS), pp. 1–3 (2016)
29. Kumar, S., Spezzano, F., Subrahmanian, S.V., Faloutsos, C.: Edge weight prediction in weighted signed networks. In: Proceedings of the IEEE International Conference on Data Mining (ICDM), pp. 221–230 (2016)
30. Gómez, V., Kaltenbrunner, A., López, V.: Statistical analysis of the social network and discussion threads in slashdot. In: Proceedings of the International Conference on World Wide Web (WWW), pp. 645–654 (2008)

31. Massa, P., Avesani, P.: Controversial users demand local trust metrics: an experimental study on epinions. com community. In: Proceedings of the AAAI Conference on Artificial Intelligence (AAAI), pp. 121–126 (2005)
32. Kipf, T.N., Welling, M.: Semi-supervised classification with graph convolutional networks. In: Proceedings of the International Conference on Learning Representations (ICLR), pp. 1–14 (2017)
33. Velickovic, P., Cucurull, G., Casanova, A., Romero, A., Liò, P., Bengio, Y.: Graph attention networks. In: Proceedings of the International Conference on Learning Representations (ICLR), pp. 1–12 (2018)
34. Chinchor, N.: MUC-4 evaluation metrics. In: Proceedings of the Conference on Message Understanding (MUC), pp. 22–29 (1992)

A Property-Based Method for Acquiring Commonsense Knowledge

Ya Wang[1,2], Cungen Cao[1], Yuting Cao[3], and Shi Wang[1](✉)

[1] Key Laboratory of Intelligent Information Processing, Institute of Computing Technology, Chinese Academy of Sciences, Beijing 100190, China
{wangya,cgcao,wangshi}@ict.ac.cn

[2] University of Chinese Academy of Sciences, Beijing, China

[3] Department of Computer Science and Information Technology, Guangxi Normal University, Guilin 541004, China

Abstract. Commonsense knowledge is crucial in a variety of AI applications. However, one kind of commonsense knowledge that has not received attention is that of properties of actions denoted by verbs. To address this limitation, we propose an approach to acquiring commonsense knowledge about action properties. In this paper, we take self-motion actions as an example to present our method. We first identify commonsense properties of actions from their definitions. We then introduce a list of dimensions for acquiring commonsense knowledge based on adjectives. Finally, we extract commonsense knowledge from text by parsing sentences that involve actions. Experiments show that our method allows to obtain high-quality commonsense knowledge.

Keywords: Commonsense knowledge · Action properties · Dimensions · Text parsing

1 Introduction

Commonsense knowledge is true statements about the world that is known to most people. It is necessary to achieve human-level intelligence in domains such as natural language processing [1, 2], computer vision [3, 4] and robotics [5]. Verbs are the most important organizers of sentences and occupy the core position in a language [6]. Actions are denoted by verbs. We will use the term *verb* and *action* interchangeably for the rest of the paper. Commonsense knowledge about action properties is an important part of human commonsense knowledge, e.g., that *a person runs with his feet* or that *a fish swims in the water*. Unfortunately, this kind of commonsense knowledge has never been systematically explored by prominent commonsense knowledge resources like Cyc [7], ConceptNet [8] and Webchild [9]. The same holds for recent research on commonsense knowledge [10–12].

To overcome the above limitation, we present a method for acquiring commonsense knowledge about action properties. In this paper, we select self-motion actions as an

H. Qiu et al. (Eds.): KSEM 2021, LNAI 12815, pp. 53–65, 2021.
https://doi.org/10.1007/978-3-030-82136-4_5

example, which are the concepts of locomotion, as in *run* and *swim*, to introduce our work. Our method is composed of three major parts.

The first part is **property identification**. In WordNet [13], semantically equivalent actions are grouped into synsets. Each synset carries synonymous information which is the definition of the actions in the synset. The definition of a concept describes its meaning and provides rich information about the properties of the concept, e.g., the definition "move fast by using one's feet, with one foot off the ground at any given time" of synset {run}. For {run}, we could identify the salient properties of *speed* (fast), *tool* (feet), *location* (ground) and *manner* (with one foot off the ground at any given time). Therefore, we extract commonsense properties of actions by reading their definitions. A goal of this paper is to build a high-quality commonsense knowledge repository of actions, so we rely on expert humans to extract the commonsense properties of actions.

The second part is **dimensions for acquiring commonsense knowledge**. The commonsense properties of an action also have their own features. Taking *run* as an example, the agent must have feet and the location must be bigger than the agent. Since humans take commonsense knowledge for granted and it is often unnecessary to express commonsense facts explicitly, commonsense knowledge acquisition is an extremely difficult task. So, we identify a list of dimensions for acquiring commonsense knowledge. These dimensions can be used to elicit commonsense knowledge from human contributors and provide a basis for acquiring commonsense knowledge about properties. Most commonsense knowledge is about properties of concepts. For example, *snow is white* (color) and *a watermelon is heavier than an apple* (weight). Thus, we consider properties of concepts as the dimensions of acquiring commonsense knowledge. Adjectives typically encode properties of concepts [14, 15]; that is, an adjective is one that ascribes a value to a property. Moreover, the number of adjectives is limited. For these reasons, we have manually summarized dimensions for acquiring commonsense knowledge based on adjectives.

The third part is **commonsense knowledge extraction**. Web text contains a huge amount of commonsense knowledge. In this paper, we employ the improved robust Earley algorithm [16] to parse a text sentence containing a verb (e.g., run) or verb phrase (e.g., run into). We can get a corresponding semantic parse tree of this sentence. Then we extract the text knowledge about action properties contained in the parse tree using a knowledge extractor. We acquire the commonsense knowledge about properties of an action using the properties identified in part 1 and dimensions determined in part 2, for instance, "*Agent* has feet" (instrument) and "The volume of *location* is larger than that of *agent*" (volume). Since the number of properties and dimensions is limited, we collect the commonsense knowledge through human computation to ensure the quality. Such commonsense knowledge can function as the templates for acquiring commonsense knowledge through substituting properties in the templates for corresponding property values extracted from Web corpora. Finally, we obtain new commonsense knowledge according to these text knowledge and commonsense knowledge acquisition templates, for instance, *a rabbit has feet* or *the volume of the park is larger than that of a person.*

The rest of the paper is organized as follows. In Sect. 2, we review previous research that is related to our work. Section 3 introduces the approach to identifying commonsense properties of actions. We describe the method for determining the dimensions of acquiring commonsense knowledge in Sect. 4. Then in Sect. 5, we propose the method for extracting commonsense knowledge and conduct an experiment to evaluate the performance of this method. Finally, we make a conclusion about our work in Sect. 6.

2 Related Work

Many attempts have been made to construct commonsense knowledge bases. The Cyc [7] project is built by a large team of humans. It manually compiles commonsense knowledge with focus on general logical axioms rather than properties particularly the properties of actions. ConceptNet [8] is a huge repository of commonsense assertions. Commonsense knowledge in ConceptNet is collected using crowdsourcing techniques. However, it just covers several generic relations that is related to action properties and does not involve the specific properties like speed, direction and path of self-motion actions. Webchild [9] presents a method for acquiring commonsense knowledge from the Web. It includes fine-grained hasProperty relations such as hasShape, hasColor and hasTaste that connect nouns with adjectives. While it contains rich object properties, it is ignorant regarding action properties. [17] extracts large amounts of comparative commonsense knowledge from the web like "cars are faster than bikes" and "houses are bigger than desks". It contains comparative commonsense knowledge about properties of actions. However, these comparisons between objects are not in the context of actions. [18] designs an on-line game to motivate players to contribute commonsense knowledge about human goals. [19] acquires part-whole commonsense knowledge from Web contents and image tags. [20] induces numerical commonsense knowledge from pre-trained language models, e.g., a bird usually has two legs. [18–20] do not consider the commonsense knowledge about action properties. Unlike these commonsense knowledge resources, our work focuses on the commonsense knowledge about action properties. This kind of commonsense knowledge would complement or expand upon commonsense knowledge available in these commonsense knowledge bases.

There is little work on commonsense knowledge acquisition about action properties. [21] presents a method for acquiring relative physical knowledge of object pairs when an action is applied to these objects from natural language text along five dimensions: size, weight, speed, strength and rigidness. For example, given a statement "Tom entered his house", we can infer that the house is bigger than Tom. However, the number of dimensions is tiny compared to the dimensions in this paper. [22] and [23] investigates recognizing previously unseen actions with verb attributes. It considers action attributes like temporal duration, motion dynamics, body involvements, indoor related, etc. [24] taps into movie scripts and other narrative texts to extract participating agent, location and time of an activity. However, these attributes in [22, 23] and [24] are too general and have a limited coverage. [11] develops an approach to acquiring commonsense evidence for action justification. The commonsense evidence is merged into six categories. It involves properties of actions like agent, location and effect. But it does not provide detailed information about these properties. [25] extracts commonsense facts from Web n-gram data. It covers action properties such as location and purpose. However, the commonsense assertions about these properties have a low accuracy, for example, location has a 57% accuracy and purpose only has a 53% accuracy. In contrast with prior research, our work conducts a comprehensive study on commonsense knowledge about action properties. Moreover, the acquired commonsense knowledge is of high quality.

3 Identifying Commonsense Properties of Actions

WordNet [13] is a popular online lexical database. In WordNet, verbs are divided into 14 semantic domains including verbs of cognition, motion, communication, change and more. Virtually all the verbs in these semantic categories denote actions. The motion verbs are derived from two roots: {move: make a movement} and {move: travel}. In this paper, we focus on the second sense, which is the meaning of locomotion. We collect 456 self-motion verbs or verb phrases such as *run*, *go out* and *head for the hills* from WordNet. These actions are grouped into 260 semantic synsets. An action synset is a group of actions with highly similar semantics, e.g. {exit, go out, get out, leave}. Each synset of WordNet carries a synonymous expression which can be considered the definition of the synset. The definition of an action usually contains clues to extract typical properties of this action. For example, the definition of {swim} is "travel through water", so we can obtain the property of the medium (water) for *swim.* Action properties are more difficult to conceptualize compared to object properties as they involve varying levels of abstractness. We aim to construct a high-quality commonsense knowledge base of action properties and the number of actions is limited, so we tap human intelligence to extract commonsense properties of actions. We extract 19 commonsense properties of self-motion actions as shown in Table 1.

Table 1. Commonsense properties of self-motion actions.

Property	Definition	Examples
Agent	The entity that causes the happening of moving	Waste, run off (run off as waste)
Location	The extended spatial location of moving	Slide (move smoothly along a surface)
Starting point	A location where a journey begins	Take off, lift off (depart from the ground)
Midpoint	A location where a journey passes	Leak (enter or escape as through a hole or crack or fissure)
End point	A location where a journey ends	Move in (move into a new house or office)
Destination	The place designated as the end of a journey	Ascend (go along towards (a river's) source)
Goal	An anticipated outcome of moving	Travel, trip, jaunt (make a trip for pleasure)
Direction	The spatial relation between Something and the course along which it moves	Hop (make a jump forward or upward)

(*continued*)

Table 1. (*continued*)

Property	Definition	Examples
Time	The time of starting to move	Decamp, skip, vamoose (leave suddenly)
Cause	A justification for moving	Break down, collapse (collapse due to fatigue, an illness, or a sudden attack)
Result	A phenomenon that is caused by moving	Leap out, rush out, sally out, burst forth (jump out from a hiding place and surprise (someone))
Speed	Distance moved per unit time	Flee, fly, take flight (run away quickly)
Tool	A device that the something uses to change location	Fly (travel in an airplane)
Medium	The surrounding environment of moving	Swim (travel through water)
Distance	Size of the gap between starting point and end point	Come (cover a certain distance)
Manner	A way of moving	Sweep, sail (move with sweeping, effortless, gliding motions)
Path	A route along which something moves	Detour (travel via a detour)
Trajectory	Shape of path	Circle (move in a circular path above (someone or something))
Frequency	The number of moving	Tumble (roll over and over, back and forth)

run (跑)
{
- **agent:** human or animal
- **location:** ground
- **direction:** front
- **speed:** fast speed
- **tool:** foot
- **medium:** air
- **manner:** manner that with one foot off the ground at any given time

}

Fig. 1. Action frame of ***run***.

An action is represented in the form of frame with the above commonsense properties as slots. Each commonsense property (frame slot) in the action frame has one or more values as illustrated in Fig. 1. A property value must be a noun or noun phrase in the singular form to facilitate commonsense knowledge acquisition. In total, we have built more than 3217 semantic frames of verbs, which cover all the Chinese verbs. This commonsense knowledge collection will be a valuable asset for tasks like action recognition, action similarity computation, action categorization, and so on.

4 Dimensions for Acquiring Commonsense Knowledge

For several decades, commonsense knowledge acquisition has been a major impediment to the development of artificial intelligence as commonsense knowledge is usually not expressed explicitly but resides in the mind of humans. In fact, we humans are not clear what kind of commonsense knowledge we possess, though we have an enormous body of commonsense knowledge. Therefore, acquiring commonsense knowledge is a challenging task even for humans *if* we are not provided with clues about it.

Most commonsense knowledge involves attributes of objects and actions, for example, *a person wants to be healthy* (goal), *a car is bigger than a bike* (size), *sugar is sweet* (taste), etc. We argue that attributes of objects and actions can be used as good clues to acquire commonsense knowledge from humans. The function of adjectives is to express values of properties. For example, *good-looking* is used to describe the appearance of a person and *red* is the color of strawberries. So, we introduce a method that collects clues about commonsense knowledge based on adjectives. These clues serve as dimensions of acquiring commonsense knowledge. However, when people use adjectives to describe something, they rarely express the properties related these adjectives. For instance, we will say "you are beautiful" to compliment a woman, but we usually do not tell her "your appearance is beautiful". Therefore, it is difficult to determine dimensions based on adjectives using automatic information extraction technology [26], but easy for us humans. Moreover, the number of adjectives is limited. People could complete this task in a short time. For these reasons, we decided to rely on human intelligence to determine dimensions of acquiring commonsense knowledge with adjectives.

We investigate all the 1067 adjectives which denote 1329 semantic items in the book "*Usage Dictionary of Chinese Adjectives*" [27] and collect 115 dimensions. Due to the inherent linguistic characteristics, one Chinese adjective may depict different facets of things at the same time, e.g., *dense* (稠密) describes both quantity and distance. Moreover, an adjective may imply different meanings in different contexts. For example, *small* (小) can denote the young age of a person or the small volume of an object. To avoid missing the dimensions, we reserve all the attributes that an adjective can denote. A dimension may be a superordinate dimension of other dimensions, e.g., "content" is a superordinate dimension of "water content" and "fat content" which can be determined from *humid* (湿润) and *greasy* (油腻) respectively. These sub-dimensions provide more refined information. In this case, these sub-dimensions are collected as well as their more general dimensions. Only a few dimensions are shown in Table 2 because of the limited space.

Table 2. Dimensions of acquiring commonsense knowledge.

Dimension	Adjectives
Age	Old, young, elderly, middle-aged,...
Color	Red, white, golden, purple,...
Shape	Square, triangular, circular, curved,...
Mood	Happy, angry, sad, anxious,...
Speed	Fast, quick, slow, rapid,...
Location	Domestic, rural, foreign, marine,...
Temperature	Hot, cold, warm, chilly,...
Area	Tiny, spacious, extensive, broad,...
Weight	Heavy, weightless, underweight, light,...
Height	Tall, high, low, short,...
Price	Cheap, expensive, pricey, luxury,...
Wealth	Rich, poor, wealthy, indigent,...
Light	Bright, dark, dim, gloomy,...
……	……

These dimensions will be used as hints to acquire commonsense knowledge about action properties. The method of acquiring commonsense knowledge with dimensions can be used not only to acquire commonsense knowledge about action attributes, but also to obtain other kinds of commonsense knowledge (Fig. 2).

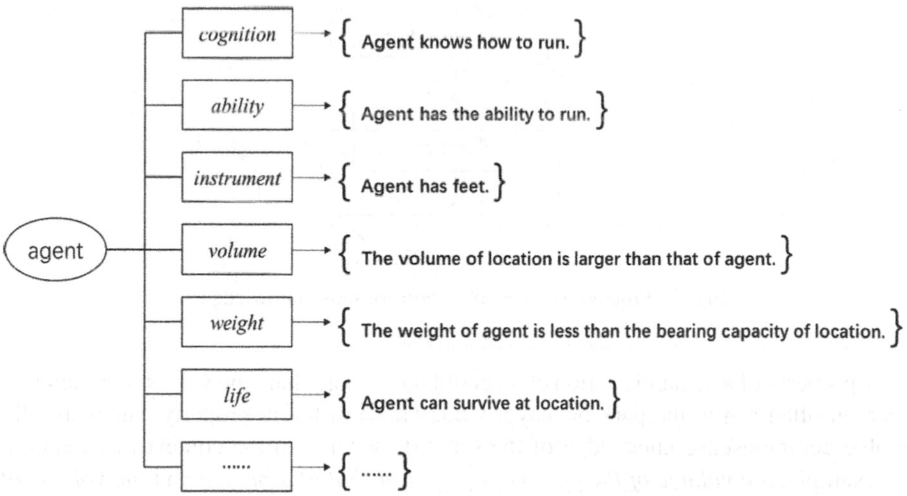

Fig. 2. Commonsense knowledge about the agent of ***run*** acquired using the dimensions.

5 Extracting Commonsense Knowledge from Text

5.1 Commonsense Knowledge Extraction

In the process of parsing text sentences, the system takes a sentence (e.g., the old man runs into the kitchen) as input and produces a parse tree as output. The next step is to extract text knowledge from the parse tree, allowing us to identify the property values included in the sentence. Consider the input sentence "the old man runs into the kitchen", we will acquire the knowledge that "the old man is *agent*" and "the kitchen is *end point*" as depicted in Fig. 4. Then we apply the extracted knowledge to the commonsense knowledge acquisition templates (i.e., the commonsense knowledge about action properties). Finally, we obtain commonsense knowledge that *the old man has feet* and *the volume of the kitchen is larger than that of the old man* by replacing the properties in a template with the property values extracted from corpora (Fig. 3).

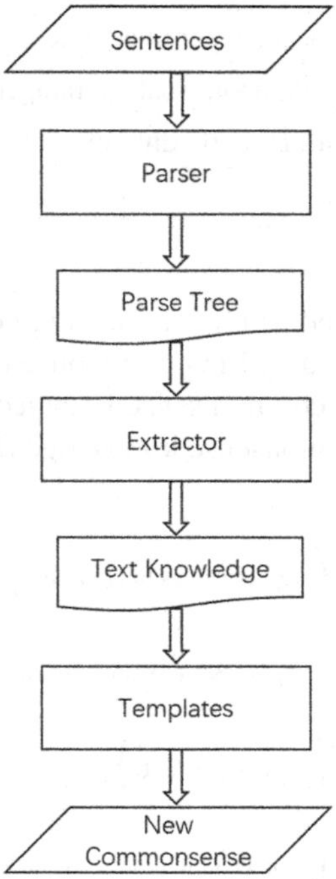

Fig. 3. Process of extracting commonsense knowledge.

A property of a semantic action class could have more than one values, for example, a person often run in the park or playground. These different property values usually involve commonsense knowledge of the same dimension in the context of an action. For example, *the volume of the park is larger than that of a person* and *the volume of the playground is larger than that of a person.* That is to say, *the volume of location is larger than that of agent* is a commonsense knowledge acquisition template. Therefore, we construct a set of commonsense knowledge acquisition templates with the properties identified in Sect. 3 and dimensions summarized in Sect. 4, thus allowing us to acquire new commonsense knowledge automatically. Manually constructed textual templates are reliable tools to acquire commonsense knowledge [28–30]. In contrast with these general templates, the templates in this paper are also commonsense knowledge themselves. In addition, instead of having humans contribute commonsense knowledge by filling the templates like [28–30], we acquire commonsense knowledge by replacing the properties automatically in these templates with property values extracted from the text. Thus, our templates are of high precision and we can exploit very large corpora to extract as much commonsense knowledge as possible.

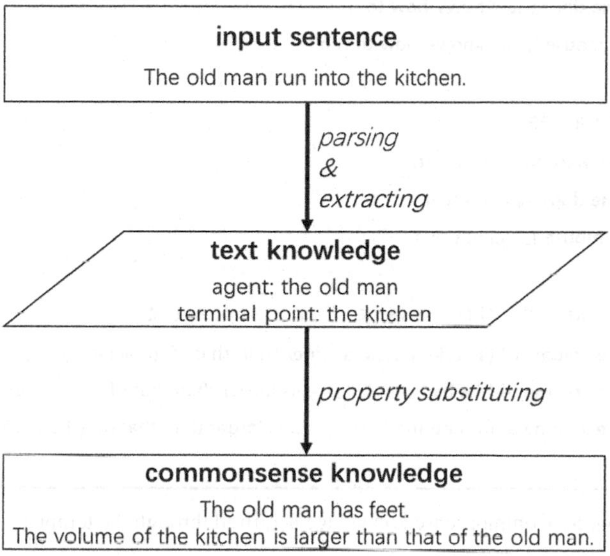

Fig. 4. An example of extracting commonsense knowledge.

We aim at extracting high-quality commonsense knowledge about properties of actions. For this purpose, we manually construct these templates as the number of properties and dimensions is limited. Some templates contain general concepts of properties, for instance, "Agent runs at a limited speed". *Speed* in this template is a general concept of speed but not the property that will be replaced by its property values to acquire commonsense knowledge. To distinguish template properties from general concepts of properties, we do not use any modifiers before template properties, e.g., "it is possible for agent to run at speed". We can obtain new commonsense knowledge of *a person runs at a limited speed* (人以有限的速度奔跑) and *it is possible for a person to run at a speed of six meters per second* (人可以以6m/s的速度奔跑) with the two templates about speed respectively.

Though the number of templates is limited, the values of a property that constituting a template are various. Thus, we can acquire a large body of commonsense knowledge with limited templates. As our goal is to gather commonsense knowledge, most knowledge we acquire will not hold as absolute universal truths, but rather be a reflection of overall tendencies. A lot of interesting commonsense knowledge can be acquired with this method like *the area of a tea table is larger than that of the ante, a dog has the memory of how to run, a person can survive in the bedroom*, etc. It is unnatural to express this commonsense knowledge in the text or communicate them with others. Therefore, it is very hard to extract them from Web contents or collect them from human contributors who are not equipped with dimensions (Fig. 5).

Agent knows how to run.

- ✓ **(A person)$_{\text{AGRNT}}$ knows how to run.**
- ✓ **(The dog)$_{\text{AGRNT}}$ knows how to run.**
- ✓ **(A mouse)$_{\text{AGRNT}}$ knows how to run.**
- ✓ ......

Agent has feet.

- ✓ **(A person)$_{\text{AGRNT}}$ has feet.**
- ✓ **(The dog)$_{\text{AGRNT}}$ has feet.**
- ✓ **(A mouse)$_{\text{AGRNT}}$ has feet.**
- ✓ ......

The volume of location is larger than that of agent.

- ✓ **The volume of (a park)$_{\text{LOCATION}}$ is larger than that of (a person)$_{\text{AGENT}}$.**
- ✓ **The volume of (the bedroom)$_{\text{LOCATION}}$ is larger than that of (a mouse)$_{\text{AGENT}}$.**
- ✓ **The volume of (a supermarket)$_{\text{LOCATION}}$ is larger than that of (the dog)$_{\text{AGENT}}$.**
- ✓ ......

Fig. 5. Commonsense knowledge acquired through the templates.

5.2 Evaluation

In order to evaluate the semantic parsing method, we have human judges annotate 250 random samples of the output action properties. For the input sentences, we choose CCL corpus [31], which is a large-scale Chinese corpus developed by the Research Center for Chinese Linguistics of Peking University, as the source of the input dataset. CCL is one of the most commonly used Chinese corpora that extracted from newspapers, literature, movie scripts, etc. The system achieves an accuracy of 94.57% for the *agent* and an accuracy of 94.59% for the *end point*.

To evaluate the quality of commonsense knowledge automatically extracted from text, we randomly select 4 self-motion actions which involves 73910 commonsense knowledge between the agent and end point. Each sentence must contain one of the 4 action verbs. We rely on expert human annotators to judge the commonsense knowledge. Commonsense knowledge is marked as correct if it makes sense to the annotators. We compute the precision as $c/c + i$, where c and i are the counts of correct and incorrect commonsense knowledge respectively. The results are reported in Table 3. We can observe from these assessments that our method achieves good precision. In some sentences, no information on agent or end point is available. This partly accounts for the low scores. Some errors are introduced in the process of parsing, where the system does not correctly identify the properties contained in the sentence. Such incorrect cases also lead to a lower precision.

Table 3. Evaluation of the commonsense knowledge.

Action	Commonsense knowledge	Precision
Run into (跑进)	11030	93.70%
Run to (跑到)	49025	92.88%
Run up (跑上)	4480	94.31%
Run back (跑回)	9375	94.61%

6 Conclusion

We develop a novel method for acquiring commonsense knowledge about action properties and extracting commonsense knowledge from web corpora based on templates. The templates are constructed by combining the commonsense properties of actions and dimensions collected using adjectives. Experiments show that the commonsense knowledge acquired with our method is of high quality and good coverage. In addition, a commonsense knowledge base of actions is established. It provides comprehensive information about commonsense properties of actions.

References

1. Chen, J., Yu, Z.: Incorporating structured commonsense knowledge in story completion. Proc. AAAI Conf. Artif. Intell. **33**, 6244–6251 (2019)
2. Wu, S., Li, Y., Zhang, D., et al.: Diverse and informative dialogue generation with context-specific commonsense knowledge awareness. In: Proceedings of the 58th Annual Meeting of the Association for Computational Linguistics, pp. 5811–5820 (2020)
3. Singh, K.K., Divvala, S., Farhadi, A., Lee, Y.J.: DOCK: detecting objects by transferring common-sense knowledge. In: Ferrari, V., Hebert, M., Sminchisescu, C., Weiss, Y. (eds.) ECCV 2018. LNCS, vol. 11217, pp. 506–522. Springer, Cham (2018). https://doi.org/10.1007/978-3-030-01261-8_30
4. Wang, P., Liu, D., Li, H., et al.: Give me something to eat: referring expression comprehension with commonsense knowledge. In: Proceedings of the 28th ACM International Conference on Multimedia, pp. 28–36 (2020)
5. Kaiser, P., Lewis, M., Petrick, R.P.A., et al.: Extracting common sense knowledge from text for robot planning. In: 2014 IEEE International Conference on Robotics and Automation (ICRA), pp. 3749–3756. IEEE (2014)
6. Fellbaum, C.: English verbs as a semantic net. Int. J. Lexicogr. **3**(4), 278–301 (1990)

7. Lenat, D.B.: CYC: a large-scale investment in knowledge infrastructure. Commun. ACM **38**(11), 33–38 (1995)
8. Liu, H., Singh, P.: ConceptNet—a practical commonsense reasoning tool-kit. BT Technol. J. **22**(4), 211–226 (2004)
9. Tandon, N., De Melo, G., Suchanek, F., et al.: Webchild: harvesting and organizing commonsense knowledge from the web. In: Proceedings of the 7th ACM International Conference on Web Search and Data Mining, pp. 523–532 (2014)
10. Gao, Q., Yang, S., Chai, J., et al.: What action causes this? towards naive physical action-effect prediction. In: Proceedings of the 56th Annual Meeting of the Association for Computational Linguistics (Volume 1: Long Papers), pp. 934–945 (2018)
11. Yang, S., Gao, Q., Saba-Sadiya, S., et al.: Commonsense justification for action explanation. In: Proceedings of the 2018 Conference on Empirical Methods in Natural Language Processing, pp. 2627–2637 (2018)
12. Romero, J., Razniewski, S., Pal, K., et al.: Commonsense properties from query logs and question answering forums. In: Proceedings of the 28th ACM International Conference on Information and Knowledge Management, pp. 1411–1420 (2019)
13. Fellbaum, C., Miller, G.: WordNet: An Electronic Lexical Database. MIT Press, Cambridge (1998)
14. Blanco, E., Cankaya, H., Moldovan, D.: Commonsense knowledge extraction using concepts properties. In: Twenty-Fourth International FLAIRS Conference (2011)
15. Raskin, V., Nirenburg, S.: An applied ontological semantic microtheory of adjective meaning for natural language processing. Mach. Transl. **13**(2), 135–227 (1998)
16. Fang, F., Wang, Y., Zhang, L., Cao, C.: Knowledge extraction from Chinese records of cyber attacks based on a semantic grammar. In: Lehner, F., Fteimi, N. (eds.) KSEM 2016. LNCS (LNAI), vol. 9983, pp. 55–68. Springer, Cham (2016). https://doi.org/10.1007/978-3-319-47650-6_5
17. Tandon, N., De Melo, G., Weikum, G.: Acquiring comparative commonsense knowledge from the web. In: Proceedings of the Twenty-Eighth AAAI Conference on Artificial Intelligence (AAAI 2014), pp. 166–172. AAAI Press (2014)
18. Lieberman, H., Smith, D., Teeters, A.: Common consensus: a web-based game for collecting commonsense goals. In: ACM Workshop on Common Sense for Intelligent Interfaces (2007)
19. Tandon, N., Hariman, C., Urbani, J., Rohrbach, A., Rohrbach, M., Weikum, G.: Commonsense in parts: mining part-whole relations from the web and image tags. In: Proceedings of the Thirtieth AAAI Conference on Artificial Intelligence (AAAI 2016). AAAI Press, pp. 243–250 (2016)
20. Lin, B.Y., Lee, S., Khanna, R., et al.: Birds have four legs?! NumerSense: probing numerical commonsense knowledge of pre-trained language models. arXiv preprint arXiv:2005.00683 (2020)
21. Forbes, M., Choi, Y.: Verb physics: relative physical knowledge of actions and objects. Meeting of the Association for Computational Linguistics, pp. 266–276 (2017)
22. Zellers, R., Choi, Y.: Zero-shot activity recognition with verb attribute induction. In: Empirical Methods in Natural Language Processing, pp. 946–958 (2017)
23. Liu, J., Kuipers, B., Savarese, S.: Recognizing human actions by attributes. In: Proceedings of the 2011 IEEE Conference on Computer Vision and Template Recognition (CVPR 2011). IEEE Computer Society, pp. 3337–3344 (2011)
24. Tandon, N., De Melo, G., De, A., et al.: Knowlywood: mining activity knowledge from hollywood narratives. In: Proceedings of the 24th ACM International on Conference on Information and Knowledge Management, pp. 223–232 (2015)
25. Tandon, N., De Melo, G., Weikum, G., et al.: Deriving a web-scale common sense fact database. In: National Conference on Artificial Intelligence, pp. 152–157 (2011)

26. Kondreddi, S.K., Triantafillou, P., Weikum, G.: Combining information extraction and human computing for crowdsourced knowledge acquisition. In: 2014 IEEE 30th International Conference on Data Engineering, pp. 988–999. IEEE (2014)
27. Usage Dictionary of Chinese Adjectives. Commercial Press (2003)
28. Singh, P., Lin, T., Mueller, E.T., Lim, G., Perkins, T., Zhu, W.L.: Open mind common sense: knowledge acquisition from the general public. In: Meersman, R., Tari, Z. (eds.) OTM 2002. LNCS, vol. 2519, pp. 1223–1237. Springer, Heidelberg (2002). https://doi.org/10.1007/3-540-36124-3_77
29. Kuo, Y., Hsu, J.Y., Shih, F., et al.: Contextual commonsense knowledge acquisition from social content by crowd-sourcing explanations. In: National Conference on Artificial Intelligence (2012)
30. Collell, G., Van Gool, L., Moens, M.F.: Acquiring common sense spatial knowledge through implicit spatial templates. In: Thirty-Second AAAI Conference on Artificial Intelligence (2018)
31. Zhan, W., Guo, R., et al.: Development of CCL corpus of Peking University. Corpus Linguist. (001), 71–86 (2019)

Multi-hop Learning Promote Cooperation in Multi-agent Systems

Xingyu Liu[1], Runyu Guan[1,2], Tao Wang[1(✉)], Le Han[1], Yu Qin[1], and Yi Wang[1]

[1] College of Computer Science and Electronic Engineering, Hunan University, Changsha, China
wangtao@hnu.edu.cn

[2] University of Southern California, Los Angeles, USA

Abstract. The behavior of individuals maximizing their own benefits in some systems leads to decline of system performance. A challenge remains to promote and maintain cooperation between selfish individuals in multi-agent systems. We propose a multi-hop learning method to promote cooperation in multi-agent system. Based on spatial evolutionary dilemma game, agents can learn strategies from multi-hop neighbors on grid network to improve overall system's fitness. We investigate the system's cooperation rate with different hop learning ability in the Prisoner's Dilemma game, the Snowdrift game and the Stag-hunt game. Experiments show that for Stag-hunt game and Prisoner's Dilemma game, multi-hop learning is a fairly good way to promote cooperation in multi-agent systems.

Keywords: Evolutionary game · Game theory · Multi-agent system · Coordination · Nash equilibrium · Pareto optimality

1 Introduction

Cooperation makes single-cell organisms becoming complex animals and the prosperity of human society depends on countless relationships [1]. However it seems not preferred by Darwinian selection, since a cooperator incurs a cost to benefit others making defectors an evolutionary advantage [2,3]. Selfish individuals often mess the system to maximize their own interests, especially in some multi-agent systems such as P2P systems, wireless sensor networks and so on [4]. Therefore how to promote and maintain cooperation among selfish individuals in multi-agent systems is not only helpful for understanding the existence of cooperation in the real world, but also important for practical applications [5–7].

The emergence of evolutionary game theory has become a powerful tool for studying inter-group cooperative behavior [8,9]. Common dilemma models in evolutionary game include Prisoner's Dilemma Game [10,11], Snowdrift Game [12,13], Stag-hunt Game [14,15], and Public Goods Game [16–18]. So far, the researchers have proposed several mechanisms to define interactions between

H. Qiu et al. (Eds.): KSEM 2021, LNAI 12815, pp. 66–77, 2021.
https://doi.org/10.1007/978-3-030-82136-4_6

intelligence and explain the persistence of cooperation, such as kin selection, direct reciprocity [19], indirect reciprocity [20], group selection [21], and network reciprocity [22], which can effectively promote the initiation and maintenance of cooperative behavior [23,24].

In the past few decades, there are lots of work on the function and structure of network. The earliest on network structure is fully connected network, which assumes that game agents are evenly mixed. Then comes the lattice network [25], the small world network [26], the scale-free network [27] and other complex networks [28,29], discussing the impact of different network structures in the evolutionary game. Many mechanisms can effectively promote cooperation, such as the strategy update mechanism [30–32], memory mechanism [33–35], tax mechanism [36], reward and punishment mechanism [37], prior cooperation belief mechanism, and reputation mechanism [38].

Previous researchers proposed increasing the size of the neighborhood to study its impact on cooperation. Margarita et al. studied the continuous prisoner's dilemma on lattice and found that the mean-field limit of no cooperation is reached for a neighborhood size of about five-hop, where player gamed and updated rule with five-hop neighbors. They also found that cooperation does not depend on network size, but only on the network topology [39]. Wang et al. studied the Prisoner's Dilemma game on a grid, showed that the cooperation depends on the noise and cost-effectiveness ratio, and cooperation can be significantly enhanced by increasing the size of the interactive neighborhood [40]. Wang et al. found that cooperation is best enhanced when the interaction neighborhood is two-hop. In general, these works suggested that the individual's learning range and game range are increased synchronized. They tried to find new mechanisms such as reputation, cooperative belief, network type or imitation rule, etc. to foster cooperation. Nevertheless, to the best of our knowledge, no research has considered the heterogeneous learning range with game range in the framework of network reciprocity.

We proposed a multi-hop learning with one-hop game mechanism: by increasing the learning hop of the agent, its scope of comparing and adopting strategy is not confined to the nearest neighborhood. We introduced trigger conditions on two common strategy updating rules, and then conducted a series of experiments.

This article is scheduled as follows. In the second section, we introduce common models of evolutionary game, several common strategy updating rules, and put forward our multi-hop learning mechanism. In the third section, we selected two common strategy updating rules to carry on the experiments and analyze the result. Finally, we summarize the main conclusion of the full paper.

2 Model

2.1 Game Model

There are several classic game dilemmas, such as Prisoner's Dilemma Game, Snowdrift Game, Stag-hunt Game, Boxed Pig Game etc. In this paper, we selected the first three dilemma game models for our experiments. Let's start by introducing these three common models.

The payoff matrix of the 2×2 matrix game is $\begin{bmatrix} R\ S \\ T\ P \end{bmatrix}$, the reward for each of two cooperating participants is R; the mutual punishment of the two participants who betrayed each other is P. When an agent choosing to cooperate with a defector, the cooperator's payoff is S and the temptation for the defector is T. There are three kinds of well-known dilemma games mentioned above: Prisoner's Dilemma Game (T−R>0, P−S>0, can be abbreviated as PD game), Snowdrift Game (T−R>0, can be abbreviated as SD game, also called chicken game or eagle pigeon game) and Stag-hunt Game (P−S>0, can be abbreviated as SH game). Without losing universality, we simplified the 4 - parameter matrix to 1 - parameter matrix: the parameter r is called defection reward. So the payoff matrix of Prisoner's Dilemma Game is $\begin{bmatrix} 1 & 0 \\ 1+r & 0.1 \end{bmatrix}$ (1>r>0) (This is a strict Prisoner's Dilemma Game, and its result is similar to $\begin{bmatrix} 1 & 0 \\ b & 0.1 \end{bmatrix}$ (2>b>1)); the payoff matrix of Snowdrift Game is $\begin{bmatrix} 1 & 1-r \\ 1+r & 0 \end{bmatrix}$ (1>r>0); the payoff matrix of Stag-hunt Game is $\begin{bmatrix} 1 & -r \\ r & 0 \end{bmatrix}$ (1>r>0).

2.2 Strategy Updating Rules

In the iteration of evolutionary gaming, the agent may decide to imitate the neighbor's strategy based on the comparison between its own payoff and the neighbor's payoff after a game round. Different strategy updating rules can determine various evolution directions and having completely different influences on the results. In this paper, we used two classical strategy updating rules: unconditional imitation rule and replicator dynamic rule.

(1)Unconditional imitation rule: after a game round, the agent learns the strategy from the one with the largest payoff among its neighbors. The precondition must be satisfied is that the neighbor's payoff is greater than itself. Take the example of agent a and agent b to describe the imitation probability formula:

$$p\left(S_a \rightarrow S_b\right) = \begin{cases} 1, & I_b > I_a \\ 0, & I_b < I_a \end{cases} \tag{1}$$

Among them, $p\left(S_a \rightarrow S_b\right)$ is the probability that agent a imitates agent b, S_a and S_b is the current policies of agent a and agent b, I_a and I_b is the cumulative payoff of a and b after a game round.

(2)Replicator dynamic rule: replicator dynamic rule is the updating rule closest to replication dynamics. Agent a will select a neighbor randomly (assuming it's agent b) after a round of game. If payoff of a is greater than that of the neighbor b, a will still stick to its own strategy instead of adopting neighbor b's strategy. If the income of b is greater than that of a, agent a will imitate b's strategy with a certain probability.

$$p\left(S_a \rightarrow S_b\right) = \begin{cases} \frac{I_b - I_a}{\phi}, & I_b > I_a \\ 0, & I_b < I_a \end{cases} \tag{2}$$

In order to guarantee the learning probability p within (0,1), making ϕ satisfies the equation.

$$\phi = max(k_a, k_b)(max(R, T) - min(P, S)) \tag{3}$$

In this formula, k_a,k_b respectively represents the number of direct neighbors of agent a and agent b. Similar to unconditional imitation rule, for the replicator dynamic rule, agent can only learn strategies that are better than its own after a game round. However, under the replicator dynamic rule, the strategy adopting is conditional and based on a certain probability, making it closer to the reality.

2.3 Multi-hop Learning Mechanism

Based on the above evolutionary game theory, we proposed a mechanism that can promote cooperation in the system——multi-hop learning mechanism. In usual game model, agents study the nearest neighbor. In this paper, we considered increasing the scope of learning so that the scope of learning was extended to its neighbor's neighbor, or further.

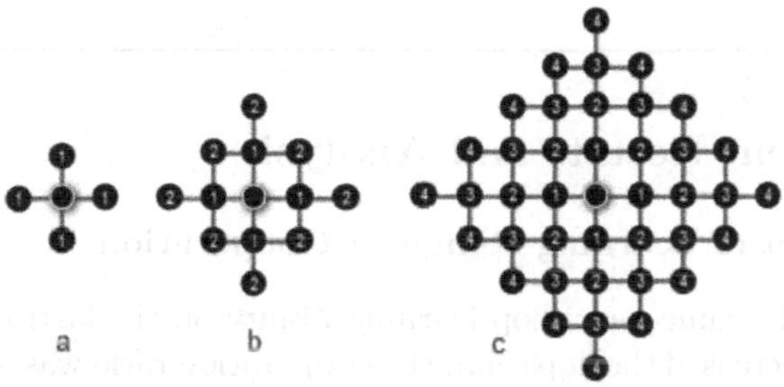

Fig. 1. Neighbor range under different learning hops

We defined learning hop as an individual's learning range. First of all, establishing a quadrilateral borderless lattice network with the size of N=L*L, L is the number of agents on a quadrilateral edge. As Fig. 1 shows, each square corresponds to a game individual, two squares adjacent to each other are a pair of game players and an agent can only game with nearest neighbors. The parameter S is defined to represent the learning hop. As Fig. 1(a) shows, when S=1, it represents classic Von Neumann Neighborhood (VNN), so the learning hop is 1. When the range is extended to a neighbor's neighbor (learning hop S=2), The size of the whole range is shown in Fig. 1(b). Figure 1(c) shows the learning range when S=4. According to this rule, we can obtain the relationship between S and the number of all neighbors in the corresponding range: sum=2S∗(S+1).

2.4 The Experimental Process

All data were bases on 100 samples as the following algorithm, which described the main simulation experiment:

Algorithm 1: experimental process

```
Input: 10000 agents was placed on 100 * 100 periodic boundary lattic network
for game ∈ { Prisoner's Dilemma game,Snowdrift game,Stag-hunt game } do
    for payoff parameter r ∈ { 0,0.1,0.2 ... 1 } do
        for hop=1 to 5 do
            for each agent do
                Initialize the strategy randomly
                payoff ← 0
            end
            for i=1 to 1000 generations do
                Each two adjacent agents played the game at the same time
                Calculating payoff based on the current payoff matrix
                Accumulate the payoff of all their games
                Adjusted their strategy according to hops and updating rules
                Agent had a probability of p=0.01 mutation rate to reverse its
                strategy
                Count and save system cooperation ratio
            end
        end
    end
end
```

3 Experiment Results and Analysis

3.1 The Effect of Learning Range to Cooperation

All agents had the same multi-hop learning ability on the lattice network, then they gradually increased the hops, and the cooperation ratio was observed. Cooperation ratio is defined as follows:

$$R_c = N_c/(N_c + N_d) \tag{4}$$

where Nc represented the number of agents that choose to cooperate, and Nd represented the number of agents that choose to defect.

The result was in Fig. 2. Overall, multi-hop learning greatly promoted cooperation in the Stag-hunt game, slightly in the Prisoner's Dilemma game and had no obvious effect on the Snowdrift game.

In the Stag-hunt game with replicator dynamic rule, cooperation rate changed smoothly. As the learning hops increased, the cooperation rate increased significantly. While with unconditional imitation rule, when the learning range is more than 1 hop, cooperation was greatly promoted and defectors almost disappeared. In the Prisoner's Dilemma game with replicator dynamic rule, the cooperation rate with multi-hop was higher than 1-hop significantly. While with unconditional imitation rule, the rate of cooperation with multi-hop was higher than 1-hop except for defection reward r =0.4 and 0.5.

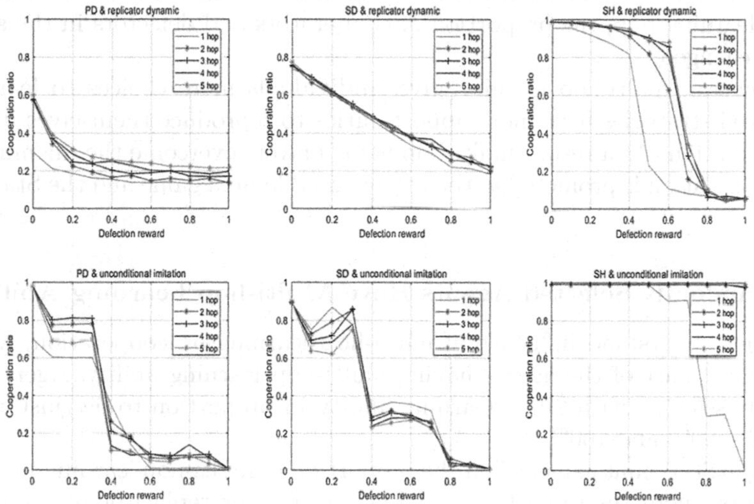

Fig. 2. The effect of different learning hops to cooperation. For several different hops of 1, 2, 3, 4, and 5, the cooperation rate is a function of defection reward r. Column 1, 2, 3 are the PD, SD and SH game respectively; line 1, 2 display replicator dynamic and unconditional imitation updating rule respectively.

For the Stag-hunt game, its Nash equilibrium is (C, C) and (D, D) (C for cooperating and D for defecting). When r<0.5, agents in well-mixed population are dominated by (C, C); when r>0.5, they are dominated by (D, D). When r>0.5, lattice network promotes cooperation with traditional one-hop learning in Fig. 2(c, f). For replicator dynamic rule with multi-hop learning, pairs of cooperative agents with high payoffs are learned by more defectors around, which leading to the increases of cooperators. For unconditional imitation rule, it is interesting that defectors almost disappear with multi-hop learning. This is because agents increase the range of learning, small numbers of (C, C) pairs can be learned by defectors in "defector ocean".

For the Prisoners' Dilemma game in Fig. 2(a, d), with multi-hop learning, agents randomly select a neighbor to learn in the increased group. Since the Nash equilibrium for the Prisoner's Dilemma game is (D, D) but (C, C) can provide a higher payoff for each player, in the case of standard one-hop learning, cooperative agents can form many small clusters in the lattice network. Around them is a large "ocean" formed by defectors. The payoffs of agents that in the "ocean" are all zero because all their opponents choose to defect. However, in the cluster since everyone is cooperative, they can get payoffs much higher than zero. As a result, cooperators in the cluster can have a better cumulative payoff than defectors in the "ocean". When the agents increase their learning range, defectors in the ocean can learn from cooperative agents which are their indirect neighbors, and they will change to cooperate, thus increasing cooperation rate.

For the Snowdrift game in Fig. 2(b, e), the Nash equilibrium is (C, D), which lead the cooperators and the defectors being mixed in the network. After increasing the learning hop, the proportion of cooperators and defectors in the system has not changed.

In general, multi-hop learning gives individuals more choices to learn and high-payoff strategies have more opportunities to reproduce themselves into the next generation. As a result, multi-hop helps players overcome the dilemma and more cooperation is promoted in the Prisoner's dilemma game and the Stag-hunt game.

3.2 Randomly Selected Agents Have Multi-hop Learning Ability

To further understand influence of multi-hop learning on cooperation, we randomly made part of the agents having multi-hop learning ability. Agents were randomly selected with 2-hop learning ability in proportion to 0%(just 1-hop), 30%, 60%, 90% and 100%.

For the Stag-hunt game, when the proportion of multi-hop learning increases, cooperation increases respectively in Fig. 3(c, f). For replicator dynamic rule, with rising of multi-hop learning agents, the range of high cooperation area has been extended to higher defection reward area. For unconditional imitation rule, when 30% have a multi-hop learning ability, it is obvious to promote cooperation and almost all agents choose to cooperate when the proportion of multi-hop learning ability reaches 90%. This is because the Nash equilibrium of Stag-hunt game is (C, C) and (D, D), and (C, C) is the balance state with higher payoffs for each side which is the best strategy pair leading to the choice of each agent tends to be the same in continuous evolution. The more agents can multi-hop learn, the more helpful for (C, C) being discovered and learned.

For the Snowdrift game, with both rules, the distinction between curves is very small in Fig. 3(b, e), which is consistent with the previous analysis. The Nash equilibrium of the Snowdrift game is (C, D), the stable state of the system is mainly determined by the value of the Defection reward.

For the Prisoner's Dilemma game, cooperation also increases with 2-hop learning ability in Fig. 3(a, d). For replicator dynamic rule the difference between curves is small. There is no perfect "win-win" strategy for Prisoner's Dilemma game. The most profitable combination is when you choose to defect and your opponent chooses to cooperate. But soon the opponent will change the strategy because of the reduction of payoffs, and then the (D, D) strategy will have very low payoffs. At this time, the (C, C) strategy will become worth learning for the agents, so the agent's choice of strategy is quite confusing. For unconditional imitation rule, the distinction between curves is obvious. When there are more agents with multi hop learning ability, there are more cooperators. The unconditional imitation rule is a simpler and more idealistic updating rule. It can be clearly seen that multi-hop learning has a catalytic effect on the rate of system cooperation.

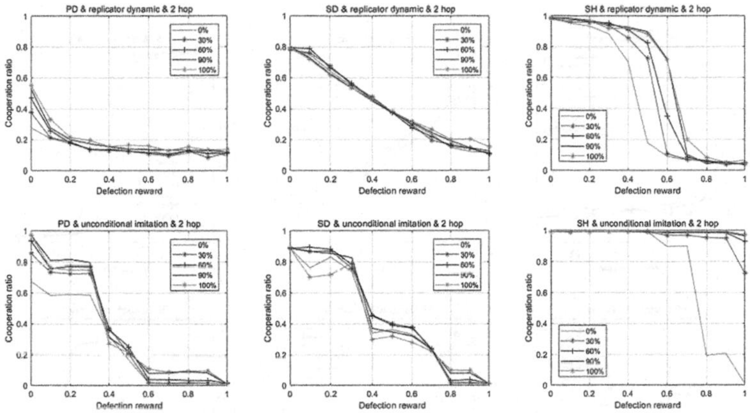

Fig. 3. Randomly selected agents have 2-hop learning ability. For different proportion (0%, 30%, 60%, 90%, and 100%) of agents with 2-hop learning capabilities, the cooperation rate is a function of defection reward r. Column 1, 2, 3 are the PD, SD and SH game respectively; line 1, 2 display replicator dynamic and unconditional imitation rule respectively.

3.3 Agents Have Multi-hop Learning Ability According to Their Own Payoff

In this section, we discuss another important issue. In real world, individual's learning ability may be related to his income or possessions. On the one hand, the rich are more able to get more information. On the other hand, the rich may be content with the status, while the poor may try harder to get more information. It is not clear how the players' payoff affect their learning ability and further affect system cooperation. We let the possibility of agents have multi-hop learning ability depend on their own accumulative payoffs. There are two cases: the agents whose payoff is lower than the average of its neighbors getting 2/3/4 hops learning ability (marked as "lower-2/3/4" in Fig. 3) and the agents whose payoff is higher than the average getting 2/3/4 hops learning ability (marked as "higher-2/3/4" in Fig. 3).

For the Stag-hunt game, cooperation is promoted in both cases, and higher-payoff getting multi-hop learning promote cooperation more strongly than lower-payoff. The result with unconditional imitation rule (Fig. 4(f)) is more obvious than that with replicator dynamic rule (Fig. 4(c)). As we explained in Sect. 3.2, (C, C) is the best pair of strategies in Stag-hunt game with the highest payoff which most agents will prefer. High-payoff agents getting multi-hop learning ability help the cooperator to consolidate their cooperation strategy.

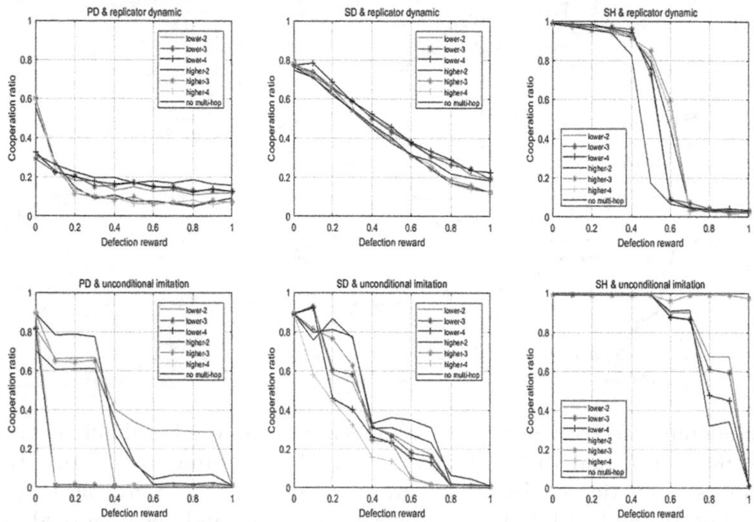

Fig. 4. Agents have multi-hop learning ability according to their own payoffs, and the cooperation rate is a function of defection reward r. There are two cases in each subgraph: the agents whose payoff is lower than the average of its neighbors getting 2/3/4 hops learning ability (marked as "lower-2/3/4") and the agents whose payoff is higher than the average getting 2/3/4 hops learning ability (marked as "higher-2/3/4"). Column 1, 2, 3 are the PD, SD and SH game respectively; line 1, 2 display replicator dynamic and unconditional imitation rule respectively.

For the Prisoner's Dilemma game, with replicator dynamic rule (Fig. 4(a)), when the defection reward is lower than 0.1, the higher-payoff agents getting multi-hop learning can promote cooperation; otherwise, lower-payoff agent getting multi-hop learning ability can promote cooperation. But in general, rates of cooperation are lower than the original no-hop situation. For the unconditional imitation rule, the conclusion is not obvious.

Our hypothesis in Sect. 3.1 can explain the phenomenon in replicator dynamic rule (Fig. 4(a)), when the Defection reward is greater than 0.1, most of lower-payoff agents choose the defection strategy. Increasing their range of learning can help some defectors near the "ocean" edge to learn from cooperative agents. When higher-payoff agents getting multi-hop learning ability, some of the higher-payoff cooperative agents that form cooperative clusters may learn further defectors on the boundary of clusters which benefit from (C, D).

For the Snowdrift game, in replicator dynamic rule (Fig. 4(b)), the cooperation rate of lower-payoff getting multi-hop learning is slightly higher than the higher-payoff. For this game, lower-payoff agents are mainly cooperators in the mixed Nash equilibrium, and the one-hop neighbors of these agents are mainly defectors. Multi-hop learning increases their probability to learn from cooperators which are not around them, while for higher-payoff agents getting multi-hop learning ability, increasing the scope of learning does not bring additional advantages. The result with unconditional imitation rule is not obvious (Fig. 4(e)).

4 Conclusion

For Stag-hunt game and Prisoner's Dilemma game, multi-hop learning is a fairly good way to promote cooperation in multi-agent systems and for Snowdrift game, its effect is not obvious, which is mainly due to the mixed Nash equilibrium of Snowdrift game.

Among the three dilemma games, cooperation rate of the Stag-hunt game is most obviously promoted by multi hop learning, which is because in this game (C, C) is not only the Nash equilibrium with highest payoffs, but also the highest overall-payoff strategy pair. Agents tend to this perfect win-win strategy and multi-hop learning ability can help it spread faster.

The Prisoner's dilemma game and the Snowdrift game has been studied a lot, while for the Stag-hunt game, the mechanism to promote cooperation is not the same sometimes. It is valuable to make further study for the Stag-hunt game.

Acknowledgement. This work was supported by the National Natural Science Foundation of China under Grant No.61672215.

References

1. Wang, Z., et al.: Onymity promotes cooperation in social dilemma experiments. Sci. Adv. **3**(3), e1601444 (2017)
2. Szolnoki, A., Perc, M.: Evolutionary dynamics of cooperation in neutral populations. New J. Phys. **20**(1), 013031 (2018)
3. Li, X., et al.: Punishment diminishes the benefits of network reciprocity in social dilemma experiments. Proc. Nat. Acad. Sci. **115**(1), 30–35 (2018)
4. Huang, K., Chen, X., Yu, Z., Yang, C., Gui, W.: Heterogeneous cooperative belief for social dilemma in multi-agent system. Appl. Math. Comput. **320**, 572–579 (2018)
5. Chen, M., Zhang, Y., Qiu, M., Guizani, N., Hao, Y.: SPHA: smart personal health advisor based on deep analytics. IEEE Commun. Mag. **56**(3), 164–169 (2018)
6. Tao, L., Golikov, S., Gai, K., Qiu, M.: A reusable software component for integrated syntax and semantic validation for services computing. In: 2015 IEEE Symposium on Service-Oriented System Engineering, pp. 127–132. IEEE (2015)

7. Gai, K., Qiu, M.: Reinforcement learning-based content-centric services in mobile sensing. IEEE Netw. **32**(4), 34–39 (2018)
8. Smith, J.M.: Evolution and the Theory of Games. Cambridge University Press, Cambridge (1982)
9. Hofbauer, J., Sigmund, K., et al.: Evolutionary Games and Population Dynamics. Cambridge University Press, Cambridge (1998)
10. Tanimoto, J.: Dilemma solving by the coevolution of networks and strategy in a 2× 2 game. Phys. Rev. E **76**(2), 021126 (2007)
11. Tanimoto, J., Sagara, H.: A study on emergence of alternating reciprocity in a 2× 2 game with 2-length memory strategy. BioSystems **90**(3), 728–737 (2007)
12. Doebeli, M., Hauert, C.: Models of cooperation based on the prisoner's dilemma and the snowdrift game. Ecol. Lett. **8**(7), 748–766 (2005)
13. Wang, B., Pei, Z., Wang, L.: Evolutionary dynamics of cooperation on interdependent networks with the prisoner's dilemma and snowdrift game. EPL Europhys. Lett. **107**(5), 58006 (2014)
14. Diebold, J., Tari, S., Cremers, D.: The role of diffusion in figure hunt games. J. Math. Imaging Vis. **52**(1), 108–123 (2015)
15. Büyükboyacı, M.: Risk attitudes and the stag-hunt game. Econ. Lett. **124**(3), 323–325 (2014)
16. Szolnoki, A., Chen, X.: Benefits of tolerance in public goods games. Phys. Rev. E **92**(4), 042813 (2015)
17. Archetti, M., Scheuring, I.: Game theory of public goods in one-shot social dilemmas without assortment. J. Theor. Biol. **299**, 9–20 (2012)
18. Liu, P., Liu, J.: Contribution diversity and incremental learning promote cooperation in public goods games. Physica A Stat. Mech. Appl. **486**, 827–838 (2017)
19. Nowak, M.A.: Five rules for the evolution of cooperation. Science **314**(5805), 1560–1563 (2006)
20. Berger, U.: Learning to cooperate via indirect reciprocity. Games Econ. Behav. **72**(1), 30–37 (2011)
21. Crowley, P.H., Baik, K.H.: Variable valuations and voluntarism under group selection: an evolutionary public goods game. J. Theor. Biol. **265**(3), 238–244 (2010)
22. Boccaletti, S., et al.: The structure and dynamics of multilayer networks. Phys. Rep. **544**(1), 1–122 (2014)
23. Yan, L.J., Cercone, N.: Bayesian network modeling for evolutionary genetic structures. Comput. Math. Appl. **59**(8), 2541–2551 (2010)
24. Wang, C., Wang, L., Wang, J., Sun, S., Xia, C.: Inferring the reputation enhances the cooperation in the public goods game on interdependent lattices. Appl. Math. Comput. **293**, 18–29 (2017)
25. Wu, Z.-X., Rong, Z.: Boosting cooperation by involving extortion in spatial prisoner's dilemma games. Phys. Rev. E **90**(6), 062102 (2014)
26. Wu, Z.-X., Xu, X.-J., Chen, Y., Wang, Y.-H.: Spatial prisoner's dilemma game with volunteering in newman-watts small-world networks. Phys. Rev. E **71**(3), 037103 (2005)
27. Santos, F.C., Santos, M.D., Pacheco, J.M.: Social diversity promotes the emergence of cooperation in public goods games. Nature **454**(7201), 213–216 (2008)
28. Li, D., Ma, J., Tian, Z., Zhu, H.: An evolutionary game for the diffusion of rumor in complex networks. Physica A Stat. Mech. Appl. **433**, 51–58 (2015)
29. Zhu, Y., Zhang, J., Sun, Q., Chen, Z.: Evolutionary dynamics of strategies for threshold snowdrift games on complex networks. Knowl.-Based Syst. **130**, 51–61 (2017)

30. Rong, Z., Wu, Z.-X., Chen, G.: Coevolution of strategy-selection time scale and cooperation in spatial prisoner's dilemma game. EPL Europhys. Lett. **102**(6), 68005 (2013)
31. Chen, X., Wang, L.: Promotion of cooperation induced by appropriate payoff aspirations in a small-world networked game. Phys. Rev. E. **77**(1), 017103 (2008)
32. Li, Y., Lan, X., Deng, X., Sadiq, R., Deng, Y.: Comprehensive consideration of strategy updating promotes cooperation in the prisoner's dilemma game. Physica A Stat. Mech. Appl. **403**, 284–292 (2014)
33. Chen, Z.-G., Wang, T., Xiao, D.-G., Xu, Y.: Can remembering history from predecessor promote cooperation in the next generation? Chaos Solitons Fractals **56**, 59–68 (2013)
34. Wang, T., Chen, Z., Li, K., Deng, X., Li, D.: Memory does not necessarily promote cooperation in dilemma games. Physica A Stat. Mech. Appl. **395**, 218–227 (2014)
35. Wang, T., Chen, Z., Yang, L., Zou, Y., Luo, J.: Memory boosts turn taking in evolutionary dilemma games. BioSystems **131**, 30–39 (2015)
36. Xu, L., Cao, X., Du, W., Li, Y.: Effects of taxation on the evolution of cooperation. Chaos, Solitons Fractals **113**, 63–68 (2018)
37. Song, Q., Cao, Z., Tao, R., Jiang, W., Liu, C., Liu, J.: Conditional neutral punishment promotes cooperation in the spatial prisoner's dilemma game. Appl. Math. Comput. **368**, 124798 (2020)
38. Quan, J., Zhou, Y., Wang, X., Yang, J.-B.: Information fusion based on reputation and payoff promotes cooperation in spatial public goods game. Appl. Math. Comput. **368**, 124805 (2020)
39. Ifti, M., Killingback, T., Doebeli, M.: Effects of neighbourhood size and connectivity on the spatial continuous prisoner's dilemma. J. Theor. Biol. **231**(1), 97–106 (2004)
40. Wang, J., Xia, C., Wang, Y., Ding, S., Sun, J.: Spatial prisoner's dilemma games with increasing size of the interaction neighborhood on regular lattices. Chin. Sci. Bull. **57**(7), 724–728 (2012)

FedPS: Model Aggregation with Pseudo Samples

Mulin Xu(✉)

Fudan University, Shanghai 200433, China
mlxu18@fudan.edu.cn

Abstract. Federated learning (FL) is an emerging machine learning task that allows many clients to train a global model collaboratively while keeping their respective data nondisclosure. The regular method of federated learning is to average the parameters of client models, which may only work in the cases of few client models with same architectures and initialized parameters. Moreover, this strategy has a heavy communication burden as it requires a lot of communication rounds to reach acceptable performance. In this work, we propose a novel model aggregation method for federated learning (FedPS), which generate pseudo samples from each client model to train the global model on the server. The proposed method could support the aggregation of more than twenty heterogeneous models simultaneously, only requires a single round of communication and can achieve an improved aggregation performance than state-of-the-art federated learning methods.

Keywords: Federated learning · Model aggregation · Pseudo samples · Data-free

1 Introduction

Federated learning (FL), as an emerging machine learning task, has become more and more important in the field of distributed training. Clients send their model architectures and parameters to the server instead of sending their private training data, thus ensuring the privacy safety of clients. In contrast, ensemble learning methods combine multiple heterogeneous weak classifiers by averaging the prediction results of each single model. However, due to the large number of participating clients, the direct application of ensemble learning methods in the scene of federated learning is not feasible in practice.

Classical federated learning algorithms, such as FedAvg [10] and related algorithms, are based on directly weighted averaging client model parameters, so they can only be applied when all client models have the same size and architecture. And the more client models participate in aggregation, the worse is the performance of the aggregation algorithm. Furthermore, these methods require lots of communication rounds to achieve a certain performance level, so the communication cost is usually very high. In reality, many scenarios are too complicated

H. Qiu et al. (Eds.): KSEM 2021, LNAI 12815, pp. 78–88, 2021.
https://doi.org/10.1007/978-3-030-82136-4_7

to deal with for these methods. For example, some clients have more landscape photos while others have more food photos, in this case the categories are imbalanced; the dogs in some client devices are black while the dogs of the same category in other client devices are white, in this case the data distribution is non-identical. To summarize, the challenges of these federated learning methods include:

- **Heterogeneous model architectures.** It is impossible to directly average the parameters of models with different model architectures or output nodes.
- **High communication overhead.** A parameter average is equivalent to an iterative step in SGD, so multiple iterations are needed to make the global model converge.
- **Performance degradation with more clients.** The more client models, the more difficult to find the intersection of the low-loss area of the parameter space by optimization.

In order to alleviate the limitations of the classical federated learning method and further improve the aggregation performance, we propose a model aggregation algorithm based on pseudo samples. Specifically, we generate pseudo samples for each client model starting from random noise, without using any additional information about clients, and collect all of them to construct a pseudo dataset to train the global model. This aggregation method is model-agnostic [2], and is not only suitable to homogeneous models, but also to heterogeneous models. Moreover, in the process of model aggregation, the client only needs to send model parameters to the server once, and there is no need to communicate afterwards, which greatly reduces the communication overhead.

In this paper, we propose a novel federated learning framework to aggregate homogeneous and heterogenous client models. The proposed aggregation method only requires a single round of communication and can achieve an improved aggregation performance than state-of-the-art federated learning methods. To summarize, our main contributions are as follows:

- Almost all federated learning methods perform model aggregation from the perspective of generating model parameters, and there is currently no method for model aggregation from the perspective of generating pseudo samples. Our proposed FedPS model aggregation method based on pseudo samples fills this gap.
- Our proposed FedPS algorithm allows for heterogenous models aggregation, and could support the aggregation of more than twenty client models simultaneously, only requires a single round of communication.
- We conduct a large number of numerical experiments on various datasets and settings, showing that our federated learning method based on pseudo samples performs well when the client dataset categories are imbalanced or the data distributions are non-identical.

2 Methodology

First of all, we need to generate a batch of corresponding pseudo samples for each client model without using any additional information about the client. The procedure is shown in Fig. 1: Input random noise into the client model to obtain a response at the output node of the client model, and calculate the gradient of the loss function to the input sample through backpropagation to update the pseudo sample. The generated pseudo samples do not necessarily have visual meanings, but can be used to help train global model. However, the quality of pseudo samples is uneven, so we add a quality detection module to help select high-quality pseudo samples, which greatly improves the performance of model aggregation.

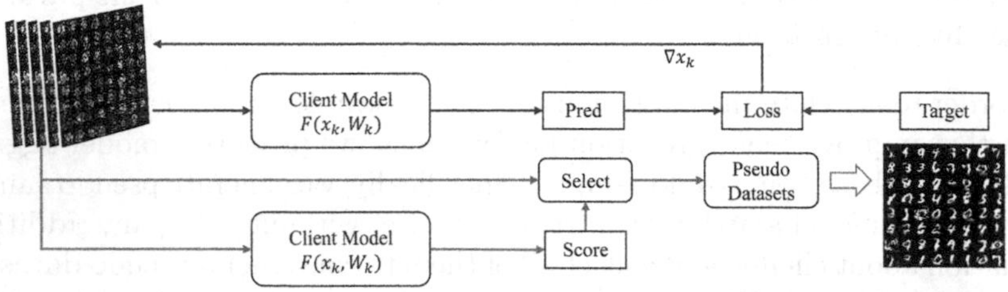

Fig. 1. The method of generating pseudo samples. We first randomly initialize a batch of pseudo samples (the module in the upper left corner), and input them into the client model. Then calculate the derivative of the loss function to the input tensor, to update the pseudo samples. When the pseudo samples converge, we send them to the client model again to get the model's score on the sample quality, and pick some samples with better quality into the pseudo dataset.

Give a randomly initialized input $\mathbf{x} \in \mathcal{R}^{H \times W \times C}$ (H, W, an C denote the height, width, and number of color channels) and a category target label $\mathbf{y}$ for each client model. At each SGD iteration step t, the pseudo sample $(\mathbf{x}_t, \mathbf{y})$ will be input into the client model for forward propagation, and then backward propagation to calculate the gradients:

$$\nabla \mathbf{x}_t = \frac{\partial(\mathcal{L}(F(\mathbf{x}_t, W), \mathbf{y}) + \mathcal{R}(\mathbf{x}_t))}{\partial \mathbf{x}_t} \tag{1}$$

where W is the parameter set of client model, $\mathcal{L}(\cdot)$ is a classification loss such as cross-entropy, and $\mathcal{R}(\cdot)$ is an image regularization term. We follow DeepDream [1,11] to use an image prior to steer $\mathbf{x}_t$ away from unrealistic images with no discernible visual information:

$$\mathcal{R}_{\text{prior}}(\mathbf{x}_t) = \alpha_{\text{tv}} \mathcal{R}_{\text{TV}}(\mathbf{x}_t) + \alpha_{\ell_2} \mathcal{R}_{\ell_2}(\mathbf{x}_t) \tag{2}$$

where R_{TV} and R_{ℓ_2} penalize the total variance and ℓ_2 norm of $\hat{x}$, respectively, with scaling factors α_{tv} and α_{ℓ_2}. As both prior work and we empirically observe, image prior regularization provides more stable convergence to valid images.

As for the category loss $\mathcal{L}(\cdot)$, we discusses two classification losses according to the application scenarios of the image classification model: single-label and multi-label. For the scene of single-label classification, we uses CrossEntropy and Softmax to calculate the single-label classification loss:

$$\mathcal{L}(o, \mathbf{y}) = -\frac{1}{n}\sum_{i}^{n}(\mathbf{y}_i * log(o_i)) \tag{3}$$

And for the scene of multi-label classification, we use BinaryCrossEntropy and Sigmoid to calculate the multi-label classification loss:

$$\mathcal{L}(o, \mathbf{y}) = -\frac{1}{n}\sum_{i}^{n}(\mathbf{y}_i * log(o_i) + (1 - \mathbf{y}_i) * log(1 - o_i)) \tag{4}$$

After the back propagation, we calculates the gradient of the loss function to the pseudo sample $\nabla \mathbf{x}_t$, the pseudo sample is updated accordingly. Then, the pseudo samples are updated by

$$\mathbf{x}_{t+1} = \mathbf{x}_t - \eta \nabla \mathbf{x}_t \tag{5}$$

where η is the learning rate of updating pseudo samples. After a series of iterations, we can obtain a batch of better quality pseudo samples, as shown in Fig. 2. Our pseudo sample generation algorithm basically recovers the five data distribution without obtain the original data. The sample which generated by the client model for single-label classification is also single-label; if the client model is trained in a multi-label dataset, the generated samples are also multi-label.

As one can see, the image quality of some pseudo samples is high, but there are also a small number of pseudo samples with low quality. These low-quality pseudo samples may have negative effect on model aggregation, so we add a quality detection module to help select high-quality pseudo samples. Specifically, we input the generated pseudo samples into the client model again for inference, and let the client model score the batch of pseudo samples. We discard the pseudo samples with low scores, and merge the pseudo samples with high scores into a dataset for this client.

Thus, we define an important concept under our framework of federated learning, the **pseudo dataset**, which is constructed using pseudo samples:

$$\mathcal{D}_k = \{\mathbf{x}_i \mid h(F(\mathbf{x}_i, W_k)) > \epsilon\} \tag{6}$$

where $h(\cdot)$ is the function to score the model output, W_k is the parameter of client model k, and ϵ is the threshold for selecting pseudo samples. A higher threshold can filter out better quality pseudo samples, but it will also increase the time to generate a sufficient amount of pseudo samples, vice versa.

$$h(\cdot) = 1 - sigmoid(\mathcal{H}_{cross}(\cdot, \arg\max_{j}(y_j^i))) \tag{7}$$

After getting all the client models, we use the above methods to generate pseudo samples for these models in parallel and select the pseudo samples with

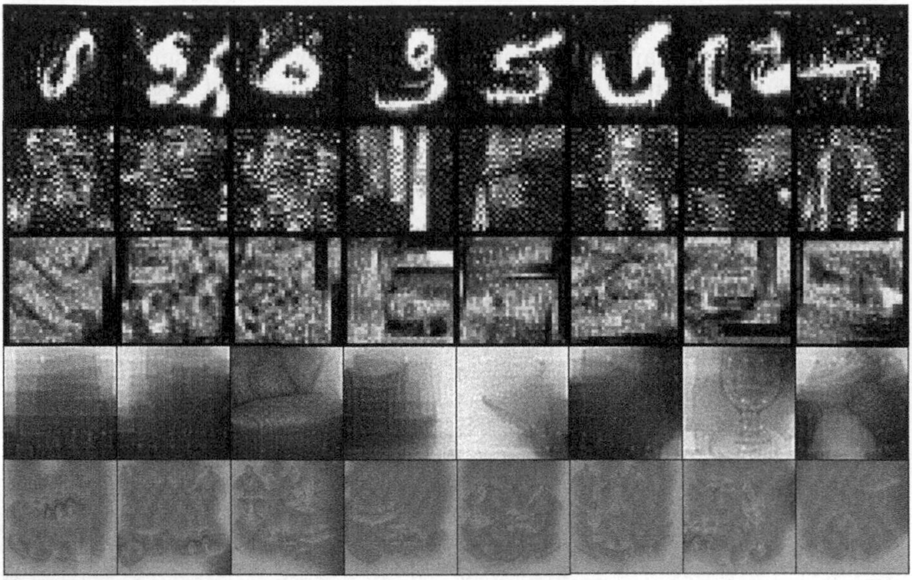

Fig. 2. Visualization of pseudo samples generated from the client models, which trained on MNIST, FMNIST, CIFAR-10, ImageNet and COCO, respectively.

better quality. After that, we put these pseudo sample $\{(\mathbf{x}_i, \mathbf{y}_i)\}_{i=1}^n$ into a universal dataset $\mathcal{U}$ in real time, until the size of $\mathcal{U}$ is enough to train a global model.

Based on $\mathcal{U}$, we build the global model $\mathcal{N}$, whose architecture can be either consistent or inconsistent with the architecture of the client model. Next, the parameters W of global model $\mathcal{N}$ are randomly initialized, which is suitable for homogeneous and heterogeneous model aggregation.

After setting the architecture of the global model $\mathcal{N}$ and its parameters, we shuffle the universal dataset $\mathcal{U}$, and continuously sample a mini-batch pseudo samples $\{(\mathbf{x}_i, \mathbf{y}_i)\}_{i=1}^n \leftarrow \mathcal{U}$ to feed into the global model $\mathcal{N}$ for training, obtain the output $\mathbf{z}_i$ of global model $\mathcal{N}$, and calculate the cross-entropy loss function:

$$\mathcal{L} = \frac{1}{n}\sum_{i}^{n}\mathcal{H}(\mathbf{z}_i, \mathbf{y}_i) \quad (8)$$

which is a normal classification loss function. Finally, the derivative of the loss function to the model parameters W is calculated to iteratively update the global model $\mathcal{N}$.

3 Experiments

In this section we demonstrate the effectiveness of our proposed federated learning method. We perform a number of ablations experiments to better understand the contributions of each component in our method. We will show the successful application of our FedPS method to homogenous client models and heterogenous client models with imbalanced category datasets and non-identical distribution datasets, which can validate that our FedPS algorithm can effectively solve the challenges of federated learning mentioned in Sect. 1. Two special methods will appear in the following:

- **Supremum model.** The supremum model is a model that combines all real client data to train a global model in a non-distributed training scenario. This does not exist in the federated learning scenario, but the performance of the supremum model will be used as the upper bound of all aggregation algorithms.
- **Ensemble model.** The ensemble model is often used as the object to be compared by the federated learning algorithm. It merges the output results of all client models and uses a method similar to voting to obtain classification results. Compared with federated learning, ensemble learning is usually better in performance, but it is the result of all models inferring together, rather than using an aggregated model for inference.

3.1 Category Imbalance

In this experiment, we use the Dirichlet random number as in [4,7,12] to create the category imbalanced client training data. The value of α controls the degree of imbalance: $\alpha = 10$ means identical local data distributions, and the smaller α is, the more likely the clients hold samples from only one randomly chosen category.

We set up the experiment in the above environment. We have 20 clients, each client uses ResNet-18 [3] as the classification model. We will aggregate 2 models and 20 models on the MNIST dataset [6] of 28×28 pixel images with 10 classes selected according to different α values. Compared with other federated learning algorithm, our FedPS does not need to have a large number of communication rounds. We aggregate client models only in a single communication round. So we conduct the following experiments in one communication round and evaluate the Top-1 accuracy of aggregated models.

The compared results are reported in Table 1. As the imbalance α decreases, the performance of each client model on the entire testset gradually decreases, indicating that when the categories are imbalanced, each client model only learns part of the knowledge of the category, which also make the model aggregation more difficult. Although the category imbalance continues to increase, the aggregation model based on our FedPS algorithm always keeps a high top-1 accuracy, while the other compared methods have more or less reduced performance.

The results of aggregating 20 client models are reported in Table 2. As the number of clients increases, it will become increasingly difficult to aggregate models from the perspective of parameters. These algorithms performed poorly in the experiment of simultaneous aggregation of 20 models. For our FedPS algorithm, as the number of client models increases, there will be more reference

Table 1. Top-1 acc. (%) under varying degrees of imbalance in two client models aggregation, which are trained on MNIST. The smaller the α, the greater the degree of imbalance.

	2 Clients				
Imbalance α	10.0	1.0	0.75	0.5	0.25
Client average	98.89%	97.76%	95.96%	92.30%	55.28%
Ensemble	99.26%	99.09%	98.63%	89.90%	74.36%
FedAvg	97.66%	**97.66%**	97.38%	90.01%	51.27%
PFNM	64.12%	64.66%	52.46%	54.52%	51.24%
FedMA	50.23%	46.48%	48.61%	33.66%	34.38%
OT	96.23%	81.48%	81.61%	70.66%	56.38%
FedPS (**ours**)	**98.04%**	97.39%	**97.44%**	**97.12%**	**96.25%**

Table 2. Top-1 acc. (%) under varying degrees of imbalance in 20 client models aggregation, which are trained on MNIST.

	20 Clients				
Imbalance α	10.0	1.0	0.75	0.5	0.25
Client average	98.48%	97.69%	95.96%	92.39%	77.81%
Ensemble	99.47%	99.48%	99.37%	99.03%	98.57%
FedAvg	8.92%	9.74%	9.74%	9.74%	10.09%
PFNM	14.33%	19.22%	13.60%	11.45%	17.27%
FedMA	13.60%	12.87%	13.60%	12.87%	16.92%
OT	16.92%	21.74%	12.87%	13.60%	11.33%
FedPS (**ours**)	**98.85%**	**98.63%**	**98.39%**	**98.25%**	**97.64%**

models that we can use to generate pseudo samples, and the data distribution for generating pseudo samples will be more comprehensive and diverse. Therefore, for the FedPS algorithm, the larger the number of clients, the better the model aggregation performs.

This experiment demonstrates that our FedPS outperforms the compared methods in all cases and leads to consistent performance improvements in most scenarios. Especially in scenarios with imbalanced categories and multiple clients, our method even performs better than the ensemble model.

3.2 Distribution Non-identicalness

In different clients, the data distribution of the same category may be nonidentical. For example, the photos labeled "dogs" in some devices are black dogs, while the photos with the same label in other devices are white dogs. We first consider a toy data distribution of a 3-classification task with a 3-layer MLP as in [7] and display the decision boundaries (over RGB channels) on the input space in Fig. 3. We build two different data distributions for each category, train MLP models respectively, and then use different algorithms to aggregate these two models.

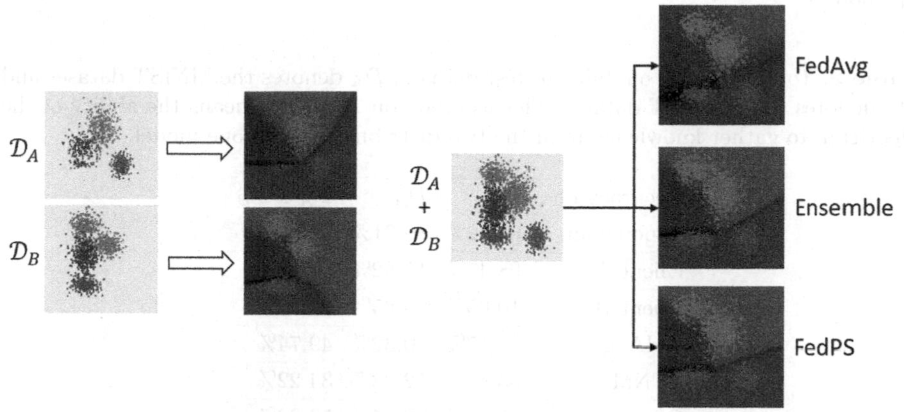

Fig. 3. The limitation of FedAvg. The averaged model results in much blurred decision boundaries, while our FedPS performs much better.

This figure provides insights on the limitation of FedAvg and the advantage of our FedPS. The model based on FedAvg produces blurred decision boundaries, while our FedPS method performs much better. It shows that aggregating models only from the perspective of parameters will make the aggregated model lack a clear decision boundary, which is fatal for the discriminant model. On the contrary, our FedPS algorithm uses a method similar to training to obtain the aggregated model, which makes it easy to learn a distinct decision boundary for the discriminative model.

Subsequently, we conduct more detailed experiments to test the effect of our aggregation algorithm on models with different data distributions (trained on non-identical distribution datasets). In order to reflect the inconsistency of the data distributions of the same category, we merge the MNIST dataset and the FMNIST dataset (both of them have 28×28 pixel images and 10 classes) as a new dataset. In this way, each category of the new test dataset contains two data distributions, we mark them as $\mathcal{D}_A$(MNIST) and $\mathcal{D}_B$(FMNIST). And then, we use ResNet-18 as client neural network models. The client Model A is trained on the MNIST dataset and the client Model B is trained on the FMNIST dataset. At this time, we use different algorithms to aggregate the two client models to compare the aggregation capabilities of each algorithm for different distributions of knowledge.

The results are reported in Table 3. $\mathcal{D}_A$ denotes the MNIST dataset and $\mathcal{D}_B$ denotes the FMNIST dataset. The accuracy on $\mathcal{D}_A \cup \mathcal{D}_B$ means the ability of the algorithm to gather knowledge from the two distributions into one model.

Furthermore, we use all the data of both MNIST and FMNIST dataset to train superemum model, which represents the upper bound of the performance that ResNet-18 can perform in such a data set with two data distributions. Through the comparison with the superemum model, the performance difference between the federated learning algorithm and the non-distributed training method can be seen.

Table 3. Top-1 acc. (%) on different test dataset. $\mathcal{D}_A$ denotes the MNIST dataset and $\mathcal{D}_B$ denotes the FMNIST dataset. The accuracy on $\mathcal{D}_A \cup \mathcal{D}_B$ means the ability of the algorithm to gather knowledge from the two distributions into one model.

Accuracy on	$\mathcal{D}_A$	$\mathcal{D}_B$	$\mathcal{D}_A \cup \mathcal{D}_B$
Superemum	98.82%	89.31%	94.06%
Client A	98.47%	15.82%	57.14%
Client B	10.65%	89.85%	50.25%
FedAvg	39.17%	60.32%	49.74%
PFNM	55.64%	12.83%	34.22%
OT	45.82%	72.65%	59.23%
FedMA	42.31%	31.67%	36.99%
FedPS (**ours**)	94.22%	88.43%	**91.32%**

From Table 3, we can see that client Model A performs well on $\mathcal{D}_A$ and has fully learned the knowledge of the MNIST dataset, but it has poor performance on $\mathcal{D}_B$ because it has not seen the data distribution of the FMNIST dataset. Client Model B is just the opposite. At this time, different algorithms are used to aggregate the above two client models. It can be seen that other aggregation methods based on model parameters are less effective (because of the blurred decision boundaries), and our method makes the global model have higher accuracy.

3.3 Aggregate Heterogenous Models

Here we consider heterogeneous model aggregation, which is very difficult for model aggregation algorithms based on parameters. Since we use the method of generating pseudo samples to train a new neural network to obtain the aggregated model, this method is model-agnostic and can generate pseudo samples for any neural network models, so heterogeneous client models can be easily aggregated.

We prepare five data sets for the experiment: MNIST, FMNIST, CIFAR 10/100 [5] and CelebA [8] (following the settings in [9] to classify the most balanced attribute in CelebA). For the experiment on each dataset, we randomly divide the training data into two parts and place them in two different clients to train the neural network model. We provide LeNet-5 [6], ResNet and AlexNet [5] as the classification model for clients and guarantee that the model architectures of the two clients are different. After training on their respective datasets, we use our FedPS method to aggregate these two client models. The experimental results are shown in Table 4.

Table 4. Top-1 acc. (%) of aggregated heterogeneous client models. In each experiment, each client model uses only half of the data in the dataset, and we use FedPS algorithm to aggregate them.

Dataset	MNIST	FMNIST	CIFAR-10	CIFAR-100	CelebA
Client model A	ResNet-18	LeNet-5	ResNet-34	ResNet-34	AlexNet
	96.23%	86.22%	84.24%	77.84%	77.59%
Client model B	LeNet-5	ResNet-18	ResNet-18	ResNet-50	ResNet-50
	95.91%	92.89%	83.99%	70.47%	81.32%
Aggregated model	ResNet-18	ResNet-18	ResNet-34	ResNet-50	AlexNet
	96.31%	90.71%	81.36%	71.66%	76.56%

From Table 4, we can see that on the same data set, different model architectures have different performance. Using our FedPS model aggregation algorithm, we can easily realize the aggregation of heterogeneous models, and the performance of the aggregation model does not decrease compared with each client model.

4 Conclusion

In this paper, we propose a novel federated learning framework, which could support the aggregation of more than twenty heterogeneous client models simultaneously. The proposed aggregation method only requires a single round of communication and can achieve an improved aggregation performance than state-of-the-art federated learning methods. Then we find a way to estimate the amount of novel knowledge contained in each client model, and select only a subset of models for aggregation by avoiding aggregating redundant knowledge for further improving efficiency.

References

1. Bhardwaj, K., Suda, N., Marculescu, R.: Dream distillation: a data-independent model compression framework. arXiv preprint arXiv:1905.07072 (2019)
2. Finn, C., Abbeel, P., Levine, S.: Model-agnostic meta-learning for fast adaptation of deep networks. arXiv preprint arXiv:1703.03400 (2017)
3. He, K., Zhang, X., Ren, S., Sun, J.: Deep residual learning for image recognition. In: Proceedings of the IEEE Conference on Computer Vision and Pattern Recognition, pp. 770–778 (2016)

4. Hsu, T.M.H., Qi, H., Brown, M.: Measuring the effects of non-identical data distribution for federated visual classification. arXiv preprint arXiv:1909.06335 (2019)
5. Krizhevsky, A., Hinton, G., et al.: Learning multiple layers of features from tiny images. Master's thesis, Computer Science Department (2009)
6. LeCun, Y., Bottou, L., Bengio, Y., Haffner, P.: Gradient-based learning applied to document recognition. Proc. IEEE **86**(11), 2278–2324 (1998)
7. Lin, T., Kong, L., Stich, S.U., Jaggi, M.: Ensemble distillation for robust model fusion in federated learning. arXiv preprint arXiv:2006.07242 (2020)
8. Liu, Z., Luo, P., Wang, X., Tang, X.: Deep learning face attributes in the wild. In: Proceedings of the IEEE International Conference on Computer Vision, pp. 3730–3738 (2015)
9. Lopes, R.G., Fenu, S., Starner, T.: Data-free knowledge distillation for deep neural networks. arXiv preprint arXiv:1710.07535 (2017)
10. McMahan, B., Moore, E., Ramage, D., Hampson, S., y Arcas, B.A.: Communication-efficient learning of deep networks from decentralized data. In: Artificial Intelligence and Statistics, pp. 1273–1282 (2017)
11. Mordvintsev, A., Olah, C., Tyka, M.: Inceptionism: going deeper into neural networks (2015). https://research.googleblog.com/2015/06/inceptionism-going-deeper-into-neural.html (2015)
12. Yurochkin, M., Agarwal, M., Ghosh, S., Greenewald, K., Hoang, T.N., Khazaeni, Y.: Bayesian nonparametric federated learning of neural networks. arXiv preprint arXiv:1905.12022 (2019)

Dense Incremental Extreme Learning Machine with Accelerating Amount and Proportional Integral Differential

Weidong Zou[1], Yuanqing Xia[1], Meikang Qiu[2], and Weipeng Cao[3](✉)

[1] School of Automation, Beijing Institute of Technology, Beijing 100081, China
[2] Department of Computer Science, Texas A&M University-Commerce, Commerce, TX 75428, USA
[3] College of Computer Science and Software Engineering, Shenzhen University, Shenzhen 518060, China
caoweipeng@szu.edu.cn

Abstract. Incremental Extreme Learning Machine (I-ELM) has been widely concerned in recent years because of its ability to automatically find the best number of hidden layer nodes and non-iterative training mechanism. However, in big data scenarios, I-ELM and its variants face great challenges because the least squares method is used to calculate their output weights in the training process, which is time-consuming and unstable. To alleviate this problem, we propose a novel Dense I-ELM based on the Accelerating Amount and the Proportional Integral Differential techniques (AA-PID-DELM) in this paper. For AA-PID-DELM, the dense connection architecture can exert the maximum utility of each hidden layer node, and the accelerating amount and PID techniques can make the model achieve better generalization ability and stability in big data scenarios. Extensive experimental results on the approximation of 2D nonlinear function and several UCI data-sets have proved the effectiveness of AA-PID-DELM.

Keywords: Incremental extreme learning machine · Accelerating amount · Proportional integral derivative · Neural network architecture

1 Introduction

With the development of our society, machine learning techniques had been used widely in various areas, such as services [1–3], health care [4], transportation [5], resource allocation [6], and mobile applications [7]. In recent years, Extreme Learning Machine (ELM) has gained increasing attention and has been applied in many fields, such as active learning from imbalanced data [8], domain adaptation [9], data stream mining [10], and batch-mode reinforcement learning [11].

As an important variant of ELM, Incremental ELM (I-ELM) [12] provides a simple and efficient method to train a constructive single hidden layer feed-forward neural network. The parameters of hidden layer nodes for I-ELM are

H. Qiu et al. (Eds.): KSEM 2021, LNAI 12815, pp. 89–100, 2021.
https://doi.org/10.1007/978-3-030-82136-4_8

selected randomly and kept frozen throughout its training process and only its output weights need to be calculated by using the least squares method. This training mechanism enables I-ELM to achieve a much faster training speed than traditional constructive neural networks. However, to meet high performance requirements, it often needs a large number of hidden layer nodes. To alleviate this problem, many improved methods are proposed, such as enhanced I-ELM [13], error minimized ELM [14], bidirectional ELM [15] and its variants [16,17], orthogonal I-ELM [18], and dynamic adjustment ELM [19].

However, when dealing with big data problems, the above algorithms still suffer from the high computational complexity problem because they have to use the least squares method to calculate the generalized inverse of the hidden layer output matrix. To address the problem, some researchers exploited distributed method to calculate the output weights of ELM, such as distributed ELM with alternating direction method of multiplier [20], maximally split and relaxed alternating direction method of multiplier for regularized ELM [21], and distributed subgradient-based ELM [22].

Different from the existing practice, we propose a new solution in this paper. Specifically, we construct a dense I-ELM model, which connects each hidden layer node to every other hidden layer node. Then, we integrate the accelerating amount technique to I-ELM for accelerating its training efficiency and improving the generalization performance of the model. Moreover, we use Proportional Integral Derivative (PID) instead of the least squares method to improve the adaptability of the model to big data processing scenarios. We call the new method Dense Incremental Extreme Learning Machine with Accelerating Amount and Proportional Integral Differential (AA-PID-DELM).

The remainder of this paper is organized as follows. I-ELM and PID are briefly introduced in Sect. 2. In Sect. 3, the details of the proposed AA-PID-DELM is given. The experimental results and discussion are presented in Sect. 4. Section 5 is the conclusion of this paper.

2 Preliminaries

2.1 I-ELM

I-ELM is essentially a constructive single hidden layer feed-forward neural network. One can use a linear combination of n continuously differentiable functions to represent an I-ELM model with n additive hidden layer nodes:

$$\mathbf{f}_n(\mathbf{x}) = \sum_{i=1}^{n} \beta_i g(\mathbf{a}_i \cdot \mathbf{x} + b_i), \mathbf{a}_i \in \mathbf{R}^d, \beta_i, b_i \in \mathbf{R}. \quad (1)$$

where $\mathbf{a}_i$, b_i, and β_i refer to the input weight, hidden bias, and output weight of the i-th hidden node, respectively. $g(\mathbf{a}_i \cdot \mathbf{x} + b_i)$ denotes the output of the i-th hidden node, which is additive.

The number of the hidden node for I-ELM can dynamically increase according to the feedback of the model prediction error. The target function and the residual error function are expressed as $\mathbf{f} \in \mathbf{L}^2(\mathbf{X})$ and $\mathbf{e}_n = \mathbf{f} - \mathbf{f}_n$, respectively. The I-ELM model with n additive hidden nodes can be expressed as a linear combination of functions:

$$\mathbf{f}_n(\mathbf{x}) = \mathbf{f}_{n-1}(\mathbf{x}) + \beta_n g(\mathbf{a}_n \cdot \mathbf{x} + b_n). \tag{2}$$

2.2 Proportional Integral Differential

PID is a commonly used universal control technique in control systems. The error between the set value and the actual value can be minimized by adjusting the coefficients of PID model [23]. The learning pipeline of PID is shown in Fig. 1. Suppose that u is the output of PID, then it can be represented by using a linear combination of the proportional, integral, and differential error between the actual value and the set value:

$$u(k) = k_p E(k) + k_i \sum_{j=1}^{k} E(j) + k_d(E(k) - E(k-1)). \tag{3}$$

where k is sample time. k_p, k_i and k_d are the parameters of PID.

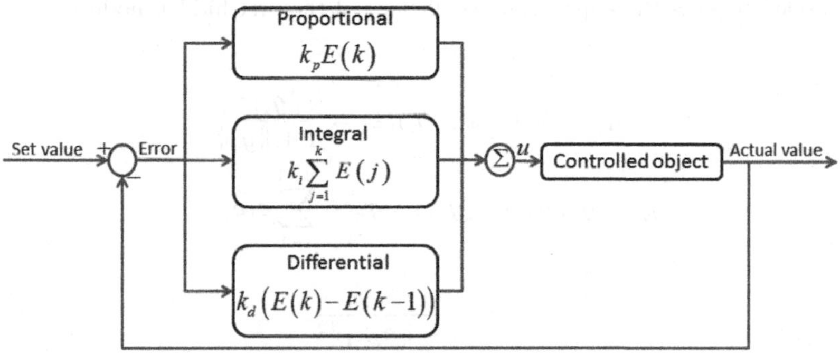

Fig. 1. The learning pipeline of PID

3 Dense I-ELM with Accelerating Amount and Proportional Integral Differential

The topological structure of the proposed AA-PID-DELM is shown in Fig. 2.

Given a training data set $D = \{\boldsymbol{x}, \boldsymbol{y}\} \in \mathbf{R}^{n \times M}$, the activation function of AA-PID-DELM is required to be piecewise and continuous. The AA-PID-DELM model with n hidden layer nodes can be expressed as a linear combination of equations:

$$\mathbf{f}_n(\boldsymbol{x}) = \sum_{i=1}^{n} (\beta_i \tilde{\mathbf{g}}_i + \alpha_{i-1} \boldsymbol{e}_{i-1}), \tag{4}$$

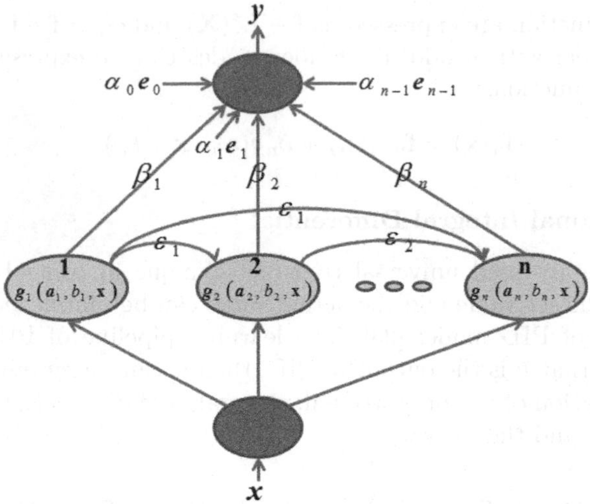

Fig. 2. The network structure of AA-PID-DELM. (Note: β_n refers to the output weight of the n-th hidden node, which is calculated by using the PID method. $\boldsymbol{f}_{n-1}$ denotes the output of the model with $n-1$ hidden nodes, and the current residual error can be represented as $\boldsymbol{e}_{n-1} = \boldsymbol{y} - \boldsymbol{f}_{n-1}$. α_{n-1} is the compression factor [24] of the n-th hidden node and ε_1 is the appropriate coefficient of the first hidden node.)

$$\boldsymbol{g}_i = \phi(\boldsymbol{a}_i \cdot \boldsymbol{x} + b_i), \varepsilon_i = \frac{\|\boldsymbol{g}_i\|^2}{1 + \|\boldsymbol{g}_i\|},$$
$$\tilde{\mathbf{g}} = [\boldsymbol{g}_1, \boldsymbol{g}_2 + \varepsilon_1 \boldsymbol{g}_1, ..., \boldsymbol{g}_n + \sum_{i=1}^{n-1} \varepsilon_i \boldsymbol{g}_i], \tag{5}$$

$$\alpha_{i-1} = \frac{\|\boldsymbol{e}_{i-1}\|}{1 + \|\boldsymbol{e}_{i-1}\|^2}. \tag{6}$$

The output weight of the i-th hidden layer node is calculated as follows:

$$\begin{aligned}\beta_i =& \beta_{i-1} + k_p \times (\|\boldsymbol{e}_{i-1}\| - \|\boldsymbol{e}_{i-2}\|) + k_i \times \|\boldsymbol{e}_{i-1}\| \\ &+ k_d \times (\|\boldsymbol{e}_{i-1}\| - 2 \times \|\boldsymbol{e}_{i-2}\| + \|\boldsymbol{e}_{i-3}\|).\end{aligned} \tag{7}$$

The pseudo-code of the proposed AA-PID-DELM can be summarized as Algorithm 1.

4 Experiments and Discussions

All the experiments are conducted in PC with Intel(R) Core(TM) i7-3520M CPU with NVIDIA NVS 5400M and 8 GB RAM. The parameters of the hidden layer nodes in AA-PID-DELM are randomly generated from $[-1, 1]^d \times [-1, 1]$

Algorithm 1. AA-PID-DELM

Input: A training set $D = \{\boldsymbol{x}, \boldsymbol{y}\} \in \mathbf{R}^{n \times M}$, $\boldsymbol{e}_0 = \boldsymbol{y}$ and $E_1 = \|\boldsymbol{y}\|$.
Output: The parameters of the model.
for $p = 1$; $p \leq n$ **do**
  Randomly assign the parameters of hidden layer node: $(\boldsymbol{a}_p, b_p)$;
  Calculate the output of the hidden layer node: $\boldsymbol{g}_p = \phi(\boldsymbol{a}_p \cdot \boldsymbol{x} + b_p)$;
  Calculate the appropriate coefficient of the p-th hidden layer node: $\varepsilon_p = \frac{\|\boldsymbol{g}_p\|^2}{1+\|\boldsymbol{g}_p\|}$;
end for
Calculate the output matrix of dense hidden layer nodes: $\tilde{\boldsymbol{g}} = [\boldsymbol{g}_1, ..., \boldsymbol{g}_n + \sum_{i=1}^{n-1} \varepsilon_i \boldsymbol{g}_i]$;
Key phase: Use the PID algorithm to calculate the output weight of dense hidden layer nodes.
Given intermediate variables $\|\boldsymbol{e}_{i-2}\| = eck1 = 0$, $\|\boldsymbol{e}_{i-3}\| = eck2 = 0$, and $\beta_0 = 0$.
Parameters (k_p, k_i, k_d) in PID are determined by hand.
for $j = 1$; $j \leq n$ **do**
  Calculate the compression factor of the j-th hidden layer node:
  $\alpha_{j-1} = \frac{\|\boldsymbol{e}_{j-1}\|}{1+\|\boldsymbol{e}_{j-1}\|^2}$;
  Calculate the output weight of the j-th hidden layer node:
  $u_j = k_p \times (E_j - eck1) + k_i \times E_j + k_d \times (E_j - 2 \times eck1 + eck2)$;
  $\beta_j = \beta_{j-1} + u_j$;
  Calculate the output of the model with j hidden layer nodes:
  $\boldsymbol{y}_j = \sum_{k=1}^{j} (\beta_k \tilde{\boldsymbol{g}}_k + \alpha_{k-1} \boldsymbol{e}_{k-1})$
  Calculate the residual error:
  $\boldsymbol{e}_j = \boldsymbol{y} - \boldsymbol{y}_j$
  $E_{j+1} = \|\boldsymbol{e}_j\|$;
  $eck2 = eck1$;
  $eck1 = E_j$;
end for
Set the output weights of hidden layer nodes: $\boldsymbol{\beta} = [\beta_1, ..., \beta_n]$.

based on a uniform sampling distribution. The activation function of AA-PID-DELM is the hyperbolic tangent function. The parameters of PID are set to $k_p = 0.000011$, $k_i = 0.000002$, and $k_d = 0.002$.

The performance evaluation indexes include mean absolute error (MAE), mean absolute percentage error (MAPE), root mean square error (RMSE), relative root mean square error (rRMSE), and absolute fraction of variance (R^2), which can be calculated as follows [18–22]:

$$MAE = \frac{1}{m} \sum_{i=1}^{m} |\hat{u}_i - u_i|, \tag{8}$$

$$MAPE = \frac{1}{m} \sum_{i=1}^{m} |\frac{\hat{u}_i - u_i}{\hat{u}_i}| \times 100\%, \tag{9}$$

$$RMSE = \sqrt{\frac{1}{m} \sum_{i=1}^{m} (\hat{u}_i - u_i)^2}, \tag{10}$$

$$rRMSE = \sqrt{\frac{m\sum_{i=1}^{m}(\hat{u}_i - u_i)^2}{(m-1)\sum_{i=1}^{m}(\hat{u}_i)^2}}, \tag{11}$$

$$R_2 = 1 - \sqrt{\frac{\sum_{i=1}^{m}(\hat{u}_i - u_i)^2}{\sum_{i=1}^{m}(\hat{u}_i)^2}}, \tag{12}$$

where u_i and $\hat{u}_i$ refer to the predicted value and the true value respectively. m denotes the number of samples.

4.1 Experiments on the Approximation of 2-D Nonlinear Function

We used the 2-D nonlinear function approximation problem to evaluate the performance of AA-PID-DELM, broad learning system (BLS) [25], and fuzzy broad learning system (FBLS) [26]. The dataset is composed of 1500 samples, 67% of which is used for training and the remaining is used for testing. In our experiments, Gaussian white noise was added to the training samples. The 2-D nonlinear function can be visualized as Fig. 3 and can be expressed as [27]:

$$y = -c_1 e^{(-0.2\sqrt{\frac{1}{n}\sum_{j=1}^{n} x_{1j}^2})} - e^{(\frac{1}{n}\sum_{j=1}^{n} cos(2\pi x_{2j}))} + wgn(0,1) \tag{13}$$
$$(c_1 = 20, e = 2.7282, n = 2).$$

For BLS, the number of the feature nodes is set to $N_f = 2$, and the number of the mapping groups is set to $N_m = 10$. For FBLS, the searching range for fuzzy rules is set to 2, and the searching range for the number of fuzzy subsystems is set to 10. The regularization parameter for the sparse regularization of BLS and FBLS is set to $\lambda = 0.001$. The hyperbolic tangent function is chosen as the activation function of their enhancement nodes. The number of the enhancement nodes for BLS and FBLS, and the number of hidden layer nodes for AA-PID-DELM are decided from $\{10, 12, 14, 16, 18, 20, 22, 24, 26, 28\}$. The source codes of BLS and FBLS are downloaded from the website: https://www.fst.um.edu.mo/en/staff/pchen.html.

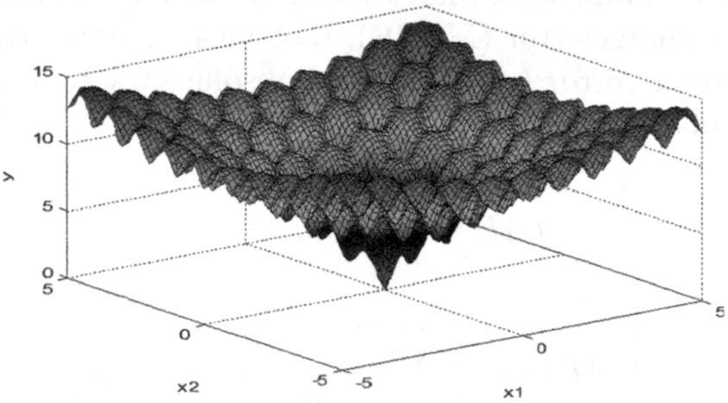

Fig. 3. The visualization of the 2-D nonlinear function

The values of rRMSE and R_2 on testing samples are shown in Fig. 4. In our experiment, we found that changing the number of enhancement nodes has no significant impact on the testing rRMSE and R_2 when the number of feature nodes or fuzzy subsystems is fixed. The testing rRMSE decreases and the testing R_2 increases with the increase of hidden layer nodes for AA-PID-DELM.

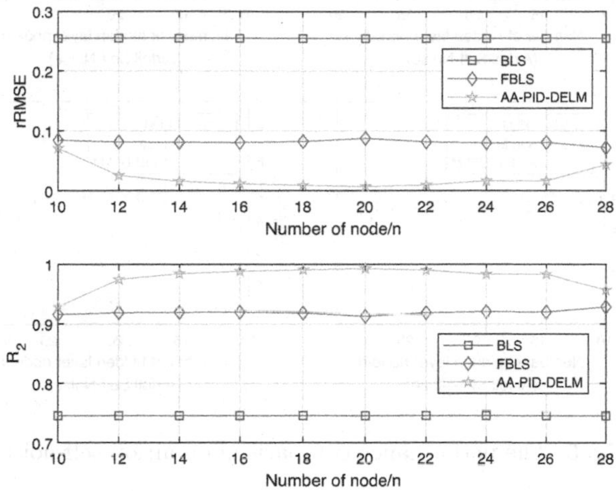

Fig. 4. The experimental results on the approximation of 2-D nonlinear function

From Fig. 4, one can observe that the proposed AA-PID-DELM achieves the lowest testing rRMSE and the highest R_2 on approximation of 2D nonlinear function, which means AA-PID-DELM can achieve better generalization performance and stability than other algorithms.

4.2 Experiments on UCI Data-Sets

Four regression problems from UCI database are chosen for evaluating the performance of AA-PID-DELM in this section. For all the regression problems, the average results are obtained over 10 runs of 10-fold cross validation. The details of the regression problems is shown in Table 1.

In this experiment, Sigmoid function $\mathbf{H}(\mathbf{a}, b, \mathbf{x}) = \frac{1}{1+exp(-(\mathbf{a}\cdot\mathbf{x}+b))}$ is selected as the activation function of B-ELM and I-ELM. AA-PID-DELM, B-ELM, and I-ELM recruit input weights and hidden biases randomly from the $[-1,1]^d \times [-1,1]$ based on a uniform sampling distribution probability. The number of hidden layer nodes for AA-PID-DELM, B-ELM, and I-ELM is decided from $\{10, 12, 14, 16, 18, 20, 22, 24, 26, 28, 30\}$. The experimental results are shown in Figs. 5, 6, 7 and 8.

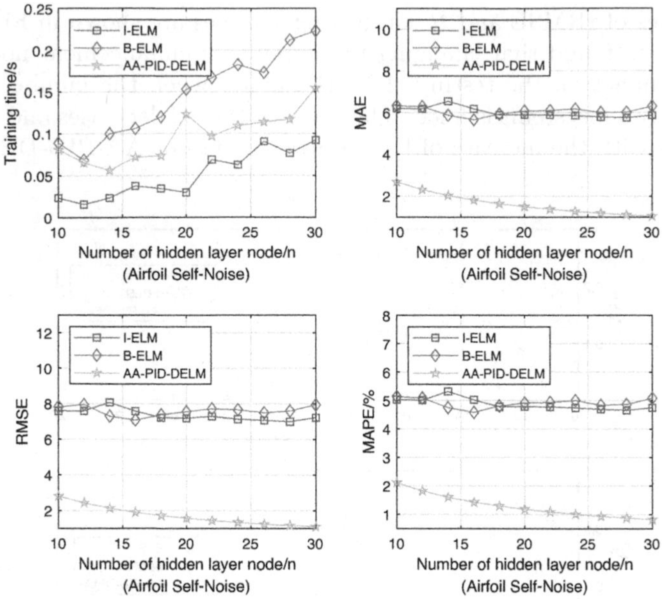

Fig. 5. The performance comparison on airfoil self-noise

It can be observed from Figs. 5, 6, 7 and 8, the values of RMSE, MAE, and MAPE of the AA-PID-DELM model are the lowest on all data sets, which means that the AA-PID-DELM model has better prediction ability and stability than other models.

Further, we compared the performance of the proposed AA-PID-DELM with SVM [28], SCN [29], and HELM [30]. For SVM, the kernel function is $\mathbf{K}(\mathbf{x}_i, \mathbf{x}_j) = e^{-\gamma\|\mathbf{x}_i - \mathbf{x}_j\|^2}$, $C = 150$, and $\gamma = 0.24$. For SCN, the maximum times for random configuration is $T_{max} = 10$, the maximum number of hidden nodes is $L_{max} = 30$, and the expected error tolerance is $\epsilon = 0.02$. The source code of SCN is downloaded from the website: http://www.deepscn.com. For HELM, we set $C_{HELM} = 0.1$, and the number of hidden nodes are $N1 = 10$, $N2 = 50$, and $N3 = 10$. The number of hidden layer nodes for AA-PID-DELM is set to 30.

Table 1. Details of regression problems

Data-sets	Instance	Attributes
Appliances energy prediction	19735	29
Beijing multi-site air-quality data	420768	18
SGEMM GPU kernel performance	241600	18
3D road network (North Jutland, Denmark)	434874	4

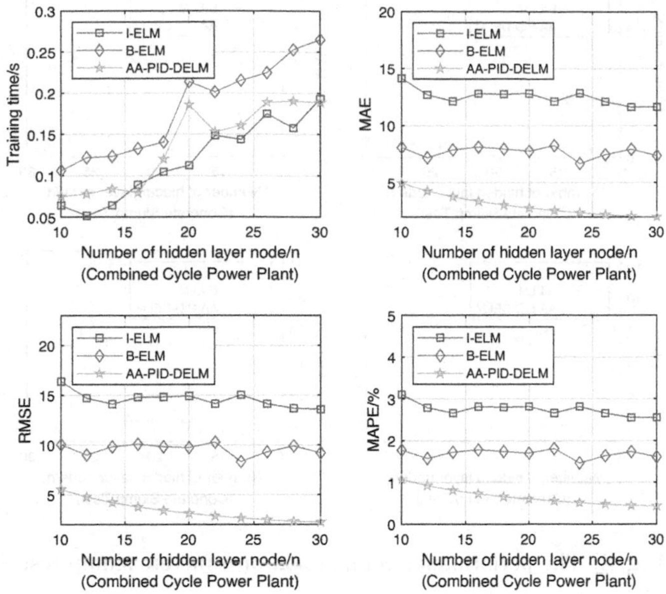

Fig. 6. The performance comparison on combined cycle power plant

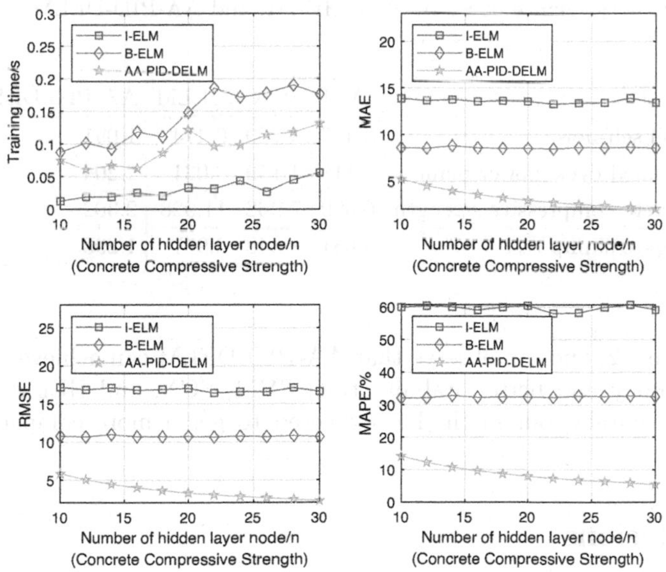

Fig. 7. The performance comparison on concrete compressive strength

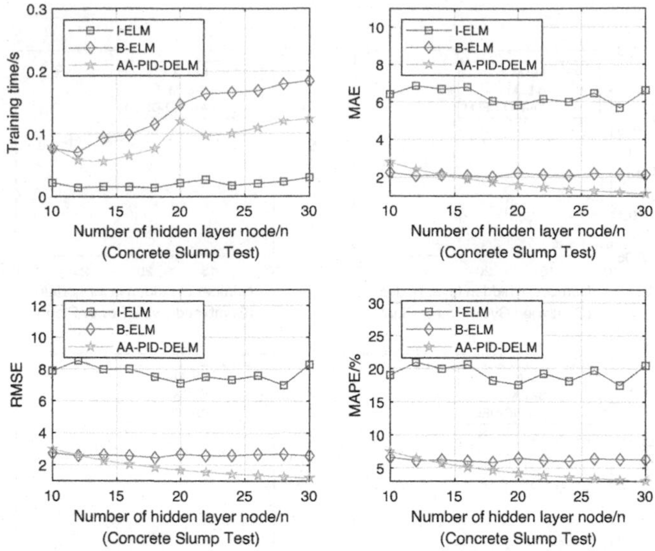

Fig. 8. The performance comparison on concrete slump test

The average results are obtained over 10 runs of 10-fold cross validation, which are shown in Table 2.

Table 2. The performance of SVM, SCN, HELM, and AA-PID-DELM on regression problems

Data-sets	SVM	SCN	HELM	AA-PID-DELM
Airfoil self-noise	3.453	3.769	6.474	1.091
Combined cycle power plant	4.111	4.159	8.031	2.204
Concrete compressive strength	6.599	7.962	11.928	2.302
Concrete slump test	3.031	2.048	2.957	1.293

From Table 2, one can observe that AA-PID-DELM can achieve higher prediction accuracy and better stability than SVM, SCN, and HELM. Given an acceptable accuracy, our method is expected to get a more compact network structure.

5 Conclusions

In order to reduce the network structure complexity of I-ELM and accelerate its training efficiency, we proposed an improved I-ELM called AA-PID-DELM algorithm based on the accelerating amount and PID techniques in this paper.

AA-PID-DELM adopts a novel dense connection architecture so that each hidden layer node can exert its maximum utility, so as to achieve the goal of reducing the network structure complexity of the model. Moreover, AA-PID-DELM uses the accelerating amount and PID techniques to replace the least squares method to calculate the output weights of the model, which effectively improves the stability and computational efficiency of the model in dealing with big data problems. Extensive experimental results on the approximation of 2D nonlinear function and four benchmark regression problems have proved the effectiveness of the AA-PID-DELM.

Acknowledgement. This work was supported by National Natural Science Foundation of China (61906015, 61836001, 61836005) and Guangdong Science and Technology Department (2018B010107004).

References

1. Tao, L., Golikov, S., Gai, K., Qiu, M.: A reusable software component for integrated syntax and semantic validation for services computing. In: IEEE Symposium on Service-Oriented System Engineering, pp. 127–132 (2015)
2. Qiu, M., Ming, Z., Wang, J., Yang, L.T., Xiang, Y.: Enabling cloud computing in emergency management systems. IEEE Cloud Comput. **1**(4), 60–67 (2014)
3. Gai, K., Qiu, M.: Optimal resource allocation using reinforcement learning for IoT content-centric services. Appl. Soft Comput. **70**, 12–21 (2018)
4. Chen, M., Zhang, Y., Qiu, M., Guizani, N., Hao, Y.: SPHA: smart personal health advisor based on deep analytics. IEEE Commun. Mag. **56**(3), 164–169 (2018)
5. Zhu, M., et al.: Public vehicles for future urban transportation. IEEE Trans. Neural Netw. Learn. Syst. **17**(12), 3344–3353 (2016)
6. Dai, W., Qiu, L., Wu, A., Qiu, M.: Cloud infrastructure resource allocation for big data applications. IEEE Trans. Big Data **4**(3), 313–324 (2016)
7. Gai, K., Qiu, M.: Reinforcement learning-based content-centric services in mobile sensing. IEEE Netw. **32**(4), 34–39 (2018)
8. Yu, H.L., Yang, X.B., Zheng, S., Sun, C.Y.: Active learning from imbalanced data: a solution of online weighted extreme learning machine. IEEE Trans. Neural Netw. Learn. Syst. **30**(4), 1088–1103 (2019)
9. Li, S., Song, S.J., Huang, G., Wu, C.: Cross-domain extreme learning machines for domain adaptation. IEEE Trans. Syst. Man Cybern. Syst. **49**(6), 1194–1207 (2019)
10. Cao, W.P., Ming, Z., Xu, Z.W., Zhang, J.Q., Wang, Q.: Online sequential extreme learning machine with dynamic forgetting factor. IEEE Access **7**, 179746–179757 (2019)
11. Liu, J.H., et al.: Efficient batch-mode reinforcement learning using extreme learning machines. IEEE Trans. Syst. Man Cybern. Syst. **51**(6), 3664–3677 (2021). https://doi.org/10.1109/TSMC.2019.2926806
12. Huang, G.B., Chen, L., Siew, C.K.: Universal approximation using incremental constructive feedforward networks with random hidden nodes. IEEE Trans. Neural Netw. **17**(4), 879–892 (2006)
13. Huang, G.B., Chen, L.: Enhanced random search based incremental extreme learning machine. Neurocomputing **16–18**(71), 3460–3468 (2008)

14. Feng, G., Huang, G.B., Lin, Q., Gay, R.: Error minimized extreme learning machine with growth of hidden nodes and incremental learning. IEEE Trans. Neural Netw. Learn. Syst. **8**(20), 1352–1357 (2009)
15. Yang, Y., Wang, Y., Yuan, X.: Bidirectional extreme learning machine for regression problem and its learning effectiveness. IEEE Trans. Neural Netw. Learn. Syst. **9**(23), 1498–1505 (2012)
16. Cao, W., Ming, Z., Wang, X., Cai, S.: Improved bidirectional extreme learning machine based on enhanced random search. Memetic Comput. **11**(1), 19–26 (2017). https://doi.org/10.1007/s12293-017-0238-1
17. Cao, W.P., Gao, J.Z., Wang, X.Z., Ming, Z., Cai, S.B.: Random orthogonal projection based enhanced bidirectional extreme learning machine. In: International Conference on Extreme Learning Machine, pp. 1–10 (2018)
18. Ying, L.: Orthogonal incremental extreme learning machine for regression and multiclass classification. Neural Comput. Appl. **27**(1), 111–120 (2014). https://doi.org/10.1007/s00521-014-1567-3
19. Feng, G.R., Lan, Y., Zhang, X.P., Qian, Z.X.: Dynamic adjustment of hidden node parameters for extreme learning machine. IEEE Trans. Cybern. **45**(2), 279–288 (2015)
20. Luo, M.N., Zhang, L.L., Liu, J., Guo, J., Zheng, Q.H.: Distributed extreme learning machine with alternating direction method of multiplier. Neurocomputing **261**, 164–170 (2017)
21. Lai, X.P., Cao, J.W., Huang, X.F., Wang, T.L., Lin, Z.P.: A maximally split and relaxed ADMM for regularized extreme learning machines. IEEE Trans. Neural Netw. Learn. Syst. **31**(6), 1899–1913 (2019). https://doi.org/10.1109/TNNLS.2019.2927385
22. Vanli, N.D., Sayin, M.O., Delibalta, I., Kozat, S.S.: Sequential nonlinear learning for distributed multiagent systems via extreme learning machines. IEEE Trans. Neural Netw. Learn. Syst. **28**(3), 546–558 (2017)
23. An, W., Wang, H., Sun, Q., Xu, J., Dai, Q., Zhang, L.: A pid controller approach for stochastic optimization of deep networks. In: IEEE Conference on Computer Vision and Pattern Recognition, Utah, USA, pp. 8522–8531 (2018)
24. Sara, S., Nicholas, F., Geoffrey, E.H.: Dynamic routing between capsules. In: Thirty-first Conference on Neural Information Processing Systems, California, USA, pp. 1–11 (2017)
25. Chen, C.L.P., Liu, Z.L., Feng, S.: Universal approximation capability of broad learning system and its structural variations. IEEE Trans. Neural Netw. Learn. Syst. **30**(4), 1191–1204 (2019)
26. Shuang, F., Chen, C.L.P.: Fuzzy broad learning system: a novel neuro-fuzzy model for regression and classification. IEEE Trans. Cybern. **50**(2), 414–424 (2020)
27. Wen, C.J., Xia, B., Liu, X.: Solution of second order ackley function based on SAPSO algorithm. In: IEEE International Conference on Control Science and Systems Engineering (ICCSSE) (2017)
28. Lin, H.J., Zhu, L.L., Mehrabankhomartash, M., Saeedifard, M., Shu, Z.L.: A simplified SVM-based fault-tolerant strategy for cascaded H-Bridge multilevel converters. IEEE Trans. Power Electron. **35**(11), 11310–11315 (2020)
29. Wang, D.H., Li, M.: Stochastic configuration networks: fundamentals and algorithms. IEEE Trans. Cybern. **47**(10), 3466–3479 (2017)
30. Tang, J., Deng, C., Huang, G.B.: Extreme learning machine for multilayer perceptron. IEEE Trans. Neural Netw. Learn. Syst. **27**(4), 809–821 (2016)

Knowledge-Based Diverse Feature Transformation for Few-Shot Relation Classification

Yubao Tang[1,2], Zhezhou Li[1,2], Cong Cao[2(✉)], Fang Fang[2], Yanan Cao[2], Yanbing Liu[2], and Jianhui Fu[3]

[1] School of Cyber Security, University of Chinese Academy of Sciences, Beijing, China
[2] Institute of Information Engineering, Chinese Academy of Sciences, Beijing, China
{tangyubao,lizhezhou,caocong,fangfang0703,caoyanan,liuyanbing}@iie.ac.cn
[3] Shandong Institutes of Industrial Technology, Jinan, China

Abstract. Few-shot relation classification is to classify novel relations having seen only a few training samples. We find it is unable to learn comprehensive relation features with information deficit caused by the scarcity of samples and lacking of significant distinguishing features. Existing methods ignore the latter problem. What's worse, while there is a big difference between the source domain and the target domain, the generalization performance of existing methods is poor. And existing methods can not solve all these problems. In this paper, we propose a new model called Knowledge-based Diverse Feature Transformation Prototypical Network (KDFT-PN) for information deficit, lacking of significant distinguishing features and weak generalization ability. To increase semantic information, KDFT-PN introduces the information of knowledge base to fuse with the sample information. Meanwhile, we propose a novel Hierarchical Context Encoder based on prototypical network, which can enhance semantic interaction and improve cross-domain generalization ability. Moreover, this method has been evaluated on cross-domain and same-domain datasets. And experimental results are comparable with other state-of-the-art methods.

Keywords: Few-shot relation classification · Relation classification · Few-shot learning · Domain adaption · Knowledge fusion

1 Introduction

Relation classification is one of important steps to construct knowledge base and support intelligent systems. When facing a new field, labeled samples are likely to be few, or the labeling cost is very high. Therefore, it is necessary to carry out the research of few-shot relation classification. Few-shot relation classification (Few-shot RC) is proposed by [8], which aims to achieve novel relation classification having seen few training samples for each class. It is challenging since

H. Qiu et al. (Eds.): KSEM 2021, LNAI 12815, pp. 101–114, 2021.
https://doi.org/10.1007/978-3-030-82136-4_9

the method for Few-shot RC must have the capability of learning from deficient information caused by the scarcity of samples and cross-domain adaption.And existing methods can not solve all these problems.

As for the first challenge, each class uses very few samples for supervised learning. Thus, the sample information is not enough to provide comprehensive features, which makes the model unable to learn enough information. What's worse, some samples are lack of significant distinguishing features, which are difficult to be classified. In Table 1, each instance includes one sentence and a pair of target entities. Both instance relations are "spouse". As for instance S1, the semantic meaning of S1 itself makes it hard to be classified to "spouse". "Bill Hayes" and "Susan Seaforth Hayes" are couples in real life. But there is no way to know such background information from the sentence only. In contrast, we can tell the accurate relation of instance S2 for the word "wife" in the sentence. But samples such as S1 which lacks of significant distinguishing features, are accounts for a large proportion. It can not be ignored in Few-shot RC that the model only uses several instances to learn for each relation class, so such samples lacking significant distinguishing features cause a severe damage to this task. Existing methods ignore this problem. In order to solve information deficit and the above problem, we introduce the knowledge base information corresponding to target entities with Entity-level Knowledge Fusion Module, which can help to provide more semantic features.

Table 1. Support instances for training

No.	Relation	Instance
S1	Spouse	Doug is portrayed by Bill Hayes and Julie is portrayed by **Susan Seaforth Hayes**
S2	Spouse	His niece **Yang Yan** was Emperor Wu's first wife and empress

Table 2. Instances for few-shot RC domain adaption

No.	Domain	Relation	Instance
S	Source	Subordinate to	Jong Batu is located in the **Brunei River** to the east of the Istana Nurul Iman
T	Target	Ingredient of	Cellulose gel membranes have been prepared By a pre-gelation method employing **cellulose** solutions

As for the second challenge, while there is a big difference between the source domain and the target domain, the existing methods [5,8] are poor in cross domain generalization.And existing methods can not solve all these problems.

During training, models usually focus too much on source domain features and ignore deeper common features of the whole task, which makes it hard to generalize. When domain difference becomes larger, the feature space learned by the encoder is not applicable for the target domain. Such as Table 2, the model will pay too much attention to feature words such as "river" or "island" for relation "subordinate to" in source domain. The model is evaluated on relation "ingredient of" in target biomedical domain. Although the semantics of these two relations is different, both still have the common point of subordination. Therefore, subordination is a deeper common feature for the whole classification task, which is benefit for generalization ability. Based on this idea, we improved prototypical network with inserting Diverse Feature Transformation Layers (DFT layers) in the encoder. DFT layers can offset features of source domain to simulate the data distribution of multiple domains. Thus, the model can learn a wider range of features instead of focusing only one domain.

In this paper, to solve information deficit caused by the scarcity of samples,lacking of significant distinguishing features and domain adaptation in Few-shot RC, we propose a new method called Knowledge-based Diverse Feature Transformation Prototypical Network (KDFT-PN). We also open source on github page[1]. Our contributions are as follows.

- For information deficit, We propose an Entity-level Knowledge Fusion Module in KDFT-PN to fuse knowledge corresponding to target entities with sample information via entity-level attention fusion mechanism. This module provides well-directed external knowledge to make up information deficit.
- For better information interaction and improving domain adaption in prototypical network, we also propose a Hierarchical Context Encoder in KDFT-PN, which includes Context Purification Sub-encoder and Diverse Feature Transformation Layer. The former can purify sample representation and make semantics interact. The latter can simulate and learn multiple data domains for improving generalization ability in Few-shot RC.
- The method is evaluated on CrossFewRel and SameFewRel datasets built for Few-shot RC. And experimental results show that our model is comparable with other state-of-the-art methods.

The whole paper includes five parts. The first part is this introduction, and the second part is related work including relation classification and few-shot relation classification. The third part is the approach details we proposed. The forth part are experiments and results, and the final part is the conclusion.

2 Related Work

Relation Classification (RC) is a key task for information extraction and has many research work [10,17,19]. It aims to classify the relation of target entity pairs in digital text with the predefined relation set and output entity relation

[1] "https://github.com/lightningbaby/kdft-pn-backup.git".

triplets. Those triplets can be used to construct knowledge base and support intelligent systems.

Few-shot Relation Classification (Few-shot RC) is proposed by [8] and is a cross task of RC and Few-shot Learning. Few-shot learning [3,9] is to learn with few training samples, and then to identify unseen data points. Many researchers studied Few-shot RC. Existing methods can be classified five types: metric-based methods, pre−trained model methods, adversarial learning [7] based methods, meta-learning methods [4] and KNN [1] methods.

Metric-based methods which only focus on information deficit include prototypical network [15] based methods [5,18], such as **PN-(CNN)**[5] and Graph Neural Networks [6] based method, such as **GNN** [5]. Pre-trainded model methods include BERT [2] series [5,16], such as **PN(BERT)** [5] which only focuses on cross-domain generalization and Transformer series [18]. Adversarial learning based methods have **PN-ADV(CNN)** and **PN-ADV(BERT)** [5], which also only focus on cross-domain generalization. Meta-learning methods have **SNAIL** [5,11] and **Meta Networks** [8,12]. **KNN** method [5] is also used to solve FSL-RC. All these existing methods only focus on one problem, the information deficit or cross-domain generalization. They can not solve both problems, and they ignore the problem of lacking of significant distinguishing features. Our KDFT-PN consider these problems together.

Prototypical networks [15] is one of metric-based methods in Few-shot RC. It learns embedding representations and feature space to distinguish unseen categories. Firstly, the encoder encodes support set and query set independently. Then the class mean of support instance representations is as the prototype vector. Each support set has one prototype vector. Finally, it predicts query class in terms of the minimal euclidean distance between prototype vectors and the query instance, so as to predict unseen data points.

3 Approach

3.1 Task Definition

The setting of Few-shot RC is roughly following meta-learning's. There are meta-training and meta-testing stages, corresponding to datasets $D_{meta-train}$ and $D_{meta-test}$. Those relation classes have no intersection. In the meta-training phase, there are multiple classification tasks. For each task, the dataset is divided into support set $D_i^{support}$ and query set D_i^{query}. $D_{meta-train} = \{(D_1^{support}, D_1^{query}) ,..., (D_L^{support}, D_L^{query})\}$. L is the number of classification tasks. Support set $D_i^{support}$ follows N-way K-shot settings, which means N relation classes, denoted as $R_i = \{r_1, r_2, .., r_N\}$, and K samples for each class, denoted as s_k^n, with known label r_n. $D_i^{support} = (s_k^n, r_n)$, $S_i = \{s_k^n\}$, where $1 \le i \le L$, $1 \le n \le N$, $1 \le k \le K$. Query set $D_i^{query} = (q_j, r_j)$, where $1 \le i \le L$, $1 \le j \le M$, $r_j \in R$. M is the number of query samples.

We evaluate model on batches of data sampled from $D_{meta-test}$. Each batch contains (R, S, q, r). q is a query sample and its real label is $r \in R$. The goal is

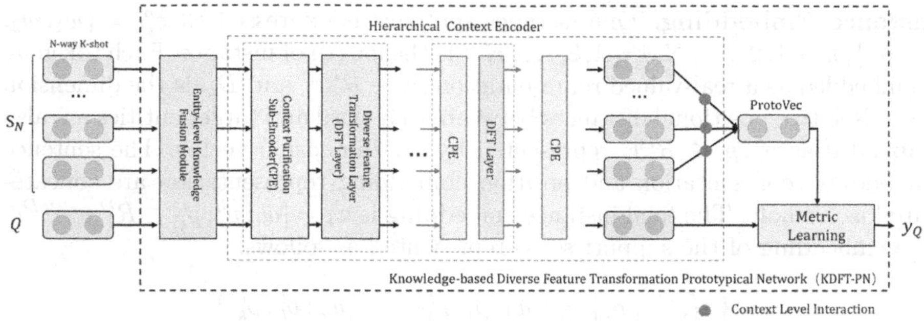

Fig. 1. KDFT-PN Overview: The input includes support set and query set. Each support set follows N-way K-shot settings. The model includes (1) Entity-level Knowledge Fusion Module, integrating knowledge description corresponding to target entities. (2) Context Purification Sub-encoder (CPE), purifying single sample in word-level, and enhancing information interaction between support and query samples in context-level. (3) Diverse Feature Transformation Layer (DFT), simulating and learning multiple data distributions to improve generalization ability.

to predict the class $y \in R$ of the query sample given support set S and relation set R. The optimization objective is to minimize loss with loss function f:

$$Loss = \frac{1}{M} \sum_{j}^{M} f(P(q_j|S, R), r)$$

3.2 Model Overview

The model structure (Fig. 1) includes Entity-level Knowledge Fusion Module (Fig. 2), Hierarchical Context Encoder (E) and metric learning module. E includes Purification Sub-encoder (CPE) (Fig. 3) and Diverse Feature Transformation Layer (DFT layer) (Fig. 4). Based on prototypical network, the main process is still to calculate the prototype vector of each class, and predict the query class by the similarity between prototype vectors and the query vector. In this work, Entity-level Knowledge Fusion Module enhances semantic information and provides prior knowledge. E is used to purify and offset features on support set and query set, expressed as $E(s)$, $E(q)$. Hierarchical Context Encoder can have multiple CPEs and DFT layers. One linear layer is used as metric Learning M to measure the similarity between prototype vectors and the query vector. M outputs query's label according to the label of support instance r_s and $E(s)$, $E(q)$. The process can be expressed as:

$$y = M(r_s, E(s), E(q))$$

The final training objective is to minimize the classification error of query instances with cross entropy loss function and the label of query instance r_q:

$$Loss(r_q, y) = cross\_entropy(r_q, y)$$

Instance Embedding. One instance sentence is expressed as $x_i^n = \{w_1, w_2, \ldots, w_l\}, n = 1, 2, \ldots, N, i = 1, 2, \ldots, K$. l is the length of instance. Each token w_i is embedded as a real-valued representation $\hat{w}_i \in R^{D_w}$, and D_w is the dimension of $\hat{w}_i$. Relative positional distances between each word and target entities are also embedded as $p_i^h, p_i^t \in R^{D_p}$, represented by D_p dimension vector. The sentence embedding representation and position embedding representation are concatenated as a whole. The final instance embedding is $\hat{x}_i = [\hat{w}_i; p_i^h; p_i^t] \in R^{D_w + 2\times D_p}$. The embedding of the support set is represented as follows.

$$\{\hat{x}_1, \ldots, \hat{x}_k\} = \{[\hat{w}_1; p_1^h; p_1^t], \ldots, [\hat{w}_k; p_k^h; p_k^t]\}$$

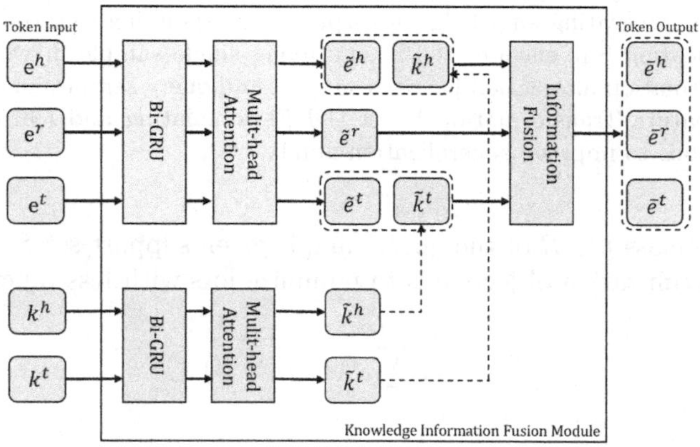

Fig. 2. Entity-level Knowledge Fusion Module: instance entities (green part) and knowledge entities (pink part) are the input. Then independent Bi-GRUs and multi-head attention mechanism (yellow part) encode and optimize the input, and two forward feedback layers (blue part) are used to fuse instance and knowledge features. (Color figure online)

3.3 Entity-Level Knowledge Fusion Module

To solve information deficit caused by the scarcity of samples and the lack of significant distinguishing features of some samples, we introduce Entity-level Knowledge Fusion Module to enrich samples' semantic features (Fig. 2). Firstly, we choose the most match candidate entity knowledge description with target entities of one sample via pre-trained BERT [2]. Target entity descriptions obtained from the knowledge base are expressed as k_i^h and k_i^t, corresponding to the head entity and tail entity. One instance $\hat{x}_i$ has three types entity, expressed as head entity e_i^h, tail entity e_i^t, and rest entities e_i^r. Firstly, entity information and instance are calculated by Bi-GRU to obtain each token representation. Secondly, these token are calculated by three multi-head self-attention module independently. Finally, the fusion method of head and tail entity information follows as Eq. 1 and Eq. 2 respectively. Rest entities are calculated as Eq. 3.

$$h_i^h = W_i^{eh} e_i^h + W_i^h k_i^h + b_i^{eh}; \quad \bar{e}_i^h = \sigma(W_i^{hh} h_i^h + b_i^{hh}). \tag{1}$$

$$h_i^t = W_i^{et} e_i^t + W_i^t k_i^t + b_i^{et}; \quad \bar{e}_i^t = \sigma(W_i^{ht} h_i^t + b_i^{ht}). \tag{2}$$

$$h_i^r = W_i^{er} + b_i^{er}; \quad \bar{e}_i^r = \sigma(W_i^{hr} h_i^r + b_i^{hr}). \tag{3}$$

After fused with knowledge information, the word of one instance is expressed as $\bar{w}_i = [\bar{e}_i^h, \bar{e}_i^r, \bar{e}_i^t]$. Finally, one instance is expressed as

$$\{\bar{x}_1, \ldots, \bar{x}_k\} = \{[\bar{w}_1; p_1^h; p_1^t] \ldots, [\bar{w}_k; p_k^h; p_k^t]\}$$

3.4 Context Purification Sub-encoder

In order to improve information interaction and the quality of prototype vectors in prototypical network, we proposes a Context Purification Sub-encoder, which is divided into two levels on the basis of the prototypical network. Word level optimizes the feature representation of a single sample, and then context level optimizes the prototype vector quality.

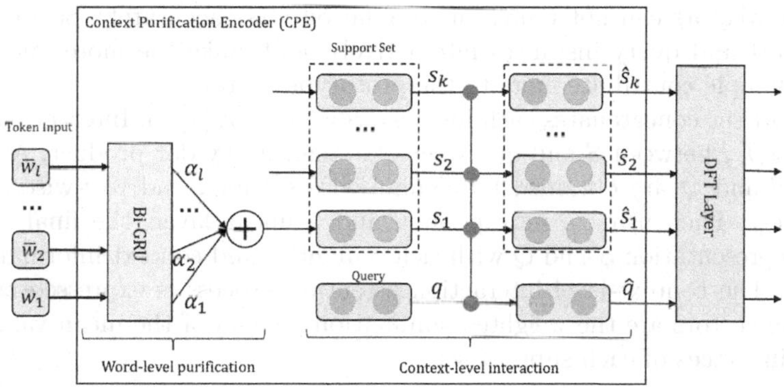

Fig. 3. Context Purification Sub-encoder Structure: (1) Word-level purification: we use Bi-GRU (the yellow rectangle) to encode each instance to get each token representation. Then multi-head self-attention mechanism is used to weight each token, and α is the weight coefficient. Finally each instance (s or q) is the weighted summation of every token. (2) Context-level interaction: support instances (green rectangles with two solid circles) interacts with query instances (orange rectangles with two solid circles) with multi-head attention mechanism (orange and green solid circles). (Color figure online)

Word-Level Purification. In order to make more informative words to contribute more in instance features, we use word-level multi-head self-attention mechanism to achieve. Firstly, for better fusion, we use Bi-GRU again to obtain each token's hidden representation $h_{\bar{w}_i}$. Then we use multi-head self-attention to get the weight of each token. Finally the weighted summation of all tokens in one sentence is used as the instance feature representation $\tilde{x}_{word-att}$. This process is expressed as Eq. 4.

$$\begin{aligned} h_{\bar{w}_i} &= [\overrightarrow{GRU}([\bar{w}_i; p_i^h; p_i^t]); \overleftarrow{GRU}([\bar{w}_i; p_i^h; p_i^t])]; \\ \tilde{x}_z^{word-att} &= \textstyle\sum_i^L \alpha_{\bar{w}_i,z} h_{\bar{w}_i}; \\ \tilde{x}_{word-att} &= concat(\tilde{x}_z^{word-att}) W_{MH}. \end{aligned} \tag{4}$$

$\alpha_{\bar{w}_i}$ is the weight coefficient of the word $\bar{w}_i$ and z is the heads number. W_α, W_s are parameters to be learned, seen as Eq. 5.

$$\begin{aligned} \alpha_{\bar{w}_i,z} &= \frac{exp(W_Z^\alpha score_i)}{\sum_j^L exp(W_Z^\alpha score_i)}; \\ score_{i,z} &= \tanh(W_z^s h_{\bar{w}_i} + b_z^s). \end{aligned} \tag{5}$$

Context-Level Interaction. In original prototypical network, after encoding support set and query set independently, prototype vectors are the mean value of each support set. If one support set has instances lacking significant distinguishing features, those instances will cause a severe damage to prototype vectors. Prototype vectors can not represent its relation class accurately. So we encode the support and query instances interactively, and make the more informative support sample contribute more to the prototype vector.

Support set concatenates each instance $S = concat(\{s_k^n\})$. Interaction attention score $\beta_{i,j}$ between S and query set Q is realized by dot product. Attention weights $\bar{S}$ and $\bar{Q}$ are obtained by column-wise softmax and row-wise softmax respectively. Then using a max pooling and a linear layer, the final instance feature representation $\hat{S}$ and $\hat{Q}$ with rich semantics and context information are obtained. The context-level interaction attention process is expressed as Eq. 6. Prototype vectors are the weighted summation instead of the mean value of all support instances of each support set.

$$\begin{aligned} \beta_{i,j} &= S_i \odot Q_j; \\ \beta_i^{Q2S} = softmax(\beta_{1,t}, ..., \beta_{NK,t}), &\quad \beta_i^{S2Q} = softmax(\beta_{t,1}, ..., \beta_{t,M}); \\ \bar{S} = \sum_i^{NK} \beta_i^{Q2S} S_i, &\quad \bar{Q} = \sum_i^{M} \beta_i^{S2Q} Q_i; \\ \hat{S} = W_{col}\bar{S} + b_{col}, &\quad \hat{Q} = W_{row}\bar{Q} + b_{row}. \end{aligned} \tag{6}$$

3.5 Diverse Feature Transformation Layer

In order to improve the generalization ability in Few-shot RC, we insert the Diverse Feature Transformation Layer (DFT layer) (Fig. 4) into the Hierarchical

Context Encoder to offset sample features, so as to simulate the distribution of multiple data domains. Therefore, the model can learn deeper common features among multiple simulated data domains, instead of focusing too much on one source domain.

Our work divides training dataset into pseudo-seen and pseudo-unseen datasets. we use pseudo-seen dataset to update the classification model. After one CPE, instance features $\hat{S}$ and $\hat{Q}$ with rich context and semantic information are obtained. Then we add a DFT layer f_θ between CPEs, each Layer is

$$\begin{aligned} \tilde{S} = f_\theta(\hat{S}) = \varphi \times \hat{S} + \psi; \\ \tilde{Q} = f_\theta(\hat{Q}) = \varphi \times \hat{Q} + \psi. \end{aligned} \tag{7}$$

The output of the support set through a certain CPE layer is $\hat{S} \in R^{B \times N \times K \times D_C}$ and $\hat{Q} \in R^{B \times N \times M/N \times D_C}$, which is the input of DFT layer. One DFT layer transforms features with scaling weight $\varphi \in R^{B \times N \times K \times 1}$ and bias $\psi \in R^{B \times N \times K \times 1}$, and outputs $\tilde{S} \in R^{B \times N \times K \times D_C}$ and $\tilde{Q} \in R^{B \times N \times M/N \times D_C}$. B is the batch size. We train the classification model with the pseudo-seen dataset. φ and ψ are initially sampled from Gaussian distribution $\varphi \sim N(1, softplus(\theta_\varphi))$ and $\psi \sim N(1, softplus(\theta_\psi))$, and they do not update with the model. After the classification model trained, the pseudo-unseen data set is used to optimize φ and ψ, so that DFT layer can be adapted to the whole relation classification task, rather than the limited adaptation to the training set.

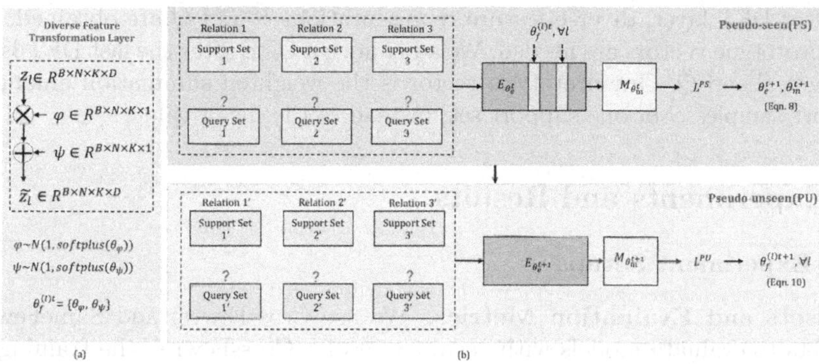

Fig. 4. Diverse Feature Transformation Layer Overview. (a) DFT layer is a affine function with the scaling and bias terms parameterized by the hyper-parameters θ_φ and θ_ψ sampled from Gaussian distribution. (b) We use a learning-to-learn algorithm to optimize the hyper-parameters of DFT layers by maximizing the performance on the pseudo-unseen domain (bottom) after the model optimized on the pseudo-seen domain (top).

Learning Diverse Feature Transformation Layer. To improve performance in the unseen domain, after training the model using the seen domains, we use meta-learning to learn DFT layer parameters. During training, at each iteration t, pseudo-seen domain task set T^{PS} and pseudo-unseen Tasks T^{PU} are sampled from the seen domain set $\{T_1^{seen}, T_2^{seen}, \ldots, T_N^{seen}\}$. Hierarchical Context Encoder without DFT layers and metric Learning module are denoted by $E_{\theta_e^t}$, $M_{\theta_m^t}$ respectively. $\theta_f^t = \{\theta_\varphi, \theta_\psi\}$ are hyper-parameters of DFT layer. E integrated with DFT layers is expressed as $E_{\theta_e^t, \theta_f^t}$. Firstly, with pseudo-seen task $T^{PS} = \{(s^{PS}, r_s^{PS}), (q^{PS}, r_q^{PS})\}$, we optimize parameters of the classification model:

$$L(*) = Loss(r_q^{PS}, M_{\theta_m^t}((r_s^S, E_{\theta_e^t, \theta_f^t}(s^{PS})), E_{\theta_e^t, \theta_f^t}(q^{PS}))$$
$$(\theta_e^{t+1}, \theta_m^{t+1}) = (\theta_e^t, \theta_m^t) - \alpha \nabla_{\theta_e^t, \theta_m^t} L(*) \quad (8)$$

After updated with Eq. 8, the model generalization ability can be measured. After removing DFT layers, we use pseudo-unseen task $T^{PU} = \{(s^{PU}, r_s^{PU}), (q^{PU}, r_q^{PU})\}$ to calculate the query loss based on the updated model, expressed as:

$$L^{PU} = Loss(r_q^{PU}, M_{\theta_m^{t+1}}((r_q^{PU} E_{\theta_e^{t+1}}(s^{PU})))) \quad (9)$$

L^{PU} represents the effectiveness of the DFT layer, and is used to update DFT layer parameters θ_f^t. During training phase, the classification model and DFT layer are updated jointly.

$$\theta_f^{t+1} = \theta_f^t - \alpha \nabla_{\theta_f^t} L^{PU} \quad (10)$$

After DFT layer, diverse feature representations $\tilde{S}$ and $\tilde{Q}$ are obtained, and then prototype vectors are needed. We add another CPE after the last DFT layer, then get $\hat{S}$ and $\hat{Q}$. One prototype vector is the weighted summation among all support samples $\hat{S}$ of one support set, instead of the mean value.

4 Experiments and Results

4.1 Experiment Setups

Datasets and Evaluation Metrics. We use CrossFewrel and SameFewRel datasets to evaluate models with accuracy. As for CrossFewrel, the training set is from Wikipedia, and the testing set is from UMLS (biomedical field). It is used to evaluate the cross domain generalization performance. There are 64 relations in the training set, and each relation has 700 instances. And the test set has 20 relations, and each relation has 100 instances. As for SameFewRel, both training set and testing set are from Wikipedia. The number of relation type and instance is same with CrossFewrel. We investigate four few-shot learning settings: 5-way 5-shot, 5-way 1-shot, 10-way 5-shot, and 10-way 1-shot, which are the same as [8].

Baselines and Competitive Approaches. Following the setting of [5], we use the following models as baseline models for cross domain experiments.

Prototypical Networks [15]. In terms of the selection of encoders and whether to use adversarial learning, four baseline models are derived. **PN-(CNN)** uses CNN as encoder only. **PN-ADV(CNN)** uses adversarial learning and CNN encoder. **PN(BERT)** uses pre-trained BERT as encoder only. **PN-ADV(BERT)** uses pre-trained BERT encoder and adversarial learning.

Following the setting of [8], we use the following models as baseline models for same domain experiments.

SNAIL [11] is to simulate the process of human reading, and read the subsequent text with previous article information. Query samples are concatenated behind support samples. Then one-dimensional CNN is used to capture features to gather information.

Meta Networks [12] is a meta-learning algorithm. Its idea is to use a high-level meta learner to supervise the learning process of base learner. And the base learner is a base CNN classification model.

GNN [14] takes the support sample and its corresponding label together as the node of the graph, and takes the query sample as the node of the graph. The label of the query sample can be predicted through the graph information dissemination.

Model Details. As a combination, CPE and DFT layers can be used several times in turn, and we use them twice in order to fully capture various features in the experimental stage. And an extra CPE is set as the last layer. All hyper-parameters are listed in Table 3. We adopt pre-trained Glove word embeddings [13].

Table 3. Hyper-parameters used in our experiments

Parameter	Value
Word embedding dimension	50
Position embedding dimension	5
Bi-GRU hidden size	230
Head (Multi-head attention)	3
Batch size	4
Sentence length	128
Learning rate	1e–3
Optimizer	SGD

4.2 Results

Table 4 is the accuracy result of the proposed model and other comparative experiments in four experimental settings on CrossFewRel dataset. Compared

Table 4. Experiment results on Cross-domain dataset

No.	Model	5-way 5-shot	5-way 1-shot	10-way 5-shot	10-way 1-shot
1	**KDFT-PN**	**81.92**	**58.01**	**59.42**	**46.24**
2	KDFT-PN w/o DFT	73.8	53.24	51.8	38.43
3	KDFT-PN w/o DFT w/o CPE	63.52	46.94	47.62	35.27
4	PN+ADV	59.32	43.51	45.6	29.04
5	PN-ADV(BERT)	56.36	42.68	38.73	27.42
6	PN(BERT)	53.42	41.35	38.1	27.96
7	PN(CNN)	48.85	36.16	36.2	21.27

with the prototypical network and other methods, our model KDFT-PN achieves the best results in four settings. The accuracy is improved by an average of 14%, which verifies that our model has good generalization performance for the domain adaptation problem of Few-shot RC. Meanwhile, through the group 2 KDFT-PN w/o DFT in the table, we can see that the generalization performance of the model greatly reduces if remove DFT layers. Compared with KDFT-PN, the accuracy of KDFT-PN w/o DFT is dropped by an average of 7%, by which the effectiveness of DFT layer is also proved. Group 3 KDFT-PN w/o DFT w/o CPE means that KDFT-PN only integrates the information of knowledge base. Compared with group 2 KDFT-PN w/o DFT, the accuracy of KDFT-PN w/o DFT w/o CPE is dropped by an average of 6%, but it is still much better than other baseline models, which also verifies the effectiveness of introducing knowledge base for cross-domain Few-shot RC. Meanwhile, it can be found from results of other baseline models that adversarial learning also plays a role in this task.

Table 5. Experiment results on SameFewRel dataset

No.	Model	5-way 5-shot	5-way 1-shot	10-way 5-shot	10-way 1-shot
1	**KDFT-PN**	**89.96**	**81.4**	**85.88**	**70.44**
2	PN(CNN)	86.01	70.94	75.2	58.96
3	SNAIL	77.2	64.58	65.06	50.36
4	Meta-Net	79.63	61.37	64.94	50.3
5	GNN	79.33	63.92	61.48	44.75
6	KNN	68.96	52.79	53.68	39.62

For further exploration, we also evaluate our model on SameFewRel dataset, and results are shown as Tabel 5. Compared with other methods, the accuracy is improved by an average of 9%. We find our model surprisingly achieves competitive performance when compared with other state-of-the-art Few-shot RC methods, which verifies the effectiveness of KDFT-PN for Few-shot RC.

5 Conclusions

This paper focuses on the task of few-shot relation classification. In order to solve problems of information deficit caused by the scarcity of samples and poor generalization effect, this paper proposes Knowledge-based Diverse Feature Transformation Prototypical Network (KDFT-PN), which includes Entity-level Knowledge Fusion Module, Context Purification Sub-encoder and Diverse Feature Transformation Layer. Entity-level Knowledge Fusion Module integrates the entity information of knowledge base to enrich semantic features. Context Purification Sub-encoder improves semantic interaction and the quality of prototype vectors. And Diverse Feature Transformation Layer simulates and learns multiple data domains to improve generalization ability. Experiment results show that our model can deliver accuracy comparable to other state-of-the-art algorithms on cross-domain and same-domain datasets, which verifies the effectiveness of our model in Few-shot RC.

Acknowledgements. This research is supported by the National Key RD Program of China (No.2017YFC0820700, No.2018YFB1004700).

References

1. Cover, T., Hart, P.: Nearest neighbor pattern classification. IEEE Trans. Inf. Theory **13**(1), 21–27 (1967)
2. Devlin, J., Chang, M.W., Lee, K., Toutanova, K.: Bert: pre-training of deep bidirectional transformers for language understanding, pp. 4171–4186 (2019). https://doi.org/10.18653/v1/N19-1423, https://www.aclweb.org/anthology/N19-1423
3. Fink, M.: Object classification from a single example utilizing class relevance metrics. In: Advances in Neural Information Processing Systems 2004, pp. 449–456 (2004). http://papers.nips.cc/paper/2576-object-classification-from-a-single-example-utilizing-class-relevance-metrics
4. Finn, C.: Model-agnostic meta-learning for fast adaptation of deep networks. In: Proceedings of the 34th International Conference on Machine Learning, vol. 70, pp. 1126–1135. PMLR (2017). http://proceedings.mlr.press/v70/finn17a.html
5. Gao, T.: FewRel 2.0: towards more challenging few-shot relation classification. In: Proceedings of the 2019 Conference on Empirical Methods in NLP, pp. 6250–6255. Association for Computational Linguistics (2019). https://doi.org/10.18653/v1/D19-1649, https://www.aclweb.org/anthology/D19-1649
6. Garcia, V., Bruna, J.: Few-shot learning with graph neural networks (2018). https://openreview.net/forum?id=BJj6qGbRW
7. Goodfellow, I.J., Shlens, J., Szegedy, C.: Explaining and harnessing adversarial examples. In: Computer Science (2014)
8. Han, X.: FewRel: a large-scale supervised few-shot relation classification dataset with state-of-the-art evaluation. In: Proceedings of the 2018 Conference on Empirical Methods in Natural Language Processing, pp. 4803–4809. Association for Computational Linguistics, Brussels (2018)
9. Li, F., Fergus, R., Perona, P.: One-shot learning of object categories. IEEE Trans. Pattern Anal. Mach. Intell. **28**(4), 594–611 (2006). http://papers.nips.cc/paper/6996-prototypical-networks-for-few-shot-learning.pdf

10. Mintz, M.: Distant supervision for relation extraction without labeled data. In: Proceedings of the 47th Annual Meeting of the Association for Computational Linguistics and the 4th International Joint Conference on Natural Language Processing of the AFNLP (2009)
11. Mishra, N., Rohaninejad, M., Chen, X., Abbeel, P.: A simple neural attentive meta-learner. In: 6th International Conference on Learning Representations (2018). https://openreview.net/forum?id=B1DmUzWAW
12. Munkhdalai, T., Yu, H.: Meta networks (2017)
13. Pennington, J., Socher, R.: Glove: global vectors for word representation. In: Proceedings of the 2014 Conference on Empirical Methods in NLP (2014)
14. Satorras, V.G., Estrach, J.B.: Few-shot learning with graph neural networks. In: 6th International Conference on Learning Representations, ICLR 2018 (2018). https://openreview.net/forum?id=BJj6qGbRW
15. Snell, J., Swersky, K., Zemel, R.S.: Prototypical networks for few-shot learning. In: Advances in Neural Information Processing Systems, vol. 30 (2017)
16. Soares, L.B.: Matching the blanks: distributional similarity for relation learning. pp. 2895–2905. Association for Computational Linguistics (2019). https://doi.org/10.18653/v1/p19-1279
17. Surdeanu, M.: Multi-instance multi-label learning for relation extraction. In: Joint Conference on Empirical Methods in Natural Language Processing & Computational Natural Language Learning (2012)
18. Wang, Y.: Learning to decouple relations: few-shot relation classification with entity-guided attention and confusion-aware training (2020)
19. Zhou, P.: Attention-based bidirectional long short-term memory networks for relation classification (2016)

Community Detection in Dynamic Networks: A Novel Deep Learning Method

Fan Zhang[1], Junyou Zhu[1], Zheng Luo[1], Zhen Wang[2], Li Tao[1], and Chao Gao[1,2(✉)]

[1] College of Computer and Information Science, Southwest University, Chongqing 400715, China
cgao@swu.edu.cn

[2] School of Artificial Intelligence, Optics, and Electronics (iOPEN), Northwestern Polytechnical University, Xi'an 710072, China

Abstract. Dynamic community detection has become a hot spot of researches, which helps detect the revolving relationships of complex systems. In view of the great value of dynamic community detection, various kinds of dynamic algorithms come into being. Deep learning-based algorithms, as one of the most popular methods, transfer the core ideas of feature representation to dynamic community detection in order to improve the accuracy of dynamic community detection. However, when committing feature aggregation strategies, most of methods focus on the attribute features but omit the structural information of networks, which lowers the accuracy of dynamic community detection. Also, the differences of learned features between adjacent time steps may be large, which does not correspond with the real world. In this paper, we utilize the node relevancy to measure the varying importance of different nodes, which reflects the structural information of networks. Having acquired the node representations at each time step, the cross entropy is used to smoothen adjacent time steps so that the differences between adjacent time steps can be small. Some extensive experiments on both the real-world datasets and synthetic datasets show that our algorithm is more superior than other algorithms.

Keywords: Community detection · Dynamic networks · Graph convolutional networks · Smoothing measures

1 Introduction

In the real world, various complex systems can be abstracted as networks, where nodes denote the entities and edges the relationship between different nodes. Based on the abstracted networks, the community detection is implemented to detect the potential relationships and it has been applied to various areas. For instance, community detection can help reveal the potential relationship between

H. Qiu et al. (Eds.): KSEM 2021, LNAI 12815, pp. 115–127, 2021.
https://doi.org/10.1007/978-3-030-82136-4_10

traffic networks distribution and economic circles [1]. In the Internet era, community detection can help evaluate the influence of information diffusion [2]. Thus, community detection owns great value of researches. However, the relationships in networks are changeable and dynamic community detection gains more and more popularity, which can help detect the evolving relationships.

In view of the enormous value carried by dynamic community detection, more and more researchers are dedicated to improving the effects of dynamic community detection. The feature extraction is a typical example transferred to the field of community detection. The first phase of such a method is a process of low-dimensional representation by mapping reconstruction. In the second phase, the node representation is used for community detection. The methods for feature extraction can be divided into two general kinds, that is, the traditional feature extraction methods [3] and neural networks-based extraction methods [4]. A traditional feature extraction method, the Histogram of Oriented Gradient (HOG) constitutes features by calculating the histogram of oriented gradient in the local area of graph [5]. Combined with Support Vector Machine (SVE), HOG has been widely used in the graph recognition area. Such kind of methods often rely on some prior knowledge. Different from traditional methods, neural networks-based extraction methods are a kind of self-learning feature representation methods which owns better representation effects [6]. However, there still exist some problems when applying feature extraction to dynamic community detection. Firstly, since such kind of methods just commit simple aggregation of attribute information, they fail to consider the structural information of networks, which is of great significance for networks. In addition, they transfer feature extraction to dynamic community detection without considering the dynamism of networks. Consequently, the accuracy of dynamic community detection suffers and there still exists improvement space.

As described above, most methods transferred from deep learning area concentrate on static networks and omit the dynamism of networks. In addition, the structural information is often ignored when aggregating nodes on one time step. The structural information and attribute information can reflect the network to a degree. The ignorance of either of these two information can greatly affect the effects of dynamic community detection. Moreover, the differences of node representations between adjacent time steps may be large, which violates the real-world rules [7]. Since the dynamic community detection aims to help guide the real world, the incorrespondence can affect the ground application. Thus, the capture of dynamism is also important for its application in the real world. The main problems can be concluded as follows:

(1) The structural information of networks is often ignored, which makes the accuracy of node representations suffer.
(2) The accuracy of node representations on one single time step has a large improvement space since the reconstruction error can not well reflect the goodness of learned features.
(3) The node representations between adjacent time steps may have large differences, which does not correspond with the real society.

Focused on these problems, we intend to optimize the existing feature extraction methods on static networks and apply them to dynamic community detection. When committing feature extraction at one specific time step, the structural information of networks is taken into account. In addition, we utilize the mutual information maximum strategy to better reflect the goodness of learned features. Having acquired the features at each time step, the cross entropy loss function is utilized to smoothen the learned features between adjacent time steps. The learned features of dynamic communities can be used to commit dynamic community detection with lower cost and higher accuracy. Thus, the main contributions of our paper are as follows:

(1) To take the structural information of networks into account, the similarity matrix is constructed to measure the importance of different nodes for a specific target node.
(2) At one specific time step, the mutual information maximum is taken in order to better reflect the goodness of learned features.
(3) The cross entropy is added into loss function to smoothen the learned feature matrixes between different time steps so that the differences between adjacent time steps can be small.

The rest of this paper is organized as follows. Firstly, Sect. 2 introduces the related work on dynamic community detection and feature representation. Then, Sect. 3 describes our novel feature extraction method on dynamic networks in detail. Sect. 4 illustrates the used data sets and comparison experiments. Finally, Sect. 5 concludes this paper.

2 Related Work

2.1 Dynamic Community Detection

Dynamic networks are such a kind of network that changes over time, where nodes and edges can be added to or removed from the network [8]. That is, the relationships between nodes keep changing. In our experiments, we assume the number of nodes in a network is constant. In another sentence, we still take the nodes which lose contact with others of a network into account. Since the relationships between nodes keep changing, dynamic community detection aims to find the community division at each time step. In essence, dynamic community detection is to cluster nodes with close contacts together and those with sparse contacts into different groups at each time step as shown in Fig. 1.

In general, dynamic community detection methods can be divided into two kinds. The first kind concentrates on the fixed clustering on networks and directly applies the traditional community detection algorithms at each time step independently. The other kind aims to optimize the loss function. For instance, multi objective discrete particle swarm optimization for community detection in dynamic networks (DYNMOPSO) proposed by Gao is a dynamic community

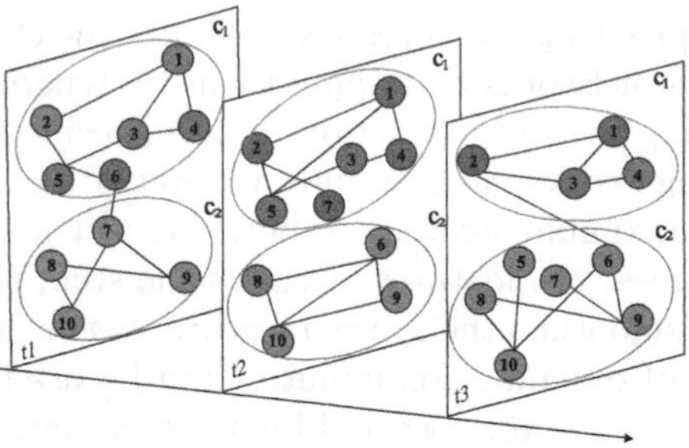

Fig. 1. Simple process of dynamic community detection. In the graph, the ten different nodes are labeled from 1 to 10. The dynamic community detection method aims to divide nodes with high relevancy together at all time steps. The nodes clustered into the same group are given the same color. From this graph, the evolution of communities can be viewed and applied to real-life guidance. (Color figure online)

detection which utilizes the swarm intelligence [9]. In addition, a novel evolutionary clustering model HDPHTM proposed by Xu studies the size and structure of communities automatically utilizing the prior knowledge [10]. DYNMOPSO is a dynamic community detection which utilizes the swarm intelligence pattern to solve such a community detection problem in dynamic networks [9]. Such kind of community detection methods is biologically inspired, which has efficiently improved the accuracy of community detection [11]. S-ENMF leverages the non-negative matrix factorization when committing dynamic community detection [16]. Genlouvain Identifies communities from multiplex biological networks [17]. DECS is a novel multi-objective evolutionary clustering algorithm [18]. Timers proposes an optimized incremental Singular Value Decomposition approaches to process newly changed nodes and edges in dynamic networks [19]. These methods directly commit dynamic community detection based on the original data, which not only increases the cost but also affects the accuracy. Thus, feature extraction measures are taken before dynamic community detection in order to cut the cost and improve the accuracy.

2.2 Networks Based Feature Extraction on Graphs

Networks based feature extraction applies deep learning methods to dynamic communities [12]. One of the most popular methods is utilizing graph convolutional networks to learn the low-dimensional representations of nodes [13]. By utilizing graph convolutional operations, the attribute information of neighboring nodes can be aggregated into the target node and help update the corresponding features. The acquired features are input as the final low-dimensional representation. Such kind of methods are based on the locality strategies and apply to large-scale networks. The learned low-dimensional representations can be used to commit dynamic community detection. In this way, the computational cost can be cut and the community division results can be more accurate.

In addition, graph attention networks compute the hidden representations of each node in graphs and utilize the attention mechanism to calculate neighboring nodes [14]. In the end, it outputs the features of each node and helps aggregate the information of networks. However, most of these methods are only used for static networks and they ignore the dynamism of networks. Thus, in our method, we commit feature extraction at each time step and then smoothen node representations between adjacent time steps to capture dynamism.

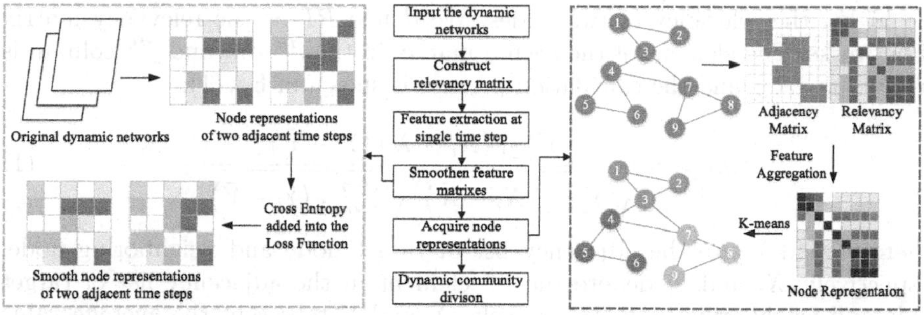

Fig. 2. The simple processes of NNFE. Firstly, we input the information of dynamic communities. Then, the adjacency matrix and relevancy matrix can be calculated. Based on these two matrixes, the node representations at each time step can be acquired. Following that, the cross entropy of node representations between adjacent time steps is used to smoothen the node representations. Finally, the node representations are input to the K-means algorithm to commit dynamic community detection.

3 The Proposed NNFE Method

To improve the efficiency of dynamic community detection, we propose a Novel Networks Feature Extraction method (NNFE). The core ideas of our NNFE method are introduced as follows. Firstly, the relevancy matrix is constructed, which ensures that the structural information of networks is taken into account. Then, the method takes the mutual information maximum strategies at single time step. Such technology can help improve the accuracy of node representation at single time step. Finally, the smoothing strategy is taken between two adjacent time steps. The detailed flowchart of our NNFE is shown in Fig. 2.

3.1 The Relevancy Matrix Construction

In our proposed NNFE, the structural information of networks is taken into account and this can help improve the accuracy of feature learning. For a target node, the neighboring nodes can have different importance and we utilize the relevance between target node and neighboring node to measure the importance of different nodes. Specifically, the pearson coefficient is used to measure the relevancy of different nodes [15]. Based on the method of covariance, the pearson coefficient is known as the best method of measuring the association between variables of interest. It evaluates the similarity of vectors and then outputs a value ranging from −1 to 1. In our proposed method, the adjacency relationship of one node with all other nodes constitutes the feature vector of the target node, which is composed of a series of 0 and 1. Based on the feature vector, the pearson value between each two nodes can be measured. The higher the pearson value, the higher the relevancy of two nodes. We define RL as the relevancy matrix of networks. The element of the such a matrix in the ith row and j^{th} column is denoted as RL_{ij} and the calculation process is shown in Eq. (1).

$$RL_{(i,j)} = \frac{\sum_{i=1}^{n}\left(X_i - \bar{X}\right)\left(Y_i - \bar{Y}\right)}{\sqrt{\sum_{i=1}^{n}\left(X_i - \bar{X}\right)^2}\sqrt{\sum_{i=1}^{n}\left(Y_i - \bar{Y}\right)^2}} \tag{1}$$

where X and Y are the adjacency list of target node and neighboring node, respectively. X_i and Y_i denote the ith element in the adjacency list of target node and neighboring node respectively. $\bar{X}$ and $\bar{Y}$ represent the average value of the corresponding list.

3.2 The Mutual Information Maximum

The feature representation of networks can be used for community detection. However, most methods focus on the reconstruction error of feature learning to train parameters. That is, they first encode the original matrixes and obtain the feature representation of networks. Then they utilize the learned features to reconstruct the original graph and compare the differences between the original graph and the reconstructed graph. However, the small reconstruction error cannot ensure the accuracy of learned features. In this paper, we utilize the mutual information maximum strategy to mine the features of dynamic networks.

The proposed NNFE method aims to maximize the mutual information between the local representations and global representations. Firstly, the eigenvector of nodes is taken as the local representations of each node. For one target node, we leverage the Graph Convolutional Networks to aggregate the information of the neighboring nodes.

$$H = \mathcal{E}(\mathbf{A_t}, \mathbf{F_t}) = \sigma\left(\mathbf{D_t}^{-\frac{1}{2}}\hat{\mathbf{A}}_\mathbf{t}\mathbf{D_t}^{-\frac{1}{2}}\mathbf{F_t}\Theta\right) \tag{2}$$

where $\mathbf{A_t}$ and $\mathbf{F_t}$ are the adjacency matrix and feature matrix at one time step, respectively. $\mathbf{D_t}$ represents the current degree matrix where each element denotes the degree of the corresponding node. $\boldsymbol{\Theta}$ denotes the weight matrix at current time step. $\sigma(.)$ is the activation function. However, $\hat{\mathbf{A}}_\mathbf{t}$ is different from the traditional adjacency matrix. The $\hat{\mathbf{A}}_\mathbf{t}$ not only considers the adjacency relationship but also the relevancy of different nodes as defined in Eq. (3). In this way, the structural information of networks can be taken into account and this helps improve the accuracy of feature extraction at one time step.

$$\hat{\mathbf{A}}_t = \mathbf{A}_t + \alpha \mathbf{RL}_t \quad (3)$$

where the parameter α adjusts how we consider the relevancy between the target node and neighboring nodes. $\mathbf{RL}_t$ represents the relevancy matrix of current time step. $\hat{\mathbf{A}}_t$ is the adjusted adjacency matrix added with the relevancy.

Having acquired the local representations, the proposed method combines all the local representations to acquire a global representation. Inspired by Deep Graph Infomax, the average function is chosen as the readout function to aggregate all the local representations, which is defined in Eq. (4). Then, the proposed NNFE maximizes the mutual information between the local representations and global representations in order to increase the accuracy of feature extraction at one time step.

$$\mathcal{H}(\mathbf{P}) = \frac{1}{N}\sum_{i=1}^{N} \boldsymbol{h}_i \quad (4)$$

At last, when we obtain the local representations and global representations, we commit row perturbation to generate the negative samples. Then, a discriminator $\mathcal{D}$ is defined to contrast the true samples and negative samples. By leveraging the JensenShannon divergence, the loss function is defined for maximizing the mutual information between local and global representations as shown in Eq. (5).

$$\mathcal{L}_{\text{loss}} = \sum_{i=1}^{n} \log \mathcal{D}\left(\mathbf{h}_i^t, \mathbf{g}^t\right) + \sum_{j=1}^{n} \log\left(1 - \mathcal{D}\left(\tilde{\mathbf{h}}_j^t, \mathbf{g}^t\right)\right) \quad (5)$$

where $\mathcal{D}$ is the discriminator. $\mathrm{h_i^t}$ and $\mathrm{h_j^t}$ represent the true and false local representations at each time step, respectively, while $\mathbf{g}^t$ stand for the global representations.

3.3 The Cross Entropy-Based Smoothing

Since we commit network feature extraction at each time step independently, the differences between adjacent time steps may be large. However, the communities do not change dramatically between two adjacent time steps. In this way, the acquired dynamic community division results may not correspond with the real division. Therefore, how to smooth the feature matrix between two adjacent time steps is of great significance.

In our proposed NNFE method, the cross entropy is utilized to smooth feature matrixes. We assume that the probability distribution of the last time step is y_1 and the distribution of current time step is y_2. Then, the cross entropy is defined as shown in Eq. (6). The higher the cross entropy, the more similar the two adjacent feature matrixes. To minimize the differences between adjacent time steps, the value of cross entropy is added into the loss function. When training weight networks, the value of cross entropy between adjacent time steps increases with the decline of loss function. In this way, the differences of node representations between two adjacent time steps can be smaller. By leveraging the cross entropy smoothing measures, the experimental results can more correspond with the real world.

$$L = -[y_1 \log y_2 + (1 - y_1) \log(1 - y_2)] \tag{6}$$

4 Experiments

4.1 Datasets and Evaluation Metric

Datasets. In our experiments, both the real-world networks and synthetic networks are utilized to confirm the contributions of our novel feature extraction on networks for dynamic community detection. The specific information of these datasets is listed in Table 1.

Table 1. The used dynamic networks with real community divisions. V denotes how many nodes the network has at each time step. T stands for the total time steps of each dynamic network.

	Dataset	V	T
G_1	CollegeMsg	1899	7
G_2	WildBird	202	6
G_3	Bitcoinotc	6005	20
G_4	Email	2029	29
G_5	SYN-FIX	1024	10

Real-world datasets: The real-world datasets used are CollegeMsg[1], WildBird[2], Bitcoinotc[3] and email[4]. The scale of these four datasets spans largely. In detail, the smallest dataset owns 202 nodes and the largest one has 6005 nodes.

Synthetic datasets: The SYN-FIX datasets are utilized as the synthetic datasets in our experiments.

[1] https://snap.stanford.edu/data/CollegeMsg.html.
[2] http://networkrepository.com/aves-wildbird-network.php.
[3] http://snap.stanford.edu/data/soc-sign-bitcoin-otc.html.
[4] http://networkrepository.com/dynamic.php.

Evaluation Metric and Parameter Setting. The Normalized Mutual Information (NMI) is one of the most popular evaluation metrics for dynamic community detection, which requires both the experimental division and the real division. Differently, the modularity Q only needs the experimental division to evaluate the divided community structure. Since we are equipped with the real division of networks, we choose NMI as the main metrics for dynamic community detection.

$$\text{NMI} = \frac{-2\sum_{i=1}^{C_A}\sum_{j=1}^{C_B} C_{ij} \cdot \log\left(\frac{C_{ij} \cdot N}{C_i \cdot C_j}\right)}{\sum_{i=1}^{C_A} C_i \cdot \log\left(\frac{C_i}{N}\right) + \sum_{j=1}^{C_B} C_{ij} \cdot \log\left(\frac{C_j}{N}\right)} \tag{7}$$

Where N denotes the total number of nodes in networks. C_{ij} represents the number of nodes which not only belong to the community i but also j. Also, C_i and C_j denote how many nodes one specific community owns. C_A and C_B are the experimental division and real division, respectively. The value of NMI ranges from 0 to 1 and a higher value indicates a more accurate community division.

In our proposed method, two parameters α and γ describe how to consider the smoothness of dynamic networks and structural information of networks, respectively. The higher the α is, the more the smoothness between adjacent time steps is considered. Similarly, a higher value of γ indicates we consider structural information of networks with higher degree. Specifically, after experiencing parameter modifications many times, we set α as 0.01 and γ as 0.1, respectively.

4.2 Comparison Results

We compare our algorithm with some traditional algorithms, that is, DYNMOPSO [9], S-ENMF [16], Genlouvain [17], DECS [18] and Timers [19] on both real-world and synthetic networks. The specific NMI comparison results are shown in Table 2.

Table 2. The NMI value of different dynamic community detection algorithms on real-world datasets

	G_1	G_2	G_3	G_4
NNFE	**0.7077**	**0.8961**	**0.8596**	**0.8482**
DYNMOPSO	--------	0.5882	--------	--------
S-ENMF	0.3061	0.5054	0.4543	0.4999
Genlouvain	0.2422	0.5855	0.0921	0.1876
DECS	0.2423	0.5855	--------	0.0812
Timers	0.1222	0.4970	0.5912	0.5561

In Table 2, the short stripes denote the computational time is so large that the results cannot be acquired in reasonable time. It's easy to find that our algorithm surpasses the comparison algorithms on all four real-world datasets, that is, G_1, G_2, G_3 and G_4.

For synthetic networks, we implement experiments on G_5 and calculate the corresponding NMI value. To test the robustness of our algorithm, we increase the value of Z, which denotes the noise level in synthetic networks. The detailed comparison results are shown in Fig. 3.

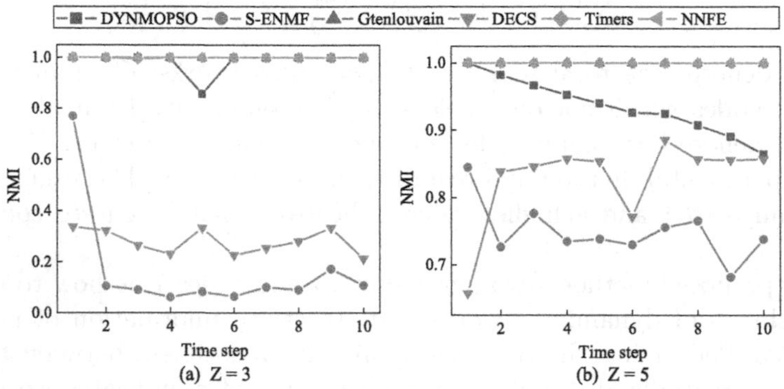

Fig. 3. Comparison results on SYN-FIX networks: The y-axis represents the NMI value of community detection and x-axis denotes the time step. (a) describes the results on SYN-FIX networks when $Z = 3$ and (b) describes the results on SYN-FIX networks when $Z = 5$

Judging from Fig. 3, we can find that our algorithm also takes lead on synthetic networks. At each single time step, the NMI value of our community detection results is the highest among all the comparison algorithms. Although the value of Z increases, that is, the noise level of networks becomes higher, the efficiency of our algorithm does not suffer at all. This proves the strong robustness of our algorithm. In total, our algorithm can achieve both the high efficiency and the strong robustness.

4.3 Ablation Studies

To prove the effectiveness of design choices, we conduct ablation studies on G_2 and G_3 respectively. Since G_2 and G_3 are the largest and smallest datasets in our experimental datasets, they can be the most representative. On each time step, our algorithm leverages the mutual information maximum to improve the accuracy of feature learning on each time step. Then, our algorithm constructs the relevancy matrix to take the structural information into account when aggregating nodes. Having acquired the node representations of each time step, the cross entropy is used to smooth between adjacent time steps. Thus, our ablation studies remove the relevancy matrix construction and cross entropy smoothing respectively in order to analyze our design choices. The specific results can be seen in Table 3.

Table 3. Ablation study

Framework	Community detection	
	G_2	G_3
Basic	0.8845	0.8486
Basic + RMC	0.8856	0.8517
Basic + CES	0.8855	0.8507
Basic + RMC+CES (ours)	**0.8961**	**0.8596**

In Table 3, *Basic* represents the feature extraction method transferred to dynamic networks without any optimization strategies. *RMC* and *CES* denote the measures of relevancy matrix construction and cross entropy-based smoothing measures. It is easy to find that the NNFE with *RMC* and *CES* modules obtains the best NMI value. When we add either of these two modules, the effects of NNFE gains improvement. This reflects that our built-in modules can better the performance of our proposed NNFE. The *NMC* measure helps the NNFE mine the global structural information and *CES* smooths the adjacent time steps in order to match the real world. Equipped with these strategies, the performance of our NNFE gains further improvement.

5 Conclusion

To optimize the traditional deep learning based dynamic community detection algorithms, this paper proposes a novel networks feature extraction method in order to improve the accuracy of dynamic community detection. Firstly, we take the structural information into account when aggregating features so that the node representations can be more accurate. Then, the mutual information maximum is taken. Having acquired the learned node representations at each time step, the cross entropy loss is applied to smooth the node representations between two adjacent time steps so that the experimental division can better correspond with the real world. The detected rule of dynamic community evolution can be used to localize current hot topics and predict future directions of many events. Some extensive experiments on both the real-world datasets and synthetic datasets prove that the accuracy and robustness of our algorithm are better than many state-of-the-art algorithms. In our work, we mainly optimize the feature extraction before community detection. Thus, in the future, we aim to further optimize the community detection algorithm we use after finishing feature extraction so that the accuracy of dynamic community detection can be higher.

Acknowledgment. Prof. Chao Gao and Dr. Li Tao are corresponding authors of this paper. This work was supported by the National Key R&D Program of China (No. 2019YFB2102300), National Natural Science Foundation of China (Nos. 61976181, 11931015, 61762020), Fok Ying-Tong Education Foundation, China (No. 171105), Key Technology Research and Development Program of Science and Technology Scientific and Technological Innovation Team of Shaanxi Province (No. 2020TD-013) and National Municipal Training Program of Innovation and Entrepreneurship for Undergraduates (No. 202010635053).

References

1. Sun, Y., Mburu, L., Wang, S.: Analysis of community properties and node properties to understand the structure of the bus transport network. Physica A **450**, 523–530 (2016)
2. Gao, C., Su, Z., Liu, J., Kurths, J.: Even central users do not always drive information diffusion. Commun. ACM **62**(2), 61–67 (2019)
3. Li, J., Guo, J.: A new feature extraction algorithm based on entropy cloud characteristics of communication signals. Math. Probl. Eng. **2015**, 1–8 (2015)
4. Lerner, B., Guterman, H., Aladjem, M., Dinstein, I.H.: A comparative study of neural network based feature extraction paradigms. Pattern. Recogn. Lett. **20**(1), 7–14 (1999)
5. Shu, C., Ding, X., Fang, C.: Histogram of the oriented gradient for face recognition. Tsinghua Sci. Technol. **16**(2), 216–224 (2011)
6. Mao, J., Jain, A.K.: Artificial neural networks for feature extraction and multivariate data projection. IEEE Trans. Neural Netw. **6**(2), 296–317 (1995)
7. Du, N., Jia, X., Gao, J., Gopalakrishnan, V., Zhang, A.: Tracking temporal community strength in dynamic networks. IEEE Trans. Knowl. Data Eng. **27**(11), 3125–3137 (2015)
8. Kuhn, F., Oshman, R.: Dynamic networks: models and algorithms. ACM Sigact. News **42**(1), 82–96 (2011)
9. Wang, C., Deng, Y., Li, X., Chen, J., Gao, C.: Dynamic community detection based on a label-based swarm intelligence. IEEE Access **7**, 161641–161653 (2019)
10. Xu, T., Zhang, Z., Philip, S.Y., Long, B.: Evolutionary clustering by hierarchical dirichlet process with hidden Markov state. In: Proceedings of the 8th IEEE International Conference on Data Mining (DMIN), pp. 658–667 (2008)
11. Gao, C., Liang, M., Li, X., Zhang, Z., Wang, Z., Zhou, Z.: Network community detection based on the physarum-inspired computational framework. IEEE ACM T. Comput. Bi. **15**(6), 1916–1928 (2016)
12. Wang, H., et al.: Medication combination prediction using temporal attention mechanism and simple graph convolution. IEEE J. Biomed. Health Inform. (2021). https://doi.org/10.1109/JBHI.2021.3082548
13. Taguchi, H., Liu, X., Murata, T.: Graph convolutional networks for graphs containing missing features. Future Gener. Comput. Syst. **117**, 155–168 (2021)
14. Song, W., Xiao, Z., Wang, Y., Charlin, L., Zhang, M., Tang, J.: Session-based social recommendation via dynamic graph attention networks. In: Proceedings of the 12th ACM International Conference on Web Search and Data Mining (WSDM), pp. 555–563 (2019)
15. Benesty, J., Chen, J., Huang, Y., Cohen, I.: Pearson correlation coefficient. In: Noise Reduction in Speech Processing, pp. 1–4 (2009)

16. Ma, X., Dong, D.: Evolutionary nonnegative matrix factorization algorithms for community detection in dynamic networks. IEEE Trans. Knowl. Data Eng. **29**(5), 1045–1058 (2017)
17. Mucha, P.J., Richardson, T., Macon, K., Porter, M.A., Onnela, J.P.: Community structure in time-dependent, multiscale, and multiplex networks. Science **328**(5980), 876–878 (2010)
18. Liu, F., Wu, J., Xue, S., Zhou, C., Yang, J., Sheng, Q.: Detecting the evolving community structure in dynamic social networks. World Wide Web **23**(2), 715–733 (2019). https://doi.org/10.1007/s11280-019-00710-z
19. Zhang, Z., Cui, P., Pei, J., Wang, X., Zhu, W.: Timers: error-bounded SVD restart on dynamic networks. In: 32nd Proceedings of the AAAI Conference on Artificial Intelligence(AAAI), pp. 224–231 (2018)

Additive Noise Model Structure Learning Based on Rank Statistics

Jing Yang[1,2], Gaojin Fan[1,2(✉)], Kai Xie[1,2], Qiqi Chen[1,2], and Aiguo Wang[3]

[1] Key Laboratory of Knowledge Engineering With Big Data, Hefei University of Technology, Ministry of Education, Hefei 230009, Anhui, People's Republic of China

[2] School of Computer Science and Information Engineering, Hefei University of Technology, Hefei 230009, Anhui, People's Republic of China

[3] School of Electronic and Information Engineering, Foshan University, Foshan, Guangdong, China

Abstract. To examine the structural learning of the additive noise model in causal discovery, a new algorithm RCS (Rank-Correlation-Statistics) is proposed in combination with the rank correlation method. This algorithm can effectively process the multivariate linear Non-Gaussian data, and multivariate nonlinear non-Gaussian data. In this article, combined with hypothesis testing, a constraint method is proposed to select the potential neighbors of the target node, which greatly reduces the search space and obtains good time performance. Then the method is compared with the existing technology on 7 networks on the additive noise structure model. The results show that the RCS algorithm is superior to existing algorithms in terms of accuracy and time performance. Finally, it shows that the RCS algorithm has a good application on real data.

Keywords: Causal discovery · Rank statistics · Additive noise model · Arbitrary distribution · Real data

1 Introduction and Related Work

With the development of big data and machine learning [22, 23], the understanding of relationships among data with greatly affect the cost and performance of various applications [24]. The purpose of causal structure learning is to discover the causal relationships contained in the data. Identifying this relationship will help people understand the nature and laws of the problem when making decisions [1]. Bayesian Network (BN) [2] and Structural Equation Modeling (SEM) [3] are widely used in fault diagnosis, genetic data analysis and event prediction [4]. In recent years, many algorithms related to learning the Bayesian Network structure have emerged. The first hybrid algorithm to appear is the CB [5] algorithm, other algorithms such as the SC algorithm [6], MMHC algorithm [7], L1MB algorithm [8], PCB [9] and PCS [10] algorithm.

At present, these algorithms have relatively good effects on the multivariate linear model, but they often violate this assumption in practical applications. For example, analyzing stock data helps financial development, but stock data does not necessarily

H. Qiu et al. (Eds.): KSEM 2021, LNAI 12815, pp. 128–139, 2021.
https://doi.org/10.1007/978-3-030-82136-4_11

follow a linear distribution [11]. In the medical field, patient monitoring data sets can help medical diagnosis and treatment, but the data sets obtained from monitoring equipment do not necessarily follow a linear distribution [12, 13]. The analysis of factory machinery and equipment data can be helpful for failure prediction, but the data obtained by sensors does not necessarily follow a linear distribution [14]. The above data may have linear non-Gaussian properties or nonlinear non-Gaussian properties. To solve this type of data problem, therefore, Shimizu et al. proposed a Linear Non-Gaussian Acyclic Model (LiNGAM) [15] for causal discovery. Hoyer et al. gave a description of a causal model for arbitrarily distributed data from the perspective of a Bayesian network model [16]. An additive noise model and an algorithm for identifying causal structures are proposed. The algorithm uses nonlinear regression and a statistical independence test based on HSIC (Hilbert-Schmidt Independence Criterion) standards. HSIC is a nuclear-based independence test standard. The time complexity of the algorithm is an exponential function of the number of variables.

Tillman et al. proposed weakly additive noise models on the basis of the additive noise model [17], which extends the framework to the case where the additive noise model is reversible and does not exist additive noise in any distribution. Then they proposed the kPC algorithm [18]. The kPC algorithm uses the Kernel-Based Conditional Dependence Measure to test the conditional independence. The algorithm combines the PC style search with the partial search of the additional noise model in the substructure of the Markov equivalence class to obtain the equivalence classes of such models from the data. The algorithm still needs more conditional independence tests. This constitutes an effective alternative to the traditional method, which assumes authenticity and only recognizes the Markov equivalence classes of the graph so that some edges are directionless.

For model estimation, a Gaussian Process Partial Observable Model (GPPOM) [19] is proposed, and independence is forced into it to learn the potential parameters related to each observation. Huang found that when encountering heterogeneous or non-stationary data, its potential generation process will change across domains or over time. Furthermore, it is called the constraint-based causal discovery (CD-NOD) [20] from heterogeneous/non-stationary data to find the causal framework and direction, and estimate the nature of the mechanism change. Determine the causal orientation by using the independent changes in the data distribution implied by the latent causal model, and benefiting from the information carried by the change distribution. Most of the structure learning algorithms for arbitrarily distributed data are methods based on dependency analysis, and most of them require more independence tests. So far, the computational complexity still needs to be improved.

In order to reduce the computational complexity, for linear non-Gaussian data, Yang proposed partial correlation statistics based on local learning, based on partial correlation, and other algorithms. While achieving higher accuracy, the complexity of the algorithm is significantly reduced. However, it cannot be effectively solved when dealing with non-linear data. Therefore, it is expected to construct a fast and effective causal structure learning algorithm model of additive noise model by identifying the implied causality from arbitrarily distributed continuous numbers. We propose the RCS algorithm.

2 RCS Algorithm

The rank correlation coefficient is a statistical analysis index that reflects the degree of rank correlation. Here we use the Spearman correlation coefficient. It is a non-parametric index that measures the dependence of two variables. It uses a monotonic equation to evaluate the correlation of two statistical variables. Rank the complete data set $D = \{X^1, \ldots, X^2 X^m\}$ and all the data to obtain a new data set $D' = \{X^{1'}, \ldots, X^{m'}\}$. In a variable set V, any two variables $X_i, X_j \in \mathbf{V}$, and the j-th variable X_j and X_i are calculated as follows:

$$r_{ij} = 1 - \frac{6 \sum_{k=1}^{m} (d_{ij}^k)^2}{m(m^2 - 1)} \tag{1}$$

Where d_{ij} represents the level difference between variables X_i and X_j, where $d_{ij}^k = X_i^{k'} - X_j^{k'}$, and it represents the level difference between variables X_i and X_j between the k-th sample.

The research object of the RCS algorithm is an observable complete data set, there are no hidden variables, and the data is continuous linear or nonlinear data.

Theorem 2.1. [21] For two variables X_i and X_j, no matter whether the overall distribution of the two variables is normal or not, r_{ij} represents the Spearman correlation coefficient between the two variables X_i and X_j, m is the sample size, m > 100. Then the statistic t on the Spearman correlation coefficient r_{ij} obeys the student t distribution with m − 2 degrees of freedom.

$$t = \frac{r_{ij}}{\sqrt{(1 - r_{ij}^2)/(m - n)}} \tag{2}$$

The true value of the rank correlation coefficient r_{ij} can be tested by hypothesis testing. The hypothesis is as follows:

$$H_0 : r_{ij} = 0 \quad H_1 : r_{ij} \neq 0; \tag{3}$$

Through the previous discussion, if the Spearman correlation coefficient is zero, it means that the variables are independent of each other, so we set it to 0 here. If the assumption is true, it means that the variables are independent of each other, otherwise, it means that the variables are related. By calculating the p-value, it is judged to accept and reject the hypothesis. When the p-value is less than the significance level K_α, the null hypothesis is often rejected. In this article, we use the significance level of 0.005. Defining r_{ij}^{act} represents the rank correlation coefficient calculated on real data, Z^{act} represents the value of the actually calculated statistic, and $\Pr_{H_0}$ represents the probability calculated under the premise of the null hypothesis. We conduct a two-sided test on it. The p value is:

$$p - value(X_i, X_j) = \Pr_{H_0}\left(\left|\frac{\hat{r}_{ij} - r_{ij}}{(1 - \hat{r}_{ij}^2)/(m-2)}\right| > \left|\frac{\hat{r}_{ij}^{act} - r_{ij}}{(1 - \hat{r}_{ij}^2)/(m-2)}\right|\right) = (1 - \Phi(Z^{act})) * 2 \tag{4}$$

Based on the p-value, give the definition of strong correlation and weak correlation:

Definition 2.1: Strong correlation: $\forall X_i, X_j \in \mathbf{V}$, X_i and X_j have a strong correlation if and only if $p - value(X_i, X_j) < K_\alpha$

Definition 2.2. Weak correlation: $\forall X_i, X_j \in \mathbf{V}$, X_i and X_j have a weak correlation if and only if $p - value(X_i, X_j) \geq K_\alpha$

Therefore, by comparing the value of p and K_α by Definitions 2.1 and 2.2, if the value of p is bigger than K_α, the null hypothesis is accepted, and there is a weak correlation between X_i and X_j, otherwise there is a strong correlation between X_i and X_j. The above threshold K_α is the significance level in probability statistics, and is also the degree of confidence.

The algorithm description is shown in Table 1:

Table 1. Pseudo code description of RCB algorithm

Algorithm RCS(Rank-Correlation-Statistics)
Input: Data set, Significance level
Output: Directrd Acyclic Graph
1./*step 1. Restriction Step : Get the skeleton of the Bayesian network,
2.set of candidate neighbor nodes PN (X_j) for each variable X_j ,candidate neighbor matrix PNM.*/
3.PN (X_j)=∅, ($X_j \in V$, j=1 to n)
4.PNM(i, j)=0 (i=1 to n, j=1 to n)
5.for $X_j \in V$, j=1 to n do
for $X_i \in V$, i=1 to j , i≠j do
Calculation r(X_i , X_j)
p-value(X_i , X_j) = (1-φ(Z^{act}))*2
if p-value< K_α
PN (X_j)= PN (X_j)∪ X_i , PNM (i, j) =1
else
PNM (i, j) =0
end
14. end for
15.end for
16.get PN (X_j) and PNM
17./*step 2. Constrained Search Step : get the final Bayesian network*/
18.Establish an empty net G.
19.Use constrained hill search according to PN (X_j) and PNM. Test all the operations
20.of adding edges, deleting edges, and inverting edges, and perform the operation that
21.makes the MDL scores drop the most.
22.Output DAG

Input data set $D = \{D^1, \ldots, D^m\}$ and significance level K_α, each column of the data set corresponds to a variable, each row is a sample instance. The output is a directed acyclic graph.

Step 1 (lines 4–17), introduction to the constraint phase: First initializes PN (X_j) to be empty, and all elements of PNM are 0. Then we select the candidate neighbor set for each variable and obtain the final candidate neighbor matrix. Since the Spearman correlation coefficient is symmetric, that is, $r(X_i, X_j) = r(X_i, X_j)$ (i $< j$). If X_i and X_j have a strong correlation, then X_j and X_i also have a strong correlation. The selection of candidate neighbors itself has no directionality. In the search stage, it includes the operation of inverting the edge. After greedy search, the direction of the edge can be finally determined. Therefore, we set PNM(i,j) to 1. PNM is the upper triangular matrix and the diagonal elements are all 0. Through this operation, the efficiency can be improved in the search phase.

Step 2 (Lines 19–23) Search phase: After the constraint phase, we can get a skeleton diagram of the primary Bayesian network. This skeleton limits our search range and greatly reduces the search space in the greedy search stage. That is to say, the edges on the final network structure must be within this skeleton range, and they are all finalized through the search stage. In the search phase, we perform restricted greedy search based on the scoring function. In the space constrained by the Bayesian network skeleton, the greedy hill-climbing search method is used to perform operations such as adding edges, deleting edges, and changing the direction of edges to find the network with the best score.

3 Experimental Research

In this section, we experiment with the RCS algorithm and some Bayesian network structure learning algorithms under different data sets and different network conditions. We use eight algorithms: KPC, PCB, LIMB, TC, BESM, Two_phase, RCS and CD-NOD algorithm. And then The Friedman test and Nemenyi follow-up test were used to compare the time efficiency and structure recognition quality of these algorithms with that of existing structure learning algorithms.

3.1 Network and Data Set

The network used in our experiment is obtained from a real decision support system that covers many real-world applications (such as medicine, agriculture, insurance). Because the true structure of each network is known, these networks form a strict standard for evaluating the performance of each algorithm. These networks include Alarm, Carpo, Factors, Insurance, Mildew, Water, Chain. These networks include Alarm, Carpo, Factors, Insurance, Mildew, Water, Chain, among which the Factors are artificial. The data set used in our experiment is generated by the additive noise structural equation model. We use the following two types of structural equation model ANM, where each variable of the formula <1> is defined as the linear function of its parent nodes and disturbance variable. Each variable in formula <2> is defined as a non-linear function of its parent node and disturbance.

3.2 Performance Evaluation Index

First, the ten-fold cross-validation method is used to obtain the test results of each algorithm on each data set. We use two indicators to measure the performance of the algorithm. It includes two aspects: the first is the running time, which indicates the time efficiency of the algorithm. The time required for all calculations performed by the algorithm can be captured. The second indicator accuracy is an indicator for evaluating structural errors and has been widely used to compare the quality of graph reconstruction. Structural errors include: missing edges, extra edges, missing direction and wrong direction. The number of structural errors is the number of incorrect edges of the estimated model compared to the real model.

The weights are usually randomly generated. The weight is generated by the function $\pm 1 + \mathrm{N}\ (0, 1)/4$. On each data set, ten-fold cross-validation is performed on each data set to obtain ten well-trained networks. The statistics for each report are the average of ten runs of each algorithm.

$<1>\ x_i = \mathbf{w}_{X_i}^T \mathbf{pa}(X_i) + \exp(rand(0, 1))$

$<2>\ x_i = \sin(\mathbf{pa}(X_i)) + rand(0, 1)$

3.3 Experimental Results and Analysis on Linear Data

In this experiment, RCS (0.005) is used. And then compare it with KPC, PCB (0.1), LIMB, TC (0.005), BESM (0.005), and Two_phases. These algorithms are compared.

Figures 1 and 2 are the result graph of the continuous data of the linear multivariate non-Gaussian distribution generated by ANM <1>. The X axis in the two graphs represents the sample size (100, 500, 1000, 5000, 10000, and 20000), and the Y axis represents the number of structural errors or running time. In all the results, some statistical information is missing because some implementations cannot be performed correctly on a specific data set under the tenfold cross-validation procedure or failed to complete their calculations within 12 h. On the linear data, we use the data generated by ANM <1> to carry out the experiment. We use the ten-fold crossover method to obtain the test results of the structural errors and time lengths of these seven algorithms on different data sets and different networks.

Then sort them according to the test performance from good to bad, and assign the order value 1, 2, 3…; if the test performance of the algorithm is the same, the order value is divided equally. Then, use Friendman test to determine whether the performance of these algorithms is the same. In order to show the above test more intuitively, use the Friedman test chart in Fig. 3 to display it.

The final result of the experiment: Analyze the Friedman test chart in Fig. 3. This data is generated by ANM <1>, which is linear multivariate non-Gaussian continuous data. From the structural error inspection graph, we can get that the three algorithms of RCS, BESM, and PCB are significantly better than the four algorithms of KPC, L1MB, TC, and Two-phase. Then from the time performance test chart, we can get that RCS is significantly better than the five algorithms of BESM, PCB, KPC, TC, and Two-phase. Through comparison, it is known that the accuracy of the three algorithms of RCS, BESM, and PCB are similar and there is no significant difference, but the RCS algorithm is significantly better than these two algorithms in terms of time performance.

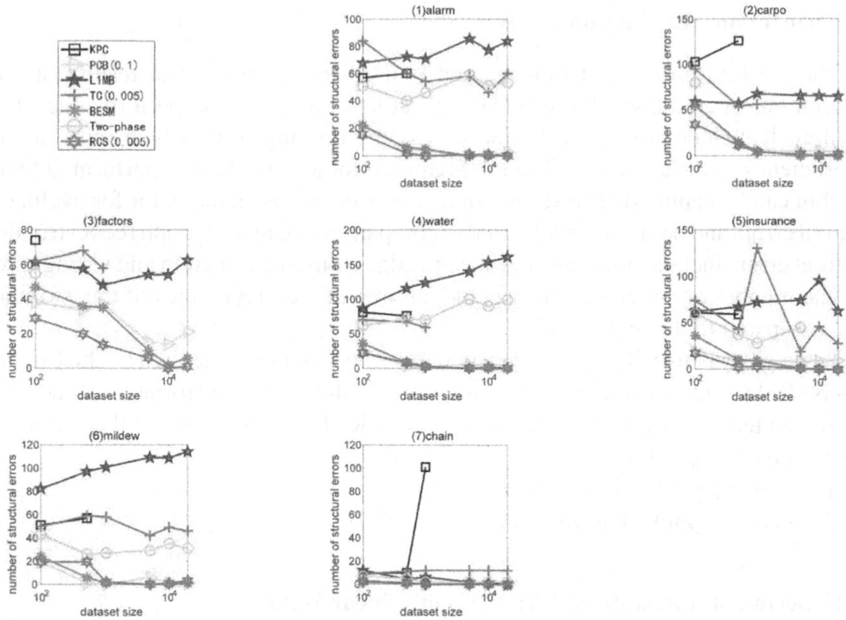

Fig. 1. For ANM <1>, the structural errors of the seven algorithms in different networks and data sets

In short, the RCS algorithm has better time performance and fewer structural errors than other algorithms on linear data.

3.4 Experimental Results and Analysis on Nonlinear Data

On the nonlinear data, we use the multivariate nonlinear non-Gaussian data generated by ANM <2> to conduct experiments. Figures 4 and 5 show the structural error and time performance of the three algorithms of RCS, KPC, and CD-NOD under different networks and different data sets. The X axis in the figure represents the sample size (100, 500, 1000, 5000, 10000 and 20000), and the Y axis represents the number of structural errors or running time. In all the results, some statistical information is missing because some implementations cannot be performed correctly on a specific data set under the tenfold cross-validation procedure or failed to complete their calculations within 12 h.

From Figs. 4 and 5, we can get the comparison results shown in Table 2. Table 2 shows the comparison between RCS and other algorithms in terms of structural error and time performance. The first term represents the number of networks where RCS is better than the algorithm to be compared. The second term represents the number of RCS networks with similar structural errors or running times. The similarity is defined here between 85% and 115%. The third term represents the number of networks where RCS is inferior to the algorithm to be compared.

From Fig. 4 and Fig. 5 and Table 2, we can understand that the RCS algorithm has better time performance and fewer structural errors on multivariate nonlinear non-Gaussian data. Especially in terms of time performance, it has great advantages compared

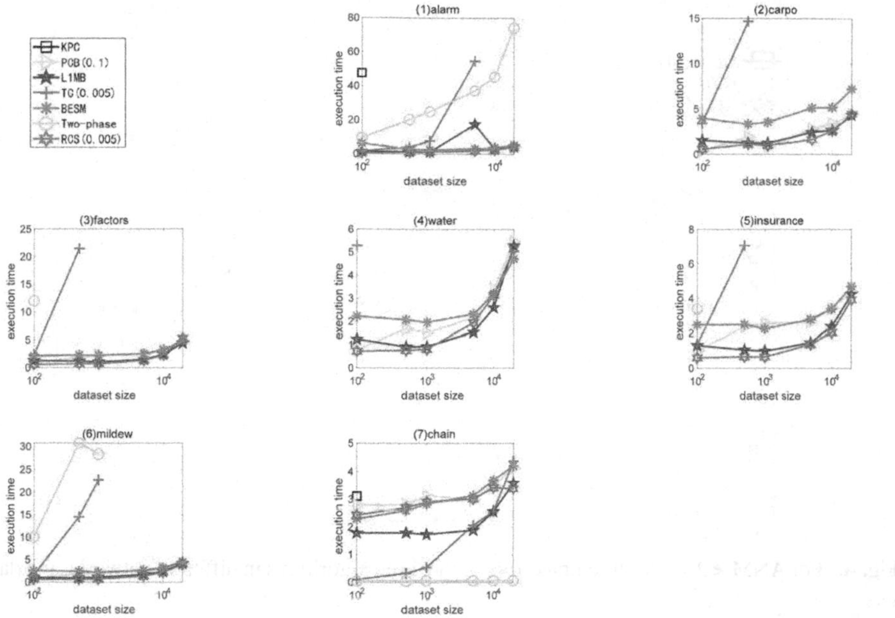

Fig. 2. For ANM <1>, the execution time of the seven algorithms in different networks and data sets

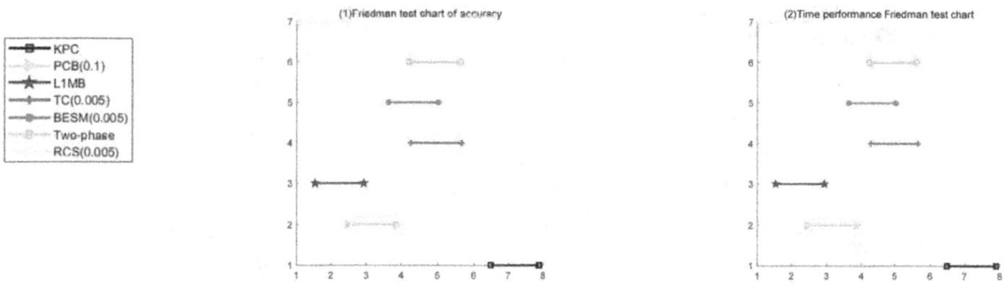

Fig. 3. For ANM <1>, the Freeman test chart of the structural error and time performance of the seven algorithms under different networks and data sets

to CD-NOD and KPC algorithms. The time performance of these two algorithms will increase exponentially for conditional independence testing. For high-dimensional and complex networks, the time efficiency is low.

Generally speaking, regardless of whether the data is linear or conforms to the Gaussian distribution, the RCS algorithm has high accuracy. This characteristic is very good, indicating that the RCS algorithm has good adaptability. Especially in the nonlinear field, the RCS algorithm has a huge advantage in time performance compared with other algorithms.

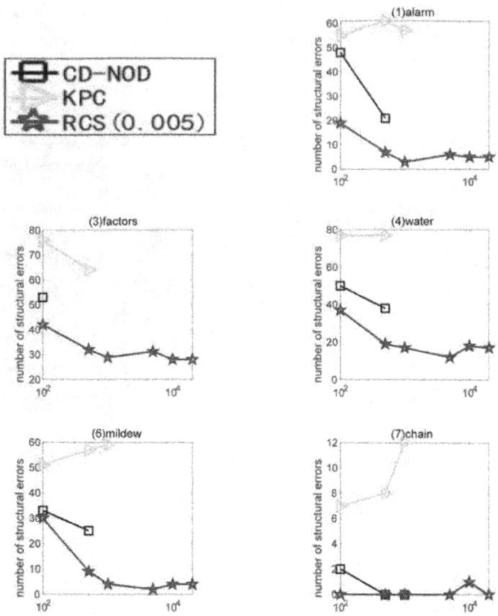

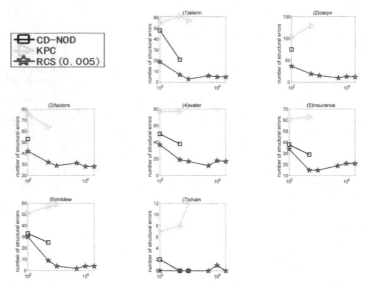

Fig. 4. For ANM <2>, the structural errors of the three algorithms in different networks and data sets

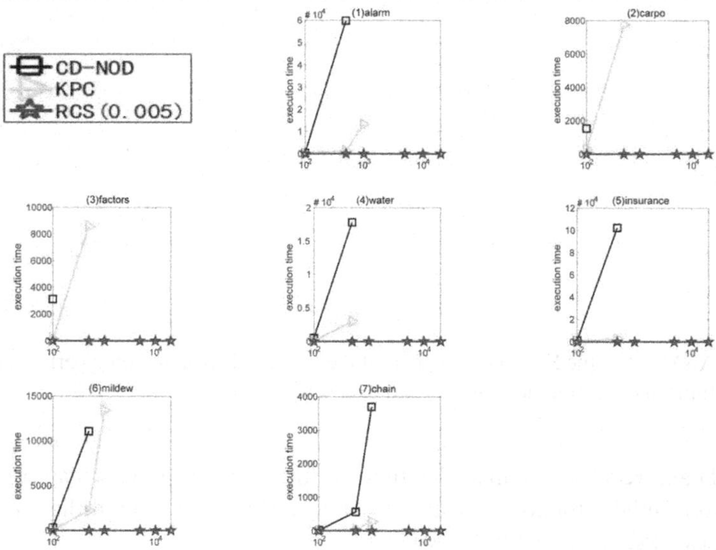

Fig. 5. For ANM <2>, the execution time of the three algorithms in different networks and data sets

3.5 Application in Power Plant Data

In this experiment, the data comes from the real production environment, which is the data recorded by Unit 1 of Tengzhou Power Plant in 2017. The RCS algorithm was run on 62 measurement points to construct the causality diagram of the system. Then

Table 2. Accuracy comparison between RCS and other algorithms

Algorithm	Structural error	Time performance
CD-NOD	7/0/0	7/0/0
KPC	7/0/0	7/0/0

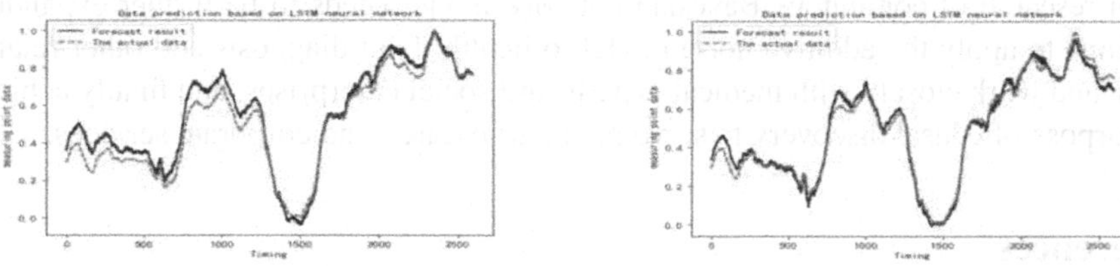

(a) (b)

Fig. 6. Comparison before and after using RCS algorithm at No. 7 measuring point (Color figure online)

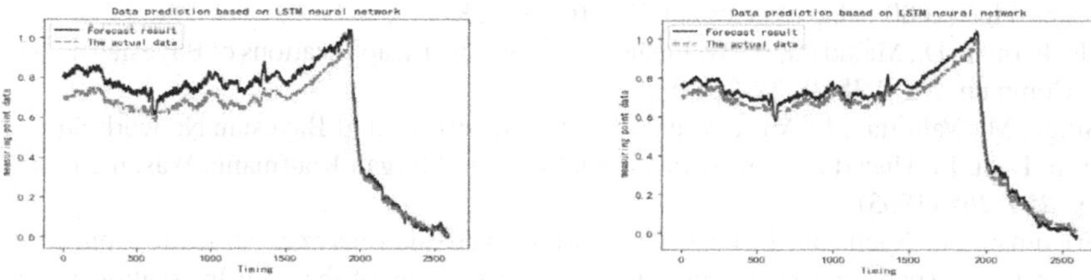

(a) (b)

Fig. 7. Comparison before and after using RCS algorithm at No. 20 measuring point (Color figure online)

we apply the Long Short Memory Network (LSTM) to the Markov equivalence classes of some measurement points and predict possible trends. Only the experimental results of measurement points 7 and 20 are given here. The experimental results are shown in Fig. 6 and Fig. 7. The black line is the predicted value, and the red line is the observed value. Figure (a) shows all the measuring points predicted by the model, and figure (b) uses the RCS algorithm to make model predictions for the measuring points.

Result analysis: The model predictions of the above two measuring points (7, 20) show that our RCS algorithm can effectively remove the influence of irrelevant measuring points on the observation measuring points. The causality obtained through the algorithm will help to better predict and diagnose the fault model. Therefore, the RCS algorithm model can effectively identify the non-linear causality of the multivariate system, and has a good prospect in practical applications.

4 Conclusion and Future Work

In this article, we study the structure learning of the additive noise model in causal discovery. We propose a new algorithm RCS, which can be applied to multivariate linear non-Gaussian data and multivariate nonlinear non-Gaussian data. The validity of the algorithm is proved theoretically and experimentally. Experimental results show that the algorithm has higher accuracy and better time performance.

We will further carry out the application research of additive noise model. The application research of continuous Bayesian network model needs to be further expanded. Continue to apply the additive noise model to health, fault diagnosis and other related fields, and work closely with medical experts and social enterprises, and finally achieve the purpose of causal discovery to serve medical research and corporate services.

References

1. Yang, J., Guo, X., An, N.: Streaming feature-based causal structure learning algorithm with symmetrical uncertainty. J. Inf. Sci. **467**, 708–724 (2018)
2. Bollen, K.A.: Structural Equations with Latent Variables. John Wiley, New York (1989)
3. Pearl, J.: Causality: Models, Reasoning, and Inference. Cambridge University Press, Cambridge (2000). singapore.cs.ucla.edu/BOOK-2K/
4. Heckerman, D., Mamdani, A., Wellman, M.P.: Real-world applications of Bayesian networks. J. Commun. ACM **38**(3), 24–26 (1995)
5. Singh, M., Valtorta, M.: An Algorithm for the Construction of Bayesian Network Structures from Data. In: Uncertainty in Artificial Intelligence. Morgan Kaufmann, Washington D. C., pp. 259–265 (1993)
6. Friedman, N., Nachman, I., Peer, D.: Learning Bayesian network structure from massive datasets: the sparse candidate algorithm, In: Proceedings of the 15th International Conference on Uncertainty in Artificial Intelligence. Morgan Kaufmann Publishers, San Francisco, pp. 206–215 (1999)
7. Tsamardinos, I., Brown, L.E., Aliferis, C.F.: The max-min hill-climbing Bayesian network structure learning algorithm J. . Mach. Learn. **65**(1), 31–78 (2006). https://doi.org/10.1007/s10994-006-6889-7
8. Schmidt, M., Niculescu-Mizil, A., Murphy, K.: Learning graphical model structure using L1-regularization paths, In: Proceedings of the Association for the Advancement of Artificial Intelligence, pp. 1278–1283 (2007)
9. Yang, J., Li, L., Wang, A.: A partial correlation-based Bayesian network structure learning algorithm under linear SEM. J. Knowl. Based Syst. **24**(7), 963–976 (2011)
10. Yang, J., An, N., Alterovitz, G.: A partial correlation statistic structure learning algorithm under linear structural equation models. IEEE Trans. Knowl. Data Eng. **28**(10), 2552–2565 (2016)
11. English, T.S., Ledwith, M.J., Davis, G.M.: The application of Bayesian networks to approximate the probability distribution of returns of equities. In: Proceedings of the IEEE Systems and Information Engineering Design Symposium, pp. 177–182 (2009)
12. Krizmaric, M., Mertik, M.: Application of Bayesian networks in emergency medicine. In: Proceedings of Central European Conference on Information and Intelligent Systems, Faculty of Organization and Informatics Varazdin, p. 1 (2008)
13. Chen, M., Zhang, Y., Qiu, M.: SPHA: smart personal health advisor based on deep analytic. IEEE Commun. Mag. **56**(3), 164–169 (2018)

14. Cai, B., Liu, Y., Xie, M.: A dynamic-Bayesian-network-based fault diagnosis methodology considering transient and intermittent faults. IEEE Trans. Autom. Sci. Eng. **14**(1), 276–285 (2016)
15. Shimizu, S., Inazumi, T., Sogawa, Y.: DirectLiNGAM: a direct method for learning a linear non-Gaussian structural equation model. J. Mach. Learn. Res. **12**, 1225–1248 (2011)
16. Hoyer, P.O., Janzing, D., Mooij, J.M.: Nonlinear causal discovery with additive noise models. J. Adv. Neural Inf. Process. Syst. **21**, 689–696 (2008)
17. Tillman, R.E., Gretton, A., Spirtes, P.: Nonlinear directed acyclic structure learning with weakly additive noise models. In: Conference on Neural Information Processing Systems, pp. 1847–1855 (2009)
18. Zhang, K., Peters, J., Janzing, D.: Kernel-based conditional independence test and application in causal discovery. arXiv preprint: arXiv:1202.3775 (2012)
19. Hu, S., Chen, Z., Nia, V.P.: Causal inference and mechanism clustering of a mixture of additive noise models. arXiv preprint: arXiv:1809.08568 (2018)
20. Huang, B., Zhang, K., Zhang, J.: Causal discovery from heterogeneous/nonstationary data with independent changes. arXiv e-prints: arXiv:1903.01672 (2019)
21. Zar, J.H.: Significance testing of the Spearman rank correlation coefficient. J. Am. Stat. Assoc. **67**(339), 578–580 (1972)
22. Gai, K., Qiu, M.: Reinforcement learning-based content-centric services in mobile sensing. IEEE Netw. **32**(4), 34–39 (2018)
23. Li, C., Qiu, M.: Reinforcement Learning for Cyber-Physical Systems: with Cybersecurity Case Studies. CRC Press, Boca Raton (2019)
24. Qiu, M., Jiang, Y., Dai, W.: Cost minimization for heterogeneous systems with Gaussian distribution execution time. In: 2015 IEEE 17th International Conference on High Performance Computing (2015)

A MOOCs Recommender System Based on User's Knowledge Background

Yibing Zhao, Wenjun Ma(✉), Yuncheng Jiang(✉), and Jieyu Zhan

Guangzhou Key Laboratory of Big Data and Intelligent Education, School of Computer Science, South China Normal University, Guangzhou, China
yibingzhao@m.scnu.edu.cn, {mawenjun,ycjiang,zhanjieyu}@scnu.edu.cn

Abstract. Massive open online courses (MOOCs) are becoming a novel and flexible way for education. Learning on the MOOCs platform is a continuous process with multiple independent selections of courses. Meanwhile, students' choices of subsequent courses are affected by their knowledge background, i.e., their historical courses and their learning performance on these courses. However, existing MOOC recommender systems often neglect students' knowledge background. To fill this gap, in this paper we propose a knowledge-aware recommendation model which incorporates users' historical enrolled courses and learning feedback. Specifically, we first construct a Course Knowledge Graph to represent the learning sequence between MOOCs and a Keyword Knowledge Graph to model the relation between course titles. With these two knowledge graphs and the course titles, we can extract the content feature and knowledge graph feature of courses. Second, we combine the extracted features with the user's learning feedback to learn the representation of his knowledge background according to his historical enrollments. Third, to model the different impacts of historical courses, we use an attention module to calculate the weights of these courses and aggregate the user's historical representation, and finally predict the probability of the user enrolling a course. We conduct a series of experiments compared with state-of-the-art baseline methods across multiple popular metrics. The promising results show that our proposed method can effectively recommend MOOCs to students.

Keywords: Recommender system · Knowledge graph · Personalized learning · MOOCs · Educational resource · Attention networks

1 Introduction

Nowadays, MOOCs platforms such as Coursera, edX and Udacity have provided low-cost opportunities for anyone to access courses from worldwide universities online. It is a major challenge faced by MOOCs platforms to recommend the most suitable course from numerous courses for different students with various learning experiences.

H. Qiu et al. (Eds.): KSEM 2021, LNAI 12815, pp. 140–153, 2021.
https://doi.org/10.1007/978-3-030-82136-4_12

In general, course recommendation is quite different from other recommendation tasks as it highlights the importance of student's knowledge background. A student's knowledge background, including his learned courses and his learning performance, will directly affect his choice of subsequent courses. First, unlike other activities such as watching movies or reading news, learning courses is a continuous process with multiple independent selections. Hence, there is a learning sequence between courses. For example, before learning the course "Machine Learning", students need to master the knowledge of "Calculus" and "Probability Theory". Second, a student will be accustomed to using the knowledge he has learned to help study a new course, which is called the *transfer of learning* [13]. So the student's learning performance on previously learned courses will influence the efficiency of the transfer of learning. It may lead to repulsion if a new course involves much knowledge that the student is not skilled in.

Unfortunately, the existing MOOCs recommendation models [1,2,4,8,18,26] neglect knowledge background. Considering the above challenges, we propose a knowledge-aware MOOCs recommendation framework based on users' knowledge background. In detail, for an input course, we first enrich its information by associating words in the course title with relevant entities in an external knowledge graph and construct a knowledge sub-graph called Keyword Knowledge Graph (KKG). We also apply the contextual relations of each course (i.e., prerequisite, successor, and parallel courses) to construct a Course Knowledge Graph (CKG). The CKG provides more complementary information including the learning sequence of the user's historical courses and the category of courses. Inspired by the theory of the transfer of learning, we learn a knowledge background portrait for each user according to his historical enrollments with the combination of CKG and his learning feedback. To model the impact of different historical courses on a candidate course, we use an attention module to aggregate the different weights of historical courses. Finally, we process the user embeddings and candidate course embeddings with a deep neural network to calculate the probability of the user enrolling a candidate course. Experimental results on a real-world dataset show that our method outperforms several baseline models, and proves the efficacy of introducing users' knowledge background in MOOCs recommendation scenario.

The key contributions of this paper can be summarized as follows:

- We highlight the importance of user's knowledge background in course recommendation, which is often neglected by the existing MOOCs recommendation systems.
- We develop a novel model for recommending courses in MOOCs, which applies rich side information including Keyword Knowledge Graph and Course Knowledge Graph.
- We conduct numerous experiments with real-world data collected from XuetangX. The results demonstrate the effectiveness of the proposed model compared with a series of strong baselines.

The rest of the paper is organized as follows. Section 2 summarizes the related work on knowledge-based recommender systems. Section 3 introduces the preliminary concepts of our model. Section 4 gives an overview of our framework and explains the implementation details. The experiment results are discussed in Sect. 5, followed by the conclusion and future work of this paper in Sect. 6.

2 Related Work

Traditional recommendation strategies such as collaborative filtering (CF) have achieved great success in many recommendation tasks. CF-based methods apply user-item matrix to find users with potential common preferences. Many studies combine CF with other strategies, such as topic model [9], matrix factorization [3], and attention mechanism [6]. However, most users only enrolled in a few courses in MOOCs platforms, which leads to the sparsity of user-item matrix and limits the performance of CF-based methods.

To overcome this problem, knowledge graphs are introduced into recommender systems as side information. For example, embedding-based methods such as CKE [25] and DKN [20] generally use the representation of items or users from knowledge graphs, and KGAT [21] combines attention technique with knowledge graphs. To model the continuity of learning, multiple efforts are proposed such as association algorithm [1], reinforcement learning [26] and RNN-based method [8], Bayesian methods [2] and heterogeneous information networks (HINs) [4,18]. But these efforts only extract users' interest from their historical enrollment behaviors but neglect their learning performance.

Different from previous methods, ours applies two knowledge graphs: KKG considers the connections of knowledge concepts contained in the course title, while CKG models the relationship between courses, unified with users' learning feedback in our model.

3 Problem Formulation

In this section, we first introduce the definitions of the two knowledge graphs we designed and then formulate the problem of course recommendation.

Keyword Knowledge Graph. Usually, each course title consists of a sequence of words, where each word may be associated with an entity in the knowledge graph, and the entities in different titles may relate to each other in the knowledge graph. We organize these entities and relations in the form of knowledge graph $\mathcal{K}$ called Keyword Knowledge Graph (KKG), which is a directed graph composed of entity-relation-entity triples $(h^{\mathcal{K}}, r^{\mathcal{K}}, t^{\mathcal{K}})$. Each triplet describes that there is a relationship $r^{\mathcal{K}}$ from head entity $h^{\mathcal{K}}$ to tail entity $t^{\mathcal{K}}$.

Course Knowledge Graph. Here we define the concept of CKG. We believe that there are relationships between the courses, and different courses belong to different categories. We describe courses and their relationships in the form of knowledge graph $\mathcal{C}$, represented in entity-relation-entity triples $(h^{\mathcal{C}}, r^{\mathcal{C}}, t^{\mathcal{C}})$, where $h^{\mathcal{C}}$, $t^{\mathcal{C}}$ represent courses, and $r^{\mathcal{C}}$ represents relations.

Knowledge-Based MOOCs Recommendation. Given a user and his historical enrollments in the MOOCs platform, we aim to predict the enrollment probability about the user and a candidate course and recommend a top-K list of courses. More formally, let $U = \{u_1, u_2, \ldots, u_m\}$ be a set of users and $C = \{c_1, c_2, \ldots, c_n\}$ be a set of courses, where m is the number of users and n is the number of courses. Given a target user u, we denote his historical enrolled courses as $\{c_1^u, c_2^u, \ldots, c_k^u\}$, where $c_i^u \in C$ is the i-th course enrolled by user u, linked with an entity $e^{\mathcal{C}}$ in CKG $\mathcal{C}$. Each course title is composed of a sequence of words, i.e., $t = [w_1, w_2, \ldots]$, where each word may associate with an entity $e^{\mathcal{K}}$ in KKG $\mathcal{K}$. The goal is to learn a predict function f and use it to generate a list of recommended courses, i.e., $f : u \rightarrow \{c_i | c_i \in C, i < |C|\}$.

4 Proposed Method

This section introduces the details of how we learn the representation of knowledge graphs, courses, and users, and how we perform course recommendation based on extracted knowledge background.

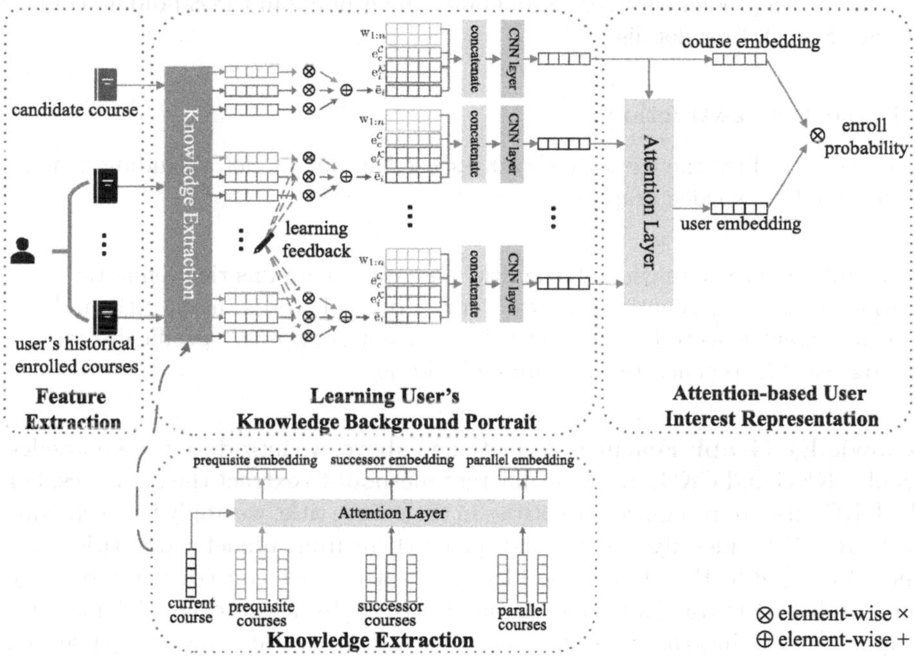

Fig. 1. Illustration of our proposed model. The sub-graph above shows the main structure of our model, and the sub-graph below presents the Knowledge Extraction layer.

The framework of our model is illustrated in Fig. 1. It consists of the following components:

- **Feature Extraction.** First, we learn the word embedding words in course titles as content feature. Then we extract the knowledge graph features of KKG and CKG. For KKG, we associate keywords in course titles with relevant entities in an external knowledge graph and construct a knowledge sub-graph. For CKG, we construct it by modeling the contextual relations of each course (i.e., prerequisite, successor, and parallel courses). Finally, we use TransH to train the embedding vectors of KKG and CKG, and these vectors are kept fixed as knowledge graph features for our model. (See Sect. 4.1 for details.)
- **Knowledge Background Portrait Learning.** In this module, we learn a knowledge background representation for each user. We first learn the context embeddings of historical enrollments through a knowledge extraction layer. Then we merge the context embeddings with the user's learning feedback with the combination of the previously extracted features. These embeddings are regarded as the user's knowledge background for the input of the next component. (See Sect. 4.2 for details.)
- **User Interest Representation.** After generating the representations of the user's knowledge background, we adopt an attention network to model the different impacts of the user's knowledge background on the candidate course. Finally, we predict the user's probability in enrolling in the candidate course. (See Sect. 4.3 for details.)

4.1 Feature Extraction

Here we introduce the extracted features used in our model, including content feature and knowledge graph feature.

Content Feature. In general, the title of a course contains rich semantic information. Hence, we generate the word embedding of words in the title and use it as a content feature for the knowledge concept keywords. Specifically, we use Word2Vec [12] to generate the word embedding.

Knowledge Graph Feature. As motioned above, we introduce two knowledge graphs, KKG and CKG, so we use different methods to extract their features. For the KKG, first, to recognize the entities in the course title, we apply the technique of NER [15] to identify entities and query them from predefined entities in a knowledge graph. Based on these identified entities, we construct a knowledge sub-graph and extract all relations among them from the original knowledge graph. Considering the relations among identified entities may be sparse and lack diversity, we expand the knowledge sub-graph by incorporating the entities in the original knowledge graph that are one hop of the identified ones.

For the CKG, we treat each course as an entity and introduce the sequential relation between courses. Usually, the MOOC platform will introduce the preparation knowledge of other courses that are necessary before learning a certain course. These courses are called *prerequisite courses*, indicating that there is a learning sequence relationship between courses. To acquire prerequisite courses, we first construct the corpus of prerequisite information and course titles, then train the corpus with LSI [14] model, calculate the similarity between course titles and prerequisite information, and finally chose one to three most similar courses as prerequisite courses. Inspired by the theory of the *transfer of learning*, we propose extracting additional context course information for each entity: prerequisite course, successor course, and parallel course. Prerequisite course and successor course are defined as the set of its immediate neighbors of *prerequisite* relation in the knowledge graph, i.e.,

$$prerequisite(e) = \{e_i | (e, r, e_i) \in \mathcal{C}\}, \tag{1}$$

$$successor(e) = \{e_i | (e_i, r, e) \in \mathcal{C}\}, \tag{2}$$

where r is the *prerequisite* relation in CKG $\mathcal{C}$.

The parallel course is defined as

$$parallel(e) = \{e_i | (e_i, r, e_c) \in \mathcal{C} \; and \; (e, r, e_c) \in \mathcal{C}\}, \tag{3}$$

where r is the *category* relation and e_c is the category entity in CKG.

Many knowledge graph embedding methods can be applied for KKG and CKG. Such embeddings will be taken as a knowledge graph feature, which is used as the input of our model.

4.2 Knowledge Background Portrait Learning for User

Given the context course embeddings of CKG, one straightforward way is to average the embeddings of all the context courses. Take prerequisite course as an example,

$$\bar{\mathrm{e}}_{pre} = \frac{1}{|prerequiste(e)|} \sum_{e_i \in prerequiste(e)} e_i, \tag{4}$$

where e_i is the entity embedding of CKG.

However, the context courses of an enrolled course have different positions relative to the enrolled course in CKG, so the enrolled course is supposed to have different impacts on its context courses. Hence, we apply the *knowledge extraction* layer, which uses an attention network to model the importance of different context courses. Specifically, take prerequisite courses as an example, for one of user u's enrolled courses c_i and its each prerequisite courses c_k^i, we first look up their entity embeddings e_i and e_k^i, then parameterize the attention coefficient a_{ik} as a function with e_i and e_k^i as inputs and then aggregate the embeddings according to their attentions:

$$\mathrm{e}_{pre}^i = \sum_{k=1}^{K_i} att(e_k^i, e_i) e_k^i, \tag{5}$$

where K_i is the number of prerequisite courses of c_i, and $att(\cdot)$ can be instantiated by a multi-layer perception on the concatenation or the element-wise product of the two embeddings e_i and e_k^i.

Likewise, the attention coefficients of successor courses c_m^i and parallel courses c_n^i are

$$\mathrm{e}_{suc}^i = \sum_{m=1}^{M_i} att(e_m^i, e_i)e_m^i, \tag{6}$$

$$\mathrm{e}_{par}^i = \sum_{n=1}^{N_i} att(e_n^i, e_i)e_n^i, \tag{7}$$

where e_m^i and e_n^i are the entity embeddings of c_m^i and c_n^i of CKG. M_i and N_i are the number of successor and parallel courses.

A user's knowledge background including his learned courses and the learning feedback of these courses. We calculate the correct rate s_T and error rate s_F of the tests of user's enrolled courses, and regard them as the penalty coefficients of context course embedding $\bar{e_i}$:

$$\bar{\mathrm{e}}_i = s_F \mathrm{e}_{pre}^i + s_T \mathrm{e}_{suc}^i + 0.5 \times \mathrm{e}_{par}^i. \tag{8}$$

We take 0.5 as the penalty coefficient of the parallel course embeddings because we consider that they have the same weight compared with the current course[1].

Following the notations used in Sect. 3, for course c in MOOCs, its entity embedding of CKG is denoted as $e_c^{\mathcal{G}_2} \in \mathbb{R}^{m\times 1}$, where m is the dimension of entity embedding. We use $t = [w_1, w_2, \ldots, w_n]$ to denote the input sequence of title t of length n, and $\mathrm{w}_{1:n} = [\mathrm{w}_1\ \mathrm{w}_2\ \ldots\ \mathrm{w}_n] \in \mathbb{R}^{d\times n}$ to denote the word embedding matrix of the title, which can be generated by Word2Vec. These words may be associated with k entities in KKG. For the i-th entity, we denote it as $\mathrm{e}_i^{\mathcal{K}} \in \mathbb{R}^{m\times 1}$, where m is the dimension of entity embedding.

Given the input above, we concatenate them as

$$\mathrm{W} = [\mathrm{w}_1\ \mathrm{w}_2\ \ldots\ \mathrm{w}_n\ \mathrm{e}_c^{\mathcal{C}}\ \mathrm{e}_1^{\mathcal{K}}\ \mathrm{e}_2^{\mathcal{K}}\ \ldots\ \mathrm{e}_k^{\mathcal{K}}\ \bar{\mathrm{e}}_c] \in \mathbb{R}^{d\times n}. \tag{9}$$

Similar to TextCNN [10], we apply multiple filter $h \in \mathbb{R}^{d\times l}$ with varying window sizes l to extract local patterns in the concatenate embedding. The local activation of sub-matrix $\mathrm{W}_{i:i+l-1}$ with respect to h can be written as

$$\mathrm{o}_i^h = ReLU(h * \mathrm{W}_{i:i+l-1} + b_1) + b_2, \tag{10}$$

then we use max-over-time pooling to choose the largest feature:

$$\tilde{\mathrm{o}}^h = \max\left\{\mathrm{o}_1^h, \mathrm{o}_2^h, \ldots, \mathrm{o}_{n-l+1}^h\right\}. \tag{11}$$

All features $\tilde{\mathrm{o}}^h$ will be concatenated and taken as the representation $\mathrm{v}(c)$ of the input course c, i.e.,

$$\mathrm{v}(c) = [\tilde{\mathrm{o}}^{h_1}\ \tilde{\mathrm{o}}^{h_2}\ \ldots\ \tilde{\mathrm{o}}^{h_z}], \tag{12}$$

where z is the number of filters.

Given user u with his enrolled history $\{c_1^u, c_2^u, \ldots, c_k^u\}$, his knowledge background portrait, i.e., the embeddings of his enrolled courses can be represented as $\mathrm{v}(c_1^u), \mathrm{v}(c_2^u), \ldots, \mathrm{v}(c_k^u)$.

[1] For candidate courses, we average e_{pre}^i, e_{suc}^i, and e_{par}^i in this step because candidate courses do not have learning feedback.

4.3 Attention-Based User Interest Representation

Considering a user's requirement in courses may be various, user u's historical courses should have different impacts on the candidate course c_j. Here we also adopt an attention network to model the different impacts of the user's enrolled courses on the candidate course. For one of user u's enrolled course c_i^u and a candidate course c_j, we first concatenate their embeddings $\mathrm{v}(c_i^u)$ and $\mathrm{v}(c_j)$ respectively as discussed in Sect. 4.2, then apply the attention method and use a softmax function to calculate the normalized attention weight:

$$\pi(u,j) = \mathrm{softmax}\Big(att\big(\mathrm{v}(c_i^u), \mathrm{v}(c_j)\big)\Big) = \frac{\exp\Big(\big(att\big(\mathrm{v}(c_i^u), \mathrm{v}(c_j)\big)\big)\Big)}{\sum_{n=1}^{k} \exp\Big(\big(att\big(\mathrm{v}(c_n^u), \mathrm{v}(c_j)\big)\big)\Big)}. \quad (13)$$

Thus, the embedding of user u concerning the candidate course c_j can be calculated as the weighted sum of his enrolled course embeddings:

$$\mathrm{v}(u) = \sum_{n=1}^{k} \pi(u,j)\mathrm{v}(c_n^u). \quad (14)$$

Finally, we conduct the inner product of user and course representations to predict the probability of user u enrolling course c_j:

$$\hat{y}(u,j) = \mathrm{v}(u)^{\mathrm{T}}\mathrm{v}(c_j). \quad (15)$$

5 Experiments

5.1 Dataset Description

Table 1. Description of dataset.

Type	Number
#users	168664
#courses	6410
#activity logs	325563
#course categories	24
#entites (in KKG)	255957
#relations (in KKG)	4359
#triples (in KKG)	630429

"#" denotes "the number of".

We collected real-world data from XuetangX[2] MOOCs platform. We select user activities from August 1st, 2015 to August 1st, 2017. Since the original dataset[3]

[2] http://www.xuetangx.com.

[3] The original dataset is available at http://moocdata.cn/data/user-activity.

does not have prerequisite information, we crawled the prerequisite information from course detail pages. Additionally, we search all occurred entities in the dataset as well as the ones within their one hop in the DBpedia[4] knowledge graph and extract all triples among them. We split the dataset into a training set and a test set in a ratio of 8:2. For each sequence in the dataset, we treat the last enrolled course as the target course, and the rest is regarded as the historical courses. During the training process, for each positive instance, we generate 4 negative instances by replacing the target course with each of 4 randomly sampled courses from its context course, while each positive instance in the test set is paired with 49 negative instances. Many methods [23,24] can be used for preprocessing the dataset.

The basic statistics and distributions of the dataset are shown in Table 1 and Fig. 2, respectively.

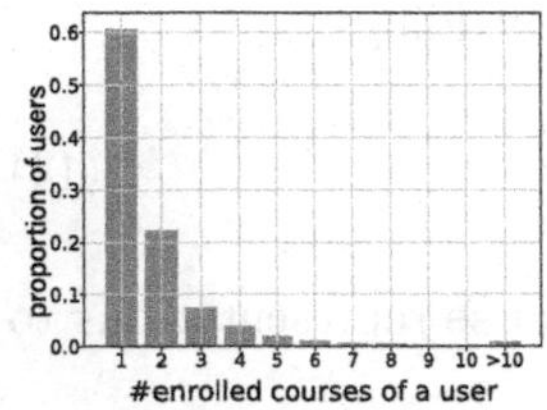

(a) The number of enrolled courses of a user.

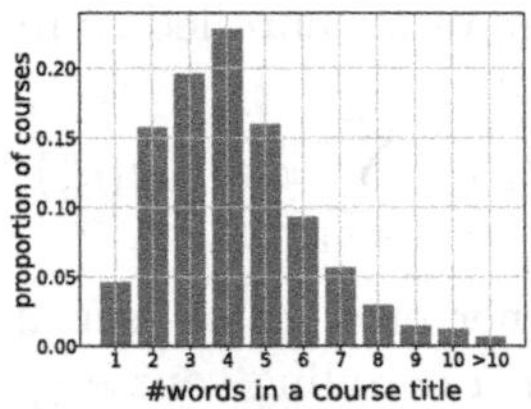

(b) The number of words in a course title.

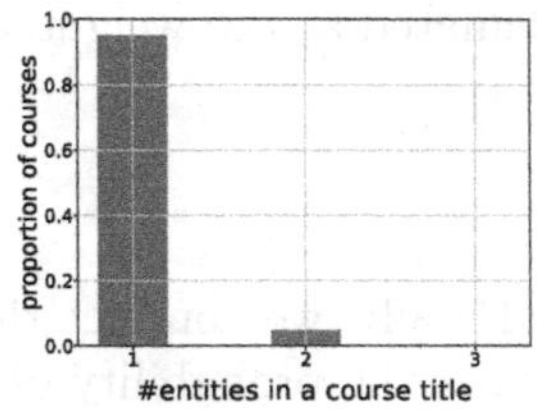

(c) The number of entities in a course title.

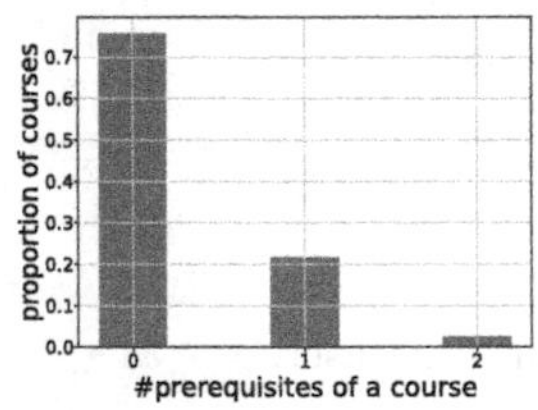

(d) The number of prerequisites of a course.

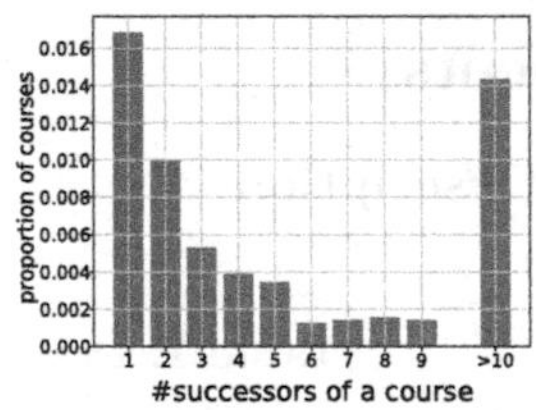

(e) The number of successors of a course.

Fig. 2. Data distributions in dataset and knowledge graph.

5.2 Baselines

The comparison methods include:

- **BPR-MF** [17]**:** It optimizes a pairwise ranking loss for the recommendation task in a Bayesian way.
- **FM** [16]**:** This is a state-of-the-art feature-based factorization model that can easily incorporate any heuristic features. For a fair comparison, we only use the embeddings of users and courses.

[4] http://wiki.dbpedia.org.

- **MLP** [7]: It applies a multi-layer perception to a pair of user representation and corresponding course representation to learn the probability of recommending a course to the user.
- **NAIS** [6]: This is an item-to-item collaborative filtering algorithm. It distinguishes the weights of different historical courses by an attention mechanism.
- **CKE** [25]: This is a KG-based representative regularization-based method, which exploits semantic embedding to enhance matrix factorization.
- **KGAT** [21]: It is a recommendation framework tailored to a knowledge-aware personalized recommendation. Built upon the graph neural network framework, KGAT explicitly models the high-order relations in the collaborative knowledge graph to provide a better recommendation with item side information.
- **DKN** [20]: The method takes a knowledge graph as side information, whose key component is a knowledge-aware CNN. In this paper, we adapt DKN to the MOOCs recommendation scenario.
- **HRL** [26]: This is a hierarchical reinforcement learning model for course recommendation in MOOCs platform, which jointly trains a profile reviser and a basic recommendation model.

5.3 Experiment Setup

We choose TransH [22] to learn the knowledge graph entity embeddings. The dimension of both word embeddings and entity embeddings are set as 100. The number of filters in Sect. 4.2 is set as 100 for each of the window sizes 1, 2. We use Adam [11] to train our model by optimizing the cross-entropy loss, where the learning rate is set as 0.0001 and batch size is fixed at 512.

We evaluate all the methods with widely used metrics, including the Area Under The Curve (AUC), Hit Ratio of top-K items (HR@K), Normalized Discounted Cumulative Gain of top-K items (NDCG@K), and mean reciprocal rank (MRR) [5]. We set K to 5 and 10, and report the average metrics for all users in the test set. The final recommendation list for user u is $R_u = \{r_u^1, r_u^2, \ldots, r_u^K\}$, where r_u^i denotes the rank at the ith position in R_u based on the predicted score.

5.4 Results

This section presents the results of different models. Table 2 shows the overall performance of all the comparison methods.

We can observe that:

- Our proposed model outperforms the comparison baselines in most cases. We improves 17.16%, 29.17%, and 32.39% concerning HR@10, NDCG@10, and MRR over the strongest baselines. Particularly, our model performs competitively to other KG-based models such as CKE, KGAT, and DKN. It is because not only do we consider the knowledge concepts and keywords contained in course titles, but also apply the CKG to learn students' knowledge background.

Table 2. Comparison of different models.

Methods	AUC	HR@5	HR@10	NDCG@5	NDCG@10	MRR
BPR-MF	0.7186	0.2369	0.3092	0.1683	0.1932	0.1579
FM	0.6916	0.1748	0.2336	0.1279	0.1477	0.1116
MLP	0.8454	0.4736	0.5973	0.3333	0.3733	0.3197
NAIS	0.8766	0.5209	0.6631	0.3298	0.3760	0.3466
CKE	0.7093	0.2344	0.3002	0.1702	0.1931	0.1526
KGAT	0.7179	0.1992	0.2635	0.1468	0.1687	0.1217
DKN	0.7082	0.3170	0.5561	0.2034	0.2802	0.2193
HRL	**0.9143**	0.6343	0.7498	0.5024	0.5398	0.4859
Our model	0.8772	**0.8269**	**0.8785**	**0.6808**	**0.6973**	**0.6433**

- Traditional methods such as BPR-MF and FM perform worse among all the methods. Because in MOOCs platforms, most of the users only enrolled in a few courses. Thus, the embeddings of users cannot be sufficiently inferred from the sparse data. Besides, traditional methods cannot model students' knowledge background from the user-item matrix, while deep learning methods such as MLP and NAIS perform better because they can extract the features of user enrolling courses from the user-item matrix.
- Compared with other KG-based methods, KGAT does not perform as well as expected. One possible reason is that KGAT requires a one-to-one correspondence between items and entities, while only CKG satisfies this condition. So we use CKG instead of KKG when running KGAT.
- HRL performs best among all baselines especially in AUC, it is probably because in reinforcement learning, when transitioning to another state, the environment will give the agent a reward, which is similar to students' learning feedback. But our model introduces knowledge graphs, which leads to overall better performance than HRL.

6 Conclusion and Future Work

In this work, we explore the task of MOOCs recommendation. Our proposed model is a knowledge-based deep model that naturally incorporates users' knowledge background into course recommendations. We design two knowledge graphs: a Keyword Knowledge Graph that contains the entities associated with words in course titles, and a Course Knowledge Graph to model the relationship between MOOCs. Then we apply a convolution neural network to learn the representation of user's knowledge background via their historical enrollment and learning feedback. To model the different impacts of a user's historical enrollment on the current candidate course, we use an attention module to explore and aggregate the user's historical representation. We conduct extensive experiments on real-world data collected from XuetangX. The results demonstrate the rationality and effectiveness of our proposed method.

In the future, a valuable direction is to model the relationship between knowledge concepts with knowledge graphs. Then we can conduct more fine-grained recommendations such as and recommending courses or exercises based on knowledge concepts and users' learning feedback. Moreover, we consider applying our model as a software component [19] into MOOCs platforms.

Acknowledgments. The works described in this paper are supported by The National Natural Science Foundation of China under Grant Nos. 61806080, 61772210, 62006085 and U1911201; Humanities and Social Sciences Foundation of Ministry of Education of China under Grant No. 18YJC72040002; Guangdong Province Universities Pearl River Scholar Funded Scheme (2018); The Project of Science and Technology in Guangzhou in China under Grant No. 202007040006; Key Projects of the National Social Science Foundation of China (No. 19ZDA041); Guangzhou Key Laboratory of Big Data and Intelligent Education (No. 201905010009); Doctoral Startup Project of Natural Science Foundation of Guangdong Province of China under Grant No. 2018A030310529.

References

1. Bendakir, N., Aïmeur, E.: Using association rules for course recommendation. In: Proceedings of the AAAI Workshop on Educational Data Mining, vol. 3, pp. 1–10 (2006)
2. Bulathwela, S., Perez-Ortiz, M., Yilmaz, E., Shawe-Taylor, J.: TrueLearn: a family of Bayesian algorithms to match lifelong learners to open educational resources. In: Proceedings of the 34th AAAI Conference on Artificial Intelligence, vol. 34, pp. 565–573 (2020)
3. Elbadrawy, A., Karypis, G.: Domain-aware grade prediction and top-n course recommendation. In: Proceedings of the 10th ACM Conference on Recommender Systems, pp. 183–190 (2016)
4. Gong, J., et al.: Attentional graph convolutional networks for knowledge concept recommendation in MOOCs in a heterogeneous view. In: Proceedings of the 43rd International ACM SIGIR Conference on Research and Development in Information Retrieval, pp. 79–88 (2020)
5. Gunawardana, A., Shani, G.: Evaluating recommender systems. In: Ricci, F., Rokach, L., Shapira, B. (eds.) Recommender Systems Handbook, pp. 265–308. Springer, Boston, MA (2015). https://doi.org/10.1007/978-1-4899-7637-6_8
6. He, X., He, Z., Song, J., Liu, Z., Jiang, Y.G., Chua, T.S.: NAIS: neural attentive item similarity model for recommendation. IEEE Trans. Knowl. Data Eng. **30**(12), 2354–2366 (2018)
7. He, X., Liao, L., Zhang, H., Nie, L., Hu, X., Chua, T.S.: Neural collaborative filtering. In: Proceedings of the 26th World Wide Web Conference, pp. 173–182 (2017)
8. Jiang, W., Pardos, Z.A., Wei, Q.: Goal-based course recommendation. In: Proceedings of the 9th International Conference on Learning Analytics & Knowledge, pp. 36–45 (2019)
9. Jing, X., Tang, J.: Guess you like: course recommendation in MOOCs. In: Proceedings of the International Conference on Web Intelligence, pp. 783–789 (2017)

10. Kim, Y.: Convolutional neural networks for sentence classification. In: Proceedings of the 2014 Conference on Empirical Methods in Natural Language Processing, pp. 1746–1751 (2014)
11. Kingma, D.P., Ba, J.: Adam: a method for stochastic optimization. In: Proceedings of the 3rd International Conference on Learning Representations, pp. 1–15 (2015)
12. Mikolov, T., Corrado, G., Chen, K., Dean, J.: Efficient estimation of word representations in vector space. In: Proceedings of the International Conference on Learning Representations, pp. 1–12 (2013)
13. Ormrod, J.: Human Learning. Pearson (2011)
14. Papadimitriou, C.H., Raghavan, P., Tamaki, H., Vempala, S.: Latent semantic indexing: a probabilistic analysis. J. Comput. Syst. Sci. **61**(2), 217–235 (2000)
15. Qi, P., Zhang, Y., Zhang, Y., Bolton, J., Manning, C.D.: Stanza: a Python natural language processing toolkit for many human languages. In: Proceedings of the 58th Annual Meeting of the Association for Computational Linguistics: System Demonstrations (2020)
16. Rendle, S.: Factorization machines with libFM. ACM Trans. Intell. Syst. Technol. **3**(3), 1–22 (2012)
17. Rendle, S., Freudenthaler, C., Gantner, Z., Schmidt-Thieme, L.: BPR: Bayesian personalized ranking from implicit feedback. In: Proceedings of the 25th Conference on Uncertainty in Artificial Intelligence, pp. 452–461 (2009)
18. Sheng, D., Yuan, J., Xie, Q., Luo, P.: MOOCRec: an attention meta-path based model for top-k recommendation in MOOC. In: International Conference on Knowledge Science, Engineering and Management, pp. 280–288 (2020)
19. Tao, L., Golikov, S., Gai, K., Qiu, M.: A reusable software component for integrated syntax and semantic validation for services computing. In: Proceedings of the 2015 IEEE Symposium on Service-Oriented System Engineering, SOSE 2015, pp. 127–132. IEEE Computer Society, USA (2015)
20. Wang, H., Zhang, F., Xie, X., Guo, M.: DKN: deep knowledge-aware network for news recommendation. In: Proceedings of the 27th World Wide Web Conference, pp. 1835–1844 (2018)
21. Wang, X., He, X., Cao, Y., Liu, M., Chua, T.S.: KGAT: knowledge graph attention network for recommendation. In: Proceedings of the 25th International Conference on Knowledge Discovery & Data Mining, pp. 950–958 (2019)
22. Wang, Z., Zhang, J., Feng, J., Chen, Z.: Knowledge graph embedding by translating on hyperplanes. In: Proceedings of the 28th AAAI Conference on Artificial Intelligence, pp. 1112–1119 (2014)
23. Yin, H., Gai, K.: An empirical study on preprocessing high-dimensional class-imbalanced data for classification. In: 2015 IEEE 17th International Conference on High Performance Computing and Communications, 2015 IEEE 7th International Symposium on Cyberspace Safety and Security, and 2015 IEEE 12th International Conference on Embedded Software and Systems, pp. 1314–1319 (2015)
24. Yin, H., Gai, K., Wang, Z.: A classification algorithm based on ensemble feature selections for imbalanced-class dataset. In: 2016 IEEE 2nd International Conference on Big Data Security on Cloud (BigDataSecurity), IEEE International Conference on High Performance and Smart Computing (HPSC), and IEEE International Conference on Intelligent Data and Security (IDS), pp. 245–249 (2016)

25. Zhang, F., Yuan, N.J., Lian, D., Xie, X., Ma, W.Y.: Collaborative knowledge base embedding for recommender systems. In: Proceedings of the 22nd International Conference on Knowledge Discovery & Data Mining, pp. 353–362 (2016)
26. Zhang, J., Hao, B., Chen, B., Li, C., Chen, H., Sun, J.: Hierarchical reinforcement learning for course recommendation in MOOCs. In: Proceedings of the 33rd AAAI Conference on Artificial Intelligence, pp. 435–442 (2019)

TEBC-Net: An Effective Relation Extraction Approach for Simple Question Answering over Knowledge Graphs

Jianbin Li[1], Ketong Qu[1(✉)], Jingchen Yan[1], Liting Zhou[2], and Long Cheng[1,2]

[1] School of Control and Computer Engineering, North China Electric Power University, Beijing, China
{lijb87,120192227066,lcheng}@ncepu.edu.cn

[2] Insight SFI Research Centre for Data Analytics, Dublin City University, Dublin, Ireland

Abstract. Knowledge graph simple question answering (KGSQA) aims on answering natural language questions by the lookup of a single fact over a knowledge graph. As one of the core tasks in the scenarios, relation extraction is critical for the quality of final answers. To improve the accuracy of relation extraction in KGSQA, in this paper, we propose a new deep neural network model called TEBC-Net, which is constructed based on the combination of **T**ransformer **E**ncoder, **B**iLSTM and **C**NN **Net** in a seamless way. We give the detailed design of our approach and have conducted an experimental evaluation with a benchmark test. Our results demonstrate that TEBC-Net can achieve higher accuracy on relation extraction and question answering tasks in KGSQA, compared to some current methods including the state-of-the-art.

Keywords: Knowledge graph simple question answering · Relation extraction · Natural language processing · Deep learning · TEBC-Net

1 Introduction

The knowledge graph (KG) can be viewed as an abstract for the interlinked descriptions of entities in our real world. It is normally represented by a semantic network [7], in which each node has several attributes, and the edges between nodes indicates their relationships [15,25]. Generally, KGs usually contains a huge amount of data and it is always hard for general users to retrive valuable information from them in an effective way [5], unless for the ones who are familiar with the relevant query syntax (e.g., SPARQL [6]). To cope with this problem, knowledge graph question answering (KGQA [8,12]), which aims to use facts in KGs to answer natural language questions, has been proposed to bridge the semantic gap.

In fact, with large-scale KGs (e.g., Freebase [10], DBpedia [14] and YAGO [21]) being used in a wide range of applications, as well as the advancing of natural language processing (NLP) technology, KGQA has become a hot

H. Qiu et al. (Eds.): KSEM 2021, LNAI 12815, pp. 154–165, 2021.
https://doi.org/10.1007/978-3-030-82136-4_13

research topic in both academia and industry [3,16,17]. Specifically, KG simple question answering (KGSQA) is a typical research problem in domain of KGQA. It focuses on answering simple questions by the lookup of a single fact in a KG. For example, a simple natural language question like "`Where was Michael Jordan born?`" can be answered by searching the property `place of birth` of the entity `Michael Jordan` over the responsible KG.

Similar to many other NLP problems, relation extraction (RE), which can extract semantic relationships between two or more entities of a certain type, is also one of the most important tasks in KGSQA. Specifically, it can be used to extract original structure information contained in a natural language question and on that basis to construct a query over KGs. For instance, we can get the relation `place of birth` for the above example with RE. To perform relation extraction in the context of KGSQA in an effective way, various neural network based approaches have been proposed in recent years (e.g., based on CNN [30]). However, they are shown to be not accurate enough for KGQA [31].

To improve the accuracy of RE in KGSQA, in this paper, we propose a new approach using a deep neural network we called TEBC-Net. The model is constructed based on the combination of **T**ransformer **E**ncoder, **B**iLSTM and **C**NN **Net** in a seamless way. Specifically, we introduce a knowledge graph embedding (KGE) algorithm to encode the facts in KGs. Then, for a given question, we use BiLSTM to capture its context information, and employ the self-attention mechanism of the encoding module in Transformer to extract the key information. After that, we use CNN to capture the character information of the question and employ the self-attention mechanism again to extract key information to complete the relation extraction. Our experimental evaluation shows that the proposed method is very effective for relation extraction in simple question answering over knowledge graphs.

Generally, the main contributions of this paper can be summarized as follows:

- We introduce a new and effective model TEBC-Net, which aims to improve the accuracy of the relation extraction for KGSQA.
- We present the detailed design and implementation of the proposed TEBC-Net, with open source code available.
- Our experimental results demonstrate that TEBC-Net is very effective on relation extraction in the context of KGSQA. Specifically, compared to some current approaches including the state-of-the-art, TEBC-Net can achieve higher accuracy on RE and KGSQA tasks with a benchmark test.

The reminder of this paper is organized as follows: Sect. 2 reports the related work of this paper; Sect. 3 presents the detailed structure and implementation of the proposed TEBC-Net; Sect. 4 presents the experimental results of our method; and Sect. 5 concludes this work and also discusses a few directions for the future research.

2 Related Work

In this section, we report the works in relation to knowledge graph question answering and relation extraction.

2.1 Knowledge Graph Question Answering

Template-based question answering is one of the core methods for KGQA, which focuses on matching questions using pre-defined templates to obtain formal queries [29,30]. As a typical example, the work [4] presents an approach to solve the question-query template construction problem in different environments. In each condition, the proposed system can use query workload and a question repository as input to match the query that best captures the semantics of the question, and then summarize each pair into a template. Although the template-based method can be used for KGQA, it always meets various problems like high cost for template generation, limited number of templates, etc.

To remedy the above problems, with the advancing of machine learning technology, the end-to-end deep-learning based KGQA approach has become popular [19,27]. For example, the work [9] introduces a comprehensive system which uses multi-channel CNN to extract relations and maps relation phrases to knowledge base predicates. Although various effective methods have been proposed in recent years [3,8,9,13,30], as we will show in this paper, our proposed model can further improve their accuracy including the state-of-the-art.

2.2 Relation Extraction

Relation extraction is one of the most important tasks in information extraction [31]. For the traditional research in RE, a small pre-defined relation set with a given text and two entities is usually employed. The goal is to find out whether the text can denote any types of relation between the two entities. In this case, RE is always known as a classification task. With the rapid development of deep learning, various advanced techniques have been used in RE, such as word embedding [11,18], CNNs and LSTMs [20,23], attention models [24,32], etc. Within the scope of this paper, RE in KGSQA is different from a general RE, since it begins with Feature-Rich methods [2,28], and then towards to deep learning [8,29] and attention models [9]. Although the deep learning models mentioned above can support large RE in KGSQA tasks, how to achieve high accuracy in the question answering is still challenging current approaches. In this work, we will focus on proposing a new model to improve the problem.

3 The Proposed TEBC-Net for KGSQA

For all questions that a knowledge graph can answer, the vector representation of the relation must be projected into the relation embedding space in advanced. In this case, we divide the process of our KGSQA into three steps: (1) we represent each entity and relation in a KG as a low-dimensional vector using knowledge graph embedding (KGE); (2) we use the TEBC-Net to take a question as input and return a mapped vector. The vector space distance between the two vectors will be calculated and ranked to complete the RE; and (3) we perform KGSQA based on the extracted relation in the question. The details of each step are given as follows. Specifically, we will mainly focus on the second step for the purpose of this work.

3.1 Knowledge Graph Embedding

Embedding KGs using low-dimensional vectors is a typical data pre-processing method for KGSQA. Motivated by the effectiveness of KGE [25] in many NLP applications, we have used the approach to solve the pre-trained embedding problem of KG in KGSQA. Generally, KGE represents each entity and relation in a KG as a low-dimensional vector and can keep the original structure and relation of the KG in the form of a numerical vector. Currently, various translation models (e.g., TransE, TransH and TransR) have been proposed and have shown to be able to achieve good prediction performance [4,26]. In this work, among them we have employed the model TransE [4] to vectorize the entities and relations in KGs. The main reason is that we focus on simple questions, the data sets in which contain only one head entity and one relation, which is easier to train with TransE, compared to other approaches [13]. Readers can refer to the work [13] for more details as well as the performance of TransE.

3.2 TEBC-Net Model

To perform relation extraction for a given question, we have considered three core factors in our method: the global features of words, the character features of words, and the importance of words. Specifically, based on the commonly used Transformer model [22], we use the self-attention mechanism in the Transformer encoding layer to filter and encode the importance of words. In the meantime, we use a CNN model to characterize the features of the questions to be encoded.

To correctly encode the generated word context sequence, we use the bi-directional mechanism of BiLSTM to replace the trigonometric position encoding used in Transformer. There are two motivations for this design:

- Compared to the absolute position encoding used in the original Transformer model, our method can express both the relative position and absolute position in the word order encoding process.
- Although the trigonometric function position embedding used in Transformer can check the distance between two words, it ignores the direction of the word on the left or the right [27].

The neural network architecture of the proposed TEBC-Net is demonstrated in Fig. 1. For the purpose of our presentation, we divide the architecture of our model into two parts: the left-hand side and right-hand side part. The left part focuses on extracting global features with importance from encoding while the right one can extract character features with importance.

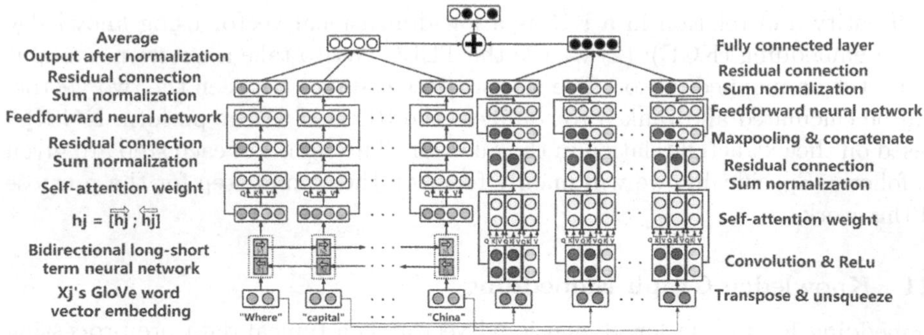

Fig. 1. The proposed TEBC-Net model for relation extraction[1] (For readability, all the figures used in this work with a high resolution are also available with the provided source code link in Sect. 4.).

Global Features with Importance. The left-hand side of our model shows how to encode questions using a combination of BiLSTM and self-attention mechanism. Firstly, we decompose a question into a set of word sequence x_j ($j = 1, 2, \ldots, M$). Then, we use the pre-trained model GloVe [19] to embed each word, and use BiLSTM to learn the forward and the backward hidden layer state sequence. Taking the forward direction as an example, the computation process can be represented as.

$$f_j = \sigma(W_{xf}x_j + W_{hf}\overrightarrow{h_{j+1}} + b_f) \quad (1)$$

$$i_j = \sigma(W_{xi}x_j + W_{hi}\overrightarrow{h_{j+1}} + b_i) \quad (2)$$

$$o_j = \sigma(W_{xo}x_j + W_{ho}\overrightarrow{h_{j+1}} + b_o) \quad (3)$$

$$c_j = \sigma(f_j \cdot c_{j+1} + i_j \tanh(W_{xc}x_j + W_{hc}\overrightarrow{h_{j+1}} + b_c)) \quad (4)$$

$$\overrightarrow{h}_j = o_j \cdot \tanh(c_j) \quad (5)$$

where f_j, i_j, and o_j are the output vectors of the forget gate, input gate and output gate respectively, c_j is the unit state vector, σ is the sigmoid function.

We combine the state vectors of the forward and backward hidden layers to obtain the output vector of BiLSTM, i.e., the word context information is recorded as $h_j = [\overrightarrow{h}_j : \overleftarrow{h}_j]$. Then, we pass the obtained h_j vector to the self-attention module. Since the h_j generated by BiLSTM contains the sequence information of the context position of the words, it can be directly used for self-attention calculation. The self-attention mechanism requires attention calculations between all words, and the process can be formulated as:

$$L_i = \sum_{j=1}^{M} \alpha_{ij} \times h_j \quad (6)$$

$$Attention(Q, K, V) = softmax(\frac{Q \cdot K^T}{\sqrt{d_k}}) \cdot V \quad (7)$$

$$d_k = hidden_{size} \times 2/n_{heads} \tag{8}$$

Here, the Q, K and V are all from the same sequence output by BiLSTM. The result of the dot product between K^T and Q will be used as the attention weight α_{ij} in Eq. 6, and the value of V is used as h_j. During the training of the attention weight, the gradient will decrease with increasing the value of Q, K. Therefore, we add d_k to prevent the gradient from disappearing. On all these basis, we link the output of the self-attention layer with the BiLSTM using a residual connection, and then pass the result to the normalization layer.

The normalized result will be sent to a feed forward neural network (FFN) represented by the Eq. 9 below. Moreover, we also link the input and output of the FFN as a residual connection, and then perform a sum and normalization operation on that basis. For all the words processed by the above operations, the mean of the outputs, based on the dimension of the question length, will be treated as the final output of the left-hand part of our network model.

$$FFN(x) = max(0, xW_1 + b_1)W_2 + b_2 \tag{9}$$

Character Features with Importance. For the right-hand side of our model, we encode questions using a combination of CNN and self-attention mechanism. Generally, the pre-trained embedded 3D vectors are first transformed into 4D vectors by adding an input channel. Then, the 4D vectors are handled by three 2D convolution operations with the kernel size (2, 300), (3, 300), and (4, 300), respectively, and a ReLu nonlinear transformation is used to adjust the dimensionality. Followed by that, each vector of each word is processed by the self-attention layer, the result of which is concatenated with the original vector as a residual. With that, the three vectors corresponding to each word are Max-pooled, and the third dimensional vector representing the question length will be removed. Moreover, the three vectors are merged according to the second dimension after the concatenate operation. Finally, we can get the output with the processing of FFN and residual connection operations as well as the fully connected layer.

In detail, our processing is based on the following formulas:

$$C_i = f(w_i \cdot x_{j:j+g-1} + b) \tag{10}$$

$$T = [C_1, C_2, \ldots, C_{M-g+1}] \tag{11}$$

$$Maxpooling = max[C_1, C_2, ..., C_{M-g+1}] = max(T) \tag{12}$$

$$Linear = \{Maxpooling_1, Maxpooling_2, \ldots, Maxpooling_{M-g+1}\} \tag{13}$$

where C_i denotes the extraction of question features by convolution, w_i is the convolution kernel, g is the convolution kernel size, $x_{(j:j+g-1)}$ is the question vector, which is composed of the words from the j-th to $(j + g - 1)$-th position in a question, and T represents the feature matrix obtained by the convolution operation.

With the vectors obtained from the left-hand and right-hand sides of our model, we can then obtain the final question representation result. As presented by the Eq. 14 and 15, we train our model by minimizing the mean square error between the relation representation (P_l), which is embedded by the pre-trained TransE model, and the question representation ($\hat{P}_l$).

$$\hat{P}_l = \frac{1}{M}\sum\nolimits_{j=1}^{M} r_j^T \tag{14}$$

$$Loss = \frac{1}{n}\sum i = 1^m w_i(P_{li} - \hat{P}_{li})^2 \tag{15}$$

3.3 KGSQA Execution Based on TEBC-Net

To evaluate the performance of TEBC-Net in the presence of different RE and question answering tasks, we have integrated the developed TEBC-Net model into KEQA [13], which is the state-of-the-art framework for KGSQA. Generally, with the KEQA framework, we can performs three main tasks in related to simple question answering over knowledge graphs: head entity recognition, relation extraction and head entity detection (HED). Specifically, we use TEBC-Net to replace the original model used in KEQA to implement head entity recognition and relation extraction tasks, respectively. In terms of HED, since it aims to determine whether the words contained in a question are entities, we just need to adjust the output of TEBC-Net in KEQA, as demonstrated in Fig. 2.

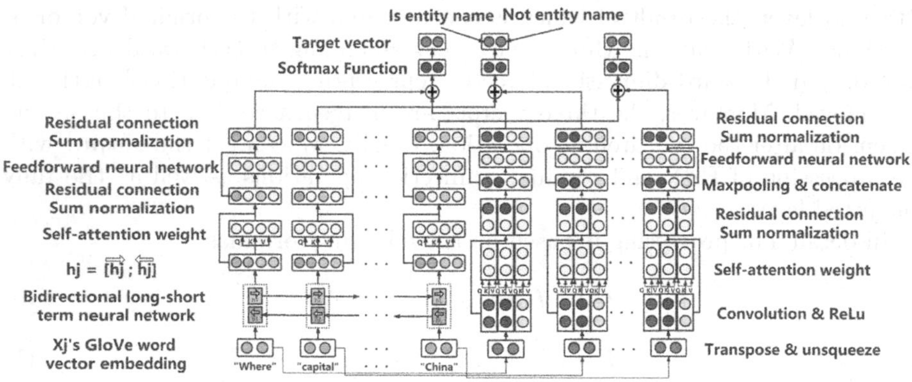

Fig. 2. The structure of TEBC-Net HED model.

4 Experimental Evaluation

In this section, we present an experimental evaluation of our approach in the presence of RE tasks and KGSQA tasks respectively.

4.1 Experimental Setup

Similar to some current works [13], we have used two typical public available datasets from Freebase in our experiments, with the detailed statistical information as presented in Table 1. In detail, FB5M [10] is used as a knowledge graph, and SimpleQuestions [3], which contains more than 10,000 simple questions related to the facts in Freebase, is used as the question answering dataset. For the training, validation and test sets, we have used the same configurations as the original design of the datasets.

Table 1. The detailed information of the used datasets in our experiments

	FB5M	SimpleQuestions
Training set	17,872,174	75,99
Validation set	N.A	9,811
Test set	N.A	10,487
Relation (M)	7,523	1,837
Entity (N)	3,988,95	131,481
Dictionary size	3,988,95	18,8

In our tests, we first use FB5M as the knowledge graph and apply KGE algorithm to learn the entity embedding set and relation embedding set. Next, we adopt TEBC-Net model to extract the head entity and relation of each question. The performance is measured by the accuracy of correctly extracted head entities and relations. The TEBC-Net HED model is used to determine whether the entity in the question is a head entity, and the evaluation criteria of KGSQA tasks refer to the accuracy of predicting new questions. The embedding dimension d of the TransE is set to 250, and the embedding dimension is set to 300 for the pre-trained word embedding based on GloVe. The source code used in our evaluation is available at https://github.com/oldbark/TEBC-Net.

4.2 Relation Extraction Tasks

To demonstrate the effectiveness of our method on relation extraction, we have compared TEBC-Net with other three methods over the FB5M dataset: CNN, BiLSTM and BiLSTM-Attention. The CNN is used as the baseline and the BiLSTM-Attention used in the work [13] can be seen as the state-of-the-art.

The RE results are reported in Table 2. There, we can see that TEBC-Net can perform around 10% better than CNN, and around 2% than the BiLSTM-Attention method, in terms of accuracy. The main is that CNN can learn the vector representation of questions and extract the character information. However, it is not suitable for learning the context information of words and cannot well represent the global features of sentences. In comparison, BiLSTM, as a global feature extraction model, can perform better than CNN in the cases of either using attention mechanism or not. Nevertheless, it is obvious that encoding the questions based on character features alone is not sufficient, so the global features should also be learned. With integrating the self-attention mechanism and residual learning, our proposed TEBC-Net model can extract both character features and global features in an effective way.

Since our TEBC-Net is more complex than other three models, it is interesting to see whether it can converge in a quick way. To this end, we have compared the values of accuracy and loss of TEBC-Net with other three methods by varying the number of epochs during the training process. As we can see from Fig. 3 and Fig. 4, TEBC-Net converges at a similar rate with other models, which means that our model can actually replace others in practical applications.

Table 2. The accuracy of relation extraction on the SimpleQuestions.

Models	FB5M (Accuracy)
CNN	0.72328
BiLSTM	0.80313 (+7.985%)
BiLSTM-Attention	0.80295 (+7.947%)
TEBC-Net	0.82014 (+9.686%)

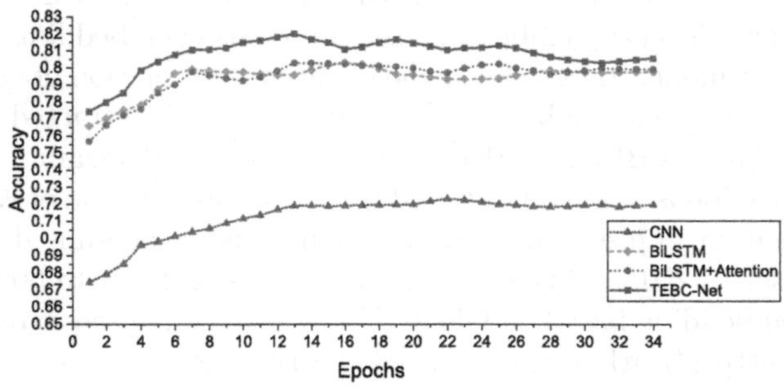

Fig. 3. Comparison of accuracy of TEBC-Net with the other three models.

4.3 KGSQA Tasks

To show that TEBC-Net can indeed improve the accuracy of simple question answering over knowledge graphs, we have compared our model with 6 other deep-learning based KGSQA algorithms, including the state-of-the-art [13]. The performance results over SimpleQuestions dataset are reported in Table 3. There, we can see that the accuracy rate of TEBC-Net applied to KGSQA can reach 75.6%, which is the best among all the methods. Specifically, its accuracy rate is around 31.7% higher compared to the method proposed in the work [3], and it can perform slightly better than the state-of-the-art approach [13].

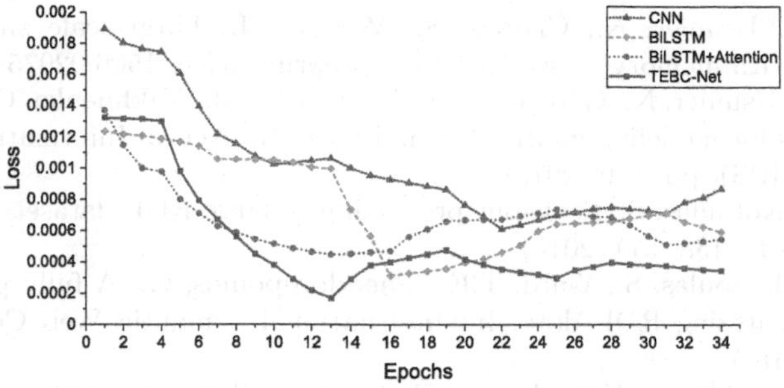

Fig. 4. Comparison of loss of TEBC-Net with the other three models.

Table 3. The performance comparison on the SimpleQuestions dataset.

Methods	FB5M (Accuracy)
Bordes et al. [3]	0.43900
Dai et al. [8]	0.18700
Yin et al. [30]	0.47200 (+3.3%)
Golub and He [9]	0.70300 (+26.4%)
Bao et al. [1]	0.72800 (+28.9%)
Xiao Huang et al. [13]	0.74000 (+30.1%)
TEBC-Net-KGSQA	0.75600 (+31.7%)

5 Conclusion

In this work, we have proposed an effective relation extraction approach for simple question answering over knowledge graphs. Specifically, we first use BiLSTM to capture the context information of a question, and employ the self-attention mechanism of the encoding module in Transformer to extract key information. On that basis, we then use CNN to capture the character information of the question, and use the self-attention mechanism to extract key information to complete the relation extraction for KGSQA. We have given the detailed design of our method and our experiments demonstrate that the proposed TEBC-Net can perform better than the current approaches including the state-of-the-art, in the presence of relation extraction and simple question answering tasks.

References

1. Bao, J., Duan, N., Yan, Z., Zhou, M., Zhao, T.: Constraint-based question answering with knowledge graph. In: Proceedings of the 26th International Conference on Computational Linguistics, pp. 2503–2514 (2016)
2. Bast, H., Haussmann, E.: More accurate question answering on freebase. In: Proceedings of the 24th ACM International on Conference on Information and Knowledge Management, pp. 1431–1440 (2015)

3. Bordes, A., Usunier, N., Chopra, S., Weston, J.: Large-scale simple question answering with memory networks. arXiv preprint arXiv:1506.02075 (2015)
4. Bordes, A., Usunier, N., Garcia-Duran, A., Weston, J., Yakhnenko, O.: Translating embeddings for modeling multi-relational data. In: Neural Information Processing Systems (NIPS), pp. 1–9 (2013)
5. Cheng, L., Kotoulas, S.: Scale-out processing of large RDF datasets. IEEE Trans. Big Data **1**(4), 138–150 (2015)
6. Cheng, L., Kotoulas, S., Ward, T.E., Theodoropoulos, G.: A fully parallel framework for analyzing RDF data. In: International Semantic Web Conference, pp. 289–292 (2014)
7. Cheng, L., Malik, A., Kotoulas, S., Ward, T.E., Theodoropoulos, G.: Fast compression of large semantic web data using X10. IEEE Trans. Parallel Distrib. Syst. **27**(9), 2603–2617 (2016)
8. Dai, Z., Li, L., Xu, W.: CFO: conditional focused neural question answering with large-scale knowledge bases. arXiv preprint arXiv:1606.01994 (2016)
9. Golub, D., He, X.: Character-level question answering with attention. arXiv preprint arXiv:1604.00727 (2016)
10. Google: Freebase data dumps (2018). https://developers.google.com/freebase
11. Gormley, M.R., Yu, M., Dredze, M.: Improved relation extraction with feature-rich compositional embedding models. arXiv preprint arXiv:1505.02419 (2015)
12. Hao, Y., et al.: An end-to-end model for question answering over knowledge base with cross-attention combining global knowledge. In: Proceedings of the 55th Annual Meeting of the Association for Computational Linguistics, pp. 221–231 (2017)
13. Huang, X., Zhang, J., Li, D., Li, P.: Knowledge graph embedding based question answering. In: Proceedings of the 12th ACM International Conference on Web Search and Data Mining, pp. 105–113 (2019)
14. Lehmann, J., et al.: Dbpedia-a large-scale, multilingual knowledge base extracted from Wikipedia. Semant. Web **6**(2), 167–195 (2015)
15. Lin, Y., Liu, Z., Sun, M., Liu, Y., Zhu, X.: Learning entity and relation embeddings for knowledge graph completion. In: Proceedings of the AAAI Conference on Artificial Intelligence, vol. 29 (2015)
16. Lukovnikov, D., Fischer, A., Lehmann, J., Auer, S.: Neural network-based question answering over knowledge graphs on word and character level. In: Proceedings of the 26th International Conference on World Wide Web, pp. 1211–1220 (2017)
17. Mohammed, S., Shi, P., Lin, J.: Strong baselines for simple question answering over knowledge graphs with and without neural networks. arXiv preprint arXiv:1712.01969 (2017)
18. Nguyen, T.H., Grishman, R.: Employing word representations and regularization for domain adaptation of relation extraction. In: Proceedings of the 52nd Annual Meeting of the Association for Computational Linguistics, pp. 68–74 (2014)
19. Pennington, J., Socher, R., Manning, C.D.: GloVe: global vectors for word representation. In: Proceedings of the 2014 Conference on Empirical Methods in Natural Language Processing (EMNLP), pp. 1532–1543 (2014)
20. Santos, C.N., Xiang, B., Zhou, B.: Classifying relations by ranking with convolutional neural networks. arXiv preprint arXiv:1504.06580 (2015)
21. Suchanek, F.M., Kasneci, G., Weikum, G.: Yago: a core of semantic knowledge. In: Proceedings of the 16th International Conference on World Wide Web, pp. 697–706 (2007)
22. Vaswani, A., et al.: Attention is all you need. arXiv preprint arXiv:1706.03762 (2017)

23. Vu, N.T., Adel, H., Gupta, P., Schütze, H.: Combining recurrent and convolutional neural networks for relation classification. arXiv preprint arXiv:1605.07333 (2016)
24. Wang, L., Cao, Z., De Melo, G., Liu, Z.: Relation classification via multi-level attention CNNs. In: Proceedings of the 54th Annual Meeting of the Association for Computational Linguistics, pp. 1298–1307 (2016)
25. Wang, Q., Mao, Z., Wang, B., Guo, L.: Knowledge graph embedding: a survey of approaches and applications. IEEE Trans. Knowl. Data Eng. **29**(12), 2724–2743 (2017)
26. Wang, Z., Zhang, J., Feng, J., Chen, Z.: Knowledge graph embedding by translating on hyperplanes. In: Proceedings of the AAAI Conference on Artificial Intelligence, vol. 28 (2014)
27. Yan, H., Deng, B., Li, X., Qiu, X.: TENER: adapting transformer encoder for named entity recognition. arXiv preprint arXiv:1911.04474 (2019)
28. Yao, X., Van Durme, B.: Information extraction over structured data: question answering with freebase. In: Proceedings of the 52nd Annual Meeting of the Association for Computational Linguistics, pp. 956–966 (2014)
29. Yih, S.W., Chang, M.W., He, X., Gao, J.: Semantic parsing via staged query graph generation: question answering with knowledge base (2015)
30. Yin, W., Yu, M., Xiang, B., Zhou, B., Schütze, H.: Simple question answering by attentive convolutional neural network. arXiv preprint arXiv:1606.03391 (2016)
31. Yu, M., Yin, W., Hasan, K.S., Santos, C., Xiang, B., Zhou, B.: Improved neural relation detection for knowledge base question answering. arXiv preprint arXiv:1704.06194 (2017)
32. Zhou, P., et al.: Attention-based bidirectional long short-term memory networks for relation classification. In: Proceedings of the 54th Annual Meeting of the Association for Computational Linguistics, pp. 207–212 (2016)

Representing Knowledge Graphs with Gaussian Mixture Embedding

Wenying Feng[1,2], Daren Zha[1], Xiaobo Guo[1,2(✉)], Yao Dong[1,2], and Yuanye He[1,2]

[1] Institute of Information Engineering, Chinese Academy of Sciences, Beijing, China
{fengwenying,zhadaren,guoxiaobo,dongyao,heyuanye}@iie.ac.cn
[2] School of Cyber Security, University of Chinese Academy of Sciences, Beijing, China

Abstract. Knowledge Graph Embedding (KGE) has attracted more and more attention and has been widely used in downstream AI tasks. Some proposed models learn the embeddings of Knowledge Graph (KG) into a low-dimensional continuous vector space by optimizing a customized loss function. However, these methods either ignore the polysemy of entities/relations in KG, or cannot model the uncertainty of them. Therefore, we propose **KG2GM** (**K**nowledge **G**raph to **G**aussian **M**ixture), a *density-based* KGE method, for modeling the polysemy and uncertainty of KG simultaneously. Each entity/relation in KG is represented by a Gaussian mixture probability distribution. Each Gaussian component of the mixed distribution represents one kind of semantics, where the mean vector denotes its space position, and the covariance matrix denotes its uncertainty. In this way we can model the polysemy and uncertainty of KG simultaneously. We employ symmetrized KL divergence and EL (Expected Likelihood) to measure the component similarities and make their probabilistic combination as the score function of the triplet. We conduct experiments on link prediction with two benchmark datasets (WN18RR and FB15k-237). The results show that our method can effectively model the polysemy and uncertainty of entities and relations in KG.

Keywords: Knowledge Graph Embedding · Gaussian Mixture Model · Distributed representation · Knowledge graph completion · Link prediction

1 Introduction

Knowledge Graphs (KGs) such as WordNet, Freebase and Yago have been widely used in various AI tasks including expert system, semantic search, and Q&A [1–3]. KG usually describes knowledge as many relational data and represents them as subject-property-object (SPO) triple facts [4]. In a triple fact (h, r, t), h and t represent head entity and tail entity, respectively, and r represents the relationship between them. Knowledge Graph Embedding (KGE) is the main method

H. Qiu et al. (Eds.): KSEM 2021, LNAI 12815, pp. 166–178, 2021.
https://doi.org/10.1007/978-3-030-82136-4_14

for KG representation. A series of methods, including translation-based, bilinear, and neural network-based models, are proposed for KGE and achieve excellent performance on KG datasets.

However, these models are most *point-based*, focus on embedding entities and relations of KG as points in vector space. They can only capture a certain specific semantics of entity/relation, and lack the capability to deal with the entity/relation that contains multiple meanings. For example, the entity *Apple* denotes a kind of fruit or a company, and the relation *PartOf* denotes *Location* for triplet (*New York, PartOf, US*) and *Composition* for triplet (*Monitor, PartOf, Television*). Thus, TransG [5] is proposed to address this issue of multiple relation semantics by generating semantic components dynamically.

Another problem of the most KGE methods is that different entities and relations often share the same margin (a crucial parameter during training KGE model) when separating a positive triplet and its corresponding negative triplet, and the (un)certainties of entities and relations in KGs are totally neglected [4]. For example, we can easily deduce a person by giving his *spouse* (a relation), but hardly do that by giving his *nationality* (another relation). Because the uncertainty of *nationality* is greater than that of *spouse*. To overcome this limitation, *density-based* embedding is proposed, which uses probability distribution to represent KG. Specifically, KG2E [4] represents each entity/relation with multi-dimensional Gaussian distribution, where the mean vector denotes its position and the covariance matrix can properly represent its uncertainty. According to the statistics in KG2E, for a relation r in triplet (h, r, t), the more uncertain it is, the greater the determinant and trace of its Gaussian distribution. Hence probability distribution representation based on density can model the uncertainty of entity/relation effectively.

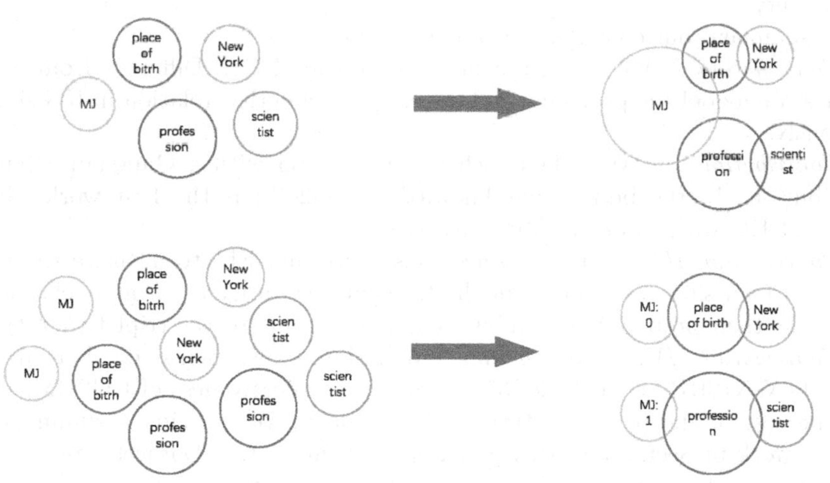

Fig. 1. Illustrations of KG2E (top) and KG2GM (bottom).

Although KG2E can model the uncertainty of entity/relation by distribution embedding, its single Gaussian component can only capture one certain semantics, and lacks the capability to representing entity/relation which contains multiple meanings. Inspired by multimodal distribution of word [6], which aims to model multiple word meanings and uncertainty information for words by mixing multiple Gaussian components, we introduce **KG2GM** (**K**nowledge **G**raph to **G**aussian **M**ixture) to model the polysemy and uncertainty of KG.

As shown in Fig. 1, Each circle is a 2D display of Gaussian distribution for the entity/relation in KG, whose center is specified by the mean vector and radius specified by the covariance, reflecting the space position of the semantics and its uncertainty. The two subfigures on the top is the illustration of single Gaussian distribution embedding, namely KG2E. For the example triplet (*Michael_Jordan, place_of_birth, New_York*) and (*Michael Jordan, profession, scientist*), *Michael Jordan* (shorted as *MJ* in the figure) in the former triplet indicates the basketball star *Michael Jordan*, and an expert of machine learning in the latter triplet. Despite the uncertainty retained, KG2E cannot model the multiple meanings of entity/relation, so *Michael Jordan* would be regarded as one kind of entity semantics and its covariance is more likely to be unnecessarily large in order to hold the two triplets at the same time (see top right figure of Fig. 1). To overcome the limitation of single Gaussian distribution with reserving uncertainty information, we introduce KG2GM. Specifically, we represent each entity/relation with mixed Gaussian distributions. Each kind of semantics of entity/relation is represented by a Gaussian component. The number of components can be specified before training. For the entity *Michael Jordan* in the example above, the two kinds of semantics is assigned two independent Gaussian components (see the two subfigures at the bottom of Fig. 1). Then the mixed probability distributions can represent the multiple meanings of entity/relation with reserving their uncertainty.

In summary, our contributions are as follows:

Contribution I: We propose a new method for KGE. Different from other models, we model the polysemy and uncertainty of entity/relation in KG simultaneously.

Contribution II: We embed each entity/relation with a Gaussian Mixture distribution. To the best of our knowledge, KG2GM is the first work which represent KG with Gaussian Mixture Model.

Contribution III: We use two methods (SKL and EL) to measure the similarity of Gaussian components of the transformed entity $t - h$ and relation r, and make their probabilistic combination as the score for the triplet (h, r, t).

Contribution IV: Through link prediction experiments on benchmark datasets WN18RR and FB15k-237, we prove the effectiveness of KG2GM.

The rest of the paper is structured as follows. We provide a summary of related work in Sect. 2 and then our approach in Sect. 3. Dataset descriptions and experimental results are reported in Sect. 4, followed by our conclusion and future research directions in Sect. 5.

2 Related Work

Almost all the related works for KGE take efforts on embedding each entity/relation of KG into a low-dimensional continuous real-valued vector. The related models can be classified into the following three categories.

Translation Based Models. TransE [7] is the first translation-based model for KGE, which represents relation as a vector r, to indicate the semantic translation from head entity h to tail entity t. TransE has few parameters and low computational complexity, and achieves excellent performance on *1-1* relationship. But it performs poorly while dealing with complex relation types such as *1-N*, *N-1* and *N-N*. To remedy the limitation of TransE, TransH [8] projects head/tail entity onto the hyperplane of the relation, which makes one entity have different representations for different relations. Furthermore, TransR [9] makes the entity projection into the semantic spaces corresponding to different relations. TransD [10] projects head entity and tail entity into the relational space respectively on the basis of TransR. TransM [11] takes the structure of KG into consideration by pre-calculating the distinct weight for each training triplet according to its relational mapping property.

Bilinear Models. RESCAL [12] is the first bilinear model for KGE, which models the pairwise interactions between latent factors by representing each relation as a matrix. Since the large computational complexity caused by the large number of parameters in RESCAL, DistMult [13] simplify RESCAL by restricting relation matrix to diagonal matrix. Afterwards, ComplEx [14] extends DistMult by introducing complex-valued embedding so as to better model asymmetric relations. HolE [15] combines the representation capability of RESCAL with the simplicity and efficiency of DistMult.

Neural Network Based Models. Various KGE methods based on neural network have been proposed in recent years. ConvE [16] introduces multi-layer convolution network to model the interaction between entity and relation. ConvKB [17] concatenates head, tail and relation vectors into a convolution network. ParamE [18] utilizes translational property and nonlinearity fitting capability simultaneously. InteractE [19] enhances the representation capability by feature permutation, feature reshaping and circular convolution.

In addition, some *density-based* models represents KG with probability distribution. Luke Vilnis firstly propose density-based Gaussian embedding model for learning the representations of words [20], which inspired KG2E. KG2E [4] learns the representations of KG in the space of multi-dimensional Gaussian distributions to model the uncertainty of entities and relations. Ben Athiwaratkun extends Gaussian embedding of words to multimodal distributions for modeling word polysemy [6]. Inspired by Gaussian mixture distributions for words, we proposed multimodal distribution representation model KG2GM for KG.

3 Methodology

To capture the polysemy and uncertainty simultaneously, we represent each entity/relation in KG as a Gaussian mixture distribution and combine the weighted similarity score of each component pair as the score of the triplet. We use h, r and t to denote the head entity, relation and tail entity in a triplet fact (h, r, t). Mathematical symbols $\mathcal{H}$, $\mathcal{R}$ and $\mathcal{T}$ correspond to the Gaussian mixture distribution of h, r and t. In a Gaussian distribution $\mathcal{N}(\boldsymbol{\mu}, \boldsymbol{\Sigma})$, $\boldsymbol{\mu}$ is the mean vector, and $\boldsymbol{\Sigma}$ is the covariance matrix of the Gaussian distribution.

3.1 Gaussian Mixture Embeddings of Entity and Relation

In KG2GM, each entity/relation of KG is represented as a mixture distribution of multiple Gaussian components. Each component is an independent Gaussian distribution, which represents a kind of semantics of entity/relation. Since distribution-based representation is more likely to capture the uncertainty of semantics, and mixed components can represent the polysemy, the way of mixed distribution has a stronger representation capability for KG. Specifically, we represent each entity/relation as mixed Gaussian distribution like follows:

$$\mathcal{H} \sim \sum_{i=1}^{M} \pi_{h,i} \mathcal{N}(\boldsymbol{\mu}_{h,i}, \boldsymbol{\Sigma}_{h,i}) \; \mathcal{R} \sim \sum_{j=1}^{M} \pi_{r,j} \mathcal{N}(\boldsymbol{\mu}_{r,j}, \boldsymbol{\Sigma}_{r,j}) \; \mathcal{T} \sim \sum_{k=1}^{M} \pi_{t,k} \mathcal{N}(\boldsymbol{\mu}_{t,k}, \boldsymbol{\Sigma}_{t,k}) \tag{1}$$

$$\|\boldsymbol{\mu}\| \leqslant 1 \quad c_{min} \boldsymbol{I} \leqslant \boldsymbol{\Sigma} \leqslant c_{max} \boldsymbol{I} \tag{2}$$

$$\theta = \{\pi_{h,i}, \pi_{r,j}, \pi_{t,k}, \boldsymbol{\mu}_{h,i}, \boldsymbol{\mu}_{r,j}, \boldsymbol{\mu}_{t,k}, \boldsymbol{\Sigma}_{h,i}, \boldsymbol{\Sigma}_{r,j}, \boldsymbol{\Sigma}_{t,k}\} \tag{3}$$

In formula 1, M is the number of mixed components, which is shared by entities and relations. $\pi_{h,i}$, $\pi_{r,j}$, $\pi_{t,k}$ are the weights of each component, which need to be trained, and $\sum_{i=1}^{M} \pi_{h,i} = 1$, $\sum_{j=1}^{M} \pi_{r,j} = 1$, $\sum_{k=1}^{M} \pi_{t,k} = 1$. $\boldsymbol{\mu}_{h,i}$, $\boldsymbol{\mu}_{r,j}$ and $\boldsymbol{\mu}_{t,k}$ are the mean vectors of the i_{th}, j_{th}, k_{th} component of head entity, relation and tail entity respectively. $\boldsymbol{\Sigma}_{h,i}$, $\boldsymbol{\Sigma}_{r,j}$, $\boldsymbol{\Sigma}_{t,k}$ are their corresponding covariance matrices. The same as KG2E, We restrict norm of $\boldsymbol{\mu}$ less than 1 and $\boldsymbol{\Sigma}$ to diagonal matrix for computing efficiency, see formula 2. $\boldsymbol{I}$ is diagonal matrix and c_{min}, c_{max} is the coefficients of $\boldsymbol{I}$ for constraint of $\boldsymbol{\Sigma}$. The training goal is to learn all the parameters in formula 3, including the weight, mean vector and covariance matrix for each component of entities and relations.

3.2 Energy Function

$$f(h, r, t) = \sum_{i=1}^{M} \sum_{j=1}^{M} \sum_{k=1}^{M} \pi_{h,i} \pi_{r,j} \pi_{t,k} \varepsilon(h_i, r_j, t_k) \tag{4}$$

We follow the *energy-based* framework like most models. The core of this framework is an energy function $\varepsilon_\theta(x)$, which is defined to calculate the score of input x. The training goal is to learn the optimal parameters θ^* by making the score difference of positive and negative samples meet with the hyperparameter margin γ. We define the energy function for triplet (h, r, t) as formula 4, which is the probabilistic combination of each component score function of h, r and t. We use two score functions for calculating $\varepsilon(h_i, r_j, t_k)$: Symmetrized KL divergence (SKL) and Expected Likelihood (EL). They are introduced in detail in the next section.

3.3 Component Similarity Measure

Following the concept of KG2E [4], we consider the difference between the transformation from head entity h to tail entity t and r as measurement metric. We use simple subtraction operation to express this transformation: $\mathcal{T}_k - \mathcal{H}_i$, which corresponds to the probability distribution $\mathcal{P}_{e_{i,k}} \sim \mathcal{N}(\boldsymbol{\mu}_{t,k} - \boldsymbol{\mu}_{h,i}, \boldsymbol{\Sigma}_{t,k} + \boldsymbol{\Sigma}_{h,i})$. This transformation denotes the difference of the i_{th} component of head entity h and the k_{th} component of tail entity t. The probability distribution of the j_{th} component of relation r is expressed as $\mathcal{P}_{r_j} \sim \mathcal{N}(\boldsymbol{\mu}_{r,j}, \boldsymbol{\Sigma}_{r,j})$. Then the most important step is to calculate the similarity of $\mathcal{P}_{e_{i,k}}$ and $\mathcal{P}_{r_j}$. There are two ways to achieve this:

Symmetrized KL Divergence. KL divergence (Kullback–Leibler divergence) is an asymmetric measurement of the difference between two probability distributions. Formula 5 is the KL divergence between $\mathcal{P}_{e_{i,k}}$ and $\mathcal{P}_{r_j}$, $tr(\boldsymbol{\Sigma})$ and $\boldsymbol{\Sigma}^{-1}$ indicate the trace and inverse of the covariance matrix respectively, and D is the embedding dimension.

$$\begin{aligned}\varepsilon_{kl}(h_i, r_j, t_k) &= \mathcal{D}_{kl}(\mathcal{P}_{e_{i,k}}, \mathcal{P}_{r_j}) \\ &= \int_{x \in \mathcal{R}^{\mathcal{D}}} \mathcal{N}(x; \boldsymbol{\mu}_{r,j}, \boldsymbol{\Sigma}_{r,j}) \log \frac{\mathcal{N}(x; \boldsymbol{\mu}_{e_{i,k}}, \boldsymbol{\Sigma}_{e_{i,k}})}{\mathcal{N}(x; \boldsymbol{\mu}_{r,j}, \boldsymbol{\Sigma}_{r,j})} dx \\ &= \frac{1}{2}\{tr(\boldsymbol{\Sigma}_{r,j}^{-1}\boldsymbol{\Sigma}_{e_{i,k}}) + (\boldsymbol{\mu}_{r,j} - \boldsymbol{\mu}_{e_{i,k}})^T \boldsymbol{\Sigma}_{r,j}^{-1}(\boldsymbol{\mu}_{r,j} - \boldsymbol{\mu}_{e_{i,k}}) \\ &\quad - \log \frac{\det(\boldsymbol{\Sigma}_{e_{i,k}})}{\det(\boldsymbol{\Sigma}_{r,j})} - D\}\end{aligned} \tag{5}$$

$$\varepsilon_{skl}(h_i, r_j, t_k) = \frac{1}{2}(\mathcal{D}_{kl}(\mathcal{P}_{e_{i,k}}, \mathcal{P}_{r,j}) + \mathcal{D}_{kl}(\mathcal{P}_{r,j}, \mathcal{P}_{e_{i,k}})) \tag{6}$$

In order to eliminate the influence of asymmetry, we employ symmetrized KL divergence (SKL) to measure the similarity of two Gaussian components, following formula 6.

Expected Likelihood. Expected Likelihood (EL) is a symmetric similarity measurement for two probability distributions. EL is defined as the logarithm of the inner product of two distributions. Therefore, we take logarithm inner product of $\mathcal{P}_{e_{i,k}}$ and $\mathcal{P}_{r_j}$ as their similarity measure metric as follows:

$$\begin{aligned}
\varepsilon_{el}(h_i, r_j, t_k) &= \mathcal{D}_{el}(\mathcal{P}_{e_{i,k}}, \mathcal{P}_{r_j}) \\
&= \log \int_{x \in \mathcal{R}^{\mathcal{D}}} \mathcal{N}(x; \boldsymbol{\mu}_{e_{i,k}}, \boldsymbol{\Sigma}_{e_{i,k}}) \mathcal{N}(x; \boldsymbol{\mu}_{r,j}, \boldsymbol{\Sigma}_{r,j}) dx \\
&= \log \mathcal{N}(0; \boldsymbol{\mu}_{e_{i,k}} - \boldsymbol{\mu}_{r,j}, \boldsymbol{\Sigma}_{e_{i,k}} - \boldsymbol{\Sigma}_{r,j}) \\
&= \frac{1}{2}\{(\boldsymbol{\mu}_{e_{i,k}} - \boldsymbol{\mu}_{r,j})^T (\boldsymbol{\Sigma}_{e_{i,k}} + \boldsymbol{\Sigma}_{r,j})^{-1} (\boldsymbol{\mu}_{e_{i,k}} - \boldsymbol{\mu}_{r,j}) \\
&\quad + \log \det(\boldsymbol{\Sigma}_{e_{i,k}} + \boldsymbol{\Sigma}_{r,j}) - D \log(2\pi)\}
\end{aligned} \tag{7}$$

The calculation derivation for the integral in line 2 of formula 5 and formula 7 refers to [4], and we obtain the line 3 of formula 5 and line 4 of formula 7. Notice that the similarity score of formula 6 and 7 is the measurement for single component distributions of mixed represented h, r and t, the final score for triplet (h, r, t) are obtained by weighted combination calculation following formula 4.

3.4 Learning

We define the following margin-based loss function for training the embeddings. The training goal is to minimize the loss of formula 8 on training set. Once this goal is achieved, the positive and negative samples can be separated clearly, and the difference between them will be close to the margin γ. Then we will get a good representation of the KG, namely trained parameters in θ.

$$\mathcal{L} = \sum_{(h,r,t) \in \Gamma} \sum_{(h',r',t') \in \Gamma'} [f(h,r,t) + \gamma - f(h',r',t')]_+ \tag{8}$$

In the formula above, $[x]_+ \triangleq max(0, x)$ means to get the maximum between 0 and x, γ is the margin to separate the positive and negative samples. (h, r, t) indicates a positive sample that belongs to positive sample set Γ. (h', r', t') is the negative sample corresponding to (h, r, t), which can be obtained by negative sampling operation for (h, r, t). There are two common methods for negative sampling: *unif* and *bern* [8], we take *bern* as default setting because it tends to give more chance to replacing the head entity if the relation is *1-N*, and give more chance to replacing the tail entity if the relation is *N-1*. In this way, the chance of generating false negative labels is reduced. High-quality negative samples lead to better trained model and experiment results.

The training process is shown in Algorithm 1. Given training set and hyperparameters of input, one can get mixed Gaussian embeddings of each entity and relation in KG as output. First, entity set $\mathcal{E}$ and relation set $\mathcal{R}$ is generated from training set Γ. Then we normalize each component of all entities and relations. In each epoch, we need to construct negative sample for each triplet with a negative sampling strategy called *bern*. After that we can update the model

Algorithm 1: The Learning Algorithm of **KG2GM**

Input: Training Set $\Gamma = \{(h, r, t)\}$, number of mixed components M, embedding dimension D, margin γ, covariance matrix restriction $[c_{min}, c_{max}]$, learning rate α, epoch number n.

Output: Mixed Gaussian embeddings (mean vectors, covariance matrices, weights of components) of each entity and relation in KG.

Generate entity set $\mathcal{E}$ and relation set $\mathcal{R}$ from Γ;
foreach *item* $\in \mathcal{E} \cup \mathcal{R}$ **do**
    foreach *component c of item* **do**
        Uniform(c.mean);
        Uniform(c.covariance);
        regularize c.mean and c.covariance with constraint 2;
    end
end
epoch $\leftarrow$ 0;
while *epoch* $<n$ **do**
    $\Gamma_{batch} \leftarrow$ Sample(Γ,b); //sample a minibatch of size b from Γ
    $T_{batch} \leftarrow \emptyset$; //pairs of triplets for learning
    foreach *triplet* $\in \Gamma_{batch}$ **do**
        $triplet' \leftarrow$ negSample($triplet$); //negative sampling with *bern*
        $T_{batch} \leftarrow \Gamma_{batch} \cup (triplet, triplet')$;
    end
    Update paremeters in θ with optimizer w.r.t. formula 8;
    Regularize the mean and covariance for each component of entities and relations in T_{batch} with constraint 2;
end

parameters by minimizing loss of formula 8. The mean and covariance of each component need to be regularized at the end of each epoch.

4 Experiments

4.1 Implementation

We use *Adam* to optimize parameters in mini-batch while learning embeddings. We set the learning rate α for *Adam* to 0.01, the margin γ to 0.8, the dimension of entity/relation to 200, the batch size b to 128, and the pair of restriction values (c_{min}, c_{max}) to (0.05, 5.0). Some KGE models are implemented by an open source project called *Pykg2vec*. We rerun several baselines including TransE, TansH, TransR, TransD, TransM and KG2E. We train all the models for 100 epochs and follow default parameter settings in *Pykg2vec* for the sake of fairness. We compare the model performances on link prediction with two benchmark datasets. According to [6], mixed mode with M = 3 does not generally offer significant performance difference to that with M = 2. Hence, we implement KG2GM of two mixed components for computing efficiency.

4.2 Datasets

We use two datasets for our experiments: WN18RR and FB15k-237. WN18 is a subset of WordNet, containing lexical relational data of synsets. FB15k is filtered from Freebase, containing general facts. Since WN18 and FB15K suffer from test leakage through inverse relations, we use modified version of them, namely WN18RR and FB15k-237, for evaluation. WN18RR and FB15k-237 are obtained by removing reciprocal triplets and further filtering of WN18 and FB15K. The statistical information of the two datasets are listed in Table 1.

Table 1. Statistics of datasets

Dataset	#Ent	#Rel	#Train	#Valid	#Test
WN18RR	40943	11	86835	3034	3134
FB15k-237	14541	237	272115	17535	20466

4.3 Link Prediction

Link prediction is used to evaluate the performance of KGE model. The task aims to predict the missing h given $(?, r, t)$, or t given $(h, r, ?)$. For each test triplet (h, r, t) in test set, we replace the tail entity t with each entity e in entity set $\mathcal{E}$, and calculate the score of triplet (h, r, e) with the defined energy function $f(h, r, e)$. Then we rank all the triplets by score, the right triplet (h, r, e_t) should get a higher score and be ranked at a higher position than others.

There are two main metrics to indicate the results of link prediction: *Mean Rank* (MR) and Hits@n. MR calculates the average value of all ranked numbers of test triplets. *Mean Reciprocal Rank* (MRR) is a transformation form of MR, which is the mean of reciprocals of the ranked numbers. Hits@n counts the number of right entities in test set that are ranked in top n. A good model should obtain lower MR and higher MRR and Hits@n. We evaluate the baseline models and KG2GM on MR, MRR, Hits@[1,3,5,10] for a careful comparison.

However, these evaluation metrics may obtain worse results than the model can actually achieve. Because the replacement operation for triplet may get truth triplets other than the test triplet (h, r, t), and those truth triplets might be ranked in front of (h, r, t), thus make a worse statistical result. A common practice is to remove those truth triplets that already appeared in training, validation and test set in statistics to get a more reasonable result. The original setting is named as *raw* and the removement operation as *filter*. We take *filter* as default setting in the experiments.

4.4 Results

The results of link prediction are reported in Tables 2 and 3. We only compare several translation based models including TransE, TransH, TransR, TransD,

TransM and KG2E, and no bilinear or neural network based models are included in the comparison. The reason is that our proposed model is translation-based, so we just compare it with similar models, and we do not aim at achieving the best performance by long-time training and parameter adjustment. We only focus on the effect of the structure and representation capability of the model, so we employ our experiments with the same parameter settings and train all the models for the same fewer epochs.

Table 2. Experimental results of link prediction on WN18RR

Model	MR	MRR	Hits@1	Hits@3	Hits@5	Hits@10
TransE [7]	6629	0.0988	0.0051	0.1559	0.2064	0.2618
TransH [8]	6433	0.1045	0.0032	0.1728	0.2224	0.2770
TransR [9]	6918	0.0890	0.0029	0.1471	0.1835	0.2278
TransD [10]	6763	0.0920	0.0036	0.1302	0.1779	0.2401
TransM [11]	**5865**	**0.1110**	0.0056	0.1597	0.1934	0.2301
KG2E [4]	7521	0.0542	**0.0070**	0.0770	0.1020	0.1330
KG2GM-SKL	6297	0.0875	0.0046	**0.1820**	**0.2358**	**0.2961**
KG2GM-EL	5963	0.1086	0.0039	0.1752	0.2269	0.2805

On WN18RR, KG2GM does not achieve the best in terms of MR, MRR and Hits@1, but outperforms other approaches on Hits@3, Hits@5 and Hits@10. KG2GM with SKL outperforms other baseline models, including KG2GM with EL. The reason of the lower MR and MRR may be that WN18RR only contains a very small number of relations, and the density of each relation is very high. So KG2GM can judge the correct tail entity but cannot rank it at the top position. Since MR is easily decreased by a few obstinate triplets, we consider Hits@n is more reasonable to indicate the performance of models.

Table 3. Experimental results of link prediction on FB15k-237

Model	MR	MRR	Hits@1	Hits@3	Hits@5	Hits@10
TransE [7]	331	0.1548	0.0793	0.1687	0.2223	0.3070
TransH [8]	325	0.1535	0.0773	0.1672	0.2211	0.3071
TransR [9]	360	0.1620	**0.0904**	0.1733	0.2253	0.3062
TransD [10]	459	0.1537	0.0851	0.1657	0.2166	0.2928
TransM [11]	327	0.1533	0.0853	0.1638	0.2124	0.2909
KG2E [4]	569	0.1082	0.0420	0.1150	0.1725	0.2490
KG2GM-SKL	**295**	**0.1681**	0.0903	**0.1823**	**0.2390**	**0.3259**
KG2GM-EL	302	0.1595	0.0854	0.1770	0.2231	0.3194

On FB15k-237, KG2GM consistently achieves the best performance except Hits@1. Since FB15k-237 contains more relations, it has greater density diversity than WN18RR, so the density-based KG2GM can handle it better. This improvement indicates that uncertainty diversity of FB15k-237 is greater than that of WN18RR, which is consistent with the experiment conclusion of KG2E. The consistent improvements indicate that KG2GM captures more polysemy and uncertainty of entities/relations in KG.

In addition, we can see that KG2E performs poorly on both WN18RR and FB15k-237, even worse than most other translation based models. The reason is that KG2E usually takes more epochs to achieve better performance. In comparison, KG2GM takes less epochs when a considerable performance is achieved because of its polysemy handing mechanism. From the experimental results above, we can draw the following conclusions: 1) Gaussian mixture embedding can learn valid representation for KG. 2) Density-based KG2GM can handle the polysemy and uncertainty of entity/relation simultaneously. 3) KG2GM-SKL performs better than KG2GM-EL, which indicates that symmetrized KL divergence is an effective indicator for measuring the similarity of Gaussian components.

5 Conclusion

We propose KG2GM, a new *density-based* method for learning embeddings of KG with Gaussian Mixture Model. Each entity and relation in KG is represented by a probabilistic combination of multiple Gaussian distributions, which aims to model the polysemy and uncertainty of entity/relation. We use two metrics (SKL and EL) to measure the similarities of each component pair, and take their probabilistic combination as the energy function of the triplet. Experiments on link prediction with two benchmark datasets demonstrate the effectiveness of the proposed method. However, there is a limitation in this model: component mixing mechanism increases the complexity of the algorithm, thus limits the model for practical application. In addition, most entities and relations in KG have only one semantic but would be assigned more than one component distribution in KG2GM. This increases unnecessary parameters and computation overhead. We leaves the two problems as our future work.

Acknowledgements. This work is supported by the Youth Innovation Promotion Association, Chinese Academy of Sciences (No. 2017213). In addition, we would like to thank the anonymous reviewers for their valuable comments and suggestions that help improving the quality of this paper.

References

1. Chen, M., Zhang, Y., Qiu, M., et al.: SPHA: smart personal health advisor based on deep analytics. IEEE Commun. Mag. **56**(3), 164–169 (2018)

2. Tao, L., Golikov, S., Gai, K., et al.: A reusable software component for integrated syntax and semantic validation for services computing. In: 2015 IEEE Symposium on Service-Oriented System Engineering (SOSE), pp. 127–132. IEEE (2015)
3. Gai, K., Qiu, M.: Reinforcement learning-based content-centric services in mobile sensing. IEEE Netw. **32**(4), 34–39 (2018)
4. He, S., Liu, K., Ji, G., Zhao, J.: Learning to represent knowledge graphs with Gaussian embedding. In: Proceedings of the 24th ACM International on Conference on Information and Knowledge Management, pp. 623–632. ACM (2015)
5. Xiao, H., Huang, M., Zhu, X.: TransG: a generative model for knowledge graph embedding. In: Proceedings of the 54th Annual Meeting of the Association for Computational Linguistics (Volume 1: Long Papers), Berlin, pp. 2316–2325. ACL (2016)
6. Athiwaratkun, B., Wilson, A.: Multimodal word distributions. In: Proceedings of the 55th Annual Meeting of the Association for Computational Linguistics (Volume 1: Long Papers), Berlin, pp. 1645–1656. ACL(2017)
7. Bordes, A., Usunier, N., Garcia-Duran, A., et al.: Translating embeddings for modeling multi-relational data. In: Advances in Neural Information Processing Systems, pp. 2787–2795 (2013)
8. Wang, Z., Zhang, J., Feng, J., et al.: Knowledge graph embedding by translating on hyperplanes. In: 28th AAAI Conference on Artificial Intelligence (2014)
9. Lin, Y., Liu, Z., Sun, M., et al.: Learning entity and relation embeddings for knowledge graph completion. In: 29th AAAI Conference on Artificial Intelligence (2015)
10. Ji, G., He, S., Xu, L., et al.: Knowledge graph embedding via dynamic mapping matrix. In: Proceedings of the 53rd Annual Meeting of the Association for Computational Linguistics and the 7th International Joint Conference on Natural Language Processing (Volume 1: Long Papers), pp. 687–696 (2015)
11. Fan, M., Zhou, Q., Chang, E., et al.: Transition-based knowledge graph embedding with relational mapping properties. In: Proceedings of the 28th Pacific Asia Conference on Language, Information and Computation, pp. 328–337 (2014)
12. Nickel, M., Tresp, V., Kriegel, H P.: A three-Way model for collective learning on multi-relational data. In: Proceedings of the 54th International Conference on Machine Learning, pp. 809–816 (2011)
13. Yang, B., Yih, W T., He, X., et al.: Embedding entities and relations for learning and inference in knowledge bases. In: Proceedings of the 3rd International Conference on Learning Representations (2015)
14. Trouillon, T., Welbl, J., Riedel, S., et al.: Complex embeddings for simple link prediction. In: Proceedings of the 33rd International Conference on Machine Learning, pp. 2071–2080 (2016)
15. Nickel, M., Rosasco, L., Poggio, T.: Holographic embeddings of knowledge graphs. In: Proceedings of the 30th AAAI Conference on Artificial Intelligence, pp. 1955–1961 (2016)
16. Dettmers, T., Minervini, P., Stenetorp, P., et al.: Convolutional 2D knowledge graph embeddings. In: Proceedings of the 32nd AAAI Conference on Artificial Intelligence (2018)
17. Nguyen, D.Q., Nguyen, T.D., Nguyen, D.Q., et al.: A novel embedding model for knowledge base completion based on convolutional neural network. In: Proceedings of the 2018 Conference of the North American Chapter of the Association for Computational Linguistics: Human Language Technologies (Volume 2: Short Papers) (2018)

18. Che, F., Zhang, D., Tao, J., et al.: ParamE: regarding neural network parameters as relation embeddings for knowledge graph completion. In: Proceedings of the AAAI Conference on Artificial Intelligence, pp. 2774–2781 (2020)
19. Vashishth, S., Sanyal, S., Nitin, V., et al.: InteractE: improving convolution-based knowledge graph embeddings by increasing feature interactions. In: Proceedings of the AAAI Conference on Artificial Intelligence, pp. 3009–3016 (2020)
20. Vilnis, L., McCallum, A.: Word representations via gaussian embedding. In: Proceedings of the International Conference on Learning Representations (2015)

A Semi-supervised Multi-objective Evolutionary Algorithm for Multi-layer Network Community Detection

Ze Yin[1], Yue Deng[1], Fan Zhang[1], Zheng Luo[1], Peican Zhu[2], and Chao Gao[1,2(✉)]

[1] College of Computer and Information Science, Southwest University, Chongqing 400715, China
cgao@nwpu.edu.cn
[2] School of Artificial Intelligence, Optics, and Electronics (iOPEN), Northwestern Polytechnical University, Xi'an 710072, China

Abstract. In the real world, many complex systems can be abstracted as multi-layer networks. Recently, community detection for multi-layer networks plays a vital role in multi-relationship complex system analysis, thus gradually gaining popularity especially in the optimization algorithms. The multi-objective optimization (MOOP) methods attract attention owing to the flexibility in solving community detection problems. Nevertheless, most of the MOOP methods pay little attention to the prior information, which cannot ensure the high-level accuracy and robustness against networks with complicated community structures. To address the problem, this paper proposes a semi-supervised multi-objective evolutionary algorithm for multi-layer community detection (SS-MOML). The SS-MOML mainly consists of two steps: First, it extracts the prior information from the network. Second, based on the prior information, the prior layer is constructed by creating virtual connections and the high-quality initial population is generated. And then the optimization process begins, in which the genetic operation based on the prior information is committed to guiding the evolutionary direction of chromosomes. Some extensive experiments are implemented and the results prove that the proposed SS-MOML stands out in accuracy and robustness than 7 state-of-the-art multi-layer community detection algorithms.

Keywords: Community detection · Multi-layer network · Semi-supervised multi-objective optimization · Prior information

1 Introduction

Networks have become effective tools for processing complex systems in the real world such as social networks, biological networks and technological networks [10]. In a network, nodes represent the entities, and edges stand for the connections between entities. The traditional single-layer network can only represent a

H. Qiu et al. (Eds.): KSEM 2021, LNAI 12815, pp. 179–190, 2021.
https://doi.org/10.1007/978-3-030-82136-4_15

single relationship. However, the relationship of entities is diversified. Therefore, multi-layer networks, which can address multi-relationship more effectively, have gradually been a research hot spot [11].

Communities are one of the most essential attributes of networks, which can reveal the potential structure characteristics of networks [10]. Generally speaking, a community (module or cluster) is a series of nodes with closer connections or more similar attributes [6]. Up to now, single-layer network based community detection algorithms have made great achievements, for example, Gao et al. propose a physarum-based framework [5] and Yang et al. propose a semi-supervised framework [17]. However, because of the particular structure of multi-layer networks, traditional single-layer based methods cannot address multi-layer networks effectively. In the past decades, some multi-layer community detection algorithms have been proposed, among which multi-objective optimization algorithm (MOOP) is one of the most effective methods. Due to the local and global search capabilities of the evolutionary algorithm, the multi-objective evolutionary algorithm (MOEA), one of the most classical MOOP methods, has attracted great attention [9]. MOEAs achieve good performance because they can balance the information of each layer by optimizing different objective functions. However, this kind of algorithms pays much attention to the topological information rather than taking prior information into full consideration.

Yang et al. suggest that only considering the topological information is not adequate for algorithms [17]. The prior information can further improve the accuracy and robustness of the algorithm by dividing the preknown similar nodes into the same community despite the weak relationship of the topological information. For example, the prior information can be added to the non-negative matrix factorization-based (NMF) or spectral clustering-based (SC) algorithm as a graph regularization [17]. However, there are few researches for incorporating the prior information into the MOEA. This is because it is difficult to extract the consensus prior information due to the complex structure of multi-layer networks. Besides, unlike the NMF and SC methods, MOEAs find the optimal community partition by imitating the population evolution, which brings difficulties in applying the guidance of prior information.

To address the problem mentioned above, this paper proposes a novel **S**emi-**S**upervised **M**ulti-**O**bjective evolutionary algorithm for **M**ulti-**L**ayer network community detection (named SS-MOML). The main idea of SS-MOML is to incorporate the prior information into the MOEA from beginning to end. More specifically, it aims to construct the prior layer, initialization and prior information based genetic operation, which incorporates the prior information into networks and optimization process, respectively. The prior layer, high-quality initialization and modified genetic operation can guide the evolution of the population by dividing similar nodes into the same community as far as possible. The contributions are listed as follows.

- Instead of only paying attention to the topological information like the traditional MOEAs, the SS-MOML neatly combines the idea of semi-supervised methods and MOEA methods on different aspects, so as to further improve the accuracy and robustness.

- In order to extract the prior information for multi-layer networks with various structures, this paper proposes DeepWalk-based method and $S\phi rensen-Dice's$ similarity-based method, where a novel density-based aggregation strategy is added into the DeepWalk to adapt to various network structures.
- In order to get the utmost of the prior information and MOEA, this paper proposes a SS-MOML algorithm, which utilizes the prior information to generate the prior layer, initial population and guide the population evolution.

The paper is organized as follows. Sect. 2 introduces the problem definition of multi-layer network community detection. The proposed SS-MOML algorithm is presented in detail in Sect. 3. The extensive experiments are elucidated in Sect. 4. Finally, Sect. 5 concludes the paper.

2 Problem Definition

A multi-layer network can be represented as a graph $G = (V, E_l\ (l = 1, \ldots, L))$, which consists of L layers. Each layer has the same node set $V = \{v_1, v_2, \ldots, v_N\}$ which satisfies $|V| = N$ and N represents the number of nodes. E_l stands for the edge set of the l_{th} layer which represents a kind of relationship. Existing approaches formulate the multi-layer network as a set of matrices, $A^{(l)} \in \mathbb{R}_+^{N\times N}(l = 1, \cdots, L)$, which is used to encode the information of each layer.

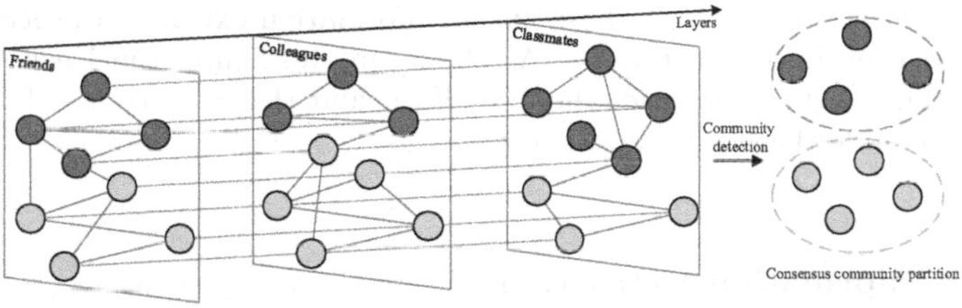

Fig. 1. An example of multi-layer networks. The network consists of 3 layers, and different layers represent different relationships (i.e., friends, colleagues, and classmates). Nodes pertaining to different communities are colored differently.

A multi-layer network has multiple layers, where each layer represents one relationship, which is shown in Fig. 1. The complex structure of multi-layer networks leads to the diversity of the community structure in each layer. The ultimate goal of the multi-layer network community detection algorithm is to find a consensus community partition that best adapts to each layer of the multi-layer network.

3 Proposed Method

The proposed SS-MOML algorithm is introduced in this section. The flowchart of the proposed algorithm is shown in Fig. 2. The algorithm mainly consists of two components, namely, the prior information extraction and the optimization process. In the former part, two prior information extraction methods are proposed, that is, DeepWalk-based method (shown in (a)) and $S\phi rensen-Dice's$-similarity-based method (shown in (b)). The optimization process is based on the NSGA-II, and the prior information is incorporated into the optimization section in each step. The main components of the optimization process are shown in (c), and each of them is introduced as follows.

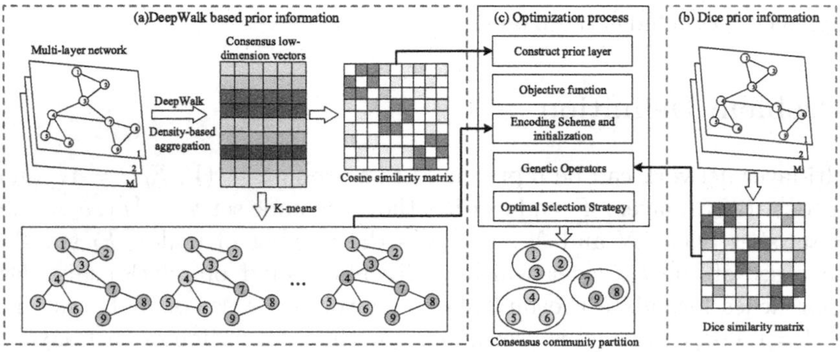

Fig. 2. The flowchart of the SS-MOML algorithm. (a) and (b) represent the DeepWalk-based and the $S\phi rensen - Dice's$-based prior information extraction process, respectively. (c) is the optimization process. As shown in the figure, the DeepWalk-based information is utilized to construct the prior layer and the $S\phi rensen - Dice's$-based information to guide the genetic operation.

3.1 Prior Information Extraction

As mentioned above, the prior information is used to guide the algorithm to divide the similar nodes into the same community. Therefore, the prior information plays a key role in algorithm since high accurate prior information can provide a correct guidance. For example, Ma et al. believe that the subgraph composed of closely connected nodes should be the prior information and they find such prior information through a greedy search method [10]. In this paper, we extract the prior information by applying DeepWalk (DW for short) [14] and $S\phi rensen - Dice's$ (Dice for short) similarity [16] because the DW can extract the relatively high-order information and Dice can eliminate the effect of node degree. Firstly, the DeepWalk algorithm is applied in each network layer to acquire the low-dimensional representation vectors of each one. Due to the particularity of multi-layer network structure (i.e., each network layer represents a certain kind of relationship), the low-dimensional vectors need to be merged into a consensus vector as the consensus prior information of the network. The most intuitive way is to compute the average of each vector. However, the quantity of information and the importance of each layer are different, so calculating the average of vectors may lead to low accuracy. To overcome the problem, we propose the density-based aggregation strategy, which quantizes the amount of information in each layer using density, which functions as the weight to merge vectors from different layers [8]. Since the increase of density means the decrease of information quantity on the contrary, it is inconvenient to calculate the weight. To address this problem, the equation is converted to Eq. (1).

$$density = \frac{M_c}{N(N-1)/2} \tag{1}$$

where M_c represents the number of connections within communities, and N is the number of nodes. The density means the proportion of connections and nodes within a community. We regard a network layer as a community, so that the density can be used to quantize the information quantity of a network layer.

The second method is to extract the prior information by applying Dice similarity. The equation is shown in Eq. (2).

$$\mathbf{S}\left(v_i, v_j\right) = \frac{2ComNeighbours\left(v_i, v_j\right)}{Length\left(v_i\right) + Length\left(v_j\right)} \tag{2}$$

where v_i and v_j represent the nodes, $ComNeighbours(v_i, v_j)$ means the number of common neighbours of nodes v_i and v_j. $Length(v_i)$ is the degree of the node v_i. To preserve the structure of the multi-layer network, the neighbours of all layers are considered when calculating the number of neighbours of nodes, which ensures the connection information of all layers are considered.

After that, the prior information contains the similarity between every two nodes. To construct the prior layer, we retain a part of node pairs with the highest DW-based cosine similarity as virtual edges according to a predefined threshold θ. Finally, the collection of virtual edges constitutes the prior layer. The prior layer contains accurate information of community structure because the connected nodes are more likely to belong to the same community (they are more similar). In addition, the Dice-based prior information is incorporated into the genetic operation, which is described in Sect. 3.4.

3.2 Objective Functions

The MOEA can be represented as $F = \{F_1, F_2, \ldots, F_t\}$, where F_i is the i_{th} objective function, and t means the number of functions. The MOEA optimizes each objective function to find the optimal solution. In this paper, we choose two widely-used objective functions, Modularity (Q) [12] and Normalized Cut (Nc) [3], which are shown in Eq. (3) and Eq. (4).

$$Q = \frac{1}{2M}\sum_{i,j}^{N}\left(A_{ij} - \frac{d_i \times d_j}{2M}\right)\delta\left(C^i, C^j\right) \tag{3}$$

where M is the number of edges, A represents the corresponding adjacent matrix and d_i means the degree of node i. C stands for the community and C^i represents the node i that belongs to C. When $C^i = C^j$, $\delta\left(C^i, C^j\right) = 1$, and 0 otherwise. In this paper, the first objective function is the average of Q for each layer.

$$Nc\left(\{C_k\}_{k=1}^{K}\right) = \frac{1}{K}\sum_{k=1}^{K} Nc_k \tag{4}$$

where $Nc_k = \frac{W_k^o}{2 \cdot W_k^i + W_k^o} + \frac{W_k^o}{2 \cdot (W_k^a - W_k^i) + W_k^o}$, and C_k is the k_{th} community. W_k^i, W_k^o and W_k^a are the sum of edge weights within communities, between communities, and total edges of community k, respectively. To adapt to the structure of multi-layer networks, the W_k^i, W_k^o and W_k^a are calculated for all layers.

3.3 Encoding Scheme and Initialization

The encoding scheme will affect the computational cost of the algorithm. Label-based and locus-based methods are two widely-used encoding approaches. However, the label-based method may cause redundancy, which leads to space consuming. For example, the encoding sequence {1 1 1 2 2 2 2} and {2 2 2 1 1 1 1} represent the same community partition. Therefore, the locus-based encoding scheme is selected in the proposed algorithm.

To generate the high-quality initial population, we apply the k-means algorithm to the consensus low-dimensional vector (calculated by DW-based method). Then the clustering result is transformed to the locus-based encoding, which is the initial population. The flowchart of initialization is also shown in Fig. 2.

3.4 Genetic Operators

Genetic operation is one of the most critical components, which is helpful to break the local optimality and find the optimal solution. In this paper, the crossover and mutation operations are used to increase the population diversity.

The crossover operation can generate various offspring chromosomes. The uniform crossover is selected in this paper because it is more random. Firstly, a binary mask, having the same length as the chromosome, is generated randomly. The offspring is generated by choosing the gene of parents according to the value of the binary mask. More specifically, at a gene, when the value of the mask is 0, the offspring chooses the first parent, otherwise another parent.

To make full use of the guiding ability of Dice-based prior information (calculated in Sect. 3.1), we propose the Dice-based mutation strategy. Simultaneously, to ensure the utilization of the local information (i.e., neighbours of nodes), we design a mutation strategy consisting of two parts as shown in Fig. 3.

There are two mutation strategies, and 50% of parent chromosome conducts the neighbour-based mutation strategy and others perform the Dice-based mutation strategy to take full advantage of the local information and prior information. For neighbour-based strategy, a gene of a parent chromosome is selected

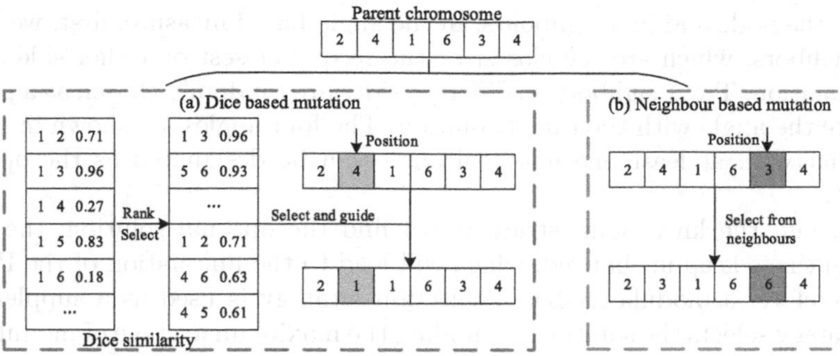

Fig. 3. The diagram of mutation operation. The mutation consists of two components, which are neighbour-based (red dotted line) and Dice-based strategy (blue dotted line). (Color figure online)

randomly according to a predefined probability. Then, the value of the selected gene mutates to the value of one of its neighbours. As for the Dice-based strategy, some genes are selected randomly with a predefined probability and the value of genes is selected from the Dice similarity table randomly. Similar to DW similarity mentioned in Sect. 3.1, the Dice similarity table is constructed by a part of node pairs with the highest Dice similarity according to a predefined reservation threshold ϵ. Figure 3 illustrates the processes of genetic operation.

3.5 Optimal Selection Strategy

As mentioned above, MOEAs can find a collection of solutions. Finding an appropriate way to extract the optimal solution is important for the algorithm. The knee point strategy is a useful method [1]. The idea of the knee point refers to a little improvement of one objective function leading to a significant reduction of other objective functions. For a two-fitness-function MOEA, an angle-based method is applied to find the knee point of the solution set [1].

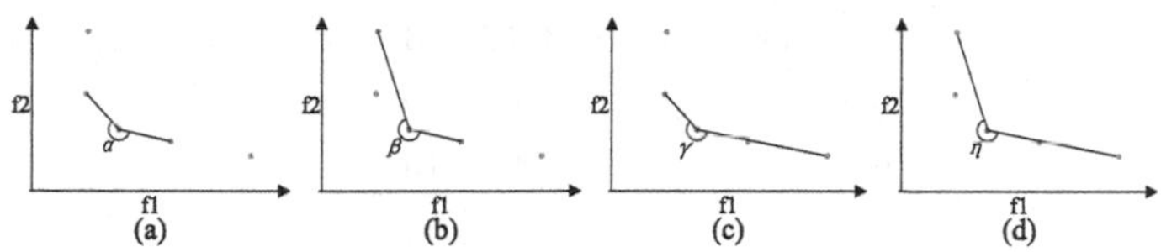

Fig. 4. An example of knee point strategy. The red point represents the target node and green points are four neighbours of the target node. α, β, γ and η are four angles. (Color figure online)

The angle-based method estimates the trades-offs of two objective functions by measuring the slopes of two lines, where the line is constructed by passing through the node and its neighbours. In the angle-based measure, first, we select four neighbors, which are the closest or the second closest on either side of the target solution. Two neighbors on different sides are randomly chosen as a pair to calculate the angle with the target solution. The four angles are shown in Fig. 4. The point with at least one maximal angle can be designated as the optimal solution.

Although the knee point strategy can find the optimal solution, the total iteration times keep unchanged, which will lead to the fluctuation of the Pareto set. Therefore, a modularity-based selection strategy is used as a supplement. The strategy selects the solutions by finding the maximum average of modularity.

4 Experiment

4.1 Datasets and Metrics

Various synthetic and real-world datasets are used to validate the performance of the proposed algorithm. The basic information of datasets is shown in Table 1. The synthetic datasets are generated by the multi-layer LFR benchmark (mLFR) [2]. The mLFR benchmark controls the structure of the network by changing the mixing parameter (μ) and the degree change chance (Dc). Both the μ and Dc range in (0, 1). With the increase of μ and Dc, the community structure of the multi-layer network becomes more complicated. The real-world networks with different types and scales (i.e., SND [7], MPD [7], WTN [7], CoRA [7], Citeseer [7]) are used to ensure the comprehensiveness of the experiment.

Table 1. The summary of datasets. The first five are real-world datasets and the last two are generated by the mFLR benchmark.

Network	Layers	Nodes	Clusters
SND	3	71	3
MPD	3	87	6
WTN	14	183	10
CoRA	2	1662	3
CiteSeer	2	3312	3
Syn1	3	5000	9
Syn2	3	10000	16

Besides the datasets, metrics are also significant for experiments. In this paper, two widely-used metrics are used to evaluate the accuracy of the detected communities, namely, Normalized Mutual Information (NMI) [7] and Adjusted Rand Index (ARI) [7]. Both two metrics evaluate the similarity between partition C and Ω, where Ω represents the ground truth and C stands for the partition calculated by the proposed algorithm. The range of NMI and ARI is [0,1]. The larger the both metrics, the more accurate the community partition.

Table 2. The experimental results on various datasets. The $\mathcal{A}_1 - \mathcal{A}_8$ represent SS-MOML (our proposed algorithm), MOEA-MultiNet, SC-ML, MIMOSA, S2-jNMF, COMCLUS, CSNMF and GMC algorithm, respectively. The '-' represents that the algorithm cannot run successfully on this network.

	Algorithms	$\mathcal{A}_1$	$\mathcal{A}_2$	$\mathcal{A}_3$	$\mathcal{A}_4$	$\mathcal{A}_5$	$\mathcal{A}_6$	$\mathcal{A}_7$	$\mathcal{A}_8$
SND	*NMI*	**0.721**	0.437	0.681	0.132	0.582	0.555	0.681	0.597
	ARI	**0.747**	0.201	0.493	0.088	0.452	0.480	0.493	0.428
MPD	*NMI*	**0.591**	0.494	0.495	0.096	0.516	0.421	0.504	0.451
	ARI	**0.468**	0.385	0.379	0.01	0.396	0.365	0.394	0.248
WTN	*NMI*	**0.316**	0.140	0.231	0.065	0.157	0.183	0.284	0.203
	ARI	**0.197**	0.052	0.129	0.007	0.069	0.105	**0.197**	0.015
CoRA	*NMI*	**0.886**	0.317	0.480	0.011	0.796	0.471	0.514	0.519
	ARI	**0.924**	0.243	0.485	0.001	0.813	0.447	0.491	0.426
CiteSeer	*NMI*	**0.345**	-	0.191	-	0.149	0.182	0.237	0.042
	ARI	**0.337**	-	0.169	-	0.147	0.119	0.207	0.012
Syn1	*NMI*	0.965	-	0.950	0.855	0.772	0.950	**1**	0.999
	ARI	0.972	-	0.902	0.896	0.602	0.902	**1**	0.999
Syn2	*NMI*	0.953	-	**1**	0.098	0.452	0.894	0.946	0.963
	ARI	0.895	-	**1**	0.01	0.074	0.814	0.874	0.954

4.2 Baselines and Parameter Settings

In SS-MOML, the parameter settings of DeepWalk are the same as the source paper. The number of iterations and populations are both 500. Besides, θ and ϵ, which are used to control the proportion of retaining prior information, are set as 0.3 and 0.1, respectively. The analysis of parameters is shown in Sect. 4.4.

To verify the performance of our algorithm, various kinds of algorithms are selected as the comparison algorithms, namely, MOEA based method (MOEA-MultiNet [9]), spectral clustering based methods (SC-ML [4] and MIMOSA [3]), matrix factorization based approaches (S2-jNMF [10], COMCLUS [13] and CSNMF [7]) and multi-view clustering based method (GMC [15]). The parameter settings of comparison algorithms are consistent with the source paper.

4.3 Experimental Results

The results of comparison experiments are shown in Table 2. The experiment consists of seven comparison algorithms mentioned above running on five real-world datasets and two synthetic datasets (Syn1 and Syn2).

The results show that the proposed SS-MOML performs better than other state-of-the-art methods on most of the datasets. Since the prior information guides the algorithm to divide similar nodes into the same community, the proposed algorithm can keep a high-level performance on Citeseer, WTN and MPD, which have a complicated community structure. Moreover, we find that the SS-MOML has a higher accuracy than another classical MOEA-based method

(MOEA-MultiNet) on most networks due to the utilization of prior information. On Syn1 and Syn2 (large scale synthetic network), the accuracy of SS-MOML is slightly lower than some comparison algorithms because the structure of synthetic networks is simpler compared with real-world networks and the objective function values are not linearly related to the accuracy. In general, the performance of SS-MOML surpasses other algorithms on various kinds of multi-layer networks.

4.4 Parameter Analysis

In this section, some experiments of threshold θ and ϵ are implemented to verify the effects of two parameters on our algorithm. The results are shown in Fig. 5.

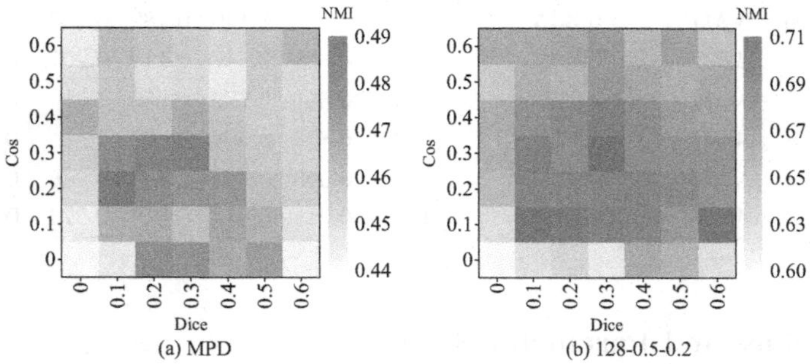

Fig. 5. The experimental results of parameter analysis. The x-axis and y-axis represent the threshold of Dice (ϵ) and cosine similarity (θ), which controls the reservation proportion of prior information. To ensure the comprehensiveness of experiments, a real-world network (MPD) and synthetic network (128-0.5-0.2) are chosen as experimental datasets. To avoid the fluctuation of knee point selection strategy, the experiments take the second optimal selection strategy (maximize the average modularity).

The experimental results indicate that the NMI value drops to the minimum on both two datasets when $\theta = 0$ and $\epsilon = 0$, which means there is no prior information incorporated into the algorithm. With θ and ϵ increase, the NMI value rises because the prior information guides the algorithm to find better solutions. As shown in (a), when the values of θ and ϵ surpass 0.5, the reserved quantity of prior information grows up, leading to the decrease of the accuracy for prior information (the similarity between nodes declines). The experiments prove the positive impact of prior information on the algorithm.

4.5 Robustness Analysis

As mentioned above, the prior information can improve the robustness of the algorithm. This section validates the robustness of the proposed SS-MOML algorithm. The experiment, as shown in Fig. 6, consists of two sub-experiments, which change the network structure and number of layers respectively.

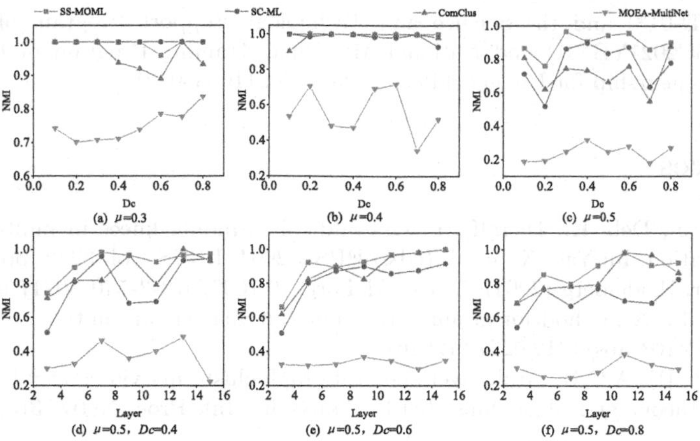

Fig. 6. The analysis of robustness. (a)–(c) are designed to validate the stability of algorithms for various network structures. (d)–(f) represent the experimental results running on networks with different layers.

The results show that the proposed SS-MOML performs better than other state-of-the-art methods in terms of accuracy and stability on various synthetic networks with different structure and number of layers. Compared with MOEA-MultiNet, the proposed algorithm owns a remarkable advantage. In addition, we can find that the NMI has less volatility than the other state-of-the-art methods with high robustness. It is because that the prior information participates in the initialization and each step of the MOEA, which can ensure the nodes with high similarity are distributed into the same community.

5 Conclusion

This paper proposes a novel semi-supervised multi-objective evolutionary algorithm for multi-layer network community detection, called SS-MOML. SS-MOML first extracts the prior information using DW-based strategy and Dice-based strategy. Then, it constructs the prior layer based on the DW-based strategy and the optimization process begins. In each iteration step, the Dice-based mutation strategy will guide the population evolution based on the Dice-based prior information. Moreover, the prior information can evaluate the similarity between nodes, and guide them into the same community despite the weak relationship on topological information. A series of extensive experiments prove our SS-MOML performs superiorly to other state-of-the-art algorithms on most datasets.

Acknowledgement. This work was supported by the National Key R&D Program of China (No. 2020AAA0107700), National Natural Science Foundation of China (Nos. 61976181, 11931015), Key Technology Research and Development Program of Science and Technology Scientific and Technological Innovation Team of Shaanxi Province

(No. 2020TD-013) and the Science and Technology Support Program of Guizhou (No. QKHZC2021YB531) and National Municipal Training Program of Innovation and Entrepreneurship for Undergraduates (No. S202110635042).

References

1. Branke, J., Deb, K., Dierolf, H., Osswald, M.: Finding knees in multi-objective optimization. In: Yao, X., et al. (eds.) PPSN 2004. LNCS, vol. 3242, pp. 722–731. Springer, Heidelberg (2004). https://doi.org/10.1007/978-3-540-30217-9_73
2. Bródka, P.: A method for group extraction and analysis in multilayer social networks. CoRR abs/1612.02377 (2016)
3. Chen, P., III, A.O.H.: Multilayer spectral graph clustering via convex layer aggregation: theory and algorithms. IEEE Trans. Sig. Inf. Proc. Netw. **3**(3), 553–567 (2017)
4. Dong, X., Nefedov, N.: Clustering on multi-layer graphs via subspace analysis on Grassmann manifolds. IEEE Trans. Sig. Process. **62**(4), 905–918 (2014)
5. Gao, C., Liang, M., Wang, Z., Zhou, Z.: Network community detection based on the Physarum-inspired computational framework. IEEE ACM Trans. Comput. Biol. Bioinform. **15**(6), 1916–1928 (2018)
6. Gao, C., Liu, J., Kurths, J.: Even central users do not always drive information diffusion. Commun. ACM **62**(2), 61–67 (2019)
7. Gligorijevic, V., Zafeiriou, S.: Non-negative matrix factorizations for multiplex network analysis. IEEE Trans. Pattern Anal. Mach. Intell. **41**(4), 928–940 (2019)
8. Leskovec, J., Lang, K.J., Mahoney, M.W.: Empirical comparison of algorithms for network community detection. In: The 19th International Conference on World Wide Web, Raleigh, pp. 631–640. ACM (2010)
9. Liu, W., Wang, S., Gong, M., Zhang, M.: An improved multiobjective evolutionary approach for community detection in multilayer networks. In: The 2017 IEEE Congress on Evolutionary Computation, Donostia, pp. 443–449. IEEE (2017)
10. Ma, X., Dong, D., Wang, Q.: Community detection in multi-layer networks using joint nonnegative matrix factorization. IEEE Trans. Knowl. Data Eng. **31**(2), 273–286 (2019)
11. Mucha, P.J., Richardson, T., Onnela, J.P.: Community structure in time-dependent, multiscale, and multiplex networks. Science **328**(5980), 876–878 (2010)
12. Newman, M.E., Girvan, M.: Finding and evaluating community structure in networks. Phys. Rev. E **69**(2), 026113 (2004)
13. Ni, J., Cheng, W., Fan, W., Zhang, X.: ComClus: a self-grouping framework for multi-network clustering. IEEE Trans. Knowl. Data Eng. **30**(3), 435–448 (2018)
14. Perozzi, B., Al-Rfou, R., Skiena, S.: DeepWalk: online learning of social representations. In: The 20th ACM SIGKDD International Conference on Knowledge Discovery and Data Mining, New York, pp. 701–710. ACM (2014)
15. Wang, H., Yang, Y., Liu, B.: GMC: graph-based multi-view clustering. IEEE Trans. Knowl. Data Eng. **32**(6), 1116–1129 (2020)
16. Xie, Y., Gong, M., Wang, S., Yu, B.: Community discovery in networks with deep sparse filtering. Pattern Recognit. **81**, 50–59 (2018)
17. Yang, L., Cao, X., Meng, D.: A unified semi-supervised community detection framework using latent space graph regularization. IEEE Trans. Cybern. **45**(11), 2585–2598 (2015)

Named Entity Recognition Based on Reinforcement Learning and Adversarial Training

Shi Peng, Yong Zhang(✉), Yuanfang Yu, Haoyang Zuo, and Kai Zhang

Hubei Provincial Key Laboratory of Artificial Intelligence and Smart Learning, Computer School, National Language Resources Monitoring and Research Center for Network Media, Central China Normal University, Wuhan, People's Republic of China
{pengshi,zhy740645146,yuyuanfang}@mails.ccnu.edu.cn, {ychang, zhangkai}@ccnu.edu.cn

Abstract. In this paper, we propose a new model that combines reinforcement learning and adversarial training to exploit the data generated by distant supervision for named entity recognition. Our model can not only reduce the influence of noise in generated data, but also find more informative instances for training. In the pre-training stage of the model, in order to make full use of the data generated by distant supervision, we use reinforcement learning to select reliable instances to pre-train a classifier. In the training stage of the model, we introduce the adversarial training mechanism, which can not only find more reliable instances to enhance the ability of the classifier, but also use noise data to improve the ability of the model to resist noise. To evaluate the performance of the model, we conduct experiments on two public datasets, Species800 dataset in biology and EC dataset in e-commerce domain. The experimental results show that in Species800 dataset, the F1 score of our model is 1.68% higher than that of baseline, and in EC dataset, the F1 score of our model is 6.32% higher than that of baseline. Compared to the state of art models, our model can achieve comparable performance just using word2vec embedding.

Keywords: Distant supervision · Reinforcement learning · Adversarial training · Named entity recognition · Partial annotation

1 Introduction

Named Entity Recognition (NER) aims at identifying named entities in the given text, which is an important component in information extraction task [1–3, 25]. Previously, Hidden Markov Models (HMM) and Conditional Random Fields (CRF) are usually used for named entity recognition. In recent years, many models based on neural network have been designed for this task. For example, BiLSTM is used to encode words, and then CRF is adopted to determine the final tag for each word in the sentence [1, 4]. As we all know, NER needs large amount of annotated data for training. Meanwhile, in some specific fields, the human-annotated data is relatively small, which affects the accuracy of the

H. Qiu et al. (Eds.): KSEM 2021, LNAI 12815, pp. 191–202, 2021.
https://doi.org/10.1007/978-3-030-82136-4_16

model. Considering that distant supervision is already widely used in some tasks, such as relation extraction [5, 6] and entity recognition [7], we can apply distant supervision to automatically generate large amount of training data, which makes human-cost very low.

However, distant supervision inevitably brings some problems. Firstly, distant supervision may produce noisy data, which can have a negative effect on the model. Secondly, there are a lot of incomplete annotated data in the auto-labeled data, and the standard CRF can't learn the incomplete annotated data well.

Inspired by the research of Wang et al. [8], we decide to build a large-scale dataset which can provide more instances to improve the performance of NER. According to their research, we propose an entity-based latent instance discovery strategy. It can be described that if a given word in a sentence is marked as an entity, then this word can be marked as an entity of the same type if it appears in other sentences.

Inspired by the researches of Yang et al. in 2018, Jun et al. in 2018 and Wang et al. in 2019 [6, 8, 9], we propose a method that combines reinforcement learning and adversarial training, which can not only obtain informative instances from candidate set, but also filter out the noise instances for NER as shown as Fig. 1. Our model is mainly divided into two parts. The left part adopts the adversarial mechanism, and the right part uses reinforcement learning to pre-train discriminator. In order to make full use of the existing data, we use small-scale data and auto-labeled data to pre-train discriminator. However, auto-labeled data has the following problems: incomplete annotation and noisy annotation [9]. For incomplete annotation problem, we adopt CRF-PA model to learn partial annotations [9, 10], and for noisy annotation problem, we exploit reinforcement learning to select positive instance for training [6]. So that discriminator has a certain ability to identify the corresponding entity type. For reinforcement learning, the instance selector selects sentences according to the action, and then uses the selected sentences to train discriminator, which in turn generates a reward for updating the relevant parameters of the policy function.

After the pre-training, we will conduct the adversarial training. Excessive noise in the automatically labeled data will affect the effect of reinforcement learning, then, we will use adversarial training to select some relatively reliable instances from the unreliable set to construct a new unreliable set. Before the adversarial training, we divide the data set into two parts: reliable set and unreliable set. The function of discriminator is to determine whether the instance picked by generator is informative and annotated correctly. Generator's role is to confuse discriminator by selecting data form unreliable set, thus inducing discriminator to make wrong judgments. After the adversarial training starts, discriminator selects data from reliable set and unreliable set respectively for training, generator uses the data from the unreliable set for training, and then selects instances from the unreliable set to confuse discriminator. With the progress of training, generator should try its best to pick out large number of noise instances to confuse discriminator, so as to improve discriminator's ability to distinguish noise data, and at same time, discriminator can also promote generator to select more informative instances. When the two components reached the balance, the accuracy and noise-resolving ability of discriminator were significantly enhanced, and the capability of generator selection of informative instances was also improved. At this point, the relatively reliable instances will also be selected out of unreliable set, and we will use these instances to construct a new unreliable set. Finally, we will use reinforcement learning to retrain a classifier discriminator on reliable set and new unreliable set.

In summary, our contribution in this paper is that we propose a novel method combining reinforcement learning with adversarial training for NER for the first time. In this model, CRF-PA model is used to learn the partial annotation data, which can not only reduce the influence of noise data generated by remote supervision, but also can find more informative instances to train the model. At the same time, we also propose the entity-based latent instance discovery strategy, which has simple rules and can quickly help us construct more instances from raw text. Experimental results show that the method performs well.

In Sect. 2, we will discuss related works on named entity recognition. Next, we will discuss our model in Sect. 3. We will present the results of our experiment in Sect. 4. And finally, we will make a summary of the article and discuss the future work in Sect. 5.

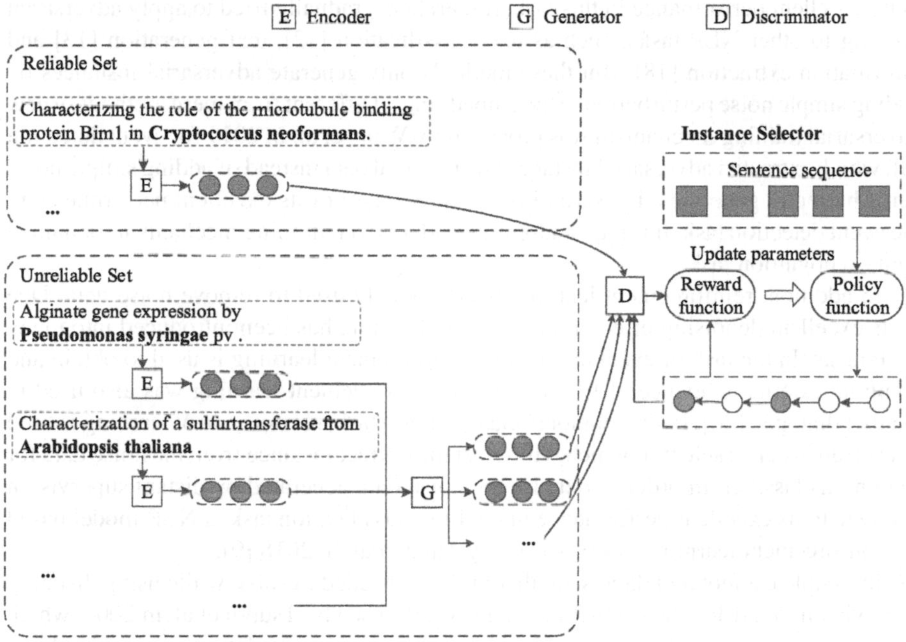

Fig. 1. The overall structure of the model

2 Related Work

Named entity recognition task has attracted a lot of attention in recent years, which is a key component of many other NLP tasks. Previously, Hidden Markov Models (HMM) and Conditional Random Fields (CRF) are the traditional models for named entity recognition tasks [11, 16], where some complex feature functions should be provided for different scenarios. With the rapid development of neural network, many neural network based models have been designed to deal with the named entity recognition since the neural network has powerful ability of feature extraction. For example, BiLSTM-CRF [1, 4] have become the well-known model for NER and performs better than HMM and CRF.

Although these models work well, they require a lot of manually annotated data to train them. In some specific areas, the model is difficult to perform well due to the lack of manually annotated data. To alleviate the problem, distant supervision has been introduced to construct large-scale training data. In other tasks, such as relation extraction [5, 6], distant supervision has achieved good results. Distant supervision has also been used for named entity recognition task [7], and achieved good results. However, due to the lack of effective denoising mechanism, the data generated by distant supervision may have noise, which will affect the accuracy of the model. Researchers come up with many ways to solve this problem, such as reinforcement learning and adversarial training. Many researchers have tried to apply the Adversarial training mechanism to deep learning [22–24]. Adversarial training was first applied to the task of image classification [17]. Due to its excellent performance in this task, researchers gradually tried to apply adversarial training to other NLP tasks, such as text classification [12], text generation [13] and information extraction [18]. But these methods only generate adversarial instances by adding simple noise perturbation to the embeddings. Different from these methods, a new adversarial training mechanism was proposed by Wang et al. in 2019 for event detection [8], which extracted adversarial instances from actual data instead of adding simple noise perturbation to generate adversarial instances. Because of its excellent performance in the event detection task, this paper adopts this adversarial training mechanism for named entity recognition task.

In addition, reinforcement learning is also widely used to remove noise data. Due to its excellent denoising effect, reinforcement learning has been introduced into many NLP tasks. In the task of event extraction, reinforcement learning is used to obtain and combine external evidence [19]. Later, Deep reinforcement learning was also used in chatbot dialogue [20]. In the relational classification task, reinforcement learning is used to train an instance selector, which will select the correct instance from the noise data for training a classifier, in order to denoise the noise data generated by distant supervision [6]. Due to its excellent performance in relation classification task, a NER model based on reinforcement learning was proposed by Yang et al. in 2018 [9].

Incomplete annotated data is another problem needed to solve while using distantly supervision for NER. The CRF-PA model was proposed by Tsuboi et al. in 2008, which extends the standard CRF model and can be learned using incomplete annotated data [10]. Since distant supervision will produce incomplete annotated data, researchers decide to use CRF-PA model to learn incomplete annotated data in NER task [9].

So in this paper we propose a novel model for NER, where combine confrontation training and reinforcement learning are used to enhance the performance of the model, and CRF-PA model is adopted to learn partial labeled data.

3 Methodology

In this section, we will describe the overall framework of our model in detail. The right part of Fig. 1 is pre-training discriminator based on reinforcement learning, and the main module of this part is instance selector. Assuming that each input sentence is x_{ii}, each sentence corresponds to an action a_i. The value of the policy function is calculated from action a_i and state $s_{i.}$ The instance selector decides whether to pick x_i to train discriminator based on the value of a_i. A reward is generated to update the relevant parameters of the policy function after training with x_i.

In the left part of Fig. 1, we will introduce adversarial training mechanism. First, we will divide the dataset into two parts: reliable set and unreliable set. Then, we use the partitioned dataset for adversarial training. In the training process, generator uses instances in the unreliable set to train its ability to select confusing instances, while discriminator uses data in the reliable set to train its classification ability and uses instances recommended by generator to train its ability to resist noise. When the training is balanced, discriminator will score all the instances in the unreliable set. By setting a threshold, we pick out those informative instances whose scores are higher than the threshold to construct a new unreliable set.

The overall training process is as follows. We first construct a large candidate set based on the entity-based latent instance discovery strategy. We call the data labeled with small scale as reliable set R and the candidate set as unreliable set U. Then we use reinforcement learning to pre-train a discriminator on R and U. Since too much noise data in U will affect the effect of reinforcement learning, we will carry out adversarial training. When the adversarial training is balanced, the instances recommended by generator from U that discriminator considers to be reliable will be selected. We use these selected instances to construct a new unreliable set, and finally retrain a classifier discriminator by reinforcement learning on R and new U.

3.1 Entity-Based Latent Instance Discovery Strategy

To make full use of untagged raw data, we propose an instance discovery strategy. We assume that if a given word in a sentence is marked as an entity, then this word can be marked as an entity of the same type if it appears in other sentences. For example, there is a species named '*human cytomegalovirus*' in the text '*Identification of binary interactions between human cytomegalovirus virion proteins*'. So all other sentences containing the phrase '*human cytomegalovirus*' will be selected as a candidate instance and the phrase will be marked as a species.

3.2 Instance Encoder

In this paper, we use BiLSTM as an instance encoder, whose function is to transform the input instances into corresponding embedding. After instance x passes through BiLSTM, each character c corresponds to an output feature h_t. h_t is concatenated by $\overrightarrow{h_t}$ and $\overleftarrow{h_t}$, which respectively represent left and right context.

All the tags on each position t correspond to a score. To calculate this score, we add an MLP layer after the Instance Encoder, and we mark the score as o_t:

$$
\begin{aligned}
h_t^{\mathrm{mlp}_1} &= W^{\mathrm{mlp}_1} h_t + b^{\mathrm{mlp}_1} \\
o_t &= W^{\mathrm{mlp}_2} h_t^{\mathrm{mlp}_1} + b^{\mathrm{mlp}_2}
\end{aligned}
\tag{1}
$$

In the above formula, W^{mlp_1}, W^{mlp_2}, b^{mlp_1} and b^{mlp_2} are the parameters.

3.3 Discriminator

When giving an instance x, its corresponding tag sequence is y, and the function of discriminator is to judge whether the given instance expresses its corresponding tag sequence. Similar to CRF, we use conditional probability to express the probability that a given instance x corresponds to a tag sequence y. We implement discriminator according to the following formula:

$$p(y|x) = \frac{e^{score(x,y)}}{\sum_{\tilde{y}\in Y_x} e^{(x,\tilde{y})}}$$
$$score(x, y) = \sum_{t=0}^{n} \left(o_{t,y_t} + T_{y_{t-1},y_t}\right) \tag{2}$$

In the above formula, we denote the transmission score from y_{t-1} to y_t as T_{y_{t-1},y_t}, and denote Y_x for all possible tag sequences of instance x.

Similar to paper of Wang et al., in 2019, a well-trained discriminator will give high scores to data from a reliable set and low scores to data from an unreliable set [8]. Therefore, we define the loss function of discriminator as follows:

$$L_D = -\sum_{x\in R} \frac{1}{R} \log(p(y|x)) - \sum_{x\in U} P_u(x)\log(1 - p(y|x)) \tag{3}$$

In the above formula, R is the reliable set and U is the unreliable set.

3.4 Generator

The purpose of generator is to confuse discriminator by selecting data from an unreliable set, thus tricking discriminator into making a wrong judgment. Generator calculates a confusion score for all instances of the unreliable set, which we call the confusing probability P_U. Generator selects instances from unreliable sets by optimizing P_U. Hence, we use the following formula to calculate P_U:

$$f(x) = W \cdot x + b$$
$$p_U(x) = \frac{e^{f(x)}}{\sum_{x\in U} e^{f(x)}} \tag{4}$$

In the above formula, W and b are parameters.

For the instance in the unreliable set, generator will select the instance in the unreliable set to train discriminator, and discriminator will calculate a score for each instance of the selected instance. The higher the score is, the more confusing the instance is, so it is easier to induce discriminator to make a wrong judgment. Generator can optimize P_U to pick out the more deceptive instances from the unreliable set. Therefore, we define the loss function of generator as follows:

$$L_G = -\sum_{x\in U} p_U(x) log(p(y|x)) \tag{5}$$

In the above formula, $p(y|x)$ is computed by discriminator.

3.5 Instance Selector

Before reinforcement learning, we first merge the data from the reliable set and the data from the unreliable set into set C. The instance selector then decides whether to select an instance from C based on the value of the action. It is worth noting that data from the reliable set in C is selected by default. At the end of each training round, discriminator will generate a reward to generator, and generator will update relevant parameters according to this reward.

State. Following the paper of Yang et al. in 2018, state represents the current instance and its corresponding label sequences. We represent State as a vector S_t, which contains the following information: (1) The vector representation of the current sentence, which we use the output of BiLSTM to represent this vector. (2) The score calculated from the output of the MLP layer [9].

Policy Function. The action a_t has two values, 0 and 1. 0 indicates that the current instance is not selected. In contrast, 1 means to select the current instance. We sample the value of a_t by A_θ, where θ is the parameter of MLP layer. Therefore, we adopt a logistic function as the policy function [9]:

$$A_\theta(s_t, \alpha_t) = \alpha_t\sigma(W^*s_t + b) + (1 - \alpha_t)(1 - \sigma(W^*s_t + b)) \quad (6)$$

In the above formula, S_t is the State vector and σ is sigmoid function.

Reward. We use reward to judge whether the sentence selected by the instance selector is of high quality, that is, whether the sentence can promote the training of discriminator. We believe that after the instance selector completes the instance selection, the model will get a final reward. Before this, the reward corresponding to each action is zero. For a batch, it is composed of two parts of data, which are respectively: instance $\tilde{R}$ in the reliable set and instance $\tilde{U}$ in the unreliable set. Noting that all instances in $\tilde{R}$ are selected by default. Reward can be calculated by the following formula:

$$r = \frac{1}{\left|\tilde{U}_s\right| + \left|\tilde{R}\right|}\left(\sum\nolimits_{x_j, z\in\tilde{U}_s} \log p(z|x_j) + \sum\nolimits_{x_k, y\in\tilde{R}} logp(y|x_k)\right) \quad (7)$$

In the above formula, $\tilde{U}_s$ represents the instances selected from $\tilde{U}$.

As mentioned above, in the process of pre-training discriminator, in order to solve incomplete annotation problem, we use the CRF-PA model to calculate the conditional probability of the instance in $\tilde{U}_s$. Instead of treating them as non-entities, we consider that in an instance of auto-labeled, characters that are not matched can be any other appropriate label. Therefore, we believe that the automatically labeled data has a set of appropriate label sequences z. We define the conditional probability of an instance in $\tilde{U}_s$ to be the sum of the conditional probabilities of all the label sequences in z. The conditional probabilities of the instances in $\tilde{U}_s$ are as follows:

$$p(z|x) = \sum\nolimits_{\tilde{y}} p(\tilde{y}|x) = \frac{\sum_{\tilde{y}\in z} e^{score(x,\tilde{y})}}{\sum_{\tilde{y}\in Yx} e^{(x,\tilde{y})}} \quad (8)$$

Selector Training. Following the paper of Yang et al. in 2018, we use the following formula to calculate the gradient and update the instance selector [9]:

$$\theta = \theta + \partial \sum_{t=1}^{|\tilde{U}|} r(\alpha_t)\nabla_\theta logA_\theta(s_t, \alpha_t) \tag{9}$$

4 Experiment

4.1 Datasets

In order to evaluate the effect of our model, we conducted experiments on Species800 corpus and EC corpus respectively.

Species800 Corpus. This corpus is associated with biological species and contains 800 abstracts from PubMed. In order to make the corpus more diverse, the researchers extracted abstracts from eight categories, with about 100 abstracts from each category. The training set of the corpus contains 5733 sentences, the development set contains 830 sentences, and the test set contains 1630 sentences. In addition, in order to construct a large candidate set, we randomly selected 15,000 sentences from PubMed to construct the candidate set.

EC Corpus. This corpus is a Chinese dataset of e-commerce. The training set of the corpus contains 1200 sentences, the development set contains 400 sentences, and the test set contains 800 sentences. We use the 2500 sentences provided by Yang et al. in 2018 as the raw data [9].

4.2 Settings

In order to evaluate the effect of this experiment, we use Precision (P), Recall (R) and F1 score as the evaluation criteria.

Our model's hyper-parameters are set as follows. For reinforcement learning, our Settings are the same as those of paper of Yang et al. in 2018 [9]. For the adversarial training, we set the learning rate of Discriminator and Generator as $1*10^{-3}$, and the other Settings are basically the same as that the paper of Wang et al. in 2019 [8]. In this experiment, we use pre-trained word vectors to initialize the embedding layer of the BiLSTM. We use a 200-dimensional word vector, which is trained using PubMed abstracts, all PubMed Central (PMC) articles and English Wikipedia.

4.3 Results

Table 1 shows the results of the model on the Species800 dataset. NER represents BiLSTM model, PA represents CRF-PA model, ADV represents adversarial training, and RL represents reinforcement learning. The results for lines 3 to 7 are reported by Lee et al. in 2020 [21]. As shown in Table 1, NER+PA+RL+ADV performed better than the baseline model BiLSTM-CRF, with the value of F1 increased by about 1.68%.

Meanwhile, this model performed better than Bert, BioBERT v1.0(+PubMed), BioBERT v1.0 (+PMC) and BioBERT v1.1 (+PubMed +PMC), with the value of F1 increased by 2.61%,1.16%,1.15% and 0.18%, respectively. Even compared to the state of art model BioBERT V1.0 (+PubMed +PMC), our mode still can achieve a comparable performance and the F1 value is decreased by 1.07%, but the Precision increased by about 1.62%. It should be noted that BioBERT V1.0 (+PubMed +PMC) uses a large number of biomedical texts for retraining of BERT specially, and on the contrast our model just uses the word2vec as embedding, which need much less memory.

Table 1. Results on the Species800 dataset. The result of italics are reported by Lee et al. in 2020 [21]

Model	Training data	Precision (%)	Recall (%)	F1 score (%)
BiLSTM-CRF	R	75.95	69.47	72.56
BERT(wiki+Books)	R	69.35	74.05	71.63
BioBERT v1.0(+PubMed)	R	70.60	75.75	73.08
BioBERT v1.0(+PMC)	R	71.54	74.71	73.09
BioBERT v1.1(+PubMed +PMC)	R	72.80	75.36	74.06
BioBERT v1.0(PubMed +PMC)	R	72.84	77.97	**75.31**
NER+PA	R+U	66.03	72.40	69.07
NER+PA+ADV	R+U	72.69	73.53	73.10
NER+PA+RL	R+U	71.63	72.75	72.19
NER+PA+RL+ADV	R+U	74.46	74.15	74.24

By comparing NER+PA and NER+PA+ADV, it can be seen that the value of F1 increases by 4.03% when the adversarial training is added in the experiment, which means that the model has selected more informative instances for training after the adversarial training. By comparing NER+PA and NER+PA+RL, the value of F1 increases by 3.10% when reinforcement learning is added in the experiment, which means that adding reinforcement learning in the experiment can eliminate the influence of noise more effectively and make more full use of incomplete annotated instances. When we add reinforcement learning and adversarial training in the experiment at the same time, the Precision is improved by 8.43%, 1.75% for recall and 5.17% for F1. It can be found that both adversarial training and reinforcement learning can improve the performance respectively. However, when adversarial training and reinforcement learning are added in our model together, the performance is improved significantly, where we can not only pick out more informative instances through adversarial training, but also eliminate the influence of noise on them, so as to improve the effect of the model.

Table 2 shows the results of the models on the EC dataset. The results of BiLSTM-CRF and NER+PA+RL are reported by Yang et al. in 2018 [11]. As can be seen from the Table 2, compared with baseline model BiLSTM-CRF, NER+PA+RL+ADV model has the greatest improvement, with the value of F1 increased by 6.32%. It can be found that the introduction of adversarial training and reinforcement learning can not only eliminate the influence of noise data and incomplete annotated data, but also pick out more informative instances to promote the training of the model. In addition, F value of NER+PA+ADV and NER+PA+RL are increased by 4.6% and 2.26%, respectively, compared to the baseline model BILSTM-CRF.

Table 2. Results on the EC dataset.

Model	Training data	Precision (%)	Recall (%)	F1 score (%)
BiLSTM-CRF	R	59.93	58.46	59.19
NER+PA	R+U	59.63	60.82	60.08
NER+PA+ADV	R+U	62.08	65.61	63.79
NER+PA+RL	R+U	61.57	61.33	61.45
NER+PA+RL+ADV	R+U	64.93	66.09	**65.51**

In order to explore the influence of different sizes of reliable data and unreliable data on the model, we randomly selected 25%, 50% and 75% sentences from the reliable set and unreliable set respectively for training. Table 3 shows the results of the model with different sizes of reliable data and unreliable data on EC dataset. From the Table 3, we can see that the performance of NER+PA+RL+ADV is better than that of baseline system at different sizes of data, which shows 5.67% F1 improvement on 25%, 3.24% F1 improvement on 50% and 2.55% F1 improvement on 75%, respectively. Although performance improved on reliable data of different sizes, the improvement was particularly significant on 25%, with the value of F1 increasing by 5.67%. This shows that even if we use less reliable data, we can still make relatively large improvements. This is because the discriminator can improve its classification ability by picking out reliable instances from the unreliable set.

Table 3. Results of different percentages of training data on the species800 dataset.

Model	Training data	Precision (%)	Recall (%)	F1 score (%)
BILSTM-CRF	25%R	69.96	49.07	57.68
NER+P+RL+ADV	25%R+25% U	59.86	67.28	63.35
BILSTM-CRF	50%R	71.66	65.73	68.57
NER+PA+RL+ADV	50%R+50% U	72.57	71.06	71.81
BILSTM-CRF	75%R	70.84	68.67	69.74
NER+PA+RL+ADV	75%R+75% U	73.71	70.93	72.29
BILSTM-CRF	100%R	75.95	69.47	72.56
NER+PA+RL+ADV	100%R+100% U	74.46	74.15	74.24

5 Conclusion and Future Work

This paper presents a new method to solve the noise problem of distant supervision. For the first time, we combined reinforcement learning with adversarial training and applied it to NER tasks. We adopted CRF-PA model to learn incomplete annotated data generated by distant supervision, and we introduced reinforcement learning to reduce the impression of noise data on the model, and at the same time added adversarial training mechanism to select more informative instances from U for training. In addition, we also propose an entity-based latent instance discovery strategy, which is simpler and faster to construct candidate sets from raw text compared to other complex methods. We conducted experiments on two datasets in different domains, and the experimental results show that the performance of our model is better than the comparison model.

For future research, we will refine our model by following directions: (1) For the embedding, we will try to construct more effective vector representation of words through pre training for specific domain like BioBERT. (2) As a key component in our model, the instance selector will be sophisticated designed in the future since it is critical for the quality of the generated data.

Acknowledgement. We thank our anonymous reviewers for their work. This work was supported by National Natural Science Foundation of China (No.61977032, No.62077018), the 13th five-year plan of the State Language Commission (ZDI135-99) and the Fundamental Research Funds for the Central Universities (CCNU20CG008).

References

1. Lample, G., Ballesteros, M., Subramanian, S., et al.: Neural architectures for named entity recognition. In: Proceedings of NAACL-HLT, pp. 260–270 (2016)
2. Peters, M.E., et al.: Deep contextualized word representations. In: Proceedings of NAACL-HLT (2018)
3. Liu, L., Shang, J., Ren, X., et al.: Empower sequence labeling with task-aware neural language model. In: Proceedings of the AAAI Conference on Artificial Intelligence, vol. 32(1) (2018)
4. Huang, Z., Xu, W., Yu, K.: Bidirectional LSTM-CRF models for sequence tagging. arXiv preprint: arXiv:1508.01991 (2015)
5. Mintz, M., Bills, S., Snow, R., et al.: Distant supervision for relation extraction without labeled data. In: ACL/IJCNLP (2009)
6. Feng, J., Huang, M., Zhao, L., et al.: Reinforcement learning for relation classification from noisy data. In: Thirty-Second AAAI Conference on Artificial Intelligence (2018)
7. Shang, J., Liu, L., Ren, X., et al.: Learning named entity tagger using domain-specific dictionary. In: EMNLP (2018)
8. Wang, X., Han, X., Liu, Z., et al.: Adversarial training for weakly supervised event detection. In: Proceedings of NAACL-HLT, pp. 998–1008 (2019)
9. Yang, Y., Chen, W., Li, Z., et al.: Distantly supervised ner with partial annotation learning and reinforcement learning. In: Proceedings of the 27th International Conference on Computational Linguistics, pp. 2159–2169 (2018)
10. Tsuboi, Y., Kashima, H., Mori, S., et al.: Training conditional random fields using incomplete annotations. In: Proceedings of the 22nd International Conference on Computational Linguistics (Coling 2008), pp. 897–904 (2008)

11. Ratinov, L., Roth, D.: Design challenges and misconceptions in named entity recognition. In: Proceedings of the Thirteenth Conference on Computational Natural Language Learning (CoNLL-2009), pp. 147–155 (2009)
12. Miyato, T., Maeda, S., Koyama, M., et al.: Distributional smoothing with virtual adversarial training.
13. Xie, Z., Wang, S.I., Li, J., et al.: Data noising as smoothing in neural network language models. arXiv preprint: arXiv:1703.02573 (2017)
14. Sharma, S., Daniel, R., Jr.: BioFLAIR: pretrained pooled contextualized embeddings for biomedical sequence labeling tasks. arXiv preprint: arXiv:1908.05760 (2019)
15. Giorgi, J.M., Bader, G.D.: Towards reliable named entity recognition in the biomedical domain. Bioinformatics **36**(1), 280–286 (2020)
16. Passos, A., Kumar, V., McCallum, A.: Lexicon infused phrase embeddings for named entity resolution. In: CoNLL-2014, p. 78 (2014)
17. Goodfellow, I.J., Shlens, J., Szegedy, C.: Explaining and harnessing adversarial examples. Stat **1050**, 20 (2015)
18. Hong, Y., Zhou, W., Zhang, J., et al.: Self-regulation: employing a generative adversarial network to improve event detection. In: Proceedings of the 56th Annual Meeting of the Association for Computational Linguistics (Volume 1: Long Papers), pp. 515–526 (2018)
19. Narasimhan, K., Yala, A., Barzilay, R.: Improving information extraction by acquiring external evidence with reinforcement learning. In: EMNLP (2016)
20. Li, J., Monroe, W., Ritter, A., et al.: Deep reinforcement learning for dialogue generation. arXiv preprint: arXiv:1606.01541 (2016)
21. Lee, J., Yoon, W., Kim, S., et al.: BioBERT: a pre-trained biomedical language representation model for biomedical text mining. Bioinformatics **36**(4), 1234–1240 (2020)
22. Qiu, H., Dong, T., Zhang, T., et al.: Adversarial attacks against network intrusion detection in IoT systems. IEEE Internet Things J. **8**, 10327–10335 (2020)
23. Li, Y., Song, Y., Jia, L., et al.: Intelligent fault diagnosis by fusing domain adversarial training and maximum mean discrepancy via ensemble learning. IEEE Trans. Ind. Inf. **17**, 2833–2841 (2020)
24. Zeng, Y., Qiu, H., Memmi, G., Qiu, M.: A data augmentation-based defense method against adversarial attacks in neural networks. In: Qiu, M. (ed.) ICA3PP 2020. LNCS, vol. 12453, pp. 274–289. Springer, Cham (2020). https://doi.org/10.1007/978-3-030-60239-0_19
25. Ma, X., Hovy, E.: End-to-end sequence labeling via bi-directional LSTM-CNNs-CRF. In: Proceedings of the 54th Annual Meeting of the Association for Computational Linguistics (Volume 1: Long Papers), pp. 1064–1074 (2016)

Improved Partitioning Graph Embedding Framework for Small Cluster

Ding Sun[1], Zhen Huang[1,2(✉)], Dongsheng Li[1,2], Xiangyu Ye[1], and Yilin Wang[1]

[1] National University of Defense Technology, Changsha 410073, Hunan, China
{sunding,huangzhen,dsli,xyye,wangyilin14}@nudt.edu.cn
[2] National Key Laboratory of Parallel and Distributed Processing, Changsha, China

Abstract. Graph embedding is a crucial method to produce node features that can be used for various machine learning tasks. Because of the large number of embedded parameters in large graphs, a single machine cannot load the entire graph into GPUs at once, so a partitioning strategy is required. However, there are some problems with partitioning strategies. Firstly, partitioning introduces data I/O and processing overhead, which increases training time, especially on the cluster with a small number of sites. Secondly, partitioning can affect the performance of the model. For multi-relation graphs, this effect is often negative. To address these problems, we propose the training pipeline and random partitions recombination methods. The training pipeline can reduce the time overhead by masking data loading time to GPU computation, and partitions recombination can effectively improve multi-relation model performance. We conducted experiments on multi-relation graphs and social networks, and the results show that both methods are effective.

Keywords: Graph embedding · Knowledge graphs · Partitioning graph framework · GPU · Distributed graph algorithms

1 Introduction

In recent years, the study of graph-structured data has attracted a great deal of attention. Graph-structured data is a representation of relations between entities in the real world. Two essential types of graph-structured data are network data and knowledge graph(KG). Network data has been widely used in various fields such as social networks [11], citation networks [15], e-commerce [17], and knowledge graphs have been widely used for structured search, question answering [7]. However, it is difficult to work with graph-structured data directly. Hence, an essential technique for graph-structured data is graph embedding. The graph embedding technique creates vector representations for each node in a graph. The distance between these vectors predicts the occurrence of edges in the graph. Graph embedding has proven to be a valuable feature for downstream tasks [2].

Currently, there are many effective graph embedding methods for graph-structured data [1,13,16,18]. However, for large size graph data, training its

H. Qiu et al. (Eds.): KSEM 2021, LNAI 12815, pp. 203–215, 2021.
https://doi.org/10.1007/978-3-030-82136-4_17

embedding is still a difficult task. A key factor limiting the training of large graphs is memory. For example, a graph with 2 billion nodes and an embedding dimension of 100 would require 800G of memory to store the embeddings. During training, the relational embeddings, the edge data, and the embeddings' gradients also need to be stored, so much more than 800G of memory is required. Large-scale models are often trained using GPUs, and modern GPUs usually have 12 GB or 16 GB capacity, which is not enough for large graph sizes [4,12,20].

There are currently two main approaches to scale graph embedding methods to large graphs. One is multi-level methods [3,10], which reduce the size of the graph by coarsening it and then train the embedding on the coarsened graph. However, multi-level methods suffer from performance loss compared to training graph embeddings on the original graph. Moreover, such methods do not support distributed training and cannot be applied to huge graphs. Another approach is the partitioning methods [9,21], which divides all nodes into non-overlapping partitions so that the whole graph is divided into different subgraphs, and then different subgraphs are trained. The partitioning supports models that are too large to fit in GPU memory on a single machine and allows for the model's distributed training.

However, there are some problems with the partitioning method. Firstly, although partitioning reduces memory consumption, it requires additional data loading overheads because training has to switch between multiple subgraphs. When the number of machines is small, the extra overhead caused by partitioning is more pronounced because the gains from parallelism are reduced. Secondly, we find that for multi-relation graph embedding models, partitioning causes a degradation in model performance. We found in our experiments that when the number of partitions was increased from 1 to 4, the MRR dropped by 6% on FB15K.

To solve these problems, we propose a training pipeline and partition recombination methods based on the PBG(Pytorch BigGraph) framework [9]. We divide the algorithm into two parallel parts in the training pipeline, loading the data required for the next step in memory while performing the GPU computation. In the partitions recombination method, we split the whole graph into more sub-partitions and buckets and recombine the sub-partitions into larger granularity partitions randomly at each epoch, thus increasing the randomness of the training data.

Our contributions in this paper can be summarized as follows:

(1) We implement a pipelined distributed partition training framework that accelerates the partitioning train process.
(2) We propose a random partitions recombination method to address the performance degradation of multi-relation models due to partitioning.

The rest of the paper is organized as follows: Sect. 2 reviews existing graph embedding models and the partitioning schemes. Section 3 introduces our proposed training pipeline and random partitions recombination methods in detail. In Sect. 4, we show the experimental results, and we conclude this paper in Sect. 5.

2 Related Work

2.1 Graph Embedding Models

The goal of graph embedding is to project all nodes (entities) and relations into a low-dimensional space while preserving the semantic information represented by all edges. There are several different graph embedding methods. For node embedding of homogeneous graphs such as social networks, a common approach is the random walk based approach. This kind of models include DeepWalk [13], node2vec [5], etc. For heterogeneous graphs such as multi-relation graphs, the main graph embedding methods are geometric models and tensor decomposition models [14]. The geometric model interprets relations as geometric transformations in the latent space.This kind of methods include TransE [1],TransD [8], etc. The tensor decomposition model implicitly treats the KG as a 3D adjacency matrix, which is only partially observable due to the KG's incompleteness. Representatives of this type of method are DistMult [19], ComplE [16], etc.

In this paper, we continue the definition of the graph embedding model in PBG. PBG decomposes the entire model into a relational operator and a comparator. Relational operators transform the raw vectors of entities into a specific space, and then comparators calculate scores between pairs of given vectors in the specific space. This combination of relation operators and comparators allows PBG to train RESCAL, DistMult, TransE, and ComplEx models [9].

2.2 Partitioning Framework

For large graphs, It is difficult to apply the above model directly to obtain embeddings, and a partitioning framework is required. Entities are split into P parts. After entities are partitioned, each edge (h, r, t) is divided into a bucket based on their head(h) and tail(t) entities' partitions. Thus all edges are divided into P^2 buckets. For edge bucket (p_i, p_j), partitions i and j respectively are swapped from disk, and then the edges are loaded and subdivided among the threads for training [9].

The main partitioning frameworks are Graphvite and PBG. Graphvite is a graph embedding framework that enables multi-GPUs training at a large scale. It is a single-machine training framework. PBG is a large-scale graph embedding system, and similar to Graphvite, it is also based on a partitioning strategy. Compared to Graphvite, it supports multi-machines parallel training. Figure 1 shows the parallelization scheme of PBG. Ranks indicate the sites in the cluster, and the lock sever ensures that no simultaneously trained buckets share the same partitions, and the parameter server is used to synchronize a small number of global parameters that are not partitioned (relation embeddings).

We propose the training pipeline and random partitions recombination methods based on the PBG framework. The pipelining approach is optimized for GPU training of PBG, reducing the time overhead due to data I/O and processing and accelerating the distributed training process of graph embedding models. The partitions recombination method increases the randomness of the training data

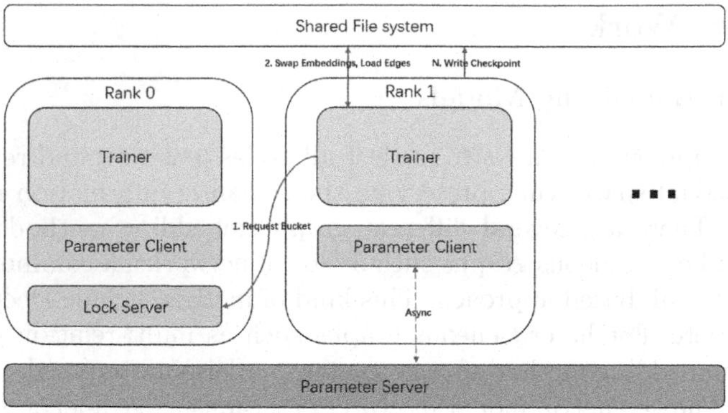

Fig. 1. The parallelization scheme of PBG.

by obtaining random combinations of buckets at different epochs, thus improving partitioned training models' performance.

3 Proposed Methodology

In this section, we first analyze the time overhead caused by partitioning and then detail the implementation of the training pipeline and random partitions recombination.

3.1 Training Pipeline

Partitioning causes each training bucket to require data loading first. Thus the total time overhead can be divided into two parts.

$$Time_{total} = Time_{load} + Time_{train} \tag{1}$$

$Time_{load}$ indicates the time overhead of data loading, and $Time_{train}$ indicates the training time overhead. Since our method only changes the data loading process and does not change the training process afterward, we analyze $Time_{load}$, and for $Time_{train}$, no further analysis is performed.

The data loading time overhead can be divided into the following components.

$$Time_{load} = Conn + EmbdIO + EdgeIO \tag{2}$$

where $Conn$ is the time to communicate with the lock server, $EmbdIO$ is the embeddings I/O time, and $EdgeIO$ is the edges transfer time. The relationship between them and the number of partitions P: $Conn = k1 * P^2/N$, $EmbdIO = k2 * P$, $EdgeIO = C$, k1, k2 and C are constants that are independent of P, N is the number of sites used. To reduce $Time_{load}$ caused by partitioning, we propose a pipeline-based approach to data loading. We divide the whole

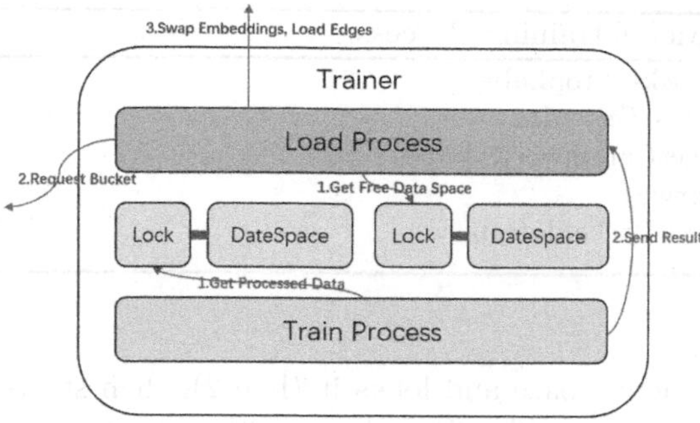

Fig. 2. The workflow of training pipeline. The green one is the data loading process, and the blue one is the training process; both processes are working on different data spaces simultaneously. (Color figure online)

procedure into two parts, the data loading part, and the model training part. We have implemented the two parts of the program in separate processes.

The data processing process is responsible for data loading, and the model training process is responsible for controlling the GPU training. As shown in Fig. 2, the two processes alternate between the two data spaces to complete the pipeline. To prevent data access conflicts, each data space has a shared lock, and only the process that acquires the lock for that data space can use the data in that data space.

Algorithm 1: Data Loading Process

Input: G, epoch, SharedLocks, StopLabel
1 BucketScheduler=getBucketScheduler(G)
2 **for** *from i = 0 to epoch-1* **do**
3   remain = StartNewEpoch(BucketScheduler)
4   **while** *remain ¿ 0* **do**
5   dataspace=getDataSpace(SharedLocks)
6   remain,bucket=getBucket(BucketScheduler)
7   LoadBucket(bucket,dataspace)
8   SetAndReleaseLocks(dataspace)
9   SaveModel()
10 StopLabel=True

Algorithm 1 presents the data loading process. The data loading process first acquires the free space and locks it (line 5), requests a bucket from the lock server (line 6), loads the relevant data from the shared file system into the free data space (swap embedding, load edge) after successful acquisition (line 7), and finally marks the parameter space as trainable and releases the lock(line 8); Algorithm 2 presents the training process. The training process first acquires

Algorithm 2: Model training Process

Input: SharedLocks, StopLabel
1 **while** *StopLabel is False* **do**
2 dataspace=getDataSpace(SharedLocks)
3 Train(dataspace)
4 SetAndReleaseLocks(dataspace)

the trainable parameter space and locks it (line 2), then starts training on the data in the parameter space (line 3) and marks the parameter space as free after training is completed (line 4).

With the pipelined approach, we can perform data loading and model training simultaneously. As shown in Fig. 3, the pipelining can eliminate the $Time_{load}$ in (1) so that we can achieve good acceleration when P is large, and N is small.

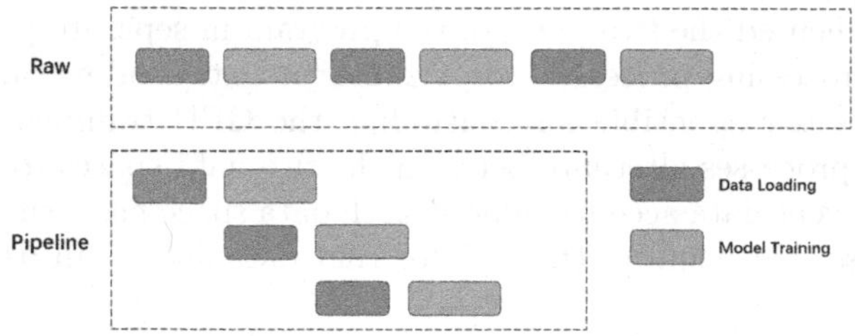

Fig. 3. Comparison of the training process of the training pipeline and the raw PBG. The blue and yellow colors represent data loading and model training, respectively. Compared to the serial approach of the raw method, the pipeline makes the two processes parallel and thus reduces the time. (Color figure online)

3.2 Random Partitions Recombination

Another problem associated with partitioned training is that partitioning can have an impact on multi-relation model performance. In the partitioned training framework, edges are no longer sampled i.i.d. but are grouped by partition. Therefore, convergence under SGD may be slower [9]. In Sect. 4.3, we test the quality of the embeddings of the PBG in two multi-relation benchmarks with different numbers of partitions and find that the quality of the embeddings decreases when the number of partitions increases. We also test the quality of the embedding on LiveJournal and find that the embeddings' quality is quite robust to partitioning in the social network.

So we propose the partitions recombination method to improve the quality of the embeddings with multi-relation graphs. First, we divide the graph at a finer granularity. For example, when setting the number of partitions to 2 and the

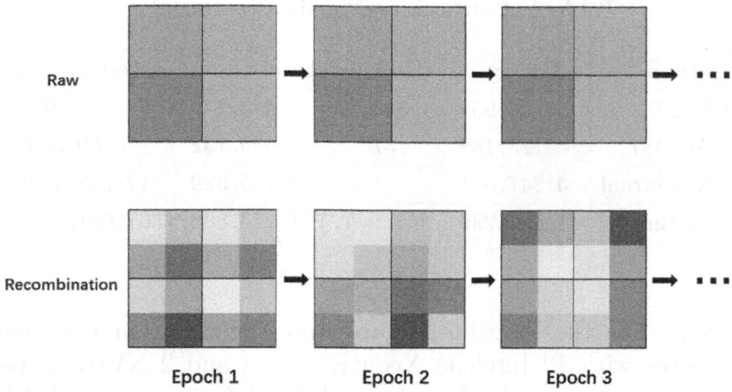

Fig. 4. Training process of the raw PBG and the random partitions recombination. The black box represents a bucket, and different colors represent different data distributions. Between epochs, each bucket of the recombination method has a different data distribution. (Color figure online)

number of sub-partitions per partition to 2, so that the whole actual graph of nodes is divided into 4 sub-partitions, and all edges form 16 sub-buckets. Then, in each epoch, we recombine the sub-partitions into 2 partitions in random order and train on the new partitions. If required, we can set a more significant number of sub-partitions.

As shown in Fig. 4, by random recombination, we obtain different distributions of buckets between epochs, increasing the randomness of the sub-datasets. Although training is still performed on separate sub-datasets for the whole model at each epoch, the distribution of these sub-datasets and the previous sub-datasets are not the same between epochs, so the model does not fit the distribution of the particular sub-datasets.

4 Experiments

In this section, we evaluate the performance of our two methods. Firstly, we test the speed-up effect of the training pipeline, and then we verify the model's performance improvement by random partitions recombination.

4.1 Experiments Settings

Datasets. For the multi-relation model performance experiments, we used the knowledge base datasets FB15K, YAGO37 [6]. FB15K is a subset of the well-known knowledge base Freebase. YAGO37 is extracted from the core facts of YAGO3 and is a new dataset proposed in recent years. In the pipeline effect experiments, we used the medium-sized social network LiveJournal and the large social network Twitter. we extracted 0.75 of the data from LiveJournal and Twitter as training data. Table 1 show the statistics of these datasets.

Table 1. Datasets used in the experiments

Dataset	#Ent	#Rel	#Train	#Test
FB15K	14,951	1,345	483,142	59,071
YAGO37	123,189	37	989,132	50,000
LiveJournal	4,847,571	1	51,745,329	17,248,444
Twitter	41,652,230	1	1,101,273,886	367,091,296

Basic Setup. For the distributed pipelining acceleration experiments, we requested 4 sites with 12 Intel(R) Xeon(R) cores and 2 NVIDIA Tesla P100 GPUs per site on a cluster. We directly used the default settings of PBG on the social network data. We set the embedding dimension to 128 and adapted the batch size to the training data size, which was 5000 for LiveJournal and 50000 for Twitter. For random partitions recombination experiment, since accuracy tests do not need to consider the effect of hardware on training speed, we used a local standalone machine for convenience. On FB15K, we used the optimal settings in PBG, i.e., embedding dimension is 400, the number of negative samples is 1000, and the regularization factor is 0.001. On YAGO37, we used the same settings. On both FB15K and YAGO37 data, we used the ComplEx model, trained for 50 epochs. We perform random initialization of the relation embeddings, which improves the performance compared to PBG.

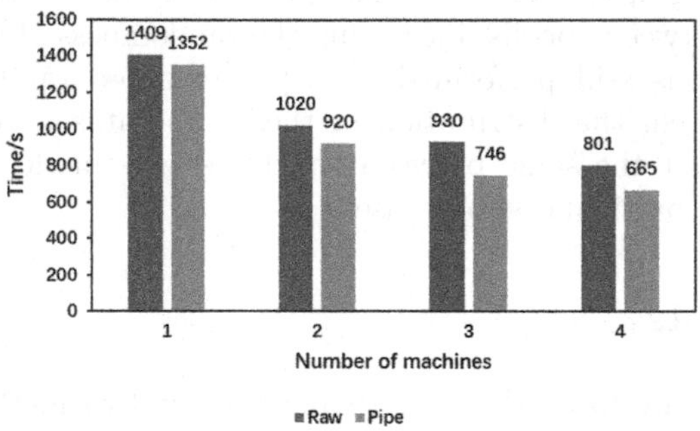

Fig. 5. When the number of machines reaches the maximum parallel number supported by the partitions, the training time on LiveJournal (epochs = 30).

4.2 Time Efficiency of Training Pipeline

Meet the Maximum Number of Parallelism. For small-sized and medium-sized graphs, where the model itself is small, the purpose of partitioning is for parallel speedup, where the number of partitions is determined by the number of machines, regardless of memory overhead. On the dataset LiveJournal, we tested the acceleration of the pipeline when the number of machines meets the maximum parallelism required for the partitioning. We use 2 and 4 machines for parallelism, respectively, where the PBG algorithm requires the graph to be partitioned into 4, 6, and 8 partitions, respectively. If the same number of machines is used, the pipelining method requires more partitions to work, so we further partition the graph into 8 and 16 partitions and then use the pipelining method for training.

The training times are shown in Fig. 5, and the pipelined approach effectively improves the training speed when the number of machines meets the maximum parallelism required for the partitions. Although the increase in the number of partitions brings about an increase in GPU scheduling time, the pipelining method can still reduce the loading time of partitions from the storage node to the training node. Therefore, pipelining still delivers significant performance gains, with speedups of 4%, 9%, 19.7%, and 16.9% for machine counts of 1, 2, 3, and 4, respectively.

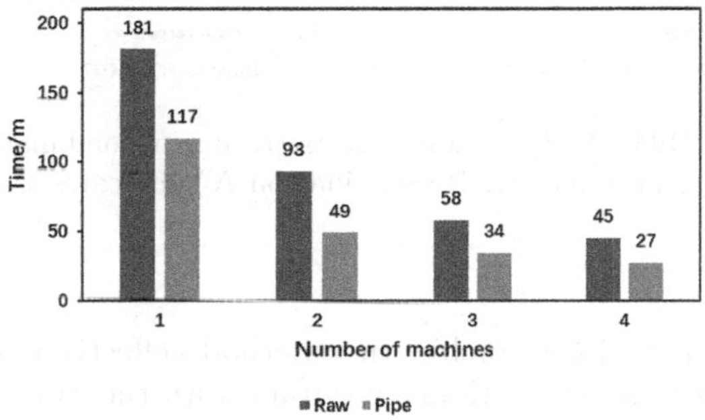

Fig. 6. When the number of machines is less than the maximum parallel number supported by the partitions, the training time on Twitter (epochs = 10).

Less Than the Maximum Number of Parallelism. In many cases, huge graphs require more partitioning due to the total amount of GPU memory on a single machine, but the number of machines does not meet the maximum parallelism required for partitioning. We tested the pipeline acceleration of partitioned training in this case on the Twitter dataset, which has 41,652,230 entities and 1,101,273,886 edges in the training set. We limited the GPU memory to 1/4 of the entire graph model, and to meet the memory limit, we partitioned it into 16 partitions of 2,603,264 entities each, resulting in 256 buckets of approximately 4,301,851 edges each, at a time when the original PBG supported a maximum of 8 machines in parallel. However, the actual number of available machines is 4. The training time is shown in Fig. 6. With a machine count of 1, 2, 3, and 4, we achieved a speed-up of 35%, 47%, 41%, and 40%, respectively. The results show that the training process can be effectively accelerated by the pipeline when the number of machines does not meet the maximum number of parallelism.

4.3 Effectiveness of the Random Partitions Recombination

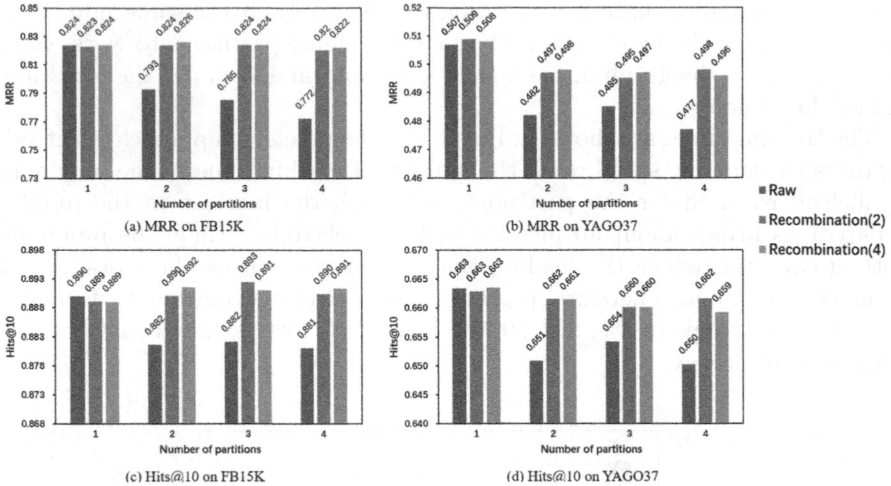

Fig. 7. MRR and Hit@10 of the random partitions recombination and the raw method on FB15K and YAGO37. Recombination(N) indicates that the number of sub-partitions is N.

To validate the partition recombination method's effectiveness, We conducted experiments to compare our method's accuracy with the raw PBG partitioning training algorithm. We use Mean Reciprocal Rank (MRR) and Hits@10 to evaluate the quality of embeddings. MRR represents the mean reciprocal rank of original triples. Hits@10 is the percentage rate of original triples ranked at the top 10 in prediction. For testing, following the approach in previous work, we use filtered ranking metrics [1]. For the filtered metrics, the edges present in the training, validation, or test sets are removed from the set of negatively sampled edges for sorting, which avoided artificially undesirable results. We used the ComplEx model, which is the most effective model in the PBG framework for multi-relation graphs. After 50 epochs of training, the test results are shown in Fig. 7. MRR decreased by about 6% on both FB15K and YAGO37, when the number of partitions was increased from 1 to 4. In contrast, when the partitions recombination method is used with 4 sub-partitions, MRR dropped by 0.3% on FB15K with almost no drop and about 1.5% on YAGO37. The results show that the embedding performance is not sensitive to the number of partitions when we adopt the random partitions recombination. In addition, we conducted experiments using different numbers of sub-partitions, and the results show that the number of sub-partitions does not significantly impact the results. Therefore, we can use a smaller number of sub-partitions during training to reduce partitions recombination time.

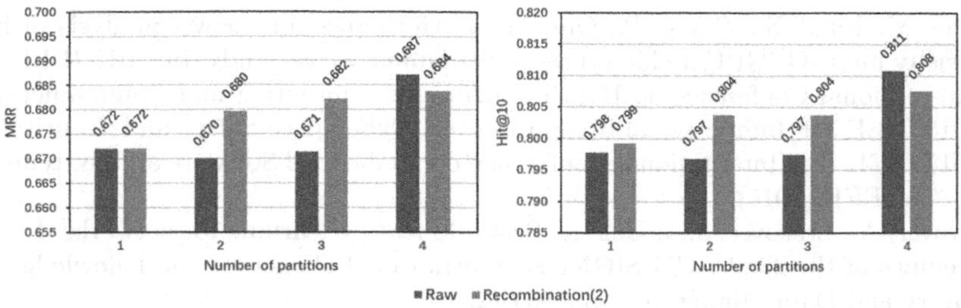

Fig. 8. MRR and Hit@10 of the random partitions recombination and the raw method on LiveJournal. Recombination(N) indicates that the number of sub-partitions is N.

We also tested the effect of partitioning on the social network. Because it is difficult to test filtered metrics on the entire test set, we randomly selected 10,000 samples from the test set for testing. As shown in Fig. 8, in contrast to multi-relation graphs, the effect of partitioning on embedding quality on social networks is small, and even better results can be achieved with a larger number of partitions.

5 Conclusion

Based on the existing partitioning framework, this paper proposed the training pipeline and random partitions recombination. We showed that the pipelining method could speed up the partitioning training of graph embeddings. In particular, the speed-up effect is more significant for the training of super-large graphs in a small cluster, where the number of machines does not meet the maximum number of parallelism of partitions. We also showed that the partitions recombination method could reduce the impact of partitioning on the multi-relation graph model and improve the quality of multi-relation graph embedding under partitioning training effectively.

Acknowledgment. This work is supported by the National Key R&D Program of China under Grants (No. 2018YFB0204300).

References

1. Bordes, A., Usunier, N., Garcia-Duran, A., Weston, J., Yakhnenko, O.: Translating embeddings for modeling multi-relational data. In: Neural Information Processing Systems (NIPS), pp. 1–9 (2013)
2. Cai, H., Zheng, V.W., Chang, K.C.C.: A comprehensive survey of graph embedding: problems, techniques, and applications. IEEE Trans. Knowl. Data Eng. **30**(9), 1616–1637 (2018)
3. Deng, C., Zhao, Z., Wang, Y., Zhang, Z., Feng, Z.: Graphzoom: a multi-level spectral approach for accurate and scalable graph embedding. arXiv preprint arXiv:1910.02370 (2019)

4. Gao, Y., Iqbal, S., Zhang, P., Qiu, M.: Performance and power analysis of high-density multi-GPGPU architectures: a preliminary case study. In: 2015 IEEE 17th International Conference on High Performance Computing and Communications, 2015 IEEE 7th International Symposium on Cyberspace Safety and Security, and 2015 IEEE 12th International Conference on Embedded Software and Systems, pp. 66–71. IEEE (2015)
5. Grover, A., Leskovec, J.: node2vec: Scalable feature learning for networks. In: Proceedings of the 22nd ACM SIGKDD International Conference on Knowledge Discovery and Data Mining, pp. 855–864 (2016)
6. Guo, S., Wang, Q., Wang, L., Wang, B., Guo, L.: Knowledge graph embedding with iterative guidance from soft rules. In: Proceedings of the AAAI Conference on Artificial Intelligence, vol. 32 (2018)
7. Huang, X., Zhang, J., Li, D., Li, P.: Knowledge graph embedding based question answering. In: Proceedings of the Twelfth ACM International Conference on Web Search and Data Mining, pp. 105–113 (2019)
8. Ji, G., He, S., Xu, L., Liu, K., Zhao, J.: Knowledge graph embedding via dynamic mapping matrix. In: Proceedings of the 53rd Annual Meeting of the Association for Computational Linguistics and the 7th International Joint Conference on Natural Language Processing, vol. 1: Long papers, pp. 687–696 (2015)
9. Lerer, A., et al.: Pytorch-biggraph: a large-scale graph embedding system. arXiv preprint arXiv:1903.12287 (2019)
10. Liang, J., Gurukar, S., Parthasarathy, S.: Mile: a multi-level framework for scalable graph embedding. arXiv preprint arXiv:1802.09612 (2018)
11. Mislove, A., Marcon, M., Gummadi, K.P., Druschel, P., Bhattacharjee, B.: Measurement and analysis of online social networks. In: Proceedings of the 7th ACM SIGCOMM Conference on Internet Measurement, pp. 29–42 (2007)
12. Niu, J., Liu, C., Gao, Y., Qiu, M.: Energy efficient task assignment with guaranteed probability satisfying timing constraints for embedded systems. IEEE Trans. Parallel Distrib. Syst. **25**(8), 2043–2052 (2013)
13. Perozzi, B., Al-Rfou, R., Skiena, S.: Deepwalk: online learning of social representations. In: Proceedings of the 20th ACM SIGKDD International Conference on Knowledge Discovery and Data Mining, pp. 701–710 (2014)
14. Rossi, A., Barbosa, D., Firmani, D., Matinata, A., Merialdo, P.: Knowledge graph embedding for link prediction: a comparative analysis. ACM Trans. Knowl. Disc. Data (TKDD) **15**(2), 1–49 (2021)
15. Sen, P., Namata, G., Bilgic, M., Getoor, L., Galligher, B., Eliassi-Rad, T.: Collective classification in network data. AI Mag. **29**(3), 93–93 (2008)
16. Trouillon, T., Welbl, J., Riedel, S., Gaussier, É., Bouchard, G.: Complex embeddings for simple link prediction. In: International Conference on Machine Learning, pp. 2071–2080. PMLR (2016)
17. Wang, J., Huang, P., Zhao, H., Zhang, Z., Zhao, B., Lee, D.L.: Billion-scale commodity embedding for e-commerce recommendation in alibaba. In: Proceedings of the 24th ACM SIGKDD International Conference on Knowledge Discovery & Data Mining, pp. 839–848 (2018)
18. Xu, W., Zheng, S., He, L., Shao, B., Yin, J., Liu, T.Y.: Seek: segmented embedding of knowledge graphs. arXiv preprint arXiv:2005.00856 (2020)
19. Yang, B., Yih, W.T., He, X., Gao, J., Deng, L.: Embedding entities and relations for learning and inference in knowledge bases. arXiv preprint arXiv:1412.6575 (2014)

20. Zhao, H., Chen, M., Qiu, M., Gai, K., Liu, M.: A novel pre-cache schema for high performance android system. Future Gener. Comput. Syst. **56**, 766–772 (2016)
21. Zhu, Z., Xu, S., Tang, J., Qu, M.: Graphvite: a high-performance CPU-GPU hybrid system for node embedding. In: The World Wide Web Conference, pp. 2494–2504 (2019)

A Framework of Data Fusion Through Spatio-Temporal Knowledge Graph

Xiaohan Zhang, Xinning Zhu(✉), Jie Wu, Zheng Hu, and Chunhong Zhang

School of Information and Communication Engineering,
Beijing University of Posts and Telecommunications, Beijing, China
zhuxn@bupt.edu.cn

Abstract. Data fusion aims to integrate data from different sources that represent the same real-world object from different views. The fusion of multi-source data can reduce the uncertainty and supplement the missing information of single-source knowledge. However, when data is generated from heterogeneous resources, it would be difficult to merge them straightforwardly by traditional data integration methods. So in this paper, we propose a knowledge graph based data fusion framework to integrate spatio-temporal information extracted from two different sources, i.e., travel notes and mobile phone data respectively, which record human travelling behaviors from different views. Firstly, we introduce a method of constructing a path-based spatio-temporal knowledge graph from different sources. Then, a long-path-based knowledge graph embedding is applied to learn entity representations of different knowledge graphs jointly, which can eliminate the heterogeneity of the information from different sources. An attenuation mechanism for modeling the long path relation is proposed in order to improve the representation learning for long path based knowledge graph. Finally, the entities are aligned considering context information to obtain the travelling knowledge in a unified and enhanced form. The experimental results show that compared with the baselines, the long-path-based knowledge graph embedding method is more suitable for the knowledge graph constructed in this paper. And through entity alignment, the two knowledge graphs can be fused to offer more information for subsequent applications.

Keywords: Data fusion · Knowledge graph · Spatio-temporal information · Entity embedding · Entity alignment

1 Introduction

A large-scale knowledge base has become of great importance in various applications such as intelligent search, question answering and recommendation. When building a knowledge base, uneven quality and incompleteness among different heterogeneous sources expects an appropriate data fusion method to obtain more accurate and complete information from more than one single sources.

H. Qiu et al. (Eds.): KSEM 2021, LNAI 12815, pp. 216–228, 2021.
https://doi.org/10.1007/978-3-030-82136-4_18

Spatial and temporal information are crucial for a variety of applications in the fields of urban computing, tourism planning and so on. With spatio-temporal information incorporated in knowledge graphs, the reconstruction and analytics of events can be facilitated. In [1], the concept of a temporal knowledge graph that interconnects entities and events using temporal relations is formalized. A spatial knowledge graph is proposed in [2] to demonstrate semantic connectivities between spatial entities. However, for events or entities, their time and location information is often missing or incomplete [1], which limits the use of these knowledge bases. Different data sources that represent the same objects but record information of objects from different views may contain various amounts of time and location information of objects. However, traditional data fusion methods can not be applied straightforwardly to integrate spatio-temporal information when data is generated from heterogeneous sources.

In this paper, we propose a knowledge graph based fusion framework to merge and align spatial-temporal information spreading across heterogeneous sources. Two data sets, i.e. travel notes and mobile phone data, which containing rich but different spatio-temporal information, can be merged by applying the fusion framework to provide more accurate and complete spatio-temporal information about travelling behaviors. We first construct two spatio-temporal KG from two sources respectively, with locations as entities and time transitions between locations as relations. Then a new knowledge graph embedding method Long-Path-TransE (LPTransE) is presented to learn the entities' low-dimensional vector representation of different knowledge graph jointly. By adding attenuation factor and learning path representation by an iteration method, LPTransE is more suitable to learn long relation paths. Finally, through the transform of two vector spaces and measuring the similarity between entity embedding pairs considering context information, two knowledge graphs are aligned to get the final unified and enhanced travelling knowledge graph.

In summary, our key contributions are presented as follows:

- We present an spatio-temporal knowledge graph to model the spatio and temporal information of human trajectory.
- We propose Long-Path-TransE (LPTransE) to specific long relation paths in knowledge graph embedding.
- Through entity alignment, two knowledge graphs are fused to complement the missing or incomplete time and semantics informations.

2 Related Work

2.1 Knowledge Graph Embedding

Knowledge graph embedding can be divided into two categories: translatation-based model and path-based reasoning model. In the translatation-based model TransE [5], the relation is treated as the translation from the head to tail entity. It is simple and effective, but it does not perform well in solving 1-to-n, n-to-1, and n-to-n relations. To solve this problem, TransM [6] calculates a weight for each relation. TransH [7] projects an entity into a hyperplane determined by the relation. TransR [8] embeds entities and relations into different vector spaces.

In order to solve the problem of multi-hop reasoning, some work introduces path reasoning algorithm based on embedding model. PTransE [4] represents the multi-step relation path as a vector in a low-dimensional vector space. RTransE [9] forms a relation path of length 2 by simply adding a translation vector. RKRL [10] considers the intermediate entities on the path when embedding the relation path. However, simply combining relation vectors to construct multi-hop path vector is not conducive to embed longer relation paths.

2.2 Entity Alignment

Recently, knowledge graph embedding has become the most popular solution for entity alignment. JE [11] combines different KGs into a unified vector space to align the entities. MTransE [12] learns to transform an embedded vector of each entity into a corresponding vector in another space. GCN-align [13] is a new graph-based model for knowledge graph alignment through GCN. KECG [14] proposes a semi-supervised entity alignment method based on joint knowledge embedding model and cross graph model. BootEA [17] proposes a bootstrap method based on embedded entity alignment, which iteratively marks possible entity alignments as training data for learning alignment-oriented embedding.

3 Model

In this work, we focus on spatio-temporal knowledge fusion from different source, especially in the tourism scene for our real needs. Therefore, two datasets containing spatial-temporal information of human mobility are used. The knowledge graph constructed from travel notes dataset [3] consists of rich semantic information, but often lacks time information for transfers between locations. While mobile phone dataset can provide abundant spatial-temporal trajectories, but suffers from a lack of semantic information. So fusing spatio-temporal knowledge of these two data sets effectively will be beneficial for subsequent applications. The framework of spatio-temporal knowledge fusion is shown in Fig. 1.

First, travel notes and CDR data are respectively used to construct spatio-temporal knowledge graphs with location as entity and transfer time between locations as relation. The travel notes KG G_1 takes POI(point of interest) as entity, while the CDR KG G_2 takes base station as entity. After constructing two KGs, we proposes LPTransE, a long-path based knowledge graph embedding learning algorithm, to learn the low-dimensional vector representation of entities and relations. Finally, considering the context information, entity alignment is carried out by comparing the distance of different entity pairs in vector spaces.

3.1 Construction of Knowledge Graph

A knowledge graph is represented by $G = (E, R)$, where E and R are the sets of entities and relations. Given a triple (h, r, t) in the knowledge graph, h and

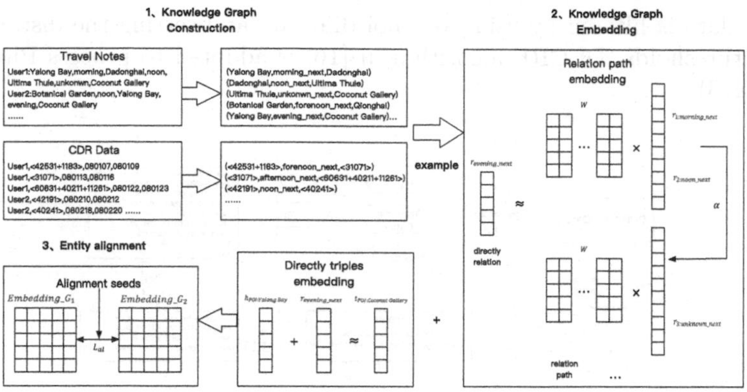

Fig. 1. Framework of spatio-temporal knowledge fusion

t are head and tail entity respectively, where $h, t \in E$, and $r \in R$, represents a relation between h and t. In this article, we focus more on multiple-step relation paths than traditional triples. Given a path, we take the location that the path passed through as the entity, and the transfer-time as relation for the following considerations: In a spatio-temporal KG, multiple-step relation paths between entities represent a travelling trip. So a path-based representation learning can better model transition relations between entities, i.e. locations in this work.

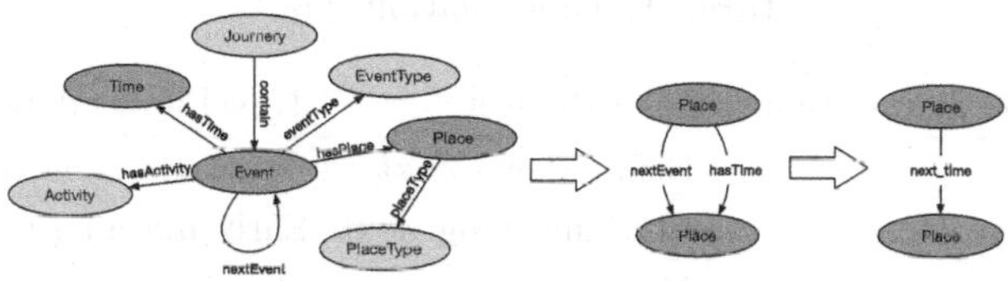

Fig. 2. Travel notes knowledge graph construction

Travel Notes Knowledge Graph. Wu J. et al. propose an Event-centric Tourism Knowledge Graph (ETKG) [3] that interconnects tourist activities using temporal relations in chronological order. As shown in Fig. 2, each event consists of activity, place, time and some other properties in the event. We extract time and place attributes of event from ETKG, then construct a new graph which contains only places as entities, time transitions between places as relations. As shown in Table 1, we extend the nextEvent relation to eight more specific time transition relations.

CDR Knowledge Graph. The preprocess of CDR data refers to [15]. We delete the invalid data, including missing, duplicate, and incorrect data. And the drift data is filtered by using voronoi diagram and setting the distance and velocity thresholds. DECRE algorithm in [16] is adopted to process Ping-Pong data (Fig. 3).

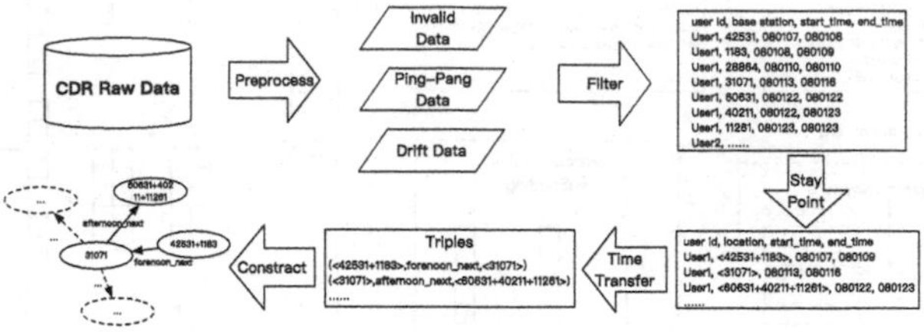

Fig. 3. Framework of CDR knowledge graph construction

We use a stay points extraction method [15] to get the potentially meaningful locations in the trip. The combination of multiple base stations is retained to better represent the stay area. Finally, we construct the CDR KG according to these spatio-temporal trajectory sequences, in which the anonymous base station IDs within the stay area are represented as entities, the time of leaving the current stay area is used as the time transition relation between entities. The time information is discretized into several time periods as shown in Table 1.

Table 1. Time relation types

Time division(hour)	CDR dataset	Travel notes dataset
0–4	Before_dawn_next	Before_dawn_next
5–6	Early_morning_next	Early_morning_next
7–8	Morning_next	Morning_next
9–11	Forenoon_next	Forenoon_next
12–13	Noon_next	Noon_next
14–17	Afternoon_next	Afternoon_next
18–23	Evening_next	Evening_next
Unkonwn time		Unkonwn_next

3.2 Knowledge Graph Representation Learning

There are three steps: representing entities and relations as vectors, defining the scoring function for triples, learning entity and relation representations. Through the optimization problem that triples in the KG tend to have lower scores than those not in, the entity and relation representations can be learned. On the basis of PTransE [4], we propose a Long-Path-based TransE(LPTransE) to model multi-step relation paths in spatio-temporal knowledge graph. The scoring function and optimization objective used in this paper are described below.

Suppose $P(h,t) = \{p_1, ..., p_N\}$ indicates a set of relation paths connecting the head entity h and tail entity t, where each relation path p_i can be expressed as $h \xrightarrow{r_1} ... \xrightarrow{r_l} t$. And the scoring function of each triple (h,r,t) is defined as:

$$G(h,r,t) = E(h,r,t) + E(h,P,t) \tag{1}$$

According to TransE [5], the score of triple is $E(h,r,t) = ||\mathbf{h} + \mathbf{r} - \mathbf{t}||$. And $E(h,P,t)$ focus on the multiple-step relation path triples, which is defined as

$$E(h,P,t) = 1/Z \sum_{p \in P(h,t)} R(p|h,t)E(h,p,t) \tag{2}$$

where $R(p|h,t)$ is the reliability of the relation path p, $Z = \sum_{p \in P(h,t)} R(p|h,t)$ is a normalization factor, and $E(h,p,t) = ||\mathbf{p} + \mathbf{h} - \mathbf{t}||$ is the scoring function of the path triple. Since $E(h,r,t) = ||\mathbf{h} + \mathbf{r} - \mathbf{t}||, \mathbf{r} \approx \mathbf{t} - \mathbf{h}$, then $E(h,p,t) = ||\mathbf{p} - (\mathbf{t} - \mathbf{h})|| = ||\mathbf{p} - \mathbf{r}|| = E(p,r)$, which means that the score is lower when the path embedding $\mathbf{p}$ is closer to the direct relation embedding $\mathbf{r}$.

Relation Path Reliability. In PTransE [4], the original resource in h is set to be 1, and the reliability $R(p|h,t)$ of path p is defined as the proportion of resource that eventually flows to tail entity t.

Relation Path Representation. The embedding $\mathbf{p}$ of relation path p is obtained by the following iteration method. Given the path $p = \{r_1, ...r_l\}$:

$$\begin{aligned} q_0 &= W \cdot [r_1 : r_2] \\ q_1 &= W \cdot [(\alpha \cdot q_0) : r_3] \\ &\cdots \\ q_{(l-2)} &= W \cdot [(\alpha \cdot q_{(l-3)}) : r_l] \end{aligned} \tag{3}$$

where $W \in R^{d \times 2d}$ is the parameter matrix to be learned, and d is the dimension of relation vector. α is an attenuation factor that measures the reduction of the influence of the previous relation on the tail entity as the length of the relation path increases. $[a:b]$ represents the concatenation of two vectors. By initializing q_0 and performing recursively along the relation path, we will finally obtain the d dimensional path vector $\mathbf{p} = q_{(l-2)}$, where l is the length of relation path p.

Objective Function. The optimization objective is:

$$L(G) = \sum_{(h,r,t) \in S} [L(h,r,t) + 1/Z \sum_{p \in P(h,t)} R(p \mid h,t)L(p,r)] \tag{4}$$

where $L(h, r, t)$ and $L(p, r)$ are margin-based loss functions for triple (h, r, t), path and direct-relation pair (p, r) respectively:

$$L(h, r, t) = \sum_{(h',r',t') \in S^-} [\gamma_1 + E(h, r, t) - E(h', r', t')]_+ \tag{5}$$

$$L(p, r) = \sum_{(h,r',t) \in S^-} [\gamma_2 + E(p, r) - E(p, r')]_+ \tag{6}$$

where $[x]_+ = max(0, x)$, γ_1, γ_2 are the margins, and S is the set of triples in KG. While $S^- = \{(h', r, t)\} \cup \{(h, r, t')\} \cup \{(h, r', t)\}$, consisting of the original triple (h, r, t) with one component being replaced.

3.3 Entity Alignment

The objective of the alignment model is to construct the transitions between vector spaces of two knowledge graphs G_1 and G_2. We propose an entity alignment method tending to align entity pairs and relation pairs instead of triples as used in MTransE [12]. We define the aligned entity and relation sets, $E_{al} = \{(e, e') \in G_1 \times G_2 | e \sim e'\}$, $R_{al} = \{(r, r') \in G_1 \times G_2 | r \sim r'\}$. The loss function is:

$$L_{al} = \sum_{(e,e') \in E_{al}} ||e' - f_1(e)|| + \sum_{(r,r') \in R_{al}} ||r' - f_2(r)|| \tag{7}$$

Where $f_1(\cdot)$ and $f_2(\cdot)$ are the transform fuctions of entity and relation respectively. Based on MTransE [12], the transform fuctions are defined as follows.

- **Linear Transform** It models the transitions using linear transformation. The transform fuctions are $f_1(e) = W^1 \cdot e$ and $f_2(r) = W^2 \cdot r$.
- **Linear Transform with bias** It is obtained by linear transformation with bias. The transform fuctions are $f_1(e) = W^1 \cdot e + b_1$ and $f_2(r) = W^2 \cdot +b_2 r$.
- **Distance based** It correct axes of vector spaces to make the embeddings of aligned pairs coincident. The transform fuctions are $f_1(e) = e$ and $f_2(r) = r$.
- **Translation Vector** It adds the translation vector in two vector spaces. The transform fuctions are $f_1(e) = e + b_1$ and $f_2(r) = r + b_1$.

where $W^1, W^2 \in R^{d \times d}$ are transform matrixs, d is the dimension of embedding vectors. And $b_1, b_2 \in R^{d \times 1}$ are the biases. The overall objective function of the joint learning of two knowledge graph embeddings with entity alignment is:

$$L = L(G_1) + L(G_2) + L_{al} \tag{8}$$

After the learning of entity embeddings, we compute the similarity between unaligned entities in G_2 and all entities in G_1 to find the correct alignment. With the context of entity considered, the similarity definition of entities is:

$$dis_{context}(e', e) = dis(e', f_1(e)) + dis(e'^{in}, f_1(e)) + dis(e'^{out}, f_1(e)) \tag{9}$$

where $dis(\cdot,\cdot)$ is the Euclidean distance of two vectors. And the inlinks and outlinks embedding e^{in}, e^{out} of entity e are the average of its contextual entities:

$$e_i^{in} = \frac{1}{|In(e_i)|} \sum_{e_j \in In(e_i)} e_j \tag{10}$$

$$e_i^{out} = \frac{1}{|Out(e_i)|} \sum_{e_j \in Out(e_i)} e_j \tag{11}$$

where $In(e) = \{e_j | (e_j, r, e) \in G\}$ denotes inlink entities where e_j acts as head entity while e acts as tail entity. $Out(e) = \{e_j | (e, r, e_j) \in G\}$ is on the opposite.

For each unaligned entity in G_2, we calculate the distance with all transformed entities embeddings in G_1. And the closest one is regarded as aligned entity. We will compare the effect of adding context in Sect. 4.

4 Experiments

Datasets. We use two data sets in this paper, CDR dataset and travel notes dataset, to verify the model. The CDR dataset is composed of 4 months call data from Hainan province provided by a Chinese operator, where the CDR raw data format is (anonymous user ID, anonymous base station ID, start time, end timc). The travel notes dataset [3] captures users' travel notes about Hainan from Ctrip (https://www.ctrip.com), one of the largest travel websites in China. The details of two datasets are shown in Table 2.

Table 2. Statistics of datasets

Dataset	Relations	Entities	Paths	Triples	Triples with time information	Triples without time information
CDR	7	927	6447	7749	7749	0
Travel notes	8	144	2783	6736	1338	5398

Baseline. For knowledge graph representation:

- TransE [5]: It treats the relation as translation between head and tail entity.
- TransH [7]: It interprets a relation as a translating operation on a hyperplane.
- TransR [8]: It projects entities to corresponding relation space.
- PTransE(ADD) [4]: The path embedding is expressed as the sum of all relation embeddings passing through, in the form of $\mathbf{p} = \mathbf{r}_1 + ... + \mathbf{r}_l$.
- PTransE(MUL) [4]: The path embedding is expressed by multiplying all the relation embeddings passing through, in the form of $\mathbf{p} = \mathbf{r}_1 \cdot ... \cdot \mathbf{r}_l$.

For entity alignment:

- MTransE [12]: It provides transitions for each embedding vector to its cross-lingual counterparts in other spaces.
- BootEA [17]: It iteratively labels likely entity alignment as training data for learning alignment-oriented KG embeddings.

Settings. In optimization, stochastic gradient descent (SGD) is used to minimize the loss function. The entity and relation embedding vector dimension $d = 200$, the learning rate is 0.001. The knowledge graph embedding goes through 500 rounds of training, and $\gamma_1 = 1.0, \gamma_2 = 0.5$. For the attenuation factor α, We test it in (0,1) and find the best performance can be achieved when α is 0.4.

For entity alignment, we randomly select about 60% golden entity mappings between the target and source KG as the seeds used for cross KG-training [18]. Due to the relation consistency of two knowledge graphs, the seven relation types are regarded as aligned relation pairs. The training rounds is 1000. The similarity threshold for BootEA is 0.05. Other settings are the same as before. We use two measures as the evaluation metrics: the mean of correct entity ranks (Mean Rank,MR) and the proportion of valid entities ranked in top-k (Hits@k).

5 Results

The Effect of Knowledge Graph Representation. We use tail entity prediction task and 80% of triples in each relation type are used for train while 20% for test. Two cases are compared. Raw indicates that all but the triple currently being tested are considered to be incorrect, while Filter means to filter out other correct triples before sorting. Evaluation results are shown in Table 3. TransE performs worst because there are 1-to-n relation types in the dataset. And translation-based methods perform worse than path-based methods. Compared with LPTransE, the paths in PTransE are obtained by random walk in the knowledge graph, which can not get reliable path information. The cumulative and multiplicative methods only apply to short paths, and once the path length increases, it makes all the relations that pass through the same weight. LPTransE performs the best compared to other algorithms. This is because LPTransE is constructed on the basis of long path which length is longer than 3 mostly, and the attenuation factor is added when calculating the path embedding vector.

Table 3. Evaluation results on entity prediction

	Model	Raw			Filter		
		Hit@5	Hit@10	MR	Hit@5	Hit@10	MR
Translation-based	TransE	20.34%	40.10%	20.59	54.06%	71.05%	10.76
	TransH	25.12%	44.08%	18.82	74.53%	82.70%	7.36
	TransR	27.99%	49.90%	16.54	82.61%	86.89%	5.67
Path-based	PTransE(Add-2-hop)	28.23%	51.41%	15.37	79.28%	86.96%	5.59
	PTransE(Add-3-hop)	29.19%	52.28%	14.94	83.19%	89.61%	5.08
	PTransE(Mul-2-hop)	28.32%	52.40%	14.88	82.73%	88.47%	4.99
	PTransE(Mul-3-hop)	29.71%	52.09%	15.09	82.61%	88.53%	5.12
	LPTransE	**31.07%**	**54.34%**	**14.57**	**84.49%**	**89.95%**	**4.72**

Table 4. Evaluation results on entity alignment

Model	Hit@5	Hit@10	Hit@20	MR
MTransE(Linear transform)	26.85%	35.23%	50.28%	31.0
MTransE(Linear transform with bias)	29.90%	44.19%	59.80%	26.58
MTransE(Distance based)	38.66%	51.04%	64.38%	24.20
MTransE(Translation vector)	42.85%	54.47%	64.38%	21.95
BootEA(Distance based)	39.80%	55.23%	69.52%	22.42
BootEA(Translation vector)	43.80%	60.95%	71.61%	21.41
MTransE$^+$(Linear transform)	27.61%	39.23%	56.38%	28.95
MTransE$^+$(Linear transform with bias)	35.04%	49.71%	64.38%	25.26
BootEA$^+$(Distance based)	47.61%	62.09%	74.09%	20.48
BootEA$^+$(Translation vector)	48.76%	63.61%	73.71%	20.26
MTransE$^+$(Distance based)	50.09%	63.80%	71.42%	20.97
MTransE$^+$(Translation vector)	**53.90%**	**66.28%**	**75.42%**	**19.47**

The Effect of Entity Alignment. The results of entity alignment are shown in Table 4. We develop the variants of entity alignment methods with $^+$ tagged, which add contextual information to measure similarities between entities. The normal methods only compare the similarity $dis(e', f_1(e))$ in Eq. (9). Considering the results with no contextual information added, BootEA performs better than MTransE for the bootstrapping approach. Besides, Translation Vector and Distance based methods perform better than Linear Transform, that is because of the high similarity of the structure of two knowledge graphs. Due to the aligned seeds, two vector spaces can be consistent easily.

Considering the results with contextual information added, it indeed improves the alignment performance. Since the alignment type between base station and POI is one-to-many, which means that one POI in G_1 may corresponding to several base stations in G_2, adding the contextual base stations which are likely to be close and belong to the same POI helps to alignment. BootEA$^+$ in this condition is worse than MTransE$^+$, because we only add the contextual information in the distance calculation after the joint learning, which means that the iteration process is still only based on the similarity of the entities themselves.

The Effect of Attenuation Factor. The performance is shown in Fig. 4. The influence of first-hop relation in the path is weakened if α is too small while it does not highlight the importance of the last-hop on a long path if α is too big. We finally take α to be 0.4 in our model which performs best.

Case Study. As shown in Fig. 5(a), we randomly choose ten POI entities in travel notes KG and their aligned entities in CDR KG according to the valid set.

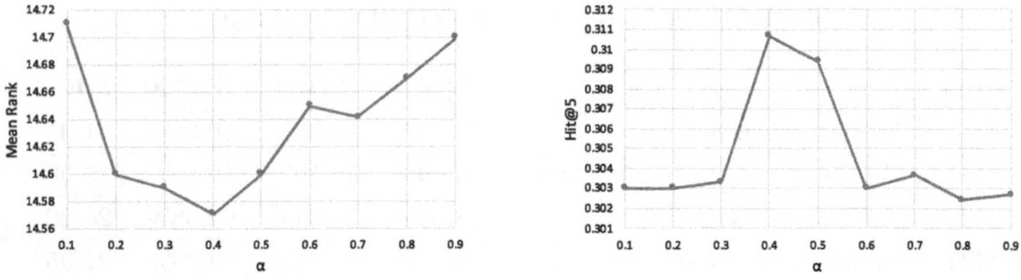

Fig. 4. The influence of attenuation factor

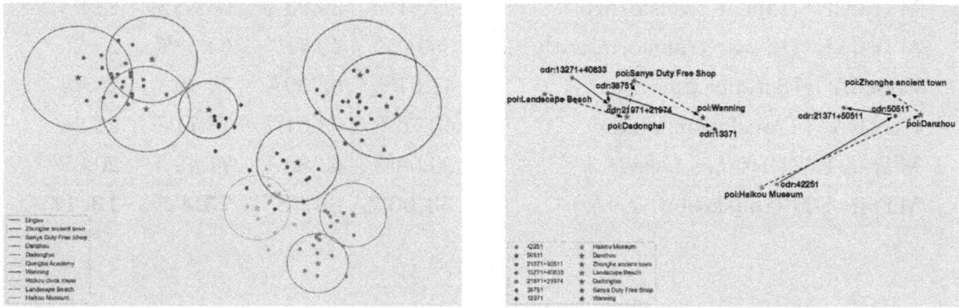

(a) Visualization of aligned pairs (b) An example of fusion

Fig. 5. A visualization example of aligned entities

And the t-SNE algorithm [19] is used to visualize the embeddings in a low dimensional space. As expected, the t-SNE algorithm tends to map the representations of similar entities to nearby points. The center of each circle which represented by the star marker is the entity in travel notes KG, while the points across it in same color are the groud truth of the aligned entities in CDR KG, which means that they represent same locations in the real world. As we can see, points in different colors were basically separated and close to the their own center POI entity points which means they are more similar, so our framework performs well in alignment. In addition, we randomly choose two paths constructed by these ten groups of aligned entities in CDR KG to provide some cases in Fig. 5(b). The solid lines represents the path in CDR KG while dashed lines means the path in travel notes KG. The star markers and points in the same color are aligned entitiy pairs. For example, the path $42251 \xrightarrow{morning\_next} 30861 + 60463 \xrightarrow{afternoon\_next} 21371 + 50511$ turns to $Haikou\ Museum \xrightarrow{morning\_next} Danzhou \xrightarrow{afternoon\_next} Zhonghe\ ancient\ town$. The POI entity complements the semantics of the CDR entity while the CDR path which make supplements for the missing or incomplete time informations in travel notes KG.

6 Conclusion

This paper propose a framework of fusing spatio-temporal datas which describe the same facts through knowledge graph construction, representation learning and entity alignment. Due to the applicability of LPTransE in our path-based knowledge graph, the evaluations show the great performance compared with other methods. It means that we can fuse path-based spatio-temporal datas with a small number of aligned entity seeds, which offers a possibility for other similar scenarios. At present, this paper only fuses two cross-source knowledge graphs in tourism together, and the application after fusion is our next research.

Acknowledgements. This work was supported by the Guangdong Province Science and Technology Project 2021A0505080015.

References

1. Gottschalk, S., Demidova, E.: EventKG - the hub of event knowledge on the web - and biographical timeline generation. In: Semantic Web (2019)
2. Wang, P., Liu, K., et al.: Incremental mobile user profiling: reinforcement learning with spatial knowledge graph for modeling event streams. In: KDD (2020)
3. Wu, J., Zhu, X., Zhang, C., Hu, Z.: Event-centric tourism knowledge graph-a case study of hainan. In: KSEM (2020)
4. Lin, Y., Liu, Z., Luan H., et al.: Modeling relation paths for representation learning of knowledge bases. In: Computer Science (2015)
5. Bordes, A., Usunier, N., et al.: Translating embeddings for modeling multi-relational data. In: Proceedings of NIPS, pp. 2787–2795 (2013)
6. Fan, M., Zhou, Q., Chang, E., et al.: Transition-based knowledge graph embedding with relational mapping properties. In: PACLIC, Information and Computing (2014)
7. Wang, Z., Zhang, J., Feng, J., et al.: Knowledge graph embedding by translating on hyperplanes. In: AAAI (2014)
8. Lin, Y., Liu, Z., Sun, M., Liu, Y., Zhu, X.: Learning entity and relation embeddings for knowledge graph completion. In: AAAI, pp. 2181–2187 (2015)
9. García-Durán, A., Bordes, A., Usunier, N.: Composing relationships with translations. In: EMNLP (2015)
10. Seo, S., Oh, B., Lee, K.H.: Reliable knowledge graph path representation learning. IEEE Access (99), 1 (2020)
11. Hao, Y., Zhang, Y., He, S., Liu, K., Zhao, J.: A joint embedding method for entity alignment of knowledge bases. In: CCKS (2016)
12. Chen, M., Tian, Y., Yang, M., Zaniolo, C.: Multilingual knowledge graph embeddings for cross-lingual knowledge alignment. In: IJCAI (2017)
13. Wang, Z., Lv, Q., Lan, X., Zhang, Y.: Cross-lingual knowledge graph alignment via graph convolutional networks. In: EMNLP (2018)
14. Li, C., Cao, Y., Hou, L.: Semi-supervised entity alignment via joint knowledge embedding model and cross-graph model. In: EMNLP-IJCNLP (2019)
15. Zhu, X., Sun, T., Yuan, H., et al.: Exploring group movement pattern through cellular data: a case study of tourists in Hainan. IJGI **8**(2), 74 (2019)
16. Shad, S.A., Chen, E., Bao, T.: Cell oscillation resolution in mobility profile building. Int. J. Comput. Sci. Issues **9**(3), 205–213 (2012)

17. Sun, Z., Hu, W., Zhang, Q., et al.: Bootstrapping entity alignment with knowledge graph embedding. In: IJCAI (2018)
18. Cai, P., Li, W., Feng, Y., et al.: Learning knowledge representation across knowledge graphs. In: AAAI-17 Workshop (2017)
19. Van der Maaten, L.J.P., Hinton, G.E.: Visualizing high-dimensional data using t-SNE. Mach. Learn. Res. **9**, 2579–2605 (2008)

SEGAR: Knowledge Graph Augmented Session-Based Recommendation

Xinyi Xu, Yan Tang(✉), and Zhuoming Xu

College of Computer and Information, Hohai University, Nanjing 210036, China
{xy.xu.hhu,tangyan,zmxu}@hhu.edu.cn

Abstract. Predicting the next interaction item in the session-based recommendation system is an emerging and challenging research task. Existing studies model a session as a sequence or graph of items for predicting the next-click item. However, these approaches ignore the global graph-based relations between the session items and the local neighborhood-based item relevance to external knowledge bases, thus fail to encode rich semantic knowledge between items for achieving comprehensive and accurate recommendations. To overcome the current shortcomings, we proposed a novel knowledge graph augmented model called SEGAR (Knowledge Graph Augmented Session-based Recommendation) by leveraging graph convolutional network and knowledge graph attention network. When integrating the static local attributes and the knowledge about all the last session items encoded in their k-hop neighborhoods in the knowledge graph, SEGAR models all sessions as a session graph and captures the dynamic global temporal and popularity-aware information from the session context. The model encodes a comprehensive semantic knowledge between items for achieving more accurate recommendation. Extensive experiments on two benchmark datasets show that SEGAR outperforms four state-of-the-art models on the session-based recommendation task.

Keywords: Session-based recommendation · Attention network · Graph convolutional network · Knowledge graph

1 Introduction

In recent years, more and more researches are paying attention to the new research field of session-based recommender systems [2,3,6,15]. A session-based recommender system provides recommendations solely based on a user's interactions in an ongoing session, and which does not require the existence of user-profiles or their entire historical preferences. Such system aim to capture short-term but dynamic user preferences to provide more timely and accurate recommendations sensitive to the evolution of users' session contexts.

Numerous studies focus on modeling the user sessions and on leveraging deep learning models such as Recurrent Neural Networks (RNNs) [13] to capture users' general interests from the session of user actions. [6] uses the encoder-decoder

H. Qiu et al. (Eds.): KSEM 2021, LNAI 12815, pp. 229–241, 2021.
https://doi.org/10.1007/978-3-030-82136-4_19

structure and the attention mechanism for the recommendation, which cannot model complex session patterns. Current RNN-based methods only focus on the current session and the transition to the last-clicked item and ignore the dynamic information contained in the item's neighborhood in the session.

A Knowledge Graph (KG) is the source of factual knowledge, depicted in the form of a graph of entities and their relationships. KG is a semantic-rich computational model that maps entities and relations to low-dimensional representation vectors through KG embedding methods to obtain a semantic-rich item presentation [4]. The KG domain can associate item entities, and uses local semantic neighborhood knowledge to improve the precision of recommendation predictions. The representation of the item entity in the knowledge graph contains the structural information and feature information on its $k-hop$ neighbors, which is useful for the recommendation. However, there are few studies that take advantage of KG to assist the session-based recommendation task.

In this paper, we proposed the SEGAR (Knowledge Graph Augmented Session-based Recommendation) to overcome the current research limitations mentioned above. As shown in Fig. 1. Firstly, SEGAR models all sessions as a session graph to obtain the embedding of every session node through a Graph Convolutional Network that integrates both time and popularity weights into the session node global embedding. The embedding of the session is then obtained by means of an attention mechanism. Secondly, SEGAR makes use of the one-to-one mapping between the item entity in the external knowledge graph to the last item in the session to be predicted. It uses the Knowledge Graph Attention Network [12] to aggregate the $k - hop$ neighborhood knowledge of the item entity to obtain the local embedding for the last session item. Lastly, SEGAR jointly combines the global embedding of the session and the local embedding of last session item to generate the final session embedding for predicting the next-step clicking likelihood of each candidate item. Extensive experiments and a case study on two benchmark datasets show that SEGAR outperforms four state-of-the-art session-based models. As far as we know, this is one of the first research attempts that aims to simultaneously taking into account the dynamic global relationship and static knowledge of local neighborhoods for session-based recommendations. To summarize, the major contributions to this study are as follows:

- We propose a graph-based session node embedding method based on graph convolutional neural network that considers the weights of item's temporal and popularity factors to jointly obtain the session item's dynamic global embedding. This method helps to improve the recommendation accuracy.

- We leverage the state-of-the-art knowledge graph attention network on external KG by associating item entity in KG with the last session item to obtain $k - hop$ neighborhood semantic knowledge. This encodes the static local neighborhood-based item relevancy for further improving the accuracy of session-based recommendation.

- Extensive experiments are conducted on two real-world data sets for our proposed model, the results show that the performance of SEGAR is better than the four SOTA models.

2 Related Work

Common session-based recommendation methods include conventional methods, latent representation methods, and deep neural networks. FPMC [9] is a session prediction method based on Markov chains. It also has the problem that it can only deal with uncomplicated datasets. Nowadays, there are more researches using deep neural networks to solve the session-based recommendation problem. The model STAMP [8] obtains the users' general interest in the long-term memory of the session context, while taking into account that the users' current interest comes from the short-term memory of the last click. NARM [6] only captures general interest, and combines the main purpose and sequential behavior to get a session representation. However, our model clearly emphasizes the mixture feature of current interest and general interest in the last click. The SR-GNN [14] transforms sessions into a graph structure and constructs a directed graph based on historical sessions using graph neural network but does not encode the local relations between items in external knowledge bases and does not explicitly consider the impact on time and item popularity. RippleNet [10] uses KG and takes user's favorite items as a starting point, and distributes it on KG through multiple layers such as ripples to achieve user feature extraction but the importance of item relations to RippleNet is sparse and difficult to converge. In short, SEGAR can combine dynamic global knowledge and static local knowledge and learn at the same time in a unified model to achieve more accurate recommendations.

3 Problem Definition

In this section, we give the following problem definition. Let $V = \{v_1, v_2 \dots v_n\}$ represents the total set of items contained in all sessions. The session S can be sorted by time stamp as the list $S = [v_{s,1}, v_{s,2} \dots v_{s,n-1}]$, where $v_{s,i} \in V$ means an item is interacted by the user for the i-th time in the session S. $k_{s,i}$ represents the total number of occurrences of the item node $v_{s,i}$ in all sessions, and $t_{s,i}$ represents the time stamp of the item node $v_{s,i}$ in all sessions. Our task of the session-based recommendation is to predict the next clicked item of session S, denoted as $v_{s,n+1}$. Given a session S, the SEGAR outputs the probabilities $\hat{Y}$ of all candidate items where the value of $\hat{Y}$ is the score that the corresponding item may be recommended. We select the item with the highest score of the recommendation.

Session Graph: Each session S can be modeled as a directed graph $G = (V, E)$, where $v_{s,i} \in V$ represents an item node. Edge $(v_{s,i-1}, v_{s,i}) \in E$ represents that the user clicks on the item $v_{s,i}$ after $v_{s,i-1}$ in the session S. Then, we can get the adjacency matrix A of the session graph, which can be used as the input of GCN when generating the embedding of the session node. Each session S can be represented as a vector $\mathbf{S}$ composed of the node vectors.

Knowledge Graph: The knowledge graph is composed of a large number of entities and the relationships between entities. In this task, the entities we filter out are mainly items that appear in the sessions and extract the triples associated with the item entities, represented as (h, r, t), where h and t represent the head entity and the tail entity, respectively, and r represents the relationship between the head entity and the tail entity, such as item attributes.

4 The Proposed Model

The schematic illustration of the SEGAR model is presented in Fig. 1. Firstly, we model all sessions which composed of items as session graphs and use the GCN to obtain the dynamic global session embedding $\mathbf{S_g}$ that integrates the temporal and popularity weights of each session node. Secondly, we use the Knowledge Graph Attention Network [12] to aggregate the $k-hop$ neighborhood knowledge of the item entity to obtain the local embedding $\mathbf{S_l}$ for the last session item. Lastly, SEGAR jointly combines the dynamic global embedding $\mathbf{S_g}$ of the session and the local embedding $\mathbf{S_l}$ of last session item to generate the final session embedding $\mathbf{S}$ for predicting the next-step clicking likelihood of each candidate item. In this section, we describe the SEGAR model in three steps: Global Embedding, Local Embedding, and Recommendation Generation.

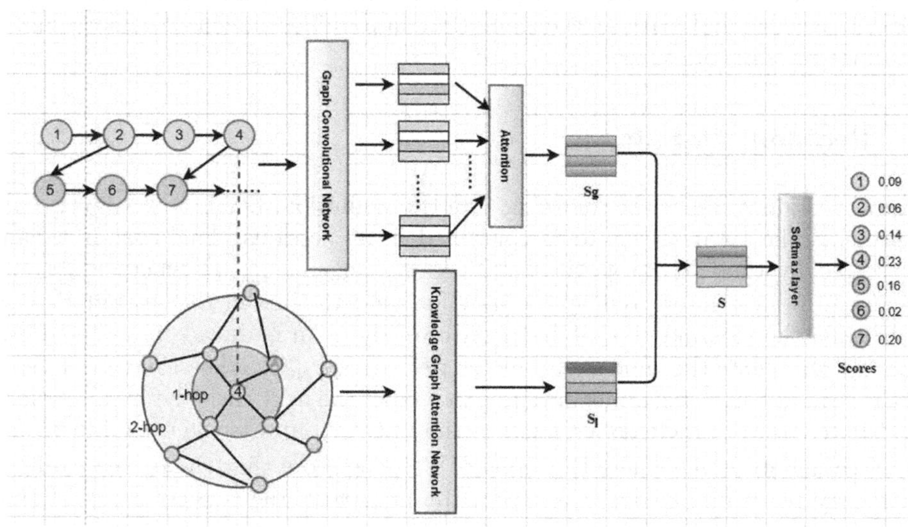

Fig. 1. The schematic illustration of our proposed model

4.1 Global Embedding

After establishing the session graph, SEGAR obtains the embedding of the session node. The structure of the graph is usually irregular. The ingenious design of GCN provides feature extraction and calculation capabilities from graphic data, and finally obtains a vectorized representation of the graph. There are n nodes in the session graph. We randomly initialize the characteristics of these nodes to form a matrix X. Then the relationship between each node forms an adjacency matrix A. The matrix X and A are inputs to the GCN model. We first show the learning process of node embeddings in the session graph. Formally, the nodes in the graph G update function is defined as follows:

$$v_{s,i}^{(l+1)} = \sigma\left(\hat{D}^{-\frac{1}{2}}\hat{A}\hat{D}^{-\frac{1}{2}}v_{s,i}^{(l)}W^{(l)} + b^{(l)}\right) \tag{1}$$

$v_{s,i}^{(l+1)}$ represents the node at the layer of $l+1$ of the GCN. For the input layer, $v_{s,i}$ is represented as X and $\hat{A}$ represents $A+I$, where I is the identity matrix. $\hat{D}$ represents the corresponding degree matrix of $\hat{A}$. σ is a non-linear activation function. This operation obtains the initial embedding vector of the item node.

The popularity weight of our item is the number of times each item is clicked divided by the total number of all candidate nodes. The item popularity weight of a session node is defined as Eq. (2):

$$W_{p,i} = \frac{k_{s,i}}{\sum_{i=1}^{n-1} k_{s,i}} \tag{2}$$

In addition, the time span between the nodes in the session indicates the temporal distance from two items in the session S. Common sense tells us items with long temporal distance from the current session node tend to have a weaker impact on the interaction of the next item. Therefore, SEGAR uses the time stamp of each node in the session graph to calculate the session node item temporal weight. The equation for calculating the temporal weight of a session node is as defined as Eq. (3):

$$W_{t,i} = \frac{|t_{s,i} - t_{s,n-1}|}{t_{s,n-1}} \tag{3}$$

As a result, the weight of a session node combining both popularity and temporal factors is defined as Eq. (4):

$$W_{s,i} = W_{p,i} \cdot W_{t,i} \tag{4}$$

Lastly, the global embedding of the session node in the session graph $\mathbf{V_{s,i}}$ combined both popularity and temporal factors is defined as Eq. (5):

$$\mathbf{V_{s,i}} = v_i^{(l+1)} \cdot W_{s,i} \tag{5}$$

Finally, we use the attention mechanism to obtain the global embedding $\mathbf{S_g}$.

$$\alpha_i = \mathbf{q}^\top \sigma\left(W_1 \mathbf{V}_{\mathbf{s,n-1}} + W_2 \mathbf{V}_{\mathbf{s,i}} + c\right) \tag{6}$$

$$\mathbf{S}_{\mathrm{g}} = \sum_{i=1}^{n-1} \alpha_i \mathbf{V}_i \tag{7}$$

where parameters $\mathbf{q} \in \mathbb{R}^d, W_1, W_2 \in \mathbb{R}^{d \times d}$ control the embedding of session node and $\mathbf{S}_{\mathrm{g}} \in \mathbb{R}^d$ represents the global embedding vectors.

4.2 Local Embedding in SEGAR

After getting the session nodes' dynamic global embedding, SEGAR leverages external knowledge graph to obtain the session node's static local embedding that encodes the neighborhood knowledge. First, SEGAR forms an one-to-one mapping relationship between the entities in the item KG and the last session node in the session. Then, KGAT(Knowledge Graph Attention Network) [12] is used to aggregate the attribute and neighborhood knowledge of the item entity in the KG to obtain the local embedding of the last session item in the session.

The initial embedding layer of the KG is a vector representation of the structural nodes and edges of the KG using TransR [7]. The practice of multi-layered attention embedding propagation is the same as that of the first layer, except that the operation is repeated multiple times. The first layer of propagation is divided into three steps: message propagation, knowledge-based attention, and information aggregation [12]. The whole process recursively propagates the node neighborhood embeddings to update their representations and uses the attention mechanism to learn the weights of each neighbor in the propagation process.

Message Propagation: For a node n, record the set of triples with its head node as N_h represented as (h, r, t), then the message from the neighborhood is $e_t \in \mathbb{R}^d$. Here, we use TransR [7] to get tail entity embedding denoted as e_t.

$$e_{N_h} = \sum_{(h,r,t) \in N_h} \pi(h, r, t) e_t \tag{8}$$

$\pi(h, r, t)$ represents the weight of the neighborhood and controls the decay factor on each propagation on edge r, indicating how much information being propagated from t to h conditioned to relation r.

Knowledge-Based Attention: The weight of the neighborhood is obtained through the relational attention mechanism, which is defined as Eq. (9):

$$\pi(h, r, t) = \left(W_r e_t\right)^\top \tanh\left(\left(W_r e_h + e_r\right)\right) \tag{9}$$

We choose tanh as the non-linear activation function.

Attention score depends on the distance between e_h and e_r under relation r. Finally, SEGAR uses softmax normalization on the weight of the neighborhood, which is defined as Eq. (10):

$$\pi(h,r,t) = \frac{\exp(\pi(h,r,t))}{\sum_{(h,r',t')\in\mathcal{N}_h} \exp\left(\pi\left(h,r',t'\right)\right)} \tag{10}$$

Information Aggregation: Then, an Information aggregator is used to aggregate the entity representation. According to KGAT [12], there exists three types of aggregator functions: *GCN Aggregator, GraphSage Aggregator* and *Bi-Interaction aggregator*. Among them, we choose the Bi-Interaction aggregators since it works best for session-based recommendation tasks by considering both interaction directions. The Bi-Interaction aggregator is defined in Eq. (11):

$$f = LeakyReLU\left(W\left(e_h + e_{N_h}\right)\right) + LeakyReLU\left(W\left(e_h \odot e_{N_h}\right)\right) \tag{11}$$

We choose the LeakyReLU activation function, which introduces a small slope to keep the updates process alive with the ability to retain some degree of the negative values that flow into it.

The advantage of the embedding propagation layer lies in explicitly exploiting the first-order connectivity information. The equation for the k_{th} hops Information propagation is defined in Eq. 12:

$$e_{s,n-1}^{(k)} = e_h^{(k)} = f\left(e_h^{(k-1)}, e_{N_h}^{(k-1)}\right) \tag{12}$$

After the information aggregation, SEGAR iteratively aggregates multi-hop neighborhood information to obtain a richer and more complete representation of the last session node. Finally, the local embedding vector $\mathbf{S_l}$ of the last session node is represented in Eq. 13:

$$\mathbf{S_l} = \mathbf{V_{s,n-1}} = e_{s,n-1}^{(0)} \| \cdots \| e_{s,n-1}^{(k)} \tag{13}$$

where $\|$ represents the concatenation operation.

4.3 Recommendation Generation

After generating both global and local session node embeddings, then we consider the embedding $\mathbf{S}$ of the session graph G_s by combining all session node embeddings. The overall session representation $\mathbf{S}$ is then obtained by jointly combing the local and global session embeddings:

$$\mathbf{S} = W_3\left[\mathbf{S_l}; \mathbf{S_g}\right] \tag{14}$$

where $\mathbf{S_l} \in \mathbb{R}^d$ represents the local embedding in our model, $W_3 \in \mathbb{R}^{d\times 2d}$ compresses the local embedding and the global embedding.

After obtaining the embedding for the entire session, we calculate the score $\hat{\mathbf{y}}_i$ for each candidate item:

$$\hat{\mathbf{y}}_i = \mathbf{S}^\top \mathbf{V}_{s,i} \tag{15}$$

Then, we apply the softmax function to obtain the prediction output vector $\hat{\mathbf{Y}}$ of the model:

$$\hat{\mathbf{Y}} = softmax(\hat{\mathbf{y}}) \tag{16}$$

where $\hat{\mathbf{Y}}$ represents a probability distribution over the items $v_{s,i} \in V$, each element $\hat{y_i} \in \hat{\mathbf{Y}}$ denotes the probability of item $v_{s,i}$ appearing as the next-click in the session.

For each session graph, the loss function is defined as the cross entropy of $\hat{\mathbf{Y}}$:

$$\mathcal{L}(\hat{\mathbf{Y}}) = -\sum_{i=1}^{m} \mathbf{Y}_i \log\left(\hat{\mathbf{Y}}_i\right) + (1 - \mathbf{Y}_i)\log\left(1 - \hat{\mathbf{Y}}_i\right) \tag{17}$$

5 Experiments

In this section, we first introduce the experimental data set, then we describe the experimental setup, and finally analyze and compare the performance of the SEGAR model with four SOTA baselines.

5.1 Experiments Setup

Datasets and Data Preparation: We evaluate the proposed models on two datasets. There are no publicly available session recommendation datasets that also have corresponded session item KG. Therefore, we use benchmark datasets in the field of music and movie recommendation, namely Last.fm [11], MovieLens 1M[1] We then linked the item in the datasets with the Freebase [1] entity preserving the user interactions with the linked items in the experimental dataset. We group interaction records by users and sort them according to time stamps and form a session. We also filter out rarely visited items with less than two clicks, and we filter out clicks (items) that did not appear in training set.

Same as [8], we use a session splitting preprocess to generate sessions and corresponding labels by segment the input session for training and testing for both datasets. For example, for an input session,$s = [v_{s,1}, v_{s,2}, \ldots, v_{s,n}]$, we generate a series of sessions and labels $([v_{s,1}, v_{s,2}, \ldots, v_{s,n-1}], v_{s,n})$. In this session, $[v_{s,1}, \ldots, v_{s,n-1}]$ is the generated session, and $v_{s,n}$, represents the next clicked item as the label of the session. The statistics of two benchmark datasets, namely Last.fm and MovieLens 1M, and their corresponding KGs built from Freebase are shown in Table 1 and Table 2.

Evaluation Metrics: We use the following two metrics for evaluation of the performance of the Session-based Recommendation model, which is also widely used in related studies.R@20 is the proportion of correctly recommended items in the test cases amongst the top-20 items.MRR@20 is the average of the reciprocal rank of the recommended items.

[1] https://grouplens.org/datasets/movielens/1m/.

Table 1. Statistics of datasets

Statistics	Last.fm	MovieLens 1M
#clicks	21,074	916,714
#items	3,846	3,952
#sessions	3,009	13,633
#average length	5.67	19.06

Table 2. Statistics of KGs

Statistics	Last.fm	MovieLens 1M
#interactions	42,346	756,684
#data density	3.704%	0.268%
#entities	9,366	18,920
#relations	60	81
#KG Triples	15,518	968,038

Parameters: We construct training set and test set by randomly splitting the dataset with the ratio of 7 : 3. In the SEGAR model, we set the dimension of the latent vector d as 128 for both datasets. The mini-batch Adam [5] optimizer is exerted to optimize these parameters, where the initial learning rate is set to 0.001. The initial learning rate is in $\{0.001, 0.0005, 0.0001\}$, and it will decay by 0.1 every three cycles. The batch size is 128, and the epoch is 30. The embedding size is 128. All the local items embeddings are initialized using TransR [7].

Baselines: The following models, including the state-of-art and closely related works, namely:SR-GNN, NARM, FPMC and RippleNet. They are used as baselines to evaluate the performance of SEGAR:

5.2 Comparison with Baseline Models

In this study, we compared SEGAR with four SOTA baselines mentioned above. The overall performance of R@20 and MRR@20 is shown in Table 3. From the experiment results, it is observed that SEGAR consistently achieves the best performance on both benchmark datasets in terms of R@20 and MRR@20, expect for obtaining a bit lower the MRR values on Last.fm dataset compared to NARM. These results verify the effectiveness of the proposed model.

Table 3. The comparison of SEGAR with four SOTA baselines over two datasets

Method	Last.fm		MovieLens 1M	
	R@20(%)	MRR@20(%)	R@20(%)	MRR@20(%)
SR-GNN	12.007	2.844	25.000	6.232
NARM	11.990	**3.370**	21.137	5.370
FPMC	7.437	0.801	16.742	3.676
RIPPLENET	7.910	1.903	23.560	5.138
SEGAR(1hop)	**14.490**	2.899	**34.375**	**9.983**

The neural network-based method such as NARM and SR-GNN achieves decent performance, proving the effectiveness of deep learning in the session-based recommendation. For the FPMC method, the main disadvantage of the Markov chain-based model is that the independence assumption is too strong, which limits the accuracy of the prediction. Short-term/long-term memory model such as NARM uses recurring units to capture the user's overall interest. This method has the disadvantage of ignoring the transition to distant objects. That is why NARM has a strong performance on short sessions as for Last.fm datasets, but performs not so well on datasets with long sessions such as Movielens. In contrast, the local and global embedding of SEGAR ensures a steadily accurate performance on both short and long sessions-based recommendation. For RippleNet, which like SEGAR that also uses KGs to make recommendations, the importance of the relationship is weak, because the embedded matrix of the relationship is sparse and slow to converge. Besides, as the size of KG increases, the size of the fluctuation set may grow unexpectedly, which not only leads to calculation and storage overhead but also reduces the accuracy.

5.3 Ablation Study

To evaluate how much can the introduction of knowledge graph enhance the session-based recommendation, and to study how many hops of the node neighborhood aggregation are sufficient for achieving accurate results, we perform ablation study and present the results and findings in this section. The following methods are used in this study:

Table 4. Results of the ablation experiment

Method	Last.fm		MovieLens 1M	
	R@20(%)	MRR@20(%)	R@20(%)	MRR@20(%)
SRGAR(w/o KG)	12.145	2.807	28.125	6.812
SRGAR(KG-1hop)	**14.490**	**2.899**	**34.375**	**9.983**
SRGAR(KG-2hop)	14.445	2.844	33.082	7.737
SRGAR(KG-3hop)	14.253	2.849	31.250	7.406

SEGAR-without KG: This method removes the part of the model that uses KGs to generate local session embeddings, and only uses graph convolutional neural networks and temporal and popularity weights to update session node embeddings.

SEGAR-KG (k hop): This method is controlled by the number of hops of node neighborhoods aggregated into the static local item embedding.

Combining Table 3 and Table 4, we find that the overall effect of SEGAR with KG is better, which proves that the GCN, the temporal weight, and popularity weights indeed help update session nodes with dynamic global knowledge and assist in achieving more accurate prediction. Moreover, the popularity weight has a greater influence on the musical dataset. So, it will have a slightly better result. In another dataset, the variance of the length of the sessions in the MovieLens 1M dataset is large, so this has a certain impact on the model results which are not as close as the Last.fm dataset. Because of the large number of sessions in the MovieLens 1M dataset, the Recall and MRR values are higher.

Furthermore, the model with the KG allows an additional improvement of the results. It shows that 1-hop neighborhood aggregation performs better than 2-hop and 3-hop neighborhood aggregation. This demonstrates that information directly related to the node has more significant impact in the session-based recommendation. The 1-hop neighborhood is a key entity related to items. More neighborhood may reduce and dilute the distinguishing features of the local integration vector, thus reducing the prediction accuracy. In summary, this study show that the SEGAR with KG performs better than the model without KG. The knowledge graph plays an important role in helping the session based recommendation.

5.4 Comparison Between Long and Short Sessions

The last comparative experiment aims to verify the effectiveness of the model over long and short sessions. On the Last.fm dataset, we represent short sessions with a session length less than or equal to 6, and those with a session length of larger than 6 are regarded as long sessions. Their proportions are 55.44% and 44.56%, respectively. The division is based on the average length. Similarly, on the MovieLens 1M dataset, we represent those with a session length of less than or equal to 19 as short sessions and those with a session length of more than 19 are regarded as long sessions. Their proportions are 37.43% and 62.57%, respectively. The experimental results are shown in Fig. 2.

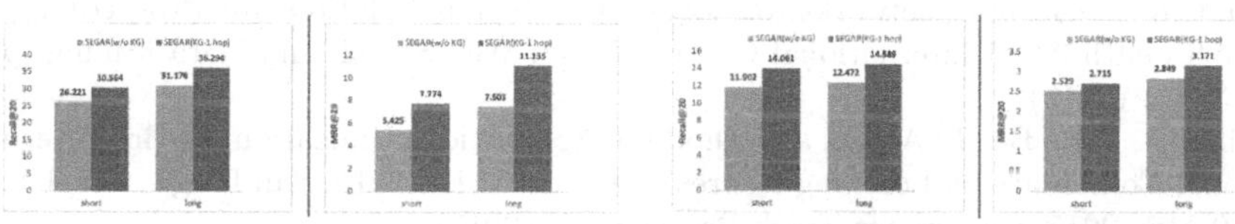

(a) Last.fm (b) MovieLens 1M

Fig. 2. The results of comparison between long and short sessions

We find that the model has a better recommendation effect on long sessions. This is because, as the length of the session grows, the model can capture more complete user interaction information, generating better the recommendation results. In addition, the overall result of the Last.fm dataset is not as good as MovieLens 1M, because the average session length of the Last.fm is much shorter. There is also a large gap in the ratio of session length distribution.

6 Conclusions

Current session-based recommendation models ignore the dynamic global connection between the items and the static local neighborhood-based item relevancy from external knowledge bases, which encode a complete semantic knowledge between items for a more comprehensive and accurate recommendation. To address these issues, we proposed a novel model called SEGAR by leveraging the convolutional graph network and knowledge graph attention network. SEGAR has a unique collaborative knowledge integration mechanism that incorporates static, local and dynamic representations of global session entities with time and popularity factors. Extensive experiments on two benchmark datasets show that SEGAR outperforms four state-of-the-art methods in the accuracy for session-based recommendations. We plan to reduce the time complexity of this model for broader applications in the future.

Acknowledgments. The work was supported by Key Technologies Research and Development Program of China (2017YFC0405805-04) and Basal Research Fund of China (2018B57614).

References

1. Chen, D., Zhao, H.: Research on the method of extracting domain knowledge from the freebase RDF dumps. IEEE Access **6**, 50306–50322 (2018)
2. Chen, M., Zhang, Y., Qiu, M., Guizani, N., Hao, Y.: SPHA: smart personal health advisor based on deep analytics. IEEE Commun. Mag. **56**(3), 164–169 (2018)
3. Gu, P., Han, Y., Gao, W., Xu, G., Wu, J.: Enhancing session-based social recommendation through item graph embedding and contextual friendship modeling. Neurocomputing **419**, 190–202 (2021)
4. Huang, J., Ren, Z., Zhao, W.X., He, G., Wen, J.R., Dong, D.: Taxonomy-aware multi-hop reasoning networks for sequential recommendation. In: Proceedings of the Twelfth ACM International Conference on Web Search and Data Mining, pp. 573–581 (2019)
5. Kingma, D.P., Ba, J.: Adam: a method for stochastic optimization. In: 3rd International Conference on Learning Representations, ICLR 2015, San Diego, CA, USA, 7–9 May 2015, Conference Track Proceedings (2015)
6. Li, J., Ren, P., Chen, Z., Ren, Z., Lian, T., Ma, J.: Neural attentive session-based recommendation. In: Proceedings of the 2017 ACM on Conference on Information and Knowledge Management, pp. 1419–1428 (2017)
7. Lin, Y., Liu, Z., Sun, M., Liu, Y., Zhu, X.: Learning entity and relation embeddings for knowledge graph completion. In: Proceedings of the Twenty-Ninth AAAI Conference on Artificial Intelligence, 25–30 January 2015, pp. 2181–2187 (2015)
8. Liu, Q., Zeng, Y., Mokhosi, R., Zhang, H.: Stamp: short-term attention/memory priority model for session-based recommendation. In: Proceedings of the 24th ACM SIGKDD International Conference on Knowledge Discovery & Data Mining, pp. 1831–1839 (2018)
9. Rendle, S., Freudenthaler, C., Schmidt-Thieme, L.: Factorizing personalized markov chains for next-basket recommendation. In: Proceedings of the 19th international conference on World wide web, pp. 811–820 (2010)

10. Wang, H., et al.: Ripplenet: Propagating user preferences on the knowledge graph for recommender systems. In: Proceedings of the 27th ACM International Conference on Information and Knowledge Management, pp. 417–426 (2018)
11. Wang, H., Zhao, M., et al.: Knowledge graph convolutional networks for recommender systems. In: The World Wide Web Conference, WWW 2019, San Francisco, CA, USA, 13–17 May 2019, pp. 3307–3313. ACM (2019)
12. Wang, X., He, X., Cao, Y., Liu, M., Chua, T.: KGAT: knowledge graph attention network for recommendation. In: Proceedings of the 25th ACM SIGKDD International Conference on Knowledge Discovery & Data Mining, KDD 2019, Anchorage, AK, USA, 4–8 August 2019, pp. 950–958. ACM (2019)
13. Wu, C., Wang, J., Liu, J., Liu, W.: Recurrent neural network based recommendation for time heterogeneous feedback. Knowl.-Based Syst. **109**, 90–103 (2016)
14. Wu, S., Tang, Y., Zhu, Y., Wang, L., Xie, X., Tan, T.: Session-based recommendation with graph neural networks. Proc. AAAI Conf. Artif. Intell. **33**, 346–353 (2019)
15. Zhang, C., Nie, J.: Spatio-temporal attentive network for session-based recommendation. In: Li, G., Shen, H.T., Yuan, Y., Wang, X., Liu, H., Zhao, X. (eds.) KSEM 2020. LNCS (LNAI), vol. 12275, pp. 131–139. Springer, Cham (2020). https://doi.org/10.1007/978-3-030-55393-7_13

Symbiosis: A Novel Framework for Integrating Hierarchies from Knowledge Graph into Recommendation System

Haizhou Du(✉) and Yue Tang

School of Computer Science and Technology, Shanghai University of Electric Power, Shanghai, China
duhaizhou@shiep.edu.cn

Abstract. Integrating knowledge graphs into recommendation systems is promising as knowledge graphs can be side information to address cold start and data sparsity issues in recommendation systems. However, existing methods largely assume that knowledge graphs are under a closed-world assumption, this may lead to suboptimal performances. Furthermore, many existing approaches fail to model semantic hierarchies, which are common in real-world applications. Therefore, it is crucial to consider the incomplete nature of knowledge graphs as well as to represent hierarchical structure when incorporating it into recommendation system. In this paper, we propose Symbiosis, which is an end-to-end model that utilizes link prediction task in knowledge graphs to assist recommendation task. A general motivation for Symbiosis is that the two tasks automatically share the latent features between items and entities. We also incorporated a hierarchical structure method that maps entities into the polar coordinate system into the Symbiosis. Under this framework, not only users can get better recommendations but also knowledge graphs can be completed as these two tasks have a mutual effect. To evaluate the performance of each component, we conduct extensive experiments with two real-world datasets from different scenarios. The extensive results show that Symbiosis can be trained substantially improving F1-score by 59.7% on movie dataset and MR by 59.3% on music dataset compared to state-of-the-art methods.

Keywords: Recommendation systems · Knowledge graph embedding · Hierarchical structure · Collaborative joint learning · Multi-task learning

1 Introduction

With the development of big data and deep learning, knowledge graph(KG) has attracted great attention in many fields such as recommendation systems(RS), dialogue systems and search engines. Among which recommendation systems have been widely adopted to help the users to obtain the favorite item, advice

H. Qiu et al. (Eds.): KSEM 2021, LNAI 12815, pp. 242–254, 2021.
https://doi.org/10.1007/978-3-030-82136-4_20

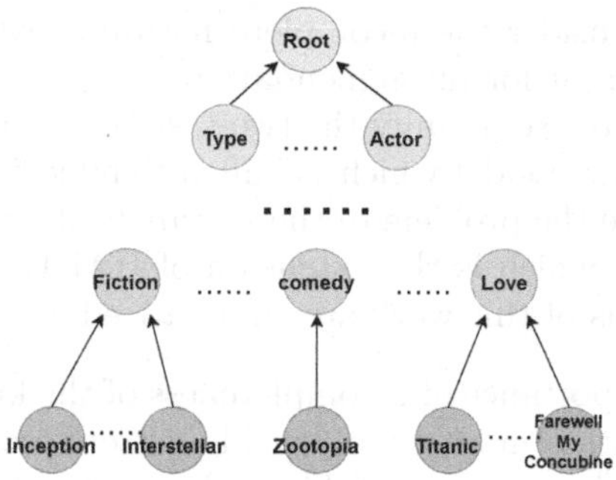

Fig. 1. The hierarchical structure in recommendation systems. The items are first categorized into different categories (*e.g.*,the movie type and the actors of the movie), and then each category is divided into several sub-categories (*e.g.*,Fiction in the movie type and Co-star in the actors of the movie), while each sub-category includes multiple items (*e.g.*,Inception, Interstellar in the Fiction movie).

[4] or services [17]. Early recommendation systems mainly used collaborative filtering(CF) to recommend items.

However, CF often suffers from data sparsity and cold start problems in real-world recommendation scenarios. To solve these problems, researchers suggest integrating side information into CF, such as introducing social networks [7], Context-related comment information [5], knowledge graph [12,20]. KG can enhance the performance of the recommendation system from three aspects: 1)From the perspective of nodes, KG introduces semantic associations between items, which can help to discover potential associations between items and improve the accuracy of recommended items. 2)From the edge point of view, KG is composed of various types of relationships, which is conducive to rationally expanding users' interests, and increasing the diversity of recommended items. 3)KG connects the user's history with the recommendation path, which brings the interpret ability for the recommendation systems [19,20]. Taken these advantages of KG, the recommendation system can solve the problems that cannot be solved by CF method before.

Whereas, there are also problems in KG. The current KG assumed that it is complete and there are no missing nodes or edges, which limits the benefits of the transferred knowledge. Apart from this, existing knowledge graph embedding models mainly focus on modeling relation patterns such as symmetry/antisymmetry, inversion, and composition. However, many existing approaches fail to model semantic hierarchies, which are common in real-world applications. As shown in Fig. 1. Such a hierarchical graph essentially reveals the rich relations behind items. For example, two items(*i.e.*,actors and directors) from different but closely related categories are very likely to have complementary relations w.r.t. their functions. Such hierarchy relations between items can greatly improve the performance of recommendations. As such, we believe that it is critical to consider the incomplete nature of KG as well as the data construction when using it for recommendation.

In this paper, we propose to unify the two tasks of item recommendation and link prediction in a joint model which is called Symbiosis for mutual enhancements. In order to solve the problem of the hierarchical structure in the dataset, we use HiRec method, which is the extension of HAKE [25] in the embedding layer. The contributions of this work are summarized as follows:

- We highlight the importance of incompleteness of the knowledge graph which is a mutual information in order to provide better recommendation.
- We emphasize the importance of hierarchical structure in the real-world dataset so that to systematically analyze the data complexities and characteristics in RS.
- We develop a new method Symbiosis, which achieves jointly training item recommendation task as well as link prediction task in an explicit and end-to-end manner.
- We conduct extensive experiments on two public benchmarks, demonstrating the effectiveness of Symbiosis.

In the rest of this paper, we first review some related work in Sect. 2. Then we introduce the design and analysis of Symbiosis in Sect. 3. Next we describe the experimental settings and results for verifying the performance of Symbiosis in terms of link prediction and item recommendation in Sect. 4. Finally, we conclude the work and discuss the limitations of the work in Sect. 5.

2 Related Work

There are two tasks in our paper to get a joint-learning model, one is link prediction in KG, and the other is item recommendation in recommendation systems. In this section, we will first introduce related work for each of them and then show the correlation between these two tasks.

2.1 Link Prediction in KG

Early methods in solving link prediction contain translation-based model and Matrix Decomposition model.

TransE [2] first proposed the core idea of Translation-based model. It performs well in modeling 1-1 relations. TransH [21] learns different representations for an entity conditioned on different relations. TransR [8] models entities and relations in entity space and relation space respectively. RESCAL [9] represents each relation as a matrix to capture the compositional semantics between entities, and ComplEx [18] introduces complex-value for asymmetric relations.

2.2 Item Recommendation in Recommendation Systems

Early methods such as collaborative filtering algorithms [15] may cause cold-start problem, also, they suffer from the data sparsity issue.

To this end, content-based methods make use of various side information such as the contextual reviews [1], relational data [6] and knowledge graphs [12,20] to improve RS. Piao and Breslin [11] extracted lightweight features drived from KG for factorization machines. Zhang et al. [24] constructed a unified graph by adding a buy relation between users and items. KGAT [20] first applies TransR to obtain the initial representation for entities. CoFM [12] first takes into account the refinements of entity embeddings from user-item modeling as another transferring task. CKE [23] is a representative regularization-based method, which exploits semantic embeddings derived from TransR [8] to enhance matrix factorization.

2.3 Relationship Between Two Tasks – Collaborative Joint Learning

Items in RS usually correspond to entities in many fields, making it possible to transfer knowledge between different fields, thus we can apply the strategy of multi-task learning to jointly train the recommendation module along with the link prediction task to improve the quality of recommendation.

KTUP [3] is proposed to jointly learn the task of RS and KG completion. Hence, embeddings of items and preferences can be enriched by transferring knowledge of entities, relations and preferences in each module under the framework of KTUP. MKR [19] consists of a recommendation module and a KGE module. These two parts are connected with a cross & compress unit to transfer knowledge and share regularization of items in the RS module and entities in the KG. RCF [22] introduces a hierarchical description of items, including both the relation type embedding and relation value embedding.

Our work can be seen as a multi-task learning framework, in which we aim to utilize the connection between RS and KG to help improve their performance. With the joint training of the RS module and the KG module, combined with hierarchical embedding, Symbiosis effectively get better predictions.

3 Approach

In this section, we first formalize the problem, then give an overall architecture for our solution, and introduce the details of the framework.

3.1 Problem Statement

Symbiosis. The input contains KG, user-item interactions and a set of item entity alignments $\mathcal{A} = \{(i, e) \mid i \in \mathcal{I}, e \in \mathcal{E}\}$.

Symbiosis is able to output not only item recommendation results, but also link prediction results. Now let's talk about these two tasks respectively.

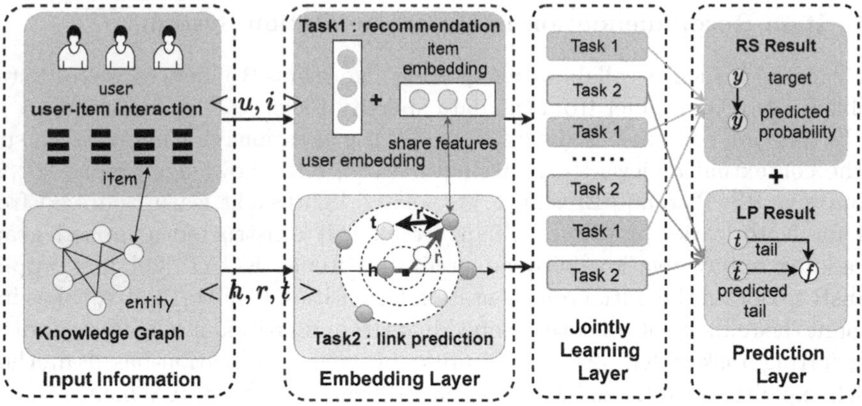

Fig. 2. The architecture of the joint model.

Link Prediction in Knowledge Graphs. We define a KG as a labeled, directed multi-graph KG = $(\mathcal{E}, \mathcal{R}, \mathcal{G})$, where $\mathcal{E}$, $\mathcal{R}$ and $\mathcal{G}$ represent entities, relations, and edges respectively. Link prediction over a knowledge graph aims to predict the missing head entities h or tail entities t or missing relations r for a triple (h, r, t).

Item Recommendation in Recommendation Systems. The recommendation task is to recommend one or a series of unobserved items to a given user.

- Input: User-Item Interaction Matrix and Knowledge Graph.
- Output: One prediction function that predict the probability $\hat{y}_{i,j}$ that user u would adopt item i.

Based on the above two prediction tasks, we can integrate them into one model through the Symbiosis.

3.2 The Proposed Framework

We designed a novel end-to-end jointly architecture, called Symbiosis, as shown in Fig. 2, which consists of three main components, *i.e.*,embedding layer, jointly learning layer and prediction layer.

Embedding Layer. Here we use HiRec(Hierarchy structure in Recommendation Systems), which is the extension of HAKE [25] as the embedding model for recommendation task. As shown in Fig. 3. To be more specific, it maps entities into the polar coordinate system. As far as we know, we are the first to employ the hierarchy structure from KG to RS.

HiRec consists of two partsthe modulus part and the phase partwhich aim to model items in the two different categories, respectively.

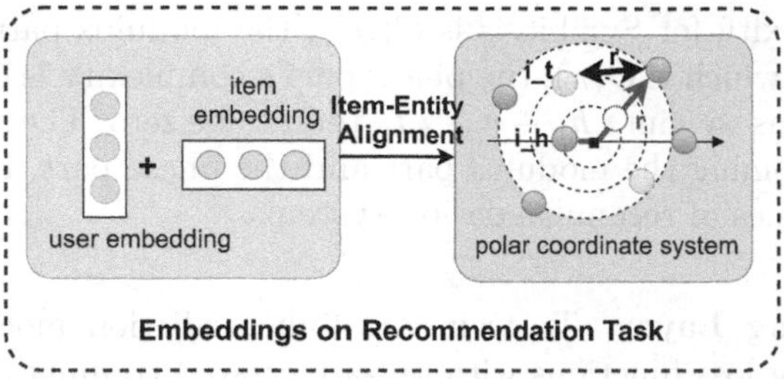

Fig. 3. Embeddings transfer from kg to RS.

- **The Modulus Part** aims to model the items at different levels of the hierarchy. Follow the idea of RotatE [16], which regards the relation **r** as a scaling transformation between $\boldsymbol{h}$ and $\boldsymbol{t}$, We can formulate the modulus part as follows:

$$\boldsymbol{i\_h}_m \circ \boldsymbol{r}_m = \boldsymbol{i\_t}_m \tag{1}$$

where $\boldsymbol{i\_h}_m, \boldsymbol{i\_t}_m \in \mathbb{R}^k$, and $\boldsymbol{r}_m \in \mathbb{R}^k_+$.
The corresponding distance function is:

$$d_{r,m}(\boldsymbol{i\_h}_m, \boldsymbol{i\_t}_m) = \| \boldsymbol{i\_h}_m \circ \boldsymbol{r}_m - \boldsymbol{i\_t}_m \|_2 \tag{2}$$

where $\boldsymbol{i\_h}$, $\boldsymbol{r}$ and $\boldsymbol{i\_t}$ denote the embedding representation of head, relation and tail in RS, and the index m represents modulus part.
- **The Phase Part** aims to model the items at the same level of the semantic hierarchy. We can formulate the phase part as follows:

$$(\boldsymbol{i\_h}_p + \boldsymbol{r}_p) \mod 2\pi = \boldsymbol{i\_t}_p \tag{3}$$

where $\boldsymbol{i\_h}_p, \boldsymbol{r}_p, \boldsymbol{i\_t}_p \in [0, 2\pi)^k$.
The corresponding distance function is:

$$d_{r,p}(\boldsymbol{i\_h}_p, \boldsymbol{i\_t}_p) = \| \sin((\boldsymbol{i\_h}_p + \boldsymbol{r}_p - \boldsymbol{i\_t}_p)/2) \|_1 \tag{4}$$

Specifically, we formulate HiRec as follows:

$$\begin{cases} \boldsymbol{i\_h}_m \circ \boldsymbol{r}_m = \boldsymbol{i\_t}_m \\ (\boldsymbol{i\_h}_p + \boldsymbol{r}_p) \mod 2\pi = \boldsymbol{i\_t}_p \end{cases} \tag{5}$$

where $\boldsymbol{i\_h}_m$, $\boldsymbol{i\_t}_m \in \mathbb{R}^k$, $\boldsymbol{r}_m \in \mathbb{R}^k_+$, $\boldsymbol{i\_h}_p$, $\boldsymbol{r}_p$, $\boldsymbol{h\_t}_p \in [0, 2\pi)^k$.
The distance function of HiRec is:

$$d_r(\boldsymbol{i\_h}, \boldsymbol{i\_t}) = \lambda_1 d_{r,m}(\boldsymbol{i\_h}_m, \boldsymbol{i\_t}_m) + \lambda_2 d_{r,p}(\boldsymbol{i\_h}_p, \boldsymbol{i\_t}_p) \tag{6}$$

where λ_1, $\lambda_2 \in \mathbb{R}$ are parameters that learned by the model. The corresponding score function is:

$$f_r(\boldsymbol{i\_h}, \boldsymbol{i\_t}) = d_r(\boldsymbol{i\_h}, \boldsymbol{i\_t}) = -(\lambda_1 d_{r,m}(\boldsymbol{i\_h}, \boldsymbol{i\_t}) + \lambda_2 d_{r,p}(\boldsymbol{i\_h}, \boldsymbol{i\_t})) \tag{7}$$

The time complexity for Symbiosis is $O(n^3)$, the modulus part's complexity is the same as [16], which is $O(n)$, the phase part's complexity is $O(n^3)$ due to the taylor expansion as we aim $\boldsymbol{i\_h}_p + \boldsymbol{r}_p$ - $\boldsymbol{i\_t}_p$ tend to be zero. The space complexity is $O(n)$. By combining the modulus part and the phase part, HiRec can model semantic hierarchies of recommendation systems.

Jointly Learning Layer. To train the link prediction module, we use the negative sampling loss functions with self-adversarial training [16]:

$$\mathcal{L}_1 = -\log\sigma(\gamma - d_r(\boldsymbol{h}, \boldsymbol{t})) - \sum_{i=1}^{n} p(h_i^{'}, r, t_i^{'}) \log\sigma(d_r(\boldsymbol{h}_i^{'}, \boldsymbol{t}_i^{'}) - \gamma) \tag{8}$$

where γ is a fixed margin, σ is the sigmoid function, and $(h_i^{'}, r, t_i^{'})$ is the ith negative sample.

To train the recommendation module, we use bprLoss:

$$\mathcal{L}_2 = -\sum_{i \in RS} \sum_{i' \notin RS} \log\sigma(g(u, i) - g(u, i^{'})) \tag{9}$$

where (u, i) is positive sample and $(u, i^{'})$ is negative sample. $g(u, i)$ and $g(u, i^{'})$ represent the score of each (u, i) and $(u, i^{'})$, respectively. Notice the i in Eq.(9) is divided into two parts(*i.e.*,the modulus part and the phase part) as the embedding layer described to model the hierarchical structure of recommendation systems, finally we use BPRMF to calculate $g(u, i)$ and $g(u, i^{'})$.

We train Symbiosis using the overall objective function as follows:

$$\mathcal{L} = \lambda\mathcal{L}_1 + (1 - \lambda)\mathcal{L}_2 \tag{10}$$

where $\mathcal{L}_1$ and $\mathcal{L}_2$ represent the loss in link prediction task and loss in recommendation task, respectively. λ is a hyperparameter to balance the two tasks.

Thus, the enhanced item embeddings contain the relational knowledge among entities that are complementary to user-item interactions, and improves item recommendation.

Prediction Layer. The final item recommendation for a user u is given according to the following ranking criterion:

$$u : i_1 > i_2 > ... > i_n \rightarrow \boldsymbol{U}_u^T \boldsymbol{e}_{j1} > \boldsymbol{U}_u^T \boldsymbol{e}_{j2} > ... > \boldsymbol{U}_u^T \boldsymbol{e}_{jn} \tag{11}$$

where i is item in recommendation systems, $\boldsymbol{U}_u$ is the embedding of user u, and $\boldsymbol{e}_{jn}$ is the embedding of item n.

4 Evaluations

In this section, we evaluate our proposed framework on two real-world datasets for both movie and music recommendation scenarios.

We aim to answer the following research questions:

- How does Symbiosis perform compared with state-of-the-art item recommendation methods?
- How does Symbiosis perform compared with state-of-the-art knowledge graph completion methods?

4.1 Datasets Introduction

To evaluate the effectiveness of Symbiosis, we utilize two benchmark datasets: MovieLens-1m [10] and Last.FM [19]. For each dataset, the ratio of training, validation, and test set is 7 : 1 : 2.

Table 1 shows the statistics of MovieLens-1m and Last.FM datasets.

Table 1. Information of two datasets.

Model	Attribute	MovieLens-1m	Last.FM
RS	Users	6040	1893
	Items	3240	17633
	Ratings	998539	42346
	Avg. ratings	165	22
KG	Entity	14708	9367
	Relation	20	60
	Triple	434189	1551

4.2 Experimental Settings

For hyperparameters, the learning rate is 0.001 and 0.0001 on movie and music dataset, respectivly. We use Adam as our optimization methods. The λ is set to 0.7, for that we found as the higher the λ is, the worse the link prediction performs.

Competing Methods

We will verify the efficiency of our model in two parts: Item Recommendation in Recommendation Systems and Link Prediction in Knowledge Graphs.

Item Recommendation in Recommendation Systems

- Typically CF Model. FM [13] and BPRMF [14] are two typically collaborative filtering models, they are the foundations of other baselines.
- CKE. CKE [23] exploits semantic embeddings derived from TransR to enhance matrix factorization.
- CFKG. CFKG [24] applies TransE on the unified graph, casting the recommendation task as the plausibility prediction of (u, buy, i) triplets.
- CoFM. CoFM [12] jointly trains FM and TransE by sharing parameters or regularization of aligned items and entities.

- MKR. MKR [19] consists of a recommendation module and a KGE module. The former learns latent representation for users and items, while the latter learns representation for item associated entities with th KGE model.
- KTUP. KTUP [3] jointly learn the task of RS and KG completion. The bridge is that items can be aligned with corresponding entities in the KG.

Link Prediction in Knowledge Graphs

- Translation Model. Such as TransE [2], TransH [21], TransR [8] etc. These models describe relations as translations from source entities to target entities, can model the inversion and composition patterns.
- HAKE. HAKE [25] can model the semantic hierarchies in knowledge graphs as well as symmetry/antisymmetry, inversion, and composition relation patterns.

Effectiveness of the Item Recommendation task

In this section, we evaluate our models and the state-of-the-art methods on the task of item recommendation based on two datasets.

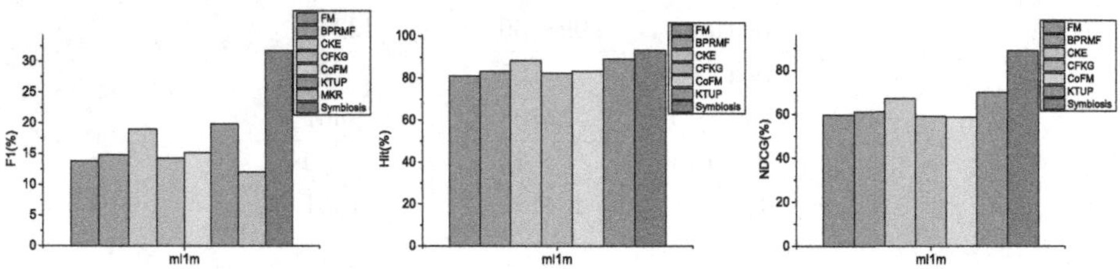

(a) F1 (b) Hit (c) NDCG

Fig. 4. The item recommendation performances on movie dataset.

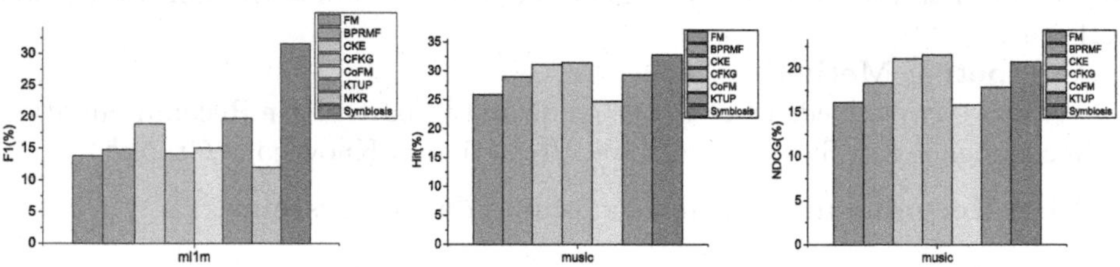

(a) F1 (b) Hit (c) NDCG

Fig. 5. The item recommendation performances on music dataset.

- Metrics. We evaluate the item recommendation performance with F1-Score, Hit and NDCG metrics.
- Ablation experiments. For item recommendation results, we can divide them into two parts: one is single model for improving the performance in recommendation system, the methods contain FM, BPRMF, the other is the multi-task learning model of recommendation system and link prediction, these method contain CKE, CFKG, CoFM, KTUP, MKR and Symbiosis .
- Findings. We test the performances of FM, BPRMF, CKE, CFKG, CoFM, KTUP, MKR and Symbiosis in this paper on two datasets. Which results are illustrated in Fig. 4 and Fig. 5. We can see that our proposed Symbiosis have improved all metrics on dataset ml1m and last.fm, especially it improves F1-score by 59.7% and precision by 47.2% on ml1m compared to state-of-the-art methods in recommendation systems. This is due to the end-to-end learning of Symbiosis obtains the hierarchical structure than other methods that focuses on preference induction. As a conclusion, Symbiosis performs better compared with state-of-the-art item recommendation methods.

Effectiveness of the Link Prediction task

In this section, we evaluate our models as well as the baseline methods on the task of link prediction based on two datasets.

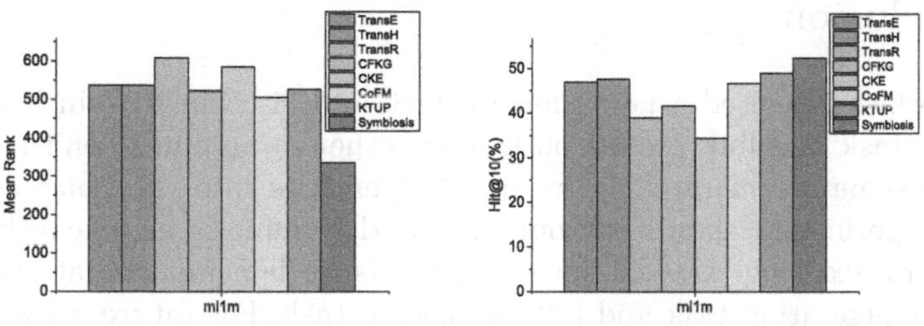

(a) Mean Rank (b) Hit@10

Fig. 6. The link prediction performances on ml1m dataset.

- Metrics. We evaluate the link prediction performance with MeanRank and Hit@10 metrics.
- Ablation experiments. For link prediction results, we divide them into two parts: one is single model for improving the link prediction performance in knowledge graph, the methods contain TransE, TransH, TransR, the other is the multi-task learning model of recommendation system and link prediction, these method contain CKE, CFKG, CoFM, KTUP and Symbiosis .
- Findings. We test the performances of Translation models (*i.e.*,TransE, TransH, TransR), CFKG, CKE, CoFM, KTUP and Symbiosis in this paper on two datasets. Which results are illustrated in Fig. 6 and Fig. 7. We can see that our proposed Symbiosis have improved all metrics on these two dataset.

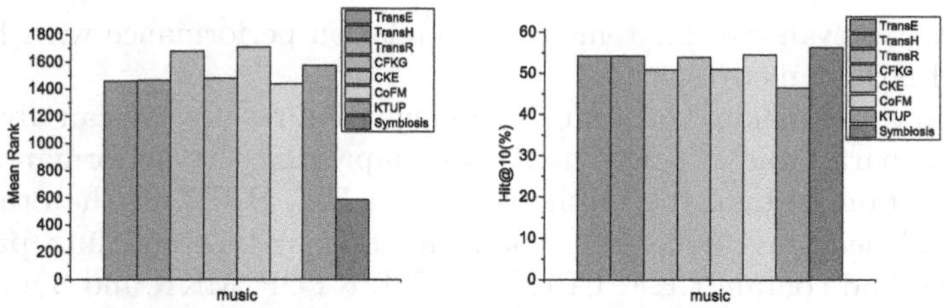

(a) Mean Rank (b) Hit@10

Fig. 7. The link prediction performances on music dataset.

This is due to Symbiosis is a joint learning model which can benifit both tasks in item recommendation and link prediction, we can see that translation-based models are the worst as they train link prediction task only, the Symbiosis perform best among these method as it consider the incompleteness as well as the hierarchical structure between entities than other methods. As a conclusion, Symbiosis performs better compared with state-of-the-art knowledge graph completion methods.

5 Conclusion

In this work, we devised a new framework Symbiosis, which train item recommendation task and link prediction task together in an end-to-end fashion. To model the semantic hierarchies, we mapped entities into the polar coordinate system. Experiments show that our proposed Symbiosis significantly outperforms several existing state-of-the-art methods on benchmark datasets for the both recommendation task and link prediction task. For future works, we plan to investigate how to balance the importance in these two tasks in Symbiosis framework. We will also incorporate other KGE methods as the implementation of KGE module in Symbiosis as users in RS may have special structure.

References

1. Beidas, R.S., Kendall, P.C.: Training therapists in evidence-based practice: a critical review of studies from a systems-contextual perspective. Clin. Psychol. Sci. Pract. **17**(1), 1–30 (2010)
2. Bordes, A., Usunier, N., Garcia-Duran, A., Weston, J., Yakhnenko, O.: Translating embeddings for modeling multi-relational data. In: Advances in Neural Information Processing Systems, Lake Tahoe, pp. 2787–2795 (2013)
3. Cao, Y., Wang, X., He, X., Hu, Z., Chua, T.S.: Unifying knowledge graph learning and recommendation: towards a better understanding of user preferences. In: WWW, San Francisco, pp. 151–161 (2019)
4. Chen, M., Zhang, Y., Qiu, M., Guizani, N., Hao, Y.: Spha: smart personal health advisor based on deep analytics. IEEE Commun. Mag. **56**(3), 164–169 (2018)

5. Cheng, Z., Ding, Y., Zhu, L., Kankanhalli, M.: Aspect-aware latent factor model: rating prediction with ratings and reviews. In: Proceedings of the 2018 World Wide Web Conference, Lyon, France, pp. 639–648 (2018)
6. Feng, F., He, X., Wang, X., Luo, C., Liu, Y., Chua, T.S.: Temporal relational ranking for stock prediction. ACM Trans. Inf. Syst. (TOIS) **37**(2), 1–30 (2019)
7. Jamali, M., Ester, M.: A matrix factorization technique with trust propagation for recommendation in social networks. In: Proceedings of the Fourth ACM Conference on Recommender Systems, Barcelona, Spain, pp. 135–142 (2010)
8. Lin, Y., Liu, Z., Sun, M., Liu, Y., Zhu, X.: Learning entity and relation embeddings for knowledge graph completion. In: AAAI, Austin, Texas, USA (2015)
9. Nickel, M., Tresp, V., Kriegel, H.P.: Factorizing yago: scalable machine learning for linked data. In: WWW, pp. 271–280 (2012)
10. Noia, T.D., Ostuni, V.C., Tomeo, P., Sciascio, E.D.: Sprank: semantic path-based ranking for top-n recommendations using linked open data. ACM Trans. Intell. Syst. Technol. (TIST) **8**(1), 1–34 (2016)
11. Piao, G., Breslin, J.G.: Factorization machines leveraging lightweight linked open data-enabled features for top-n recommendations. In: Bouguettaya, A., et al. (eds.) WISE 2017. LNCS, vol. 10570, pp. 420–434. Springer, Cham (2017). https://doi.org/10.1007/978-3-319-68786-5_33
12. Piao, G., Breslin, J.G.: Transfer learning for item recommendations and knowledge graph completion in item related domains via a co-factorization model. In: Gangemi, A., et al. (eds.) ESWC 2018. LNCS, vol. 10843, pp. 496–511. Springer, Cham (2018). https://doi.org/10.1007/978-3-319-93417-4_32
13. Rendle, S.: Factorization machines. In: 2010 IEEE International Conference on Data Mining, Sydney, pp. 995–1000. IEEE (2010)
14. Rendle, S., Freudenthaler, C., Gantner, Z., Schmidt-Thieme, L.: Bpr: bayesian personalized ranking from implicit feedback. arXiv preprint arXiv:1205.2618 (2012)
15. Schafer, J.B., Frankowski, D., Herlocker, J., Sen, S.: Collaborative filtering recommender systems. In: Brusilovsky, P., Kobsa, A., Nejdl, W. (eds.) The Adaptive Web. LNCS, vol. 4321, pp. 291–324. Springer, Heidelberg (2007). https://doi.org/10.1007/978-3-540-72079-9_9
16. Sun, Z., Deng, Z.H., Nie, J.Y., Tang, J.: Rotate: knowledge graph embedding by relational rotation in complex space. arXiv preprint arXiv:1902.10197 (2019)
17. Tao, L., Golikov, S., Gai, K., Qiu, M.: A reusable software component for integrated syntax and semantic validation for services computing. In: 2015 IEEE Symposium on Service-Oriented System Engineering, pp. 127–132. IEEE (2015)
18. Trouillon, T., Welbl, J., Riedel, S., Gaussier, É., Bouchard, G.: Complex embeddings for simple link prediction. In: ICML, New York (2016)
19. Wang, H., Zhang, F., Zhao, M., Li, W., Xie, X., Guo, M.: Multi-task feature learning for knowledge graph enhanced recommendation. In: WWW, San Francisco, pp. 2000–2010 (2019)
20. Wang, X., He, X., Cao, Y., Liu, M., Chua, T.S.: Kgat: knowledge graph attention network for recommendation. In: Proceedings of the 25th ACM SIGKDD International Conference on Knowledge Discovery & Data Mining, Alaska, USA, pp. 950–958 (2019)
21. Wang, Z., Zhang, J., Feng, J., Chen, Z.: Knowledge graph embedding by translating on hyperplanes. In: AAAI, Canada (2014)
22. Xin, X., He, X., Zhang, Y., Zhang, Y., Jose, J.: Relational collaborative filtering: modeling multiple item relations for recommendation. In: SIGIR, Paris, France, pp. 125–134 (2019)

23. Zhang, F., Yuan, N.J., Lian, D., Xie, X., Ma, W.Y.: Collaborative knowledge base embedding for recommender systems. In: Proceedings of the 22nd ACM SIGKDD International Conference on Knowledge Discovery and Data Mining, San Francisco, pp. 353–362 (2016)
24. Zhang, Y., Ai, Q., Chen, X., Wang, P.: Learning over knowledge-base embeddings for recommendation. arXiv preprint arXiv:1803.06540 (2018)
25. Zhang, Z., Cai, J., Zhang, Y., Wang, J.: Learning hierarchy-aware knowledge graph embeddings for link prediction. In: AAAI, New York, vol. 34, pp. 3065–3072 (2020)

An Ensemble Fuzziness-Based Online Sequential Learning Approach and Its Application

Wei-Peng Cao[1], Sheng-Dong Li[2], Cheng-Chao Huang[3], Yu-Hao Wu[1], Qiang Wang[4], Da-Chuan Li[4(✉)], and Ye Liu[1(✉)]

[1] College of Computer Science and Software Engineering, Shenzhen University, Shenzhen, China
ly@szu.edu.cn
[2] China Electronics Cloud Brain (Tianjin) Technology CO., LTD., Tianjin, China
[3] Nanjing Institute of Software Technology, ISCAS, Nanjing, China
[4] Department of Computer Science and Engineering, Southern University of Science and Technology, Shenzhen, China
lidc3@mail.sustech.edu.cn

Abstract. Traditional deep learning algorithms are difficult to deploy on most IoT terminal devices due to their limited computing power. To solve this problem, this paper proposes a novel ensemble fuzziness-based online sequential learning approach to support the local update of terminal intelligent models and improve their prediction performance. Our method consists of two modules: server module and terminal module. The latter uploads the data collected in real-time to the server module, then the server module selects the most valuable samples and sends them back to the terminal module for the local update. Specifically, the server module uses the ensemble learning mechanism to filter data through multiple fuzzy classifiers, while the terminal module uses the online neural networks with random weights to update the local model. Extensive experimental results on ten benchmark data sets show that the proposed method outperforms other similar algorithms in prediction. Moreover, we apply the proposed method to solve the network intrusion detection problem, and the corresponding experimental results show that our method has better generalization ability than other existing solutions.

Keywords: Extreme learning machine · Fuzzy classifier · Ensemble learning · Online learning · Intrusion detection system

1 Introduction

Traditional deep learning models have made breakthroughs in many fields, especially in computer vision and natural language processing. However, the training of such models often requires strong computing power, which is impossible for most terminal devices in industrial IoT scenarios [1–3]. To alleviate this issue,

H. Qiu et al. (Eds.): KSEM 2021, LNAI 12815, pp. 255–267, 2021.
https://doi.org/10.1007/978-3-030-82136-4_21

researchers have proposed many solutions from the perspective of model compression and the design of lightweight neural networks, this study focuses on the latter one, specifically, the design of a new Neural Network with Random Weights (NNRW) [4], which is expected to be able to support the model's effective training and updating on devices with limited computing power [5,6].

Taking Extreme Learning Machine (ELM) [7], a typical NNRW, as an example, it believes that not all parameters in the neural network require to be iteratively updated. Therefore, in ELM, some parameters are randomly assigned under certain rules, then they remain unchanged throughout the subsequent model training process. This training mechanism greatly reduces the size of parameters to be learned. ELM also adopts a non-iterative training mechanism to further accelerate the training efficiency of the model. Traditional ELM and its variants mainly adopt the batch learning mode, so it is difficult for them to effectively deal with the problem of data stream mining in real-life scenarios.

To solve this problem, Liang NY et al. [8] proposed the Online Sequential ELM algorithm (OS-ELM), which was latterly improved and applied to many scenarios by other researchers [9–14]. OS-ELM inherits the advantages of ELM, such as high training efficiency and good generalization ability. The training of OS-ELM can be completed efficiently without the help of GPUs, so it is suitable for many edge devices. Some representative OS-ELM-based works include: Mao WT et al. [9] combined a hybrid sampling strategy with OS-ELM to handle the imbalance problem of online sequential learning. Zhang HG et al. [10] and Cao WP et al. [11] considered the timeliness of sequential data and used the forgetting factor to weigh the importance of new samples and old samples. Chen YT et al. [12] combined the idea of federated learning with OS-ELM and proposed a federated online learning framework. In their method, OS-ELM is used to accelerate computational efficiency, and the federal learning mechanism is used to protect the privacy of local data in edge devices. Jiang XL et al. [13] applied OS-ELM to solve the indoor localization problem and achieved an acceptable accuracy. Wong PK et al. [14] used OS-ELM to do engine air-ratio prediction and achieved good results. The innovation of these algorithms and applications is enlightening and demonstrates the great potential of OS-ELM.

However, OS-ELM and the above-mentioned algorithms will face great challenges when the data stream for the model update is on large scale. This is because these algorithms have to calculate the generalized inverse of the output matrix of the hidden layer [15] in the process of model training. In big data scenarios, the dimension of this matrix is extremely high, calculating its generalized inverse will suffer from the problem of high instability and low precision, leading to the uncertainty of the model.

To avoid this problem, we previously proposed a Fuzziness-based OS-ELM algorithm (FOS-ELM) [16] based on the output fuzziness of samples, which can filter the relatively valuable samples from the whole data stream. In this way, one can effectively reduce the scale of the data stream from extremely large to relatively small. Then, one can use the filtered samples to update local models, avoiding the inaccuracy problem caused by calculating the generalized inverse of the huge matrix. Specifically, FOS-ELM first trains a fuzzy classifier based on the initial data and then uses it to evaluate the quality of new samples according to their corresponding fuzziness. Our study reveals that the samples with high output fuzziness can effectively improve the generalization ability of online models. Therefore, FOS-ELM uses the fuzzy classifier to filter out such samples and applies them to update the online model, thus improving the stability and prediction accuracy of the model. At the same time, the reduction in data size allows the model to be effectively trained on various terminal devices.

However, FOS-ELM has a disadvantage: the performance of the online model depends heavily on the reliability of the fuzzy classifier. Since the fuzzy classifier of FOS-ELM is only trained with the initial data and cannot be updated with the new data, so any change in the data stream will make the model face the risk of paralysis. Moreover, a single fuzzy classifier inevitably has a certain "blind zone" due to its inductive bias.

To solve this problem, we improve FOS-ELM from the perspective of ensemble learning and propose a novel ensemble FOS-ELM algorithm (EFOS-ELM). EFOS-ELM has two major innovations: First, inspired by the idea of ensemble learning, we adopt three methods to train three fuzzy classifiers respectively and combine them to predict the output fuzziness of new samples. Second, we use the framework of "server module + terminal module" to divide and conquer all the samples in the data stream. Specifically, EFOS-ELM uploads all the new samples to the server module for the update of three fuzzy classifiers. Meanwhile, the samples filtered by the server module were provided for the update of the terminal model. The contributions of this paper can be summarized as follows:

(1) The introduction of the ensemble learning strategy into the fuzziness based online learning paradigm effectively improves the prediction accuracy of the output fuzziness of new samples, so one can more accurately and stably filter out small-scale and high-quality samples from the data stream;
(2) The online learning framework of "server module + terminal module" is explicitly constructed. The relatively powerful computing ability of the server module is utilized to train the large model, which is used to select the most valuable samples for the terminal model update, so that the local model can be effectively updated under the original hardware configuration;
(3) We evaluated the performance of EFOS-ELM on ten benchmark data sets and applied it to solve a typical network intrusion detection problem. The experimental results show that EFOS-ELM can achieve higher recognition accuracy than other machine learning algorithms.

The organization of this paper are organized as follows: in Sect. 2, we take OS-ELM as an example to briefly review the learning mechanism of online NNRWs. In Sect. 3, the details of the proposed EFOS-ELM algorithm are introduced. In Sect. 4, we show our experimental configuration and the corresponding results. We conclude this paper in Sect. 5.

2 Preliminaries

In this section, we take OS-ELM as an example to review the learning mechanism of online NNRWs. OS-ELM is an ELM-based online learning algorithm for data stream mining, which inherits the non-iterative training mechanism of ELM and has high training efficiency. Compared with traditional online neural networks such as the online backpropagation method [17], it can achieve higher training efficiency and better generalization ability in many scenarios. OS-ELM and ELM have the same network structure, as shown in Fig. 1.

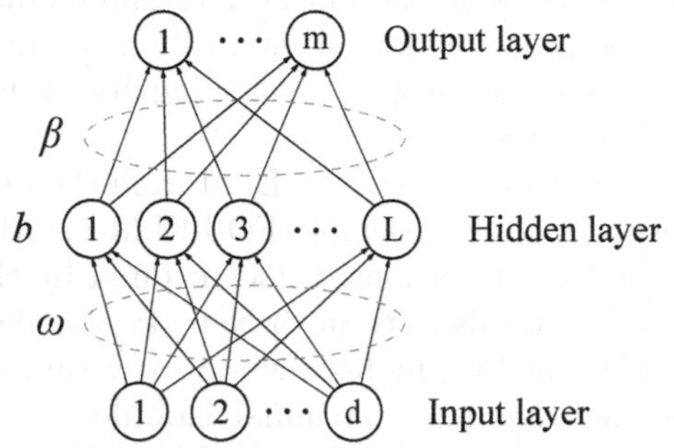

Fig. 1. The network structure of OS-ELM.

The original OS-ELM has only one hidden layer. L refers to the number of hidden layer nodes. Input weights ω and hidden biases b are randomly assigned from $[-1, 1]$ according to a uniform distribution. Details of the training mechanism of OS-ELM are as follows.

Given an initial training dataset $D_0 = \{(x_i, t_i)|x_i \in R^d, t_i = R^m\}_{i=1}^{N_0}$, where N_0, d, and m refer to the number of samples, the feature dimensions, and the number of classes, respectively. The initial model M_0 can be calculated through the following three steps:

Step 1. Randomly generate input weights ω and hidden biases b from $[-1, 1]$ according to a uniform distribution;

Step 2. Calculate the output matrix of the hidden layer:

$$H_0 = \begin{pmatrix} G(\omega_1 \cdot x_1 + b_1) & \cdots & G(\omega_L \cdot x_1 + b_L) \\ \vdots & \ddots & \vdots \\ G(\omega_1 \cdot x_{N_0} + b_1) & \cdots & G(\omega_L \cdot x_{N_0} + b_L) \end{pmatrix}_{N_0 \times L}$$

where $G(\cdot)$ is the activation function of the hidden layer;

Step 3. Calculate the output weights $\beta_0 = H_0^{+} T_0 = (H_0^T H_0)^{-1} H_0^T T_0$, where T_0 is the label matrix.

When new training data arrive, OS-ELM adopts the following steps to update the model parameters:

Let $k = 0$ and $P_0 = (H_0^T H_0)^{-1}$;

Step 4. Update the output matrix of the hidden layer after the same preprocessing for the new data of the $(k+1)$ block:

$$H_{k+1} = [H_k^T, H_{k+1}^T]^T$$

where H_{k+1} represents the random feature mapping matrix corresponding to the new data.

Step 5. Update the current output weights: $\beta_{k+1} = \beta_k + P_{k+1}H_{k+1}^T(T_{k+1} - H_{k+1}\beta_k)$ where $P_{k+1} = P_k - P_k H_{k+1}^T(I + H_{k+1}PH_{k+1}^T)^{-1}H_{k+1}P_k$, and T_{k+1} represents the label matrix corresponding to the new data.

Step 6. Set $k = k + 1$. Repeat steps 4–6 until all new data has been learned.

In this study, we assume that OS-ELM is the local model in terminal devices. Since many IoT terminal devices collect data in real-time, the amount of data used for model updating is huge. To address the challenge of learning massive data to local models, we propose an online learning framework with the linkage of "server module + terminal module", which uses the computing power of the server module to train large models and selects the most valuable samples for the update of the terminal module, so that the local model can be effectively updated under the original hardware configuration. Details of the proposed algorithm will be given in the next section.

3 Ensemble Fuzziness Based Online Sequential Extreme Learning Machine

In this section, we introduce details of the proposed EFOS-ELM algorithm. The learning pipeline of EFOS-ELM is shown in Fig. 2.

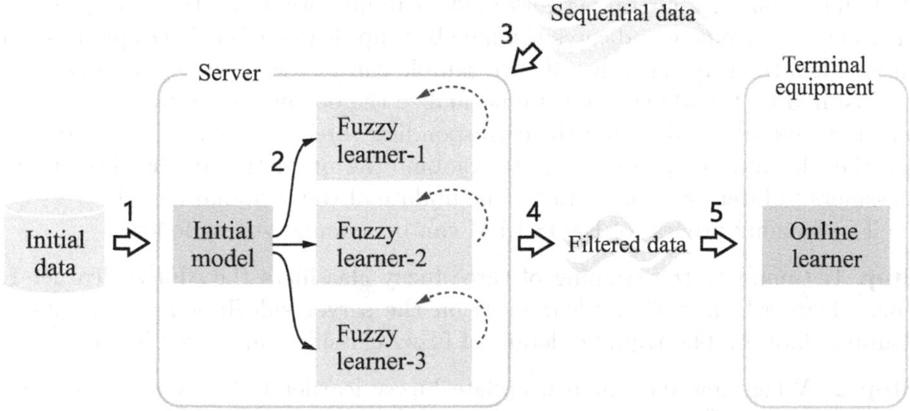

Fig. 2. The learning framework of EFOS-ELM.

Our method mainly includes two modules: server module and terminal module. Specifically, we deploy three fuzzy classifiers on the server side and use the voting mechanism to filter the most valuable samples in the data stream. At the same time, all the new data will also be used to update the three fuzzy classifiers to ensure that they can adapt to the changes of data in time. The terminal equipment deploys the online learner module (OS-ELM was used in this experiment), which will use the filtered data to update the local model, so as to make the model better adapt to the changes of the environment without changing the hardware of the terminal platform.

Next, we briefly introduce the key techniques of the three fuzzy classifiers on the server side. In real life, people do not have clear boundaries for some concepts such as "tall" and "short", "fat" and "thin". To describe this situation with unclear boundaries, fuzzy set theory was proposed [18,19]. On this basis, the authors of [20] proposed the concept of fuzzy entropy to describe the fuzziness of a fuzzy set. Later, other researchers also proposed several new methods to calculate the fuzzy entropy. Here we introduce three most commonly used methods.

Given a fuzzy set $\mu = \{\mu_1, \mu_2, ..., \mu_m\}$, the fuzziness of μ can be calculated by the following three formulas respectively:

$$F(\mu) = -\frac{1}{m}\sum_{i=1}^{m}(\mu_i log\mu_i + (1-\mu_i)log(1-\mu_i)) \tag{1}$$

$$F(\mu) = \frac{2}{m}\sum_{i=1}^{m}\left|\mu_i - \left[\mu_i \geq \frac{1}{2}\right]\right| \tag{2}$$

$$F(\mu) = \sum_{i=1}^{m}(\mu_i(1-\mu_i)) \tag{3}$$

For the properties and rationality of (1), (2), and (3), please refer to [20–22].

The combination of fuzzy set theory and machine learning technology has drawn tremendous attention in recent years. In [23], the authors pointed out that the output of a neural network model can be normalized to a fuzzy vector, in which each element indicates the membership degree of each sample to each class. Then the learning value of each sample can be evaluated by its fuzziness.

Inspired by the above work, we normalize the output of the three classifiers on the server side and obtain the corresponding three fuzzy classifiers. Then we use the idea of ensemble learning to combine the prediction of the three fuzzy classifiers to filter valuable data for the update of the terminal model.

The training process of EFOS-ELM can be summarized as follows:

Step 1. Complete the training of three fuzzy classifiers (i.e., Fuzzy learner-1, Fuzzy learner-2, and Fuzzy learner-3) on the server side based on the initial training dataset. The training details of fuzzy classifiers are given in [16].

Step 2. When new data arrive, update Fuzzy learner-1, Fuzzy learner-2, and Fuzzy learner-3. Then use the three fuzzy classifiers to calculate the fuzziness of each sample respectively, and then filter out the samples with relatively high fuzziness based on the voting mechanism. In our experiment, we chose the top 1/3 of the samples ranked by fuzziness.

Step 3. Update the local model (i.e., OS-ELM) on terminal devices based on the filtered samples.

Step 4. Repeat steps 2–4 regularly to improve the adaptability of the server module and the terminal model to the environment.

Compared with FOS-ELM and OS-ELM, EFOS-ELM has the following characteristics:

(1) Ensemble learning mechanism enables the fuzzy classifiers to filter out valuable samples more accurately;
(2) The server module can utilize massive new data to ensure the timely update and good generalization ability of the fuzzy classifiers;
(3) The data used for the update of terminal models are only the samples with high fuzziness, so the updating efficiency of the local model is very high.

4 Experimental Setting and Results

In our experiments, we evaluated the performance of EFOS-ELM on ten benchmark classification problems and one network intrusion detection problem.

4.1 Experimental Setting

All the experiments were conducted on Windows 10 OS with CPU I5-5300 and 8 GB RAM. The simulation software is Matlab R2014a. The number of hidden layer nodes in all neural networks was set to 50, and the Sigmoid function (i.e., $G(z) = 1/(exp(-z)))$ was chosen as the activation function. Each experiment was conducted thirty times independently and the final experimental result was the average of these thirty experimental results.

4.2 Experimental Results on the Benchmark Datasets

The ten benchmark classification datasets are from the UCI data database [24] and the relevant details are shown in Table 1.

For each dataset, we divided it into a training dataset and a testing dataset according to 7:3, and then the training dataset was further divided into an initial dataset and a sequential dataset according to 3:7 to simulate the process of online learning. We standardized the features of these datasets to mitigate the negative effects of dimension differences on the learner.

We simulated three of the most common online learning scenarios: learning new samples one-by-one (scenario #1), learning new samples chunk-by-chunk (a fixed chunk size, > 1) (scenario #2), and learning new samples chunk-by-chunk (a randomly varying chunk size) (scenario #3). The experimental results

Table 1. The details of ten benchmark datasets.

Dataset	Attributes	Classes	Samples number
Pima	8	2	768
Credit	6	2	690
Sonar	60	2	208
Musk	166	2	476
Spambase	57	2	458
AU1_21	20	2	1000
Wilt	5	2	500
Abalone	7	3	1379
Wine_QW	11	3	4535
Page	10	3	532

Table 2. The experimental results on benchmarks (case #1).

Datasets	Accuracy	OS-ELM	FOS-ELM	EFOS-ELM
Pima	Training	0.8225	0.8099	0.8551
	Testing	0.6864	0.7034	**0.7500**
Credit	Training	0.8224	0.8132	0.8093
	Testing	0.6715	0.6908	**0.7005**
Sonar	Training	0.9600	0.9079	0.9605
	Testing	0.7206	0.8088	**0.8235**
Musk	Training	0.8914	0.8994	0.8686
	Testing	0.6871	0.7347	**0.7619**
Spambase	Training	0.9341	0.9401	0.9481
	Testing	0.8531	0.8811	**0.9021**
Au1_21	Training	0.7059	0.7754	0.7888
	Testing	0.6833	0.7200	**0.7267**
Wilt	Training	0.7606	0.7819	0.9006
	Testing	0.7267	0.7667	**0.7933**
Abalone	Training	0.6125	0.6360	0.6653
	Testing	0.5429	0.5690	**0.5714**
Wine_QW	Training	0.6015	0.6040	0.5979
	Testing	0.5770	0.5880	**0.5916**
Page	Training	0.9347	0.9235	0.9392
	Testing	0.8261	0.8571	**0.8634**

Table 3. The experimental results on benchmarks (case #2, chunk size = 20).

Datasets	Accuracy	OS-ELM	FOS-ELM	EFOS-ELM
Pima	Training	0.7535	0.7887	0.7840
	Testing	0.7203	0.7331	**0.7712**
Credit	Training	0.8496	0.7967	0.8132
	Testing	0.7101	0.7198	**0.7295**
Sonar	Training	0.9342	0.9692	0.9737
	Testing	0.6912	0.7500	**0.7941**
Musk	Training	0.8914	0.8971	0.9029
	Testing	0.7483	0.7619	**0.7823**
Spambase	Training	0.9193	0.9042	0.9255
	Testing	0.8601	0.8671	**0.8741**
Au1_21	Training	0.7807	0.7655	0.7861
	Testing	0.7133	0.7167	**0.7300**
Wilt	Training	0.8421	0.8830	0.9468
	Testing	0.7200	0.8200	**0.8533**
Abalone	Training	0.6238	0.6200	0.6429
	Testing	0.6184	0.6119	**0.6310**
Wine_QW	Training	0.5819	0.5872	0.5908
	Testing	0.5652	0.5689	**0.5887**
Page	Training	0.9397	0.9317	0.9415
	Testing	0.8696	0.9006	**0.9255**

corresponding to these three scenarios are shown in Table 2, Table 3, and Table 4, respectively.

It can be observed from Table 2, 3 and 4 that the proposed EFOS-ELM can achieve higher testing accuracy than OS-ELM and FOS-ELM. This experimental phenomenon implies that:

(1) Ensemble learning strategy is effective for the performance improvement of FOS-ELM;
(2) The combination of different fuzziness calculation methods can filter out valuable samples more accurately;
(3) The proposed algorithm has better generalization ability than OS-ELM and FOS-ELM.

Table 4. The experimental results on benchmarks (case #3, chunk size ∈ [10, 20]).

Datasets	Accuracy	OS-ELM	FOS-ELM	EFOS-ELM
Pima	Training	0.8225	0.8099	0.8188
	Testing	0.6864	0.7034	**0.7288**
Credit	Training	0.8410	0.8093	0.8366
	Testing	0.7488	0.7536	**0.7778**
Sonar	Training	0.9368	0.9238	0.9305
	Testing	0.6471	0.6912	**0.7500**
Musk	Training	0.8892	0.8994	0.8686
	Testing	0.7279	0.7347	**0.7619**
Spambase	Training	0.9341	0.9479	0.9401
	Testing	0.8531	0.8811	**0.9021**
Aul_21	Training	0.7032	0.7914	0.8070
	Testing	0.6267	0.6633	**0.6800**
Wilt	Training	0.7713	0.9574	0.9704
	Testing	0.6867	0.8067	**0.8200**
Abalone	Training	0.6514	0.6204	0.6536
	Testing	0.6095	0.6190	**0.6333**
Wine_QW	Training	0.5896	0.5994	0.6071
	Testing	0.5660	0.5770	**0.5814**
Page	Training	0.9356	0.9296	0.9497
	Testing	0.8385	0.8758	**0.8944**

4.3 Experiments on Network Intrusion Detection Problem

Intrusion detection is one of the most important research topics in the field of network security [25,26]. Intrusion Detection System (IDS) is a kind of network security protection equipment or software that can monitor, recognize, and deal with network intrusion or suspicious activities in real-time. In recent years, machine learning-based IDS has been proposed continuously. NSL-KDD [27] is currently one of the most commonly used benchmark datasets to evaluate the performance of IDS. This study also uses NSL-KDD to evaluate the performance of the proposed algorithm for the intrusion detection problem.

NSL-KDD contains 41 attributes and the specific meaning of each dimension is described in [28]. The class label of NSL-KDD indicates whether a sample is a suspicious activity. In our experiment, the preprocessing method for NSL-KDD is the same as in [28].

Considering the feature complexity and the number of samples in NSL-KDD are much higher than those in the above benchmark datasets, in this experiment, we set the number of hidden layer nodes of fuzzy classifiers and online learners to 300 and 100, respectively. The size of the data chunk for online model updates is set to be a random integer between 30 and 50. The details of the corresponding experimental results are shown in Table 5.

Table 5. The experimental results on the network intrusion detection problem.

Algorithms	Accuracy
J48	0.6397
Naive Bayes	0.5577
NB tree	0.6616
Random forests	0.6325
Random tree	0.5851
Multi-layer perceptron	0.5734
SVM	0.4229
Ashfaq' method	0.6882
OS-ELM	0.5836
FOS-ELM	0.6570
EFOS-ELM	**0.6902**

Note: Except for OS-ELM, FOS-ELM, and EFOS-ELM, other experimental results are obtained from [28].

It can be observed from Table 5 that compared with the other ten machine learning methods, EFOS-ELM can achieve a higher prediction accuracy. This experiment verifies the effectiveness of EFOS-ELM and implies the potential of EFOS-ELM in network intrusion detection scenarios.

Remark: Here we discuss the advantages and disadvantages of EFOS-ELM. The advantages of EFOS-ELM are as follows. First, the generalization ability of the original FOS-ELM is effectively improved by using the ensemble learning mechanism. Second, the learning architecture of "server module + terminal module" provides an effective solution for the intellectualization of various platforms with limited computing power. The disadvantage of EFOS-ELM is that the data collected by the terminal equipment need to be transmitted to the server side for screening, and this process has higher requirements on the security and transmission speed of the data. To alleviate this issue, one may upgrade our solution based on "5G + federated learning". Specifically, with the popularization of the 5G infrastructure, the transmission speed of data will be improved qualitatively. Meanwhile, the federated learning mechanism [29] can be considered to improve the security of local data.

5 Conclusions

To make full use of the information of the data stream and support the update of terminal intelligent models, we proposed a novel ensemble online learning method (i.e., EFOS-ELM) based on the fuzzy theory, ensemble learning, and neural network with random weights in this study. The learning framework of EFO-ELM consists of the server module and the terminal module. On the server side, EFO-ELM uses the ensemble learning mechanism to fuse the outputs of three fuzzy classifiers and filters out the samples with high learning value. Then it sends these samples to the terminal side for local model updating. Since the updating of the terminal model uses relatively small-scale samples with high-quality, it can not only have high learning efficiency but also guarantee the good generalization ability of the local model. Extensive experimental results show that our proposed EFOS-ELM is effective and can achieve better generalization ability than other similar algorithms. EFOS-ELM is expected to be widely used in various scenarios of the industrial IoT.

Acknowledgement. This work was supported by National Natural Science Foundation of China (61836005) and Guangdong Science and Technology Department (2018B010107004).

References

1. Gai, K., Qiu, M., Zhao, H., Sun, X.: Resource management in sustainable cyber-physical systems using heterogeneous cloud computing. IEEE Trans. Sustain. Comput. **3**(2), 60–72 (2017)
2. Guo, Y., Zhuge, Q., Hu, J., Qiu, M., Sha, E.H.M.: Optimal data allocation for scratch-pad memory on embedded multi-core systems. In: IEEE International Conference on Parallel Processing (ICPP), pp. 464–471 (2011)
3. Zhang, L., Qiu, M., Tseng, W.C., Sha, E.H.M.: Variable partitioning and scheduling for MPSoC with virtually shared scratch pad memory. J. Signal Process. Syst. **58**(2), 247–265 (2010)
4. Cao, W., Wang, X., Ming, Z., Gao, J.: A review on neural networks with random weights. Neurocomputing **275**, 278–287 (2018)
5. Niu, J., Liu, C., Gao, Y., Qiu, M.: Energy efficient task assignment with guaranteed probability satisfying timing constraints for embedded systems. IEEE Trans. Parallel Distrib. Syst. **25**(8), 2043–2052 (2013)
6. Gao, Y., Iqbal, S., Zhang, P., Qiu, M.: Performance and power analysis of high-density multi-GPGPU architectures: a preliminary case study. In: International Conference on High Performance Computing and Communications, pp. 66–71 (2015)
7. Huang, G.B., Zhu, Q.Y., Siew, C.K.: Extreme learning machine: theory and applications. Neurocomputing **70**(1–3), 489–501 (2006)
8. Liang, N.Y., Huang, G.B., Saratchandran, P., Sundararajan, N.: A fast and accurate online sequential learning algorithm for feedforward networks. IEEE Trans. Neural Netw. **17**(6), 1411–1423 (2006)
9. Mao, W., Wang, J., He, L., Tian, Y.: Online sequential prediction of imbalance data with two-stage hybrid strategy by extreme learning machine. Neurocomputing **261**, 94–105 (2017)
10. Zhang, H., Zhang, S., Yin, Y.: Online sequential ELM algorithm with forgetting factor for real applications. Neurocomputing **261**, 144–152 (2017)

11. Cao, W., Ming, Z., Xu, Z., Zhang, J., Wang, Q.: Online sequential extreme learning machine with dynamic forgetting factor. IEEE Access **7**, 179746–179757 (2019)
12. Chen, Y.T., Chuang, Y.C., Wu, A.Y.: Online extreme learning machine design for the application of federated learning. In: IEEE International Conference on Artificial Intelligence Circuits and Systems (AICAS), pp. 188–192 (2020)
13. Jiang, X., Liu, J., Chen, Y., Liu, D., Gu, Y., Chen, Z.: Feature adaptive online sequential extreme learning machine for lifelong indoor localization. Neural Comput. Appl. **27**(1), 215–225 (2016)
14. Wong, P.K., Wong, H.C., Vong, C.M., Xie, Z., Huang, S.: Model predictive engine air-ratio control using online sequential extreme learning machine. Neural Comput. Appl. **27**(1), 79–92 (2014). https://doi.org/10.1007/s00521-014-1555-7
15. Chen, C.P., Liu, Z.: Broad learning system: an effective and efficient incremental learning system without the need for deep architecture. IEEE Trans. Neural Netw. Learn. Syst. **29**(1), 10–24 (2017)
16. Cao, W., Gao, J., Ming, Z., Cai, S., Shan, Z.: Fuzziness-based online sequential extreme learning machine for classification problems. Soft Comput. **22**(11), 3487–3494 (2018). https://doi.org/10.1007/s00500-018-3021-4
17. Duffner, S., Garcia, C.: An online backpropagation algorithm with validation error-based adaptive learning rate. In: de Sá, J.M., Alexandre, L.A., Duch, W., Mandic, D. (eds.) ICANN 2007, Part I. LNCS, vol. 4668, pp. 249–258. Springer, Heidelberg (2007). https://doi.org/10.1007/978-3-540-74690-4_26
18. Zadeh, L.A.: Fuzzy sets as a basis for a theory of possibility. Fuzzy Sets Syst. **1**(1), 3–28 (1978)
19. Zadeh, L.A.: Probability measures of fuzzy events. J. Math. Anal. Appl. **23**(2), 421–427 (1968)
20. De Luca, A., Termini, S.: A definition of a nonprobabilistic entropy in the setting of fuzzy sets theory. Inf. Control **20**(4), 301–312 (1972)
21. Kaufmann, A.: Introduction to the theory of fuzzy subsets: fundamental theoretical elements. Academic Press (1975)
22. Ebanks, B.R.: On measures of fuzziness and their representations. J. Math. Anal. Appl. **94**(1), 24–37 (1983)
23. Wang, X.Z., Xing, H.J., Li, Y., Hua, Q., Dong, C.R., Pedrycz, W.: A study on relationship between generalization abilities and fuzziness of base classifiers in ensemble learning. IEEE Trans. Fuzzy Syst. **23**(5), 1638–1654 (2014)
24. Lichman, M.: UCI machine learning repository. University of California, School of Information and Computer Science, Irvine. [OL] (2021). http://archive.ics.uci.edu/ml
25. Qiu, M., Ming, Z., Wang, J., Yang, L.T., Xiang, Y.: Enabling cloud computing in emergency management systems. IEEE Cloud Comput. **1**(4), 60–67 (2014)
26. Dai, W., Qiu, M., Qiu, L., Chen, L., Wu, A.: Who moved my data? privacy protection in smartphones. IEEE Commun. Mag. **55**(1), 20–25 (2017)
27. NSL-KDD Data Set, [OL] (2021). http://nsl.cs.unb.ca/NSL-KDD/
28. Ashfaq, R.A., Wang, X.Z., Huang, J.Z., Abbas, H., He, Y.L.: Fuzziness based semi-supervised learning approach for intrusion detection system. Inf. Sci. **378**, 484–497 (2017)
29. Cheng, Y., Liu, Y., Chen, T., Yang, Q.: Federated learning for privacy-preserving AI. Commun. ACM **63**(12), 33–36 (2020)

GASKT: A Graph-Based Attentive Knowledge-Search Model for Knowledge Tracing

Mengdan Wang[1], Chao Peng[1(✉)], Rui Yang[1], Chenchao Wang[1], Yao Chen[1], and Xiaohua Yu[2]

[1] Institute of Software Engineering, East China Normal University, Shanghai, China
51194501177@stu.ecnu.edu.cn, cpeng@sei.ecnu.edu.cn

[2] Department of Education Information Technology, East China Normal University, Shanghai, China
xhyu@deit.ecnu.edu.cn

Abstract. Knowledge tracking (KT) is a fundamental tool to customize personalized learning paths for students so that they can take charge of their own learning pace. The main task of KT is to model the learning state of the students, however the process is quite involved. First, due to the sparsity of real-world educational data, the previous KT models ignore the high-order information in question-skill; second, the long sequence of student interactions poses a demanding challenge for KT models when dealing with long-term dependencies, and the last, due to the complexity of the forgetting mechanism. To address these issues, in this paper, we propose a Graph-based Attentive Knowledge-Search Model for Knowledge Tracing (GASKT). The model divides problems and skills into two types of nodes, utilizing R-GCN to thoroughly incorporate the relevance of problem-skill through embedding propagation, which reduces the impact of sparse data. Besides, it employs the modified attention mechanism to address the long-term dependencies issue. For the attention weight score between questions, on the basis of using the scaled dot-product, the forgetting mechanism is fully considered. We conduct extensive experiments on several real-world benchmark datasets, and our GASKT outperforms the state-of-the-art KT models, with at least 1% AUC improvement.

Keywords: Knowledge tracing · Relational graph convolutional networks · Attention · LSTM · Forgetting mechanism

1 Introduction

Each student has his own pace of learning, but it is difficult to achieve personalized education in a traditional classroom. To address the distinct learning

C. Peng—Supported by the Scientific and Technological Innovation 2030 Major Projects under Grant 2018AAA0100902, the Shanghai Science and Technology Commission under Grant No. 20511100200 and OneSmart Education Group.

H. Qiu et al. (Eds.): KSEM 2021, LNAI 12815, pp. 268–279, 2021.
https://doi.org/10.1007/978-3-030-82136-4_22

needs, the computer-aided education (CAE) system breaks fresh ground with its advanced technology. Knowledge tracing (KT), as a fundamental task in CAE systems, aims at evaluating the dynamic changes of students' knowledge states based on historical learning interactions.

There has been extensive research in the field of KT. However, the recent KT models mainly have the following three drawbacks. First, due to the sparseness of educational data, the high-order information between problems and skills has not been fully utilized. Second, because the student's interaction is a long sequence, it is generally appreciated that recurrent neural networks are not good at capturing such long-term dependencies. Finally, the complexity of the human brain's forgetting mechanism remains a major challenge.

Deep Knowledge Tracing (DKT) [1] is the first deep KT method, which exploits the Long Short-Term Memory (LSTM) [2] to predict the students' future performance. Since DKT uses one hidden variable to represent the knowledge state, it's difficult to trace the dynamic learning process of students. To address this limitation, Dynamic Key-Value Memory Networks (DKVMN) [3] extends on the memory-augmented neural networks (MANNs), using key matrix to store the representation of the skills, and the value matrix to characterize the knowledge state of each skill.

However, neither DKT nor DKVMN fully utilizes the high-order information in problem-skill, or adequately takes into account the forgetting behavior of students. Moreover, they are based on RNN mode and fail to effectively capture long-term dependencies between exercises.

DKT-forget [4] takes the memory mechanism into account based on DKT, adding three forgetting features, but still suffers from the remaining two shortcomings. Exercise-Enhanced Recurrent Neural Network (EERNN) [5] obtains embeddings of exercises from their textual information, aiming to obtain rich information to address the challenge of the scarcity of education data. However, in reality, textual information about the problem is difficult to obtain and EERNN fails to sufficiently consider the forgetting mechanism. Graph-based Interaction model for Knowledge Tracing (GIKT) [6] uses graph convolutional network (GCN) [7] to get the high-order embedding of the problems and skills, and introduces a history recap module to select the top-k most relevant problems by the attention score. However, in GIKT, insufficient consideration is given to the memory mechanism. For example, although question e_τ is close to the current question e_t, it will be filtered out due to its low score, which is inconsistent with the fact that recent information is clearer in short term memory.

To address the issues in current KT models, inspired by DKT-forget [4], EERNN [5] and GIKT [6], our Graph-based Attentive Knowledge-Search Model for Knowledge Tracing (GASKT) combines the strengths of the memory mechanism and high-order embedding. Specifically, unlike EERNN which uses bidirectional LSTM to encode textual information, we leverage the graph neural network to get the embedding of the exercises. Moreover, observing that the problems and skills belong to two different types of nodes, we transform the relationship between them into a heterogeneous graph, and utilize Relational Graph

Convolutional Network (R-GCN) [8] instead of GCN (in GIKT) to extract high-order information. Based on the use of LSTM to model the knowledge state of students, the attention mechanism is applied to further enhance the model's ability of capturing long-term dependencies, which is thoroughly incorporated with forgetting behavior.

In summary, in this paper, we propose a deep KT framework GASKT. Our main contributions are as follows:

1. We use R-GCN to extract high-order information about problems and skills, and divide problems and skills into two types of nodes, then construct a corresponding heterogeneous graph.
2. We give adequate consideration to the forgetting mechanism and employ the modified attention mechanism to evaluate students' future performance. Based on the similarity computed by the scaled dot-product, we combine two more features into the attention weight scores between questions: time distance and past trial counts.
3. We conduct experiments on three benchmark datasets, and the results show that GASKT has better performance and higher interpretability compared with existing solutions.

2 Related Work

Knowledge tracing (KT) is the task of capturing the dynamic changes of students' knowledge state based on their historical learning interactions.

The existing knowledge tracing methods can be roughly categorized into three main types, Bayesian knowledge tracing (BKT), factor analysis models, and deep learning models.

BKT. [9] models the student's knowledge state as a binary-valued variable, and uses the hidden Markov model to update and maintain the variable based on the student's practice. Several studies have integrated some other factors, such as individual student's prior knowledge [10], slip and guess probabilities [11] and item difficulty [12].

Factor Analysis. Among the factor analysis models, The additive factor model (AFM) [13] considers the number of students' attempts to the question, while the performance factor analysis model (PFA) [14] counts the positive and negative attempts separately.

Deep Learning Methods. In deep KT models, Deep Knowledge Tracing (DKT) [1] is the first model that applies deep learning to KT. Another notable model is Dynamic Key-Value Memory Networks (DKVMN) [3], which extends on memory-augmented neural networks (MANNs), using key matrix to store the representation of skills and value matrix to represent and update students' knowledge acquisition ability. DKT-forget [4] builds on DKT by incorporating three forgetting properties in the input of the model. And DKT+ [15] is an improved version of DKT that takes into account the regularization of prediction consistency.

However, both DKT and DKVMN are based on RNN [16], these models and their variants suffer from impoverished capturing capabilities when dealing with long sequences. To tackle this issue, the attention mechanism has been extensively used in many studies. Self Attentive Knowledge Tracing (SAKT) [17] is the first model to incorporate the self-attention mechanism in the KT. Given that people's memory declines exponentially over time, and repetitive practices deepen the user's memory, it's clear that the plain attention mechanism fails to satisfy the requirements of KT, so our GASKT modifies the attention mechanism by combining the forgetting features of the learner: the time distance and the past trial counts.

To cope with the challenges of spare data, some models incorporate the textual content of exercises, such as Exercise-Enhanced Recurrent Neural Network (EERNN) [5] extracts textual features via a bidirectional LSTM. Another way to resolve this issue is to leverage graph neural networks. Graph-based Interaction Model for Knowledge Tracing (GIKT) [6] is the first KT model that uses GCN to learn high-order information in problem-skill. Considering that it is difficult to obtain the textual information of the exercise in reality, we utilize graph neural networks to learn the embedding of the nodes. Different from the GIKT, our proposed GASKT employs R-GCN rather than GCN to extract high-order information between nodes, by constructing the problem-skill relationship graph into a heterogeneous graph.

3 Problem Definition

The problem of knowledge tracing (KT) can be described as follows: when a student is answering the question e_t, given his historical learning record $X = (x_1, x_2, ..., x_{t-1})$, where $x_i = (e_i, r_i)$, $r_i \in \{0,1\}$ is the correctness of the student's answer to the question e_i. The goal is to predict the probability that the student will answer the current question e_t correctly. Particularly, in our work, we denote the total length of questions as $|E|$, the total number of skills as $|S|$, and the number of questions answered by each student is unified as l.

Question embedding matrix: $\widetilde{\mathbf{E}} \in \mathbb{R}^{|E| \times d}$, where d denotes the embedding dimension. For a problem e_i its node embedding is $\tilde{e}_i$, corresponding to row i in the matrix $\widetilde{\mathbf{E}}$. Similarly, $\widetilde{\boldsymbol{E}} \in \mathbb{R}^{l \times d}$ represents the embedding matrix of the questions answered by the student.

Skill embedding matrix: $\widetilde{\mathbf{S}} \in \mathbb{R}^{|S| \times d}$, where d is the same embedding dimension as question embedding matrix. For a skill s_i its node embedding is $\tilde{s}_i$, corresponding to row i in the matrix $\widetilde{\mathbf{S}}$.

Student's knowledge states matrix: $\mathbf{H} \in \mathbb{R}^{|l| \times d_h}$, where d_h represents the embedding dimension of the student's knowledge state. Here, row i of the $\mathbf{H}$

matrix represents the embedding representation of the student's knowledge state at timestamp i.

Student's attention scores matrix: $\mathbf{A} \in \mathbb{R}^{|l| \times d_h}$. In the $\mathbf{A}$ matrix, row i represents the embedding representation of the student's attention score at timestamp i.

4 The GASKT Method

This section will clarify our framework in detail. GASKT comprises four components, embedding module, knowledge evolution module, knowledge search module, and the response prediction module. Figure 1 visualizes the overall framework of the model.

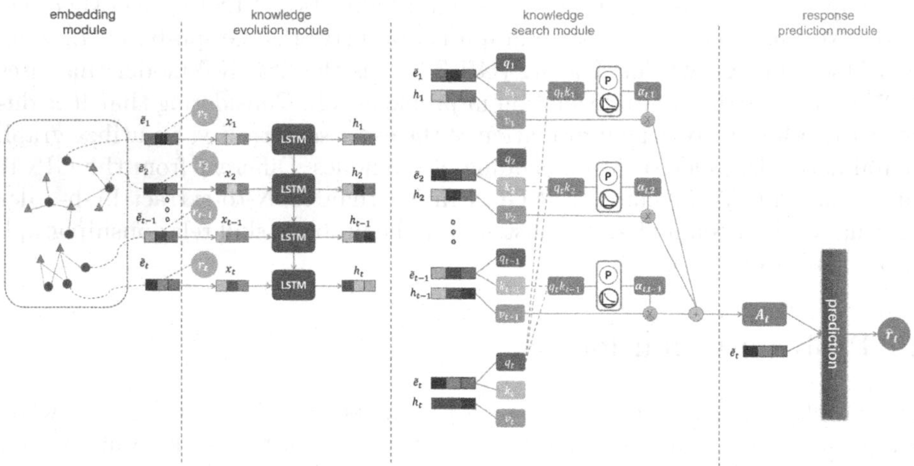

Fig. 1. The overall framework and workflow of GASKT

4.1 Embedding Module

The correctness of students' responses to the new question predominantly depends on their mastery states of the similar questions and skills. Consequently, the feature embedding between questions and skills is particularly important. However, the sparsity of available educational data brings a demanding challenge to the predictions for KT. In this model, to meet the challenge, we use the R-GCN [8] to fully extract question-skill correlations.

R-GCN [8] is an extension to GCN [7] that aims at handling large-scale multi-relational data. The key difference between them is that GCN contains the same type of nodes and edges, so they share the same weight parameters; while R-GCN has different types of nodes and edges, they will share the same parameters only if they belong to the same type. Obviously, the problems and skills belong to different types of nodes, so we choose R-GCN to represent the relationship map among them in the form of a heterogeneous graph.

We construct a directed and labeled multi-graph $\mathcal{G} = (\mathcal{V}, \mathcal{E}, \mathcal{R})$, where node $v_i \in \mathcal{V}$, labeled edge (relation) $(v_i, r, v_j) \in \varepsilon$, $r \in \mathcal{R}$ is the relationship type. In this model, there are two types of nodes, problem nodes e and skill nodes s; two types of edges, that is, $(problem, contain, skill)$, $(skill, contain - by, problem)$.

The calculation of R-GCN consists of the following two steps. First, it calculates and aggregates the messages for each relation r, and second, it aggregates the results from multiple relations. The R-GCN formula for the l level of node v_i can be expressed as follows:

$$h_i^l = \sigma(\sum_{r \in \mathcal{R}} \sum_{j \in \mathcal{N}_i^r} \frac{1}{c_{i,r}} W_r^{(l-1)} h_j^{(l-1)} + W_o^{(l-1)} h_i^{(l-1)}) \tag{1}$$

where $\mathcal{N}_i^r$ denotes all neighbor nodes of node v_i under relation $r \in \mathcal{R}$. W_r, W_o is the weight parameter of the network, $c_{i,r}$ is a normalization constant, and σ is a nonlinear transformation.

4.2 Knowledge Evolution Module

We concatenate the student's answer r_t with the embedding feature $\tilde{e}_t$ of exercise e_t, besides, the r_t is extended to $\mathbf{r_t} = [r_t, r_t, ..., r_t] \in \mathbb{R}^d$.

$$x_t = [\tilde{e}_t, \mathbf{r_t}] \tag{2}$$

The sequence dependencies between exercises in the interactions will severely affect the learning state of students. In order to capture these dependencies, we use a Long Short-Term Memory Network (LSTM) [2] to model the learning process of students.

$$i_t = \sigma(W_i[x_t, h_{t-1}, c_{t-1}] + b_i) \tag{3}$$

$$f_t = \sigma(W_f[x_t, h_{t-1}, c_{t-1}] + b_f) \tag{4}$$

$$o_t = \sigma(W_o[x_t, h_{t-1}, c_{t-1}] + b_o) \tag{5}$$

$$c_t = f_t c_{t-1} + i_t \tanh(W_c[x_t, h_{t-1}] + b_c) \tag{6}$$

$$h_t = o_t \tanh(c_t) \tag{7}$$

Where i_t, f_t, o_t, c_t, and h_t represents input gate, forget gate, output gate, cell state, and hidden state respectively. Finally, we get the student's knowledge state matrix $\mathbf{H} \in \mathbb{R}^{|l| \times d_h}$.

4.3 Knowledge Search Module

In the knowledge evolution module, we use LSTM [2] to model the student's knowledge state. However the LSTM has limited capacity to capture long-term dependencies when dealing with long sequences. To tackle this limitation, we apply the modified attention mechanism to enhance the model's ability to capture information.

Same as the basic scaled dot-product attention mechanism, we need three inputs as Q, K and V. In this model, we map the embedding matrix $\widetilde{\boldsymbol{E}} \in \mathbb{R}^{l \times d}$ of the questions answered by the student to Q, K respectively (the dimensions of them are d_q, d_k, where$d_q = d_k$), and map the student's knowledge mastery state $\mathbf{H} \in \mathbb{R}^{|l| \times d_h}$ to V (the dimension is d_v).

With the basic scaled dot-product attention mechanism, we compute the attention distribution as follows:

$$\alpha_{t,\tau} = Softmax(\frac{Q_t K_\tau^T}{\sqrt{d_k}}) = \frac{exp(\frac{Q_t K_\tau^T}{\sqrt{d_k}})}{\sum_{\tau'} exp(\frac{Q_t K_{\tau'}^T}{\sqrt{d_k}})} \in [0,1] \tag{8}$$

As we know the current state of knowledge is obtained based on the student's historical performance. Therefore, when calculating the attention score, for the question e_t, we only consider questions e_τ that satisfies $\tau < t$.

Intuitively, Q_t indicates the mapping of $\tilde{e}_t$, which is the embedding representation of the question e_t answered at time t, and K_τ indicates the mapping of $\tilde{e}_\tau$. Where $\alpha_{t,\tau}$ represents the effect of question e_τ on question e_t, that is, the similarity between them. Exactly, the closer the $\alpha_{t,\tau}$ is to 1, the greater the similarity between the two questions.

H. Ebbinghaus [18] has mentioned in his early research that people's memory declines exponentially over time, and repeated practice can deepen users' memory. Given the forgetting mechanism of the human brain, the basic attention mechanism fails to satisfy the requirements of KT. Therefore, combined with [4,18], we add two forgetting factors to the basic attention formula, one is the time distance, and the other is the past trial counts.

- **time distance**: time distance between two arbitrary problems.
- **past trial counts**: the number of questions that student has previously answered with the same skills as the current one.

According to the human brain's forgetting mechanism, the influence between e_t and e_τ tends to decrease exponentially with time. Additionally, considering that repetition deepens the human brain's memory, the influence between them should be greater when problems shared with the same skills as e_τ have been trained repeatedly. Combining the above memory mechanisms, we redefine the attention formula as follows:

$$\alpha_{t,\tau} = Softmax(\frac{e^{-\theta D_{t-\tau}} \cdot e^{\beta P_\tau} \cdot Q_t K_\tau^T}{\sqrt{d_k}}) \in [0,1] \tag{9}$$

Where $D_{t-\tau}$ is $D_t - D_\tau$, which denotes the distance between problem e_t and problem e_τ. θ, β are decay factors. $e^{-\theta D_{t-\tau}}$ denotes the factor of the distance. P_τ represents the total number of practiced exercises that share the same skill as question e_τ before time τ. And $e^{\beta P_\tau}$ denotes the factor of the past trial counts.

Moreover, we incorporate the multi-head attention mechanism to jointly focus on different parts of the input information, allowing the model to summarize the learner's past learning performance in multiple time dimensions. More specifically, we use h independent attention heads (where $d_q = d_k = d/h, d_v = d_h/h$), and concatenate the final output into a $1\times(h{\cdot}d_v)$ vector, where $h{\cdot}d_v = d_h$.

The final attention score matrix for all problems that answered by a student is as follows.

$$\mathbf{A} = Attention(Q, K, V) = \sum_{t}\sum_{\tau}\alpha_{t,\tau}v_\tau \tag{10}$$

Where $\mathbf{A} \in \mathbb{R}^{l\times d_h}$, represents the student's attention scores matrix.

4.4 Response Prediction Module

The response prediction module is a fully connected network with sigmoid function. To predict the probability that a student will answer question e_t correctly, we concatenate A_t (student's attention score of the current question e_t) with $\tilde{e}_t$ (embedding of the current question e_t) as the input to the response prediction module.

$$\hat{r}_t = \sigma(W_r[A_t, \tilde{e}_t] + b_r) \tag{11}$$

The parameters of the entire model GASKT can be optimized by minimizing the cross-entropy loss $\mathcal{L}$ between the predicted probability of the correctness $\hat{r}_t$ and the true label of the student's answer r_t.

$$\mathcal{L} = -\sum_{t}(r_t \log \hat{r}_t + (1 - r_t)\log(1 - \hat{r}_t)) \tag{12}$$

5 Experimental

5.1 Datasets

Table 1. Datasets

	ASSIST09	ASSISTChall	Statics
Users	3841	1708	333
Ques	15911	2210	-
Skills	123	101	1223
Inter	258896	864711	189297

Table 2. Performance comparison

Model	ASSIST09	ASSISTChall	Statics
BKT	0.6571	0.7301	0.7300
DKT	0.8024	0.7263	0.8233
DKT+	0.8236	0.7339	0.8175
DKVMN	0.8093	0.7073	0.8195
GIKT	0.8108	0.7586	0.8230
GASKT	**0.8301**	**0.7800**	**0.8271**

To verify the effectiveness of the GASKT model, we conduct a series of experiments on three benchmark datasets. Table 1 illustrates the statistics of the datasets.

- **ASSIST09**[1]: This dataset was collected by ASSISTment online tutoring platform in 2009-2010. Refer to the standard processing of the previous work [19], we delete users with less than 3 interactions and remove the problem of empty skills and scaffolding, besides.
- **ASSISTChall**[2]: This dataset was obtained from the 2017 data mining competition. The data processing method is the same as ASSIT09.
- **Statics**[3]: This dataset was collected from a one-semester Statics course through an online educational system. We process the dataset the same as ASSIST09.

5.2 Baseline

To validate the performance of the model, we select the following models as the baseline.

- **BKT** [9] models the student's knowledge state as a set of binary variables on the basis of Bayesian theory.
- **DKT** [1] is the first model that applies deep learning methods to KT. It uses LSTM to model the knowledge states of students.
- **DKT+** [15] adds the regularization of prediction consistency on the basis of DKT.
- **DKVMN** [3] extends on memory augmentation networks (MANNs) by using a key matrix to store the concepts of knowledge and a value matrix to update the student's knowledge state.
- **GIKT** [6] aggregates problems and skills embeddings by using graph convolutional networks.

5.3 Implementation Details

To set up the experimental conditions, we randomly split the dataset into 3:1:1, with 60% for training, 20% for validation, and 20% for testing.

To improve computational ability, we refer to previous work [3] and uniformly set the length of student interaction to 200. For the multi-skilled questions (ASSIST09) [1,3], we present the questions multiple times, each corresponding to a skill. In the embedding module, the dimension of the embedding size d is set to 128, and the maximum number of the sampling layers L is set to 3. Next in the knowledge evolution module, set the output dimension d_h of LSTM to 128, representing the size of student's knowledge state dimension.

To prevent overfitting, we used a dropout with probability 0.2. In addition, Adam optimizer is utilized to find the optimal parameters of the model, with the learning rate at 0.001 and the batch size of 24. Except for the Statics, since it is small, we set its batch size to 12.

---

[1] https://sites.google.com/site/assistmentsdata/home/assistment-2009-2010-data/skill-builder-data-2009-2010.

[2] https://sites.google.com/view/assistmentsdatamining.

[3] https://pslcdatashop.web.cmu.edu/DatasetInfo?datasetId=507.

5.4 Overall Performance

Table 2 records the AUC performances of all KT models involved in the comparison. As can be seen from the table, our proposed GASKT achieves the best performance for predicting students' future knowledge state over three benchmark datasets, which verifies the effectiveness of GASKT.

In conclusion, we have the following observations. First, all deep KT models perform better than BKT. Second, the latest deep KT methods show greater improvements than DKT, suggesting that it is insufficient to represent the knowledge state with only one hidden variable. Thrid, our proposed GASKT achieves an average performance improvement of 1.90% compared to GIKT. In our experimental setting, multi-skilled problems are repeated multiple times, with each corresponding to a skill. However, in GIKT, joint skills are used as skill representation of the problem. To standardize the criteria, the same experimental setup as ours is used for GIKT, and we observe that the AUC performance of GIKT on the ASSIST09 is 0.8108, slightly better than its work report of 0.7896. On ASSIST09 and ASSISTChall, our GASKT significantly outperforms GIKT, which illustrates that taking forgetting mechanisms into account is more conducive to simulating the knowledge states of students. More importantly, on Statics, since it only contains skills, both GASKT and GIKT perform random assignments to the nodes of this dataset. In this setting, our GASKT has a slight performance improvement over GIKT, which shows that in small datasets, the effect of the modified attention mechanism is not significan compared with large data sets.

5.5 Ablation Studies

Effect of R-GCN Layer. Table 3 lists the performance of GASKT with changes of L. In particular, when $L = 0$, the node embedding is initialized randomly.

Table 3. Effect of R-GCN layer

	ASSIST09	ASSISTChall
0	0.8125	0.7760
1	0.8291	0.7768
2	0.8294	0.7783
3	**0.8301**	**0.7800**

Table 4. Effect of the modified attention

Model	ASSIST09	ASSISTChall	Statics
GASKT-O	0.8171	0.7686	0.8197
GASKT-D	0.8286	0.7789	0.8263
GASKT-N	0.8187	0.7720	0.8206
GASKT	**0.8301**	**0.7800**	**0.8271**

The experimental results show that with an increase of L, the performance of GASKT gradually improves over the datasets. When $L = 3$, the model achieves the highest AUC performance, which proves the effectiveness of high-order aggregation to the model. Notably, on the ASSIST09 dataset, the greatest improvement in model performance is seen with successive increases of L. More specifically, when $L = 0$, the AUC performance of GASKT is 0.8125, and when $L = 3$, the performance is 0.8301, with a significant improvement of 2.17%. However, the model performance improves marginally by 0.52% on the ASSISTChall. Based on phenomenon mentioned above, it can be inferred that it is because ASSIST09 contains the most number of problems and skills in these datasets and has multi-skilled problems, which allows the graph neural network to outperform the random initialization in learning node embedding.

Effect of the Modified Attention. To verify the effectiveness of the two forgetting factors, we perform the following experiments. The detailed results of the experiment can be found in Table 4.

- **GASKT-O** Based on the original attention formula, which fails to consider the forgetting mechanism.
- **GASKT-D** The effect of the time distance is added to the original attention function.
- **GASKT-N** The influence of the past trial counts is added to the original attention function.
- **GASKT** Taking the forgetting mechanism into consideration, adding two elements: time distance and the past trial counts.

From the table, it can be found that GASKT-D and GASKT-N show greater improvement over GASKT-O, verifying that the forgetting factors facilitate the model performance, which is consistent with the pattern of memory mechanisms. Furthermore, taking GASKT-O as reference, the AUC performance of GASKT-D has considerably improved by an average of 1.18% over three datasets, while the performance of GASKT-N has slightly increased by an average of 0.25%, signifying that time distance has a greater impact on the current knowledge state compared to the past trial counts.

6 Conclusion

In this paper, we proposed the GASKT model, which focused on predicting the learner's mastery of the current exercise. Our method extracted high-order information between questions and skills via R-GCN, and combined the attention mechanism with the LSTM to deeply explore the dependencies between the current exercise and the previous exercises. Furthermore, to take forgetting mechanisms into account, we incorporated two forgetting factors, time distance and past trial counts. The experimental results demonstrated that our method outperformed the most previous KT models on three benchmark datasets, and exhibited outstanding interpretability.

References

1. Piech, C., et al.: Deep knowledge tracing. In: Advances in Neural Information Processing Systems, vol. 28, pp. 505–513 (2015)
2. Hochreiter, S., Schmidhuber, J.: Long short-term memory. Neural Comput. **9**(8), 1735–1780 (1997)

3. Zhang, J., Shi, X., King, I., Yeung, D.-Y.: Dynamic key-value memory networks for knowledge tracing. In: Proceedings of the 26th International Conference on World Wide Web, pp. 765–774 (2017)
4. Nagatani, K., Zhang, Q., Sato, M., Chen, Y.-Y., Chen, F., Ohkuma, T.: Augmenting knowledge tracing by considering forgetting behavior. In: The World Wide Web Conference, pp. 3101–3107 (2019)
5. Su, Y., et al.: Exercise-enhanced sequential modeling for student performance prediction. In Proceedings of the AAAI Conference on Artificial Intelligence, vol. 32, no. 1 (2018)
6. Yang, Y., et al.: Gikt: a graph-based interaction model for knowledge tracing. In: Joint European Conference on Machine Learning and Knowledge Discovery in Databases (2020)
7. Kipf, T.N., Welling, M.: Semi-supervised classification with graph convolutional networks. arXiv preprint arXiv:1609.02907 (2016)
8. Schlichtkrull, M., Kipf, T.N., Bloem, P., van den Berg, R., Titov, I., Welling, M.: Modeling relational data with graph convolutional networks. In: Gangemi, A., et al. (eds.) ESWC 2018. LNCS, vol. 10843, pp. 593–607. Springer, Cham (2018). https://doi.org/10.1007/978-3-319-93417-4_38
9. Corbett, A.T., Anderson, J.R.: Knowledge tracing: modeling the acquisition of procedural knowledge. User Model. User-Adap. Inter. **4**(4), 253–278 (1994). https://doi.org/10.1007/BF01099821
10. Pardos, Z.A., Heffernan, N.T.: Modeling individualization in a Bayesian networks implementation of knowledge tracing. In: De Bra, P., Kobsa, A., Chin, D. (eds.) UMAP 2010. LNCS, vol. 6075, pp. 255–266. Springer, Heidelberg (2010). https://doi.org/10.1007/978-3-642-13470-8_24
11. Baker, R.S.J., Corbett, A.T., Aleven, V.: More accurate student modeling through contextual estimation of slip and guess probabilities in Bayesian knowledge tracing. In: Woolf, B.P., Aïmeur, E., Nkambou, R., Lajoie, S. (eds.) ITS 2008. LNCS, vol. 5091, pp. 406–415. Springer, Heidelberg (2008). https://doi.org/10.1007/978-3-540-69132-7_44
12. Pardos, Z.A., Heffernan, N.T.: KT-IDEM: introducing item difficulty to the knowledge tracing model. In: Konstan, J.A., Conejo, R., Marzo, J.L., Oliver, N. (eds.) UMAP 2011. LNCS, vol. 6787, pp. 243–254. Springer, Heidelberg (2011). https://doi.org/10.1007/978-3-642-22362-4_21
13. Cen, H., Koedinger, K., Junker, B.: Learning factors analysis – a general method for cognitive model evaluation and improvement. In: Ikeda, M., Ashley, K.D., Chan, T.-W. (eds.) ITS 2006. LNCS, vol. 4053, pp. 164–175. Springer, Heidelberg (2006). https://doi.org/10.1007/11774303_17
14. Pavlik Jr, P.I., Cen, H., Koedinger, K.R.: Performance factors analysis-a new alternative to knowledge tracing. Online Submission (2009)
15. Yeung, C.-K., Yeung, D.-Y.: Addressing two problems in deep knowledge tracing via prediction-consistent regularization. In: Proceedings of the Fifth Annual ACM Conference on Learning at Scale, pp. 1–10 (2018)
16. Williams, R.J., Zipser, D.: A learning algorithm for continually running fully recurrent neural networks. Neural Comput. **1**(2), 270–280 (1989)
17. Pandey, S., Karypis, G.: A self-attentive model for knowledge tracing. arXiv preprint arXiv:1907.06837 (2019)
18. Ebbinghaus, H.: Memory: a contribution to experimental psychology. Ann. Neurosci. **20**(4), 155 (2013)
19. Xiong, X., Zhao, S., Van Inwegen, E.G., Beck, J.E.: Going deeper with deep knowledge tracing. International Educational Data Mining Society (2016)

Fragile Neural Network Watermarking with Trigger Image Set

Renjie Zhu[1], Ping Wei[1], Sheng Li[1], Zhaoxia Yin[2], Xinpeng Zhang[1(✉)], and Zhenxing Qian[1]

[1] School of Computer Science and Technology, Fudan University, Shanghai, China
{19210240144,17110240026,lisheng,zhangxinpeng,zxqian}@fudan.edu.cn
[2] School of Computer Science and Technology, Anhui University, Anhui, China
Yinzhaoxia@ahu.edu.cn

Abstract. Recent studies show that deep neural networks are vulnerable to data poisoning and backdoor attacks, both of which involve malicious fine tuning of deep models. In this paper, we first propose a black-box based fragile neural network watermarking method for the detection of malicious fine tuning. The watermarking process can be divided into three steps. Firstly, a set of trigger images is constructed based on a user-specific secret key. Then, a well trained DNN model is fine-tuned to classify the normal images in training set and trigger images in trigger set simultaneously in a two-stage alternate training manner. Fragile watermark is embedded by this means while keeping model's original classification ability. The watermarked model is sensitive to malicious fine tuning and will produce unstable classification results of the trigger images. At last, the integrity of the network model can be verified by analyzing the output of watermarked model with the trigger image set as input. The experiments on three benchmark datasets demonstrate that our proposed watermarking method is effective in detecting malicious fine tuning.

Keywords: Neural network · Fragile watermarking · Model integrity protection · Malicious tuning detection · Data poisoning · Backdoor defense

1 Introduction

Deep neural networks (DNN) have been widely used in all areas, such as computer vision [1], natural language processing [2], etc. In addition, a variety of learning methods have been proposed, such as reinforcement learning [3,4], federated learning [5], and so on. Then comes into our sight not only the security of data [6], but also the security of models. These well-trained deep models are valuable assets to the owners. However, they may be possessed or tampered illegally. For example, customers who buy a DNN model might distribute it beyond the license agreement, or attackers may inject backdoor into the models.

H. Qiu et al. (Eds.): KSEM 2021, LNAI 12815, pp. 280–293, 2021.
https://doi.org/10.1007/978-3-030-82136-4_23

Some malicious attacks like adversarial examples [7], data poison [8] and backdoor attack [8] are very common in deep learning. Correspondingly, some measures have been taken to solve these security issues. Among them, neural network watermarking is a promising research area. Digital watermarking is a traditional technique used for copyright protection or integrity authentication of digital products. Neural network watermarking is the extension of traditional watermarking concept for neural networks. And neural network watermarking techniques can be classified into two types: robust and fragile watermarking.

So far, most of the published researches are robust watermarking techniques used for protecting the copyright of DNN models. The word robust means these methods are insensitive to changes that aim to remove the embedded watermark. The robust watermarking techniques can roughly be divided into two categories: weight-parameter-based methods [9–13] and trigger-set-based methods [14–18]. The former ones are white-box schemes, in which the details of network parameters are needed. While the latter ones are black-box watermarking methods requiring no inner parameters of the models. In these methods, a trigger image set is built in advance and these images may be assigned with false labels that are irrelevant to their contents. In the verification process, the watermarked model's classification results of trigger set can be used for authentication directly.

Fragile watermarking [19] is originally designed for multimedia authentication, which is sensitive to content modification and is usually transparent in terms of perception. Now we migrate the concept of traditional fragile watermarking to neural networks. For DNN fragile watermarking, the following properties should be considered. First, it should require low training cost and be easy to embed and extract from the model. Second, the embedded watermark should be imperceptible and has no much impact on model's original performance. Third, there should be some quantifiable metrics for malicious tampering authentication. Fourth, it should be extensible and can be widely applied to other networks and datasets.

Formally, image classifier $\mathcal{C}_\theta$ is a supervised learning task aiming at finding a classification function $\mathcal{F}$ to classify the images in training set Tra with the classification loss $\mathcal{L}_{cla}$, i.e., $\mathcal{C}_\theta = \mathcal{L}_{cla}(\mathcal{F}(Tra))$. Usually, the trigger-set-based watermarking methods need a trigger image set Tri apart from training set, where images in Tri are stamped with preset labels according to some rules. And watermarked classifier $\mathcal{C}_{\theta_w}$ tries to classify the images in both the training set and trigger set, i.e., $\mathcal{C}_{\theta_w} = \mathcal{L}_{cla}(\mathcal{F}(Tra \ \cup \ Tri))$. Watermarked models gain the ability to recognize both normal images and trigger images by training the network from scratch or fine tuning trained models. For unmodified watermarked models, $\mathcal{C}_{\theta_w}$ is supposed to output the predefined labels for input trigger images.

DNN models are vulnerable to malicious attacks like data poisoning attacking. Now many DNN models need multi-parties training, the participants might inject backdoor into the network while updating parameters. Typical data poisoning behaviors can be classified into three kinds as follows:

1) Simple data poisoning [8]: attackers attempt to reduce the model performance by introducing lots of mislabeled samples to the training set, which can be expressed as: $\mathcal{C}_{\theta p} = \mathcal{L}_{cla}(\mathcal{F}(Tra \cup Mislabeled\ Samples))$.
2) Backdoor data poisoning [8]: it is a more imperceptible way of model tampering by adding some poisoned samples with a fixed backdoor pattern to the training set, that is, $\mathcal{C}_{\theta b} = \mathcal{L}_{cla}(\mathcal{F}(Tra \cup Backdoor\ Samples))$. Through training, this backdoor pattern can be added to normal samples to obtain the expected output label y_b, i.e., $\mathcal{C}_{\theta b}(x \oplus Backdoor\ pattern) = y_b$. This data poisoning method is difficult to be found, for only a small number of backdoor samples are needed and the injected backdoor has little impact on model's performance.
3) Label-consistent data poisoning [20]: label consistency means there is no tampering with image labels. This kind of attacking method often use adversarial example or GANs to recreate the samples in training set, making DNN more difficult to learn the features of image content. So, the backdoor attacking can succeed because networks focus on the backdoor pattern more than often. And traditional backdoor samples with wrong labels are easy to be detected by checking the training set, therefore, the label-consistency data poisoning methods have drawn much attention.

Some approaches have been proposed to detect the malicious tampering of DNN models. In [21], a detection and mitigation system for DNN backdoor attacks is proposed, where the backdoor can be identified and even some mitigation techniques are proved to remove the embedded backdoors. And in [22], a black-box based backdoor detection scheme is presented with minimal prior knowledge of the model. Both of them are solutions of detecting the existence of backdoors afterwards, and no precautions are taken to prevent backdoor inserting. In [13], a reversible watermarking algorithm for integrity authentication is proposed, in which the parameters of the model can be fully recovered after extracting the watermarking and the integrity of the model can be verified by applying the reversible watermarking. However, it's a white-box method requiring the details of networks, which is inconvenient for watermarking embedding and extraction. Therefore, we proposed a black-box based integrity authentication method with fragile watermarking technique, in which a trigger set is used and no model inner parameter is revealed. Let's call it: fragile neural network watermarking with trigger image set.

The contributions of this paper are summarized as follows:

- We firstly proposed a black-box based fragile watermarking method for authenticating the integrity of DNN classifiers.
- A novel loss function, $\mathcal{L}_{var}$ and an alternate two-stage training strategy were put forward elaborately, with which fragile watermark can be embedded easily into the neural network. Meanwhile, two easily accessible metrics are designed for model authentication, which can be obtained quickly by only checking the classification outputs of trigger images.

- Our proposed watermarking method is of good compatibility and extensibility, and experiments on three benchmark datasets showed that the embedded watermark have little impact on the prior task of the network.

The rest of this paper is organized as follows: Sect. 2 describes the proposed fragile watermarking and authentication metrics. Then, the properties of our scheme are demonstrated in Sect. 3. At last, conclusion is given in Sect. 4.

2 Fragile Watermarking

2.1 Application Scenario

Before introducing our proposed watermarking method, let us describe the application scenario with the following scenes. Consider three parties: model trainer, consumer, and attacker. The training of a complex network requires multiple stages of adjustment, and an attacker among the trainers may use the convenience of accessing training data for poisoning, resulting in network backdoored or performing worse than expected. And attackers could even poison models delivered to consumers. To this end, we introduce a fragile watermarking method suitable for neural networks to verify the integrity of watermarked models.

2.2 Watermarking Methodology

Figure 1 shows the overview of the proposed watermarking method. The whole process is divided into three steps: the first step is to construct a trigger image set using a secret key; and the second step is to embed a fragile watermark in a two-stage training procedure; the last step is the authentication process determining whether a neural model is tampered through two proposed metrics.

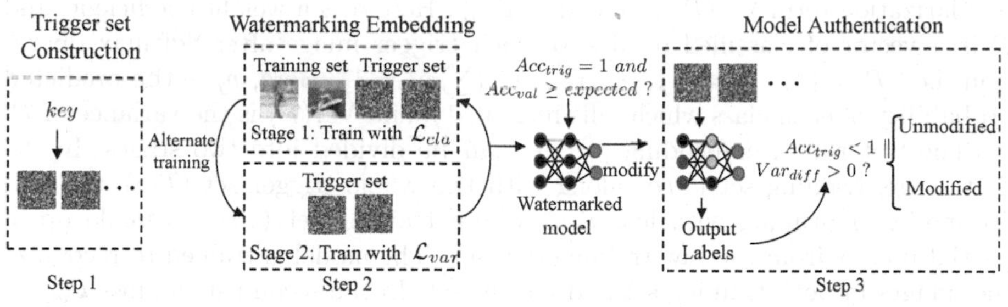

Fig. 1. An overview of the proposed fragile neural network watermarking method. The process of our scheme is divided into 3 steps. The fragile watermark is embedded by fine tuning the well-trained models in a two-stage alternate training manner, until the fine-tuned models satisfy the following condition: $Acc_{trig} = 1$ and $Acc_{val} \geq$ *expected value*. At last, the integrity of fragile watermarked model can be authenticated by evaluating two metrics, namely $Acc_{trig} < 1$ or $Var_{diff} \geq 0$.

The first step of our scheme is to generate L pseudo-random trigger images with the secret key *key* specified by the model trainer. Each trigger image is assigned with a fix label, which can be expressed as follows:

$$\{Image_i, Label_i\} \leftarrow \{(I_i,\ i\%C) \mid i = 0, 1, \cdots, L-1\}, \tag{1}$$

where $Image_i$ or I_i represents a trigger image and $Label_i$ is its preset label $i\%C$. Here, % is the Mod operation of math, and C is the total number of classes in training dataset. Figure 2 shows three trigger samples used in our experiments.

Fig. 2. Three examples of trigger images.

The second step of our method is watermarking embedding process. Our proposed fragile watermark is usually embedded in the well-trained models by a two-stage fine tuning procedure, with the classification loss $\mathcal{L}_{cla}$ and fragile watermarking loss $\mathcal{L}_{var}$, which are defined as follows:

$$\mathcal{L}_{cla} = -\sum_{j=0}^{C-1} y_j \log(p_j), \tag{2}$$

$$\mathcal{L}_{var} = \mathcal{L}_{cla} + \alpha \cdot \mathrm{Var}(\mathcal{P}), \tag{3}$$

where $\mathcal{L}_{cla}$ is the cross entropy loss for multi-class classification. For fragile watermarking, the watermarked model should be sensitive to modification. Thus, a regularization term $\mathrm{Var}(\mathcal{P})$ is added in $\mathcal{L}_{var}$. Here α is a weight coefficient, and $\mathcal{P}$ is a vector of classified results for each trigger image after Softmax operation, i.e., $\mathcal{P} = \{p_j \mid j = 0, 1, \cdots, C-1\}$ $(\sum p_j = 1)$. Here, p_j is the predicted probability of each class which falls into (0, 1), and $\mathrm{Var}(\mathcal{P})$ is the variance of $\mathcal{P}$.

The watermark embedding process can be divided into two stages. In the first stage, training set (Tra) along with the whole trigger set (Tri) are used for model fine-tuning with loss $\mathcal{L}_{cla}$, where training set (Tra) is made up of partial images from the raw training dataset. The model is trained to recognize the images in both training set and trigger set. In the second stage, loss $\mathcal{L}_{var}$ is used to fine-tune the model only on the trigger set, with the purpose of reducing the variance of predicted probability vector and classifying all the trigger images rightly. This watermark embedding process would not stop until two conditions are satisfied: 1). The classification accuracy on trigger samples is equal to 1, i.e., $Acc_{trig} = 1$; 2). The classification accuracy on normal samples in validation set is equal to or greater than the expected value, that is, $Acc_{val} \geq expected$. By using this alternate training method, the proposed fragile watermark are embedded easily into the DNN models. And the classification accuracy on normal images are usually not lower than the original un-watermarked models.

Here, we also defined the concept $\mathcal{C}_{\theta robust}$ as the classifier with a robust watermark. It is trained on both training set and trigger set with loss $\mathcal{L}_{cla}$, which means only the first stage of watermarking embedding is used. It can be expressed as: $\mathcal{C}_{\theta robust} = \mathcal{L}_{cla}(\mathcal{F}(Tra \cup Tri))$. This is also the way that many previous methods [14–18] embed robust watermarks. By doing so, the output of the watermarked model to the trigger set will not be easily changed by fine-tuning the model, in other words, the watermark is not fragile.

The performance of fragile watermarked model has a close relation to the size of Tra, which reflects the trade-off between watermarking embedding efficiency and model performance. When the size of Tra declines, it takes less time for watermark embedding, yet the classification accuracy on normal images will also decrease. Hence, we randomly take 10% of the images in raw training database as the training set Tra. The sensibility of watermark is enhanced gradually as α increases, but a too large value can also lead to performance degradation. Here we limit α ranging from 0 to several hundreds in our experiments.

The last step of our scheme is model authentication. After acquired, the DNN model's predicted labels of trigger images will be quantified into two authentication metrics to decide whether the model has been modified or not.

2.3 Authentication Metrics

Two novel authentication metrics are proposed to verify whether a watermarked model has been modified in our scheme. The first one is Acc_{trig}, which is the classification accuracy on the input trigger images. If $Acc_{trig} < 1$, it indicates that the model has been modified. The stronger the malicious attack is, the more Acc_{trig} will drop. If a model is modified, the trigger images may be classified into different classes as follows:

$$\mathcal{N} = \{n_0, n_1, \ldots, n_i, \ldots, n_{C-1}\}, \tag{4}$$

where n_i means the number of trigger samples that are classified as the i-th class image, and the summation of n_i is equal to the image number of trigger set. Similarly, $\mathcal{N}_0$ is the corresponding statistical result of unmodified model. Based on these two values, the second metric of our scheme is given:

$$Var_{dif} = \mathrm{Var}(\mathcal{N}) - \mathrm{Var}(\mathcal{N}_0), \tag{5}$$

where Var_{dif} is used to measure the difference of classification results before and after the watermarked model is tampered. The value of Var_{dif} reflects the degree to which the model has been modified. Var_{dif} is always greater than or equal to zero and a great value means the watermarked model is modified severely.

3 Experiments

In our paper, watermarking experiments are conducted with resnet18 [23] and resnet50 [23], which were trained on datasets cifar-10 & cifar-100, and Caltech101, respectively. The information of these datasets is showed in Table 1. We trained the classifiers from scratch with the following configurations: the optimizer of resnet18 is SGD with momentum with the learning rate of 0.1, which decreases ten times every twenty epochs; the optimizer of resnet50 is Adam, and the learning rate is 1e−4, which is reduced to 1e−5 in the last 20 epochs. Then fragile watermarking is embedded by fine-tuning the trained classifiers above. During the process of watermarking or attacking, the optimizer remains unchanged, and the learning rate is set to value in the final stage of training.

Table 1. Dataset information

Dataset	cifar-10	cifar-100	Caltech101	Our *Tri*
Classes (C)	10	100	101	-
Image size	32,32,3	32,32,3	300,200,3	32,32,3
Dataset size	60000	60000	9145	≥36
Training size	45000	45000	6583	-
Testing size	10000	10000	1830	-
Val size	5000	5000	732	-

3.1 Visualization of Watermarking

In this part, we compared the outputs of fragile watermarked models by some visual methods. Figure 3 records the classification accuracy of images during the watermark embedding fine-tuning process, in which Val Acc and Trigger Acc means classification accuracy on validation set and trigger set, respectively.

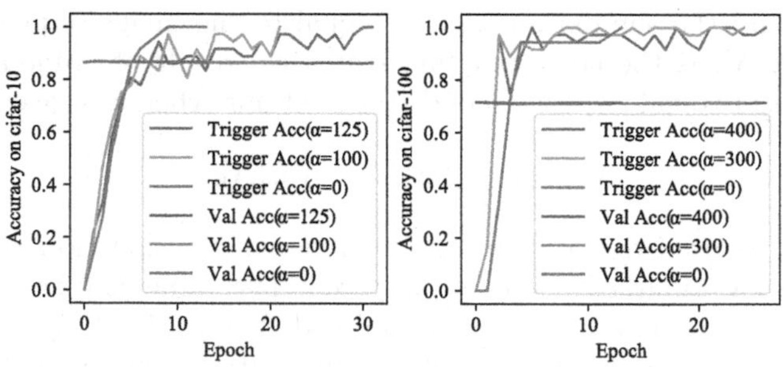

Fig. 3. The accuracy curves with different α values used during watermarking embedding. Val Acc and Trigger Acc means classification accuracy on validation set and trigger set, respectively.

When α is 0, a robust watermark instead of a fragile watermark is embedded, and with the increase of α, the sensibility of watermark increases and it will take more epochs for fragile watermark embedding. However, from Fig. 3, we can see that the increase of α has little effect on the performance of classifiers, for the watermarking embedding fine-tuning process would not stop until two conditions are satisfied, i.e., $Acc_{trig} = 1$ and $Acc_{val} \geq expected$. Thus, we can pick α ranging from zero to several hundreds casually for watermark embedding.

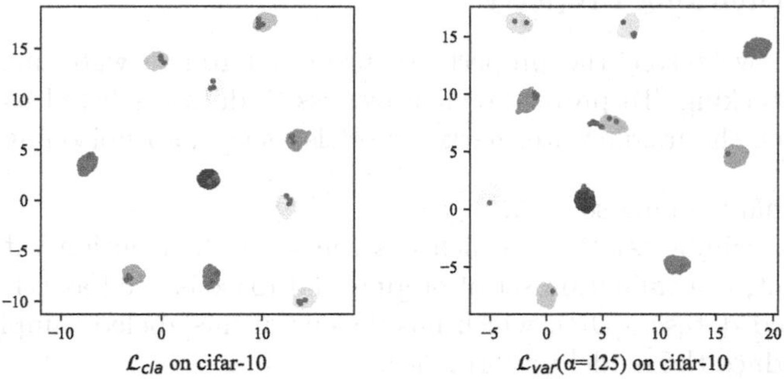

Fig. 4. Comparison of feature projection extracted by different models. The figures on the left and right are results of robust and fragile watermarked model trained on cifar-10, respectively.

The model's last convolution layer's output tensor were projected onto a two-dimension plane as demonstrated in Fig. 4 by a visualization tool UMAP. The left and right figures illustrate the projected features extracted by classifiers with robust and fragile watermark trained on cifar-10, respectively, where 10 larger colored circles represent the projected feature points of 5,000 normal samples, and the purple dots inside the circles are projected feature points of 36 trigger images, which all belong to 10 image classes. As shown in Fig. 4, once the model is embedded with fragile watermark, the projected feature points of trigger samples will deviate from the center to classification boundary.

3.2 Perceptual Transparency

The existence of fragile watermark has little influence on original classification ability of model. Table 2 lists the testing accuracy of un-watermarked models and fragile watermarked models when varying the value of α. Results show that the reduction of accuracy is less than 0.3% after watermark is embedded, and in some cases the accuracy of watermarked model even increase slightly compared to that of the clean model.

Table 2. The accuracy of un-watermarked classifier and fragile watermarked classifier for normal images in testing set when varying the value of α

Dataset	Un-water, Acc	α	Watermarked, Acc
cifar-10	86.40%	[0, 125]	[86.36%, 86.54%]
cifar-100	72.55%	[0, 400]	[72.31%, 72.57%]

3.3 Watermarking Property

In this part, we tested the property of proposed fragile watermarking under malicious attacking. To prove the effectiveness, 5 datasets listed as follows are used to attack the fragile watermarked models using data poisoning method.

1. The original training set (T).
2. An extra training set (ET), which has the same distribution with T. In our experiment, the validation set of original database is used as ET.
3. A poisoned dataset (DP), which has dozens of mislabeled samples with the aim to reduce the model performance.
4. A simple backdoor poisoned dataset (SB), which contains the images in training set (T) as well as some mislabeled samples with backdoor patterns.
5. A label-consistent poisoned dataset (LCB) constructed according to [20].

Five datasets above are created on the basis of a image database, such as cifar-10 and cifar-100. As [20] demonstrates, the minimum number of poisoned samples for backdoor attacking should not be lower than 0.15% of the training set size. Thus, for dataset cifar-10, we only added 75 (0.15% of the size) poisoned

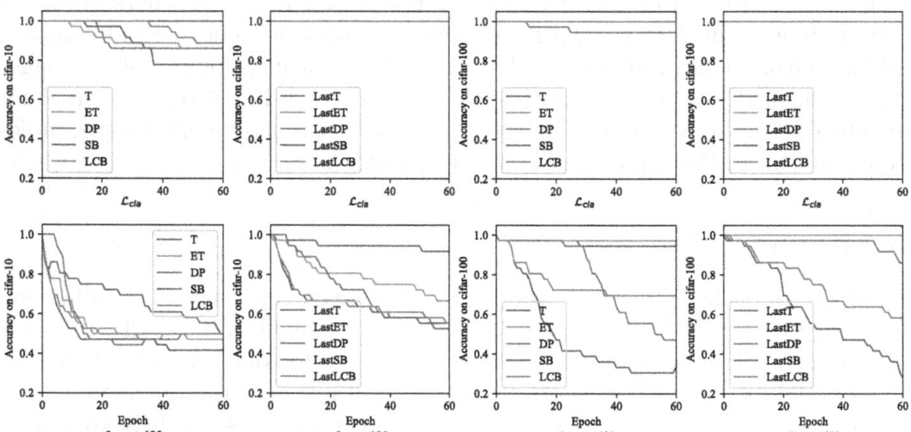

Fig. 5. The classification accuracy of trigger set (Acc_{trig}) when the robust watermarked models (the first row) and fragile watermarked models (the second row) are fine-tuned with 5 datasets (T, ET, DP, SB, and LCB) on cifar-10 or cifar-100, respectively. If the curve's label is prefixed with Last, it means only the last layer of model is fine-tuned, otherwise all layers are fine-tuned.

samples to dataset DP, SB, and LCB. In our experiment, the backdoor pattern is a $3 \times 3 \times 3$ white-and-black square block, which is superimposed on the lower right corner of normal samples.

Figure 5 illustrates the mean accuracy of trigger set when watermarked models are fine-tuned with 5 datasets above. The malicious attacking experiments are conducted either on all the layers, or only on the last layer of the watermarked models. In Fig. 5, the first and second row are respectively the attacking results of models with robust watermarks and fragile watermarks. It can be easily seen that the fragile watermarked models are vulnerable to all kinds of modifications compared to the robust watermarked models. The accuracy on trigger set Acc_{trig} declines rapidly when the fragile watermarked models are fine-tuned with poisoned datasets. And the more different the poisoned data is, the faster Acc_{trig} goes down. Thus, the accuracy curves of DP, SB, and LCB decline more quickly than the curves of T and ET.

Table 3. Value of Var_{dif} when the fragile watermarked model has been fine-tuned with 5 different datasets for ten epochs

Dataset	T	ET	DP	SB	LCB
Var_{dif}(cifar-10)	0.40	1.80	4.60	24.40	13.80
Var_{dif}(cifar-100)	0.00	0.00	0.02	0.30	0.30

Table 3 lists the Var_{dif} values, when the fragile watermarked model is fine-tuned with 5 datasets mentioned above. As can be seen, the Var_{dif} value of T and ET are much smaller than the values of other three poisoned datasets, with the reason that the images in T and ET are the same or similar to the images in raw training set. When fragile watermarked models are maliciously fine-tuned with poisoned dataset DP, SB, and LCB, Var_{dif} will be much greater than zero. The Var_{dif} values of cifar-10 are much larger than the values of cifar-100, mainly because that cifar-10 owns less images classes and is sensitive to modification.

In order to view the variation of Var_{dif} more intuitively, we depicted the heat maps of classified trigger image numbers according to $\mathcal{N}$ in equation (4). As shown in Fig. 6, the well trained model is fine-tuned with four datasets T, DP, SB, and LCB. The horizontal and vertical axis are the class number and the epoch number of fine tuning, respectively. For each block, the intensity of the color is proportional to the predicted number of trigger samples falling into the corresponding image categories. In the heat maps of poisoned datasets DP, SB, and LCB, the distribution of colored blocks are more uneven compared to blocks of T. This is because the embedded fragile watermark is damaged greatly when model is fine-tuned by these three poisoned datasets.

After a model is embedded with proposed fragile watermark, it may be upload to cloud or sent to the users directly. To verify the integrity of acquired model, we can apply the two metrics Acc_{trig} and Var_{dif} with the trigger image set offered

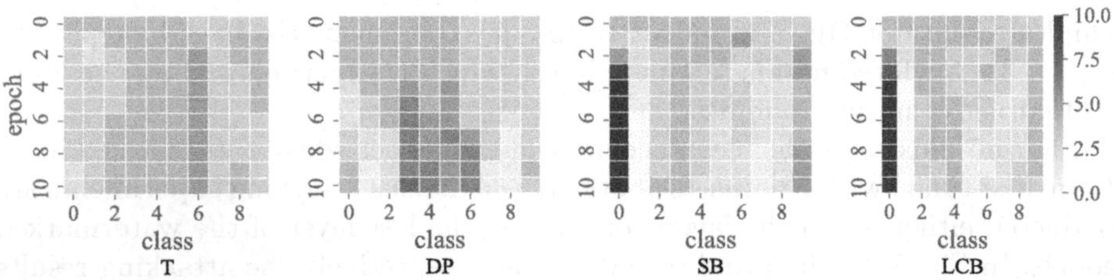

Fig. 6. The numbers of trigger samples being classified into each class during the malicious fine-tuning process carried on 4 datasets. The horizontal axis here is the image classes and vertical axis is the epochs. The color depth of blocks means the numbers of trigger images that are predicted as the corresponding image class.

Table 4. The classification accuracy of fragile watermarked models on normal images in testing set with different sizes of trigger set used in fragile watermarking

Trigger set size	Accuracy (cifar-10)	Accuracy (cifar-100)
0	86.40%	73.22%
36	86.54%	73.11%
100	86.38%	73.03%
200	86.21%	72.91%

by the model owner. As long as $Acc_{trig} < 1$ or $Var_{dif} > 0$, we can believe that the received models have been tampered.

3.4 Extensibility

Here, we explored the influence of trigger image set size on model performance. First, we constructed several trigger sets of size ranging from 0 to 200, and then each trigger set is used to embed fragile watermark individually. At last, the classification accuracy on the testing set are tested in Table 4. It can be seen that the size of trigger image set has no influence on the prediction consequences of fragile watermarked models.

The fragile watermarking method is also experimented on dataset Caltech101. In our experiments, classifier resnet50 is first embedded with fragile watermark, and then be fine-tuned with 5 datasets (T, ET, DP, SB, and LCB). Caltech101 is a 101-class dataset with the image size of about $300 \times 200 \times 3$ pixels, and the backdoor pattern for Caltech101 is a $9 \times 9 \times 3$ block. As a result, the testing set accuracy of the un-watermarked classifier resnet50 is 94.46%, and the accuracy of fragile watermarked classifiers is between 94.23% and 94.49%. The classification ability of DNN model is proved to be almost unaffected by watermarking.

The performance of watermarked resnet50 is also tested by fine tuning the model with 5 datasets on the basis of Caltech101, and the results are presented in Fig. 7. The left two and right two figures are separately the fine-tuned results

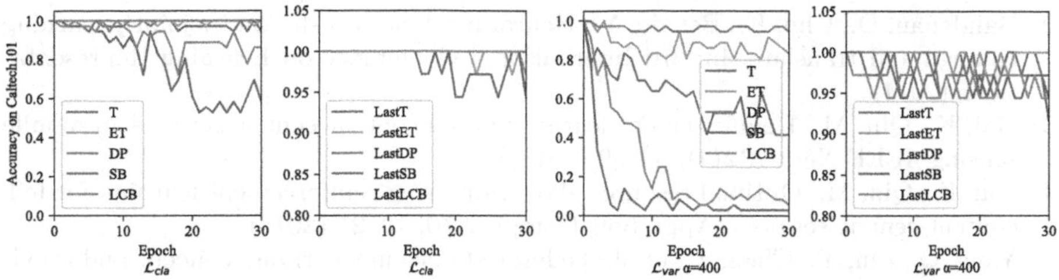

Fig. 7. The classification accuracy of trigger set (Acc_{trig}) when 5 datasets (T, ET, DP, SB, LCB) are used to fine-tune robust watermarked resnet50 and fragile watermarked resnet50 respectively on dataset Caltech101.

of robust and fragile watermarked resnet50. As illustrated in Fig. 7, fragile watermarked resnet50 is sensitive to all kinds of fine tuning, especially when fine-tuned with poisoned datasets DP, SB, and LCB. When all the layers of watermarked resnet50 are fine-tuned, the curves of poisoned datasets DP, SB, and LCB goes down more quickly than other curves. When only the last layer of model is fine-tuned, accuracy curves fluctuate wildly. But in general, our proposed fragile watermarking method is sensitive to malicious fine-tuning and can be used to detect model tampering carried on various datasets.

4 Conclusion

In this paper, we proposed a black-box based fragile neural network watermarking method with trigger image set for authenticating the integrity of DNN models. In our approach, models are trained to fit both the training set and the trigger set simultaneously in a two-stage alternate training process, which aims to embed fragile watermark while keeping the original classification performance. The embedded fragile watermark is sensitive to model tampering, and thus can be used to verify the integrity of models. Two meaningful metrics are provided to determine whether the fragile watermarked model has been modified as well as assess the distribution difference between the training set and the data used for malicious attacking. The experiments on three benchmark datasets have shown that our proposed fragile watermarking method is widely applicable to various classifiers and datasets. We leave the research on more sensitive semi-fragile neural network watermarking to future work.

Acknowledgment. This work was supported in part by the National Natural Science Foundation of China under Grants U1936214, U20A20178, 62072114, U20B2051, 61872003.

References

1. Deng, J., Berg, A., Satheesh, S., et al.: Imagenet large scale visual recognition competition 2012. See net. org/challenges/LSVRC, p. 41 (2012)

2. Bahdanau, D., Cho, K., Bengio, Y.: Neural machine translation by jointly learning to align and translate. In: 3rd International Conference on Learning Representations (2014)
3. Gai, K., Qiu, M.: Reinforcement learning-based content-centric services in mobile sensing. IEEE Netw. **32**(4), 34–39 (2018)
4. Gai, K., Qiu, M.: Optimal resource allocation using reinforcement learning for IoT content-centric services. Appl. Soft Comput. **70**, 12–21 (2018)
5. Yang, Q., Liu, Y., Chen, T., et al.: Federated machine learning: concept and applications. ACM Trans. Intell. Syst. Technol. (TIST) **10**(2), 1–19 (2019)
6. Dai, W., Qiu, M., Qiu, L., et al.: Who moved my data? privacy protection in smartphones. IEEE Commun. Mag. **55**(1), 20–25 (2017)
7. Szegedy, C., Zaremba, W., Sutskever, I., et al.: Intriguing properties of neural networks. arXiv preprint arXiv:1312.6199 (2013)
8. Gu, T., Dolan-Gavitt, B., Garg, S.: Badnets: Identifying vulnerabilities in the machine learning model supply chain. arXiv preprint arXiv:1708.06733 (2017)
9. Uchida, Y., Nagai, Y., Sakazawa, S., et al.: Embedding watermarks into deep neural networks. In: Proceedings of the 2017 ACM on International Conference on Multimedia Retrieval, pp. 269–277 (2017)
10. Wang, T., Kerschbaum, F.: Attacks on digital watermarks for deep neural networks. In: ICASSP 2019–2019 IEEE International Conference on Acoustics, Speech and Signal Processing (ICASSP), pp. 2622–2626 (2019)
11. Fan, L., Ng, K., Chan, C.: Rethinking deep neural network ownership verification: embedding passports to defeat ambiguity attacks. In: Advances in Neural Information Processing Systems, pp. 4714–4723 (2019)
12. Feng, L., Zhang, X.: Watermarking neural network with compensation mechanism. In: Li, G., Shen, H.T., Yuan, Y., Wang, X., Liu, H., Zhao, X. (eds.) KSEM 2020, Part II. LNCS (LNAI), vol. 12275, pp. 363–375. Springer, Cham (2020). https://doi.org/10.1007/978-3-030-55393-7_33
13. Guan, X., Feng, H., Zhang, W., et al.: Reversible watermarking in deep convolutional neural networks for integrity authentication. In: Proceedings of the 28th ACM International Conference on Multimedia, pp. 2273–2280 (2020)
14. Adi, Y., Baum, C., Cisse, M., et al.: Turning your weakness into a strength: watermarking deep neural networks by backdooring. In: 27th {USENIX} Security Symposium ({USENIX} Security 18), pp. 1615–1631 (2018)
15. Zhang, J., Gu, Z., Jang, J., et al.: Protecting intellectual property of deep neural networks with watermarking. In: Proceedings of the 2018 on Asia Conference on Computer and Communications Security, pp. 159–172 (2018)
16. Guo, J., Potkonjak, M.: Watermarking deep neural networks for embedded systems. In: 2018 IEEE/ACM International Conference on Computer-Aided Design (ICCAD), pp. 1–8 (2018)
17. Le Merrer, E., Pérez, P., Trédan, G.: Adversarial frontier stitching for remote neural network watermarking. Neural Comput. Appl. **32**(13), 9233–9244 (2019). https://doi.org/10.1007/s00521-019-04434-z
18. Zhu, R., Zhang, X., Shi, M., Tang, Z.: Secure neural network watermarking protocol against forging attack. EURASIP J. Image Video Process. **2020**(1), 1–12 (2020). https://doi.org/10.1186/s13640-020-00527-1
19. Zhang, X., Wang, S.: Fragile watermarking with error-free restoration capability. IEEE Trans. Multimed. **10**(8), 1490–1499 (2008)
20. Turner, A.l., Tsipras, D., Madry, A.: Label-consistent backdoor attacks. arXiv preprint arXiv:1912.02771 (2019)

21. Wang, B., Yao, Y., Shan, S., et al.: Neural cleanse: identifying and mitigating backdoor attacks in neural networks. In: 2019 IEEE Symposium on Security and Privacy (SP), pp. 707–723 (2019)
22. Chen, H., Fu, C., Zhao, J., et al.: Deepinspect: a black-box trojan detection and mitigation framework for deep neural networks. In: International Joint Conferences on Artificial Intelligence Organization, pp. 4658–4664 (2019)
23. He, K., Zhang, X., Ren, S., et al.: Deep residual learning for image recognition. In: Proceedings of the IEEE Conference on Computer Vision and Pattern Recognition, pp. 770–778 (2016)

Introducing Graph Neural Networks for Few-Shot Relation Prediction in Knowledge Graph Completion Task

Yashen Wang(✉) and Huanhuan Zhang

National Engineering Laboratory for Risk Perception and Prevention (RPP), China Academy of Electronics and Information Technology of CETC, Beijing, China
yswang@bit.edu.cn

Abstract. Relation prediction is a key problem for graph-structured data, to many applications such as knowledge graph completion (KGC), while embedding-based methods, effective for relation prediction in KGs, perform poorly on relations that only have a few associative triples. Nowadays, many works focus on leveraging Graph Neural Network (GNN) for alleviating few-shot learning problems in relation prediction task. However, existing work usually only averages the neighbors of the target nodes, which limits model's performance and capability. Besides, although the Graph Attention Network (GAT) can generate more powerful feature representations through the expansion of multi-head attention, unfortunately it only considers the relationship between neighbors in the same layer, and does not make full use of hierarchical information (e.g., layer-wise information), resulting in excessive over-smoothing problem. Hence, this paper develops a novel GNN-based model for few-shot relation prediction, by leveraging intra-layer neighborhood attention and inter-layer memory attention, to alleviate over-smoothing tendencies of deep GNNs. Empirical studies on two real-world datasets confirm the superiority of the proposed model. The proposed model addresses the few-shot relation prediction and outperforms competitive state-of-the-art models.

Keywords: Relation prediction · Few-shot learning · Graph Neural Networks · Representation learning

1 Introduction

A Knowledge Graph (KG) is composed by a large amount of triples in the form of (h, r, t), wherein h and t represent head entity and tail entity respectively and r indicates the corresponding relation between h and t [20,22,39]. Large-scale Knowledge Graphs (KG) such as FreeBase [3], YAGO [30], Wikipedia [8], WordNet [21] and Probase [41], provide effective basis for many important AI tasks such as semantic search [35], recommendation [46], relation prediction [38], question answering [49], etc. Despite their effectiveness, knowledge graphs are

H. Qiu et al. (Eds.): KSEM 2021, LNAI 12815, pp. 294–306, 2021.
https://doi.org/10.1007/978-3-030-82136-4_24

still far from being complete. This problem motivates the task of Knowledge Graph Completion (KGC), which is targeted at assessing the plausibility of triples not present in a knowledge graph.

Given the ubiquitous existence of networks, Relation Prediction (RP) is to predict new triples based on existing ones [1,5,19,36], is an important task for KGC, as well as other applications including such as recommendation system [50] and metabolic network reconstruction [24].

For relation prediction, KG embedding methods [4,22,32,37] are promising ways. As we all known, the effectiveness of kg embedding method is guaranteed by enough training instances, so the results are much worse for elements with a small number of instances during training procedure [5,48]. Such a challenge presents in *few-shot* learning [14,29]. The goal of few-shot learning is to learn a classifier that generalizes well even when trained with a limited number of training instances per class.

Many methods have been proposed towards few-shot learning task, including meta-learning [5,26] and metric-learning [11]. Recently, Graph Neural Networks (GNN) has demonstrated its superior performance in few-shot learning task [16,27,47]. However, over-smoothing [23,25] get serious when learning GNN models that become deep [10,18,25]. This is because: (i) Existing work usually *only* averages the neighbors of the target nodes, which limits model's performance; (ii) Although the Graph Attention Network (GAT) [33] can generate more powerful feature representations through the expansion of multi-head attention, unfortunately it *only* considers the relationship between neighbors in the same layer, and does *not* make full use of hierarchical information (e.g., layer-wise information), resulting in excessive over-smoothing problem. Hence, this paper attempts to address these challenge on GNN based methods for few-shot learning by leveraging novel graph attention methodology, to alleviate the problems of over-smoothing. Especially, we propose a relational Graph Convolutional Network (RGCN) based model for few-shot relation prediction task, by leveraging two kind of graph attention mechanism: (i) intra-layer neighborhood attention for attending to the most relevant neighbor node, and (ii) inter-layer memory attention for maintaining earlier memory.

Our contributions could be summarized as follows: This paper addresses the aforementioned limitation of GNN models for few-shot relation prediction regime, by introducing two graph attention modules aiming at alleviating over-smoothing situations.

2 Task Definition

Definition 1 (Knowledge Graph $\mathcal{G}$): A knowledge graph $\mathcal{G} = \{\mathcal{E}, \mathcal{R}, \mathcal{T}\}$. $\mathcal{E}$ indicates the set of entities and $\mathcal{R}$ indicates the set of relation types, respectively. (h, r, t) indicates the triple which is viewed as the basic unit of knowledge graph, wherein $h, t \in \mathcal{E}$ and $r \in \mathcal{R}$. $\mathcal{T} = \{(h, r, t)|h, t \in \mathcal{E}, r \in \mathcal{R}\}$ represents the set of triples.

Definition 2 (Few-Shot Relation Prediction Task)**:** With a knowledge graph $\mathcal{G} = \{\mathcal{E}, \mathcal{R}, \mathcal{T}\}$, given a support set $\mathcal{S}_r = \{(h,t) \in \mathcal{E} \times \mathcal{E} | (h,r,t) \in \mathcal{T}\}$ about relation $r \in \mathcal{R}$, where $|\mathcal{S}_r| = K$[1], predicting the tail entity linked with relation r to head entity h, formulated as $(h, r, ?)$, is called K-shot relation prediction.

3 Methodology

This section overviews the proposed relational Graph Convolutional Network (RGCN) based model for few-shot relation prediction task, which is integrated with two graph attention modules: (i) intra-layer neighborhood attention (Sect. 3.2), and (ii) inter-layer memory attention (Sect. 3.3). Wherein, intra-layer neighborhood attention aims at attending to the most related neighbor entity nodes, and inter-layer memory attention aims at maintaining earlier memory from previous RGCN layer. The following experimental sections will prove that both intra-layer neighborhood attention and inter-layer memory attention surely contribute to few-shot relation prediction.

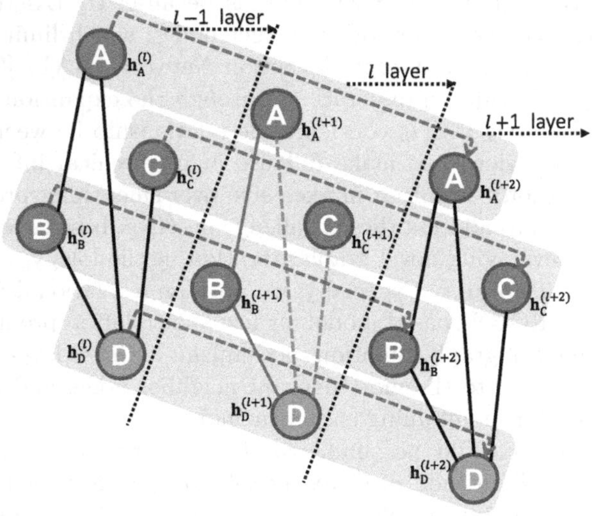

Fig. 1. The overall architecture of the proposed few-shot relation prediction model with intra-layer neighborhood attention and inter-layer memory attention.

3.1 Relation Prediction Based on RGCN

This paper adopts a multi-stage RGCN [9,13,28] for relation prediction task. The RGCN extends the graph convolution operation [17] to heterogenous graphs.

[1] Usually the value of K is very small in application situations.

Generally, a RGCN model consists of a sequence of RGCN layers. l-th layer computes i-th entity node representation $\mathbf{h}_i^{(l+1)}$:

$$\mathbf{h}_i^{(l+1)} = \sigma(\sum_{r=1}^{|\mathcal{R}|} \sum_{j \in \mathcal{N}_i^r} a_{r;(i,j)}^{(l)} \mathbf{h}_j^{(l)} \mathbf{W}_r^{(l)}) \tag{1}$$

Wherein, $a_{r;(i,j)}^{(l)}$ indicates the element of the weighted adjacency matrix $\mathbf{A}_r^{(l)} \in \mathbb{R}^{|\mathcal{E}| \times |\mathcal{E}|}$, which indicates whether and how strong entity i and entity j are directly connected under relation type r. There exit different methods to construct $\mathbf{A}_r^{(l)}$, e.g., its element $a_{r;(i,j)}^{(l)}$ can be defined as the similarity or distance between entity i and entity j. Here, $\mathcal{N}_i^r$ represents the neighborhoods of entity i under relation type r. $\mathbf{W}_r^{(l)} \in \mathbb{R}^{d_l \times d_{l+1}}$ is a matrix associated with the r-th relation type. Function $\sigma(\cdot)$ is a non-linear function, e.g., ReLU or Leaky-ReLU. We could observe from Eq. (1) that, the output of each conventional RGCN layer for entity node i is a non-linear combination of the hidden representations of its neighboring nodes (in $\mathcal{N}_i^r$) weighted according to the relation type r.

Each entity node i is assigned with a initial representation vector $\mathbf{x}_i \in \mathbb{R}^{d_x}$, which could be pre-trained by traditional KGE models, e.g., TrasnE [4] and DistMult [44], etc. Note that, for entity i, its input of the first layer in the proposed RGCN model, is formulated as: $\mathbf{h}_i^{(0)} = \mathbf{x}_i$.

The RGCN based model for relation prediction task here is supervised by DistMult model [44]. The loss function can be defined as follows:

$$\mathcal{L} = \sum_{(i,r,j) \in \mathcal{T}^+ \cup \mathcal{T}^-} \log(1 + \exp(-y \times \mathbf{h}_i^\top \mathrm{D}(\mathbf{h}_r) \mathbf{h}_j)) \tag{2}$$

Here, $\mathrm{D}(\cdot)$ denotes a diagonal matrix. $\{\mathbf{h}_i, \mathbf{h}_r, \mathbf{h}_j\}$ are the representation vector of the head entity i, relation type r and the tail entity j, respectively: (i) For entity's representation vectors (i.e., $\mathbf{h}_i$ and $\mathbf{h}_j$), they are obtained by the ultimate layer of the aforementioned RGCN; (ii) For relation's representation vectors (i.e., $\mathbf{h}_r$), they are trained directly from Eq. (2), which is the main difference compared with normal KGE model, similar to [5]. $\mathcal{T}^+$ and $\mathcal{T}^-$ are the positive and negative sets of triples. Apparently, many tactics can be adopted here for constructing $\mathcal{T}^-$, however this is not central to our discussion. $y = 1$ if the triple is a positive example, and $y = -1$ otherwise. $\mathbf{h}_i^\top \mathrm{D}(\mathbf{h}_r) \mathbf{h}_j$ (in Eq. (2)) denotes the score of triple (i, r, j) [44].

However, the paradigm of aforementioned model becomes fragile when only a few training edges are available for a particular relation type. Unfortunately, such few-shot problem widely exists in KGs. Hence, we attempt to modify such RGCN based relation prediction model for adapting few-shot learning scene, by utilizing the following attention mechanisms.

3.2 Intra-layer Neighbor Attention

Problem: Current GNN based models based on node feature propagation usually are shallow. Mainly because if we set a larger number of propagation steps, the problem of feature *over-smoothing* [7,10] becomes worse. Usually, such over-smoothing phenomenon happens when the number of layers of GNN model becomes larger. Because traditional GNN fuses semantic signals from all the neighbor nodes and ultimately converges to a stationary point in training procedure.

Solution: To overcome this problem, this paper proposes a novel *intra-layer neighbor attention* mechanism with sparsity constraint to help the model to attend to the most relevant entity nodes. We aims at imposing sparsity on the weighted adjacency matrix $\mathbf{A}_r^{(\cdot)}$, to focus on the most related neighbor entity node. Similar to [14] and other recent successful GNN application, we also introduce MLP to learn the weighted adjacency matrix $\mathbf{A}_r^{(l)}$, as follows:

$$\hat{\mathbf{A}}_r^{(l)} = \arg\min_{\mathbf{A}_r^{(l)}} \|\mathbf{A}_r^{(l)} - \mathbf{O}_r^{(l)}\|_F \tag{3}$$

Here, $\mathbf{O}_r^{(l)}$ indicates the original adjacency matrix with the intra-layer neighbor attention. For each pair of entity node i and entity node j, the sparsity constraint is defined as follows:

$$o_{r;(i,j)}^{(l)} = \mathrm{MLP}^{(l)}(|\mathbf{h}_i^{(l)} - \mathbf{h}_j^{(l)}|) \tag{4}$$

$$\| \mathbf{A}_{r;(i;\cdot)}^{(l)} \|_0 \leq \eta \times |\mathcal{E}| \tag{5}$$

Wherein, $o_{r;(i,j)}^{(l)}$ is the element of the adjacency matrix $\mathbf{O}_r^{(l)}$, and $\mathbf{A}_{r;(i;\cdot)}^{(l)} \in \mathbb{R}^{1\times|\mathcal{E}|}$ indicates the i-th row of $\mathbf{A}_r^{(l)}$. $\eta \in (0,1]$ indicates the entity node maintaining ratio for representation update. $|\cdot|$ represents absolute function. The projection onto a l_0 unit ball [2,40] could be used for solve Eq. (3) added with sparsity constraints (Eq. (4) and Eq. (5)), by keeping the $\eta \times |\mathcal{E}|$ elements of each row of $\mathbf{O}_r^{(l)}$ with the largest magnitudes. Especially, in each epoch, $\mathbf{O}_r^{(l)}$ is updated based on back-propagation mechanism firstly, and then we apply Eq. (3) to update $\mathbf{A}_r^{(l)}$.

3.3 Inter-layer Memory Attention

Problem: Existing GNN based relation prediction work usually averages the neighbors of the target entity nodes, which limits its performance.

As we all know, the conventional Graph Attention Network (GAT) only considers the relationship among neighbors in the same layer, while ignoring the beneficial layer-wise information, which also easily leads to the challenge of over-smoothing.

Solution: To overcome this problem, this paper proposes an *inter-layer memory attention* mechanism, by leveraging "previous memory" of intermediate features at earlier layers [12,15,27,43]. We attempt to densely connect the output of each RGCN layer, because the intermediate RGCN node represents a consistent and common representation on different RGCN layers [6]. Especially, this paper combines the transition function based on Eq. (1) and graph self-loop (i.e., identity matrix $\mathbf{I}$), for capturing self information. Therefore, Eq. (1) could be reformed as follows:

$$\mathbf{h}_i^{(l+1)} = \sigma(\sum_{r=1}^{|\mathcal{R}|} \sum_{j \in \mathcal{N}_i^r} [a_{r;(i,j)}^{(l)} \mathbf{h}_j^{(l)} \| \mathbb{I}_{r;(i,j)}^{(l)} \mathbf{h}_j^{(l)}] \mathbf{W}_r^{(l)}) \tag{6}$$

Wherein, $\|$ denotes concatenation operation, and $\mathbb{I}_{r;(i,j)}^{(l)} \in \mathbf{I}$. $\mathbf{W}_r^{(l)} \in \mathbb{R}^{2d_l \times d_{l+1}}$ is a learnable matrix corresponding to the r-th relation type.

Moreover, instead of using $\mathbf{h}_i^{(l+1)}$ in Eq. (6) as the input to $(l+1)$-th layer directly, we leverage "previous memory" by the entity node representation at the current l-th layer, as follows:

$$\mathbf{h}_i^{(l+1)} = [\mathbf{h}_i^{(l)} \| \sigma(\sum_{r=1}^{|\mathcal{R}|} \sum_{j \in \mathcal{N}_i^r} [a_{r;(i,j)}^{(l)} \mathbf{h}_j^{(l)} \| \mathbb{I}_{r;(i,j)}^{(l)} \mathbf{h}_j^{(l)}] \mathbf{W}_r^{(l)})] \tag{7}$$

4 Experiments

We conducted extensive experiments to evaluate the effectiveness of the proposed model for few-shot learning.

4.1 Datasets and Evaluation Metrics

We use two datasets: (i) NELL, derived from; and (ii) Wiki, derived from [34], in the experiments. Following [42], we select the relations with less than 500 but more than 50 triples as few-shot tasks. There are 67 and 183 tasks in NELL dataset and Wiki dataset, respectively. In addition, we utilize 51/5/11 task relations for training/validation/testing in NELL dataset, and the division is set to 133/16/34 in Wiki dataset. Table 1 lists the statistics of two datasets. Wherein, "$|\mathcal{E}|$" denotes the number of all unique entities, and "$|\mathcal{T}|$" denotes the number of all relational triples. "$|\mathcal{R}|$" represents the number of all relations and "$|\mathcal{R}_{\text{FS}}|$" represents the number of relations selected as few-shot tasks. Moreover, "#Train", "#Dev" and "#Test" indicates the number of relations in training, validation and test set.

Table 1. Statistics of NELL and Wiki datasets.

Dataset	$\lvert\mathcal{E}\rvert$	$\lvert\mathcal{T}\rvert$	$\lvert\mathcal{R}\rvert$	$\lvert\mathcal{R}_{\text{FS}}\rvert$	#Train	#Dev	#Test
NELL	68,545	181,109	358	67	51	5	11
Wiki	4,838,244	5,859,240	822	183	133	16	34

This paper utilizes two traditional metrics to evaluate different methods on these datasets, i.e., MRR and HITS@N. MRR indicates the mean reciprocal rank, and HITS@N is the proportion of correct entities ranked in the top N in relation prediction task. The value of N is set to 1, 5 and 10 in our experiments. The few-shot size K is set as $\{1, 5, 10\}$ for the following experiments. Moreover, experiments to analyze the impact of K are also conducted.

4.2 Baselines

For verifying the proposed model, we consider different categories of the state-of-the-art few-shot relation prediction models: (i) KGE models, including **ComplEx** [32] and **DistMult** [44]; (ii) Meta-learning models, including **GMatching** [42], **MetaR** [5], **FSRL** [45]; (iii) GNN based few-shot relation prediction models, including **RGCN** [28], **GNN** [27], **RA-GCN** [31], and **I-GCN** [14].

- **ComplEx:** [32] proposes to solve relation prediction problem through latent factorization and makes use of complex valued embeddings.
- **DistMult:** [44] utilizes the learned relation embeddings for mining logical rules.
- **GMatching:** [42] introduces a local neighbor encoder to model the vector representations for entities and relations.
- **MetaR:** [5] solves few-shot relation prediction by focusing on transferring relation-specific meta information, to make model learn the most important knowledge.
- **FSRL:** [45] performs joint optimization of relation-aware heterogeneous neighbor encoder, recurrent auto-encoder aggregation network and matching network, for few-shot relational learning.
- **RGCN:** [28] introduces relational graph convolutional networks, which is developed specifically to handle the highly multi-relational data characteristic of realistic KGs.
- **GNN:** [27] explores graph neural representations for few-shot, semi-supervised and active learning.
- **RA-GCN:** [31] proposes a relational aggregation GCN, which extracts the topological relationship features of KGs based on a GCN.
- **I-GCN:** [14] proposes an inductive RGCN for learning informative relation embeddings in the few-shot learning regime.

4.3 Experimental Settings

For all the comparative models, for each relation r from the few-shot relation set $\mathcal{R}_{\text{FS}}$, we train with only K triples about relation r (i.e., $\mathcal{S}_r$) as well as all the triples from the other kinds of relations. And we then test on the rest edges of the few-shot relation r. Following [5], trained model is applied on validation tasks each 1,000 epochs, the current model parameters and corresponding performance will be recorded. After stopping, the model that has the optimal

Table 2. Performance comparison of different models on the NELL datasets.

Model	HITS@1			HITS@5			HITS@10			MRR		
	1-shot	5-shot	10-shot	1-shot	5-shot	10-shot	1-shot	5-shot	10-shot	1-shot	5-shot	10-shot
DistMult	0.136	0.163	0.215	0.220	0.307	0.479	0.260	0.376	0.571	0.162	0.232	0.343
ComplEx	0.108	0.130	0.172	0.162	0.225	0.351	0.189	0.274	0.416	0.130	0.186	0.275
Gmatching	0.119	0.143	0.189	0.260	0.362	**0.564**	0.313	0.453	**0.688**	0.186	0.267	**0.395**
MetaR	0.170	0.168	0.183	0.336	0.350	0.408	0.401	0.437	0.500	0.250	0.261	0.281
FSRL	0.215	0.212	0.230	0.417	0.434	0.506	0.468	0.510	0.584	0.306	0.319	0.343
R-GCN	0.141	0.139	0.151	0.332	0.346	0.404	0.392	0.427	0.489	0.259	0.270	0.290
GNN	0.142	0.140	0.152	0.337	0.351	0.410	0.414	0.451	0.516	0.261	0.273	0.294
RA-GCN	0.146	0.144	0.157	0.344	0.358	0.414	0.406	0.442	0.506	0.268	0.280	0.301
I-GCN	0.143	0.142	0.154	0.339	0.353	0.412	0.400	0.436	0.498	0.264	0.275	0.296
Ours	**0.221**	**0.218**	**0.233**	**0.429**	**0.442**	0.516	**0.479**	**0.518**	0.592	**0.322**	**0.336**	0.350

performance on HITS@10 will be treated as final model to be reported in this section. Besides, for number of training epoch, this section uses early stopping with 30 patient epochs, which indicates that the train procedure stops when the performance on HITS@10 drops 30 times continuously. For the proposed model, we tune hyper-parameters on the validation dataset. Each entity and relation are assigned with a representation vector initially, which is pre-trained by traditional DistMult [44]. Apparently, other tactics can be adopted here for entity (or relation) representation initialization, however this is not central to our discussion.

4.4 Performance Summary

Tables 2 and 3 report the HITS@1, HITS@5, HITS@10 and MRR scores of the baseline models along with the proposed **GCN**, in the task of few-shot relation prediction for the NELL and Wiki datasets, respectively. Wherein, **Bold** numbers are the best results of all and underline numbers are the second best results. From the experimental results, we could conclude that, the proposed model significantly outperforms the alternative methods in few-shot scenario. Specifically, for 1-shot link prediction, the proposed model increases by 2.79%,

Table 3. Performance comparison of different models on the Wiki datasets.

Model	HITS@1			HITS@5			HITS@10			MRR		
	1-shot	5-shot	10-shot	1-shot	5-shot	10-shot	1-shot	5-shot	10-shot	1-shot	5-shot	10-shot
DistMult	0.065	0.069	0.083	0.155	0.157	0.168	0.189	0.197	0.237	0.111	0.114	0.123
ComplEx	0.081	0.086	0.104	0.117	0.118	0.126	0.140	0.146	0.175	0.105	0.108	0.116
Gmatching	0.120	0.128	0.154	0.272	0.275	0.295	0.336	0.351	0.422	0.200	0.205	0.221
MetaR	**0.152**	**0.178**	**0.236**	0.233	0.264	0.317	0.280	0.302	0.375	0.193	0.221	0.266
FSRL	0.134	0.157	0.208	0.289	0.328	0.394	0.378	0.408	**0.506**	0.214	0.245	0.295
RGCN	0.120	0.141	0.187	0.274	0.310	0.372	0.325	0.351	0.435	0.203	0.233	0.280
GNN	0.122	0.143	0.189	0.279	0.316	0.380	0.338	0.365	0.453	0.205	0.235	0.283
RA-GCN	0.125	0.146	0.193	0.283	0.321	0.386	0.337	0.364	0.451	0.211	0.241	0.290
I-GCN	0.123	0.144	0.196	0.279	0.317	0.393	0.332	0.358	0.469	0.208	0.238	0.293
Ours	0.138	0.161	0.200	**0.300**	**0.338**	**0.400**	**0.390**	**0.420**	0.467	**0.220**	**0.252**	**0.301**

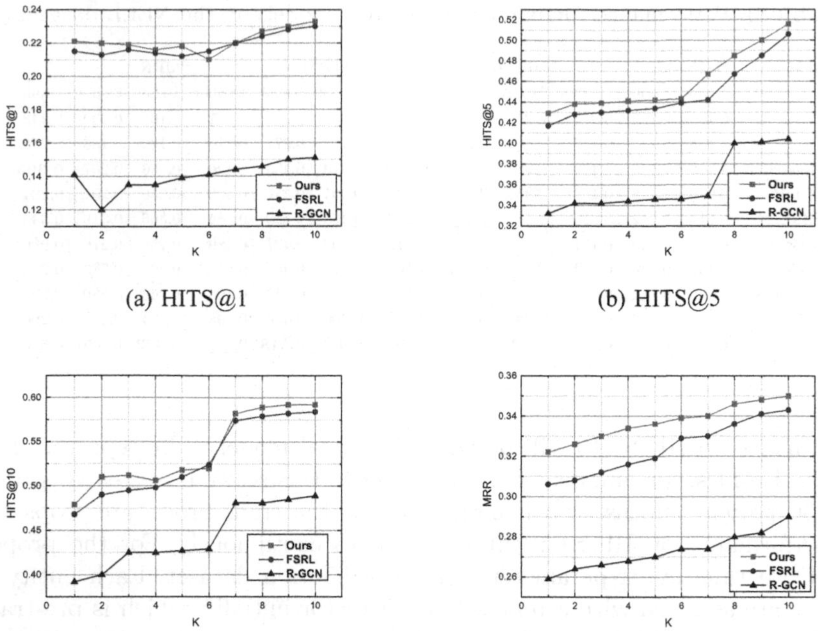

(a) HITS@1 (b) HITS@5

(c) HITS@10 (d) MRR

Fig. 2. Impact of few-shot size K in NELL dataset.

2.87%, 2.35% and 5.23% on HITS@1, HITS@5, HITS@10 and MRR on NELL dataset, and 3.81%, 3.17% and 2.80% HITS@5, HITS@10 and MRR on Wiki dataset. For 5-shot, our model increases by 2.85%, 1.84%, 2.57% and 5.33% on HITS@1, HITS@5, HITS@10 and MRR on NELL dataset, and 3.05%, 2.94% and 2.86% HITS@5, HITS@10 and MRR on Wiki dataset. The overall results indicate that the proposed attentive RGCN based model has the capability of few-shot relation prediction. In parallel, the impressive improvement compared with conventional **R-GCN** (as well as recent **RA-GCN** and **I-GCN**) demonstrates that the key idea of our model, attending to the most related neighbor node (discussed in Sect. 3.2) and maintaining earlier memory from previous GCN layer (discussed in Sect. 3.3), works well on few-shot relation prediction task.

4.5 Parameter Optimization

This paper studies few-shot relation prediction for knowledge graph completion, thus we analyze the impact of few-shot size K. Figure 2 shows the performances of the proposed model (**Ours**), **FSRL** and **I-GCN** in NELL dataset with different values of few-shot size K. Form experimental figures we could conclude that: With the increment of K, (i) performances of all models increase; and (ii) the proposed model consistently outperforms the comparative models in different values of K, demonstrating the stability of the proposed model. Overall, it intuitively shows that *larger* reference set can produce better reference set embedding for the relation.

Hyper-parameter η in Eq. (4) controls the sparsity ratio in the proposed intra-layer neighbor attention (detailed in Sect. 3.2). Figure 3 shows how varying η affects the relation prediction performance in NELL dataset (HITS@5). From the experimental results, $\eta = 0.7$ releases the optimal results in most cases.

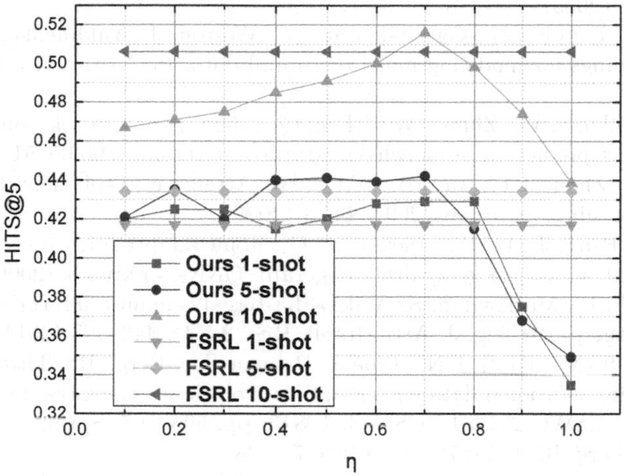

Fig. 3. Impact of sparsity ratio hyper-parameter η in NELL dataset.

5 Conclusion

Few-shot learning aims to learn latent patterns from few training examples and has shown promises in practice. Unlike the most current few-shot learning researches studying computer vision, imitation learning, spatiotemporal analysis, sentiment analysis domains, little researches leverage few-shot learning to predict relations for completing KGs. In this paper, we develop a novel GCN based relation prediction model with addition of intra-layer neighborhood attention and inter-layer memory attention, which can be applied for few-shot scenario. The experimental results on real-world datasets report that, the proposed model significantly outperforms the GNN based and state-of-the-art KGE based models in few-shot learning relation prediction task.

Acknowledgements. We thank anonymous reviewers for valuable comments. This work is funded by: (i) the National Natural Science Foundation of China (No. U19B2026); (ii) the New Generation of Artificial Intelligence Special Action Project (No. AI20191125008); (iii) the National Integrated Big Data Center Pilot Project (No. 20500908, 17111001, 17111002).

References

1. Baek, J., Lee, D., Hwang, S.J.: Learning to extrapolate knowledge: Transductive few-shot out-of-graph link prediction. arXiv abs/2006.06648 (2020)
2. Bernardi, C.A.D., Vesely, L.: Intersection properties of the unit ball. J. Math. Anal. Appl. **475**, 1108–1129 (2019)
3. Bollacker, K.D., Evans, C., Paritosh, P., Sturge, T., Taylor, J.: Freebase: a collaboratively created graph database for structuring human knowledge. In: Sigmod Conference (2008)
4. Bordes, A., Usunier, N., Garcia-Duran, A., Weston, J., Yakhnenko, O.: Translating embeddings for modeling multi-relational data. In: NIPS 2013, pp. 2787–2795 (2013)
5. Chen, M., Zhang, W., Zhang, W., Chen, Q., Chen, H.: Meta relational learning for few-shot link prediction in knowledge graphs. arXiv abs/1909.01515 (2019)
6. Cheng, H., Zhou, J.T., Tay, W., Wen, B.: Attentive graph neural networks for few-shot learning. arXiv abs/2007.06878 (2020)
7. Chien, E., Peng, J., Li, P., Milenkovic, O.: Joint adaptive feature smoothing and topology extraction via generalized pagerank GNNs. arXiv abs/2006.07988 (2020)
8. Gabrilovich, E., Markovitch, S.: Wikipedia-based semantic interpretation for natural language processing. J. Artif. Intell. Res. **34**(4), 443–498 (2014)
9. Schlichtkrull, M., Kipf, T.N., Bloem, P., van den Berg, R., Titov, I., Welling, M.: Modeling relational data with graph convolutional networks. In: Gangemi, A., et al. (eds.) ESWC 2018. LNCS, vol. 10843, pp. 593–607. Springer, Cham (2018). https://doi.org/10.1007/978-3-319-93417-4_38
10. Hasanzadeh, A., et al.: Bayesian graph neural networks with adaptive connection sampling. arXiv abs/2006.04064 (2020)
11. He, J., Hong, R., Liu, X., Xu, M., Zha, Z., Wang, M.C.: Memory-augmented relation network for few-shot learning. arXiv abs/2005.04414 (2020)
12. Huang, G., Liu, Z., Weinberger, K.Q.: Densely connected convolutional networks. 2017 IEEE Conference on Computer Vision and Pattern Recognition (CVPR), pp. 2261–2269 (2017)
13. Huang, Z., Li, X., Ye, Y., Ng, M.K.: MR-GCN: multi-relational graph convolutional networks based on generalized tensor product. In: IJCAI (2020)
14. Ioannidis, V.N., Zheng, D., Karypis, G.: Few-shot link prediction via graph neural networks for covid-19 drug-repurposing. arXiv abs/2007.10261 (2020)
15. Ji, F., Yang, J., Zhang, Q., Tay, W.: GFCN: a new graph convolutional network based on parallel flows. In: ICASSP 2020–2020 IEEE International Conference on Acoustics, Speech and Signal Processing (ICASSP), pp. 3332–3336 (2020)
16. Kim, J., Kim, T., Kim, S., Yoo, C.: Edge-labeling graph neural network for few-shot learning. In: 2019 IEEE/CVF Conference on Computer Vision and Pattern Recognition (CVPR), pp. 11–20 (2019)
17. Kipf, T.N., Welling, M.: Semi-supervised classification with graph convolutional networks. CoRR abs/1609.02907 (2016)
18. Li, Q., Han, Z., Wu, X.M.: Deeper insights into graph convolutional networks for semi-supervised learning. arXiv abs/1801.07606 (2018)
19. Liben-Nowell, D., Kleinberg, J.: The link-prediction problem for social networks. J. Assoc. Inf. Sci. Technol. **58**, 1019–1031 (2007)
20. Lin, Y., Liu, Z., Sun, M., Liu, Y., Zhu, X.: Learning entity and relation embeddings for knowledge graph completion. In: AAAI 2015, pp. 2181–2187 (2015)

21. Miller, G.: Wordnet: a lexical database for English. Commun. ACM **38**, 39–41 (1995)
22. Nickel, M., Rosasco, L., Poggio, T.: Holographic embeddings of knowledge graphs. In: Thirtieth AAAI Conference on Artificial Intelligence, pp. 1955–1961 (2016)
23. Oono, K., Suzuki, T.: Graph neural networks exponentially lose expressive power for node classification. arXiv: Learning (2020)
24. Oyetunde, T., Zhang, M., Chen, Y., Tang, Y.J., Lo, C.: BoostGAPFILL: improving the fidelity of metabolic network reconstructions through integrated constraint and pattern-based methods. Bioinformatics **33**, 608–611 (2017)
25. Rong, Y., Huang, W., Xu, T., Huang, J.: Dropedge: towards deep graph convolutional networks on node classification. In: ICLR (2020)
26. Rusu, A.A., et al.: Meta-learning with latent embedding optimization. arXiv abs/1807.05960 (2019)
27. Satorras, V.G., Bruna, J.: Few-shot learning with graph neural networks. arXiv abs/1711.04043 (2018)
28. Schlichtkrull, M., Kipf, T., Bloem, P., Berg, R.V., Titov, I., Welling, M.: Explorer modeling relational data with graph convolutional networks (2018)
29. Snell, J., Swersky, K., Zemel, R.: Prototypical networks for few-shot learning. arXiv abs/1703.05175 (2017)
30. Suchanek, F.M., Kasneci, G., Weikum, G.: Yago: a core of semantic knowledge. In: International Conference on World Wide Web (2007)
31. Tian, A., Zhang, C., Rang, M., Yang, X., Zhan, Z.: RA-GCN: relational aggregation graph convolutional network for knowledge graph completion. In: Proceedings of the 2020 12th International Conference on Machine Learning and Computing (2020)
32. Trouillon, T., Welbl, J., Riedel, S., Gaussier, É., Bouchard, G.: Complex embeddings for simple link prediction (2016)
33. Velickovic, P., Cucurull, G., Casanova, A., Romero, A., Liò, P., Bengio, Y.: Graph attention networks. CoRR abs/1710.10903 (2017)
34. Vrandečić, D., Krötzsch, M.: Wikidata: a free collaborative knowledgebase. Commun. ACM **57**(10), 78–85 (2014)
35. Wang, Y., Yan Huang, H., Feng, C.: Query expansion with local conceptual word embeddings in microblog retrieval. IEEE Trans. Knowl. Data Eng. **33**, 1737–1749 (2021)
36. Wang, Y., Liu, Y., Zhang, H., Xie, H.: Leveraging lexical semantic information for learning concept-based multiple embedding representations for knowledge graph completion. In: Shao, J., Yiu, M.L., Toyoda, M., Zhang, D., Wang, W., Cui, B. (eds.) APWeb-WAIM 2019, Part I. LNCS, vol. 11641, pp. 382–397. Springer, Cham (2019). https://doi.org/10.1007/978-3-030-26072-9_28
37. Wang, Y., Zhang, H., Shi, G., Liu, Z., Zhou, Q.: A model of text-enhanced knowledge graph representation learning with mutual attention. IEEE Access **8**, 52895–52905 (2020)
38. Wang, Y., Zhang, H.: Harp: a novel hierarchical attention model for relation prediction. ACM Trans. Knowl. Discov. Data **15**, 17:1–17:22 (2021)
39. Wang, Z., Zhang, J., Feng, J., Chen, Z.: Knowledge graph embedding by translating on hyperplanes. In: AAAI 2014, pp. 1112–1119 (2014)
40. Wen, B., Ravishankar, S., Bresler, Y.: Structured overcomplete sparsifying transform learning with convergence guarantees and applications. Int. J. Comput. Vision **114**, 137–167 (2014). https://doi.org/10.1007/s11263-014-0761-1

41. Wu, W., Li, H., Wang, H., Zhu, K.Q.: Probase: a probabilistic taxonomy for text understanding. In: Proceedings of the 2012 ACM SIGMOD International Conference on Management of Data, pp. 481–492 (2012)
42. Xiong, W., Yu, M., Chang, S., Guo, X., Wang, W.Y.: One-shot relational learning for knowledge graphs. In: EMNLP (2018)
43. Xu, K., Li, C., Tian, Y., Sonobe, T., Kawarabayashi, K., Jegelka, S.: Representation learning on graphs with jumping knowledge networks. In: ICML (2018)
44. Yang, B., Tau Yih, W., He, X., Gao, J., Deng, L.: Embedding entities and relations for learning and inference in knowledge bases. CoRR abs/1412.6575 (2014)
45. Zhang, C., Yao, H., Huang, C., Jiang, M., Li, Z., Chawla, N.V.: Few-shot knowledge graph completion. arXiv abs/1911.11298 (2020)
46. Zhang, F., Yuan, N.J., Lian, D., Xie, X., Ma, W.: Collaborative knowledge base embedding for recommender systems. In: Proceedings of the 22nd ACM SIGKDD International Conference on Knowledge Discovery and Data Mining (2016)
47. Zhang, J., Zhang, M., Lu, Z., Xiang, T., Wen, J.: AdarGCN: Adaptive aggregation GCN for few-shot learning. arXiv abs/2002.12641 (2020)
48. Zhang, M., Chen, Y.: Link prediction based on graph neural networks. arXiv abs/1802.09691 (2018)
49. Zhang, Y., Dai, H., Kozareva, Z., Smola, A.J., Song, L.: Variational reasoning for question answering with knowledge graph. CoRR abs/1709.04071 (2018)
50. Zhao, Y., Gao, S., Gallinari, P., Guo, J.: A novel embedding model for relation prediction in recommendation systems. IEICE Trans. Inf. Syst. **100-D**, 1242–1250 (2017)

A Research Study on Running Machine Learning Algorithms on Big Data with Spark

Arpad Kerestely, Alexandra Baicoianu, and Razvan Bocu(✉)

Faculty of Mathematics and Informatics, Transilvania University of Brasov, Brasov, Romania
{arpad.kerestely,a.baicoianu,razvan.bocu}@unitbv.ro

Abstract. The design and implementation of proactive fault diagnosis systems concerning the bearings during their manufacturing process requires the selection of robust representation learning techniques, which belong to the broader scope of the machine learning techniques. Particular systems, such as those that are based on machine learning libraries like Scikit-learn, favor the actual processing of the data, while essentially disregarding relevant computational parameters, such as the speed of the data processing, or the consideration of scalability as an important design and implementation feature. This paper describes an integrated machine learning-based data analytics system, which processes the large amounts of data that are generated by the bearings manufacturing processes using a multinode cluster infrastructure. The data analytics system uses an optimally configured and deployed Spark environment. The proposed data analytics system is thoroughly assessed using a large dataset that stores real manufacturing data, which is generated by the respective bearings manufacturing processes. The performance assessment demonstrates that the described approach ensures the timely and scalable processing of the data. This achievement is relevant, as it exceeds the processing capabilities of significant existing data analytics systems.

Keywords: Big data · High performance computing · Spark · Fault detection · Representation techniques · Machine learning

1 Introduction

The scientific developments that have been achieved during the past few years imply that the valuable knowledge that can be extracted from the analysis of large scale data sets has produced the development of the so-called "Big Data" field. Thus, the clusters and computational grids [10] allow for the analysis of big data to occur in a cost effective way [12].

This article presents an integrated data analytics system, which considers an assessment model that aims to optimize the big data analytics processes, with a focus on the automotive industry and the necessary car parts manufacturing

H. Qiu et al. (Eds.): KSEM 2021, LNAI 12815, pp. 307–318, 2021.
https://doi.org/10.1007/978-3-030-82136-4_25

processes. The contribution's relevance is enhanced by the fact that real-world data is used in order to evaluate the validity of the described model.

The results of the performance assessment stage of the research that is reported in this paper, and also the relevant contributions that are reported in the existing literature demonstrate that Spark exhibits a great potential to scale. Thus, the design decision to consider Spark for the processing core of the data analytics system is completely justified. Additionally, the availability of the Hadoop Distributed File System (HDFS) optimizes the creation of the storage resources, and it also provides very high aggregate bandwidth across the multinode cluster infrastructure. Furthermore, the utilization of Spark alleviates the memory problems that are present on similar data analytics systems, which do not consider a multinode cluster infrastructure.

The paper is structured considering the following sections. The next section discusses about essential technical concepts, which are required in order to accurately understand the contribution that is reported in this paper, and it also describes the industrial dataset that is used. Furthermore, the experimental setup and the integrated data analytics system are described. Moreover, the processing of the available real-world data is described, and the proper analysis is made. The last section discusses on the open problems, and it also concludes the paper.

2 The Experimental Dataset

The experimental evaluation that is reported in this paper considers a dataset concerning the bearings' fault detection. Furthermore, vibrations and acoustic signals were measured on an electric engine mounted on bearings, with four different bearing conditions: healthy, inner and outer race fault, and ball defect. The bearing condition marks the class of each entry, enabling the utilization of supervised learning. Concerning the classification process, we can talk about a multi-class classification problem, which considers four classes.

The dataset was generated using a fault machine simulator from SpectraQuest, and it was subsequently used by the authors of the work that is reported in [6] in order to compute results on vibrations and acoustic signals under medium rotational speeds. It is worth pointing out that only parts of the dataset were used in their study, and that the choice of their algorithms is inclined towards the ones that require engineering expertise. This contrasts with the work that is reported in [1], where the authors report typical, general purpose classification algorithms.

The bearing fault detection dataset originally came split into 336 MATLAB files, with a total size of 19.69 GB. After the decompression has been applied, the size of the dataset increased to 28.3 GB. Considering the purposes of efficient storage and easier data processing, the 336 MATLAB files were converted into the same number of Apache Parquet files, with a total size of 9.75 GB. While there is no general agreement concerning the threshold for a dataset to be categorized as big, let us consider the suggestions in [5]. Thus, this dataset falls into the medium category, as its size belongs to the range 10 GB-1 TB, and it can be stored on a machine's storage drive, rather than in its memory. This assertion considers the specifications of a typical end user computer.

The dataset contains 14 float64 and an int32 columns (features), and about 262 million rows (entries/samples). The features are as follows: BL_[X, Y, Z] (Left bearing - axis X, Y and Z), BR_[X, Y, Z] (Right bearing - axis X, Y and Z), MR_[X, Y, Z] (Motor - axis X, Y and Z), [BL, BR]_AE (Left bearing and Right bearing Acoustic Emission), [BL, BR]_Mic (Left bearing and Right bearing Microphone), defect_type. The last column represents the class and can take four different values: Healthy, Ball, Inner, Outer. These are stored as integer numbers, which take the values 0, 1, 2, 3, respectively. The speed feature is also interesting, as it depicts the motors' rotation per minute (rpm) parameter, and it has its values clustered in the vicinity of $300, 420, 540, ..., 2580, 2700$, with an increment of 120 rpm.

It has already been stated that the data was converted to the Parquet [3] format, which is a columnar format supported by a number of data processing frameworks, including Pandas [7] and Spark. This conversion allowed for the input data to be easily read considering both the Scikit-learn and Spark tests. The Parquet format is also an efficient file format, which provides good compression levels and fast access to the data. The supplementary increase in the read speed of the parquet files is achieved by using Apache Arrow [9] as the processing engine, considering both the evaluated frameworks. Thus, Apache Arrow speeds up the communication between the multiple frameworks, as a parquet file is read with Pandas, and then transformed into a Spark dataframe without worrying about the conversion. Additionally, it takes advantage of a columnar buffer in order to reduce input-output (IO) operations. Furthermore, it accelerates the performance of the data analytics processes [2].

3 Comparative Analysis of Spark and Scikit-Learn

The consideration of Scikit-learn in order to run the tests on large datasets can be an issue for two reasons. First, if the data is loaded with Pandas, as its usually the case, the data won't fit into memory. Second, if the testing process is conducted on the whole dataset, the computation of the results takes a long time. Thus, the reaction and the improvement can take a significant amount of time. Consequently, in an attempt to overcome these issues, four smaller datasets were generated. First, 10^2 lines were randomly sampled from each of the 336 files, each of them originally containing 780800 lines, thus resulting in a dataset of uncompressed data with the size of 3.71 MB, which represents approximately 0.01% of the entire dataset. For further reference, the name of this dataset will be *data100*. Moreover, 10^3, 10^4 and 10^5 lines were extracted in the same manner, which produced three datasets with the sizes of 37.17 MB ($\approx$0.12%), 371.7 MB ($\approx$1.28%), and 3,62 GB ($\approx$12.8%). These datasets will be referred as *data1k*, *data10k* and *data100k*. These subsets of the initial dataset enable the quick assessment of some initials setups, but they also enable the progressive comparison of the results of the two frameworks on larger datasets. This intends to determine the threshold, assuming there was one, where Spark becomes faster than Scikit-learn. The assumption is that for small datasets Scikit-learn would always run faster.

The proper preparation of the datasets allows for the tests, measurements and comparison of the classification jobs to be conducted on both Scikit-learn and Spark.

3.1 The Scikit-Learn Tests

Scikit-learn is a framework that provides a high level application programming interface (API) in order to easily specify and run standard machine learning models, such as Logistic Regression, SVM, and so on. It is usually used for running classification, regression and clustering algorithms on datasets that fit into the system's memory. The scikit-learn models require as input a two-dimensional data structure, which consists of numeric values. The Pandas data frames (DataFrame) are widely used in order to satisfy this requirement, while the consideration of NumPy arrays under the hood also determines a really good computational performance.

The scikit-learn tests consider the following runtime environment: Python 3.8.2, Pandas 1.0.3, SciPy 1.4.1, and scikit-learn 0.22.1.

Considering the algorithms that are evaluated by the authors of [1] on the same data set, K-Nearest Neighbors was randomly chosen in order to be tested on the scenarios required for this paper. However, after running some initial tests, the immediate concern was to see if K-Nearest Neighbor was implemented in Spark. The answer was immediate after looking up the list of possible algorithms, and came to confirm that Spark covers most of the common classification algorithms, but not the selected one. As a result, looking at the list of algorithms from [1] and the list of algorithms implemented in Spark, the decision was to choose the Artificial Neural Networks, which are also known as Multilayer Perceptrons, with the assumption that Spark would validly equate Scikit-learn, and exhibit no further limitations.

Before outlining the results of the tests from the current study, there are some aspects to consider regarding how the Scikit-learn version of the Multilayer Perceptron (MLPClassifier) was used. The considered network is composed of a 14 neuron input layer, three hidden layers with 50, 100 and 50 neurons respectively, and a four-neuron output layer. Scikit-learn required only the hidden layer setup, as the input and output were inferred from the training dataset. The maximum number of iterations was empirically fine tuned at 500. Additionally, while the rest of the hyperparameters were left at their default values, it is worth mentioning a few of them. Thus, the activation function was relu, the solver was adam, the L2 regularization term was 1e−4, the learning rate was constant throughout the training and had a value of 1e−3. Finally, if the score did not improve for ten consecutive iterations by at least 1e−4, the training process was stopped. Some of these hyperparameters were showcased just for easier reference, while some other ones will be important later for the comparative analysis with the Spark implementation.

The training process of the model involves that 80% of the dataset was used, while the rest of the 20% is left for testing, while shuffling and stratifying were considered during the split operations. The assessment of the model's performance involves the usage of accuracy metric, as the dataset is balanced.

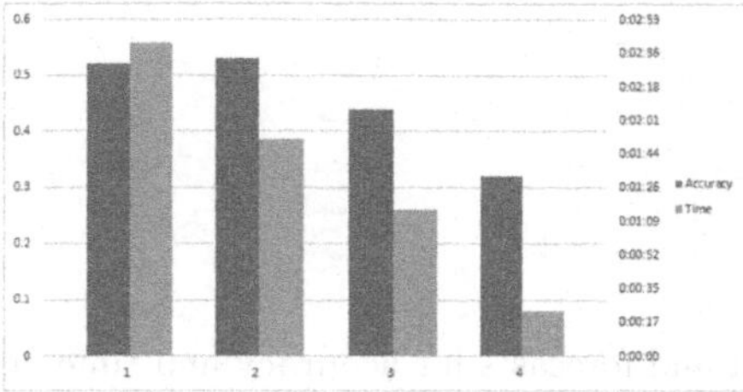

Fig. 1. Accuracy and time measurements on the *data100* dataset.

It is relevant to note that the Scikit-learn algorithms and the results they generate in comparison with the Spark results, suggest that they may take advantage of the parallel computing power of multicore machines. Some of the Scikit-learn algorithms are naturally linear. Therefore, they cannot be calculated in parallel, but in the case of the MLPClassifier, one can talk about parallelization, as this benefits from the optimized BLAS implementation, which ensures the occurrence of multithreaded calls for different linear algebra routines, such as matrix multiplications. The proper implementation of this parallelization, as it is observed during the training process, implies that there are times when almost all cores of the central processing unit (CPU) are used. In Fig. 1, it can be observed that there are 4 runs on 4 different *data100* datasets, the median accuracy is 48%, while the maximum accuracy is around 53%. Furthermore, the mean time is 1 min and 33 s, and the time varies between runs, but it is almost always directly proportional to the values of the accuracy. The last result is somewhat odd relative to the other results, and it is probably caused by applying the split operations on the training and test datasets, and also by the consideration of the MLP training. In Fig. 2, two of the best time and accuracy measurements can be observed for the datasets *data100*, *data1k*, and *data10k*. It can be observed that the accuracy, but also the training time increase for larger datasets, which is somehow obvious. Considering an empirical point of view, the accuracy increases logarithmically, while the time increases exponentially. The figure shows the actual increase with a solid line, and the forecast with a dotted line. The memory constraints measurements for *data100k* could not be conducted, but the forecast suggests that the accuracy could have reached nearly 70%, while the training time could have ranged between 19 and 28 h, with an average value of 24 h.

The scikit-learn experiments provided a solid base of comparison with Spark, although they also brought to surface a notable limitation in the form of the memory constraints. Consequently, this approach is not scalable. Considering a

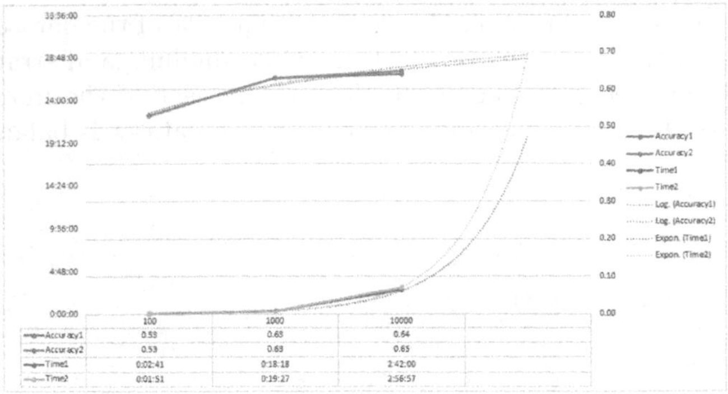

Fig. 2. Assessment and forecasts for accuracy and time on larger datasets.

project that requires scaling, it can be asserted that a cloud solution could be a better choice. Therefore, the switch to Spark appears as an optimal research direction.

3.2 The Spark Tests

Considering the measurements and comparisons that are applied on the classification jobs, it is worth to use Apache Spark for the large-scale data processing operations since it offers a full stack of libraries, including the Apache Spark DataFrame API to preprocess the data, and the Spark ML API for the construction of machine learning pipelines that are built on top of DataFrames, all of which can be programmed using Python. Furthermore, Spark offers the possibility to be run in standalone or cluster mode. The additional boost of the input-output operations, and the actual data processing speed, is determined by the consideration of the Apache Arrow.

The tests that consider Spark used the following runtime environment: Java 1.8.0_181, Spark 3.0.0-preview2, PyArrow 0.16, and Python 3.8.2. It is relevant to note that running in cluster mode, the Python code should be submitted with the same environment as the master and workers use, even when using the Jupyter Notebook.

The usage of Spark in cluster mode considers a master/slave architecture. This means that the work needs to be submitted to the master, which will distribute the proper jobs to the workers. The process that submits the work is called a driver. Each of these three processes must benefit of the same runtime environment setup. Furthermore, the workers also represent a variation of manager processes, as they span executors in accordance with the driver request. The number of executors, as well as the number of cores and the amount of memory that an executor is able to use can be configured from the driver, usually through a *SparkSession* object. Thus, a *SparkSession* example can be seen in the provided source code.

Before outlining the results of the tests from the current study, there are some aspects to consider regarding how the Spark version of the Multilayer Perceptron (MultilayerPerceptronClassifier) was used. The considered network has the same architecture in the Scikit-learn tests. Spark requires specifying also the number of neurons of the input and output layer, besides the hidden layer. The number of input neurons is equal to the number of features in the training set minus one, as obviously, we don't use the defect_type column as input. The number of output neurons is four, as there are four possible defect types (outcome classes). The maximum number of iterations again 500, as for the Scikit-learn tests. Additionally, while the rest of the hyperparameters were left at their default values, it is worth mentioning a few of them. Thus, the solver was l-bfgs, the learning rate, called *stepSize*, was constant throughout the training and had a value of 0.03, finally, the tolerance value was 1e−6. Some of these hyperparameters were showcased just for easier reference, while some other ones will be important later for the comparative analysis with the Scikit-learn implementation.

The training process of the model involves that 80% of the dataset was used, while the rest of the 20% is left for testing, while shuffling was considered during the split operations. The assessment of the model's performance involves the usage of accuracy metric.

Considering the remaining part of this section, several scenarios are described, analyzed, discussed and compared with the Scikit-learn baseline from a performance perspective. The validity of the comparison is ensured by the usage of one computer with Spark in cluster mode. This means that the driver, master and worker are deployed on the same computer. The input file(s) are on the local filesystem. The scenarios cascade from one another because of certain limitations that are encountered along the way, but the results get better with each scenario, until they reach an optimal configuration.

Scenario 1: Spark was configured to run one executor, with one core, and with 30 GB of associated memory. Although the amount of allocated memory seems to be overestimated, previous research findings prov that it is a good practice to allocate all the available memory [8]. The input was one parquet file for each of the datasets *data100*, *data1k*, *data10k*, and *data100k*. The import of the data from a parquet file into a Spark DataFrame does not imply that all the data is loaded into memory, but only the subsets that are needed considering an on demand model.

This scenario tried to replicate the Scikit-learn setup as closely as possible, assuming that the Scikit-learn algorithms ran on a single thread. Considering the two selected samples, as they are presented in Table 1, it can be observed that there is a big discrepancy in runtime between this scenario and the one that pertains to the Scikit-learn implementation, which led to some investigations. It turned out that Scikit-learn's implementation of MLP uses multithreading for most of its computation so, in order to be aligned to the next scenario, multiple cores will be allocated to the Spark executor.

Table 1. Comparison of Scikit-learn and Spark in Scenario 1.

	data100		*data1k*		*data10k*		*data100k*	
	Acc.	Time	Acc.	Time	Acc.	Time	Acc.	Time
Scikit-learn	0.53	0:02:41	0.63	0:18:18	0.64	2:42:00	N/A	N/A
Spark S1	0.35	0:10:53	0.35	1:40:16	0.32	18:18:19	0.355	181:19:35

Table 2. Comparison of the Spark Scenario 1 and Spark Scenario 2.

	data100		*data1k*		*data10k*		*data100k*	
	Acc.	Time	Acc.	Time	Acc.	Time	Acc.	Time
Spark S1	0.35	0:10:53	0.35	1:40:16	0.32	18:18:19	0.355	181:19:35
Spark S2	0.36	0:11:00	0.33	1:34:02	0.35	17:03:22	0.35	176:29:48

Scenario 2: Spark was configured to run with a similar configuration as in Scenario 1, with the only difference that instead of one core, the executor was allowed to use all the twelve cores available on the machine.

The expectation from this scenario was to obtain similar results as compared to the Scikit-learn implementation. Nevertheless, the results that are displayed in Table 2 suggest an odd behaviour. Thus, the results are nearly the same as in the case of Scenario 1. Moreover, the inspection of the processor usage while the tests are performed, confirms that only one core was actively running. Consequently, further research and investigation efforts defined the third scenario, which aims to find a proper solution that effectively makes use of the available multiple cores. It is significant to analyze the multiple test measurements that are done in the context of both Scenario 1 and Scenario 2, as it can be observed in Fig. 3. It is immediate to observe that the time required to run a test grows proportionally with the size of the data. Thus, let us note that the bubble sizes grow proportionally with the time, too. Unfortunately, the same cannot be said about the accuracy, which seems to be in the same interval, regardless of how much data is used, more specifically around 35% and 25%. It is important to note that in the case of the 25%, one could say that learning didn't even occur, as it is the same as the random choice of a class out of the four that are available. Moreover, in the case when the accuracy is around 25%, it can be observed that the run time is significantly less compared to the 35% case. This is probably a consequence of an early termination of the neural network's training process. To design of a valid comparison with Scikit-learn implies that this aspect was considered during the selection process of the samples, which have already been described, using the results from the 35% accuracy pool.

Scenario 3: Spark was configured to run with the same configuration as in Scenario 2, but instead of one parquet file, multiple parquet files were used as input. This resulted in Spark running jobs on multiple cores. While it may

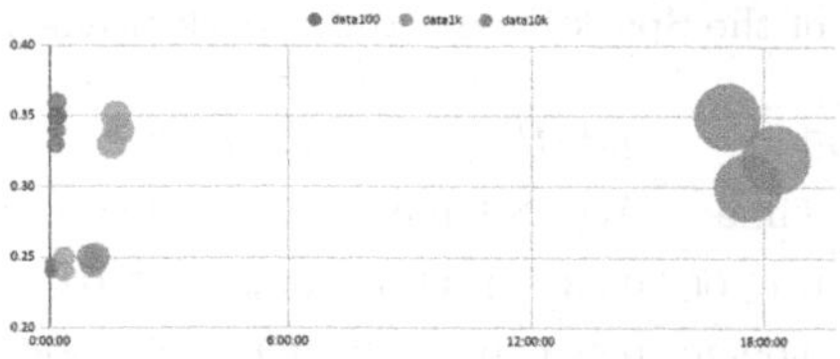

Fig. 3. Comparative overview regarding the Spark tests on one CPU core in Scenario 1 and Scenario 2.

sound strange, initially it was just a trial and error subject, but later it turned out that Spark cannot run jobs in parallel on a monolithic parquet file. The author of [4] also specifies that this behavior only happens when the data is on the local system and not on a HDFS (Hadoop Distributed File System). Due to this shortcoming, some exploration was done on splitting data, in the following ways:

- based on the defect_type feature, which resulted in 4 splits, which in turn allowed only 4 parallel jobs at a time, while the available core were 12
- by grouping the speed in discrete values, and split by speed, with the disadvantage of loosing information (regarding speed)
- introducing a new column which would contain the remainder of dividing the index by 12, then split based on this new column, with the disadvantage of having an extra column
- using the maxRecordsPerFile parameter like in Listing 1, available from Spark 2.2+

Listing 1. Method for splitting data

```
sp_df:DataFrame = spark.read.load(data_path)
count = sp_df.count()
sp_df.write.format("parquet")
  .option("maxRecordsPerFile", count//12)
  .save(r"data\split")
```

Considering also the cases where more tasks would access the same file, the last solution was used for splitting the data, into not 12, but 20 chunks to avoid concurrent file access.

The results were outlined in Table 3, and depict that Spark now indeed runs multi-cored, outperforming the speed of Spark Scenario 1 five times, and also matching the speed of Scikit-learn. The noticeable difference in accuracy between Scikit-learn and Spark is due to the different solvers used by the two, but it is the closest comparison to what we can get. It is necessary to note that the levels of the accuracy, which are displayed in Table 3, are justified by the consideration of the training time optimization over the accuracy in the current version of the data analytics system.

Table 3. Comparison of the Spark Scenario 2, Spark Scenario 3 and Scikit-learn.

	data100		*data1k*		*data10k*		*data100k*	
	Acc.	Time	Acc.	Time	Acc.	Time	Acc.	Time
Spark S2	0.36	0:11:00	0.33	1:34:02	0.35	17:03:22	0.35	176:29:48
Spark S3	0.354	0:02:36	0.354	0:18:37	0.308	3:43:26	0.352	36:43:53
Scikit-learn	0.53	0:02:41	0.63	0:18:18	0.64	2:42:00	N/A	N/A

Scaling with Spark. As demonstrated in the previous section, Spark can run as fast as Scikit-learn on a single machine, utilizing the full power of the CPU. Naturally the next step, out of curiosity but also for scalability purposes, is to try to get a new speed record in terms of training time. Along with this, another target is to break the barrier of how much data can be processed. Both of these objectives could theoretically be achieved by growing the processing power of Spark, with the addition of new computers (nodes) to the cluster. Using the setup mentioned in the previous section, switching to a multi-node cluster setup is straightforward as Spark is already running in cluster mode.

Running Spark on multiple computers can be done in a few simple steps. On each computer the same Java and Spark versions should be installed, and in the case of running PySpark, python should be also available on the systems. Spark needs to know the path to the Java and Python installations either through the system path or specific environment variables. Next, it is recommended to run Spark on one of the computers as master and as worker on the rest of the computers. The Spark driver can be on the same computer as the master.

The dataset is stored on each of the computers. Moreover, it has to be in the same location, because the driver cannot indicate to each worker individually, where to search for the data, it will pinpoint a single location, be it a local folder, a shared folder on the network, a path on a distributed filesystem, etc. While the most scalable solution would normally have been to store the data in a distributed filesystem like the Hadoop Distributed File System (HDFS), this would have introduced overhead to the network, thus biasing the speed results, the main objective of these tests. For testing the performance of Spark, the input dataset consisted of the initially mentioned 336 parquet files.

Table 4. Comparison of a seven node Spark cluster with Scenario 3.

	data100		*data1k*		*data10k*		*data100k*		*all*	
	Acc.	Time	Acc.	Time	Acc.	Time	Acc.	Time	Acc.	Time
Spark S3	0.354	0:02:36	0.354	0:18:37	0.308	3:43:26	0.352	36:43:53	N/A	N/A
Spark cluster	0.35	0:09:17	0.35	0:18:14	0.3	1:17:45	0.346	9:49:37	0.352	44:29:34

At this point it is also worth mentioning that Spark natively handles the cases when a worker drops by whatever reasons, by assigning the unfinished tasks to other workers. With the default setup, the driver or master are still single point of failures (SPOF), but Spark can be configured to have a temporary replacement for the master or the driver, so undesirable fails in either of them can be handled without stopping the processing or loosing the already computed results. The cluster for the following tests was deployed considering seven workstations with the same hardware configuration. Thus, they use hard disk drives for the local storage, 16 GB of RAM memory, eight CPU cores, which are connected physically to a switch with a 100 Mpbs link speed. One computer was configured as the master and driver host, and the rest as worker machines. Each worker was configured to spawn two executors with 3 GB of RAM memory, and 4 CPU core. The results from Table 4 show that, considering this new setup, Spark proves to be slower for small datasets than the setup form *Scenario 3*, but things get progressively better as the size of the data grows, considering a logarithmic curve. The table also shows that the training on the whole dataset is possible using the integrated data analytics system on multiple machines, and it takes approximately 45 h.

4 Conclusions and Open Problems

The contribution that is presented in this paper is significant in several respects. Thus, it describes an integrated data analytics system, which is capable to fully process the large datasets that are generated during the bearings manufacturing processes using a multinode cluster setup. This achievement is significant considering that most of the existing similar approaches are able to process only subsets of the existing large datasets. Moreover, while the data analytics system that is presented in this paper is equally efficient to other similar approaches on small datasets of up to 10 MB, it is more efficient on larger datasets that are able to use the efficient machine learning-based data processing core, and the multinode cluster infrastructure.

The current version of the system is designed in order to optimize the training phase of the data analytics process. Furthermore, it is important to note that the architecture of the data analytics system allows for relevant data processing routines to be re-engineered. This allows for the future optimized iterations of the system to be implemented in an efficient way, so that useful improvements, such as the stronger consideration of the accuracy, will become available. The software system that was considered in order to conduct the research is available at this address: https://github.com/akerestely/hpc-hadoop-spark.

The work on the data analytics system is planned to be continued in several respects. Thus, the accuracy will be considered with a higher importance during the analysis processes. Additionally, interesting hypotheses will be checked, such as whether the processing of larger amounts of data may imply the increase of the accuracy levels. Several research pathways will be considered. Thus, other training and processing models will be designed and tested, which consider more efficient hyper-parameters that use grid search and cross validation. Additionally, the confusion matrix will be thoroughly studied, so that the classes that produce the prediction errors are identified. Furthermore, it is possible that the lower levels of the accuracy may be generated by an early stop of the relevant processes, which is possibly determined by the backpropagation that reached a local minimum. This hypothesis will also be attentively analyzed.

Acknowledgments. The authors wish to extend their gratitude to Siemens Industry Software Romania for their kind support and for the industrial experimental dataset, and also to the Transilvania University of Brasov for the provision of the necessary hardware infrastructure.

References

1. Baicoianu, A., Mathe, A.: Diagnose bearing failures with machine learning models (2021). In review process
2. Cachuan, A.: A gentle introduction to apache arrow with apache spark and pandas (2020). https://towardsdatascience.com
3. Databricks: Parquet files (2020). https://docs.databricks.com/data/data-sources/read-parquet.html
4. Davis, C.: Big data on a laptop: Tools and strategies - part 3 (2018). https://tech.popdata.org
5. Driscoll, M.: Winning with big data: Secrets of the successful data scientist (2010). https://conferences.oreilly.com/datascience/public/schedule/detail/15316
6. Freitas, C., Cuenca, J., Morais, P., Ompusunggu, A., Sarrazin, M., Janssens, K.: Comparison of vibration and acoustic measurements for detection of bearing defects. In: International Conference on Noise and Vibration Engineering 2016 and International Conference on Uncertainty in Structural Dynamics 2016, vol. 1 (2016)
7. Nagpal, A., Gabrani, G.: Python for data analytics, scientific and technical applications. In: 2019 Amity International Conference on Artificial Intelligence (AICAI), pp. 140–145. IEEE (2019)
8. Pedapatnam, R.: Understanding resource allocation configurations for a spark application (2016). http://site.clairvoyantsoft.com/
9. Spark, A.: Pyspark usage guide for pandas with apache arrow (2020). https://spark.apache.org/docs
10. Case Western Reserve University: The case western reserve university bearing data center website (2020). https://csegroups.case.edu/bearingdatacenter
11. Zhang, R., Tao, H., Wu, L., Guan, Y.: Transfer learning with neural networks for bearing fault diagnosis in changing working conditions. IEEE Access **5**, 14347–14357 (2017)
12. Zhang, S., Zhang, S., Wang, B., Habetler, T.G.: Machine learning and deep learning algorithms for bearing fault diagnostics-a comprehensive review. arXiv preprints arXiv:1901.08247 (2019)

Attentional Neural Factorization Machines for Knowledge Tracing

Xiaowu Zhang and Li Li(✉)

School of Computer and Information Science, Southwest University, Chongqing, China
xiaohuangren@email.swu.edu.cn, lily@swu.edu.cn

Abstract. To promote the quality and intelligence of online education systems, knowledge tracing becomes a fundamental and crucial task. It models knowledge state and predicts performance based on student's learning records. Recently, factorization machine based approaches have been proposed to fit student's learning behavior by generating interactions between underlying features. However, there are two major unresolved issues: (1) quantities of interactions are introduced along with different features involved in. Nevertheless, the redundant interactions do not effectively contribute to the model training. There is a need to extract the most important and relevant interactions. (2) The widely employed factorization machines simply process with second order interactions, leading to insufficiently expressive representations, which is not beneficial to prediction. To this end, we propose a novel Attentional Neural Factorization Machines (ANFMs) to address the above problems. First, we leverage attention mechanisms to suppress the interference of interactions redundancy by distinguishing the importance of different interactions. To be specific, explicit and implicit attention strategies are utilized respectively. Secondly, to facilitate expressive capability, we apply neural networks to the transformed interactions after attention propagation, which is able to capture high order representations. Extensive experiments on two real-world datasets clearly show that ANFMs outperforms baselines with significant margins, which demonstrates the effectiveness of our work.

Keywords: Knowledge tracing · Factorization machines · Attention mechanism

1 Introduction

In recent decades, massive online open courses (MOOCs) [2], which provide an open access to class instruction and diverse resources for students worldwide, show an alternative view on educational concept. In contrast to conventional education, they significantly reduce the cost of learning and release burden on both teachers and students. Especially under circumstances of the epidemic of intelligent tutoring systems [5], we rather expect an effective technique that track

H. Qiu et al. (Eds.): KSEM 2021, LNAI 12815, pp. 319–330, 2021.
https://doi.org/10.1007/978-3-030-82136-4_26

and estimate the knowledge state of students for individualized recommendation [6]. To achieve this goal, researchers introduced *knowledge tracing* (KT) [16] into this task.

In literature, many efforts have been done in KT [9,10,21]. The prior well-known strategies are *item response theory* (IRT) [22] and *bayesian knowledge tracing* (BKT) [25], which have been proved efficacious in many scenarios. More than this, with the emergence and large-scale adoption of neural networks, researchers also developed neural based methods to explore KT task. Among which, the first and most representative work is *deep knowledge tracing* (DKT) [12,24], which exceeds most of traditional methods. Another method deserving to be mentioned is *dynamic key and value memory network* (DKVMN) [1,26], it dynamically writes to the *value* matrix where knowledge state stored while reading from the *key* matrix where knowledge concepts stored, which is consistent with people's cognition and even performs better than DKT. More recently, *knowledge tracing machine* (KTM) [20] employs factorization machine (FM) [14] and attains excellent results, which inspires our work.

Though productive achievements have been obtained by these methods, there are further problems underexplored. In general, existing factorization based methods have a dissatisfied performance resulting from the following grounds. First, the introduction of redundant features do not effectively contribute to the model training. Secondly, factorization machines simply process with second-order interactions, which leads to insufficient expressions.

To solve problems above, we propose *attentional neural factorization machines* (ANFMs). Specifically, we first introduce a Bi-interaction layer [7] to preliminarily encode interactions between features. Then, we transfer the informative but redundant encodings to an attention layer for solving the deficiency caused by interactive operations. In other words, we intend to distinguish the importance of these primary interactions, meanwhile, restrain defects of redundancy. Then, we convey the weighted results to neural layers for high-order representations. The main contributions are summarized as follows:

1. We integrate factorization machine into knowledge tracing for effectively capturing relation between features.
2. We first introduce two attentional strategies to solve negative effects brought by Bi-interaction, which presents a new view for factorization machines.
3. Extensive experiments on real-world data demonstrate the effectiveness of ANFMs.

2 Related Work

2.1 Bayesian Knowledge Tracing

Bayesian knowledge tracing (BKT) [25] occupies the mainstream of predicting student's performance chronically before large-scale application of deep learning techniques. It infers student's knowledge state by fitting hidden markov model

(HMM) where several latent variables included (e.g., initial knowledge, probability of learning, guess and slip). Thanks to Corbett's work, a lot of extensions to BKT prevailed including but not limited to contextual estimation of slipping and guessing probabilities [3], introduction of student-specific parameters or forgetting hypotheses [13]. However, BKT-based models inevitably suffer from lack of expression which motivates us to promote model's representation in our approach.

2.2 Deep Knowledge Tracing

As deep learning techniques show a remarkable performance in sequential tasks, researchers also attempted to use such deep models for KT task. Among these models, deep knowledge tracing (DKT) [12] first leverages RNN where the hidden units are deemed as student knowledge state to predict student's performance. What's more, performance has been greatly improved compared to BKT-based models. Another effective deep-based method, dynamic key-value memory network (DKVMN) [26], simulates student's learning activities by leveraging a pair of key-value matrix, where *key* matrix represents the knowledge concepts while *value* matrix represents the knowledge state. By continuously updating the *value* matrix through reading and writing process at each timestamp, DKVMN effectively tracks a student's knowledge state. We have to point out that DKT and DKVMN are the classic model in knowledge tracing using deep techniques. However, additional attributes affiliated to students and questions actually contributes to prediction a lot. Therefore, we introduce more features into our model than deep based models.

2.3 Knowledge Tracing Machines

Since factorization machines (FMs) [14] have demonstrated a powerful performance in many tasks (e.g., click-through rating), there has been several attempts to introduce this model into KT. *Knowledge tracing machines* (KTMs) [20] is one of the representative works, which takes observed temporal triplets and customized side information (e.g., *win* and *fail*) as input and achieved performance no less than DKT. Unfortunately, some of inessential interactions internally lessen the model's performance. As the key idea of this paper, we attempt to decrease this defect on maximum degree.

3 Methodology

The task of knowledge tracing can be defined as predicting the performance of $|S|$ students over $|P|$ questions, each question may contain one or several skills and each student may attempt a question multiple times. Assuming that we have observed triplets $(s, q, r) \in |S| \times |P| \times \{0, 1\}$, which represents student s attempted question q correctly ($r = 1$) or not ($r = 0$). Then, given the student's next attempt pair $(\tilde{s}, \tilde{q})$, we are supposed to predict the probability of $\tilde{s}$ will gets $\tilde{q}$ correctly.

3.1 Factorization Component

Inspired by Knowledge Tracing Machines (KTMs) [20], we similarly refer student, question and extra information as features in the context. Specifically, we have to declare that each feature is either numerical (e.g., *student* = 1) or categorical (e.g., *answer_type* = algebra). Formally, let L be the total number of all features, we concatenate all feature's one-hot encodings into a sparse vector $\boldsymbol{x} \in \mathbb{R}^L$, where each entry takes either 1 or 0. Here, we first give the equation of FM:

$$y(\hat{x}) = w_0 + \sum_{i=1}^{L} w_i x_i + \sum_{i=1}^{L} \sum_{j=i+1}^{L} v_i^T v_j \cdot x_i x_j \tag{1}$$

where w_0 is a global bias, w_i is the linear coefficient, x_i is the i-th binary entry in $\boldsymbol{x}$, $v_i^T v_j$ denotes dot product between v_i and v_j, d represents the embedding size. It is worth noting that due to the $x_i x_j$ term, only interactions of non-zero features are taken into consideration when computing the last term.

FM has a strong power in prediction, it enhances linear regression (LR) by adding a second-order factorized interaction term. Besides, previous work have shown that especially FM outperforms naive matrix factorization (MF) and SVM in many predictive tasks [17,18]. As effective as it is, unfortunately, it suffers from expressive limitations because of its linearity [15] when dealing with complex real-world data. In this view, we propose ANFMs to make better use of second-order interactions rather than directly execute dot product. Specifically, ANFMs takes $\boldsymbol{x} \in \mathbb{R}^L$ as input and estimates prediction as:

$$\hat{y}_{ANFMs}(\boldsymbol{x}) = w_0 + \sum_{i=1}^{L} w_i x_i + h(\boldsymbol{x}) \tag{2}$$

where the former two terms are inherited from the original FM, denoting global bias and linearity. The last term $h(\boldsymbol{x})$ is the core of ANFMs that we proposed for boosting prediction performance, in which interactive and attentional manipulation are involved in as shown in Fig. 1. In the following, we will elaborate $f(\boldsymbol{x})$ layer by layer.

Embedding. As mentioned above, each entry of input $\boldsymbol{x}$ is mapped to an embedding vector. Specifically, we initialize a set of dense vectors $\mathcal{V}_{\boldsymbol{x}}' = \{v_1, \ldots, v_L\}$ as an embedding lookup table, after that, we can acquire the embedding vector $\mathcal{V}_{\boldsymbol{x}} = \{x_1 v_1, \ldots, x_L v_L\}$ of input $\boldsymbol{x}$. Note that $\boldsymbol{x}$ consists of binary entries entirely. Therefore, we only need to consider the embedding for non-zero entries. In the following, we still use $\mathcal{V}_{\boldsymbol{x}} = \{x_i v_i\}(x_i \neq 0)$ to represent the embedding vectors.

Interaction. To extract the correlation between features, we transmit the embedding vectors $\mathcal{V}_{\boldsymbol{x}}$ to the interaction layer, which converts the embeddings

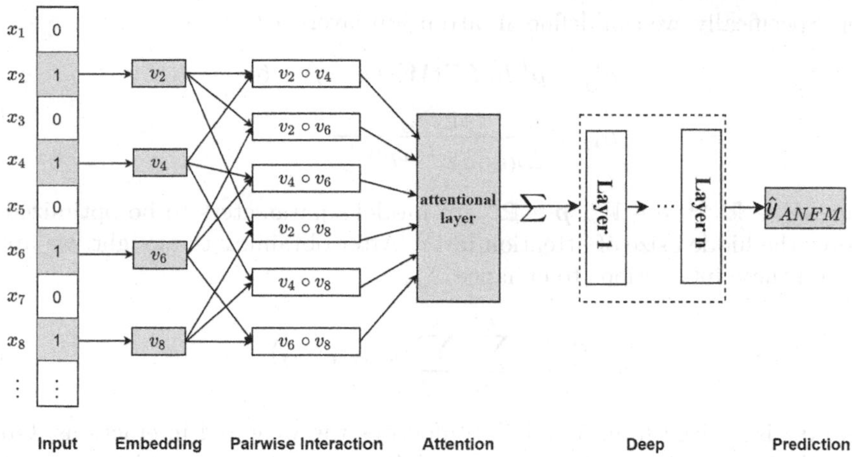

Fig. 1. Flowchart of ANFMs

to pairwise interaction vectors:

$$\mathcal{Z}'_x = \sum_{i=1}^{L}\sum_{j=i+1}^{L} x_i v_i \circ x_j v_j \tag{3}$$

Be aware that each entry of input is either 0 or 1. Therefore, we omit x_i in $\mathcal{V}_x$ to simplify $\mathcal{Z}'_x$:

$$\mathcal{Z}_x = \sum_{i=1}^{L}\sum_{j=i+1}^{L} v_i \circ v_j \tag{4}$$

where $\circ$ denotes the element-wise product of pair embedding vectors. So far, we have obtained the encoded second-order pairwise interactions $\mathcal{Z}_x$.

3.2 Attention Component

Attention mechanism plays an important role in many tasks, the main idea of attention is to identify the importance of different constituents when compressing them into a single vector. Due to different pairwise interactions contribute to the prediction differently, we introduce attention to our proposal by employing two different types of mechanisms—*explicit attention* and *implicit attention*.

Explicit Attention. By explicitly figuring out the weight of each interaction, we can identify the importance of them. Similar to [23], we compute the weight by an end-to-end way in the process of minimizing the prediction loss as shown in Fig. 1. To achieve the goal, we input the pairwise interactions into the attention layer. Specifically, we can define an attention layers as:

$$\begin{aligned}\alpha'_{ij} &= \boldsymbol{p}^T ReLU(\boldsymbol{W}(v_i \circ v_j) + \boldsymbol{b}) \\ \alpha_{ij} &= \frac{exp(\alpha'_{ij})}{\sum_{(i,j)\in \mathcal{Z}_x} exp(\alpha'_{ij})}\end{aligned} \tag{5}$$

where $\boldsymbol{W} \in \mathbb{R}^{k\times d}$, $\boldsymbol{b} \in \mathbb{R}^k$, $\boldsymbol{p} \in \mathbb{R}^k$ are model's parameters to be optimized, k denotes the hidden size of attention layer. After obtaining the weight, we apply them on these interactions to enhance $\mathcal{Z}_{\boldsymbol{x}}$:

$$\mathcal{Z}_{\boldsymbol{x}}^{exp} = \sum_{i=1}^{L} \sum_{j=i+1}^{L} \alpha_{ij}(v_i \circ v_j) \tag{6}$$

where a_{ij} is derived from 5 and $\mathcal{Z}_{\boldsymbol{x}}^{exp}$ denotes the weighted interactions. Obviously, the output of attention layer is a d dimensional vector, which compresses the whole feature interactions by identifying their importance. Afterwards, we take this output to the deep layer. However, before that, we introduce another attention mechanism.

Implicit Attention. Since the success of self attention mechanism has achieved, more and more researchers bring it into different fields. In this paper, we also leverage it into our model as an attention method. Specifically, we take the same notation as Vaswani described in [19]:

$$\mathcal{Z}_{\boldsymbol{x}}^{imp} = Attention(Q, K, V) = softmax\Big(\frac{QK^T}{\sqrt{d_k}}\Big)V \tag{7}$$

where $\mathcal{Z}_{\boldsymbol{x}}^{imp}$ denotes the pairwise interactions with attention, due to there is no explicit weight coefficient appeared in this attention mechanism, we mention it as implicit attention layer.

It is worth pointing out that when removing the attention layer, the FM component can be computed in linear time due to there is no extra parameter introduced. On this condition, we can reformulate 3 as:

$$\mathcal{Z}_{\boldsymbol{x}} = \frac{1}{2}\Big[(\sum_{i=1}^{L} v_i)^2 - \sum_{i=1}^{L} {v_i}^2\Big] \tag{8}$$

we will utilize this equation in our experiments when attention layer is removed.

In summary, we abbreviate our model as ANFM when *explicit attention* is employed while SANFM if *implicit attention* were applied. They are both involved in for distinguishing the importance between pairwise interactions, we will take a further step on analysing their performance in following sections.

3.3 Deep Component

Be aware that both Eq. 6 and 7 obtain a d dimensional weighted interaction vector. For higher expression purpose, we pass the vector to a stack of fully connected neural networks. Specifically, the equation is:

$$\begin{aligned} \boldsymbol{o}_1 &= \sigma(\boldsymbol{W}_1 \mathcal{Z}_x^a + \boldsymbol{b}_1), \\ \boldsymbol{o}_2 &= \sigma(\boldsymbol{W}_2 \boldsymbol{o}_1 + \boldsymbol{b}_2), \\ &\cdots\cdots \\ \boldsymbol{o}_n &= \sigma(\boldsymbol{W}_n \boldsymbol{o}_{n-1} + \boldsymbol{b}_n) \end{aligned} \tag{9}$$

where $\mathcal{Z}_x^a$ jointly denotes the weighted interaction vectors with explicit or implicit attention, n denotes the number of deep layers, $\boldsymbol{W}_n$, $\boldsymbol{b}_n$ and σ respectively denote the weight, bias and activation function for the n-th layer. Due to the rich expressiveness of neural networks, we are able to learn high-order interactions [4,11].

Finally, we need to transform o_n to the prediction probability:

$$h(\boldsymbol{x}) = \boldsymbol{q}^T \boldsymbol{o}_n \tag{10}$$

where $\boldsymbol{q}^T$ denotes the weight of the prediction layer. In general, we can fuse above components into the conclusive form as:

$$\hat{y}(\boldsymbol{x}) = w_0 + \sum_{i=1}^{L} w_i x_i + \boldsymbol{q}^T(\sigma(\ldots\sigma(\boldsymbol{W}_1 \mathcal{Z}_{\boldsymbol{x}} + \boldsymbol{b}_1)\ldots) + \boldsymbol{b}_n) \tag{11}$$

3.4 Optimization

Remind that we have observed the triplets (s, q, r) of a student and figured out the student's probability $\hat{y}$ of the correctness about question q. Therefore, we apply cross entropy as the objective function to estimate parameters as:

$$Loss = -\sum r \log(\hat{y}) + (1 - r) \log(1 - \hat{y}) \tag{12}$$

The *Loss* function is minimized by stochastic gradient descent (SGD) on mini-batches and some excellent techniques (e.g., batch normalization) are utilized to facilitate optimization. We will interpret this process in detail to prove the feasibility and effectiveness of our model in next section.

4 Experiment

We conduct several experiments[1] for ablation and comparison with baselines to answer the following questions:

Q1 Our model is divided into several components (factorization, attention, deep) as illustrated in Sect. 3, how dose these components influence our model respectively?

Q2 Attention size, another hyper-parameters with a default value 32, appears in attention component, what is its impact on prediction?

[1] https://github.com/xiaohuangrener/ANFMs.

Q3 We compared our model with different baselines to show the superiority of our model, how does our model perform?

In the rest of this section, we first introduce the experimental settings. Then, we will give the results and analysis.

4.1 Experimental Settings

Parameter Settings. Here, we point out the relevant parameters in our experiments. Firstly, we minimize *Loss* function with mini-batch stochastic gradient descend (SGD) where the batch size was set to 256 while learning rate to 0.1. By default, we show the results under embedding size 32 and attention size 32. Besides, in the neural network component, we choose one layer with 32 hidden units. Secondly, to prevent overfitting and speed up the training process, we bring batch normalization (BN) [8] into our model.

Datasets. We conduct experiments on two public datasets: ASSISTment2009[2] and ASSISTment2017[3] , and we extracted 5 features for interactive operation as shown in Table 1. We randomly split the dataset into training (60%), validation (20%) and test (20%) sets. The validation set is used for tuning hyper-parameters and all the final prediction and comparison is conducted on the test set.

Table 1. Statistics of dataset

Feature	#Students	#Questions	#Skills	#Original	#Answer_type
ASSISTment2009	4163	17751	123	2	5
ASSISTment2017	1709	2095	91	2	15

Baselines. We conducted experiments to evaluate the effectiveness of our model by comparing with the following previous models:

- BKT [25] was proposed for predicting student's performance, it achieved a considerable performance before deep techniques applied into this task.
- DKT[4] [12] first leverages deep techniques (RNNs) into knowledge tracing and achieved state-of-the-art performance, causing plenty of succeeding work based on DKT rising up rapidly.
- KTM[5] [20] treated the inputs as sparse data, and utilized factorization machines (FM) [14] to practicably predict student's performance.

[2] https://sites.google.com/site/assistmentsdata/home/assistment-2009-2010-data.
[3] https://sites.google.com/view/assistmentsdatamining/dataset?authuser=0.
[4] https://github.com/chrispiech/DeepKnowledgeTracing.
[5] https://github.com/jilljenn/ktm.

4.2 Experimental Results and Analysis

Embedding Size and Components Effects (Q1). We initialized the embedding vectors for each feature with embedding size 32. However, it has been empirically proved that this hyper-parameter affects the performance to some extent. Therefore, we explore the performance under different embedding size. Meanwhile, some components may be removed for ablation.

Ensure that other parameters fixed, we tune the embedding size in 16, 32, 64 for FM (remove attention and deep components), NFM (remove attention component), ANFM and SANFM. Afterwards, we uniformly select 6 points in 200 epochs as shown in Fig. 2.

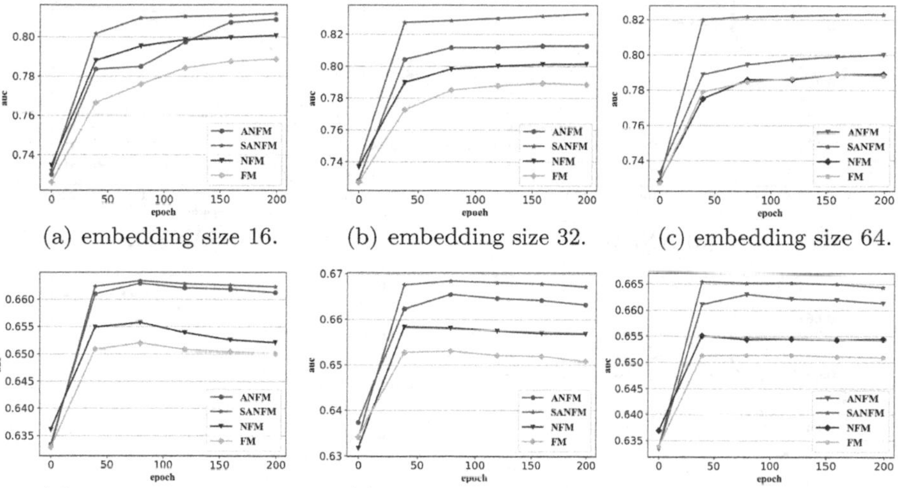

(a) embedding size 16. (b) embedding size 32. (c) embedding size 64.

(d) embedding size 16. (e) embedding size 32. (f) embedding size 64.

Fig. 2. SANFM, ANFM, NFM and FM with embedding size 16, 32, 64 under ASSISTment2009 (a, b, c) and ASSISTment2017 (d, e, f).

As we clearly see that, regardless of the embedding size, SANFM generally outperforms ANFM, NFM and FM, ANFM performs second and NFM is somewhat lower while FM relatively worst. Further, we have a reason believe that our model is effective because of the more components involved in, the higher performance it will be. However, when it comes to the embedding size, Fig. 2(b) and Fig. 2(c) surpass Fig. 2(a) as well as Fig. 2(e) and Fig. 2(f) outperform Fig. 2(d), which indicates our model has a better performance under embedding size 32 and 64. In addition, we found that in Fig. 2(d), Fig. 2(e) and Fig. 2(f), a downward trend occurred in the last few points, which means our model slightly suffers overfitting in ASSISTment2017 though batch normalization (BN) used.

Attention Size (Q2). In the attention component, whether explicit or implicit, different attention size will lead to different performance. From Fig. 3(a) and Fig. 3(b), we can clearly observe that ANFM and SANFM have a different sensitivity to this hyper-parameter when attention size altered. In Fig. 3(a), ANFM obtains the best performance when the attention size is set to 32 while SANFM gets its best when it is set to 64 in Fig. 3(b), the same happened to Fig. 3(c) and Fig. 3(d). We are not strange to this result due to they are two completely different attentional mechanisms. In terms of results, SANFM outperforms ANFM, it shows a stronger power in our model.

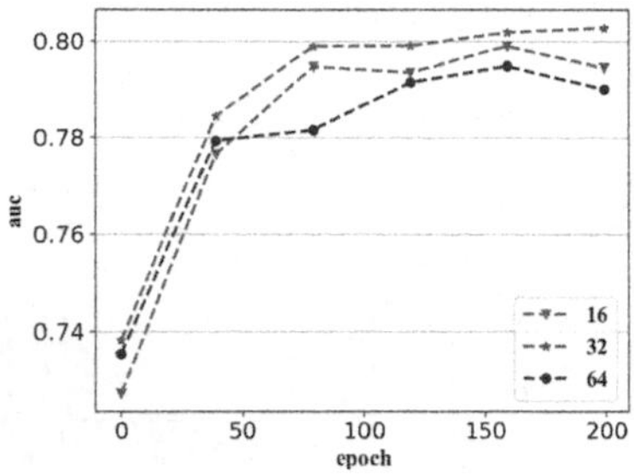

(a) ANFM.

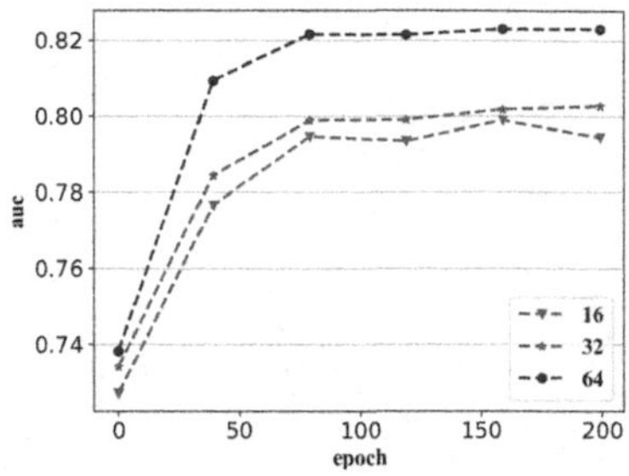

(b) SANFM.

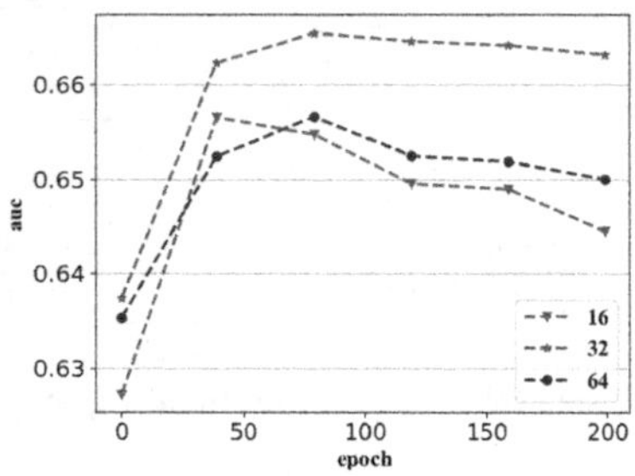

(c) ANFM.

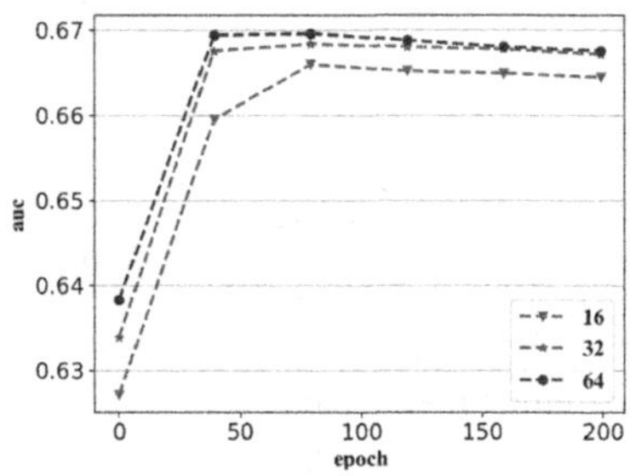

(d) SANFM.

Fig. 3. SANFM,ANFM with different attention size under ASSISTment2009 (a, b) and ASSISTment2017 (c, d).

Comparison with Baselines (Q3). We also conducted experiments to compare our model's performance with baselines. From Table 2, we can see that our model, particularly SANFM, substantially outperforms other models, meanwhile, ANFM performs marginally higher than KTM, but considerably higher than DKT and BKT in ASSISTment2017, which confirms the effectiveness and validity of our approach.

Table 2. Comparison between our model and baselines. 'e.dim' and 'a.size' represent embedding size and attention size respectively.

	ASSISTment2009			ASSISTment2017		
Model	AUC	e.dim	a.size	AUC	e.dim	a.size
BKT	0.670	–	–	0.545	–	–
DKT	0.801	32	–	0.651	32	32
KTM	0.819	32	–	0.642	32	–
FM	0.79	32	32	0.653	32	32
NFM	0.801	32	32	0.658	32	32
ANFM	**0.825**	32	32	0.664	32	32
SANFM	**0.832**	32	64	0.668	32	64

5 Conclusion

In this paper, we proposed a novel attentional neural factorization machines for knowledge tracing, which brings the factorization machine with attention and neural networks. The key idea of our model is the attentional manipulation for interactions, it ensures that our model can discriminate the importance of different pairwise interactions, and the neural network allows us to learn complex information from pairwise interactions. Experiments on two datasets demonstrate that ANFMs outperforms BKT, DKT and KTM.

Acknowledgements. This research was supported by NSFC (Grants No. 61877051). Li Li is the corresponding author for the paper.

References

1. Abdelrahman, G., Wang, Q.: Knowledge tracing with sequential key-value memory networks. In: SIGIR, pp. 175–184. ACM (2019)
2. Anderson, A., Huttenlocher, D.P., Kleinberg, J.M., Leskovec, J.: Engaging with massive online courses. In: WWW, pp. 687–698. ACM (2014)
3. Baker, R.S.J., Corbett, A.T., Aleven, V.: More Accurate student modeling through contextual estimation of slip and guess probabilities in Bayesian knowledge tracing. In: Woolf, B.P., Aïmeur, E., Nkambou, R., Lajoie, S. (eds.) ITS 2008. LNCS, vol. 5091, pp. 406–415. Springer, Heidelberg (2008). https://doi.org/10.1007/978-3-540-69132-7_44
4. Blondel, M., Fujino, A., Ueda, N., Ishihata, M.: Higher-order factorization machines. In: NIPS, pp. 3351–3359 (2016)
5. Bradác, V., Kostolanyova, K.: Intelligent tutoring systems. In: eLEOT. Lecture Notes of the Institute for Computer Sciences, Social Informatics and Telecommunications Engineering, vol. 180, pp. 71–78. Springer (2016)
6. Chen, Y., et al.: Tracking knowledge proficiency of students with educational priors. In: CIKM, pp. 989–998. ACM (2017)

7. He, X., Chua, T.: Neural factorization machines for sparse predictive analytics. In: SIGIR, pp. 355–364. ACM (2017)
8. Ioffe, S., Szegedy, C.: Batch normalization: accelerating deep network training by reducing internal covariate shift. In: ICML, JMLR Workshop and Conference Proceedings, vol. 37, pp. 448–456. JMLR.org (2015)
9. Khajah, M., Lindsey, R.V., Mozer, M.: How deep is knowledge tracing? In: EDM, International Educational Data Mining Society (IEDMS) (2016)
10. Nagatani, K., Zhang, Q., Sato, M., Chen, Y., Chen, F., Ohkuma, T.: Augmenting knowledge tracing by considering forgetting behavior. In: WWW, pp. 3101–3107. ACM (2019)
11. Novikov, A., Trofimov, M., Oseledets, I.V.: Exponential machines. In: ICLR (Workshop). OpenReview.net (2017)
12. Piech, C., et al.: Deep knowledge tracing. In: NIPS, pp. 505–513 (2015)
13. Qiu, Y., Qi, Y., Lu, H., Pardos, Z.A., Heffernan, N.T.: Does time matter? Modeling the effect of time with Bayesian knowledge tracing. In: EDM, pp. 139–148. www.educationaldatamining.org (2011)
14. Rendle, S.: Factorization machines. In: ICDM, pp. 995–1000. IEEE Computer Society (2010)
15. Rendle, S.: Factorization machines with libFM. ACM Trans. Intell. Syst. Technol. **3**(3), 57:1–57:22 (2012)
16. Corbett, A.T., Anderson, J.R.: Knowledge tracing: modeling the acquisition of procedural knowledge. User Model. User-Adapted Interact. **4**, 253–278 (1994). https://doi.org/10.1007/BF01099821
17. Thai-Nghe, N., Drumond, L., Krohn-Grimberghe, A., Schmidt-Thieme, L.: Recommender system for predicting student performance. In: RecSysTEL@RecSys. Procedia Computer Science, vol. 1, pp. 2811–2819. Elsevier (2010)
18. Toscher, A., Jahrer, M.: Collaborative filtering applied to educational data mining. In: KDD Cup (2010)
19. Vaswani, A., et al.: Attention is all you need. In: NIPS, pp. 5998–6008 (2017)
20. Vie, J., Kashima, H.: Knowledge tracing machines: factorization machines for knowledge tracing. In: AAAI, pp. 750–757. AAAI Press (2019)
21. Wang, F., et al.: Neural cognitive diagnosis for intelligent education systems. In: AAAI, pp. 6153–6161. AAAI Press (2020)
22. Wilson, K.H., Karklin, Y., Han, B., Ekanadham, C.: Back to the basics: Bayesian extensions of IRT outperform neural networks for proficiency estimation. In: EDM, pp. 539–544. International Educational Data Mining Society (IEDMS) (2016)
23. Xiao, J., Ye, H., He, X., Zhang, H., Wu, F., Chua, T.: Attentional factorization machines: learning the weight of feature interactions via attention networks. In: IJCAI, pp. 3119–3125. ijcai.org (2017)
24. Xiong, X., Zhao, S., Inwegen, E.V., Beck, J.: Going deeper with deep knowledge tracing. In: EDM, pp. 545–550. International Educational Data Mining Society (IEDMS) (2016)
25. Yudelson, M.V., Koedinger, K.R., Gordon, G.J.: Individualized Bayesian knowledge tracing models. In: Lane, H.C., Yacef, K., Mostow, J., Pavlik, P. (eds.) AIED 2013. LNCS (LNAI), vol. 7926, pp. 171–180. Springer, Heidelberg (2013). https://doi.org/10.1007/978-3-642-39112-5_18
26. Zhang, J., Shi, X., King, I., Yeung, D.: Dynamic key-value memory networks for knowledge tracing. In: WWW, pp. 765–774. ACM (2017)

Node-Image CAE: A Novel Embedding Method via Convolutional Auto-encoder and High-Order Proximities

Di Qiao(✉), Wu Yang, and Wei Wang

Harbin Engineering University, Harbin, HLJ, People's Republic of China
{yangwu,w_wei}@hrbeu.edu.cn

Abstract. The network embedding method, which mainly aims to generate low-dimensional embedding vectors for nodes in a network, has received great passion from researchers and provides excellent tools for application and research. Various models have been applied to this field to gain high-quality embedding vectors and got prodigious success, such as Matrix Factorization, Multilayer Perceptron, Recurrent Neural Network, Generative Adversarial Networks, Graph Convolutional Network, and so on. However, a very powerful model—Convolutional Neural Network, which plays a significant role in Digital Image Processing, Natural Language Processing, etc.—has not been widely used (except whole-graph embedding). CNN is thought inappropriate to embed nodes into vectors because traditional CNN can only work on grid-like data such as images while a graph generally has a irregular structure. And with the development of the embedding method, high-order proximities are gradually found playing a crucial role in exploring the network's underlying structure. However, many existing embedding methods can only preserve **fixed-order** proximities, limiting the scope of their application. In this paper, we try to explore a viable way to apply CNN on node-embedding task. We first build an image for each node that can flexibly preserve different order proximities and feed them into a variation of the Convolutional Neural Network, the Convolutional Auto-Encoder (CAE), to generate embedding vectors. Experiments show that our method outperforms state-of-the-art embedding methods.

Keywords: Graph embedding · High-order proximity · Convolutional Auto-Encoder

1 Introduction

Nowadays, networks are ubiquitous and provide an excellent way to organize a diverse set of real-world information. Network analysis, which aims to mine useful information in networks, is an ideal tool for gaining insights into our increasingly connected world. Because most machine learning methods are more willing to process data depicted by vectors, representing network data (nodes, edges, etc.) in vectors is a crucial problem for network analysis tasks. Graph embedding, or network embedding, whose central idea is to find a mapping function, which converts nodes or edges in the network to a latent low-dimensional representation, has been widely recognized as an effective approach to analyze networks.

H. Qiu et al. (Eds.): KSEM 2021, LNAI 12815, pp. 331–345, 2021.
https://doi.org/10.1007/978-3-030-82136-4_27

According to [20], commonly used models in network embedding can be divided into three main sub-categories: Matrix Factorization Family, Random Walk Family, and Deep Neural Network Family. Arguably, most of these embedding models can be viewed as a two-phase system: the network investigation part and the feature extraction part, as was shown below (Fig. 1):

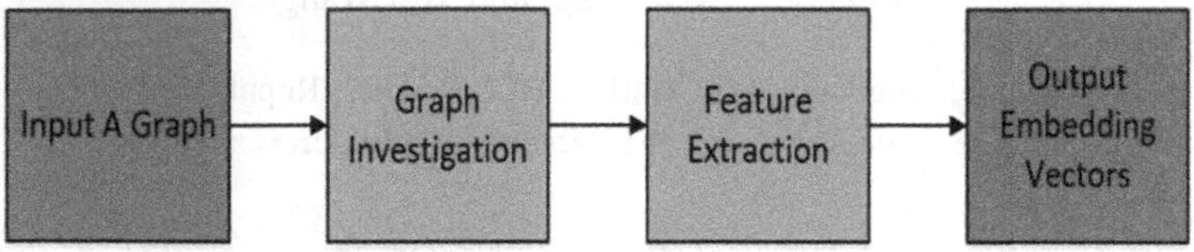

Fig. 1. Two-phase perspective of the embedding methods.

Given the examples from the most influential Random Walk Family [1, 3, 26], etc. – we see, these methods first use a truncated random walk strategy or enhanced truncated random walk strategy to generate a set of sequences of nodes. Then they feed these sequences into a neural network [23] to produce embedding vectors. So in this process, node sequence generation can be seen as an investigation of the network because random walk reveals this network's inner structure, and vectors are node features extracted from corpora of node sequences. This perspective makes sense. Network data is always of high-dimension. To make a better embedding result, we first need to get a more accurate and profound understanding of it. According to this perspective, in Matrix Factorization and deep learning model family, an adjacent matrix is regarded as a description of network and matrix factorization and deep neural network extract information.

Except for node sequences and adjacent matrix, the high-order proximities between nodes are of decisive importance in exploring the interior structure of the network [4, 21, 27], and thus can provide valuable information for learning the embedding vectors. However, a problem of methods using high-order proximities, as was discussed in [27], is that many of them can only preserve fixed-order proximities. But due to the complexity of the structure of networks, fixed-order proximities may not fit well to process varied networks, say, with different degrees of sparsity. So the capability of a model to shift from one order of proximities to another to find out the best result can bring huge advantages.

As to feature extraction, deep learning models are powerful tools among which convolutional neural network (CNN) has achieved great success in many applications. Therefore, applying CNN on graph tasks is appealing. However traditional CNN works in Euclidean space while graphs are non-Euclidean space data, which pose a great challenge to use regular convolutional operations on generic graphs.

In view of these things, we hereby propose Node-Image CAE, a novel embedding method employing high-order proximities and Convolutional Auto-Encoder. Because Convolutional Auto-Encoder is more prone to tackle the data in grid-like form, we try to make an image for each node in the network via combining high-order proximities whose details will be expanded shortly later. Extensive experiments on several social networks dataset are conducted. The experimental results demonstrate the embedding performance of our proposed method on a variety of tasks, including network reconstruction, link prediction, and visualization. We must make it clear that we neither put the whole adjacent matrix in to CAE nor are we GCN-based embedding methods. To summarize, the main contributions of our work are as follows:

- We propose a novel deep network embedding model Node-Image CAE with Convolutional Auto-Encoders, to learn vertex representations and hence show CNN can also work in network embedding, even though it has been used in whole-graph embedding [17].
- We creatively draw a 'picture' for each node by employing high-order proximities, which can serve as a straightforward way to show each node's structural characteristic in a network for deep learning model analysis. And our node image can preserve different order of proximities, which overcome the problem of some method which can only preserve fixed-order proximities.
- We conduct several experiments on network reconstruction tasks, link prediction, and visualization using real-world and synthetic social network datasets. Experimental results demonstrate that our proposed method, most of the time, outperforms some state-of-the-art network embedding or never performs worse than them. So the effectiveness and efficiency of our Node-Image CAE model are justified.

The rest of this paper is organized as follows. Section 2 summarizes the related works which use Auto-Encoder or Convolutional Auto-Encoder as feature extractors in other fields. In Sect. 3, we introduce our proposed method. Section 4 presents the experimental results. Finally, we make a conclusion in Sect. 5.

2 Related Works

Auto-Encoder [25] is used in miscellaneous tasks. A traditional Auto-Encoder comprises an encoder and a decoder, including an input layer, some hidden layers, and an output layer. A three-layer auto-encoder is shown in Fig. 2: the output layer contains the same number of neurons as the input layer, and the hidden layer has a smaller number of neurons than the input layer. The loss function is made following the difference between input and output, so the training process is to make the output as consistent as possible with the original input. After training, the outcomes of hiding layers can make a perfect feature representation for input data.

Convolutional Auto-Encoder [12] uses the substitution of convolutional layers and deconvolutional layers for the fully-connected layers. As shown in Fig. 3, the convolutional encoding and decoding substructure are of symmetrical form, including the same number of convolution layers and deconvolution layers, respectively, so that the output and the input have the same shape.

Traditional Auto-Encoder and Convolutional Auto-Encoder have already been used in a wide range of research fields to acquire better experiment result. In [22], by using a user score matrix on a film rating data set, CAE is used as a substitution of Matrix Factorization in a collaborative filtering algorithm to make recommendations more precise and sensible. [15] uses the CAE model to detect a defect on the surface of mobile phone logos. Both of these two work add noise to original input data to make their model more

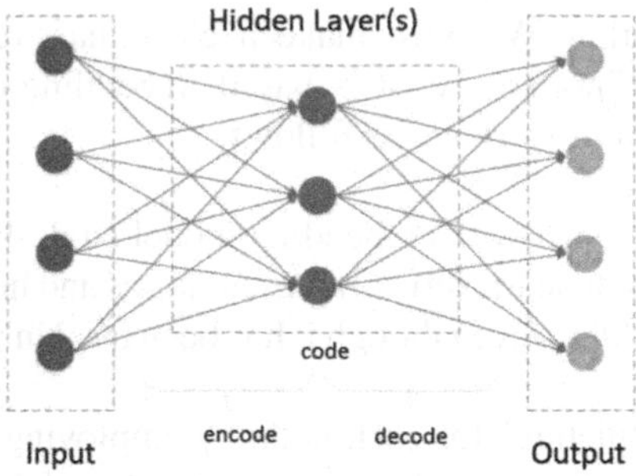

Fig. 2. A simple auto-encoder with three layers.

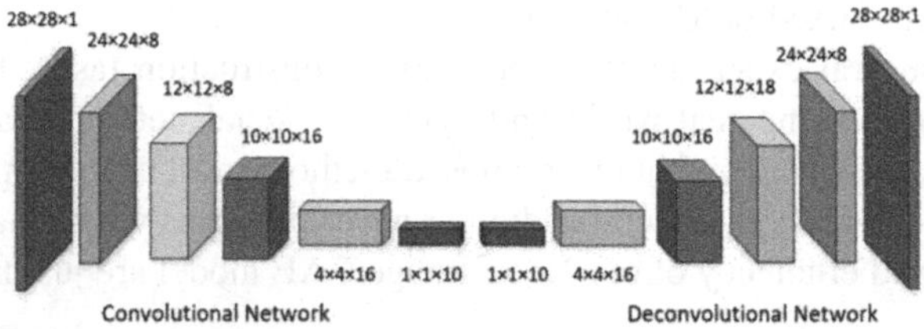

Fig. 3. A convolutional auto-encoder.

robust. In [16], they use a three-layer CAE to extract features from pictures created by a Micro-Doppler Radar device for recognition of human activities, and so the system can tell whether these activities are aided or unaided. Silent Speech Interface (SSI) was introduced almost a decade ago t. These devices record human organ movement in speech communication using only non-acoustic sensors. In this system, features extracted from ultrasound tongue images and lip images play a crucial role. [10] and [2] use Denoising Auto-Encoder and Denoising CAE, respectively, to lower Word Error Rate.

3 Node-Image CAE Model

In this section, we give some details about implement of our model. We first discuss the creation of an image for each node in the network, and then we explore the optimization of the Convolutional Auto-Encoder.

3.1 Problem Definition

To begin with, we first give some relevant definitions for better understanding.

Definition 1: (Graph) A graph is denoted as $G = (V, E)$ where V represents all vertices $\{n_1, n_2, \ldots, n_{|V|}\}$ in a graph, and E is set of all edges in a graph. Each edge e is associated with a weight, and weights equal 1 or 0 if the graph is a simple undirected graph.

Definition 2: (Adjacency Matrix) The adjacency matrix A for a graph is an $n \times n$ matrix, where n denotes the number of nodes in the graph and $A_{ij} = 1$ if V_i and V_j share a link in a simple undirected graph. Note that unless otherwise stated, graph and network are synonyms, and both are referred to as simple undirected graphs.

Definition 3: (High-Order Proximity) Given an adjacency matrix A of a graph, k-order proximity is defined as a k-th power of A: $A^k = \underbrace{A \cdot A \cdot \ldots \cdot A}_{k}$. And we may also refer to the combination of high-order proximities from 1 to k as k-order proximity if don't cause any confusion.

Definition 4: (Graph Embedding) Given Graph G, graph embedding is a mapping function $\Phi : V \mapsto R^{|v| \times d}$, where $d \ll |V|$. The objective of the function is to try to make two mapping results as similar as possible if two vertices share greatly common traits.

3.2 Make an Image for Each Node

In this section, we detail the process about how to make node images. When we get an adjacent matrix $A_{m \times m}$ and a series power of it: A^1, A^2,..., A^k, we will not treat them separately as [21] do, or add them together as a polynomial function of A in [27]. We just simply stack one power of A on the top of another to form a tensor with the shape of $m \times m \times k$. Here we give an example in Figs. 4, 5 and 6. Given an adjacent matrix A (red layer) of size 9×9, we calculate A^2 (green layer), A^3 (blue layer) and put them on the top of A, and we get a tensor with size of $9 \times 9 \times 3$.

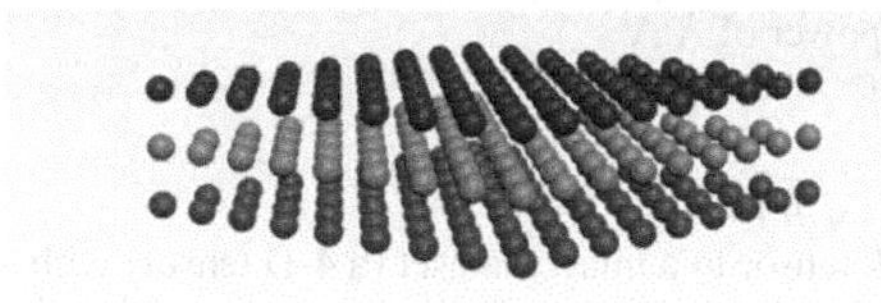

Fig. 4. A tensor combining different power of A. (Color figure online)

If we see this tensor from another perspective(left or right), we will get 9 2-D arrays of size 9×3:

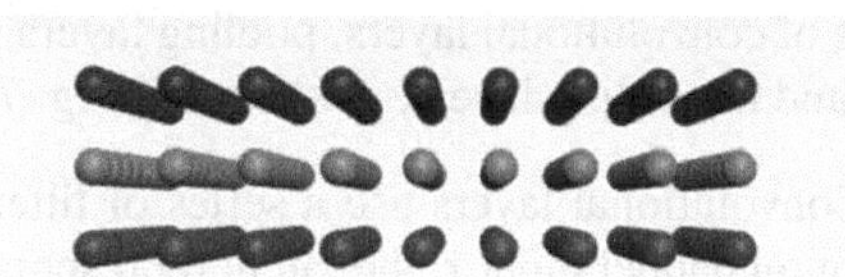

Fig. 5. Another perspective of the above tensor. (Color figure online)

Now that every slice of this tensor is corresponding to a node, we reshape each 2-D slice to a tensor with size of $3 \times 3 \times 3$ and get a 3-channel, 3×3 image for the node:

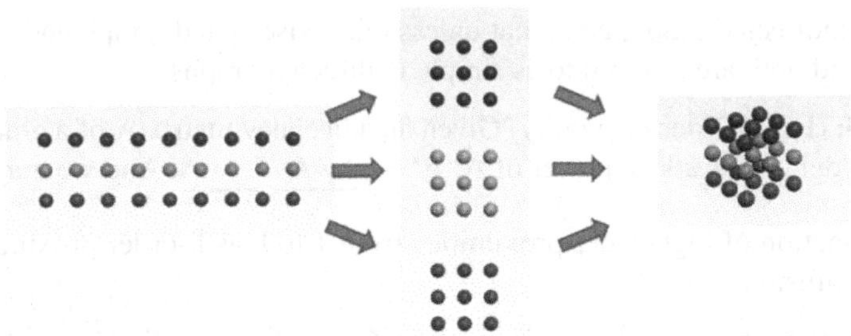

Fig. 6. Reshape a slice of tensor to a 3-channel image. (Color figure online)

After this reshape operation, we can get a 9-image dataset where each image posses a shape of 3 × 3 × 3. And in this way, we can see the k-order information of a node is well fitted into the image's k-th channel. We summarize the above things in Algorithm 1:

Algorithm 1: Make a image for each node in graph

Input: Adjacent matrix of graph: A
Parameter:order of proximity k
Output: A images dataset

```
1:  Create a blank tensor with form of m×m×k.
2:  for i in 1:k
3:      Calculate i-th power of A:A^i.
4:      tensor(:,:,i)=A^i.
5:  end
6:  Calculate l = ceil(√m)
7:  Reshape the m×m×k tensor to a image dataset (a 4-D tensor) with size of m × l × l × k .
8:  return image dataset
```

3.3 Convolutional Auto-Encoder

As has been described above, CAE combines the benefits of convolutional neural network with the structure of auto-encoder and make an excellent tool for unsupervised tasks. Our CAE model consists of convolutional layers, pooling layers, full-connection layers, deconvolutional layers, and unpooling layers, as shown in Fig. 7.

Convolution Layers. Convolutional layers use a series of filters to generate different feature images. For a mono-channel input x, the latent representation of the k-*th* feature map can be described by the Eq. 1:

$$h_j^k = \sigma\left(x \otimes W_j^k + b_j^k\right) \tag{1}$$

where σ is an activation function (we choose the ReLU), and $\otimes$ denotes the convolutional operation. W_j^k and b_j^k are weights for k-*th* filter and k-*th bias* in j-*th layer.* Result of this operation is the feature map h_j^k.

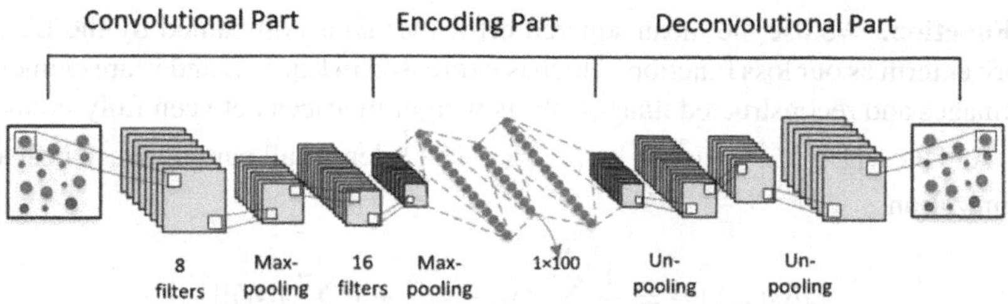

Fig. 7. CAE model as a feature extractor.

Pooling Layers. Pooling operation is used to make reduced feature maps to lessen the redundancy, so the CNN can focus on the main features of the input. Before pooling operation, a feature map is firstly divided into several non-overlapping small regions whose shape is commonly 2×2 or 3×3. We use the max-pooling method:

$$o_j^i = max\left(r_j^i\right) \tag{2}$$

where r_j^i represent the i-*th* small region in j-*th* feature map;and o_j^i represent i-*th* single scalar element in j-*th* reduced feature map.

Fully-Connected Layers. Fully-connected layers are the same as those in traditional Auto-Encoder. Its computation is conducted according to Eq. 3:

$$e_i = \sigma(\mathrm{W_i} x_i + b_i) \tag{3}$$

W_i and b_i denote the weight matrix and bias between two fully-connected layers; x_i and e_i are the input and output. We choose outputs of one fully-connected layer as embedding vectors.

Unpooling Layers. Due to the irreversibility of pooling operation, many ways have been contrived to undo its effect, which can be called unpooling. To form an expanded feature map, we also need to divide it into small regions. One way of the unpooling operation is mapping the values of elements in the present feature map to randomly prescribed locations in corresponding small regions and zeroing the rest.

Deconvolution Layers. Deconvolution is the inverse operation of convolution and is used for the reconstruction of initial input x. The reconstruction result is obtained using Eq. 4:

$$\mathrm{y} = \sigma\left(\sum_{k \in H} \mathrm{h_j^k} \otimes \widetilde{\mathrm{W}}_\mathrm{j}^\mathrm{k} + \mathrm{c_j}\right) \tag{4}$$

In this formula, H identifies all feature maps in j-th layer and $\widetilde{\mathrm{W}}$ means the flip operation over both dimensions of the weights, c_j is the only bias used to get the output y in this layer.

Loss Function. We use the mean squared error (MSE) accompanied by the L2-norm regularizer term as our loss function, which is expressed in Eq. 5. x_i and y_i are elements of input images and reconstructed images. W_i is weight matrices between fully-connected layers. And $\theta = \left\{\left(w_1^1, b_1^1\right), \left(w_1^2, b_1^2\right), \ldots, \left(w_j^k, b_j^k\right)\right\}$ denote all parameters to be learned in optimization:

$$Loss(x, y|\theta) = \frac{1}{N}\sum_{i=1}^{N}(x_i - y_i)^2 + \nu\sum_{i=1}^{k}||W_i||_2^2 \tag{5}$$

Optimization. Thus in optimization, Eq. 5 is deemed as a function of θ, and we use the adaptive moment estimation (ADAM) [5] as an optimization algorithm. ADAM algorithm calculates the gradient of $Loss(\theta)$:

$$g_t = \nabla_\theta Loss_t(\theta_{t-1}) \tag{6}$$

In the above formulas, t is time-step; g_t is the gradient of the loss function at t time-step. Then ADAM gets first-order moment estimation m_t and second-order moment estimation v_t using Eq. 7 and Eq. 8:

$$m_t = \beta_1 m_{t-1} + (1 - \beta_1)g_t \tag{7}$$

$$v_t = \beta_2 v_{t-1} + (1 - \beta_2)g_t^2 \tag{8}$$

β_1 is m's exponential decay rate, and β_2 is v's, g_t^2 means the element-wise square of g_t Then because moment estimates are biased towards zero, especially during the initial time steps, ADAM uses Eq. 9 to solve the problem:

$$\alpha_t = \alpha \cdot \sqrt{1 - \beta_2^t}/\left(1 - \beta_1^t\right) \tag{9}$$

β_1^t and β_2^t denote the t power of β_1 and β_2; α is step size; So the parameters can be updated in Eq. 10:

$$\theta_t = \theta_{t-1} - \alpha_t \cdot m_t/\left(\sqrt{v_t} + \hat{\varepsilon}\right) \tag{10}$$

θ_t is parameters vector at t time-step; β_1,$\beta_2 \in [0,1.0)$; m and v are both initialized to zero. The process of optimization in Algorithm 2:

Algorithm 2: Optimization of CAE

Input: Node-Image data set from Algorithm1
Output: Network embedding vectors

1: Randomly initialize all parameters $\boldsymbol{\theta}$.
2: **repeat**
3:     **for** each image X **in** Data set
4:       Use X and $\boldsymbol{\theta}$,according to Eq. (1)~(4),calculate reconstruction image Y.
5:       Use X and Y,according to Eq. (5),calculate loss function *Loss*.
6:       Update $\boldsymbol{\theta}$ according to Eq.(6)~(10).
7:     **end for**.
8: **until** converge or exceed running times limit
9: **return** embedding vectors

4 Experiments

In this section, we evaluate the performance of Node-Image CAE[1] on a series of real-world datasets. Specifically, we choose three application scenarios for experiments which are reconstruction, link prediction, and visualization.

4.1 Experiment Setup

Datasets. In order to make evaluation more comprehensive, we utilize four datasets in our experiments, including one social network, two citation networks, and one synthetic network. Some details of these datasets are as follows:

- ARXIV CONDMAT is a collaboration network from arXiv about Condense Matter category [11]. The dataset contains 23133 nodes and 186936 edges, so it's a sparse network to some degree. We only use this dataset for reconstruction tasks.
- BLOGCATALOG is a widely used social network dataset to assess the performance of embedding algorithms. It has 10312 nodes and 667966 edges. Except for reconstruction, this dataset is also used for link prediction tasks.
- ARXIV GR-QC is a paper collaboration network in the field of General Relativity and Quantum Cosmology from arXiv.This graph has 5242 vertices and 28980 edges. We only use this dataset for reconstruction tasks.
- SYN-SBM is a synthetic network. It is generated by [19] using Stochastic Block Model. The network has 1024 nodes, 42090 edges, and 3 communities, which can be seen as labels for each node. We use it to visualize the embedding result.

Baseline Algorithm. To validate the performance of our approach, we compare it against the following baseline algorithms:

- *GraphGAN* [9] uses a generative adversarial network to fit a graph's underlying true connectivity distribution, and uses the generative model's parameters as embedding vectors. GraphGAN unifies two categories of graph embedding models: generative models and discriminative models.
- *SDNE* [7] employ a deep auto-encoder to preserve the first-order and second-order proximities. *SDNE* first puts a row of the adjacent matrix into auto-encoder and then tries to reconstruct it. Embedding vectors are produced in the middle of the auto-encoder.
- *GraRep* [21] create a positive log probability matrix for different orders of proximity and uses the SVD to train the model.*GraRep* directly concatenates the representation of different orders.
- *LINE* [13] proposes first and second-order proximity among nodes and defines loss function according to them. After optimization of the loss function, it concatenates these representations as final embedding vectors.

[1] The code is available at https://github.com/CuteKittyhoho/Node-Image-CAE.

- *DeepWalk* [3] sees network embedding from an NLP perspective. It regards nodes as words and truncated random walks as sentences. So the word-embedding model skip-gram can be applied to learn embedding vectors.

Experimental Environment. We conduct all experiments on a single PC with one 9th Gen Core i7 processor, 16 GB of memory and NVIDIA GTX 1650 GPU. The CAE model presented in this paper is implemented using TensorFlow-GPU-1.15.0, an open-source platform for machine learning.

4.2 Node Images

After algorithm 1, each network dataset has been converted to a corresponding image dataset whose statistics we show in Table 1. N, S, C represent the number, size, and channel of images in each dataset, respectively; P means the order of proximity when we get the best performance.

Table 1. Statistics of the image datasets.

Image dataset	P	N	S	C
Blog-Image	3	10312	102 × 102	3
Gr-Qc-Image	2	5242	73 × 73	3
CondMat-Image	2	23133	157 × 157	2
SBM-Image	1	1024	32 × 32	1

We also randomly pick one image from SBM-Image **(1)**, CondMat-Image **(2)**, Blog-Image **(3)**, respectively, and show them in Fig. 8.

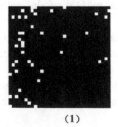

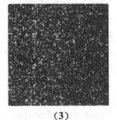

(1) (2) (3)

Fig. 8. A example of node images.

4.3 Reconstruction

In the reconstruction task, we first calculated the dot-similarity for each node-pairs and restored the network according to the assumption that node-pairs with higher dot-similarity are more likely to form an edge. We use two citation networks ARXIV GR-QC, ARXIV CONDMAT, and a social network BLOGCATALOG, in this experiment. We use precision@k as the evaluation metrics (Fig. 9).

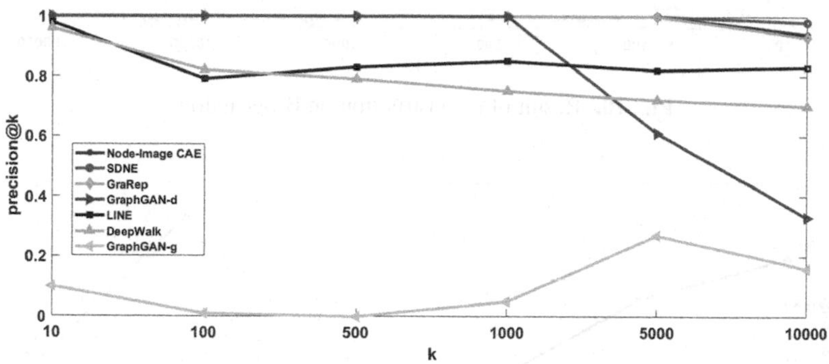

Fig. 9. Result of reconstruction on arXiv Gr-Qc.

While [7] states that they use the generative model's parameters as embedding vectors, *GraphGAN* actually also yields embedding vectors from its discriminative model. We use both of them to show the performance of GraphGAN and denote them as *GraphGAN-g* and *GraphGAN-d* respectively. The result shows that on the small-scale dataset ARXIV GR-QC all methods perform well. However, on the BlogCatalog dataset, which has 10312 nodes, the performance of *GraRep, LINE,* and *DeepWalk* begin to degrade drastically, and *SDNE* also shows some degree of incompetence, but our method can still maintain relatively steady and good performance. On the above two datasets we can see that *GraphGAN*'s discriminative model's embedding vectors have a better performance than its generative model's, and its precision drop suddenly and drastically when k is large. It is also worth mentioning that *GraphGAN's* training time is far longer than other methods. On dataset ARXIV CONDMAT (23133 nodes), we have a similar observation. Due to the limitation of our PC's memory, algorithm *GraRep* and *GraphGAN* can not run on our PC. And we can tell that even though all methods' performance worsens as the network's scale expands, our model still remains the best. And we guess the main contribution to the degradation of *SDNE* performance is the network's increasing sparsity (Figs. 10 and 11).

4.4 Link Prediction

In this section, we still use the BlogCatalog dataset to conduct the link prediction task. We randomly hide 4000 edges and use the remained network to train the embedding model. We use the same method and the criteria as in the reconstruction task and results are reported in Table 2. Some observations and analysis are listed as follows:

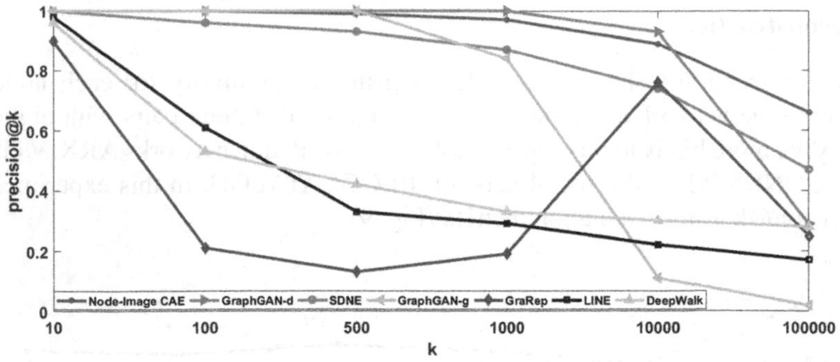

Fig. 10. Result of reconstruction on Blogcatalog.

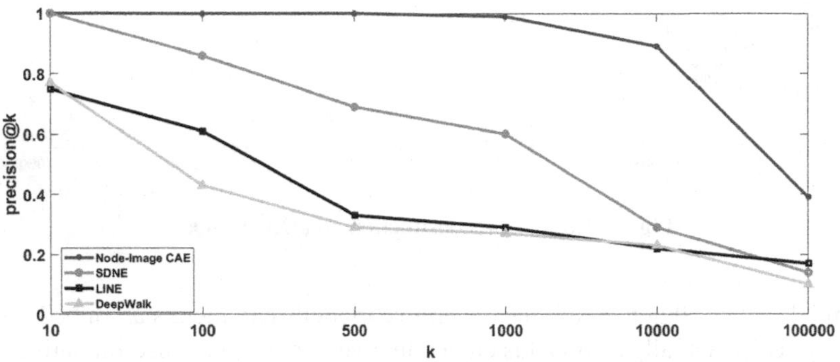

Fig. 11. Result of reconstruction on arXiv CondMat.

In the link prediction task out model, *SDNE* and *LINE* have a relatively good performance, and our model is still the best among all the baseline. In this task performance of *GraRep* and *GraphGAN* is not convincing. As for *DeepWalk*, the impact of removing edges is not as remarkable. The randomness of selecting the next node in a truncated random walk may sometimes successfully circumvent these removed edges. As to our model and *SDNE*, because one of the important auto-encoder applications is denoising, auto-encoder-based methods surely have a better fault-tolerant capability.

4.5 Visualization

The process of visualization is to project the node embedding vectors into a two-dimensional plane. If the embedding result truly reflects the properties of the network, nodes of the same category should be projected closer. In this paper, we employ the well-developed tool t-SNE to visualize node representations of the SYN-SBM network. The visualization result is shown in Fig. 12.

From Fig. 12, we find out that the results of *SDNE* and *GraphGAN-d* are not satisfactory because while the clusters of different categories are formed, the peripheral part of these clusters is still mixed a little bit. For our method, *GraRep* and *LINE,* the result looks well because points of the same color form clear clusters. Obviously, the

Table 2. Result of link prediction on BlogCatalog

Model	P@10	P@100	P@500	P@1000	P@10000
Node-Image CAE	**1.00**	**0.84**	**0.64**	**0.57**	**0.34**
SDNE	1.00	0.58	0.44	0.38	0.20
LINE	0.89	0.42	0.29	0.17	0.07
DeepWalk	0.60	0.30	0.14	0.05	0.01
GraphGAN-d	0.00	0.02	0.02	0.02	0.02
GraRep	**0.00**	**0.00**	**0.00**	**0.00**	**0.00**
GraphGAN-g	**0.00**	**0.00**	**0.00**	**0.00**	**0.00**

results of *DeepWalk* and *GraphGAN-g* is the lowest, the cause of this may be that purely random walk in *DeepWalk* and BFS-tree in *GraphGAN* may miss some important traits about this network, while other methods can capture more comprehensive information in different ways.

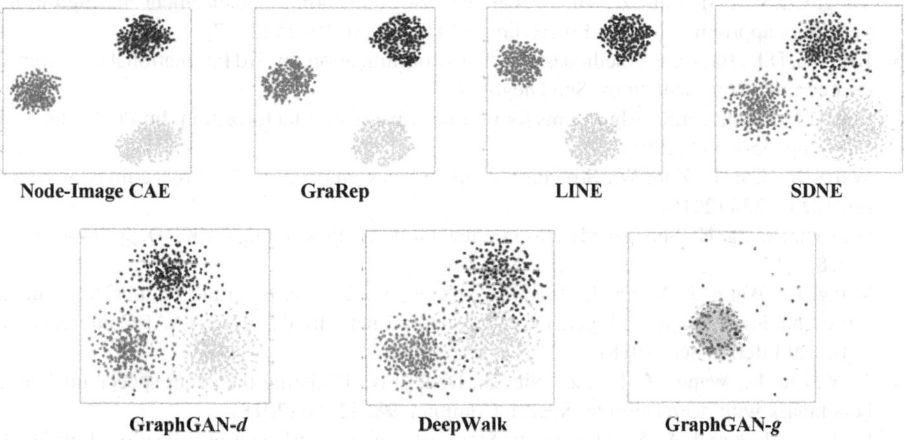

Fig. 12. Result of visualization on SYN-SBM. (Color figure online)

5 Conclusions

This paper proposed Node-Image CAE, a new network embedding method that conformed well to the network embedding model's two-phase paradigm. We first used high-order proximities to create an image for each node in a network. Then these images were fed into a Convolutional Auto-Encoder to encode every image. Thus the result could be seen as network embedding vectors. Empirical results showed that our model had a steady and excellent performance in a variety of network datasets. More importantly, we believe our model has high extensibility. An image is a vast container that can accommodate rich information about a node in the network. So our creation of node-images may not be the best (the power of an adjacent matrix can be time consuming when graphs are very large) and are definitely not the only way to map this information into images. In addition to that, state-of-the-art convolutional neural network research may be applied to make the Convolutional Auto-Encoder a better feature extractor.

Acknowledgments. This work was supported by NSFC-Xinjiang Joint Fund Key Program (grant No.U2003206) and National Natural Science Foundation of China (grant No.61972255).

References

1. Grover, A., Leskovec, J.: node2vec: Scalable feature learning for networks. In: Proceedings of KDD, pp. 855–864 (2016)
2. Li, B., Xu, K., Feng, D., Mi, H., Wang, H., Zhu, J.: Denoising convolutional auto-encoder-based B-mode ultrasound tongue images feature extraction. In: ICASSP (2019)
3. Perozzi, B., Al-Rfou, R., Skiena, S.: Deepwalk: Online learning of social representations. In: Proceedings of KDD, pp. 701–710 (2014)
4. Yang, C., Sun, M., Liu, Z., Tu, C.: Fast network embedding enhancement via high order proximity approximation. In: Proceedings of IJCAI, pp. 19–25 (2017)
5. Kingma, D.P., Ba, J.L.: A method for stochastic optimization. In: 3rd International Conference on Learning Representations, San Diego (2015)
6. Lee, D.D., Seung, H.S.: Algorithms for non-negative matrix factorization. In: Proceedings of NIPS, pp. 556–562 (2001)
7. Wang, D., Cui, P., Zhu, W.: Structural deep network embedding. In: Proceedings of KDD, pp. 1225–1234 (2016)
8. Gao, H., Huang, H.: Self-paced network embedding. In: Proceedings of KDD, pp. 1406–1415 (2018)
9. Wang, H., Wang, J., Wang, J., Zhao, M., Zhang, W., Zhang, F., et al.: GraphGAN: Graph representation learning with generative adversarial nets. In The 23th AAAI Conference on Artificial Intelligence (2018)
10. Ji, Y., Liu, L., Wang, H., Liu, Z., Niu, Z., Denby, B.: Updating the silent speech challenge benchmark with deep learning. Speech Commun. **98**, 42–50 (2018)
11. Leskovec, J., Krevl, A.: SNAP datasets: Stanford large network dataset collection, June 2014. http://snap.stanford.edu/data
12. Masci, J., Meier, U., Ciresan, D., Schmidhuber, J.: Stacked convolutional auto-encoders for hierarchical feature extraction. In: Honkela, T., Duch, W., Girolami, M., Kaski, S. (eds.) Artificial Neural Networks and Machine Learning. LNCS, vol. 6791, pp. 52–59. Springer, Heidelberg (2011). https://doi.org/10.1007/978-3-642-21735-7_7
13. Tang, J., Qu, M., Wang, M., Zhang, M., Yan, J., Mei, Q.: Line: Large-scale information network embedding. In: Proceedings of WWW, pp. 1067–1077 (2015)
14. Adamic, L.A., Glance, N.: The political blogosphere and the 2004 US election: divided they blog. In: Proceedings of the 3rd international workshop on Link discovery, pp. 36–43 (2005)
15. Ke, M., Lin, C., Huang, Q.: Anomaly detection of logo images in the mobile phone using convolutional auto-encoder. In: ICSAI (2017)

16. Seyfioglu, M.S., Ozbayoglu, A.M., Gurbuz, S.Z.: Deep convolutional auto-encoder for radar-based classification of similar aided and unaided human activities. IEEE Trans. Aerosp. Electron. Syst. **54**, 1709–1723 (2018)
17. Niepert, M., Ahmed, M., Kutzkov, K.: Learning convolutional neural networks for graphs. In: Proceedings of the 33rd International Conference on Machine Learning, pp. 2014–2023 (2016)
18. Riolo, M.A., Cantwell, G.T., Reinert, G., Newman, M.E.J.: Efficient method for estimating the number of communities in a network. Phys. Rev. E **96**(3), 032310 (2017)
19. Goyal, P., Ferrara, E.: Graph embedding techniques, applications, and performance: a survey. Knowl. Based Syst. **151**, 78–94 (2018)
20. Cui, P., Wang, X., Pei, J., Zhu, W.: a survey on network embedding. IEEE Trans. Knowl. Data Eng. **31**(5), 833–852 (2019)
21. Cao, S., Lu, W., Xu, Q.: GraRep: Learning graph representations with global structural information. In: Proceedings of CIKM, pp. 891–900 (2015)
22. Zhang, S.Z., Li, P.H., Chen, X.N.: Collaborative convolution auto-encoder for recommendation systems. In: ICNCC. ACM (2019)
23. Mikolov, T., Sutskever, I., Chen, K., Corrado, G.S., Dean, J.: Distributed representations of words and phrases and their compositionality. In: Proceedings of NIPS, pp. 3111–3119 (2013)
24. Von Luxburg, U.: A tutorial on spectral clustering. Stat. Comput. **17**(4), 395–416 (2007). https://doi.org/10.1007/s11222-007-9033-z
25. Bengio, Y., Lamblin, P., Popovici, D., Larochelle, H.: Greedy layer-wise training of deep networks. In: Neural Information Processing Systems (2007)
26. Dong, Y., Chawla, N.V., Swami, A.: metapath2vec: Scalable representation learning for heterogeneous networks. In: KDD (2017)
27. Zhang, Z., Cui, P., Wang, X., Pei, J., Yao, X., Zhu, W.: Arbitrary-order proximity preserved network embedding. In: Proceedings of KDD (2018)

EN-DIVINE: An Enhanced Generative Adversarial Imitation Learning Framework for Knowledge Graph Reasoning

Yuejia Wu and Jiantao Zhou(✉)

College of Computer Science, Inner Mongolia University Engineering Research Center of Ecological Big Data Ministry of Education National and Local Joint Engineering Research Center of Mongolian Intelligent Information Processing, Inner Mongolia Engineering Laboratory of Cloud Computing and Service Software, Inner Mongolia Key Laboratory of Social Computing and Data Processing, Hohhot, China

wuyuejia@imudges.com, cszjtao@imu.edu.cn

Abstract. Knowledge Graphs (KGs) are often incomplete and sparse. Knowledge graph reasoning aims at completing the KG by predicting missing paths between entities. The reinforcement learning (RL) based method is one of the state-of-the-art approaches to this work. However, existing RL-based methods have some problems, such as unstable training and poor reward function. Although the DIVINE framework, which a novel plug-and-play framework based on generative adversarial imitation learning, improved existing RL-based algorithms without extra reward engineering, the rate of policy update is slow. This paper proposes the EN-DIVINE framework, using Proximal Policy Optimization algorithms to perform gradient descent when discriminator parameters take policy steps to improve the framework's training speed. Experimental results show that our work can provide an accessible improvement for the DIVINE framework.

Keywords: Knowledge graph reasoning · Reinforcement learning · Imitation learning · Proximal Policy Optimization algorithm

1 Introduction

In essence, Knowledge Graph (KG) is a semantic network that reveals the relationship between entities and can formally describe things and their relations in the real world. Knowledge Graphs (KGs), such as Freebase [1], NELL [2] and WordNet [3], have been used to provide efficient support for many tasks, such as Natural Language Processing (NLP), Recommendation System (RS), Question Answering System (QA), etc. However, KGs performance usually affects due to incompleteness and lack of important facts.

The Knowledge Graph reasoning technology is used to solve the problems. KG reasoning uses some methods to deduce new knowledge or identify wrong

H. Qiu et al. (Eds.): KSEM 2021, LNAI 12815, pp. 346–356, 2021.
https://doi.org/10.1007/978-3-030-82136-4_28

knowledge according to KG's existing knowledge. The knowledge Graph completion task, which is a content of the KG reasoning, aims at inferring new information from existing KG facts. There are three main categories to approach to these tasks: path ranking algorithm (PRA) [4], embedding-based techniques [5], and graphical models [6].

Recent studies on KG reasoning show that Reinforcement Learning (RL) based methods can obtain state-of-the-art experiment results. DeepPath [7] first described a reinforcement learning framework for learning multi-hop relational paths. Das et al. [8] proposed a new algorithm, MINIVER, improved DeepPath by constructing learning questions as answering questions. Cheng et al. [9] presented DIVINE, a novel plug-and-play framework, to solve these issues efficiently. However, the rate of policy update is slow, which may affect the performance of training.

In this paper, we use the Proximal Policy Optimization algorithm to improve the DIVINE framework's training performance that has shown the best performance in the current reasoning method based on reinforcement learning. The structure of this paper is organized in four sections: Related Wark, Methodology, Experiments and Results, and Conclusion.

2 Related Work

Knowledge Graph (KG) is essentially the knowledge base of the semantic network. KG technologies have been widely used in semantic analysis (e.g., Dong et al., [10]), in-depth questions and answers (e.g., Hu et al., [11], Luo et al., [12]), personalized recommendations (e.g., Wang et al., [13]), and other application fields and played an important role. Although the existing KGs scale is significant, they are still quite incomplete and sparse.

KG reasoning technology is one of the efficient methods to alleviate these problems. DeepPath first brought Deep Reinforcement Learning (DRL) to KG reasoning, a path-based and controllable multi-hop reasoning method, which constructs the path learning process as a reinforcement learning process. MINIVER made some improvements on that basis, which regards the learning question as a QA question and does not require pretraining, can compete with many state-of-the-art methods. DIVINE adaptively learned reasoning strategies and reward function by imitating the demonstration, which is sampled automatically from KG. It does not need to set up the reward function manually.

To be specific, the DIVINE framework, as shown in Fig. 1, is composed of two modules: generative adversarial reasoner and demonstration sampler. The reasoner consists of a generator that can be any of the policy-based agents in existing RL-based methods and a discriminator interpreted from the self-adaptive reward function's perspective. The sampler does two parts of the job for each relation: topology filtering and semantic matching to have high-quality demonstrations.

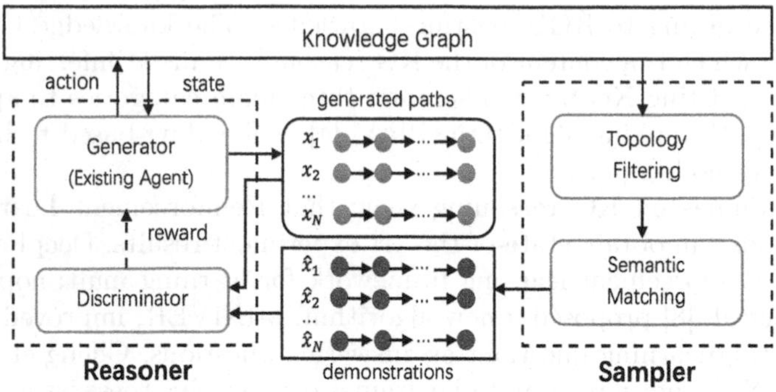

Fig. 1. Overview of the DIVINE framework

Although the DIVINE framework can learn reasoning policies and reward functions self-adaptively, there still exist some problems. First, it used a beam search to broaden the search horizon, leading to a lack of diversity among samples. Second, in the reasoner part in the DIVINE framework, it used the Trust Region Policy Optimization [14] for gradient descent when learning strategy. The TRPO is relatively complex and not compatible with architectures that contain noise (such as Dropout) or parameter sharing (Between policy and value functions, or with ancillary tasks). Also, the problem of sparse rewards still exists. This paper focuses on the second problem and proposes the EN-DIVINE framework that uses the Proximal Policy Optimization (PPO) algorithm [15].

3 Methodology

3.1 Problem Presentation

DIVINE is a path-based GAIL method that encourages the diversity of evidence paths and enables existing RL methods to self-learn reasoning strategies and reward functions, thus improving existing RL methods. However, as mentioned in the related work section, the DIVINE framework has two problems we need to solve. Firstly, it uses the TRPO for strategy learning, which needs to calculate multiple linear matrices, has a large amount of computation, and slow training speed, so it cannot be applied to large-scale problems. Second, in the DIVINE framework, the mini-batch stochastic gradient descent (SGD) was used to optimize the discriminator's loss function, and the generator was updated with the Adam algorithm [19]. When SGD randomly selects the gradient, it will introduce noise so that the weight update direction may not be correct. Besides, SGD cannot overcome the problem of the optimal local solution.

Following two sections, we first introduce the PPO algorithm as preliminaries and then introduce the solution in detail in Sect. 3.3.

3.2 Proximal Policy Optimization Algorithm

In recent years, several methods of reinforcement learning for neural network function approximation have been proposed. The three most representative methods are deep Q-learning [16], "vanilla" policy gradient methods [17], and trust region natural policy gradient methods, which is used to update the generator in GAIL [18]. Policy Gradient Methods is realized by calculating the policy gradient's estimated value and inserting it into a stochastic gradient rise algorithm. The most widely used gradient estimator has the form:

$$\hat{g} = \widehat{\mathbb{E}_t}[\nabla_\theta \log \pi_\theta(a_t|s_t)\widehat{A_t}] \tag{1}$$

where π_θ is a stochastic policy and $\widehat{A}_t$ is an estimator of the function. The estimator $\hat{g}$ is obtained by separating the objective:

$$L^{PG}(\theta) = \widehat{\mathbb{E}_t}[\log \pi_\theta(a_t|s_t)\widehat{A_t}] \tag{2}$$

Proximal Policy Optimization (PPO) algorithm introduces a family of policy optimization methods that use multiple epochs of stochastic gradient ascent to perform each policy update. In the PPO algorithm, two kinds of objectives are proposed as follows:

$$L^{CLIP}(\theta) = \widehat{\mathbb{E}_t}[\min(r_t(\theta)\widehat{A_t}, clip(r_t(\theta), 1-\epsilon, 1+\epsilon)\widehat{A_t})] \tag{3}$$

$$L^{KLPEN}(\theta) = \widehat{\mathbb{E}_t}[\frac{\pi_\theta(a_t|s_t)}{\pi_{\theta_{old}}(a_t|s_t)}\widehat{A_t} - \beta KL[\pi_{\theta_{old}}(\cdot|s_t), \pi_\theta(\cdot|s_t)]] \tag{4}$$

where $r_t(\theta)$ is a probability radio and the ϵ, β are hyperparameters. In the formula (3), by taking the minimum of the clipped and unclipped objective, the change in probability ratio is ignored to make the objective better and added when making the objective worse. The formula (4) uses the Kullback– Leibler-divergence (KL) divergence to calculate the similarity degree of the action's probability distribution and adds it to the likelihood function.

3.3 The EN-DIVINE Framework

As mentioned in Sect. 3.1, for the first problem, the GAIL algorithm used in the DIVINE framework expects to find a saddle point (Π, D) with the following formula:

$$\mathbb{E}_{\pi_E}[\log D(s,a)] + \mathbb{E}_\pi[\log(1 - D(s,a))] - \lambda H(\pi) \tag{5}$$

π_θ is a parameterized policy, and θ is the weight. D_ω is a parameterized discriminator with a weight of ω. The TRPO algorithm can make sure that the $\pi_{\theta_{i+1}}$ does not stay away from the π_{θ_i}. However, the TRPO algorithm has some defects. It uses a quadratic function to approximate the constraint conditions and uses a linear function to approximate the loss function to be optimized, which will cause difficulties in convergence. In the strategy gradient algorithm, the PPO algorithm improves the performance of TRPO, which is the best implementation of the current strategy algorithm. However, at present, the PPO algorithm has not been used in the GAIL algorithm to make gradient descent. So when calculating Q(s, a) in GAIL, we use the PPO algorithm to calculate the advantage function, that is, the advantage function uses the value in critic and C(s, a) calculated by D_ω to calculate loss, to update actor and critic network in the policy part.

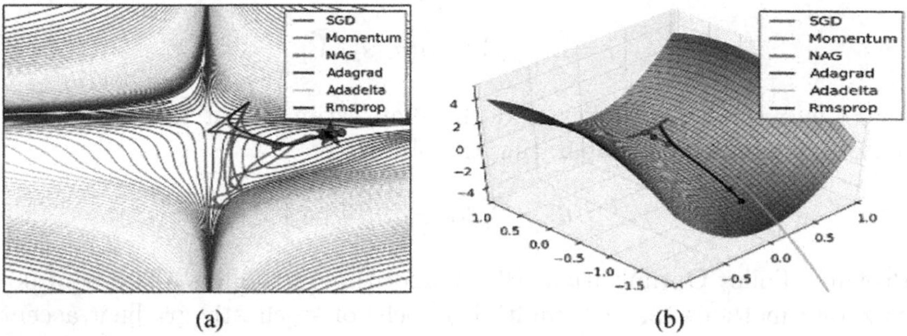

Fig. 2. The convergence process and the rate of descent of optimizers

On the second problem, several optimization algorithms can alleviate the pain (e.g., Nesterov accelerated gradient (NAG), Adam, AdaDelta). Sebastian Ruder [20] compared those standard optimization algorithms. From the results shown in Fig. 2, the AdaDelta has a short convergence trajectory and a fast running and descending speed. So, we use the AdaDelta algorithm [21] to optimize the loss function of the discriminator. The specific frame structure has shown in Fig. 3.

In detail, from the structure overview shown in Fig. 3, the EN-DIVINE framework contains two parts, which are the same as the original. However, in the reasoner, we use the PPO algorithm to update the generator G. More specifically, at the training phase, the discriminator D is trained by minimizing its loss to distinguish packages efficiently. According to the discriminator's feedback, we obtained the reward and then update the generator G with the PPO algorithm to improve training speed. In each policy update, first, we optimize the KL-penalized objective by formula (4) and then compute d as:

$$d = \widehat{\mathbb{E}_t}[KL[\pi_{\theta_{old}}(\cdot|s_t), \pi_\theta(\cdot|s_t)]] \tag{6}$$

where let $\beta = \beta/2$ if $d < \frac{d_{targ}}{1.5}$ or let $\beta = \beta \times 2$ if $d > d_{targ} \times 1.5$. In this model, we can quickly reach a specific target value of the KL deviation at each policy update by applying penalties to the KL deviation and adjusting the penalty coefficient.

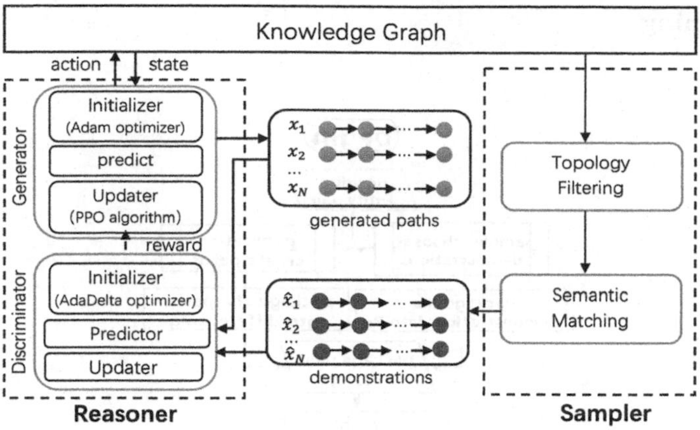

Fig. 3. Overview of the reasoner part in the EN-DIVINE framework

4 Experiments and Results

4.1 Datasets and Implementation Settings

Our experiments are based on the environment of python and implemented programmatically using TensorFlow. Based on those necessary configurations, as shown in Table 1, our experiments were conducted on NELL-995, FB15K-237, and WN18.

Table 1. Overview of the experimental datasets

Dataset	Entities' number	Relations' number	Facts' number
NELL-995	75492	200	154213
FB15K-237	14505	237	272115
WN18	40943	18	86835

In our experiments, we regard the DIVINE as a baseline. In particular, the DIVINE has two parts: GAIL-DeepPath and GAIL-MINERVA. We use the code released by Li et al. Most experiment settings are the same as the original.

4.2 Training

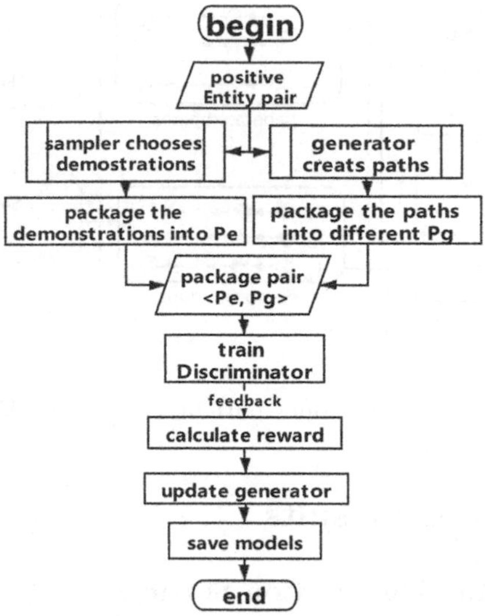

Fig. 4. Overview of the flowchart of training phase

The training phase is essential for our experimental model. The flowchart is shown in Fig. 4. At the training phase, each positive entity pair used to generate demonstration candidates Ω_E, the demonstration sampler first chooses the homologous demonstrations. It then packs them into the package $\mathscr{P}_e$; meanwhile, the generator is used to create the relational paths and packs them into different packages $\{\mathscr{P}_g|\mathscr{P}_g \subseteq \Omega_G\}$ in line with their correctness. After that, for each package pair $< \mathscr{P}_g, \mathscr{P}_e >$, the discriminator D is trained via minimizing its loss to distinguish between $\mathscr{P}_g$ and $\mathscr{P}_e$ efficiently. According to the feedback of the discriminator, the reward obtained similar to the original experiment. Then we update the generator G with the PPO algorithm to improve the speed of training. Besides, we use the AdaDelta algorithm to optimize the discriminator's loss function and the Adam algorithm to optimize the generator's loss function. The final step is to save the models.

4.3 Testing

After training, there are two main tasks in experiments at the testing phase: link prediction and fact prediction. The purpose of the link prediction task is to predict the missing head entity h, the tail entity t, or the relationship r of a triple (h, r, t). The fact prediction predicts whether an unknown fact (h, r, t) is correct. We used mean average precision (MAP), mean reciprocal rank (MRR), Hits@1, Hits@3, and Hits@10 to evaluate the performance of experiments, which are standard metrics for KG reasoning tasks. For each metric, the higher the score, the better the performance.

4.4 Results and Analysis

The overall results, including link prediction and fact prediction, on the experimental dataset, are shown in Table 2. The "D(*)" means the DIVINE framework, the "E(*)" signifies our work, the "DP" means the DeepPath algorithm, and the 'M' means the MINERVA algorithm. We used the Hits@K (K = 1, 3, 10), MAP, and MRR scores to evaluate experiments' performance.

The results shown in Table 2 reveal that the framework's performance has improved a little bit with our improvements. For this three datasets, each of them represents a situation. We can make it evident that the score of every metric in the link prediction task is higher than before. In detail, compared with NELL-995, FB15K-237 has lower scores but much improvement. While the results of WN18 are in between, and the improvement effect is similar. These improvements demonstrate better performance at both high and low data densities. Moreover, the link prediction task's growth is more evident than that in the fact prediction task. That probably is because the changes in the demonstration paths we made are small.

Table 2. Overall results on experimental datasets

Dataset	Metric	Link prediction				Fact prediction	
		D (DP)	E (DP)	D (M)	E (M)	D (DP)	E (DP)
NELL-995	Hits@1	0.749	**0.751**	0.840	**0.846**	0.701	0.701
	Hits@3	0.878	**0.883**	0.936	**0.940**	0.841	**0.842**
	Hits@10	0.948	**0.951**	0.994	**0.996**	0.933	**0.935**
	MAP	0.821	**0.823**	0.893	**0.898**	0.785	0.785
	MRR	0.811	**0.820**	0.874	**0.879**	0.774	0.774
FB15K-237	Hits@1	0.520	**0.534**	0.444	**0.473**	0.421	**0.423**
	Hits@3	0.740	**0.756**	0.590	**0.639**	**0.599**	0.592
	Hits@10	0.835	**0.884**	0.673	**0.686**	0.692	0.692
	MAP	0.658	**0.694**	0.568	**0.575**	0.558	0.558
	MRR	0.639	**0.672**	0.556	**0.558**	0.545	**0.553**
WN18	Hits@1	0.703	**0.726**	0.715	**0.719**	0.687	0.687
	Hits@3	0.832	**0.833**	0.856	**0.874**	0.698	0.698
	Hits@10	0.864	**0.873**	0.872	**0.885**	0.734	**0.741**
	MAP	0.669	**0.705**	0.634	**0.647**	0.632	0.632
	MRR	0.648	**0.651**	0.623	**0.630**	0.611	**0.614**

For each query relation, we also display the results of the link prediction task and use the MAP score to evaluate the capability of experiments on the NELL-995 dataset, which is shown in Table 3. Notably, there are seven MAP scores of query relations higher than the baseline results in the DeepPath task; two scores are the same, three scores smaller, and the average value higher. In the MINERVA task, there are nine scores higher than before, three scores lower, and the average rating more senior. The results show that our improvements are valid for most of the query relations. To sum up, although the results are modest, it can be seen that we provide an accessible development for the framework.

Table 3. Results of link prediction on NELL-995 between DIVINE and ours

Query relations	D (DeepPath)	I (DeepPath)	D (MINERVA)	I (MINERVA)
AgentBelongsToOrg	0.674	**0.678**	0.876	**0.880**
AthleteHomeStadium	**0.877**	0.875	**0.916**	0.914
AthletePlaysForteam	0.779	0.779	0.813	**0.831**
AthletePlaysInLeague	0.962	**0.973**	0.965	**0.966**
AthletePlaysSport	0.960	**0.966**	**0.986**	0.986
OrgHeadquarteredInCity	0.801	**0.807**	**0.936**	0.936
OrgHiredPerson	0.758	0.758	0.860	**0.863**
PersonBornInLocation	**0.780**	0.778	0.827	**0.836**
PersonLeadsOrg	0.810	**0.811**	0.881	**0.882**
TeampPlaysInLeague	.896	**0.899**	0.957	**0.969**
TeampPlaysSport	0.816	**0.821**	0.874	**0.881**
WorksFor	**0.741**	0.739	0.822	**0.826**
Overall	0.821	**0.823**	0.893	**0.898**

5 Conclusion

In summary, first, we proposed the EN-DIVINE framework, enhanced the DIVINE framework by using the PPO algorithm when taking policy steps, and updating the policy's actor and critic network. Second, we use the AdaDelta algorithm to optimize the loss function of the discriminator. Besides this, we also change some experimental settings to obtain well performance.

Although our work provides an accessible improvement for the DIVINE, the range of optimization is not apparent. In the future, we are interested in making more significant improvements and solving sparse rewards to improve existing methods.

Acknowlegements. This work is supported by the National Natural Science Foundation of China under Grant No.61662054, Inner Mongolia Colleges and Universities of Young Technology Talent Support Program under Grant No. NJYT-19-A02, the Major Project of Inner Mongolia Natural Science Foundation: Research on Key Technologies of Cloud Support for Big Data Intelligent Analysis under Grant No.2019ZD15,

Research and application on Key Technologies for Discipline Inspection and Supervision's Big Data under Grant No.2019GG372, Inner Mongolia Science and Technology Innovation Team of Cloud Computing and Software Engineering, and Inner Mongolia Application Technology Research and Development Funding Project "Mutual Creation Service Platform Research and Development Based on Service Optimizing and Operation Integrating".

References

1. Bollacker, K., Evans, C., Paritosh, P., Sturge, T., Taylor, J.: Freebase: a collaboratively created graph database for structuring human knowledge. In: Proceedings of the 2008 ACM SIGMOD International Conference on Management of Data (SIGMOD 2008), pp. 1247–1250. Association for Computing Machinery, New York (2008). https://doi.org/10.1145/1376616.1376746
2. Carlson, A., Betteridge, J., Kisiel, B., Settles, B., Hruschka, E.R., et al.: Toward an architecture for never-ending language learning. In: Proceedings of the Twenty-Fourth AAAI Conference on Artificial Intelligence (AAAI 2010), pp. 1306–1313. AAAI Press (2010)
3. Miller, G.: WordNet: a lexical database for English. In: Proceedings of the workshop on Human Language Technology (HLT 1993), p. 409. Association for Computational Linguistics, USA (1993). https://doi.org/10.3115/1075671.1075788
4. Lao, N., Mitchell, T.M., Cohen, W.W.: Random walk inference and learning in a large scale knowledge base. In: Proceedings of the Conference on Empirical Methods in Natural Language Processing (EMNLP 2011), pp. 529–539. Association for Computational Linguistics, USA (2011)
5. Bordes, A., Usunier, N., García-Durán, A., Weston, J., Yakhnenko, O.: Translating embeddings for modeling multi-relational data. In: NIPS (2013)
6. Richardson, M., Pedro, M.: Domingos: Markov logic networks. Mach. Learn. **62**, 107–136 (2006)
7. Xiong, W., Hoang, T., Wang, W.Y.: DeepPath: a reinforcement learning method for knowledge graph reasoning. In: EMNLP, pp. 564–573 (2017). https://doi.org/10.18653/v1/D17-1060
8. Das, R., et al.: Go for a walk and arrive at the answer: reasoning over paths in knowledge bases using reinforcement learning. arXiv abs/1711.05851 (2018)
9. Li, R., Cheng, X.: DIVINE: a generative adversarial imitation learning framework for knowledge graph reasoning. In: EMNLP/IJCNLP, pp. 2642–2651 (2019). https://doi.org/10.18653/v1/D19-1266
10. Dong, L., Lapata, M.: Coarse-to-fine decoding for neural semantic parsing. In: ACL, pp. 731–742 (2018). https://doi.org/10.18653/v1/P18-1068
11. Hu, S., Zou, L., Zhang, X.: A state-transition framework to answer complex questions over knowledge base. In: EMNLP, pp. 2098–2108 (2018). https://doi.org/10.18653/v1/D18-1234
12. Luo, K., Lin, F., Luo, X., Zhu, K.Q.: Knowledge base question answering via encoding of complex query graphs. In: EMNLP, pp. 2185–2194 (2018). https://doi.org/10.18653/v1/D18-1242
13. Wang, X., Wang, D., Xu, C., He, X., Cao, Y., Chua, T.-S.: Explainable reasoning over knowledge graphs for recommendation. arXiv:1811.04540 (2019)
14. Schulman, J., Levine, S., Abbeel, P., Jordan, M.I., Moritz, P.: Trust region policy optimization. arXiv:1502.05477 (2015)

15. Schulman, J., Wolski, F., Dhariwal, P., Radford, A., Klimov, O.: Proximal policy optimization algorithms. arXiv:1707.06347 (2017)
16. Kingma, D.P., Ba, J.: Adam: a method for stochastic optimization. CoRR abs/1412.6980 (2015)
17. Mnih, V., Kavukcuoglu, K., Silver, D., Rusu, A.A., Veness, J., et al.: Human-level control through deep reinforcement learning. Nature **518**, 529–533 (2015)
18. Mnih, V., Badia, A.P., Mirza, M., Graves, A., Lillicrap, T., et al.: Asynchronous methods for deep reinforcement learning. arXiv:1602.01783 (2016)
19. Ho, J., Ermon, S.: Generative adversarial imitation learning. arXiv:1606.03476 (2016)
20. Ruder, S.: An overview of gradient descent optimization algorithms. arXiv:1609.04747 (2016)
21. Zeiler, M.D.: ADADELTA: an adaptive learning rate method. arXiv:1212.5701 (2012)

Knowledge Distillation via Channel Correlation Structure

Bo Li[1,2], Bin Chen[1,2](✉), Yunxiao Wang[1,2], Tao Dai[1,2], Maowei Hu[3], Yong Jiang[1,2], and Shutao Xia[1,2]

[1] Tsinghua Shenzhen International Graduate School, Tsinghua University, Shenzhen, China
{l-b18,wang-yx20}@mails.tsinghua.edu.cn, cb17@tsinghua.org.cn, {jiangy,xiast}@sz.tsinghua.edu.cn

[2] PCL Research Center of Networks and Communications, Peng Cheng Laboratory, Shenzhen, China

[3] Shenzhen Rejoice Sport Tech. Co., LTD., Shenzhen, China

Abstract. Knowledge distillation (KD) has been one of the most popular techniques for model compression and acceleration, where a compact student model can be trained under the guidance of a large-capacity teacher model. The key of known KD methods is to explore multiple types of knowledge to direct the training of the student to mimic the teacher's behaviour. To this end, we aims at the knowledge exploration on channel correlation structure in terms of intra-instance and inter-instance relationship among a mini-batch, that can be extracted and transferred from the teacher's various outputs. Specifically, we propose a novel KD loss that derived from the **C**hannel **C**orrelation **S**tructure (CCS) including feature-based and relation-based knowledge. With this novel KD loss, we can align the channel correlation of both feature maps between the teacher and student model by their channel correlation matrices. Extensive experimental results are performed to verify the effectiveness of our method compared with other KD methods on two benchmark datasets.

Keywords: Deep neural networks · Knowledge distillation · Channel Correlation Structure

1 Introduction

In the past few years, deep neural networks (DNN) have been applied in various computer vision tasks such as image classification [7], object detection [4] and image processing tasks such as image compression [17,18]. DNN with thousands of layers can be easily trained on powerful GPUs that largely outperforms traditional machine learning algorithms on many popular benchmarks with millions of images. However, these deep models with millions of parameters are computationally expensive and memory intensive that make it infeasible to be deployed in resource-limited edge devices and practical applications with strict latency requirements. To reduce the model size of DNN, recent works have developed diverse strategies to obtain a lightweight model, including model pruning

H. Qiu et al. (Eds.): KSEM 2021, LNAI 12815, pp. 357–368, 2021.
https://doi.org/10.1007/978-3-030-82136-4_29

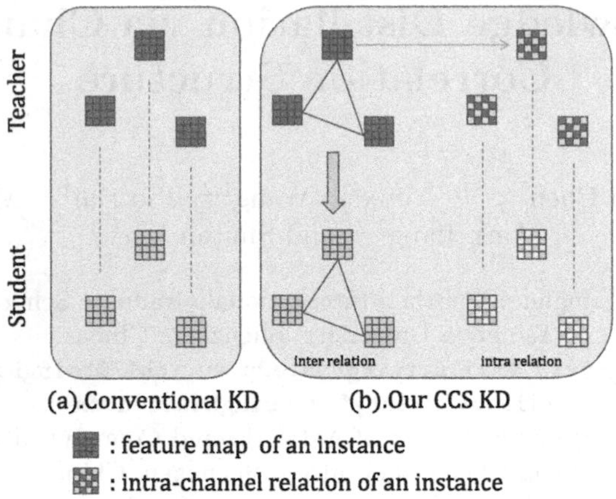

Fig. 1. Conventional KD v.s. CCS KD.

[6,13], parameter quantization [19], low-rank factorization [21], compact convolutional filters design [10] and knowledge distillation [9,15,20,26]. In this paper, we mainly focuses on the knowledge distillation methods of DNN and their application in image classification task.

Knowledge distillation consists of a pair of teacher-student models, where a lightweight student model is trained under the guidance of a well-trained larger teacher model. The guidance heavily relies on some transferable knowledge extracted from the teacher model, which can be roughly divided into response-based knowledge, feature-based knowledge and relation-based knowledge as shown in [5]. Hinton *et al.* [9] break new ground in response-based knowledge distillation that trains a student model mimics the teacher's real predicted probabilities instead of using actual ground-truth labels. Except for the previous knowledge of final predicted probabilities, some feature-based KD methods [8,20,26] have confirmed that the output of the last layer or the intermediate layers, i.e., feature maps can also be utilized as knowledge to supervise the training of the student model since they contains more abstract and high-level information. Both response-based and feature-based knowledge neglect the knowledge of mutual relations of data, current relation based knowledge distillation [15,25] further consider structural relations of outputs and transfer the relational knowledge to the student model. Nevertheless, previous work neglects the channel-level intra-instance and inter-instance correlation knowledge that contains rich semantic information for subsequent downstream tasks such as the attention mechanism proposed in [24].

This paper continues the exploration of novel knowledge to supervise the training of the student model as shown in Fig. 1. Specifically, we first take the channel correlation structure as a mix type of both feature-based and relation based knowledge embedded in a teacher model. For its concrete realizations, we propose two kinds of channel correlation structures: (1) channel correlation for

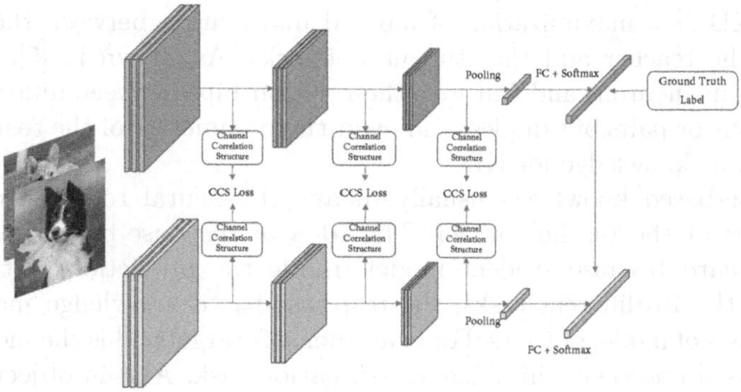

Fig. 2. Overall framework of our proposed CCS method.

intra-instance relationship across different channels. (2) channel correlation for inter-instance across different channels. Compared with past KD methods, we can obtain more concise and diverse intermediate feature maps. By introducing a novel regularization loss to minimize the difference of the channel relationship between teacher and student model, we force the student network to preserve the channel relation structure learned by the teacher model. Extensive experiments on CIFAR10 and CIFAR100 datasets validate the effectiveness of our proposed method under various settings.

Overall, our contributions can be summarized as follows:

1. We introduce two kinds of channel relationships in KD and propose a novel KD loss via channel correlation structure, namely, CCS KD.
2. Experiments and ablation studies conducted on CIFAR10 and CIFAR100 both verify the effectiveness of our proposed method.

The remainder of the paper is organized in as follows: Sect. 2 introduces common knowledge distilling methods. In Sect. 3, we introduce a novel channel based loss that considers channel correlations of different feature maps. We evaluate our methods in Sect. 4 using current architectures on public benchmarks.

2 Related Work

2.1 Knowledge Distillation

The main idea of knowledge distillation is to transfer the information from cumbersome model into training a small model without a significant drop in accuracy. The cumbersome model can be a single large model or an ensemble of several pre-trained models. Bucilua *et al.* [2] first proposed model compression that the student model mimic the teacher model to learn the competitive or even superior performance. Then, Hinton *et al.* [9] popularized the method of learning a small model from a large model as the knowledge distillation. The key of knowledge distillation is how the knowledge is defined. Ahn *et al.* [1] and Tian *et al.* [22]

formulate KD as a maximization of mutual information between the representations of the teacher and the student networks. As shown in [5], the logits, the activations, neurons and features, the relationships between different activations/neurons or pairs of samples, and even the parameters of the teacher model can be used as knowledge for KD.

Response-based knowledge usually means the neural response of the last output layer of the teacher model. The idea of response-based knowledge is straight-forward because student model mimic the prediction of the teacher model directly. In different tasks, the response-based knowledge may indicate different types of model outputs. For example, soft targets [9] is the most popular response-based knowledge in image classification task. And in object detection task, response contains both logits and the offset of bounding boxes [3]. From another perspective, the principles behind soft targets and label-smoothing [12] are similar. They both play the role of a regularization term in loss function [14].

Feature-based knowledge refers to the output of intermediate layers. The student model is trained to match the features or the activations directly or indirectly with some transformations. And there are lots of works using feature-based knowledge for distillation. Romero *et al.* [20] distill a teacher using additional linear projection layers as hints to directly match the feature maps between the teacher and the student. Instead of imitating output activations of the teacher, Zagoruyko *et al.* [26] defined the attention map from the original feature maps as knowledge. Huang and Wang [11] generalized it via neuron selectivity transfer.

Relation-based knowledge also use the output of intermediate layers but it focus on the relationships between different data samples and layers. Yim *et al.* [25] proposed the flow of solution process (FSP) matrix for KD. FSP matrix is defined as the Gram matrix between two layers. Tung *et al.* [23] propose a similarity-preserving knowledge distillation method based on the observation that semantically similar inputs tend to elicit similar activation patterns. Park *et al.* [15] propose Relational Knowledge Distillation using distance-wise and angle-wise distillation losses. Tian *et al.* [22] further introduced the contrastive loss to transfer pair-wise relationship across different modalities.

3 Methodology

In this section, we first review traditional KD framework. Then we propose two types of channel correlation structure for KD. Finally, we integrate the channel correlation structure into the overall loss function to regularize the training of the student model.

3.1 Knowledge Distillation

We referred a well-trained teacher model as T and a student model as S. Given a set of N training samples $\mathcal{X} = \{x_i\}_{i=1}^{N}$, we denote the outputs of any layer of T and S as $f^T(\cdot)$ and $f^S(\cdot)$, respectively, e.g., the probability vector after the softmax layer, intermediate layer's feature maps, etc. Most of recent works on

KD for training the student model can be unified into the following overall loss $\mathcal{L}$:

$$\mathcal{L} = \mathcal{L}_{task} + \alpha\mathcal{L}_{KD}, \tag{1}$$

where $\mathcal{L}_{task}$ is a task-related loss, e.g., cross-entropy (CE) loss for classsification task, $\mathcal{L}_{KD}$ is the KD loss that penalizes the difference between the teacher and the student based on different types of knowledge and α is a hyperparameter that adjusts the impotance of the distillation. The well-known individual knowledge distillation (IKD) proposed by Hinton *et al.* [9] can be specified as follows.

$$\mathcal{L} = \mathcal{L}_{CE} + \alpha\mathcal{L}_{IKD} \tag{2}$$

where $\mathcal{L}_{CE}$ is the common CE loss and $\mathcal{L}_{IKD}$ is realized by the pre-softmax outputs $f^T(x_i)$ and $f^S(x_i)$ with temperature $\mathcal{T}$ under the Kullback-Leibler (KL) divergence, i.e.,

$$\mathcal{L}_{IKD}=\sum_{x_i\in\mathcal{X}} \mathrm{KL}\left(\mathrm{softmax}\left(\frac{f^T(x_i)}{\mathcal{T}}\right), \mathrm{softmax}\left(\frac{f^S(x_i)}{\mathcal{T}}\right)\right) \tag{3}$$

Given a mini-batch $\mathcal{B} \subseteq \mathcal{X}$ containing B samples, we can formulate the relation-based KD (RKD) similar to IKD as follows.

$$\mathcal{L} = \mathcal{L}_{CE} + \alpha\mathcal{L}_{RKD}, \tag{4}$$

where

$$\mathcal{L}_{RKD}=\frac{\sum_{x_i,x_j\in\mathcal{B}} l\left(\Gamma(f^S(x_i), f^S(x_j)), \Gamma(f^T(x_i), f^S(x_j))\right)}{B^2}. \tag{5}$$

Here function $\Gamma(\cdot,\cdot)$ describes the relation between two outputs, and $l(\cdot)$ is a loss to measure the difference between teacher's and student's extracted relation.

3.2 Channel Correlation Structure (CCS) Based KD

Rather than simply utilizing IKD and RKD to direct the training of a student model, we aims to explore fine-grained relationship between channels from an individual and pairwise perspective. In current large-scale CNNs, convolutional layer plays an important role in extracting different kinds of features by different learnable filters. Note that each filter can generate an output channel of the whole feature map that contributes to both the final representation and prediction vector via a full connected (FC) layer, thus the correlation structure of different channels is crucial for the resulting performance of a teacher model, which can be regarded as a new type of knowledge for KD, and provides a novel understanding of the roles of different filters and internal mechanism that helps to direct the training of DNNs.

Based on the intuitive idea above, we propose two kinds of channel correlation for KD as follows:

1. Channel correlation for intra-instance relationship refers to the relationship between different channels of an individual instance that contributes to more fine-grained representation of an instance's feature map.
2. Channel correlation for inter-instance relationship refers to the relationship between channels of distinct instances in a mini-batch, which contains more discriminative information for better classification.

Channel Correlation Matrix. Given two samples x_i and x_j, we specify the inter-instance channel correlation of the intermediate feature maps $f^T(\cdot)$ by an **inter-instance correlation matrix** $M^T(x_i, x_j) \in \mathbb{R}^{C \times C}$, whose element $M^T_{s,t}(x_i, x_j)$ $(s, t \in \{1, 2, \ldots, C\})$ can be calculated by

$$\begin{aligned} M^T_{s,t}(x_i, x_j) &\triangleq \Gamma\left(f(x_i)_s, f(x_j)_t\right), \\ &= \frac{Cov\left(vec\left(f(x_i)_s\right), vec\left(f(x_j)_t\right)\right)}{\sqrt{Var\left(vec\left(f(x_j)_s\right)\right)} \cdot \sqrt{Var\left(vec\left(f(x_j)_t\right)\right)}} \end{aligned} \tag{6}$$

where $\Gamma(\cdot, \cdot)$ first reshapes the two-dimensional feature maps $f(x_i)_s, f(x_j)_t$ into two vectors, and calculates their correlation coefficients.[1]

Note that when $x_i = x_j$, we can similarly obtain the corresponding **intra-instance correlation matrix** $M^T(x_i, x_i)$.

Alignment Step for Unmatched Feature Maps. Note that the number of the channels between T and S is not necessarily equal, i.e., $C \neq C'$, so we need to transform the S' s feature maps to align the dimension of the T's. Following the strategy proposed in [20], we apply the 1×1 convolution layer to realize the alignment step for unmatched feature maps, i.e.,

$$f'^S_l(x_i) = \mathrm{Conv}_{1\times 1\times C}\left(f^S_l(x_i)\right) \in \mathbb{R}^{H' \times W' \times C}, \tag{7}$$

where $\mathrm{Conv}_{1\times 1\times C}$ denotes the 1×1 convolution layer with C filters so that the transformed output has the same dimension with the T's. Then we can also obtain the student's intra-instance correlation matrix $M^S(x_i, x_j)$ and inter-instance correlation matrix $M^S(x_i, x_i)$ by (7).

Overall Loss. Based on the intra-instance correlation matrix $M^T(x_i, x_i)$ and $M^S(x_i, x_i)$, we define a loss $\mathcal{L}_{intra}$ that penalizes intra-instance channel relation per instance $x_i \in \mathcal{B}$:

$$\mathcal{L}_{intra} = \sum_{k=1}^{K} \sum_{i=1}^{B} \sum_{s,t=1, s\neq t}^{C} \|M^T_{s,t}(x_i, x_i) - M^S_{s,t}(x_i, x_i)\|_F^2 \tag{8}$$

where K is the total number of stages to deploy KD and $l = \|\cdot\|_F$ is the Frobenius norm.

[1] Cov and Var denotes covariance and variance, respectively.

Similarly, we introduce a loss $\mathcal{L}_{inter}$ that penalizes inter-instance channel relation for two instances $x_i, x_j \in \mathcal{B}$, where

$$\mathcal{L}_{inter} = \sum_{k=1}^{K} \sum_{i,j=1,i\neq j}^{B} \sum_{s,t=1}^{C} \|M_{s,t}^{T}(x_i, x_j) - M_{s,t}^{S}(x_i, x_j)\|_F^2 \tag{9}$$

Then we can integrate the loss $\mathcal{L}_{intra}$ and $\mathcal{L}_{inter}$ into a novel Channel Correlation Structure (CCS) distillation loss $\mathcal{L}_{CCS}$, where

$$\mathcal{L}_{CCS} = w_{intra} * \mathcal{L}_{intra} + w_{inter} * \mathcal{L}_{inter} \tag{10}$$

where w_{intra} and w_{inter} are the weights of $\mathcal{L}_{intra}$ and $\mathcal{L}_{inter}$ Finally, we can obtain the overall objective for training the student model as follows.

$$\mathcal{L} = \mathcal{L}_{CE} + \alpha\mathcal{L}_{IKD} + \beta\mathcal{L}_{CCS}, \tag{11}$$

where α and β are tunable hyperparameter to balance the loss terms. And the overall framework of CCS was shown in Fig. 2.

4 Experiments

In this section, we conduct ablation studies to verify the effectiveness of different combinations of CCS. Then we conduct experiments to validate the effectiveness of our proposed CCS method on CIFAR100 and CIFAR10 dataset compared with eight KD methods including traditional knowledge distillation (TKD) proposed in [9], FitNets [20] based on intermediate features, attention transfer (AT) [26] based on attention map, relational knowledge distillation (RKD) [15] based on the relation graph, correlation congruence (CC) [16] based on the correlation between instance of data, variational information distillation (VID) [1] based on the mutual information between teacher and student, similarity preserving (SP) [23] based on the similar activations of input pairs in the teacher networks. Finally we conduct self-distillation with CCS loss.

4.1 Performance Comparisons

Dataset and Implementation Details

CIFAR100 has 100 classes, each of which contains 600 images including 500 training images and 100 testing images per class. Follow the setting in [7], we randomly crop 32×32 images from zero-padded 40×40 image, and apply random horizontal flipping as data augmentation. We use SGD to optimize the model parameters. Batch size is 64, momentum is 0.9 and weight decay is 5×10^{-4}. The student network was trained for 240 epochs, the learning rate start at 0.1 and decayed at 150, 180, 210 epochs. We choose four different pairs of ResNet-like teacher-student models. For teacher network, the accuracy of ResNet56, ResNet110, ResNet32 $\times$ 4 are 72.34%, 74.34% and 79.42%. We set $\alpha = 1$ and

Table 1. Top-1 accuracy of different teacher-student network pairs on CIFAR100.

Teacher Net	ResNet56	ResNet110	ResNet110	ResNet32 × 4
Student Net	ResNet20	ResNet20	ResNet32	ResNet8 × 4
Teacher	72.34	74.31	74.31	79.42
Baseline	69.64	69.64	72.11	72.62
TKD	71.03	70.89	73.1	73.4
FitNets	69.3	69.4	70.92	73.55
AT	70.22	70.19	72.73	73.56
CC	69.71	69.5	71.61	72.77
VID	70.92	70.05	72.34	73.46
SP	70.42	70.95	72.98	73.36
RKD	69.77	69.34	71.83	72.41
CRD	71.37	71.07	73.40	74.87
CCS	**71.65**	**71.23**	**73.76**	**74.94**

$\beta = 1$ for CCS loss. As for other KD methods, we follow the settings as [22] in general and make some fine tuning.

CIFAR10 consists of 60000 32×32 color images in 10 classes and 6000 images per class including 50000 training images and 10000 testing images. We choose Resnet20 as teacher models and use three different networks ResNet20 × 0.5, ResNet14 × 0.5 and ResNet20 × 0.375 as our student model. ResNet20 × 0.5 has the same number of layers as ResNet20 while the channels is reduced by half. When following the same teacher-student settings as CIFAR100, we find that the performance gap between the accuracy of ResNet20 and ResNet110 is non-obvious, thus, we choose smaller-capacity networks as our student model.

Evaluation Results on CIFAR100 and CIFAR10. In Table 1, we make a comparison of CCS methods with some individual knowledge distillation methods such as TKD [9], FitNets [20], AT [26] and some relation-based knowledge distillation methods such as RKD [15], CC [8], SP [23] on CIFAR100. It can be seen that our CCS KD method consistently outperforms other IKD methods and most relation-based KD methods under four different teacher-student pairs by a considerable improvement. To be concrete, CCS outperforms IKD methods with 0.84% improvement on average. And CCS outperforms CRD in three pairs of teacher-student settings, which is comparable to the state-of-the-art methods.

In Table 2, we also make a comparison of CCS methods with other methods conducted on CIFAR10. Our CCS KD method also outperforms other methods under the same teacher-student settings. However, we observed that the improvement of CCS is not as obvious as that on CIFAR100. This phenomenon may boil down to the larger weight decay parameter with 5×10^{-4} rather than 1×10^{-4} so that the influence of weights regularization is too much. Nevertheless, our CCS still achieves better performance consistently than other methods.

Table 2. Top-1 accuracy of different teacher student network pairs on CIFAR10.

Teacher	ResNet20			
Student	ResNet20 × 0.5	ResNet14 × 0.5	ResNet20 × 0.375	ResNet14 × 0.375
Teacher Acc	92.37	92.37	92.37	92.37
Baseline	89.20	87.86	87.03	84.43
TKD	89.85	88.58	87.53	84.13
FitNets	89.25	87.42	87.27	84.04
AT	89.37	87.55	87.60	83.59
CC	88.6	86.44	86.19	84.28
VID	89.15	87.26	86.07	83.88
SP	88.96	86.51	86.58	83.64
RKD	89.71	87.94	87.74	83.53
CRD	87.36	85.10	85.89	83.52
CCS	**90.2**	**88.78**	**88.07**	**84.48**

Table 3. Distillation with different losses and positions

Loss	Block	Top-1 acc
Baseline	–	59.81
L_{CCS}	$rb2$	60.45
L_{CCS}	$rb3$	60.37
L_{CCS}	$rb2 + rb3$	61.79
$L_{CCS} + L_{IKD}$	$rb2$	**62.14**
$L_{CCS} + L_{IKD}$	$rb3$	61.61
$L_{CCS} + L_{IKD}$	$rb2 + rb3$	61.64

Table 4. Top-1 accuracy of student model trained with self distillation

KD loss	w_{intra}	w_{inter}	Top-1 acc
$\mathcal{L}_{IKD}$	0	0	73.40
$\mathcal{L}_{intra}$	10	0	74.08
	1	0	**74.58**
	0.1	0	74.04
	0.01	0	74.21
$\mathcal{L}_{inter}$	0	0.01	73.69
	0	0.1	**74.61**
	0	1	74.07
	0	10	74.21

4.2 Ablation Study

The Effectiveness of CCS Loss. To verify the effectiveness and choosing the appropriate strategy for our distillation, we conduct ablation studies on CIFAR100 datasets. ResNet20 and ResNet20×0.5 are taken as the teacher model and the student model, respectively. The backbone are divided into three stages from residual block 1 to residual block 3 ($rb1$–$rb3$). The layers close to input usually extract low-level features, while the layers close to output usually extract high-level features. So we try to add distillation loss on $rb2$ and $rb3$. In Table 3, we can find that our CCS loss indeed improve the accuracy of the student model. When the distillation performed at the residual block2, the student network achieves the best accuracy.

Impact of Hyper-parameters. To explore the impact of inter and intra channel correlation, we try different w_{inter} and w_{intra} for ResNet8×4 on CIAFR100. When $w_{inter} = 0$ and $w_{intra} = 0$, The overall loss degenerates into $\mathcal{L}_{IKD}$. It can be seen that CCS loss improves IKD consistently according from the results in Table 4.

4.3 Combination with Other KD Methods

In this part, we further explore whether CCS loss can serve as a plugin term to train together with other KD methods on CIFAR100 datasets. We train student network with a single KD method. Then we add a CCS loss term to other known kinds of KD loss, e.g., we combine CCS loss with other relation-based KD loss. For the CCS term, we set the weight coefficient as 1, and for another KD method, we also follow the settings in [22] with some fine tuning. We use ResNet32 × 4 as the teacher model and ResNet8 × 4 as the student model. The accuracy of the teacher is 79.42%. Table 5 shows that CCS loss can indeed be used as a plugin into other KD methods to improve the performance.

Table 5. Top-1 accuracy of students trained with/without CCS loss

Generation	Resnet32 × 4	Resnet110
0	79.42	74.31
1	79.68	**76.11**
2	80.18	75.42
3	**80.29**	75.49
4	79.33	74.51
5	79.43	75.33

Table 6. Top-1 accuracy of student model trained with self distillation

Generation	Resnet32 × 4	Resnet110
0	79.42	74.31
1	79.68	**76.11**
2	80.18	75.42
3	**80.29**	75.49
4	79.33	74.51
5	79.43	75.33

4.4 Self Distillation

As shown above, CCS loss helps training a small student model from its teacher, so we conduct self-distillation experiments to obtain further verification whether CCS loss can improve a student neural networks whose architecture is identical to the teacher's. Each network is trained for 5 generations. And in each generation, the student from the previous generation is used as a new teacher. Table 6 shows that different network can achieve their best performance at different generations.

5 Conclusion

In this paper, we proposed a novel kind of knowledge based on the channel correlation structure for knowledge distillation. Comparing with known conventional KD methods, it was advantaged in directing the training of the student model under the fine-grained supervision of intra-instance and inter-instance relation embedded in the teacher model and providing new perspective on KD. And it could achieve comparable performance compared with state of the art. Extensive experimental results on CIFAR10 and CIFAR100 demonstrated that our proposed method yields significant improvements over previous KD techniques under various settings. We believed that channel correlation structure of a DNN can be further explored from the theoretical aspect or other explanatory viewpoints that are helpful to improve current knowledge distillation methods. Applying channel correlation structure proposed in this paper in other application is also a promising and interesting problem in future work.

Acknowledgment. This work is supported in part by the National Natural Science Foundation of China under Grant 61771273, and the R&D Program of Shenzhen under Grant JCYJ20180508152204044.

References

1. Ahn, S., Hu, S.X., Damianou, A., Lawrence, N.D., Dai, Z.: Variational information distillation for knowledge transfer. In: Proceedings of the IEEE/CVF Conference on Computer Vision and Pattern Recognition, pp. 9163–9171 (2019)
2. Buciluǎ, C., Caruana, R., Niculescu-Mizil, A.: Model compression. In: Proceedings of the 12th ACM SIGKDD International Conference on Knowledge Discovery and Data Mining, pp. 535–541 (2006)
3. Chen, G., Choi, W., Yu, X., Han, T., Chandraker, M.: Learning efficient object detection models with knowledge distillation. In: Proceedings of the 31st International Conference on Neural Information Processing Systems, pp. 742–751 (2017)
4. Girshick, R.: Fast R-CNN. In: Proceedings of the IEEE International Conference on Computer Vision, pp. 1440–1448 (2015)
5. Gou, J., Yu, B., Maybank, S.J., Tao, D.: Knowledge distillation: a survey. arXiv preprint arXiv:2006.05525 (2020)
6. Han, S., Mao, H., Dally, W.J.: Deep compression: compressing deep neural networks with pruning, trained quantization and Huffman coding. arXiv preprint arXiv:1510.00149 (2015)
7. He, K., Zhang, X., Ren, S., Sun, J.: Deep residual learning for image recognition. In: Proceedings of the IEEE Conference on Computer Vision and Pattern Recognition, pp. 770–778 (2016)
8. Heo, B., Kim, J., Yun, S., Park, H., Kwak, N., Choi, J.Y.: A comprehensive overhaul of feature distillation. In: Proceedings of the IEEE International Conference on Computer Vision, pp. 1921–1930 (2019)
9. Hinton, G., Vinyals, O., Dean, J.: Distilling the knowledge in a neural network. arXiv preprint arXiv:1503.02531 (2015)
10. Howard, A.G., et al.: MobileNets: efficient convolutional neural networks for mobile vision applications. arXiv preprint arXiv:1704.04861 (2017)
11. Huang, Z., Wang, N.: Like what you like: knowledge distill via neuron selectivity transfer. arXiv preprint arXiv:1707.01219 (2017)
12. Kim, S.W., Kim, H.E.: Transferring knowledge to smaller network with class-distance loss (2017)
13. Liu, Z., Sun, M., Zhou, T., Huang, G., Darrell, T.: Rethinking the value of network pruning. arXiv preprint arXiv:1810.05270 (2018)

14. Müller, R., Kornblith, S., Hinton, G.: When does label smoothing help? arXiv preprint arXiv:1906.02629 (2019)
15. Park, W., Kim, D., Lu, Y., Cho, M.: Relational knowledge distillation. In: Proceedings of the IEEE Conference on Computer Vision and Pattern Recognition, pp. 3967–3976 (2019)
16. Peng, B., et al.: Correlation congruence for knowledge distillation. In: Proceedings of the IEEE/CVF International Conference on Computer Vision, pp. 5007–5016 (2019)
17. Qiu, H., Zheng, Q., Memmi, G., Lu, J., Qiu, M., Thuraisingham, B.: Deep residual learning-based enhanced jpeg compression in the internet of things. IEEE Trans. Industr. Inf. **17**(3), 2124–2133 (2020)
18. Qiu, M., Qiu, H.: Review on image processing based adversarial example defenses in computer vision. In: 2020 IEEE 6th International Conference on Big Data Security on Cloud (BigDataSecurity), IEEE International Conference on High Performance and Smart Computing, (HPSC) and IEEE International Conference on Intelligent Data and Security (IDS), pp. 94–99. IEEE (2020)
19. Rastegari, M., Ordonez, V., Redmon, J., Farhadi, A.: XNOR-Net: ImageNet classification using binary convolutional neural networks. In: Leibe, B., Matas, J., Sebe, N., Welling, M. (eds.) ECCV 2016. LNCS, vol. 9908, pp. 525–542. Springer, Cham (2016). https://doi.org/10.1007/978-3-319-46493-0_32
20. Romero, A., Ballas, N., Kahou, S.E., Chassang, A., Gatta, C., Bengio, Y.: FitNets: hints for thin deep nets. arXiv preprint arXiv:1412.6550 (2014)
21. Sainath, T.N., Kingsbury, B., Sindhwani, V., Arisoy, E., Ramabhadran, B.: Low-rank matrix factorization for deep neural network training with high-dimensional output targets. In: 2013 IEEE International Conference on Acoustics, Speech and Signal Processing, pp. 6655–6659. IEEE (2013)
22. Tian, Y., Krishnan, D., Isola, P.: Contrastive representation distillation. In: International Conference on Learning Representations (2019)
23. Tung, F., Mori, G.: Similarity-preserving knowledge distillation. In: Proceedings of the IEEE/CVF International Conference on Computer Vision, pp. 1365–1374 (2019)
24. Wang, Q., Wu, B., Zhu, P., Li, P., Zuo, W., Hu, Q.: ECA-NET: efficient channel attention for deep convolutional neural networks. In: Proceedings of the IEEE/CVF Conference on Computer Vision and Pattern Recognition, pp. 11534–11542 (2020)
25. Yim, J., Joo, D., Bae, J., Kim, J.: A gift from knowledge distillation: fast optimization, network minimization and transfer learning. In: Proceedings of the IEEE Conference on Computer Vision and Pattern Recognition, pp. 4133–4141 (2017)
26. Zagoruyko, S., Komodakis, N.: Paying more attention to attention: improving the performance of convolutional neural networks via attention transfer. arXiv preprint arXiv:1612.03928 (2016)

Feature Interaction Convolutional Network for Knowledge Graph Embedding

Jiachuan Li, Aimin Li(✉), and Teng Liu

Qilu University of Technology (Shandong Academy of Sciences), Jinan 250353, China
{1043119704,1043119226}@stu.qlu.edu.cn, lam@qlu.edu.cn

Abstract. Due to the general incompleteness of knowledge graphs, knowledge graph link prediction is a hot research topic for knowledge graph completion. The low-dimensional embedding of entities and relations can be realized through link prediction methods, and then inference can be made. The previous link prediction methods mainly used shallow and fast models of the knowledge graph, such as TransE, TransH, TransA and other models. The feature extraction capabilities of these models are insufficient, which affects the performance of prediction. The recently proposed method ConvE uses embedded two-dimensional convolution and multi-layer nonlinear features to model the knowledge graph, which increases the interaction between entities and relations to a certain extent. In this paper, we propose a Feature Interaction Convolutional Network (FICN) for knowledge graph embedding, which uses three methods: Random Permutation, Chequer Reshaping and Circular Convolution to increase the feature interaction capability of the model, thereby effectively improving the link prediction performance. We verified the feasibility and effectiveness of FICN on the FB15K-237, WN18RR and YAGO3-10 data sets. Through experiments, we found that on these three data sets, FICN has a certain degree of improvement in MRR score compared to ConvE, and it is also stronger than ConvE in MR, HIST@10 and HIST@1 indicators. In addition, our model increases the training speed by adding the Batch Normalization preprocessing method during convolution training. Compared with ConvE model, our model has about a 50% reduction in training time.

Keywords: Knowledge graph · Feature interaction · Link prediction · Graph embedding · Convolutional network

1 Introduction

Knowledge graphs (KGs) are knowledge bases with a graph structure, where nodes represent entities and edges represent relations between entities. These

This work was supported by National Key R&D Program of China (No.2019YFB 1404700).

H. Qiu et al. (Eds.): KSEM 2021, LNAI 12815, pp. 369–380, 2021.
https://doi.org/10.1007/978-3-030-82136-4_30

relations are expressed in the form of (s, r, o) triples, (for example: entity s = Yao Ming, relation r = nationality, entity o = China). KGs are used in many aspects, such as information retrieval, natural language understanding, question answering systems, recommendation systems, etc. In mobile communication, resource outsourcing through resource allocation can reduce the local workload and the self-learning process can achieve the best allocation [7]. A large amount of information resources in the Internet of Things need to be allocated with high precision through knowledge learning [6]. The NP problem of task assignment in cloud computing can lead to service latency. The system sustainability can be improved by solving the problem of task assignment [8].

Although the knowledge graph contains millions of entities and triples, they are far from complete compared with the existing facts and newly added knowledge in the real world. Therefore, the completion of knowledge graph is very important. Link prediction accomplishes this task by inferring missing facts based on known facts in KG. The current dominant approach is to learn low-dimensional representations of all entities and relations (called embedding) and use them to predict new facts. Given a scoring function to learn the embedded KGs, the scoring function assigns a higher score to a true fact than to an invalid one. From the initial model of TransE [1], many knowledge graphs embedding models have been proposed, such as TransH [25], DistMult [27], TransR [14], TransD [12], and TransA [26].

However, these shallow models have limited ability to extract the number of features. The only way to increase the number of features (and their expressiveness) in a shallow model is to increase the embedding size, but this will lead to an increase in the number of parameters, thereby limiting its scalability to a larger knowledge graph. Convolutional Neural Networks (CNN) [10] have the advantage of using multiple layers, thereby increasing their expressive power while maintaining parameter efficiency. Dettmers [4] uses these characteristics to propose a 2D convolution model-ConvE, which applies convolution filters to entity and relation embedding. They aim to increase the number of interactions between embedded components, but ConvE cannot maximize the interaction between entities and relations.

In this paper, we improved the performance of link prediction by increasing the number of such interactions. On the basis of ConvE, we improve it to further enhance the interaction between relation embedding and entity embedding.

Our contributions are as follows:

- Based on ConvE, we proposed the Feature Interactive Convolutional Network (FICN). To increase interactive expression capabilities, we added three operations: Random Permutation, Chequer Reshaping, and Circular Convolution.
- By adding a Batch Normalization (BN) preprocessing algorithm, the training speed of the model is greatly improved, and overfitting is alleviated to a certain extent.

We verified the effectiveness of FICN on the standard FB15K-237, WN18RR and YAGO3-10 data sets. The MRR scores are all higher than ConvE, and the MR, HITS@1 and HITS@10 scores also have good results.

In this paper, we analyze the previous link prediction model (Sect. 2), improve the FICN model according to its shortcomings. The model increases the feature interaction ability through random permutation, chequer reshaping and circular convolution, and adds BN preprocessing algorithm to improve the computing ability of the model (Sect. 3). We get better results than ConvE by conducting experiments on three common datasets (Sect. 4).

2 Related Work

Knowledge graph embedding learning is directly applied to knowledge base completion (ie link prediction) and relation extraction. The embedding methods can be roughly divided into the following three categories:

Non-Neural: TransE [1] did this work by projecting entities and relations into the same embedded vector space. TransE along with subsequent methods such as TransH [25] et al., used translational targets as scoring functions. DistMult [27] and ComplEx [23] use a model based on bilinear diagonals.

Neural Networks: Neural tensor network [20] combines entity and relation embedding through a tensor of specific relations, which is used as the input of the nonlinear hidden layer to calculate the score function. Multilayer perceptrons are also used to model score functions [5,17].

Convolutional Neural Networks (CNN): ConvE [4] uses a convolution filter to filter the reshaped entity and relation embedding to calculate the output vector and compare it to all other entities in the knowledge graph. ConvKB [15] is another convolution-based approach that applies a convolutional filter of width 1 to stacked subject, relation, and object embedding to calculate scores. However, the performance of ConvKB is inconsistent across data sets, so we do not compare it.

Recent methods [16,27] indicate that the expressive power of the model can be enhanced by increasing the interaction between entity and relation embedding. Based on this principle, ConvE [4] uses convolution in 2D shaping embedding to achieve it.

3 Our Method

Increasing the interaction between entity and relation embedding can enhance the link prediction performance. We proposed a Feature Interaction Convolutional Network for Knowledge Graph Embedding, called FICN. FICN introduced three operations: Random Permutation, Chequer Reshaping, and Circular Convolution. Batch Normalization algorithm is also used to increase training speed of this model. In this section, we will introduce the components of FICN. The overall architecture of FICN is shown in Fig. 1.

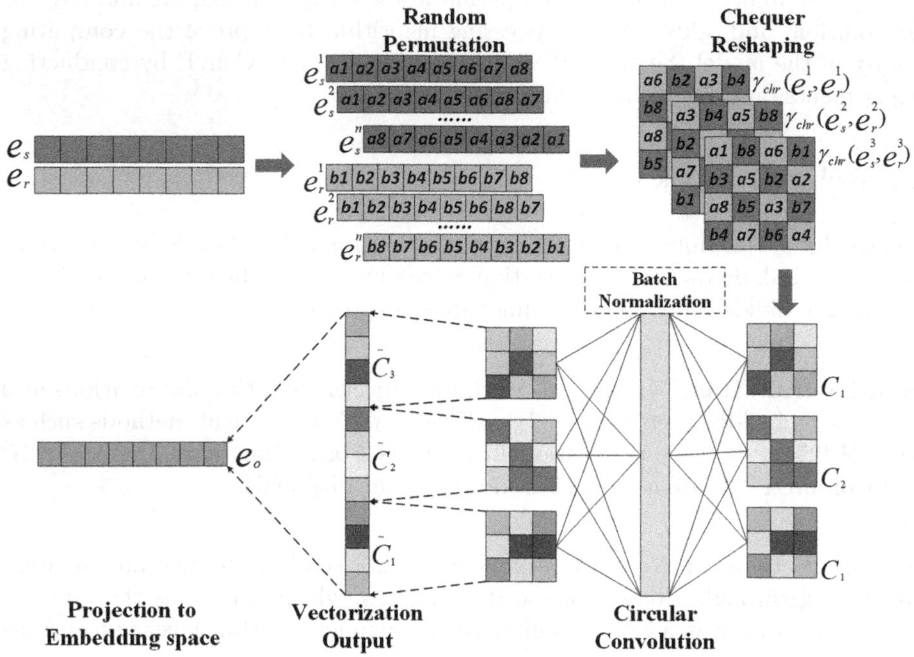

Fig. 1. Overview of FICN. We define entity and relation embedding as e_s and e_r , then generate random permutations of these embeddings and reshape them with chequer reshaping function (γ_{chr}). We add batch normalization (BN) processing to circular convolution. Each shaped data (C_i) is convoluted by circular convolution, and then they are vectorized output ($\widetilde{C}_i$) and fed back to a fully connected layer to generate a prediction object (e_o).

3.1 Random Permutation

The order in which we input is not fixed, but rather generates multiple permutations by random permutations to capture more interaction. The FICN model first generates random permutations of e_s and e_r, which we express as $\Lambda_r = [(e_s^1, e_r^1); (e_s^2, e_r^2); \dots (e_s^n, e_r^n)]$. In most cases, the interaction sets contained in $\mu(e_s^i, e_r^i)$ for different i are disjoint. We know from our knowledge of permutations and combinations that in all the permutations, the number of different interactions is huge, and for n different permutations, we have n times as many interactions as we have in a single permutation.

3.2 Chequer Reshaping

The reshaping function $\gamma : \mathbb{R}^d \times \mathbb{R}^d \rightarrow \mathbb{R}^{m \times n}$ can transform the embedding vectors e_s and e_r into a matrix $\gamma(e_s, e_r)$, where $m \times n = 2d$. We compared three kinds of reshaping functions and finally decided to apply the chequer reshaping function to our model. We use function $\gamma_{chr}(e_s^i, e_r^i), \forall i \in \{1, \ldots, \text{n}\}$ to apply to the definition $\Lambda_r = [(e_s^1, e_r^1); (e_s^2, e_r^2); \ldots (e_s^n, e_r^n)]$ in the previous section. The reshaping function used in ConvE [4] is $\gamma_{stk}(\cdot)$, which has limited ability to capture the interaction. We use $\gamma_{chr}(\cdot)$ to capture the largest heterogeneous interaction between entities and relations. Three kinds of reshaping functions are introduced as follows:

- Stack (γ_{stk}) reshapes e_s and e_r into a matrix of $(m/2) \times n$ shape, and then simply stacks them along the height to form a matrix of $m \times n$.
- Alternate (γ_{alt}^{λ}) reshapes e_s and e_r into a matrix of $(m/2) \times n$ shape, and then stacks them alternately to form a $m \times n$ matrix.
- Chequer (γ_{chr}) arranges the elements in e_s and e_r into a matrix of $m \times n$, all the adjacent elements in the matrix are not from the same embedded component.

3.3 Circular Convolution

Our training model does not use standard convolution, but uses circular convolution with stronger interaction ability. Circular convolution has been successfully applied to image recognition and other tasks [24]. The circular convolution on the two-dimensional input matrix $A \in \mathbb{R}^{m \times n}$ with filter $\upsilon \in \mathbb{R}^{l \times l}$ is defined as:

$$[A * \upsilon]_{x,y} = \sum_{a=-[l/2]}^{[l/2]} \sum_{b=-[l/2]}^{[l/2]} A_{[x-a]_m, [y-b]_n} \upsilon_{a,b} \tag{1}$$

Where $[z]_n$ denotes z modulo n and $[\cdot]$ is floor function.

FICN stacks each reshaped permutation into a single channel. We apply deep circular convolution [3], and different filter banks can adopt different filter arrangement. In practical operation, we use a better cross-channel shared filter, which can input more instances to train a set of kernel weights.

3.4 Batch Normalization Pretreatment

In the training process of the middle layer of the network, the distribution of data will change, and this change is called the Internal Covariate Shift. Therefore, we include the Batch Normalization (BN) algorithm [11] in the convolutional network. The algorithm preprocesses the input data, and the formula is defined as follows:

$$\hat{x}^{(l)} = \frac{x^{(l)} - E[x^{(l)}]}{\sqrt{Var[x^{(l)}]}} \tag{2}$$

Where $E[x^{(l)}]$ represents the average value of neuron $x^{(l)}$ in each batch of training data, and $\sqrt{Var[x^{(l)}]}$ represents a standard deviation of the activation degree of neuron $x^{(l)}$ in each batch of training data.

Only using normalization processing will destroy the feature distribution of the upper layer network learning, so two learnable parameters δ, η are introduced here:

$$y^{(l)} = \delta^{(l)}\hat{x}^{(l)} + \eta^{(l)} \tag{3}$$

Each neuron has parameters δ and η. Therefore, when:

$$\delta^{(l)^-} = \sqrt{Var[x^{(l)^-}]}; \eta^{(l)} = E[x^{(l)}] \tag{4}$$

We can recover the features learned at the original level. Then, the forward conduction formula of BN network layer is given as follows:

$$\mu_{\mathrm{B}} \leftarrow \frac{1}{m}\sum_{i=1}^{m} x_i \tag{5}$$

$$\sigma_{\mathrm{B}}^2 \leftarrow \frac{1}{m}\sum_{i=1}^{m} (x_i - \mu_{\mathrm{B}})^2 \tag{6}$$

$$\overset{\wedge}{\underset{i}{x}} \leftarrow \frac{x_i - \mu_{\mathrm{B}}}{\sqrt{\sigma_{\mathrm{B}}^2 + \varepsilon}} \tag{7}$$

$$y_i \leftarrow \delta \overset{\wedge}{\underset{i}{x}} + \eta \equiv BN_{\delta,\eta}(x_i) \tag{8}$$

Where m stands for mini-batch size. μ, σ is the mean and the standard deviation respectively. We use this data to calculate the mean and standard deviation required in the test phase:

$$E[x] \leftarrow E_{\mathrm{B}}[\mu_{\mathrm{B}}] \tag{9}$$

$$Var[x] \leftarrow \frac{m}{m-1} E_{\mathrm{B}}[\sigma_{\mathrm{B}}^2] \tag{10}$$

Therefore, the BN formula of the test phase is as follows:

$$y = \frac{\delta}{\sqrt{Var[x] + \varepsilon}} \cdot x + (\eta - \frac{\delta E[x]}{\sqrt{Var[x] + \varepsilon}}) \tag{11}$$

We normalized each feature graph as a processing unit. With this method, we did not need to adjust parameters such as learning rate, Dropout and $L2$ in the training process. The algorithm has the characteristics of fast convergence and improving the network generalization ability, which greatly improves the training speed of our model. In the training process, BN will thoroughly disrupt the training data to prevent the repetition of the same sample in each batch of training, and further improve the interactive ability of FICN.

3.5 Score Function

Table 1 shows some scoring functions. We flatten and connect the output of each cyclic convolution into a vector, and then project the vector into the embedded space ($\mathbb{R}^d$). We define the scoring function used in FICN as follows:

$$\varphi(e_s, e_r, e_o) = h(vec(f(\gamma(\Lambda_r)\Theta\omega))W)e_o \tag{12}$$

$vec(\cdot)$ represents vector link, Θ represents circular convolution with BN preprocessing, W represents a weight matrix that can be learned, and e_o represents the embedded matrix of object entities. Our functions h and f use *sigmoid* and *ELU*.

Table 1. The score functions defined by the various link prediction models and the score functions we used.

Model	Scoring Function $\varphi(e_s, e_r, e_o)$
TransE	$\|\|e_s + e_r - e_o\|\|_p$
DistMult	$\langle e_s, e_r, e_o \rangle$
HolE	$\langle e_r, e_s * e_o \rangle$
ComplEx	$\text{Re}(\langle e_s, e_r, e_o \rangle)$
RotatE	$-\|\|e_s \circ e_r - e_o\|\|^2$
ConvE	$f(vec(f([\bar{e_s}; \bar{e_r}] * \omega))W)e_o$
FICN	$\boldsymbol{h(vec(f(\gamma(\Lambda_r)\Theta\omega))W)e_o}$

4 Experiment

4.1 Datasets

We evaluated the performance of link prediction using three public benchmark data sets (FB15K-237, WN18RR and YAGO3-10) in reference to the ConvE model. Table 2 shows the summary statistics for the data set.

Table 2. Summarized data for the data set used.

Dataset	$\|\varepsilon\|$	$\|\mathcal{R}\|$	#Triples		
			Train	Valid	Test
FB15K-237	14,541	237	272,115	17,535	20,466
WN18RR	40,943	11	86,835	3,034	3,134
YAGO3-10	123,182	37	1,079,040	5,000	5,000

FB15K-237. [22] data set, which contains textual references to knowledge base relational triples and Freebase entity pairs, is an improved version of the FB15K [1] data set in which all reverse relations are removed to prevent direct inference of test triples from reverse training triples.

WN18RR. [4] was created from WN18 [1], which is a subset of WordNet. However, many of its text triples are obtained by reversing triples from the training set. Therefore, the WN18RR data set was created to ensure that there is no inverse relation between the evaluation data set.

YAGO3-10. is a subset of YAGO3 [21] and consists of entities with at least 10 relations. A triple consists of descriptive attributes of a person.

4.2 Experiment Parameter

The range of super parameters in our FICN model is as follows: learning rate {0.0001,0.001}, number of convolution filters {64,96}, kernel size {7,9,11}, number of feature rearrangement {1,2,4}, label smoothing {0.1}, batch size {128,256}, hidden layer dropout{0.3,0.5}, feature dropout{0.2,0.5}.

We set different parameters for different data sets: For FB15K-237, the learning rate is set to 0.0001, the number of convolution filters is set to 96, and the kernel size is set to 9; For WN18RR, learning rate is set to 0.001, feature rearrangement number is set to 4, kernel size is set to 11, hidden layer dropout is set to 0.3, feature dropout is set to 0.2; For YAGO3-10, the number of convolution filters is set to 64, the size of the kernel is set to 7, the number of feature rearrangement is set to 2, the hidden layer dropout is set to 0.3, and the feature dropout is set to 0.2. Since we have added BN preprocessing algorithm into the model, there is no need to consider the problem of adjusting the learning rate. Adaptive Moment (Adam) algorithm [13] was used to train the model. Our model is implemented by PyTorch.

4.3 Benchmark

In our experiment, we compared our result with the following models:

- Non-Neural: A method that uses simple vector-based operations to calculate the score. Examples include DistMult [27], ComplEx [23], KBGAN [2] and KBLRN [9].
- Neural: The method based on nonlinear neural network architecture is used in the scoring function. Such as R-GCN [18], ConvE [4] and ConvTransE [19].

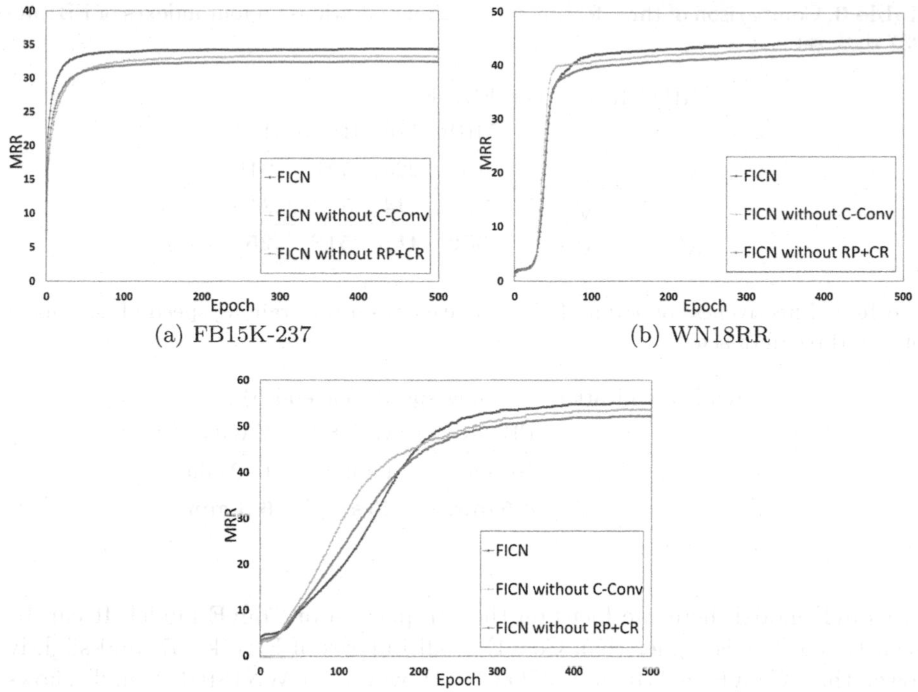

(a) FB15K-237 (b) WN18RR

(c) YAGO3-10

Fig. 2. Comparison of three feature interaction operations on MRR index of three data sets.

4.4 Ablation Study

In this section, we compare the impact of three feature interaction operations on the performance improvement of FICN model. Since Random Permutation (RP) and Chequer Reshaping (CR) need to work together, we use these two operations as one module, and Circular Convolution (C-Conv) as the other module. As shown in the Fig. 2 and Table 3. The effect of BN pretreatment on the time spent in training an epoch was also compared. As shown in the Table 4. The experimental results prove that the three feature interaction operations can help improve the model link prediction performance, and the addition of BN can greatly reduce the model calculation time.

4.5 Performance Comparison

Our experiment was evaluated using MRR, MR, HIST@10 and HIST@1 four evaluation criteria. We compare FICN with the knowledge graph embedding method mentioned in Sect. 4.3. Table 5 lists the scores of the knowledge graph embedding model on three link prediction data sets. The other benchmarks listed in this table are from papers [2,4,9,19]. Because our model is an improvement

Table 3. Comparison of three feature interaction operations on four indexes of FB15K-237 data set.

RP+CR	C-Conv	FB15K-237			
		MRR	MR	H@10	H@1
√		.326	225	.509	.241
	√	.315	214	.5	.24
√	√	**.336**	**186**	**.518**	**.25**

Table 4. Effectiveness of adding BN pretreatment on the training speed of the model on the three data sets.

Batch Normalization	Training speed (one epoch)		
	FB15K-237	WN18RR	YAGO3-10
	10 min	1 min	14.2 min
√	**4.5 min**	**45 s**	**6.3 min**

of ConvE model, here, we focus on the comparison of ConvE model. It can be seen that FICN is higher than ConvE in all indexes of FB15k-237, and slightly lower than ConvE in MR in YAGO3-10. However, in WN18RR, ConvE shows better performance in MR indexes, and the other three indexes are similar to our model. Overall, our method is verified by the fact that we can improve link prediction performance by adding feature interactions.

Table 5. Link prediction evaluation of FICN and other models on three data sets.

Model	FB15K-237				WN18RR				YAGO3-10			
	MRR	MR	H@10	H@1	MRR	MR	H@10	H@1	MRR	MR	H@10	H@1
DistMult	.241	254	.419	.155	.430	5100	.49	.39	.34	5926	.54	.24
ComplEx	.247	339	.428	.158	.44	5261	.51	.41	.36	6351	.55	.26
R-GCN	.248	–	.417	.151	–	–	–	–	–	–	–	–
KBGAN	.278	–	.458	–	.214	–	.472	–	–	–	–	–
KBLRN	.309	209	.493	.219	–	–	–	–	–	–	–	–
ConvTransE	.33	–	.51	.24	**.46**	–	.52	**.43**	–	–	–	–
ConvE	.325	244	.501	.237	.43	**4187**	.52	.40	.44	**1671**	.62	.35
FICN	**.336**	**186**	**.518**	**.25**	.452	4956	**.522**	.429	**.549**	1866	**.655**	**.379**

5 Conclusion

In order to improve the performance of knowledge graph link prediction, we proposed a Feature Interaction Convolutional Network (FICN), which increases the interaction between entities and relations embedding by adding Random Permutation, Chequer Reshaping and Circular Convolution operations. At the same time, by adding Batch Normalization (BN) preprocessing, the model training time is shortened greatly. Experiments show that our method has achieved a certain degree of link prediction performance improvement on three public data sets. Compared with the ConvE model, our method is in a leading state in both the evaluation index score and the model training speed. In our future work, we consider using more methods to increase interaction or do processing of data sets to make our model have better prediction performance.

References

1. Bordes, A., Usunier, N., Garcia-Duran, A., Weston, J., Yakhnenko, O.: Translating embeddings for modeling multi-relational data. In: Neural Information Processing Systems (NIPS), pp. 1–9 (2013)
2. Cai, L., Wang, W.Y.: Kbgan: Adversarial learning for knowledge graph embeddings. arXiv preprint arXiv:1711.04071 (2017)
3. Chollet, F.: Xception: deep learning with depthwise separable convolutions. In: Proceedings of the IEEE Conference on Computer Vision and Pattern Recognition, pp. 1251–1258 (2017)
4. Dettmers, T., Minervini, P., Stenetorp, P., Riedel, S.: Convolutional 2d knowledge graph embeddings. In: Proceedings of the AAAI Conference on Artificial Intelligence, vol. 32 (2018)
5. Dong, X., et al.: Knowledge vault: a web-scale approach to probabilistic knowledge fusion. In: Proceedings of the 20th ACM SIGKDD International Conference on Knowledge Discovery and Data Mining, pp. 601–610 (2014)
6. Gai, K., Qiu, M.: Optimal resource allocation using reinforcement learning for IoT content-centric services. Appl. Soft Comput. **70**, 12–21 (2018)
7. Gai, K., Qiu, M.: Reinforcement learning-based content-centric services in mobile sensing. IEEE Network **32**(4), 34–39 (2018)
8. Gai, K., Qiu, M., Zhao, H., Sun, X.: Resource management in sustainable cyber-physical systems using heterogeneous cloud computing. IEEE Trans. Sustain. Comput. **3**(2), 60–72 (2017)
9. Garcia-Duran, A., Niepert, M.: Kblrn: end-to-end learning of knowledge base representations with latent, relational, and numerical features. arXiv preprint arXiv:1709.04676 (2017)
10. Gu, J., et al.: Recent advances in convolutional neural networks. Pattern Recognit. **77**, 354–377 (2018)
11. Ioffe, S., Szegedy, C.: Batch normalization: accelerating deep network training by reducing internal covariate shift. In: International Conference on Machine Learning, pp. 448–456. PMLR (2015)
12. Ji, G., He, S., Xu, L., Liu, K., Zhao, J.: Knowledge graph embedding via dynamic mapping matrix. In: Proceedings of the 53rd Annual Meeting of the Association for Computational Linguistics and the 7th International Joint Conference on Natural Language Processing (vol. 1: Long papers), pp. 687–696 (2015)

13. Kingma, D.P., Ba, J.: Adam: a method for stochastic optimization. arXiv preprint arXiv:1412.6980 (2014)
14. Lin, Y., Liu, Z., Sun, M., Liu, Y., Zhu, X.: Learning entity and relation embeddings for knowledge graph completion. In: Proceedings of the AAAI Conference on Artificial Intelligence, vol. 29 (2015)
15. Nguyen, D.Q., Nguyen, T.D., Nguyen, D.Q., Phung, D.: A novel embedding model for knowledge base completion based on convolutional neural network. arXiv preprint arXiv:1712.02121 (2017)
16. Nickel, M., Rosasco, L., Poggio, T.: Holographic embeddings of knowledge graphs. In: Proceedings of the AAAI Conference on Artificial Intelligence, vol. 30 (2016)
17. Ravishankar, S., Talukdar, P.P., et al.: Revisiting simple neural networks for learning representations of knowledge graphs. arXiv preprint arXiv:1711.05401 (2017)
18. Schlichtkrull, M., Kipf, T.N., Bloem, P., van den Berg, R., Titov, I., Welling, M.: Modeling relational data with graph convolutional networks. In: Gangemi, A., et al. (eds.) ESWC 2018. LNCS, vol. 10843, pp. 593–607. Springer, Cham (2018). https://doi.org/10.1007/978-3-319-93417-4_38
19. Shang, C., Tang, Y., Huang, J., Bi, J., He, X., Zhou, B.: End-to-end structure-aware convolutional networks for knowledge base completion. In: Proceedings of the AAAI Conference on Artificial Intelligence, vol. 33, pp. 3060–3067 (2019)
20. Socher, R., Chen, D., Manning, C.D., Ng, A.: Reasoning with neural tensor networks for knowledge base completion. In: Advances in Neural Information Processing Systems, pp. 926–934. Citeseer (2013)
21. Suchanek, F.M., Kasneci, G., Weikum, G.: Yago: a core of semantic knowledge. In: Proceedings of the 16th international conference on World Wide Web, pp. 697–706 (2007)
22. Toutanova, K., Chen, D.: Observed versus latent features for knowledge base and text inference. In: Proceedings of the 3rd Workshop on Continuous Vector Space Models and their Compositionality, pp. 57–66 (2015)
23. Trouillon, T., Welbl, J., Riedel, S., Gaussier, É., Bouchard, G.: Complex embeddings for simple link prediction. In: International Conference on Machine Learning, pp. 2071–2080. PMLR (2016)
24. Wang, T.H., Huang, H.J., Lin, J.T., Hu, C.W., Zeng, K.H., Sun, M.: Omnidirectional cnn for visual place recognition and navigation. In: 2018 IEEE International Conference on Robotics and Automation (ICRA), pp. 2341–2348. IEEE (2018)
25. Wang, Z., Zhang, J., Feng, J., Chen, Z.: Knowledge graph embedding by translating on hyperplanes. In: Proceedings of the AAAI Conference on Artificial Intelligence, vol. 28 (2014)
26. Xiao, H., Huang, M., Hao, Y., Zhu, X.: Transa: An adaptive approach for knowledge graph embedding. arXiv preprint arXiv:1509.05490 (2015)
27. Yang, B., Yih, W.t., He, X., Gao, J., Deng, L.: Embedding entities and relations for learning and inference in knowledge bases. arXiv preprint arXiv:1412.6575 (2014)

Towards a Modular Ontology for Cloud Consumer Review Mining

Emna Ben Abdallah[1(✉)], Khouloud Boukadi[1], and Rima Grati[2]

[1] Mir@cl Laboratory, Sfax University, Sfax, Tunisia
[2] Zayed University, Abu Dhabi, United Arab Emirates

Abstract. Nowadays, online consumer reviews are used to enhance the effectiveness of finding useful product information that impacts the consumers' decision-making process. Many studies have been proposed to analyze these reviews for many purposes, such as opinion-based recommendation, spam review detection, opinion leader analysis, etc. A standard model that presents the different aspects of online review (review, product/service, user) is needed to facilitate the review analysis task. This research suggests SOPA, a modular ontology for cloud Service OPinion Analysis. SOPA represents the content of a product/service and its related opinions extracted from the online reviews written in a specific context. The SOPA is evaluated and validated using cloud consumer reviews from social media and using quality metrics. The experiments revealed that the SOPA-related modules exhibit a high cohesion and a low coupling, besides their usefulness and applicability in real use case studies.

Keywords: Modular ontology · Cloud services · Online reviews · Social media · Opinion analysis

1 Introduction

Online reviews are an essential source of information for consumers to evaluate different services and products before deciding which provider to choose. They have a significant power to influence consumers' purchasing decisions. Through Social Media platforms (SMPs), such as Facebook and Amazon, consumers can freely give feedback, exhibit their reactions to a post or product, share their opinions with other peers, and share their grievances with the companies. However, SMPs were mainly built to be exploited by humans making their content harder to interpret by machines. Hence, it is essential to use the semantic web to present the social media content precisely and facilitate information readability by the machine, which allows web-based applications to interact syntactically and semantically between users and resources [21].

Several ontologies have been proposed in the literature [1,2,5,21] to solve the problem of information extraction from social media platforms and online review based product/service analysis. However, limited information has been

H. Qiu et al. (Eds.): KSEM 2021, LNAI 12815, pp. 381–394, 2021.
https://doi.org/10.1007/978-3-030-82136-4_31

considered to support context-aware analysis to provide a personalized product/service analysis from online reviews. Although, in the area of cloud service, context cannot be ignored; as observed in [17], cloud research should not only analyze opinions about cloud services but also a personalized experience influenced by consumer context. For example, the service availability depends on the user location and the user requirements, which differ according to their industries and use cases. Thus, the service qualities observed by one user in different contexts will vary significantly. Hence, we believe that it is interesting to analyze cloud services based on the experiences and feedback of other users who acquired the cloud services in a context similar to that of the end-user. This paper presents a modular ontology for cloud Service OPinion Analysis (SOPA) that aims at representing the content of a product/service and its related opinions, which are extracted from the consumer's reviews written in a specific context. The use of modular ontologies allows the treatment of data from each of the disparate sources in an autonomous manner, an adequate population of ontologies, and distributed reasoning with the data, providing a solution to manage and reason with data within peer-to-peer systems. We represent all the involved domains in separate modules, namely cloud service, user context, social media, and opinion modules. Then we integrate them to promote the reusability of each module separately. Furthermore, the different modules are based on the upper-level ontology named Basic Formal Ontology (BFO) [3] to ensure the semantic interoperability of ontological modules and the reuse of existing ontologies. In particular, the proposed ontology has the merit to be used for the analysis of any product/service since the cloud service module is aligned with the reference ontology Product-Service System (PSS) ontology.

The rest of the paper is organized in the following manner. Related works are presented in Sect. 2. Section 3 details our proposal, namely the construction of a modular ontology for cloud service analysis. Section 4 is devoted to the ontology instantiation and the ontology evaluation before concluding remarks and future work in Sect. 5.

2 Related Work

The semantic web has achieved great success in the social media and opinion mining fields. Bojrs et al. [5] demonstrated that applying semantic web frameworks to the social web, such as SIOC (Semantically Interlinked Online Communities) [8] and FOAF (Friend-of-a-Friend) [11], can create a network of interlinked and semantically rich knowledge. Besides, the work presented in [21] also examined the use of semantic modeling techniques to represent knowledge on the social media platform for product recommendation purposes. The model has been validated using Twitter (as a social media data source) and based on an automotive industry expert to define the products' rules and characteristics in the created ontology. Besides, several studies [1,24] have applied ontologies for feature-based opinion mining. The main goal of these works was to compute the polarity by considering the features of a concept. In these works, the authors first built ontologies that model the texts' content and then extracted features and associated opinions from texts using the proposed ontologies. Zhuang et al. [24] proposed a semi-automatic domain ontology builder for aspect-based sentiment analysis (SOBA) to improve the performance of feature-based sentiment analysis. SOBA semi-automates the ontology building process for the objective of ensuring the quality of the resulting ontology. Ali et al. [1] proposed an ontology and latent Dirichlet allocation (OLDA)-based topic modeling and word embedding approach for sentiment classification. The proposed system retrieves transportation content from social networks, removes irrelevant content to extract meaningful information, and generates topics and features from extracted data using a fuzzy domain ontology. Moreover, the authors in [2] relied on a product review ontology to bring a link between the middle of life phase to the beginning of life phase in the closed-loop product lifecycle management.

The proposed ontologies contain important entities (i.e., concepts, relationships, and axioms) that can be reused to provide necessary grounds and understanding of the social media-based analysis. However, limited information has been provided for the relationships between the different domains and how that can be used to evaluate cloud services through online reviews and latent opinions. Furthermore, existing ontologies lack lightweight and modular mechanisms that can be utilized to exploit information existing in social media effectively. Our study aims to develop a semantic ontology-based model that can infer the context-aware analysis of cloud services based on user's opinions.

3 The Proposed SOPA Ontology

Cloud consumer review mining involves reasoning belonging to different domains, namely cloud service domain, social media domain, user context domain, and opinion domain. Indeed, we propose in this study to build a modular ontology, namely SOPA, by integrating a set of ontologies, considered as modules, presenting the different domains involved. According to [12], an ontology module can be considered as a loosely coupled and self-contained component of an ontology maintaining relationships with other modules.

To build the SOPA ontology, we adopt the Agile methodology for developing Ontology Modules (AOM) [13]. The key steps in a single iteration include the definition of competency questions (CQ). We use an upper-level ontology, BFO, to guarantee the semantic interoperability of ontological modules and re-use several existing ontologies.

3.1 AOM Methodology

Building a modular ontology is not a straightforward task, especially when ontologies become more significant and more complex [23]. Therefore, a methodology that guides and manages modular ontology development is necessary. In this work, we adopt AOM [13] since it enables the development of the proposed modules incrementally and iteratively, whereas other methodologies are used to develop ontologies in one step. AOM includes four phases: exploration, planning, module development, and finally release phases [13]. The development life-cycle begins with the exploration phase, in which we identified the ontology requirements and objectives. We defined a set of Competency Questions (CQs) according to the studied domains and experts' needs. The CQs refer to a set of questions expressed in natural language so that the ontology must be able to answer them correctly [15]. The planning phase consists of extracting stories given the set of CQs to represent the requirements that should be considered to design the different domains. Accordingly, stories present the different scenarios from which facts can be obtained, which will be used to build the ontology. After that, the next phase, namely module development, aims to design a semi-formal module using the extracted stories related to each module. Finally, the modules are formalized, implemented, and evaluated to be combined in the release phase. This phase notably requires a modular ontology formalism to combine the different modules. This will be addressed in the next Section.

3.2 CIMOn

To define and specify modular ontology, several popular formalisms are proposed, e.g. the Contextual Integration for Modular Ontology method (CIMOn) [23], E-Connection [14], IDDL [25], etc. In our work, we use the CIMOn method [23], which allows a safe/clean manual integration and reuse of different ontology modules. Using "context", extra information is only needed when ontologies are about to be integrated, such as extra relations, which can be stored independently. Thus, original ontology modules are kept intact and can be reused for different purposes in different contexts at the same time. CIMOn is compatible with owl:imports, while it introduced a "filter" to achieve partly importing, which means that the ontology's content can be partly integrated into context, and this feature makes ontology reuse more flexible.

3.3 BFO as an Upper-Level Ontology

The Basic Formal Ontology (BFO) is a small, upper-level ontology designed to support information retrieval, analysis, and integration in scientific and other domains. Besides, BFO is in the process of being ISO standard (ISO 21838-2). More than 250 ontology-driven endeavors use it throughout the world [3]. The two main categories of BFO classes are "Continuant", which are entities that continue to exist over time such as objects and locations (forests, water, etc.), and "Occurrent" which are event entities, processes, and temporal region such as rain, earthquakes, etc.

3.4 PSS as a Reference Ontology

Reference ontologies are often built to capture the fundamental concepts of a domain. The common Product Service System (PSS) ontology is a reference ontology that provides a cohesive delivery of products and services. It enables collaborative consumption of both products and services, which can be used as a reference ontology in the manufacturing domain [9]. The PSS ontology includes products, services, PSS, PSS lifecycle, process, stakeholders, etc. It uses the BFO as a starting point for categorizing entities and relationships in the specific research domain.

3.5 Reused Ontologies

To build our ontology, we reused concepts from some existing ontologies that are relevant for describing the SOPA ontology, such as CONON [22], CSO [18] and FoaF (Friend-of-a-Friend) [11]. We chose these ontologies for two reasons: reduce duplicate work and promote interoperability between ontologies. CONON is an ontology-based context model in which a hierarchical approach is adopted for designing context ontologies. The context model supports multiple semantic contextual representations like classification, dependency, and quality of context. CSO (Cloud Service Ontology) is developed in [18] which integrates service descriptions obtained from heterogeneous sources. The ontology model accounts for the functional and non-functional properties, attributes, and infrastructure relations, platform, and software services. The CSO relies on cloud standards such as NIST, OCCI, CIMI, etc. The SIOC [8] Core Ontology provides the imported concepts and properties required to represent information from online communities on the semantic web.

3.6 Competency Questions (CQs)

CQs consist of a set of questions stated and replied (the replies are often also neglected during ontology specification) in natural language. The ontology must be able to answer them correctly [15]. CQs play an essential role in the ontology development life cycle, as they represent the ontology requirements. This section presents some defined CQs in the context-aware opinion-based cloud service analysis domain to which SOPA should give the right answers. Table 1 summarizes some examples of CQs which will be used to evaluate the ontology at the end of the process.

3.7 Overview of the SOPA Ontology

The proposed ontology comprises a set of modules covering the four domains related to cloud consumer review mining: cloud service module, social media module, user context module, and opinion module. Each module is defined as follows:

- Cloud service module: This module describes the various cloud service pertinent information in a homogeneous model. It accounts for the functional and non-functional properties, attributes, relations of infrastructure, platform, and software services. To build this module, we reuse cloud service concepts defined in CSO ontology [18].

Table 1. Competency questions examples

Competency questions		Ontology
CQ1	Which cloud services have high availability in Tokyo?	Global ontology
CQ2	Which virtual machine has a price per hour less or equal to 1$ and has Memory at least 7GO?	Cloud service ontology
CQ3	What are the reviews that discussed a particular item characteristics of a given item category?	Social media ontology
CQ4	What are the items that have a high opinion level?	Opinion ontology
CQ5	In which context the cloud users said that the availability of Amazon is high?	Global ontology

- Social media module: This module is the conceptualization of the social media domain focusing on online reviews. It is conceptualized to be generic enough to be used for many other purposes such as reviews/feedback discovering a particular item (product/service), and recommending items.
- User context module: Context can be defined as any information used to identify the situation of an entity [10]. According to this definition, an entity can be a person, a place, or an object that can be considered important in the interaction between the user and the application. Moreover, we rely on two reference ontologies FoaF and CONON, to correctly model context information.
- Opinion module: This module aims to store users' opinions and infer the item state according to these opinions.

Each module is referenced by the main class called "pivotal class" and linked to other classes by a hierarchical "subClassOf" or non-hierarchical relations. The ontological modules are not independent. Each module has at least one inter-module relationship (R_{inter}) with other modules. For instance, the "CloudUser" concept in the cloud service module is equivalent to the "User" concept in the user context module, which is, in turn, equivalent to the "User" concept in the social media module. Indeed, in the modular ontology, a cloud user has a context and a set of reviews. Besides, a cloud service has a set of opinions extracted from a set of reviews about it. This is by defining: the R_{inter} "isAbout" between "OpinionTerm" and "Cloud Service" concepts, the R_{inter} "talkAbout" between "review" and "Cloud Service" concepts, and the R_{inter} "extractedFrom" between "OpinionTerm" and "Review" concepts. The SOPA ontology includes 69 classes, 41 object properties, and 273 axioms (logical statements) defining, interconnecting and interrelating classes.

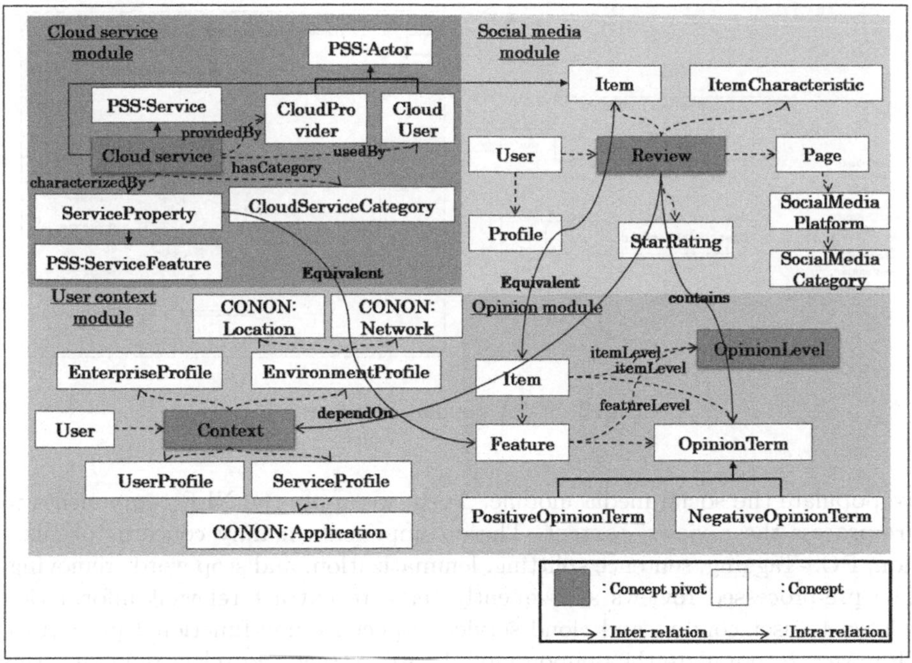

Fig. 1. Partial view of SOPA modules

4 Ontology Population and Evaluation

4.1 Ontology Population

The SOPA population consists in creating new instances of the concepts related to the cloud service, user context, social media, and opinion modules. As illustrated in Fig. 2, the SOPA population mainly concerns three main phases: cloud service collection phase, user context collection phase, and online review collection phase. The cloud service collection is built to prepare the SOPA ontology to extract relevant information related to the cloud service module (service properties, pricing model, operating systems, etc.) from consumers' reviews. For this purpose, we rely on a focused crawler for cloud service discovery [6] that aims to collect cloud service features. The user context collection consists of populating the usage context module to be able to extract relevant information related to this module from consumers' reviews such as the service use case, the used tools, and the user job type (Fig. 1).

The review collection phase starts with the consumer review gathering from different social media platforms such as Trustradius, G2CROWD, and Facebook. For doing so, we propose a dedicated crawler that aims to extract the content and the metadata (ratings, date, etc.) of the reviews and the consumers' profiles (enterprise, job type, career level, etc.). The Table 2 presents statistics about the collected reviews as well as consumers' contexts. Based on the reviews' metadata,

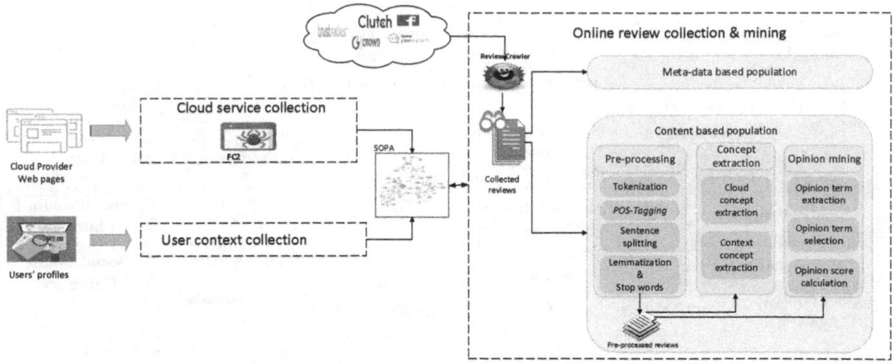

Fig. 2. SOPA population process

we populate the social media module. Then, we apply the NLP components to pre-process the reviews' content. These components mainly concern tokenization, POS-Tagging, sentence splitting, lemmatization, and stop words removing. The pre-processed reviews subsequently serve to extract relevant information related to user context and cloud service, especially non-functional properties. Moreover, to populate the opinion module, we extract and select opinion terms associated with the retrieved non-functional property by relying on the Point-wise Mutual Information (PMI) [7]. Subsequently, each opinion term's polarity score is established based on the SentiWordNet dictionary [4].

Table 2. Social media platform dataset description

Dataset	Trust radius	G2CRO WD	Clutch	Gartner peer insights	Facebook	All
#Reviews	2500	1500	1500	3000	1500	10000
%Reviews with contextual information	85%	72%	83%	91%	64%	79.4%

4.2 Ontology Quality Evaluation

The evaluation step using metrics aims to check each module's consistency and between modules and the global ontology and provide an insight to the ontology users about the granularity of each module. Firstly, we check the modules' consistency through the reasoner Pellet, an OWL2 reasoner, integrated into the Protégé software. Ontology inconsistency refers to the fact that logical incoherence or modeling problems arise if the primitives given by the ontology implementation language are not used correctly (such as contradictory relations). Secondly, we evaluate the different modules in comparison with specific criteria.

For this purpose, we rely on the criteria and metrics defined by Khan [16]. These metrics are mainly grouped into four categories of criteria:

1. The structural criteria are calculated based on the structural and hierarchical properties of the module. Calculating structural criteria involves evaluating the size and the atomic size of the different modules and the global ontology.
2. The logical criteria include correctness, clarity, and completeness metrics. The first one evaluates if every axiom that exists in the module also exists in the global ontology. While the clarity determines how effectively the ontology communicates the defined terms' intended meaning, measured by the Class/relation ratio (CRR). The completeness implies that every entity in a module is preserved as in the source ontology. Completeness also covers the granularity and richness of the ontology. Each module's completeness is measured using the Axiom/Class Ratio (ACR), which describes the ratio between axioms and classes. Moreover, the evaluation of the global ontology completeness is achieved while relying on different case studies presented in Sect. 4.3.
3. The relational criteria deal with the relations and behavior that modules exhibit with each other such as the inter-Module Distance (IMD), the cohesion, and the coupling. The IMD in a set of modules has been described as the number of modules that have to be considered to relate two entities. Cohesion refers to the degree to which the elements in a module belong together. It is obtained by computing the number of relations between different classes in a module. Lastly, coupling measures the degree of interdependence of a module.
4. Richness criteria aim to measure ontologies' richness in terms of attributes, relations, and subclasses. It includes the following metrics : Attribute Richness (AR), Inheritance Richness (IR), and Relationship Richness (RR).

We evaluate the different modules including: Cloud service module ($M_{CloudService}$), User context module ($M_{UserContext}$), Social media module ($M_{SocialMedia}$), Opinion module ($M_{Opinion}$) and the SOPA ontology.

Table 3. Ontology evaluation results

Module	Structural metrics				Richness metrics		Relational metrics			Logical metrics		
	Number of classes	Number of properties	Number of axioms	Atomic size	IR	RR	Coh	IMD	Coupling	Correctness	ACR	CRR
$M_{CloudService}$	143	112	5044	13.69	0.811	0.491	0.113	14101	0.0016	True	58.687	0.627
$M_{UserContext}$	67	73	296	2.39	0.850	0.561	0.136	1236	0.003	True	4.418	0.475
$M_{SocialMedia}$	75	84	10758	3.0	0.986	0.532	0.232	4875	0.007	True	143.44	0.474
$M_{Opinion}$	42	13	77	3.15	0.976	0.240	0.548	100	0.009	True	1.83	0.778
SOPA	79	123	14612	9.05	0.974	0.615	0.175	575	–	True	184.962	0.395

According to the metric results applied to SOPA, we can draw the following conclusions:

- As shown in Table 3, all the proposed modules and the SOPA ontology have IR values comprised between 0.8 and 0.9, which represent high IR values, which implies that knowledge is well grouped into different categories and subcategories in the modules. We can also consider the different modules and the SOPA ontology as horizontal ontologies by relying on this measure. Indeed, the various modules represent a wide range of knowledge with a low level of detail. Accordingly, they are more open to evolving and being specified. This evolution corresponds to our objective to enrich the ontology with further information in other development iterations.

- An ontology that contains only inheritance relationships conveys less information than an ontology that contains various sets of relationships. According to the RR values, we can conclude that the global ontology (SOPA) has more information compared to the modules (RR = 0.615). Also, compared to the other modules, $M_{UserContext}$ (RR = 0.561) and $M_{SocialMedia}$ (RR = 0.532) modules have the highest ones.
- The completeness metric, ACR, aims to analyze the degree of coverage of the designed domain. In other words, it shows whether the ontology has a rich formalization of conceptual choices and motivations. A high ACR value indicates that the ontology can cover the relevant properties of the domain of interest. In this regard, we notice that the $M_{SocialMedia}$ module has a high degree of coverage of the designed domain (ACR = 143.44) and subsequently the SOPA ontology (ACR = 184.962), which can be explained by the fact that these two ontologies are instantiated using 1000 consumers' reviews. Consequently, around 1000 instances are automatically created for each class for these two ontologies.
- By comparing the cohesion values ($coh(M_o)$), we found that $M_{SocialMedia}$ and $M_{Opinion}$ have the highest cohesion values due to the strong relatedness of different classes of each module. The SOPA has a great cohesion value (coh = 0.175), which implies that the various concepts belonging in SOPA are linked together sufficiently to achieve the common goal of mining cloud consumer reviews.
- As shown in Table 3, the coupling between the different modules is weak. Each ontological module is loosely coupled with other modules. Indeed, the SOPA ontology modules are sufficiently independent and easier to understand, modify, and reuse.
- The different modules are also evaluated in terms of extensibility and interoperability. First, the extensibility metric aims to assess the ontology's capability to be easily extended by other ontologies. In this regard, our ontology has been designed by using the BFO upper-level ontology and the reuse of existing ontologies. Besides, since our proposal is modular, new modules and ontologies can be easily integrated. Second, interoperability examines how the ontology is aligned to the upper level or other ontologies. The consistent use of an upper-level ontology and existing ontologies such as PSS is a significant step towards enabling interoperability among ontologies.

4.3 Stories Based Evaluation: Analysis Results

This section presents some useful analysis generated by SOPA ontology.

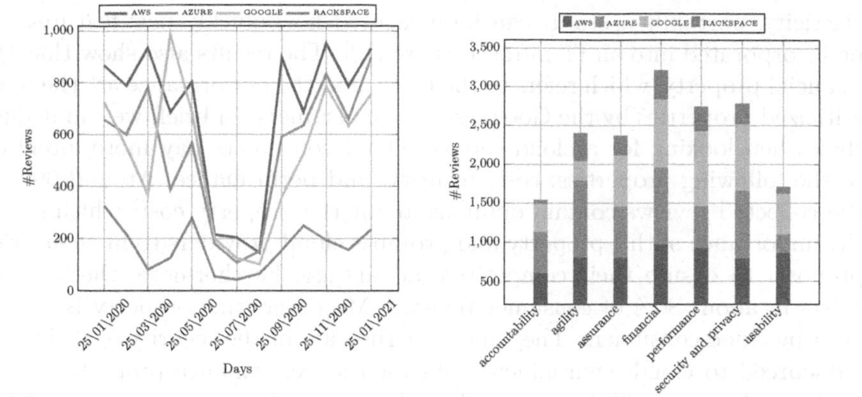

(a) Analysis of reviews that talk about AWS, Azure, Google and Rackspace providers per days.

(b) Analysis of reviews that talk about SMI based service properties

Fig. 3. Consumer review analysis per day and per service property

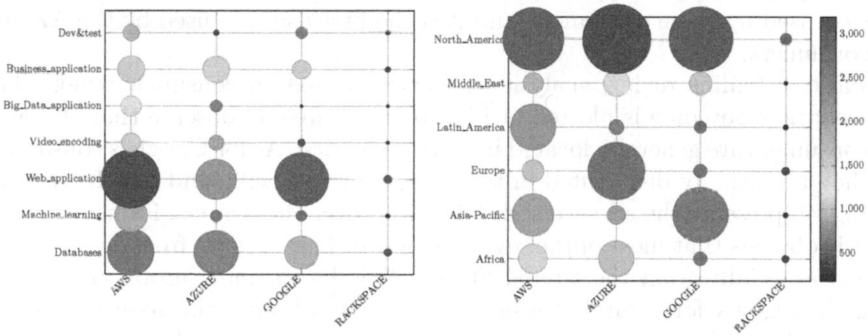

(a) Analysis of cloud service reviews per use case

(b) Analysis of cloud service reviews per Region

Fig. 4. Consumer review analysis per user case and per region

Scenario 1: Consumer opinion evolution analysis per service using a sample of dates. The outcome of this scenario is depicted in Fig. 3a. We notice that the review number decreases in the summer, especially between June and August. It can be explained by the fact that the reviewers post reviews about the used cloud services during their works.

Scenario 2: Online review analysis per service based on service properties. The purpose of this scenario is to show the most criticized cloud service properties. To this end, we consider the top seven cloud service properties concepts of the SMI standard [20]. The answers to this scenario are plotted in Fig. 3b. We can notice that agility is the property the most criticized by consumers regarding the AZURE service. It should be noted that agility depends on adaptability, elasticity, portability, etc. It can be measured how quickly new features can be incorporated into an IT infrastructure [19]. The results also show that the financial property, which refers to the price, and the performance are the most criticized properties by the Google service consumers. In brief, we can deduce that when looking for a cloud service, cloud consumers pay more intention to the following properties: cost, security, and performance. Around 90% of the collected reviews contain opinions about the property cost, which shows the importance of this property and prompts cloud providers to fit their price proposal to ensure their competitive advantage. Furthermore, the security exists in about 80% of consumer reviews. Moreover, this property is sought after by cloud consumers. They are concerned about the security of their data outsourced to cloud environments. As for the performance property, it was criticized by about 78% of the collected reviews. This property depends on suitability, interoperability, accuracy, service response time, and functionality.

Scenario 3: Online review analysis per service based on service use case. The objective of this scenario is to identify the most mentioned use cases. In this regard, we can see that most AWS and Google consumers use virtual machines to deploy their web applications. After that, the Database is the second use case used by these consumers, and it is the first use case used by the AZURE consumers.

Scenario 4: Online review analysis per service based on consumer region. This scenario's outcome is plotted in Fig. 4b where we can observe that the AWS consumers are generally located in North America. As for Google's consumers, they are usually distributed in two regions Asia-Pacific and North America. Fig. 4b presents the reviewers' distributions over the regions. From the figure, it is obvious that most of the reviewers write their reviews from North America, especially from the United States. This latter and Europe are the two main regions for Azure's consumers. We also observe the reduced number of Rackspace's consumers compared to other services in all regions. On the other hand, the findings reveal that North American consumers are the most active as they frequently post new reviews on online platforms. Contrariwise, the results show consumers' inaction in the Middle East and Africa regions, which is maybe due to consumer culture in each of these regions.

In conclusion, several kinds of analysis can be established using SOPA for the different cloud actors. Using SOPA, the cloud provider can identify influential parameters on the users' demands and capture their variations. Hence, he/she could enhance service quality to satisfy the users' needs to maintain his/her excellent reputation. The SOPA offers a personalized QoS analysis of cloud services according to his context and requirements for the user side.

5 Conclusion

The integration and the use of many consumers' reviews need a semantic representation as a prerequisite for their unambiguous and precise interpretation and advanced analytical processing. Ontology can be deemed as a lethal weapon by containing detailed definitions of concepts regarding cloud service, social media, user context, and opinion, as well as their properties. For this reason, we proposed a modular ontology named SOPA, which supports context-aware cloud service analysis through consumers' reviews. The SOPA ontology allows the representation of knowledge over social media platforms, the cloud service, and a user context starting from the semantical information extracted from social media. Besides, the model enables a characterization through keywords upon the content from users' context, cloud services, social media, and the users' opinions about cloud services to be represented. Furthermore, the model enables the cloud service analysis through property-based opinions extracted from the review content. The primary benefits of the SOPA are the flexibility of connecting four independent modules such as cloud service, user context, social media, and opinion modules, which can be easily reused or integrated into other ontologies. Moreover, this ontology has the merit to be used for analyzing any type of product/service since the cloud service module is aligned with the reference ontology Product-Service System (PSS).

We plan to use the developed ontology to analyze cloud services based on the QoS requirements and the end-user context to help him select the service that meets his needs.

References

1. Ali, F., et al.: Transportation sentiment analysis using word embedding and ontology-based topic modeling. Knowl.-Based Syst. **174**, 27–42 (2019)
2. Ali, M.M., Doumbouya, M.B., Louge, T., Rai, R., Karray, M.H.: Ontology-based approach to extract product's design features from online customers' reviews. Comput. Ind. **116**, 103175 (2020)
3. Arp, R., Smith, B., Spear, A.D.: Building Ontologies with Basic Formal Ontology. Mit Press, Cambridge (2015)
4. Baccianella, S., Esuli, A., Sebastiani, F.: Sentiwordnet 3.0: an enhanced lexical resource for sentiment analysis and opinion mining. In: Lrec. vol. 10, pp. 2200–2204 (2010)
5. Bojārs, U., Breslin, J.G., Peristeras, V., Tummarello, G., Decker, S.: Interlinking the social web with semantics. IEEE Intell. Syst. **23**(3), 29–40 (2008)
6. Boukadi, K., Rekik, M., Rekik, M., Ben-Abdallah, H.: Fc4cd: a new soa-based focused crawler for cloud service discovery. Computing **100**(10), 1081–1107 (2018)
7. Bouma, G.: Normalized (pointwise) mutual information in collocation extraction. In: Proceedings of GSCL, pp. 31–40 (2009)
8. Breslin, J.G., Decker, S., Harth, A., Bojars, U.: Sioc: an approach to connect web-based communities. Int. J. Web Based Communities **2**(2), 133–142 (2006)
9. Correia, A., Stokic, D., Siafaka, R., Scholze, S.: Ontology for colaborative development of product service systems based on basic formal ontology. In: 2017 International Conference on Engineering, Technology and Innovation (ICE/ITMC), pp. 1173–1180 (June 2017)
10. Dey, A.K.: Understanding and using context. Pers. Ubiquit. Comput. **5**(1), 4–7 (2001)

11. Ding, L., Zhou, L., Finin, T., Joshi, A.: How the semantic web is being used: an analysis of FOAF documents. In: Proceedings of the 38th Annual Hawaii International Conference on System Sciences, p. 113c. IEEE (2005)
12. d'Aquin, M., et al.: Neon formalisms for modularization: syntax, semantics. Technical report, algebra (2008)
13. Gobin, B.A.: An agile methodology for developing ontology modules which can be used to build modular ontologies (2013)
14. Cuenca Grau, B., Parsia, B., Sirin, E.: Ontology Integration Using ε-Connections. In: Stuckenschmidt, H., Parent, C., Spaccapietra, S. (eds.) Modular Ontologies. LNCS, vol. 5445, pp. 293–320. Springer, Heidelberg (2009). https://doi.org/10.1007/978-3-642-01907-4_14
15. Grüninger, M., Fox, M.S.: The role of competency questions in enterprise engineering. In: Rolstadås, A. (ed.) Benchmarking—Theory and Practice. IAICT, pp. 22–31. Springer, Boston, MA (1995). https://doi.org/10.1007/978-0-387-34847-6_3
16. Khan, Z.C.: Applying evaluation criteria to ontology modules (2018)
17. Qu, L., Wang, Y., Orgun, M.A., Liu, L., Bouguettaya, A.: Context-aware cloud service selection based on comparison and aggregation of user subjective assessment and objective performance assessment. In: 2014 IEEE International Conference on Web Services, pp. 81–88 (June 2014)
18. Rekik, M., Boukadi, K., Ben-Abdallah, H.: Cloud description ontology for service discovery and selection. In: 2015 10th International Joint Conference on Software Technologies (ICSOFT), vol. 1, pp. 1–11 (July 2015)
19. Siegel, J., Perdue, J.: Cloud services measures for global use: The service measurement index (smi). In: 2012 Annual SRII Global Conference. pp. 411–415 (July 2012). https://doi.org/10.1109/SRII.2012.51
20. Siegel, J., Perdue, J.: Cloud services measures for global use: the service measurement index (smi). In: SRII Global Conference (SRII), 2012 Annual, pp. 411–415. IEEE (2012)
21. Villanueva, D., González-Carrasco, I., López-Cuadrado, J., Lado, N.: Smore: Towards a semantic modeling for knowledge representation on social media. Sci. Comput. Program. **121**, 16–33 (2016), special Issue on Knowledge-based Software Engineering
22. Wang, X.H., Zhang, D.Q., Gu, T., Pung, H.K.: Ontology based context modeling and reasoning using owl. In: Proceedings of the Second IEEE Annual Conference on Pervasive Computing and Communications Workshops, 2004, pp. 18–22 (March 2004)
23. Xu, D.: Contribution to the elaboration of a decision support system based on modular ontologies for ecological labelling. Ph.D. thesis (2017)
24. Zhuang, L., Schouten, K., Frasincar, F.: Soba: Semi-automated ontology builder for aspect-based sentiment analysis. J. Web Seman. **60**, 100544 (2019)
25. Zimmermann, A.: Integrated distributed description logics. In: Proceedings of 20th International workshop on description logic (DL), pp. 507–514. Bolzano University Press (2007)

Identification of Critical Nodes in Urban Transportation Network Through Network Topology and Server Routes

Shihong Jiang[1], Zheng Luo[1], Ze Yin[1], Zhen Wang[2], Songxin Wang[3], and Chao Gao[1,2](✉)

[1] College of Computer and Information Science, Southwest University, Chongqing 400715, China
cgao@nwpu.edu.cn

[2] School of Artificial Intelligence, Optics, and Electronics (iOPEN), Northwestern Polytechnical University, Xi'an 710072, China

[3] School of Information Management and Engineering, Shanghai University of Finance and Economics, Shanghai 200433, China

Abstract. The identification of critical nodes has great practical significance to the urban transportation network (UTN) due to its contribution to enhancing the efficient operation of UTN. Several existing studies have discovered the critical nodes from the perspectives of network topology or passenger flow. However, little attention has been paid to the perspective of service routes in the identification of critical stations, which reflects the closeness of the connection between stations. In order to address the above problem, we propose a two-layer network of UTN to characterize the effects of server routes and present a novel method of critical nodes identification (BMRank). BMRank is inspired by eigenvector centrality, which focuses on network topology and mutual enhancement relationship between stations and server routes, simultaneously. The extensive experiments on the UTN of Shanghai illustrate that BMRank performs better in the identification of critical stations compared with baseline methods. Specifically, the performance of BMRank increases by 12.4% over the best of baseline methods on a low initial failure scale.

Keywords: Critical nodes · Urban transportation network · Network topology · Server routes

1 Introduction

Urban transportation network (UTN) is an essential part of urban infrastructure, which plays a significant role in public traffic with the advantages of efficiency, safety, environmental protection [3]. However, the stations of urban public transportation are often disrupted by some incidents, such as severe weather, sudden disasters, and terrorist attacks [4]. Besides, the cascading failures on the metro network indicate that the disruption of several critical nodes will seriously reduce

H. Qiu et al. (Eds.): KSEM 2021, LNAI 12815, pp. 395–407, 2021.
https://doi.org/10.1007/978-3-030-82136-4_32

the transmission efficiency of the entire network [6]. Therefore, it is significant to identify the critical nodes of UTN. For example, the reliability and quality of service provided by the UTN can be improved through the formulation of protection strategies for critical nodes. Meanwhile, since the traffic system can be managed in several parts [2], it is necessary to determine the management priority of each part, which can be obtained by the number of critical nodes.

In recent years, the methods of identifying the critical nodes in UTN can be divided into topology-based and passenger flow-based. The topology-based methods tend to abstract UTN into a connected network, in which a node represents a station (i.e., bus station or metro station), and an edge means a road that connects two neighboring stations. In this way, Yang et al. have analyzed critical nodes based on a new weighted composite index [14], founding that the betweenness with a high weigh value is appropriate for Beijing metro network. Wu et al. have introduced NOP measures to evaluate the importance of metro stations [11]. The result shows that the New York metro network has better performance in the topological efficiency when critical nodes are under attack.

The passenger flow-based pay attention to the characteristics of passenger flow based on the collected traffic data and focus on the network topology. For example, Xia et al. have proposed SIRank metrics that reflect the importance of stations from the perspective of passenger flow and network topology [12]. The results indicate that passenger flow makes greater contributions to the identification of the critical nodes in the Shanghai metro network. Du et al. have utilized the ITPE method to measure station importance based on a weighted network, in which the edge weight is estimated according to passenger flow volume in metro lines [3]. In their results, passenger flow has the advantage of effectively identifying critical nodes while network topology methods cannot completely recognize. Jing et al. have measured the critical nodes in the Shanghai metro network by using the route redundancy approach and the passenger flow of each station [8], through which they have found that the transfer stations or high degree stations are not necessarily critical nodes.

Relevant works aforementioned generally do not consider the relationship between stations and routes. However, the case is that many critical stations possibly constitute an important route, and also a critical station is likely on many important routes [13]. Furthermore, the node criticality is related to the number and importance of neighboring nodes. Among them, the neighbors closely connected to the node will have a more significant influence, and the closeness between the nodes can be determined by the number of service routes shared by them. Meanwhile, the existing methods generally regard UTN as a single-layer network. However, The bus and the subway are two primary modes in UTN that play complementary roles in improving urban transportation efficiency [9]. Therefore, this study constructs a UTN as a two-layer network to identify critical nodes, where each layer represents the bus sub-layer and the metro sub-layer, respectively.

Therefore, in order to illustrate the interdependent patterns in the UTN and the closeness of connections between stations, we construct a two-layer network model based on network topology and service routes, where the nodes represent bus or subway stations, and the edge weight denotes the number of service routes between adjacent stations. Then, we propose a new method, namely BMRank, which discovers critical nodes based on both the network topology and server routes. Specifically, BMRank reflects the influence of closely connected neighbor stations through the improved two-layer network. Meanwhile, it captures the mutual enhancement relationship between stations and server routes through a bipartite graph constructed according to the two-layer network. In addition, BMRank also focuses on the transfer relationship of passenger flow between service routes, which contributes to the accuracy of critical node identification. On the whole, the major contributions of this paper are summarized as follows:

- An extended two-layer network model is proposed to describe the interdependent patterns in the UTN and the closeness of connections between stations. The advancement of the proposed network model compared with the existing network model is that the service routes is taken into consideration.
- A new algorithm for identifying the critical nodes called BMRank is proposed, which is based on both the network topology and server routes. Meanwhile, BMRank also takes into account the transfer relationship of passenger flow between service routes.

The rest of this paper is structured as follows. First, Sect. 2 describes the two-layer network and proposes the method of critical node identification. Subsequently, Sect. 3 illustrates the datasets and the comprehensive experiments. Finally, Sect. 4 concludes this paper.

2 Proposed Method

2.1 Constructing the BM Network

The metro system and bus system, as the main components of urban transportation network (UTN), are essential for residents' daily travel. They are not isolated systems but interact with each other through some transfer stations to improve transmission efficiency. Therefore, this paper constructs a two-layer network, called BM network, to characterize such interaction between metro system and bus system based on the transfer nodes. The conceptions of the bus network, metro network, and two-layer network are introduced as follows.

Definition 1: As shown in Fig. 1(a), a bus network is formulated as a weighted graph $G^B = (V^B, E^B, W^B)$. $V^B = \{v_i^B \mid i \in [1, N^B]\}$ is a set of nodes corresponding to bus stations. $E^B = \{e_{ij}^B = (v_i^B, v_j^B) \mid i, j \in [1, N^B], i \neq j\}$ represents a set of edges which connect two neighboring stations on the same server route. $N^B = |V^B|$ denotes the number of bus stations. $W^B = \{w_{ij}^B \mid i, j \in [1, N^B], i \neq j\}$ indicates a set of edge weights, in which $w_{i,j}^B$ is established by the number of server route. For example, $w_{1,2}^B = 2$ because there are two server routes (i.e., Route 1 and Route 2) between station v_1^B and station v_2^B.

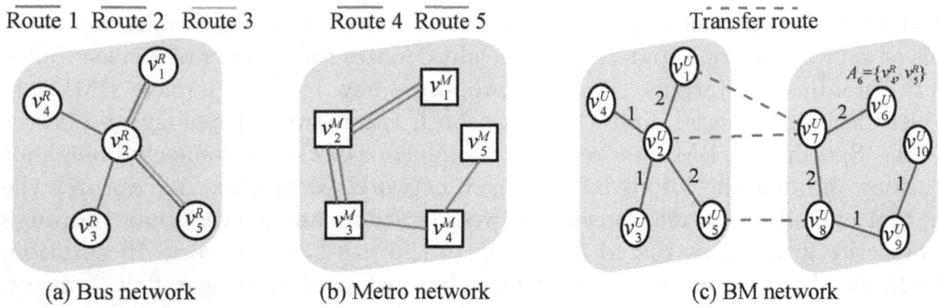

Fig. 1. A schematic illustration of (a) the bus network, (b) the metro network, and (c) the BM network. BM network is a two-layer network constructed by bus network and metro network, in which geographically adjacent bus and metro stations form inter-edges that connect different transportation system, and the node attributes record the server routes through such node. For instance, node attribute of v_6^U is denoted as $A_6 = \{v_4^R, v_5^R\}$, since it is located on route 4 and route 5 in the metro network.

Definition 2: As shown in Fig. 1(b), the metro network is denoted as a weighted graph $G^M = (V^M, E^M, W^M)$, where $V^M = \{v_i^M \mid i \in [1, N^M]\}$, $E^M = \{e_{ij}^M = (v_i^M, v_j^M) \mid i, j \in [1, N^M], i \neq j\}$ and $W^M = \{w_{ij}^M \mid i, j \in [1, N^M], i \neq j\}$ refer to a set of nodes, edges, and edge weights, respectively. $N^M = |V^M|$ denotes the number of metro stations.

Definition 3: As shown in Fig. 1(c), the two-layer network can be described as $G^U = (V^U, E^U, W^U)$, where $V^U = \{V^B, V^M\} = \{v_i^U \mid i \in [1, N^B + N^M]\}$ is a set of node, and $E^U = \{E^B, E^M, E^I\} = \{e_{ij}^U = (v_i^U, v_j^U) \mid i, j \in [1, N^B + N^M], i \neq j\}$ represents a set of edges. Specifically, $E^I = \{e_{ij}^I = (v_i^B, v_j^M)\}$ refers to a set of inter-edges. For instance, there exists an edge $e_{1,2}^U$ between bus station v_1^B and metro station v_2^M, since v_1^B and v_2^M each other as transfer stations. $W^U = \{W^B, W^M, W^I\} = \{w_{ij}^U \mid i, j \in [1, N^B + N^M], i \neq j\}$ is a set of edge weights, in which $W^I = \{w_{ij}^I\}$ denotes the weight of inter-edges. Besides, the node attributes is defined by $\{A_i \mid i \in [1, N^B + N^M]\}$, where A_i is a set that contains the routes passing through v_i^U. Figure 1(c) depicts $A_6 = \{v_4^R, v_5^R\}$ since station v_6^U is traversed by route 4 and route 5.

2.2 Proposed BMRank Method

This paper proposes the BMRank method based on the HITS algorithm [5] to improve the accuracy for the identification of critical nodes in UTN. The main idea is inspired by two factors. For one thing, the neighbors that are closely connected to a node have a greater influence on the criticality of this node. For another, there exists a mutual enhancement relationship between stations and server routes. A instance is presented in Fig. 2(a), the node v_4^U has a more significant influence on the importance of node v_5^U than node v_6^U, since node

v_4^U is connected to node v_5^U more closely. In addition, a critical station would have many important routes through it, and an important route would traverse many critical stations as well [13]. The BMRank is proposed based on network topology and server routes according to the above revelations. Specifically, the server routes are utilized to describe the closely connected relationship between nodes and mutual enhancement relationship between stations and server routes. Besides, The BMRank also considers the transfer relationship of passenger flow between service routes. According to the above analysis, the BMRank improves the performance of identifying critical nodes because it combines network topology, server routes, and passenger flow to obtain critical nodes. The process of BMRank is as follows.

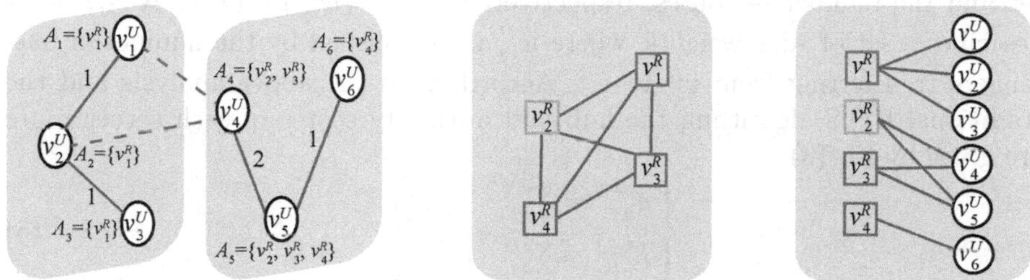

(a) BM network (b) Route network (c) Bipartite graph

Fig. 2. (a) The BM network. (b) The route network, where the squares represent the server routes, between which the edge represents the transfer relationship of passenger flow. And (c) the bipartite graph, where the square and circle represents server route and station, respectively. The edge (r_1, u_1) connected station u_1 and server route r_1, since station u_1 is located on server route r_1.

Firstly, BMRank identifies critical nodes based on their neighbors, among which the closely connected nodes have more significant influence. As shown in Fig. 2(a), BM network captures the connections between nodes which represent metro station and bus station respectively. Similar to the HITS algorithm, the node importance is determined by BMRank through an iterative calculation. Besides, BMRank also considers the edge weight defined by the number of server routes between stations, which describes the closeness of the connections between nodes. Thus, the hub and authority scores of each node are given by Eq. (1).

$$\begin{cases} a_{v_i^U}^{t+1} = \sum_j^{N^B+N^M} w_{ij}^U h_{v_j^U}^t \\ h_{v_i^U}^{t+1} = \sum_j^{N^B+N^M} w_{ij}^U a_{v_j^U}^{t+1} \end{cases} \quad (1)$$

where $a_{v_i^U}^{t+1}$ and $h_{v_i^U}^{t+1}$ denote the authority score and the hub score of node v_i^U at time step $t+1$, respectively. The initial values of both $a_{v_i^U}^{t+1}$ and $h_{v_i^U}^{t+1}$ are equal to 1. When the iteration terminates at time step t, the importance of node v_i^U calculated by the influence of neighbors as shown in Eq. (2).

$$NI(v_i^U) = a_{v_i^U}^t + h_{v_i^U}^t \tag{2}$$

Next, the importance of the server route is an essential auxiliary information in BMRank, which can be applied in the mutually reinforcing relationship between station and server route to improve the accuracy of BMRank. Thus, in order to calculate the importance of server routes, we construct a route network according to the node attributes of BM network and passenger transfer behavior. As shown in Fig. 2(b), the node of route network corresponds to a server route of UTN and the edge records the behavior of passengers transferring from one line to another. Therefore, the route network is formulated as a weighted graph $G^R = (V^R, E^R, W^R)$. $V^R = \{v_i^R \mid i \in [1, N^R]\}$, $E^R = \{e_{ij}^R = (v_i^R, v_j^R) \mid i, j \in [1, N^R], i \neq j\}$ and $N^R = |V^R|$ denote the node set, edge set and the number of routes, respectively. $W^R = \{w_{ij}^R \mid i, j \in [1, N^R], i \neq j\}$ describes a set of edge weights, where w_{ij}^R is established by the number of passengers transferring from v_i^R to v_j^R. According to the above analysis and the traditional HITS algorithm, the hub and authority scores of each server route are given by Eq. (3).

$$\begin{cases} a_{v_i^R}^{t+1} = \sum_j^{N^R} w_{ij}^R h_{v_j^R}^t \\ h_{v_i^R}^{t+1} = \sum_j^{N^R} w_{ij}^R a_{v_j^R}^{t+1} \end{cases} \tag{3}$$

where $a_{v_i^R}^t$ and $h_{v_i^R}^t$ are authority scores and hub scores of node v_i^R at time step t, respectively. The initial values of both $a_{v_i^R}^t$ and $h_{v_i^R}^t$ are equal to 1. When the iteration process is terminated, the importance of server route v_i^R determined by passenger flow is expressed as the sum of $a_{v_i^R}^t$ and $h_{v_i^R}^t$ based on Eq. (4)

$$RI(v_i^R) = a_{v_i^R}^t + h_{v_i^R}^t \tag{4}$$

Then, the mutually reinforcing relationship between server routes and stations is utilized by BMRank to discover critical nodes. Mutually reinforcing relationship refers to a critical station will have many important server routes through it, and an important server route will traverse many critical stations [13]. To accurately capture the mutually reinforcing relationship, we introduce the bipartite graph to formulate BM network in which one kind of nodes represents station, namely station nodes, while the other type of nodes means server route, namely route nodes. If a server route traverses a station, there would be an edge between the corresponding route node and station node in the bipartite graph. As shown in Fig. 2(c), the bipartite graphs of BM network is formulated as $G^{UR} = (V^U \cup V^R, E^{UR}, W^{UR})$, where $E^{UR} = \{e_{ij}^{UR} = (v_i^U, v_j^R) \mid i \in [1, N^B + N^M], j \in [1, N^R]\}$ represents edge set. $W^{UR} = \{w_{ij}^{UR} \mid i \in [1, N^B + N^M], j \in [1, N^R]\}$ refers to a set of edge weights, where $w_{ij}^{UR} = 1$ indicates that there is an edge e_{ij}^{UR}, otherwise $w_{ij}^{UR} = 0$. According to the bipartite graph, the mutually reinforcing relationships between server routes and stations are

$$\begin{cases} I_{v_i^U}^{t+1} = \sum_j^{N^R} w_{ij}^{UR} I_{v_j^R}^t \\ I_{v_i^R}^{t+1} = \sum_j^{N^N+N^B} w_{ij}^{UR} I_{v_j^U}^{t+1} \end{cases} \tag{5}$$

where $I_{v_i^U}^t$ and $I_{v_i^R}^t$ represent the importance of station nodes and route nodes at time step t, respectively. The initial values of $I_{v_i^U}^t$ and $I_{v_i^R}^t$ are equal to 1.

Finally, BMRank integrates the neighbor's influence and the route importance as the prior information into Eq. (5). The combined method has the advantage of using the prior information to guide the calculated process [7] from the perspective of network topology and server route. According to the above analysis, the node importance can be acquired by Eq. (6).

$$\begin{cases} I_{v_i^U}^{t+1} = (1-\beta)NI(v_i^U) + \beta \sum_j^{N^R} w_{ij}^{UR} I_{v_j^R}^t \\ I_{v_i^R}^{t+1} = (1-\alpha)RI(v_i^R) + \alpha \sum_j^{N^M+N^B} w_{ij}^{UR} I_{v_j^U}^{t+1} \end{cases} \tag{6}$$

where β and $\alpha \in [0, 1]$ are hyper-parameters which balance the roles of the prior information and the mutually reinforcing relationship. When the iteration calculation terminates at time step t, the importance of node v_i^U is defined as Eq. (7)

$$I(v_i^U) - I_{v_i^U}^t. \tag{7}$$

In addition, based on the node importance, we redefine the server route importance as the sum of the importance of the stations on the server route, which is calculated as Eq. (8)

$$SRI(v_j^R) = \sum_i^{N^B+N^M} w_{ij}^{UR} I\left(v_i^U\right) \tag{8}$$

where a high value of $SRI(v_j^R)$ indicates a strong importance of route v_j^R.

3 Experimental Analysis

3.1 Dataset

We evaluate the proposed method by Shanghai's UTN, including the metro system, the bus system, and the smart card data. The details of three datasets are elaborated below.

Dataset 1 (Metro system): The data set is collected from the Shanghai Metro[1] in April 2015. The dataset records 209 stations and 12 server routes of the Shanghai Metro in detail.

[1] http://service.shmetro.com/.

Dataset 2 (Bus system): By API services provided by Amap[2], we collected 2933 stations and 386 server routes of the bus system in downtown areas in Shanghai.

Dataset 3 (Smart card data): The smart card data in this paper is provided by the organizing committee of Shanghai Open Data Apps[3]. More specifically, these data contain 123 million trip records during April 2015.

3.2 Evaluation Metrics

According to the complex network, the removal of critical nodes will result in a substantial decline in the structure and function of a network [3]. Therefore, this paper verifies the performance of the proposed algorithm by estimating the robustness of a network under the node attack and route attack. Specifically, we evaluate network robustness through the total number of failed nodes [6], the relative size of the giant component [9] and the global efficiency [9].

Definition 4: The cumulative number of failed nodes ($F(t)$) describes the change in the number of failed nodes over time step, which is defined as $F(t) = \sum_{i=1}^{N} s_i^t$. where $s_i^t = 1$ indicates that the node i failed at or before the time step t, otherwise $s_i^t = 0$. N represents the size of network.

Definition 5: The relative size of the giant component (S) reflects the ratio of the network scale before and after the node disrupt, which is calculated by $S = \frac{N'}{N}$, where N' denotes the scale of the giant component after some nodes are removed. N represents the size of initial network.

Definition 6: The global efficiency (E) refers to the connected closeness among nodes in a network, which is defined as $E = \frac{2}{N(N-1)} \sum_{i<j \in N} \frac{1}{d_{ij}}$, where d_{ij} denotes the shortest distance between node i and node j in a network.

3.3 Parameter Setting

BMRank includes two hyper-parameters β and α, which are used to balance the effects of the prior information and the mutually reinforcing relationship. According to the detailed analysis of parameters which is shown in Sect. 3.5, we set $\beta = 0.1$ and $\alpha = 0.2$ to obtain the best experimental performance.

In order to evaluate the performance of the BMRank method in identifying key nodes, we compare our method with five baseline methods, which are classic or available approaches that recently published (i.e., LC [1], CC [10], HITS [5], GIN [16], ECRM [15]). The parameters of these baseline approaches are set according to the source paper.

---

[2] https://lbs.amap.com/.

[3] http://data.sh.gov.cn/.

3.4 Experimental Results

This paper conducts robustness experiments based on the route attack to verify the effectiveness of the proposed method. In the traditional robustness experiments, some nodes are removed to simulate the station disruption. Nevertheless, on account of the higher occurrence of line interruptions in UTN, we remove nodes belonging to the same route when performing robustness experiments in this work. More specifically, routes are first sorted from large to small according to Eq. (8), which is constructed based on the node importance identification method. And then, the nodes belonging to the top k routes are removed. Finally, the relative size of the giant component S and the global efficiency E are used to evaluate the robustness of networks. The smaller the values of E and S, the better the performance of the corresponding node importance identification method.

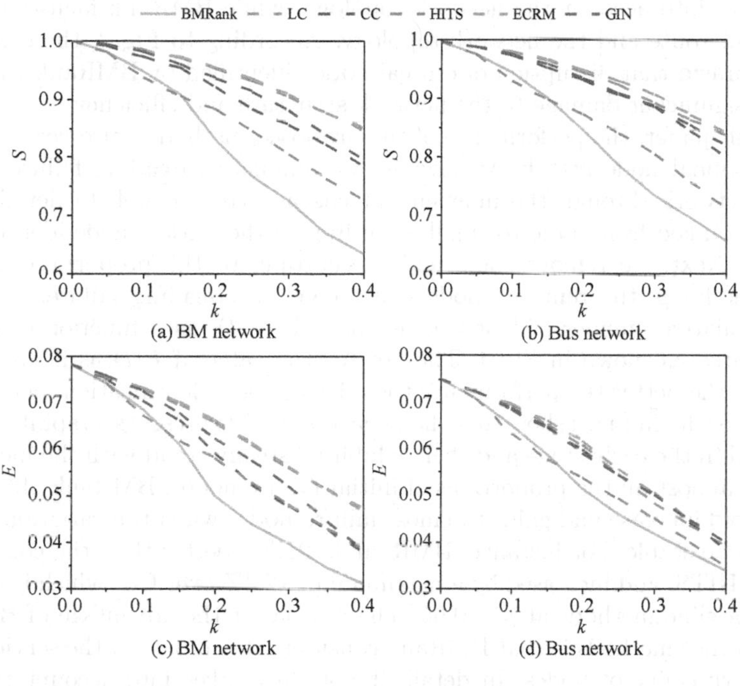

Fig. 3. Comparison of the average network efficiency E and the relative size of giant component S of top-k server routes ranked by different methods on BM network and bus network. These results indicate that BMRank presents a more obvious declining trend because it takes into account the role of the server route.

As shown in Fig. 3, the robustness experiments are implemented by comparing BMRank with baselines on the BM network and the bus network respectively. The result indicates that as the value of k increases, the values of E and S descend in a clear trend. In particular, BMRank has achieved better performance than the baseline methods in terms of both E and S, especially on the BM network. Since only the local structure of a network is considered, the value of E and S about classic algorithm LC shows the larger. CC and GIN based on the global network structure overcome the disadvantage of LC. Although their performance has improved, they are inferior compared with BMRank. Since BMRank takes the role of server route into consideration when identifying critical nodes, the performance of BMRank on the BM network for E and S is improved by 34.0% and 28.6% at $k = 0.4$, respectively, compared to ECRM. Although BMRank is proposed based on HITS, it is clear that with the increase of k, BMRank gradually obtains better results. On the bus network, the performance of BMRank increased by 7.7% over HITS in terms of S at $k = 0.4$. The reason is that HITS only takes into account the network topology, while BMRank focuses on both the server route and the network topology. According to Fig. 3, the conclusion can be drawn that disruption of critical nodes identified by BMRank will cause a more significant damage to the network structure and efficiency.

In this paper, the performance of the proposed method is also verified based on traditional node attack. Meanwhile, we simulate cascading failure process in the network through the independent cascade (IC) model. In detail, nodes are first ranked from large to small according to the critical node identification method. Next, we remove some nodes according to the proportion of initial failure nodes p, the removed node will trigger a cascading failure. And then the cumulative number of failed nodes, namely $F(t)$, as a function of time, is investigated as shown in Fig. 4. The greater the value of $F(t)$ as it approaches stability, the better the performance the critical node identification method has.

The results in Fig. 4 show that the variation in $F(t)$ presents a rapidly increasing trend in the early stage and then exhibits a steady trend with the increase of time. In almost all the proportions of initial failure nodes, BMRank obtains the most rapid increase and gains the most failure nodes when the variation in $F(t)$ tends to be stable. For instance, BMRank is 21.9% better than the comparison method HITS, and increased by a maximum of 12.4% over CC, which is the best of the baseline methods at $p = 0.05$. The reason for the advantage of BMRank over all other methods is that BMRank considers the impact of the service route on the criticality of nodes. In detail, it not only takes into account the edge weight calculated by the number of server routes but also pays attention to the transfer relationship of passenger flow between the service routes.

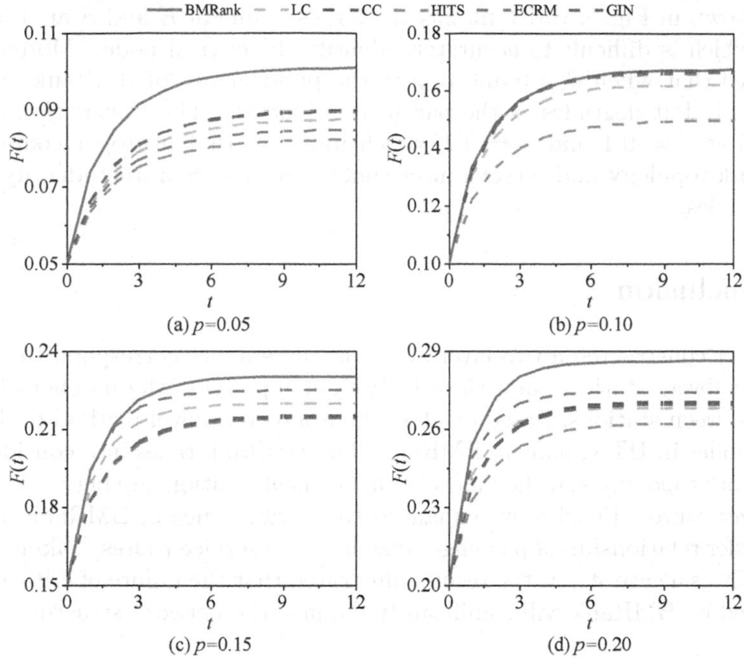

Fig. 4. The cumulative number of failed nodes $F(t)$ corresponding to various methods in the different proportions of initial failure nodes p. Since BMRank focuses on both the server route and the network topology, the cumulative number of failed nodes corresponding to BMRank has the fastest growth, leading to more failed nodes.

3.5 Parameter Analysis

In the section, we conduct some robustness experiments to analyze the effect of parameters β and α on BMRank. The results are shown in Fig. 5.

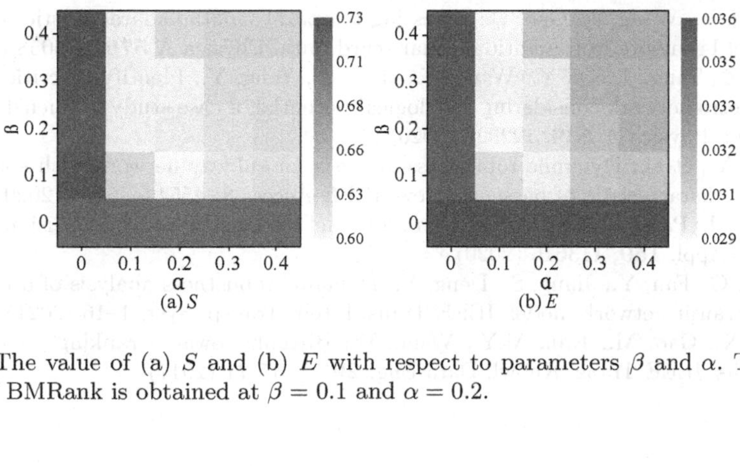

Fig. 5. The value of (a) S and (b) E with respect to parameters β and α. The best result of BMRank is obtained at $\beta = 0.1$ and $\alpha = 0.2$.

As shown in Fig. 5, BMRank has the largest value of E and S at $\beta = 0$ and $\alpha = 0$, which is difficult to accurately identify the critical nodes. Moreover, we discovered that when $\beta \neq 0$ and $\alpha \neq 0$, the performance of BMRank improves significantly but degrades as the parameters increase. The best performance is obtained at $\beta = 0.1$ and $\alpha = 0.2$, which indicates that a proper combination of network topology and server routes contributes to accurately identifying the critical nodes.

4 Conclusion

This paper constructed a two-layer network where nodes correspond to bus stations or subway stations, and the edge weight represents the number of server routes between stations. Based on this, we proposed a novel method to discover critical nodes in UTN, namely BMRank. The BMRank takes into consideration the network topology and the mutual enhancement relationship between stations and server routes. Besides, we enhanced the performance of BMRank utilizing the transfer relationship of passenger flow between service routes. Taking Shanghai's UTN as a case study, the results illustrated that the failure of critical nodes discovered by BMRank will significantly damage the network structure.

Acknowledgement. This work was supported by the National Key R&D Program of China (Grant No. 2019YFB2102300), National Natural Science Foundation of China (Nos. 61976181, 11931015, 61762020), Key Technology Research and Development Program of Science and Technology Scientific and Technological Innovation Team of Shaanxi Province (No. 2020TD-013), the Science and Technology Foundation of Guizhou (No. QKHJC20181083) and the Science and Technology Support Program of Guizhou (No. QKHZC2021YB531).

References

1. Chen, D., Lü, L., Shang, M.S., Zhang, Y.C., Zhou, T.: Identifying influential nodes in complex networks. Physica A **391**(4), 1777–1787 (2012)
2. Deng, Y., Wang, J., Gao, C.: Assessing temporal−spatial characteristics of urban travel behaviors from multiday smart-card data. Physica A **576**, 126058 (2021)
3. Du, Z., Tang, J., Qi, Y., Wang, Y., Han, C., Yang, Y.: Identifying critical nodes in metro network considering topological potential: a case study in Shenzhen city–China. Physica A **539**, 122926 (2020)
4. Fan, Y., et al.: Dynamic robustness analysis for subway network with spatiotemporal characteristic of passenger flow. IEEE Access **8**, 45544–45555 (2020)
5. Fang, J., Partovi, F.Y.: A HITS-based model for facility location decision. Expert Syst. Appl. **159**, 113616 (2020)
6. Gao, C., Fan, Y., Jiang, S., Deng, Y.: Dynamic robustness analysis of a two-layer rail transit network model. IEEE Trans. Intell. Transp. Syst. 1–16 (2021)
7. He, X., Gao, M., Kan, M.Y., Wang, D.: BiRank: towards ranking on bipartite graphs. IEEE Trans. Knowl. Data Eng. **29**(1), 57–71 (2017)

8. Jing, W., Xu, X., Pu, Y.: Route redundancy-based approach to identify the critical stations in metro networks: a mean-excess probability measure. Reliab. Eng. Syst. Saf. **204**, 107204 (2020)
9. Li, X., Guo, J., Gao, C., Su, Z.: Network-based transportation system analysis: a case study in a mountain city. Chaos Solitons Fractals **107**, 256–265 (2018)
10. Sabidussi, G.: The centrality index of a graph. Psychometrika **31**(4), 581–603 (1966)
11. Wu, X., Dong, H., Tse, C.K., Ho, I.W., Lau, F.C.: Analysis of metro network performance from a complex network perspective. Physica A **492**, 553–563 (2018)
12. Xia, F., Wang, J., Kong, X., Zhang, D., Wang, Z.: Ranking station importance with human mobility patterns using subway network datasets. IEEE Trans. Intell. Transp. Syst. **21**(7), 2840–2852 (2020)
13. Xu, M., Wu, J.: Discovery of critical nodes in road networks through mining from vehicle trajectories. IEEE Trans. Intell. Transp. Syst. **20**(2), 583–593 (2019)
14. Yang, Y., Liu, Y.: Robustness assessment of urban rail transit based on complex network theory: a case study of the Beijing subway. Saf. Sci. **79**, 149–162 (2015)
15. Zareie, A., Sheikhahmadi, A.: Finding influential nodes in social networks based on neighborhood correlation coefficient. Knowl. Based Syst. **194**, 105580 (2020)
16. Zhao, J., Wang, Y., Deng, Y.: Identifying influential nodes in complex networks from global perspective. Chaos Solitons Fractals **133**, 109637 (2020)

Graph Ensemble Networks for Semi-supervised Embedding Learning

Hui Tang, Xun Liang(✉), Bo Wu, Zhenyu Guan, Yuhui Guo, and Xiangping Zheng

School of information, Renmin University, Beijing, China
{huitang,xliang,wubochn,zhenyu_guan,yhguo,xpzheng}@ruc.edu.cn

Abstract. Recently, semi-supervised graph learning has attracted growing research interests. Since the Graph Convolutional Network (GCN) was formulated, some studies argue that shallow architectures fall through over-fitting and have limited ability to aggregate information from high-order neighbors. However, although deep GCNs have powerful nonlinear fitting ability, problems such as over-smoothing still exist with the expansion of layer depth. In this paper, we explore such an ignored question that whether a shallow GCN can achieve significant improvement over deep GCNs. Motivated by this curiosity, we propose an effective graph learning framework—Graph Ensemble Network (GENet) for semi-supervised learning tasks. We combine ensemble learning with data augmentation, which samples multi-subgraphs by randomly removing some edges to generate different topology spaces, and knowledge distillation is introduced to make the multi-subnetworks learn collaboratively. The central idea is that employ attention mechanism and consistency constraint to learn adaptive importance weights of the embeddings from the ensemble model, and then transfer learned knowledge to a shallow GCN. Extensive experiments on graph node classification verify the superiority of the proposed GENet compared with the state-of-the-art methods.

Keywords: Graph Convolutional Network · Semi-supervised learing · Data augmentation · Ensemble learning · Attention mechanism · Knowledge distillation

1 Introduction

Graph neural network is a very promising research field, which is widely used in image recognition [25], social network [23], recommendation system [6], etc. Graph Convolution Network (GCN) [16], as an important branch of graph neural network, is inspired by Convolutional Neural Network (CNN) to extract high-level features from high-order neighbors of nodes with message passing and aggregation strategies [8]. According to the number of GCN layers, it can be divided into two categories: shallow and deep. Generally, less than three layers is

H. Qiu et al. (Eds.): KSEM 2021, LNAI 12815, pp. 408–420, 2021.
https://doi.org/10.1007/978-3-030-82136-4_33

considered as a shallow network. We review the vanilla GCN [13], which has two layers and is difficult to generate powerful representation embedding alone for complex graph-structured data owing to limited layers. Inspired by deep CNNs, some researches tried to design deep GCNs. As we all know, the more layers of a deep learning model, the better its performance. However, this rule does not seem to be suitable for graph data. When the number of layers is beyond three, GCNs fall down two misfortunes: over-fitting [16] and over-smoothing [15]. Over-fitting is a common deep learning problem, which is that the trained model performs well in the training set but poor in the test set. Especially in semi-supervised learning, there are only a few labeled training data compared to full-supervised and the problem is more noteworthy. Another problem is over-smoothing, which is a peculiar defect of deep GCNs when tacking directly many layers results in losing each node's own characteristics and finally generate the indistinguishable embeddings for all nodes.

Nowadays, many researchers have noticed these obstacles and put forward some solutions, such as skipping connection strategy. Skipping connection with residual mapping, is effective for training deep neural networks. Jknet [21] connected each hidden layer closely with the last layer, so the high-level layers still have sufficient low-level features to learn representations of different high-order nodes. Unfortunately, adding skipping connections in deep GCNs merely slows down the over-smoothing but not eliminated. Shallow models are very sensitive to noise data and have limited ability to perform well in the face of complex data. In machine learning, It has been shown that ensemble of classifiers are more accurate than any of its individual members. Due to stacking multiple layers of GCN, the last layer outputs indistinguishable embedding, which the effect is inferior to a shallow GCN. The weakness of deep GCNs is identified, a natural question is, "Can we shy away the weakness and utilize a new type of shallow GCN that attains the advantages of the state-of-the-art GCNs?" Inspired by the above, we combine ensemble learning with removing some edges randomly. On the one hand, we leverage the ensemble learning to improve the robustness and generalization ability of multiple shallow GCNs. On the one hand, in order to capture different properties we use randomly drop some edges to construct subgraphs of different topological spaces.

In short, the main contributions of our paper can be summarized as follows: (i) We construct the Graph Ensemble Convolutional Networks (GENet) framework, which links ensemble learning with dropedge mechanism. By dropping out a certain rate of edges randomly, the multi-subgraphs includes more diversity into the input data to prevent over-fitting. Each member in ensemble model generate individual embedding from different topology spaces and have powerful capacity to resist against noise perturbations in graph data. (ii) Combined with knowledge distilation and attention mechanism, multi-GCNs in the ensemble model (teacher) are able to learn each other instead of alone by knowledge distilation, and attention mechanism can adequately transfer embeddings generated by the teacher model into a shallow GCN (student). Finally, with the help of consistency constraint the student model has the same or superior to the teacher model, which proves that a shallow GCN also has marvelous performance on graph data. (iii) Extensive experiments are performed and the results demonstrated that GENet model achieves state-of-the-art performance across six publicly available nodes classification benchmarks.

2 Related Work

Graph convolution networks was first presented by [3] and have prominent improvements based on spectral graph theory. A vanilla GCN has two layers and directly performs convolution operation on graph-structured data by aggregating information from high-order neighbors of nodes. The formula is defined as

$$H^{(l+1)} = \sigma(AH^{(l)}W^{(l)}) \tag{1}$$

A denotes the adjacency matrix of G, H^l and H^{l+1} represent the embedding vectors of the l and $l+1$ layers, respectively. W is the weight matrix that needs to be learned for each layer. σ is a nonlinear activation function, such that Sigmoid, ReLU. However, shallow GCNs are lack of extracting high-order nodes information because of limited non-linear fitting ability. Some researchers argue that the performance of model can be enhanced by expanding layers of GCN. Klicpera et al. [14] proposed Personalized PageRank strategy to derive a fixed filter of order, which preserved locality and thus was suitable for classification tasks by generalizing an arbitrary graph diffusion process. Inspired by the residual mechanism, GCNII [5] expanded the vanilla GCN to 64 layers with initial residual and identity mapping. Though the experimental results had made some progress, a lot of computational overhead were required.

Some works are devoted to improving the performance of shallow models. GAT [20] used two layers with attention mechanism to allow for assigning different importances to different nodes and do not depend on knowing the entire graph structure upfront. Mixhop [1] showed that the vanilla GCN cannot learn general neighborhood mixing functions and proposed a mixhop model to learn a general class of neighborhood relationships. Although over-fitting is eliminated in shallow GCNs, how to prevent over-fitting and improve the robustness of shallow networks has not been well solved. Several sampling-based methods have been proposed for improving graph representation learning, including the node-wise sampling methods and the edge-wise methods. Grand model [7] proposed to randomly remove some nodes features with a binary mask as removal probability. Rong et al. [17] put forward to randomly drop out a certain rate of edges from A and sampled a new subgraph $G^{'}$.

Ensemble Learning has shown considerable improvements in model generalization and produces excellent results compared with a single model. Super Learner [12] and Stochastic Depth [11] generally create exponent numbers with shared weights during training and then average them to explicitly select reliable prediction at test time. Similar to [19], which trained an ensemble of 16 CNN models and compressed the learned function into shallow multi-layer perceptrons containing 5 layers. But the subnetworks are very complex, which is not feasible for SSGL task, and the subnetworks were trained independently and cannot learn from each other. Knowledge Distillation (KD) aims at learning a light-weight student network such that it can mimic the behavior of a complicated teacher network. [2] was the first to introduce knowledge distillation by minimizing L2 distance between the features from the last layers of two networks. Recently, [24] proposed a simple and universal method to improve the performance of deep neural network by queue training with peers and mutual distillation.

3 The Proposed Method

In this section, we introduce the details about building the GENet model. The architecture can be seen in Fig. 1.

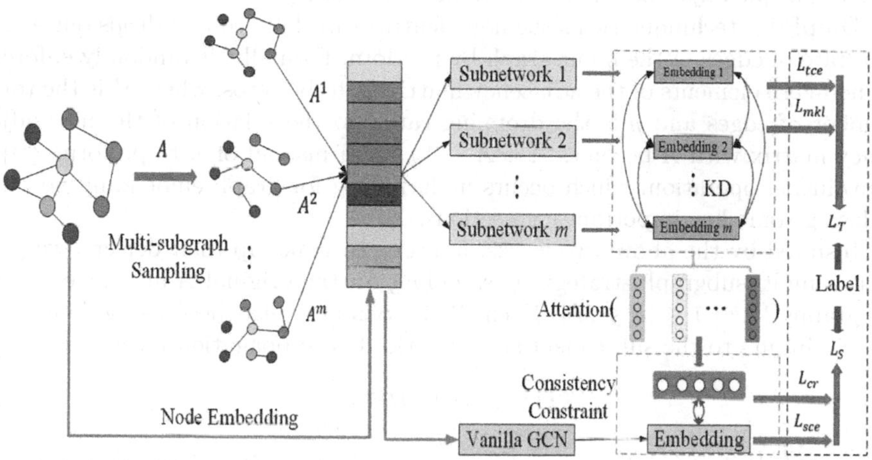

Fig. 1. Overview of GENet framework. We input multiple subgraphs sampled by deleting randomly some connections. For the ensemble model, each subnetwork is trained collaboratively to obtain knowledge provided by peer networks. GENet employs attention mechanism dynamically to transfer optimal embeddings to the vanilla GCN.

3.1 Multi-subgraph Sampling

Data augmentation is a general paradigm to prevent overfitting and upgrade robustness. Augmentation needs to satisfy a hypothesis that ensures the sampled data distribution is basically consistent with the original data. However, from the perspective of Eq. 1, A determines the topology structure of G and H contains the all feature information for nodes. We can either utilize A or H to enlarge data samples: (1) apply a transformation $f : A \rightarrow A_m$ such that A_m replaces A for both training and inference, or (2) apply many transformations $f_i : X \rightarrow$

X_i for $i = 1...N$ to build multiple feature input spaces, such that $\{X_i\}_1^N$ are used in training, but only X is used as input for inference. We call (1) the dropedge setting, and (2) the DropNode setting. One might ask: which strategy is preferable?

The strategy of DropNode keeps the graph topology structure unchanged and use a binary mask $\zeta_i \sim Bernoulli(1\text{-}\delta)$ randomly samples a new node feature matrix. After dropnode, the perturbed feature matrix $\tilde{X}$ is fed into the propagation layer to perform message passing. So predict class distribution is

$$\bar{Z} = \frac{1}{N+1}\sum_{i=1}^{N} P(Y|\tilde{X}^i;\theta) \tag{2}$$

where $\tilde{X}^i = \frac{1}{K+1}\sum_{j=1}^{K} A^j X^i, X^i = \zeta_i X$. However, DropNode coupled the propagation from feature transformation and increase much computational overhead when multiple adjacency matrices are directly multiplied.

DropEdge technique keeps the node features unchanged and drops out a certain rate of edges of the input graph by random. Formally, it randomly enforces V_p non-zero elements of the adjacency matrix A to be zeros, where V is the total number of edges and p is the dropping rate. So the relation of the new adjacency matrix with A becomes $\hat{A} = A - A_{drop}$, $\hat{A}$ instead of A to perform graph convolution operation, which occurs underfitting for graph embedding because of losing some key important connections.

Inspired by the above two works, in order to make up their defects, we propose a multi-subgraph strategy by sampling on the original A and generate M subgraphs $\{\hat{A^m}|\ 1 \le m \le M\}$. Each $\hat{A^m}$ associated with the same node feature matrix inputs to the subsequent subnetwork. The propagation formula is

$$H_m^{(l+1)} = \sigma(\hat{A^m} H_m^{(l)} W^{(l)}) \tag{3}$$

where $H_m^{(l+1)}$ denotes the feature representation of the $(l+1)$ layers on the mth sampled A^m. $Z = \{P(Y|X, A^m;\Theta), 1 \le m \le M\}$ denotes the prediction output of M different models, where $Z \in R^{M\times N\times C}$, so we can obtain more accurate and effective prediction results to increase the robustness of the ensemble model.

3.2 Objective Function

GENet mainly includes two parts: (i) The ensemble model consists of multiple subnetworks jointly learning. (ii) The vanilla GCN distills the knowledge produced by all subnetworks. T and S represent the ensemble model and the vanilla GCN respectively. In order to make the two models perform better, we introduce 3 loss functions: (1) the cross-entropy loss, (2) the distillation loss, and (3) the consistency regularization loss.

For semi-supervised nodes classification setting, the cross entropy is a commonly used loss function to measure the difference between two probability distributions of truth labels and prediction. Suppose the training set is I, for each node $i \in I$ the real label is Y_i and the prediction label is $\hat{Y}_i$. The teacher model has multi-subnetworks and its cross entropy loss is defined as:

$$L_{tce} = -\sum_{m}^{M}\sum_{i \in I} Y_{mi} log(softmax(Z_{mi})) \quad (4)$$

Similarly, denote the output embedding of the student model as Z_s and its cross entropy loss as follows:

$$L_{sce} = -\sum_{i \in I} Y_i log(softmax(Z_s)) \quad (5)$$

For the ensemble model, we use multiple models jointly for the same task but in different domains by sampling different topology spaces. Except using binary cross entropy L_{ce} to monitor prediction and true label, we hope that each subnetwork also obtains training experience provided by another peer networks. We exploit the Kullback Leibler (KL) divergence to match the probability estimate of its peers and learn collaboratively throughout the training process. The KL distance loss of mutual learning between subnetworks is computed as:

$$L_{mkl} = \sum_{i=1}^{m}\sum_{j=1, j \neq i}^{m} Z_j * (log(softmax(Z_j)) - log(softmax(Z_i))) \quad (6)$$

We employ the attention mechanism to adaptively select the most relevant embedding components from different subnetworks of the teacher model. Review our goal, let the lightweight student model perform the same or exceed the teacher model. For the output embeddings $\hat{Z}$ and Z_s of the teacher model and the student, despite the two models have different performance discrepancy, here we design a consistency constraint to further enhance their commonality. Firstly, we employ L_2-normalization to scale the two embeddings as $\hat{Z}_{tnor}$ and Z_{snor}, and then the two normalized matrix can be used to capture the similarity of n nodes by multiplying their own transposed matrices. The consistency implies that the two matrice distributions should be similar, which gives rise to the following regularization:

$$L_{cr} = ||\hat{Z}_{tnor}\hat{Z}_{tnor}^T - Z_{snor}Z_{snor}^T||_2 \quad (7)$$

As mentioned above, we have three constraints for our GENet model to produce better performance. Combining the node classification task and constraints, we have the following overall objective functions for the teacher and student models:

$$L_T = L_{tce} + \alpha L_{mkl} \quad (8)$$

$$L_S = L_{sce} + \beta L_{cr} \quad (9)$$

where α and β are parameters of the joint distillation and consistency constraint terms. The L_{cr} is utilized to transfer the knowledge learned by the teacher model to the student model. Both two losses are optimized simultaneously and iteratively to learn the embedding of nodes for classification through end-to-end training.

4 Experimental Analysis

In this section, we evaluate the performance of GENet against the state-of-the-art graph models on six open graph datasets, which proves that our model has excellent performance in semi-supervised nodes classification task.

4.1 Datasets

We conduct experiments on three standard citation network benchmark datasets: Cora, Cite seer and Pubmed [18]. For citation network graphs, nodes and edges represent documents and citation relationships (undirected) respectively. Node features correspond to elements of a bag-of-words representation of a document. We use exactly the same settings of features and data splits on the three benchmark datasets as literature on semi-supervised graph learning [22]. Similarly, in order to inspect that whether our model still performs well on large-scale datasets, we also verify the curiosity on three larger and more complex datasets: social networks (BlogCatalog, Flickr) and protein-protein interactions (PPI), we follow the semi-supervised setting in [9] for train/validation/test splitting. Summary statistics for each dataset are shown in Table 1.

Table 1. Summary of the benchmark datasets statistics

Attributes	Cora	Citeseer	Pumbed	BlogCatalog	Flickr	PPI
Nodes	2708	3327	19717	5196	7575	10076
Edges	5429	4732	44338	171743	239738	157213
Features	1433	3703	500	8189	12047	50
Training set	140	120	60	519	757	1007
Validation set	500	500	500	1039	1515	2015
Testing set	1000	1000	1000	3638	5303	7054
Classes	7	3	6	6	9	121

4.2 Baselines

We evaluate the performance of GENet comprehensively using eight state of the art methods as baselines for semi-supervised node classification: GCN [13], GAT [20], JKNet [21], Mixhop [1], Graphsage [10], FastGCN [4], Grand [7] and GCNII [5]. These methods are variants of GCN and can be divided into two types: shallow and deep methods. Shallow methods include GAT, Mixhop and Grand, and the rest can be regarded as deep methods. In semi-supervised learning, the trainset is relatively small compared to the validset and the testset, and it is prone to overfitting. In order to overcome this problem, we employ early stopping strategy with a patience of 100 epochs on validsets to alleviate this problem. We perform a grid search strategy to tune the hyper-parameters of learning rates, the number of neurons and the probability of deleting edges, and use Accuracy (ACC) and macro F1-score (F1) to evaluate performance of models on testsets.

4.3 Node Classification Results

We exhibit comparative node classification results against current baselines in Table 2, which shows that the proposed GENet model consistently improves the performance over other methods. We have the following observations:

Table 2. Node classification results (%). (Bold: best)

Method	Metrics	Cora	Citeseer	Pumbed	BlogCatalog	Flickr	PPI
GCN	ACC	81.5	71.1	79.0	75.0	61.2	53.4
	F1	80.1	73.1	78.9	71.8	46.5	47.9
GAT	ACC	83.1	70.8	78.5	63.8	46.9	52.5
	F1	82.2	71.6	77.1	69.0	37.3	52.7
JKNet	ACC	81.1	69.8	78.1	70.0	56.7	49.1
	F1	81.4	66.7	79.3	67.6	55.9	41.7
Mixhop	ACC	81.9	71.4	80.8	71.6	61.2	53.4
	F1	79.4	69.3	81.1	76.3	60.7	53.8
Graphsage	ACC	80.7	67.4	77.8	73.4	46.9	50.5
	F1	81.6	62.7	79.3	72.1	48.2	50.7
FastGCN	ACC	81.4	68.8	77.6	75.9	58.7	52.1
	F1	82.7	68.3	76.7	77.3	55.2	50.6
Grand	ACC	85.4	75.4	**82.7**	80.4	61.5	60.5
	F1	83.5	74.4	82.2	80.8	61.7	62.6
GCNII	ACC	85.5	73.5	80.2	81.0	63.9	63.2
	F1	85.6	73.7	80.3	81.2	**63.8**	62.1
GENet	ACC	**86.9**	**76.7**	81.2	**84.1**	**65.2**	**66.7**
	F1	**86.6**	**75.3**	**82.6**	**83.8**	63.6	**65.9**

Compared with all baselines, the proposed GENet generally achieves the best performance on five datasets. Especially, for ACC, GENet achieves maximum relative improvements of 3.1% on BlogCatalog and 3.2% on Citeseer. The results demonstrate the effectiveness of GENet. For Pumbed, GENet is inferior slightly to the Grand method in ACC, but keep ahead in F1.

GENet consistently outperforms GCN on all the datasets, indicating the effectiveness of the ensemble learning in GENet. The output of GENet comes from the student model, which is also a two layer GCN. However, with the help

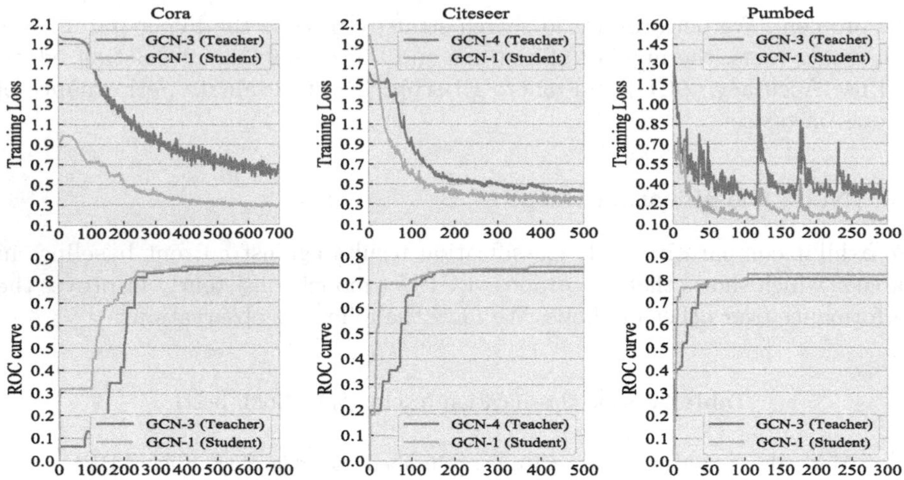

Fig. 2. Training loss and ROC curves on three datasets

of the ensemble learning and attention mechanism, a shallow GCN still behavior better than deep GCNs, and it allows us to regain confidence in the shallow GCNs for graph node classification.

The excellent performance of GENet comes from the teacher model, which learns valuable information in various topological spaces by randomly removing edges with a certain probability, and then transfers the learned knowledge to the student model. To further comprehend the relationship between teacher and learning models, we record their training loss and ROC curves during training process. As depicted in Fig. 2, due to the space limitation, we only post the result of three datasets. The training loss of the student model decreases faster than that of the teacher model, which is in line with our cognition, because the lightweight model is easier to converge. Moreover, the larger the area represented by the ROC curve, the better the performance of the model. Obviously, the student model really benefits from the teacher model.

For a more intuitive comparison and to further show the superiority of the proposed model. We conduct the task of visualization on Citeseer and BlogCatalog datasets. We employ t-TSNE to plot the output embedding of GENet (or GCN, GAT) before softmax and the results are showed in Fig. 3. Apparently, GENet performs best and has widened the intra-class similarity to distinguish different classes.

4.4 Model Analysis

In order to comprehensively evaluate the proposed GENet, we conduct an ablation study to examine the contribution of some details: sampling methods and the size of teacher model.

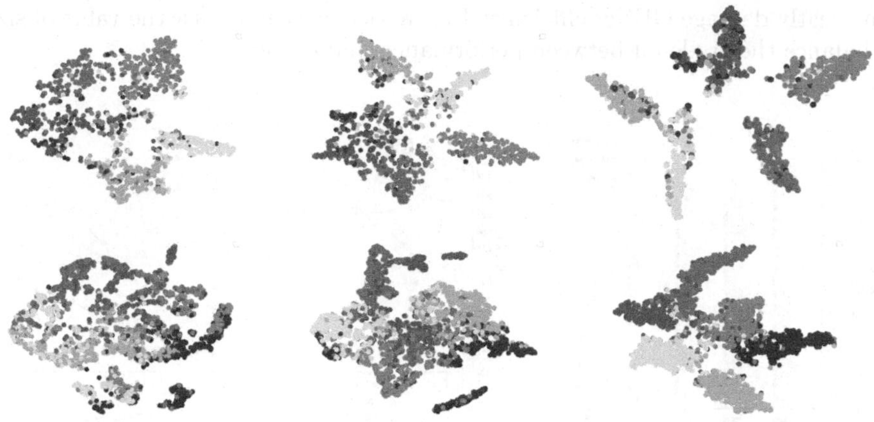

Fig. 3. Visualization of the learned node embeddings on Citeseer (first row) and BlogCatalog (second row)

In Subsect. 3.1, we introduce two current mainstream sampling methods that can increase the graph data diversity and enhance the model robustness for semi-supervised graph learning. One is to create a new topology space from the adjacency matrix A by removing some edges and the other is to sample a new node feature matrix H by deleting some node features. We have such questions: Is the sampling process necessary? and which of the two sampling methods is more suitable? To answer these, we analyze the model's prediction accuracy on all datasets with respect to three sampling methods: dropedge sampling and dropnode sampling and no sampling. As can be seen from the histogram in Fig. 4, dropedge sampling is obviously superior to dropnode sampling and produces better results. Moreover, we can observe the significant gap between sampling and no sampling, indicating that sampling is equally important for graph learning on ensemble models. The teacher model is composed of several shallow GCNs and the size of subnetworks mainly determines the efficiency of GENet. Figure 5 reports the details about the average per-epoch training time and classification accuracy of GENet on all datasets, which shows that the efficiency of GENet is not positively correlated with the size of subnetworks. We deeply analyze the situation and come to this conclusion that with the size increasing, the output embeddings of the teacher model become more consistent and general, which not only transfers more valuable knowledge to the student model, but also brings bad performance to its. The optimal size is related to the scale of the datasets. Large datasets generally require more subnetworks to achieve optimal performance. In addition, we observe that increasing size can significantly improve the GENet's classification accuracy at the cost of its training efficiency. Especially for large-scale datasets, integrating too many subnetworks in the teacher model can greatly damage GENet efficiency. In practice, we can adjust the value of size to balance the trade-off between performance and efficiency.

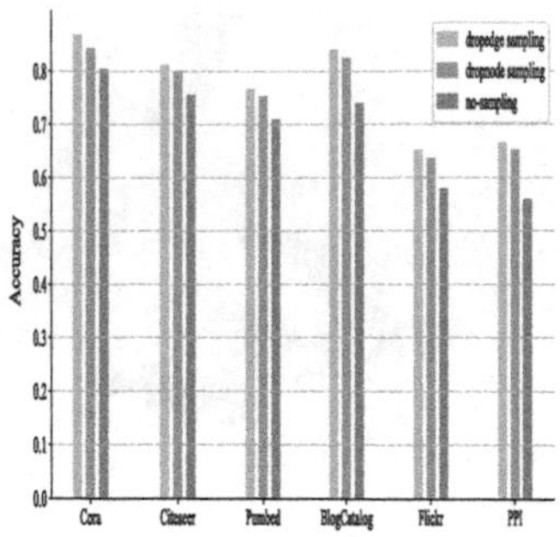

Fig. 4. Comparison of sampling methods

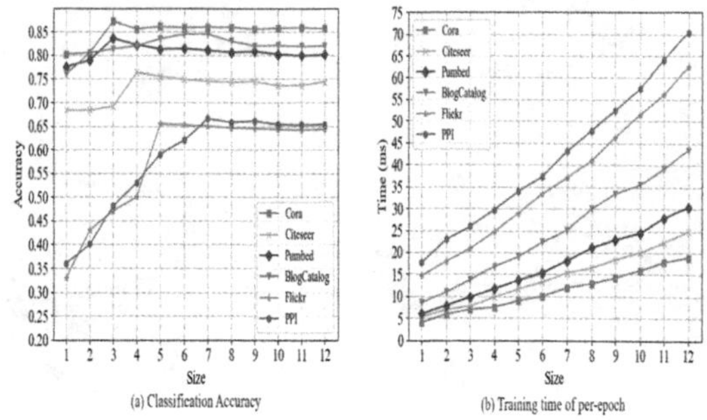

Fig. 5. Efficiency Analysis for GENet

5 Conclusion

In this paper, we rethinked the over-smoothing problem existed in deep GCNs and discover that stacking multiple shallow GCNs still perform well. Motivated by this findings, we proposed the GENet model for semi-supervised graph representation learning, which includes the teacher model and the student model. The teacher model combines data augmentation with knowledge distillation, so multiple GCNs not only have input multiple topology spaces by multi-subgraph sampling, but also learn collaboratively to prevent over-fitting and enhance robustness. To further transfer knowledge from the ensemble model to the student model, we introduce attention mechanism and consistency constraint to learn adaptive importance weights of the embeddings. More importantly, GENet has significant efficiency and provides a new perspective to avoid over-smoothing and overcome over-fitting in GCNs.

References

1. Abu-El-Haija, S., Perozzi, B., Kapoor, A.: Mixhop: higher-order graph convolutional architectures via sparsified neighborhood mixing. In: Proceedings of the 36th International Conference on Machine Learning, ICML, pp. 21–29 (2019)
2. Ba, J., Caruana, R.: Do deep nets really need to be deep? Adv. Neural Inf. Process. Syst. **27**, 2654–2662 (2014)
3. Bruna, J., Zaremba, W., Szlam, A., LeCun, Y.: Spectral networks and locally connected networks on graphs. In: 2nd International Conference on Learning Representations, ICLR (2014)

4. Chen, J., Ma, T., Xiao, C.: FastGCN: fast learning with graph convolutional networks via importance sampling. In: 6th International Conference on Learning Representations, ICLR 2018, Vancouver, 30 April–3 May 2018, Conference Track Proceedings (2018). OpenReview.net
5. Chen, M., Wei, Z., Huang, Z., Ding, B., Li, Y.: Simple and deep graph convolutional networks. In: Proceedings of ICML, pp. 1725–1735 (2020)
6. Fan, W., et al.: Graph neural networks for social recommendation. In: Proceedings of WWW, pp. 417–426 (2019)
7. Feng, W., et al.: Graph random neural networks for semi-supervised learning on graphs. In: NeurIPS (2020)
8. Gilmer, J., Schoenholz, S.S., Riley, P.F., Vinyals, O., Dahl, G.E.: Neural message passing for quantum chemistry. arXiv preprint arXiv:1704.01212 (2017)
9. Goyal, P., et al.: Graph representation ensemble learning. In: Atzmüller, M., Coscia, M., Missaoui, R. (eds.) IEEE/ACM International Conference on Advances in Social Networks Analysis and Mining, ASONAM 2020, pp. 24–31. IEEE (2020)
10. Hamilton, W.L., Ying, Z., Leskovec, J.: Inductive representation learning on large graphs. In: Guyon, I., et al. (eds.) Advances in Neural Information Processing Systems 30: Annual Conference on Neural Information Processing Systems 2017, 4–9 December 2017, Long Beach, CA, USA, pp. 1024–1034 (2017)
11. Huang, G., Sun, Yu., Liu, Z., Sedra, D., Weinberger, K.Q.: Deep networks with stochastic depth. In: Leibe, B., Matas, J., Sebe, N., Welling, M. (eds.) ECCV 2016. LNCS, vol. 9908, pp. 646–661. Springer, Cham (2016). https://doi.org/10.1007/978-3-319-46493-0_39
12. Ju, C., Bibaut, A., van der Laan, M.: The relative performance of ensemble methods with deep convolutional neural networks for image classification. J. Appl. Stat. **45**(15), 2800–2818 (2018)
13. Kipf, T.N., Welling, M.: Semi-supervised classification with graph convolutional networks. arXiv preprint arXiv:1609.02907 (2016)
14. Klicpera, J., Bojchevski, A., Günnemann, S.: Predict then propagate: graph neural networks meet personalized pagerank. In: Proceedings of the 36th International Conference on Machine Learning, ICLR (2019)
15. Li, Q., Han, Z., Wu, X.M.: Deeper insights into graph convolutional networks for semi-supervised learning. In: Proceedings of the AAAI Conference on Artificial Intelligence (2018)
16. Li, R., Huang, J.: Learning graph while training: an evolving graph convolutional neural network. CoRR abs/1708.04675 (2017)
17. Rong, Y., Huang, W., Xu, T., Huang, J.: DropEdge: towards deep graph convolutional networks on node classification. In: Proceedings of the 37th International Conference on Machine Learning, ICLR (2020)
18. Sen, P., Namata, G., Bilgic, M., Getoor, L., Gallagher, B., Eliassi-Rad, T.: Collective classification in network data. AI Mag. **29**(3), 93–106 (2008). https://doi.org/10.1609/aimag.v29i3.2157
19. Urban, G., et al.: Do deep convolutional nets really need to be deep and convolutional? arXiv preprint arXiv:1603.05691 (2016)
20. Velickovic, P., Cucurull, G., Casanova, A., Romero, A., Liò, P., Bengio, Y.: Graph attention networks. In: 6th International Conference on Learning Representations, ICLR (2018). OpenReview.net
21. Xu, K., Li, C., Tian, Y.: Representation learning on graphs with jumping knowledge networks. In: Proceedings of ICML, pp. 5449–5458 (2018)
22. Yang, Z., Cohen, W.W., Salakhutdinov, R.: Revisiting semi-supervised learning with graph embeddings. CoRR abs/1603.08861 (2016)

23. Zhang, C., Song, D., Huang, C., Swami, A., Chawla, N.V.: Heterogeneous graph neural network. In: Proceedings of the 25th ACM SIGKDD International Conference on Knowledge Discovery & Data Mining, pp. 793–803 (2019)
24. Zhang, Y., Xiang, T., Hospedales, T.M., Lu, H.: Deep mutual learning. In: Proceedings of the IEEE Conference on Computer Vision and Pattern Recognition, pp. 4320–4328 (2018)
25. Zhou, J., et al.: Graph neural networks: a review of methods and applications. CoRR abs/1812.08434 (2018)

Rethinking the Information Inside Documents for Sentiment Classification

Xinyu Jiang[1], Chongyang Shi[1(✉)], Shufeng Hao[2], Dequan Yang[1], and Chaoqun Feng[1]

[1] Beijing Institute of Technology, Beijing, China
{cy_shi,yangdequan,fengcq}@bit.edu.cn
[2] Taiyuan University of Technology, Taiyuan, China
haoshufeng@tyut.edu.cn

Abstract. Document-level sentiment classification aims to predict the sentiment rating of a particular document. Most of the methods take word embeddings as the inputs of a neural network. However, most existing methods fail to account for the fact that a specific word usually contains a certain amount of redundant information, and generally different words contain different amounts of redundancy. Such ambiguous word representation will cause models to misunderstand a text, and thus to incorrectly predict the sentiment, meanwhile simply treating words with different amounts of redundancy equally is not appropriate. Moreover, these methods take the user ratings as the training target, which leads to the fact that the information selected by the model is usually limited to the rating itself and there is no obvious sentiment tendency. Accordingly, we propose a Rethinking mechanism (R-TM) to rethink the information inside documents. More specifically, R-TM filters out redundancy contained in different words from different levels, and selects information from positive and negative two different perspectives. Our experimental results demonstrate that the proposed mechanisms can achieve consistent improvements compared to state-of-the-art methods.

Keywords: Sentiment classification · Rethinking mechanism · Multi-level filtering · Double-perspective selection · Hierarchical architecture

1 Introduction

Sentiment analysis is a critical task in the field of natural language processing. Most researchers approach sentiment analysis as a classification task in which sentiment ratings are taken as categories and text features are used to train a classifier [9–11].

However, most existing methods fail to account for the fact that a specific word usually contains a certain amount redundant information, such as different senses that coexist in a word embedding, and generally different words contain different amounts of redundancy. As depicted in Fig. 1(a), the word "of"

H. Qiu et al. (Eds.): KSEM 2021, LNAI 12815, pp. 421–432, 2021.
https://doi.org/10.1007/978-3-030-82136-4_34

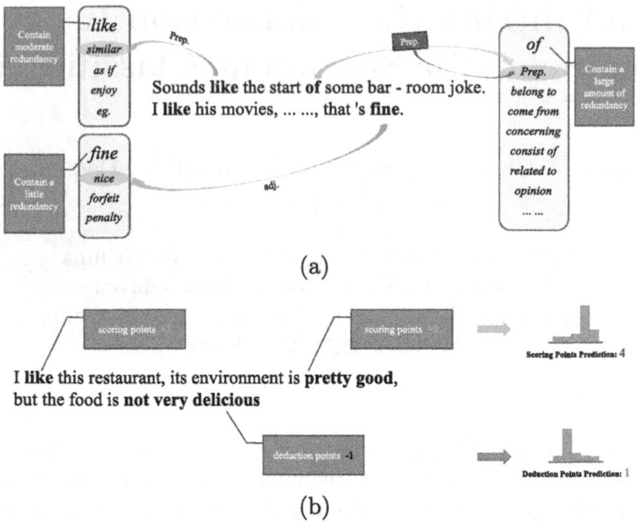

Fig. 1. Cases of different amount of redundancy in different words (a) and selecting information from positive and negative two different perspectives (b).

has many different senses, so its representation will contains a large amount of redundancy; while the word "fine" has less senses, so its representation will contains a little redundancy. If an ambiguous word representation of this kind is taken as the input of a neural network, the models will be unable to obtain the user's real sentiments or opinions. Moreover, most of the existing methods take the user ratings as the training target, which leads to the information selected by the model usually has no obvious sentiment tendency. For example, when the user rating is 3 or 4 (up to 5), words that express user's strong satisfaction will not be extracted successfully. This paper aims to address above challenges.

We observed that the category of words can be used to identify the real meaning of words, and words with different amounts of redundancy can be processed in different ways. As depicted in Fig. 1(a), for the words "like" and "fine", it is easy to identify the real meaning of them by using the category information; for the word "of", since it has a large number of senses, there is a huge amount of redundancy in it. A single category or even multiple categories information can not accurately locate its meaning. Therefore, this paper proposes to use the category itself to replace the original word "of" to reduce the amount of redundant information. Because word "of" is a function word and its meaning is not clear, such a replacement method will not have much influence on the understanding of the text. Moreover, the final score is usually obtained by the user considering the scoring points (the part that the user is satisfied with) and deduction points (the part that the user is not satisfied with) of the product, and all the words with different sentiment polarity will contribute to the final rating. As depicted in Fig. 1(a), the words "like" and "pretty good" contribute to the scoring points; while the words "not very delicious" contribute to the deduction points. Integrating the scoring and deduction points, we can infer the final rating.

Accordingly, we propose a Rethinking mechanism (R-TM) to rethink the information inside documents, which consists of two modules, namely a Multi-level Filtering (M-LF) module and a Double-perspective Selection (D-PS) module. The M-LF module filters out redundancy contained in different words from different levels, namely weak, medium and strong, to identify the real meaning of words. The D-PS module selecting information from two different perspectives, namely positive (correspond to the scoring point) and negative (correspond to the deduction point). These extracted information is used to predict the score value and deduction value respectively, and the final sentiment rating is obtained by integrating the score points and deduction points. The main contributions of our paper can be summarized as follows:

- We propose a Multi-Level Filtering (M-LF) mechanism that uses the corresponding category to filter out redundant information from three different levels, namely weak, medium and strong; while retaining the relatively salient and precise information within the word.
- We propose a Double-perspective Selection (D-PS) mechanism that selects information from two different perspectives, namely positive (correspond to the scoring point) and negative (correspond to the deduction point), in this way, we can extract words with more explicit sentiment polarity.
- We conduct experiments on IMDB and Yelp datasets to verify the effectiveness of R-TM mechanisms. Experimental results demonstrate that our model achieves consistent improvement over various state-of-the-art methods.

2 Related Work

The rapid development of online review sites has attracted an increasing number of researchers to participate in the study of document-level sentiment classification. Compared with the traditional method, neural network based model does not need to artificially extract text features, and a well-designed neural architecture can achieve excellent classification results.

Glorot et al. [6] study the domain adaptation problem in sentiment classification and apply a Autoencoder to extract text features in an unsupervised manner. Socher et al. [12] train the Recursive Neural Tensor Network (RNTN) on a new Sentiment Treebank and achieve very impressive results. Tang et al. [13] introduce Convolutional Neural Networks (CNN) into sentiment classification, and enrich document representations with user and product information.

Besides, Recurrent Neural Network (RNN) and attention mechanism are also widely used for sentiment classification. Yang et al. [15] propose an attention mechanism, which is based on randomly initialized context word vector and sentence vector. Chen et al. [3] indicate that user and product information can be used for key words extraction, so they propose an attention mechanism based on user and product embeddings. Wu et al. [14] observe that user information and product information present different characteristics when extracting key words of the text, so they propose two attention mechanisms, which are based on user information and product information respectively and applied to two independent hierarchical networks. Du et al. [4] propose a Convolution-Based Attention Mechanism, which takes the result of convolution operations as the importance of corresponding text segment, and applied it to the word and sentence level of a hierarchical network. Amplayo [1] further proposed that the attention mechanism could be used to incorporate user and product information as additional biases, and subsequently opted to represent user and product information as chunk-wise importance weight matrices.

However, the methods discussed above embed words as input to a neural network and typically focus on words with higher attention weights, while failing to consider that a certain amount of redundant information can exist in words; and these methods take the user ratings as the training target, which leads to the extracted information usually has no obvious sentiment tendency.

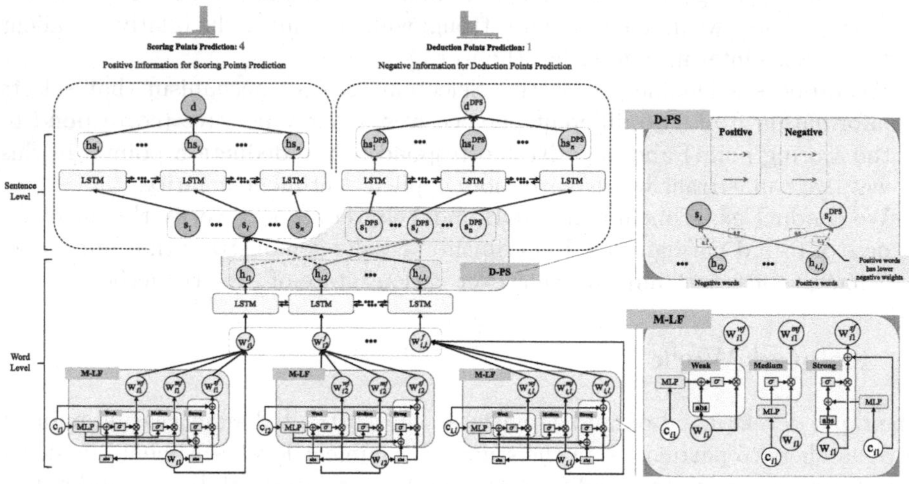

Fig. 2. Rethinking mechanism (R-TM) for sentiment classification

3 Methods

In this section, we will provide a detailed description of the proposed model.

3.1 Architecture and Double-Perspective Selection (D-PS) Mechanism

The architecture of our proposed Rethinking mechanism (R-TM) is illustrated in Fig. 2. The R-TM mechanism contains two modules, namely a Multi-level Filtering (M-LF) module and a Double-perspective Selection (D-PS) module. The

M-LF module filters out redundant information contained in different words from different levels to retain the relatively salient and precise information within the word; and the D-PS module selects information from two different perspectives to extract words with more explicit sentiment polarity:

(1) Firstly, the word embeddings $[\mathbf{w}_{i1}, ..., \mathbf{w}_{i,l_i}]$ within a sentence s_i (where l_i is the length of the sentence s_i) and the corresponding category representations $[\mathbf{c}_{i1}, ..., \mathbf{c}_{i,l_i}]$, are passed through the M-LF mechanism. This allows us to obtain the final filtered representations $[\mathbf{w}^f_{i1}, ..., \mathbf{w}^f_{i,l_i}]$, which will be further passed through the LSTM layer to obtain the hidden states $[\mathbf{h}_{i1}, ..., \mathbf{h}_{il_i}]$.
(2) Secondly, we use two different attention mechanisms to encode these hidden states to obtain the sentence representation $\mathbf{s}_i$ and the negative sentence representation $\mathbf{s}_i^{DPS}$. The former one is trained as a collection of positive words in the sentence, while the latter one is trained as a collection of negative words.
(3) Thirdly, the sentence representations $[\mathbf{s}_1, ..., \mathbf{s}_n]$ within a document d (where n is the length of d) are further passed through the LSTM layer to obtain the hidden states $[\mathbf{hs}_1, ..., \mathbf{hs}_n]$. And the negative sentence representations $[\mathbf{s}_1^{DPS}, ..., \mathbf{s}_n^{DPS}]$ are used to obtain the negative hidden states $[\mathbf{hs}_1^{DPS}, ..., \mathbf{hs}_n^{DPS}]$.
(4) Finally, the hidden states $[\mathbf{hs}_1, ..., \mathbf{hs}_n]$ and $[\mathbf{hs}_1^{DPS}, ..., \mathbf{hs}_n^{DPS}]$ are used to generate the document representation $\mathbf{d}$ and the negative document representation $\mathbf{d}^{DPS}$ respectively, via the sentence-level attention mechanism. The document representation $\mathbf{d}$ is used to predict the scoring value and the negative document representation $\mathbf{d}^{DPS}$ is used to predict the deduction value.

Note that, our R-TM has two different train target, one is for scoring points prediction called positive target, and the other is for deduction points prediction called negative target. The sum of these two values is the maximum value of the sentiment. For example, the user rating of a document is 4 (up to 5), the former train target (positive target) is 4 and the latter train target (negative target) is 1 (= 5 − 4).

In the training stage, we minimize the cross-entropy $\mathcal{L}(\theta)$ between the predicted positive probability distribution $P(y|d;\theta)$ and the positive one-hot target Y (for scoring points prediction), and the cross-entropy $\mathcal{L}^{DPS}(\theta)$ between the predicted negative probability distribution $P(y^{DPS}|d;\theta)$ and the negative one-hot target Y^{DPS} (for deduction points prediction).

In the testing stage, the final predicted probability distribution $P(y^f|d;\theta)$ is obtained by integrating the predicted positive probability distribution $P(y|d;\theta)$ and the predicted negative probability distribution $P(y^{DPS}|d;\theta)$, as follows:

$$P(y^f|d;\theta) = P(y|d;\theta) + Reverse(P(y^{DPS}|d;\theta)), \tag{1}$$

where the *Reverse*() is a operation that reverses vectors. The final predicted sentiment is determined by $P(y^f|d;\theta)$.

The following sections will present the details of M-LF mechanisms.

3.2 Multi-level Filtering (M-LF) Mechanism

Simply treating words with different amount of redundancy equally is not appropriate. Therefore, we propose a Multi-Level Filtering (M-LF) mechanism to filter out redundancy from three different levels: weak, medium and strong.

For words with a little redundancy, we filtering them from the weak level to retain a lot of original word information; for words with moderate redundancy, we filtering them from the medium level; for words with a large amount of redundancy, we filtering them from the strong level and meanwhile introduce the corresponding categories information for the words to ensure the information enrichment of the filtered results.

The filtering procedures (M-LF) are illustrated in the bottom right parts of Fig. 2. At each time step t, the category representation $\mathbf{c}_{it}$ is passed through the linear layer, as follows:

$$\mathbf{c}_{it}^{f} = \mathbf{W}^{f}\mathbf{c}_{it} + \mathbf{b}^{f}, \tag{2}$$

where $\mathbf{W}^{f} \in \mathbb{R}^{d_w \times d_c}$ and $\mathbf{b}^{f} \in \mathbb{R}^{d_w}$ denote the weight matrix and bias of the linear layer, respectively. $\mathbf{c}_{it}^{f} \in \mathbb{R}^{d_w}$ will be further used in the three-level filtering procedure, which enables us to obtain the weak-level filtered result $\mathbf{w}_{it}^{wf}$, the medium-level filtered result $\mathbf{w}_{it}^{mf}$ and the strong-level filtered result $\mathbf{w}_{it}^{sf}$.

Weak-Level Filtering: For words with a little redundancy, we filter out redundant information from the weak level and retain a lot of original word information. As depicted in the "weak" part of Fig. 2, we introduce the original word embedding $\mathbf{w}_{it}$ to weaken the filtering degree according to different feature in $\mathbf{w}_{it}$. The more salient features there are in $\mathbf{w}_{it}$, the less likely they are to be filtered out.

More concretely, the absolute value $|\mathbf{w}_{it}|$ is employed as a bias for $\mathbf{c}_{it}^{f}$ to implement the weak-level filtering process (the larger the element in $|\mathbf{w}_{it}|$, the more salient the corresponding feature is in $\mathbf{w}_{it}$), as follows:

$$\mathbf{w}_{it}^{wf} = \sigma(\mathbf{c}_{it}^{f} + |\mathbf{w}_{it}|) \otimes \mathbf{w}_{it}, \tag{3}$$

where σ is the logistic sigmoid function, while $\mathbf{w}_{it}^{wf}$ is the weak-level filtered result. The greater the relative size of the elements in the absolute value $|\mathbf{w}_{it}|$, the more likely it is that the sigmoid result will be 1; as such the corresponding feature in the original word embedding $\mathbf{w}_{it}$ will be retained.

Medium-Level Filtering: For words with moderate redundancy, as depicted in the "medium" part of Fig. 2, we filter out redundancy using only the category information $\mathbf{c}_{it}^{f}$, as follows:

$$\mathbf{w}_{it}^{mf} = \sigma(\mathbf{c}_{it}^{f}) \otimes \mathbf{w}_{it}, \tag{4}$$

where $\mathbf{w}_{it}^{mf}$ is the medium-level filtered result.

Strong-Level Filtering: For words with a large amount of redundancy or the categories can replace the corresponding words to some extent, we filtering them from the strong level and meanwhile introduce the corresponding categories information for the words.

As depicted in the "strong" part of Fig. 2, we also introduce the word embedding $\mathbf{w}_{it}$ to strengthen the degree of filtering according to different features in $\mathbf{w}_{it}$. The more salient features there are in the original word embedding, the more likely they are to be filtered out.

More concretely, the negative absolute value $-|\mathbf{w}_{it}|$ is employed as a bias for $\mathbf{c}_{it}^{f}$ to implement the strong-level filtering process. To ensure the information enrichment of the strongly filtered results, we introduce the category representation $\mathbf{c}_{it}$, as follows:

$$\mathbf{w}_{it}^{sf} = \sigma(\mathbf{c}_{it}^{f} - |\mathbf{w}_{it}|) \otimes \mathbf{w}_{it} + \mathbf{c}_{it}, \tag{5}$$

where $\mathbf{w}_{it}^{sf}$ is the strong-level filtered result. The greater the relative size of the elements in the absolute value $|\mathbf{w}_{it}|$, the more likely it is that the sigmoid result will be 0, and such the corresponding feature in the original word embedding $\mathbf{w}_{it}$ will be filtered out.

Filtering from Which Level?: We concatenate the word embedding $\mathbf{w}_{it}$ and the three filtering results, i.e. $[\mathbf{w}_{it}; \mathbf{w}_{it}^{wf}; \mathbf{w}_{it}^{mf}; \mathbf{w}_{it}^{sf}]$, and pass the result through a linear layer, as follows:

$$\mathbf{wd}_{it} = \mathbf{W}_{w}[\mathbf{w}_{it}; \mathbf{w}_{it}^{wf}; \mathbf{w}_{it}^{mf}; \mathbf{w}_{it}^{sf}] + \mathbf{b}_{w}, \tag{6}$$

where $\mathbf{W}_{w} \in \mathbb{R}^{4\times 4*d_w}$ and $\mathbf{b}_{w} \in \mathbb{R}^{4}$ denote the weight matrix and the bias of the linear layer, while the output $\mathbf{wd}_{it} \in \mathbb{R}^{4}$ represents the probability distribution of the word embedding and the three filtering results.

Note that, if the probability of the word embedding $\mathbf{w}_{it}$ (or the weak-level filtering result $\mathbf{w}_{it}^{wf}$/the medium-level filtering result $\mathbf{w}_{it}^{mf}$/the strong-level filtering result $\mathbf{w}_{it}^{sf}$) is higher than all other probabilities, this indicates that the word w_{it} most likely contains no (or a little/moderate/a large amount of) redundant information.

We then obtain the final filtered representation $\mathbf{w}_{it}^{f} \in \mathbb{R}^{d_w}$ for each word, as follows:

$$\mathbf{w}_{it}^{'} = \epsilon([\mathbf{w}_{it}; \mathbf{w}_{it}^{wf}; \mathbf{w}_{it}^{mf}; \mathbf{w}_{it}^{sf}]); \tag{7}$$

$$\mathbf{w}_{it}^{f} = (\mathbf{wd}_{it}^{T}\mathbf{w}_{it}^{'})^{T}, \tag{8}$$

where $\epsilon(.)$ denotes the reshape function, $\mathbf{w}_{it}^{'} \in \mathbb{R}^{4\times d_w}$, $\mathbf{wd}_{it}^{T} \in \mathbb{R}^{1\times 4}$ is the transpose of the probability distribution $\mathbf{wd}_{it} \in \mathbb{R}^{4}$, and $(.)^{T}$ is the transpose procedure.

The final filtered representation $\mathbf{w}_{it}^{f} \in \mathbb{R}^{d_w}$ will be further passed through the LSTM layer to obtain the t-th hidden state $\mathbf{h}_{it}$.

4 Experiments

In this section, we carry out experiments on three sentiment classification datasets in order to validate the effectiveness of our proposed model.

Table 1. Statistics of IMDB, Yelp2013 and Yelp2014 datasets

Datasets	Classes	Docs	Docs/user	Docs/product	Sens/doc	Words/sen
IMDB	10	84,919	64.82	51.94	16.08	24.54
Yelp 2013	5	78,966	48.42	48.36	10.89	17.38
Yelp 2014	5	231,163	47.97	55.11	11.41	17.26

4.1 Datasets and Metrics

The IMDB and Yelp datasets, which were constructed by [13], are widely used in document-level sentiment classification tasks. The statistics of these datasets are summarized in Table 1. In the present research, the datasets are split into three parts: 80% is used for training, 10% for validation, and the remaining 10% is used for testing.

We use *Accuracy* and *RMSE* as metrics for evaluating the performance of these models. *Accuracy* is used to measure the overall sentiment classification performance, while *RMSE* is used to evaluate the difference between the predicted sentiment rating pre_i and the ground truth labels lab_i, as follows:

$$Accuracy = \frac{M}{N}, \qquad RMSE = \sqrt{\frac{\sum_{i=1}^{N}(lab_i - pre_i)^2}{N}}, \tag{9}$$

where M represents the number of predicted sentiment ratings that are identical with the ground truth, while N indicates the number of documents.

4.2 Experimental Settings

Basic Settings: We pre-train 200-dimensional word embeddings on each dataset using SkipGram [8]; these word embeddings are not fine-tuned during the training stage. We then randomly initialize the user and product embeddings from a uniform distribution U (−0.01, 0.01), and the dimensions are set to 200. We further set the number of hidden state dimensions in the LSTM cell to 100 and apply bidirectional LSTM. Finally, the initial learning rate is set to 0.005 and utilize the Adam optimizer [7] to update the parameters during training.

M-LF Mechanism Settings: We select the parts-of-speech and position as word categories to conduct our experiments.

For *Part-Of-Speech:* We utilize the Natural Language Toolkit (NLTK) [2] to tokenize the documents and determine which part-of-speech the words should be categorized as. We randomly initialize the representation of parts-of-speech from a uniform distribution U (−0.01, 0.01), and the dimensions are set to 200.

For *Position:* we limit each sentence has no more than 50 words, and each position of the sentence has its own category embedding.

Table 2. Document-level sentiment classification results.

Models	IMDB		Yelp 2013		Yelp 2014	
	Acc.(%)	RMSE	Acc.(%)	RMSE	Acc.(%)	RMSE
Majority	19.6	2.495	41.1	1.060	39.2	1.097
AvgWordvec+SVM	28.5	1.901	52.4	0.886	50.8	0.933
CNN (Trigram)	41.6	1.547	61.2	0.736	60.0	0.737
UPNN	46.3	1.509	59.5	0.789	59.4	0.762
HAN (GRU)	49.1	1.344	65.3	0.672	64.8	0.666
H-CRAN	49.1	1.372	64.7	0.687	65.1	0.665
NSC+UPA	53.3	1.245	66.5	0.671	66.7	0.653
HUAPA	54.8	1.189	68.0	0.642	68.6	0.629
CHIM	56.4	1.161	67.8	0.646	69.2	0.629
R-TM (position)	56.5	1.175	68.1	0.638	69.1	0.625
R-TM (part-of-speech)	**57.0**	**1.160**	**68.6**	**0.635**	**69.4**	**0.621**

4.3 Baselines

We compare our model with the following popular baseline methods: **Majority** takes the majority sentiment rating in the training set as the sentiment rating of all documents in the test set. **AvgWordvec** averages all word vectors in a review to create its feature, then uses an SVM classifier to predict sentiment. **CNN (Trigram)** uses three different convolution kernels to obtain the semantic information of the unigrams, bigrams and trigrams in a sentence for classification purposes. **UPNN** [13] utilizes user and product information to enrich the results of **CNN (Trigram)**. **HAN (GRU)** [15] utilizes a hierarchical network with a new attention mechanism based on two randomly initialized context vectors. **H-CRAN** [4] proposes a Convolution-Based Attention Mechanism that uses the convolution results as the attention weights of corresponding text segments. **NSC+UPA** [3] proposes a hierarchical network containing an attention mechanism based on user and product information. **HUAPA** [14] builds two individual hierarchical neural networks that use user attention and product attention separately. **CHIM** [1] represents user and product information as chunk-wise importance weight matrices. We present the experimental results reported by [1].

4.4 Model Comparison

The experimental results are presented in Table 2. From the table, we can conclude the following:

- User and product attention mechanisms are more effective at sentiment classification than other attention methods; **NSC+UPA** achieves considerable improvement compared to **HAN** and **H-CRAN**. However, attention mechanisms are only able to obtain keywords from among all words, and cannot obtain the important information inside a certain word (or sentence). This is also a critical reason behind our decision to utilize the Multi-Level Filtering (M-LF) mechanism to filter out redundancy inside a word.

- Our proposed model, **R-TM** (part-of-speech), achieves performance improvements relative to the various baselines. More specifically, **R-TM** (part-of-speech) outperforms the previous state-of-the-art method **CHIM** by 0.8% on the small dataset Yelp2013, by 0.6% on the other small dataset IMDB, and by 0.2% on the large dataset Yelp2014 in terms of accuracy. The RMSE of our model is also smaller compared to other baselines.
- Evidently, the results obtained by **R-TM** (part-of-speech) are noticeably better than those of **R-TM** (position) on all three datasets. More specifically, **R-TM** (part-of-speech) outperforms the **R-TM** (position) by 0.5% on the small dataset Yelp2013, by 0.5% on the other small dataset IMDB, and by 0.3% on the large dataset Yelp2014 in terms of accuracy. This indicates that filtering redundancy using the category *parts-of-speech* is more effective than using *position* in terms of Sentiment Classification.

Table 3. Classification accuracy of several baselines with and without R-TM.

Models	IMDB	Yelp 2013	Yelp 2014
HAN (GRU)	0.491	0.653	0.648
HAN (R-TM)	0.540	0.668	0.673
H-CRAN	0.491	0.647	0.651
H-CRAN (R-TM)	**0.546**	**0.667**	**0.678**
NSC+UPA	0.533	0.665	0.667
NSC+UPA (R-TM)	**0.546**	**0.671**	**0.679**

4.5 Ablation Study

To further validate the efficiency and applicability of **R-TM**, we introduce our method for several different baselines.

The performances of these baselines with or without a **R-TM** are shown in Table 3. From the table, we can observe that:

- Each baseline that incorporates our R-TM mechanism achieves significant performance improvements, which demonstrates the applicability and efficiency of our method.
- In particular, the NSC+UPA (R-TM) outperforms the NSC+UPA by 1.3%/0.6%/1.2% on the datasets IMDB/Yelp2013/Yelp2014 in terms of accuracy, while the HAN (R-TM) outperforms the HAN by 4.9%/1.5%/2.5% on the datasets IMDB/Yelp2013/Yelp2014 in terms of accuracy.

4.6 Case Study

We pass the word embeddings through the M-LF mechanism and obtain the more explicit word embeddings. We then visualize the word and sense embeddings of five different categories. In more detail, we use TSNE to map the dimensions of embeddings to 2 for visualization purposes.

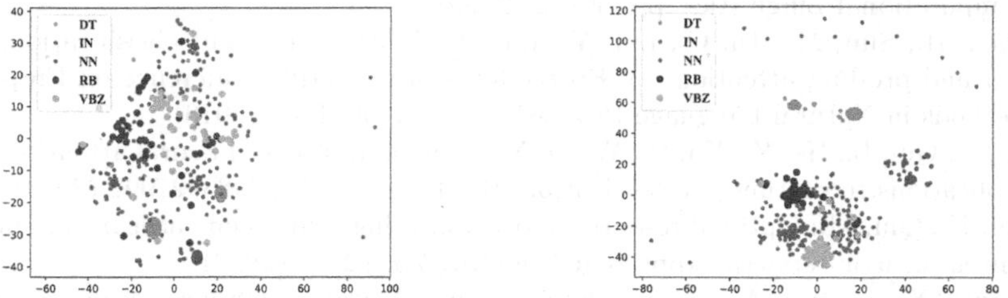

(a) Word Embedding (b) More Explicit Word Embedding

Fig. 3. Word embedding distribution with and without the M-LF mechanism.

The word embedding distributions with and without the M-LF mechanism is presented in Fig. 3. From the table, we can observe the following:

Different colors represent the embeddings of words with different categories. The original pre-trained word embedding distribution (word embedding without the M-LF mechanism) is chaotic, and the embeddings of different categories are difficult to distinguish, as shown in Fig. 3a; By contrast, the more explicit word embeddings (word embedding with the M-LF mechanism) of the same category exhibit a clustering phenomenon, as shown in Fig. 3b.

The above indicates that the proposed M-LF mechanism can filter out the redundant senses of words to a certain extent while retaining more precise (i.e., category-related) senses of the words.

5 Conclusion

Most existing methods fail to account for the fact that a specific word usually contains a certain amount of redundant information, and generally different words contain different amounts of redundancy. And the information extracted by these methods usually without obvious sentiment tendency. To solve these problems, we proposed a Rethinking mechanism (R-TM) to rethink the information inside documents. The proposed model filters out redundant information contained in different words from different levels and is able to extract words with more explicit sentiment polarity. We go on to evaluate our model on several sentiment classification datasets. Our experimental results demonstrate that our model achieves consistent improvements compared to other baseline methods.

Acknowledgement. This work is supported by the National Key Research and Development Program of China (No. 2019YFB1406302).

References

1. Amplayo, R.K.: Rethinking attribute representation and injection for sentiment classification. In: Proceedings of the 2019 Conference on Empirical Methods in Natural Language Processing, pp. 5601–5612 (2019)
2. Bird, S.: NLTK: the natural language toolkit. In: 21st International Conference on Computational Linguistics and 44th Annual Meeting of the Association for Computational Linguistics, pp. 69–72 (2006)
3. Chen, H., Sun, M., Tu, C., Lin, Y., Liu, Z.: Neural sentiment classification with user and product attention. In: Proceedings of the 2016 Conference on Empirical Methods in Natural Language Processing, pp. 1650–1659 (2016)
4. Du, J., Gui, L., He, Y., Xu, R., Wang, X.: Convolution-based neural attention with applications to sentiment classification. IEEE Access **7**, 27983–27992 (2019)
5. Gai, K., Qiu, M.: Optimal resource allocation using reinforcement learning for IoT content-centric services. Appl. Soft Comput. **70**, 12–21 (2018)
6. Glorot, X., Bordes, A., Bengio, Y.: Domain adaptation for large-scale sentiment classification: a deep learning approach. In: Proceedings of the 28th International Conference on Machine Learning, pp. 513–520 (2011)
7. Kingma, D.P., Ba, J.: Adam: a method for stochastic optimization. In: 3rd International Conference on Learning Representations, Conference Track Proceedings, pp. 1–15 (2015)
8. Mikolov, T., Sutskever, I., Chen, K., Corrado, G.S., Dean, J.: Distributed representations of words and phrases and their compositionality. In: 27th Annual Conference on Neural Information Processing Systems, pp. 3111–3119 (2013)
9. Pang, B., Lee, L., Vaithyanathan, S.: Thumbs up? Sentiment classification using machine learning techniques. In: Proceedings of the 2002 Conference on Empirical Methods in Natural Language Processing, pp. 79–86 (2002)
10. Socher, R., Huval, B., Manning, C.D., Ng, A.Y.: Semantic compositionality through recursive matrix-vector spaces. In: Proceedings of the 2012 Joint Conference on Empirical Methods in Natural Language Processing and Computational Natural Language Learning, pp. 1201–1211 (2012)
11. Socher, R., Pennington, J., Huang, E.H., Ng, A.Y., Manning, C.D.: Semi-supervised recursive autoencoders for predicting sentiment distributions. In: Proceedings of the 2011 Conference on Empirical Methods in Natural Language Processing, pp. 151–161 (2011)
12. Socher, R., et al.: Recursive deep models for semantic compositionality over a sentiment treebank. In: Proceedings of the 2013 Conference on Empirical Methods in Natural Language Processing, pp. 1631–1642 (2013)
13. Tang, D., Qin, B., Liu, T.: Learning semantic representations of users and products for document level sentiment classification. In: Proceedings of the 53rd Annual Meeting of the Association for Computational Linguistics, pp. 1014–1023 (2015)
14. Wu, Z., Dai, X., Yin, C., Huang, S., Chen, J.: Improving review representations with user attention and product attention for sentiment classification. In: Proceedings of the Thirty-Second AAAI Conference on Artificial Intelligence, pp. 5989–5996 (2018)
15. Yang, Z., Yang, D., Dyer, C., He, X., Smola, A.J., Hovy, E.H.: Hierarchical attention networks for document classification. In: The 2016 Conference of the North American Chapter of the Association for Computational Linguistics: Human Language Technologies, pp. 1480–1489 (2016)

Dependency Parsing Representation Learning for Open Information Extraction

Li Zekun, Ning Nianwen, Peng Chengcheng, and Wu Bin(✉)

Beijing University of Posts and Telecommunications,
Beijing 100876, People's Republic of China
{lizekun,nianwenning,chengchengpeng,wubin}@bupt.edu.cn

Abstract. Open information extraction (OIE) aims to extract structured information from text. Specifically, it extracts arguments and their logical relationships from a sentence. However, as a syntactic feature commonly used in OIE, the tree structure of dependency parsing (DP) is often overlooked. In this paper, we propose a dependency parsing representation learning model for OIE. This model can fully represent the tree structure and edge information of DP. Then we fuse the learned DP embedding in a Graph Convolutional Network-based OIE model. The experiments show that the proposed OIE model outperforms four baselines on three open-sourced data sets.

Keywords: Information extraction · Representation learning · Dependency parsing · BERT · Natural language processing

1 Introduction

Open information extraction (OIE) aims to extract structured information from natural language text. The result is a triplet (or fact), it can be represented in the form of <argument1, relation, argument2>. We can also call the argument or relation the "extraction". Unlike traditional relation extraction, OIE does not need to define any relationship types in advance but extract a relation indicator from the sentence. Therefore, OIE is domain-independent, which makes it suitable for large-scale Internet text. OIE can be applied in converting unstructured text data to structured information, constructing an open-domain knowledge graph, and contributes to other downstream tasks such as Q&A task, reading comprehension, and entity relation extraction [16].

Revealing the syntactic dependency between sentence components, dependency parsing (DP) has become the most common syntactic feature used by traditional OIE methods such as [5] and [3]. However, recent neural methods such as [6] and [18] rarely take the tree structure of DP into account. The embedding of dependencies is randomly initialized and optimized during the training process of the target task. [23] found that the randomly initialized DP embedding even reduces their model's performance. Therefore, we need to design a more accurate and informative DP embedding method.

H. Qiu et al. (Eds.): KSEM 2021, LNAI 12815, pp. 433–444, 2021.
https://doi.org/10.1007/978-3-030-82136-4_35

Graph Convolutional Network (GCN) [12] is a neural network that operates directly on graph structures. It can aggregate the information of a node's neighborhoods in the graph structure. Some of the previous works [24], and [7] uses GCN to learn the feature of the DP tree and have made considerable improvements. Inspired by these works, we come up with the idea of using GCN in the OIE model to extract the information from the dependency tree. However, GCN only considers the weight of edges. The critical dependency relation information on the edges is ignored.

To address these problems, we present a new dependency representation learning model. The advantage of our model is that using attention-guided GCN (AGGCN [7]) for extracting the words' neighbor information from the DP tree structure and using TransD [9] model to learn an embedding of dependency relation. The learned DP embedding completes the information of the edges that AGGCN ignores and improves our OIE model's performance.

In conclusion, the main contributions of this paper are:

1. We present a new dependency representation learning model, which has a stronger ability to represent the dependency relationships.
2. Based on the informative dependency embedding, we present an open information extraction model, which can make full use of the DP tree information.
3. Our model is proved to have a good performance on both Chinese and English data in the experiments.

2 Related Work

Traditional OIE methods are generally based on unsupervised or self-supervised learning. They match the sentences' components according to patterns defined manually or learned from a small corpus to generate triplets. Representative traditional OIE methods include TextRunner [4], Reverb [5], OLLIE [15], Clausie [3]. These methods are usually unable to cope with complex and long sentences, the extraction effect is limited by the quality of patterns.

Researchers have paid much more attention to open information extraction recently. With the release of large-scale open-sourced data sets such as Reverb [5], OIE-2016 [19], SAOKE [21], COER [10], there are more and more deep learning-based methods in the field of OIE. These methods mainly formulate OIE as two kinds of tasks: sequence labeling and text generation.

Sequence Labeling. We can mark the arguments and relation words with special labels. For example, the most well-known "BIO" tag scheme, in which we use the "B" tag to mark the start of extraction, "I" to mark the following part of the extraction, and "O" to mark non-extraction words. The model predicts the label with the highest probability for each word to extract the sentence's tuple. This kind of methods include NST [11], RnnOIE [20], LOREM [8], OpenIE6 [13] and Multi2OIE [17].

Text Generation. Given the original sentence, these Seq2Seq models first encode the words into a vector space and then decode the embedding to generate triplets. This kind of method includes Logician [21] and IMojie [14].

As we mentioned earlier, most previous neural methods overlooked the tree structure of DP and its embedding is often randomly initialized. The ability of aggregating nodes' information of GCN and the effectiveness of TransD on graph representation inspired us. So we use them to represent the DP relation. How they work in our model will be described in the next section.

3 Methods

The whole workflow of this paper is shown in Fig. 2. When applying this method, we first train a DP representation learning model on the whole corpora. The weights in the relation embedding layer of TransD are saved as the dependency embedding. Then fuse the DP embedding with the tokens' embedding in the OIE model and train the OIE model to extract arguments and relations.

In the following subsections, we will describe the DP representation learning model and open information extraction model in details.

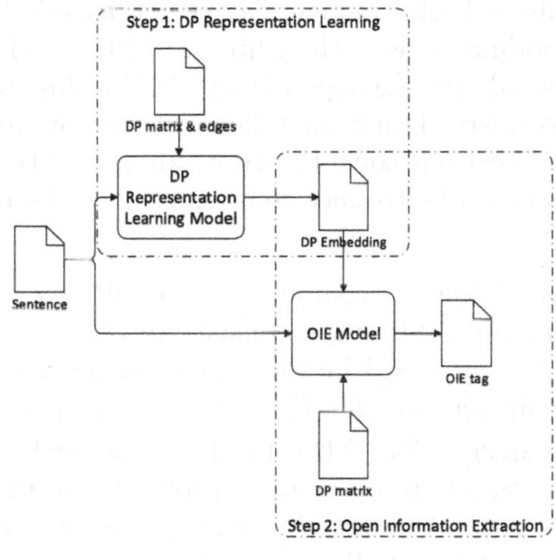

Fig. 1. Overall procedure of this work

3.1 DP Representation Learning

We use the DP representation learning model to learn a more informative representation of dependency relationships. Its architecture is shown in Fig. 2.

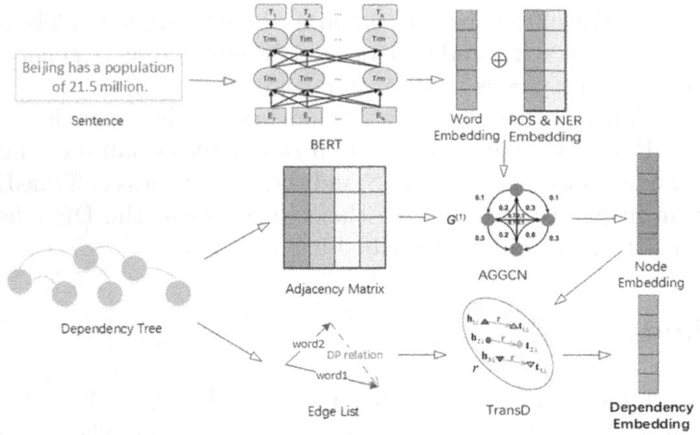

Fig. 2. Architecture of DP representation learning model

Pre-processing. First, we use LTP[1] to obtain the DP tree as well as Part-of-Speech (POS) and Named Entity Recognition (NER) tags of the sentences in our training sets. LTP cuts the sentence into words when conducting dependency parsing, while the Chinese BERT model takes tokens as units. Therefore, we have made the following modifications to the Chinese DP trees: (1) The tokens in one word share the headword and the dependency relationship of the original word; (2) If the headword consists of multiple tokens, we take its first character as the new head. These modifications solve the contradiction between DP and BERT in granularity but inevitably introduce some noise into the DP tree structure.

Sample Generation. Then we combine all the DP trees of the sentences to form a large directed graph, this graph consists all the edges of every DP trees. Formally, let $S = \{s_1, ..., s_i, ..., s_n\}$ be the sentences in our data set, R_{dp} be the dependency relationship set, and $DPT_i = \{< w_j^h, r_k, w_j^t >, ...\}$ be the DP tree of s_i, where $w_j^h, w_j^t \in s_i, r_k \in R_{dp}$. Then the large directed graph is an edge list $DP_G = \{< w_h, r_k, w_t >, ...\}$. In order to improve the accuracy of learning, we refer to the idea of comparative learning and add some non-existent edges as negative samples in the data set. We use $DP_G{}' = \{< w_h', r_k, w_t' >, ...\}$ denotes the negative samples, where w_h', w_t' are random words that have no dependency. The loss of samples in DP_G will be minimized in training, while the loss of samples in $DP_G{}'$will be maximized.

BERT Layer. The word embedding is initialized by BERT, a pre-trained language model. It can generate a dynamic embedding for every word according to the given sentence. The $BERT_{base}$ that we use consists of 12 fully connected

[1] http://ltp.ai/.

layers. Each layer consists of 768 Transformer encoders. Each encoder performs 12 head self-attention computation, which can be expressed as:

$$\begin{aligned} head_h &= Attention(Q_h, K_h, V_h) \\ &= softmax(\frac{Q_h K_h^T}{\sqrt{d_k}})V_h \end{aligned} \tag{1}$$

$$\text{MultiHead}(Q, K, V) = (head_1 \oplus head_2 \oplus ... \oplus head_h)W^O \tag{2}$$

where d_k is the number of parameters in the Q, K, V matrix, and $softmax$ $(QK^T/\sqrt{d_k})$ is the weight of each word in the feature representation of the entire sentence. $head_h$ is the result of the self-attention function of Q, K, V which are all come from token embedding.

AGGCN Layer. Attention guided GCN [7] is a leading improvement of GCN. The achievement of AGGCN on close-domain relation extraction motivated us. The adjacency matrix used by the original GCN is a 0–1 matrix. When applied to a DP tree, the adjacency matrix becomes very sparse. According to [22], a shallow GCN model may not be able to capture non-local interactions of a sparse graph. Therefore, AGGCN transforms the original adjacency matrix into a weight matrix, and the nonexistent edges are also given a small weight. Thus, the original sparse dependency tree is transformed into a weighted, fully connected graph. Then AGGCN uses a self-attention mechanism to learn the weights of the edges and aggregate the graph's information to every single node.

The word embedding of a sentence is concatenated with the POS and NER tag embeddings, and then input to AGGCN as the node embedding to learn the information of its neighbors. AGGCN can be expressed as:

$$\mathbf{g}_j^{(l)} = [\mathbf{x}_j; \mathbf{h}_j^{(1)}; ...; \mathbf{h}_j^{(l-1)}] \tag{3}$$

$$\tilde{\mathbf{A}}^{(t)} = \text{softmax}(\frac{Q\mathbf{W}_i^Q \times (K\mathbf{W}_i^K)^T}{\sqrt{d}})V \tag{4}$$

$$\mathbf{h}_{t_i}^{(l)} = \rho(\sum_{j=1}^{n} \tilde{\mathbf{A}}_{ij}^{(t)} \mathbf{W}_t^{(l)} \mathbf{g}_j^{(l)} + \mathbf{b}_t^{(t)}) \tag{5}$$

where $\mathbf{g}_j^{(l)}$ is the concatenation of the initial node embedding $\mathbf{x}_j$ and the node embedding produced by former layer $1, ..., l-1$, $\tilde{\mathbf{A}}$ is the fully connected graph and each entry $\tilde{\mathbf{A}}_{ij}$ is the weight of the edge going from node i to node j, $\mathbf{h}_j^{(l)}$ is the embedding of ith word in lth layer, $t = 1, ..., N$ which selects the weight matrix and bias term associated with the tth attention guided matrix $\tilde{\mathbf{A}}^{(t)}$.

TransD Layer. First proposed by TransE [1], the translating embedding model is originally designed for graph representation learning. The main idea of this method is as follows: let h, r, t be the embedding of head entity, relation, and tail entity, the distance of $h+r$ and t in the vector space should be as low as possible.

TransD [9] is one of the main improvements of TransE. It introduces a unified projection space for h, r, t to deal with N-to-N relations and the ambiguity of relationships with a few extra parameters.

So in the final layer, the output of AGGCN is the input node embedding of TransD. The final loss function for this model is:

$$\mathrm{E}_{in}(\mathbf{x}) = \mathrm{AGGCN}(\mathrm{BERT}(\mathbf{x}) \oplus \mathrm{E}_{pos} \oplus \mathrm{E}_{ner}) \tag{6}$$

$$\mathbf{h}_{\perp} = \mathbf{M}_{rh}\mathrm{E}_{in}(\mathbf{h}), \mathbf{t}_{\perp} = \mathbf{M}_{rt}\mathrm{E}_{in}(\mathbf{t}) \tag{7}$$

$$score(\mathbf{h}, \mathbf{r}, \mathbf{t}) = -\left\| \mathbf{h}_{\perp} + \mathbf{r} + \mathbf{t}_{\perp} \right\|_2^2 \tag{8}$$

$$L = \begin{bmatrix} \gamma + score_{h,t \in DP_G}(\mathbf{h}, \mathbf{r}, \mathbf{t}) \\ -score_{h',t' \in DP_{G'}}(\mathbf{h}', \mathbf{r}, \mathbf{t}') \end{bmatrix}_+ \tag{9}$$

where BERT($\mathbf{x}$), AGGCN($\mathbf{x}$) denotes the encode function of BERT and AGGCN model, $\mathbf{M}_{rh}$, $\mathbf{M}_{rt}$ are the projection matrix and bias terms which project node embedding to the vector space of dependency relations, γ is the margin value, it's the gap in score of positive and negative examples, and $[x]_+ \triangleq \max(0, x)$.

During the training process, the model will read a batch size number of sentences at a time, and take the DP tree (both real edges and the negative samples) of these sentences as the samples for training. At last, the model's final embedding for each dependency relation will be saved.

3.2 Open Information Extraction Model

The open information extraction model is trained to predict the OIE label sequence of the sentence. Its architecture is shown in Fig. 3.

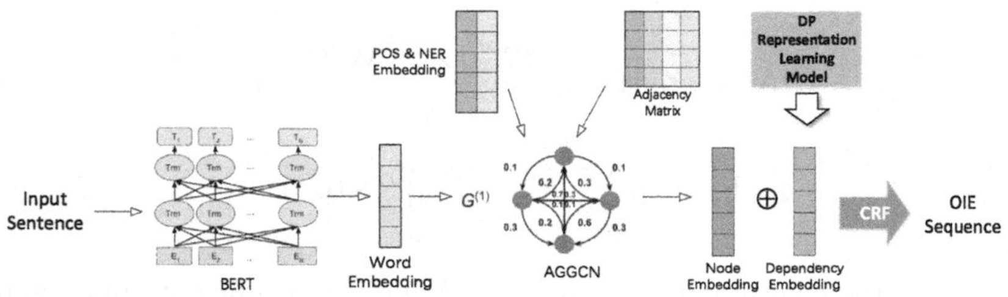

Fig. 3. Architecture of open information extraction model

Embedding Layers. The features of the sentence that we use include word, dependency relation, POS tag, and NER tag. The word is still encoded by BERT, and the embedding of POS and NER are randomly initialized in the embedding layers. The DP embedding is pre-trained by the model we described in Subsect. 3.1. It is loaded as the initial weight of the DP embedding layer in this model.

AGGCN Layer. Same to the DP representation learning model, we also use the AGGCN layer to learn the information of tree structure. The output of AGGCN is used as the input word embedding of the CRF layer.

CRF Layer. Finally, the word embedding is concatenated with the embedding of its dependency embedding. The final embedding then inputs into the CRF decoder layer and predicts the tag sequence with the highest probability.

The loss function of OIE model is shown in the Formula (10–11), where $\mathbf{x}$ is the input words, E_{dp} is the learned DP embedding, y is the target label sequence.

$$\mathrm{E}_{word} = \mathrm{AGGCN}(\mathrm{BERT}(\mathbf{x}) \oplus \mathrm{E}_{pos} \oplus \mathrm{E}_{ner}) \tag{10}$$

$$L = \mathrm{CRF}(\mathrm{E}_{word} \oplus \mathrm{E}_{dp}, y) \tag{11}$$

The time complexity of BERT, AGGCN, and the Viterbi decoding algorithm for CRF are all $O(n^2)$, where n is the max length of the sentence. So the time complexity of the whole method is also $O(n^2)$.

4 Experimental Setup

4.1 Data

We conducted experiments on the following three data sets:

NeuralOpenIE[2]**:** NeuralOpenIE is an English data set created by [2] using only high-confidence extractions of an existing relation extractor [16] from Wikipedia sentences. The total data size is more than 8GB.

SAOKE[3]**:** A human-annotated public Chinese OIE data set containing more than 40 thousand Chinese sentences and the corresponding facts. Many of them are **complex sentences and multivariate relation tuples**. In our experiment, only complete triplets (contains the relation word and at least two arguments) are taken out and transformed into the form of sequence labeling.

COER[4]**:** A high-quality Chinese knowledge base, which contains more than 100M relation triples. It is created by an unsupervised open extractor from diverse and heterogeneous web text, including encyclopedias and news.

The scale of **NeuralOpenIE** and **COER** is much larger than that of **SAOKE**. To eliminate the affect of the difference of data scale, we randomly sampled our experimental data of a scale matching the size of **SAOKE**. The number of the examples and the split for train, valid and test set of them is shown in Table 1.

[2] https://1drv.ms/u/s!ApPZx_TWwibImHl49ZBwxOU0ktHv.

[3] https://ai.baidu.com/broad/download?dataset=saoke.

[4] https://github.com/TJUNLP/COER.

Table 1. Number of examples of the datasets

Datasets	Number of examples		
	Train	Valid	Test
NeuralOpenIE	40000	5000	5000
SAOKE	44024	5503	5486
COER	40056	5007	5007

4.2 Baselines

We choose the following four baseline methods. Each of them is an open-sourced representative OIE method based on neural networks in recent years.
RnnOIE [20]**:** An English OIE method based on BiLSTM and CRF, one of the earliest neural OIE model. Since this method is mainly designed for English, we only reproduce the English data experiment.
LOREM [8]**:** Based on a CNN-LSTM based model NST [11], the embedding layer of LOREM is improved to make it suitable for multi-language and cross-lingual transfer learning. We add the Chinese Fasttext[5] model into LOREM and extend its applicability to Chinese data.
Span-OIE [23]**:** A neural OIE method that aims to select extraction spans from the sentence. Also, we replace the pre-trained word2vec model file to transform it into a Chinese-compatible model. A tag sequence is generated according to the span results to adapt to the metrics.
Multi²OIE [17]**:** A BERT-based OIE method, which extracts the relation first and then takes the relation as one of the inputs to extract the arguments.

4.3 Evaluation Metrics

Our evaluation metrics consist of the three most widely used metrics: precision, recall, and F1. Assume that True Positive (TP) is the number of correctly extracted tokens; False Positive (FP) is the number of miss-extracted tokens; False Negative (FN) is the number of tokens that should be extracted but the model doesn't. The calculation formula of the metrics is as Formula (12–14). Note that the F1 value equally reflects both the precision and the recall and is the most important metric of an ORE method.

$$precison = \frac{TP}{TP + FP} \tag{12}$$

$$recall = \frac{TP}{TP + FN} \tag{13}$$

$$F1 = \frac{2 \times Precision \times Recall}{Precision + Recall} \tag{14}$$

[5] https://fasttext.cc/.

Table 2. Comparison with baseline methods

Models	NeuralOpenIE			SAOKE			COER		
	P(%)	R(%)	F1(%)	P(%)	R(%)	F1(%)	P(%)	R(%)	F1(%)
RnnOIE	**79.74**	80.75	80.24	–	–	–	–	–	–
LOREM	70.09	82.81	75.93	**64.01**	27.34	38.32	78.07	79.24	78.65
SpanOIE	51.67	48.96	50.28	52.92	37.29	43.75	76.43	43.63	55.54
Multi^{2}OIE	57.36	**91.22**	70.43	24.69	**69.68**	36.46	40.57	81.96	54.27
Ours*	78.04	84.09	**81.28**	62.08	42.25	**50.28**	**84.74**	**86.06**	**85.40**

5 Result and Analysis

5.1 Model Comparison

We compared our model with the baseline models mentioned earlier on three data sets, the result is shown in Table 2. We can see that our model takes the highest F1 score on all three data sets. Moreover, our model has an improvement in recall than the baseline models not based on BERT. Multi2OIE has the highest recall on NeuralOpenIE and SAOKE, but it is not comparable to our model on precision and F1 score.

The experimental results show that the performance of our model is better than the baseline models on the three data sets. None of the four baseline models have considered the information of DP tree, which is believed to be the main reason why our method outperforms the baselines.

5.2 Ablation Studies

To explore the contribution of our main innovations to the improvement of model performance, we continue to conduct some ablation experiments. We set up two groups of control experiments.

BERT+GCN: In this group, we did not load the dependency embedding learned from the representation learning model but let the model initialize the embedding **randomly**.

BERT: In this group, we further remove the AGGCN layer. The POS and NER embedding is preserved as a part of the sentence features.

Table 3. Ablation experiment results

Groups	NeuralOpenIE			SAOKE			COER		
	P(%)	R(%)	F1(%)	P(%)	R(%)	F1(%)	P(%)	R(%)	F1(%)
Ours	**78.04**	84.09	**81.28**	**62.08**	42.25	**50.28**	**84.74**	**86.06**	**85.40**
BERT+GCN	75.42	**87.17**	80.87	50.13	**47.04**	48.53	82.91	86.62	84.72
BERT	79.53	81.79	80.65	57.69	41.91	48.55	82.26	86.34	84.25

The results of ablation experiments are shown in Table 3. When comparing our model with the BERT+GCN group, we can see that the learned dependency embedding mainly improved the precision, which in turn improves the F1 score. The improvements are greater for the Chinese data set, especially for SAOKE. When comparing the BERT+GCN with the BERT group, AGGCN has a better performance on higher-quality data sets, but it doesn't perform well on SAOKE which contains more complex sentences. This result may come as no surprise. AGGCN extracts the information of the dependency parsing tree. However, the LTP dependency parser is likely to fail when dealing with complex sentences, and the error will be passed to the GCN layer. This error propagation finally leads to the poor performance of the BERT+GCN group.

5.3 Error Analysis

ENG Example	A graph of dependencies is program specific and generated by a programmer .
Gold	<A graph of dependencies; is; program specific> <A graph of dependencies; is; generated by a programmer>
Prediction	<A graph of dependencies; is; program specific and generated by a programmer>
CHN Example	黑龙江省委书记吉炳轩、省长王宪魁出席会议
Gold	< 黑龙江; 省委书记; 吉炳轩 > < 黑龙江; 省长; 王宪魁 >
Prediction	< 黑龙江省委; 书记; 吉炳轩; 王宪魁 >

Fig. 4. Examples of bad predictions

To find out the parts of our model that can be improved in the future, we analyzed the model's misjudged prediction results on the test set. We found that misjudgments mostly occur in sentences containing multiple triplets. Seeing the ENG Example in Fig. 4, from which we can extract a triplet <a graph of dependencies; is; program specific> and a triplet <a graph of dependencies; is; generated by a programmer>. However, the model cannot solve the compound-complex sentence and take "program-specific and generated by a programmer" as the second argument. Similar mistakes also occur in the Chinese data set.

For most machine learning models, the same input only leads to the same output. For sentences with multiple triplets, it is difficult for the model to obtain information indicating multiple triplets. Therefore, generating multiple triplets from one sentence is a major difficulty of the OIE task at present. In future work, we will try to improve our OIE model to solve the multi-triplet problem.

6 Conclusion

In this paper, we propose an open information extraction method that can capture more information from the dependency tree. First, we present a new DP representation learning model to get a strong dependency embedding. Then,

AGGCN is used to learn the neighborhood information on the DP tree. With the help of the DP tree's information, our OIE model's effect has been improved. The model comparison experiment shows that our OIE model outperforms some mainstream works. The ablation studies show that the embedding learned by the DP representation learning model provides a considerable improvement to our OIE model. Hence, the strong learning ability of this model for DP information is proved. Finally, we will try to improve our OIE model to solve the multi-triplet problem in future work.

References

1. Bordes, A., Usunier, N., Garcia-Duran, A., Weston, J., Yakhnenko, O.: Translating embeddings for modeling multi-relational data. In: Advances in Neural Information Processing Systems, pp. 2787–2795 (2013)
2. Cui, L., Wei, F., Zhou, M.: Neural open information extraction. In: Proceedings of the 56th Annual Meeting of the Association for Computational Linguistics (Volume 2: Short Papers), pp. 407–413. Association for Computational Linguistics, Melbourne, Australia, July 2018. https://doi.org/10.18653/v1/P18-2065
3. Del Corro, L., Gemulla, R.: ClausIE: clause-based open information extraction. In: Proceedings of the 22nd International Conference on World Wide Web, pp. 355–366. WWW 2013. Association for Computing Machinery, New York, NY, USA (2013). https://doi.org/10.1145/2488388.2488420
4. Etzioni, O., Banko, M., Soderland, S., Weld, D.S.: Open information extraction from the web. Commun. ACM **51**, 68–74 (2008)
5. Etzioni, O., Fader, A., Christensen, J., Soderland, S., Mausam, M.: Open information extraction: the second generation. In: Proceedings of the Twenty-Second International Joint Conference on Artificial Intelligence - Volume Volume One, pp. 3–10. IJCAI 2011. AAAI Press (2011)
6. Gashteovski, K., Gemulla, R., del Corro, L.: MinIE: minimizing facts in open information extraction. In: Proceedings of the 2017 Conference on Empirical Methods in Natural Language Processing, pp. 2630–2640. Association for Computational Linguistics, Copenhagen, Denmark, September 2017. https://doi.org/10.18653/v1/D17-1278
7. Guo, Z., Zhang, Y., Lu, W.: Attention guided graph convolutional networks for relation extraction. In: Proceedings of the 57th Annual Meeting of the Association for Computational Linguistics, pp. 241–251 (2019)
8. Harting, T., Mesbah, S., Lofi, C.: LOREM: language-consistent open relation extraction from unstructured text. Proc. Web Conf. **2020**, 1830–1838 (2020)
9. Ji, G., He, S., Xu, L., Liu, K., Zhao, J.: Knowledge graph embedding via dynamic mapping matrix. In: Proceedings of the 53rd Annual Meeting of the Association for Computational Linguistics and the 7th International Joint Conference on Natural Language Processing (volume 1: Long papers), pp. 687–696 (2015)
10. Jia, S., Shijia, E., Li, M., Xiang, Y.: Chinese open relation extraction and knowledge base establishment. ACM Trans. Asian Low Resource Lang. Inf. Process. **17**(3), 1–22 (2018)
11. Jia, S., Xiang, Y.: Chinese user service intention classification based on hybrid neural network. J. Phys. Conf. Ser. **1229**, 012054 (2019)
12. Kipf, T.N., Welling, M.: Semi-supervised classification with graph convolutional networks. arXiv preprint arXiv:1609.02907 (2016)

13. Kolluru, K., Adlakha, V., Aggarwal, S., Mausam, Chakrabarti, S.: OpenIE6: iterative grid labeling and coordination analysis for open information extraction. In: Proceedings of the 2020 Conference on Empirical Methods in Natural Language Processing (EMNLP), pp. 3748–3761. Association for Computational Linguistics, Online, November 2020
14. Kolluru, K., Aggarwal, S., Rathore, V., Mausam, M., Chakrabarti, S.: IMoJIE: iterative memory-based joint open information extraction. In: The 58th Annual Meeting of the Association for Computational Linguistics (ACL), Seattle, U.S.A, July 2020
15. Mausam, Schmitz, M., Bart, R., Soderland, S., Etzioni, O.: Open language learning for information extraction. In: Proceedings of the 2012 Joint Conference on Empirical Methods in Natural Language Processing and Computational Natural Language Learning, pp. 523–534. EMNLP-CoNLL 2012. Association for Computational Linguistics, USA (2012)
16. Mausam, M.: Open information extraction systems and downstream applications, pp. 4074–4077. IJCAI 2016. AAAI Press (2016)
17. Ro, Y., Lee, Y., Kang, P.: Multi^{2}OIE: multilingual open information extraction based on multi-head attention with BERT. In: Proceedings of the 2020 Conference on Empirical Methods in Natural Language Processing: Findings, pp. 1107–1117 (2020)
18. Roy, A., Park, Y., Lee, T., Pan, S.: Supervising unsupervised open information extraction models. In: Proceedings of the 2019 Conference on Empirical Methods in Natural Language Processing and the 9th International Joint Conference on Natural Language Processing (EMNLP-IJCNLP), pp. 728–737. Association for Computational Linguistics, Hong Kong, China, November 2019. https://doi.org/10.18653/v1/D19-1067
19. Stanovsky, G., Dagan, I.: Creating a large benchmark for open information extraction. In: Proceedings of the 2016 Conference on Empirical Methods in Natural Language Processing (EMNLP) (to appear). Association for Computational Linguistics, Austin, Texas, November 2016
20. Stanovsky, G., Michael, J., Zettlemoyer, L., Dagan, I.: Supervised open information extraction. In: Proceedings of the 2018 Conference of the North American Chapter of the Association for Computational Linguistics: Human Language Technologies, vol. 1 (Long Papers), pp. 885–895 (2018)
21. Sun, M., Li, X., Wang, X., Fan, M., Feng, Y., Li, P.: Logician: a unified end-to-end neural approach for open-domain information extraction. In: Proceedings of the Eleventh ACM International Conference on Web Search and Data Mining, pp. 556–564. WSDM 2018. Association for Computing Machinery, New York, NY, USA (2018). https://doi.org/10.1145/3159652.3159712
22. Xu, K., Li, C., Tian, Y., Sonobe, T., Kawarabayashi, K.I., Jegelka, S.: Representation learning on graphs with jumping knowledge networks. In: International Conference on Machine Learning, pp. 5453–5462. PMLR (2018)
23. Zhan, J., Zhao, H.: Span model for open information extraction on accurate corpus. In: Proceedings of the AAAI Conference on Artificial Intelligence, vol. 34(05), pp. 9523–9530, April 2020. https://doi.org/10.1609/aaai.v34i05.6497, https://ojs.aaai.org/index.php/AAAI/article/view/6497
24. Zhang, Y., Qi, P., Manning, C.D.: Graph convolution over pruned dependency trees improves relation extraction. In: Proceedings of the 2018 Conference on Empirical Methods in Natural Language Processing, pp. 2205–2215 (2018)

Hierarchical Policy Network with Multi-agent for Knowledge Graph Reasoning Based on Reinforcement Learning

Mingming Zheng(✉), Yanquan Zhou, and Qingyao Cui

Beijing University of Posts and Telecommunications, Beijing 100876, China
{mingmingzheng,zhouyanquan,cuiqingyao}@bupt.edu.cn

Abstract. Multi-hop reasoning on Knowledge Graphs (KGs) aims at inferring the triplets that not in the KGs to address the KGs incompleteness problem. Reinforcement learning (RL) methods, exploiting an agent that takes incremental steps by sampling a relation and entity (called an action) to extend its path, has yielded superior performance. Existing RL methods, however, cannot gracefully handle the large-scale action space problem in KGs, causing dimensional disaster. Hierarchical reinforcement learning is dedicated to decomposing a complex reinforcement learning problem into several sub-problems and solving them separately, which can achieve better results than directly solving the entire problem. Building on this, in this paper, we propose to divide the action selection process in each step into three stages: 1) selecting a pre-clustered relation cluster, 2) selecting a relation in the chosen relation cluster, and 3) selecting the tail entity of the relation selected by the previous stage. Each stage has an agent to determine the selection, which formulated a hierarchical policy network. Furthermore, for the environment representation of KGs, the existing methods simply concatenate the different parts (the embedding of start entity, current entity and query relation), which ignore the potential connections between different parts, so we propose a convolutional neural network structure based on inception network to better extract features of the environment and enhance the interaction across different parts of the environment. The experimental results on three datasets demonstrate the effectiveness of our proposed method.

Keywords: Knowledge graph reasoning · Hierarchical reinforcement learning · Data mining

1 Introduction

KGs organize human knowledge into a structured system through triplets, which plays an important role in downstream tasks such as search engine, recommendation system and so on. Due to the fact that world knowledge is updated constantly, the KGs are always incomplete. However, some triplets that are not

H. Qiu et al. (Eds.): KSEM 2021, LNAI 12815, pp. 445–457, 2021.
https://doi.org/10.1007/978-3-030-82136-4_36

directly stored in KGs can be inferred from the triplets that are, which leads to a task called KGs reasoning, which can handle the incompleteness of KGs. Figure 1 shows an example, assuming that a triple (Alexander, athlete plays for team, Yankees) and (Yankees, team plays in league, ncaa) are already stored in KGs, then we can answer the query (Alexander, player plays in league, ?) with "ncaa". In doing so, we can infer a triplet (Alexander, player plays in league, ncaa) that does not exist in KGs.

The existing methods include rule-based methods such as Neural LP [13], embedding-based methods such as TransE [1], and path-based methods like PRA [8]. Although these methods are effective to some extent, each method has its own shortcomings. Rule-based methods are hard to scale up to large KGs, embedding-based methods can't explain the reasoning process well, path-based methods generate the paths that are gathered by random walks, which might be inferior and noisy. More recently, leveraging RL methods to reason on KGs make up for all the shortcomings of the above-mentioned methods [2,17]. The RL agent can walk conditioned by the policy network in the KGs with multi-hops and reach the target entity in a certain number of steps, which can be formulated as a Markov decision process.

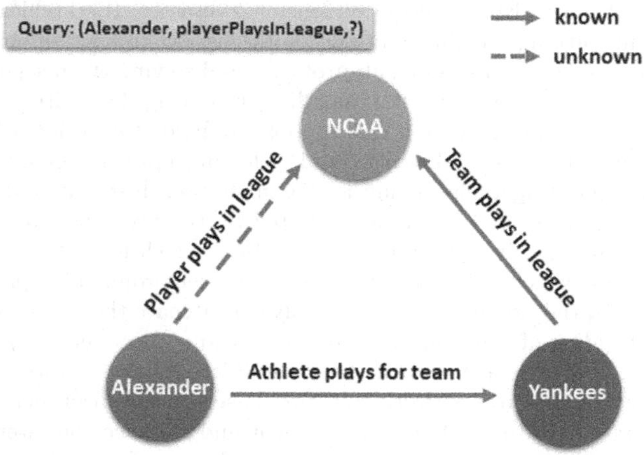

Fig. 1. A small fragment of knowledge graph. The solid line indicates an existing relation, dashed line means inferred relationship from prior, which depicts the reasoning process.

However, the existing RL-based methods take all the relations and entities that connected to the current entity as action space, which cannot handle the large-scale discrete action space problem, where the number of action space can be up to hundreds, causing dimensional disaster.

To tackle this problem, inspired by the idea of hierarchical reinforcement learning which decomposes a complex reinforcement learning problem into several sub-problems and solving them separately, we divide the selection of action in each step into three stages and propose a hierarchical policy network, as depicts in Fig. 2. Firstly, we classify the out-edges (relations) of each entity using clustering algorithm based on the pre-trained embedding of relations. We take the relation clusters as action space of the first stage which means that the agent is responsible for choosing a relation cluster. Secondly, the agent in second stage selects a relation from the relation cluster chosen by the first stage. Finally, the last stage's agent only need to choose an action from the greatly reduced action space which only includes a relation and its tail entities. In this way, a complex selection process is decomposed into several sub-problems and solving them separately, where the action space that are required to process has been greatly reduced, avoiding dimensional disaster.

In addition, the existing approaches that represent the KGs environment as an input to the policy network simply concatenate the different parts of the representation (start entity, current entity and query relation), which ignore the potential interaction between different parts. Based on this, we use the inception-based convolutional neural network for the feature extraction of environment representation to enhance the interaction of different parts. We conduct experiments on three mainstream datasets using the proposed methods, and demonstrate the superior performance over the past work.

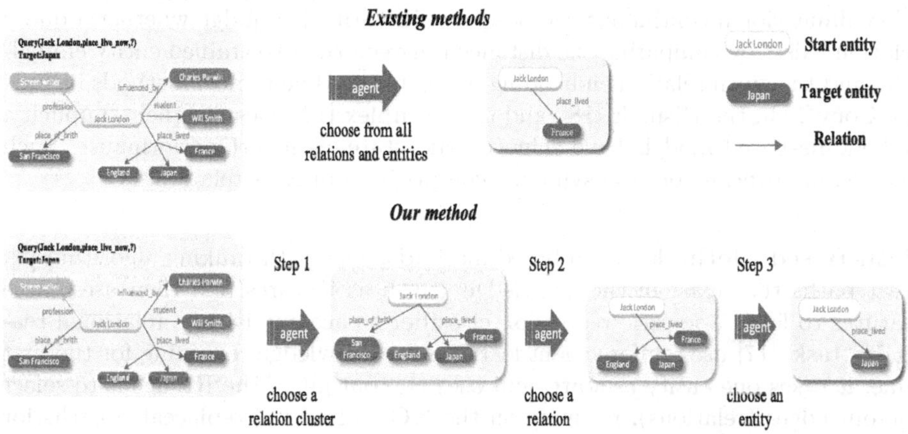

Fig. 2. The overall structure of our proposed method. The top part describes the current methods, directly select from hundreds of actions. The bottom part describes our hierarchical policy network, which divides the entire problem of action selection into three stages, where relation in same color means belonging to the same relation cluster.

In summary, our contributions are twofold:

- We divide the selection of action in each step into three stages and propose a hierarchical policy network with multi-agent based on the idea of hierarchical reinforcement learning, which effectively solves the problem of dimension disaster.

- For the state representation of the KGs environment, we consider the interaction between different parts and use a fine-grained convolution kernel based on inception network to obtain the refined features.

2 Related Work

2.1 Knowledge Graph Reasoning

Numerous approaches have been proposed for knowledge graph reasoning. They can be mainly divided into three categories: the rule-based methods, the embedding-based methods, and the path-based methods.

Rule-Based Methods. Rule based methods manually or mathematically summarize the logic of reasoning rules, then use these rules to reason on KG completion task, e.g., ProPPR [13] and Neural LP [19]. Such methods, unfortunately, are not well suited for knowledge graphs in a large-scale setting.

Embedding-Based Methods. Embedding-based methods capture the characteristics of the distance between entities and relations by mapping them into a low dimensional continuous vector space. In turn, they judge whether a query relation exists by comparing the distance between the two trained entity embedding and the given relation embedding of the query. The typical methods include the ConvE [3], the Dismult [18], and the Complex [12]. Despite their simplicity, embedding-based models have achieved the state-of-the-art performance. Such models, however, ignore the symbolic composition of KGs relations.

Path-Based Methods. Path based methods, e.g., path ranking algorithm [8], treat paths that exist in the knowledge graph as features and then uses these features to learn a logistic regression classifier to accomplish the relational reasoning task. [17] use reinforcement learning for knowledge reasoning for the first time, it takes one entity as start, and uses the output of the RL agent to select the out edges (relations), navigate on the KG to find the replaceable paths for a particular relation. [2] introduce historical path information into environment representation. [10] improved the reward mechanism. However, the existing RL-based methods cannot handle the problem of large-scale action space in the knowledge graph very well.

2.2 Hierarchical Reinforcement Learning Method

Traditional reinforcement learning methods conduct trial-and-error through interaction with the environment, thereby the policies are continuously being optimized, include [5,6], etc. However, an important shortcoming of reinforcement learning is that it cannot solve the large scale action space problem, which causes dimension disaster. The hierarchical reinforcement learning decomposes a complex problem into several sub-problems, and solves the sub-problems one by one through the divide-and-conquer method to finally solve a complex problem. The existing hierarchical reinforcement learning methods include [4,7,11], etc. These methods are very promising for large scale action space tasks, but they might require access to goal-reaching reward systems that are not defined in the original Markov decision process. HIPPO [9], which includes a high level policy and a low level policy using off-policy training method. Although they are effective, they cannot be directly used in knowledge reasoning tasks.

3 Method

3.1 Task Definition

Given a KGs $\mathcal{G} = \{(h, r, t)\} \subseteq \mathcal{E} \times \mathcal{R} \times \mathcal{E}$, where $\mathcal{E}$ and $\mathcal{R}$ are the entity set and the relation set, the (h, r, t) denotes the triplets in the KGs. The $(\boldsymbol{h}, \boldsymbol{r}, \boldsymbol{t})$ denotes the embedding of the entity and relation. For the task of KG reasoning, which is described in Fig. 1, given a head entity and a query relation $(h, r_q, ?)$, we need to find the tail entity in the knowledge graph, when (h, r_q, t) does not exist in the KGs.

3.2 Reinforcement Learning Formulation

We formulate the reasoning problem as a Markov Decision Process, which can be defined as a tuple (S, A, P, R, γ), where S is the continuous state space, $A = a_1, a_2, \cdots, a_n$ is the set of all available actions for each entity, $P(S_{t+1} = s' \mid S_t = s, A_t = a)$ is the transition probability matrix and $R(s, a)$ is the reward function of each (s, a) pair. γ is the discount factor for the reward which has a range of 0 to 1.

State. States is the representation of the environment. In KGs, the state is the representation of current environment of KGs. At time step t, we formulate the state representation as $(e_t, (e_s, r_q))$, where e_t denotes the current entity, e_s means the start entity, r_q is the query relation. Also, we follow the setting of [10], take the path history information $h_t = (e_s, r_1, \ldots, r_t, e_t)$, which conclude the sequence of actions taken up to step t as the representation of KGs environment.

$$h_0 = LSTM(0, [r_0; e_s]) \tag{1}$$

$$h_t = LSTM(h_{t-1}, [r_t, e_t]) \tag{2}$$

Action. $a \in A$, where A is the set of all available actions that the agent can take. In KGs, the action set includes the current entity's all out edges (relations). At each step, the agent takes the state representation as input and outputs an action to extend its reasoning path.

Transition. Transition model $P(s^{'}|s, a)$ means the probability of the state transformation from s to $s^{'}$ after taking an action a. In our task, the transition probability is determined by the KGs.

Reward. The reward indicates the immediate feedback after the agent takes an action, to evaluate the quality of the action being taken. We follow the reward settings in [10], when the target entity is reached, we set the reward to 1. When the target is not reached, we use the result of the scoring function f of the knowledge representation model as the reward, which effectively solves the problem of sparse reward, [10] introduced this in detail.

$$reward = \begin{cases} 1, & e_T = e_a \\ f(e_s, r_q, e_T), & e_T \neq e_a, \end{cases} \tag{3}$$

where e_a denotes the correct target entity, e_T denotes the entity that the agent actually arrives, and f denotes the scoring function following [10].

3.3 The Proposed Method

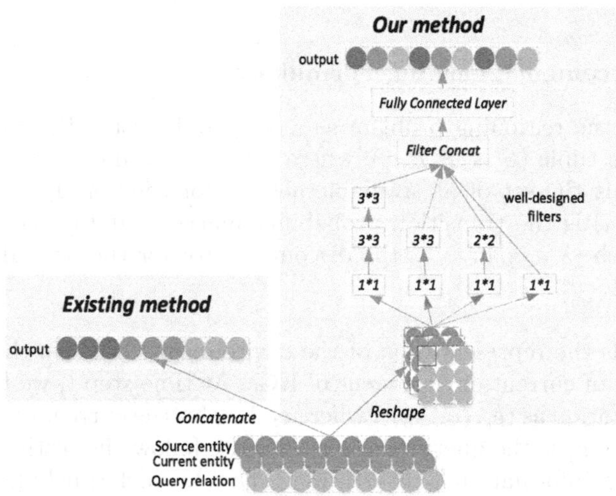

Fig. 3. The proposed inception-based state encoder of environment, the left part depicts current methods which simply concatenate different parts of the environment representation, the right part depicts our inception-based state encoder.

Hierarchical Policy Network with Multi-agents. To handle the large-scale action space problem, which cause dimension disaster, following the idea of hierarchical reinforcement learning, we divide the action selection process of each step into three stages, and we use a hierarchical policy network with multi-agents for action selection. For the first stage, we pre-cluster the relations according to the pre-trained knowledge graph embedding model. After clustering, we obtain

k relation clusters for each entity, formulated as $G_1, G_2, \ldots, G_k$, and $r_{i_j} \in G_i$ represent that r_{i_j} is an relation belong to relation cluster G_i, also, we take every cluster center's embedding G_m as an representation of every relation cluster. The agent in the first stage is responsible for choosing a relation cluster with the input of the environment representation,

$$G \sim \pi_{\theta_1}(\cdot \mid s_t), G \in G_1, G_2, \ldots, G_k \tag{4}$$

where G is the chosen cluster, and implemented using a fully connected neural network, which output the probability of selecting each relationship cluster.

For the second stage, we choose a relation from the cluster selected from previous. We take the relation cluster from the top layer and choose a relation:

$$\pi_{\theta_2}(r_t, s_t) = \sigma(G_t \times W_1(Relu(W_2 s_t))), r \in G \tag{5}$$

where the action space G_t is encoded by stacking the embeddings of the reduced actions in it, $A_t \in |A_t| \times 2d$, σ is the softmax function.

For the agent in the bottom layer, we take the tail entities of relation chosen from the middle layer as action space which is greatly reduced, and finally choose an entity to form the path. As such, given the environmental state and guided by the policy networks, a top-down selection is performed from the top to the bottom and form the corresponding path in the knowledge graph.

$$\pi_{\theta_3}(a_t, s_t) = \sigma(A_t \times W_1(Relu(W_2 s_t))), \tag{6}$$

where the action space A_t is encoded by stacking the embeddings of the reduced actions in it, $A_t \in |A_t| \times 2d$, σ is the softmax function.

Inception-Based State Encoder. As mentioned above Fig. 3, the existing state representation methods directly concatenate different parts of the environment representation (start entity, current entity and query relation) into the policy network as environmental information, ignoring the interaction between those parts. Inspired by the ConvE and the InceptionE [16] which uses 2D convolution operation to model the head entity and relation, we introduce a convolutional neural network into the state encoding module to enhance the interaction. We use several well-designed filters with different scales to enhance the interaction between each input part by using different parts of the information as multiple channels of the input, while keeping the parameter efficient. To be more specific, given a current state information, we first concatenate the input including the embeddings of head entity, query relation and current entity on the channel dimension, denoted as v_h, v_q, v_{e_t}. Then we take the 1*1 filter to increase the interaction between the start entity, query relation and the current entity embeddings, which can be denoted as:

$$v_{1*1} = Relu([v_h || v_q || v_{e_t}] * w_{1*1}), \tag{7}$$

where Relu is a non-linear activation function, the operator $||$ means the concatenation, $*$ denote the convolution operation and w is the weight matrix of the $1*1$ convolution filter, and the output v_{1*1} is the output containing the interaction features following the first $1*1$ convolution layer. Subsequently, as depicted in [16], we take the filters with different sizes, like $2*2$, $3*3$, to capture higher level features. As a result, we obtain two feature matrices v_{2*2} and v_{3*3}. We use a similar operation, using two $3*3$ convolution filters and generate the output.

$$v_{2(3*3)} = Relu(Relu(v_{1*1} * w^{1}_{1*1}) * w^{2}_{3*3}), \tag{8}$$

where w^{2}_{3*3} is the feature matrix. The final output is composed of different levels of interaction filters, denoted as v_s, then we feed the v_s into a fully connected network, and concatenate it with the history information:

$$v_s = Inception(v_h, v_q, v_{e_t}) = Relu(vec(v_{1*1}||v_{2*2}||v_{3*3}||v_{2(3*3)})\mathbf{W}), \tag{9}$$

where W is the parameter of the fully connected layer.

$$v = [v_s||h], \tag{10}$$

where h is the history information. Then we take v as input into the hierarchical policy network.

3.4 Training

The hierarchical policy network with multi-agent work collaboratively, choose relation cluster, relation and entity respectively and finally reach the correct target entity or fail to reach it within a certain number of steps, eventually obtain a reward that is used to update three agents' parameters. We take the REINFORCE [14] algorithm to training, maximizing the expected reward:

$$J(\theta) = E_{(e_s,r,e_o)\in g}[E_{(a_1,\ldots,a_T\sim\pi_\theta)}(R(s_T \mid e_s, r_q))] \tag{11}$$

and updates θ with the following stochastic gradient:

$$\nabla_\theta J(\theta) \approx \nabla_\theta \sum_{t=1}^{T} R\left(s_T \mid e_s, r\right) \log \pi_\theta\left(a_t \mid s_t\right). \tag{12}$$

Table 1. Description of the datasets used in our experiments. #Ent and #Rel describes the total number of entities and relations in the KG respectively. #Fact denotes the total number of triplets concluded in the KG used as training set and dev set, and #query denotes the triplets as the test set.

Dataset	#Ent	#Rel	#Fact	#Query
WN18RR	40,493	11	86,835	3,134
FB15K-237	14,541	237	272,115	20,466
NELL-995	75,492	200	154,213	3,992

4 Experiments

4.1 Datasets and Settings

Datasets. WN18RR and FB15K-237, are subsets of WN18 and FB15K, solving the test set leakage problem of the raw datasets. Details are in Table 1 We follow the setup of [10], using the same train/dev/test splits for three datasets.

Also, to enhance the policy network the ability to roll back, like previous work, we add the reverse edge (t, r^{-1}, h) to datasets, and add "no op" relation for each entity between the entity and itself, which adapts the long reasoning path, allowing the agent to loop multiple consecutive steps over the same entity. An overview of both datasets can be found in Table 1.

Table 2. Question answering results on the WN18RR, FB15k-237 and NELL-995. The top part is embedding-based methods, the bottom part is path-based methods. Specially, [10] and is reinforcement learning based method as our baseline.

	WN18RR			FB15K-237			NELL-995		
	H@1	H@10	MRR	H@1	H@10	MRR	H@1	H@10	MRR
DistMult	**43.1**	52.4	**46.2**	32.4	60.0	41.7	55.2	78.3	64.1
ComplEx	41.8	48.0	43.7	32.8	61.6	42.5	64.1	86.0	72.6
ConvE	40.3	**54.0**	44.9	**34.1**	**62.2**	**43.5**	**67.8**	**88.6**	**76.1**
NeuralLP	37.6	65.7	46.3	16.6	34.8	22.7	-	-	-
MINERVA	41.3	51.3	44.8	21.8	45.6	29.3	66.3	83.1	72.5
[10]	41.8	51.7	45.0	32.7	56.4	40.7	**65.6**	84.4	72.7
Ours	**43.8**	**53.9**	**47.3**	**33.2**	**59.1**	**42.2**	65.5	**84.7**	**73.1**

Settings. We experiment with our hierarchical structured policy network and inception-based encoder on three datasets. To get the best result, we take pre-trained knowledge graph embedding model TKRL [15] to cluster and we use KNN(K-Nearest Neighbors) based clustering algorithm. Also, we set the embedding size of entity and relation as 100 and 100 respectively. For the LSTM module, we set the hidden layer to 3. The learning rate we set 0.001. We take the Adam optimization method and mini-batch strategy. The evaluation criteria are hits@k where k = 1, 10 and Mean Reciprocal Rank (MRR). We selected the best model with the highest MRR score on the corresponding validation set.

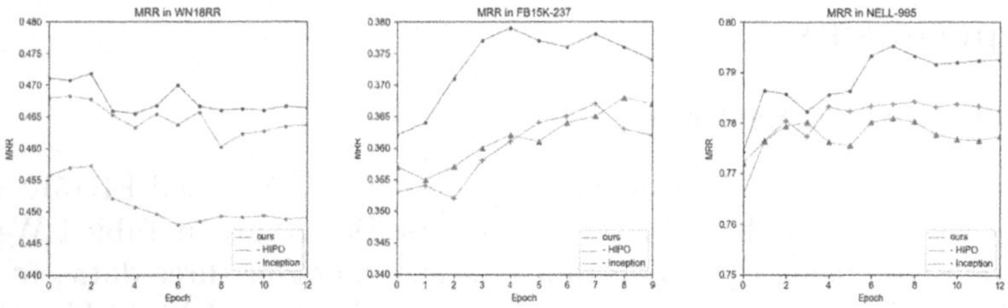

Fig. 4. Ablation study on three datasets, and we take the MRR metric to demonstrate the effectiveness of our proposed method.

4.2 Overall Results

The evaluation results of our proposed approach and the baselines are shown in Table 2. The top part presents the embedding-based approaches, and the bottom part presents the path-based approaches. On several datasets, we find that embedding-based models perform strongly, achieving the overall best evaluation metrics on FB15K-237 and NELL-995 dataset, despite their simplicity. While previous path based approaches achieve comparable performance on some of the datasets(WN18RR, NELL-995), they perform significantly worse than the embedding based models on the other datasets (14.2 absolute points lower on FB15K-237). [10] is the first path-based reasoning approach which is consistently comparable or better than embedding based approaches on three datasets, so, we experimented with our proposed method based on [10].

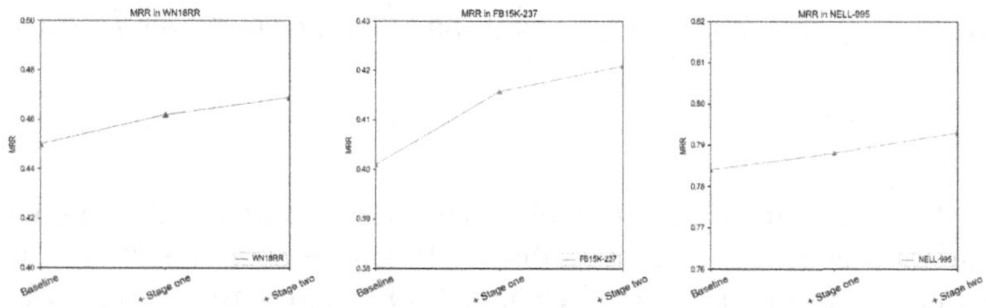

Fig. 5. This shows the experimental results when we gradually add each selection stage.

From the results, we can observe that:

In addition to the small improvement in the NELL-995 model (0.3 on hits@10 and 0.4 on MRR), the model is effective on the other two datasets, especially on the dataset with a relatively large average out degree of FB15K-237, the improvement of the model is more obvious, which can be up to 2.7 on hits@10, the reason we speculate should be that the average out degree of the entities in this dataset is much higher than that of the other two datasets, our hierarchical policy network divided the entire selection process into three stages, which avoids choosing from hundreds of actions and avoids the problem of dimensional disasters in reinforcement learning.

4.3 Ablation Study

For comparison, we perform an ablation study where we remove the hierarchical policy network structure (– HIPO) and the inception-based encoder (– Inception) from the entire model, and compare the MRR metric on the validation set. From Fig. 4, we can observe that:

More specifically, for the effect of hierarchical policy network structure, on FB15K-237 dataset, because of its high average degree, the large action space has more influence on the result, and our method improved the results significantly. Moreover, for the WN18RR dataset, the hierarchical policy network model has some improvement, for the NELL-995 dataset, the improvement is slight. Furthermore, for the encoder of inception network, the three datasets show their effectiveness respectively. The reason should be that the policy network has gained the more refined representation characteristics of KGs by the Inception-based encoder. Also, to validate the effectiveness of every stage, We adopt a method of gradually add each stage to verify the effectiveness of each stage. In this way, to see how each stage influences the performance, we record the corresponding results. And we can observe from Fig. 5: when we gradually add each stage, the policy network becomes more effective. Specifically, for the dataset WN18RR and FB15K237, the first stage(firstly choose an relation cluster) plays a more important role, for the dataset NELL-995, the second stage plays a more important role.

4.4 Case Study

Accordingly, in this section, we present a few representative example cases to demonstrate the effectiveness of our proposed method, which can be seen in Tables 3 and 4. Since the hierarchical policy network decomposes the complex action selection process into three stages, it works better for large action spaces (corresponding to entities with too many relations in the knowledge graph), and

Table 3. Example question for query *organizationhiredperson* from NELL-995, incorrectly answered by [10] and correctly answered by our policy network, the query entity's degree is 320 and the dataset median degree is 1.

	Reasoning path
[10]	$person\_mexico\_ryan\_whitney \xrightarrow{organizationhiredperson^{-1}}$ $country\_us \xrightarrow{personleadsorganization^{-1}} personus\_warren\_buffet$ $\xrightarrow{personleadsorganization} non\_gov\_organization\_us$
Ours	$person\_mexico\_ryan\_whitney \xrightarrow{worksfor}$ $government\_organization\_capitol$

we analyzed some paths not found by [10] but found by our model. In the two examples, we identified the degree of the start entity, and found that the policy network of hierarchical structure is very effective for large-scale action space queries.

Table 4. Example question for query *worksfor* from NELL-995, incorrectly answered by [10] and correctly answered by our policy network, the query entity's degree is 4 and the dataset median degree is 1.

	Reasoning path
[10]	$coach\_mike\_martz \xrightarrow{coachesteam} sportsteam\_st\_louis\_rams \xrightarrow{worksfor^{-1}}$
	$coach\_mike\_martz \xrightarrow{coachwontrophy} award\_trophy\_tournament\_super\_bowl\_xlii$
Ours	$coach\_mike\_martz \xrightarrow{coachesteam} sportsteam\_rams$

5 Conclusion and Future Work

In conclusion, we proposed a hierarchical multi-agent policy network to address the issue of large-scale action space in KGs reasoning, and experimentally demonstrated that our method has better results for high-degree entities. In addition, we further enhanced the interaction between different parts of the representation of the KGs environment by using an Inception-based network. In the future, we will try a hierarchical clustering algorithm to replace the current KNN clustering algorithm, in order to perform better classification on the outgoing edges of each entity.

References

1. Bordes, A., Usunier, N., Garcia-Duran, A., Weston, J., Yakhnenko, O.: Translating embeddings for modeling multi-relational data. In: Advances in Neural Information Processing Systems, pp. 2787–2795 (2013)
2. Das, R., et al.: Go for a walk and arrive at the answer: reasoning over paths in knowledge bases using reinforcement learning. arXiv preprint arXiv:1711.05851 (2017)
3. Dettmers, T., Minervini, P., Stenetorp, P., Riedel, S.: Convolutional 2d knowledge graph embeddings. arXiv preprint arXiv:1707.01476 (2017)
4. Eysenbach, B., Gupta, A., Ibarz, J., Levine, S.: Diversity is all you need: learning skills without a reward function. arXiv abs/1802.06070 (2019)
5. Gai, K., Qiu, M.: Optimal resource allocation using reinforcement learning for IoT content-centric services. Appl. Soft Comput. **70**, 12–21 (2018)
6. Gai, K., Qiu, M.: Reinforcement learning-based content-centric services in mobile sensing. IEEE Netw. **32**(4), 34–39 (2018)
7. Kulkarni, T.D., Narasimhan, K., Saeedi, A., Tenenbaum, J.: Hierarchical deep reinforcement learning: integrating temporal abstraction and intrinsic motivation. arXiv abs/1604.06057 (2016)

8. Lao, N., Mitchell, T., Cohen, W.: Random walk inference and learning in a large scale knowledge base. In: Proceedings of the 2011 Conference on Empirical Methods in Natural Language Processing, pp. 529–539 (2011)
9. Li, A.C., Florensa, C., Clavera, I., Abbeel, P.: Sub-policy adaptation for hierarchical reinforcement learning. arXiv preprint arXiv:1906.05862 (2019)
10. Lin, X.V., Socher, R., Xiong, C.: Multi-hop knowledge graph reasoning with reward shaping. arXiv preprint arXiv:1808.10568 (2018)
11. Nachum, O., Gu, S., Lee, H., Levine, S.: Data-efficient hierarchical reinforcement learning. arXiv abs/1805.08296 (2018)
12. Trouillon, T., Welbl, J., Riedel, S., Gaussier, É., Bouchard, G.: Complex embeddings for simple link prediction. In: International Conference on Machine Learning (ICML) (2016)
13. Wang, W.Y., Cohen, W.W.: Learning first-order logic embeddings via matrix factorization. In: IJCAI, pp. 2132–2138 (2016)
14. Williams, R.J.: Simple statistical gradient-following algorithms for connectionist reinforcement learning. Mach. Learn. **8**, 229–256 (2004)
15. Xie, R., Liu, Z., Sun, M.: Representation learning of knowledge graphs with hierarchical types. In: IJCAI (2016)
16. Xie, Z., Zhou, G., Liu, J., Huang, X.: ReinceptionE: relation-aware inception network with joint local-global structural information for knowledge graph embedding. In: ACL (2020)
17. Xiong, W., Hoang, T., Wang, W.Y.: DeepPath: a reinforcement learning method for knowledge graph reasoning. arXiv preprint arXiv:1707.06690 (2017)
18. Yang, B., Yih, W., He, X., Gao, J., Deng, L.: Embedding entities and relations for learning and inference in knowledge bases. arXiv preprint arXiv:1412.6575 (2014)
19. Yang, F., Yang, Z., Cohen, W.W.: Differentiable learning of logical rules for knowledge base reasoning. In: Advances in Neural Information Processing Systems, pp. 2319–2328 (2017)

Inducing Bilingual Word Representations for Non-isomorphic Spaces by an Unsupervised Way

Shaolin Zhu[1], Chenggang Mi[2(✉)], and Linlin Zhang[3]

[1] Zhengzhou University of light industry, Zhenghzou, China
[2] Northwestern Polytechnical University, Xi'an, China
michenggang@nwpu.edu.cn
[3] Zhejiang University, hangzhou, China

Abstract. Bilingual word representations (BWRs) play a very key role in many natural language processing (NLP) tasks, especially cross-lingual applications such as machine translation and cross-lingual information retrieval et al. Most existing methods are based on offline unsupervised methods to learn BWRs. Those offline methods mainly rely on the isomorphic assumption that word representations have a similar distribution for different languages. Several authors also question this assumption and argue that word representation spaces are non-isomorphic for many language pairs. In this paper, we adopt a novel unsupervised method to implement joint training BWRs. We first use a dynamic programming algorithm to detect continuous bilingual segments. Then, we use the extracted bilingual data and monolingual corpora to train BWRs jointly. Experiments show that our approach improves the performance of BWRs compared with several baselines in the real-world dataset.(By unsupervised, we mean that no cross-lingual resources like parallel text or bilingual lexicons are directly used.)

Keywords: Bilingual word representation · Natural language process · Joint training · Unsupervised · Dynamic programming

1 Introduction

Bilingual word representations (BWRs) are the representations of words of two languages in one common continuous vector space. BWRs benefits a lot in many cross-lingual natural language processing (NLP) tasks, such as bilingual lexicon induction [3,14,28], machine translation [15,26], cross-lingual information retrieval [16,17] and other applications [6–8].

Recent efforts in learning BWRs have predominantly focused on fully unsupervised approaches that project two trained monolingual representations into a shared space (so-called offline mapping) without any bilingual signals [3,14,24,27].

Supported by Northwestern Polytechnical University and Zhejiang University.

H. Qiu et al. (Eds.): KSEM 2021, LNAI 12815, pp. 458–466, 2021.
https://doi.org/10.1007/978-3-030-82136-4_37

The offline mapping methods can train two monolingual word representations only on two monolingual data. Then, they based on the isomorphic assumption that two equivalent words in different languages should have similar distributions to map two monolingual word representations into a shared space. However, several authors [20,22,27] questioned this isomorphic assumption (subsequently referred to as the orthogonality assumption). [23] demonstrated that the pre-trained representations are non-isomorphic for many language pairs. The non-isomorphic spaces mean that the distribution of clusters of word representations are similar, but miss out within the clusters. This means that although some words can be aligned by the assumption, many words may obtain miss alignment information.

Recently, [22,27] use parallel data to jointly training BWRs. However, Although they demonstrated that joint training can effectively relieve the limitation of the non-isomorphic issue in BWEs, the method heavily dependent on bilinugal parallel data. Our method is motivated by those works, the main difference is that we solve the limitation of supervision signals (parallel data) for jointly training BWRs.

In this paper, we propose a new unsupervised method how jointly training BWRs by using monolingual corpora. We first use adopt the unsupervised cross-lingual word representations training initializing BWRs. After that, we propose a dynamic programming algorithm that unsupervised finding parallel data from monolingual corpora for jointly training BWEs based on nearest-neighbors method. Our method can effectively relieve the limitation of supervision parallel data of existing approaches. Finally, we propose a joint method to use obtained bilingual parallel data to jointly train BWEs. The experimental results on real-world datasets show that our method learns better BWRs for cross-lingual tasks compare with several strong baseline models.

The rest of the paper is organized as follows: In Sect. 2, we introduce what is the non-isomorphic space and how to evaluate. In Sect. 3, we mainly describe our proposed method. Section 4 gives the experimental datasets and settings, while Sect. 5 analyzes its result. Finally, we end with a discussion and conclusion.

2 Non-isomorphic Spaces

The isomorphic assumption means that there is an orthogonal mapping matrix to map one representation space to another. We can be formally defined as follows:

$$||I - W^T W||^2 = 0 \tag{1}$$

where W is a matrix from the source representation X mapping to the target representation Y as $WX = Y$. concurrently, the above equation means that if the two representation spaces are isomorphic, there is an orthogonal mapping matrix. If the above equation is not satisfied, the representation spaces are non-isomorphic [23]. To evaluate the validity of non-isomorphism, we use the Gromov Hausdorff (GH) distance in this paper, The distance is mainly to check two vactor spaces are aligned or not. The GH distance between two metric spaces is a measure of the worst-case or diametric distance between the spaces. For the detail, we use two metric spaces X, and Y with a distance function $d(.,.)$, the GH distance is defined as:

$$d(X,Y) = max\{H(x,y), H(y,x)\} \tag{2}$$

$H(x,y)$ provides a quantitative estimate of the isometry of two spaces from X to Y, and $H(y,x)$ is from y to x. In experiments as Sect. 5, we can find the values of $||I - W^T W||$ and GH distances are bigger for etymologically distant language pairs than close language pairs[1]. This means the non-isomorphic spaces are existing in many language pairs, especially for etymologically distant language pairs.

3 Methodology

We aim to create a BWRs space where each source word representation has closely the nearest neighbor among the target. In this paper, we propose an unsupervised joint method to train BWRs by mining monolingual corpora. Our proposed method consists of three sequential steps: (1) We firstly use a fully unsupervised initialization heuristic scheme that creates an initial BWRs; (2) Then, we use the BWEs to mine bilingual signals from monolingual corpora by a dynamic programming algorithm based on nearest-neighbors searching; (3) Finally, we use a joint method to refine the BWRs.

3.1 Unsupervised Initial BWRs

In this section, we need to map pre-trained source and target word representations into a share vector space. Firstly, we use Word2Vec[2] to build monolingual word representations.

Previous methods for learning BWRs can be roughly divided into two categories [22], i.e., offline mapping and jointly learning methods. As the second category, the skip-gram [18] for example, requires bilingual corpus during training, current methods for unsupervised BWEs mainly fall into the first category. [3] showed that excellent quality BWEs can be trained without any bilingual supervision. They used an unsupervised self-learning method that initial BWRs obtained from singular value decomposition (SVD) as follows:

$$W^* = \underset{(W_X,W_Y)}{argmax} \sum_i \sum_j D_{i,j}((X_i W_X).(Y_j W_Y)), \quad \textbf{with} \quad USV^T = X^T DZ \tag{3}$$

[1] We mean that the etymologically close languages are closely-related languages such as English-French. The distant languages are etymologically different such as English-Chinese.

[2] https://code.google.com/p/word2vec/.

where $D_{i,j}$ is a sparse matrix if the jth source word is a translation of the ith target word. An optimal solution is given by $w_X = U$ and $w_Y = V$. Then, a similarity matrix of all words in the vocabulary can be calculated by $Xw_Xw_Y^TY^T$. In this paper, we follow the approach of [3] to create the initial BWRs. At the same time, we use orthographic information to improve the initial BWRs in rare words as [4].

3.2 Parallel Continuous Bilingual Phrase Pairs Detection

In fact, various algorithms for extracting parallel sentences were proposed [11,13,19]. Although those methods all can extract some good quality parallel sentences, one major disadvantage is that sentence pairs which have similar meanings but are not exactly parallel are often extracted. To overcome this problem, [12] proposed to aligned words in the candidate sentence pairs to detect parallel phrases similarly. They argue continuous phrases are more related, candidates having long enough segments are parallel. Our method is motivated by the work, the main difference is that we mine continuous parallel phrases rather than sentences. The main reason[3] is that we hope to mine good quality bilingual data (words or phrases) for jointly training BWRs.

We iterate over the source sentences from left to right and greedily align each source word to the most nearest-neighbors target word that was not already aligned. In detecting aligned words, we don't use word similarity to filter. We design a dynamic programming algorithm as follows:

$$\begin{aligned} max \sum_{i=0}^{N}\sum_{j=0}^{M}[m_t](w_i^x.w_j^y), \\ \textbf{s.t.} \quad [m_t = 1] \\ w_i^x \in NN_k^{target}(w_j^y) \\ w_j^y \in NN_k^{source}(w_i^x) \end{aligned} \tag{4}$$

For a length N of source x phrase, we search the translation of every source word in the length M of the target y phrase[4]. If a target word w_j^y is in the k nearest-neighbors ($k = 10$) of the source word w_i^x, we set $[m_t = 1]$ to represent the two words are aligned, otherwise $[m_t = 0]$. We use $w_i^x \in NN_k^{target}(w_j^y)$ to represent the k nearest-neighbors. Similarly, target words could be aligned as well, as $w_j^y \in NN_k^{source}(w_i^x)$. We argue that if every word in the source continuous phrase all has the nearest neighbors in target, it is more likely aligned. In our process, we don't calculate an alignment similarity score for each position

[3] Most of the related works extract parallel sentences to improve machine translation system. Recall of extracted parallel data also is important. Ours only consider obtaining some (rather than all) good quality parallel data (words or phrases), parallel sentences are not necessary.

[4] In this paper, we define a phrase that contains three words at least. We also test the different number of words how to affect the results in the experimental section.

of the source and target sentences respectively. Instead, we emphasize that the nearest-neighbor words must be in continuous phrases. In detail, we look for continuous phrases on both source and target sides by looking for sequences of indices where the nearest-neighbors are existing.

3.3 Jointly Training BWRs

In the above, we design an unsupervised method to extract parallel phrases. Then, we use the mined parallel phrases and monolingual corpora to jointly train BWRs. Jointly training BWRs has proven to be an effective strategy for mitigating the non-isomorphic issue [20,22,27]. The offline method is to learn a linear transformation matrix W to map the source to the target. The joint method is simultaneously learning the BWRs in different languages with cross-lingual supervision. [5] proposed the multivec[5] [5] to training our BWRs on parallel data demonstrated that the joint method can solve the non-isomorphic issue for many language pairs. In this paper, we mainly solve the limitation of cross-lingual supervision to train the BWRs model jointly. From the above section, we have already obtain bilingual data by our proposed method. Therefore, we use the multivec[6] [5] to training our BWEs on our unsupervised extracted parallel phrases and monolingual corpora. When jointly training BWRs, we normalize the embeddings and mean centers of each dimension. This process has been demonstrated to be beneficial by [1].

[22] showed that linguistic divergences cause strong mismatches in BWRs for offline methods. However, it is not clear whether this is an inherent limitation of non-isomorphic spaces or an insurmountable obstacle that arises from the linguistic divergences across languages, and hence a more general issue when learning BWRs. In experiments, we will carefully analyze those factors. The results show that non-isomorphic spaces are an inherent limitation for offline methods, linguistic divergences can cause the spaces are more non-isomorphic.

4 Experimental Setting

We next describe the datasets and evaluation measures used in our experiments.

4.1 Datasets

To jointly train our BWRs, we need to obtain monolingual corpora. We extract monolingual corpora from Wikipedia that is widely used by previous works in training BWRs. More concretely, we use WikiExtractor[7] to extract plain text from Wikipedia which contains comparable corpora. We obtain 100 million sentences for six languages separately English, German, Russian, Chinese, Italian,

[5] https://github.com/alex-berard/multivec.
[6] https://github.com/alex-berard/multivec.
[7] https://github.com/attardi/wikiextractor.

Turkey. When training BWRs, we use the six languages to make up 3 relatively close language pairs(English-German, English-Italian, German-Italian) and 3 distant language pairs (English-Russian, English-Turkey, English-Chinese).

4.2 Evaluation Setting

Blingual Lexicon Induction(BLI): It is by far the most popular evaluation task for BWRs used by previous work [9]. We use the nearest neighbor with cosine similarity (NN) to induce a bilingual lexicon. In order to evaluate the quality of the induced translations, we compare them with existing bilingual dictionaries, which we call MUSE[8]. It consists of another 1,500 test entries and was compiled by [14] using internal translation tools.

Table 1. Average accuracies (%) are trained on the wikipedia corpora.

Methods	En-De	En-It	De-It	En-Ru	En-Tr	En-Zh
$\|\|I - W^T W\|\|$	0.13	4.81	5.13	5.32	7.63	13.86
GH	0.18	0.41	0.43	0.46	0.80	0.92
Methods with bilingual supervision						
[21]	60.7	58.32	53.69	32.15	33.2	32.63
[25]	72.8	70.57	64.72	41.6	40.65	38.3
[2]	72.62	71.31	64.4	43.86	46.06	36.41
Methods without bilingual supervision						
[14]	68.49	70.86	65.32	29.13	41.66	37.5
[3]	73.02	73.42	64.52	45.66	47.6	40.6
[10]	73.23	72.13	66.18	43.7	46.64	42.13
Proposed method	**74.15**	**72.33**	**67.07**	**50.06**	**51.81**	**50.7**

5 Results and Discussion

In this section, We give the results of baselines and our method. We first present the main results of BWRs. Then, we summarize and discuss the main findings across several dimensions of comparison.

We report the results of the BLI task on Wikipedia. At the same time, we use the work of [3] to initialize our BWRs. The results are average accuracies (%) of word translation, as shown in Table 1. We compare ours with supervised and unsupervised methods to test the performance.

As it can be seen from Table 1, we find the proposed method performs at par with or outperforms the baselines in three close language pairs English-German, English-Italian and German-Italian. At the same time, we find the

[8] https://github.com/facebookresearch/MUSE.

proposed method gets substantially better results in the more challenging distant language pairs English-Russian, English-Turkey and English-Chinese. However, all baselines have an obvious drop in distant languages. The offline unsupervised methods are all based on the assumption that word representations in different languages have isomorphic distribution in vector space. [27] have demonstrated that the similarity is less when two languages are distant. Moreover, we use $||I - W^T W||$ and GH to compute correlations against an empirical measure of the orthogonality and similarity of two word representation spaces. We can easily find that etymologically close language pairs have lower values of $||I - W^T W||$ and GH than other language pairs. In contrast, we find that the accuracies of word translation are disproportional to the values of $||I - W^T W||$ and GH. This means that the non-isomorphic issue is more serious for etymologically distant language pairs. As our unsupervised joint method does not rely on the isomorphic assumption, we get better results than baselines.

From Table 1, we also can see that the proposed method is more robust. While the other baselines succeed in some cases and fail in others, our method can get a good performance in all cases. Moreover, our method is not sensitive to linguistic and data itself differences. The situations are difficult to tune without a development set, which is critical in realistic unsupervised conditions. In addition to being more robust, our proposed method also obtains substantially better accuracies. We surpass previous methods by at least 10 points in close-relatively language pairs and more in distant language pairs. Our analysis reveals that the proposed unsupervised joint training obtains substantially better BWEs than offline mapping. So we obtain stronger results on BLI. Moreover, our results show that the non-isomorphic issue across languages can be effectively mitigated by the proposed unsupervised jointly training. However, offline mapping methods are relatively poor as they rely on the isomorphic assumption. A similar distribution assumption is not strictly consistent for all language pairs.

6 Conclusion

In this paper, we proposed an unsupervised method that leverage jointly training BWRs to mitigate the non-isomorphic issue, contrasting with the main current offline unsupervised methods. Our method contained a dynamic programming algorithm that can effectively mine monolingual information to connect two monolingual corpora for jointly training BWRs. Then, we proposed a cross-lingual regularization to jointly train BWRs. In the experiments, the results show that our method significantly and consistently outperforms the baselines. In particular, we demonstrated that the performance of our method is still good in distant language pairs. The results are still significant in all cases.

Note that our joint training needs the help of an offline unsupervised method to initialize BWRs. Future work should consider alternative approaches to try to overcome the limitations of this situation.

Acknowledgments. This work is supported by the National Natural Science Foundation of China (61906158), the Project of Science and Technology Research in Henan Province (212102210075).

References

1. Artetxe, M., Labaka, G., Agirre, E.: Learning principled bilingual mappings of word embeddings while preserving monolingual invariance. In: Proceedings of the 2016 Conference on Empirical Methods in Natural Language Processing, pp. 2289–2294 (2016)
2. Artetxe, M., Labaka, G., Agirre, E.: Learning bilingual word embeddings with (almost) no bilingual data. In: Proceedings of the 55th Annual Meeting of the Association for Computational Linguistics, vol. 1: Long Papers), pp. 451–462 (2017)
3. Artetxe, M., Labaka, G., Agirre, E.: A robust self-learning method for fully unsupervised cross-lingual mappings of word embeddings. In: Proceedings of the 56th Annual Meeting of the Association for Computational Linguistics, vol. 1: Long Papers), pp. 789–798 (2018)
4. Braune, F., Hangya, V., Eder, T., Fraser, A.: Evaluating bilingual word embeddings on the long tail. In: Proceedings of the 2018 Conference of the North American Chapter of the Association for Computational Linguistics: Human Language Technologies, vol. 2 (Short Papers), pp. 188–193 (2018)
5. Bérard, A., Servan, C., Pietquin, O., Besacier, L.: MultiVec: a Multilingual and Multilevel Representation Learning Toolkit for NLP. In: The 10th edition of the Language Resources and Evaluation Conference (LREC 2016), May 2016
6. Gai, K., Qiu, M.: Optimal resource allocation using reinforcement learning for IoT content-centric services. Appl. Soft Comput. **70**, 12–21 (2018)
7. Gai, K., Qiu, M.: Reinforcement learning-based content-centric services in mobile sensing. IEEE Netw. **32**(4), 34–39 (2018)
8. Gai, K., Qiu, M., Zhao, H., Sun, X.: Resource management in sustainable cyber-physical systems using heterogeneous cloud computing. IEEE Trans. Sustain. Comput. **3**(2), 60–72 (2017)
9. Glavaš, G., Litschko, R., Ruder, S., Vulić, I.: How to (properly) evaluate cross-lingual word embeddings: on strong baselines, comparative analyses, and some misconceptions. In: Proceedings of the 57th Annual Meeting of the Association for Computational Linguistics, pp. 710–721 (2019)
10. Grave, E., Joulin, A., Berthet, Q.: Unsupervised alignment of embeddings with Wasserstein procrustes. In: The 22nd International Conference on Artificial Intelligence and Statistics, pp. 1880–1890 (2019)
11. Hangya, V., Braune, F., Kalasouskaya, Y., Fraser, A.: Unsupervised parallel sentence extraction from comparable corpora (2018)
12. Hangya, V., Fraser, A.: Unsupervised parallel sentence extraction with parallel segment detection helps machine translation. In: Proceedings of the 57th Annual Meeting of the Association for Computational Linguistics, pp. 1224–1234 (2019)
13. Keung, P., Salazar, J., Lu, Y., Smith, N.A.: Unsupervised bitext mining and translation via self-trained contextual embeddings. arXiv preprint arXiv:2010.07761 (2020)
14. Lample, G., Conneau, A., Ranzato, M., Denoyer, L., Jégou, H.: Word translation without parallel data. In: International Conference on Learning Representations (2018)

15. Lample, G., Ott, M., Conneau, A., Denoyer, L., Ranzato, M.: Phrase-based & neural unsupervised machine translation. In: Proceedings of the 2018 Conference on Empirical Methods in Natural Language Processing, pp. 5039–5049 (2018)
16. Litschko, R., Glavaš, G., Ponzetto, S.P., Vulić, I.: Unsupervised cross-lingual information retrieval using monolingual data only. In: The 41st International ACM SIGIR Conference on Research & Development in Information Retrieval, pp. 1253–1256 (2018)
17. Litschko, R., Glavaš, G., Vulic, I., Dietz, L.: Evaluating resource-lean cross-lingual embedding models in unsupervised retrieval. In: Proceedings of the 42nd International ACM SIGIR Conference on Research and Development in Information Retrieval, pp. 1109–1112 (2019)
18. Luong, M.T., Pham, H., Manning, C.D.: Bilingual word representations with monolingual quality in mind. In: Proceedings of the 1st Workshop on Vector Space Modeling for Natural Language Processing, pp. 151–159 (2015)
19. Marie, B., Fujita, A.: Efficient extraction of pseudo-parallel sentences from raw monolingual data using word embeddings. In: Proceedings of the 55th Annual Meeting of the Association for Computational Linguistics, vol. 2: Short Papers, pp. 392–398 (2017)
20. Marie, B., Fujita, A.: Unsupervised joint training of bilingual word embeddings. In: Proceedings of the 57th Annual Meeting of the Association for Computational Linguistics, pp. 3224–3230 (2019)
21. Mikolov, T., Sutskever, I., Chen, K., Corrado, G.S., Dean, J.: Distributed representations of words and phrases and their compositionality. In: Advances in Neural Information Processing Systems, pp. 3111–3119 (2013)
22. Ormazabal, A., Artetxe, M., Labaka, G., Soroa, A., Agirre, E.: Analyzing the limitations of cross-lingual word embedding mappings. In: Proceedings of the 57th Annual Meeting of the Association for Computational Linguistics, pp. 4990–4995 (2019)
23. Patra, B., Moniz, J.R.A., Garg, S., Gormley, M.R., Neubig, G.: Bilingual lexicon induction with semi-supervision in non-isometric embedding spaces. In: Proceedings of the 57th Annual Meeting of the Association for Computational Linguistics, pp. 184–193 (2019)
24. Ren, S., Liu, S., Zhou, M., Ma, S.: A graph-based coarse-to-fine method for unsupervised bilingual lexicon induction. In: Proceedings of the 58th Annual Meeting of the Association for Computational Linguistics, pp. 3476–3485 (2020)
25. Smith, S.L., Turban, D.H., Hamblin, S., Hammerla, N.Y.: Offline bilingual word vectors, orthogonal transformations and the inverted softmax. arXiv preprint arXiv:1702.03859 (2017)
26. Sun, H., Wang, R., Chen, K., Utiyama, M., Sumita, E., Zhao, T.: Unsupervised bilingual word embedding agreement for unsupervised neural machine translation. In: Proceedings of the 57th Annual Meeting of the Association for Computational Linguistics, pp. 1235–1245 (2019)
27. Vulić, I., Glavaš, G., Reichart, R., Korhonen, A.: Do we really need fully unsupervised cross-lingual embeddings? In: Proceedings of the 2019 Conference on Empirical Methods in Natural Language Processing and the 9th International Joint Conference on Natural Language Processing (EMNLP-IJCNLP), pp. 4398–4409 (2019)
28. Zhao, X., Wang, Z., Zhang, Y., Wu, H.: A relaxed matching procedure for unsupervised BLI. In: Proceedings of the 58th Annual Meeting of the Association for Computational Linguistics, pp. 3036–3041 (2020)

A Deep Learning Model Based on Neural Bag-of-Words Attention for Sentiment Analysis

Jing Liao and Zhixiang Yi(✉)

School of Computer Engineering and Science, Hunan University of Science and Technology, Xiangtan, China

Abstract. In the field of Natural Language Processing, sentiment analysis is one of core research directions. The hot issue of sentiment analysis is how to avoid the shortcoming of using fixed vector to calculate attention distribution. In this paper, we proposed a novel sentiment analysis model based on neural bag-of-words attention, which utilizes Bidirectional Long Short-Term Memory (BiLSTM) to capture the deep semantic features of text, and fusion these features by attention distribution based on neural bag-of-words. The experimental results show that the proposed method has improved 2.53%–6.46% accuracy compared with the benchmark.

Keywords: Sentiment analysis · Deep learning · Attention mechanism · Neural bag-of-words

1 Introduction

With the development of the internet and mobile internet, people are accustomed to express their opinions or sentiments on internet, which can produce a large amount of high value text data. For example, customer reviews in e-commerce platforms can not only help other customers to make a decision, but also help merchants to understand user demands and improve service quality. However, it is a time-consuming and labor-intensive work to manually extract useful information from a mass of reviews. Sentiment analysis can automatically summarize the sentiments or opinions expressed in the text, so it has received extensive attention.

Sentiment analysis is one of the fundamental task in Natural Language Processing (NLP), which detects, extracts and classifies the opinions, sentiments and attitudes expressed in the language by computation [1]. Sentiment analysis is a classification task, which aims to assign labels to textual units (sentences, documents, etc.) such as dividing sentiment categories into positive polarity, negative polarity and neural polarity or using rating (e.g. 1–5) to assess sentiment level.

The keys to predict sentiment category are how to recognize opinion words or sentiment words contained in the text and how to analysis the sentiment of these words. In recent years, deep learning models have become a popular solution to solve the problem of sentiment analysis. Deep learning models utilize neural networks to automatically capture deep hidden features, and use low-dimensional vectors to implicitly represent

H. Qiu et al. (Eds.): KSEM 2021, LNAI 12815, pp. 467–478, 2021.
https://doi.org/10.1007/978-3-030-82136-4_38

the semantic or syntactic features. For example, Convolutional Neural Network (CNN) can capture local features such as n-gram [2, 3], while Recurrent Neural Network (RNN) can capture global features such as word order information and context dependencies [4, 5].

Although deep learning model is effective in feature extraction, it is a black box model with poor interpretability, while attention mechanism can improve the ability to extract features and interpretability. Attention mechanism was originally applied to learn alignments between different languages in neural machine translation task [6]. Attention mechanism can help models to pay more attention to these inputs related to the task. Inputting a query vector and a set of value vectors, attention mechanism will calculate the correlation score between query vector and each value vector to acquire a weight distribution named attention distribution, and calculate the weighted sum of these value vectors using attention distribution. For sentiment analysis, the heavier the weight, the larger the possibility that the word is a sentiment word or opinion word, the more important the information that the word contains. Because there is lack of extra information in sentiment analysis, the query vector of attention mechanism is a fixed vector in some cases [7–9]. The fixed vector is randomly initialized by the model and jointly learned during the training process, to recognize the key words. The query vector is an important parameter in attention mechanism, while it is possible that attention mechanism will output improper attention distribution because of fixed query vector can not provide it with sentiment features of current input text, which might lead models to ignore some sentiment words or regard some irrelevant words as sentiment words and result in false decision.

In this paper, to avoid the shortcoming of using fixed vector to calculate attention distribution, we propose a novel sentiment analysis model based on neural bag-of-words attention (NBOW-Att). This model utilizes Bidirectional Long Short-Term Memory (BiLSTM) to mine semantic features, takes neural bag-of-words as query vector to calculate attention distribution, and aggregates these features according to attention distribution. Different from fixed vector, neural bag-of-words can implicitly represent the sentiment features of the text and provide attention mechanism with sentiment features of current input text [10]. So that, it can provide model with sentiment features of current input text, improve the ability to recognize sentiment words and classification performance.

The rest of the paper is organized as follows. Section 2 presents the related work. Section 3 introduces the structure of NBOW-Att. Section 4 describes the tested datasets, baseline methods and experiment settings. Section 5 discusses the experimental results. Conclusion is made in Sect. 6.

2 Related Work

As one of the fundamental and vital task in NLP, sentiment analysis has received extensive attention. Methods of sentiment analysis can be categorized into three directions: rule based methods, machine learning based methods and deep learning based methods. Rule based methods classify text into different categories using pre-defined dictionary, but it requires domain knowledge and the systems are difficult to maintain. Machine learning based methods usually extract some hand-crafted features (bag-of-words, n-gram, etc.) from the text at first, and then fed these features to a classifier such as Naive Bayes, Support Vectors Machines etc. However, feature extracting is time-consuming and costly. In recent years, deep learning based methods have become popular in the field of sentiment analysis, they can automatically capture the features from input with different neural networks.

CNN and RNN are frequently-used deep learning methods in NLP. CNN is good at capturing the local relationship in temporal or spatial structures, for example, Kim [2] and Conneau et al. [3] proposed the text classification models based CNN which can extract the local features of different parts of text like n-gram. However, CNN is insensitive to long-term relationships. In contract to CNN, RNN is able to capture the global features of sequence. As the variants of RNN, Long Short-Term Memory Networks (LSTM) [11] and Gated Recurrent Network (GRU) [12] can effectively deal with the problems of gradient vanishing or exploding that RNN suffered to, so that, they are ideal alternative to RNN in the field of sentiment analysis. For instance, Xu et al. [13] and Sharfuddin et al. [5] proposed the sentiment analysis model based LSTM, Tang et al. [4] adopted GRU to predict the sentiment categories of documents. These methods treat text as a sequence composed of words and extract context dependencies and word order information from text. Since the methods only contain LSTM or GRU probably ignores the local features, Kowsari et al. [14] proposed HDLtex which leveraged RNN and CNN to learn the features at different levels from the document. Zhao et al. [15] created a serial hybrid model of BiLSTM and CNN, using multiple filters with varying sizes to extract local features from the output of BiLSTM. These models tried to preserve the local features as much as possible while capturing the global features.

All these methods mentioned above can capture the semantic features effectively, but they are black box model with poor interpretability. Recently, attention mechanism has attracted extensive attention because of the ability to increase the interpretability of deep learning model. For example, Yang et al. [7] proposed Hierarchical Attention Networks (HAN), using attention mechanism to recognize the important words and sentences, and combine their semantic features captured by bidirectional GRU into text representation. Based on HAN, Zeng at el. [16] proposed hierarchical double-attention neural networks, using CNN and attention mechanism to generate sentence representation and using attention mechanism and bidirectional GRU to integrate document representation. Chen et al. [17] combined attention mechanism and bidirectional slice GRU to augment local attention. Lin et al. [8] employed a self-attentive sentence embedding model (SASE), leveraging multi-head attention mechanism to extract the semantic of multiple important aspects of text. Schoene et al. [9] predicted the fine-grained emotions of tweets with bidirectional dilated LSTM and attention mechanism, which could increase the range of temporal dependencies that can be modeled by LSTM.

Because there is little extra information in input data, the query vector of attention mechanism in these models mentioned above is mostly a fixed vector. We argue that the fixed vector fails to provide semantic features of the current input text for the attention mechanism, which weakens its ability to recognize sentiment words. To address this drawback, we use the neural bag-of-words of text as the query vector to compute attention distribution and improve its ability to recognize sentiment words.

3 Model

Given a textual unit, sentiment analysis is to predict the sentiment category of this text. Formally, we define the text with n words as $S = \{w_1, w_2, \ldots, w_n\}$, the set of sentiment categories with c labels as $L = \{l_1, l_2, \ldots, l_c\}$. The goal of sentiment analysis is to calculate the sentiment category distribution $p = \{p_1, p_2, \ldots, p_c\}$ and assign the highest probability label l to the sentiment category of S.

In this section, we introduce the proposed method NBOW-Att, which is a sentiment analysis model based on neural bag-of-words attention. The structure of NBOW-Att is shown in Fig. 1, it consists of input layer, BiLSTM layer, attention layer and classification layer. In our model, Input layer encodes the words into vector representations, BiLSTM layer produces a hidden state matrix which can represent contextual semantic features, attention layer aims to recognize the important parts of the text and aggregates these semantic features into text representation, classification layer predicts the sentiment category of the text based on text representation. The details of these components are introduced in the following parts.

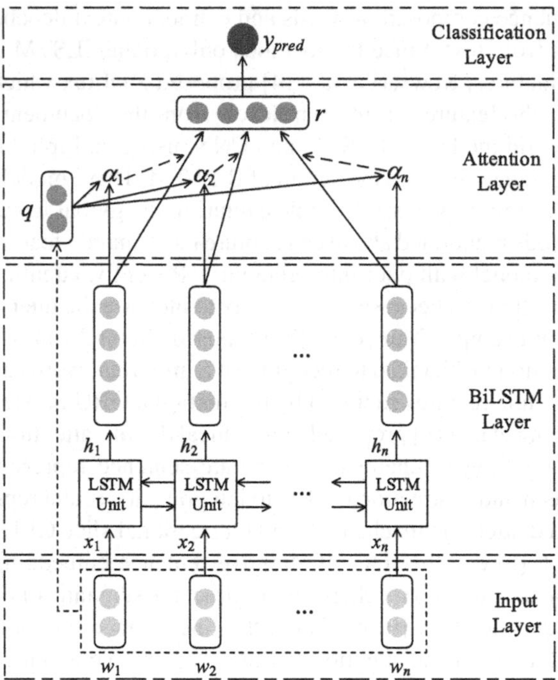

Fig. 1. The structure of NBOW-Att

3.1 Input Layer

In input layer, we use an embedding matrix E to encode the words in textual unit S into word vectors which can provide lexical-semantic features, and obtain a vector matrix

$X = \{x_1, x_2, \ldots, x_n\} \in R^{d \times V}$, where x_i $(1 \leq i \leq n)$ is the vector of w_i, V is the size of vocabulary, d is the dimension of word vector.

3.2 BiLSTM Layer

As a variant of RNN, LSTM is suitable for handling sequence with arbitrary length, it also can capture global semantic features such as word order information and long-term dependencies. Compared with RNN unit, LSTM unit has a memory cell and three gates (input gate, forget gate and output gate) which ensure the gradient of the long-term dependencies will not disappear, so that LSTM can address the gradient vanishing or gradient exploding problems occurred in the training stage of RNN. At the t-th time step, the LSTM unit is updated with the following equations [11]:

$$i_t = \sigma(W_i x_t + U_i h_{t-1} + b_i) \tag{1}$$

$$f_t = \sigma\left(W_f x_t + U_f h_{t-1} + b_f\right) \tag{2}$$

$$o_t = \sigma(W_o x_t + U_o h_{t-1} + b_o) \tag{3}$$

$$c_t = f_t \odot c_{t-1} + i_t \odot tanh(W_a x_t + U_a h_{t-1} + b_a) \tag{4}$$

$$h_t = o_t \odot tanh(c_t) \tag{5}$$

where, x_t is the input vector, h_t is the hidden state of current time step, c_t is the memory cell, i_t, f_t and o_t represent input gate, forget gate and output gate respectively, W_i, W_f, W_o, U_i, U_f, U_o are weights, b_i, b_f, b_o are bias, σ represents sigmoid function, $\odot$ denotes element-wise product. In the following parts, the size of h_t is set to be k.

Because sequence information can only be transmitted one-way in LSTM, we use BiLSTM to capture the semantic features in order to obtain the context semantic information of the sequence for every time step. BiLSTM is comprised of forward LSTM and backward LSTM, the former processes sequence from left to right and produces the forward hidden state, while the latter processes sequence in the reverse order and produces the backward hidden state. The hidden state of BiLSTM is the concatenation of the forward hidden state and backward hidden state of every word. The hidden state of t-th word is shown in following equation:

$$h_t = h_{l \to r} \oplus h_{r \to l} \tag{6}$$

where, $h_{l \to r}$ is the forward hidden state, $h_{r \to l}$ is the backward hidden state,$h_t \in R^{2k}$ is the hidden state concatenated by $h_{l \to r}$ and $h_{r \to l}$, $\oplus$ denotes the concatenation operation.

3.3 Attention Layer

In this layer, we apply attention mechanism to recognize the sentiment words and combine the hidden representations produced by BiLSTM layer to generate the text representation. For attention mechanism, we use neural bag-of-words instead of fixed vector to query which words are important to the classification decision. The neural bag-of-words is the average sum of all word vectors in the text, and the successful application of Deep Averaging Network [10] has demonstrated that neural bag-of-words can effectively represent the sentiment features of text. In that, we use neural bag-of-words to provide attention mechanism with the sentiment features of current input text and improve the ability of model to recognize the sentiment words. Formally, the query vector q is:

$$q = \frac{1}{n}\sum_{i=1}^{n} x_i \tag{7}$$

Similar to the computational process of [7], after obtaining query vector and the hidden vector representation of each word (value vector), we firstly feed the word annotation h_i through MLP to get u_i as a hidden representation of h_i, and evaluate the probability that i-th word is sentiment word by calculating the similarity s_i between u_i and q. Next, we use softmax function to transform the similarity score s_i into the normalized weight α_i, and get attention distribution $\alpha = (\alpha_1, \alpha_2, \cdots, \alpha_n)$. Finally, we get the text representation r by computing the weighted sum of the word annotations based on the attention distribution α. The whole process can be formulated as follows:

$$u_i = tanh(W_m h_i + b_m) \tag{8}$$

$$s_i = q^T \bullet u_i \tag{9}$$

$$\alpha_i = \frac{exp(s_i)}{\sum_{j=1}^{n} s_j} \tag{10}$$

$$r = \sum_{i=1}^{n} \alpha_i h_i \tag{11}$$

where $q \in R^d$, $r \in R^{2k}$, $\bullet$ denotes dot product, $W_m \in R^{d \times 2k}$ and $b_m \in R^d$ are learnable parameters in MLP.

3.4 Classification Layer

In this layer, we feed the text representation r into a fully connected layer to get a vector with c dimensions. Then, we feed this vector to the softmax layer to obtain the probability distribution p of sentiment categories, and output the predicted sentiment category y_{pred} corresponding to largest probability:

$$p = softmax(W_s r + b_s) \tag{12}$$

$$y_{pred} = argmax(p) \tag{13}$$

where $p \in R^c$, $W_s \in R^{2k \times c}$ and $b_s \in R^c$ are the parameters of fully connected layer.

3.5 Loss Function

Since sentiment analysis task is a classification problem, we choose cross entropy function as loss function and use L2 regularization to avoid overfitting.

$$L(\theta) = \frac{1}{N}\sum\nolimits_{i=1}^{N} y_i \log(p) + \beta\|\theta\|_2^2 \tag{14}$$

where, $y_i \in R^c$ is the one-hot vector of truth label, β is the L2 regularization factor and N is the total number of training samples. The details of training will be introduced in Sect. 4.1.

4 Experiment

4.1 Experimental Settings

There are several preliminaries need to been done before training. Firstly, we tokenize the textual unit into words by NLP tool Spacy[1]. Then, for each dateset, we choose the 50,000 most frequent words from the training set and two special token UNK and PAD to build the vocabulary, where UNK represents those words that do not exist in the vocabulary and PAD is used to fill the text. Next, we unify the input length via filling the text using PAD when the length is shorter than 400 and cutting the text when the length is longer than 400.

Performance of deep learning model heavily depends on the hyper parameters used in training. In the experiment, we select the optimal set of hyper parameters from different combinations of hyper parameters. We set word vector (*d*) to 300 dimensions and set the hidden state of LSTM (*k*) to 300 dimensions. Training is done via Adam optimizer [18] with the default parameters. In addition, the size of mini-batch is 64, the dropout rate is 0.5 and L2 regularization parameter (β) is 0.00001. Our model is implemented by PyTorch[2], all the weights and bias are given the initial value by sampling from the uniform distribution U [−0.1,0.1]. To improve the classification performance, we use pre-trained word vectors[3] trained by Glove [19] to initialize the embedding matrix E, those words that do not have pre-trained vector are initialized by uniform distribution U [−0.1,0.1], the parameters in matrix E can be fine-tuned during the training.

4.2 Datasets

We use three datasets to test the proposed model in this experiment.

IMDB [20] is a binary sentiment analysis dataset about movie reviews, including 25000 train samples and 25000 test samples. The sentiment categories are divided into positive polarity and negative polarity.

Yelp [4] is the dataset summarized from the Yelp Dataset Challenge in 2013, 2014, 2015. Yelp is divided into two sub-dataset Yelp-2 and Yelp-5. Yelp-2 is the binary datasets

1 https://spacy.io/.
2 https://pytorch.org/.
3 http://nlp.stanford.edu/data/glove.6B.zip.

with positive polarity and negative polarity, it has 560000 train samples and 38000 test samples. Yelp-5 is a fine-grained dataset with 5 sentiment categories, which are very negative, negative, neutral, positive, very positive. Yelp-5 has 650000 train samples and 50000 test samples.

Since these datasets do not include development set, we randomly select 30% of the test data as the development set from IMDB, and select 10% of the train data as the development set from Yelp-2 and Yelp-5. Summary statistics of these datasets are concluded in Table 1.

Table 1. Statistics of datasets

Dataset	Train	Dev	Test	L	C	Proportion
IMDB	25000	7500	17500	269.4	2	1:1
Yelp-2	504000	56000	38000	157.2	2	1:1
Yelp-5	595000	65000	50000	158.7	5	1:1:1:1:1

Notes: Train represents the number of samples in training set, Dev represents the number of samples in development set, Test represents the number of samples in testing set, L represents the average length of text, C represents the number of categories, Proportion represents the ratio of the number of different categories in testing set.

4.3 Baselines

We compare our method with following baseline methods.

DAN [10] uses neural bag-of-words to represent text and augments the weak differences between different text representation vectors through a multi-layer feedforward neural network.

TextCNN [2] is a text classification model based on CNN, it uses multiple filers (with varying window sizes) to extract different local features from text.

SASE [8] firstly uses BiLSTM to extract semantic features from text, and then obtains multiple representation vectors that can represent different aspects from these semantic features by multi-head attention mechanism. In the last, SASE outputs the average sum of these vectors as text representation.

BiLSTM contains two sub-method BiLSTM-Last and BiLSTM-AP. BiLSTM-Last takes the hidden state of the last time step as text representation, while BiLSTM-AP takes the average sum of the hidden states of all time steps as text representation.

BiLSTM-Att uses the fixed query to calculate attention distribution, the rest structure of BiLSTM-Att is the same as NBOW-Att.

5 Result and Discussion

5.1 Experimental Result

We use accuracy to evaluate the performance of these methods. In all experiments, the number of epoch for training is 20. In training process, we evaluate the performance on development set in every epoch and save the trained parameters in the epoch with highest validation accuracy. After training, we load the saved parameters and evaluate the accuracy on the testing set. We also apply early stopping in training and the patience is 5. To minimize the influence of initial parameters, we repeat training process 5 times and report the average results.

Table 2. Experimental results on datasets

Models	IMDB	Yelp-2	Yelp-5
DAN	87.21%	92.61%	61.37%
TextCNN	89.42%	95.75%	64.73%
BiLSTM-Last	87.28%	96.55%	67.21%
BiLSTM-AP	88.10%	96.61%	67.27%
SASE	89.10%	96.71%	67.49%
BiLSTM-Att	89.23%	96.71%	67.38%
NBOW-Att	**89.74%**	**96.84%**	**67.83%**

The experimental results are shown in Table 2 and there are some findings can be concluded. (1) DAN achieves worst performance among all test methods in the three datasets, which indicate that neural bag-of-words is a shallow representation. The lack of word order information and the weakness of sentiment features caused by average operation restrict the classification performance of DAN. (2) The accuracy of BiLSTM-Last and BiLSTM-AP are better than TextCNN, which indicates that CNN pays more attention to local features and has little ability to capture global features like long-term dependencies or context information. (3) When using BiLSTM to handling super long text, BiLSTM-Last may forget some information preserved at the front of sequence, though BiLSTM-AP can keep this information to some extend via average sum operation (The results of BiLSTM-AP are better than BiLSTM-Last in all datasets infers it). (4) Compared to BiLSTM-AP, the models that contain attention mechanism, such as SASE, BiLSTM-Att and NBOW-Att, have better performance, it indicates that the fusion of features captured by BiLSTM affects the reservation of pivotal information. The process of average pooling may weak the sentiment features because of the noise caused by irrelevant words, while attention mechanism can allocate different weights for different words to recognize the sentiment words and preserves their features. (5) NBWO-Att achieves the best result in all datasets indicates the effectiveness of using neural bag-of-words to compute attention distribution. The shallow sentiment features exist in neural bag-of-words can provide model with sentiment features of current input text and improve the ability to recognize the sentiment words.

5.2 The Comparison of Neural Bag-of-Words and Fixed Vector

In this section, we use the average model of trained BiLSTM-Att and trained NBOW-Att to compare the difference between neural bag-of-words and fixed vector.

Firstly, we evaluate the precision, recall and F1 score on testing set of all datasets, results are displayed in Table 3. There is no significant difference between BiLSTM-Att and NBOW-Att in Yelp-2 dataset. But in IMDB and Yelp-5 datasets, the precision, recall and F1 value of NBOW-Att are slightly higher than BiLSTM-Att, which indicate that using the neural bag-of-words instead of fixed vector to compute the attention distribution can improve the ability to recognize sentiment words and improve the classification performance of the model.

Table 3. The comparison with NBOW-Att and BiLSTM-Att

Dataset	NBOW-Att			BiLSTM-Att		
	Precision	Recall	F1	Precision	Recall	F1
IMDB	0.898	0.898	0.898	0.894	0.891	0.890
Yelp-2	0.967	0.967	0.967	0.967	0.967	0.967
Yelp-5	0.673	0.677	0.674	0.671	0.674	0.671

Besides, we visualize the attention weights to intuitively compare the differences between NBOW-Att and BiLSTM-Att. We visualize the attention weights via background-color, the color strength shows the importance degree of the word, the darker the more important. The color intensity of i-th word is computed by following equation:

$$I_i = \frac{w_i^a}{w_{max}^a - w_{min}^a} \tag{15}$$

where, w_i^a is the attention weight of i-th word, w_{max}^a]and w_{min}^a are the maximum weight and minimum weight in attention distribution respectively.

The results are shown in Table 4, in this experiment, we randomly select some reviews with the length up to 100 words from IMDB testing set. The visualization results show that NBOW-Att labels the words which have strong background color in the test text, these labelled words contain strong sentiment tendencies, such as 'good', 'funny', 'mess'. BiLSTM-Att also can label words with strong sentiment tendencies, however, part of words labelled by BiLSTM-Att do not contain strong sentiment tendencies. Besides, the maximum weight of BiLSTM-Att is smaller than 0.1 in most long text case. Because of the way of calculating weight of sentiment words and the influence of noise words, attention mechanism cannot fully preserve the semantic features of all sentiment words, which leads to misjudgment of the model. For example, BiLSTM-Att cannot identify the sentiment category of text 3.

In addition, NBOW-Att makes a wrong decision for text 4, its attentions focus on these words with positive polarity words like 'good', 'funny', while the truth label of this text is negative. This indicates that when processing the text that does not contain obvious emotional tendencies or uses ironic expressions, NBOW-Att may misjudge their sentiment categories.

Table 4. Visualization of attention weights and sentiment prediction results

Model	Text	w^a_{max}	P	G
BiLSTM-Att	The biggest heroes , is one of the greatest movies ever . A good story , great actors and a brilliant ending is what makes this film the jumping start of the director Thomas 's great carrier .	0.07	1	1
NBOW-Att	The biggest heroes , is one of the greatest movies ever . A good story , great actors and a brilliant ending is what makes this film the jumping start of the director Thomas 's great carrier .	0.27	1	1
BiLSTM-Att	What a script , what a story , what a mess !	0.43	0	0
NBOW-Att	What a script , what a story , what a mess !	0.89	0	0
BiLSTM-Att	This movie makes you wish imdb would let you vote a zero . One of the two movies I 've ever walked out of . It 's very hard to think of a worse movie with such big name actors . Well ... Armageddon almost takes it , but not quite .	0.09	1	0
NBOW-Att	This movie makes you wish imdb would let you vote a zero . One of the two movies I 've ever walked out of . It 's very hard to think of a worse movie with such big name actors . Well ... Armageddon almost takes it , but not quite .	0.31	0	0
BiLSTM-Att	If you like bad movies (and you must to watch this one) here 's a good one . Not quite as funny as the first , but much lower quality .A must see for fans Jack Frost as well as anyone up for a good laugh at the writing .	0.06	1	0
NBOW-Att	If you like bad movies (and you must to watch this one) here 's a good one . Not quite as funny as the first , but much lower quality . A must see for fans of Jack Frost as well as anyone up for a good laugh at the writing .	0.26	1	0

Notes: P represents the prediction labels of text, G represents the truth labels of text.

6 Conclusion

In this paper, we have proposed a novel sentiment analysis model based on neural bag-of-words attention, which utilizes BiLSTM to capture the deep semantic features of text, and fuses these features by attention distribution based on neural bag-of-words. The experimental results show that, compared with other baselines, NBOW-Att achieves the best classification accuracy on three sentiment analysis datasets. In addition, we further compared the differences of attention mechanism based on neural bag-of-words and fixed vector, and the visualization results show that the former can identify the sentiment words in the text better than the latter. However, the performance of NBOW-Att on identifying the sentiment of the text that contains little obvious emotional tendencies or uses ironic expressions is not very well which need to be improved in the next step.

Acknowledgement. This research is partially supported by the Outstanding Youth Project of Hunan Provincial Education department (No.18B228).

References

1. Pang, B., Lee, L.: Opinion mining and sentiment analysis. Found. Trends Inf. Retr. **2**, 1–135 (2008)
2. Kim, Y.: Convolutional neural networks for sentence classification. In: EMNLP, pp. 1746–1751 (2014)
3. Conneau, A., Schwenk, H., Yann, L.C.: Very deep convolutional networks for text classification. In: Proceedings of the 15th Conference of the European Chapter of the Association for Computational Linguistics, pp. 1107–1116 (2017)
4. Tang, D., Qin, B., Liu, T.: Document modeling with gated recurrent neural network for sentiment classification. In: EMNLP, pp. 1422–1432 (2015)
5. Sharfuddin, A.A., Tihami, M., Islam, M.: A deep recurrent neural network with BiLSTM model for sentiment classification. In: Proceedings of the 2018 International Conference on Bangla Speech and Language Processing, pp. 1–4 (2018)
6. Bahdanau, D., Cho, K., Bengio, Y.: Neural machine translation by jointly learning to align and translate. In: Proceedings of the 3rd International Conference on Learning Representations (2015)
7. Yang, Z., Yang, D., Dyer, C., He, X., Smola, A., Hovy, E.: Hierarchical attention networks for document classification. In: HLT-NAACL, pp. 1480–1489 (2016)
8. Lin, Z., et al.: A structured self-attentive sentence embedding. arXiv preprint arXiv:1703.03130 (2017)
9. Schoene, A., Alexander, P., Dethlefs, N.: Bidirectional dilated LSTM with attention for fine-grained emotion classification in tweets. In: Proceedings of the 3rd Workshop on Affective Content Analysis, pp. 100–117 (2020)
10. Lyyer, M., Manjunatha, V., Jordan, B., Daume, H.: Deep unordered composition rivals syntactic methods for text classification. In: ACL, pp. 1681–1691 (2015)
11. Hochreiter, S., Schmidhuber, J.: Long short-term memory. Neural Comput. **9**(8), 1735–1780 (1997)
12. Cho, K., et al.: Learning phrase representations using RNN encoder-decoder for statistical machine translation. In: EMNLP, pp. 1724–1734 (2014)
13. Xu, G., Meng, Y., Qiu, X., Yu, Z., Wu, X.: Sentiment analysis of comment texts based on BiLSTM. IEEE Access **7**, 51522–51532 (2019)
14. Kowsari, K., Brown, D., Heidarysafa, M., Meimandi, K., Gerber, M., Barnes, L.: HDLTex: Hierarchical deep learning for text classification. In: Proceedings of the 16th IEEE International Conference on Machine Learning and Applications, pp. 364–371 (2017)
15. Zhao, H., Wang, L., Wang, W.: Text sentiment analysis based on serial hybrid model of bi-directional long short-term memory and convolutional neural network. J. Comput. Appl. **40**(1), 16–22 (2020)
16. Zeng, B., Han, X., Wang, S., Zhou, W., Yang, H.: Hierarchical double-attention neural networks for sentiment classification. CAAI Trans. Intell. Syst. **15**(3), 460–467 (2020)
17. Chen, H., Gao, B., Chen, L., Yu, C.: Sentiment classification model combining attention mechanism and bidirectional slice GRU. J. Chinese Comput. Syst. **41**(9), 1793–1799 (2020)
18. Kingma, D., Ba, J.: Adam: a method for stochastic optimization. arXiv preprint arXiv:1412.6980 (2014)
19. Pennington, J., Socher, R., Manning, C.D.: GloVe: Global vectors for word representation. In: EMNLP, pp. 1532–1543 (2014)
20. Maas, A., Daly, R., Pham, P., Huang, D., Andrew, Y., Potts, C.: Learning word vectors for sentiment analysis. In: ACL, pp. 142–150 (2011)

Graph Attention Mechanism with Cardinality Preservation for Knowledge Graph Completion

Cong Ding, Xiao Wei(✉), Yongqi Chen, and Rui Zhao

School of Computer Engineering and Science, Shanghai University, Shanghai, China
{mollydc,xwei,MrChenYQ,zhaorui1513}@shu.edu.cn

Abstract. Embedding knowledge graph with graph attention network has become a novel research topic in the field of knowledge graph completion. However, the current graph attention network generates the same embeddings for different structures and different entities when generating entity embeddings for knowledge graph. The quality of embedding directly contributes the effective of completion. We analyze the reason why graph attention network cannot distinguish structure, because the aggregation based on attention GNN ignores the cardinality information, which is the mapping of diverse features, and helps to distinguish the contributions of different nodes in the domain. Therefore, we propose the graph attention preserving (KBCPA) model. Cardinality information is added into the attentional mechanism based aggregation to generate different representations for different entities, thus improving the discrimination ability of the model. Our experiments present that our model is effective and competitive, and it obtains better performance than previous state-of-the-art embedding models for knowledge graph completion on two benchmark datasets WN18RR and FB15k-237.

Keywords: Cardinality preservation · Knowledge graph · Graph attention mechanism

1 Introduction

Knowledge graph has received more and more attention and research due to its inclusion of real-world knowledge and structured knowledge representation. Many downstream applications revolve around knowledge graph, such as knowledge question answering, recommendation systems, knowledge reasoning, and so on. These applications are involved in different fields. So far, the industry represented by Google and the academia represented by Carnegie Mellon University have built several large-scale knowledge graph, such as Freebase [2], Wikidata [20], Nell [4], DBpedia [1], etc. Although knowledge graphs are very as an acceptable way to express knowledge, most knowledge graphs are not complete. For example, in the Freebase Knowledge Graph, 71% of people don't have an exact date of birth and 75% don't have any information about their nationality [6].

H. Qiu et al. (Eds.): KSEM 2021, LNAI 12815, pp. 479–490, 2021.
https://doi.org/10.1007/978-3-030-82136-4_39

The incompleteness of the knowledge graph has become a major concern, and more and more people are devoting their efforts to it.

Knowledge graph completion, also known as relational prediction, knowledge reasoning, etc. [7]. Generally, the normal triples are (H, R, T), and the knowledge graph completion task can be described as: given the missing triples, the column is $(h, r, ?)$, $(h, ?, r)$ and $(?, r, t)$ [8], the missing part can be predicted through the algorithm model. The translation model tries to use distance scoring function to build module of triples, and the tensor decomposition model uses Tri-Linear Dot to calculate the score of each triple. All models strive to make the correct triples score higher and the wrong triples score lower, as do neural network-based approaches [19]. Both the translation model and the CNN-based model deal with each triple independently, and therefore cannot encapsulate the rich semantics and underlying relationships inherent in the proximity of a given entity in knowledge graph. The graph neural network model solves the above problems by embedding the information of the surrounding nodes.

The current graph neural network model is not sensitive to the change of structural information, it is difficult to capture the subtle change of structural information, and lacks the ability to distinguish different multisets (subgraphs) [22]. Most GNNs are constrained by the 1-Weisfeiler-Lehman (WL) test, so it is possible to generate the same representation for actually different structures and figures. The discriminative power means how well an attention-based GNN can distinguish different elements (local or global structures). Therefore, in the completion task, when two central nodes have the same or similar distribution of neighbor nodes, the structural information of the node set will change slightly, which will cause the semantic change of the central node. However, the current model lacks the ability to distinguish the above structural changes.

Motivated by the several components, we propose a method based on cardinality preserving graph attention model – KBCPA. We reveal the reason for the current graph neural network model lacking of discrimination ability is the ignorance of cardinality information in aggregation. Cardinality information is a mapping of the quantitative characteristics of multiplicity elements in multiset. The addition of cardinality information can help the model to further distinguish the contribution of the central node and the distant node, so as to identify the structural features of the similar subgraph. Therefore, KBPCA improves the attention mechanism via cardinality preservation. Our ideas are as follows:

1. Encapsulate multi-hop relations by a given node;

2. Obtain cardinality information to improve the discrimination ability of the attention mechanism;

3. End-to-end model, the encoder uses an improved graph attention mechanism KBCPA to strengthen the link prediction ability of the decoder ConvKB. Our model achieves the above objectives by assigning different attention coefficients to nearby nodes and iteratively updating them. At the same time, we adopted an end-to-end training approach, and ConvKB was the most suitable decoder for our model, ensuring the accuracy of the prediction.

Our contributions are as follows:

1. We use cardinality information to improve the link prediction;

2. We extend the graph attention mechanism and add cardinality information to iteration training on the premise of acquiring the characteristics of nodes and relationships.

3. We have carried out relationship prediction experiments on FB15K-237 and WN18RR, and the experimental results show that our model has improved in Hit @1, Hit @3 and Hit @10 compared with the most advanced model KBGAT. In particular, we achieved 92% accuracy on hit@1 on the Kinship dataset.

2 Related Work

At present, the most advanced knowledge graph completion method is knowledge representation learning, which is mainly divided into translation model, tensor decomposition model and neural network model [14].

Bordes et al. proposed the Transe model [3], which regards the relationship in the knowledge base as a kind of translation vector between entities. For each triple (H, R, T), TransE uses the vector LR of relation R as the translation between the head entity vector LH and the tail entity vector LT. We can also regard LR as the translation of LH from LT, so TransE is also called the translation model. But TransE cannot solve the problem of more than a one-to-many relationship.

The translation model tries to use the distance scoring function to build the module for the triples, while the tensor decomposition model uses Tri-Linear Dot to calculate the score of each triple. Well-known tensor decomposition models include Hole [13], ProjE [17], and Dismult [21]. All models strive to make the correct triples score higher and the wrong triples score lower, as do neural network-based approaches. Both the translation model and the CNN-based model deal with each triple independently, and therefore cannot encapsulate the rich semantics and underlying relationships inherent in the proximity of a given entity in knowledge graph.

CNN is used to learn deep expression features. ConvE [5] adopts embedded two-dimensional convolution and multi-layer nonlinear features to model the interaction between entities and relations, reshapes head entities and relations into two-dimensional matrix vectors, and gets the corresponding feature map through several filters. ConvKB [12] is an improvement on the ConvE model. ConvE inputs two entities and relationships, whereas ConvKB inputs the entire triple. Compared with the ConvE which captures the local relationship, the ConvKB maintains the transition characteristics and shows better experimental performance.

R-GCN [15] is the first attempt to use graph neural network model for representation learning of knowledge graph, and has achieved success. SACN introduced weighted GCN [16] to define the strength of two adjacent nodes with the same relationship type, and used node structure, node attributes and relationship type to capture structural information in the knowledge graph. The decoding module Conv-TransE adopts the ConvE model as the semantic matching metric and retains its translational characteristics. Subsequently, KBGAT [11] tried to use graph attention network again, and trained relationship features and node features together, and the effect was improved.

At present, it has become a new trend to use graph-neural network to embed knowledge graph, but there is a problem of graph discrimination when learning nodes embedded based on graph-neural network: the representation vectors obtained by subgraphs with different structures are the same or similar, which affects the efficiency of graph-neural network representation learning.

3 Background

Notations. Knowledge graph $G = (V, E)$, where V is the set of nodes and E is the set of edges. The neighbor node of node i is defined as $n(i)$, $N(i) = n(i) \cup \{i\}$. For triples t_{ijk} in $N(i)$. Their feature vectors are came from a multiset $M(i) = (S_i, u_i)$, $S_i = s_1, s_2, ..., s_n$ is the ground set of $M(i)$, $u_i : S_i \rightarrow N$ is the multiplicity function that gives the multiplicity of each s $\in$ S_i . The cardinality $|M|$ of a multiset is the number of elements (with multiplicity) in the multiset.

3.1 General Attention-Based GNNs in Knowledge Graph

Graph neural networks (GNNs) adopt element (node or edge) feature X and graph structure A as input to learn the representation of each element h_i or each graph h_G for different tasks.

In this study, we study GNN under the framework of information aggregation, which follows a neighborhood aggregation scheme, in which the representation vector of a node is calculated by recursively aggregating and transforming the representation vector of its neighboring nodes. To get the new embedding of the entity e_i, we learned the representation of each triple associated with e_i. We learn these embedding results by conducting a linear transformation on the connection of entities and relational eigenvectors of a specific triplet $t_{ijk} = (e_i, r_k, e_j)$:

$$\boldsymbol{t_{ijk}} = \mathbf{W}_1 \left[\boldsymbol{h}_i \,\|\boldsymbol{h}_j\|\, \boldsymbol{g}_k\right] \tag{1}$$

where $\boldsymbol{t_{ijk}}$ is the vector representation of a triple t_{ijk} vectors. And Vectors $\boldsymbol{h_i}$, $\boldsymbol{h_j}$ and $\boldsymbol{r_k}$ is embeddings of entities e_i, $e_j$and relation r_k, espectively. Additionally, W_1 denotes the linear transformation matrix.

We need learn the importance of each triple t_{ijk} by b_{ijk}, attention value same as (Velickovic et al. 2018) [9]. We perform a parameterized linear transformation with a weight matrix W_2 and apply the LeakyRelu nonlinearity to obtain the absolute attention values of the triples.

$$b_{ijk} = LeakyReLU\left(\mathrm{W}_2 t_{ijk}\right) \tag{2}$$

Compute the relative attention values a_{ijk} for a single triple by applying softmax over b_{ijk},

$$\alpha_{ijk} = softmax_{jk}\left(b_{ijk}\right) = \frac{\exp\left(b_{ijk}\right)}{\sum_{n \in \mathcal{N}_i} \sum_{r \in \mathcal{R}_{in}} \exp\left(b_{inr}\right)} \tag{3}$$

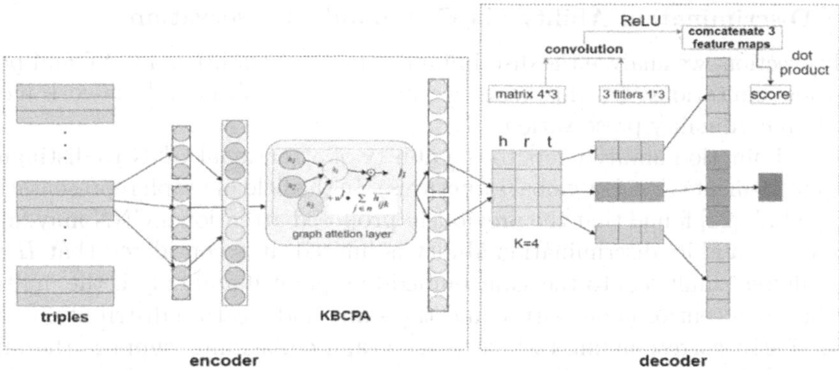

Fig. 1. The encoder is our proposed KBCPA, a triplet trained by the model that outputs related entities and relation vectors. The decoder is composed of ConvKB, and the vector output by the encoder is used as input to form a matrix of K * 3, where K is the vector dimension (K = 4 is taken as an example in the figure). After the convolution layer, the characteristic vector obtained is splice into a vector of 3k * 1, and finally multiplied by a weight matrix to get the final triple score. The higher the score, the higher the trueness of the triple.

where N_i denotes the neighborhood of entity e_i and $\mathcal{R}_{ij}$ denotes the set of relations connecting entities $e_i$and e_j The new embedding of the entity e_i is the sum of each triple representation weighted by their attention values as shown in Eq. 4.

$$\overrightarrow{h_i'} = \sigma\left(\sum_{j\in\mathcal{N}_i}\sum_{k\in\mathcal{R}_{ij}} \alpha_{ijk} t_{ijk}\right). \tag{4}$$

In our architecture, we extend the notion of an edge to a directed path by introducing an auxiliary relation for n-hop neighbors between two entities. The introduction of the auxiliary edge of relation enriches the information transmission mechanism. However, the addition of relation edge increases the difficulty of graph neural network to identify the structure and single node. It may even appear that the mapping vectors of the triples composed of different entity nodes and relational edges are the same. Therefore, we are more interested in improving the discrimination of the model.

4 Our Approach

In this section, we introduce the end to end model for knowledge completion. The encoder is our proposed KBCPA, the decoder is composed of ConvKB [12]. As shown in Fig. 1.

4.1 Discrimination Ability via Cardinality Preservation

In this section, we analyze the discriminant ability of traditional GAT and point out their limitations. On this basis, we propose a graph neural network model based on cardinality preservation.

Discrimination ability refers to the ability of attentional GNN to distinguish different elements (local or global structures). In the field of graph representation, Zhang et al. [22] found that the previously proposed attentional GNN may fail in some cases, and its discrimination ability is limited. It is considered that H will map different multisets to the same embedding point if and only if the multiset has the same central node feature and the same node feature distribution.

Similarly, corresponding to knowledge graph embedding, suppose the input is a countable space R. Given a base set multiset $X \in \mathbb{R}$ the node characteristic of the central node is c. Information transfer function: $H(c, X) = \sum_{x \in X} \sum_{k \in \mathcal{R}_{cx}} \partial_{cxk} f(x)$. f is a mapping of the input feature vectors. And ∂_{cxk} is the attention weight between $f(x)$ and $f(c)$ calculated by the attention function *Att* in Eq. 4. For all f and *Att*, $H(c_1, X_1) = H(c_2, X_2)$, if and only if $c_1 = c_2, X_1 = (S, u)$ and $X_2 = (S, ku)$.

Since all h cannot distinguish between multiset multisets sharing the same node feature distribution, we can say that h ignores the multiplicity information of each identical element in the multiset. Therefore, the cardinality of multiset is not preserved.

4.2 Encoder–KBCPA

Our goal is to modify the attention mechanisms so that they capture cardinality information. To achieve our purpose, we modify the weighted summation function in Eq. 4 to add cardinality information without changing the attention function, so as to maintain its original expressive power, this is aggregation of our KBCPA model:

$$\overrightarrow{h_i'} = \sigma\left(\sum_{j \in n_i \in R_{ij}} \alpha_{ijk} \overrightarrow{t_{ijk}} + w^l \odot \sum_{j \in n_i} \overrightarrow{t_{ijk}}\right), \tag{5}$$

where w^l is a non-zero vector $\in \mathbb{R}^n$, $\odot$ denotes the elementwise multiplication.

In the model, each element in the multiset contributes to the preservation of cardinality information. Although it is a multiset with the same distribution characteristics, it can also obtain different h with different cardinality multiset. However, it is worth noting that we did not change the *Att* function, so on the basis of retaining the learning ability of the original attention mechanism, we increased the discrimination ability of the attention mechanism. As show Fig. 2: An illustration of attention-based aggregators on different multiset of node features. Assuming that two different multisets, $H1$ and $H2$, have the same central node feature and the same node feature distribution, Aggregators will map h_i to h_{i1} and h_{i2} for $H1$ and $H2$. The original model would get $h_{i1}' = h_{i2}'$ without making any distinction, while our model KBCPA gets the result that $h_{i1}'' \neq h_{i2}''$. It's successful in differentiating between $H1$ and $H2$.

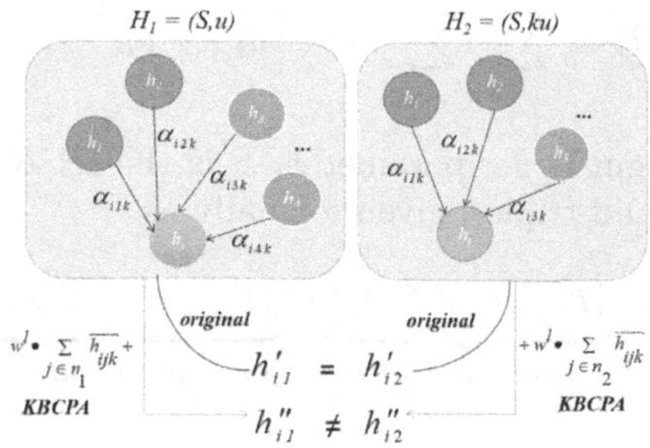

Fig. 2. The original model would get $h'_{i1} = h'_{i2}$ without making any distinction, KBCPA gets the result: $h''_{i1} \neq h''_{i2}$.

4.3 Decoder

Our model uses ConvKB [21] as the decoder. The model uses neural network addition operation instead of Transe to complete the translation of head entity + relation = tail entity. In the convolutional layer, different filters are used to extract the global features of triple t_{ijk} on each dimension. Extract the global relationships among same dimensional entries of the embedding triple. The feature maps are concatenated into a single feature vector which is then computed with a weight vector via a dot product to produce a score for the triple (h, r, t). This score is used to infer whether the triple (h, r, t) is valid or not. The score function with multiple feature mappings can be formally written:

$$f\left(t_{ij}^{k}\right) = \left(\prod_{m=1}^{\Omega} ReLU\left([\boldsymbol{h}_i, \boldsymbol{g}_k, \boldsymbol{h}_j] * \omega^{m}\right)\right) \cdot \mathrm{W} \tag{6}$$

where ω_m represents the m_{th}convolutional filter, Ω is a hyper-parameter denoting number of filters used, $*$ is a convolution operator, and $\mathbf{W} \in \mathbb{R}^{\Omega k \times 1}$ represents a linear transformation matrix used to compute the final score of the triple. The model is trained using soft-margin loss as:

$$\begin{gathered} \mathcal{L} = \sum_{t_{ij}^{k} \in \{S \cup S'\}} \log\left(1 + \exp\left(l_{t_{ij}^{k}} \cdot f\left(t_{ij}^{k}\right)\right)\right) + \frac{\lambda}{2} \| \mathrm{W}\|_2^2 \\ wherel_{t_{ij}^{k}} = \begin{cases} 1 & fort_{ij}^{k} \in S \\ -1 & fort_{ij}^{k} \in S' \end{cases} \end{gathered} \tag{7}$$

4.4 Training Objective

Our model learn from the idea of TransE about translational scoring function, which learns embeddings such that for a given golden triple $t_{ij}^{k} = (e_i, r_k, e_j)$, the condition $\boldsymbol{h}_i + \boldsymbol{g}_k \approx \boldsymbol{h}_j$ holds. In our model, we learn entity and relation embeddings by minimizing the L1-norm dissimilarity measure given by $d_{t_{ij}} = \left\|\overrightarrow{h_l} + \overrightarrow{g_k} - \overrightarrow{h_j}\right\|_1$ We also use hinge-loss training our model given by the following expression:

$$L(\Omega) = \sum_{t_{ij} \in S} \sum_{t'_{ij} \in S'} \max \left\{ d_{t'_{ij}} - d_{t_{ij}} + \gamma, 0 \right\} \tag{8}$$

where $\gamma > 0$ is a margin hyper-parameter, S is the set of valid triples, and S' denotes the set of invalid triples, given formally as

$$S' = \underbrace{\left\{ t^k_{i'j} \mid e'_i \in \mathcal{E} \backslash e_i \right\}}_{replaceheadentity} \cup \underbrace{\left\{ t^k_{ij'} \mid e'_j \in \mathcal{E} \backslash e_j \right\}}_{replacetailentity}. \tag{9}$$

5 Experimental Results

5.1 Dataset

To evaluate our proposed approach, we used three benchmark datasets: WN18RR [5], FB15K-237 [18], and Kinship [10]. WN18RR and FB15K-237 are Correspondingly subsets of two common datasets WN18 and FB15K and as shown one can use a simple inversion rule based model to get the latest results. We used the data segmentation provided by Nguyen et al. [12].

5.2 Evaluation Protocol

In the relational prediction task, the goal is to predict a triplet (e_i, r_k, e_j) without e_i or e_j, By replacing each entity e_i, we generate a set of (N,1) corrupted triples for each entity e_i. Then we assign a score to each of these triples. We then sort the scores in ascending order to get a correct triple ranking(e_i, r_k, e_j). Repeat the whole process by replacing the tail entity e_j and reporting the average index. We report the mean reciprocal rank (MRR), mean rank (MR) and the proportion of correct entities in the first N hits for $N = 1$, 3 and 10 (Hits@N).

5.3 Training Protocol

We create two sets of invalid triples, replacing the head or tail of the triple with one invalid entity at a time. We randomly select the same number of invalid triples from these two sets to ensure robust detection performance for head and tail entities.

We use entity and relationship embedding generated by Transe to initialize our embedding. We follow a two-step training process, we first train our KBCPA to encode information about graph entities and relationships, and then train a decoder model like ConvKB to perform the relationship prediction task. To learn our model parameters, including entity embedding and relationship embedding, filter ω and weight vector w. The last level of entity and relationship embedding is set to 200. We used Adam to optimize all the parameters and select its initial learning rate $\in \{5e{-}6, 1e{-}5, 5e{-}5, 1e{-}4, 5e{-}4\}$. We use ReLU as the activation function g. We choose the number of filters $\tau \in \{50, 100, 200, 400, 500\}$. We run ConvKB up to 200 epoch.

5.4 Result Analysis

We have seven currentstate-of-art methods: DisMult [21], ComplEx [19], ConvE [5], TransE [3], ConvKB [12], R-GCN [15], KBGAT [11] compared with our methods. The Table 1, 2 and 3 show the result of the comparison experiment using the same evaluation protocol. The best results are shown in bold. The experimental results show that our model performs better than the state-of-the-art method on four metrics for kinship, and two metrics for WN18RR, and five metrics for FB15k-237.

Table 1. Experiment on dataset kinship.

	Kinship				
			Hits@N		
	MR	MRR	@1	@3	@10
DisMult	5.26	0.516	36.1	58.1	86.7
ComplEx	2.48	0.832	73.3	89.9	97.11
ConvE	2.03	0.833	73.8	91.7	**98.14**
TransE	6.8	0.309	0.9	64.3	84.1
ConvKB	3.3	0.614	43.62	75.5	95.3
R-GCN	25.92	0.109	3	8.8	23.9
KBGAT	1.94	0.904	85.9	94.1	98
Our work	**1.84**	**0.9274**	**92.1**	**94.2**	98

KBCPA does better than the closely related model KBGAT on three experimental datasets, especially on kinship. That's a six percent improvement on the hit@1 metrics. And KBCPA obtains the best MR, MRR, hit@1 and hit@3. The result show KBCPA is good at processing dataset with high in-degree small types of nodes and edges.

WN18RR and FB15k-237 are created to reflect real world data without reversible relations. Therefore, the experiment on this database has more practical significance and attracts more attention. Happily, the experimental results of KBCPA on WN18RR and FB15k-237 validate the validity of our model. So far, KBGAT is the best baseline. Our model get higher hit@3 and hit@10 scores on WN18RR with 2% improvement compared with KBGAT. For FB15k-237, our model get more better result, MR, MRR, hit@n($n = 1, 2, 3$) scores are the best in our experiment where KBCPA gains significant improvement of $237-194 = 43$ in MR (which is about 18+% relative improvement) compared with KBGAT.

Our model is not inferior to the excellent baseline model such as KBGAT, or the powerful baseline model such as TransE. This is all due to the excellent discrimination ability of KBCPA, which makes different structures and entities map to different vector representations completing is not only a task of practical significance, but also a means to test the embedding effect. Our model optimizes the embedding expression ability of the model, and introduces the auxiliary

Table 2. Experiment on dataset WN18RR.

	WN18RR				
			Hits@N		
	MR	MRR	@1	@3	@10
DisMult	7000	0.444	41.2	47	50.4
ComplEx	7882	0.449	40.9	46.9	53
ConvE	4464	**0.456**	**41.9**	47	53.1
TransE	2300	0.243	4.27	44.1	53.2
ConvKB	**1295**	0.265	5.82	44.5	55.8
R-GCN	6700	0.123	20.7	13.7	8
KBGAT	1940	0.440	36.2	48.3	58.1
Our work	1980	0.454	36.9	**50.1**	**60.2**

Table 3. Experiment on dataset FB15k-237.

	FB15k-237				
			Hits@N		
	MR	MRR	@1	@3	@10
DisMult	512	0.281	19.9	30.1	44.6
ComplEx	546	0.278	19.4	29.7	45
ConvE	245	0.312	22.5	34.1	49.7
TransE	323	0.279	19.8	37.6	44.1
ConvKB	216	0.289	19.8	32.4	47.1
R-GCN	600	0.289	10	18.1	30
KBGAT	237	0.446	37.1	49.5	59.7
Our work	**194**	**0.466**	**38.8**	**50.1**	**61.6**

edge of the relationship side to conduct training at the same time. The excellent experimental results also verify the effectiveness of our idea.

6 Conclusion

In this paper, a graph attention network model for knowledge graph completion was proposed to solve the problem that the previous model's discrimination ability was not strong. On the basis of embedding relational features, this model also retained cardinality features, so as to improve the discrimination ability of the model. We also proved that our model has reached the most advanced experimental performance to date. In the future, we will consider the time knowledge graph and introduce the auxiliary edge of time to better improve the efficiency of completion.

Acknowledgements. This work was supported by the National Key Research and Development Program of China (No. 2018YFB0704400).

References

1. Auer, S., Bizer, C., Kobilarov, G., Lehmann, J., Cyganiak, R., Ives, Z.: DBpedia: a nucleus for a web of open data. In: Aberer, K., et al. (eds.) ASWC/ISWC -2007. LNCS, vol. 4825, pp. 722–735. Springer, Heidelberg (2007). https://doi.org/10.1007/978-3-540-76298-0_52
2. Bollacker, K., Evans, C., Paritosh, P., Sturge, T., Taylor, J.: Freebase: a collaboratively created graph database for structuring human knowledge. In: Proceedings of the 2008 ACM SIGMOD International Conference on Management of Data, pp. 1247–1250 (2008)
3. Bordes, A., Usunier, N., Garcia-Duran, A., Weston, J., Yakhnenko, O.: Translating embeddings for modeling multi-relational data. In: Neural Information Processing Systems (NIPS), pp. 1–9 (2013)
4. Carlson, A., Betteridge, J., Kisiel, B., Settles, B., Hruschka, E., Mitchell, T.: Toward an architecture for never-ending language learning. In: Proceedings of the AAAI Conference on Artificial Intelligence, vol. 24 (2010)
5. Dettmers, T., Minervini, P., Stenetorp, P., Riedel, S.: Convolutional 2D knowledge graph embeddings. In: Proceedings of the AAAI Conference on Artificial Intelligence, vol. 32 (2018)
6. Dong, X., et al.: Knowledge vault: a web-scale approach to probabilistic knowledge fusion. In: Proceedings of the 20th ACM SIGKDD International Conference on Knowledge Discovery and Data Mining, pp. 601–610 (2014)
7. Ji, S., Pan, S., Cambria, E., Marttinen, P., Philip, S.Y.: A survey on knowledge graphs: representation, acquisition, and applications. IEEE Trans. Neural Netw. Learn. Syst. (2021)
8. Kadlec, R., Bajgar, O., Kleindienst, J.: Knowledge base completion: baselines strike back. arXiv preprint arXiv:1705.10744 (2017)
9. Kipf, T.N., Welling, M.: Semi-supervised classification with graph convolutional networks. arXiv preprint arXiv:1609.02907 (2016)
10. Lin, X.V., Socher, R., Xiong, C.: Multi-hop knowledge graph reasoning with reward shaping. arXiv preprint arXiv:1808.10568 (2018)
11. Nathani, D., Chauhan, J., Sharma, C., Kaul, M.: Learning attention-based embeddings for relation prediction in knowledge graphs. arXiv preprint arXiv:1906.01195 (2019)
12. Nguyen, D.Q., Nguyen, T.D., Nguyen, D.Q., Phung, D.: A novel embedding model for knowledge base completion based on convolutional neural network. arXiv preprint arXiv:1712.02121 (2017)
13. Nickel, M., Rosasco, L., Poggio, T.: Holographic embeddings of knowledge graphs. In: Proceedings of the AAAI Conference on Artificial Intelligence, vol. 30 (2016)
14. Paulheim, H.: Knowledge graph refinement: a survey of approaches and evaluation methods. Semant. Web **8**(3), 489–508 (2017)
15. Schlichtkrull, M., Kipf, T.N., Bloem, P., van den Berg, R., Titov, I., Welling, M.: Modeling relational data with graph convolutional networks. In: Gangemi, A., et al. (eds.) ESWC 2018. LNCS, vol. 10843, pp. 593–607. Springer, Cham (2018). https://doi.org/10.1007/978-3-319-93417-4_38

16. Shang, C., Tang, Y., Huang, J., Bi, J., He, X., Zhou, B.: End-to-end structure-aware convolutional networks for knowledge base completion. In: Proceedings of the AAAI Conference on Artificial Intelligence, vol. 33, pp. 3060–3067 (2019)
17. Shi, B., Weninger, T.: ProjE: embedding projection for knowledge graph completion. In: Proceedings of the AAAI Conference on Artificial Intelligence, vol. 31 (2017)
18. Toutanova, K., Chen, D., Pantel, P., Poon, H., Choudhury, P., Gamon, M.: Representing text for joint embedding of text and knowledge bases. In: Proceedings of the 2015 Conference on Empirical Methods in Natural Language Processing, pp. 1499–1509 (2015)
19. Trouillon, T., Welbl, J., Riedel, S., Gaussier, É., Bouchard, G.: Complex embeddings for simple link prediction. In: International Conference on Machine Learning, pp. 2071–2080. PMLR (2016)
20. Vrandečić, D., Krötzsch, M.: Wikidata: a free collaborative knowledgebase. Commun. ACM **57**(10), 78–85 (2014)
21. Yang, B., Yih, W.t., He, X., Gao, J., Deng, L.: Embedding entities and relations for learning and inference in knowledge bases. arXiv preprint arXiv:1412.6575 (2014)
22. Zhang, S., Xie, L.: Improving attention mechanism in graph neural networks via cardinality preservation. In: IJCAI: Proceedings of the Conference, vol. 2020, p. 1395. NIH Public Access (2020)

Event Relation Reasoning Based on Event Knowledge Graph

Tingting Tang[1], Wei Liu[1(✉)], Weimin Li[1], Jinliang Wu[2], and Haiyang Ren[2]

[1] School of Computer Engineering and Science, Shanghai University, Shanghai, China
liuw@shu.edu.cn

[2] The 54th Research Institute of China Electronics Technology Group, Shijiazhuang, China

Abstract. Natural language text contains numerous event-based, and a large number of semantic relations exist between events. Event relations express the event rationality logic and reveal the evolution process of events, which is of great significance for machines to understand the text and the construction of event-based knowledge base. Event relation discovery includes extracting event relation from text and obtaining event relation by reasoning. Event relation extraction focuses on the recognition of explicit relations, while event relation reasoning can also discover implicit relations, which is more meaningful and more difficult. In this paper, we propose a model combining LSTM and attention mechanism for event relation reasoning, which uses the attention mechanism to dynamically generate event sequence representation according to the type of relation and predicts the event relation. The macro-F1 value in the experimental result reaches 63.71%, which shows that the model can effectively discover implicit event-event relation.

Keywords: Event knowledge graph · Event relation · Bi-LSTM · Attention mechanism

1 Introduction

Events and event relations in natural language contain advanced semantic information. Events do not occur in isolation, and the occurrence of the event is logically related to other events. The event relation is different from the classification relation between traditional concepts. It is often used to describe the higher-level semantic relations between events, such as causality, follow, concurrency, and composite. Discover event relations from text helps machines understand text better, and facilitate the construction of event-based knowledge bases from text.

Supported by the National Key Research and Development Program of China (No. 2017YFE0117500), the National Natural Science Foundation of China (No. 61991410), the research project of the 54th Research Institute of China Electronics Technology Group (No. SKX192010019).

H. Qiu et al. (Eds.): KSEM 2021, LNAI 12815, pp. 491–503, 2021.
https://doi.org/10.1007/978-3-030-82136-4_40

Event relation discovery includes event relation extraction and event relation reason. Recent research work on event relation extraction mainly aims at temporal event relation detection [17], subevent relation recognition [1,10], and causality relation extraction [7]. These methods are mainly divided into pattern matching method and machine learning method. The pattern matching method generally uses the rule template to match the keywords of the relation, and the machine learning method constructs the model to capture the semantics and features of the text for relation extraction. Existing methods focus on the extraction of explicit relations and cannot predict event relations from event-event sequence, while event relation reasoning can also discover implicit relations, which is more meaningful and difficult.

In this paper, we aim at reasoning implicit relations of events from text. Event relation reason is a task to obtain the pairs of event sequences and classify the relation (causality, follow, concurrency, and composite) between them. Existing methods of event relation discovery based on machine learning generally use models such as RNN and GCN [5,6,21] to obtain the representation of the event. However, the text contains redundant information unrelated to the event, resulting in the weakness of semantic information in the event feature vector. Event knowledge graph is event-based knowledge base for specific application domain. It is usually constructed by domain experts iteratively through manual or automatic methods. Event knowledge graph describes important events with related elements (such as action, objects, time and place) in a specific domain in the form of RDF triples, and also contains the description of rationality relationship between events. So we can generate the event representation sequence from it and take it as a priori knowledge base for event relation reasoning.

In this paper, we propose a model combining LSTM and attention mechanism for event relation reasoning. We obtain event information from the event knowledge graph and use the attention mechanism to dynamically generate event sequence representation according to the type of relation. To verify the effectiveness of the proposed event relational reasoning method, we annotate a new text set about COVID-19 on the basis of CEC[1] corpus, and construct an event knowledge graph about COVID-19 from the annotated texts.

The remainder of this paper is organized as follows: Sect. 2 introduces and discusses relevant works about the recognition model of different event relations. Section 3 introduces the event knowledge graph. Section 4 describes our proposed model. Section 5 demonstrates relevant experiments and analyzes the results. Finally, Sect. 6 concludes by summarizing our proposed method and pointing out directions for future work.

2 Related Work

Recent research work on event relation extraction tasks mainly aims at causality relation extraction, temporal relation detection and subevent relation recognition.

[1] https://github.com/daselab/CEC-Corpus.

Causality relation is the most important semantic relation between events, Girju [7] constructed a template to identify causality relations and used it to match the keywords of the relation. Peng [18] proposed a method to measure causality on event triggers by using pointwise mutual information. Recently, Mirza [14] presented a data-driven approach with rules to extract causal relations between events. Kriengkrai [9] extracted the original sentence of the causal candidate from the network text and the multi-column CNN is used to determine whether there is a causal relation between event pairs.

Event temporal relations specify how different events in a paragraph relate to each other in terms of time sequence. Current work aimed at representing event pairs based on linguistic features and using statistical learning methods (such as logistic regression [12] and SVM [15]) to capture the relations. With the development of deep learning technology, Cheng [5] and Xu [21] extracted the shortest dependency path of the event context and classified the event temporal relation with neural network based on LSTM. Dai [6] combined LSTM and GCN to capture features and correlation syntax for event temporal relation detection.

Besides, some research aims at the extraction of event hierarchical relations. This task attempts to extract hierarchical structure where the parent event contains child events described in the same document. To cope with this task, Araki [2] introduced a multi-class logistic regression model to detect subevent relations. Glavaš [8] constructed rich set of features for subevent relation classification. Zhou [24] constructed a common temporal sense language model Tacolm and predicted subevent relations on this basis.

Existing research works obtain event features and representations from text and uses different models to learn a particular relation between events, individually. These methods mainly aim at the extraction of explicit relations of texts, while a large number of semantic relations are implicit. Moreover, they are primarily developed at the sentence level and hence it is easy to omit relational event pairs scattered in different sentences or even in different documents.

In this paper, we construct the event knowledge graph and generate the event sequence based on it. Then we use a neural network model to learn the relation characteristics between events and predict the event relation.

3 Event Knowledge Graph

Based on the event model and event ontology concept proposed by Liu [11], we propose the event knowledge graph. Event knowledge graph is an event-based knowledge base accumulated in knowledge application, which contains event-based knowledge in different fields.

To construct the event knowledge graph, from the perspective of knowledge representation, we define an event as

$$E := < A, P, O, L, T > \quad (1)$$

where A, P, O, L, T represents the trigger, participant, object, location, and time of the event, respectively. The event knowledge graph includes event ontology models and event instances, which is described as

$$EKG := < EOs, EIs > \tag{2}$$

where EOs is event ontology set and EIs is event instance set. The event ontology is a shared, formal and explicit specification of the event class system model. It contains event class concepts, rules for event knowledge inference and relations between event classes (including causality, follow, concurrency, and composite).

An event instance is an instantiation of an event class, representing a specific event. We extend the RDF triples to represent the basic elements in the event knowledge graph. For example, the relation between the event instance and the event class can be described as $< e_1, type, ec_1 >$, where e_1 is an event instance and ec_1 is an event class. Event relations describe the rationality relation between events, represented as $< e_1, event\_relation, e_2 >$. Event elements is the description of the event, which is defined as: $< e_1, element\_relation, element\_entity >$, where $element\_relation$ is selected from {*hasParticipant, hasObject, hasLocation, hasTime*} and $element\_entity$ represents the event element entity.

Event knowledge graph is usually constructed by domain experts iteratively through manual or automatic methods. Machine learning methods are widely used in the automatic construction of event knowledge graph, such as GNN [16] is used to extract event trigger, and K-means is used to identify event elements.

Proof. "Since the COVID-19 epidemic spread in Europe and the world, the European Commission will continue to restrict travel to Europe from mid-March to 15 June this year." The event knowledge graph from the text is shown in Fig. 1.

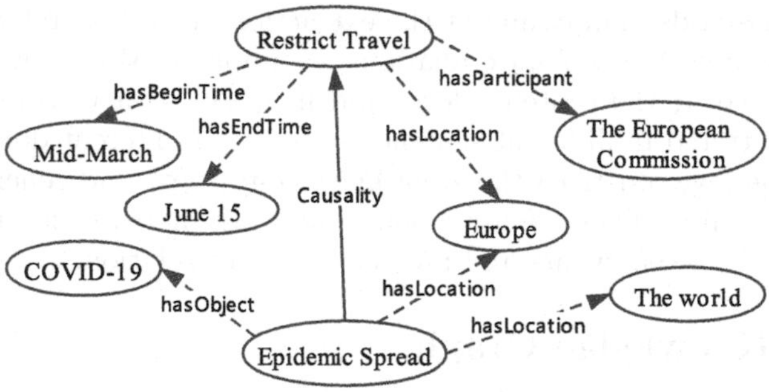

Fig. 1. A simple subgraph of the event knowledge graph.

4 Proposed Method

In this model, word2vec is used to map element words into low-dimensional vectors space, and LSTM is used to model event sequence. In addition, Attention mechanism assigns different weights to event element vectors.

4.1 Event Representation

In this paper, the event sequence is generated from the event knowledge graph. In CEC, we find that the average length of event sequence is 4.85, and 96.63% of event elements (trigger, participant, object, location and time) can be covered completely when the length of the event sequence is twelve. So we set the length of the event sequence as twelve. In a Chinese sentence, events are usually described in the order of time, participants, triggers, objects, and place. Therefore, we obtain the event trigger and related elements from the event knowledge graph in order. The event sequence contains six words filled forward and five words filled backward in the above order based on the event trigger. We use "⟨pad⟩" to mark paddings to ensure that the length of event sequence is equal.

4.2 LSTM

We use LSTM, a special RNN, to process sequence data and learn long-term dependencies. As shown in Fig. 2, the LSTM layer runs on a vector sequence of event sequences. LSTM has three gates (input i, forget f and output o) and a cell storage vector. The forget gate decides what information to throw away from the cell state. The input gate determines how the input vector $x(t)$ changes the cell state. The output gate allows the cell state to affect the output.

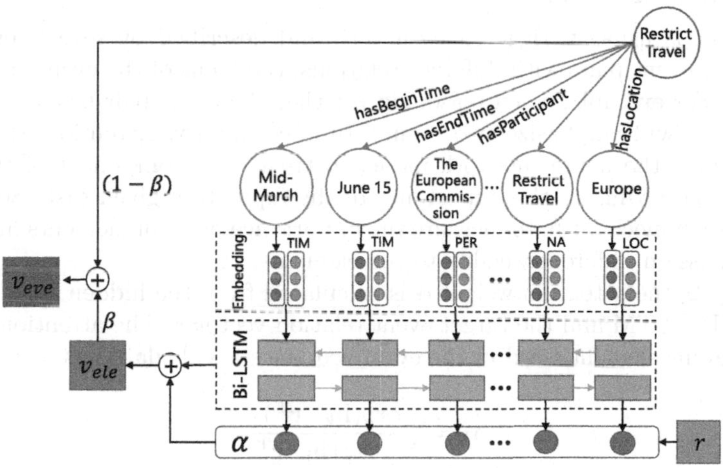

Fig. 2. The event-event relation reason model based on Bi-LSTM and attention mechanism. The input consists of two parts: an event sequence with NER tags and a target event-event relation. v_{ele} and v_{eve} are embedding vectors of the event and event element. The weight vector α is calculated based on the target event-event relation.

4.3 Word Encoder

Word embeddings learned from a large amount of unlabeled data can capture the semantics of words. In this paper, we use word2vec [13] to learn word embeddings on the corpus. Considering the effect of event element type on event representation, we concatenate the word vector e_{word} and the type vector e_{type} to represent each word.

$$w_t = e_{word} \oplus e_{type} \tag{3}$$

As the reversed order of event sequence also carries rich information, we can feed the reverse event sequence into LSTM to obtain the backward representation. Bidirectional LSTM uses two LSTMs to obtain the semantics of the forward and backward sequences, respectively. Therefore, for an event represented by sequence w_t, $t \in [0, T]$, the calculation is described simply as follows:

$$\overrightarrow{h}_t = \overrightarrow{LSTM}(w_t), t \in [1, T] \tag{4}$$

$$\overleftarrow{h}_t = \overleftarrow{LSTM}(w_t), t \in [T, 1] \tag{5}$$

We concatenate the forward hidden state $\overrightarrow{h}_t$ and the backward hidden state $\overleftarrow{h}_t$ to contain the semantics of the event, which is described as $event_i = [\overrightarrow{h}_t, \overleftarrow{h}_t]$.

4.4 Attention Layer

Each event is usually triggered by a verb and described by several event elements. For event pairs with different relations, the focus of the event elements is different. For example, when reasoning whether the event pair has a concurrent relation, we will emphasize two events' time continuity. Attention Mechanism [3] can guide the neural network model to treat each component of the input unequally according to the importance of the input to a given task. So, we use the attention mechanism to measure the importance of event elements in relation type and assign different weights to the elements.

In Fig. 2, the attention weight α is calculated from the hidden state h calculated by Bi-LSTM and the target event relation vector r. The attention score of the kth event element word in the event sequence is calculated as:

$$\alpha_k = \frac{exp(\mathbf{h}_\mathrm{k} \cdot \mathbf{r}^\mathrm{T})}{\sum_i exp(\mathbf{h}_\mathrm{i} \cdot \mathbf{r}^\mathrm{T})} \tag{6}$$

$$v_{element} = \alpha^\mathrm{T}\mathbf{H} \tag{7}$$

where $\mathbf{H} = [\mathbf{h}_1, ..., \mathbf{h}_T]$ is a matrix and $v_{element}$ is the vector of event elements which integrates all event element of the event. The vector of event sequence is defined as the weighted sum of $v_{trigger}$ and $v_{element}$, which is described as

$$v_{event} = (1 - \beta) \cdot v_{trigger} + \beta \cdot v_{element} \tag{8}$$

where $\beta \in [0, 1]$ trades off event trigger and elements and $v_{trigger}$ is the hidden vector of the trigger word token in Bi-LSTM.

4.5 Event-Event Relation Reason

Inspired by the translation model in the knowledge graph, such as TransE [4] and TransH [20], we regard the event as a special entity and assume that the distance of event-event with relation in vector space is close. Considering that events and relations are in different semantic spaces, we map the event vector into the relation semantic space through the relation matrix. The score of event pairs under the relation is calculated as follows:

$$g(event_1, r, event_2) = ||W_r v_{event_1} + r - W_r v_{event_2}|| \quad (9)$$

The objective is to minimize the maximum interval loss function. The main idea of this method is that we should maximize the score interval between each positive sample $T_i = (event_1, r, event_2)$ and the negative sample $T_i^{'}$ generated by replacing an event in the triple randomly. The loss function is expressed as

$$J = \sum_{T_i \in S} \sum_{T_i^{'} \in S'} max(0, 1 - g(T_i) + g(T_i^{'})) \quad (10)$$

where S and $S^{'}$ represent the set of positive and negative examples, respectively.

5 Experiments

In this section, we present the experiments on event relation reason. Specifically, we conduct evaluation for event relation extraction based on CEC corpus (Sect. 5.1–Sect. 5.4). We demonstrate the effects of event elements on event relation reasoning by adjusting the parameter β (Sect. 5.5). Finally, a detail ablation study is given to explain the significance of attention mechanism (Sect. 5.6).

5.1 Dataset

In experiments, we use CEC, a Chinese event-based dataset, to generate the event knowledge graph. Figure. 3 shows the annotation content of corpus by taking the event *travel restriction to Europe* as an example. Besides, we use 92 representative reports about COVID-19 and mark the event triggers, event elements (such as participants, time, location), and event relations semi-automatically. We add 3459 event instances and 1616 event relations to the CEC in total.

5.2 Experimental Settings

The dimension of the word vector is 128 dimensions, which word2vec trains. The vector of event element type is a 32-dimensional vector initialized randomly. The size of the LSTM is 128 (256 for Bi-LSTM), and the number of layers in the LSTM is 2. During the training process, we used gradient descent and the Adam optimizer algorithm to update the parameters. The batch size is 64. The learning rate is 0.02, and we use the exponential slowing method to make the learning rate decrease exponentially with the increase of the training step. To prevent neural networks from over-fitting, we adopt dropout [19] and L2 regularization.

```
<Event eid="e5">
    <Participant sid="s5" type="agent">欧盟(the European Commission)
</Participant>将继续(will continue to)
    <Denoter did="d5" type="operation">限制(restrict)</Denoter>赴
    <Location lid="l5">欧洲(Europe)</Location>
    <Object oid="o5">旅行(travel)</Object>, 从(from)
    <Time tid="t5" type="relTime">今年3月中旬(mid-March this year)</Time>至(to)
    <Time tid="t5" type="relTime">6月15日(15 June)</Time>
</Event>
```

Fig. 3. The annotation of *travel restriction to Europe* event in the corpus. For ease of reading, the English translation of the Chinese text is added in the brackets.

5.3 Evaluation Metrics

We use precision (P), recall (R) and F_1-measure (F_1) to evaluate the results. **Precision:** the percentage of correctly predicted event relations in total predicted event relations.

Recall: the proportion of correctly predicted event relations in the relation samples.

F_1-measure: $F_1 = \frac{2*P*R}{P+R}$

5.4 Result and Discussion

To verify the effectiveness of the model, we compare with the following methods:

- **word+PoS+SVM:** For the event sequence, we spliced word vectors based on the bag-of-words model and part of speech tags as event features and used SVM as a classifier.
- **word+PoS+KNN:** We use the same feature engineering above but use KNN as the classifier.
- **Yang:** Yang et al. [22] proposed an event-based Siamese Bi-LSTM network to model events and applied it to the learning of causality.
- **Zhang:** Zhang [23] used deep LSTM with average pooling in the last layer to obtain the average vector value and learn the event temporal relation.

Table 1. Performance comparison with different methods

Method	Causality	Follow	Concurrency	Composite	Overall
word+PoS+SVM	61.67	38.93	30.98	50.45	45.51
word+PoS+KNN	64.89	46.44	34.67	57.84	50.96
Yang's model	70.59	42.82	41.19	69.21	55.95
Zhang's model	71.16	45.96	39.79	72.50	57.35
our model	**73.18**	**50.75**	**48.16**	**82.76**	**63.71**

Table 1 reveals the performance comparison of the five models on the dataset. The macro-average F_1 vlaue of our method is 63.71%. Our model achieves better performance on the relations of *causality* and *composite*, compared with *follow* and *concurrency*. There are two possible reasons. Firstly, event pairs with *causality* and *composite* relations have a strong logical connection with event triggers, and their distribution is relatively concentrated. Secondly, the *follow* and *concurrency* relation focus on the time element of event pair. However, the model does not distinguish well between two relations.

From Table 1, we can find that the overall performance of our model is better than the four benchmarks in macro-average F_1 value. Compared with the machine learning-based methods, our neural network model significantly improves the F_1 value. These results further verify the effectiveness of the neural network in the task of event relation reason.

The comparison of model performances on individual relation types also proves the improvement on the F_1 score. Our model achieves the greatest performance improvement (72.5 vs. 82.76) on *composite* relation. The relations of *follow* and *concurrency* are so difficult to distinguish that the traditional methods cannot recognize them well. However, the BiLSTM can capture the semantic features of event sequences, and the attention mechanism assigns different weights to event elements. Hence, our model significantly improves the performance of two relations. These results prove the validity of our model.

5.5 The Effect of β

Table 2 lists the detailed performance of our model with different parameters β. We select numbers from $\{0, 0.1, 0.2, 0.3, 0.4\}$ as the parameter β to verify the effect of event elements on event relation reason. From the table, we can find that it is better to add event elements to the event representation than to take the event trigger's hidden vector as the event's representation. When β is 0.2, the model is most suitable for the event relation reason task and achieves the best performance. When β is greater than 0.2, the model becomes less effective. It is likely that the lack of event trigger information and the emphasis on event element information resulting in insufficient semantic coherence of the event. These results indicate that integrating event trigger and elements to represent event semantic information is more suitable for event-event relation reason.

Table 2. The effect of β on experimental performance

β	Precision (%)	Recall (%)	F1-score (%)
0.0	60.27	61.25	60.65
0.1	62.23	62.91	62.52
0.2	**64.05**	**63.74**	**63.71**
0.3	61.54	61.90	61.46
0.4	60.40	61.22	60.69

5.6 Analysis of Attention Weight α

We design two sets of comparative experiments to confirm the impact of the attention mechanism. In the first set of experiments, we use the attention mechanism to assign different weights to event elements in a specific relation and take the weighted summation result as the event's element representation. In the second set of experiments, we only add the average vectors of event elements. The experimental results are shown in Fig. 4. In general, the model combining the attention mechanism has a better experimental result. The attention mechanism can dynamically assign weights to elements according to the type of relation and capture the features of specific event elements.

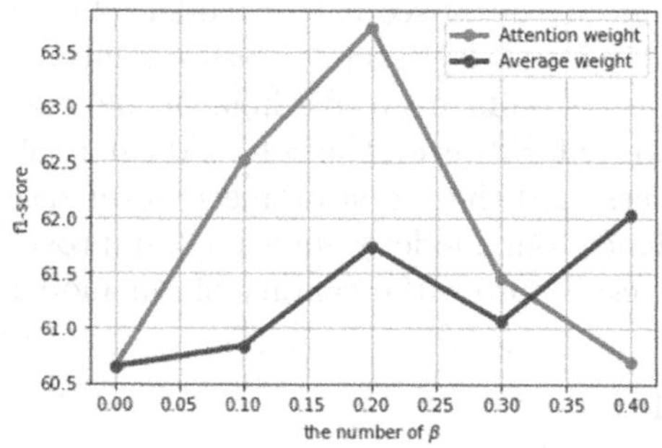

Fig. 4. Influence of attention mechanism. **Red line**: the representation of event elements obtained by the attention mechanism. **Blue line**: the representation of the event element obtained by adding the average element vectors. (Color figure online)

Figure 5 shows several examples of the attention vector α learned by our model. In the first example, the *causality* relation focuses on the logical connection between event pairs, and the model assigns similar attention scores to event elements. The time element and the continuity of the event occurrence are important clues to the *follow* relation. In the second example, the model focuses not only on time but also on the continuity of the event pairs. Therefore it assigns high attention scores to key elements of the event, such as "fire" and "fireman". Furthermore, the *concurrency* relation refers to the occurrence of two events simultaneously or one after the other. The third example is a negative sample. However, to explore the *concurrency* relation between events, the model tries to capture this feature by assigning a high attention score to the time element.

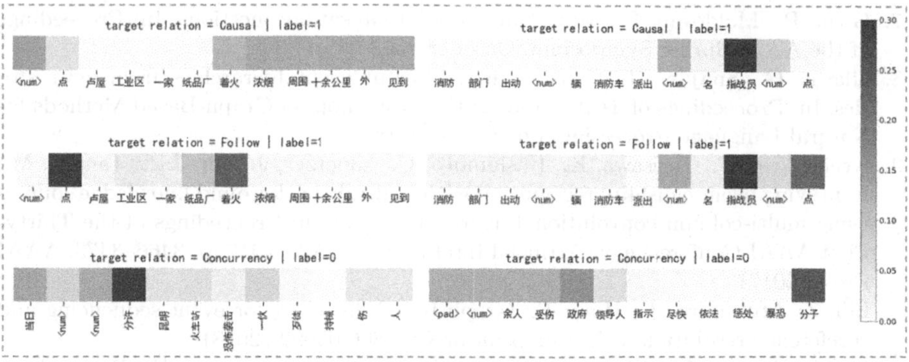

Fig. 5. Visualization of attention weight vector α of sample event instances learned by our model.

6 Conclusion

In this paper, we proposed an event relation reason model based on LSTM and attention mechanism. The event knowledge graph is introduced as a priori knowledge base and we obtain the event sequence from it. The model learns features for relation reasoning iteratively along the event representation sequence. We leverage LSTM for event information propagation and integration. Meanwhile, attention mechanism assigns different weights to event elements dynamically. Experimental results show that the model achieves a better performance on the reasoning of event causality and composition relation. In future work, we will improve the reasoning of concurrency and follow relation between events.

References

1. Aldawsari, M., Finlayson, M.A.: Detecting subevents using discourse and narrative features. In: Proceedings of the 57th Annual Meeting of the Association for Computational Linguistics (2019)
2. Araki, J., Liu, Z., Hovy, E.H., Mitamura, T.: Detecting subevent structure for event coreference resolution. In: LREC, pp. 4553–4558 (2014)
3. Bahdanau, D., Cho, K., Bengio, Y.: Neural machine translation by jointly learning to align and translate. arXiv preprint arXiv:1409.0473 (2014)
4. Bordes, A., Usunier, N., Garcia-Duran, A., Weston, J., Yakhnenko, O.: Translating embeddings for modeling multi-relational data. In: Neural Information Processing Systems (NIPS) pp. 1–9 (2013)
5. Cheng, F., Miyao, Y.: Classifying temporal relations by bidirectional LSTM over dependency paths. In: Proceedings of the 55th Annual Meeting of the Association for Computational Linguistics (Volume 2: Short Papers), pp. 1–6 (2017)
6. Dai, Q., Kong, F., Dai, Q.: Event temporal relation classification based on graph convolutional networks. In: Tang, J., Kan, M.-Y., Zhao, D., Li, S., Zan, H. (eds.) NLPCC 2019. LNCS (LNAI), vol. 11839, pp. 393–403. Springer, Cham (2019). https://doi.org/10.1007/978-3-030-32236-6_35

7. Girju, R., Moldovan, D.: Mining answers for causation questions. In: Proceedings of the AAAI Spring Symposium, October 2002
8. Glavaš, G., Šnajder, J.: Constructing coherent event hierarchies from news stories. In: Proceedings of TextGraphs-9: the Workshop on Graph-Based Methods for Natural Language Processing, pp. 34–38 (2014)
9. Kruengkrai, C., Torisawa, K., Hashimoto, C., Kloetzer, J., Oh, J.H., Tanaka, M.: Improving event causality recognition with multiple background knowledge sources using multi-column convolutional neural networks. In: Proceedings of the Thirty-First AAAI Conference on Artificial Intelligence, AAAI 2017, p. 3466–3473. AAAI Press (2017)
10. Liu, Z., Mitamura, T., Hovy, E.: Graph-based decoding for event sequencing and coreference resolution. arXiv preprint arXiv:1806.05099 (2018)
11. Liu, Z., Huang, M., Zhou, W., Zhong, Z., Fu, J., Shan, J., Zhi, H.: Research on event-oriented ontology model. Comput. Sci. **36**(11), 189–192 (2009)
12. Mani, I., Verhagen, M., Wellner, B., Lee, C., Pustejovsky, J.: Machine learning of temporal relations. In: Proceedings of the 21st International Conference on Computational Linguistics and 44th Annual Meeting of the Association for Computational Linguistics, pp. 753–760 (2006)
13. Mikolov, T., Chen, K., Corrado, G., Dean, J.: Efficient estimation of word representations in vector space. arXiv preprint arXiv:1301.3781 (2013)
14. Mirza, P.: Extracting temporal and causal relations between events. In: Proceedings of the ACL 2014 Student Research Workshop, pp. 10–17 (2014)
15. Mirza, P., Tonelli, S.: Classifying temporal relations with simple features. In: Proceedings of the 14th Conference of the European Chapter of the Association for Computational Linguistics, pp. 308–317 (2014)
16. Nguyen, T., Grishman, R.: Graph convolutional networks with argument-aware pooling for event detection. In: Proceedings of the AAAI Conference on Artificial Intelligence, vol. 32 (2018)
17. Ning, Q., Subramanian, S., Roth, D.: An improved neural baseline for temporal relation extraction. arXiv preprint arXiv:1909.00429 (2019)
18. Peng, H., Song, Y., Roth, D.: Event detection and co-reference with minimal supervision. In: Proceedings of the 2016 Conference on Empirical Methods in Natural Language Processing, pp. 392–402 (2016)
19. Srivastava, N., Hinton, G., Krizhevsky, A., Sutskever, I., Salakhutdinov, R.: Dropout: a simple way to prevent neural networks from overfitting. J. Mach. Learn. Res. **15**(1), 1929–1958 (2014)
20. Wang, Z., Zhang, J., Feng, J., Chen, Z.: Knowledge graph embedding by translating on hyperplanes. In: Proceedings of the AAAI Conference on Artificial Intelligence, vol. 28 (2014)
21. Xu, Y., Mou, L., Li, G., Chen, Y., Peng, H., Jin, Z.: Classifying relations via long short term memory networks along shortest dependency paths. In: Proceedings of the 2015 Conference on Empirical Methods in Natural Language Processing, pp. 1785–1794 (2015)
22. Yang, Z., Liu, W., Liu, Z.: Event causality identification by modeling events and relation embedding. In: Cheng, L., Leung, A.C.S., Ozawa, S. (eds.) ICONIP 2018. LNCS, vol. 11303, pp. 59–68. Springer, Cham (2018). https://doi.org/10.1007/978-3-030-04182-3_6

23. Zhang, Y., Li, P., Zhou, G.: Classifying temporal relations between events by deep bilstm. In: 2018 International Conference on Asian Language Processing (IALP), pp. 267–272. IEEE (2018)
24. Zhou, B., Ning, Q., Khashabi, D., Roth, D.: Temporal common sense acquisition with minimal supervision. arXiv preprint arXiv:2005.04304 (2020)

PEN4Rec: Preference Evolution Networks for Session-Based Recommendation

Dou Hu[1], Lingwei Wei[2,3], Wei Zhou[2(✉)], Xiaoyong Huai[1], Zhiqi Fang[1], and Songlin Hu[2,3]

[1] National Computer System Engineering Research Institute of China, Beijing, China
[2] Institute of Information Engineering, Chinese Academy of Sciences, Beijing, China
zhouwei@iie.ac.cn
[3] School of Cyber Security, University of Chinese Academy of Sciences, Beijing, China

Abstract. Session-based recommendation aims to predict user the next action based on historical behaviors in an anonymous session. For better recommendations, it is vital to capture user preferences as well as their dynamics. Besides, user preferences evolve over time dynamically and each preference has its own evolving track. However, most previous works neglect the evolving trend of preferences and can be easily disturbed by the effect of preference drifting. In this paper, we propose a novel Preference Evolution Networks for session-based Recommendation (PEN4Rec) to model preference evolving process by a two-stage retrieval from historical contexts. Specifically, the first-stage process integrates relevant behaviors according to recent items. Then, the second-stage process models the preference evolving trajectory over time dynamically and infer rich preferences. The process can strengthen the effect of relevant sequential behaviors during the preference evolution and weaken the disturbance from preference drifting. Extensive experiments on three public datasets demonstrate the effectiveness and superiority of the proposed model.

Keywords: Recommender systems · Session-based recommendation · Graph neural networks · Sequential behavior · User preference

1 Introduction

With the rapid development of online platforms, *Recommender Systems* [1,2] have received increasing concern recently. In many real-world services, user identification is not always available and only the historical user-item interactions during an ongoing session can be accessed easily. In such scenario, *Session-based Recommendation* (SBRS) [3] emerges by focusing on an anonymous session of user-item interactions (e.g., purchases of items) within a certain period. Exploring user preferences as well as their dynamics behind user-item interactive behaviors in the session is the key to advance the performance of SBRS.

H. Qiu et al. (Eds.): KSEM 2021, LNAI 12815, pp. 504–516, 2021.
https://doi.org/10.1007/978-3-030-82136-4_41

Traditionally, similarity-based [4] and matrix factorization [5,6] methods are not suitable for the session-based scene because of ignoring the order of the user's behaviors. Some methods [7,8] deal with dependencies between adjacent behaviors successively and equally. Intuitively, not all behaviors are strictly dependent on each adjacent behavior. Each user has diverse preferences, and each preference has its own evolution. That is, the user's intentions can be very different in adjacent visits, and one behavior of a user may depend on the behavior that takes a long time ago. Such a phenomenon can be named *preference drifting*, caused by the diversity and dynamics of user preferences. Recently, many works [9–13] apply an attention mechanism to integrate relative behaviors. Although they can capture diverse preferences, they still ignore sequential patterns in different preferences and obtain one fixed preference evolving trajectory. Thereby, they can be disturbed by the preference drifting.

In this paper, we propose a novel two-stage **P**reference **E**volution **N**etworks **for** session-based **Rec**ommendation (short for **PEN4Rec**), to model preference evolving process based on historical contexts. Following graph-based models [12, 13], we first encode user-item behaviors in a session graph to capture complex item transitions under multi-hop neighbor connections. After that, different from taking behaviors as preferences directly, we extract user preferences via a well-designed two-stage retrieval.

Specifically, the first-stage process integrates relevant behaviors from historical contexts according to the recent items via the attention mechanism. And the second-stage process models the preference evolving trajectory over time dynamically and reasons diverse preferences. There are two key layers in the second-stage process, i.e., a session reader layer and a preference fusion layer. The former layer applies an adaptive bidirectional gated recurrent unit (Bi-GRU) to sufficiently gather the contextual information for each item in two directions of the ongoing sequential session. Then, the latter layer combines the attention mechanism and gated recurrent unit (GRU) to capture more relevant preferences during the preference evolution. The attention weights are applied to strengthen the above relevant behaviors' influence on the preference evolution and weaken irrelevant behaviors' effect that results from preference drifting. Through the above two-stage retrieval, we can produce more diverse preferences and make precise recommendations.

To assess the proposed model, we compare with typical baselines on three public benchmark datasets. Experimental results demonstrate the effectiveness of the proposed model. The main contributions are summarized as follows:

- We investigate the preference drifting phenomenon for session-based recommendations, and propose a new two-stage PEN4Rec to model preference evolving process based on historical contexts.
- We design a novel second-stage retrieval process to strengthen the effect of relevant sequential behaviors during the preference evolution and weaken the disturbance from preference drifting.

- We conduct extensive experiments on three real-world benchmark datasets. The results consistently demonstrate the effectiveness and superiority of the proposed model[1].

2 Related Work

2.1 Conventional Recommendation Methods

Similarity-based methods [4] recommended items similar to the previously clicked item in the session. Matrix factorization methods [5,6] represented user preferences by factorizing a user-item matrix consisting of the whole historical behaviors. These methods are not suitable for the session-based scene because of ignoring the order of the user's behaviors. Then, Rendle et al. [7] combined Markov chain and matrix factorization to simulate the sequential behavior between two adjacent interactions while ignoring long-term dependencies.

2.2 Deep Learning Based Recommendation Methods

In recent years, many deep learning based methods are proposed for SBRS. Particularly, Hidasi et al. [8] first employed recurrent neural networks (RNNs) [14] to simply treat the data as time series. The work had facilitated the investigation of RNN-based models [15] in SBRS. Li et al. [9] applied an attention mechanism on RNN to capture sequential features and main intents. Liu et al. [11] used an attentive network to capture short-term and long-term preferences. Wang et al. [10] exploited the key-value memory networks [16] to consider information from the current session and neighborhood sessions. More recently, some graph-based works [12,13,17–19] apply graph neural networks (GNNs) [20–22] to learn complex item transitions based on the session graph. Especially, Wu et al. [12] and Xu et al. [13] extracted preferences after a gated graph neural network (GGNN) [20] by using the attention layer to capture long-term preferences.

Although these methods show promising performance, almost all the above approaches neglect the evolving trend of preferences and can be easily disturbed by the effect of preference drifting. Different from them, the proposed PEN4Rec can strengthen the effect from relevant sequential behaviors during the preference evolution and weaken the disturbance effect that results from preference drifting.

3 Problem Definition

In this section, We will define the task of session-based recommendation.

Formally, let $\mathcal{V} = \{v_1, v_2, ..., v_{|\mathcal{V}|}\}$ denote the set of all unique items involved in all sessions. We define an anonymous session sequence s as a sequence of items $s = [v_1, v_2, ..., v_n]$ ordered by timestamp, where $v_i \in \mathcal{V}$ represents a user-clicked item at time step i within the session s. The goal of **session-based**

[1] The source code is available at https://github.com/zerohd4869/PEN4Rec.

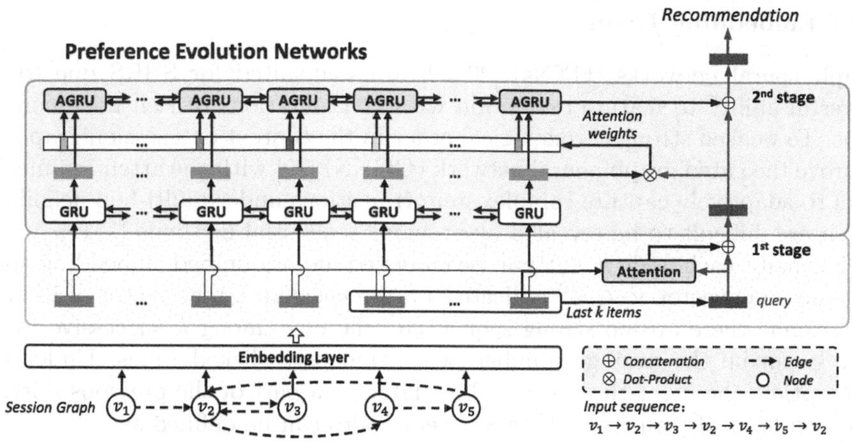

Fig. 1. The architecture of the proposed model. PEN4Rec builds a directed session graph for each session sequence and encode items into a unified embedding space by the embedding layer. Then, in the first-stage process, irrelevant behaviors are integrated according to the last k items from historical contexts. In the second-stage process, the model retrieves diverse preferences and reasons the preference evolving trajectory that is relevant to the updated query. Finally, PEN4Rec generates a vector representation with diverse preferences to make recommendations.

recommendation is to predict the next item, i.e., v_{n+1}, given the session s. Generally, we design and train a model to output a probability distribution $p(v|s)$ over the entire item set $\mathcal{V}$. The items with top-c probabilities will be in candidate items for recommendation.

4 The Proposed Model

In this section, we propose **P**erference **E**volution **N**etworks for session-based **Rec**ommendation (**PEN4Rec**), as shown in Fig. 1.

4.1 Session Graph Construction

Firstly, given an input session sequence $s = [v_1, v_2, ..., v_n]$, we build a directed session graph $\mathcal{G} = (\mathcal{V}, \mathcal{E})$. In the session graph, we treat each item $v_i \in \mathcal{V}$ as a node. Each edge $(v_{i-1}, v_i) \in \mathcal{E}$ is formulated as a directed edge to represent a user clicks item v_{i-1} and v_i consecutively. The connection matrix $\mathbf{A} \in \mathbb{R}^{n \times 2n}$ is defined as the concatenation of two adjacency matrices, which are denoted weighted connections of outgoing and incoming edges in $\mathcal{G}$, respectively. Since several items may appear in the session sequence repeatedly, we assign each edge with normalized weighted. The value is computed as the occurrence of the edge divided by the out-degree of that edge's start.

4.2 Embedding Layer

Graph neural networks (GNNs) [20–22] are well-suited for SBRS due to the powerful ability to feature extraction with considerations of rich node connections. To weaken strong chronological order in the context of a session graph, we improve the gated graph neural network (GGNN) [20] with the attention mechanism to adaptively capture complex item transitions under multi-hop neighbors, which are difficult to be revealed by previous sequential methods [7–11].

Formally, each node $v_i \in \mathcal{V}$ can be embeded into an unified embedding space and the node vector $\mathbf{v}_i \in \mathbb{R}^d$ indicates a d-dimensional latent vector of item v_i. We assume there are no strong sequential relations among k successive items, e.g., k can be the average number of continuously clicked items. Under this assumption, the $k+1$-th item may be related to a part of the previous k items. The t-th layer of transitions between item nodes can be defined as:

$$\begin{aligned} \mathbf{a}_{c,i}^t &= \mathbf{A}_{c,i:}[\mathbf{v}_1^{t-1}, ..., \mathbf{v}_n^{t-1}]^\top \mathbf{W}_a + \mathbf{b}_a, \\ \alpha_c &= softmax((\mathbf{W}_\alpha \mathbf{a}_{c,i}^t)^\top \mathbf{v}^t), \\ \mathbf{a}_i^t &= \sum\nolimits_c \alpha_c \mathbf{a}_{c,i}^t, \end{aligned} \tag{1}$$

where $\mathbf{A}_{c,i:} \in \mathbb{R}^{1\times 2n}$ are the two columns of blocks in $\mathbf{A}$ under c-hop neighbors corresponding to v_i, $c = k-1$. $\mathbf{W}_a \in \mathbb{R}^{d\times 2d}$ and $\mathbf{b}_a \in \mathbb{R}^d$ are learnable parameters. $\mathbf{a}_i^t$ adaptively extracts the contextual information of multi-hop neighbors for v_i. Then, the final output $\mathbf{v}_i^t$ of the embedding layer is computed by:

$$\begin{aligned} \mathbf{z}_i^t &= \sigma(\mathbf{W}_z \mathbf{a}_i^t + \mathbf{U}_z \mathbf{v}_i^{t-1}), \\ \mathbf{r}_i^t &= \sigma(\mathbf{W}_r \mathbf{a}_i^t + \mathbf{U}_r \mathbf{v}_i^{t-1}), \\ \widetilde{\mathbf{v}}_i^t &= tanh(\mathbf{W}_o \mathbf{a}_i^t + +\mathbf{U}_o(\mathbf{r}_i^t \odot \mathbf{v}_i^{t-1})), \\ \mathbf{v}_i^t &= (1-\mathbf{z}_i^t) \odot \mathbf{v}_i^{t-1} + \mathbf{z}_i^t \odot \widetilde{\mathbf{v}}_i^t, \end{aligned} \tag{2}$$

where $\mathbf{z}_i^t$ and $\mathbf{r}_i^t$ are reset and update gates to determine the preserved and discarded information, respectively. $\mathbf{W}_z, \mathbf{W}_r, \mathbf{W}_o \in \mathbb{R}^{2d\times d}$, $\mathbf{U}_z, \mathbf{U}_r, \mathbf{U}_o \in \mathbb{R}^{d\times d}$ are learnable parameters. $\sigma(\cdot)$ is the sigmoid function. $\odot$ is the element-wise multiplication.

4.3 Preference Evolution Networks

Due to joint influence from the external environment and internal cognition, user preferences evolve over time dynamically. PEN4Rec aims to capture user preferences and models preference evolving process by transitively retrieving relevant information in the two-stage process. The advantages are two points. First, the model can supply the representation of recent preferences with more relative history information. Also, it is better to predict the next item by following the preference evolution trend.

The First-Stage Process. We design the first-stage process to integrate relevant behaviors from historical contexts according to the local preference. We regard recent k items as the local preference since the next item may be related to a part of the previous k items. Thus, the query is defined as $\mathbf{q}^{(0)} = [\mathbf{v}_{n-k+1}; ...; \mathbf{v}_n]$. Then, we aggregate relevant behaviors by adopting the soft-attention mechanism to better represent the global preference $\mathbf{p}^{(0)}$:

$$\begin{aligned} \beta_i &= \sigma(\mathbf{W}_1 \mathbf{q}^{(0)} + \mathbf{W}_2 \mathbf{v}_i + \mathbf{b}), \\ \mathbf{p}^{(0)} &= \sum\nolimits_{i=n-k+1}^{n} \beta_i \mathbf{v}_i, \end{aligned} \tag{3}$$

where $\mathbf{W}_1 \in \mathbb{R}^{d \times kd}$ and $\mathbf{W}_2 \in \mathbb{R}^{d \times d}$ controls the weights of item embedding vectors, and $\mathbf{b} \in \mathbb{R}^d$ is the bias parameter. After the first-stage process, the query can be updated as:

$$\mathbf{q}^{(1)} = \mathbf{W}_q[\mathbf{p}^{(0)}; \mathbf{q}^{(0)}] + \mathbf{b}_q, \tag{4}$$

where $\mathbf{W}_q \in \mathbb{R}^{d \times 2d}$ and $\mathbf{b}_q \in \mathbb{R}^d$ are parameters.

The Second-Stage Process. The second-stage process is designed to retrieve diverse preferences and reason the preference evolving trajectory that is relevant to the updated query via a *session reader layer* and a *preference fusion layer*.

For **the session reader layer**, we utilize an adaptive bidirectional GRU (Bi-GRU) to record the contextual information for each item in two directions. Bi-GRU allows for message propagation from neighboring contexts, capturing spatial information in the ongoing sequential session. Formally, given the item embedding $\mathbf{v}_i$, the retrieval can be formulated as:

$$\begin{aligned} \overrightarrow{\mathbf{m}}_i &= \overrightarrow{GRU}(\mathbf{v}_i, \overrightarrow{\mathbf{m}}_{i-1}), \\ \overleftarrow{\mathbf{m}}_i &= \overleftarrow{GRU}(\mathbf{v}_i, \overleftarrow{\mathbf{m}}_{i+1}), \end{aligned} \tag{5}$$

where $\overrightarrow{\mathbf{m}}_i, \overleftarrow{\mathbf{m}}_i \in \mathbb{R}^d$ indicates the hidden states of the forward GRU and the backward GRU. Then we adopt a residual connection by concatenating them and combine the input to enable sufficient interaction between items.

$$\mathbf{m}_i = tanh(\mathbf{W}_m[\overrightarrow{\mathbf{m}}_i; \overleftarrow{\mathbf{m}}_i] + \mathbf{b}_m) + \mathbf{v}_i, \tag{6}$$

where $\mathbf{W}_m \in \mathbb{R}^{d \times 2d}$ and $\mathbf{b}_m \in \mathbb{R}^d$ are learnable parameters.

The preference fusion layer retrieves the information to adaptively extract key information in complex queries, which is inspired by dynamic memory networks [23]. It is formed by modifying the GRU by embedding information from the attention mechanism. Specifically, we update the internal state of a normal GRU with the attention weights to strengthen the effect of relevant behaviors on the preference evolution and weaken irrelevant behaviors' effect. The attention weights and modified updated gated are computed as follows, respectively.

$$\gamma_i = \frac{exp((\mathbf{q}^{(1)})^\top \mathbf{m}_i)}{\sum_i exp((\mathbf{q}^{(1)})^\top \mathbf{m}_i)}, \tag{7}$$

$$\mathbf{h}_i = \gamma_i \circ \widetilde{\mathbf{h}}_i + (1 - \gamma_i) \circ \mathbf{h}_{i-1}, \tag{8}$$

where $\mathbf{h}_{i-1}$ represents the previous hidden state and $\widetilde{\mathbf{h}}_i$ represents the internal state of a normal GRU.

After that, the Bi-GRU is advantageous for retaining the positional and ordering information of contexts. The final hidden state of this layer serve as the contextual vector to refine the representation of the query, i.e., $\mathbf{p}^{(1)} = \mathbf{h}_n$. Then, the query can be updated by:

$$\mathbf{q}^{(2)} = \mathbf{W}_s[\mathbf{p}^{(1)}; \mathbf{q}^{(1)}] + \mathbf{b}_s, \tag{9}$$

where $\mathbf{W}_s \in \mathbb{R}^{d \times 2d}$ and $\mathbf{b}_s$ are the learnable parameters. Finally, we adopt the hybrid embedding to represent the rich preference, denoted as $\mathbf{s}$, i.e., $\mathbf{s} = \mathbf{q}^{(2)}$.

4.4 Recommendation

For each session, we predict the next click for all candidate items by multiplying the corresponding item embedding $\mathbf{v}_i$.

$$\hat{\mathbf{y}}_i = softmax(\mathbf{s}^\top \mathbf{v}_i), \tag{10}$$

where $\hat{\mathbf{y}}_i$ is the probability of the candidate item $v_i \in \mathcal{V}$ to be the next interacted in the session s. For each session graph, the loss function $\mathcal{L}$ is defined as the cross-entropy of the prediction and the ground truth:

$$\mathcal{L}(\hat{\mathbf{y}}) = -\sum_{i=1}^{l} \mathbf{y}_i log(\hat{\mathbf{y}}_i) + (1 - \mathbf{y}_i) log(1 - \hat{\mathbf{y}}_i), \tag{11}$$

where $\mathbf{y}$ denotes the one-hot encoding vector of the ground truth item, and l is the number of all candidate items.

5 Experimental Setups

5.1 Datasets and Preprocessing

We conduct the experiments on three public benchmark datasets, i.e., Yoochoose, Diginetica and LastFM datasets. The statistics are summarized in Table 1.

Yoochoose[2] is a challenging dataset for RecSys Challenge 2015. It contains a stream of user clicks on an e-commerce website within 6 months. Following [9,12], we take the recent fractions 1/64 of training sessions and filter out all sessions of length 1 and items that occur less than 5 times. For generating training and test sets, sessions of the subsequent day are used for testing. **Diginetica**[3] comes from CIKM cup 2016. We again follow [9,12] and filter out all sessions of length 1 and items that occur less than 5 times. Sessions of the subsequent week are

[2] https://2015.recsyschallenge.com/challenge.html.
[3] https://cikm2016.cs.iupui.edu/cikm-cup/.

used as test datasets. **LastFM**[4] is a music recommendation dataset released by [24]. Following [10], we select the top 40,000 most popular artists as the item set and filter out sessions that are shorter than 2 and longer than 50 items. The splitting of the dataset is the same as the previous work [10].

Table 1. Summary of the three benchmark datasets.

Datasets	All the clicks	Train sessions	Valid sessions	Test sessions	All the items	Avg. length
Yoochoose	557,248	332,873	36,986	55,898	16,766	6.16
Diginetica	982,961	647,532	71,947	60,858	43,097	5.12
LastFM	3,804,922	26,984	5,996	5,771	39,163	13.52

5.2 Evaluation Metrics

We evaluate the recommender system with two commonly-used metrics, P@20 and MRR@20. **P@20** (Precision calculated over top-20 items) computes the proportion of correctly recommended items amongst the top-20 items in an unranking list. **MRR@20** (Mean Reciprocal Rank calculated over top-20 items) is the average of reciprocal ranks of the desired items. The reciprocal rank is set to 0 when the rank exceeds 20.

5.3 Comparison Methods

We compare our model **PEN4Rec** with the following baselines: **POP** and **S-POP** always recommend the most popular items in the whole training set or the current session, respectively. **BPR-MF** [5] uses matrix factorization for recommendation. **FPMC** [7] is a hybrid model for next-basket recommendation. To adapt it to SBRS, we ignore user latent representations when computing recommendation scores. **Item-KNN** [4] recommends items similar to the existing items in the session, where similarity is based on the co-occurrence number of two items. **GRU4Rec** [8] uses RNN with GRUs and session-parallel mini-batch training process. **NARM** [9] further improves GRU4Rec with a neural attention mechanism to capture users' main intent and sequential behaviors. **STAMP** [11] uses the attention mechanism to capture general preference and the recent focus. **CSRM** [10] applies key-value memory networks to consider information from the current session and neighbor sessions. **SR-GNN** [12] encodes the session graph with GGNN and uses an attention layer to represent preferences. **GC-SAN** [13] applies self-attention layers after GGNN to capture long-range dependencies.

5.4 Implementation Details

Following [12], we set the number of layers for GGNN to 1, the dimension of latent vectors to 100. Besides, we select other hyper-parameters on a validation

[4] https://www.dtic.upf.edu/ocelma/MusicRecommendationDataset/lastfm-1K.html.

set. All parameters are initialized using a Gaussian distribution with a mean of 0 and a standard deviation of 0.1. The model is trained with the mini-batch Adam optimizer. We set the batch size to 100, the dropout to 0.5, and the L_2 penalty to 10^{-6}. The hyper-parameter k is set with range [1, 5] and the best settings are 3, 2, and 4 for Yoochoose, Diginetica, and LastFM, respectively.

6 Experimental Results and Analysis

6.1 Results and Analysis

The general results are presented in Table 2. We **bold** the best performance and underline the state-of-the-art result of baselines. The scores on Diginetica dataset differ from results reported in [9,11] because they did not sort the session items according to "timeframe" field, which ignores the sequential information.

Table 2. Experimental results (%) on three datasets.

Methods	Yoochoose		Diginetica		LastFM	
	P@20	MRR@20	P@20	MRR@20	P@20	MRR@20
POP	6.71	1.65	0.89	0.20	4.43	1.15
S-POP	30.44	18.35	21.06	13.68	22.38	8.73
BPR-MF [5]	31.31	12.08	5.24	1.98	13.38	5.73
FPMC [7]	45.62	15.01	26.53	6.95	24.08	8.23
Item-KNN [4]	51.60	21.81	35.75	11.57	11.59	4.19
GRU4Rec [8]	60.64	22.89	29.45	8.33	21.42	8.21
NARM [9]	68.32	28.63	49.70	16.17	25.64	9.18
STAMP [11]	68.74	29.67	45.64	14.32	-	-
CSRM [10]	69.85	29.71	51.69	16.92	<u>27.55</u>	9.71
SR-GNN [12]	70.57	<u>30.94</u>	50.73	17.59	26.20	10.43
GC-SAN [13]	<u>70.66</u>	30.04	<u>51.70</u>	<u>17.61</u>	26.61	<u>10.62</u>
PEN4Rec	**71.53**	**31.71**	**52.50**	**18.56**	**28.82**	**11.33**
Improve	**1.2%**	**2.5%**	**1.5%**	**5.4%**	**4.6%**	**6.7%**

From the table, we have the following observations:

1) **PEN4Rec** obtains the best performance on three datasets, which demonstrates the effectiveness of the proposed model. This mainly contributes to the embedding of the session graph and the two-stage modeling of preference evolving process.
2) All deep learning based methods in the second block that make full use of user-item interactions to represent user preferences, are superior to conventional methods in the first block that cannot effectively use the time order.

3) Graph-based models, **PEN4Rec**, **SR-GNN**, and **GC-SAN** consistently outperform most RNN-based models like **GRURec** and **NARM**, and the attention-based model **STAMP**. This proves the graph structure is more suitable for SBRS than the sequence structure, the RNN modeling, or a set structure, the attention modeling.
4) Although RNN-based **CSRM** obtains worse results than **SR-GNN** and **GC-SAN** on most datasets, **CSRM** outperforms them under the P@20 metric on LastFM dataset. This may be due to the supplement of collaborative neighborhood information.

6.2 Ablation Study

In this part, we first compare with the following variants to analyze the key components of **PEN4Rec**.

- **GNN-Last** and **AGNN-Last** remove the two-stage modeling and recommend based on the embedding of the last item. They use GGNN and attention-based GGNN to encode the session graph, respectively.
- **PEN4Rec-Non** removes the second-stage process and recommends based on the output of the first-stage process.

Besides, we compare with some two-stage variants to show the superiority of the proposed model.

- **PEN4Rec-ATT** replaces the second-stage process with the attention mechanism where the query is the output of the first-stage process.
- **PEN4Rec-GRU** replaces the second-stage process with GRU.
- **PEN4Rec-ATT-GRU** applies GRU with attentional input to reason preference instead of updated vectors in the second-stage process.

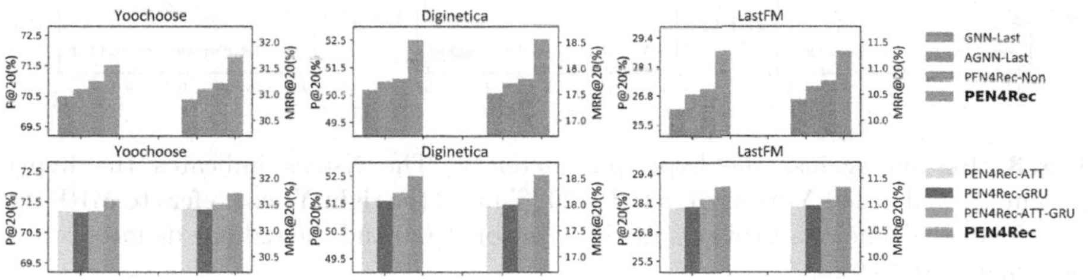

Fig. 2. Results (%) of ablation study on three datasets.

As shown in the top three subgraphs of Fig. 2, **PEN4Rec** obtains the best performance. **PEN4Rec-Non** is more powerful than **AGNN-Last** and **GNN-Last** which ignore the special modeling of user preferences. The results reveal the effectiveness of the first-stage process. However, **PEN4Rec-Non** removes the second-stage retrieval and cannot fully explore latent preferences behind explicit behaviors. Its inferior performance than the full model proves the effectiveness of the proposed second-stage process. Moreover, **AGNN-Last** outperforms **GNN-Last**, which proves the effectiveness of the introduction of multi-hop neighbors.

As shown in the down three subgraphs of Fig. 2, compared with all two-stage variants, **PEN4Rec** obtains better results. **PEN4Rec-GRU** deals with dependencies between adjacent behaviors successively and equally, which are not suitable for capturing diverse preferences since the preference has its own evolving track. The method would be disturbed by the preference drifting. While **PEN4Rec-ATT** ignores the sequential features in preferences and suffers from the understanding of evolving preferences. Although **PEN4Rec-ATT-GRU** activates relative preferences during preference evolution by the attention score, the variant ignores sequential patterns in different preferences and obtains sub-optimal performance. Because even zero input can also change the hidden state of GRU, so the less relative preferences also affect the learning of preference evolving. Different from these variants, we design the second-stage process to combine the local activation ability of the attention mechanism and sequential learning ability from GRU seamlessly. In this way, **PEN4Rec** effectively strengthens the effect of relative sequential behaviors and weakens the disturbance from preference drifting, which boosts modeling the preference evolution.

6.3 Parameter Analysis

We analyze the effect of the vital hyper-parameter k in PEN4Rec. It determines how many recent items are used to form the query that retrieves the relevant behaviors from historical contexts.

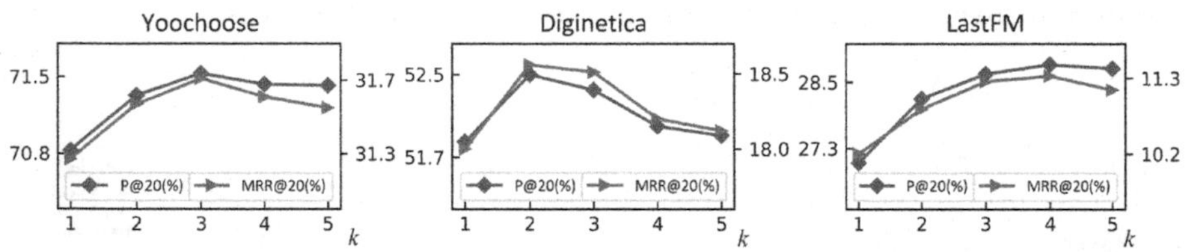

Fig. 3. Results against the hyper-parameter k. The X-axis indicates the hyper-parameter k. The left Y-axis refers to P@20 (%) and the right Y-axis refers to MRR@20 (%). The green line represents results in terms of P@20 and the red line denotes results in terms of MRR@20.

Figure 3 shows results against the hyper-parameter k on three datasets. We observe that the best settings are 3, 2, and 4 on Yoochoose, Diginetica, and PHEME, respectively. This demonstrates that adequate history information indeed contributes to retrieving rich contextual features and providing more clues to reason the preference evolving trajectory. Thereby, more expressive preferences can be captured for more precise recommendations.

7 Conclusion

In this paper, we propose a novel PEN4Rec to model preference evolving process by a well-designed two-stage retrieval from historical contexts for session-based recommendation. Specifically, the first-stage process integrates relevant behaviors according to recent items. Then, the second-stage process retrieves diverse preferences and models the preference evolving trajectory over time dynamically. The process effectively strengthens the effect of relevant sequential behaviors during the preference evolution and overcomes the disturbance from preference drifting. Experimental results on three benchmark datasets demonstrate the effectiveness and superiority of the proposed model.

References

1. Liu, Y., Ren, Z., Zhang, W., Che, W., Liu, T., Yin, D.: Keywords generation improves e-commerce session-based recommendation. In: WWW, pp. 1604–1614 (2020)
2. Zhang, L., Liu, P., Gulla, J.A.: Dynamic attention-integrated neural network for session-based news recommendation. Mach. Learn. **108**(10), 1851–1875 (2019). https://doi.org/10.1007/s10994-018-05777-9
3. Schafer, J.B., Konstan, J.A., Riedl, J.: Recommender systems in e-commerce. In: EC, pp. 158–166 (1999)
4. Sarwar, B.M., Karypis, G., Konstan, J.A., Riedl, J.: Item-based collaborative filtering recommendation algorithms. In: WWW, pp. 285–295 (2001)
5. Rendle, S., Freudenthaler, C., Gantner, Z., Schmidt-Thieme, L.: BPR: bayesian personalized ranking from implicit feedback. In: UAI, pp. 452–461 (2009)
6. Koren, Y., Bell, R.M.: Advances in collaborative filtering. In: Recommender Systems Handbook, pp. 145–186 (2011)
7. Rendle, S., Freudenthaler, C., Schmidt-Thieme, L.: Factorizing personalized Markov chains for next-basket recommendation. In: WWW, pp. 811–820 (2010)
8. Hidasi, B., Karatzoglou, A., Baltrunas, L., Tikk, D.: Session-based recommendations with recurrent neural networks. In: ICLR (Poster) (2016)
9. Li, J., Ren, P., Chen, Z., Ren, Z., Lian, T., Ma, J.: Neural attentive session-based recommendation. In: CIKM pp. 1419–1428. ACM (2017)
10. Wang, M., Ren, P., Mei, L., Chen, Z., Ma, J., de Rijke, M.: A collaborative session-based recommendation approach with parallel memory modules. In: SIGIR, pp. 345–354 (2019)
11. Liu, Q., Zeng, Y., Mokhosi, R., Zhang, H.: STAMP: short-term attention/memory priority model for session-based recommendation. In: KDD, pp. 1831–1839 (2018)
12. Wu, S., Tang, Y., Zhu, Y., Wang, L., Xie, X., Tan, T.: Session-based recommendation with graph neural networks. In: AAAI, pp. 346–353 (2019)
13. Xu, C., et al.: Graph contextualized self-attention network for session-based recommendation. In: IJCAI, pp. 3940–3946 (2019)
14. Jordan, M.I.: Serial order : a parallel distributed processing approach. Institute for Cognitive Science Report (1986)
15. Ren, P., Chen, Z., Li, J., Ren, Z., Ma, J., de Rijke, M.: Repeatnet: a repeat aware neural recommendation machine for session-based recommendation. In: AAAI, pp. 4806–4813. AAAI Press (2019)

16. Miller, A.H., Fisch, A., Dodge, J., Karimi, A., Bordes, A., Weston, J.: Key-value memory networks for directly reading documents. In: EMNLP, pp. 1400–1409 (2016)
17. Chen, T., Wong, R.C.: Handling information loss of graph neural networks for session-based recommendation. In: KDD, pp. 1172–1180 (2020)
18. Pan, Z., Cai, F., Chen, W., Chen, H., de Rijke, M.: Star graph neural networks for session-based recommendation. In: CIKM, pp. 1195–1204 (2020)
19. Qiu, R., Li, J., Huang, Z., Yin, H.: Rethinking the item order in session-based recommendation with graph neural networks. In: CIKM, pp. 579–588 (2019)
20. Li, Y., Tarlow, D., Brockschmidt, M., Zemel, R.S.: Gated graph sequence neural networks. In: ICLR (Poster) (2016)
21. Scarselli, F., Gori, M., Tsoi, A.C., Hagenbuchner, M., Monfardini, G.: The graph neural network model. IEEE Trans. Neural Networks **20**(1), 61–80 (2009)
22. Velickovic, P., Cucurull, G., Casanova, A., Romero, A., Liò, P., Bengio, Y.: Graph attention networks. In: ICLR (Poster). OpenReview.net (2018)
23. Xiong, C., Merity, S., Socher, R.: Dynamic memory networks for visual and textual question answering. ICML **48**, 2397–2406 (2016)
24. Bertin-Mahieux, T., Ellis, D.P., Whitman, B., Lamere, P.: The million song dataset. In: ISMIR (2011)

HyperspherE: An Embedding Method for Knowledge Graph Completion Based on Hypersphere

Yao Dong[1], Xiaobo Guo[1,2](✉), Ji Xiang[1], Kai Liu[1], and Zhihao Tang[1]

[1] Institute of Information Engineering, Chinese Academy of Sciences, Beijing, China
{dongyao,guoxiaobo,xiangji,liukai,tangzhihao}@iie.ac.cn

[2] School of Cyber Security, University of Chinese Academy of Sciences, Beijing, China

Abstract. Knowledge graph completion (KGC) aims to predict missing facts by mining information already present in a knowledge graph (KG). A general solution for KGC task is embedding facts in KG into a low-dimensional vector space. Recently, several embedding models focus on modeling *isA* relations (i.e., ***instanceOf*** and ***subclassOf***), and produce some state-of-the-art performance. However, most of them encode instances as vectors for simplification, which neglects the uncertainty of instances. In this paper, we present a new knowledge graph completion model called HyperspherE to alleviate this problem. Specifically, HyperspherE encodes both instances and concepts as hyperspheres. Relations between instances are encoded as vectors in the same vector space. Afterwards, HyperspherE formulates *isA* relations by the relative positions between hyperspheres. Experimental results on dataset YAGO39K empirically show that HyperspherE outperforms some existing state-of-the-art baselines, and demonstrate the effectiveness of the penalty term in score function.

Keywords: Knowledge graph embedding · Hypersphere · Link prediction · Instance · Concept · IsA relations

1 Introduction

Knowledge graph (KG) consists of structured facts in the real world. Some large-scale KGs such as WordNet [10], YAGO [16], Freebase [2] and Nell [11] are built in recent years. These KGs find application in a variety of fields including machine translation [25], conversation generation [26], relation extraction [19] and recommender systems [24]. Each KG may include millions of triples. Given that most existing KGs are incomplete, a fundamental problem is to predict missing links. Therefore, knowledge graph completion (KGC), which is also known as link prediction, receives enormous research attention. Link prediction task exploits the existing facts in KG to predict missing ones. A general method for link prediction is knowledge graph embedding (KGE), which encodes each element (entities

H. Qiu et al. (Eds.): KSEM 2021, LNAI 12815, pp. 517–528, 2021.
https://doi.org/10.1007/978-3-030-82136-4_42

and relations) in KG into a continuous low-dimensional real-value vector space, and completes KG by evaluating the scores of facts.

State-of-the-art KGE models can be broadly categorised as translational models [3,8,21], bilinear models [7,18,23] and deep learning models [4,13,20]. TransE [3] is the most famous translational models. Many translational models can be regarded as the extensions of TransE. The key of a translational model is regarding relations between entities as translations, which is a simple, effective and intuitive design. On the other hand, bilinear models represented by DistMult [23] and ComplEx [18] achieve better performance on metric Hits@1 by matching latent semantics of entities and relations. Recently, deep learning models for KGC have received increasing research attention. Many kinds of neural networks are applied to link prediction and achieve significant performance.

Most existing methods achieve significant performance, however, the previous methods always encode entities as vectors in embedding space and consider both instances and concepts as entities, which ignores the uncertainty of entities and lack transitivity of *isA* relations. To address the second issue, TransC [9] is proposed, which differentiates concepts and instances by encoding concepts and instances as hyperspheres and vectors, respectively. Even if TransC encodes concepts as hyperspheres, instances and relations are still encoded as vectors. Besides, one of the score functions in TransC is entirely based on TransE, which may limit the representation ability. Considering that each instance may have many meanings (i.e., polysemy) and contain rich information in the real world, it is insufficient to model instances as vectors.

To address the above issue, we propose a new translational model **HyperspherE** that encodes both instances and concepts as hyperspheres. Relations in HyperspherE are encoded as vectors. The difference between the radii of instances is used as a penalty term to obtain more interactions, and alleviate the defects casued by using a score function similar to TransE. Moreover, HyperspherE utilizes relative positions between instances and concepts to model *isA* relations. For ***instanceOf*** relation and ***subclassOf*** relation, we enumerate four relative positions betweeen hyperspheres and define the corresponding score functions for three non-target cases: **disjoint**, **intersect** and **inverse**. In summary, our contributions are listed as follows:

- We propose HyperspherE, to the best of our knowledge, the first method using hyperspheres to encode both instances and concepts.
- Different from the existing approaches, HyperspherE can capture more information and obtain more interactions when distinguishing concepts and instances.
- Experiments on the benchmark dataset YAGO39K empirically show that HyperspherE achieves the state-of-the-art performance on most metrics.

2 Background and Notations

A knowledge graph is denoted by $\mathcal{G} = \{\mathcal{I}, \mathcal{C}, \mathcal{R}, \mathcal{S}\}$, where $\mathcal{I}$ and $\mathcal{C}$ are the sets of instances and concepts, respectively. Relation set $\mathcal{R} = \{r_i, r_c\} \cup \mathcal{R}_r$, where r_i

and r_c represent ***instanceOf*** relation and ***subclassOf*** relation, respectively, and $\mathcal{R}_r$ denotes the set of other relations. Following [9] , the triple set $\mathcal{S}$ can be divided into three disjoint subsets according to relation type:

- Relational triple set $\mathcal{S}_r = \{(h, r, t)_n\}_{n=1}^{n_r}$, where $h, t \in \mathcal{I}$ are instances, $r \in \mathcal{R}_r$ is a relation between instances and n_r is the size of $\mathcal{S}_r$.
- ***InstanceOf*** triple set $\mathcal{S}_i = \{(i, r_i, c)_n\}_{n=1}^{n_i}$, where $i \in \mathcal{I}$ is an instance, $c \in \mathcal{C}$ is a concept and n_i is the size of $\mathcal{S}_i$.
- ***SubclassOf*** triple set $\mathcal{S}_c = \{(c_1, r_c, c_2)_n\}_{n=1}^{n_c}$, where $c_1, c_2 \in \mathcal{C}$ are concepts, c_1 is a subclass of c_2 and n_c is the size of $\mathcal{S}_c$.

Given a knowledge graph $\mathcal{G}$, HyperspherE aims at predicting the missing links in $\mathcal{G}$ by learning embeddings for instances, concepts and relations in the same vector space $\mathbb{R}^k$, where k denotes the dimension of vector space. For relation $r \in \mathcal{R}_r$, we learn a k-dimensional vector $\mathbf{r} \in \mathbb{R}^k$. For each instance $i \in \mathcal{I}$ and each concept $c \in \mathcal{C}$, we learn a hypersphere $s_i(\mathbf{O}_i, p_i)$ and $s_c(\mathbf{O}_c, p_c)$, respectively, where $\mathbf{O}_i, \mathbf{O}_c \in \mathbb{R}^k$ denote the centers of hyperspheres, $p_i, p_c \in \mathbb{R}$ denote the radii of hyperspheres.

3 Related Work

In this section, we give an overview of KGC models for link prediction, and divide existing methods into three categories.

Translational Models. TransE [3], the first translational model, encodes both entities and relations as vectors in embedding space based on the translational principle $\mathbf{h} + \mathbf{r} = \mathbf{t}$, where $\mathbf{h}$, $\mathbf{r}$, $\mathbf{t}$ represents head entity, relation and tail entity, respectively. TransE is a simple model and achieves promising performance on link prediction, but it still has a few drawbacks when modeling 1-N, N-1 and N-N relations. Thus, several extensions including TransH [21], TransR [8], and TransD [6], are proposed to break through the limitations of TransE. TransH alleviates N-N relations problem by modeling relations on the relational hyperplanes; TransR focuses on different aspects of entities in relations by using separate entity space and relation spaces; TransD takes types of entities and relations into account simultaneously when mapping into relational vector spaces. On the other hand, ManifoldE [22] also aims at alleviating the N-N problem in TransE by using manifold-wise modeling instead of point-wise modeling. Different from most existing translational models, TorusE [5] firstly embeds entities and relations based on the same principle in TransE on a Non-Euclidean space: torus. TransC [9] makes the first attempt to differentiate concepts and instances by using hyperspheres to encode concepts. No longer limited to principle in TransE, RotetE [17] models each relation as a rotation in the complex vector space, which can infer more relation patterns.

Table 1. Computational complexity of several embedding models.

Model	Space complexity	Time complexity
TransE	$\mathcal{O}(nd + md)$	$\mathcal{O}(d)$
TransH	$\mathcal{O}(nd + md)$	$\mathcal{O}(d)$
TransR	$\mathcal{O}(nd_e + md_e d_r)$	$\mathcal{O}(d_e d_r)$
TransD	$\mathcal{O}(nd_e + md_r)$	$\mathcal{O}(\max(d_e, d_r))$
HolE	$\mathcal{O}(nd + md)$	$\mathcal{O}(d \log d)$
DistMult	$\mathcal{O}(nd + md)$	$\mathcal{O}(d)$
ComplEx	$\mathcal{O}(nd + md)$	$\mathcal{O}(d)$
SimplE	$\mathcal{O}(nd + md)$	$\mathcal{O}(d)$
TorusE	$\mathcal{O}(nd + md)$	$\mathcal{O}(d)$
RotatE	$\mathcal{O}(nd + md)$	$\mathcal{O}(d)$
TransC	$\mathcal{O}(nd + md)$	$\mathcal{O}(d)$
HyperspherE	$\mathcal{O}(nd + md)$	$\mathcal{O}(d)$

Bilinear Models. RESCAL [15] is the first bilinear model that can perform collective learning via matching the latent semantics hidden between entities and relations. However, RESCAL has a large number of parameters than translational models. To reduce the space complexity, DistMult [23] simplifies RESCAL by restricting a diagonal matrix, which also limits the performance. Since DistMult can only model symmetric relations, ComplEx [18] extends DistMult to the complex domain. Moreover, HolE [14] combines the representation power of tensor product and the simplicity of TransE by using circular correlation to create compositional representations. Recently, many research works in this field focuses on different forms of decomposition. For example, SimplE [7] presents a simple enhancement of Canonical Polyadic (CP) decomposition to learn embeddings dependently, and TuckER [1] is based on Tucker decomposition.

Deep Learning Models. The expressiveness limit of shallow methods like TransE gives birth to applying the neural networks in KGC. ConvE [4] as the first convolutional neural network (CNN) for link prediction, captures the interactions between entities and relations by using a 2D convolution over the reshaped embeddings. ConvKB [13] can be regarded as an extension of ConvE, which models the relations among same dimensional entries of the embeddings to obtain more interactions. For the same motivation, InteractE [20] augments the expressive power of ConvE by using three key methods: feature permutation, feature reshaping and circular convolution. Unlike most models using one kind of neural network, KBGAT [12] uses an encoder-decoder architecture, which learns graph attention-based feature embeddings by a *generalized* graph attention network (GAT) and a convolutional neural network.

Our method HyperspherE belongs to the translational models. Table 1 summarizes the space complexity and time complexity of most state-of-the-art models described above as well as HyperspherE. From Table 1, we can find that the computational complexity of HyperspherE is similar to most translational models, which indicates the high efficiency of HyperspherE. Our model shares some similarities with TransC. Both HyperspherE and TransC encode concepts as hyperspheres. However, HyperspherE also encodes instances as hyperspheres in order to capture more information and obtain more interactions between instances and concepts. The main differences between HyperspherE and TransC are listed as follows:

- *Modeling.* HyperspherE encodes each instance as a hypersphere instead of a vector, which is used in TransC.
- *Scoring.* The score function of relational triples in TransC is entirely based on TransE, where HyperspherE uses a extra penalty term to strengthen representation power.

4 HyperspherE Model

In this section, we introduce a novel embedding method, called HyperspherE. First, we define three score functions according to the category of triples and the relative positions of hyperspheres. Afterwards, we present the training method, including loss functions and the negative sampling strategy.

4.1 Score Functions

Different score functions are defined for ***instancOf***, ***subclassOf*** and relational triples.

Relational Triples. Each relational triple denoted as (h, r, t) consists of one relation and two instances. HyperspherE learns a k-dimensional vector for each relation and a hypersphere $s(\mathbf{O}, p)$ for each instance. An example of relational triples is showed in Fig. 1. According to the translational characteristic, we define a score function as follows:

$$f_r(h,t) = \|\mathbf{O}_h + \mathbf{r} - \mathbf{O}_t\|^2. \tag{1}$$

Generally, if a triple (h, r, t) holds, entity h and entity t should have some properties in common. Thus, we narrow the difference between p_h and p_t by adding a penalty term in Eq. 1. The modified score function is as follows:

$$f_r(h,t) = \|\mathbf{O}_h + \mathbf{r} - \mathbf{O}_t\|^2 + m, \tag{2}$$

where $m = |p_h - p_t|^2$, is the penalty term, which penalizes the difference between p_h and p_t.

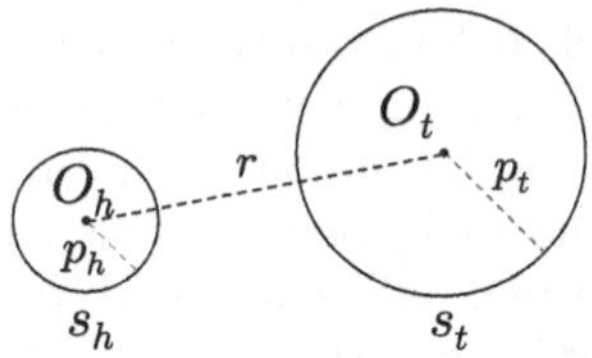

Fig. 1. A relational triple.

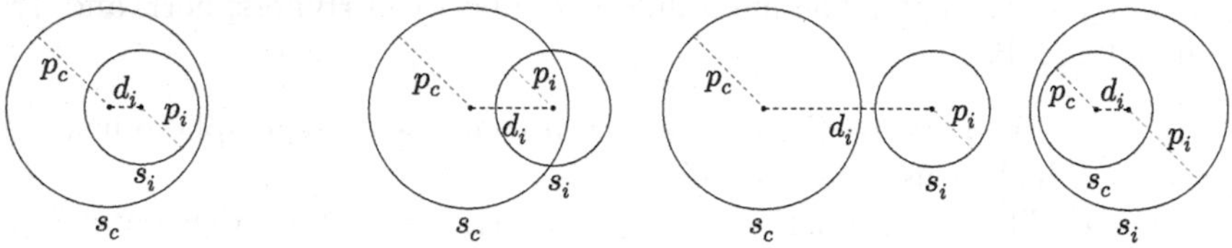

(a) $d_i \leq p_c - p_i$(**GOAL**) (b) $p_c - p_i < d_i < p_i + p_c$ (c) $d_i \geq p_i + p_c$ (d) $p_i > p_c$

Fig. 2. Objective and the three extra relative positions between hypersphere s_i and s_c. All subfigures are shown in 2D for convenience.

InstanceOf Triples. Given a ground truth of ***instancOf*** triple (i, r_i, c), the hypersphere s_i should be inside the hypersphere s_c (as shown in Fig. 2(a)). However, there are three extra relative positions between hypersphere s_i and s_c: **disjoint**, **intersect**, and **inverse**.

We define the distance d_i between the centers of s_i and s_c as follows:

$$d_i = ||\mathbf{O}_i - \mathbf{O}_c||, \tag{3}$$

where $\mathbf{O}_i$ and $\mathbf{O}_c$ denote the center of hypersphere s_i and s_c, respectively.

Afterwards, we define a specific score function for each condition.

- **Intersect.** s_i intersects with s_c (as shown in Fig. 2(b)). In this case, s_i should move into s_c. Hence, the score function is defined as follows:

$$f_i(i, c) = d_i + p_i - p_c, \tag{4}$$

where p_i and p_c denote the radii of s_i and s_c, respectively.
- **Disjoint.** s_i is disjoint from s_c (as shown in Fig. 2(c)). In this condition, we need to make these two hyperspheres closer in optimization. Similarly, we define the score fuction as follows:

$$f_i(i, c) = d_i + p_i - p_c. \tag{5}$$

- **Inverse.** s_i is inside s_c (as shown in Fig. 2(d)). This condition is exactly the opposite of our optimization objective, so we define the following score function to reduce the difference between p_i and p_c:

$$f_i(i, c) = p_i - p_c. \tag{6}$$

We observe that: (1) **Intersect** and **disjoint** have the same score function. (2) The score function of **intersect** can also achieve the optimization goal of **inverse**. Thus, we use Eq. 1 as the overall score function for non-target relative positions of ***instancOf*** triples.

SubclassOf Triples. Given a ground truth of ***subclassOf*** triple (c_1, r_c, c_2), the hypersphere s_{c1} should be inside the hypersphere s_{c2}. Therefore, we define the distance d_c between the centers of s_{c_1} and s_{c_2}, and define the similar score functions like ***instanceOf*** triples as follows:

$$d_c = ||\mathbf{O}_{c_1} - \mathbf{O}_{c_2}||, \tag{7}$$

where $\mathbf{O}_{c_1}$ and $\mathbf{O}_{c_2}$ denote the center of hypersphere s_{c_1} and s_{c_2}, respectively.

- **Intersect.** s_{c_1} intersects with s_{c_2}.

$$f_c(c_1, c_2) = d_c + p_{c_1} - p_{c_2}, \tag{8}$$

  where p_{c_1} and p_{c_2} denote the radii of s_{c_1} and s_{c_2}, respectively.
- **Disjoint.** s_{c_1} is disjoint from s_{c_2}.

$$f_c(c_1, c_2) = d_c + p_{c_1} - p_{c_2}. \tag{9}$$

- **Inverse.** s_{c_1} is inside s_{c_2}.

$$f_c(c_1, c_2) = p_{c_1} - p_{c_2}. \tag{10}$$

We use Eq. 8 as the overall score function for non-target relative positions of ***SubclassOf*** triples.

In experiments, we enforce constraints on embeddings, i.e., $||\mathbf{r}||_2 \leq 1$, $||\mathbf{O}||_2 \leq 1$, $p \leq 1$.

4.2 Training Method

We use a margin-based ranking loss function for optimizing relational triples as follows:

$$\mathcal{L}_r = \sum_{\xi \in \mathcal{S}_r} \sum_{\xi' \in \mathcal{S}'_r} [\gamma_r + f_r(\xi) - f_r(\xi')]_+, \tag{11}$$

where $[x]_+ \triangleq \max(0, x)$, ξ and ξ' denote a positive triple and a negative triple, respectively, $\mathcal{S}_r$ is the set of positive triples, $\mathcal{S}'_r$ is the set of negative triples and γ_r is the margin between positive triples and negative triples. Similarly, we define the loss function for ***instanceOf*** triples and ***subclassOf*** triples as follows:

$$\mathcal{L}_i = \sum_{\xi \in \mathcal{S}_i} \sum_{\xi' \in \mathcal{S}'_i} [\gamma_i + f_i(\xi) - f_i(\xi')]_+, \tag{12}$$

$$\mathcal{L}_c = \sum_{\xi \in \mathcal{S}_c} \sum_{\xi' \in \mathcal{S}'_c} [\gamma_c + f_c(\xi) - f_c(\xi')]_+. \tag{13}$$

We adopt stochastic gradient descent (SGD) to minimize these loss functions and learn the embeddings of triples iteratively.

The margin-based ranking loss function requires negative triples for optimizing, however, most existing large scale knowledge graphs only contain positive triples. Therefore, we sample negative triples by corrupting the positive ones. For each relational triple (h, r, t), following [9], we randomly replace h or t to generate a negative triple (h', r, t) or (h, r, t'). For instance, we obtain t' by randomly sampling from a *brother* set $\mathcal{M}_t = \mathcal{M}_1 \cup \mathcal{M}_2 \cup \ldots \cup \mathcal{M}_j$, where j is the number of concepts that t belongs to and $\mathcal{M}_j = \{a | a \in \mathcal{I} \wedge (a, r_i, c_j) \in \mathcal{S}_i \wedge (t, r_i, c_j) \in \mathcal{S}_i \wedge t \neq a\}$. For the other two kinds of triples, we follow the same policy to construct negative triples.

5 Experiments

We evaluate our approach and baseline models on link prediction task using a benchmark dataset YAGO39K.

5.1 Dataset

Most existing research work conducts experiments on FB15K and WN18, or the corresponding subsets FB15K-237 and WN18RR. However, FB15K mainly contains instances and WN18 mainly contains concepts. Such serious imbalance between instances and concepts makes all the four benchmark datasets inapplicable to demonstrate the importance of distinguishing concepts and instances. Hence, we run experiments on YAGO39K, which introduced by [9] and extracted from YAGO [16]. Note that YAGO contains a large number of instances from Wikipedia and concepts from WordNet. To the best of our knowledge, YAGO39K is the only current public dataset which the quantity of concepts and instances are at the same level. It contains 39374 instances, 46110 concepts and 39 relations. The splits of train/test/valid sets are listed in Table 2.

Table 2. Details of the dataset.

	#InstanceOf			#SubclassOf			#Relational		
DataSet	Train	Test	Valid	Train	Test	Valid	Train	Test	Valid
YAGO39K	442,836	5,000	5,000	30,181	1,000	1,000	354,997	9,364	9,341

5.2 Link Prediction

Link prediction task aims at predicting the missing instances or concepts in facts. For each relational triple (h, r, t) in test set, we either replace head instance h or tail instance t by all instances in KG, and then we calculate a dissimilarity score f_r. Afterwards, the scores are ranked in ascending order.

Evaluation Protocol. Similar to most recent works, we choose Mean Reciprocal Rank (MRR) and Hits@N as evaluation metrics. MRR is the mean reciprocal rank of correct triples, and Hits@N is the proportion of correct triples whose rank is not larger than N. Higher MRR or higher Hits@N indicates better performance. Following Bordes et al. [3], we report the *filtered* results on all metrics. In fact, we also report results on MRR with *raw* setting. Compared to the *raw* setting, *filtered* results remove all other candidates appeared in KG at ranking.

Baselines. We compare HyperspherE with several state-of-the-art baselines. Specificly, we report the first four *Translational models*: TransE [3], TransH [21], TransR [8], TransD [6] and three recent extentions, TorusE [5], TransC [9], and RotatE [17]; For *Bilinear models*, we report DistMult [23], ComplEx [18] and HolE [14] and two recent methods, SimplE [7] and TuckER [1]; For *Deep learning models*, we report KBGAT [12], which uses graph attention network (GAT) and convolutional neural network (CNN) as encoder and decoder, respectively.

Implementation. We implement HyperspherE in C++ and use CPU for both training and testing. The hyperparameters of HyperspherE are determined by grid search. We select learning rate λ for SGD among $\{0.1, 0.01, 0.001\}$, the dimensionality of embedding space k among $\{20, 50, 100\}$, the three margins γ_r, γ_i and γ_c among $\{0.1, 0.3, 0.5, 1, 2\}$. The best configurations are determined according to the *filtered* MRR on valid set. The optimal configurations are: $\gamma_r = 1$, $\gamma_i = 0.1$, $\gamma_c = 1$, $\lambda = 0.001$, $k = 100$ and taking L_1 as distance measure in score functions. For fairness: (1) We train each model for 1000 epoches. In KBGAT, we train graph attention network (GAT) layer and convolutional layer for 1000 epoches and 100 epoches, respectively. (2) Given that TorusE uses a non-Euclidean embedding space, which is totolly different from the Euclidean space, we set $k = 10000$ following the default setting in [5], so that TorusE can achieve competitive performance compared to other baseline models.

Results. Link prediction results of relational triples are shown in Table 3. Note that we report two versions of HyperspherE: with/without the penalty term when scoring the relational triples, and we use publicly available source codes to reimplement other baseline models, i.e., SimplE, TorusE, TuckER, KBGAT, and RotatE. Other results are taken from [9]. From Table 3, we conclude that: (1) HyperspherE performs extremely competitively compared to the existing state-of-the-art models across most metrics. Specificly, HyperspherE outperforms all baseline models on MRR and Hits@N with the *filter* setting apart from Hits@1, where HyperspherE obtains second best overall result. The reason is that we select the best configuration only according to the *filtered* MRR over valid set. Experimental results prove that HyperspherE is more prone to model *isA* relations than baseline models, and distinguishing instances and concepts plays a crucial part in learning embeddings for KGC. (2) HyperspherE performs a little bit worse than DistMult on MRR with the *raw* setting. In fact, most recent

Table 3. Link prediction results on YAGO39K. The best score is in **bold**, while the second best score is in underline. Results of Hits@N use the *filter* setting. [Hypersphere[1]]: without penalty term; [HyperspherE[2]]: with penalty term.

Model	MRR		Hits@N(%)		
	Raw	Filter	1	3	10
TransE [3]	0.114	0.248	12.3	28.7	51.1
TransH [21]	0.102	0.215	10.4	24.0	45.1
TransR [8]	0.112	0.289	15.8	33.8	56.7
TransD [6]	0.113	0.176	8.9	19.0	35.4
HolE [14]	0.063	0.198	11.0	23.0	38.4
DistMult [23]	**0.156**	0.362	22.1	43.6	66.0
ComplEx [18]	0.058	0.362	29.2	40.7	48.1
SimplE [7]	0.060	0.392	28.3	45.6	59.0
TorusE [5]	-	0.351	29.5	38.8	44.9
TuckER [1]	-	0.270	18.7	29.0	42.8
KBGAT [12]	-	0.469	35.1	53.9	69.2
RotatE [17]	-	0.504	**41.3**	56.0	66.8
TransC [9]	0.112	0.420	29.8	50.2	69.8
HyperspherE[1] (ours)	0.100	0.510	38.8	59.5	73.0
HyperspherE[2] (ours)	0.101	**0.518**	39.8	**60.2**	**73.2**

work only reports experimental results with the *filter* setting, which is more resonable and robust than *raw*. Besides, reporting *filtered* results can avoid possibly flawed evaluation. Note that HyperspherE significantly outperforms DistMult on MRR with the *filter* setting. (3) HyperspherE[2] outperforms HyperspherE[1] on all mertrics, which indicates that penalizing the difference of the radii between instances is a effective way to strengthen the representation power on link prediction.

Comparison with TransC. HyperspherE achieves significant performance improvement compared to TransC. Specificly, the improvement is 0.518–0.420 = 0.098 on *filtered* MRR and +10% on Hits@1 over TransC, which validates our motivation that taking the uncertainty of instances into consideration is essential.

Comparison with RotatE. Both RotatE and HyperspherE can be regarded as the extensions of TransE. Since relative positions between hyperspheres can naturally represent *isA* relations, HyperspherE outperforms RotatE on most metrics (except Hits@1), which indicates that HyperspherE infers composition pattern better than RotatE.

6 Conclusion

In this paper, we proposed a knowledge graph completion model HyperspherE, which encodes both instances and concepts as hyperspheres. With the help of the nested structure, which hyperspheres can naturally represent, HyperspherE is prone to model *isA* relations. The ability of distinguishing instances and concepts empowers HyperspherE to improve the relational triple prediction performance. Experimental results show that HyperspherE outperforms baseline models in most cases on YAGO39K, and prove that the design of penalty term is effective. In our future work, we plan to evaluate HyperspherE on more applicable datasets that have instances, concepts and *isA* relations, and we will also explore the novel use of hyperspheres for KGC.

Acknowledgments. This work is supported by the Youth Innovation Promotion Association, Chinese Academy of Sciences (No. 2017213).

References

1. Balazevic, I., Allen, C., Hospedales, T.: TuckER: tensor factorization for knowledge graph completion. In: EMNLP, pp. 5185–5194 (2019). https://doi.org/10.18653/v1/D19-1522, https://www.aclweb.org/anthology/D19-1522
2. Bollacker, K., Evans, C., Paritosh, P., Sturge, T., Taylor, J.: Freebase: a collaboratively created graph database for structuring human knowledge. In: SIGMOD, pp. 1247–1250 (2008)
3. Bordes, A., Usunier, N., Garcia-Duran, A., Weston, J., Yakhnenko, O.: Translating embeddings for modeling multi-relational data. NeurIPS **26**, 2787–2795 (2013)
4. Dettmers, T., Minervini, P., Stenetorp, P., Riedel, S.: Convolutional 2d knowledge graph embeddings. In: AAAI, vol. 32 (2018)
5. Ebisu, T., Ichise, R.: Toruse: knowledge graph embedding on a lie group. In: AAAI, vol. 32 (2018)
6. Ji, G., He, S., Xu, L., Liu, K., Zhao, J.: Knowledge graph embedding via dynamic mapping matrix. In: ACL, pp. 687–696 (2015)
7. Kazemi, S.M., Poole, D.: Simple embedding for link prediction in knowledge graphs. In: NeurIPS, pp. 4284–4295 (2018)
8. Lin, Y., Liu, Z., Sun, M., Liu, Y., Zhu, X.: Learning entity and relation embeddings for knowledge graph completion. In: AAAI, vol. 29 (2015)
9. Lv, X., Hou, L., Li, J., Liu, Z.: Differentiating concepts and instances for knowledge graph embedding. In: EMNLP, pp. 1971–1979 (2018)
10. Miller, G.A.: Wordnet: a lexical database for English. Commun. ACM **38**(11), 39–41 (1995)
11. Mitchell, T., Cohen, W., Hruschka, E., Talukdar, P., Yang, B., Betteridge, J., Carlson, A., Dalvi, B., Gardner, M., Kisiel, B., et al.: Never-ending learning. Commun. ACM **61**(5), 103–115 (2018)
12. Nathani, D., Chauhan, J., Sharma, C., Kaul, M.: Learning attention-based embeddings for relation prediction in knowledge graphs. In: ACL, pp. 4710–4723 (2019)
13. Nguyen, T.D., Nguyen, D.Q., Phung, D., et al.: A novel embedding model for knowledge base completion based on convolutional neural network. In: NAACL, pp. 327–333 (2018)

14. Nickel, M., Rosasco, L., Poggio, T.: Holographic embeddings of knowledge graphs. In: AAAI, vol. 30 (2016)
15. Nickel, M., Tresp, V., Kriegel, H.P.: A three-way model for collective learning on multi-relational data. ICML **11**, 809–816 (2011)
16. Suchanek, F.M., Kasneci, G., Weikum, G.: Yago: a core of semantic knowledge. In: WWW, pp. 697–706 (2007)
17. Sun, Z., Deng, Z.H., Nie, J.Y., Tang, J.: Rotate: knowledge graph embedding by relational rotation in complex space. In: International Conference on Learning Representations (2018)
18. Trouillon, T., Welbl, J., Riedel, S., Gaussier, É., Bouchard, G.: Complex embeddings for simple link prediction. In: ICML (2016)
19. Vashishth, S., Joshi, R., Prayaga, S.S., Bhattacharyya, C., Talukdar, P.: Reside: Improving distantly-supervised neural relation extraction using side information. In: EMNLP, pp. 1257–1266 (2018)
20. Vashishth, S., Sanyal, S., Nitin, V., Agrawal, N., Talukdar, P.P.: Interacte: improving convolution-based knowledge graph embeddings by increasing feature interactions. In: AAAI, pp. 3009–3016 (2020)
21. Wang, Z., Zhang, J., Feng, J., Chen, Z.: Knowledge graph embedding by translating on hyperplanes. In: AAAI. vol. 28 (2014)
22. Xiao, H., Huang, M., Zhu, X.: From one point to a manifold: knowledge graph embedding for precise link prediction. In: IJCAI, pp. 1315–1321 (2016)
23. Yang, B., Yih, W.t., He, X., Gao, J., Deng, L.: Embedding entities and relations for learning and inference in knowledge bases. arXiv preprint arXiv:1412.6575 (2014)
24. Zhang, F., Yuan, N.J., Lian, D., Xie, X., Ma, W.Y.: Collaborative knowledge base embedding for recommender systems. In: SIGKDD, pp. 353–362 (2016)
25. Zhao, Y., Zhang, J., Zhou, Y., Zong, C.: Knowledge graphs enhanced neural machine translation. In: IJCAI, pp. 4039–4045 (2020)
26. Zhou, H., Young, T., Huang, M., Zhao, H., Xu, J., Zhu, X.: Commonsense knowledge aware conversation generation with graph attention. In: IJCAI, pp. 4623–4629 (2018)

TROBO: A Novel Deep Transfer Model for Enhancing Cross-Project Bug Localization

Ziye Zhu[1], Yu Wang[1], and Yun Li[1,2(✉)]

[1] Jiangsu Key Laboratory of Big Data Security and Intelligent Processing, Nanjing University of Posts and Telecommunications, Nanjing, People's Republic of China
{2016070251,2017070114,liyun}@njupt.edu.cn

[2] State Key Laboratory for Novel Software Technology, Nanjing University, Nanjing, People's Republic of China

Abstract. Bug localization, which aims to locate buggy files in the software project by leveraging bug reports, plays an important role in software quality control. Recently, many automatic bug localization methods based on historical bug-fix data (i.e., bug reports labeled with corresponding buggy code files) have been proposed. However, the lack of bug-fix data for software projects in the early stages of development limits the performance of most existing supervised learning methods. To address this issue, we propose a deep transfer bug localization model called TROBO, which can transfer shared knowledge from label-rich source project to the target project. Specifically, we accomplish the knowledge transfer on both the bug report and code file. For processing bug reports, which belong to informal text data, we design a soft attention-based module to alleviate the noise problem. For processing code files, we apply an adversarial strategy to learn the project-shared features, and additionally extract project-exclusive features for each project. Furthermore, a project-aware classifier is introduced in TROBO to avoid redundancy between shared and exclusive features. Extensive experiments on four large-scale real-world projects demonstrate that our model significantly outperforms the state-of-the-art techniques.

Keywords: Bug localization · Transfer learning · Adversarial training · Attention mechanism · Bug-fix data

1 Introduction

Locating bugs during software development is an extremely essential and time-consuming task in software quality control. Recently, the automatic bug localization task is treated as a structure learning problem to capture the correlation between bug reports and their corresponding buggy code files. Specifically, bug reports record various information of errors or unexpected results (i.e., bugs)

H. Qiu et al. (Eds.): KSEM 2021, LNAI 12815, pp. 529–541, 2021.
https://doi.org/10.1007/978-3-030-82136-4_43

reported by developers, testers, and end-users. Table 1 shows a bug report from SWT project recorded in the online Bugzilla system. In the last decade, various supervised learning approaches have been proposed for automatic bug localization [6,7,21], which have proven to be effective and efficient. However, these approaches cannot perform well when are applied to locate bugs in early development or immature projects. The main reason is that there is not sufficient bug-fix data (i.e., bug reports labeled with corresponding buggy code files) for training such supervised models.

Table 1. A sample of SWT bug report from Bugzilla.

Item	Content
Bug id	395411
Summary	CTabFolderRenderer created too many times
Description	The default CTabFolderRenderer can be created too many times when calling CTabFolder.setRenderer (null) - which is valid. We need to have some way to know that we are using the default renderer already and not recreate it every time setRenderer gets called.
Report time	11.29.2012 16:28:20

A promising solution is the cross-project bug localization, which introduces transfer learning to address the bug-fix data insufficient problem for immature projects. Several studies leverage the source-target architecture, a particular transfer learning model, to learn and transfer the shared knowledge from source project (i.e., a project with sufficient bug-fix data) to target project (i.e., a project that lacks sufficient bug-fix data). For example, Huo et al. [9] propose a deep transfer learning model named TRANP-CNN, which can jointly find common representations shared by source and target projects and then locate buggy files for target project. One issue with their model is that it ignores to filter the individual features of source project in the process of transferring knowledge contained in the code. Such individual features are useless or even harmful for building a robust model to locate bugs in the target project. Zhu et al. [22] further present an adversarial transfer learning model called CooBa to solve this issue. To be specific, they utilize the adversarial training strategy to eliminate the project-specific features from the shared representation in the code processing. In addition, they employ an individual feature extractor to learn such project-specific features from code files for each project. However, their model still suffers from the feature redundancy problem, since it is uncertain whether project-specific features include project-shared features. Both above models adopt full knowledge transfer encoder dealing with the bug report, since all bug reports are natural language and record bugs of code. However, the main content of the bug report belongs to the informal document (i.e., user-generated text). Both models neglect the effect of noise in the bug report processing.

Based on above observations, we present a novel deep transfer model named TroBo (Transfer Knowledge for both Bug reports and Code files) for enhancing cross-project bug localization. Specifically, TroBo learns the natural language knowledge by a full knowledge transfer encoder for all bug reports, and the soft attention is employed to automatically filter bug-irrelevant content in the bug report. In terms of code files, TroBo includes an exclusive feature extractor for each project to capture project-exclusive features. TroBo also leverages the adversarial training strategy, including a shared feature extractor and a project discriminator, to capture common features shared by the projects. More importantly, we construct a project-aware classifier after the code embedding layer, which aims to encourage the code embedding layer to capture the characteristic of each project. The enhanced code embedding layer will improve adversarial training performance and eliminate the feature redundancy problem. Extensive experiments on large-scale real-world projects reveal that our model significantly outperforms state-of-the-art on all evaluation measures. The main contributions of this paper are highlighted as follows,

- We present a deep bug localization model called TroBo, which satisfies the requirements of projects that lack historical bug-fix data for training.
- Our model utilizes a full transfer learning module to share knowledge for bug reports of the target project, while effectively alleviating the text noise problem.
- We construct a partial transfer learning module for learning code representation, where we also design the project-aware classifier to enhance adversarial training and avoid feature redundancy.

2 Problem Statement

Assume all code files in target project t as $C^t = \{c_1^t, c_2^t, \dots, c_{n^t}^t\}$, where n^t the number of code files; all fixed bug reports denoted as $B^t = \{b_1^t, b_2^t, \dots b_{m^t}^t\}$, where m^t the number of bug reports. Similarly, for source project s, we denote $C^s = \{c_1^s, c_2^s, \dots, c_{n^s}^s\}$ as the set of code files, and $B^s = \{b_1^s, b_2^s, \dots b_{m^s}^s\}$ as the set of bug reports, where n^s and m^s are the number of code files and bug reports, respectively. It should be mentioned that m^t is far less than m^s. Indicator matrices $W^\alpha \in \mathbb{R}^{m^\alpha \times n^\alpha}$ are used to indicate a code file is buggy or clean with respect to a bug report, where $\alpha \in \{s, t\}$. Conventionally, we denote 1 as the minority class (i.e., buggy) and 0 as the majority class (i.e., clean). For example, $W_{i,j}^s = 1$ indicates the code file c_j^s is a buggy code file to the bug report b_i^s in source project. We instantiate the cross-project bug localization problem as a structure learning task to model more universal correlations between bug reports and their corresponding buggy code files from multiple projects. During training, the model aims to learn prediction functions $f^\alpha : B^\alpha \times C^\alpha \rightarrow W^\alpha$ by input pairs (b^α, c^α) from both source and target projects with their labels, $\alpha \in \{s, t\}$. After the model is fully trained, the learned function f^t is used to predict the label (buggy or clean) of each pair (b_{new}^t, c^t) for unfixed bug report b_{new}^t during testing.

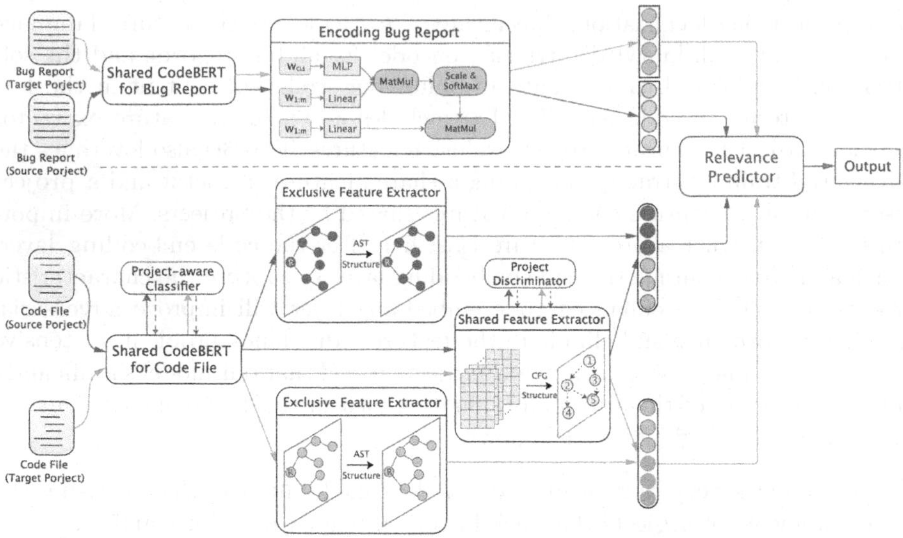

Fig. 1. Overall framework of our proposed TroBo, including bug report learning module and code file learning module, and relevance predictor.

3 The Proposed Model

In this section, we introduce the proposed model TroBo for cross-project bug localization in detail. Figure 1 depicts the overall architecture of our model, which includes three integral components: bug report learning module, code file learning module, and relevance predictor.

3.1 Learning from Bug Reports

Input Representation. We utilize CodeBERT [4], a bimodal pre-trained model based on BERT [2] suitable for both natural language and programming language, to map bug reports into corresponding embedding sequences. Specifically, we select the summary and description parts of the bug report and consider them as a sequence of words. A bug report is further represented as a word embedding sequence $\boldsymbol{w} = \{\boldsymbol{w}_1, \ldots, \boldsymbol{w}_m\}$, where m is the number of words.

Encoding Layer. In our task, bug reports from different projects are written in the same natural language (i.e., English). Considering the fixed bug reports of target project are limited, we need to apply the natural language knowledge learned from bug reports of source project to the target project. For this reason, our TroBo is designed to learn knowledge of all bug reports from both source and target projects by fully knowledge transfer.

As we mentioned before, bug reports are informal text data, normally containing some bug-irrelevant information (i.e., noise). In order to filter such noise, we employ soft attention [1] to automatically highlight the key information in bug reports. We encode a bug report as a weighted sum of all word embeddings $\{\boldsymbol{w}_1, \boldsymbol{w}_2, \ldots, \boldsymbol{w}_m\}$ by

$$\boldsymbol{v}^b = \sum_{i=1}^{m} \alpha_i \cdot \boldsymbol{w}_i^b, \tag{1}$$

where α_i is the weight of word w_i representing its importance in the input bug report. That is, words with key information have a higher weight, while words that are useless for the task have a lower weight. α_i is calculated by

$$\alpha_i = \frac{\exp(\mathrm{MLP}(\boldsymbol{w}_{[CLS]}) \cdot \boldsymbol{w}_i)}{\sum_{j=1}^{m} \exp(\mathrm{MLP}(\boldsymbol{w}_{[CLS]}) \cdot \boldsymbol{w}_j)}, \tag{2}$$

where [CLS] is a special token provided by CodeBERT, and its final hidden representation $\boldsymbol{w}_{[CLS]}$ is considered as the aggregated sequence representation for classification or ranking; MLP denotes a two-layer multilayer perceptron network. Here, we use the final hidden representation of [CLS] to represent the global information of a bug report. Note that the entire bug report learning module is shared across different projects.

3.2 Learning from Code Files

Inspired by recent work on shared–space component analysis [10], TroBo explicitly models both exclusive and shared features for each project. Specifically, we first propose a project-aware classifier after embedding layer, which can enhance the sensitivity of the embedding layer to input projects. And then we build an exclusive feature extractor for each project to capture project-exclusive features based on the Abstract Syntax Tree (AST). Simultaneously, we leverage the adversarial training strategy to extract project-shared features between source and target projects. The adversarial training strategy contains a Control Flow Graph (CFG)-based shared feature extractor and a project discriminator. In order to induce the model to produce such split features, we further add the orthogonality constraints that encourage the independence of these parts.

Input Representation. In terms of a code file, we treat it as a sequence of n code tokens, and take CodeBERT's pre-trained weights as the initialization for each token. It is worth noting that we set up two separate CodeBERTs for embedding bug reports and code files (see in Fig. 1). However, CodeBERT lacks project awareness and can not distinguish the characteristic of source project and target project. This may cause the collapse of adversarial training (especially for the project discriminator) and feature redundancy between exclusive and shared features. In response, we adapt this CodeBERT by an additional project-aware classifier to encourage the code embedding layer to capture the characteristic of each project. Specifically, we set a two-layer multilayer perceptron network as the project-aware classifier to predict project labels of the input token embedding sequence, that is, coming from the source or target project. For simplicity, the project-aware classifier can be expressed as follow,

$$\mathrm{CLF}(\boldsymbol{x}_{[CLS]}) = \mathrm{softmax}(\mathrm{MLP}(\boldsymbol{x}_{[CLS]})), \tag{3}$$

where $\boldsymbol{x}_{[CLS]}$ is the final hidden representation of the [CLS] token at the start of input code sequence. We optimize the project-aware classifier with softmax cross-entropy:

$$\mathcal{L}_{clf} = -\sum_{\alpha}\sum_{i=1}^{\mathrm{T}^{\alpha}}(y_i \log \mathrm{CLF}(\boldsymbol{x}^{\alpha}_{[CLS],i}) + (1-y_i)\log(1-\mathrm{CLF}(\boldsymbol{x}^{\alpha}_{[CLS],i})), \tag{4}$$

where $\alpha \in \{s, t\}$; y_i denotes the truly project label of the input $\boldsymbol{x}_{[CLS],i}$; T^{α} is the number of training instance of project α. In this manner, we convert a code file into a token embedding sequence $\boldsymbol{x} = \{\boldsymbol{x}_1, \boldsymbol{x}_2, \ldots, \boldsymbol{x}_n\}$ by the adapted CodeBERT, where n is the number of tokens in the code file. The token embeddings $\boldsymbol{x}$ include specific features for different projects, which enhance the downstream adversarial training and eliminate the feature redundancy problem in our task.

Exclusive Feature Extractor. For extracting exclusive features from a single project, we employ the multi-layer GCN [13] to process code files based on the AST. Specifically, the code graph $\mathcal{G}_{AST} = (\mathcal{V}_{AST}, \mathcal{E}_{AST})$ is constructed by the AST corresponding to the code file, where $\mathcal{V}_{AST}$ is the node set in the AST, each of which represents a code token; $\mathcal{E}_{AST}$ is the edge set containing the links between tokens in the AST. The corresponding node embedding matrix X is converted from token embedding sequence $\boldsymbol{x}$. Then, GCN operates directly on the AST code graph and induces the embedding vectors of nodes based on the properties of their neighborhoods, following the layer-wise propagation rule:

$$H^{l+1} = \sigma(\tilde{D}^{-\frac{1}{2}}\tilde{A}\tilde{D}^{-\frac{1}{2}}H^{l}W^{l}), \tag{5}$$

where $\tilde{A} = A + I$ is the adjacency matrix of the undirected graph $\mathcal{G}_{AST}$ with added self-connections, I is the identity matrix; $\tilde{D}_{ii} = \sum_j \tilde{A}_{ij}$; $\sigma(.)$ denotes an activation function; H^{l+1} and W^l are the node hidden representations and the trainable weight matrix in the l-th layer; $H^0 = X$. For a code file from project α, its corresponding exclusive feature extractor E^{α}_{ex} (with the same structure but no shared parameters) generates the exclusive features $\boldsymbol{g}^{\alpha}_{ex}$ as follows,

$$\boldsymbol{g}^{s}_{ex} = \mathrm{E}^{s}_{ex}(\mathcal{G}^{s}_{AST}, X^{s}); \boldsymbol{g}^{t}_{ex} = \mathrm{E}^{t}_{ex}(\mathcal{G}^{t}_{AST}, X^{t}). \tag{6}$$

Adversarial Training. Besides the exclusive features specific to each project, public features shared among different projects are effectively model more general correlations from multiple projects. In order to extract such project-invariant features, adversarial training is incorporated into our model. Generally, the adversarial training strategy [5] contains a generator and a discriminator. For our task, the target of the generator is to extract shared features, and the discriminator predicts which project the extracted features come from.

•**Shared Feature Extractor.** For generating shared representation among different projects, we adopt the combination of a CNN layer [11] and multi-layer GCN [13] to process code file based on the CFG. First, we use CNN to learning semantic information for each code statement, which is widely used for code processing and analysis tasks. We set convolution kernels with small sizes (e.g., 1, 3, 5) to extract the lexical and semantic features in code. Given a code file, CNN layer eventually provides a statement representation sequence $\boldsymbol{n} = \{\boldsymbol{n}_1, \boldsymbol{n}_2, \ldots, \boldsymbol{n}_u\}$, where u is the number of statements in the code file. Consequently, we construct the code graph $\mathcal{G}_{CFG} = (\mathcal{V}_{CFG}, \mathcal{E}_{CFG})$ based on the CFG corresponding to the code file, where $\mathcal{V}_{CFG}$ is the node set in the CFG, each of which represents a code statement; $\mathcal{E}_{CFG}$ is the edge set containing the links between statements in the CFG. The corresponding node embedding matrix N is converted from statement representation sequence $\boldsymbol{n}$. The operations on the CFG code graph are similar to the exclusive feature extractor. For simplicity, we use E_{sh} to denote the structure of CNN combined with GCN, and the shared features between different projects are extracted as follows:

$$\boldsymbol{g}_{sh}^{s} = \mathrm{E}_{sh}(\mathcal{G}_{CFG}^{s}, X^{s}); \boldsymbol{g}_{sh}^{t} = \mathrm{E}_{sh}(\mathcal{G}_{CFG}^{t}, X^{t}). \tag{7}$$

•**Project Discriminator.** The project discriminator is designed to predict project labels of the input, that is, coming from the source or target project, thereby encouraging the shared feature extractor to produce representations such that the project discriminator cannot reliably predict the project of the extracted features. The project discriminator can be expressed as follow,

$$\mathrm{D}(\boldsymbol{g}_{sh}^{\alpha}) = \mathrm{softmax}(\mathrm{MLP}(\boldsymbol{g}_{sh}^{\alpha})), \alpha \in \{s, t\}, \tag{8}$$

where MLP denotes a two-layer multilayer perceptron network. The adversarial training process is a min-max optimization and can be formalized as

$$\mathcal{L}_{adv} = \min_{\theta_{sh}}(\max_{\theta_d} \sum_{\alpha} \sum_{i=1}^{\mathrm{T}^{\alpha}} \log \mathrm{D}(\mathrm{E}_{sh}(N_i^{\alpha}))), \tag{9}$$

where T^{α} is the number of training instance of project α, θ_{sh} and θ_d denote the trainable parameters of shared feature extractor and project discriminator. By partitioning the features in such a manner, the discriminator trained on the shared representation can better generalize across projects, because its inputs are uncontaminated with the features unique to each project.

Feature Fusion. From exclusive and shared feature extractors, we obtain a exclusive and a shared representation for each code file. Due to the fact that part of the features among exclusive and shared representations might be overlapping, we adopt orthogonality constraints [3] for each project to address this issue before merging them:

$$\mathcal{L}_{diff} = \|(\boldsymbol{g}_{sh}^{s})^{T} \boldsymbol{g}_{ex}^{s}\|_F^2 + \|(\boldsymbol{g}_{sh}^{t})^{T} \boldsymbol{g}_{ex}^{t}\|_F^2, \alpha \in \{s, t\}, \tag{10}$$

where $\| \cdot \|_F^2$ is the squared Frobenius norm. Then, the representation of a code file is generated by a two-layer MLP network:

$$\boldsymbol{c}^{s} = \mathrm{MLP}^{s}(\boldsymbol{g}_{ex}^{s} \oplus \boldsymbol{g}_{sh}^{s}); \boldsymbol{c}^{t} = \mathrm{MLP}^{t}(\boldsymbol{g}_{ex}^{t} \oplus \boldsymbol{g}_{sh}^{t}), \tag{11}$$

where the $\oplus$ is the concatenate operation.

3.3 Relevance Predictor

The relevance predictor aims to learn the correlation patterns of bug reports and their related code files by the information obtained from bug report and code file encoder. Since the target project lacks sufficient labeled data for training, we construct the shared relevance predictor across the source and target projects. To predict the relevance of a bug report and a source file, we calculate the distance between their mappings in the embedding. The relevance metric is defined as

$$F(b^\alpha, c^\alpha) = \|\boldsymbol{b}^\alpha - \boldsymbol{c}^\alpha\|_2^2, \alpha \in \{s, t\}, \tag{12}$$

where $\|\cdot\|_2^2$ is the squared L2-norm. The task loss function for each project is

$$\mathcal{L}_{proj}^\alpha = \sum_{b^\alpha, c_-^\alpha, c_+^\alpha} \max(0, \tau + F(b^\alpha, c_+^\alpha) - F(b^\alpha, c_-^\alpha)), \alpha \in \{s, t\}, \tag{13}$$

where $F(\cdot,\cdot)$ is computed by Eq. 12; τ is a margin to force the related pairs should have lower distance than the unrelated ones.

3.4 Training

Giving the labeled bug-fix data of the source project s and the target project t, the final training objective is defined as follow,

$$\mathcal{L} = I(b,c)\mathcal{L}_{proj}^s + (1 - I(b,c))\mathcal{L}_{proj}^t + \lambda_1 \mathcal{L}_{adv} + \lambda_2 \mathcal{L}_{diff} + \lambda_3 \mathcal{L}_{clf}, \tag{14}$$

where λ_1, λ_2 and λ_3 are the hyper-parameters; $\mathcal{L}_{proj}^s$ and $\mathcal{L}_{proj}^t$ are computed via Eq. 13. $I(b,c) = 1$ denotes (b,c) comes from source project and vice versa. At each iteration in the training process, we alternately sample a batch of training instances from source project or target project to update the parameters. We adapt Adam [12] to directly minimize the final loss function $\mathcal{L}$ in our model.

4 Experimental Results and Analysis

4.1 Experimental Setup

Dataset. We conduct large-scale experiments on four open-source projects, including the AspectJ[1], JDT[2], SWT[3], and Eclipse Platform UI[4]. The dataset is extracted using the issue tracking system (Bugzilla) and version control system (GIT). Considering that bugs are related to different revisions, every bug report for each project has checked out a before-fix version of its source code package.

[1] https://www.eclipse.org/aspectj/.
[2] https://www.eclipse.org/jdt/.
[3] https://www.eclipse.org/swt/.
[4] https://www.eclipse.org/eclipse/platform-ui/.

Comparison Baselines. We compare our proposed model TroBo with the following baseline methods,

- BugLocator [21]: a well-known IR-based bug localization method, which considers similar bugs that have been fixed before.
- DNNLOC [14]: a model combining rVSM [21] with deep learning while considering the metadata of the bug-fixing history and API elements.
- NP-CNN [7]: a CNN-based method leveraging lexical and structure information from natural language and programming language.
- CG-CNN [8]: a CFG-based method that captures additional structural and functional information for representing the semantics of source code.
- TRANP-CNN [9]: a deep transfer model for cross-project bug localization by jointly extracting transferable features from the source and target projects.
- CooBa [22]: an adversarial transfer learning approach for cross-project bug localization, which focuses on public knowledge shared between projects.

Implementation Details. In our experiments, we use the same settings suggested in their original works, and all methods are evaluated in the cross-project context. We insert dropout layer [16] with rate 0.5 after the concatenation of outputs of the bug report and code file encoders. The initial learning rate is set to 0.008 and decreases as the training step increases. 32-sized batches are used for source project and 16-sized batches for target project. The model parameters λ_1, λ_2, and λ_3 are set as 0.5, 0.2, and 0.3, separately. We repeat the experiment 10 times in order to calculate an accurate average measurement. Followed the work of Huo et al. [9], we use only one source project and conduct one-to-one cross-project bug localization. For example, if AspectJ is selected as the target project, total three cross-project pairs are formed by treating the other three projects as the source project one by one. We consider that all bug reports of source project and 20% bug reports of target project are fixed and their corresponding bug-fix data is used as training data. The remaining 80% bug reports of the target project are unfixed and used for testing. To evaluate the performance of the TroBo, two metrics are used, Top-K Rank and Mean Average Precision (MAP), which are widely for evaluation in bug localization [9,21–23].

4.2 Effectiveness Results

The effectiveness of our proposed model is evaluated with all comparison baselines on four projects (12 cross-project tasks). The experimental results are presented in Fig. 2 and the best performance of each cross-project task is marked with "•". The horizontal coordinate points to different tasks. For example, "SWT → JDT" represents that SWT is the source project and JDT is the target project. The histograms in the first row and second row report the Top-10 Rank results and the MAP results, respectively. From Fig. 2, we can observe:

(1) Our proposed TroBo outperforms the state-of-the-art in all tasks on both metrics. Considering the Top-10 value, TroBo surpasses its

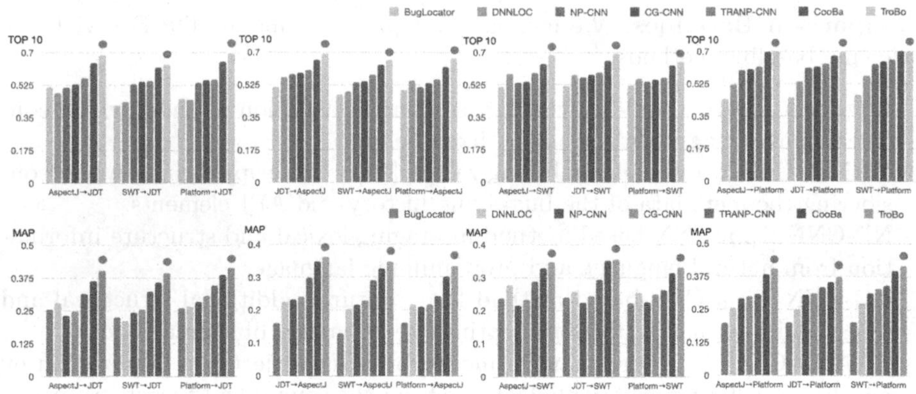

Fig. 2. Performance comparisons with bug localization models in terms of Top-10 Rank and MAP.

best competitor (i.e., CooBa) by 1.6-4.6% on JDT, 2.6-4.8% on AspectJ, 1.8-4.9% on SWT, and 3.0–4.6% on Platform, respectively. It also achieves a 7.4% average improvement over cross-project bug localization TRANP-CNN in terms of MAP on all tasks. Compared with the average results, TroBo achieves the average top-10 of 0.687 and MAP of 0.373. In summary, TroBo performs best considering cases comprising of all possible cross-project tasks and metrics. These results demonstrate that our proposed TroBo can effectively resolve the bug localization problem for projects without sufficient bug-fix data.

(2) The conventional bug localization models are not effective when directly used for label-poor projects. We can see that the performance of the best conventional bug localization model CG-CNN still lags behind all transfer learning models (i.e., TRANP-CNN, CooBa, TroBo) by an obvious gap on all tasks. Similar results can be finds all conventional models. For example, CooBa and TRANP-CNN improve NP-CNN by 11.7% and 7.6% w.r.t. MAP on project JDT. These results indicate that although conventional models used the bug-fix data of source project in training, they cannot make full use of the knowledge in the source project. In practice, it is indeed necessary to build a specialized bug localization technique for label-poor projects.

4.3 Ablation Study

In our model, we first employ an attention mechanism to automatically filter bug-irrelevant content in the bug report. Second, we introduce adversarial transfer learning to extract public features shared between source project and target project. Finally, a project-aware classifier and orthogonality constraints are leveraged to explicitly separate exclusive and shared features for each project. In order to further investigate whether the important components of TroBo are effective or not, we design multiple TroBo variants for evaluation, including (1) TroBo-attn: TroBo without attention mechanism, (2) TroBo-clf: TroBo without

Table 2. MAP of multiple TroBo variants on all tasks. In this table, A denotes Aspect, J denotes JDT, S denotes SWT, and P denotes Eclipse Platform UI.

Task	A→J	S→J	P→J	J→A	S→A	P→A	A→S	J→S	P→S	A→P	J→P	A→P
TroBo-attn	0.393	0.385	0.408	0.355	0.339	0.321	0.340	0.344	0.317	0.384	0.355	0.402
TroBo-clf	0.389	0.380	0.397	0.351	0.326	0.314	0.333	0.338	0.307	0.377	0.349	0.394
TroBo-clf-oc	0.368	0.352	0.375	0.334	0.305	0.294	0.328	0.311	0.283	0.347	0.320	0.366
TroBo-clf-oc-excl	0.342	0.332	0.358	0.317	0.299	0.275	0.302	0.303	0.279	0.328	0.304	0.342
TroBo-clf-oc-excl-pd	0.316	0.325	0.344	0.298	0.287	0.247	0.284	0.296	0.267	0.304	0.296	0.324
TroBo	**0.402**	**0.394**	**0.415**	**0.361**	**0.347**	**0.333**	**0.347**	**0.355**	**0.331**	**0.405**	**0.374**	**0.416**

project-aware classifier, (3) TroBo-clf-oc: TroBo without project-aware classifier and orthogonality constraints, (4) TroBo-clf-oc-excl: the exclusive feature extractor is further removed, that is, the model only extracts shared knowledge across projects, and (5) TroBo-clf-oc-excl-pd: only the shared feature extractor is retained to directly transfer knowledge without the project discriminator. The final experimental results in terms of MAP are presented in Table 2. One could observe that the entire TroBo model achieves better performance than other variants. Comparing the performance of TroBo and TroBo-attn, we observe that the attention mechanism is indeed effective in filtering bug-irrelevant noise in the bug report. Also, we observe that TroBo-clf-oc surpasses TroBo-clf-oc-excl on all tasks. It indicates that exclusive features of a specific project are useful for bug localization. In addition, the performances of TroBo, TroBo-clf, and TroBo-clf-oc indicate that both the project-aware classifier and orthogonality constraints have played an essential role in learning the exclusive and shared knowledge. Finally, compared with TroBo-clf-oc-excl-pd, TroBo-clf-oc-excl with adversarial training significantly improves the performance. The results demonstrate that a straight-forward application of transfer learning cannot guarantee the extraction of pure shared knowledge.

5 Related Work

Various structure learning methods have achieved decent performance on the bug localization task, including information retrieval-based and machine learning-based methods. Zhou et al. [21] proposed BugLocator based on the revised Vector Space Model (rVSM). With the advent of deep learning, many researchers presented deep bug localization techniques. Lam et al. [14] proposed a bug localization model combining rVSM [21] with Deep Neural Network (DNN). Most deep learning-based approaches [6,7,18,19] consider code files as flat sequences, and then use a neural network model to extract the feature from it to be correlated to the bug reports. Furthermore, KGBugLocator [20] apply constructed code knowledge graph based on AST to represent code files. CG-CNN [8] employ CFG to capture the additional structural and functional information for representing the semantics of source code. For finding bugs in cross-project settings, early studies predict the buggy files without considering bug reports [15].

For example, Turhan et al. [17] proposed a Nearest Neighbor (NN) Filter to select similar instances from source project to the target project, thereby building a new training set homogenous to the target project. Recently, Huo et al. [9] first proposed a cross-project bug localization method TRANP-CNN that uses bug reports to guide locating bugs in a full knowledge transfer manner. Zhu et al. [22] further presented an adversarial transfer learning method CooBa leveraging the adversarial training strategy to partially transfer code knowledge.

6 Conclusions

In this work, we proposed a novel deep transfer model TroBo for cross-project bug localization. Specifically, we designed a noise reduction and full knowledge transfer module for bug reports, and a code learning module retains the characteristic of each project while partially transferring knowledge from source project to target project. More importantly, we added a project-aware classifier after code embedding layer to enhance adversarial training and avoid feature redundancy. Extensive experiments show that our model has achieved significant improvements. For future work, we will apply TroBo to other software mining tasks and further explore cross-language bug localization.

Acknowledgements. This research was supported by State Key Lab. for Novel Software Technology (KFKT2020B21), and Postgraduate Research and Practice Innovation Program of Jiangsu Province (SJKY19_0763).

References

1. Bahdanau, D., Cho, K., Bengio, Y.: Neural machine translation by jointly learning to align and translate. arXiv preprint arXiv:1409.0473 (2014)
2. Devlin, J., Chang, M.W., Lee, K., Toutanova, K.: Bert: pre-training of deep bidirectional transformers for language understanding. In: NAACL HLT, pp. 4171–4186 (2019)
3. Edelman, A., Arias, T.A., Smith, S.T.: The geometry of algorithms with orthogonality constraints. SIAM J. Matrix Anal. Appl. **20**(2), 303–353 (1998)
4. Feng, Z., et al.: Codebert: a pre-trained model for programming and natural languages. arXiv preprint arXiv:2002.08155 (2020)
5. Ganin, Y., et al.: Domain-adversarial training of neural networks. J. Mach. Learn. Res. **17**(1), 2030–2096 (2016)
6. Huo, X., Li, M.: Enhancing the unified features to locate buggy files by exploiting the sequential nature of source code. In: Proceedings of the 26th International Joint Conference on Artificial Intelligence (IJCAI), pp. 1909–1915 (2017)
7. Huo, X., Li, M., Zhou, Z.H.: Learning unified features from natural and programming languages for locating buggy source code. In: Proceedings of the 25th International Joint Conference on Artificial Intelligence (IJCAI), pp. 1606–1612 (2016)
8. Huo, X., Li, M., Zhou, Z.H.: Control flow graph embedding based on multi-instance decomposition for bug localization. In: AAAI, pp. 4223–4230 (2020)
9. Huo, X., Thung, F., Li, M., Lo, D., Shi, S.T.: Deep transfer bug localization. IEEE Trans. Softw. Eng. (2019)

10. Jia, Y., Salzmann, M., Darrell, T., et al.: Factorized latent spaces with structured sparsity. NIPS **10**, 982–990 (2010)
11. Kim, Y.: Convolutional neural networks for sentence classification. In: Proceedings of Conference on Empirical Methods in Natural Language Processing (EMNLP), pp. 1746–1751 (2014)
12. Kingma, D.P., Ba, J.: Adam: a method for stochastic optimization. arXiv preprint arXiv:1412.6980 (2014)
13. Kipf, T.N., Welling, M.: Semi-supervised classification with graph convolutional networks. arXiv preprint arXiv:1609.02907 (2016)
14. Lam, A.N., Nguyen, A.T., Nguyen, H.A., Nguyen, T.N.: Bug localization with combination of deep learning and information retrieval. In: Proceedings of the 25th International Conference on Program Comprehension (ICPC), pp. 218–229 (2017)
15. Pan, S.J., Tsang, I.W., Kwok, J.T., Yang, Q.: Domain adaptation via transfer component analysis. IEEE Trans. Neural Networks **22**(2), 199–210 (2010)
16. Srivastava, N., Hinton, G., Krizhevsky, A., Sutskever, I., Salakhutdinov, R.: Dropout: a simple way to prevent neural networks from overfitting. J. Mach. Learn. Res. **15**(1), 1929–1958 (2014)
17. Turhan, B., Menzies, T., Bener, A.B., Di Stefano, J.: On the relative value of cross-company and within-company data for defect prediction. Empirical Softw. Eng. **14**(5), 540–578 (2009)
18. Xiao, Y., Keung, J., Mi, Q., Bennin, K.E.: Improving bug localization with an enhanced convolutional neural network. In: 2017 24th Asia-Pacific Software Engineering Conference (APSEC), pp. 338–347. IEEE (2017)
19. Xiao, Y., Keung, J., Mi, Q., Bennin, K.E.: Bug localization with semantic and structural features using convolutional neural network and cascade forest. In: Proceedings of the 22nd International Conference on Evaluation and Assessment in Software Engineering 2018, pp. 101–111 (2018)
20. Zhang, J., Xie, R., Ye, W., Zhang, Y., Zhang, S.: Exploiting code knowledge graph for bug localization via bi-directional attention. In: Proceedings of the 28th International Conference on Program Comprehension, pp. 219–229 (2020)
21. Zhou, J., Zhang, H., Lo, D.: Where should the bugs be fixed?-more accurate information retrieval-based bug localization based on bug reports. In: Proceedings of the 34th International Conference on Software Engineering (ICSE), pp. 14–24 (2012)
22. Zhu, Z., Li, Y., Tong, H., Wang, Y.: Cooba: Cross-project bug localization via adversarial transfer learning. In: Proceedings of the Twenty-Ninth International Joint Conference on Artificial Intelligence, IJCAI, pp. 3565–3571 (2020)
23. Zhu, Z., Li, Y., Wang, Yu., Wang, Y., Tong, H.: A deep multimodal model for bug localization. Data Mining Knowl. Discov., 1–24 (2021). https://doi.org/10.1007/s10618-021-00755-7

A Neural Language Understanding for Dialogue State Tracking

Yuhong He and Yan Tang(✉)

School of Computer and Information Science,
Southwest University, Chongqing, China
ytang@swu.edu.cn

Abstract. Dialogue State Tracking (DST) is an important part of the task-oriented dialogue system, which is used to predict the current state of the dialogue given all the preceding conversations. In the stage of encoding historical dialogue into context representation, recurrent neural networks (RNNs) have been proven to be highly effective and achieves significant improvements in many tasks. However, hard to model extremely long dependencies and gradient vanishing are two practical and yet concerned studied problems of recurrent neural networks. In this work, based on the recently proposed TRADE model, we have made corresponding improvements in the encoding part, explore a new context representation learning on sequence data, combined convolution and self-attention with recurrent neural networks, striving to extract both local and global features at the same time to learn a better representation on dialogue context. Empirical results demonstrate that our proposed model achieves 50.04% joint goal accuracy for the five domains of MultiWOZ2.0.

Keywords: Dialogue state tracking · Neural network · Convolution · Multi-head attention

1 Introduction

In dialog systems, "state tracking" – also called "belief tracking" – refers to accurately estimate the user's goal as dialog progress. Accurate state tracking is desirable because it determines the response method adopted by the system and thus affects the quality of dialogue. In this system, the dialogue state is usually expressed in the form of a triplet. For example, as shown in Fig. 1, domain-slot-value triplet such as restaurant-food-Italian and train-day-Sunday are extracted from the conversation.

The method of tracking dialogue status is generally based on two settings. One is to predefined ontology and given all possible slot value candidates in the domain ontology. In this case, the task can be regarded as a multi-classification task [22]. The method based on this setting can often achieve better performance at a single domain such as DSTC2 [7] and WOZ2.0 [18]. Another is based on

H. Qiu et al. (Eds.): KSEM 2021, LNAI 12815, pp. 542–552, 2021.
https://doi.org/10.1007/978-3-030-82136-4_44

Example Dialogue Segment	**domain - slot - value**
User: I am looking for an **Italian restaurant** that is **moderately priced.** Sys: Stazione restaurant and coffee bar are available.	restaurant-food-Italian restaurant-price range-moderate
....	
User: Also, I am looking for a train, the **train** should **go to Broxbourne** and should **leave on Sunday**. Sys: yes there are several trains available.	train-destination- Broxbourne train-day- Sunday

Fig. 1. An example of multi-domain dialogue state tracking in a conversation.

a multi-domain dialogue dataset (MultiWOZ) [1] which is more suitable for real scenarios due to its mixed-domain conversations. In order to predict slot-value pairs in open vocabularies, TRADE [20] leverages its context-enhanced slot gate and copy mechanism to properly track slot values mentioned anywhere in dialogue history.

As TRADE just passes historical dialogue through a layer of gated recurrent units (GRU) [2], it hard to model extremely long dependencies. Although GRU can achieve good results for processing variable-length sequences, they generate a sequence of hidden states $\mathrm{h_t}$, as a function of the previous hidden state h_{t-1} and the input for position t, cause catastrophic forgetting of previous knowledge.

To deal with this problem, we conjunct convolution for learning sequence representations from different scales with a recurrent network, striving to capture both short and long range language structures. Convolutional operation does not depend on the calculation of the previous time step and therefore allow parallelization over every element in the sequence. At the same time, we also try to add multi-headed self-attention to the model to obtain the dependency between words in the sentence. Encode the input dialogue history as an implicit vector. We equipped our model with gated linear units over the output of the GRU to eases gradient propagation.

In summary, the contributions of our work are as follows:

- We respectively conjunct convolution and multi-head attention to capture local features with a recurrent network.
- Use gated linear units (GLU) [3] to splice the output of Bi-GRU instead of direct concatenated, which can effectively eases gradient propagation and retain the non-linearity.
- We conduct experiments on the MultiWOZ 2.0 dataset. Our method achieves significant improvements over the baselines in all evaluation metrics.

2 Related Work

Predefined ontology-based DST assumes that all slot-value pairs are provided in an ontology. A neural belief tracker (NBT) [12] has been proposed which reason over pre-trained word vectors, learning to compose them into distributed representations of user utterances and dialogue context. GLAD [22] uses global modules to share parameters between estimators for different types (called slots) of dialogue states and uses local modules to learn slot-specific features. GCE [13] is based on GLAD using only one recurrent network with global conditioning. Lei [11] uses a Seq2Seq model to generate belief spans and the delexicalized response at the same time.

In generative dialogue state tracking, a simple attention-based neural network has been used to point to the slot values within the conversation [4]. SUMBT [10] learns the relations between domain-slot types and slot-value appearing in utterances through attention mechanisms based on contextual semantic vectors and predicts slot-value labels in a non-parametric way. Xu [21] proposes a model that learns to predict unknown values by using the index-based pointer network for different slots. Wu [20] applies an encoder-decoder architecture to generate dialogue states with the copy mechanism.

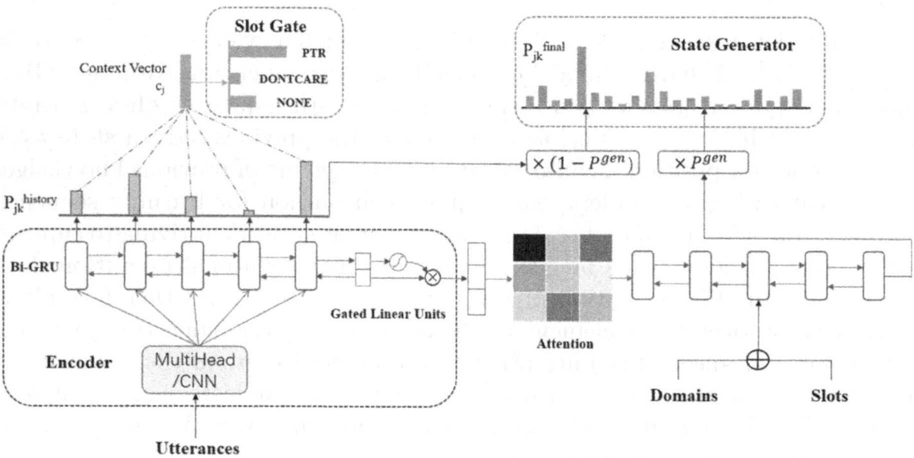

Fig. 2. A neural language understanding for dialogue state tracking

3 Our Method

In this section, we first introduce the TRADE model as background, then followed our development based on it [20] (Fig. 2). We added convolution to extract local information and multi-head attention to capture the relations between words respectively in the encoder, which can effectively make up for the shortcomings of the original model in these respects. Otherwise, gated linear units (GLU) [3] was applied to the output of the encoder to alleviate the gradient accumulation problem caused by the recurrent neural network.

3.1 Transferable Dialogue State Generator

TRADE is composed of an utterance encoder, a slot gate, and a state generator, which are shared across domains and generates dialogue states from utterances using a copy mechanism, facilitating knowledge transfer when predicting (domain, slot, value) triplets not encountered during training [9]. The encoder takes the concatenation of all words in the dialogue history as input and encodes into a sequence of fixed-length vectors which simply use bi-directional gated recurrent units (Bi-GRU) [2]. It may work fine for shorter sequences, but for longer sequences, it causes an insufficient representation of information and brings difficulty for the model to comprehend the dialogue context sequence intact. However, on the MultiWOZ 2.0 dataset, the maximum length of a dialogue context is up to 880 tokens. About 27% of instances on the test set have dialogue context sequences longer than 200 tokens, leading the joint accuracy of the model to be greatly reduced.

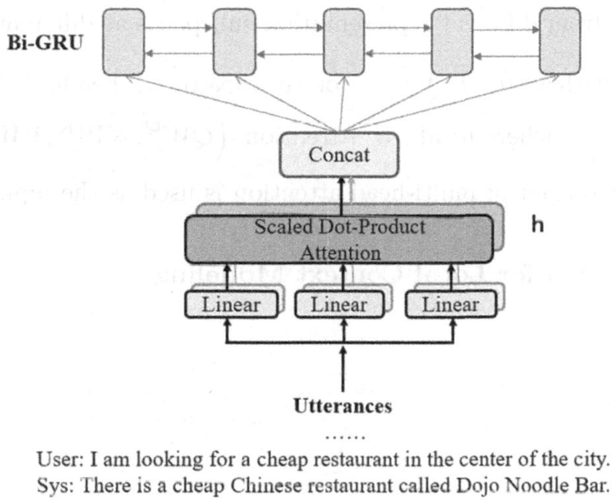

Fig. 3. Conjunct multi-head attention with Bi-GRU

3.2 Multi-head Attention for the Relation Between Words

To deal with this problem, after embedding the dialogue history, we first pass multi-headed attention instead of directly input the GRU. This mechanism was first proposed by Google *Attention Is All You Need*, which is used as a submodule of Transformer for machine translation [17]. The computational complexity of each attention layer is $O\left(n^2 \cdot d\right)$ which is faster than recurrent layer when the sequence length n is smaller than the representation dimensionality d, making it possible to better learning long-range dependencies. The coding structure of conjunct multi-head attention with Bi-GRU is shown in Fig. 3.

The input to the encoder is denoted as history $X = [U_0, R_0, \ldots, U_l, R_l] \in \mathbb{R}^{|l| \times d_{emb}}$, which is the concatenation of all words in the dialogue history, where l is the number of dialogue turns and $\mathrm{d_{emb}}$ indicates the embedding size.

It first projects X into three representations, key K, query Q, and value V. Then, it uses a self-attention mechanism to get the output representation where the self-attention operation is the dot-production between key, query, and value pairs:

$$\text{Attention}(Q, K, V) = \text{softmax}\left(\frac{QK^T}{\sqrt{d_{emb}}}\right)V \tag{1}$$

$$\text{where } Q, K, V = \text{Linear}_1(X), \text{Linear}_2(X), \text{Linear}_3(X) \tag{2}$$

We choose multi-head attention, one of the variants of attention, as our implementation. It linearly projects the queries, keys, and values h times with different instead of performing a single attention function and then concatenated the output of each head into the final result, allowing the model to jointly attend to information from different representation subspaces at different positions.

$$\begin{aligned} \text{MultiHead }(Q, K, V) &= \text{ Concat }(\text{head}_1, \ldots, \text{head}_\text{h})\, W^O \\ \text{where head }_\text{i} &= \text{ Attention }\left(QW_i^Q, KW_i^K, VW_i^V\right) \end{aligned} \tag{3}$$

At last, the output of multi-head attention is used as the input of Bi-GRU.

3.3 Convolution for Local Context Modeling

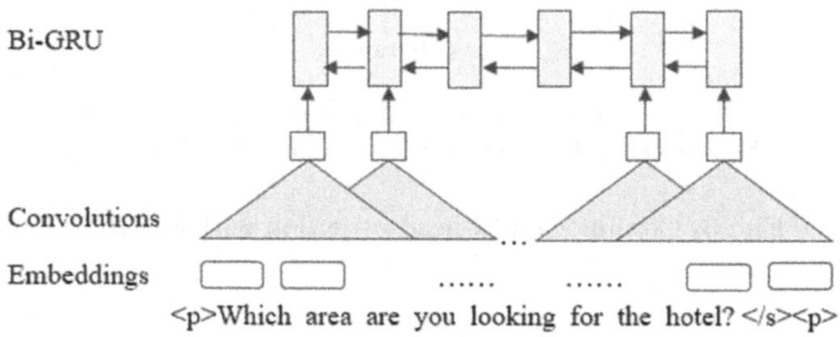

Fig. 4. Conjunct convolution with Bi-GRU

We further propose to incorporate convolution into the encoder to capture local context (Fig. 4). Each convolution sub-module contains a two-dimensional convolution with kernel size $W \in R^{k \times demb}$ followed by a non-linearity where k is kernel width. Each resulting state h_i^1 contains information over k input elements, e.g. we can obtain a feature representation capturing relationships within a window of n words by applying only $\mathcal{O}\left(\frac{n}{k}\right)$ convolutional operations for kernels of width k, compared to a linear number O(n) for recurrent neural networks. Specifically, we pad the input by $k-1$ elements on both the left and right side by zero vectors to ensure that the dimensions after the convolution operation will not change. For an input sequence X, the output O is computed as:

$$O_{i,c} = \sum_{j=1}^{k} W_{c,j} \cdot X_{i:i+k-1} \tag{4}$$

3.4 GLU for Gradient Dispersion

We choose gated linear units (GLU) [3] as non-linearity which implement a simple gating mechanism over the hidden representations $\overrightarrow{h}_t$ and $\overleftarrow{h}_t$ in two directions of the Bi-GRU:

$$\text{glu}\left[\overrightarrow{h_t}, \overleftarrow{h}_t\right] = \overrightarrow{h_t} \otimes \sigma\left(\overleftarrow{h}_t\right) \tag{5}$$

Where $\otimes$ is the point-wise multiplication and the output size is the same as the hidden size. The gates σ control which inputs of the current context are relevant. A similar non-linearity GTU (gated tanh units) has been introduced [14] but the study shows that GLU performs better in the context of language modeling [3].

4 Experiment

We evaluated our proposed methods on the public dataset.

Table 1. The dataset information of MultiWOZ2.0. In total, there are 30 (domain, slot) pairs from the selected five domains.

	Hotel	Train	Attraction	Restaurant	Taxi
Slots	price, type, parking, stay, day, people, area, stars, internet, name	destination, departure, day, arrive by, leave at, people	area, name, type	food, price, area, name, time, day, people	destination, departure, arrive by, leave by
Train	3381	3103	2717	3813	1654
Valid	416	484	401	438	207
Test	394	494	395	437	195

4.1 Dataset

Multi-domain Wizard-of-Oz2.0 (MultiWOZ2.0) [1] is a fully-labeled collection of human-human written conversations spanning over multiple domains and topics, containing 30 (domain, slot) pairs and over 4,500 possible values. Only five domains are used in our experiment because the hospital and police domains have very few dialogues and only appear in the training set. The slots in each domain and the corresponding data size are reported in Table 1.

4.2 Experimental Settings

Following Wu [20], the model is trained end-to-end using the Adam optimizer [8] with a batch size of 32, both hidden size and all word embedding dimensions are set to 400 with concatenating Glove embedding [15] and character embedding [6]. The learning rate annealing is in the range of [0.001, 0.0001] with a dropout ratio of 0.2. To enhance the generalization ability of the model, we add residual connections from the input and layer Normalized around each sub-model.

Table 2. Experimental results on the MultiWOZ 2.0 dataset.

Model	Joint accuracy	Slot accuracy
GLAD (Zhong et al., 2018)	35.57	95.44
GCE (Nouri et al., 2018)	36.27	98.42
Neural reading (Gao et al., 2019)	41.10	-
HyST (Goel et al., 2019)	44.24	-
SUMBT (Lee et al., 2019)	46.65	96.44
TRADE (Wu et al., 2019)	48.62	96.92
COMER (Ren et al., 2019)	48.79	-
-CNN	50.04	97.07
-Multi_Head	49.56	97.02

4.3 Results

Joint accuracy and slot accuracy are the two metrics used to evaluate the performance on multi-domain DST. The joint accuracy compares the dialogue state extracted by the model from the dialogue history with the label at each dialogue turn t while the slot accuracy compares each (domain, slot, value) to its ground truth.

We compared the following models that are also experimental on the MultiWOZ 2.0 dataset: GLAD [22], GCE [13], Neural Reading [4], HyST [5], SUMBT [10], TRADE [20], COMER [16], and we briefly describe these baselines models below.

- GLAD: The model uses self-attentive RNNs to learn a global tracker that shares parameters among slots and a local tracker that tracks each slot, computes semantic similarity with predefined ontology terms.
- GCE: This is the current state-of-the-art model on the single-domain WOZ dataset [19], which is a simplified and speed-up version of GLAD without slot-specific RNNs.
- Neural Reading: The model formulates dialog state tracking as a reading comprehension task, learns a question embedding for each slot, and predicts the span of each slot value.

- HyST: This is a hybrid approach for flexible and accurate dialogue state tracking which learns the appropriate method for each slot type.
- SUMBT: The model learns the relations between domain-slot-types and slot-values appearing in utterances through attention mechanisms based on contextual semantic vectors. Furthermore, the model predicts slot-value labels in a non-parametric way.
- TRADE: This is an encoder-decoder model, containing an utterance encoder, a slot gate, and a state generator, which are shared across domains. It encodes concatenated previous system and user utterances as dialogue context and generates slot value word by word for each slot exploring the copy mechanism.
- COMER: Given each turn of user utterance and system response, the model directly generates a sequence of belief states by applying a hierarchical encoder-decoder structure, leading computational complexity be a constant regardless of the number of predefined slots.

As shown in Table 2, our method significantly outperforms several previous models and achieves 50.04% of joint accuracy and 97.07% of slot accuracy with conjunct convolution on the MultiWOZ2.0. On the other hand, the model that combines multi-head attention can also achieve 49.56% of joint accuracy and 97.02% of slot accuracy.

We visualize the impact of convolution width and the number of multi-head attention heads on the joint accuracy in Fig. 5, when the convolution width is 3 and head number setting 4 can achieve the best result respectively. As the width of the convolution kernel increases, the accuracy will gradually decrease. This is because, in order to keep the output dimension unchanged after convolution, we use padding. The larger the width, the larger the padding will be, which will lead to the loss of text information to a certain extent.

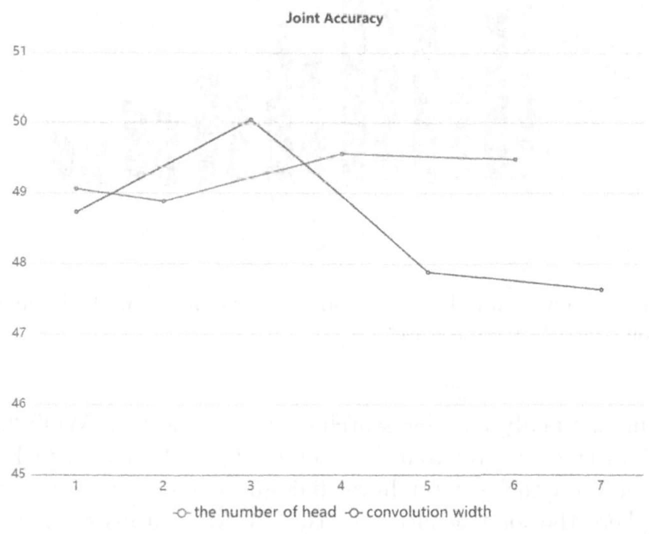

Fig. 5. The impact of the number of head and convolution width on DST joint accuracy.

Table 3. The results achieved by training on 100% single-domain data

Domain	Joint accuracy	Slot accuracy	Joint F1
Hotel	57.58	93.06	89.63
Train	77.81	95.40	94.39
Attraction	71.76	88.68	87.60
Restaurant	66.83	93.55	91.67
Taxi	75.48	89.62	86.25

4.4 Analysis

We run single domain experiments by training only one domain from the training set on the conjunct convolution model with the kernel size set 3. As shown in Table 3, the *train* domain achieves the highest performance, 77.81% on joint goal accuracy. Note that the model is better performance in *taxi* and *train* domains and poor in *hotel* and *restaurant*. It is because the slot in *hotel* and *restaurant* domains usually has a large number of possible values that is hard to recognize. However, number-related slots like *day*, *arrive by*, *leave at* and *people* in *taxi* and *train* domains can often achieve higher accuracy.

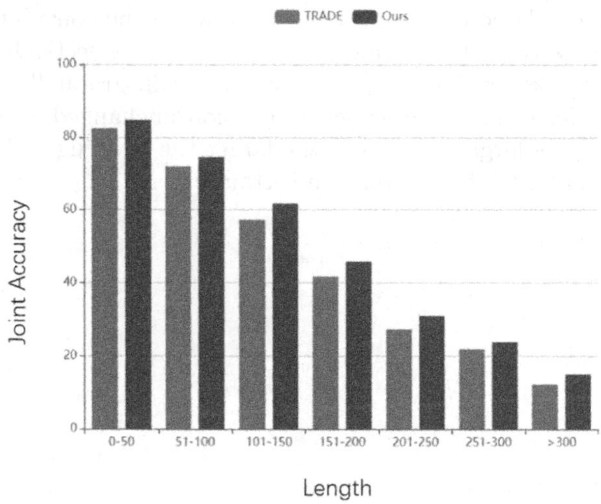

Fig. 6. The figure shows that the performance drops largely with the increase of sentence length on MultiWOZ2.0 dataset.

We have further analyzed the research results on the MultiWOZ 2.0 according to the length of the concatenated dialogue context. As shown in Fig. 6, About 27% of instances on the test set have dialogue context sequences longer than 200 tokens where the joint accuracy of the TRADE drops to lower than 30%. Our model performs better than the baseline in all cases, suggesting that GRU suffers vanishing gradient and gradient exploding problem while the proposed methods are able to make up for the shortcomings and improve modeling long dialogue context for DST.

5 Conclusion

In this paper, we have presented a conjunct multi-head and convolution layer in a multi-task learning framework to a model long dialogue context for open vocabulary-based DST. Experiments on the MultiWOZ2.0 dataset show that our model significantly outperforms the baselines and achieves over 50% of joint accuracy results.

References

1. Budzianowski, P., et al.: MultiWOZ-a large-scale multi-domain wizard-of-OZ dataset for task-oriented dialogue modelling. arXiv preprint arXiv:1810.00278 (2018)
2. Chung, J., Gulcehre, C., Cho, K., Bengio, Y.: Empirical evaluation of gated recurrent neural networks on sequence modeling. arXiv preprint arXiv:1412.3555 (2014)
3. Dauphin, Y.N., Fan, A., Auli, M., Grangier, D.: Language modeling with gated convolutional networks. In: International Conference on Machine Learning, pp. 933–941. PMLR (2017)
4. Gao, S., Sethi, A., Agarwal, S., Chung, T., Hakkani-Tur, D.: Dialog state tracking: a neural reading comprehension approach. arXiv preprint arXiv:1908.01946 (2019)
5. Goel, R., Paul, S., Hakkani-Tür, D.: HyST: A hybrid approach for flexible and accurate dialogue state tracking. arXiv preprint arXiv:1907.00883 (2019)
6. Hashimoto, K., Xiong, C., Tsuruoka, Y., Socher, R.: A joint many-task model: growing a neural network for multiple NLP tasks. arXiv preprint arXiv:1611.01587 (2016)
7. Henderson, M., Thomson, B., Williams, J.D.: The second dialog state tracking challenge. In: Proceedings of the 15th Annual Meeting of the Special Interest Group on Discourse and Dialogue (SIGDIAL), pp. 263–272 (2014)
8. Kingma, D.P., Ba, J.: Adam: a method for stochastic optimization. arXiv preprint arXiv:1412.6980 (2014)
9. Kirkpatrick, J., et al.: Overcoming catastrophic forgetting in neural networks. Proc. Nat. Aca. Sci. **114**(13), 3521–3526 (2017)
10. Lee, H., Lee, J., Kim, T.Y.: SUMBT: slot-utterance matching for universal and scalable belief tracking. arXiv preprint arXiv:1907.07421 (2019)
11. Lei, W., Jin, X., Kan, M.Y., Ren, Z., He, X., Yin, D.: Sequicity: simplifying task-oriented dialogue systems with single sequence-to-sequence architectures. In: Proceedings of the 56th Annual Meeting of the Association for Computational Linguistics (vol. 1: Long Papers), pp. 1437–1447 (2018)
12. Mrkšić, N., Séaghdha, D.O., Wen, T.H., Thomson, B., Young, S.: Neural belief tracker: data-driven dialogue state tracking. arXiv preprint arXiv:1606.03777 (2016)
13. Nouri, E., Hosseini-Asl, E.: Toward scalable neural dialogue state tracking model. arXiv preprint arXiv:1812.00899 (2018)

14. van den Oord, A., Kalchbrenner, N., Vinyals, O., Espeholt, L., Graves, A., Kavukcuoglu, K.: Conditional image generation with pixelCNN decoders. arXiv preprint arXiv:1606.05328 (2016)
15. Pennington, J., Socher, R., Manning, C.D.: Glove: global vectors for word representation. In: Proceedings of the 2014 Conference on Empirical Methods in Natural Language Processing (EMNLP), pp. 1532–1543 (2014)
16. Ren, L.: Scalable and accurate dialogue state tracking via hierarchical sequence generation. University of California, San Diego (2020)
17. Vaswani, A., et al.: Attention is all you need. arXiv preprint arXiv:1706.03762 (2017)
18. Wen, T.H., et al.: A network-based end-to-end trainable task-oriented dialogue system. arXiv preprint arXiv:1604.04562 (2016)
19. Wen, T.H., et al.: A network-based end-to-end trainable task-oriented dialogue system. In: Proceedings of the 15th Conference of the European Chapter of the Association for Computational Linguistics, Long Papers, vol. 1, pp. 438–449 (2017)
20. Wu, C.S., Madotto, A., Hosseini-Asl, E., Xiong, C., Socher, R., Fung, P.: Transferable multi-domain state generator for task-oriented dialogue systems. In: Proceedings of the 57th Annual Meeting of the Association for Computational Linguistics (Volume 1: Long Papers). Association for Computational Linguistics (2019)
21. Xu, P., Hu, Q.: An end-to-end approach for handling unknown slot values in dialogue state tracking. arXiv preprint arXiv:1805.01555 (2018)
22. Zhong, V., Xiong, C., Socher, R.: Global-locally self-attentive dialogue state tracker. arXiv preprint arXiv:1805.09655 (2018)

Spirit Distillation: A Model Compression Method with Multi-domain Knowledge Transfer

Zhiyuan Wu[1], Yu Jiang[1,2], Minghao Zhao[1], Chupeng Cui[1], Zongmin Yang[1], Xinhui Xue[1], and Hong Qi[1,2](✉)

[1] College of Computer Science and Technology, Jilin University, Changchun, China
{wuzy2118,zhaomh20,cuicp2118,yangzm2118,xuexh2118}@mails.jlu.edu.cn, {jiangyu2011,qihong}@jlu.edu.cn

[2] Key Laboratory of Symbolic Computation and Knowledge Engineering of Ministry of Education, Jilin University, Changchun, China

Abstract. Recent applications pose requirements of both cross-domain knowledge transfer and model compression to machine learning models due to insufficient training data and limited computational resources. In this paper, we propose a new knowledge distillation model, named Spirit Distillation (SD), which is a model compression method with multi-domain knowledge transfer. The compact student network mimics out a representation equivalent to the front part of the teacher network, through which the general knowledge can be transferred from the source domain (teacher) to the target domain (student). To further improve the robustness of the student, we extend SD to Enhanced Spirit Distillation (ESD) in exploiting a more comprehensive knowledge by introducing the proximity domain which is similar to the target domain for feature extraction. Persuasive experiments are conducted on Cityscapes semantic segmentation with the prior knowledge transferred from COCO2017 and KITTI. Results demonstrate that our method can boost $mIOU$ and high-precision accuracy by 1.4% and 8.2% respectively with 78.2% segmentation variance, and can gain a precise compact network with only 41.8% FLOPs.

Keywords: Knowledge transfer · Knowledge distillation · Multi-domain · Model compression · Few-shot learning

1 Introduction

Recent applications, such as self-driving cars and automated delivery robots, present the requirement of light-weight models due to limited computational resources as well as the real-time demand for recognition. At the same time, as such applications often suffer from inadequate training data [3,22], the introduction of cross-domain knowledge is urgently needed. Model compression [8,20,31],

Supported by the National Natural Science Foundation of China under Grant 62072211, 51939003, U20A20285. Full version of our article is available at arxiv.org/pdf/2103.13733.pdf.

H. Qiu et al. (Eds.): KSEM 2021, LNAI 12815, pp. 553–565, 2021.
https://doi.org/10.1007/978-3-030-82136-4_45

which compress the formed network in the back-end at the cost of a low loss of accuracy, and few-shot learning [10,25,33], which reduces the dependence of models on data through prior knowledge transfer, are presented to address these problems.

Among the various approaches, knowledge distillation and Fine-tuning-based Transfer Learning (FFT) are respectively considered as the most commonly used techniques for model compression and few-shot learning, and remarkable progress has been made in recent years [15,18,24,32,33]. However, these methods can only solve one of these two problems, and so far there has been no study to combine them.

In our work, we pioneer cross-domain knowledge transfer under the framework of feature-based knowledge distillation [29], and introduce the Spirit Distillation (SD). Different from previous approaches, SD adopts the teacher and the student networks that address problems in different domains (source and target domain, respectively). The performance of the student network is improved by exploiting the potential to extract general features with cumbersome backbone discarded through general knowledge transfer from the source domain. In addition, a more comprehensive general features extraction knowledge is transferred by extending SD to Enhanced Spirit Distillation (ESD). By introducing extra data from the proximity domain which is similar to the target domain as general feature extraction materials, the student network can learn richer and more complete knowledge and achieve a more stable performance after fine-tuning.

In general, our contributions can be summarized as follows:

- We apply knowledge distillation to both model compression and few-shot learning and propose the Spirit Distillation (SD). Through general feature extraction knowledge transfer, the compact student network is able to learn an effective representation based on the front part of the teacher network.
- We extend SD to Enhanced Spirit Distillation (ESD). By introducing the proximity domain to achieve richer supervised intermediate representation, more complete knowledge can be learned by the student network, so that robustness of the student network can be significantly boosted.
- Experiments on Cityscapes [7] semantic segmentation with the prior knowledge transferred from COCO2017 [17] and KITTI [11] demonstrate that:
  - Spirit Distillation can significantly improve the performance of the student network (by 1.8% mIOU enhancement) without enlarging the parameter size.
  - Enhanced Spirit Distillation can reinforce the robustness of the student network (8.2% high-precision accuracy boosting and 21.8% segmentation variance reduction) with comparable segmentation results attained.

2 Related Work

2.1 Knowledge Distillation

Knowledge distillation researches on the technical means of training compact student network with the prompt of cumbersome teacher network. Previous works can be mainly classified into logit-based distillation [15,21,28] and feature-based distillation [14,18,19,24], which transfer the knowledge from different stages of the teacher network to improve the performance of the student network. Pioneering works on knowledge distillation bases on logits transfer [15], which adopt a weighted average of soft and hard labels as supervisory information for student network training. Subsequent works begin to focus on transferring intermediate representation of the teacher network, like FitNet stage-wise training [24], knowledge adaptation [14], and structured knowledge distillation [18], hoping that the student network learns an effective representation based on the front part of the teacher with much fewer FLOPs.

2.2 Few-Shot Learning

Few-shot learning provides a solution to the problems in scenarios with insufficient data, utilizing prior knowledge like understanding of the dataset or models trained on other datasets to reduce the dependence of machine learning models on data [30]. Existing few-shot learning methods based on data augmentation [5,6,12], metric learning [2,26,27], and initialization [10,23,25] ameliorate the models in terms of supervised empirical growth, hypothesis space reduction, and initial parameter setting, respectively, so as to enhance the generalization ability of the models under the premise of inadequate training data.

2.3 Fine-tuning-based Transfer Learning

Fine-tuning-based transfer learning [33] proposes to splice the problem-specific feature analysis part to the first few layers of a heavy network pretrained on a large-scale dataset, and train the constructed network under the condition of freezing the weights of the front part and do further fine-tuning. Since the layers transfered from the cubersome network are able to extract features with universal properties (i.e. general features), the trained-out network tends to be of great generalization capabilities.

3 Approach

3.1 Framework of Spirit Distillation

The basic framework of SD is similar to feature-based knowledge distillation [29], which introduces both the teacher network (T) and the student network (S) in the training procedure, as shown in Fig. 1. The teacher network adopts state-of-art architecture with pre-trained weights, and the student is compact and efficient. This scheme of knowledge distillation allows the student to optimize by minimizing the distillation losses (L_D) between the hidden layer output features of the teacher (F_T) and the student (F_S), through which the student can learn a rich teacher-based intermediate representation. The optimization objective is defined as:

$$W_S^{front} \leftarrow \arg\min L_D(F_T, F_S) \tag{1}$$

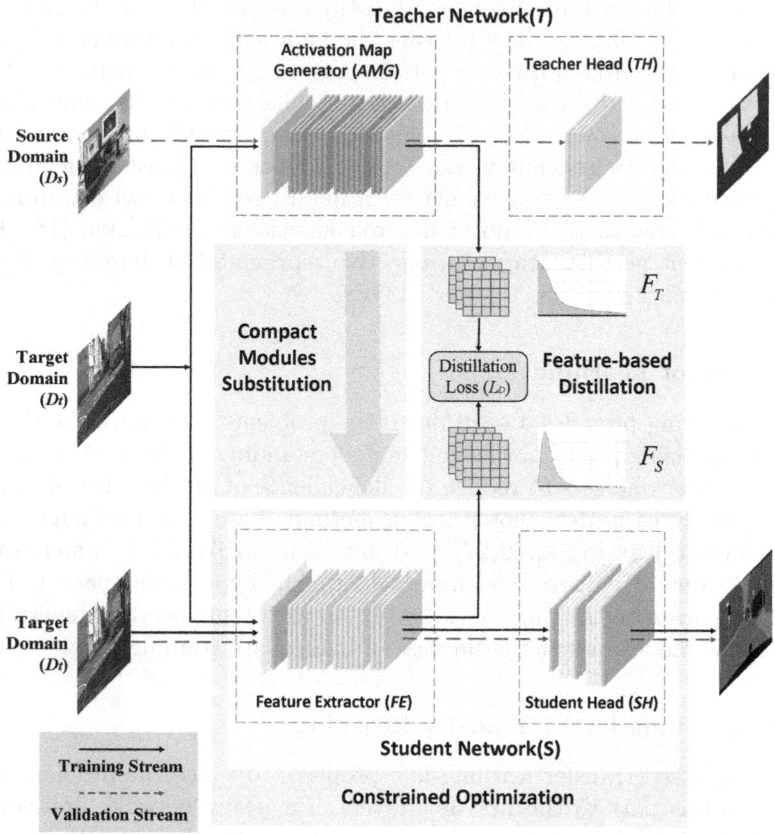

Fig. 1. Framework of Spirit Distillation. The teacher network is pretrained on the source domain (D_s), while the student network is used to solve the problem on the target domain (D_t), which is with insufficient data. Three main steps are conducted: (1) Construct the student network by compact modules substitution and designing compact SH. (2) Learn a teacher-front-based representation utilizing feature-based knowledge distillation. (3) Perform constrained optimization on the student network.

thereout, we learn the weights of the front part of the student (W_S^{front}) from its teacher.

Unlike previous knowledge distillation methods, the teacher network and the student network in this paper are solving problems in different domains. Our teacher is pretrained on the source domain (D_s), and the student is trained on the target domain (D_t). Just as there is a huge gap in sample size and scenarios between D_t and D_s, our goal is to improve the performance of S on D_t to the greatest extent, with powerful knowledge transferred from the representation of T learned from D_s. As shown in Fig. 1, SD is conducted according to the following three steps:

- Construct the student network by compact modules substitution and designing compact SH.
- Learn a teacher-front-based representation utilizing feature-based knowledge distillation.
- Perform constrained optimization on the student network.

Moreover, ESD introduces the proximity domain (D_p) that is similar to D_t and adopts data in D_p as feature extraction materials, providing richer knowledge to enhance the distillation effect.

3.2 Spirit Distillation

Student Network Construction. Given a bulky pretrained teacher network T, we divide it into two parts according to the deviation between D_s and D_t. In this way, we gain the activation map generator (AMG) which is the first part, and the teacher head (TH) to be the second one. Obtaining the S's feature extractor (FE) by replacing the convolutional layers of AMG with compact modules (e.g. group convolution [16]) to prepare the ground for efficient feature extraction. By designing the efficient feature analysis part for S (i.e., student head, denoted as SH) and stacking the part after FE, the final S is obtained. As such, the inference cost of S is much cheaper than that of T, and FE has the potential to extract general features just like AMG with even stronger generalization capability due to the smaller parameter size.

Feature-Based Distillation. We input images of D_t into AMG and gain their general features (i.e., the output of the AMG, denoted as y^{AMG}). Suppose that the general features extracted by AMG are "spirit" of the T's representation for general feature extraction. These general features are less relevant to a specific domain and a particular network architecture compared with the hidden layer output of bulky networks converged on only the D_t's training data. The rich semantic information of "spirit" for supervision is helpful knowledge to guide FE to optimize toward extracting useful features for D_t. As a result, we take y^{AMG} as the optimization objective of the feature extractor (FE, whose output is denoted as y^{FE}) and transfer the "spirit" by minimizing the distillation loss (L_D).

Constrained Optimization. After transferring the knowledge from the teacher network, further optimization is required for precise prediction. We first train S (training loss function denoted as L_P) with a frozen FE, followed by a small learning rate optimization for the overall weights, to preserve the prior knowledge in the representation of FE to the greatest extent.

3.3 Enhanced Spirit Distillation.

Since the dataset of D_t is largely undersampled from real scenes, the required diversity general features cannot be fully obtained by simply reinterpreting the images of D_t, which leads to the incomplete nature of the knowledge transferred.

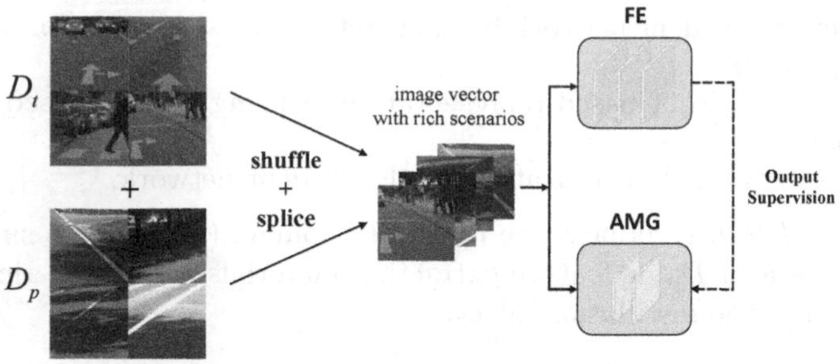

Fig. 2. The alternative strategy for images input in *ESD*. Introduce the images of the proximity domain, and shuffle them with target domain images as feature extraction materials to provide richer knowledge.

Fortunately, feature representation knowledge learned from a particular dataset tends to work well for similar domains. Therefore, introducing a large-scale dataset of D_p for feature extraction can prevent the feature extractor from overfitting to the little general features of D_t. Moreover, D_p may implicitly provide richer information of scenarios, and can compensate for the problem of insufficient data on D_t.

Based on the assumptions above, we extend SD in terms of data inputting by shuffling D_t and D_p images together, extracting their features, and allowing the student network to imitate. This method, shown in Fig. 2, expects to be executed in substitution with the input of D_t images during the feature-based distillation process, and we name the newly integrated transferring and training scheme Enhanced Spirit Distillation (ESD).

3.4 Formal Description of Enhanced Spirit Distillation

Algorithm 1 provides a formal description of the overall procedure of Enhanced Spirit Distillation. The algorithm takes the weights of pre-trained teacher network W^T (whose weights of AMG part corresponds to W^{AMG}), the weights of randomly initialized student network W^S (whose weights of FE and SH parts correspond to W^{FE} and W^{ST}), the distillation loss L_D, the prediction loss L_P, the target domain dataset D_t, the proximity domain dataset D_p, and the optimizer $optimizer_i$ of the ith stage of training (with hyper settings) as inputs, and takes trained W^S as output. Define $W_1, W_2, ...W_k$ as the weights of layers $\{W_1, W_2, ...W_k\}$, $\{W_1, W_2, ...W_k\}^X$ as the output of data X (whose label is denoted as y^X) after the transformation operation of each layer, and W^{k*} as the result of a certain iteration update of W^k.

Algorithm 1: Enhanced Spirit Distillation

Input: $W^T(W^{AMG})$, $W^S(W^{FE}, W^{ST})$, L_D, L_P, D_t, D_p, $optimizer_i$
Output: Trained W^S
Stage 1: Feature-based Distillation
while FE *not convergence* **do**
  $X_1 \leftarrow shuffle\_select(D_p, D_t)$;
  $W^{FE*} \leftarrow W^{FE} - optimizer_1(\nabla L_D(\{W^{AMG}\}^{X_1}, \{W^{FE}\}^{X_1}))$;
end
Stage 2: Frozen Training
while SH *not convergence* **do**
  $X_2, y^{X_2} \leftarrow random\_choice(D_t)$;
  $W^{SH*} \leftarrow W^{SH} - optimizer_2(\nabla L_P(\{W^S\}^{X_2}, y^{X_2}))$;
end
Stage 3: Fine-tuning
while S *not convergence* **do**
  $X_3, y^{X_3} \leftarrow random\_choice(D_t)$;
  $W^{S*} \leftarrow W^S - optimizer_3(\nabla L_P(\{W^S\}^{X_3}, y^{X_3}))$;
end

Table 1. The main properties, roles, and preprocessing methods of the datasets adopted in this paper. RC, RHF, MP, RZ in the table are abbreviations of random cropping, random horizontal flipping, maximum pooling and resizing, respectively.

Dataset	Volume	Resolution	Scenario	Domain	Preprocess
COCO2017 [17]	100K+	-	Common objects	Source	-
Cityscapes-64 [7]	64	2048 × 1024	Road Scenes	Target	RC, RHF, MP
KITTI [11]	15K	About 1224 × 370		Proximity	RZ, RC, RHP, MP

4 Experiments

4.1 Datasets

We introduce COCO2017 [17], Cityscapes [7] and KITTI [11] in our experiments, whose main properties, roles, and preprocessing methods are shown in Table 1. The subset of COCO2017 that contains the same class as Pascal VOC [9] is used to pretrain the teacher network[1]. Only the first 64 images of Aachen in Cityscapes (denoted as Cityscapes-64) are chosen for feature-based distillation and constrained optimization. What is more, the images in KITTI are randomly shuffled with Cityscapes-64 ones in the feature-based distillation process when *ESD* is adopted.

[1] The pretrained weights of the teacher network are downloaded from download.pytorch.org/models/deeplabv3_resnet50_coco-cd0a2569.pth.

4.2 Network Architecture

We adopt DeepLabV3 [4] (resnet-50 [13] backbone, pretrained on COCO2017) as the teacher network. To construct the feature extractor, we adopt the teacher's backbone with all of the convolutional layers replaced by group convolutions [16], each group being the greatest common factor of the number of input and output channels. The student head is constructed by replacing the $ASPP$ and subsequent layers with a SegNet-like [1] decoder structure, i.e., two groups of $3 \times (Conv + BN + ReLU)$ stack with bilinear up-sampling modules to achieve resolution increment and pixel-level classification. The convolution layers of the decoder also adopt group convolutions in the same setup as that adopted in the construction of FE.

4.3 Implement Details

Basic Setup. Experiments on binary segmentation on Cityscapes-64 are conducted to distinguish roads and backgrounds. Mean square error and pixel-average cross-entropy are taken as L_D and L_P, respectively.

Metrics. We adopt mean intersection over union ($mIOU$) as the index to measure the segmentation effect, the size of parameters and floating point operations in measuring the compactness and inference efficiency of the network; the prediction variance and high-precision segmentation accuracy (considered to be segmented properly when $mIOU$¿75%, denoted as (HP-Acc)) in evaluating the robustness of the model.

Hyper-parameter Settings. We take a comparison experiment on whether or not to adopt SD method. We also employ the FTT on the network that stacks AMG and the SH (denoted as constructed teacher network (CT)), and the former part is frozen in the first training stage. We directly train the student network using stochastic gradient descent (SGD) with momentum 0.9 and learning rate 10^{-2}. For distillation process, a learning rate of 3×10^{-3} and a momentum of 0.99 are adopted until convergence. Constrained optimization requires freezing weights of FE. The training of the remaining portion adopts a momentum of 0.9 with a learning rate of 10^{-2}. Further fine-tuning sets the learning rate of the entire network to 5×10^{-5} and the momentum to 0.99. l2 weight penalty is adopted in all cases, with a decay constant of 3×10^{-3}. Moreover, a data enhancement scheme with random cropping (512×512) and random horizontal flipping is adopted, with max pooling (kernel_size=2) adopted before input. To validate ESD, we set up a series of different scales to control the ratio r that the number of input D_t images to that of D_p during distillation, and conduct the experiments separately. The D_t images are preprocessed in the same way adopted for SD, except that they were previously resized to 2448×740 before cropping. All the preprocessing schemes for images in different datasets are shown in Table 1.

Table 2. The performance on the Cityscapes dataset in comparison with regular training and FTT. All the networks are trained only on the first 64 images of Cityscapes.

Method	GFLOPs	Param(M)	mIOU(%)	HP-Acc(%)
CT (FFT [33], without fine-tuning)	405.7	23.6	62.6	1.4
CT (FFT [33], with fine-tuning)	405.7	23.6	58.9	2.6
S	**169.4**	**9.5**	81.7	81.2
Ours: S (SD)	**169.4**	**9.5**	**83.5**	**84.6**

Table 3. Comparison of the results on regular training, Spirit Distillation, and Enhanced Spirit Distillation with different r values adopted.

Method		mIOU(%)	HP-Acc(%)	Var(10^{-3})
S		81.7	81.2	5.77
Ours: S (SD)		**83.5**	84.6	5.70
Ours: S (ESD)	r = 10.0	82.2	85.4	5.12
	r = 5.0	81.9	85.6	5.20
	r = 3.0	82.2	84.6	5.21
	r = 1.0	82.3	84.2	**4.52**
	r = 0.5	**83.3**	**89.2**	4.71
	r = 0.2	82.8	**89.0**	**4.48**
	r = 0	**83.1**	**89.4**	**4.51**

4.4 Results

We display the segmentation results of the student network (S) trained with SD along with the results of that trained follows regular training scheme and FTT in Table 2. To validate the effectiveness of ESD, we respectively train S under different r settings and obtain the results shown in Table 3. We also plot the comparison of *mIOU-GFLOPs*, *Var-(HP-Acc)*, and *mIOU-r* with different training settings, and calculated the distribution of segmentation effects when regular training, SD, and ESD are adopted. (see Fig. 3)

The following conclusions can be drawn from Tables 2, 3 and Figs. 3, 4.

- The S using SD outperforms normally trained S as well as the fine-tune-transferred CT. In addition, with inference efficiency significantly improved, SD also prevents the final network from over-fitting due to the large network size as well as under-fitting for the sake of freezing weights (Table 2, Fig. 3(a)).
- The segmentation effect of S is improved with either SD or ESD adopted. The S trained with ESD can perform splendid predictions in more cases, and the proportion of very poor results is significantly reduced. Hence, ESD can improve the robustness of S to a great extent (Fig. 3(b)).
- The effectiveness of introducing D_p is easily demonstrated as the final obtained S tends to gain a higher *HP-Acc* as well as *mIOU* when the value

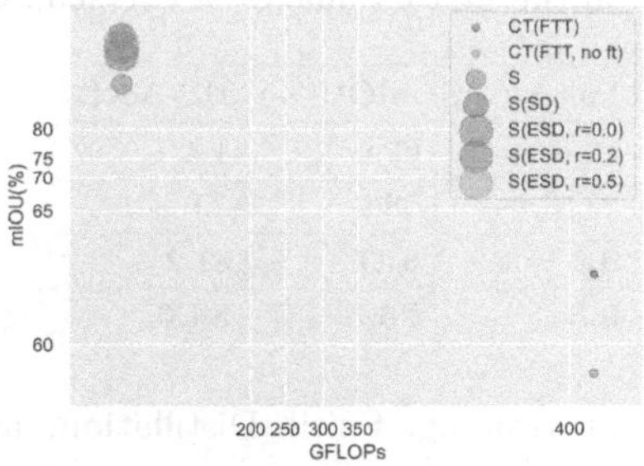

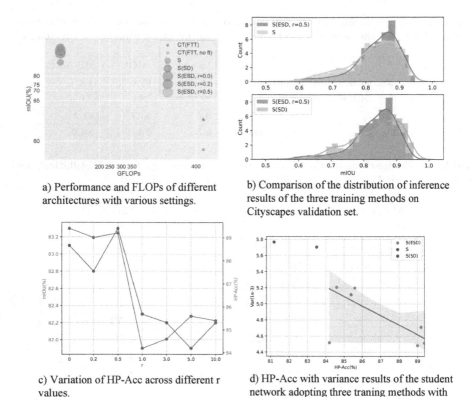

a) Performance and FLOPs of different architectures with various settings.

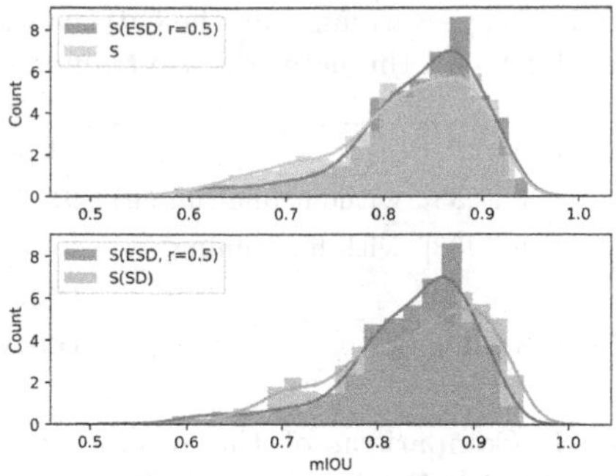

b) Comparison of the distribution of inference results of the three training methods on Cityscapes validation set.

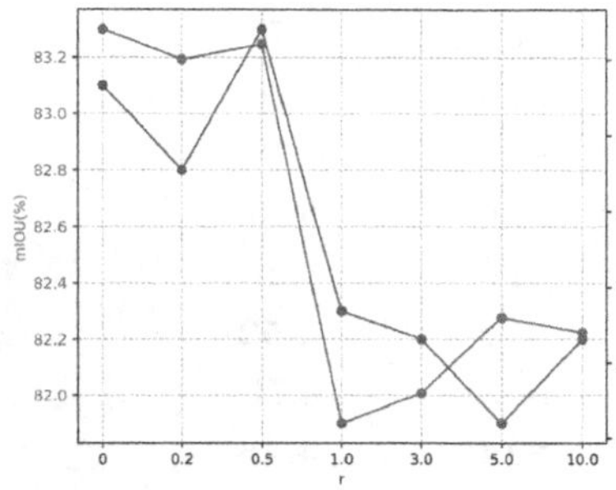

c) Variation of HP-Acc across different r values.

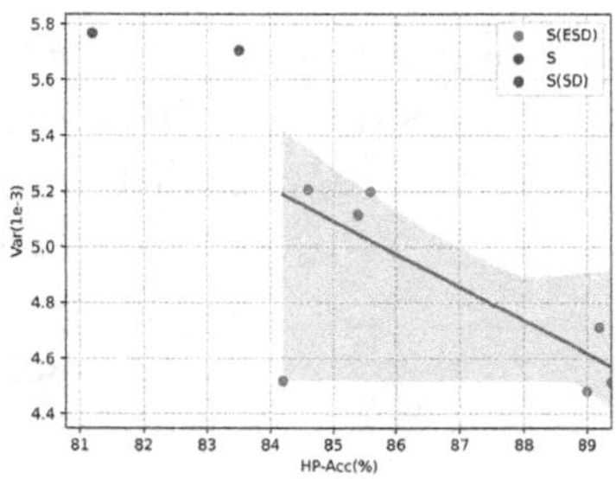

d) HP-Acc with variance results of the student network adopting three traning methods with various settings.

Fig. 3. Comparison of *mIOU-GFLOPs*, *Var-(HP-Acc)*, and *mIOU-r* with different training settings, along with the distribution of segmentation effects when regular training, *SD*, and *ESD* are adopted.

of r is set small, i.e., the proximity domain accounts for a larger proportion of the images used for feature extraction (Table 2, Fig. 3(c)).

- *ESD* effectively improves the *HP-Acc* while keeping the variances small numbers. The comprehensive learning of the general features extracted from T helps prevent unstable prediction and enhances robustness (Fig. 3(d)).
- The validity of our methods in cross-domain knowledge transfer and robustness improvement under complex scenarios is easily confirmed, as the comparison shown in Fig. 4. The obvious finding is that the segmentation results of the undistilled S are rather unsatisfactory for the shadow parts of the images. After adopting SD, the new S has improved the segmentation results of these parts, which is able to distinguish the road scene from the shadows partially. Adopting the ESD method on top of this, the S would capture the global representation for shadow segmentation more completely and can distinguish the road part with shadows of the images more as a whole. (Fig. 4)

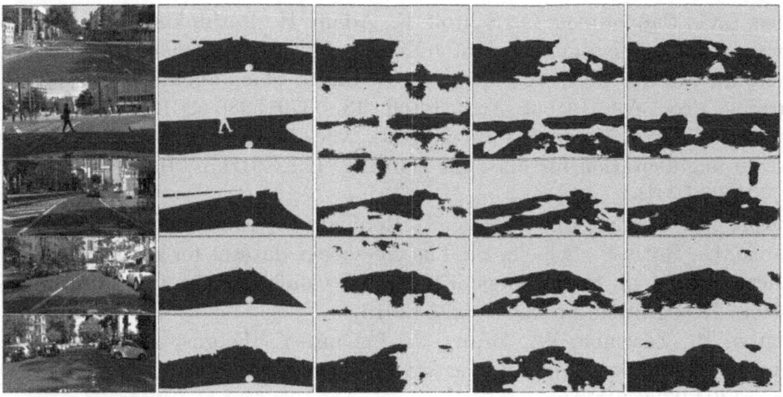

Fig. 4. Comparison of segmentation results on Cityscapes-64. (1) Input images. (2) Ground truth. (3) The segmentation results of the student network. (4) The segmentation results of the student network that adopts Spirit Distillation. (5) The result of the student network that adopts Enhanced Spirit Distillation, with r value set to be 0.5.

5 Conclusion

In order to introduce cross-domain knowledge while acquiring compressed models, a novel knowledge distillation method is proposed, which allows student networks to simulate part of the teacher's representation by transferring general knowledge from the large-scale source domain to the student network. To further boost the robustness of the student network, we introduce the proximity domain as the source of general feature extraction knowledge during feature-based distillation process. Experiments demonstrate that our methods can effectively achieve cross-domain knowledge transfer and significantly boost the performance of compact models even with insufficient training data.

Future works will include extending our approach to other visual applications and conducting domain transformation to feature extraction materials using approaches like conditional generative adversarial network training.

References

1. Badrinarayanan, V., Kendall, A., Cipolla, R.: SegNet: a deep convolutional encoder-decoder architecture for image segmentation. IEEE Trans. Pattern Anal. Mach. Intell. **39**(12), 2481–2495 (2017)
2. Bertinetto, L., Henriques, J.F., Torr, P.H., Vedaldi, A.: Meta-learning with differentiable closed-form solvers. arXiv preprint arXiv:1805.08136 (2018)
3. Biasetton, M., Michieli, U., Agresti, G., Zanuttigh, P.: Unsupervised domain adaptation for semantic segmentation of urban scenes. In: Proceedings of the IEEE/CVF Conference on Computer Vision and Pattern Recognition Workshops (2019)

4. Chen, L.C., Papandreou, G., Schroff, F., Adam, H.: Rethinking atrous convolution for semantic image segmentation. arXiv preprint arXiv:1706.05587 (2017)
5. Chen, Z., Fu, Y., Chen, K., Jiang, Y.G.: Image block augmentation for one-shot learning. Proc. AAAI Conf. Artif. Intell. **33**, 3379–3386 (2019)
6. Chen, Z., Fu, Y., Zhang, Y., Jiang, Y.G., Xue, X., Sigal, L.: Multi-level semantic feature augmentation for one-shot learning. IEEE Trans. Image Process. **28**(9), 4594–4605 (2019)
7. Cordts, M., Omran, M., Ramos, S., Rehfeld, T., Enzweiler, M., Benenson, R., Franke, U., Roth, S., Schiele, B.: The cityscapes dataset for semantic urban scene understanding. In: Proceedings of the IEEE Conference on Computer Vision and Pattern Recognition, pp. 3213–3223 (2016)
8. Denton, E., Zaremba, W., Bruna, J., LeCun, Y., Fergus, R.: Exploiting linear structure within convolutional networks for efficient evaluation. arXiv preprint arXiv:1404.0736 (2014)
9. Everingham, M., Van Gool, L., Williams, C.K., Winn, J., Zisserman, A.: The Pascal visual object classes (VOC) challenge. Int. J. Comput. Vis. **88**(2), 303–338 (2010)
10. Finn, C., Abbeel, P., Levine, S.: Model-agnostic meta-learning for fast adaptation of deep networks. In: International Conference on Machine Learning, pp. 1126–1135. PMLR (2017)
11. Geiger, A., Lenz, P., Urtasun, R.: Are we ready for autonomous driving? The KITTI vision benchmark suite. In: 2012 IEEE Conference on Computer Vision and Pattern Recognition, pp. 3354–3361. IEEE (2012)
12. Hariharan, B., Girshick, R.: Low-shot visual recognition by shrinking and hallucinating features. In: Proceedings of the IEEE International Conference on Computer Vision, pp. 3018–3027 (2017)
13. He, K., Zhang, X., Ren, S., Sun, J.: Deep residual learning for image recognition. In: Proceedings of the IEEE Conference on Computer Vision and Pattern Recognition, pp. 770–778 (2016)
14. He, T., Shen, C., Tian, Z., Gong, D., Sun, C., Yan, Y.: Knowledge adaptation for efficient semantic segmentation. In: Proceedings of the IEEE/CVF Conference on Computer Vision and Pattern Recognition, pp. 578–587 (2019)
15. Hinton, G., Vinyals, O., Dean, J.: Distilling the knowledge in a neural network. arXiv preprint arXiv:1503.02531 (2015)
16. Krizhevsky, A., Sutskever, I., Hinton, G.E.: ImageNet classification with deep convolutional neural networks. Adv. Neural Inf. Process. Syst. **25**, 1097–1105 (2012)
17. Lin, T.-Y., et al.: Microsoft COCO: common objects in context. In: Fleet, D., Pajdla, T., Schiele, B., Tuytelaars, T. (eds.) ECCV 2014. LNCS, vol. 8693, pp. 740–755. Springer, Cham (2014). https://doi.org/10.1007/978-3-319-10602-1_48
18. Liu, Y., Chen, K., Liu, C., Qin, Z., Luo, Z., Wang, J.: Structured knowledge distillation for semantic segmentation. In: Proceedings of the IEEE/CVF Conference on Computer Vision and Pattern Recognition, pp. 2604–2613 (2019)
19. Liu, Y., Shu, C., Wang, J., Shen, C.: Structured knowledge distillation for dense prediction. IEEE Trans. Pattern Anal. Mach. Intell. (2020)
20. Luo, J.H., Wu, J., Lin, W.: ThiNet: a filter level pruning method for deep neural network compression. In: Proceedings of the IEEE International Conference on Computer Vision, pp. 5058–5066 (2017)
21. Peng, B., et al.: Correlation congruence for knowledge distillation. In: Proceedings of the IEEE/CVF International Conference on Computer Vision, pp. 5007–5016 (2019)

22. Pouyanfar, S., Saleem, M., George, N., Chen, S.C.: Roads: randomization for obstacle avoidance and driving in simulation. In: Proceedings of the IEEE/CVF Conference on Computer Vision and Pattern Recognition Workshops (2019)
23. Ravi, S., Larochelle, H.: Optimization as a model for few-shot learning (2016)
24. Romero, A., Ballas, N., Kahou, S.E., Chassang, A., Gatta, C., Bengio, Y.: FitNets: hints for thin deep nets. arXiv preprint arXiv:1412.6550 (2014)
25. Rusu, A.A., Rao, D., Sygnowski, J., Vinyals, O., Pascanu, R., Osindero, S., Hadsell, R.: Meta-learning with latent embedding optimization. arXiv preprint arXiv:1807.05960 (2018)
26. Snell, J., Swersky, K., Zemel, R.S.: Prototypical networks for few-shot learning. arXiv preprint arXiv:1703.05175 (2017)
27. Sung, F., Yang, Y., Zhang, L., Xiang, T., Torr, P.H., Hospedales, T.M.: Learning to compare: relation network for few-shot learning. In: Proceedings of the IEEE Conference on Computer Vision and Pattern Recognition, pp. 1199–1208 (2018)
28. Tian, Y., Krishnan, D., Isola, P.: Contrastive representation distillation. arXiv preprint arXiv:1910.10699 (2019)
29. Wang, L., Yoon, K.J.: Knowledge distillation and student-teacher learning for visual intelligence: a review and new outlooks. IEEE Trans. Pattern Anal. Mach. Intell. (2021)
30. Wang, Y., Yao, Q., Kwok, J.T., Ni, L.M.: Generalizing from a few examples: a survey on few-shot learning. ACM Comput. Surv. (CSUR) **53**(3), 1–34 (2020)
31. Wu, J., Leng, C., Wang, Y., Hu, Q., Cheng, J.: Quantized convolutional neural networks for mobile devices. In: Proceedings of the IEEE Conference on Computer Vision and Pattern Recognition, pp. 4820–4828 (2016)
32. Xie, J., Shuai, B., Hu, J.F., Lin, J., Zheng, W.S.: Improving fast segmentation with teacher-student learning. arXiv preprint arXiv:1810.08476 (2018)
33. Yosinski, J., Clune, J., Bengio, Y., Lipson, H.: How transferable are features in deep neural networks? arXiv preprint arXiv:1411.1792 (2014)

Knowledge Tracing with Exercise-Enhanced Key-Value Memory Networks

Nan Zhang and Li Li(✉)

School of Computer and Information Science, Southwest University, Chongqing, China
kathy525@email.swu.edu.cn, lily@swu.edu.cn

Abstract. Knowledge tracing is a critical component of an intelligent tutoring system. It can track students' knowledge states and skill mastery in order to provide a more helpful learning environment for them (for example, personalized exercise recommendations). People have been trying to apply the deep learning framework in recent years to tackle the challenge of tracing knowledge. Although these deep learning models produce impressive outcomes, they do have significant drawbacks. In existing prediction models, each exercise is often represented by a basic sequence number code, and the semantic information contained in the exercise text description has not been fully mined. We introduce a new profound education method, Knowledge Tracing with Exercise-Enhanced Key-Value Memory Networks (EKVMN) in this study, that fully utilizes the text information of questions as well as the memory function of the existing deep knowledge tracing model to predict students' performance. Experiments on real-world knowledge tracing datasets reveal that our proposed model outperforms the baselines in terms of prediction performance. It also demonstrates the significance of context semantic information in the knowledge tracing task.

Keywords: Knowledge tracing · Deep learning · Word embedding · Memory network · Student assessment

1 Introduction

It is essential in an intelligent tutoring system to employ scientific ways to track students' information mastery in a focused manner. Once a student's level of knowledge is determined, individual tutoring tailored to his or her learning circumstance can be delivered [1,2]. The modeling of students' learning process can be completed based on their massive historical learning data, so that the model can automatically track students' learning status at each stage, thus achieving the purpose of adaptive learning [3]. Knowledge tracing serves to model the learning process of a student via previous encounters with issues and forecast how a student will engage in the future. The assignment might be phrased as

H. Qiu et al. (Eds.): KSEM 2021, LNAI 12815, pp. 566–577, 2021.
https://doi.org/10.1007/978-3-030-82136-4_46

a supervised learning problem: the performance of the student is anticipated in the future engagement in the light of prior interactions.

Researchers have proposed many models to improve the predictive of the knowledge tracing task. Traditional knowledge tracing models, such as Bayesian Knowledge Tracing (BKT) [4], item response theory (IRT) [5] and Performance Factor Analysis (PFA) [6] have been explored and widely used in practical intelligent teaching systems. Deep knowledge tracing (DKT) [7] has applied deep learning [8] models to the knowledge tracing task for the first time. It employs long short-term memory (LSTM) [9] to break down the constraint on separation of ability and assumption of binary state. Later on, a new model was presented to examine the interconnections between fundamental concepts and to directly output the mastery degree of each idea by a student [10]. Some academics have improved DKT's performance by examining certain side facts, like the concept prerequisite and the forgetting behavior of learners [11,12].

When building a knowledge tracing model, the first issue we have to consider is how to represent the student's historical learning trajectory data in a format that the neural network can understand [13]. Previous deep knowledge tracing models typically represent exercises with a specific number and then use straightforward one-hot encoding as the input of networks [7,10]. This approach, while convenient and straightforward, loses the rich semantic information contained in the textual description of the exercise, which plays a crucial part in modeling [14]. Based on the exercise records, we can understand the exercises from a semantic perspective and learn the semantic meaning of each part of the text using historical answer records in order to match the semantic connections.

The key to resolving this issue is to comprehend the semantics based on the exercise and then study the semantic information at the text level. In applications such as machine translation and automated question reply, semantic understanding has been applied. We propose a new knowledge tracing model to solve the problem of difficult representation of learning resources, which is inspired by these tasks. To begin, we design a semantic understanding-based exercise representation approach that maps the topic's text information to the latent space. Second, we employ a dynamic key-value memory network to model and predict students' learning processes. The following is a summary of our contributions to this work:

- We create a bi-directional self-attention module to express the semantics of each exercise by focusing on the text information of the activity.
- Based on a key-value memory network, we propose Knowledge Tracing with Exercise-Enhanced Key-Value Memory Networks, namely EKVMN to predicate and model current knowledge states of students.
- We analyze our model in three real-world datasets and observations demonstrate that the EKVMN model learns meaningful representations and exceeds baselines.

The rest of this paper is organized as follows: Sect. 2 is the details of the proposed model. Section 3 presents experimental results on three datasets. Finally, we conclude our paper in Sect. 4.

2 Methodology

In this part, we present EKVMN, a suggested model for modeling student knowledge state that incorporates question semantic information. Figure 1 illustrates the overall structure of the proposed approach.

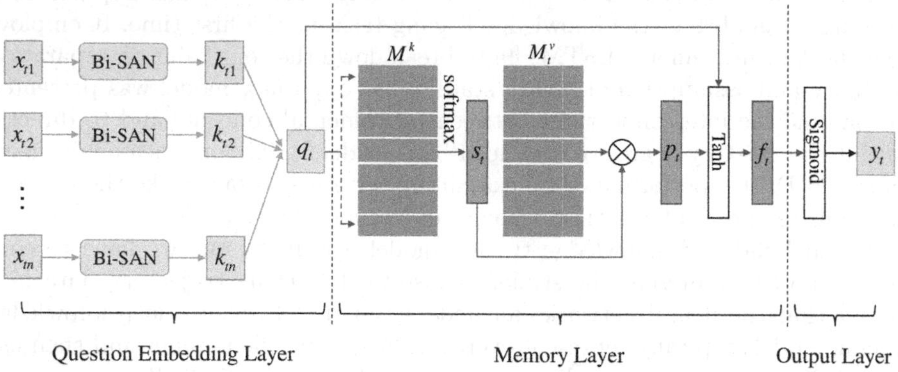

Fig. 1. The framework of EKVMN.

2.1 Question Embedding Layer

The context-aware word embeddings are combined in the question embedding layer to form the sentence encoding. The initial portion of Fig. 1 depicts it. The pre-trained word embeddings obtained from question texts using Word2Vec [15] or BERT [16] are fed into the question embedding layer.

For a particular exercise, the text content is described and coupled with a word sequence as $x = \{x_1, x_2, \ldots, x_n\}$. x_n represents the vector representation of the nth word in the sequence, and n is the number of words in each sentence. In this section, we use Google's BERT model as the pre-training language model, which is an encoder based on bi-directional Transformer [17]. It learns a decent feature representation for words from a large corpus, and we utilize the BERT output as the feature representation at the word level. To gain semantic representation at the sentence level, these vectors are fed into a bi-directional self-attention module (Bi-SAN) [18], which includes a forward self-attention network and a backward self-attention network. Bi-SAN is divided into three components: 1) intra-block self-attention, 2) inter-block self-attention, and 3) context fusion.

Intra-block Self-attention. First of all, we divide the vector representation of the input sequence into blocks, which are divided into m blocks of length α. The form of block is $[x^l]_{l=1}^{m} = [x^1, x^2, \ldots, x^m]$, where $x^1 = [x_1, x_2, \ldots, x_\alpha]$,

$x^m = [x_{n-\alpha+1}, x_{n-\alpha+2}, \ldots, x_n]$. If necessary, we will pad the last block. The output of the intra-block self-attention is:

$$h^l = g^m\left(x^l, M\right), l = 1, 2, \ldots, m \tag{1}$$

where $g^m\left(x^l, M\right)$ is a masked self-attention [19] to calculate the correlation between the two parameters. Here, the alignment score matrix is calculated by using a token2token self-attention [20]:

$$g^m\left(x^l, M\right) = \tanh\left[W^{(1)}x^l + W^{(2)}M + b^{(1)}\right] + b. \tag{2}$$

The local context characteristics can be acquired using this procedure in each block. The length α of the block is a hyperparameter that is as follows calculated: $\alpha = n/m$. We define a forward mask and a backward mask to model bi-directional information, utilized to calculate forwards attention and backward self awareness respectively:

$$M_{ij}^{fw} = \begin{cases} 0, & i < j \\ -\infty, & \text{otherwise} \end{cases} \quad M_{ij}^{bw} = \begin{cases} 0, & i > j \\ -\infty, & \text{otherwise.} \end{cases} \tag{3}$$

Inter-block Self-attention. We utilize a source2token self-attention [21] to calculate the relevance of each element in the complete phrase of a specific task for the output result of the intra-block self-attention in each block:

$$g^{s2t}(h) = W^T\sigma\left(W^{(1)}h + b^{(1)}\right) + b. \tag{4}$$

Then, the output of inter-block self-attention is:

$$u^l = g^{s2t}\left(h^l\right), l = 1, 2, \ldots, m. \tag{5}$$

Therefore, we can obtain the local context representation at the block level: $u = [u_1, u_2, \ldots, u_m]$. Then, for the local context of the block level, a masked self-attention is utilized to capture the long-distance and global connection between the blocks:

$$o = g^m(u, M). \tag{6}$$

A gate mechanism is used to dynamically integrate the local and global context features at the block level in order to merge the local and global features. The following are the output results:

$$G = \text{sigmoid}\left(W^{(g1)}o + W^{(g2)}u + b^{(g)}\right) \tag{7}$$

$$e = G \odot o + (1 - G) \odot u. \tag{8}$$

Context Fusion. For the contextual representation at the block level $e = [e_1, \ldots, e_m]$, we duplicate each element for α times to get $e^l = [e_l, e_l, \ldots, e_l]$ and let $E \triangleq [e^l]_{l=1}^m$. Afterwards, a feature fusion gate is used to combine the original sequence x, the context feature h within the block, and the long-distance global context feature E to obtain the text feature representation of the Bi-SAN:

$$F = \sigma\left(W^{(f_1)}[x; h; E] + b^{(f_1)}\right) \tag{9}$$

$$G = \text{sigmoid}\left(W^{(f_2)}[x; h; E] + b^{(f_2)}\right) \tag{10}$$

$$k = G \odot F + (1 - G) \odot x. \tag{11}$$

Two context representations based on the forward mask and the backward mask can be obtained using the preceding steps. Finally, with a source2token self-attention layer, we combine these two vectors to achieve the final context-aware embedding q of exercise.

2.2 Memory Layer

Following the work of [10], the EKVMN model is based on a key-value memory, which consists of one static matrix M^k and one dynamic matrix M^v. The exercises' concepts and the student's mastery of knowledge are stored in the two matrices, respectively.

Correlation Weight. Each latent concept's association weight is represented by the correlation weight. The softmax activation of the inner product between question embedding q_t and each key slot $M^k(i)$ was used to calculate it:

$$s_t(i) = \text{Softmax}\left(q_t^{\mathrm{T}} M^k(i)\right) \tag{12}$$

where $\text{Softmax}(z_i) = e^{z_i} / \sum_j e^{z_j}$. Both the read and write processes will use this weight vector s_t. .

Read Process The read process produces a summary of the learners' understanding of the current input exercise e_t. To begin with, the knowledge concept understanding matrix may be used to recover the students' grasp of the respective knowledge concepts. We use a read vector to represent the weighted total of the student's comprehension of the exercise's relevant knowledge concepts:

$$p_t = \sum_{i=1}^{N} s_t(i) M_t^v(i). \tag{13}$$

Then the read vector p_t and the embedding vector q_t of exercise e_t can be concatenated as the input of a fully connected layer with a Tanh activation:

$$f_t = \text{Tanh}\left(W_f^{\mathrm{T}}\left[p_t, q_t\right] + b_f\right) \tag{14}$$

where $\text{Tanh}\left(z_i\right) = \left(e^{z_i} - e^{-z_i}\right) / \left(e^{z_i} + e^{-z_i}\right)$. W_f is the weight matrix of the Tanh layer and b_f is the bias vector.

Write Process. The value matrix M^v stores the students' mastery of all knowledge concepts. When the student responds to the exercise e_t, the algorithm adjusts the value of the matrix based on whether the student answered correctly or incorrectly. We call this operation the write process as depicted in Fig. 2.

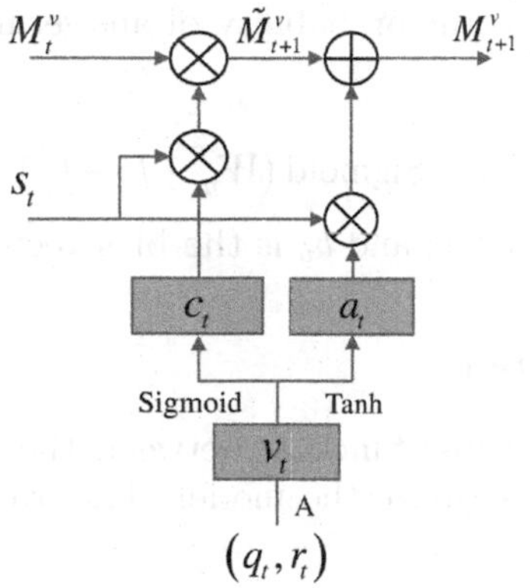

Fig. 2. The write process in memory layer.

There are two gates in the write process: an erase gate and an add gate. The former denotes the forgetting behavior that occurs during the learning process, whereas the latter denotes the rising process of knowledge that occurs after the concept has been mastered.

The tuple (q_t, r_t) is embedded with an embedding matrix A to obtain the knowledge growth v_t of the student after answering exercise e_t. The erase vector is computed as following:

$$c_t = \text{Sigmoid}\left(W_e^T \cdot v_t + b_e\right) \tag{15}$$

where $\text{Sigmoid}\left(z_i\right) = 1 / \left(1 + e^{-z_i}\right)$. W_e is the weight matrix and b_e is the bias vector. The value matrix $\tilde{M}_{t+1}^v(i)$ considering students' forgetting behavior can be obtained using correlation weight and the erase vector e_t:

$$\tilde{M}_{t+1}^v(i) = M_t^v(i)\left[1 - s_t(i)c_t\right] \tag{16}$$

where s_t is the same correlation weight used in the read process. We consider the students' knowledge growth behavior in the learning process, which is represented by the add vector, after the erase operation is completed:

$$a_t = \text{Tanh}\left(W_a^T \cdot v_t + b_a\right) \tag{17}$$

where W_e is the weight matrix of the Tanh layer and b_e is the bias vector. Finally, the value matrix will be updated by

$$M_{t+1}^v(i) = \tilde{M}_{t+1}^v(i) + s_t(i)a_t. \tag{18}$$

By erase and add vectors, the final value matrix M^v implies the forgetting behavior and knowledge growth process in the process of students' learning.

2.3 Output Layer

The output of the model is the probability of answering q_t correctly. Here, y_t is obtained as followings:

$$y_t = \text{Sigmoid}\left(W_y^T \cdot f_t + b_y\right) \tag{19}$$

where W_y is the weight matrix and b_y is the bias vector.

2.4 Model Optimization

We use the cross entropy loss function between the prediction probability y_t and the real label r_t to optimize the model. The overall objective function is described as follows:

$$\mathcal{L} = -\sum_t \left(r_t \log y_t + (1 - r_t) \log\left(1 - y_t\right)\right). \tag{20}$$

With stochastic gradient descent (SGD), the parameters can be efficiently learned [22].

3 Experiments

3.1 Experimental Setup

Datasets. To evaluate our model, we use three real-world datasets. The ASSISTments09[1] and ASSISTments12[2] datasets were collected from the ASSISTments tutoring system [23]. It's an online tutoring program that helps middle and high school students with their arithmetic challenges. If a tutoring student correctly answers a question, they are given a new one. They will be given a small tutoring session if they get the answer wrong. The ASSISTments09 dataset contains 325,637 exercises and includes 111 distinct questions

[1] https://sites.google.com/site/assistmentsdata/home/assistment-2009-2010-data.
[2] https://sites.google.com/site/assistmentsdata/home/2012-13-school-data-with-affect.

answered by 4,151 students. In the ASSISTments09 model, the textual representation of the problem is available in two languages English and Chinese, which we represent by ASSISTments09-en and ASSISTments09-zh, respectively.

The Statics2011 dataset[3] was collected from the engineering statics course at Carnegie Mellon University. We use data from the tutor mode in this experiment, which includes 1,223 different questions answered by 333 undergraduate students for a total of 189,297 exercises. We can determine the order in which students reply to these transactions because each transaction in our model has a timestamp. In addition, students with fewer than three deals were excluded.

Evaluation Methodology. To evaluate the effectiveness of the EKVMN model, we compare EKVMN with several state-of-the-art baselines.

- **Item Response Theory (IRT):** IRT [5] is used to determine whether the potential psychological characteristics can be reflected by the test questions, as well as the interaction between the test questions and the subjects.
- **Bayesian Knowledge Tracing (BKT):** BKT [4] is a Markov model with hidden variables that is one of the most widely used models. We can determine changes in learners' mastery of knowledge points by tracing changes in their knowledge.
- **Deep Knowledge Tracing (DKT):** DKT [7] is the most widely used model for knowledge tracing. It outperforms the traditional BKT model on a wide range of open-source datasets.
- **Dynamic Key-Value Memory Networks (DKVMN):** DKVMN [10] is a state-of-the-art KT model. It's a kind of memory augmented neural network (MANN) [24].

Settings. 30% of the sequences were held as a test set for each data set and 70% as a training set. We employ 5-fold cross-validation to further divide the training set (80% for training and 20% for validation), and the validation set is utilized to identify the best value of the hyperparameters. The cosine attenuation method with an initial learning rate of 0.01, 15 attenuation steps, and a minimum learning rate of 0.001 is used in the process of optimizing the algorithm in order to speed up convergence, reduce training time, and enhance solution accuracy. The size of the mini-batch for all data sets was fixed to 32 throughout the training. The training method is repeated five times for each dataset.

Furthermore, we employ the Area Under Curve (AUC) as a statistic for evaluation. The AUC value ranges from 0.5 to 1, and it can be used to evaluate the classifier's benefits and drawbacks. The higher the value, the more efficient the model is.

3.2 Performance Analysis

Prediction Accuracy. As our text encoder, we employ Google's pre-trained BERT-Base model, which we fine-tune throughout training. Bert can create

[3] https://pslcdatashop.web.cmu.edu/DatasetInfo?datasetId=507.

embeddings at the word and sentence level. EKVMN- means that the sentence-level embedding is used directly without the Bi-SAN model, while EKVMN takes the word-level embedding and gets the problem embedding through Bi-SAN.

Table 1. AUC results for all datasets.

Methods	ASSISTments09-zh	ASSISTments09-en	ASSISTments12	Statics2011
IRT	0.689	0.689	0.731	0.770
BKT	0.623	0.623	0.614	0.730
DKT	0.805	0.805	0.735	0.802
DKVMN	0.816	0.816	0.743	0.828
EKVMN-	0.838	0.835	0.767	0.843
EKVMN	**0.842**	**0.844**	**0.774**	**0.845**

Table 1 compares EKVMN's performance to the most recent state-of-the-art approaches. On all three datasets, the model has the highest AUC. On all three datasets, the reduced model EKVMN- cannot beat EKVMN, but it still beats all other baselines. The improvement from EKVMN- to EKVMN demonstrates the superiority of Bi-SAN in extracting textual information and accurately representing textual content. The performance difference between EKVMN- and EKVMN shows that textual information of embedded topics is useful in deep knowledge tracing.

The Impact of Parameters. To investigate the effect of the size of the key matrix and value matrix on model performance, we conduct a comparative experiment with EKVMN and DKVMN under varied memory slot numbers N and state dimensions d. To make a fair comparison, we employ the identical state dimensions and memory slots on three datasets for analysis: ASSISTments09, ASSISTments12, and Statics2011. For comparison, we use ASSISTments09-en from the ASSISTments09 dataset. The two models' state dimensions are set to $d = 10, 50, 100, 200$, and the number of memory slots is determined by the size of each dataset. The AUC results of the two models on three datasets are shown in Table 2.

It can be seen from Table 2 that compared with the DKVMN model, our model has better performance on all three datasets. For example, for the ASSISTments09 dataset, the EKVMN model achieved an AUC value of 0.8444 with the state dimension of 100 and the number of memory slots of 10, while the highest AUC value of the DKVMN model is 0.8157, at which time the state dimension is 50 and the number of memory slots is 20. At the same time, we can see that the number of memory slots N is 20 when ASSISTments12 obtained the optimal AUC value, which is higher than that when ASSISTments09 obtained the optimal value $N = 10$. This means that compared with ASSISTments09, the number of potential concepts in ASSISTments12 increased. We find that the

Table 2. Impact of parameters d and N

Model	ASSISTments09			ASSISTments12			Statics2011		
	d	N	AUC	d	N	AUC	d	N	AUC
DKVMN	10	10	0.8147	10	20	0.7434	10	10	0.8272
	50	20	0.8157	50	20	0.7425	50	10	0.8284
	100	10	0.8143	100	50	0.7437	100	10	0.8271
	200	20	0.8137	200	50	0.7418	200	10	0.9270
EKVMN	10	10	0.8442	10	20	0.7738	10	10	0.8435
	50	20	0.8436	50	20	**0.7742**	50	10	**0.8452**
	100	10	**0.8444**	100	50	0.7727	100	10	0.8446
	200	20	0.8439	200	50	0.7736	200	10	0.8443

number of records of students answering questions and the number of knowledge concepts contained in the system in the ASSISTments12 dataset are higher than those in the ASSISTments09 dataset, which supports our conclusion.

Embedding Visualization The EKVMN model learns exercise text embeddings. We use k-means to perform clustering analysis and t-SNE [25] to visualize the clustering results, and the reduced-dimensional clustering results are presented in two dimensions. Figure 3 depicts the visualization results of the EKVMN learning exercise representation and the exercise descriptions on the ASSISTments09 dataset. All exercises are divided into ten groups, each of which can represent one of the 111 problems in the ASSISTments09 dataset. Exercises in the same group are labeled with the same color, and these exercises are clustered together.

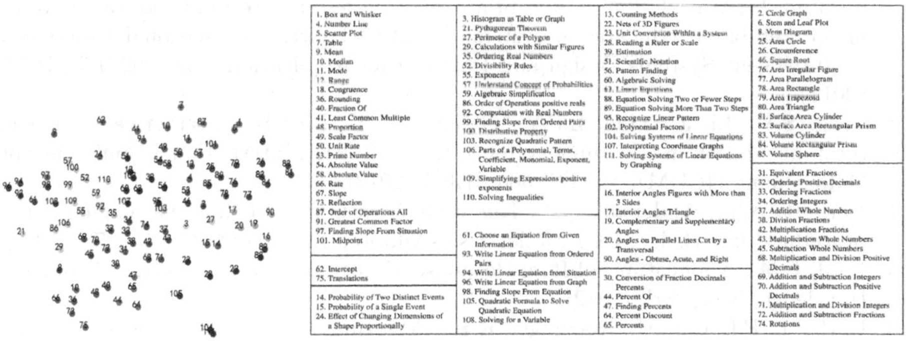

Fig. 3. Embedding visualization on the ASSISTments09 dataset.

Using the problem descriptions on the right side of Fig. 3, we can further verify the usefulness of EKVMN in detecting the underlying concepts of the exercises. For example, on the left side of Fig. 3, exercise 16, 17, and 19 fall in the same cluster in purple. They provide descriptions of "Interior Angles Figures with More than 3 Sides", "Interior Angles Triangle" and "Complementary and Supplementary Angles", which are all related to the concept of angles.

4 Conclusion

In this work, we proposed a new knowledge tracing model EKVMN to overcome the limitations of existing knowledge tracing models. To achieve the effect of dynamic learning, it employed a bi-directional self-attention module in the question embedding layer to obtain a textual representation containing semantic information and a key-value memory network to store the conceptual information of the problem and the student's knowledge mastery status in different memory units. Experimental results demonstrated that on all datasets, our proposed approach exceeded the state-of-the-art model. Also, the visualization results of question clustering proved the accuracy and usability of the question embedding, thus verifying the rationality of the semantic understanding representation.

In our future work, we will consider using knowledge graphs to build the relationship between exercises, and how to recommend appropriate study materials and exercises to students according to their cognitive level.

Acknowledgement. This research was supported by NSFC (Grants No. 61877051). Li Li is the corresponding author for the paper.

References

1. Liang, G., Weining, K., Junzhou, L.: Courseware recommendation in e-learning system. In: Liu, W., Li, Q., W.H. Lau, R. (eds.) ICWL 2006. LNCS, vol. 4181, pp. 10–24. Springer, Heidelberg (2006). https://doi.org/10.1007/11925293_2
2. Daomin, X., Mingchui, D.: Appropriate learning resource recommendation in intelligent web-based educational system. In: 2013 Fourth International Conference on Intelligent Systems Design and Engineering Applications, pp. 169–173. IEEE (2013)
3. Teng, S.Y., Li, J., Ting, L.P.Y., Chuang, K.T., Liu, H.: Interactive unknowns recommendation in e-learning systems. In: 2018 IEEE International Conference on Data Mining (ICDM), pp. 497–506. IEEE (2018)
4. Corbett, A.T., Anderson, J.R.: Knowledge tracing: modeling the acquisition of procedural knowledge. User Model. User-Adapted Interact. **4**(4), 253–278 (1994)
5. Lord, F.M.: Applications of Item Response Theory to Practical Testing Problems. Routledge, New York (2012)
6. Pavlik Jr, P.I., Cen, H., Koedinger, K.R.: Performance factors analysis-a new alternative to knowledge tracing. Online Submission (2009)
7. Piech, C., et al.: Deep knowledge tracing. In: Advances in Neural Information Processing Systems, pp. 505–513 (2015)
8. LeCun, Y., Bengio, Y., Hinton, G.: Deep learning. Nature **521**(7553), 436 (2015)
9. Hochreiter, S., Schmidhuber, J.: Long short-term memory. Neural Comput. **9**(8), 1735–1780 (1997)

10. Zhang, J., Shi, X., King, I., Yeung, D.Y.: Dynamic key-value memory networks for knowledge tracing. In: Proceedings of the 26th International Conference on World Wide Web, pp. 765–774. International World Wide Web Conferences Steering Committee (2017)
11. Chen, P., Lu, Y., Zheng, V.W., Pian, Y.: Prerequisite-driven deep knowledge tracing. In: 2018 IEEE International Conference on Data Mining (ICDM), pp. 39–48. IEEE (2018)
12. Nagatani, K., Zhang, Q., Sato, M., Chen, Y.Y., Chen, F., Ohkuma, T.: Augmenting knowledge tracing by considering forgetting behavior. In: The World Wide Web Conference, pp. 3101–3107. ACM (2019)
13. Dibello, L.V., Roussos, L.A., Stout, W.: 31A review of cognitively diagnostic assessment and a summary of psychometric models. Handbook Stat. **26**(06), 979–1030 (2006)
14. Su, Y., et al.: Exercise-enhanced sequential modeling for student performance prediction. In: Proceedings of the AAAI Conference on Artificial Intelligence, vol. 32 (2018)
15. Mikolov, T., Corrado, G., Chen, K., Dean, J.: Efficient estimation of word representations in vector space. In: Proceedings of the International Conference on Learning Representations (ICLR 2013) (2013)
16. Devlin, J., Chang, M.W., Lee, K., Toutanova, K.: BERT: pre-training of deep bidirectional transformers for language understanding (2018)
17. Vaswani, A., et al.: Attention is all you need. arXiv preprint arXiv:1706.03762 (2017)
18. Shen, T., Zhou, T., Long, G., Jiang, J., Zhang, C.: Bi-directional block self-attention for fast and memory-efficient sequence modeling. In: International Conference on Learning Representations (ICLR) (2018)
19. Shen, T., Zhou, T., Long, G., Jiang, J., Pan, S., Zhang, C.: DiSAN: directional self-attention network for RNN/CNN-free language understanding. In: Proceedings of the AAAI Conference on Artificial Intelligence, vol. 32 (2018)
20. Hu, M., Peng, Y., Huang, Z., Qiu, X., Wei, F., Zhou, M.: Reinforced mnemonic reader for machine comprehension. CoRR, abs/1705.02798 (2017)
21. Lin, Z., Feng, M., Santos, C.N.d., Yu, M., Xiang, B., Zhou, B., Bengio, Y.: A structured self-attentive sentence embedding. arXiv preprint arXiv:1703.03130 (2017)
22. Bottou, L.: Stochastic Gradient Descent Tricks. Springer, Heidelberg (2012)
23. Feng, M., Heffernan, N., Koedinger, K.: Addressing the assessment challenge with an online system that tutors as it assesses. User Model. User-Adapted Interact. **19**(3), 243–266 (2009)
24. Graves, A., et al.: Hybrid computing using a neural network with dynamic external memory. Nature **538**(7626), 471–476 (2016)
25. Laurens, V.D.M., Hinton, G.: Visualizing data using t-SNE. J. Mach. Learn. Res. **9**(2605), 2579–2605 (2008)

Entity Alignment Between Knowledge Graphs Using Entity Type Matching

Xiuting Song, Han Zhang, and Luyi Bai(✉)

School of Computer and Communication Engineering, Northeastern University (Qinhuangdao), Qinhuangdao 066004, China
baily@neuq.edu.cn

Abstract. The task of entity alignment between knowledge graphs (KGs) aims to find entities in two knowledge graphs that represent the same real-world entity. Recently, embedding-based entity alignment methods get extended attention. Most of them firstly embed the entities in low dimensional vectors space via relation structure, and then align entities via these learned embeddings combined with some entity similarity function. Even achieved promising performances, these methods are inadequate in utilizing entity type information. In this paper, we propose a novel entity alignment framework, which integrates entity embeddings and entity type information to achieve entity alignment. This framework uses encoding functions to extract the type features of entities for type matching, and combines the similarity of entity embeddings to improve the accuracy of entity alignment. Our experimental results on several real-world datasets shows that our proposed method achieves improvements on entity alignment compared with most methods, and is close to the state-of-the-art method on several metrics.

Keywords: Entity alignment · Entity type · Iterative alignment · Knowledge graph embedding · Knowledge fusion · Relation triples

1 Introduction

Knowledge graph (KG) describes various entities, concepts and their relationships in the real-world. They often serve intelligent systems such as semantic search, question answering [24], knowledge-representation system [1] and recommender systems [28] as knowledge base. Many KGs have been created separately for particular purposes. The same entity may exist in different forms in different KGs, e.g., Mount_Everest in DBpedia [11] and Q513 in Wikidata [20]. Typically, these KGs are complementary to each other in terms of completeness. We may integrate such KGs to form a larger KG for knowledge reasoning [23]. To achieve knowledge fusion, researchers have made considerable progress on the task of entity alignment.

Conventional methods for entity alignment identify similar entities based on the symbolic features, such as names, textual descriptions and attribute values. However, the computation of feature similarity often suffers from the semantic heterogeneity between different KGs. Recently, increasing attention has been paid to leveraging the KG embedding techniques for addressing this problem. As an early work, TransE [2] interprets a

H. Qiu et al. (Eds.): KSEM 2021, LNAI 12815, pp. 578–589, 2021.
https://doi.org/10.1007/978-3-030-82136-4_47

relation as the translation from its head entity to its tail entity. It expects $\mathbf{h} + \mathbf{r} \approx \mathbf{t}$ if (h, r, t) holds, where $\mathbf{h}$, $\mathbf{r}$ and $\mathbf{t}$ denote the embedding of h, r and t, respectively. Although existing embedding-based entity alignment methods have achieved promising results, they are still challenged by the following two limitations.

Firstly, the current embedding-based entity alignment methods only focuses on the vector representation of entities themselves, but do not explicitly consider the type information of the entity. For example, JE [7], MTransE [4], and IPTransE [27] only embed the relational structure of KGs for entity alignment, and JAPE [15], GCN-Align [21] and AttrE [18] complement attributes information of entities to refine the embeddings. Actually, two aligned entities also have the same type information, so the entity type can be used as a constraint to further reduce alignment errors.

Secondly, the existing entity alignment methods rely on abundant seed entity alignment as labeled training data. However, in practice, such seed entity alignment is not always accessible and very costly to obtain [8]. The limited training data would prevent the embedding-based approaches from learning accurate embeddings for entity alignment. IPTransE [27] uses an iterative method to expand the training data by adding newly aligned entities to the seed entity set. Although the iterative method will improve the effect of entity alignment, there will be the problem of error propagation, which will mislead subsequent training.

To cope with the above limitations, we propose an entity alignment framework using entity type matching, which includes three steps. The first step is to generate entity embedding using entity structural features. The second step is embed two KGs into the same vector space by using seed aligned entities as training data in order to calculate the similarity of entities, and the last step is to combine the entity similarity and entity type information to obtain the final alignment result. We summarize the main contributions of this paper as follows:

- We propose a novel entity alignment framework that integrates entity embedding and entity type information to align entities.
- We use encoding functions to extract entity type information for type matching, and then joint entity embedding similarity to obtain aligned entities.
- We evaluated the proposed approach on three real-world cross-lingual datasets. The experimental results show that our approach significantly outperformed three state-of-the-art embedding-based methods for entity alignment.

The rest of this paper is organized as follows. We discuss the related work on KG embedding and entity alignment in Sect. 2. Section 3 introduces formalization and the problem description. We describe our approach in detail in Sect. 4, and report experimental results in Sect. 5. Finally, we conclude this paper in Sect. 6.

2 Related Work

2.1 KG Embedding

Learning KG embeddings has drawn much attention in recent years. Recently emerged KG embedding models can be classified as three kinds: translation-based, semantic matching-based, and neural network-based. Translation-based models include TransE [2], and TransH [22], TransR [10] and TransD [9] extend TransE on modeling multi-mapping relations. Semantic matching models use similarity-based functions to infer relation facts, for example, the Hadamard product in DistMult [25] and ComplEx [19], and the circular correlation in HolE [12]. Considering the less expressive of translation-based models, several neural network models which exploit deep learning techniques for KG embedding are proposed. ProjE [17] uses multi-layer perceptron and ConvE [6] uses 2-D convolution over embedding for linking prediction. The neural network-based models: R-GCN [16] and attention-based model [13], which gather neighbor information of an entity to enhance entity representation.

2.2 Embedding-Based Entity Alignments

Current embedding-based entity alignment models can be classified into two kinds: translation-based entity alignment models and graph neural network (GNN)-based entity alignment models. Translation-based model MTransE [4] uses TransE to represent different KGs as independent embeddings, and learns transformation between KGs via five alignment models. IPTransE [27] and BootEA [14] are two self-training methods, which embed two KGs in a unified space and iteratively label new entity alignment as supervision. JAPE [15] and AttrE [18] employ entity attributes when learn entity embeddings. MultiKE [26] and KDCoE [3] integrate multi views of entities to learn embeddings for entity alignment. The GNN-based model GCN-Align [21] and MuGCN [5] employs graph convolutional networks to model entities based on their neighborhood information. These models exploit supplementary resource to enhance entity representations, but ignore entity type information.

3 Formalization and Problem Statement

A KG consists of a combination of relationship triples in the form of $G = (E, R, T)$, where $E = (e_1, e_2, \ldots, e_{|E|})$ represents the set of entities in the KG and the number of entities is $|E|$. $R = (r_1, r_2, \ldots, r_{|R|})$ represents the set of relationships in the KG and the number of relationships is $|R|$. $T \subseteq E \times R \times E$ denotes the set of triples in the KG, generally expressed as (h, r, t), where h and t represent the head entity and the tail entity respectively, and r represents the relationship between h and t. We consider the entity alignment task between two KGs KG_A and KG_B. Let E_A and E_B denote their entity sets, respectively. The goal is to find a set of identical entities $P = \{(e_1, e_2) \in E_A \times E_B | e_1 \equiv e_2\}$, where $\equiv$ denotes an equivalence relation in which two entities refer to the same thing. For notations, we use bold lowercase letters to represent embedding and bold uppercase letters to matrices.

4 Model

4.1 Overview

The framework of our approach is given in Fig. 1: The inputs are two KGs, KG_A and KG_B, and the outputs are aligned entity pairs. The framework consists of three modules including knowledge embedding, embedding space alignment, and entity type matching. In our approach, we propose to use entity type information for entity alignment, which will improve the accuracy of entity alignment. In the knowledge embedding module, we use TransE to embed the entities and relationships of the two KGs respectively. In the embedding space alignment module, we use seed alignment as training data to calculate entity similarity. In the entity type matching module, we first extract entity types and perform type matching, and then implement entity alignment based on entity similarity with type matching as a constraint. Furthermore, to solve the problem of less training data, we use iterative method to add newly discovered alignment entities into the training data, and provide updating methods to reduce error accumulation during iterations.

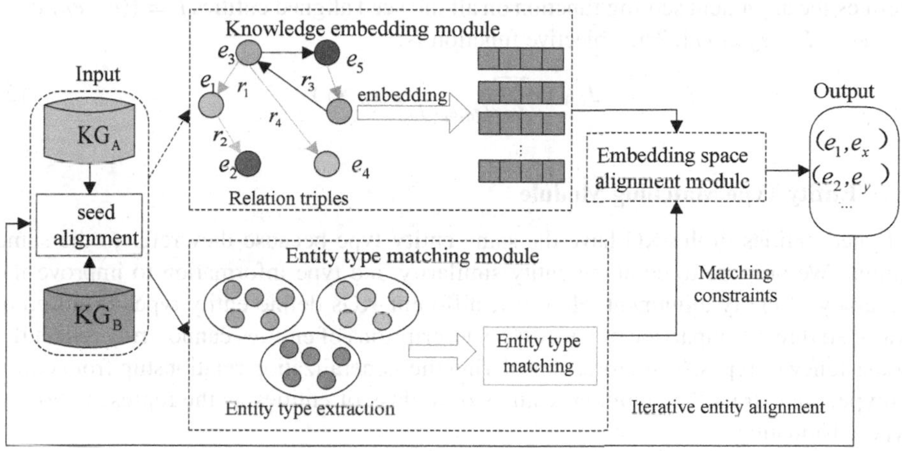

Fig. 1. Framework of our approach.

4.2 Knowledge Embedding Module

The embedding module seeks to encode a KG into a low-dimensional embedding space. To simplify the embedding process, we adopt TransE to learn the knowledge embedding for entity alignment between KGs. Given a relation fact (*h, r, t*) in KGs, we minimize the following margin-based loss function J_{KE}:

$$J_{KE} = \sum_{t_r \in T} \sum_{t'_r \in T'} max\left(0, \left[\gamma + f(t_r) - f\left(t'_r\right)\right]\right) \tag{1}$$

$$T = \{(h, r, t)|(h, r, t) \in G\}; f(t_r) = ||\boldsymbol{h} + \boldsymbol{r} - \boldsymbol{t}|| \tag{2}$$

Here, $||\boldsymbol{x}||$ is the *L1*-Norm of vector $\boldsymbol{x}, \gamma$ is a margin hyper-parameter, T is the set of valid relationship triples from the training dataset, and T' is the set of corrupted relationship triples:

$$T' = \left\{\left(h', r, t\right)|h' \in E, h' \neq h\right\} \cup \{(h, r, t')|t' \in E, t' \neq t\} \tag{3}$$

The corrupted triples are used as negative samples, which are created by replacing the head or tail entity of a valid triple in T with a random entity.

4.3 Embedding Space Alignment Module

The knowledge embedding module learns the two KG separately, namely $E_A \in \mathbb{R}_A^d$,$E_B \in \mathbb{R}_B^d$. The objective of the embedding space alignment module is to construct the transitions between the vector spaces of $\mathbb{R}_A^d$ and $\mathbb{R}_B^d$, so as to establish the connection between the two KGs. This alignment model is used in JE, IPTransE and MTransE, and the linear transformation strategy is used in our method. Its alignment score function is as follows:

$$s(e_1, e_2) = \|\boldsymbol{M}_t\boldsymbol{e}_1 - \boldsymbol{e}_2\|_2 \quad (4)$$

By learning a projection matrix $\boldsymbol{M}_t$ with dimension $d \times d$, the model can learn the alignment information between different KGs. In order to achieve this goal, this paper iterates the alignment scoring function on all the seed aligned entities $I = \{(e_a, e_b)|e_a \in E_A, e_b \in E_B, e_a \equiv e_b\}$. The objective function is:

$$J_{EA} = \sum\nolimits_{(e_a, e_b \in I)} s(\boldsymbol{e}_a, \boldsymbol{e}_b) \quad (5)$$

4.4 Entity Type Matching Module

Aligned entities in the KG have the same entity type because they refer to the same things. We propose to combine entity similarity and type information to improve the accuracy of entity alignment. However, different KGs define entity types in different ways, so direct comparison of entity type descriptions of entities cannot truly reflect the consistency of types. Therefore, considering the generalization relationship from entity to type, we extract the common features of a class of entities as the representation of type information.

For entity type z, $S_z = \{e|e \in E, e \propto z\}$ is defined as the entity set with the same type in the KG, where E is the entity set of the KG, and $e \propto z$ means that the entity e has type z. The goal is to output a vector $z_e \in \mathbb{R}^k$ representing type information with S_z as input. Since the set size $|S_z|$ of each type of entity is different, we adopt an encoding function that is insensitive to the set size:

$$z_e = \Psi(S_z) = \sigma\left(\frac{1}{|S_z|}\sum\nolimits_{e \in S_z}(\mathbf{e} \cdot \boldsymbol{W}_3 + \boldsymbol{b}_3)\right) \quad (6)$$

where $\boldsymbol{W}_3 \in \mathbb{R}^{k \times k}$ is the parameter matrix as the mapping from the entity space to its type space. $\boldsymbol{b}_3 \in \mathbb{R}^k$ is the bias parameter to be learned, and $\sigma(\cdot)$ is the nonlinear activation function, usually LeakyReLU or tanh.

The respective types z_p, z_q of the aligned entities e_a, e_b are encoded into a unified k-dimensional semantic space, and then the degree of type difference is calculated using the following distance measure function:

$$l(z_p, z_q) = \|\mathbf{z}_p - \mathbf{z}_q\|_2 \quad (7)$$

Since the entity types in the seed alignment entity set I are also aligned, similar to the embedded alignment model, we use I as supervisory information to iterate the following objective functions to learn entity type feature extraction:

$$J_{TM} = \sum\nolimits_{(e_a, e_b) \in I} l(z_p, z_q) \quad (8)$$

After obtaining the type characteristics of entities, in order to find their aligned entities in another KG more accurately, we take type matching as an additional constraint condition, and calculate the matching score of candidate entity pairs by combining entity differences and type differences:

$$\phi(e_1, e_2) = s(e_1, e_2) \cdot l(z_1, z_2) \tag{9}$$

For the unaligned entity e_1 in one KG, the entity $\widehat{e_2}$ in another KG that reaches the minimum value can be obtained, as shown in the following formula.

$$\hat{e}_2 = \arg_{e_2}\min\phi(e_1, e_2) \tag{10}$$

We set a super parameter ϵ as the matching degree threshold, and if $\phi(e_1, e_2)< \epsilon$, $\widehat{e_2}$ is the alignment entity of e_1.

4.5 Model Training and Iterative Entity Alignment

In order to learn KG representation for entity alignment, our model combines knowledge embedding, embedding space alignment and entity type matching to minimize the following objective functions:

$$J = J_{KE}+J_{EA}+J_{TM} \tag{11}$$

We use small batch gradient descent to optimize the objective function. In actual training, J_{KE}, J_{EA} and J_{TM} are alternately optimized instead of directly optimizing J. That is, for each round of epoch, $\theta \leftarrow \theta - \mu\nabla_\theta J_{KE}$, $\theta \leftarrow \theta - \mu\nabla_\theta J_{EA}$ and $\theta \leftarrow \theta - \mu\nabla_\theta J_{TM}$ are optimized in different small batches respectively, where θ represents the model parameters and μ is the learning rate. For any entity embedded vector, we force the *L2*-norm of its vector to be 1, that is, $\|e\|_2= 1, \forall e \in E$, which also shows the reversibility of the linear transformation in Formula (4). In order to avoid over-fitting of the model, the results of TransE method are used to initialize entities and relation vectors, and all parameter matrices to be learned are initialized as identity matrices.

In order to overcome the problem of insufficient training data, we use an iterative method. Although the iterative approach will improve the effect of entity alignment, there will be the problem of error accumulation, which would misguide the subsequent training. Furthermore, labeling conflicts are inevitable when we accumulate the newly-labeled alignment of different iterations. In order to improve the labeling quality and satisfy the one-to-one alignment constraint, in our iterative process, we employ a simple but effective error evaluation strategy to achieve this manner.

Let us consider the case where one entity has conflict labels in different iterations. Assume that we have two candidate alignment entities e_x and e_y for entity e_1, we would like to choose the one that provides more alignment likelihood to label e_1. Formally, we calculate the following likelihood difference:

$$SD(e_1, e_x, e_y) = s(e_1, e_x) - s(e_1, e_y) \tag{12}$$

If $SD < 0$ indicates that e_x is a candidate with a greater possibility of alignment, (e_1, e_x) is selected as the alignment entity.

Algorithm1: Model training process

Input: T_A, T_B, entity type set Z_A and Z_B, seed alignment I_{train}
Output: model parameter θ, entity alignment results A
01. $\theta_{\text{TransE}} \leftarrow$ TransE
02. $z \leftarrow (-\frac{6}{\sqrt{d}}, \frac{6}{\sqrt{d}})$ for each $z \in \{Z_A \cup Z_B\}$
03. **for** *epo* in range($epoch/k$) **do**
04.   **for** *i* in range(k) **do**
05.   optimize w.r.t J
06.   **end for**
07.   **for** $e_1 \in E_{\text{A}}$ **do**
08. $CA_{e_1} = Neighbors(E_{\text{B}}, k)$
09. $\hat{e_2} = \arg\min_{e_2 \in CA_{e_1}} \phi(e_1, e_2)$
10.   **if** $\phi(e_1, \hat{e_2}) < \epsilon$ **then**
11.   **if** $(e_1, e_x) \notin I_{\text{train}} \| SD(e_1, \hat{e_2}, e_x) < 0$ **then**
12. $A \leftarrow A \cup \{(e_1, \hat{e_2})\}$
13. $I_{\text{train}} \leftarrow I_{\text{train}} \cup \{(e_1, \hat{e_2})\}$
14.   **end if**
15.   **end if**
16.   **end for**
17. **end for**

The process of model training and iterative alignment is shown in Algorithm 1. Firstly, initialize the parameters of the knowledge embedding module (line 1) and train the model. After a certain batch of training, an iterative entity alignment is performed (lines 2–6). Select one unaligned entity e_1 in the entity set in turn, and then use formula (10) to select another entity in the KG whose matching score is less than ϵ, and mark them as newly aligned entities (lines 7–10). If the marked alignment entity conflicts with the alignment result generated in the previous iteration, use formula (12) to calculate the matching score difference of the entity pair, select a more accurate entity and add it to the training data (lines 11–13).

5 Experiments

5.1 Datasets and Evaluation Metrics

We use DBP15K as the dataset in our experiments, which are constructed in [15]. DBP15K contains three cross-lingual datasets built from the multilingual versions of DBpedia: $\text{DBP}_{\text{zh-en}}$ (Chinese to English), $\text{DBP}_{\text{ja-en}}$ (Japanese to English), $\text{DBP}_{\text{fr-en}}$ (French to English). Each dataset contains 15 thousand aligned entity pairs. Like most works using these data sets, we use 30% of these pairs as seeds and left the remaining as testing data. Table 1 lists the statistics of the three datasets.

By convention, we chose Hits@k (k = 1, 10) and mean rank (MR) as the evaluation metrics. Hits@k measures the percentage of correct alignment ranked at top *k*. MR calculate the mean of these ranks. Naturally, a higher Hits@k and lower MR scores indicate better performance. Note that, Hits@1 should be more preferable, and it is equivalent to precision widely-used in conventional entity alignment.

Table 1. Statistics of datasets.

Datasets		Entities	Relations	Attributes	Rel. triples	Attr. triples
DBP_{zh-en}	Chinese	66,469	2,803	8,113	153,929	379,684
	English	98,125	2,317	7,173	237,674	567,755
DBP_{ja-en}	Japanese	65,744	2,043	5,882	164,373	354,619
	English	95,680	2,096	6,066	233,319	497,230
DBP_{fr-en}	French	66,858	1,379	4,547	192,191	528,665
	English	105,889	2,209	6,422	278,590	576,543

5.2 Comparative Study

We compare our proposed model (JETEA) with five recent embedding-based entity alignment methods, namely JE [7], MTransE [4], IPTransE [27], JAPE [15] and GCN-Align [21]. Specifically, MTransE has five variants in its alignment model, where the fourth performs best according to the experiments. Thus, we chose this variant to represent MTransE. IPTransE is an iterative approach, we select its best variant with parameter sharing and iterative alignment. JAPE and GCN-Align combine relation and attribute embeddings for entity alignment, we use its full model. In order to show the effectiveness of the type matching constraint method in this paper more intuitively, we also compared the model (JEA) with the type matching module removed.

We use mini-batch gradient descent algorithm to optimize the objective function. We choose the entity and relationship embeddings dimensionality d among {50, 75, 100}, entity type embeddings dimensionality k among {20, 30, 40, 50}, γ_1 and γ_2 among {1, 2, 3, 4}, batch size value B among {200, 500, 1000, 1400}, and ϵ among {0.1, 0.15, 0.20, 0.25}. The learning rate μ was set to 0.005 and the training spent 500 epochs. We tuned various parameter values and set $d = 75$, $k = 30$, $\gamma_1 = 2$, $\gamma_2 = 3$, $B = 500$ and $\epsilon = 0.15$ for the best performance.

5.3 Results and Analysis

Table 2, Table 3 and Table 4 respectively shows the comparison results of JETEA and other embedding-based entity alignment methods on the three datasets of DBP15K. The results of JE, MTransE and JAPE are obtained from [15], GCN-Align are obtained from [21] and IPTransE from [14]. We found that the results of JETEA are significantly improved compared with the baseline methods JE and MTransE. For example, on the three datasets, the Hits@10 values of JETEA are 75.02, 72.42 and 71.80, respectively, which are 16.28% higher than MTransE on average. On all datasets, JTMEA's results are better than IPTransE and JAPE methods, and close to the advanced GCN-Align method on several metrics.

The result of JE method is regarded as the baseline value, because it only uses TransE for knowledge embedding and linear transformation strategy for embedding space alignment. The MTransE we selected is its fourth variant, which is the same as JE, but the result of MTransE is better than JE, because it adds a normalized constraint ($\|\boldsymbol{e}\|_2 = 1$) to the entity vector during training.

Table 2. Entity alignment results on DBP_{zh-en}.

Methods	DBP_{zh-en}		
	Hits@1	Hits@10	MR
JE	21.27	42.77	766
MTransE	30.83	61.41	154
IPTransE	35.59	68.47	121
JAPE	41.18	74.46	84
GCN-Align	41.25	74.38	–
JEA	35.06	69.23	101
JETEA	**42.69**	**75.02**	**64**

Table 3. Entity alignment results on DBP_{ja-en}.

Methods	DBP_{ja-en}		
	Hits@1	Hits@10	MR
JE	18.92	39.97	832
MTransE	27.86	57.45	159
IPTransE	37.04	70.81	98
JAPE	36.25	68.50	99
GCN-Align	39.91	74.46	–
JEA	34.04	68.91	108
JETEA	**36.44**	**72.42**	**81**

Table 4. Entity alignment results on DBP_{fr-en}.

Methods	DBP_{fr-en}		
	Hits@1	Hits@10	MR
JE	15.38	38.84	574
MTransE	24.41	55.55	139
IPTransE	31.10	68.37	89
JAPE	32.39	66.68	92
GCN-Align	37.29	74.49	-
JEA	31.09	67.02	90
JETEA	**36.46**	**71.80**	**87**

JETEA adds entity type matching module to JEA, and the results show that JETEA is better than JEA in all metrics. It shows that the similarity judgment between entities can be strengthened by joint entity type matching, thereby improving the accuracy of entity alignment. Compared with GCN-Align, JETEA has no improvement on DBP_{ja-en} and

DBP_{fr-en} datasets, which may be due to the use of entity attribute information by GCN-Align. However, the Hits@k of JETEA is similar to GCN-Align on the three datasets, and it is improved compared with GCN-Align on DBP_{zh-en}. For example, the Hits@1 and Hits@10 of GCN-Align on the DBP_{zh-en} dataset are 41.25 and 74.38, respectively, and JETEA is 42.69 and 75.02. This shows the effectiveness of our proposed model, which can approach the most advanced method in entity alignment effect.

6 Conclusion

In this paper, we introduced a KG entity alignment model JTMEA with joint entity type matching. We first used TransE to learn the entities and relationships of the two KGs respectively, and then we utilized seed alignment as supervision information, embed the two KGs into a unified semantic space and calculated the similarity of entities. Last, we extracted entity type features for type matching, and combined entity embedding similarity to select aligned entities. In addition, we also used iterative methods to enrich training data and provided updating methods to reduce error accumulation. The experiments results on three real-world datasets have shown that our proposed method achieves improvements on entity alignment compared with most methods, and is close to the state-of-the-art method on several metrics. This demonstrates the effectiveness of our method.

Acknowledgment. . The work was supported by the National Natural Science Foundation of China (61402087), the Natural Science Foundation of Hebei Province (F2019501030), the Natural Science Foundation of Liaoning Province (2019-MS-130), the Key Project of Scientific Research Funds in Colleges and Universities of Hebei Education Department (ZD2020402), the Fundamental Research Funds for the Central Universities (N2023019), and in part by the Program for 333 Talents in Hebei Province (A202001066).

References

1. Asamoah, C., Tao, L., Gai, K., Jiang, N.: Powering filtration process of cyber security ecosystem using knowledge graph. In: CSCloud, pp. 240–246 (2016)
2. Bordes, A., Usunier, N., García-Durán, A., Weston, J., Yakhnenko, O.: Translating embeddings for modeling multi-relational data. In: Proceedings of the 26th International Conference on Neural Information Processing Systems, pp. 2787–2795 (2013)
3. Chen, M., Tian, Y.N., Chang, K., Skiena, S., Zaniolo, C.: Co-training embeddings of knowledge graphs and entity descriptions for cross-lingual entity alignment. In: Proceedings of the Twenty-Seventh International Joint Conference on Artificial Intelligence, pp. 3998–4004 (2018)
4. Chen, M., Tian, Y., Yang, M., Zaniolo, C.: Multilingual knowledge graph embeddings for cross-lingual knowledge alignment. In: Proceedings of the 26th International Joint Conference on Artificial Intelligence, pp. 1511–1517 (2017)
5. Cao, Y., Liu, Z., Li, C., Liu, Z., Li, J., Chua, T.: Multi-channel graph neural network for entity alignment. In: Proceedings of the 57th Conference of the Association for Computational Linguistics, pp. 1452–1461 (2019)

6. Dettmers, T., Minervini, P., Stenetorp, P., Riedel, S.: Convolutional 2D Knowledge Graph Embeddings. In: Proceedings of the AAAI Conference on Artificial Intelligence, pp. 1811–1818 (2018)
7. Hao, Y., Zhang, Y., He, S., Liu, K. Zhao, J.: A joint embedding method for entity alignment of knowledge bases. In: China Conference on Knowledge Graph and Semantic Computing, pp. 3–14 (2016)
8. Isele, R., Bizer, C.: Active learning of expressive linkage rules using genetic programming. J. Web Semant. **23**, 2–15 (2013)
9. Ji, G., He, S., Xu, L., Liu, K., Zhao. J.: Knowledge graph embedding via dynamic mapping matrix. In: Proceedings of the 53rd Annual Meeting of the Association for Computational Linguistics and the 7th International Joint Conference on Natural Language Processing, pp. 687–696 (2015)
10. Lin, Y., Liu, Z., Sun, M., Liu, Y., Zhu X.: Learning entity and relation embeddings for knowledge graph completion. In: Proceedings of the 29th AAAI Conference on Artificial Intelligence, pp. 2181–2187 (2015)
11. Lehmann, J., Isele, R., Jakob, M., Jentzsch, A., et al.: DBpedia – a large-scale, multilingual knowledge base extracted from wikipedia. Semant. Web J. **6**(2), 167–195 (2015)
12. Nickel, M., Rosasco, L., Poggio, T.: Holographic embeddings of knowledge graphs. In: AAAI, pp. 1955–1961 (2016)
13. Nathani, D., Chauhan, J., Sharma, C., Kaul, M.: Learning attention-based embeddings for relation prediction in knowledge graphs. In: Proceedings of the 57th Conference of the Association for Computational Linguistics, pp. 4710–4723 (2019)
14. Sun, Z., Hu, W., Zhang, Q., Qu, Y.: Bootstrapping entity alignment with knowledge graph embedding. In: IJCAI, pp. 4396–4402 (2018)
15. Sun, Z., Hu, W., Li, C.: Cross-lingual entity alignment via joint attribute-preserving embedding. In: d'Amato, C., et al. (eds.) ISWC 2017. LNCS, vol. 10587, pp. 628–644. Springer, Cham (2017). https://doi.org/10.1007/978-3-319-68288-4_37
16. Schlichtkrull, M., Kipf, T.N., Bloem, P., Berg, R.V., Titov, I., Welling, M.: Modeling relational data with graph convolutional networks. In: European semantic web conference, pp. 593–607 (2018)
17. Shi, B., Weninger, T.: Proje: Embedding projection for knowledge graph completion. In: Proceedings of the Thirty-First AAAI Conference on Artificial Intelligence, pp. 1236–1242 (2017)
18. Trsedya, B.D., Qi, J., Rui, Z.: Entity alignment between knowledge graphs using attribute embeddings. In: AAAI, pp. 297–304 (2019)
19. Trouillon, T., Welbl, J., Riedel, S., Gaussier, E., Bouchard, G.: Complex embeddings for simple link prediction. In: ICML, pp. 2071–2080 (2016)
20. Vrandecic, D., Krotzsch, M.: Wikidata: a free collaborative knowledgebase. Commun. ACM **57**(10), 78–85 (2014)
21. Wang, Z., Lv, Q., Lan, X., Zhang, Y.: Cross-lingual knowledge graph alignment via graph convolutional networks. In: Proceedings of the 2018 Conference on Empirical Methods in Natural Language Processing, pp. 349–357 (2018)
22. Wang, Z., Zhang, J., Feng, J., Chen, Z.: Knowledge graph embedding by translating on hyperplanes. In: Proceedings of the 28th AAAI Conference on Artificial Intelligence, pp. 1112–1119 (2014)
23. Xiong, W., Hoang, T., Wang, W.Y.: Deeppath: A reinforcement learning method for knowledge graph reasoning. arXiv preprint arXiv:1707.06690 (2017)
24. Yih, W.T., Chang, M.W., He, X., Gao J.: Semantic parsing via staged query graph generation: question answering with knowledge base. In: Proceedings of Association for Computational Linguistics, pp. 1321–1331 (2015)

25. Yang, B., Yih, W.T., He, X., Gao, J., Deng L.: Embedding entities and relations for learning and inference in knowledge bases. arXiv preprint arXiv:1412.6575 (2014)
26. Zhang, Q., Sun, Z., Hu, W., Chen, M., Guo, L., Qu, Y.: Multi-view knowledge graph embedding for entity alignment. In: Proceedings of the Twenty-Eighth International Joint Conference on Artificial Intelligence, pp. 5429–5435 (2019)
27. Zhu, H., Xie, R., Liu, Z., Sun, M.: Iterative entity alignment via joint knowledge embeddings. In: Proceedings of the 26th International Joint Conference on Artificial Intelligence, Melbourne, pp. 4258–4264 (2017)
28. Zhang, F., Yuan, N.J., Lian, D., Xie, X., Ma W.Y.: Collaborative knowledge base embedding for recommender systems. In: Proceedings of International Conference on Knowledge Discovery and Data Mining, pp. 353–362 (2016)

Text-Aware Recommendation Model Based on Multi-attention Neural Networks

Gang Qiu[1,2(✉)], Xiaoli Yu[2], Liping Jiang[2], and Baoying Ma[2(✉)]

[1] School of Software, Shandong University, Jinan, China
[2] Changji University, Changji, China
{qiugang,mby}@cjc.edu.cn

Abstract. With the rapid development of information technology, Internet of Things and other technologies, various applications in the Internet space are emerging in an endless stream, triggering an explosive increase in data scale. Intelligent recommendation systems can efficiently filter out massive data sentiment analysis is one of the key technologies of Natural Language Processing (NLP) and intelligent recommendation systems. Finding out the reasons behind certain emotional expressions in texts through information technology has received widespread attention. Based on this, this paper proposes a text-aware recommendation model based on multi-attention neural network model to solve this problem. First, we use a modified LDA and paragraph vector learning framework to obtain the text vector representation, then capture the context information of the text through the Bi-LSTM layer, and finally input the representation into the CNN layer to classify and predict emotional factors. Experimental results show that our proposed method is significantly better than the most advanced baseline method.

Keywords: Context · Text-aware · Multi-attention mechanism · Deep learning · Recommender system · Neural networks

1 Introduction

In recent years, with the appearance of smartphone [18], intelligent transportation system [27], and tele-health [23], the growing scale of data increased significantly [5,6]. Extracting effective knowledge from massive data has received wide attention. Intelligent recommendation systems can efficiently filter out useful data from massive data, and finding out a certain sentiment expression from text is one of the key technologies of intelligent recommendation systems. At present, people use deep learning algorithms for intelligent analysis such as text key data extraction, intelligent classification, and sentiment analysis. In intelligent recommendation systems, we analyze the sentiment tendency in user comments or natural language descriptions of items to effectively improve the quality of intelligent recommendations.

H. Qiu et al. (Eds.): KSEM 2021, LNAI 12815, pp. 590–603, 2021.
https://doi.org/10.1007/978-3-030-82136-4_48

Currently, Collaborative Filtering (CF) based recommendation algorithms are more popular in intelligent recommendations, which use the historical ratings of items by users and the interactions or preferences between users and items to generate recommendation lists [20]. However, the CF approach cannot make recommendations for some new items because they never receive any feedback from users in the past, creating a cold start problem. It was found in the subsequent research that generating recommendation results based on using only user rating information does not really reflect user preferences. The recommendation method based on textual content recommendation can effectively alleviate the cold-start problem, and the recommendation effect can be improved by extracting the features of the review text or the natural able language description of the items. However, the natural language description of item content does not have enough information for computers to perform statistics, and the semantic analysis of item content is difficult.

Among deep neural networks, Hermann et al. [13] extracted the features of hidden vectors in text using the attention mechanism. Hermann et al. [19] used LSTM to parse the implicit special here in the two sentences and extended it using an attention mechanism to reason about the word-to-word and word-to-phrase inclusion relations. Li et al. [15] used word-level attention mechanism to obtain contextual corpus features and used questions to guide sentence-level attention mechanism to achieve context modeling. Chen et al. [4] propose a location-attentive RNN-based model that focuses on the location of words and incorporates the location of question words into the attentional representation of answers. Qiu et al. [7,8] used reinforcement learning methods to solve the resource allocation problem. They proposed a Smart Cloud-based Optimized Workload (SCOW) model, which was experimentally shown to be effective in improving the sustainability of the system [9]. In the above study, promising results were achieved in text and sentence analysis tasks through deep neural networks and attention mechanisms. However, they did not take into account the emotional expressions in the text, which could provide important clues for emotion recognition.

Most of the previous work ignored the emotional expressions in the text and the relevance of user comments and item descriptions. To solve the above problem, we proposed a text-aware recommendation model based on a multi-attentive mechanism neural network (TAMAN). The model first acquires word vector representation and sentence vector representation, then captures the contextual information of the text through the Bi-LSTM layer's, and finally inputs the representation to the CNN layer for classification and prediction of sentiment factors. the key contributions of our work are as follows:

- We use WLDA (word2vec Latent Dirichlet Allocation) to obtain word vector representations in short texts of user reviews, and a paragraph vector learning framework to obtain sentence vector representations of long texts of item descriptions. And the word vector representation and sentence vector representation are embedded into the Bi-LSTM layer as sentiment vectors, and the sentiment vectors and their contexts are aggregated by Bi-LSTM to be able to deeply understand the sentiment information in the text.

- We proposed a multi-attention mechanism, namely, a word vector attention mechanism guided by short textual sentiment word vectors based on user review data and a sentence vector attention mechanism guided by long textual sentiment sentence vectors based on item content, which can capture the important parts of user reviews and item description information.
- We test our proposed text-aware recommendation model based on multi-attention mechanism neural network on public dataset, and the experimental show that our proposed text-based multi-attention mechanism neural network model can more fully capture the sentiment features of different length texts and improve the recommendation effect.

The subsequent sections of this paper are organized as follows: Sect. 2 introduces related work, and Sect. 3 describes data collection and data preprocessing. In Sect. 4, we proposed Text-aware recommendation model based on multi-attention neural network model. Section 5 gives the experimental protocol and the analysis of the experimental results. Section 6 summarizes the work of this paper as well as future prospects.

2 Related Work

This section introduces related works such as content-based recommendation systems, traditionally emotional cause analysis methods, and sentiment analysis model based on text-aware attention mechanism deep neural networks.

2.1 Content-Based Recommendation System

Content-based recommendation is a recommendation method based on deep text information mining. Content-based recommendation uses user comment information as the basis for collaborative filtering recommendation, and incorporates it and content information into a factor model for mixed recommendation [21,25]. The recommendation method realizes in-depth mining of user comment recommendation factors, by integrating valuable comment information generated by users into the user modeling and recommendation process. Comment factors include the usefulness, theme, content and emotion of the comment [3,24,26]. Content-based recommendation can use deep neural networks to learn potential factors at all levels, and help users make better and faster decisions through deep learning of content [2,12]. The content-based recommendation method relies on user preferences and feature information about items, instead of rating records. It is not limited by sparse rating data, but often encounters the problem of difficulty in feature extraction.

2.2 Traditional Methods Based on Emotional Cause Analysis

The category of emotion is an important basic of the analysis of the cause of emotion.At present, many people have proposed models and methods for emotion category recognition. Ekman et al. [17] propose to classify the basic emotions into six categories, namely anger, disgust, fear, happiness, sadness, and surprise. Liu et al. [11] propose a multi-core support vector machine method based on convolution kernel, which obtains emotions from Sina city news data classification. However, due to the diversity of sentence structures, as the increasing of data dimension, extracting these features is very time-consuming. Fortunately, the neural network has a remarkable performance in extracting the emotional representation in the context.

2.3 Emotional Reason Analysis Method Based on Deep Neural Network

With the continuous development of deep learning technology, deep neural networks have been widely used, such as machine translation, natural language processing, sentiment analysis, and intelligent recommendation. Gui et al. [10] extract word-level sequence features and lexical features by building a contextual information model. Yu et al. [22] extract word position information and document features at different semantic levels through a network hierarchical utterance selection framework to improve the similarity are computed. Cai et al. [1] deal with the multi-modal information detection problem by deeply fusing the information of text features, image features and image attributes.

Although these methods can effectively extract the sentiment factors in the text, they do not consider the context of sentiment words and the correlation between user reviews and item descriptions. In this paper, a deep neural network-based multi-text sentiment analysis module is proposed to solve the problem of difficult fusion of multidimensional views of user review data, user review texts, and natural language descriptions of items. In the recommendation system, effective fusion of texts of different lengths is achieved.

3 Data Acquisition and Preprocessing

3.1 Data Acquisition

The data set we used covers about 35 million Amazon reviews, more than 6.6 million users, and more than 2.44 million items. The data set includes: item information, user information, item reviews and other information. Among them, user information includes user name, location, user level, etc. Item information includes item ID, item title, item price, item introduction, etc. Comment information includes user ID, item ID, user name, text comment, item rating, time Stamp and other information.

3.2 Data Preprocessing

The data preprocessing stage focuses on vectorizing short text information of user comments and long text information of item descriptions. We use the improved

Latent Dirichlet Allocation (LDA), that is, word2vec Latent Dirichlet Allocation (WLDA), to obtain the word vector representation of user review data, and Distributed representation of long textual information of item descriptions using a paragraph vector learning framework to obtain paragraph vector representations.

Word Vector Representation of User Comment Text. In this paper, we use vector processing of user comment data based on WLDA model and embed the generated word vectors into Bi-LSTM layer to extract more sentiment information from user comment text. At the same time, by mining the associated attributes between words, Improve the accuracy of keyword semantic representation.

LDA (Fig. 1-a) is an unsupervised generative model for modeling natural language. It can be used to identify the topic information hidden in a document set or corpus, and it can search for the hidden topic distribution in the document. Mining the hidden "topic" dimension of data from "data-word", and transforming it into a low-dimensional "data-topic" problem. However, the LDA topic generation model ignores the relationship between words in the document during the training process, and the word2vec model can effectively infer new term words. In addition, the word2vec model and the LDA topic model are trained on the corpus, the word2vec model More word vectors with similar meanings can be obtained. If the word vector is trained in the word2vec model during the Gibbs sampling stage of the topic model, then more word meanings can be used in the inference step of the LDA topic model. In view of this, we use the word2vec model to train on the long text corpus of short text splicing to obtain the word vector embedding space v_t^w. The purpose is to train word vectors that carry contextual information. The WLDA is shown in Fig. 1-b:

Where α and β are the hyper parameters of θ_i and φ_k, respectively, θ_i is the probability distribution of all topics of the i-th user review document, φ_k is the probability distribution of all words in the subject k, and the θ_i and φ_k distributions Dirichlet obeying the parameters $\acute{A}$ and $\hat{A}$ prior distribution. K is the number of topics, and M is the total number of user review documents. As shown in Fig. 1, the LDA model mainly contains two physical processes. First, the process of $\alpha \rightarrow \theta_i \rightarrow z_{i,j}$ generating the subject $z_{i,j}$ of the j-th word of the i-th user review data. Then, $\beta \rightarrow \varphi_k \rightarrow w_{i,j} \mid k = z_{i,j}$ generates a process for the j-th feature word $w_{i,j}$ of the user review data. The generation probability solving process of the j-th word $w_{i,j}$ in the i-th user review data I_i is given below. In the WLDA model, the pre-processed text is first input into the replacement word2vec model layer to obtain the trained word embedding space v. In the Gibbs sampling phase, the word ω in the LDA model is replaced with a certain probability into the word ω' output in the word2vec model layer. The goal is to supplement the word vector and add vocabulary with contextual information to the LDA model. For example, the word "*breathtaking*" can be replaced with the word "*gripping*".

Through the analysis of the WLDA topic generation model on each user's comment data, topic vectors and high-frequency word vector representations are obtained. After obtaining the k-dimensional word vector and sentence vector

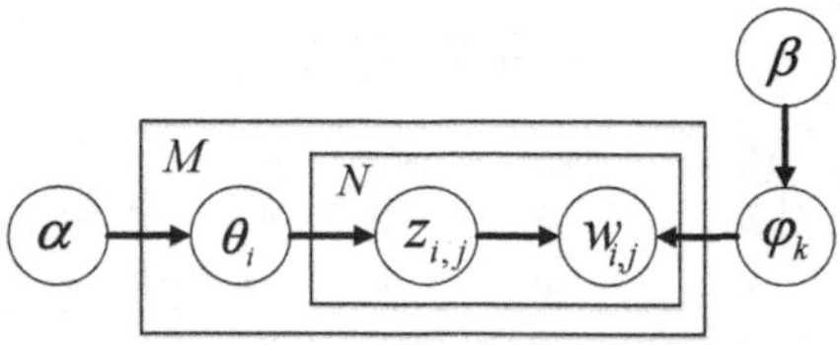

(a) LDA model structure diagram.

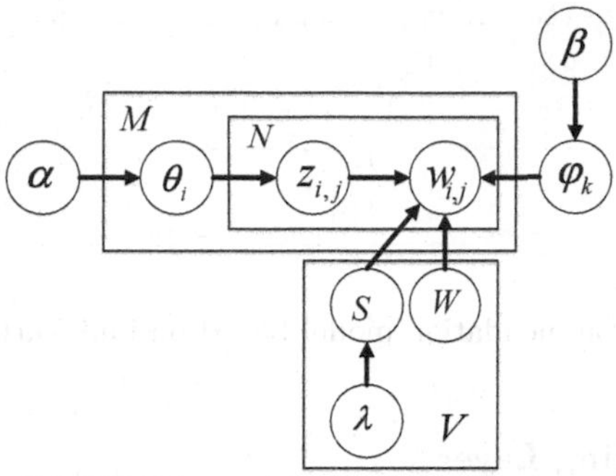

(b) WLDA model structure diagram.

Fig. 1. Comparison chart of LDA and WLDA model structure.

representations, the vectors are processed by the weighted averaging method, which enables the analysis of sentiment factors for text information of different lengths.

Paragraph Vector Representation Based on Item Content. We use a paragraph vector learning framework [14] for the distributed representation of short textual information of item descriptions. And the paragraph vectors are fed into the Bi-LSTM layer. The paragraph vector learning framework is a neural network-based model for implicit long text analysis that learns fixed-length feature representations from variable-length text fragments..

4 Text-Aware Recommendation Model Based on Multi-attention Neural Network

In this section, we proposed the TAMAN model for sentiment cause analysis. The architecture of TAMAN is shown in Fig. 2. Our model includes a text embedding layer, a Bi-LSTM layer, an attention layer, and a CNN layer. The input text of single word vectors and sentence vectors are encoded in the text embedding layer. The Bi-LSTM layer captures the contextual information of the text, while the CNN layer is used to determine the sentiment factors from the output mapping matrix and to classify and predict the sentiment factors.

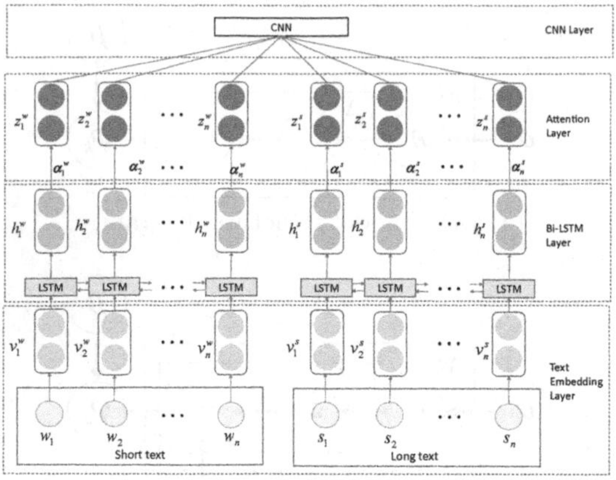

Fig. 2. Text-aware recommendation model based on multi-attention neural network

4.1 Text Embedding Layer

The text embedding layer consists of two parts, which obtain the word vector V^W and the sentence vector V^S from the user comment text and the natural language description text of the item, respectively, Where $V^W = \{v_1^w, v_2^w, \ldots, v_n^w\}$ and $V^S = \{v_1^s, v_2^s, \ldots, v_n^s\}$. The representation of high-frequency word vectors is obtained by analyzing the text of each user comment through the WLDA topic generation model. Distributed representation of long textual information of item descriptions through a paragraph vector learning framework. Finally, the word vector representation and the sentence vector representation are used as the embedding vectors of the Bi-LSTM layer.

4.2 Bi-LSTM Layer and Attention Layer

Bi-LSTM Layer. The input vector of the Bi-LSTM layer is the output vector of the text embedding layer, and the contextual information can be effectively sensed by the bi-directional LSTM. First we introduce LSTM and Bi-LSTM.

The most commonly used method for text information processing is Recurrent Neural Network (RNN), which gradient disappearance occurs when processing long sequences. To solve this problem, researchers proposed a Long and Short Term Memory (LSTM) network, which has been shown to perform better than standard RNN networks when processing textual data. LSTM enhances or forgets information by adding input gates, forgetting gates, and output gates to neurons, and one of the key extensions is that the weights of self-loops are context-dependent rather than fixed. The LSTM-based model can avoid the problem of gradient expansion and gradient disappearance by dynamically changing the values at different moments while ensuring the parameters remain unchanged. The calculation formula of each LSTM cell is as follows:

$$f_t = \sigma(W_f \cdot [h_{t-1}, x_t] + b_f) \tag{1}$$

$$i_t = \sigma(W_i \cdot [h_{t-1}, x_t] + b_i) \quad (2)$$

$$\widetilde{C} = tan(W_C \cdot [h_{t-1}, x_t] + b_C) \quad (3)$$

$$C_t = f_t * C_{t-1} + i_t * \widetilde{C} \quad (4)$$

$$O_t = \sigma(W_o \cdot [h_{t-1}, x_t] + b_o) \quad (5)$$

$$h_t = O_t * tan(C_t) \quad (6)$$

In Eqs. (1–6), f_t denotes the forgetting gate, i_t denotes the input gate, and O_t denotes the output gate, $\widetilde{C}_t$ represents the state of the cell at the previous moment, C_t represents the state of the current cell, and h_{t-1} represents the output of the cell at the previous moment, h_t indicates the output of the current unit.σ is the logistic sigmoid function, W_f,W_i,W_C,W_o,b_f,b_i,b_C,b_o is training parameters. We use bidirectional LSTM to obtain word features. $H = (h_1^w, h_2^w, \ldots, h_n^w)$ concatenated from both directions.

Bi-LSTM is a bi-directional LSTM. In Bi-LSTM information is read from forward and reverse directions respectively. The output can be generated from the past and future contexts by reading the information in the forward and reverse directions. The forward LSTM processes the word vector information from w_1 to w_n and the reverse LSTM processes the word vector information from w_n to w_1. For word vector w_1 , $\overrightarrow{h}_i^w$ and $\overleftarrow{h}_i^w$ denote the word vector features obtained from the forward LSTM and the backward LSTM, respectively. Then h can be expressed as follows $h_i^w = (\overrightarrow{h}_i^w \odot \overleftarrow{h}_i^w)$. Where h_i^w is the output of the i-th word. The $\odot$ is a concatenation function for the user to combine two outputs.

In addition, the vector of the i-th word is expressed as $\pounds^\circ$ $\overrightarrow{h}_t = \overrightarrow{LSTM}(\overrightarrow{h}_{t-1}, v_t, \theta)$, $\overleftarrow{h}_t = \overleftarrow{LSTM}(\overleftarrow{h}_{t+1}, v_t, \theta)$, Where $\overrightarrow{h}_t$,$\overleftarrow{h}_t \in \mathbb{R}^k$,$h_t \in \mathbb{R}^{2k}$, k is the number of hidden units in LSTM.

Similarly, we can obtain the hidden states $(h_t^s, t \in \{1, 2, \ldots, n\})$ of the sentence vector V^s and the emotion sentence vector representation h^s generated by Bi-LSTM according to above process.

Attention Layer. Although we embed the word vector representation and sentence vector representation into the Bi-LSTM layer, some of these information are useless, and a single Bi-LSTM network will have difficulty in filtering them effectively, which will interfere with the final prediction accuracy. Since the attention mechanism can make the connection between implicit layers closer, the importance of information can be emphasized by assigning weight coefficients to improve the prediction accuracy.

In this section, we detail the embedding of multiple attention mechanisms, which includes the Bi-LSTM attention mechanism based on word vectors and the Bi-LSTM attention mechanism based on sentence vectors. In Fig. 3, our model can selectively learn the important vector representations from the input sequences with correlations between the input and output sequences. The attention mechanism calculates the weight values corresponding to the different variables through the intermediate variables of the Bi-LSTM implicit layer, where the weight values indicate the importance of the vectors. And the key feature information will be given a higher weight value. Specifically, we obtain the relevance of the tth word of the word vector and sentence vector to the whole short text of user comments as follows:

$$a_t = \frac{exp(f(h_t^w, h_t^s))}{\sum_{i=1}^{N} exp(f(h_t^w, h_t^s))}, t \in \{1, 2, \ldots, n\} \tag{7}$$

where h_t^w and h_t^s are the representations of the tth word vector and sentence vector obtained by Bi-LSTM, and α_t is the variable weight value to indicate the degree of sentiment importance. Finally we can obtain the sentiment-oriented representation matrix $Z \in \mathbb{R}^{2k \times n}$ as a candidate value:

$$Z = [\alpha_1 * h_1, \alpha_2 * h_2, \ldots, \alpha_n * h_n] \tag{8}$$

The attention mechanism filters out some of the noise and builds a correlation model between the word vector and the sentence vector, which provides a useful representation vector for the CNN layer sentiment extraction.

4.3 CNN Layer

The CNN layer is used to automatically extract key features from the text. the CNN layer consists of a convolutional layer, a subsampling layer and a representation layer. This is shown in Fig. 4.

Experiments show that our model yields the best results with a three-layer convolutional structure, where the window size is set to (2,2), to ensure that the model is over-fitted in the future, we set the dropout value to 0.3. In the pooling layer, we use max pooling and set stride to 2 to capture the main features in the original feature map. In the fully connected layer, we used the softmax function to classify the output, producing values between 1 (positive sentiment) and 0 (negative sentiment).

5 Experiments

In this section, we evaluate the performance of the proposed TANMN model in sentiment analysis.

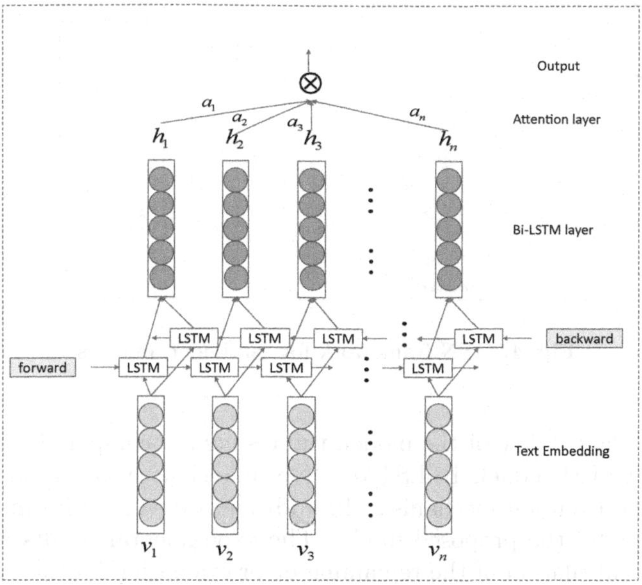

Fig. 3. Bi-LSTM with attention

5.1 Dataset

In this paper, extensive experiments are conducted on the Amazon product [16] dataset. Table 1 gives the statistics of the dataset.

5.2 Metrics

In this work, we evaluate the sentiment analysis of textual information based on user comments using the accuracy rate in information retrieval . The loss function is shown as follow:

$$MSE = \frac{1}{m}\sum_{i=1}^{m}(y_i - \hat{y}_i)^2 \tag{9}$$

where y_i and $\hat{y}_i$ denote the measured displacement value and the calculated value of the model, respectively. m is the number of the data series.

Table 1. Amazon product data statistical data table.

Data set statistics	Number
Number of user reviews	346867770
Number of users	6643669
Number of items	2441063
Timestamp	1995.07–2013.03

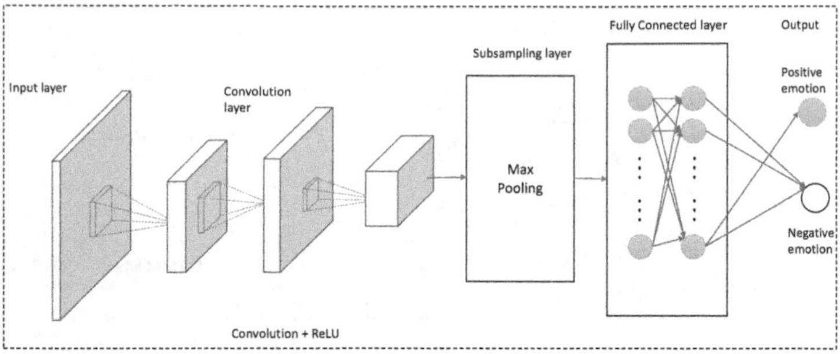

Fig. 4. CNN framework for sentiment analysis.

To verify the validity of the model, the results are compared with the knotted rows of LSTM model, Bi-LSTM, RNN model with attention mechanism, and Bi-LSTM attention mechanism. In addition, we employ Adam to optimize the parameters of the proposed model. The experimental results are shown in Table 2. The calculation of the remaining error evaluation indexes are shown as follows:

$$RMSE = \sqrt{\frac{1}{m}\sum_{i=1}^{m}(y_i - \hat{y}_i)^2} \tag{10}$$

$$SMAPE = \frac{100\%}{m}\sum_{i=1}^{m}\frac{|\hat{y}_i - y_i|}{(|\hat{y}_i| + |y_i|)/2} \tag{11}$$

$$MAPE = \frac{100\%}{m}\sum_{i=1}^{m}\left|\frac{\hat{y}_i - y_i}{y_i}\right| \tag{12}$$

$$MAE = \frac{1}{m}\sum_{i=1}^{m}|\hat{y}_i - y_i| \tag{13}$$

RMSE, MAE, MAPE, and SMAPE denote root mean square error, mean absolute error, mean absolute percentage error, and symmetric mean absolute percentage error, respectively.

In Table 2, the MSE of the Bi-LSTM model using the attention mechanism model is reduced from 1.03 to 0.69 compared to the statistical model, which is a 66.9% reduction. The MAE value in the case of Bi-LSTM with the attention mechanism model is also reduced by about 4% compared to the LSTM model, indicating that Bi-LSTM has some advantages over LSTM for long sequences. Also, the error of the Bi-LSTM model with the attention mechanism is reduced by about 0.3% compared to the Bi-LSTM model, indicating that the attention mechanism helps to improve the prediction accuracy through the weight distribution among the influencing factors.

In addition, we use Accuracy, Precision, Recall, and F-measure as performance metrics for comparative analysis. As shown in Fig. 5.

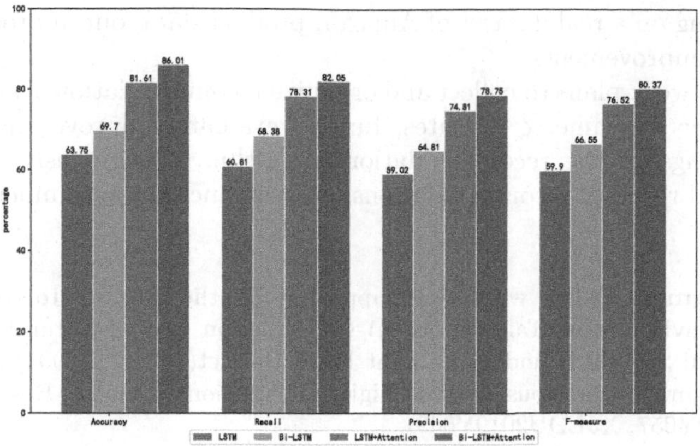

Fig. 5. Comparison of accuracy, precision, recall and F-measure in different methods.

Table 2. Statistical table of prediction models accuracy.

Method	Fuction				
	MSE	RMSE	MAE	MAPE	SMAPE
LSTM	1.06	1.03	0.81	2.56%	2.62%
Bi-LSTM	1.03	0.99	0.72	2.33%	2.38%
LSTM+Attention	0.69	0.67	0.68	2.06%	2.09%
Bi-LSTM+Attention	0.62	0.63	0.62	2.03%	2.05%

The results show that compared with other models, the Bi-LSTM model of the attention mechanism model proposed in this paper obtained the highest accuracy of 86.01%, recall of 82.05%, prediction accuracy of 78.75%, and F-measure of 80.37%.

6 Conclusion

Recommender systems are effective in solving the information overload problem. In this paper, based on the analysis of user behavior preferences, we mainly deep-mined the sentiment analysis of text information, deeply fused the short text of user review text and the long text of item content, and built a Text-aware recommendation model based on multi-attention neural network. Specifically, TAMAN first extracts vector representations of word vectors and sentence vectors by WLDA and sentence vector. Then obtains representations of words and their contextual information by Bi-LSTM, and captures important words that are more likely to contain sentiment reasons by designing a multi-attention mechanism. Finally, the lexical representations are transformed into high-level feature inputs and input to the CNN layer for sentiment reason recognition. By experimenting on a real dataset of Amazon product data, our approach achieves substantial improvements.

Our next work plans to collect and organize recommendation system datasets from Internet e-commerce websites, further evaluate, improve and parameter tuning settings of the recommendation algorithm, continuously improve the accuracy and recall of recommendations, and enhance the recommendation performance.

Acknowledgments. The work was supported by the 2021 Autonomous Region Innovation Environment (Talents, Bases) Construction Special-Natural Science Program (Natural Science Foundation) Joint Fund Project(2021D01C004) and the 2019 Xinjiang Uygur Autonomous Region Higher Education Scientific Research Project (XJEDU2019Y057, XJEDU2019Y049).

References

1. Cai, Y., Cai, H., Wan, X.: Multi-modal sarcasm detection in twitter with hierarchical fusion model. In: 57th Conference of the Association for Computational Linguistics (ACL), Florence, Italy, vol. 1, pp. 2506–2515 (2019)
2. Chen, C., Zhang, M., Liu, Y., Ma, S.: Neural attentional rating regression with review-level explanations. In: World Wide Web Conferenc on World Wide Web (WWW), Lyon, France, pp. 1583–1592 (2018)
3. Chen, L., Chen, G., Wang, F.: Recommender systems based on user reviews: the state of the art. User Model. User Adapt. Interact. **25**(2), 99–154 (2015)
4. Chen, Q., Hu, Q., Huang, J.X., He, L., An, W.: Enhancing recurrent neural networks with positional attention for question answering. In: 40th International ACM SIGIR Conference on Research and Development in Information Retrieval, Tokyo, Japan, pp. 993–996 (2017)
5. Dai, W., Qiu, L., Wu, A., Qiu, M.: Cloud infrastructure resource allocation for big data applications. IEEE Trans. Big Data **4**(3), 313–324 (2016)
6. Dai, W., Qiu, M., Qiu, L., Chen, L., Wu, A.: Who moved my data? privacy protection in smartphones. IEEE Commun. Mag. **55**(1), 20–25 (2017)
7. Gai, K., Qiu, M.: Optimal resource allocation using reinforcement learning for IoT content-centric services. Appl. Soft Comput. **70**, 12–21 (2018)
8. Gai, K., Qiu, M.: Reinforcement learning-based content-centric services in mobile sensing. IEEE Netw. **32**(4), 34–39 (2018)
9. Gai, K., Qiu, M., Zhao, H., Sun, X.: Resource management in sustainable cyber-physical systems using heterogeneous cloud computing. IEEE Trans. Sustain. Comput. **3**(2), 60–72 (2018)
10. Gui, L., Hu, J., He, Y., Xu, R., Lu, Q., Du, J.: A question answering approach to emotion cause extraction. CoRR abs/1708.05482 (2017)
11. Gui, L., Xu, R., Lu, Q., Wu, D., Zhou, Y.: Emotion cause extraction: a challenging task with corpus construction. In: 5th National Conference Social Media Processing (SMP), Nanchang, China, vol. 669, pp. 98–109 (2016)
12. Han, X., Shi, C., Wang, S., Yu, P.S., Song, L.: Aspect-level deep collaborative filtering via heterogeneous information networks. In: International Joint Conference on Artificial Intelligence (IJCAI), Stockholm, Sweden, pp. 3393–3399 (2018)

13. Hermann, K.M., et al.: Teaching machines to read and comprehend. In: Annual Conference on Neural Information Processing Systems, Montreal, Canada, pp. 1693–1701 (2015)
14. Le, Q.V., Mikolov, T.: Distributed representations of sentences and documents. In: 31th International Conference on Machine Learning (ICML), pp. 1188–1196 (2014)
15. Li, H., Min, M.R., Ge, Y., Kadav, A.: A context-aware attention network for interactive question answering. In: 23rd ACM SIGKDD International Conference on Knowledge Discovery and Data Mining, Halifax, Canada, pp. 927–935 (2017)
16. McAuley, J.J., Leskovec, J.: Hidden factors and hidden topics: understanding rating dimensions with review text. In: The Seventh Conference on Recommender Systems (RecSys), pp. 165–172 (2013)
17. Paul, E.: An-argument-for-basic-emotions. EMOT **6**(3–4), 169–200 (1992)
18. Qiu, M., Zhang, K., Huang, M.: An empirical study of web interface design on small display devices. In: IEEE/WIC/ACM International Conference on Web Intelligence (WI 2004), pp. 29–35 (2004)
19. Rocktäschel, T., Grefenstette, E., Hermann, K.M., Kociský, T., Blunsom, P.: Reasoning about entailment with neural attention. In: 4th International Conference on Learning Representations (ICLR), San Juan, Puerto Rico (2016)
20. Schafer, J.B., Frankowski, D., Herlocker, J., Sen, S.: Collaborative filtering recommender systems. In: Brusilovsky, P., Kobsa, A., Nejdl, W. (eds.) The Adaptive Web. LNCS, vol. 4321, pp. 291–324. Springer, Heidelberg (2007). https://doi.org/10.1007/978-3-540-72079-9_9
21. Wu, Y., DuBois, C., Zheng, A.X., Ester, M.: Collaborative denoising auto-encoders for top-n recommender systems. In: ACM International Conference on Web Search and Data Mining, San Francisco, USA, pp. 153–162 (2016)
22. Yu, X., Rong, W., Zhang, Z., Ouyang, Y., Xiong, Z.: Multiple level hierarchical network-based clause selection for emotion cause extraction. IEEE Access **7**, 9071–9079 (2019)
23. Zhang, Q., Huang, T., Zhu, Y., Qiu, M.: A case study of sensor data collection and analysis in smart city: provenance in smart food supply chain. Int. J. Distrib. Sensor Netw. **9**(11), 382132 (2013)
24. Zhang, W., Yuan, Q., Han, J., Wang, J.: Collaborative multi-level embedding learning from reviews for rating prediction. In: Joint Conferenc on Artificial Intelligence (IJCAI) New York, USA, pp. 2986–2992 (2016)
25. Zhang, Y., Tan, Y., Zhang, M., Liu, Y., Chua, T., Ma, S.: Catch the black sheep: unified framework for shilling attack. In: International Joint Conference on Artificial Intelligence (IJCAI), Argentina, pp. 2408–2414 (2015)
26. Zheng, L., Noroozi, V., Yu, P.S.: Joint deep modeling of users and items using reviews for recommendation. In: ACM International Conference on Web Search and Data Mining (WSDM), Cambridge, UK, pp. 425–434 (2017)
27. Zhu, M., et al.: Public vehicles for future urban transportation. IEEE Trans. Intell. Transp. Syst. **17**(12), 3344–3353 (2016)

Chinese Named Entity Recognition Based on Gated Graph Neural Network

Qing Zhong and Yan Tang(✉)

School of Computer and Information Science, Southwest University, Chongqing, China
ytang@swu.edu.cn

Abstract. Most Chinese Named Entity Recognition (CNER) models based on deep learning are implemented based on long short-term memory networks (LSTM) and conditional random fields (CRF). The serialized structure of LSTM is easily affected by word ambiguity and lack of word boundary information. In this regard, we propose a Chinese named entity recognition model based on a gated graph neural network (GGNN).We use the BERT model to generate pre-training encoding vectors of characters, and introduce global nodes to capture the global information in the sentence. Finally, we exploits multiple interactions between the characters in the graph structure, all matching words, and the entire sentence to solve the problem of word ambiguity.The comparative experimental results on the three CNER datasets show that the GGNN model has a better effect on named entity recognition.

Keywords: Chinese named entity recognition · Gated graph neural network · BERT

1 Introduction

Named Entity Recognition (NER) is a basic task in natural language processing (NLP). Its main research content is to identify proper nouns such as names of people, places, and organizations in the text to be processed. NER as one of the key technologies of natural language processing, has been widely used in information retrieval [1], relation extraction [2], question answering systems [3] and other fields. At present, the standard method of the most advanced model of English NER is to solve the task as a sequence labeling problem, and use long short-term memory network (LSTM) and conditional random field model (CRF) to capture contextual information at the word level [4]. However, compared with English, the CNER task is more complicated, there are no segmentation symbols that represent word boundaries in Chinese text, and it is more difficult to recognize entity boundaries compared to the subtasks of entity category labeling.

Therefore, for Chinese without natural separators, Chinese word segmentation (CWS) is first applied to obtain word boundaries, and then a word-level sequence labeling model similar to the English NER model is used to identify entities [5]. Moreover, most CNER models are based on LSTM and CRF to sequentially encode sentences.

H. Qiu et al. (Eds.): KSEM 2021, LNAI 12815, pp. 604–613, 2021.
https://doi.org/10.1007/978-3-030-82136-4_49

However, the underlying structure of the language is not strictly sequential [6]. The middle characters of overlapping fuzzy strings can form words with the left and right sides of the characters. Therefore, such a model will encounter the problem of word ambiguity. For example, as shown in Fig. 1, the mayor and the Yangtze River Bridge, they both contain the same character "Long", the LSTM-based model processes the characters sequentially in a serial manner, which is similar to reading Chinese, and the characters are assigned to the left word Time has a higher priority. Therefore, Ma [7] suggested that overlapping ambiguities must be resolved using sentence context information.

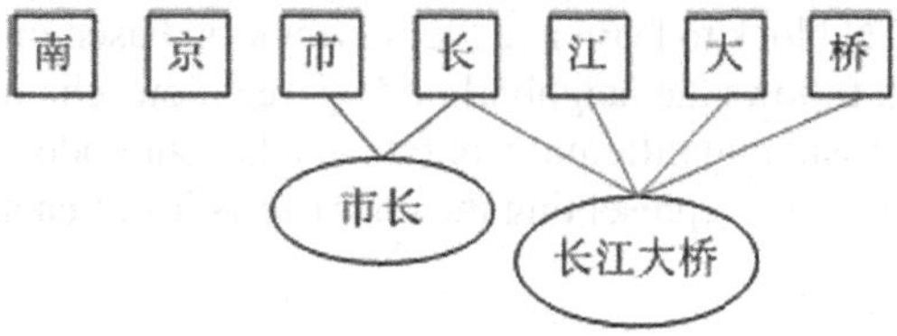

Fig. 1. Example sentences that integrate recent context words

Aiming at the problem that LSTM chain structure is prone to word ambiguity, a Chinese named entity recognition model (GGNN) based on gated graph neural network is proposed. We use the BERT model to generate pre-training encoding vectors of characters, introduce global nodes to obtain global information then construct a gated graph neural network to represent the corresponding characters and words. Through multiple interactions between the characters, all matching words and the entire sentence global node information in the graph structure, the word ambiguity problem can be solved. The comparative experimental results on the three CNER datasets show that the GGNN model has a better effect on NER.

2 Related Work

2.1 CNER Model Based on Neural Network

Recently, deep learning has developed rapidly and received increasingly attention, and neural network methods are widely used in many NLP tasks, including the CNER task [8–11].Neural network approaches, especially for BILSTM-CRF model can significantly improve the performance of the CNER task. Cao [12] applied the adversarial transfer learning framework to integrate the word boundary information shared by the task into CNER. Zhang [13] used lattice LSTM to integrate word information into a character-based model. Zhu [14] implemented CNN and Bi-GRU with a global self-attention structure to capture character-level feature information and context information. Gong [15] used the model to construct a hierarchical tree structure composed of characters, words, and predicted words from context perception to represent each sentence in CNER; Johnson [16] proposed the model combines character information, word information, and position information to obtain the dependency between them.

2.2 Graph Neural Network

The concept of graph neural network was first proposed by Gori [17]. Initially, Graph Neural Network (GNN) was a deep learning model designed to handle graphics-related tasks in an end-to-end manner. At present, graph neural networks have been successfully applied to some text classification tasks [18]. Peng [19] proposed a GCN-based deep learning model for text classification, and Zhang [20] proposed to use dependency parse trees to construct relations To extract the graph, Gui [21] exploited a rethinking mechanism to select candidate words in the dictionary, and corrects the selected word sequence through the feedback output of the upper network; and Tang [22] proposed to introduce a global attention GCN block to learn node representation based on global context. The graph neural network follows the neighborhood aggregation scheme, which aggregates node information by assigning different weights to adjacent nodes or associated edges, which is conducive to better representing the characteristics of each node.

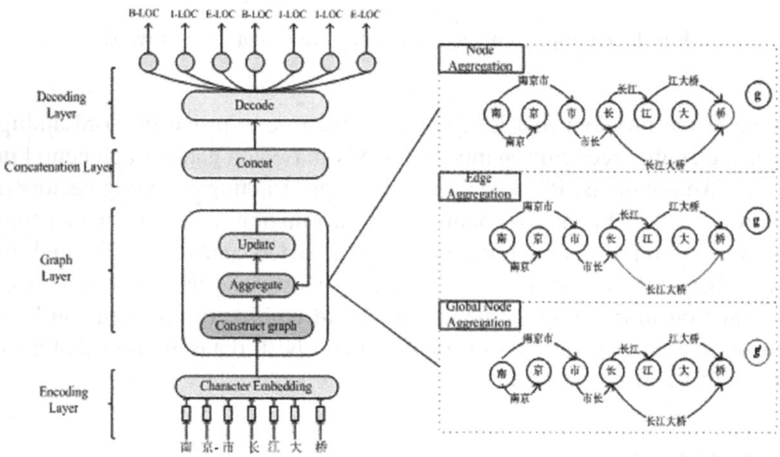

Fig. 2. Main structure of the GGNN model. The left side shows the overall architecture, including an encoding layer, a graph layer, a concatenation layer, and a decoding layer. On the right side, we show the details of graph aggregation process, we use blue lines to indicate aggregated nodes, edges and global nodes.

3 Model

The (GGNN) model is shown in Fig. 2. It consists of four parts: Encoding Layer, Graph Layer, Concatenation Layer and Decoding Layer.

3.1 Encoding Layer

The GGNN model uses BERT [23] to convert each character of the input sentence into a corresponding pre-training encoding vector. The input sentence sequence is S =

$\{c_1, c_2, ..., c_n\}$, c_i represents the i-th character in the sentence, and n represents the length of the sentence. The pre-training coding vector obtained by the BERT model is: $X = \{x_1, x_2, ..., x_n\}$, for character c_i, its corresponding pre-training coding vector is x_i.

3.2 Graph Layer

Construct Graph

we use a directed graph $G = (V, E)$ to represent a sentence, V is a collection of all nodes, each $v_i \in V$ represents a node in the graph, and the state of each node represents the characteristics of the character in the entire text sequence; E is the set of all edges, and the state of each edge represents the corresponding potential word composed of certain two nodes, a global node g is set to capture the global information.

Aggregate

Node aggregation: For node v_i, according to the neighborhood aggregation scheme, we use the relevant edge information composed of the node and the information of other nodes connected to it on these edges to aggregate the relevant information of the node. An attention mechanism is introduced to obtain the different influence of different edges and other nodes on the node. The aggregation formula for node v_i is as follows:

$$\left(v_i^t\right)' = \sigma\left(\alpha\left(v_i^t, \left\{\forall_x\left(v_x^t; e_{x,i}^t\right)\right\}\right)\right) \tag{1}$$

';' indicates the splicing operation, $e_{x,i}^t$ indicates the edge associated with the node v_i, and $\forall x\left(v_x^t; e_{x,i}^t\right)$ indicates the splicing of all the nodes connected to the node and the information of the edge. The α function represents the multi-head attention function, σ represents the sigmoid activation function.

Edge Aggregation: for edge $e_{i,j}$, consider using the information of this edge and the features $V_{i,j}^t = \left(v_i^t; ...; v_j^t\right)$ of the related nodes that make up this edge to aggregate the relevant information of this edge. The calculation formula for the aggregation of side $e_{i,j}$ is as follows:

$$\left(e_{i,j}^t\right)' = \alpha\left(e_{i,j}^t, V_{i,j}^t\right) \tag{2}$$

Global node Aggregation: Battaglia [25] proposed setting a global node to aggregate the information of each node and the edge information of the related edges, which helps to make full use of the global information. $V_{1,n}^t = \left(v_1^t; ...; v_n^t\right)$, g_c^t represents the global node and all nodes information aggregation, g_e^t represents the aggregation of the global node and all edge information, $(g_t)'$ is used to aggregate the node the edge information. The calculation formula for aggregated global information is as follows:

$g_e^t = \sigma\alpha\left(g^t, \left\{\forall e^t \in E\right\}\right), g_c^t = \sigma\alpha\left(g^t, V_{1,n}^t\right)$

$$\left(g^t\right)' = concat\left(g_c^t, g_e^t\right) \tag{3}$$

Update
For a general graph, it is a common practice to update the hidden representation of nodes based on recursion Li [26].

Representation and Update of Nodes: For node v_i, we exploit the information at the previous moment of the node to update each node in the graph in conjunction with the global node, and the formula is as follows:

$$h_{v_i}^t = concat\left(v_{i-1}^{t-1}, v_i^{t-1}\right), x_{v_i}^t = concat\left(\left(v_i^{t-1}\right)', \left(g^{t-1}\right)'\right).$$

$$m_{v^i}^t = \sigma\left(W^m x_{v_i}^t + U^m h_{v_i}^t + b^m\right), n_{v^i}^t = \sigma\left(W^n x_{v_i}^t + U^n h_{v_i}^t + b^n\right)$$

$$\tilde{v}_i^t = \tanh\left(W x_{v_i}^t + U\left(n_{v^i}^t * h_{v_i}^t\right) + b\right) // v_i^t = m_{v_i}^t * v_i^{t-1} + \left(1 - m_{v_i}^t\right) * \tilde{v}_i^t \quad (4)$$

$h_{v_i}^t$ represents the cascade of adjacent vectors of the context window,x_i^t represents the cascade of the aggregated information of the node and the aggregated information of g at time t − 1. W^m, U^m, b^m, W^n, U^n, b^n,W, V and b are all trainable parameters, the same as following, and gates $m_{v_i}^t$ and $n_{v_i}^t$ control the flow of information from the global information to v_i^t.

Representation and update of edges: For edge $e_{i,j}$, we use the information obtained after the aggregation of the edge at the last moment and the information obtained after the aggregation of the global node to update the edge. The formula is as follows:

$$x_{e_{i,j}}^t = concat\left(e_{i,j}^{t-1}, \left(g^{t-1}\right)'\right), n_{e_{i,j}}^t = \sigma\left(W^n x_{e_{i,j}}^t + U^n e_{i,j}^{t-1} + b^n\right)$$

$$\tilde{e}_{i,j}^t = \tanh\left(W x_{e_{i,j}}^t + U\left(n_{e_{i,j}}^t * e_{i,j}^{t-1}\right) + b\right), e_{i,j}^t = m_{e_{i,j}}^t * e_{i,j}^{t-1} + \left(1 - m_{e_{i,j}}^t\right) * \tilde{e}_{i,j}^t \quad (5)$$

$x_{e_{i,j}}^t$ represents the concatenation of the aggregated information of the edge and the aggregated information of the global node at time t − 1.

Representation and update of g: similarly, according to the information obtained after aggregation, the information obtained after the aggregation of the g at the last moment and the updated information of the g are used to update g. The formula is as follows:

$$m^t = \sigma\left(W^m\left(g^{t-1}\right)' + U^m g^{t-1} + b^m\right), n^t = \sigma\left(W^n\left(g^{t-1}\right)' + U^n g^{t-1} + b^n\right)$$

$$\tilde{g}^t = \tanh\left(W\left(g^{t-1}\right)' + U\left(n^t * g^{t-1}\right) + b\right), g^t = m^t * g^{t-1} + \left(1 - m^t\right) * \tilde{g}^t \quad (6)$$

$\left(g^{t-1}\right)'$ represents the g aggregated at t − 1, and g^{t-1} represents the g updated at t − 1.

3.3 Concatenation Layer

Gui proposed to construct the corresponding transposed graph [24], which has the same nodes as the original graph. G^T represents the transposition of the constructed graph. and the final output result $\hat{v}$ of node v_i is calculated as follows:

$$\hat{v}_i = concat(\overrightarrow{v_i^t}, \overleftarrow{v_i^t}) \quad (7)$$

3.4 Decoding Layer

Given the sequence of the final node state is $\hat{v} = \left(\hat{v_1}, \hat{v_2}, \ldots\ldots, \hat{v_n}\right)$, The prediction sequence is $y = (y_1, y_2, \ldots y_n)$, o_{i,y_i} represents the score of the y_i-th label of the character v_i, The conditional probability of the corresponding tag sequence y is as follows:

$$s(\hat{v}, y) = \sum\nolimits_{i=1}^{n} \left(o_{i,y_i} + T_{y_{i-1},y_i}\right)$$

$$p(y|x) = \frac{\exp^{s(\hat{v},y)}}{\sum_{\tilde{y} \in y_{\hat{v}}} \exp^{s(\hat{v},\tilde{y})}} \tag{8}$$

T is a matrix that records the scores of any two adjacent tags, and $\tilde{y}$ represents all possible tag sequences. When decoding, we use the Viterbi algorithm to find the tag sequence with the highest score as follows:

$$y^* = \underset{y \in y_{\hat{v}}}{\arg\max}\, s\left(\hat{v}, y\right), L = -\sum\nolimits_{i=1}^{n} \log p(y_i | \hat{v_i}) \tag{9}$$

4 Experiments

In order to verify the performance of the GGNN model, comparative experiments were carried out on three common Chinese named entity recognition datasets in the industry.

4.1 Experiment Settings

Evaluation Metrics and Datasets. To give an overall evaluation of models, we apply precision (P), recall (R), and F1 as our evaluation metrics in the experiments. To verify the effectiveness of our model, experiments are conducted on three datasets: Ontonotes [27], weibo NER [28] and MSRA [29]. The Ontonotes dataset and the MSRA dataset comes from Chinese news; Weibo NER comes from social media data. The statistics of each data set are shown in Table 1.

Table 1. Statistics of datasets.

Datasets	Train	Dev	Test
OntoNotes	15.7k	4.3k	4.3k
Weibo NER	1.4k	0.27k	0.27k
MSRA	46.4k	-	4.4k

Implementation Details. We use the Adam algorithm to optimize all trainable parameters, the initial learning rate is 0.005, and the Dropout rate is 0.5.

Table 2. Comparison experiment results (OntoNotes).

Input	Model	P	R	F1
Gold seg	Wang [8]	76.43	73.32	74.32
	Yang [9]	72.98	80.15	76.40
No seg	Lattice	76.35	71.56	73.88
	LSTM	76.40	72.60	74.45
	LR-CNN	75.05	72.29	73.64
	CAN-NER	67.41	62.54	64.88
	Char	64.25	61.74	63.06
	baseline	77.77	76.32	77.04
	Word	76.59	75.43	75.87
	baseline	**78.01**	**78.66**	**77.92**
	HiLSTM			
	WC-GCN			
	GGNN			

4.2 Overall Results

In this part, we compare GGNN with the following models, which are listed as follows:

Lattice LSTM [13]: This model exploited characters as the basic processing unit and the lattice structure to learn contextual information;

LR-CNN [23]: This model exploited a rethinking mechanism to select candidate words in the dictionary;

CAN-NER [14]: This model implemented CNN and Bi-GRU with a global self-attention structure to capture character-level feature information and context information;

HiLSTM [15]: The model constructed a hierarchical tree structure composed of characters, and predicted words from context perception to represent each sentence;

WC-GCN [22]: The model introduced a global attention GCN block to learn node representation based on global context.

Table 2 and Table 3 shows the results of each model on three datasets. Form the comparison, we can see that: the F1 index of the GGNN model is higher than that of the comparison model, and the effect of NER is better.

4.3 Performance Against Sentence Length

In order to evaluate the performance of the GGNN model in processing sentences of different lengths, the OntoNotes dataset is divided into six groups according to the length of the sentences for comparative experiments.

The comparison result is shown in Fig. 3. As the sentence length increases, the F1 value of Lattice LSTM and GGNN mode decreases, but when it exceeds 80, the named entity recognition effect of the GGNN model is better, which shows that the global information can be better obtained under the graph structure.

Table 3. Comparison experiment results (MSRA&&Weibo NER).

Model	MSRA			Weibo NER
	P	R	F1	F1
Cao [12]	91.73	89.58	90.64	58.70
Lattice LSTM	93.57	92.79	93.18	58.79
LR-CNN	94.50	92.93	93.74	56.64
CAN-NER	93.53	92.42	92.97	59.31
Char baseline	89.61	86.98	88.37	54.99
Word baseline	88.48	85.60	87.04	50.25
HiLSTM	94.83	93.61	94.22	63.79
WC-GCN	94.82	93.98	94.40	63.63
GGNN	**94.90**	**94.32**	**94.61**	**64.26**

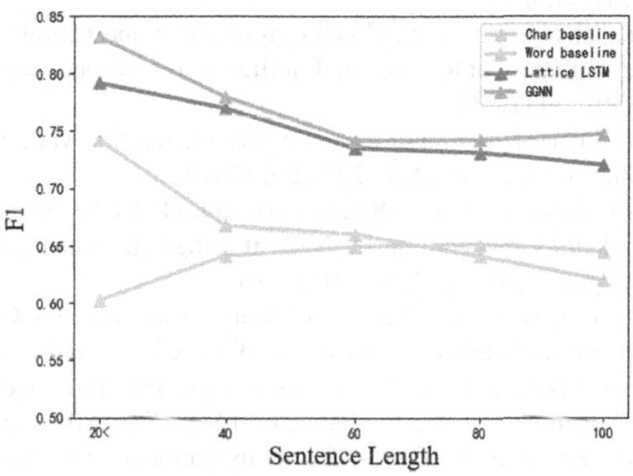

Fig. 3. The trend of F1 score with the increase of sentence length.

5 Conclusion

In this paper, we propose a Chinese named entity recognition model based on a gated graph neural network (GGNN). We construct a graph neural network to represent the relationship between characters and words. Through multiple iterations of aggregation, multiple interactions between the characters in the graph structure, all matching words and the entire sentence are used to solve the problem of word ambiguity; The comparative experiment results on the three CNER datasets show that the proposed model has better named entity recognition effect. In the future work, we consider combining the expressive power of language modeling with the large amount of knowledge contained in the semantic network to generate high-quality representations of word semantics.

References

1. Yu, C., Li, X,. et al.: Event extraction via dynamic multi-pooling convolutional neural networks. In: Proceedings of the 53rd Annual Meeting of the ACL, pp. 167–176 (2015)
2. Razvan, B., Raymond, M.: A shortest path dependency kernel for relation extraction. In: Proceedings of HLT/EMNLP, pp. 724–731 (2005)
3. Diefenbach, D,. Lopez, V., Singh, K., et al.: Core techniques of question answering systems over knowledge bases, pp. 529–569 (2018)
4. Lample, G., Ballesteros, M., Subramanian, S., et al.: Neural Architectures for Named Entity Recognition. arXiv:1603.01360 (2016)
5. He, H., Sun, X.: F-score driven max margin neural network for named entity recognition in chinese social media. arXiv:1611.04234 (2016)
6. Yi, S., Shawn, T., Alessandro, S., et al.: Ordered neurons: integrating tree structures into recurrent neural networks. In: Proceedings of ICLR (2019)
7. Ma, G., Xing, L., Keith, R.: Word segmentation of overlapping ambiguous strings during chinese reading (2014)
8. Wang, M., Che, W., Manning, C.: Effective bilingual constraints for semi-supervised learning of named entity recognizers. In: Proceedings of the AAAI Conference on Artificial Intelligence, pp. 27(1) (2013)
9. Yang, J., Teng, Z., Zhang, M., et al.: Combining discrete and neural features for sequence labeling. In: International Conference on Intelligent Text Processing and Computational Linguistics, pp. 140–154 (2016)
10. Zhou, J., Qu, W., Zhang, F.: Chinese named entity recognition via joint identification and categorization. Chin. J. Electron. **22**(2), 225–230 (2013)
11. Dong, C., Zhang, J., Zong, C., et al.: Character-based LSTM-CRF with radical-level features for Chinese named entity recognition. In: Natural Language Understanding and Intelligent Applications. Springer, Cham, pp. 239–250 (2016)
12. Cao, P., Chen, Y., Liu, K., et al.: Adversarial transfer learning for Chinese named entity recogni-tion with self-attention mechanism. In: Proceedings of the 2018 Conference on Empirical Methods in Natural Language Processing, pp. 182–192 (2018)
13. Zhang, Y., Yang, J.: Chinese NER using lattice LSTM. arXiv:1805.02023 (2018)
14. Zhu, Y., Wang, G., Karlsson, B.: CAN-NER: convolutional attention network for Chinese named entity recognition. arXiv:1904.02141 (2019)
15. Gong, C., Li, Z., Xia, Q., et al.: Hierarchical LSTM with char-subword-word tree-structure representation for Chinese named entity recognition pp. 1–15 (2020)
16. Johnson, S., Shen, S., Liu, Y.: CWPC_BiAtt: Character–Word–Position Combined BiLSTM-Attention for Chinese Named Entity Recognition. Information **11**(1) (2020)
17. Gori, M., Monfardini, G., Scarselli, F.: A new model for learning in graph do-mains. In: Proceedings of IEEE International Joint Conference on Neural Networks, pp. 729–734 (2005)
18. Veličković, P., Cucurull, G., Casanova, A., et al.: Graph attention networks. arXiv:1710.10903 (2017)
19. Peng, H., Li, J., He, Y., et al.: Large-scale hierarchical text classification with recursively regular-ized deep graph-cnn. In: Proceedings of the 2018 World Wide Web Conference, pp. 1063–1072 (2018)
20. Zhang, Y., Qi, P., Manning, C.: Graph convolution over pruned dependency trees improves relation extraction. arXiv:1809.10185 (2018)
21. Gui, T., Ma, R., Zhang, Q., et al.: CNN-Based Chinese NER with Lexicon Rethinking. In: IJCAI, pp. 4982–4988 (2019)
22. Tang, Z., Wan, B., Yang, L.: Word-Character Graph Convolution Network for Chinese Named Entity Recognition, pp. 1520–1532 (2020)

23. Devlin, J., Chang, M.W., Lee, K., et al.: Bert: pre-training of deep bidirectional transformers for language understanding. arXiv:1810.04805 (2018)
24. Gui, T., Zou, Y., Zhang, Q., et al.: A lexicon-based graph neural network for Chinese NER. In: Proceedings of the 2019 Conference on EMNLP/IJCNLP, pp. 1040--1050 (2019)
25. Battaglia, P., Hamrick, J.B., Bapst, V., et al.: Relational inductive biases, deep learning, and graph networks. arXiv:1806.01261 (2018)
26. Li, Y., Tarlow, D., Brockschmidt, M., et al.: Gated graph sequence neural networks. arXiv: 1511.05493 (2015)
27. Weischedel, R., Pradhan, S., Ramshaw, L., et al.: OntoNotes Release 2.0 (2008)
28. Peng, N,. Dredze, M.: Named entity recognition for Chinese social media with jointly trained embeddings. In: Proceedings of the 2015 Conference on EMNLP, pp. 548–554 (2015)
29. Levow, G.: The third international Chinese language processing bakeoff: word segmentation and named entity recognition. In: Proceedings of the Fifth SIGHAN Workshop on Chinese Language Processing, pp. 108–117 (2006)

Learning a Similarity Metric Discriminatively with Application to Ancient Character Recognition

Xuxing Liu[1], Xiaoqin Tang[1], and Shanxiong Chen[1,2](✉)

[1] College of Computer and Information Science, Southwest University, Chongqing 400715, China

[2] Chongqing Key Lab of Automated Reasoning and Cognition, Chongqing Institute of Green and Intelligent Technology, Chinese Academy of Sciences, Chongqing 400714, China

Abstract. The process of learning good representation in deep learning may prove difficult when the data is insufficient. In this paper, we propose a Siamese similarity network for one-shot ancient character recognition based on a similarity learning method to directly learn input similarity, and then use the trained model to establish one shot classification task for recognition. Multi-scale fusion backbone structure and embedded structure are proposed in the network to improve the model's ability to extract features. we also propose the soft similarity contrast loss function for the first time. It ensures the optimization of similar images with higher similarity and different classes of images with greater differences while reducing the over-optimization of back-propagation leading to model overfitting. A large number of experiments show that our proposed method has achieved high-efficiency discriminative performance, and obtained the best performance over the methods of traditional deep learning and other classic one-shot learning.

Keywords: Siamese network · Similarity learning · One-shot learning · Ancient character recognition

1 Introduction

Ancient characters have far-reaching research value as treasures that record ancient history, economy, culture, and scientific and technological development. After long-term efforts of paleographers, more and more ancient character materials have been sorted out. However, researchers who use computers to solve ancient character recognition are also discouraged by the lack of relevant domain knowledge. Unfortunately, even for ancient character researchers with lots of domain knowledge, it is very time-consuming to identify these unmarked ancient characters and even discover new ones. The study of ancient character recognition by computer can not only greatly improve the repetitive behavior of manual processing of character identification, but also efficiently explore the constant pattern of characters in the historical changes by means of neural networks, which can effectively help researchers to conduct further investigation of history and culture.

H. Qiu et al. (Eds.): KSEM 2021, LNAI 12815, pp. 614–626, 2021.
https://doi.org/10.1007/978-3-030-82136-4_50

In order to eliminate the dependence on a large amount of data, few shot learning is becoming a hot spot for researchers in various fields [1–3], but there is almost no application in the field of ancient character recognition. In particular, the task of using a single sample to recognize the pattern is called one shot learning [4], that is, to recognize the category matched by the test image in the support set composed of only one picture in each category. In areas where it is difficult to collect lots of training data, such as human face and ancient characters, the method of one-shot learning is very desirable.

Considering the many problems in ancient character recognition such as insufficient amount of data, more similar characters of the same kind of variants and similar characters of different classes. Drawing on the Siamese network-based one-shot image recognition method proposed by Koch [5], this paper specifically improves it based on the problems in ancient characters and proposes Siamese similarity network (SSN) for end-to-end one-shot recognition of ancient characters.

Overall, this work has two main contributions: First, this paper proposes for the first time a Siamese similarity network framework that does not rely on specific domain knowledge to solve the insufficient data and variant character recognition problems in ancient character recognition. Second, this paper proposes the soft similarity contrast loss function for the first time. It ensures the optimization of similar images with higher similarity and different classes of images with greater differences while reducing the over-optimization of back-propagation leading to model overfitting. This not only improves recognition accuracy of similar images of different classes, but also makes an important contribution to similarity models and metric learning methods.

The remainder of the paper is organized as follows. Section 2 briefly presents related previous works in ancient character recognition and one-shot learning. Section 3 explain the proposed method in detail. Datasets and experiments have been introduced in Sect. 4. We conclude the paper while discuss the future work and potential applications in Sect. 5.

2 Related Work

Currently, deep learning [6] has reached state-of-the-art performance on various pattern recognition tasks, especially on visual classification [7]. Compared with traditional methods based on rules and manually designed features, deep convolutional networks [8] have a greater advantage in terms of generalization ability and performance in processing images. Ghanim et al. [9] used hierarchical clustering techniques and ranking algorithms to rank cluster members, and finally studied the impact of six different deep convolutional neural networks on Arabic character recognition. However, when these neural network-based algorithms are forced to make predictions on a small amount of available data, they tend to crash due to severe overfitting leading to difficulty in training. Zhang et al. [10] proposed a triplet network based on deep metric learning, which maps character images to Euclidean space as feature vectors and then uses nearest neighbor classifiers for oracle recognition. Due to its triplet training approach, it is difficult to train to meaningful training samples, which leads to its slow training learning and high computational cost. And the recognition performance is not monitored during the training process thus the generated model has very poor generalization ability.

The metric-based approach of one-shot learning is simpler and more efficient, and the data will have different representations based on different tasks, especially on high-dimensional data, learning task-based representations can achieve better performance. One of the most representative achievements is the method based on Siamese network proposed by Koch et al. [5] which rank the similarity between inputs and perform classification recognition. The biggest contribution of the model is to use the ability of the verification model to distinguish the similarity, which is directly used for one-shot recognition and has a good effect on new class recognition. Later, Vinyals et al. [11] proposed to use a matching network to predict the test set category by learning embedding vectors on the support set using a cosine-based attention mechanism. The model uses segmented sampled mini-batch data to simulate the test task during training, which can reduce the difference between training and testing, thereby improving the generalization performance on the test set. Snell et al. [12] further explored the relationship between the class embedding vectors in the embedding space, and believed that there is a prototype expression for each category, and then proposed a prototype network. In the article, the class embedding vectors are closely clustered around the class representatives, which is the mean value of the embedding vector of the support set, so the classification problem becomes the category of finding the nearest neighbor of the class prototype representative of the test image, and good results have been achieved.

Compared with the traditional Siamese network, SSN mainly makes the following improvements: (1) The Siamese backbone in SSN uses a large number of multi-scale feature fusion structures and embedding structures instead of traditional simple convolution to extract image fusion features; (2) Based on the idea of deep metric learning and contrast learning, soft similarity contrast loss (SSCL) is proposed in SSN to train the model so that the similarity of similar ancient characters is higher and the similarity of different ancient characters is lower. Traditional deep network usually utilizes a model with many parameters and then use a large amount of data to prevent overfitting, while the SSN in this paper can obtain a large number of image pairs from a small amount of training data to train the parameters thus reducing model overfitting.

3 Methodology

3.1 General Strategy

Our method works by first proposing a deep metric learning method to learn a good image representation, then directly reusing the features of the network without any retraining, and finally building a one-shot task for nearest neighbor classification. Figure 1 shows the proposed recognition strategy, which constructs an end-to-end two-stage single-sample recognition framework.

In the first learning stage, by inputting a large number of image pairs as the verification task, we learn a verification model that can distinguish the sample pairs and even give similarity score, which is the Siamese similarity network (SSN) proposed in this paper. Among them, it is proposed to use a multi-scale fusion network as the backbone on SSN as well as to add embedding structures to obtain more abundant scale information. Subsequently, more accurate fusion distances can be calculated and the distance layer is simply mapped to the similarity probabilities, finally, a more efficient and accurate

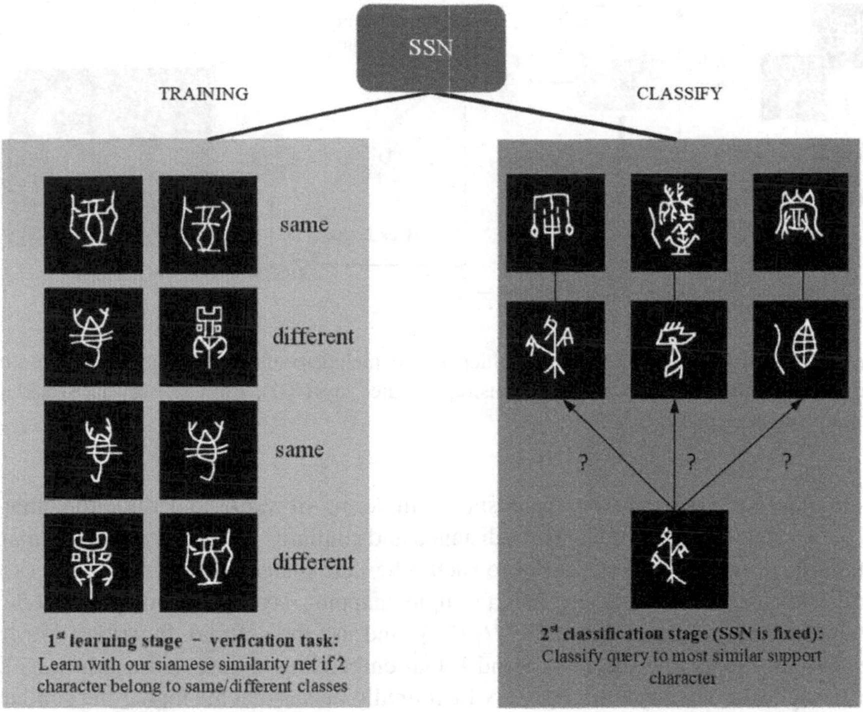

Fig. 1. The general strategy. We adopt a two-stage end-to-end recognition framework. In the learning stage, a good representation of the SSN model is obtained through a series of verification tasks, and in the classification stage, the trained model is used to perform nearest neighbor classification.

gradient value can be obtained by using the SSCL to update the parameter weights. At this stage, our SSN learned the ability to distinguish between similar or different classes of images. In the second classification stage, all parameters of the previously trained SSN are fixed and we directly use them for one-shot classification. Finally, we determine the class to which the test image belongs by solving for the highest similarity value of the input image pair. In this stage, the most similar sample classification is completed by the similarity score values output by SSN.

3.2 Network Structure

Figure 2 illustrates the structure of our SSN. It receives two character images $x^{(1)}, x^{(2)}$ of the same or different categories, Firstly, the character image features $F\left(x^{(1)}\right)$, $F\left(x^{(2)}\right)$ are extracted through the processing of Multi-Scale Backbone, and then the corresponding feature embedding representations $E\left(F\left(x^{(1)}\right)\right)$, $E\left(F\left(x^{(2)}\right)\right)$ are obtained through a special fusion embedding structure. Accordingly, these two feature vectors are passed through the proposed non-parametric fusion distance layer to obtain the semantic distance values $D\left(x^{(1)}, x^{(2)}\right)$ of the two images, at which time the fusion distance is a weighted sum of the cosine distance and the Euclidean distance, which represents

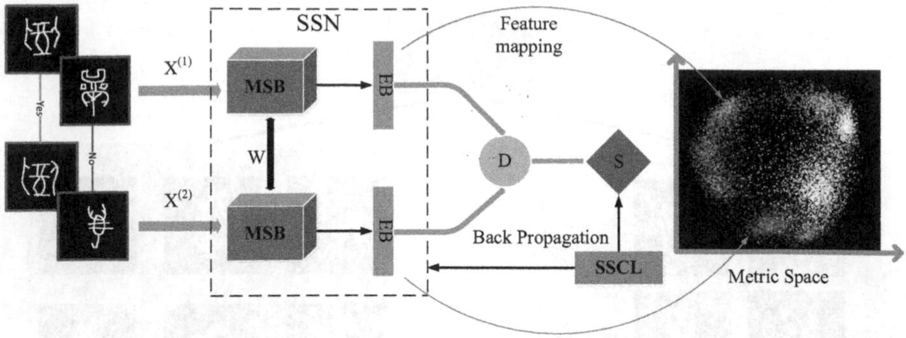

Fig. 2. The structure of proposed SSN. Which mainly includes multi-scale fusion backbone structure (MSB), embedded structure (EB), fusion distance layer (D), similarity layer (S) and soft similarity contrast loss (SSCL).

a simultaneous constraint on the distance in terms of value and direction, that is $D_{union} = \alpha D_{eul} + (1 - \alpha) D_{\cos}$ Since distance and similarity are closely related, Images with large distances are less similar to each other and images with small distances are more similar to each other. we use a simple mapping layer containing one node to obtain the final similarity score $S\left(x^{(1)}, x^{(2)}\right)$, and use the softmax function to restrict the similarity score to be between 0 and 1. Our embedding representations show a clear clustering feature in the metric space, which finally means that the higher the similarity of characters with the same category, the lower the similarity of characters with different categories.

MSB in SSN. Due to the simple convolutional layer stack used in the previous Siamese network [5] or the more traditional classical neural network [13], considering that these simple convolutional structures have limited non-linear learning capabilities in complex data sets and large variations in ancient character. Based on the network structure in Szegedy, C. et al. [14], we use the MSB module that contains a large number of multi-scale channel fusions as our feature extraction, including a large number of receptive field convolution kernels of various scales and different shapes, which play an important role in capturing multi-scale features and local features. Since increasing the network depth is proven to better extract the target features, our network will use a large number of residuals [15] to skip the connection structure, so that the network can be deepened while reducing the degradation phenomenon.

Our MSB mainly consists five consecutive multi-scale blocks, and each of which is followed by a reduction block. Figure 3 briefly illustrates the MSB module. In each multi-scale block, there are multi-scale and multi-shape convolution channels containing 4 receptive field branches of $1 * 1, 3 * 3, 5 * 5, 7 * 7$, namely C(1), C(3), C(5), C(7). The first channel is $1*1$ convolution, the second channel is $1 * 1$, $1 * 3$ and $3 * 1$ convolution, the third channel is $1 * 1$, $1 * 5$ and $5 * 1$ convolution, and the fourth channel is $1 * 1$, $1 * 7$ and $7 * 1$ convolution. The fusion of the multi-scale features of each channel is followed by the $1 * 1$ convolution to normalize the number of channels, and finally the multi-scale

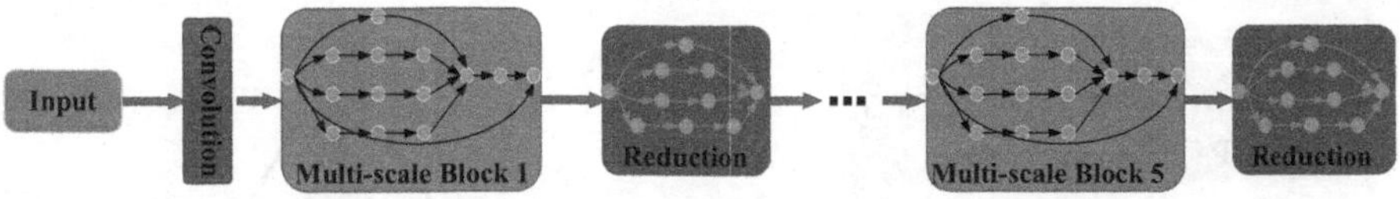

Fig. 3. The architecture of MSB module. The input of MSB is an ancient character image. The original image is first processed by a simple convolution to obtain the shallow features of the image, and then there are 5 consecutive multi-scale blocks, each of which is followed by a reduction module.

feature fusion feature is obtained through residual connection. It can be expressed as:

$$\begin{cases} R(x_{concat})=\sum c(1)+\sum c(3)+\sum c(5)+\sum c(7) \\ Y=R(x_{concat})+x \end{cases} \tag{1}$$

$R(x_{concat})$ refers to the concatenation of the feature maps produced in four multi-scale branches. x and Y denote the input and output features of the multi-scale block, respectively. The size of the feature map after passing through the multi-scale block does not change, it is subsampled by the reduction block which do convolution and pooling. Our reduction block also contains four branches. The first branch is 3 * 3 maximum pooling, the second branch is 1 * 1 and 3 * 3 convolution, and the third branch is 1 * 1 and 5 * 5 convolution. The four branches are 1 * 1, 3 * 3 and 5 * 5 convolutions.

EB in SSN. Since the traditional embedding structure only uses Fully Connected Layer (FCL) to vectorize the feature map, the structure often results in severe overfitting due to the need to optimize a large number of parameters, which results in extremely poor generalization performance of this network. Another kind of embedded structure, namely Global average pooling (GAP) [16], will lose a lot of detailed information due to its rough processing method, and may slow down the convergence speed. Inspired by the idea of residual learning in [15], we therefore use the residual structure to link the combination of FCL, GAP and Dropout [17] as our embedding structure, and three embedding structures are proposed, namely GF, GFD_IN and GFD_OUT, as shown in Fig. 4.

Unlike the residual learning of the original feature map in the residual network, our embedding structure adds a richer set of image features learned through the fully connected layer to the vector obtained after global average pooling, using the following equation.

$$\begin{cases} Y = R(x) + GAP(x) \ or \\ Y = R(x) + GAP(x) + dropout \\ R(x) = F(x) \ or \ F(x) + dropout \end{cases} \tag{2}$$

Where x and Y denote the input and output of this embedding structure, respectively, GAP(x) denotes the global average pooling of the input to obtain the original embedding representation, R(x) denotes the residual mapping to be learned, and the residual features learned from the fully connected layer are added to the embedding representation via GAP to obtain the most informative and accurate embedding representation. F(x), which means the fully connected layer, can be adjusted to represent the same number of channels as the original embedding.

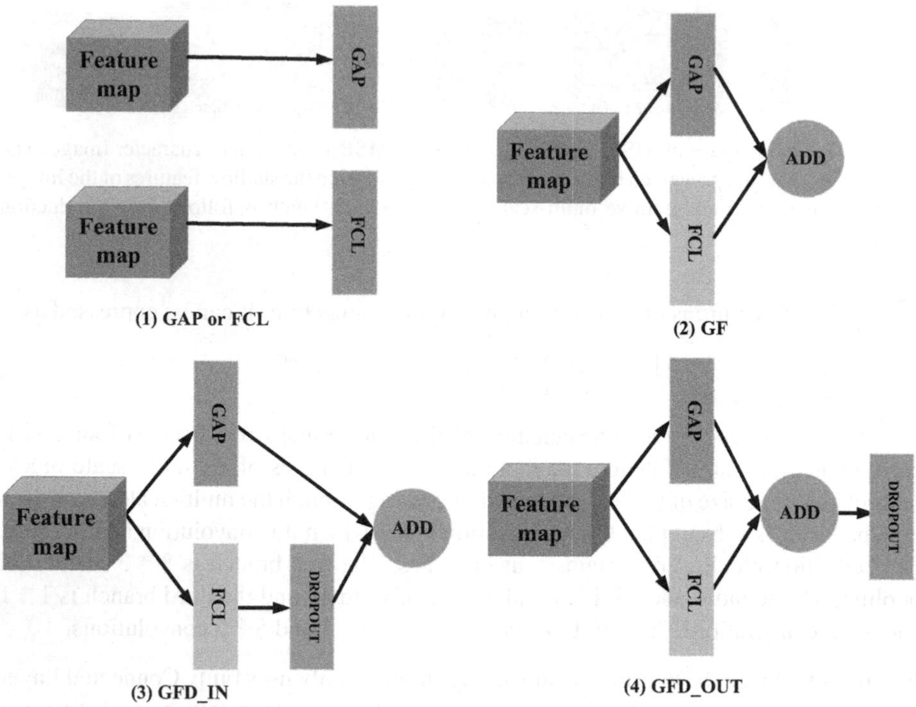

Fig. 4. Traditional embedding structure and our residual embedding structure. where (1) is the traditional embedding structure and (2) (3) (4) is our proposed residual embedding structure.

SSCL in SSN. In this paper we design a new loss function based on the traditional contrast loss (CL) [18], called the soft similarity contrast loss function (SSCL), which is expressed as shown in Eq. (3) below. The proposed loss function can not only implicitly define the similarity measure, that is, the end-to-end similarity value of the output two characters images, but also achieve the goal of metric learning, that is, the similarity of similar characters is high, while the similarity of different characters is low. In addition, we consider that contrast loss can over-optimize and thus lead to poor generalization performance. Therefore, our loss function emphasizes that the optimization object is between certain threshold values, otherwise no optimization is performed, which can prevent over-optimization from bringing overfitting, reduce problems such as incorrect optimization, and also speed up the optimization speed.

Specifically, the upper bound of similarity is set, and optimization is stopped when the similarity value of two images is higher than a certain upper bound, and similarly there is a lower bound of dissimilarity, and optimization is stopped when the dissimilarity value of two images is lower than a certain lower bound.

$$\begin{aligned} L\left(x^{(1)}, x^{(2)}\right) = {} & y^{(1)(2)} \max\left(\left(a - s\left(x^{(1)}, x^{(2)}\right)\right), 0\right) \\ & + \left(1 - y^{(1)(2)}\right)\left(s\left(x^{(1)}, x^{(2)}\right) - b\right)_{+} \end{aligned} \tag{3}$$

Where $y^{(1)(2)}$ denotes the labels of two images, if the two images are of the same category, then $y^{(1)(2)} = 1$, and $y^{(1)(2)} = 0$ if they are of different categories. The parameters a and b denote the upper bound threshold for reducing over-optimization of similar images and the lower bound threshold for over-optimization of images of different categories, respectively. $s\left(x^{(1)}, x^{(2)}\right)$ denotes the similarity score value output by SSN. As shown in Fig. 5, it is obvious that SSCL is faster and more reasonable than CL.

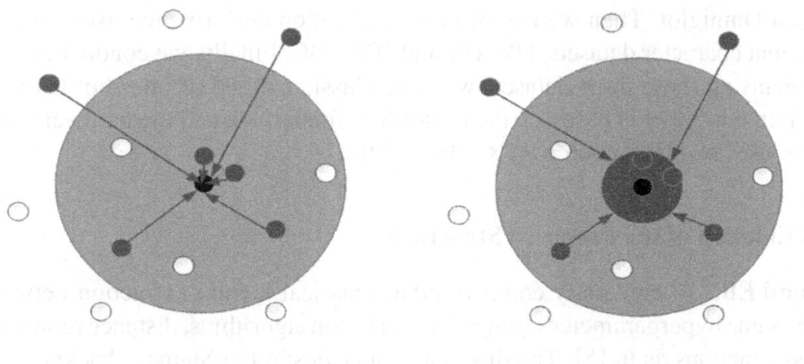

Fig. 5. Two loss functions. The blue dots indicate that similar objects need to be as close as possible in the metric space, and the black dots indicate the ideal class center representation. Where (1) denotes the traditional contrast loss, which requires the objects with high similarity to be brought infinitely close. (2) denotes our proposed soft similarity contrast loss, which stops over-optimization when the high similarity ones are brought closer to a higher threshold to speed up the convergence rate.

4 Experiment

4.1 Dataset

We conduct experiments on three datasets: Omniglot, HWAYI, HWOBC.

Omniglot: Omniglot [19] is a public dataset of handwritten characters for one-shot learning consisting of 1623 categories with a total of 32,460 images. Each category has 20 images. Each of these characters is a 105×105 binary image.

HWAYI: The HWAYI dataset [20] contains a total of 112031 handwritten ancient Yi characters in 1764 categories (27–96 images per category), and each character image has been normalized to 64×64 size.

HWOBC: The handwritten oracle dataset HWOBC [21] collected a total of 83,245 sample images in 3881 categories. (Each category has 19–24 images).

In order to obtain the best results, we did a series of pre-processing on the initial dataset of ancient character. First, considering that multi-channel color images do not affect the recognition accuracy, we first convert them into single-channel grayscale images in order to simplify the calculation. Second, in order to facilitate network training, we scaled the images to 224 × 224 uniformly. Lateral inhibition [22] is a phenomenon in which adjacent receptors are able to inhibit each other. Since the phenomenon of lateral inhibition produces a stronger visual impact on the form of images with white characters on a black background, we transformed all the pictures of the dataset into the form of white characters on a black background. Finally, we add a black bounding box with a width of 16 pixels to the image becoming a uniform 256 × 256 scale. Such a border avoids possible boundary effects during the execution of convolution and pooling.

Using SiameseNet [5] as a benchmark, we first validate our proposed MSB, EB, and SSCL on Omniglot. Then we explore the recognition performance using our SSN on two ancient character datasets, HWAYI and HWOBC. Finally, we conduct comparative experiments on these three datasets with the classic method of one-shot learning. The research in this paper is based on the tensorflow framework and the hardware operating platform uses Nvidia GeForce RTX 2080s GPUs.

4.2 Validation of the Proposed Structure

MSB and EB. To efficiently compare other classical feature extraction networks, we used the same hyperparameter settings, optimization algorithms, distance representation, and loss functions as in [5]. The difference only lies in the Siamese backbone and the embedding structures, where the Siamese backbone are the simple CNN structures in the benchmark, vgg16 [23], resnet50 [15], inceptionv3 [24] and our MSB, and the embedding structures are the traditional two structures (FCL, GAP) and our proposed three EB (GF, FGD_IN, FGD_OUT). The final EB setting of 2048 dimensions is the most appropriate in the experiment.

Table 1. Comparison of different network and embedding structure. Acc means the 20-way one-shot recognition accuracy on Omniglot dataset. The best-performing method is highlighted.

Acc (%)	Base	Vgg16	Resnet50	Inceptionv3	MSB (ours)
FCL	88.72	87.01	93.58	93.81	94.39
GAP	87.09	88.04	93.67	93.96	94.44
GF (ours)	88.94	88.25	93.91	94.58	94.93
FGD_IN (ours)	88.93	88.60	93.86	94.47	95.27
FGD_OUT (ours)	89.25	88.75	93.96	94.76	95.72

The results of the study are shown in Table 1, and the experiments demonstrate that our MSB significance outperforms other models. Meanwhile, the introduction of a more informative EB obtains a better performance than the traditional structure. The accuracy of using the simple convolutional structure model in the benchmark can reach 92%, while using the multiscale feature fusion module in this paper can exceed the original paper by 2.39%, and the accuracy after the joint proposed embedding structure reaches 95.72%, and the improvement in the Siamese branch makes our model exceed the original paper by 3.72%, achieving the best results.

SSCL. In order to achieve a better data representation to obtain higher similarity scores for similar images and lower similarity scores for dissimilar images of different classes, we propose SSCL to obtain such a good representation. This is also the most essential difference between the baseline and the method in this paper, which introduces the idea of similarity learning to improve the robustness of the model.

Following the parameter settings and the optimal structure of the joint MSB and FGD_OUT from the above experiments, the difference mainly lies in the loss function. Where the loss function contains the cross entropy in the benchmark, the CL, and our SSCL. The approach of CL combined with nearest neighbor classifier (NN) is used for recognition, while all others are tested for one-shot classification performance.

Table 2. Loss functions

Method	Error
Cross entropy	2.73%
CL + NN	2.82%
SSCL	2.19%

The experimental results are shown in Table 2. The SSCL proposed in this paper obtains better recognition performance than the cross-entropy loss function and CL. and the combination of SSCL even achieves the best performance. So far, our best model has reduced the error rate by 5.81% compared to the benchmark. Thus, we validate the proposed SSN and obtain state of the art performance.

4.3 Ancient Character Recognition

We conduct some experiments on two ancient character datasets to evaluate the efficient classification performance of our method. We use 60% of the data for training and monitoring, and the remaining 40% for testing one-shot performance. We perform 5 way one-shot and 20-way one-shot recognition tasks with a total of 550 one-shot learning trials per task, from which we calculate the classification accuracy. The dropout rate is set to 0.5 in the experiments and the fusion distance is set to 0.1 to reach the best. In order to efficiently compare our proposed structures, we will use the same hyperparameters, optimizers, and weight initialization as in the benchmark.

The experimental results are shown in Table 3. it can be seen that by using MSB and EB, there is a 1.64–2.19% improvement in the 20-way classification performance. By replacing only the distance layer metric, we find that the optimal performance is obtained using a fusion distance. From the last row, it can be seen that the proposed SSCL has a significant effect on the improvement of the model. In the HWAYI, our best model outperforms benchmark by 4.43% and 5.64% in 5-way and 20-way, respectively.

Table 3. One-shot classification performance of our method on two datasets.

Method	HWAYI(%)		HWOBC(%)	
	5-way Acc	20-way Acc	5-way Acc	20-way Acc
Base	95.32	92.18	95.27	91.81
MSB + EB + D(eul)	97.89	95.25	98.55	95.27
MSB + EB + D(cos)	97.56	94.55	98.0	94.36
MSB + EB + D(0.1)	98.12	95.5	98.75	96.18
MSB + EB + SSCL	99.75	97.82	99.25	97.5

Similarly, in the HWOBC, our best model outperforms benchmark by 3.98% and 5.69% in 5-way and 20-way, respectively. Thus, our model has a large improvement over the traditional Siamese model and achieves SOTA performance.

4.4 One-Shot Recognition Comparison Experiments

In order to further explore the proposed network, we choose other classic networks in the field of one-shot recognition to conduct comparative experiments. we choose to test the 20-way one-shot performance of Siamese networks, matching networks, prototype networks, and relation networks in the three datasets mentioned above.

Table 4. The comparison experiment of one-shot learning

Method	Accuracy (%)		
	Omniglot	HWAYI	HWOBC
SiameseNet	92.0	92.18	91.81
MatchingNet	93.8	92.7	91.35
ProtypeNet	96.0	96.5	96.3
RelationNet	97.6	97.7	97.4
SSN (our)	97.8	97.82	97.5

The above results with several excellent networks show that the proposed SSN achieves better recognition performance than mainstream methods. As shown in Table 4, our model improves about 5.64–5.8% compared to the traditional Siamese network, about 4–6.15% compared to the matching network, about 1.2–1.8% compared to the prototype network, and about 0.12–0.2% compared to the relation network. our model is not only simple and practical, but also optimal in terms of performance.

5 Conclusions

In this paper, based on the method of one-shot recognition to analyze ancient characters, we proposed a recognition method that uses SSN to calculate the similarity of image pairs for one-shot classification. In our approach, MSB and EB are used to obtain more abundant image features in order to improve the recognition of variant characters, and the proposed SSCL will result in higher similarity scores for similar images and lower scores for different classes of images. Experiments show that the proposed method achieves the best recognition accuracy than previous methods on these datasets. In future work, we will explore more methods based on deep metric learning to obtain better image representation and choose better multi-scale models to increase the recognition performance of variant characters. In addition, we may apply it to the recognition of ancient characters in more realistic scenes and recognition problems based on shapes or sketches in cases where little data is available.

Acknowledgements. This work was supported by The National Social Science Fund of China (19BYY171), China Postdoctoral Science Foundation (2015M580765), and Chongqing Postdoctoral Science Foundation (Xm2016041), the Fundamental Research Funds for the Central Universities, China (XDJK2018B020), Chongqing Natural Science Foundation (cstc2019jcyj-msxmX0130), Chongqing Key Lab of Automated Reasoning and Cognition, Chongqing Institute of Green and Intelligent Technology, Chinese Academy of Sciences(arc202003).

References

1. Yuan, G., Jiayi, M., Alan, L.: Semi-supervised sparse representation based classification for face recognition with insufficient labeled samples. IEEE Trans. Image process. **26**(5), 2545–2560 (2017)
2. Bin, P., Zhenwei, S., Xia, X.: Mugnet: deep learning for hyperspectral image classification using limited samples. ISPRS J. Photogrammetry Remote Sens. **145**, 108–119 (2017)
3. Han, A., Bharath, R., Aneesh, S.P., Vijay, P.: Low data drug discovery with one-shot learning. ACS Cent. Sci. **3**(4), 283–293 (2017)
4. Kadam, S., Vaidya, V.: Review and analysis of zero, one and few shot learning approaches. In: Abraham, A., Cherukuri, A.K., Melin, P., Gandhi, N. (eds.) ISDA 2018 2018. AISC, vol. 940, pp. 100–112. Springer, Cham (2020). https://doi.org/10.1007/978-3-030-16657-1_10
5. Gregory, K., Richard, Z., Ruslan, S.: Siamese neural networks for one-shot image recognition. In: ICML deep learning workshop, Lille, France (2015)
6. Yann, L., Yoshua, B., Geoffrey, H.: Deep learning. Nat. **521**(7553), 436–444 (2015)
7. Waseem, R., Zenghui, W.: Deep convolutional neural networks for image classification: a comprehensive review. Neural Comput. **29**(9), 2352–2449 (2017)
8. Alex, K., Ilya, S., Geoffrey, H.: Imagenet classification with deep convolutional neural networks. Commun. ACM **60**(6), 84–90 (2017)
9. Taraggy, M.G., Mahmoud, I.K., Hazem, M.A.: Comparative study on deep convolution neural networks DCNN-based offline arabic handwriting recognition. IEEE Access **8**, 95465–95482 (2020)
10. Yikang, Z., Heng, Z. Yongge, L., Qing, Y., Chenglin, L.: Oracle character recognition by nearest neighbor classification with deep metric learning.In: International Conference on Document Analysis and Recognition, Sydney, NSW, Australia, pp. 309–314. IEEE (2019)

11. Oriol, V., Charles, B., Timothy, L., Koray, K., Daan, W.: Matching networks for one shot learning. In: Proceedings of the 30th International Conference on Neural Information Processing Systems, Red Hook, NY, USA, pp. 3637–3645. Curran Associates Inc. (2016)
12. Jake, S., Kevin, S., Richard, S.Z.: Prototypical networks for few-shot learning. In: Proceedings of the 31st International Conference on Neural Information Processing Systems, pp. 4077–4087. Long Beach, CA, USA (2017)
13. Camilo, V., Qianni, Z., Ebroul, I.: One shot logo recognition based on siamese neural networks. In: International Conference on Multimedia Retrieval Dublin, ACM, Ireland (2020)
14. Christian, S., Sergey, L., Vincent, V., Alexander, A.A.: Inception-v4, inception-ResNet and the impact of residual connections on learning. In Proceedings of the 31th AAAI Conference on Artificial Intelligence, San Francisco, California, USA. AAAI Press (2017)
15. Kaiming, H., Xiangyu, Z. Shaoqing, R., Jian, S.: Deep residual learning for image recognition. In: IEEE Conference on Computer Vision and Pattern Recognition, pp. 770–778 (2016)
16. Min, L., Qiang, C., Shuicheng, Y.: Network in Network (2014)
17. Geoffrey, H., Nitish, S., Alex, K., Ilya, S., Ruslan, R.S.: Improving neural networks by preventing co-adaptation of feature detectors. Comput. Sci. **3**(4), 212–223 (2012)
18. Raia, H., Sumit, C., Yann, L.: Dimensionality reduction by learning an invariant mapping. In: IEEE Computer Society Conference on Computer Vision and Pattern Recognition, New York, NY, USA, pp. 1735–1742. IEEE (2006)
19. Simon, A.: About Omniglot (1998).https://www.omniglot.com/about.htm#langs
20. Xu, H.: Research and implementation of character detection and recognition of ancient Yi language. Dissertation, Southwest University (2020)
21. Bang, L., et al.: HWOBC-a handwriting oracle bone character recognition database. J. Phys. Conf. **1651**(1), 012050 (2020)
22. Hartline, H.K., Wagner, H.G., Ratliff, F.: Ratliff inhibition in the eye of limulus. J. Gen. Physiol. **39**, 651–673 (1956)
23. Karen, S., Andrew, Z.: Very deep convolutional networks for large-scale image recognition. In: International Conference on Learning Representations (2015)
24. Christian, S., et al.: Rethinking the inception architecture for computer vision. In: IEEE Conference on Computer Vision and Pattern Recognition, pp. 2818–2826 (2016)

Incorporating Global Context into Multi-task Learning for Session-Based Recommendation

Nan Qiu[1], BoYu Gao[1(✉)], Feiran Huang[1], Huawei Tu[2], and Weiqi Luo[1(✉)]

[1] College of Cyber Security, Jinan University, Guangzhou, China
alanqn@stu2019.jnu.edu.cn, {bygao,huangfr,lwq}@jnu.edu.cn

[2] Department of Computer Science and Information Technology, La Trobe University, Bundoora, Australia
h.tu@latrobe.edu.au

Abstract. Session-based recommendation aims to predict the potential items that user may interact with next time from given anonymous sessions. However, existing session-based recommendation models mainly utilize the current given session without considering the global context information. The models that take collaborative neighbor information into account are vulnerable to noise, and their performance is not efficient and stable enough. To provide better prediction, in this paper, we propose a novel model, namely **GCM-SR**, which incorporates **G**lobal **C**ontext into **M**ulti-task learning for **S**ession-based **R**ecommendation. Rather than directly integrating the global context information with the session-level item transition information, GCM-SR regards the global context as implicit type information and integrates it in the form of an auxiliary task to enhance recommendation performance. Then, local learning task and global learning task are joined through adjustable weights to complete prediction and recommendation. Experiments on three public datasets demonstrate the superiority of GCM-SR over the state-of-the-art models. The results may give suggestion for better performance in session-based recommendation systems.

Keywords: Session-based recommendation · Global context · Multi-task learning · Graph neural networks

1 Introduction

The purpose of session-based recommendation is to predict which items the user is most potential to interact with based on the given sessions (e.g., a series of items clicked by a user). Due to anonymous login or privacy protection, the sessions lack of user profile, so some conventional methods such as collaborative filtering [9,15] and matrix factorization [1,5] are no longer applicable. To adapt to the session-based recommendation scenario, Item K-Nearest Neighbor (KNN) [16] and Methods based on Markov chain, such as (MDPs) [17] and Factorized Personalized Markov Chain (FPMC) [14], calculate the similarity

H. Qiu et al. (Eds.): KSEM 2021, LNAI 12815, pp. 627–638, 2021.
https://doi.org/10.1007/978-3-030-82136-4_51

and transition probability, respectively, for making recommendations. However, these above models do not consider the sequence information of the session.

Most of the existing models capture sequential patterns based on recurrent neural networks (RNN), which are used to improve the recommendation performance. Furthermore, with the development of the attention mechanism, Li et al. [6] proposed NARM, which employs the attention mechanism to capture the user's main preference. To overcome the limitation that the sequential patterns can only consider adjacent item transitions, Wu et al. [21] proposed SR-GNN to apply the Graph Neural Network (GNN) to capture more complex item transitions. Subsequently, recommendation models based on graph neural networks became popular. However, almost all previous models only consider the current session information. Wang et al. [19] proposed CSRM, which improves the recommendation performance by integrating neighbor session information. Soon after, Wang et al. [20] proposed Global Context Enhanced (GCE)-GNN to use the fine-grained global context to utilize information from other sessions.

The GCE-GNN model employs the global context enhanced graph neural networks to achieve the state-of-the-art performance. GCE-GNN model directly accumulates the session-level and global-level item representation to obtain the final representation, which can reflect not only the information of the current session but also the neighbor sessions. However, with the number of neighbors in the global graph and global-level item representation learning layers increasing, the propagation of irrelevant neighbor noise information and the repeated propagation of the same neighbor information is becoming more and more obvious, which makes the representation of items in different categories inseparable. Therefore, the recommendation performance with the GCE-GNN model is not stable enough to some extent (e.g., in some datasets, GCE-GNN performs worse than a variant model without the global-level feature encoder).

The above-mentioned problem is similar to the over-smoothing issue caused by the multi-layer graph neural network to capture long-range node information mentioned in several recent works [2,7,23]. To address the issue, referring to [11, 12], we treat the global context information as an implicit type information, and use the global context as an auxiliary task to enhance recommendation through multi-task learning. Unlike [12], the global context does not require additional fields and information, and it can be directly extracted from sessions.

In this paper, we propose to incorporate **G**lobal **C**ontext into **M**ulti-task learning for **S**ession-based **R**ecommendation, which is called **GCM-SR**[1] (see Fig. 1). GCM-SR includes both local and global learning tasks. Different from GCE-GNN [20], GCM-SR first employs the global context extractor to obtain global context information, and then takes the global context information as side information and integrates it as an auxiliary task. Finally, the local and global learning tasks are jointly integrated through adjustable weight to complete the recommendation (see Sect. 3 for details). Our contributions in this paper are as follows:

[1] Code is available on https://github.com/NanQiu96/GCM-SR.

- We employ a global context extractor to generate global context information and treat it as implicit type information to enhance recommendation.
- We propose a novel model to integrate the global context information in the form of auxiliary task and incorporate it through adjustable weight, which can make the recommendation more efficient and stable.
- We conduct experiments on three public datasets, and the experimental results reveal the superiority of our model compared to the latest ones.

In the rest of this paper, we summarize related work in Sect. 2 and introduce the model in detail in Sect. 3. Then, we present the experimental results and analysis in Sect. 4 and conclude the work with the summary of future work in Sect. 5.

2 Related Work

Item-KNN [16] recommends the top K items that appear most frequently with the last interacted item to the user. Methods based on Markov chain, such as MDPs [17] and FPMC [14], use Markov chain to model the recommendation process and make predictions based on the previous interactions. However, all of them mainly consider the last interaction and ignore the information of the past interactions, which may negatively impact prediction.

To model the user's sequential behavior, Hidasi et al. [4] used the RNN constructed from gated recurrent units (GRU) to capture sequential patterns for recommendation. Considering that the user's mistakes or inadvertent operations will cause the sequential patterns to drift, Li et al. [6] proposed NARM to use the attention mechanism to capture the user's main preference. However, in many cases, the last item interacted by the user are more representative to reflect the user's current interest, hence Liu et al. [10] proposed STAMP to capture the user's preference and current interest by using long and short-term memory, respectively. Although the above recommendation methods consider the user's sequential behavior, they only model the sequential transitions of adjacent items, which may lose some transitions between non-adjacent items.

Recently, GNN has been introduced to represent complex item transitions on the graph constructed from current sessions. SR-GNN [21] obtains more accurate item embeddings for all nodes involved in session graph through Gated Graph Neural Networks (GGNNs) [8]. Furthermore, GC-SAN [22] and FGNN [13] were proposed to learn each item embedding by aggregating its neighbors' embeddings with multi-head attention. In addition to capturing the complex item transitions in sessions, TAGNN [24] also considers user interests given a certain target item by incorporating a target-aware attention module.

The information of the neighbor sessions is also beneficial to the recommendation, CSRM [19] learns to combine the information in the current session and collaborative information of the latest neighborhood sessions by fusing the gating mechanism to obtain the final representation. More recently, GCE-GNN aggregates item-level neighbor information as the global context information to enhance recommendation performance.

3 Proposed Method

3.1 Preliminaries

The purpose of a session-based recommendation is to predict which items the user is most likely to interact next based on anonymous historical interactions. We define the set of all m items as $\mathbf{V} = \{v_1, v_2, \ldots, v_m\}$. Given a session $S = \{v_{s_1}, v_{s_2}, \ldots, v_{s_n}\}$, the recommended model $\mathcal{M}$ takes S as input, and outputs $\hat{\mathbf{y}} = \{\hat{\mathbf{y}}_1, \hat{\mathbf{y}}_2, \ldots, \hat{\mathbf{y}}_m\}$. For each $\hat{\mathbf{y}}_i$, it corresponds to the probability of the user interacting on item v_i next time. Finally, model $\mathcal{M}$ takes the top K items as recommendations.

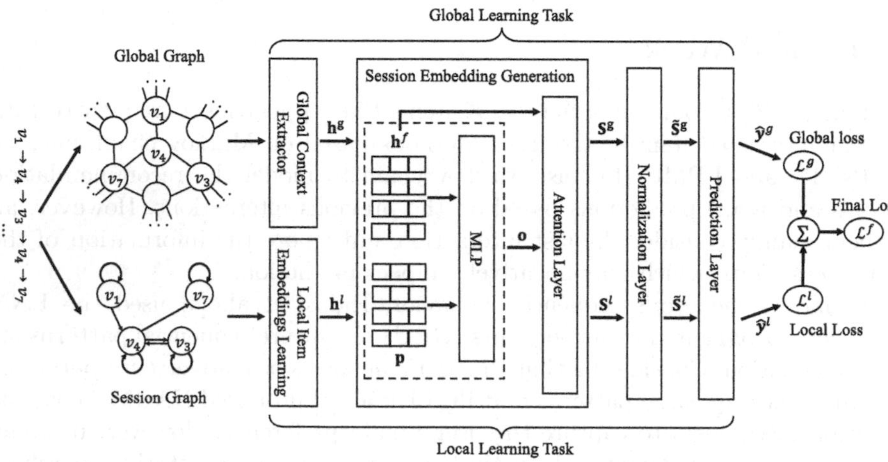

Fig. 1. Overview of the proposed model GCM-SR. First, the session and global graphs are constructed. After that, we obtain the local and global item embeddings, respectively. Then, we generate the local and global session embeddings, normalize them and apply them to calculate the probability for the candidate items. Finally, the local and global tasks are integrated to complete the recommendation.

We use the same method of constructing the session graph and the global graph (see Fig. 1) as GCE-GNN [20]. In the session graph, the edges are divided into four types, including r_{self}, r_{in}, r_{out} and r_{in-out} (r_{self} means the self-pointing of the item, r_{in} means that v_j points to v_i in edge (v_i, v_j), and so on). As for the global graph, each edge denotes the connection between the item and its neighbor, and the number of connection is defined as the weight.

3.2 Item Embeddings Learning

In this subsection, we introduce how to learn local item embeddings and global item embeddings from session graph and global graph, respectively.

Local Item Embeddings. We directly use the session-level item representation learning layer [20] to obtain the information of adjacent nodes. It can dynamically select and linearly combine the information of different adjacent nodes:

$$\mathbf{h}_i^l = \sum_{j \in \mathcal{A}_i} \alpha_{ij} \mathbf{h}_j \tag{1}$$

$$\alpha_{ij} = \frac{\exp\left(\text{LeakyReLU}\left(\mathbf{a}_{r_{ij}}^T \left(\mathbf{h}_i \odot \mathbf{h}_j\right)\right)\right)}{\sum_{k \in \mathcal{A}_i} \exp\left(\text{LeakyReLU}\left(\mathbf{a}_{r_{ik}}^T \left(\mathbf{h}_i \odot \mathbf{h}_k\right)\right)\right)} \tag{2}$$

where $\mathcal{A}_i$ is the set of adjacent nodes directly connected to node i in the session graph, $\mathbf{h}_j \in \mathbb{R}^d$ is the item embedding of node j, and α_{ij} is the importance of node j. LeakyReLU is the activation function, r_{ij} refers to the edge type in aforementioned four kinds of edges between node i and node j, and $\mathbf{a}_* \in \mathbb{R}^d$ is the learnable weight vector corresponding to the specified edge type $*$.

Global Item Embeddings. We use the global context extractor to generate global context information and output the global item embeddings. First, we aggregate the information of neighbors in the global graph for each node, and the neighbor information is linearly combined according to the session-related attention weight as [20]:

$$\mathbf{h}_i^a = \sum_{j \in \mathcal{N}_i} \beta_{ij} \mathbf{h}_j \tag{3}$$

$$\beta_{ij} = \frac{\exp\left(\mathbf{q_1}^T \text{LeakyReLU}\left(\mathbf{W}_1[(\mathbf{s} \odot \mathbf{h}_j) ; w_{ij}]\right)\right)}{\sum_{k \in \mathcal{N}_i} \exp\left(\mathbf{q_1}^T \text{LeakyReLU}\left(\mathbf{W}_1[(\mathbf{s} \odot \mathbf{h}_k) ; w_{ik}]\right)\right)} \tag{4}$$

where $\mathcal{N}_i$ is the neighbor set of the current node i, β_{ij} is the attention weight of the neighbor j to node i, w_{ij} is the number of times the current node i and node j co-occur in all sessions, $[\cdot]$ is the concatenation operation, $\mathbf{W}_1 \in \mathbb{R}^{d \times d+1}$ and $\mathbf{q}_1 \in \mathbb{R}^d$ are parameters to be trained, and $\mathbf{s}$ can be regarded as the session information which is calculated by averaging: $\mathbf{s} = \frac{1}{n}\sum_{i=1}^{n} \mathbf{h}_i$.

Second, to capture more information of neighbors related to the current node, more aggregation layers are stacked. We stack the kth-layer aggregation layer and define it as:

$$\mathbf{h}_i^{a,k} = \mathbf{agg}\left(\mathbf{h}_i^{a,k-1}, \mathbf{s}\right) \tag{5}$$

where $\mathbf{h}_i^{a,k-1}$ is the item embedding obtained by the previous aggregation layer (see Eq. (3)). Note that the input to the first aggregation layer, i.e., $\mathbf{h}_i^{a,0}$, is the initial item embedding $\mathbf{h}_i$.

Finally, to alleviate the bias and overfitting problems caused by stacking multiple layers, we employ a gated network to obtain the final global item embedding:

$$\mathbf{z} = \sigma\left(\mathbf{W}_2 \mathbf{h}_i + \mathbf{W}_3 \mathbf{h}_i^{a,k}\right) \tag{6}$$

$$\mathbf{h}_i^g = (1 - \mathbf{z}) \odot \mathbf{h}_i + \mathbf{z} \odot \mathbf{h}_i^{a,k} \tag{7}$$

where $\mathbf{W}_2, \mathbf{W}_3 \in \mathbb{R}^{d \times d}$ are the trainable parameters, and σ is the sigmoid function.

3.3 Session Embedding and Prediction

After obtaining the final item embeddings $\mathbf{h}^f$, we integrate reverse position information for the item embeddings as follows:

$$\mathbf{o}_i = \tanh\left(\mathbf{W}_4[\mathbf{h}_i^f; \mathbf{p}_{n-i+1}]\right) \tag{8}$$

where n is the length of the session, $\mathbf{p}_* \in \mathbb{R}^d$ is the position vector, and the weight matrix $\mathbf{W}_4 \in \mathbb{R}^{d\times 2d}$ is the parameters to be learned.

Then, we combine the global preference and session information to generate the final session embedding as the user's preference. We aggregate all item embeddings with different importance to generate the session embedding:

$$\mathbf{S} = \sum\nolimits_{i=1}^{n} \gamma_i \mathbf{h}_i^f \tag{9}$$

$$\gamma_i = {\mathbf{q}_2}^T \sigma\left(\mathbf{W}_5\mathbf{o}_i + \mathbf{W}_6\mathbf{s}' + \mathbf{b}_1\right) \tag{10}$$

where γ_i is the importance of node i, $\mathbf{q}_2, \mathbf{b}_1 \in \mathbb{R}^d$ and $\mathbf{W}_5, \mathbf{W}_6 \in \mathbb{R}^{d\times d}$ are trainable parameters, and $\mathbf{s}'$ is the session information calculated by: $\mathbf{s}' = \frac{1}{n}\sum_{i=1}^{n} \mathbf{h}_i^f$.

Finally, we calculate the probability of all candidate items in $\mathbf{V}$ to make prediction. First, to handle the popularity bias [3], we normalize item and session embeddings as $\tilde{\mathbf{x}}_i = \frac{\mathbf{x}_i}{\|\mathbf{x}_i\|_2}$, to obtain the final session embedding $\tilde{\mathbf{S}}$ and candidate item embedding $\tilde{\mathbf{v}}_i$. Next, we calculate the probability of each candidate item as follows:

$$\hat{\mathbf{y}}_i = \text{softmax}\left(\tau\tilde{\mathbf{S}}^T\tilde{\mathbf{v}}_i\right) \tag{11}$$

where τ is the scaling factor to solve the convergence problem.

3.4 Fusion Task and Training

In this subsection, we introduce how to integrate local learning task and global learning task for recommendation.

Local Learning Task. As shown in Subsect. 3.2, we first obtain the local item embeddings $\mathbf{h}^l$. Then we calculate the local session embedding $\mathbf{S}^l$ and the probability of the candidate items $\hat{\mathbf{y}}^l$ for the local learning task according to Subsect. 3.3.

Global Learning Task. Similar to the local learning task, we first obtain the global item embeddings $\mathbf{h}^g$, and then calculate the global session embedding $\mathbf{S}^g$ and the global learning task's probability $\hat{\mathbf{y}}^g$ for the candidate items.

Fusion Task. We use adjustable weight to integrate the prediction results $\hat{\mathbf{y}}^l$ and $\hat{\mathbf{y}}^g$, and compute the final prediction result $\hat{\mathbf{y}}^f$ as follows:

$$\hat{\mathbf{y}}^f = (1-\omega) \times \hat{\mathbf{y}}^l + \omega \times \hat{\mathbf{y}}^g \tag{12}$$

where ω is the weight of global learning task. We use the K candidate items with the highest probability as recommendations.

Training. To train our model, we use cross-entropy as the loss function of the local learning task and the global learning task as follows:

$$\mathcal{L} = -\sum_{i=1}^{m} \mathbf{y}_i \log(\hat{\mathbf{y}}_i) + (1 - \mathbf{y}_i)\log(1 - \hat{\mathbf{y}}_i) \tag{13}$$

where $\mathbf{y}_i$ is the one-hot encoding vector of the ground truth item i. After obtaining the cross-entropy loss of the local learning task $\mathcal{L}^l$ and the global learning task $\mathcal{L}^g$, we add these losses to get the final loss: $\mathcal{L}^f = \mathcal{L}^l + \mathcal{L}^g$. Finally, we use the Back-Propagation Through Time (BPTT) algorithm to train the model.

4 Experiments

We evaluate the effectiveness of the proposed model GCM-SR through experiments and answer the following questions:

- **RQ1:** Does GCM-SR have better performance than state-of-the-art methods?
- **RQ2:** Does global learning task efficiently and stably improve the performance of the GCM-SR?
- **RQ3:** How does the weight factor ω affect model performance?

4.1 Experiment Settings

Datasets. We adopt three public datasets Diginetica[2], Tmall[3] and Nowplaying[4] [25] to verify the effectiveness of our proposed model. Specifically, due to the extremely large amount of data in Tmall, we only select a specific part of the data, i.e., we filter out the sessions whose id are greater than 120,000. Also, for the Tmall and Nowplaying datasets, sessions longer than 40 and 30 are also filtered, respectively.

To be fair, we filter sessions of length less than 2 and items that appear less than 5 times across the three datasets. Similar to the previous work [18,21], for a session $S = [s_1, s_2, \ldots, s_n]$, we generate the subsequences and the corresponding labels $([s_1, s_2, \ldots, s_{n-1}], s_n)$, ..., $([s_1], s_2)$. Furthermore, the sessions of the last week or the latest are used as the test data, and the remaining data is used for training. The statistics of datasets are shown in Table 1.

Baseline Methods. We compare our method with the following baseline methods to evaluate the performance of the proposed method. (1) Conventional recommendation methods include POP, Item-KNN [16] and FPMC [14]. (2) Neural network based methods include GRU4Rec [4], NARM [6], STAMP [10] and CSRM [19]. (3) The GNN-based methods include SR-GNN [21], NISER+ [3], TAGNN [24] and GCE-GNN [20].

[2] https://competitions.codalab.org/competitions/11161.

[3] https://tianchi.aliyun.com/dataset/dataDetail?dataId=42.

[4] http://dbis-nowplaying.uibk.ac.at/#nowplaying.

Table 1. Statistics of the datasets.

Statistics	Diginetica	Tmall	Nowplaying
# clicks	982,961	818,479	1,367,963
# training sessions	719,470	351,268	825,304
# test sessions	60,858	25,898	89,824
# items	43,097	40,728	60,417
Average length	5.12	6.69	7.42

Evaluation Metrics. Following [10,20,21], we adopt the commonly used **P@N** and **MRR@N** as evaluation metrics.

Parameter Setup. For fair comparisons, both the dimension of item embeddings and batch size are set to 100. Following [20,21], the initial learning rate for Adam optimizer is set to 0.001 and decay by 0.1 after every 3 training epochs. All parameters are initialized using a Gaussian distribution with a mean of 0 and a standard deviation of 0.1. L2 penalty and the scale coefficient τ are set to $1e^{-5}$ and 12 respectively. Besides, the number of neighbors and the distance of adjacent items ε are set to 12 and 3 respectively.

4.2 Comparison with Baseline Methods (RQ1)

First, we compare our proposed method with the existing state-of-the-art methods to evaluate the effectiveness. Table 2 shows the performance of all compared methods and our method on the three datasets in terms of P@N and MRR@N (with N=10, and 20), in which the best performance highlighted in boldface.

Table 2. GCE-SR performance compared with baselines using three datasets.

Dataset	Diginetica				Tmall				Nowplaying			
Method	P@10	P@20	MRR@10	MRR@20	P@10	P@20	MRR@10	MRR@20	P@10	P@20	MRR@10	MRR@20
POP	0.76	1.18	0.26	0.28	1.67	2.00	0.88	0.90	1.86	2.28	0.83	0.86
Item-KNN	25.07	35.75	10.77	11.57	6.65	9.15	3.11	3.31	10.96	15.94	4.55	4.91
FPMC	15.43	22.14	6.20	6.66	13.10	16.06	7.12	7.32	5.28	7.36	2.68	2.82
GRU4Rec	17.93	30.79	7.73	8.22	9.47	10.93	5.78	5.89	6.74	7.92	4.40	4.48
NARM	35.44	48.32	15.13	16.00	19.17	23.30	10.42	10.70	13.6	18.59	6.62	6.93
STAMP	33.98	46.62	14.26	15.13	22.63	26.47	13.12	13.36	13.22	17.66	6.57	6.88
CSRM	36.59	50.55	15.41	16.38	24.54	29.46	13.62	13.96	13.20	18.14	6.08	6.42
SR-GNN	38.42	51.26	16.89	17.78	23.41	27.57	13.45	13.72	14.17	18.87	7.15	7.47
NISER+	40.73	53.90	17.81	18.70	30.16	36.08	16.74	17.12	16.13	21.38	7.48	7.78
TAGNN	39.03	51.83	17.17	18.08	32.87	39.76	16.71	17.49	14.18	19.10	7.45	7.72
GCE-GNN	41.16	54.22	18.15	19.04	28.01	33.42	15.08	15.42	16.94	22.37	**8.03**	**8.40**
GCM-SR	**41.49**	**54.82**	**18.27**	**19.19**	**34.01**	**40.85**	**18.03**	**18.54**	**17.90**	**24.13**	7.50	7.93

Among the conventional recommendation methods, POP performs worst, it simply recommends the K items that appear most frequently. Although Item-KNN only considers the most similar items to the last interacted item, it achieves the best performance. The performance of FPMC is worse than Item-KNN, which indicates that it is not advisable to consider only the information between adjacent items.

GRU4Rec outperforms the conventional recommendation methods, demonstrating the Effectiveness of using RNN to model the user's sequential behavior. Compared with GRU4Rec, NARM and STAMP achieve better performance in turn, indicating that the user's main intention and current interest need to be considered. CSRM performs better than STAMP, indicating that it is useful to integrate neighbor information in other sessions.

The GNN-based methods SR-GNN and NISER+ perform better than the neural network based methods, which indicates that capturing complex item transitions through GNN and alleviating popularity bias can improve the recommendation performance. Among all baselines, GCE-GNN shows better performance. The result further illustrates the effectiveness of applying GNN and fine-grained global context information.

Different from CSRM and GCE-GNN, the proposed GCM-SR uses multi-task learning to integrate the global context information, and then the local learning task and the global learning task jointly complete the recommendation. By observing the experimental results shown in Table 2, it is obvious that the proposed GCM-SR method achieves the best performance on all datasets except for MRR@N in Nowplaying, revealing the effectiveness of the proposed method, particularly for Tmall dataset.

4.3 The Effect of Global Learning Task (RQ2)

Then, we design some variant models for comparison to verify the effectiveness of global learning task. Specifically, the variant models are as follows:

- GCE-GNN w/o global: GCE-GNN without global-level feature encoder.
- GCE-GNN-k-hop: GCE-GNN with global-level feature encoder, which sets the number of hop to k.
- GCM-SR-k-hop: GCM-SR with global learning task, which sets the number of hop to k.

Here, we consider the case where k equals 1 and 2, as with [20]. The experimental results of the variant models on all datasets are shown in Table 3. Due to the noise and over-smoothing issue, the performance of GCE-GNN is not stable and efficient enough to some extent. For example, the performance of GCE-GNN-2-hop is worse than GCE-GNN-1-hop on the Tmall dataset, and on the Nowplaying dataset, GCE-GNN-1-hop and GCE-GNN-2-hop are far inferior to GCE-GNN w/o global on P@20.

To address the above-mentioned problem, we propose to incorporate the global context as an auxiliary task in GCM-SR. As our experiment shows, GCM-SR-2-hop outperforms GCM-SR-1-hop slightly. What's more, GCM-SR-k-hop achieves better performance than GCE-GNN-k-hop (with k = 1, and 2) and GCE-GNN w/o global on all datasets. Therefore, the proposed model employs global learning task to make better use of the global context and improved recommendation performance stably and efficiently.

Table 3. Variant models performance.

Dataset	Diginetica		Tmall		Nowplaying	
Variant	P@20	MRR@20	P@20	MRR@20	P@20	MRR@20
W/o global	54.08	18.76	32.96	14.72	23.11	7.55
GCE-GNN-1-hop	54.04	18.90	33.42	15.42	22.37	**8.40**
GCE-GNN-2-hop	54.22	19.04	32.58	14.83	22.45	8.29
GCM-SR-1-hop	54.69	19.15	40.31	**18.63**	**24.13**	7.93
GCM-SR-2-hop	**54.82**	**19.19**	**40.85**	18.54	24.03	7.85

4.4 The Effect of Weight Factor ω (RQ3)

The weight factor ω represents the weight of the global task. It controls the relative proportions of local and global tasks and determines the extent to which the model uses the global context to enhance recommendation.

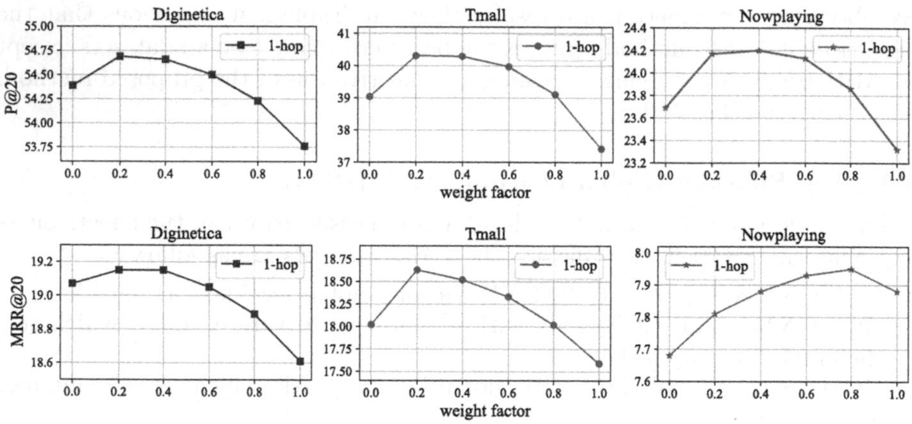

Fig. 2. P@20 and MRR@20 on three datasets.

Observing the experimental results in Fig. 2, as the proportion of global tasks increases, the performance of the model first shows a steady increase, and then gradually falling. For the Diginetica and Tmall datasets, ω between 0.2 and 0.4 achieves the better performance; and for the Nowplaying dataset, setting ω from 0.2 to 0.6 is more desirable. When ω is appropriately chosen, the performance of the GCM-SR model is significantly better than those models that only employ local learning task ($\omega = 0$) or global learning task ($\omega = 1$). The experimental results further show that the proper integration of the global context can improve the recommendation performance.

5 Conclusion

In this paper, we proposed a model which incorporates global context into multi-task learning for session-based recommendation (GCM-SR). The proposed GCM-SR model integrates global context information as an auxiliary task to efficiently and stably enhance recommendation performance and allay the influence of noise. Experiments on three public datasets revealed the superiority of our model over the state-of-the-art models.

As for future work, we would like to solve the situation where the recommendation results are not well ranked. In addition, the overfitting issue caused by stacking multiple layers in the graph is an interesting and important problem.

Acknowledgements. This work was supported by the National Science Foundation of China (61877029, 61902147) and Guangdong Province (2021A1515012629), and Guangzhou Applied and Basic Applied Foundation (202102021131).

References

1. Billsus, D., Pazzani, M.J.: Learning collaborative information filters. In: Proceedings of the 15th International Conference on Machine Learning, vol. 98, pp. 46–54 (1998)
2. Chen, D., Lin, Y., Li, W., Li, P., Zhou, J., Sun, X.: Measuring and relieving the over-smoothing problem for graph neural networks from the topological view. In: Proceedings of the AAAI Conference on Artificial Intelligence, vol. 34, pp. 3438–3445 (2020)
3. Gupta, P., Garg, D., Malhotra, P., Vig, L., Shroff, G.M.: NISER: normalized item and session representations with graph neural networks. arXiv preprint arXiv:1909.04276 (2019)
4. Hidasi, B., Karatzoglou, A., Baltrunas, L., Tikk, D.: Session-based recommendations with recurrent neural networks. arXiv preprint arXiv:1511.06939 (2015)
5. Koren, Y., Bell, R., Volinsky, C.: Matrix factorization techniques for recommender systems. Computer **42**(8), 30–37 (2009)
6. Li, J., Ren, P., Chen, Z., Ren, Z., Lian, T., Ma, J.: Neural attentive session-based recommendation. In: Proceedings of the 2017 ACM on Conference on Information and Knowledge Management, pp. 1419–1428. ACM (2017)
7. Li, Q., Han, Z., Wu, X.M.: Deeper insights into graph convolutional networks for semi-supervised learning. In: Proceedings of the AAAI Conference on Artificial Intelligence, vol. 32 (2018)
8. Li, Y., Tarlow, D., Brockschmidt, M., Zemel, R.: Gated graph sequence neural networks. arXiv preprint arXiv:1511.05493 (2015)
9. Linden, G., Smith, B., York, J.: Amazon. com recommendations: item-to-item collaborative filtering. IEEE Internet Comput. **7**(1), 76–80 (2003)
10. Liu, Q., Zeng, Y., Mokhosi, R., Zhang, H.: STAMP: short-term attention/memory priority model for session-based recommendation. In: Proceedings of the 24th ACM SIGKDD International Conference on Knowledge Discovery & Data Mining, pp. 1831–1839. ACM (2018)
11. Liu, Y., Ren, Z., Zhang, W.N., Che, W., Liu, T., Yin, D.: Keywords generation improves e-commerce session-based recommendation. In: Proceedings of the Web Conference 2020, pp. 1604–1614. ACM (2020)

12. Meng, W., Yang, D., Xiao, Y.: Incorporating user micro-behaviors and item knowledge into multi-task learning for session-based recommendation. In: Proceedings of the 43rd International ACM SIGIR Conference on Research and Development in Information Retrieval, pp. 1091–1100. ACM (2020)
13. Qiu, R., Li, J., Huang, Z., Yin, H.: Rethinking the item order in session-based recommendation with graph neural networks. In: Proceedings of the 28th ACM International Conference on Information and Knowledge Management, pp. 579–588. ACM (2019)
14. Rendle, S., Freudenthaler, C., Schmidt-Thieme, L.: Factorizing personalized Markov chains for next-basket recommendation. In: Proceedings of the 19th international conference on World Wide Web, pp. 811–820. ACM (2010)
15. Resnick, P., Iacovou, N., Suchak, M., Bergstrom, P., Riedl, J.: GroupLens: an open architecture for collaborative filtering of netnews. In: Proceedings of the 1994 ACM Conference on Computer Supported Cooperative Work, pp. 175–186. ACM (1994)
16. Sarwar, B., Karypis, G., Konstan, J., Riedl, J.: Item-based collaborative filtering recommendation algorithms. In: Proceedings of the 10th International Conference on World Wide Web, pp. 285–295. ACM (2001)
17. Shani, G., Heckerman, D., Brafman, R.I., Boutilier, C.: An MDP-based recommender system. J. Mach. Learn. Res. **6**(9), 1265–1295 (2005)
18. Tan, Y.K., Xu, X., Liu, Y.: Improved recurrent neural networks for session-based recommendations. In: Proceedings of the 1st Workshop on Deep Learning for Recommender Systems, pp. 17–22. ACM (2016)
19. Wang, M., Ren, P., Mei, L., Chen, Z., Ma, J., de Rijke, M.: A collaborative session-based recommendation approach with parallel memory modules. In: Proceedings of the 42nd International ACM SIGIR Conference on Research and Development in Information Retrieval, pp. 345–354. ACM (2019)
20. Wang, Z., Wei, W., Cong, G., Li, X.L., Mao, X.L., Qiu, M.: Global context enhanced graph neural networks for session-based recommendation. In: Proceedings of the 43rd International ACM SIGIR Conference on Research and Development in Information Retrieval, pp. 169–178. ACM (2020)
21. Wu, S., Tang, Y., Zhu, Y., Wang, L., Xie, X., Tan, T.: Session-based recommendation with graph neural networks. In: Proceedings of the AAAI Conference on Artificial Intelligence, vol. 33, pp. 346–353 (2019)
22. Xu, C., et al: Graph contextualized self-attention network for session-based recommendation. In: Proceedings of 28th International Joint Conference on Artificial Intelligence (IJCAI), pp. 3940–3946 (2019)
23. Xu, K., Li, C., Tian, Y., Sonobe, T., Kawarabayashi, K.I., Jegelka, S.: Representation learning on graphs with jumping knowledge networks. In: International Conference on Machine Learning, pp. 5453–5462. PMLR (2018)
24. Yu, F., Zhu, Y., Liu, Q., Wu, S., Wang, L., Tan, T.: TAGNN: target attentive graph neural networks for session-based recommendation. In: Proceedings of the 43rd International ACM SIGIR Conference on Research and Development in Information Retrieval, pp. 1921–1924. ACM (2020)
25. Zangerle, E., Pichl, M., Gassler, W., Specht, G.: # nowplaying music dataset: extracting listening behavior from twitter. In: Proceedings of the 1st International Workshop on Internet-Scale Multimedia Management, pp. 21–26. ACM (2014)

Exploring Sequential and Collaborative Contexts for Next Point-of-Interest Recommendation

Jingyi Liu[1,2,3], Yanyan Zhao[2], Limin Liu[1,2,3(✉)], and Shijie Jia[1,2,3]

[1] State Key Laboratory of Information Security, Institute of Information Engineering, CAS, Beijing, China
{liujingyi,liulimin,jiashijie}@iie.ac.cn

[2] School of Cyber Security, University of Chinese Academy of Sciences, Beijing, China
zhaoyanyan@iie.ac.cn

[3] Data Assurance and Communication Security Research Center, CAS, Beijing, China

Abstract. Sequential methods based on recurrent neural networks, as well as session-based long- and short-term approaches have become the state-of-the-art methods for next Point-of-Interest (POI) recommendation recently. However, most of them use spatial and temporal correlations among check-ins while they fail to model category-based sequences explicitly. Moreover, most of the session-based methods only consider users' own sessions, while they neglect the information from collaborative sessions. Besides, most of the sequential methods only consider the information in users' own sequences, while they neglect inherent similarities among POIs from a global perspective. To this end, we propose a method to explore sequential and collaborative contexts (SCC) for next POI recommendation. We simultaneously model temporal, spatial and categorical correlations among check-ins to capture sequential contexts. We generate collaborative sessions for current sessions, then leverage the collaborative information to better predict users' recent visit intents. Besides, a similarity graph is proposed to leverage collaborative information from POI side on a global scale. Finally, we combine sequential and collaborative contexts to capture preferences of users. Extensive experimental results demonstrate our model outperforms other state-of-the-art baselines consistently.

Keywords: Next POI recommendation · Location-based social networks · Collaborative session · Attention mechanism · User preference

1 Introduction

With the rapid development of location-based social networks (LBSNs) like Yelp and Foursquare, an increasing number of users would like to share their

H. Qiu et al. (Eds.): KSEM 2021, LNAI 12815, pp. 639–655, 2021.
https://doi.org/10.1007/978-3-030-82136-4_52

locations by checking in at points of interest (POIs), e.g., parks and museums. Considerable check-in data and widely distributed cloud computing environment [5,6] make it convenient to analyze preferences of users and recommend the next possible POI. Next POI recommendation aims to generate a ranked list of POIs by their distinct attractiveness to users, based on users' historical check-in sequences. Since next POI recommendation can benefit both users and service producers, it gains much more attention in recent years [3].

Various sequence based approaches have been proposed for next POI recommendation. Earlier approaches model preferences of users based on Markov Chain. For example, FPMC-LR [2] extends Factorizing Personalized Markov Chain (FPMC) by adding local region constraints for next POI recommendation. However, the existing MC based methods [2,14,17] have difficulty in capturing accurate preferences since they can not model long-range sequential contexts. Recently, in order to model long-range complex sequential interactions between users and POIs, Recurrent Neural Network (RNN) and its variants (i.e., LSTM [9] and GRU [8]) based methods [12,13,15] have been proposed and gradually become the state-of-the-art models. However, most existing RNN and its variants based methods [12,13,15] only model short-term preferences of users and they ignore the periodical regularities in users' long-term check-in sequences, resulting in inexact recommendation [10]. Session-based approaches [4,18,19] can model short-term preferences of users based on current sessions, as well as long-term preferences using the information mined from historical sessions. For example, both LSTPM [18] and DeepMove [4] achieve better performances since they use attention mechanisms and RNNs to capture long- and short-term preferences of users.

Although existing methods have made remarkable progress, there are still some sequential and collaborative contexts which are beneficial to next POI recommendation have not been effectively mined. 1) Most of the existing methods only consider temporal and spatial correlations among check-ins, while they ignore the sequential contexts mined from category-based sequences. 2) Collaborative sessions are a set of sessions which share the similar mobile patterns with the current session. They are generated by any user (not necessarily the current user). With the help of collaborative sessions, we can better predict the visit intents of current sessions. Most of the existing session-based methods only take users' own sessions into account, while they ignore the information in collaborative sessions. 3) Most of the sequential methods model preferences of users only by using their own check-in sequences. Since check-ins generated by each user are limited, and user's next possible visiting POI may never appear in his/her historical check-ins, it is important to introduce some collaborative information from POI side to tackle this problem, such as inherent similarities among POIs.

To this end, we propose a method to explore sequential and collaborative contexts (SCC) for next POI recommendation. The key insights of our proposed SCC are as follows: 1) Obviously, whether the user will like a POI is related to the category of the POI. Therefore, we argue that categorical information is essential to explore preferences of users. What's more, the density of the user-category matrix is much higher than that of user-POI matrix, it is easier to predict the categories that users may be interested in than directly predict the possible POIs. Since different categories have different distributions of time

[23], we use the sequential information mined from category-based sequences as well as correlations between time and categories to capture users' preferences of categories. Thus, we can recommend suitable POIs to users based on their categorical preferences and the current time period. 2) For some existing collaborative session based methods [7,21], they only consider item level collaborative sessions while they ignore category level collaborative sessions. However, collaborative sessions of these two levels may be different to some extent. Therefore, we generate collaborative sessions on POI and category level respectively. Then we use the information mined from them to determine the importance of each check-in in the current session. This will help better predict users' recent visit intents and make more accurate recommendation for next POI. 3) Since there are some inherent similarities among POIs, we build a global POI similarity graph to retain these similarities. Each POI in this graph has several neighbors which may be accessed successively by users. Considering different users have different mobile habits, we design a user-specific attention mechanism to generate the weights of neighbor POIs. Hence, we can recommend several similar POIs to users based on user-specific recent visit demands. This can alleviate data sparsity and accords with the intuition of collaborative filtering [20].

Our contributions can be summarized as follows:

- We propose a method to explore sequential and collaborative contexts for next POI recommendation. In our method, we explicitly model temporal, spatial and categorical correlations among check-ins to leverage sequential contexts. Moreover, we use the global information from the session and POI side to generate collaborative contexts. Both of them can help recommend more accurate POIs.
- We generate collaborative sessions of the current session and use the information from them to better predict users' recent visit intents. As a result, the intents can effectively select the most useful information from historical sessions. Besides, we build a global similarity graph to retain inherent similarities among POIs. Under the help of this graph, we can recommend similar POIs which users may be interested in based on their recent visit demands. Collaborative contexts from the session and POI side can help recommend more suitable next POI.
- We conduct extensive experiments on two public datasets. The experimental results demonstrate that our model can outperform the state-of-the-art baselines consistently.

The remainder of this paper is organized as follows. Section 2 reviews the related works. Section 3 defines the next POI recommendation task. Section 4 introduces our proposed model SCC in detail. Section 5 introduces the baselines and analyzes the experimental results. Finally, Sect. 6 concludes this paper.

2 Related Work

Early studies in POI recommendation predict preferences of users by leveraging Collaborative Filtering (CF) information from their neighbors. Matrix Factorization (MF) based methods, such as [16] and [11] have become the state-of-the-art approaches to collaborative filtering since they can capture preferences in a latent space. Then MF has been extended to introduce temporal and spatial relations among check-ins. For example, in Tensor Factorization [24], time is divided into bins and added to the factorization model as a new dimension. Tensor Factorization [27] models the spatial information via factorization for location prediction. These methods [11,16,24,27] only can model static preferences of users while they ignore using sequential relations between successive check-ins.

According to [26], users' movements have sequential patterns, considering sequential dependencies among check-ins is crucial for next POI recommendation. As a method often used in sequence prediction, Markov Chain aims to predict next POI based on consecutive check-ins of users. Factorizing Personalized Markov Chain (FPMC) [17] is a combination of Matrix Factorization and Markov Chain. FPMC-LR [2] extends FPMC for POI recommendation by adding local area constraints. However, FPMC based methods [2,17] have difficulty in capturing accurate preferences of users since they assume that all factors influence the next possible POI independently as well as they can not model long-range sequential dependencies [22].

In order to effectively model long-range complex interactions between users and POIs, Recurrent Neural Network (RNN) and its variants (i.e., LSTM [9] and GRU [8]) based methods [12,13,15] have been proposed and widely used in next POI recommendation. ST-RNN [13] adds temporal and spatial constraints to the RNN model to predict users' mobile patterns. TMCA [12] integrates contextual information including temporal, spatial and categorical relations through a two-layer attention mechanism. CARA [15] extends GRU with a Contextual Attention Gate and a Time- and Spatial-based Gate for next POI recommendation. However, most of the RNN based methods only model short-term preferences of users while they neglect the important periodical regularities and general preferences in users' long-term check-in sequences [18]. Session-based methods can capture short-term preferences by leveraging the information in current sessions, as well as long-term preferences by using the information in historical sessions. They combine long- and short-term preferences to get more accurate prediction for the next POI. DeepMove [4] uses the current status to select relevant historical check-ins for modeling long-term preferences, and uses a RNN to model short-term preferences. LSTPM [18] develops a two-layer nonlocal network to model long-term preferences, and proposes a geo-dilated RNN to capture short-term preferences.

3 Problem Formulation

Let $U = \{u_1, u_2, \ldots, u_{|U|}\}$ denote a set of $|U|$ users, $P = \{p_1, p_2, \ldots p_{|P|}\}$ denote a set of $|P|$ POIs. Each POI can be represented by a $(longitude, latitude, category)$ tuple. For each user $u \in U$, his/her check-ins can be divided into several sessions. Session is divided according to a certain time interval, which can be 24 h, 48 h etc. We use $S = \{S_1, S_2, \ldots, S_n\}$ to represent one user's check-in sequence which S_n is the current session and $\{S_1, S_2, \ldots, S_{n-1}\}$

are historical sessions. Each session S_i consists of a set of POIs in a consecutive order which can be represented as $S_i = \{p_1, p_2, \ldots, p_{|S_i|}\}$ and $p \in P$.

The next POI recommendation problem can be defined as: given a user $u \in U$, along with user's historical sessions $\{S_1, S_2, \ldots, S_{n-1}\}$ as well as his/her current session $S_n = \{p_1, p_2, \ldots, p_{t-1}\}$ where p_{t-1} is the most recent check-in in the current session, we aim to predict top-N POIs where the user u may go next at a specific timestamp t.

4 The Proposed Model

In this section, we present our model in detail. Figure 1 illustrates the architecture of SCC. SCC consists of long- and short-term preference modeling modules as well as a prediction module. In the long-term module, we use the information mined from collaborative sessions and the current session to select the most important sequential patterns from historical sessions. In the short-term module, we build a global similarity graph of POIs. Then we capture user's short-term preference by combining the user's latest check-in and its neighbors in the graph. Finally, we compute probability distributions over all POIs and all categories based on user's preferences for the prediction.

4.1 Long-Term Preference Modeling

In the long-term preference modeling, an intuitive idea is that we need to choose the most useful information from historical check-ins according to the current status. To do this, we firstly generate the time-weighted, distance-weighted and category-weighted representations of each historical session. Then we generate the representation of the current session under the help of collaborative sessions. Finally, we capture long-term preferences of users by considering the impact of each historical session on the current session.

Time-Weighted Operation. Firstly, we represent each POI p_i and its category with a POI embedding vector $l_i \in R^{d \times 1}$ and a category embedding vector $c_i \in R^{d \times 1}$, where d is the embedding dimension. Then, given a user u, in order to capture sequential dependencies, we use a LSTM layer to encode representations of POIs in historical sessions $\{S_1, S_2, \ldots, S_{n-1}\}$ as follows:

$$H_i = LSTM(l_i, H_{i-1}) \tag{1}$$

where H_i is the hidden state of POI i. We then use another LSTM layer to encode representations of POIs in the current session S_n by the same means. Then, we map one week into 48 time slots, 24 slots for weekdays and 24 slots for weekends. For each time slot, we generate a set $slot_i = (p_1, p_2, \ldots, p_{|slot_i|})$ that contains POIs have been checked-in during this time slot. After that, we measure the similarity between two time slots by the following method:

$$\tau_{i,j} = \frac{|slot_i \bigcap slot_j|}{|slot_i \bigcup slot_j|} \tag{2}$$

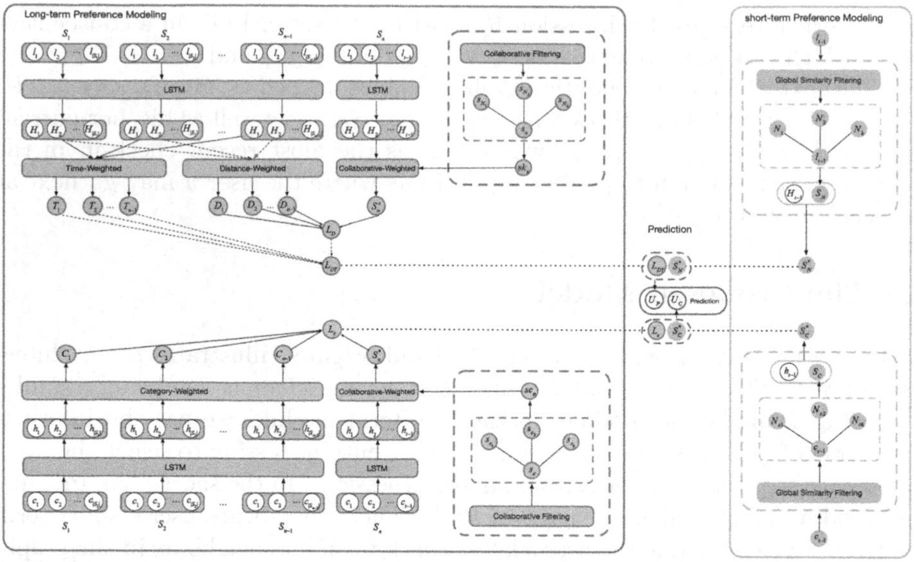

Fig. 1. The architecture of our SCC.

which means the more overlap POIs between two time slots, the more similar they are. Since preferences of users are time-sensitive, we hope those check-in records in historical sessions whose time slot is more similar to the current time slot will get a larger attention value. As for each historical session, we have got a sequence of check-in time slots $\{slot_1, slot_2, \ldots, slot_{|S_h|}\}$, where $|S_h|$ denotes the length of the session S_h. Then the time-weighted representation of each historical session can be calculated as follows:

$$T_h = \sum_{i=1}^{|S_h|} \omega_i H_i, \omega_i = \frac{\exp(\tau_{slot_c, slot_i})}{\sum_{j=1}^{|S_h|} \exp(\tau_{slot_c, slot_j})} \tag{3}$$

where $\tau_{slot_c, slot_j}$ is the similarity between the current time slot $slot_c$ and the time slot $slot_j$ of the historical check-in j in S_h. So far, we can get $n-1$ time-weighted representations $\{T_1, T_2, \ldots, T_{n-1}\}$ of historical sessions.

Distance-Weighted Operation. In the next POI recommendation, the POI a user may visit next highly relies on the distance between the latest POI and the next POI [2]. Thus, for distance-weighted operation, we want those records in historical sessions whose location is more closer to the latest check-in will get a larger attention value. Then the distance-weighted representation of each historical session can be calculated as follows:

$$D_h = \sum_{i=1}^{|S_h|} \varpi_i H_i, \varpi_i = \frac{\exp(D_{latest,i})}{\sum_{j=1}^{|S_h|} \exp(D_{latest,j})} \tag{4}$$

where $D_{latest,j}$ is the distance between the latest check-in and the historical check-in j in S_h. We can get distance-weighted representations $\{D_1, D_2, \ldots, D_{n-1}\}$ of historical sessions now.

Category-Weighted Operation. Then we process the category-based sequence. Firstly, we use two LSTM layers to encode representations of POIs' categories in historical sessions and the current session by the same means on the POI level. Then for category-weighted operation, we consider the fact that different categories have different distributions of time slots. For example, users may prefer to visit bars at night and go to restaurants during meal time. Hence, we calculate the similarity between each category and each time slot as follows:

$$\varphi_{slot_i,c_j} = \frac{|Count_{slot_i,c_j}|}{|Count_{slot_i}|} \tag{5}$$

where $Count_{slot_i}$ means the amount of categories appear in the time slot $slot_i$, and $Count_{slot_i,c_j}$ means times of category c_j appears in the time slot $slot_i$. This means the more frequently one category appears in one time slot, the more similar they are. We want those categories which are more similar to the current time slot to get a larger attention value. Therefore, the category-weighted representation of each historical session can be calculated as follows:

$$C_h = \sum_{i=1}^{|S_h|} \lambda_i h_i, \lambda_i = \frac{\exp(\varphi_{slot_c,c_i})}{\sum_{j=1}^{|S_h|} \exp(\varphi_{slot_c,c_j})} \tag{6}$$

where h_i is the hidden state of the historical check-in i's category generated from LSTM layer, and φ_{slot_c,c_j} is the similarity between the current time slot $slot_c$ and the category c_j of the historical check-in j in S_h. So far, we get category-weighted representations $\{C_1, C_2, \ldots, C_{n-1}\}$ of historical sessions.

Current Session Representation Generating. We then generate the representation of the current session by using the information mined from collaborative sessions. Collaborative sessions of the current session may be different on the POI and the category level. Thus, we need to select them respectively. Next, we will explain the process from POI level, because the same method is used on the category level.

To identify collaborative sessions of the current session, we use a k-nearest neighbor method. Specifically, for the current session, we compute the similarities between it and its neighbor sessions by calculating their jaccard similarity coefficient as follows:

$$J_{i,curr} = \frac{|N_i \bigcap N_{curr}|}{|N_i \bigcup N_{curr}|} \tag{7}$$

where N_i denotes POIs in the neighbor session s_{N_i}, and N_{curr} denotes POIs in the current session. We select k-nearest neighbor sessions $\{s_{N_1}, s_{N_2}, \ldots, s_{N_k}\}$ of the current session with highest similarities. For each neighbor session as well as the current session, we generate the representation of it by averaging representation of each check-in in it as follows:

$$s_{N_i} = \sum_{i=1}^{|s_{N_i}|} l_i, \quad s_n = \sum_{j=1}^{|S_n|} l_j \tag{8}$$

where $|s_{N_i}|$ denotes the length of the neighbor session s_{N_i}. After that, we build a graph $G_{session}$ to retain the neighborhood relationship. We then calculate the representation vector of collaborative sessions as follows:

$$sk_n = \sum_{s_{N_i} \in N_{s_n}} \delta_{s_{N_i}, s_n} s_{N_i} \tag{9}$$

where N_{s_n} denotes the collaborative session set of the current session S_n, and $\delta_{s_{N_i}, s_n}$ means the attention value between the collaborative session s_{N_i} and the current session. The attention value is computed as follows:

$$\delta_{s_{N_i}, s_n} = \frac{\exp({s_{N_i}}^T s_n)}{\sum_{s_{N_j} \in N_{s_n}} \exp({s_{N_j}}^T s_n)} \tag{10}$$

Collaborative-Weighted Operation. We use the representation vector of collaborative sessions sk_n to determine the importance of each check-in in the current session as follows:

$$\rho_i = \frac{\exp(\sigma(W_L l_i + W_C sk_n))}{\sum_{j=1}^{|S_n|} \exp(\sigma(W_L l_j + W_C sk_n))} \tag{11}$$

where $W_L \in R^{1 \times d}$ and $W_C \in R^{1 \times d}$ are trainable matrices, $\sigma(\cdot)$ is the sigmoid function. After getting the attention value of each check-in, we can generate the representation of the current session as follows:

$$S_n^+ = \sum_{i=1}^{|S_n|} \rho_i H_i \tag{12}$$

Now we have the representation S_n^+ of the current session on the POI level. Using the same method, we can get the representation S_n^* of the current session on the category level.

Long-Term Preference Modeling. After that, we capture the impact of each historical session on the current session based on the pairwise affinity between them. For POI-level, the computation process can be detailed as follows:

$$L_D = \frac{1}{D(S)} \sum_{h=1}^{n-1} \exp((S_n^+)^T D_h) \cdot W_D D_h \tag{13}$$

$$L_{DT} = \frac{1}{T(S)} \sum_{h=1}^{n-1} \exp((L_D)^T T_h) \cdot W_T T_h \tag{14}$$

where W_D and W_T are trainable weight matrices. $\exp((S_n^+)^T D_h)$ is the pairwise function to calculate the affinity score between the current session and each distance-weighted representation D_h of the historical session S_h. $\exp((L_D)^T T_h)$ is the pairwise function to compute the affinity score between the distance-based long-term user preference L_D and each time-weighted representation T_h of the historical session. $D(S) = \sum_{h=1}^{n-1} \exp((S_n^+)^T D_h)$ and $T(S) = \sum_{h=1}^{n-1} \exp((L_D)^T T_h)$ are normalization factors.

So far, we can get the long-term preference L_{DT} of the user on the POI level. By the same means, we can get long-term preference L_C on the category level.

4.2 Short-Term Preference Modeling

For the short-term preference, we firstly build a global similarity graph of POIs using all check-ins in the training dataset. Each POI in this graph has several neighbors. Secondly, we design a user-specific attention mechanism to determine the different importance of each neighbor POI. Finally, we capture the short-term preference by combining the hidden state and neighbor POIs of the latest check-in.

Global Similarity Graph Building. Here the similarity means that two POIs may be visited by one user at a specific time. Therefore, we need to measure the similarity based on recognizing which feature is pivotal for a POI to attract users. Our intuitions are as follows:

Intuition 1: Users tend to visit nearby POIs to the most recent POI [18]. Hence, for each POI, we select those POIs whose distance to it within a threshold D^* to build a spatial neighbor set.

Intuition 2: The users' preferences of POIs will vary with time in one day. Therefore, POIs always appear in the same time slot are similar to each other. We build a $|P| \times |T|$ matrix M to measure similarities between time slots and POIs. $|P|$ means the amount of POIs, $|T|$ means the number of time slots, and $M_{pt} = n$ means the POI p has been checked in n times in time slot $slot_t$. For a specific POI, to generate its temporal neighbor set, we first need to find its most similar time slot which the POI has been checked in most times. Then, we select the top T^* POIs which appear most frequently in the same time slot.

Intuition 3: Since users' check-in records demonstrate their preferences of POIs, if two POIs always co-occurrence in one user's check-ins, they are similar to each other. For a specific POI, we select the top S^* POIs that always appear together with this POI to build its semantic neighbor set.

After that, we generate the intersection of the spatial and temporal neighbor set. Then we generate the union of the intersection set and the semantic neighbor set to construct the final neighbor set of each POI. Finally, we build a global similarity graph to save the relationship.

User-Specific Attention Mechanism. We design a user-specific attention mechanism to calculate the importance of each POI in the latest check-in's neighbor set. Firstly, we generate the user representation by average pooling representations of POIs in the current session. Then we calculate the attention value of each POI in the neighbor set as follows:

$$\mu_i = \frac{\exp(\sigma(W_N l_i + W_U U))}{\sum_{j \in NB_{latest}} \exp(\sigma(W_N l_j + W_U U))} \tag{15}$$

where $W_N \in R^{1 \times d}$ and $W_U \in R^{1 \times d}$ are trainable matrices, U denotes the user representation, and NB_{latest} means the neighbor set of the latest check-in. Finally we generate the neighbor vector as follows:

$$S_N = \sum_{i \in NB_{latest}} \mu_i l_i \tag{16}$$

So far, we have got the neighbor vector S_N on the POI-level.

Short-Term Preference Modeling. Then we generate the short-term preference by combining the hidden state and the neighbor vector of user's latest check-in as follows:

$$S_N^* = \beta H_{t-1} + (1-\beta) S_N \tag{17}$$

where β is the parameter which can balance the weights of the two parts. By the same operations, we can get the short-term preference S_c^* on the category level.

4.3 Prediction

After obtaining long- and short-term preferences on the POI and category level, we calculate probability distributions of POIs and categories as follows:

$$U_p = \text{softmax}(\mathrm{W_p}(L_{DT} || \mathrm{S}_N^*)), U_c = \text{softmax}(\mathrm{W_{p_c}}(L_C || \mathrm{S}_C^*)) \tag{18}$$

where softmax($\cdot$) denotes the softmax function, and $||$ is the concatenation operation. W_p and W_{p_c} are trainable projection matrices. Then we add the probability of each POI and its category for the final prediction as follows:

$$U_{pre_i} = \text{softmax}(\alpha U_{p_i} + (1-\alpha) U_{c_i}) \tag{19}$$

where α is the parameter to balance the weights of the two parts. The next possible top-N POIs for recommendation are the ones with the largest probabilities. To learn parameters in our model, we define the objective function as the cross-entropy between the prediction result $\hat{y}$ and the ground truth y as follows:

$$L = -\sum_{n=1}^{N} y_n \log(\hat{y}_n) + (1-y_n)\log(1-\hat{y}_n) \tag{20}$$

where N is the total number of all samples, and $y_n = 1$ indicates the user visit this POI.

5 Experiments

In this section, we evaluate the recommendation performance of our proposed model SCC on two real-world LBSN datasets.

5.1 Evaluation Datasets and Evaluation Metrics

We conduct our experiments on two real-world check-in datasets which collected in New York city and Tokyo from Foursquare [25], denoted as NYC and TKY respectively. For NYC and TKY datasets, firstly we filter unpopular POIs that are visited less than five times in NYC and less than ten times in TKY. Then we generate sessions of each user by treating a user's all check-ins in one day as a single session. If there are less than three check-ins in one session, we will remove this session. Finally we filter inactive users whose check-in sessions are less than five. We use first 80% sessions of one user as train datasets, and the rest sessions as test datasets. The statistics of NYC and TKY datasets after preprocessing are shown in Table 1.

Table 1. Statistical information of NYC and TKY datasets.

Datasets	User	POI	Category	Check-in	Session
NYC	819	8149	347	161205	18253
TKY	1923	7762	292	421856	55839

To evaluate performances of recommendation models, we adopt two metrics *Recall@N* and *Normalized Discounted Cumulative Gain (NDCG@N)* which are commonly used in the previous works [1,12]. *Recall@N* is used to measure whether the ground truth POI appears in the top-N ranked list and *NDCG@N* is used to calculate the recommendation quality by considering the position of the ground truth POI in the ranked list. We choose the popular $N = \{1, 5, 10\}$ in our experiments.

5.2 Baselines and Settings

We compare the performance of SCC with the following seven methods:

Pop: This model generates recommendation list according to the popularity of POIs.

FPMC-LR [2]**:** This model extends FPMC with localized regional constraints for next POI recommendation.

GRU [8]**:** This model uses the GRU-based RNN for session-based recommendations.

LSTM [9]**:** This is a variant of RNN with a memory cell and three gates, which can effectively capture long-range dependencies between check-ins.

LTSTPI [19]**:** This session-based method models the user-specific long- and short-term preferences for sequential recommendation.

Table 2. Performance comparison on two datasets.

Dataset	Methods	Recall@N			NDCG@N		
		N = 1	N = 5	N = 10	N = 1	N = 5	N = 10
NYC	POP	0.0183	0.0406	0.0537	0.0183	0.0269	0.0311
	FPMC-LR	0.1143	0.2102	0.2363	0.1143	0.1668	0.1747
	GRU	0.1598	0.3156	0.3608	0.1598	0.2446	0.2592
	LSTM	0.1480	0.2733	0.3167	0.1480	0.2152	0.2293
	LTSTPI	0.1673	0.3429	0.3925	0.1673	0.2613	0.2794
	DeepMove	0.1688	0.3679	0.4280	0.1688	0.2733	0.2934
	LSTPM	<u>0.1801</u>	<u>0.3946</u>	<u>0.4619</u>	<u>0.1801</u>	<u>0.2929</u>	<u>0.3148</u>
	SCC	**0.1984**	**0.4135**	**0.4820**	**0.1984**	**0.3128**	**0.3341**
TKY	POP	0.0418	0.1043	0.1356	0.0418	0.0698	0.0823
	FPMC-LR	0.1482	0.2663	0.3179	0.1482	0.2109	0.2281
	GRU	0.1778	0.3390	0.4075	0.1778	0.2630	0.2852
	LSTM	0.1631	0.2930	0.3486	0.1631	0.2320	0.2500
	LTSTPI	0.1890	0.3633	0.4328	0.1890	0.2824	0.3101
	DeepMove	0.1725	0.3479	0.4066	0.1725	0.2682	0.2877
	LSTPM	<u>0.2540</u>	<u>0.4678</u>	<u>0.5475</u>	<u>0.2540</u>	<u>0.3672</u>	<u>0.3930</u>
	SCC	**0.2704**	**0.4891**	**0.5709**	**0.2704**	**0.3852**	**0.4124**

DeepMove [4]**:** This method models both the long-term preferences of users by attention mechanism, and the short-term preferences of users by a RNN module for next POI recommendation.

LSTPM [18]**:** This method uses a two-layer nonlocal network to model the long-term preferences of users, and a geo-dilated RNN module to capture the short-term preferences for next POI recommendation.

In our experiments, for a fair comparison, we set the embedding dimension and the hidden state of all baselines and our model to 500. The learning rate is chosen from $lr = \{0.1, 0.01, 0.005, 0.001\}$ and the batch size of all models is set to be 32. Besides that, we follow the reported optimal hyper-parameters of all baselines. All parameters in our model are optimized by gradient descent optimization algorithm Adam, and the optimal values of other hyper-parameters are selected by grid search.

5.3 Performance Comparisons

The results of all models are shown in Table 2. The best results of all metrics are highlighted in blodface and the suboptimal results are underlined. Compared with all baselines, our proposed SCC achieves the best performance on two datasets in terms of all metrics. SCC outperforms the strongest state-of-the-art model LSTPM by 7.06% and 5.26% on average for NYC and TKY datasets respectively, which clearly indicates the effectiveness of modeling category-based sequences and using the collaborative information from collaborative sessions and POI side.

Among baselines, the traditional method POP lags behind other models which indicates the deep learning can really boost the performance of recommendation. RNN-based models LSTM and GRU perform better than Markov Chain based method FPMC-LR which demonstrates RNN based model can capture dependencies among long sequential check-ins. Because three session-based methods LTSTPI, DeepMove and LSTPM take users' long-and short-term preferences into account and consider the distinct impact of each historical session on the final recommendation, they perform much better than other baselines on NYC dataset. Among them, the performance of LTSTPI is worse than DeepMove and LSTPM on NYC dataset since it does not consider temporal and spatial correlations among check-ins. Because the check-in sequence generated by each user in TKY dataset is longer than that in NYC dataset, it is difficult for DeepMove to capture useful history information. Therefore, the performance of DeepMove on TKY dataset drops greatly. LSTPM outperforms all other baselines on NYC and TKY datasets since it considers both temporal and spatial information among POIs and uses a geo-dilated RNN structure to model the non-consecutive check-ins. Moreover, we compare the training speeds of three session-based baselines and our proposed SCC. Since our method considers more sequential and collaborative contexts, the training efficiency of SCC is slightly lower than those of LSTPM and LTSTPI. However, the efficiency of SCC is always better than that of DeepMove. This indicates our SCC has great application values in actual POI recommendation.

5.4 Ablation Study

To verify the effectiveness of key components in SCC, we employ several variants of SCC as follows: (1) *NC* removes category-based sequences modeling from SCC. (2) *NG* removes global neighbors generating from SCC, and only use the hidden state of the latest check-in for short-term preference modeling. (3) *NCS* removes collaborative sessions generating from SCC. Then use the average pooling operation to generate the representation of the current session. (4) *NL* removes the long-term preference modeling from SCC. (5) *NS* removes the short-term preference modeling from SCC.

The performances of all variants and SCC on NYC dataset are shown in Fig. 2. We can find: (1) Compared with *NC*, SCC has better performance. This observation validates our design of modeling category-based sequences. The categorical information can help recommend more accurate next possible POI. Moreover, we find the performance of *NC* is better than the baseline LSTPM. Since both *NC* and LSTPM do not model category-based sequences, *NC* can recommend more suitable POIs under the help of the collaborative information from collaborative sessions and the POI side. (2) Compared with *NG*, SCC has better performance. This observation validates our design of the global similarity graph and the accuracy of three intuitions in our POI similarity measurement.

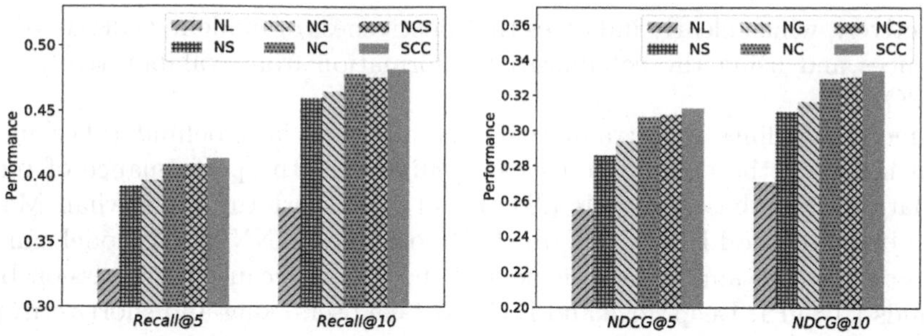

Fig. 2. Ablation study on NYC dataset.

(3) Compared with *NCS*, SCC has better performance. This observation validates collaborative sessions can help better predict the visit intent in the current session. This intent can effectively select the useful information from historical sessions. (4) Compared with *NL* and *NS*, SCC has better performance which means both the long-term and short-term preferences of users are indispensable for predicting the next possible POI.

5.5 Impact of Hyper-parameters D^*, T^* and S^*

In our model, when generating neighbor sets of POIs to build the global similarity graph, three hyper-parameters D^*, T^* and S^* are used. On NYC and TKY datasets, we set D^* as the average distance between two consecutive check-ins, which are 3.58 km and 3.67 km respectively. We set T^* used in SCC to be $\{1, 3, 5, 10\}$, and S^* to be $\{1, 2, 3, 4, 5\}$ to see the performance changes with the two hyper-parameters on NYC dataset. The experimental results are shown in the Fig. 3.

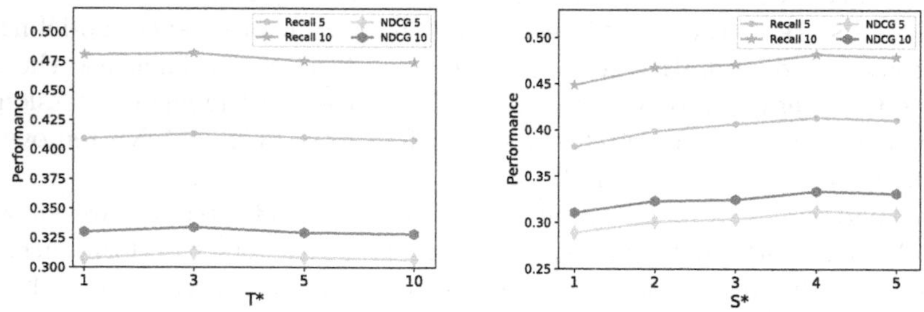

Fig. 3. Performance comparison of different T^* and S^* on NYC dataset.

For the hyper-parameter T^* and S^*, we can observe that the performance of SCC increases as T^* and S^* increase at beginning, when $T^* = 3$ and $S^* = 4$, the performance of SCC hits the peak. After that when T^* and S^* increase, the performance of SCC decreases. This makes sense because when T^* and S^* are small, similar POIs are not fully included. While when T^* and S^* become large, some POIs with low similarities are included, resulting in a slightly performance decreases.

6 Conclusion

In this paper, we proposed a method to explore sequential and collaborative contexts (SCC) for next POI recommendation. Different from the existing methods, we simultaneously modeled temporal, spatial and categorical correlations among check-ins to capture sequential contexts. We generated collaborative sessions for current sessions, then leveraged the collaborative information to better predict users' recent visit intents. Besides, a global similarity graph was proposed to leverage collaborative information from POI side on a global scale. Finally, we combined the sequential and collaborative contexts to model preferences of users. Extensive experimental results showed our model can improve the recommendation performance for next POI.

Acknowledgement. This work is supported by National Key R&D Program of China under Award No. 2018YFB0804402.

References

1. Chen, T., Yin, H., Nguyen, Q.V.H., Peng, W.C., Li, X., Zhou, X.: Sequence-aware factorization machines for temporal predictive analytics. In: 2020 IEEE 36th International Conference on Data Engineering (ICDE), pp. 1405–1416. IEEE (2020)
2. Cheng, C., Yang, H., Lyu, M.R., King, I.: Where you like to go next: successive point-of-interest recommendation. In: 23rd International Joint Conference on Artificial Intelligence (2013)
3. Cheng, W., Shen, Y., Zhu, Y., Huang, L.: Delf: a dual-embedding based deep latent factor model for recommendation. In: Proceedings of the 27th International Joint Conference on Artificial Intelligence, IJCAI-18, pp. 3329–3335. International Joint Conferences on Artificial Intelligence Organization (July 2018)
4. Feng, J., et al.: DeepMove: predicting human mobility with attentional recurrent networks. In: Proceedings of the 2018 World Wide Web Conference, pp. 1459–1468 (2018)
5. Gai, K., Qiu, M.: Optimal resource allocation using reinforcement learning for IoT content-centric services. App. Soft Comput. **70**, 12–21 (2018)
6. Gai, K., Qiu, M.: Reinforcement learning-based content-centric services in mobile sensing. IEEE Netw. **32**(4), 34–39 (2018)
7. Guo, Y., Ling, Y., Chen, H.: A neighbor-guided memory-based neural network for session-aware recommendation. IEEE Access **8**, 120668–120678 (2020)
8. Hidasi, B., Karatzoglou, A., Baltrunas, L., Tikk, D.: Session-based recommendations with recurrent neural networks. arXiv preprint arXiv:1511.06939 (2015)
9. Hochreiter, S., Schmidhuber, J.: Long short-term memory. Neural Comput. **9**(8), 1735–1780 (1997)

10. Jannach, D., Lerche, L., Jugovac, M.: Adaptation and evaluation of recommendations for short-term shopping goals. In: Proceedings of the 9th ACM Conference on Recommender Systems, pp. 211–218 (2015)
11. Koren, Y., Bell, R., Volinsky, C.: Matrix factorization techniques for recommender systems. Computer **42**(8), 30–37 (2009)
12. Li, R., Shen, Y., Zhu, Y.: Next point-of-interest recommendation with temporal and multi-level context attention. In: 2018 IEEE International Conference on Data Mining (ICDM), pp. 1110–1115. IEEE (2018)
13. Liu, Q., Wu, S., Wang, L., Tan, T.: Predicting the next location: a recurrent model with spatial and temporal contexts. In: Proceedings of the AAAI Conference on Artificial Intelligence, vol. 30 (2016)
14. Lv, Q., Qiao, Y., Ansari, N., Liu, J., Yang, J.: Big data driven hidden Markov model based individual mobility prediction at points of interest. IEEE Trans. Veh. Technol. **66**(6), 5204–5216 (2016)
15. Manotumruksa, J., Macdonald, C., Ounis, I.: A contextual attention recurrent architecture for context-aware venue recommendation. In: The 41st International ACM SIGIR Conference on Research & Development in Information Retrieval, pp. 555–564 (2018)
16. Mnih, A., Salakhutdinov, R.R.: Probabilistic matrix factorization. In: Advances in Neural Information Processing Systems, pp. 1257–1264 (2008)
17. Rendle, S., Freudenthaler, C., Schmidt-Thieme, L.: Factorizing personalized Markov chains for next-basket recommendation. In: Proceedings of the 19th International Conference on World Wide Web, pp. 811–820 (2010)
18. Sun, K., et al.: Where to go next: modeling long-and short-term user preferences for point-of-interest recommendation. In: Proceedings of the AAAI Conference on Artificial Intelligence, vol. 34, pp. 214–221 (2020)
19. Sun, K., Qian, T., Yin, H., Chen, T., Chen, Y., Chen, L.: What can history tell us? Identifying relevant sessions for next-item recommendation. In: Proceedings of the 29th ACM on Conference on Information and Knowledge Management, CIKM (2019)
20. Wang, J., De Vries, A.P., Reinders, M.J.: Unifying user-based and item-based collaborative filtering approaches by similarity fusion. In: Proceedings of the 29th Annual International ACM SIGIR Conference on Research and Development in Information Retrieval, pp. 501–508 (2006)
21. Wang, M., Ren, P., Mei, L., Chen, Z., Ma, J., de Rijke, M.: A collaborative session-based recommendation approach with parallel memory modules. In: Proceedings of the 42nd International ACM SIGIR Conference on Research and Development in Information Retrieval, pp. 345–354 (2019)
22. Wang, P., Guo, J., Lan, Y., Xu, J., Wan, S., Cheng, X.: Learning hierarchical representation model for nextbasket recommendation. In: Proceedings of the 38th International ACM SIGIR Conference on Research and Development in Information Retrieval, pp. 403–412 (2015)
23. Wu, Y., Li, K., Zhao, G., Qian, X.: Personalized long-and short-term preference learning for next poi recommendation. IEEE Trans. Knowl. Data Eng. (2020)
24. Xiong, L., Chen, X., Huang, T.K., Schneider, J., Carbonell, J.G.: Temporal collaborative filtering with Bayesian probabilistic tensor factorization. In: Proceedings of the 2010 SIAM International Conference on Data Mining, pp. 211–222. SIAM (2010)
25. Yang, D., Zhang, D., Zheng, V.W., Yu, Z.: Modeling user activity preference by leveraging user spatial temporal characteristics in LBSNs. IEEE Trans. Syst. Man Cybern. Syst. **45**(1), 129–142 (2014)

26. Zhao, P., et al.: Where to go next: a spatio-temporal gated network for next poi recommendation. IEEE Trans. Knowl. Data Eng. (2020)
27. Zheng, V., Cao, B., Zheng, Y., Xie, X., Yang, Q.: Collaborative filtering meets mobile recommendation: a user-centered approach. In: Proceedings of the AAAI Conference on Artificial Intelligence, vol. 24 (2010)

Predicting User Preferences via Heterogeneous Information Network and Metric Learning

Xiaotong Li, Yan Tang(✉), Yuan Yuan, and Yingpei Chen

School of Computer and Information Science, Southwest University, Chongqing, China
{lxt1809,y947136085,chenyingpei1}@email.swu.edu.cn,
ytang@swu.edu.cn

Abstract. Heterogeneous information network contains richer semantic information, considering multiple types of objects and relationships to more accurately determine user preferences. In addition, existing approaches usually project each user to a point in the space, it is insufficient to accurately model the intensity of the user-item relationship and the heterogeneity of different types of objects and their relationships in implicit feedback. In order to solve these problems, we propose Predicting User Preferences via Heterogeneous Information Network and Metric Learning (PUHML). First, we use heterogeneous information networks to model complex heterogeneous data, and obtain users and item node representations. Second, we construct a user-item relationship vector, and translate each user toward items according to the user-item relationship. Finally, to alleviate the limitation of inner product as a scoring function, we introduce metric learning instead of dot product, and use distance to measure user preferences. Experimental results on three datasets demonstrates the effectiveness of our proposed approach over some competitive baselines.

Keywords: Recommendation system · Heterogeneous Information Network · Metric learning

1 Introduction

Heterogeneous Information Network (HIN) as a powerful information modeling method has been proposed and used in various practical applications [12–14]. Due to the flexibility of HIN modeling data heterogeneity, many researchers have begun to use HINs in recommendation systems to describe complex and heterogeneous auxiliary information data [1]. But how to effectively extract and use heterogeneous information to assist recommendation is a huge challenge. Most of the existing recommendation algorithms based on HINs rely on the similarity of the meta-path between users and items, and use similarity to improve the effect of recommendation [2]. Similarity research reveals that between different entities The strength of the relationship can improve the recommendation effect to a certain extent. However, the connection sparsity of social information networks and the similarity based on meta-paths mainly describe the semantic relationships on HINs. Therefore, the structure and semantic information implicit in the HIN of users and items have not been fully excavated.

H. Qiu et al. (Eds.): KSEM 2021, LNAI 12815, pp. 656–665, 2021.
https://doi.org/10.1007/978-3-030-82136-4_53

Among various recommendation techniques, matrix factorization (MF) (CF) is one of the most successful models [3]. It assumes that users with similar interests in the past will tend to share similar interests in the future. More specifically, MF learns from it that the low-order vectors of users and products represent their previous interaction history, and uses the inner product to model user-item similarity. However, one of the key but not widely recognized flaws in employing inner product as a similarity metric is that it violates the triangle inequality [4]. To give a specific example, if user u_1 likes items v_1 and v_2, MF will place both items near u_1, but it is not necessary to place v_1 and v_2 near each other. That is to say, when the triangle inequality is violated, it is not guaranteed to learn the seemingly obvious item-item similarity (between v_1 and v_2) [4]. To solve those challenges, we propose a heterogeneous information network-based model to model the intensity of the user-item relationship and heterogeneity of different types of objects and their relationships.

Our contributions are summarized as follows:

- We propose Predicting User Preferences via Heterogeneous Information Network and Metric Learning (PUHML) to model the intensity of the user-item relationship and heterogeneity of different types of objects and their relationships.
- We construct a relationship vector and convert each user into multiple points according to the user-item relationship.
- We evaluate our model and results show that our PUHML model has better performance in predicting user preferences.

The rest of this paper is organized as follows: Some related work is discussed in Sect. 2. We then introduce our model in Sect. 3. Following it, Sect. 4 presents experiments results and analysis. Finally, Sect. 5 concludes this paper.

2 Related Work

2.1 Heterogeneous Information Network

Heterogeneous information network (HIN) is a special information network that contains multiple types of objects or multiple types of edges [5]. HIN is a directed graph $G = (V, E)$. Meanwhile, each node v and each link e has a type. Let A and R represent the sets of node type and link type respectively where $|A| + |R| > 2$. For each node v, we have $\phi : V \rightarrow A$; for each link e, we have $\varphi : E \rightarrow R$.

As an effective tool for semantic mining, meta-paths can specify object connection sequences and capture target semantic information at the same time. Therefore, meta-paths [6] have been widely used in various tasks in HINs.

A meta-path is defined as a path [6]. The specific form is $A_1 \xrightarrow{R_1} A_2 \xrightarrow{R_2} \cdots \xrightarrow{R_l} A_{l+1}$. It represents a compound relationship between node types A_1 and A_{l+1}.

2.2 Metric Learning

Metric Learning [7, 15] finds the appropriate distance function for the input point, such as discrete distance, Euclidean distance, etc. Metric learning plays an important role in artificial intelligence. The goal of metric learning is to learn the distance measurement of similarity between a given data, that is, similarity with a common label, and vice versa.

In order to facilitate and reduce the computational cost, we only use traditional metric learning methods. Euclidean distance and Marathon distance are the simpler methods in traditional metric learning methods. The Euclidean distance between any two data points x_i and x_j be expressed by

$$d_E^2(x_i, x_j) = \left\|(x_i - x_j)\right\|^2 = (x_i - x_j)^T (x_i - x_j)$$

$$s.t \ (x_i - x_j) \in X \tag{1}$$

3 Model

We present *Predicting User Preferences via Heterogeneous Information Network and Metric Learning*, called *PUHML*. Figure 1 represents the overall schematic illustration of PUHIN.

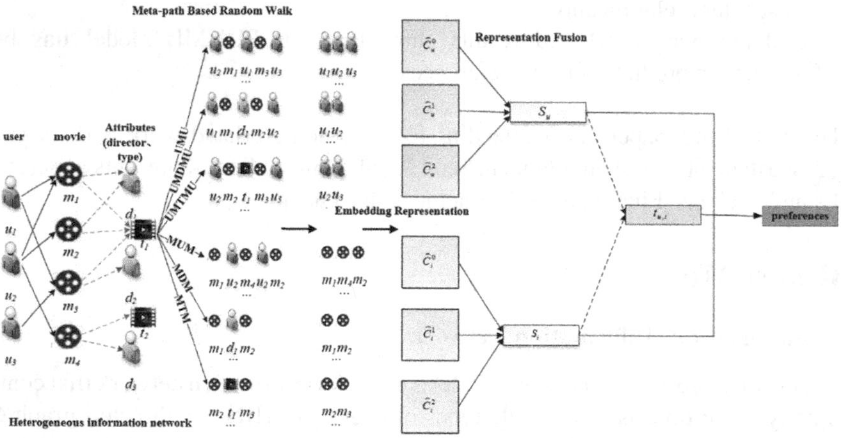

Fig. 1. The architecture of PUHML

3.1 Heterogeneous Information Network Representation Learning

Heterogeneous information network representation learning aims to generate meaningful node embedding representations. To this end, the meta-path based random walk is used to limit the walk through the meta-path. At the same time, node2vec [8] can be applied where a random walk traverses the HIN from node to node along the edge between them.

Meta-path Based Random Walk. In order to obtain rich semantic information in HINs, random walks based on meta-paths are used to generate node sequences

[5]. Given a heterogeneous information network $G = (V, E)$ and meta-path $A_1 \xrightarrow{R_1} A_2 \xrightarrow{R_2} \cdots \xrightarrow{R_l} A_{l+1}$, the random walk path will be generated by the following distribution:

$$P(n_{t+1} = v | n_t = u, p) = \begin{cases} \frac{1}{\left|N^{A_{l+1}}(u)\right|}, & (u, v) \in E \text{ and } \phi(v) = A_{l+1}; \\ 0, & \text{otherwise}, \end{cases} \tag{2}$$

where n_t is the tth node in the walk, the type of u is A_l, $N^{A_{l+1}}(u)$ is the first-order neighbor node of node u, and the type of these neighbor nodes is A_{l+1}.

Embedding Representation. Given a meta-path, we can use node2vec [8] to learn the effective representations of the nodes under the homogeneous sequence, and we can optimize the following objective to learn the representations of the nodes:

$$\max_f \sum_{u \in V} \log Pr(N(u)|f(u)) \tag{3}$$

where $f(u)$ is the current node, and $N(u)$ is the neighbor node of the node.

Representation Fusion. For our model, given a node $u \in V$, we can obtain a set of representations $\{S_u^l\}$. The S_u^l is the representation of the node u under the l meta path. In our model, we only focus on the representation of users and items, so we only select user and item nodes. In fact, for different meta-paths, different users or items have different degrees of preference. Moreover, because inactive users or items behavior data are extremely sparse, their personalized preferences for meta-paths are not obvious, and it is difficult to capture their accurate preferences. Therefore, we consider personalized weights and global weights, and utilize the non-linear function to fuse node representations:

$$\begin{aligned} S_u &= \sigma(\sum_{l=1}^{|P|} (w_u^l + w_u)(\mathbf{M_1} S_u^l + b_l)) \\ S_i &= \sigma(\sum_{l'=1}^{|P'|} (w_i^{l'} + w_i)(\mathbf{M_2} S_i^{l'} + b_{l'})) \end{aligned} \tag{4}$$

where S_u is the representation of users in HINs, S_i is the representation of items in HINs, w_u^l is the user personalized preference weight for the lth meta-path, $w_i^{l'}$ is the item personalized preference weight for the l'th meta-path, w_u and w_i are the global weight of the meta-path, $\mathbf{M}$ and b_l are the transformation matrix and bias vector under the lth meta-path, respectively.

3.2 Construct Relationship Vector

Usually each user is mapped to a point in the space, and the user will interact with multiple items, which is a one-to-many mapping. However, this is not enough to reflect the strength of the user-item relationship, because a user's implicit feedback on multiple items does not necessarily mean that user has the same preference for these items. Inspired by the translation mechanism of the knowledge graph [9], in this regard, we use the user and item representation based on the HIN to construct the relationship vector. We convert each user in the space into multiple points through the relation vector, so that the one-to-many mapping of users can be regarded as one-to-one mapping, which can reflect that users have different intensity preferences for different items. The closer the relationship between the user and the item is, the closer the converted user is to the item. Figure 2 represents the advantages of relationship vector.

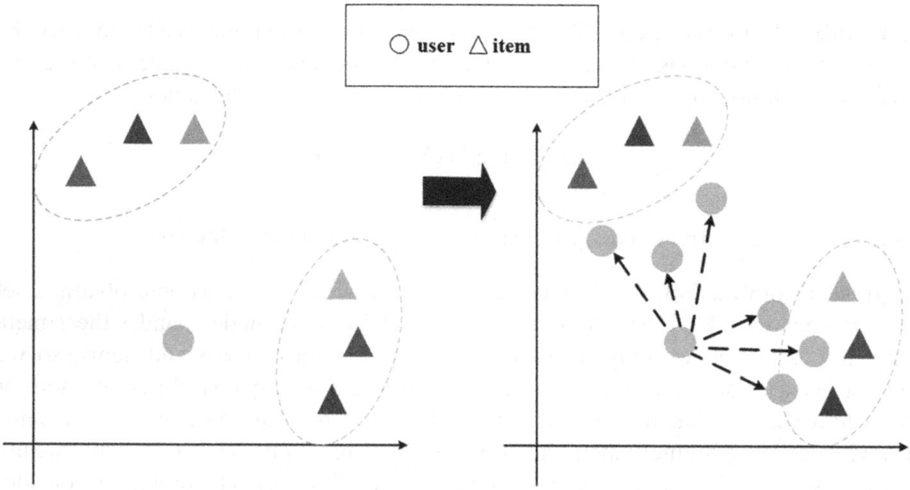

Fig. 2. The advantages of relationship vector

We use the representations S_u and S_i of the user u and the item i in the HIN obtained by (4) to construct the relation vector $t_{u,i}$:

$$t_{u,i} = f(S_u, S_i) \tag{5}$$

where $f(x, y)$ is a function used to model the interaction between the two input vectors x and y. Although various functions can be used, a simple vector product can provide high accuracy. If the relationship between the user and the project is closer, the converted user is closer to the project, reflecting that users have different strengths for different projects.

3.3 Recommendation

In order to better model the user-item heterogeneity and relationship strength in the implicit feedback, and to solve the inner product as a scoring function that violates the triangle inequality. Therefore, we introduce metric learning instead of inner product, and use Euclidean distance as a distance metric to satisfy the triangle inequality. In particular, we only use the user and item representations obtained from the HIN.

We use the Euclidean distance to calculate the distance between the user and the item, and the Euclidean distance to measure preferences:

$$\widehat{r}_{u,i} = \left\| S_u + t_{u,i} - S_i \right\|^2 \tag{6}$$

The closer the distance is, the stronger the preference, and the more likely the user will like the item. The preferences of user is obtained by calculating the Euclidean distance between $(S_u + t_u)$ and S_i.

We use e_u and e_i to represent user and item-specific feature vectors, corresponding to the representation of users and items in HINs:

$$\hat{r}_{u,i} = \alpha \cdot S_u^T \cdot e_i + \beta \cdot e_u^T \cdot S_i + \left\| S_u + t_{u,i} - S_i \right\|^2 \tag{7}$$

where α and β are adjustable parameters.

Our objective function is as follows:

$$\Psi = \sum_{u,i \in U,V} (r_{u,i} - \hat{r}_{u,i})^2 + \lambda \sum_{u} (\|S_u\|_2 + \|S_i\|_2 + \|e_u\|_2 + \|e_i\|_2) \tag{8}$$

They can be obtained by SGD.

4 Experiments

In this section, we demonstrate the effectiveness of our proposed PUHML model by comparing it with baselines on three datasets.

4.1 Experimental Setup

Datasets. For our experiments, we test on three public datasets: Douban_Movie, Douban_Book, Yelp. The statistical information of datasets is reported in Table 1.

Baselines. To demonstrate performance of our PUHML model, we take MAE and RMSE as evaluation metrics. Baselines are listed below:

PMF [10]. It is based on probabilistic matrix factorization.
SocialMF [3]. It forces the user's preferences to be similar to those of their friends.
SREE [7]. It integrates user social information into the EE model.
HERec [5]. It introduces heterogeneous information network representation of users and items, and extends the matrix factorization model.
HGCR [11]. It uses the characteristics of graph convolution neural network to automatically learn node information.

Table 1. Statistics of the datasets

Dataset (Density)	Relations(A-B)	Number of A	Number of B	Number of (A-B)
Douban_Book (0.27%)	User-Book	13,024	22,347	792,026
	User-User	12,748	12,748	169,150
	Book-Author	21,907	10,805	21,905
	Book-Publisher	21,773	1,815	21,773
	Book-Year	21,192	64	21,192
Douban_Movie (0.63%)	User-Movie	13,367	12,677	1,068,278
	User-User	2,440	2,294	4,085
	User-Group	13,337	2,753	570,047
	Movie-Director	10,179	2,449	11,276
	Movie-Actor	11,718	6,311	33,587
	Movie-Type	12,678	38	27,668
Yelp (0.08%)	User-Business	16,239	14,284	198,397
	User-User	10,580	10,580	158,590
	User-Compliment	14,411	11	76,875
	Business-City	14,267	57	14,267
	Business-Category	14,180	511	40,009

Table 2. Results of rating prediction on datasets

Dataset	Metrics	PMF	SocialMF	SREE	HERec	HGCR	PUHML
Douban_ Movie	MAE RMSE	0.6141 0.8045	0.5817 0.7680	0.5783 0.7595	0.5519 0.7053	0.5522 0.7080	**0.5516** **0.7067**
Douban_ Book	MAE RMSE	0.6074 0.7912	0.5756 0.7454	0.5664 0.7379	0.5502 0.6811	0.5511 0.7005	**0.5460** **0.6931**
Yelp	MAE RMSE	1.0791 1.3782	0.8639 1.1882	0.8385 1.1219	0.8475 1.1117	0.8400 1.1160	**0.8162** **1.0684**

4.2 Main Results

Rating Prediction. For the task of predicting user ratings, we present the results of MAE and RMSE in Table 2. Results of rating prediction on datasetsWe have the following observations:

(1) PUHML utilizes heterogeneous information outperforms those don't. The improvement on the sparse dataset Yelp is more significant. This demonstrates that the HIN is helpful in predicting the preference of users.

(2) Compared with all the baseline methods, PUHML has higher MAE and RMSE, which means a better prediction performance

Distance Analysis. In order to verify whether the relationship vector can translate each user closer to the observed item, we verify whether the change in the distance between the user and the item obtained by the PUHML model is consistent with expectations. We calculate the distance *Distance_all* between the user and the item and the distance *Distance_pos* between the user and the positive item:

$$Distance\_all = \sum_{(u,i)\in A} \left\| S_u + t_{u,i} - S_i \right\|^2 \tag{9}$$

$$Distance\_pos = \sum_{(u,i)\in S} \left\| S_u + t_{u,i} - S_i \right\|^2 \tag{10}$$

in which *Distance_all* denotes the set of items related to the user, *Distance_pos* denotes the set of users and their positive related items. The user is closer to the positive item, so during the training process, the distance between the user and the positive item should be getting smaller and smaller.

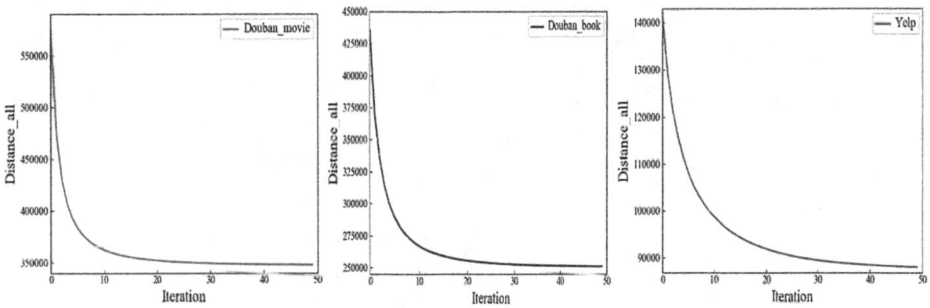

Fig. 3. The variation of the *Distance_all* as the gradient descent algorithm proceeds.

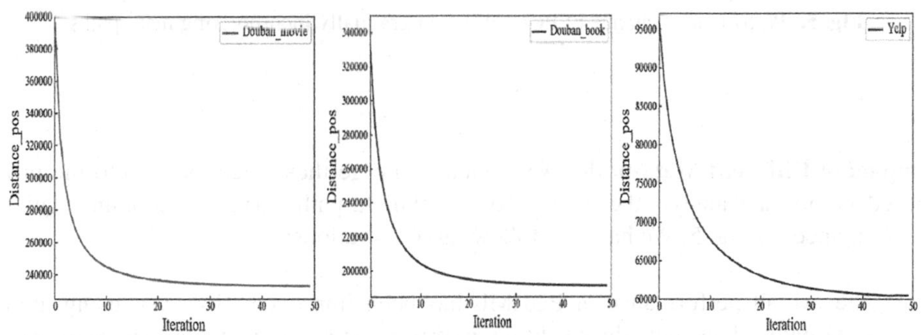

Fig. 4. The variation of the *Distance_pos* as the gradient descent algorithm proceeds.

Figure 3 and Fig. 4 shows the change of the distance curve. It can be observed that Douban_Movie, Douban_Book, and Yelp have a rapid initial decline. Douban_Movie and Douban_Book gradually reached a stable state after 30 iterations, and Yelp gradually reached a stable state after 40 iterations. The result demonstrates that the constructed relationship vector can effectively transform the user into multiple points, making the distance between the user and the item closer.

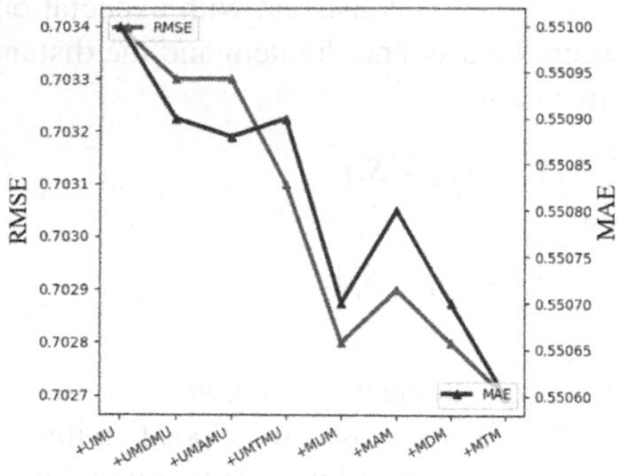

(a)Douban_Movie

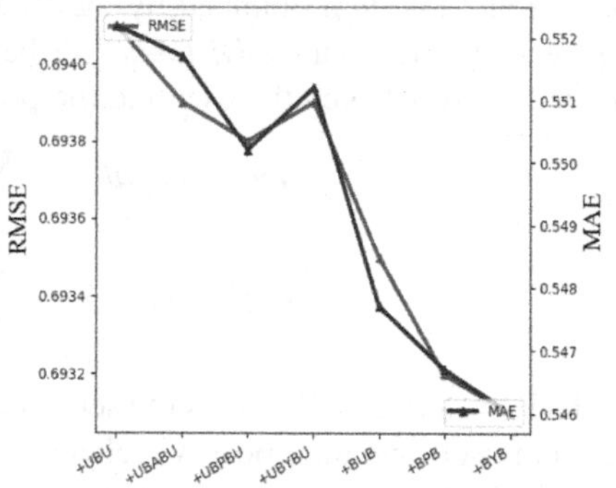

(b)Douban_Book

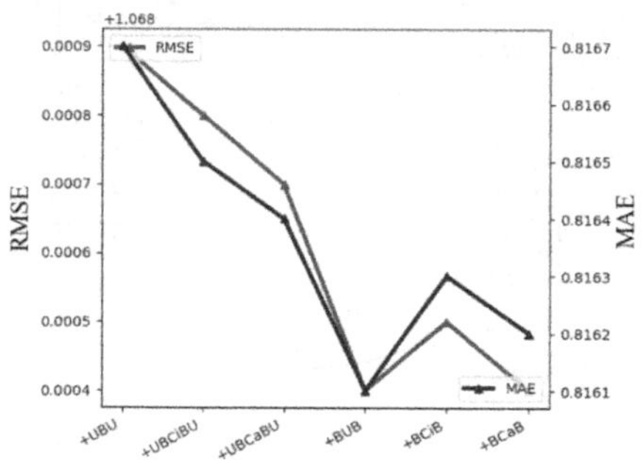

(c)Yelp

Fig. 5. Performance change of PUHML when gradually incorporating meta-paths.

Impact of Different Meta-path. We gradually merge these meta-paths into the proposed method, and analyze the impact of different meta-paths on model recommendation performance. In Fig. 5, We have the following observations:

(1) The overall performance of PUHML has been improved. However, using more meta-paths does not always bring improvements. Some meta-languages may contain information that is noisy or conflicting with the existing information.
(2) Only by merging several meta-paths, PUHML has better recommendation performance, indicating that a small number of high-quality meta-paths can bring greater performance improvements

5 Conclusions

In this work, we explore combined effects of user preferences and heterogeneous information in the recommender systems and propose a model based on heterogeneous information network and metric learning. Our model utilizes heterogeneous information network representation learning to learn effective node representations. To predict user preferences more accurately, we leverage metric learning to measure user preferences with distance. Various experiments have demonstrated that our proposed model can effectively improve the quality of recommendations. For future work, we intend to effectively use multi-source heterogeneous information and improve the interpretability of meta-path semantics for recommendation.

References

1. Shi, C., Li, Y., Zhang, J., Sun, Y., Philip, S.Y.: A survey of heterogeneous information network analysis. TKDE **29**(1), 17–37 (2016)
2. Dong, Y., Chawla, N.V., Swami, A.: metapath2vec: scalable representation learning for heterogeneous networks. In: SIGKDD, pp. 135–144. ACM (2017)
3. Jamali, M., Ester, M.: A matrix factorization technique with trust propagation for recommendation in social networks. In: RecSys, pp. 135–142. ACM (2010)
4. Park, C., Kim, D., Xie, X., Yu, H.: Collaborative translational metric learning. In: ICDM, pp. 367–376 (2018)
5. Shi, C., Hu, B., Zhao, W.X., Yu, P.S.: Heterogeneous information network embedding for recommendation. IEEE Trans. Knowl. Data Eng. **31**(2), 357–370 (2019)
6. Sun, Y., Han, J., Yan, X., Yu, P.S., Wu, T.: Pathsim: meta path-based top-k similarity search in heterogeneous information networks. PVLDB **4**(11), 992–1003 (2011)
7. Li, W., et al.: Social recommendation using Euclidean embedding. In: IJCNN, pp. 589–595 (2017)
8. Grover, A., Leskovec, J.: Node2vec: scalable feature learning for networks. In: KDD, pp. 855–864. ACM (2016)
9. Bordes, A., Usunier, N., Garcia-Duran, A., Weston, J., Yakhnenko, O.: Translating embeddings for modeling multi-relational data. In: NIPS (2013)
10. Mnih, A., Salakhutdinov, R.R.: Probabilistic matrix factorization. In: Advances in neural information processing systems, pp. 1257–1264 (2008)
11. Yin, Y., Zheng, W.: An efficient recommendation algorithm based on heterogeneous information network. Complexity **2021**(17), 1–18 (2021)
12. Gai, K., Qiu, M., Zhao, H., Sun, X.: Resource management in sustainable cyber-physical systems using heterogeneous cloud computing. IEEE Trans. Sustain. Comput. **3**(2), 60–72 (2017)
13. Gai, K., Qiu, M.: Reinforcement learning-based content-centric services in mobile sensing. IEEE Netw. **32**(4), 34–39 (2018)
14. Gai, K., Qiu, M.: Optimal resource allocation using reinforcement learning for IoT content-centric services. Appl. Soft Comput. **70**, 12–21 (2018)
15. Yu, J., Min, G., Rong, W., Song, Y., Xiong, Q.: A social recommender based on factorization and distance metric learning. IEEE Access **5**, 21557–21566 (2017)

An IoT Ontology Class Recommendation Method Based on Knowledge Graph

Xi Wang[1], Chuantao Yin[1(✉)], Xin Fan[1], Si Wu[2], and Lan Wang[2]

[1] Beihang University, Beijing, China
chuantao.yin@buaa.edu.cn
[2] Orange R&D Beijing Company Limited, Beijing, China

Abstract. Ontology is a formal representation of a domain using a set of concepts of the domain and how these concepts are related. Class is one of the components of an ontology for describing the concepts of the system. It is used to create, update, search or delete instances which are digital representations of physical things. With the development of the IoT (Internet of Things) technology, developers create and manage the corresponding IoT instances on IoT platform. With the user's query of a few key words, how to find the ontology classes accurately is a hard problem. IoT Ontology classes recommender system can help developers find the ontology classes that they want to use efficiently. In a general recommender system, user's historical usage records, background features and input keywords are used for making personalized recommendations. However, the newly established IoT platforms do not have a large number of user usage records to optimize recommendation results. And recommendation based on input words' semantics lacks relevance between the IoT ontology classes. This paper proposed a method for recommendation of IoT ontology classes based on knowledge graph building and semantics to introduce more auxiliary information and relationships for the recommendation. And the result shows that our proposed recommendation method can recommend more related IoT ontology classes and have better performance in results' accuracy.

Keywords: IoT platform · Knowledge graph · Ontology · Recommendation method · Semantic similarity

1 Introduction

An ontology is defined as "a formal, explicit specification of a shared conceptualization", and it is used to represent knowledge as a set of concepts related to each other [1]. Ontology consists of four main components namely: classes, relations, attributes and individuals [2]. Classes describe the concepts of the system and a class can have lots of subclasses. Individuals are instances of the classes. Attributes represent the features and characteristics of the classes, and relations

National Key R&D Program of China (No. 2019YFB2102200), National Natural Science Foundation of China (No. 61977003) and Orange R&D Beijing Company Limited.

H. Qiu et al. (Eds.): KSEM 2021, LNAI 12815, pp. 666–678, 2021.
https://doi.org/10.1007/978-3-030-82136-4_54

describe how the classes and individuals are related. On the IoT platform, all the ontologies are predefined by experts, developers aim to find the corresponding IoT ontology classes quickly and accurately to create, update, search or delete instances [3,4]. Our recommendation task is to recommend the ontology classes the users might want to use. In traditional recommendation methods, collaborative filtering [5] which uses the behavioral similarity between users or items is widely used to make recommendations. However, collaborative filtering methods often require the matrix of user-item interaction records. And the cold start and data sparsity are the key problem to solve. In addition, for the methods based on semantic similarity recommendation, the recommendation results will always rely on semantic similarity and lack relevance. For example, keyword matching-based recommendation use key words retrieval methods to find the similar IoT entities and the number of common words is the most important evaluation metrics of this methods [6]. In the word embedding-based recommendation methods, we use NLP (Natural Language Processing) methods, such as Word2vector [7], Glove[8], to get the embeddings of input words and the name of IoT entities. Then we calculate their similarity by cosine similarity or inner product to get the rank of recommendation results [9,10]. In recent years, recommendation based on knowledge graph has gradually become a common means to improve recommendation results [11,12]. The knowledge graph contains rich semantic associations between entities and provides auxiliary information for the recommendation system. The results of the knowledge graph are based on real connections and have strong interpretability [13], which enhances the user's credibility of the results. The knowledge graph is usually stored in the form of entity-relation-entity triples.

Therefore, this paper proposed an IoT ontology classes recommendation method based on semantics and knowledge graph building to solve the above challenges. In order to enrich the relationship between the ontology classes of the Internet of Things, this paper try to build an IoT knowledge graph and achieve the recommendation based on it. Firstly, articles related to IoT were collected from scientific and technological journals. Then by extracting entities and relationships from the text of the article, triples were constructed to form a knowledge graph. Using the constructed knowledge graph as a supplementary relationships, we proposed a recommendation mechanism which can recommend ontology classes that are semantically different from the user input text but related to them. Finally by integrating the recommendation based on semantics and recommendation based on knowledge graph, we can get the final recommended IoT ontology classes. The IoT data used in this paper is introduced in Sect. 3. Section 4 Methodology explains the algorithms of knowledge graph building and recommendation and Sect. 5 shows the experiments.

2 Related Work

2.1 General Recommender System

The collaborative filtering algorithm was first applied in the field of news recommendation in 1994 by Paul Resnick, Neophytos Iacovou [5]. The method recommend the items by similarity matrix of users or items which comes from the historical interactions. Based on this method, Sedhain proposed a recommendation algorithm that combines autoencoders and collaborative filtering algorithms [14]. Among the many collaborative filtering algorithms, the Latent factor model is the most widely used and effective method [15]. Based on FM (Factorization Machines), people combined deep learning and matrix factorization methods, and proposed the NCF (Neural collaborative filtering) method[16].

For the recommendation methods based on keyword retrieval, some of them are based on keyword matching. The number of keywords and the matching principles have an important impact on recommendation [6]. Others are based on keywords' embedding similarity with recommended items' text. Yahoo team used deep learning methods to do the embedding of users and articles, and then get the top K news by inner product of their embeddings[17].

2.2 Recommender System Based on Knowledge Graph

The recommender system based on the knowledge graph enhances the semantic information of data to further improve the accuracy of recommendation by connecting users to users, users to products and products to products. Path-based recommendation method treats the knowledge graph as a heterogeneous information network, and then constructs meta-path or meta-graph-based features between items [18]. The advantage of this type of method is that it fully and intuitively utilizes the network structure of the knowledge graph. Knowledge graph embedding-based recommendation characterize entities and relationships mainly through the method of graph embedding, and then expand the semantic information of original items and user representations. X sha proposed AKGE (Attentive Knowledge Graph Embedding) which use attention networks to learn the accurate user preferences [19]. Ma proposed Jointly Learning Explainable Rules for Recommendation with Knowledge Graph which integrates induction of explainable rules from knowledge graph with construction of a rule-guided neural recommendation model [20].

3 Data Description

The real dataset ThingInTheFuture is composed of ontologies and called ThingIn for short in the following article. The dataset is mainly involved in the field of IoT which aims to connect people and objects, objects and objects to the network.

An IoT ontology is a formal representation of a IoT domain using a set of concepts of the domain and how these concepts are related. There is a total of 40371 ontology classes (concepts) in 492 ontologies predefined by experts. For example, "public transport" is an IoT domain and there is an ontology "public transport" built for it. And "car station", "parking", "bus station", etc. are the ontology classes (concepts) in the ontology "public transport". The information of each ontology class is shown in Table 1. Name is the ontology class's semantic name which will be use to calculate the semantic embedding of class and for keyword-matching in recommendation. IRI (Internationalized Resource Identifiers) is used to find the detailed resource of the class in RDF or JSON format which will be used to create instances. Parents and Children are used to show its parent-classes and subclasses which are stored in IRI format. Among the 40,371 ontology classes, there are 20083 classes' semantic comments are empty, so it is difficult to use the comment as a complete label in the recommendation algorithm.

Table 1. Information of one ontology class

KEYS	Data storage format	Example
Name	STRING	ParkingVehicle
IRI	IRI	http://vocab.datex.org/terms#ParkingVehicle
Parents	IRI (list)	[https://w3id.org/seas/CarPark]
Children	IRI (list)	[http://opensensingcity.emse.fr/parking#TruckParkingFacility]
Comment	String	Information about one individual parking vehicle

4 Methodology

In this section, the mechanism of our proposed recommendation method based on semantics and knowledge graph building will be introduced.

4.1 Knowledge Graph Building

Collection and Preprocessing of Articles. In order to build the IoT knowledge graph, firstly IoT relevant articles are collected from scientific journals of the Internet of Things, RFIDJournal, IEEEXplore and ScienceDirect in detail. RFIDjournal is currently the world's largest and most important website focusing on RFID, one of the main technologies in IoT domain. IEEEXplore and ScienceDirect are the journals that focus on development and research on electrical, electronic, computer engineering and science-related fields. By using python library NLTK, articles are processed with sentence segmentation, word segmentation, part-of-speech tagging, and block partition. Figure 1 shows the preprocess of articles. Since many corpora in NLTK have already marked part of speech, which can be used to mark the segmented words. After getting the part of speech, the words will be divide into meaningful blocks. The main goals of chunking is to group so-called "noun phrases". Part-of-speech tags are combined with regular expressions to separate the sentence into 'VP' blocks and 'NP' blocks. The 'NP' block contains various possible combinations of nouns, and the 'VP' block contains various possible combinations of verbs. Figure 2 shows a chunk structure of an example sentence.

Constructing of Triples in Knowledge Graph. By preprocessing the IoT articles, we got the different blocks. Then the triples were built by subject-verb-object relationship. We take the first 'NP' block appearing in the sentence as

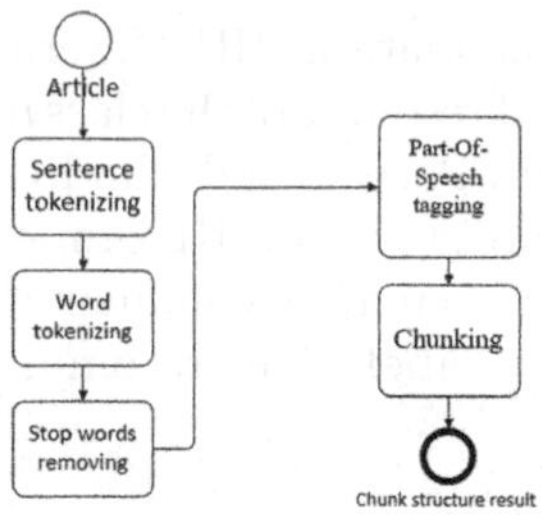

Fig. 1. Article processing

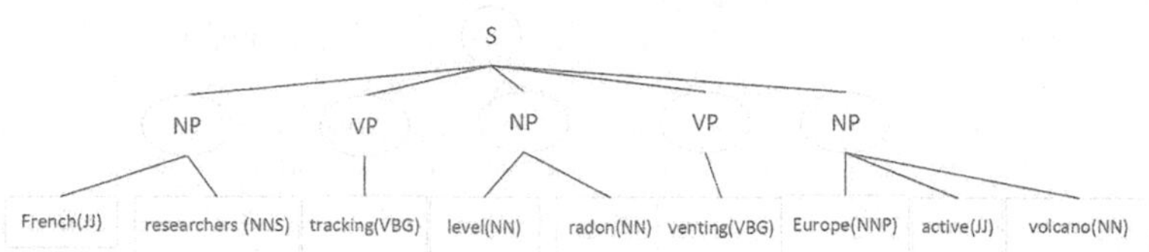

Fig. 2. The chunk structure of sentence "French researchers have been tracking the level of radon venting out of Europe's most active volcano", the abbreviation of part of speech of each word is in parentheses.

entity 1, the latter 'NP' block as entity 2, and the 'VP' block between two entities as the relationship between entities. For example, for the sentence in Fig. 2, two triples can be extracted from it. Triple 1, subject: French researchers, verb: tracking, object: level radon; Triple 2, subject: level radon, verb: venting, object: Europe active volcano. Because the stop words are removed during sentence processing, the phrases will have partial semantic incoherence problem. However, in the following part of recommendation based on knowledge graph, we use keyword matching method to recommend. Therefore, the removal of stop words has no effect on recommendation.

After obtaining the original knowledge graph (OKG) of triples, to simplify the knowledge graph for facilitating the calculation in recommendation, we use the names of the ThingIn ontology classes to filter the OKG. For example, for a triple in the knowledge graph, if the subject and object have no common words with any ontology class name, then the triple will be deleted from the knowledge graph. Then we will get the final knowledge graph (FKG). Figure 3 shows several entities and relationships of the final knowledge graph. Figure 4 shows the quantities of triples built in FKG.

4.2 Recommendation Mechanism

In the recommendation task, we have user's query, a keyword or phrase but not sentences as input words. And the recommended result is the rank of ontology classes. Then user can use the recommended classes information to create or update IoT instances.

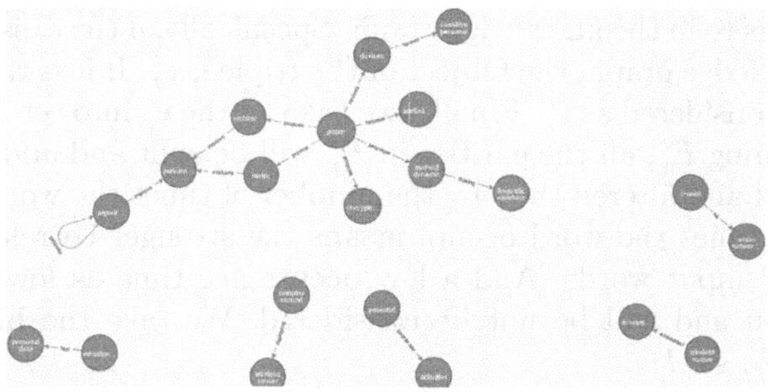

Fig. 3. Partial knowledge graph triples visualized through Neo4j. The orange nodes are the subjects or the objects of triples. Through the direction of the arrow, we can see the subject-verb-object relationship between entities. The starting entity by the arrow is the subject in the triple, the entity to which the arrow points to is the object and the verb in the middle is the relationship.

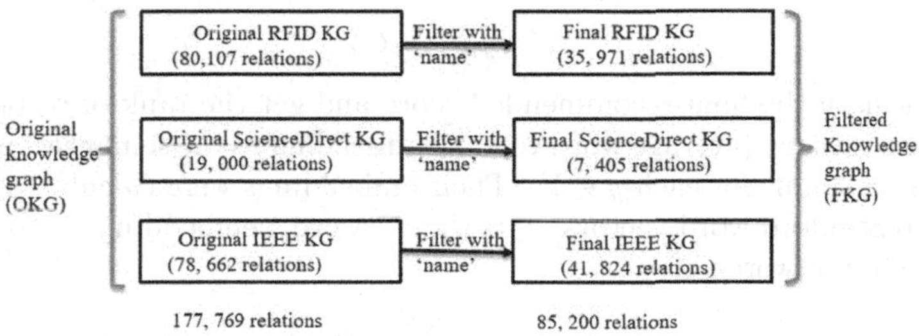

Fig. 4. Data of the final IoT knowledge graph

Recommendation Based on Knowledge Graph. In our IoT ontology class recommender system, the set of all IoT ontology classes of ThingIn dataset is named C. And E represents the set of all the entities of the final simplified knowledge graph and R represents all the relationships.

Firstly, user input text was processed by splitting words and deleting the stop words to obtain the input words list x. For example, if user's input text is "a car engine", x = ["car", "engine"]. We use words matching method to find the related entities with the input words list x in knowledge graph.

f_m is the key words matching mechanism. The entity e, in knowledge graph with $e \in E$, is also split into list, the same operation with x. And $n_e = x \cap N$ is the number of common words of x and e. For example, x = ["car", "engine"], entity e = ["old", "car", "engine"], then $n_e = 2$ because there are two words "car" and "engine" in common. If $n_e \geq 2$, we take e as related entity named e_r. If x or e only have one word, for example x = ["car"], then if $n_e \geq 1$, we take e as related entity e_r.

$$E_r = f_m(x, E) \tag{1}$$

E_r are the set of all the entities e_r collected by matching mechanism f_m in the knowledge graph E. Then, we can search the other entity e_r' of each triple that the entity e_r belongs to in the knowledge graph. Specifically, if the e_r is the Subject of a triple in knowledge graph, the Object of the triple is e'_r. If it is the Object, then the Subject is considered as e'_r. Finally, we take all the e'_r into set E'_r.

After obtaining E'_r, all the entities in E'_r will be split and added into a word list l. We sorted and filtered the l by the number of times the word occurs in the list. The more times the word occurs means the stronger correlation the word has with users' input words. And a low occurrence time as low as one means poor correlation and will be not be considered. We take the high occurrence times words into set l_f.

By apply the word matching mechanism f_m on each ontology class's name, named y, with l_f, we can find recommended IoT ontology classes. In order to enhance the relevance of the recommended results and keywords, we will take the IoT ontology classes as recommended classes if more than two words of its name occur in the set l_f. If the name has only one word, we will take it in recommended classes if it occurs in keyword list l_f. Y_r represents all the recommended ontology classes.

$$Y_r = f_m\left(l_f, C\right) \tag{2}$$

To calculate the final recommended score and get the rank of recommendation, we use the awv (average word vector) embedding as the semantic embedding of the classes' name for each $y \in Y_r$. Their embeddings were calculated with the pretrained Stanford word vectors. v_i is the ith word's embedding vector of x. n_x is the number of words of x.

$$awv\left(x\right) = \frac{\sum_{i=1}^{n_x} v_i}{n_x} \tag{3}$$

$$\widetilde{x} = awv\left(x\right) \tag{4}$$

$$\widetilde{y} = awv\left(y\right) \tag{5}$$

Finally, we take the inner product of input words' embedding and the recommended classes' as the recommended score the get the rank of IoT ontology classes.

$$score\left(\widetilde{x}, \widetilde{y}\right) = inner(\widetilde{x}, \widetilde{y}) \tag{6}$$

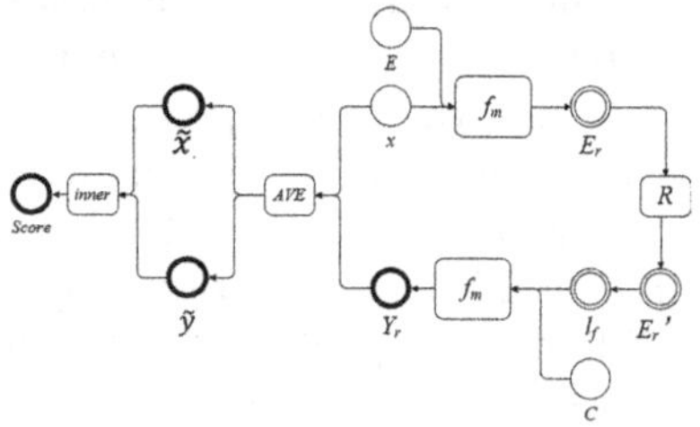

Fig. 5. Recommender system based on knowledge graph (RSBK)

From the Fig. 5, we can see the framework of RSBK (Recommender System Based on Knowledge graph). Using the constructed knowledge graph as a supplementary entity relationship network, we can recommend classes in the knowledge graph that are not only semantically similar to the user input text but also related to them.

Recommendation Based on Semantics. For the recommender system based on semantics (RSBS), firstly, we calculate the semantic embeddings of input words and each ontology class's name by average word vector method. Then we calculate the inner product of input words' embeddings $\widetilde{x}$ and each the ontology class name's embeddings $\widetilde{y}$ for each $y \in C$ as the recommended score. By the recommended score of each ontology class, we can get the rank of top N results. The calculation is the same with Eqs. (3) (4) (5) (6), but this time, we get the rank by semantic similarity of input words with all the ontology classes names, not just the classes got by knowledge graph relationships (Fig. 6).

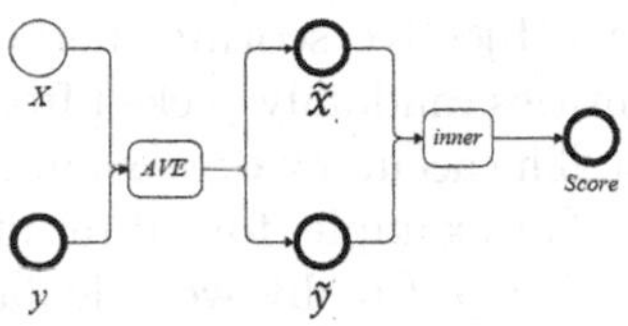

Fig. 6. Recommender system based on semantics (RSBS)

Recommendation Based on Semantics and Knowledge Graph. Recommendation based on semantics and knowledge graph is a hybrid recommendation mechanism which integrates the method RSBK and RSBS. We use the same input words as the input of the RSBK and RSBS, and calculate their recommendation results top N separately. Finally, we integrate their recommendation results and filter the repeated recommended classes. For each top N recommendation results of RSBS and RSBK, to integrate their results together, this paper propose a new evaluation method to consider the weights of both ranks in RSBS and RSBK. For the top N results of RSBS namely Y_{rsbs} and $y_{i1} \in Y_{rsbs}$ (i_1 is the rank of RSBS with $i_1 \in 1,..N$). And the results of RSBK namely Y_{rsbk} and $y_{i2} \in Y_{rsbk}$ (i_2 is the rank of RSBK with $i_2 \in 1,..N$). We calculate the final rank integrating score S:

$$S\left(Y_{rsbs}, Y_{rsbk}\right)\begin{cases}\lambda\frac{sim(y_{i1})}{i_1}+(1-\lambda)\frac{sim(y_{i2})}{i_2} & if\ y_{i1}=y_{i2}\\ \lambda\frac{sim(y_{i1})}{i_1} & if\ y_{i1}\notin Y_{rsbk}\\ (1-\lambda)\frac{sim(y_{i2})}{i_2} & if\ y_{i2}\notin Y_{rsbs}\end{cases} \tag{7}$$

$sim(y)$ is short for $score(\widetilde{x}, \widetilde{y})$ in Eq. (6), λ is the parameter to adjust the ranking weight of RSBK and RSBS results.

By calculating the final rank score S, we got the integrating final recommendation results based on semantics and knowledge graph. The whole recommendation mechanism is shown in Fig. 7.

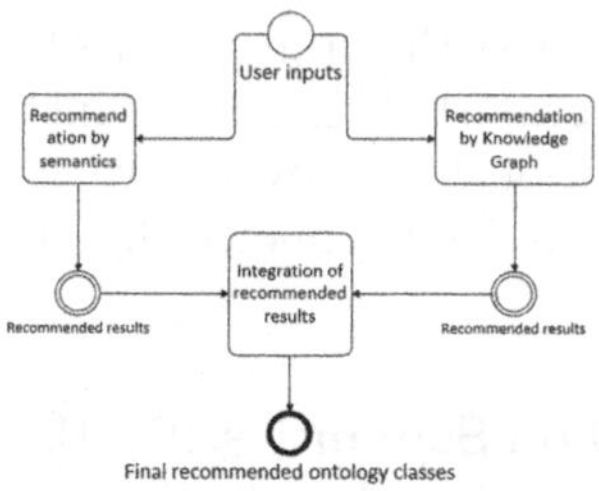

Fig. 7. Recommender system based on semantics and knowledge graph (RSBSK)

5 Experiments

5.1 Evaluations Metrics

Since there is no user's usage record and rating, we cannot use general rating indicators, such as NDCG, hit ratio for evaluation. In order to evaluate the results of our recommendations, a subjective scoring method was adopted to do the evaluations. We take 100 entities randomly picked from FKG as the input words of the recommender system. The accuracy of recommended results is normalized to a value between 0 and 1. For example, for 10 results, if 6 are judged relevant by evaluator, then accuracy is 0.6. Finally we calculate the average score of all 100 ontology classes as the final recommendation score.

5.2 Evaluation Results

Parameters. The dimension of the average word vector is 50 which is the same with the pre-trained word vector by Stanford. When integrating the results of the two algorithms RSBK and RSBS, because there are repetitive results based on semantics on both methods, in order to increase the weight of the relevant results, λ need to be less than 0.5. The experiments was done when λ equals to 0.1, 0.2, 0.3, 0.4, respectively where the effect is best when λ is 0.2 or 0.3.

Recommendation Performance. From the experimental results, we see that there is not much difference between RSBK and RSBS in the recommended accuracy. However, by integrating the two methods, the algorithm RSBSK has not significantly changed in TOP5-10, but it has 14.3% higher accuracy than RSBS in TOP 10–20, and 31.5% higher than RSBS in TOP 20–40. Therefore, with the help of knowledge graphs, we have indeed enriched and supplemented the recommendation results.

In the method RSBK, we firstly got the rough sorting result by keywords matching method, and then the final fine-gained ranking is obtained based on semantic similarity. Therefore, there will be many duplicate results got by RSBK and RSBS when the top K number is small. And the accuracy of the two recommended results is similar. The effect of integrated recommendation method

RSBSK does not have a good performance. However, as top K increases, the relevant recommendation results got by RSBK are also well considered and added to the final recommendation results, and the results of RSBSK have a better accuracy. Therefore, in the RSBSK algorithm, there are some conflicts between the recommendation ranking mechanism based on the knowledge graph and the semantics, which leads to the repetitiveness of the results. This is also a place that needs to be improved and redesigned in future work (Tables 2 and 3).

Table 2. results of RSBS and RSBK

TopK	5	10	20
RSBS	0.80	0.70	0.54
RSBK	0.80	0.68	0.50

Table 3. results of RSBSK

TopK	5–10	10–20	20–40
RSBSK	0.80	0.80	0.71

Case Study. In this section, we provide several ontology classes recommendation results (only show the names of classes in the table) of RSBS and RSBK to intuitively see the richness of recommendation results based on knowledge graphs.

Table 4. Case 1 input words: washing machine

RSBS	RSBK
WashingMachine	WashingMachine
Laundry	Laundry
Laundries_and_dry_cleaners	Laundries_and_dry_cleaners
Laundry_ball	WashingApplianceState
WashingNotification	WashingNotification
StartedWashingNotification	Carpet_cleaning
StoppedWashingNotification	Clothes_dryer
WashingApplianceState	Toilet
Rain_shower	WaterCloset
WaterStorage	shower

From the cases of Table 4 and Table 5, we can see that in the recommendation results based on the knowledge graph, we can get the related results with the

Table 5. Case 2 input words: Traffic jam

RSBS	RSBK
TrafficJam	TrafficJam
underTraffic	underTraffic
Traffic_light	Traffic_light
TrafficFlow	TrafficFlow
TrafficSpeed	TrafficLightFacility
TrafficCongestion	TrafficCongestion
combinedTraffic	TrafficData
TrafficLightFacility	AbnormalTraffic
trafficFlowExtension	Traffic_collision_avoidance_system
BusStop	TrafficHeadway

search words. For example, in the search results of the "washing machines", we got Carpet_cleaning, Clothes_dryer, Toilet and other related items commonly found in bathrooms. In the second search for "traffic jam", we got entities that are related to traffic jams, such as TrafficData, that we need to deal with traffic jams; Traffic_collision_avoidance_system of the emergency handling system; and AbnormalTraffic, the more complete description entity for traffic problems.

6 Conclusions

In this paper, we proposed a recommendation method based on semantics and knowledge graph building to enhance the relevance of recommended results. Firstly, to enrich the IoT ontology classes relationships, an IoT knowledge graph was built based on the articles collected from scientific journals. Then the triples of knowledge graph was constructed by subject-verb-object relations and filtered by the ThingIn ontology classes. Then we proposed method RSBK to get the relevant ontology classes by established knowledge graph. Finally, by integrating the two methods RSBS and RSBK, we got the final recommendation method RSBSK. Experiments were conducted on ThingIn dataset, and the results demonstrated the effectiveness and interpretability of our method. However, the method for building the knowledge based on subject-verb-object focus on only one type relation. There are still more relations that can be extracted and refined to get a better knowledge graph. And for the recommendation method based on knowledge graph, the matching mechanism is relatively basic method in this paper which can be improved with deep learning methods. These are the points to be improved in the future work.

References

1. Guarino, N., Carrara, M., Giaretta, P.: An ontology of meta-level categories. In: Principles of Knowledge Representation and Reasoning, pp. 270–280. Elsevier (1994)
2. Nambi, S.A.U., Sarkar, C., Prasad, R.V., Rahim, A.: A unified semantic knowledge base for iot. In: 2014 IEEE World Forum on Internet of Things (WF-IoT), pp. 575–580. IEEE (2014)
3. Gai, K., Qiu, M., Zhao, H., Sun, X.: Resource management in sustainable cyber-physical systems using heterogeneous cloud computing. IEEE Trans. Sustainable Comput. **3**(2), 60–72 (2017)
4. Dai, W., Qiu, L., Wu, A., Qiu, M.: Cloud infrastructure resource allocation for big data applications. IEEE Trans. Big Data **4**(3), 313–324 (2016)
5. Resnick, P., Iacovou, N., Suchak, M., Bergstrom, P., Riedl, J.: Grouplens: an open architecture for collaborative filtering of netnews. In: Proceedings of the 1994 ACM Conference on Computer Supported Cooperative Work, pp. 175–186 (1994)
6. Wartena, C., Slakhorst, W., Wibbels, M.: Selecting keywords for content based recommendation. In: Proceedings of the 19th ACM International Conference on Information and Knowledge Management, pp. 1533–1536 (2010)
7. Mikolov, T., Chen, K., Corrado, G., Dean, J.: Efficient estimation of word representations in vector space, arXiv preprint arXiv:1301.3781 (2013)
8. Pennington, J., Socher, R., Manning, C.D.: Glove: global vectors for word representation. In: Proceedings of the 2014 Conference on Empirical Methods in Natural Language Processing (EMNLP), pp. 1532–1543 (2014)
9. Khattar, D., Kumar, V., Varma, V., Gupta, M.: Weave&rec: a word embedding based 3-d convolutional network for news recommendation. In: Proceedings of the 27th ACM International Conference on Information and Knowledge Management, pp. 1855–1858 (2018)
10. Naumov, M., et al.: Deep learning recommendation model for personalization and recommendation systems, arXiv preprint arXiv:1906.00091 (2019)
11. Wang, Q., Mao, Z., Wang, B., Guo, L.: Knowledge graph embedding: a survey of approaches and applications. IEEE Trans. Knowl. Data Eng. **29**(12), 2724 2743 (2017)
12. Cao, Y., Wang, X., He, X., Hu, Z., Chua, T.-S.: Unifying knowledge graph learning and recommendation: towards a better understanding of user preferences. In: The World Wide Web Conference, pp. 151–161 (2019)
13. V. W. Anelli, T. Di Noia, E. Di Sciascio, A. Ragone, and J. Trotta, "How to make latent factors interpretable by feeding factorization machines with knowledge graphs. In: International Semantic Web Conference, pp. 38–56. Springer (2019). doi: 10.1007/978-3-030-30793-6_3
14. Sedhain, S., Menon, A.K., Sanner, S., Xie, L.: Autorec: autoencoders meet collaborative filtering. In: Proceedings of the 24th International Conference on World Wide Web, pp. 111–112 (2015)
15. Jenatton, R., Le Roux, N., Bordes, A., Obozinski, G.: A latent factor model for highly multi-relational data. In: Advances in Neural Information Processing Systems 25 (NIPS 2012), pp. 3176–3184 (2012)
16. He, X., Liao, L., Zhang, H., Nie, L., Hu, X., Chua, T.-S.: Neural collaborative filtering. In: Proceedings of the 26th International Conference on World Wide Web, pp. 173–182 (2017)

17. Okura, S., Tagami, Y., Ono, S., Tajima, A.: Embedding-based news recommendation for millions of users. In: Proceedings of the 23rd ACM SIGKDD International Conference on Knowledge Discovery and Data Mining, pp. 1933–1942 (2017)
18. Sun, Y., Han, J., Yan, X., Yu, P.S., Wu, T.: Pathsim: meta path-based top-k similarity search in heterogeneous information networks. Proc. VLDB Endowment **4**(11), 992–1003 (2011)
19. Sha, X., Sun, Z., Zhang, J.: Attentive knowledge graph embedding for personalized recommendation, arXiv preprint arXiv:1910.08288 (2019)
20. Ma, W., et al.: Jointly learning explainable rules for recommendation with knowledge graph. In: The World Wide Web Conference, pp. 1210–1221 (2019)

Ride-Sharing Matching of Commuting Private Car Using Reinforcement Learning

Junchao Lv, Linjiang Zheng(✉), Longquan Liao, and Xin Chen

Chongqing University, Shapingba District, 174 Shazheng Street, Chongqing 400044, China
Zlj_cqu@cqu.ede.cn

Abstract. Commuting private car is one of the main factors causing traffic congestion and low traffic efficiency in the morning and evening peak, and the ride-sharing matching of commuting private car is an effective measure to solve traffic problems. However, limited by the difficulty of obtaining private car trajectory data, current research in the field of transportation rarely involves private car. Electronic Registration Identification (ERI) of motor vehicles technology brings hope for the development of related research. This paper proposes a set of methods for commuting private car ride-sharing matching based on ERI data. The main research content includes two parts: commuting private car identification and commuting private car ride-sharing matching. In the commuting private car identification, information entropy and coefficient of variation are used to characterize the regularity of travel, and private cars with regular travel heights are identified as commuting private cars through random forest classification. In the commuting private car ride-sharing matching, reinforcement learning is combined with the ride-sharing matching scenes to realize the matching from a global and more foresight perspective instead of focusing on even satisfaction. Finally, we apply the ERI data of Chongqing to proposed method. The experimental results show that the method can accurately identify commuting private car, and the number of commuting private car is reduced by 21.45% and 21.01% respectively in the morning and evening peak after ride-sharing matching.

Keywords: ERI · Commuting private cars · Ride-sharing matching

1 Introduction

The rapid development of urbanization makes the rapid growth of the number of urban residents, resulting in traffic problems such as peak traffic congestion, low traffic efficiency. Commuting private car is one of the main factors causing traffic congestion and low traffic efficiency in the morning and evening peak. With the improvement of living standards, more and more residents drive private car to commute. However, the low average occupancy rate of private car increases the traffic volume of urban roads during the peak travel period caused by commuting, which exacerbates traffic problems. Ride-sharing is a mode of transportation in which individuals travel to share transportation and share travel expenses [1]. The core of ride-sharing is ride-sharing matching, which is

H. Qiu et al. (Eds.): KSEM 2021, LNAI 12815, pp. 679–691, 2021.
https://doi.org/10.1007/978-3-030-82136-4_55

to find the individuals with high ride-sharing revenue. It can bring many benefits such as reducing road congestion and overall energy use and pollution in society. Therefore, the development of ride-sharing matching for commuting private car is one of the measures to effectively solve the morning and evening peak traffic problems.

Although private car is the most important part of urban road traffic (Taking China as an example, as of the end of 2019, the car ownership of China has reached 260 million, including 207 million private cars, accounting for 79.62% of the total number of cars), the current research in the field of transportation rarely involves private car, most of the researches on commuting and ride-sharing are oriented to public transportation [2–5] and taxis [1, 6–8]. This is mainly because it is difficult to obtain private car trajectory data. This problem can be solved by ERI technology. ERI is a new type of vehicle identification and tracking technology based on radio frequency identification, which can identify vehicles including private cars with high accuracy.

This paper uses ERI data to study the ride-sharing matching of commuting private car. The main contributions of this paper are summarized as follows:

- Aiming at the problem of commuting private car identification, this paper proposes a commuting private car identification model based on random forest. The travel regularity described by information entropy and coefficient of variation is used as the identification feature of commuting private car to train the model. The AUC (Area Under ROC Curve) of the trained model reaches 94.43%, which is better than other classification models. Finally, we identified 231,190 commuting private cars, then analyzed the commuting pattern of commuting private cars and explored the impact of the commuting trip on the private car trip.
- Aiming at the problem of how to carry out commuting private car ride-sharing matching from a global and more foresighted perspective instead of focusing on instant satisfaction, this paper proposes a data-driven ride-sharing matching model based on reinforcement learning. Considering the characteristics of commuting on time, this paper chooses the trip time to define the ride-sharing benefits as a reward, which means that the greater the trip time reduced by ride-sharing, the better. We conduct an experiment on the ERI dataset in Chongqing, the results show that the number of commuting private cars in the morning and evening peaks decreases by 21.45% and 21.01% respectively after using our method.

2 Identify Commuting Private Car Using Random Forest

2.1 Problem Description

Commuting private car identification refers to the process of identifying the vehicles meet the characteristics of commuting private cars from the group of private cars. In essence, it is a binary classification problem. In this paper, the trip regularity described by information entropy and coefficient of variation is used as the feature of commuting private car, and then the random forest model is used to identify commuting private car.

Table 1. ERI trips of private car 1026.

Date	EID	Departure/arrival time	Origin/destination
2016-02-29	1026	08:05:56/08:36:03	R528/R524
2016-03-01	1026	08:09:15/08:39:00	R528/R524
2016-03-02	1026	08:03:51/08:29:53	R528/R524
2016-03-03	1026	08:03:29/08:29:22	R528/R524
2016-03-04	1026	08:03:26/08:27:36	R528/R524

2.2 Feature Extraction

For whether the trip is regular or not, this paper divides a day into two periods: 0:00 to 12:00 and 12:00 to 24:00, and then uses information entropy and coefficient of variation to measure the trip regularity in each period. Information entropy is used to measure the regularity of the whole trip, and coefficient of variation is used to measure the regularity of individual trip attributes. The reason is that before using the information entropy, the trip information needs to be discretized (the spatiotemporal information cannot be completely consistent, which will make information entropy generally large without discrimination). But this will blur out some differences in the original trip information, so the coefficient of variation is calculated for each attribute of the trip to make up for the blurred information differences. The calculation equation is as follows.

$$H(x) = -\sum_{i=1}^{n} p(xi) \log_2 p(xi),\ Cv = \frac{\sigma}{\mu} \tag{1}$$

The Regularity of the Whole Trip (Origin and Destination Information, OD)

It is almost impossible for a vehicle to have exactly the same trip in a certain period of working day, but this does not mean that the trip of the vehicle cannot be regular. As shown in Table 1, the trip of the private car 1026 doesn't appear repeatedly, but its trip is obviously regular. In order to quantitatively describe the regularity of trip, this paper uses Jaccard distance and Euclidean distance as the clustering distance measure of DBSCAN clustering algorithm, and uses the clustering results to reflect the difference of spatiotemporal information between trips. This is the discretization operation of the trip information mentioned above.

OD Information Entropy: After the discretization of trip information, the trip information entropy of individual in a certain period is calculated according to the clustering results, note as $H_{OD}(x)$. The smaller $H_{OD}(x)$, the stronger the regularity of trip.

Percentage of Days: We take the proportion of the number of travel days in a certain time period in the total number of travel days as one of the characteristics to describe the regularity of trip, note as *PoD*. The larger *PoD* is, the stronger the regularity of trip.

The Regularity of Individual Trip Attributes
DBSCAN clustering based on Jaccard distance and Euclidean distance has realized that the trips in a certain time period can be divided into multiple clusters. The trips in clusters are similar and the trips between clusters are quite different. However, clustering will blur out some differences in the original trip information, and clustering is rough, which cannot guarantee the high spatiotemporal similarity between two trips. Therefore, we need to describe the trip regularity from individual trip attributes.

In this paper, the individual trip attributes extracted from the trip include departure time, arrival time, departure place, arrival place, trip time, trip distance. According to these individual trip attributes, the following characteristics are calculated:

Temporal Difference: The average value of variation coefficient of departure time set and arrival time set, note as *TD*.

Spatial Difference: The average value of variation coefficient of departure place set and arrival place set, note as *SD*.

Difference in Trip Time: The variation coefficient of trip duration set, note as *DT*.

Difference in Trip Distance: The variation coefficient of distance set, note as *DD*.

TD and *SD* are to make up for the difference blurred by $H_{OD}(x)$. *DT* and *DD* can reflect the actual trip situation, such as different road conditions (different trip time but almost the same trip distance) and different routes (large trip distance difference).

2.3 Commuting Private Car Identification Model

Random forest has good performance in classification and regression problems and is known as "the method representing the level of ensemble learning technology". Therefore, this paper uses random forest to identify commuting private car.

Random forest has two main characteristics: random samples and random features. Random samples, that is, bootstrap sampling method, is used to sample the returned samples from the sample set until the sample set size is equal to the sample set size. Feature randomness means that when cart decision tree (base learner) divides left and right subtrees, it first randomly selects a part of features from all the features of current node, and then selects the optimal feature from these features by Eq. (2).

$$Gini(D) = 1 - \sum_{k=1}^{K} p_k^2,\ a_* = \frac{\arg\min}{a \in A} \sum_{i=1}^{I} \frac{|D^i|}{|D|} Gini(D^i) \quad (2)$$

Where K is the number of samples in D, P_k is the proportion of the k-th sample in D, a_* represents the optimal feature, I represents the value type of the sample in D, D^i represents the sample set whose value of feature a_* is equal to a_*^i.

3 Ride-Sharing Matching Method

3.1 Problem Description

Commuting private car ride-sharing matching problem is a data-driven multistage decision-making problem, and each stage is a ride-sharing matching problem.

Multistage decision-making problem is a kind of problem which can be divided into several interrelated stages according to time. Each stage needs to make a decision, the decision of each stage depends on the current stage and affects the subsequent stages.

Ride-sharing matching refers to the process of finding vehicle users with high ride-sharing revenue in a certain period of time. Ride-sharing revenue is defined as follows:

Ride-Sharing Revenue: It is defined as reduced trip distance or trip time after ride-sharing, note as *Benefit*. Suppose that there are two users A and B and the *Benefit* are defined according to the trip duration, then the *Benefit* is shown in Eq. (3).

$$Benefit = \max Benefit(A, B) = \max[Tlen(Trip^{A}) + Tlen(Trip^{B}) - Tlen(Trip^{A,B})] \quad (3)$$

Where $Tlen(Trip)$ represents trip duration, $Trip^{A}$ represents trip of A, $Trip^{A,B}$ represents shared trip of A and B. When the driver is different, $Trip^{A,B}$ may be different.

In order to solve the multistage decision-making problem of commuting private car ride-sharing matching, this paper combines reinforcement learning [9] with the application scenario of commuting private car ride-sharing. Next, show the relevant details.

3.2 Markov Decision Process Modeling

Markov decision process (MDP) is a classical form of multistage sequential decision-making [10], which is also considered as an ideal mathematical form of reinforcement learning. Next, this paper models the ride-sharing matching problem based on MDP.

Definition of Ride-sharing Matching Model Based on Markov Decision Process

State: It refers to the spatial-temporal state represented by the two-tuple of the driver's current time information t and spatial information l, note as $s = (t, l)$.

Action: There are four types of actions. In order to ensure a certain degree of comfort, this paper sets up each private car to carry up to four people (driver + passenger). The specific design of the action is given in the following section.

State Transition Probability: In the ride-sharing scenario, the driver has a definite departure place and time after each action. Therefore, the probability of taking action a from current state s to next state s' is 1, note as $P_{ss'}^{a} = 1$.

Strategy: This paper selects ε-greedy algorithm to "exploiting" the action with the highest value with 1-ε probability to maximize the expected return, and "exploring" the action with non-highest value with ε probability to improve the estimation of the value of the action. In the long run, exploration may yield greater total returns.

Rewards: That is, *Benefit*. It refers to the environmental feedback generated by the environment at time t according to the selected action a from the current state s to the next state s', which will be obtained at time $t+1$, note as R_{t+1} or $R^a_{ss'}$. Considering the characteristics of commuting on time, this paper uses the trip time to define the *Benefit* as reward, which means that the greater the trip time reduced by ride-sharing, the better.

State Value: The expected value of the sum of rewards obtained from state s at time t according to the strategy π. It's a function of strategy π and state s, denoted as $v\pi(s)$.

Action Value: The expected value of the total reward considering the action factor a. It is a function of strategy π, state s and action a, denoted as $q\pi(s, a)$.

Reward Attenuation Factor: Note as γ,$\gamma \in [0, 1][0, 1]$. When $\gamma = 0$, the value function is only determined by the current reward R_{t+1}, that is, greedy method. When $\gamma = 1$, the effect of current reward and subsequent reward on value function is the same. The decisions can be made from a long-term perspective by setting a reasonable γ.

Gain: The ride-sharing revenue after completing all the commuting trips, note as G. The goal of agent is to maximize G.

Determination of Driver in Ride-Sharing Matching Model

Since there is no clear distinction between driver and passenger in commuting private car ride-sharing, this paper determines the driver according to the following rules.

1). The trip of commuting private car is sorted in ascending order according to time. The owner of the earliest commuting trip is the driver, and its spatiotemporal information is the initial state of MDP.
2). Removes driver's trip and passenger's trip from the trip set of commuting private car after a driver chooses an action. The owner of the earliest commuting trip in the remaining set is the driver, and his spatiotemporal information is the next state.
3). Repeat operation 2) until the trip set is empty.

Four Types of Action Design in Ride-Sharing Matching Model

The Driver Does not Participate in the Ride-Sharing

The driver does not participate in the ride-sharing, only completes his original trip, directly removes the trip from the trip set of commuting private car, then determines the next driver according to the rules. The specific process is shown in Table 2.

The Driver Participation in Ride-Sharing (Three Actions).

There are two steps for drivers to participate in the ride-sharing: (1) search passengers; (2) calculate the reward. The specific processes are shown in Table 3 and Table 4. Next, we design three types of actions based on the above two steps.

a. The driver accepts to share with one passenger

After driver i is determined, passenger j is searched to obtain the set of rideable trips D composed of $Trip_{\mathrm{j}}$, and then the reward is calculated by using Eq. (3).

b. The driver accepts to share with two passengers

After driver i is determined, passenger j is searched, and then passenger k is searched continuously with passenger j as the driver to get the set D composed of $(Trip_j, Trip_k)$,and then the reward is calculated by using Eq. (3).

c. The driver accepts to share with three passengers

After driver i is determined, passenger j is searched, then passenger k is continuously searched with passenger j as the driver, and passenger l is continuously searched with passenger k as the driver again to obtain the set of rideable trips D composed of $(Trip_j, Trip_k, Trip_l)$, and then the reward is calculated by using Eq. (3).

Table 2. Algorithm of the driver doesn't participate in the ride-sharing.

Input: Sorted Trip set of commuting private car group *TRIP*.
Output: $R_{ss'}^a$ generated by current action and the next state *s'*.
Algorithm steps:
1: Select the first trip $Trip_1$ from *TRIP*
2: $t = Trip_1 \bullet R_1 \bullet t$, $l = Trip_1 \bullet R_1 \bullet rid$, $s = (t, l)$ //Initialization state s
3: $t' = Trip_1 \bullet R_{-1} \bullet t$, $l' = Trip_1 \bullet R_{-1} \bullet rid$
4: $R_{ss'}^a = -(t' - s \bullet t)$ //Calculate the reward
5: Remove $Trip_1$ from *TRIP* and select the first trip $Trip_1$ in the updated *TRIP*
6: $t = Trip_1 \bullet R_1 \bullet t$, $l = Trip_1 \bullet R_1 \bullet rid$, $s' = (t, l)$
End.

Table 3. Algorithm of searching passengers.

Input: Sorted Trip set of commuting private car group *TRIP*, longest waiting time T_{wait}.
Output: the set of rideable trips *D*.
Algorithm steps:
1: Select the first trip $Trip_1$ from *TRIP*
2: $t = Trip_1 \bullet R_1 \bullet t$, $l = Trip_1 \bullet R_1 \bullet rid$, $s = (t, l)$ //Initialization state s
3: $t' = Trip_1 \bullet R_{-1} \bullet t$, $l' = Trip_1 \bullet R_{-1} \bullet rid$
4: Remove $Trip_1$ from *TRIP*
5: Initialization $D' = \{\phi\}$, $D = \{\phi\}$
// Search for passenger trips whose departure time is between the driver's departure time and the driver's departure time + T_{wait}
6: **for** $Trip_i \in TRIP$ **do**
7: **if** $s \bullet t \le Trip_i \bullet R_1 \bullet t \le s \bullet t + T_{wait}$ **do** Add $Trip_i$ to D'
8: **if** $Trip_i \bullet R_1 \bullet t > s \bullet t$ **do** break
//Filter out passenger trips where the driver can arrive at the passenger's departure place on time from D'
9: **for** $Trip_i \in D'$ **do**
10: **if** $s \bullet t + time(s \bullet l, Tirp_i \bullet R_1 \bullet l) \le Tirp_i \bullet R_1 \bullet t$ **do** Add $Trip_i$ to D
//*time(A,B)* Indicates the time required to get from point A to point B
End.

Table 4. Algorithm of calculating rewards of ride-sharing

Input: The trip set *TRIP* of the commuting private car generated after the passenger search step and the set of rideable trips *D*.
Output: $R^a_{ss'}$ generated by current action and the next state *s'*.
Algorithm steps:

```
if D = {φ} do   Do Table 2   //Ride-sharing failure
else do   // Ride-sharing may succeed
    for Trip_i ∈ D do
        Calculate the reward R^a_{ss'} based on the current action, add (Trip_i, R^a_{ss'}) to RS
    if RS = {φ} do   Do Table 2   // Ride-sharing failure
    else do
        Select the plan with the largest R^a_{ss'} from RS as the final plan (Trip, R^a_{ss'})
        Remove Trip_1 from TRIP and select the first trip Trip_1 in the updated TRIP
        t = Trip_1 • R_1 • t , l = Trip_1 • R_1 • rid , s' = (t, l)
```

End.

3.3 Model Solving

Reinforcement learning problem solving means to find an optimal strategy $\pi*$ to make the return G greater than other strategies. G is also value (state value or action value) in essence, so to find the largest G is to find the best value, that is, Eq. (4).

$$v_{\pi*}(s) = \max_{\pi} v_{\pi}(s) \text{ or } q_{\pi*}(s, a) = \max_{\pi} q_{\pi}(s, a) \tag{4}$$

At present, there are three methods to find the optimal value in reinforcement learning, which are dynamic programming (DP), Monte Carlo (MC) and temporal difference (TD). Due to the large scale of the problem in this paper, using DP to solve it will cause Buhrmann disaster, and it is difficult to meet the requirements of MC that the sampling sequence must reach the end state. Therefore, this paper selects deep Q network [10] which is one of the TD methods to solve the model.

4 Experiment Analysis

4.1 Results of Commuting Private Car Identification

This section uses the trip set of 714,348 time periods generated by 2,718,429 trips as the dataset. The dataset doesn't contain the label information of whether it belongs to commuting private car. Therefore, we randomly selected trip set of 1000 time periods to form a sample set for random forest model, and labeled each sample with label information through manual labeling and spatiotemporal clustering method. The proportion of positive and negative samples is 534:466. 75% of the sample data is used as the training set and 25% as the test set. Finally, 231,190 commuting private cars were identified, which generated 1,158,579 commuting trips.

Model Performance Evaluation

In classification problems, precision (P, Eq. (5)), recall (R, Eq. (5)) and AUC (area under ROC curve) are usually used to measure model performance.

$$P = \frac{TP}{TP + FP}, R = \frac{TP}{TP + FN} \tag{5}$$

Table 5. The final classification effect of the model.

Evaluation index / Classification model		Precision	Recall	AUC
Simple classifier	SVM	98.51%	69.47%	84.13%
	KNN	90.32%	88.42%	88.79%
	CART	92.47%	90.53%	91.05%
	LR	93.41%	89.47%	91.12%
Ensemble learning	XGBoost	94.62%	92.63%	93.30%
	Bagging	94.68%	93.68%	93.83%
	GBDT	95.65%	92.63%	93.90%
	AdaBoost	94.74%	94.24%	94.36%
	Random forest	95.70%	93.68%	94.43%

This paper uses the above three indicators and many mature and widely used classification models to measure the performance of random forest. It can be seen from Table 5 that random forest has the highest AUC, the second highest precision and recall. When the AUC of the two models are similar, we pay more attention to the precision, that is, the commuting private car identified by the models has high reliability. The performance of random forest fully meets our expectations.

Analysis on the Characteristics of Commuting Trip of Commuting Private Cars

Spatiotemporal Characteristics (Distribution of Hot Spots in Different Periods)

According to the quartile method, this paper sets up four levels for the hot spots. Next, we extract and analyze the common highest-grade hot spots in different periods (Fig. 1) and the highest-grade hot spots in each period (Fig. 2). As shown in Fig. 1, the hot spots of common origins and destinations are similar, mainly distributed in residential areas, transportation hubs and business districts.

As shown in Fig. 1, the hot spots of common origins and destinations are similar, mainly distributed in residential areas, transportation hubs and business districts.

Figure 2(a)(b) show the hot spots of origin and destination in the morning peak commute. The origins are mainly distributed in residential areas, more in the south and less in the north. The destinations are mainly distributed in workplaces, more in the north and less in the south. Thus, the commuting traffic flow of the city shifts from south to north and from residential areas to the workplaces in the morning peak, which further proves the effectiveness of the model proposed in this paper.

Figure 2(c)(d) show the hot spots of origin and destination in the evening peak commute. There are few hot spots in this period. This is mainly because commuters' travel needs are more diversified (such as dining, entertainment) and they don't need to go home on time. However, we can still find that origins are distributed in destinations of the morning peak and destinations are distributed in origins of the evening peak. That is, there is a tidal phenomenon in the morning and evening peak.

The Influence of Commuting Trip of Commuting Private Car on the Trip of Private Car. Figure 3 shows Top20 origins and destinations distribution of private car trips. The pie chart shows the proportion of commuting trips. The pie chart's size reflects the number of trips (the larger the number of trips, the larger the pie chart). Figure 3(a)(b) shows that commuting trips account for nearly 50% of the number of private car trips in the morning peak, especially the origin; Fig. 3(c)(d) shows that the proportion of commuting trips dropped sharply (maintained at 25%) in the evening peak. It can be said that the commuting trip has great impact on private cars trips in the morning and evening peak.

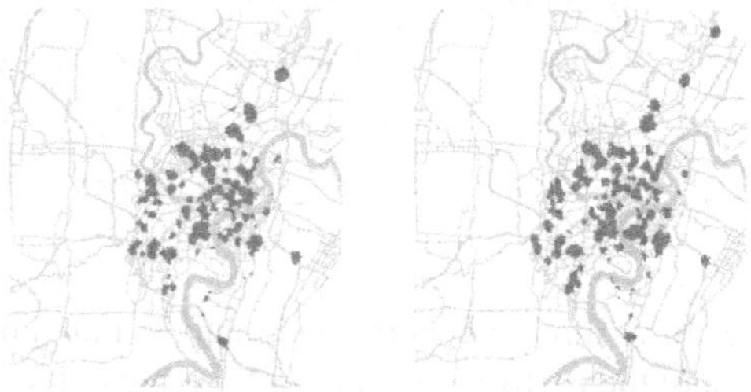

(a) Origins (b) Destinations

Fig. 1. Common hot spots.

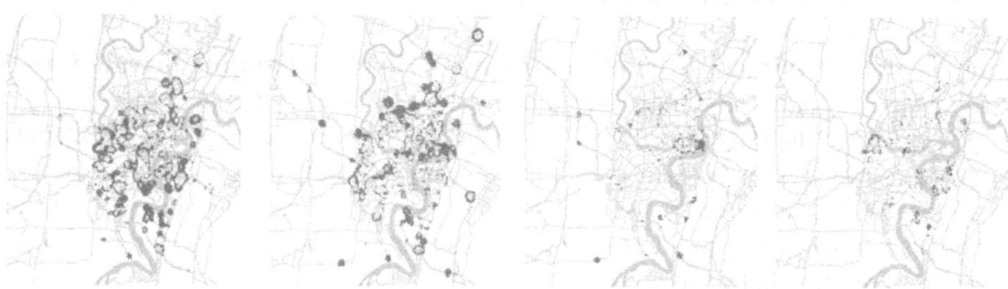

(a) O of morning peak commuting trips (b) D of morning peak commuting trips (c) O of evening peak commuting trips (d) D of evening peak commuting trips

Fig. 2. Hot spots of origin(O) and destination(D) at different times.

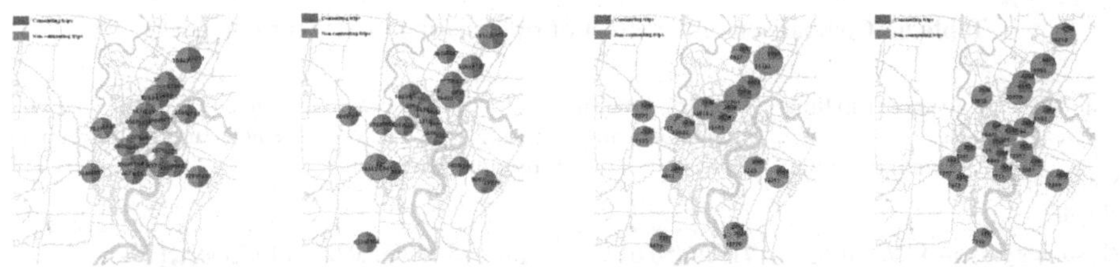

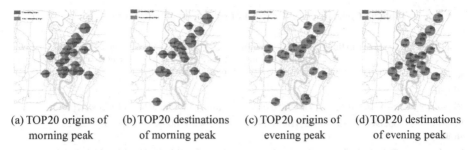

(a) TOP20 origins of morning peak (b) TOP20 destinations of morning peak (c) TOP20 origins of evening peak (d) TOP20 destinations of evening peak

Fig. 3. Origin and destination distribution of private car and proportion of commuting trips.

4.2 Results of Commuting Private Car Ride-Sharing Matching

Model Performance Evaluation

In this paper, we choose the commuting trip of private car on March 2, 2016 to carry out the ride-sharing matching experiment and select average trip time, total trip time, total trip distance and number of vehicles as the evaluation indexes to evaluate the effect of ride-sharing. And we compare fixed strategy and greedy strategy based on time information with reinforcement learning strategy.

The fixed strategies in this paper include fixed strategy 1 (the driver can share with at most one passenger), fixed strategy 2 (the driver can share with at most two passengers), fixed strategy 3 (the driver can share with at most three passengers) and fixed strategy 4 (the driver can share with as many passengers as possible).

Greedy strategy based on time information refers to that only the average trip time of ride-sharing is considered when the driver matches the passenger, and the influence on the subsequent ride-sharing is not considered. By setting the reward attenuation factor to zero in the ride-sharing matching model, the greedy strategy can be realized.

The comparison of the ride-sharing effect of reinforcement learning strategy, fixed strategy and greedy strategy is shown in Table 6. The smaller the four evaluation indexes, the better. The results show that the order of the effect of each strategy is basically the same in peaks. In the morning peak, evaluation effect from good to bad is reinforcement learning strategy, fixed strategy 1, greedy strategy, fixed strategy 4, fixed strategy 2 and fixed strategy 3. In the evening peak, except that the fixed strategy 4 is better than the greedy strategy, the order of the rest is the same as that of the morning peak. This result proves the advantage of reinforcement learning strategy.

After using reinforcement learning strategy, the number of commuting private car decreased by 38,436 (21.45%) in the morning peak, the total ride-sharing time was 11,037 h and the total ride-sharing distance was 316,887 km; In the evening peak, the number of commuting private cars decreased by 24,253 (21.01%), the total ride-sharing time was 7,819 h, and the total ride-sharing distance was 206,834 km. This greatly reduces the traffic of private car on the road, and proves the effectiveness of the ride-sharing matching model.

Table 6. Comparison of the effect of ride-sharing in the morning peak.

Evaluation index / Ride-sharing strategy	Average trip time (h, morning/evening)	Total trip time (h, morning/evening)	Total trip distance (km, morning/evening)	Number of vehicles(morning/evening)
RL strategy	54,482/39,029	71,746/50,614	1,630,734/1,055,072	140,756/91,178
Fixed strategy 1	55,596/39,992	72,418/51,173	1,633,261/1,053,734	141,815/92,323
Fixed strategy 2	70,983/51,071	74,151/52,851	1,565,230/1,006,034	171,924/111,683
Fixed strategy 3	75,321/53,507	75,516/53,686	1,553,986/1,001,610	178,718/115,032
Fixed strategy 4	60,326/42,042	72,981/51,530	1,616,630/1,046,804	150,009/95,091
Greedy strategy	61,007/44,756	72,668/51,709	1,623,726/1,042,647	145,581/96,456
Travel demand	75,655/53.845	75,655/53.845	1,554,680/1,002,751	179,192/115,431

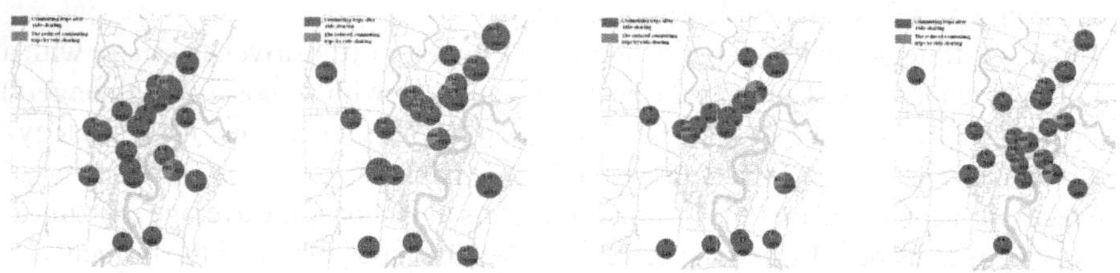

(a) TOP20 origins of morning peak (b) TOP20 destinations of morning peak (c) TOP20 origins of evening peak (d) TOP20 destinations of evening peak

Fig. 4. Origin and destination distribution of commuting trips before and after ride-sharing.

Comparison of Commuting Trips Before and After Ride-Sharing Matching
Figure 4 shows the origin and destination distribution before and after ride-sharing. The places with large differences in the number of trips before and after the ride-sharing are common hot spots, and the differences between the destinations are greater than that between the origins regardless of the morning and evening peak. That is, ride-sharing can improve the traffic conditions in common hot spots, especially in destinations.

5 Conclusion

This paper established a set of methods to achieve commuting private car sharing based on the spatiotemporal characteristics of vehicle trip contained in the ERI data. Through specific experiments, it found out the commuting travel mode of private car in the main urban area of Chongqing, and realized commuting private car ride-sharing. At the same time, it verified the effectiveness of the proposed method.

However, if the data with a longer time span is used, the commuting private car can be more accurately identified. And if the competitive relationship between agents is considered in commuting private car ride-sharing, that is, extending the framework proposed in this paper to a multi-agent environment should achieve better effects.

References

1. Furuhata, M., Dessouky, M., Ordonez, F., et al.: Ridesharing: the state-of-the-art and future directions. Transp. Res. Part B-Methodol. **57**, 28–46 (2013)
2. Hu, L., Sun, T., Wang, L.: Evolving urban spatial structure and commuting patterns: a case study of Beijing, China. Transp. Res. Part D: Transp. Environ. **59**, 11–22 (2018)
3. Long, Y., Zhang, Y., Cui, C.: Identifying commuting pattern of Beijing using bus smart card data. Acta Geogr. Sin. **67**, 1339–1352 (2012)
4. Kieu, L.M., Bhaskar, A., Chung, E.: Passenger segmentation using smart card data. IEEE Trans. Intell. Transp. Syst. **16**, 1537–1548 (2015)
5. Ma, X., Liu, C., Wen, H., et al.: Understanding commuting patterns using transit smart card data. J. Transp. Geogr. **58**, 135–145 (2017)
6. Agatz, N., Erera, A., Savelsbergh, M., et al.: Optimization for dynamic ride-sharing: a review. Eur. J. Oper. Res. **223**, 295–303 (2012)
7. Liao, Z.: Real-time taxi dispatching using global positioning systems. Commun. ACM **46**, 81–83 (2003)
8. Mahmoudi, M., Zhou, X.: Finding optimal solutions for vehicle routing problem with pickup and delivery services with time windows: a dynamic programming approach based on state-space-time network representations. Transp. Res. Part B-Methodol. **89**, 19–42 (2016)
9. Gai, K., Qiu, M.: Reinforcement learning-based content-centric services in mobile sensing. IEEE Net. 32:34–39(2018)
10. Sutton, R.S., Barto, A.G.: Reinforcement Learning: an Introduction. The MIT Press, Cambridge, Massachusetts London, England (2018)

Optimization of Remote Desktop with CNN-based Image Compression Model

Hejun Wang[1], Hongjun Dai[1(✉)], Meikang Qiu[2], and Meiqin Liu[3]

[1] School of Software, Shandong University, Jinan 250101, China
hejun_w@mail.sdu.edu.cn, dahogn@sdu.edu.cn

[2] Department of Computer Science, Texas A&M University-Commerce, Commerce, TX 75428, USA

[3] College of Electrical Engi, Zhejiang University, Hangzhou 310027, China
liumeiqin@zju.edu.cn

Abstract. Remote desktop systems become commonly used for users to enhance the efficiency of their daily tasks commonly. In this work, we propose an expanded image compression model with *convolutional neural network* (CNN) and train two jointly optimized CNN based models as the image encoder and decoder to optimize the compression of the desktop images and design a new compartmentalization of the update desktop region to fit the CNN encoder. We implement the proposed encoding on the open source *Remote Frame Buffer* (RFB) protocol. Compared with tight encoding which is dedicated to low-bandwidth remote desktop, the proposed encoding method prompts the user experience with a even lower network bandwidth consumption.

Keywords: Remote desktop · Remote frame buffer · Convolutional neural network · VNC

1 Introduction

With the development of computing power [10,11], network capability [12], big data processing [13], and artificial intelligence [14,15], remote desktop systems become commonly used for users to enhance the efficiency of their daily tasks [16]. Users are able to get access to their specific desktop environments from any location through *remote desktop client* (RDC) as long as the *remote desktop server* (RDS) is implemented. The transmission of the desktop image is a significant part in the remote desktop transportation protocol, which is directly related to the quality of the user experience. For example, *virtual network computing* (VNC) is a widely used remote desktop tool, and its RDS compresses

This work is partly supported by the Key National Natural Science Foundation of China (No. U1936203), the United Natural Science Foundation of Shandong Province (No. ZR2019LZH010), and the Open Research Project of the State Key Laboratory of Industrial Control Technology, Zhejiang University, China (No. ICT2021B13).

H. Qiu et al. (Eds.): KSEM 2021, LNAI 12815, pp. 692–703, 2021.
https://doi.org/10.1007/978-3-030-82136-4_56

the desktop image with JPEG as the compress algorithm. In this work, we propose an expanded image compression model with *convolutional neural network* (CNN) based image compression. Then, the consumption of network traffic can be further reduced with promoting user experience.

How to design a transmission protocol or remote desktop architecture across different platforms has been extensively explored in remote desktop field. WARP [6] is designed for the web client environment and the KVM server to gain better performance compared to other protocol. THINC [4] is a remote display architecture which is for remote desktop to play full-screen video and audio at full frame rate in both LAN and WAN environments. Researchers have studied remote desktop transmission protocols and architectures to allow users obtaining higher performance on low-performance devices, most researchers concentrate on how to design a remote desktop system which occupies less resources on the server side. But there exists a strong need for more research of remote desktop in various areas, which urgently need the transmission of the desktop image. What is different from a decade ago is that most current display devices have 4K or 2K, at least 1080P resolution. With the progress of display devices, the resolution is getting higher and higher, it needs lots of bandwidth to ensure that the remote desktop image is transmitted opportunely. Taking a 4K (3840×2160) resolution display device as an example. A 4K uncompressed picture has approximately 23.73 MB of data. The minimum data transfer rate required of a remote desktop with a refresh rate 60 Hz is 1.39GB/s, while the network transmission speed of general households is only 1/100 to 1/20 of that, makes it hard to guarantee the quality of user experience. Desktop images has spatial redundancy between adjacent pixels and there is frequency domain redundancy after the discrete cosine transformation. Since the human's eye is insensitive to certain signals, visual redundancy exist. Removing these redundancy can greatly reduce the storage space required. Figure 1 shows the image quality and data volume of desktop images under different compression parameters, where *quality parameters* (QP) is the JPEG major parameter.

Some researchers proposed a hybrid remote display protocol [7], improved the transmission protocol which is based on traditional video/image compression codec. Deep learning has more parameters than traditional methods, and can capture the essential information of images more effectively. It has great potential in the image processing area. The application of deep learning to the field of image compression has theoretical credibility and is of great significance for improving the image compression ratio and image restoration effect. Some image compression methods based on CNN have been proposed in recent years [2,5]. CNN has advantages in image compression. Compared with JPEG, the CNN based algorithm's compression ratio is increased and the reconstructed image presents better visual quality. While, there are some issues to be resolved in the domain of remote desktop image compression such as: (1) How to compress the image better when the resolution of the desktop image is high; (2) How to remove the blocking effects and artifacts caused by JPEG compression to improve the user experience when the user's network bandwidth is low.

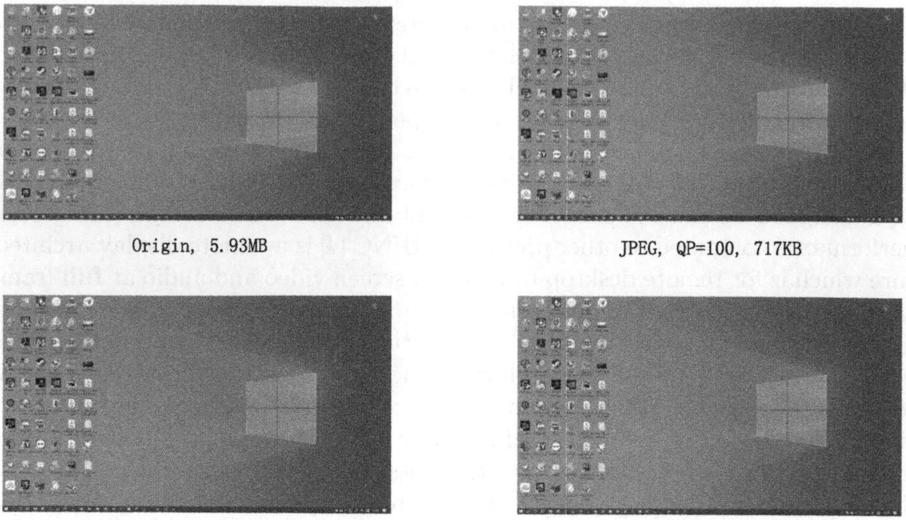

Origin, 5.93MB | JPEG, QP=100, 717KB
JPEG, QP=80, 218KB | JPEG, QP=20, 75.3KB

Fig. 1. Quality and data volume of desktop images under different QP.

In this work, we propose a new display transferring encoding for remote desktops. The newly proposed encoding is designed to detect multiple kinds update regions and utilizes a CNN based image compression method as encoder and decoder to compress and un-compress a specific kind update region. Also, there is a new method of dividing the desktop update region to fit the CNN encoder and decoder in the proposed encoding. We collect a special desktop image data set to train and optimize the performance of the CNN encoder and decoder. In experiment, the proposed encoding is compared with tight encoding, which consumes the lowest bandwidth on VNC. We use PSNR and MS-SSIM as the main performance parameters to quantify the desktop image quality of different encoding algorithms. Simultaneously, we measure the average bandwidth consumed by different encodings under their corresponding quality parameters when the remote desktop usage scenario is document editing. The experimental result indicates that the network bandwidth consumption of remote desktops can be further reduced while the desktop image quality is enhanced.

2 Related Work

This section briefly reviews the architecture of VNC and the standard encoding algorithms in *Remote Frame Buffer*(RFB) protocol 3.8 version. Then some related works about image compression bases on CNN are reviewed.

2.1 The Architecture and Encoding Standard of Remote Desktops

The architecture of VNC is briefly showed in Fig. 2. The client processes the user's input and send it to the client as a message in accordance with the RFB protocol format. The server processes the message from the client and update the frame buffer according to the input. Then the updated frame buffer is encoded following the negotiated method and is sent to the client. At last, the client decodes the frame buffer data and display on user's monitor. RFB is a simple protocol for remote access to graphical user interfaces and it works at the frame buffer level. The display side of the protocol is based around a single graphics primitive: put a rectangle of pixel data at a given x, y position. It supports 7 encoding algorithms in RFB standard that any VNC client and server.

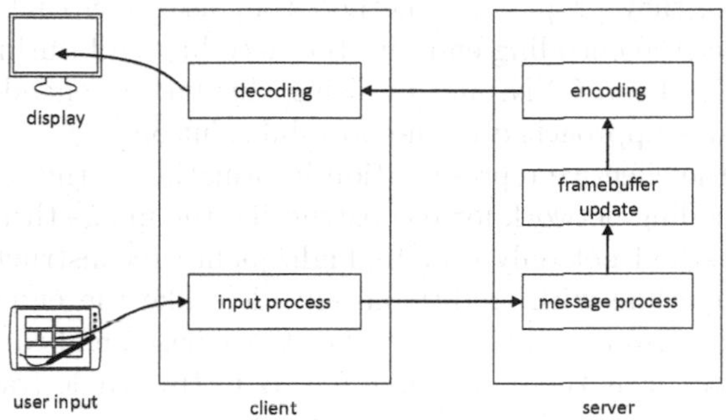

Fig. 2. Architecture of VNC

2.2 Image Compression with CNN

Image compression based on deep learning are mostly lossy image compression and rely on the powerful modeling capabilities of deep learning. The performance of image compression based on deep learning has surpassed that of JPEG, and the gap in performance is still gradually expanding. CNN has developed rapidly in the image field, especially in the field of computer vision, showing excellent performance in such directions as target detection, image classification, and semantic segmentation. The sparse connection and parameter sharing in the CNN convolution operation make CNN show its advantages in image compression.

Classical image compression methods such as JPEG and JPEG2000 usually manually optimize the three parts of change, quantization, and entropy coding. The image bit rate is calculated as discrete coefficients, and a globally differentiable function is required when using gradient descent based on CNN end-to-end optimization. For this reason, Ballé[2] et al. proposed a CNN image coding framework based on generalized divergence normalization, which makes the conversion between linear convolution and nonlinear more flexible. Later, Ballé [3] et al. proposed an image compression method based on nonlinear transformation and unified quantization. The nonlinear transformation was realized through CNN, and the local gain was realized through the previous generalized divergence normalization. This is also the first combination of CNN and image compression, laying the foundation for the feasibility of end-to-end image compression based on CNN. In order to improve the quality of reconstructed images, Jiang [5] et al. proposed an end-to-end image compression framework based on CNN. This method uses two CNN to combine the encoder and the decoder from the encoder side and the decoder side of the image at the same time. Zhao [9] et al. believe that the intuitive idea of the optimal solution to this problem is to use CNN to perfectly replace the traditional end-to-end approach of the gradient back propagation codec to improve the coding quality of the reconstructed image. Therefore, they proposed a method that uses a virtual encoder, which is used to connect the encoding end and the decoding end during training. The virtual encoder is also a CNN, and by using this virtual encoder, the CNN at the decoding end is approached to the optimal solution.

In this way, the effective representation information of the real image is projected to the decoding network for reconstructing the image through the virtual encoder. This method not only obtains high-quality reconstructed images, but also can be compatible with traditional encoders like the end-to-end network structure, and can also be extended to other CNN-based end-to-end image compression structures. But there are three CNNs in the whole framework, and it is relatively difficult to train once. Therefore, three networks need to be decomposed and trained in training.

3 Deep Encoding

We extend the RFB protocol based on RFB version 3.8 and give it a version number as 3.8d. RFB version 3.8d, a new encoding is in registration. It takes the encoding number as 24 and named as Deep encoding. Deep stands for deep learning based image compression.

The update region is split up to some tiles, each tile has 16 pixel height and 16 pixel width. The hole update region is sent and encoded as several sub-rectangles, each sub-rectangle is composed by several 16×16 tiles. This requires lower bits to indicate the boundary information of higher resolution update region. The ordering of tiles that we use is starting at the top left going in left-to-right, top-to-bottom order. If the width of the tiles on the edge of the update region is not an exact multiple of 16 then the width of them will be expanded to a multiple of 16 which is the closest to the un-expanded width. Similarly if the height of the tiles on the edge of the update region is not an exact multiple of 16 then the height of update region will be expanded to a multiple of 16.

In Deep encoding the width or height of each sub-rectangle is not larger than 256 pixels. We can utilize 32 bits to describe a sub-rectangle (16 bits for width and 16 bits for height). There is a header for each sub-rectangle that indicates the position and the width and height of the sub-rectangles. The position indicates the top left pixel's position in the sub-rectangles. The content of a header is shown in Table 1. After the header there is a byte which is a mask for the encoded sub-rectangle that indicate it is a single color sub-rectangle(mask value 0×01), a double color sub-rectangle(mask value 0×02) or a multi-color sub-rectangle(mask value 0×04).

Table 1. The header of a Deep encoding sub-rectangle.

No. of bytes	Type	Description
2	U16	x-position
2	U16	y-position
2	U16	Width of sub-rectangle
2	U16	Height of sub-rectangle
4	U32	Encoding number

The first thing to do for the RDS with Deep encoding is to detect the sub-rectangles that have simple color, because simple color sub-rectangles are easy to encode. When a single or double color sub-rectangle with a suitable size (at least 4 tile in the sub-rectangle) is detected, the server encode and send it to the client. The RDS sends the pixel value of the single color region after sending the header while encoding single color sub-rectangle. For sending double color sub-rectangles, the RDS sends a header first, and sends the pixel value of foreground and background, then encodes and sends the background pixel as bit "0" and foreground pixel as bit "1". The order of encoding double color region is left-to-right and top-to-bottom. When detecting a multi-color sub-rectangle, the RDS needs the CNN encoder to compress the sub-rectangle and send the compressed data to RDC. The RDS needs to send the length of compressed data and the compressed data follows.

4 Enhanced Decoder and Encoder

In this section we introduce the architecture and the detail of the decoder and the encoder that we implement on the RDS and RDC.

4.1 Architecture

This work implements a CNN based compression method which is proposed by Ballé [3] in our remote desktop, and its architecture is shown in Fig. 3.

Input image $\boldsymbol{x}$ in signal domain is transformed to $\boldsymbol{y}$ in code domain, which is called latent representation via the encoding network g_a. The role of g_a is to replace the DTC transformation in JPEG. In JPEG, DCT transforms the input

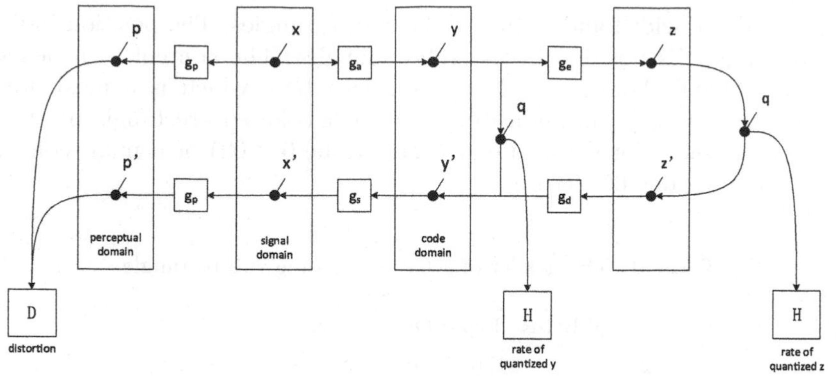

Fig. 3. Architecture of the CNN based image compression model

image signal from the spatial domain to the frequency domain. For any different image, this transformation is fixed. Therefore, there are usually block effect and shadows when reconstructing JPEG encoded images. The advantage of using the CNN to replace the DCT transformation is that the powerful feature extraction capability of the CNN can achieve the effect of approximately manually setting the transformation method according to the pixel distribution characteristics of the image, thereby block effect and shadows can be eliminated. The latent representation $\boldsymbol{y}$ generated by the encoder g_a is quantized to obtain the quantized $\boldsymbol{y}$, which is denoted as $\hat{\boldsymbol{y}}$. After $\hat{\boldsymbol{y}}$ is decoded by the decoder g_s, the output of the compressed image which is denoted as $\hat{\boldsymbol{x}}$ is obtained. g_p is a converter that transforms input x and output $\hat{x}$ to perceptual domain. The transformation result $\boldsymbol{p}$ and $\hat{\boldsymbol{p}}$ are used to evaluate the image compression quality. The entropy model H is implemented to estimate the bit rate of image compression, and the estimated bit rate is indicated as R.

The whole learning based image compression model is optimized by considering the rate-distortion trade-off in the following way:

$$L = \lambda D + R = \lambda d(\boldsymbol{x}, \hat{\boldsymbol{x}}) + H(\hat{\boldsymbol{y}}) + H(\hat{\boldsymbol{z}}) \tag{1}$$

where λ is a hyper parameter that is used for balance the bit rate and distortion and function $d(\cdot)$ calculates the distortion between the input image and the reconstructed image(mean square error or MS-SSIM [8]). H represents the bit rate for encoding latent representations $\hat{\boldsymbol{y}}$ and $\hat{\boldsymbol{z}}$.

4.2 Details

In this section we introduce the details about the image compression model. The details of the model are shown in Fig. 4. The encoder has four convolution layers with a *generative divisive normalization*(GDN) [1] layer between each two convolution layers and "IGDN" means inverse GDN. GDN is an invertible nonlinear transformation that is optimized so as to Gaussianize the data. GDN is formulated as follows:

$$\begin{aligned} \boldsymbol{y} &= g(\boldsymbol{x}, \boldsymbol{\theta}) \\ & s.t. \\ y_i &= \frac{z_i}{(\beta_i + \Sigma_j \gamma_{ij} |z_j|^{\alpha_{ij}})^{\epsilon_i}} \\ & and \\ \boldsymbol{z} &= \boldsymbol{H}\boldsymbol{x} \end{aligned} \tag{2}$$

where $\boldsymbol{\theta} = \{\boldsymbol{\alpha}, \boldsymbol{\beta}, \boldsymbol{\gamma}\}$ are parameters, as well as the matrices $\boldsymbol{H}$, $\boldsymbol{\alpha}$, and γ, for a total of $2N + 3N^2$parameters (where N is the dimensionality of the input space). The After encoding is quantization which is denoted as Q. In traditional image compression, the quantization of latent representation is described as:

$$\hat{\boldsymbol{y}} = round(\boldsymbol{y}) \tag{3}$$

However, in deep image compression, the function of quantization $round(\cdot)$ may cause the gradient of $\hat{\boldsymbol{y}}$ to desapear because the function $round(\cdot)$ is not differenciable. Thus we implement the quantization function as

$$\hat{\boldsymbol{y}} = \boldsymbol{y} + \boldsymbol{\Delta y} \tag{4}$$

where $\boldsymbol{\Delta y} \sim \boldsymbol{\mu}(\boldsymbol{0}, \boldsymbol{1})$ [2].

For arithmetic coding after quantization, the more accurate the distribution of $\hat{\boldsymbol{y}}$ is estimated, the lower the bit rate is required to encode different characters. Due to the powerful structure capture capabilities of CNN, the CNN based hyper-encoder and hyper-ecoder is implemented to capture more spatial relationship in latent representation $\boldsymbol{y}$ to reduce redundancy and to improve the compression performance. After hyper-encoder and hyper-decoder, $H(\hat{\boldsymbol{y}})$ and $H(\hat{\boldsymbol{z}})$ in formula 1 is formulated as follows:

$$\boldsymbol{H}(\hat{\boldsymbol{y}}) = E[-\log_2(p_{\hat{\boldsymbol{y}}|\hat{\boldsymbol{z}}}(\hat{\boldsymbol{y}}|\hat{\boldsymbol{z}}))] \tag{5}$$

$$\boldsymbol{H}(\hat{\boldsymbol{z}}) = E[-\log_2(p_{\hat{\boldsymbol{z}}}(\hat{\boldsymbol{z}}))] \tag{6}$$

5 Experiments and Results

5.1 Experimental Setup

We implemented the prototype with the deep image compression encoder on a server with CentOS 7 operating system and a TightVNC on another server with CentOS 7 operating system. The VNC viewer with the deep image compression decoder is implemented on a personal computer with Windows10 and the TightVNC viewer is implemented on the other Windows 10 PC. The prototype

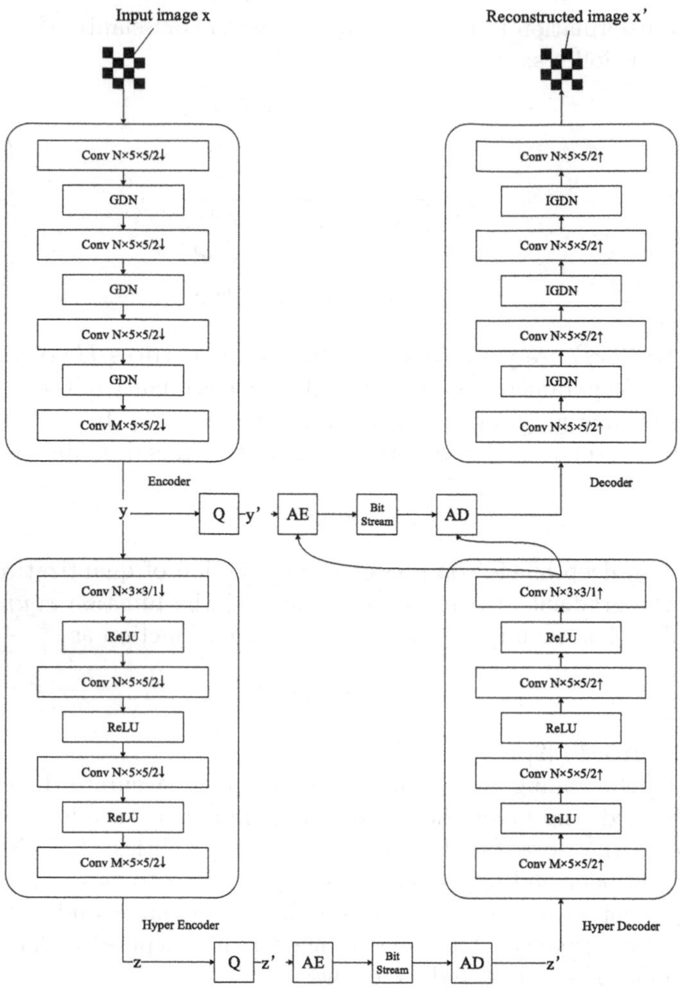

Fig. 4. Detailed architecture of the compression model. Each convolution layer is denoted by the number of filters, kernel size, and stride. ↓ indicates down-sampling, and ↑ indicates up-sampling in each convolutional layer. N and M are the hyper-parameters to set the number of channels for a specific layer. N and M were chosen dependent on λ, with $N = 128$ and $M = 192$ for the lower values of λ, and $N = 192$ and $M = 320$ for the higher values of λ. "Q" denotes quantization. "AE" and "AD" represent arithmetic encoder and arithmetic decoder. "ϕ" refers to the estimated parameters of the hyper-decoder.

is modified based on the open source code of TightVNC 1.3[1]. The two servers are DELL Precision-3640 with Intel i9-10900k processor@4.5 GHz and 64GB RAM. The graphic cards on the servers are Nvidia RTX 3090. The clients are computers that have AMD Ryzen 2600X processor@3.9 GHz with 16 GB RAM. The graphic cards on the clients are Nvidia RTX 2080ti.

In this work, we jointly optimize four CNN models, they are the encoder, the decoder, the hyper-encoder and the hyper-encoder. We set six values of λ in equation 1 as 8192, 4096, 2048, 1024, 512 and 256 to fit different compression quality parameters in VNC. For high bit rate, we firstly set $\lambda = 8192$ and train the model on one GPU with the batch size equals four and the learning rate is set to be 1×10^{-4}. For the other high bit rate $\lambda = 4096$, we adopted the model of 8192 as a pre-trained model and the training iterations are set as 500000. For low bit rate, we firstly train $\lambda = 2048$ and adopt it as the pre-trained model for other low bit rate models. The training steps of other low bit rate is the same as the high bit rate model.

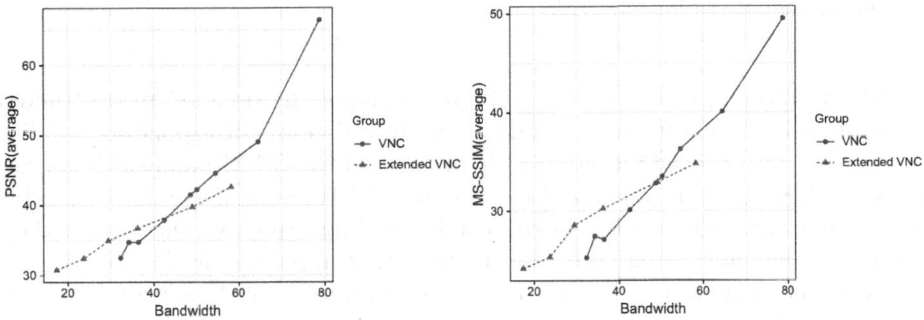

Fig. 5. Bandwidth-PSNR (on the left) and Bandwidth-MS-SSIM (on the right) curves of our proposed Extended VNC and TightVNC with tight encoding.

5.2 Results Analysis

In order to be as close as possible to the real usage scenarios of the remote desktop, we conduct experiments under the condition of simulating users to use the remote desktop for document editing. We build a python script to simulate the user's keyboard to input a fixed text at a rate of three characters per second in three minutes. During this period, we count the average bandwidth consumed by VNC and Extended VNC under different compression quality parameters. In order to evaluate the quality of desktop images, we collected a set of desktop images on the viewer and calculate the PSNR and MS-SSIM of the image sets collected from VNC and Extended VNC.

[1] TightVNC: https://www.tightvnc.com/.

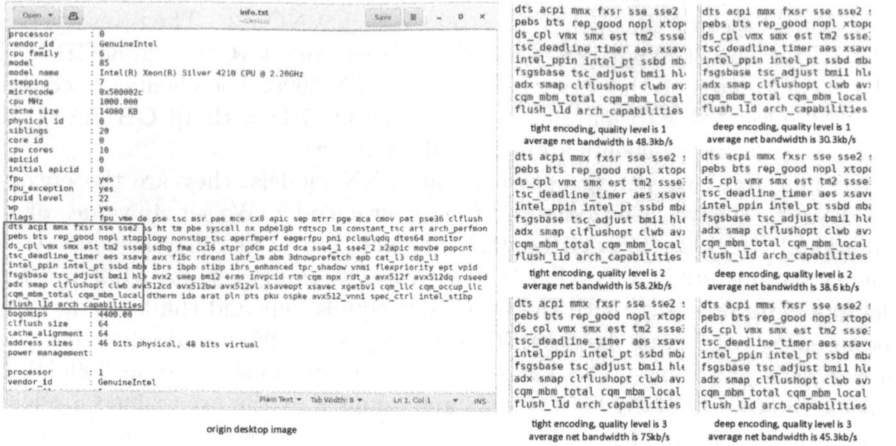

Fig. 6. Visualization of transferred desktop images with tight encoding and deep encoding, the quality level is set as 1, 2 and 3. We take "document editing" as an example for illustration.

The results are shown in Fig. 5. Figure 6 shows the detailed reconstructed desktop images of different encodings with different corresponding quality parameters with the PSNR-bandwidth curves and MS-SSIM-bandwidth curves. Figure 5 shows that the quality of reconstructed desktop image of our method is better under the same low bandwidth condition. Figure 6 shows that our method eliminates the unexpected blurs and shadows that appear under low-bandwidth environment. It indicates that our method can utilize lower bandwidth to bring users a clearer remote desktop, and make users to have a better experience.

6 Conclusions and Future Work

If there is insufficient network bandwidth when VNC is running, the display quality of the remote desktop has to be reduce to ensure the normal operation of the remote desktop. As the display quality decreases, there will be blurs and shadows on the desktop image displayed on the client, which greatly affects the user experience. We propose a new encoding method for remote desktops with deep image compression encoder and decoder implemented. The proposed remote desktop with the newly proposed CNN based image compression algorithm in recent years implemented which is able to further reduce the bandwidth required for remote desktop operation while eliminating block effect and shadows.

The desktop images are not generated randomly or by chance in remote desktop systems. The content displayed by the desktop images is very relevant to the user's operation. If some input which is generated by user's operations can be added as a part of the input to the deep image compression model, the entropy model is able to capture more prior information about latent representation y, which can further reduce the coding length of arithmetic coding and lower the compression ratio when performing arithmetic coding on quantized $\hat{y}$. In our future work, we will further explore how to use user's operation as prior information to enable remote desktops to provide a better user experience with lower bandwidth usage.

References

1. Ballé, J., Laparra, V., Simoncelli, E.P.: Density modeling of images using a generalized normalization transformation (2015)
2. Ballé, J., Laparra, V., Simoncelli, E.P.: End-to-end optimized image compression (2016)
3. Ballé, J., Minnen, D., Singh, S., Hwang, S.J., Johnston, N.: Variational image compression with a scale hyperprior (2018)
4. Baratto, R.A., Kim, L.N., Nieh, J.: Thinc: a virtual display architecture for thin-client computing, pp. 277–290 (2005)
5. Jiang, F., Tao, W., Liu, S., Ren, J., Guo, X., Zhao, D.: An end-to-end compression framework based on convolutional neural networks. .IEEE Trans. Circ. Syst. Video Technol. **28**(10), 3007–3018 (2018)
6. Ku, J., Kim, M.-S., Lee, J., Qui, P.X., Huh, E.-N.: WARP: web-based adaptive remote-desktop protocol for VDI. In: Information Science and Applications (ICISA) 2016. LNEE, vol. 376, pp. 189–194. Springer, Singapore (2016). https://doi.org/10.1007/978-981-10-0557-2_19
7. Tang, W., Song, B., Kim, M.S., Dung, N.T., Huh, E.N.: Hybrid remote display protocol for mobile thin client computing. In 2012 IEEE International Conference on Computer Science and Automation Engineering (CSAE), vol. 2, pp. 435–439 (2012)
8. Wang, Z., Simoncelli, E.P., Bovik, A.C.: Multi-scale structural similarity for image quality assessment, vol. 2, pp. 1398–1402 (2003)
9. Zhao, L., Bai, H., Wang, A., Zhao, Y.: Learning a virtual codec based on deep convolutional neural network to compress image. J. Vis. Commun. Image Represent **63**, 102589 (2019)
10. Shao, Z., et al.: Real-time dynamic voltage loop scheduling for multi-core embedded systems. IEEE Trans. Circ. Syst. II Exp. Briefs **54**(5), 445–449 (2007)
11. Guo, Y., Zhuge, Q., Hu, J., Yi, J., Qiu, M., Sha, E.H.: Data placement and duplication for embedded multicore systems with scratch pad memory. IEEE Trans. Comput.-Aided Des. Integr. Circ. Syst. **32**(6), 809–817 (2013)
12. Qiu, M., Ming, Z., Wang, J., Yang, L.T., Xiang, Y.: Enabling cloud computing in emergency management systems. IEEE Cloud Comput. **1**(4), 60–67 (2014)
13. Dai, W., Qiu, L., Ana, W., Qiu, M.: Cloud infrastructure resource allocation for big data applications. IEEE Trans. Big Data **4**(3), 313–324 (2018)
14. Gai, K., Qiu, M.: Optimal resource allocation using reinforcement learning for iot content-centric services. Appl. Soft Comput. **70**, 12–21 (2018)
15. Gai, K., Qiu, M.: Reinforcement learning-based content-centric services in mobile sensing. IEEE Netw. **32**(4), 34–39 (2018)
16. Qiu, M., Zhang, K., Huang, M.: An empirical study of web interface design on small display devices, pp. 29–35. IEEE Computer Society (2004)
17. Zhu, M., Liu, X.-Y., Tang, F., Qiu, M., Shen, R., Shu, W., Min-You, W.: Public vehicles for future urban transportation. IEEE Trans. Intell. Transp. Syst. **17**(12), 3344–3353 (2016)

Author Index